W9-CJA-696

ST/ESA/STAT/SER.G/65 (Vol. II)

Department of Economic and Social Affairs
Statistics Division

2016

International Trade Statistics Yearbook

Volume II
Trade by Product

United Nations
New York, 2017

DEPARTMENT OF ECONOMIC AND SOCIAL AFFAIRS

The Department of Economic and Social Affairs of the United Nations Secretariat is a vital interface between global policies in the economic, social and environmental spheres and national action. The Department works in three main interlinked areas: (i) it compiles, generates and analyses a wide range of economic, social and environmental data and information on which Member States of the United Nations draw to review common problems and to take stock of policy options; (ii) it facilitates the negotiations of Member States in many intergovernmental bodies on joint courses of action to address ongoing or emerging global challenges; and (iii) it advises interested Governments on the ways and means of translating policy frameworks developed in United Nations conferences and summits into programmes at the country level and, through technical assistance, helps build national capacities.

NOTE

Symbols of United Nations documents are composed of capital letters combined with figures.

The designations employed and the presentation of material in this publication do not imply the expression of any opinion whatsoever on the part of the Secretariat of the United Nations concerning the legal status of any country, territory, city or area, or of its authorities, or concerning the delimitation of its frontiers or boundaries.

Where the designation "country or area" appears in this publication, it covers countries, territories, cities or areas. In previous issues of this publication, where the designation "country" appears in the headings of tables, it should be interpreted to cover countries, territories, cities or areas.

In some tables, the designation "developed" economies is intended for statistical convenience and does not necessarily express a judgement about the stage reached by a particular country or area in the development process.

ST/ESA/STAT/SER.G/65 Vol. II

UNITED NATIONS PUBLICATION
Sales No E.17.XVII.3 H

ISBN 978-92-1-161633-0
e-ISBN 978-92-1-362931-4
Print ISSN 1010-447X
Online ISSN 2412-1355

Enquiries should be directed to
Sales and Marketing Section
Outreach Division
Department of Public Information
United Nations
New York 10017
USA

E-mail: publications@un.org
Internet: http://unp.un.org

PREFACE

The *2016 International Trade Statistics Yearbook* (2016 ITSY) is the sixty-fifth edition of this yearbook. Its objective is to inform about the detailed merchandise and services imports and exports of individual countries (areas) by commodity and service category and by partner country (volume I), the world trade in individual products (3-digit SITC groups and 11 main EBOPS categories) (volume II) and total world merchandise trade - up to the year 2016. The two volumes are prepared at different points in time during 2017: *Volume I - Trade by Country* is made electronically available in June, and *Volume II - Trade by Product,* in December, as the preparation of the tables in Volume II requires additional country data which, normally, become available later in the year.

Beginning with the 2013 edition, trade in services data was introduced to the *International Trade Statistics Yearbook: Volume I - Trade by Country and Volume II – Trade by Product*. Therefore, the content and format of the yearbook were redesigned to take into account new additions of graphs/tables and analytical text. The data used in the tables and graphs in both volumes of the yearbook are taken at a specific time (June/November 2017) from the publicly available UN Comtrade (http://comtrade.un.org). Users are advised to visit the database for additional and more current information as it is continuously updated.

The *International Trade Statistics Yearbook* is prepared by the Trade Statistics Branch of the Statistics Division, Department of Economic and Social Affairs of the United Nations Secretariat. Under the general supervision of the Chief of Branch, Ronald Jansen, the programme manager is Markie Muryawan and the chief editor is Melissa Paca, assisted by Marjorie Imperial-Damaso. Bekuretsion Amdemariam has the leading role in the processing of the data for UN Comtrade and Htu Aung for UN Service Trade. Habibur Rahman Khan, Kenneth Iversen, Nancy Snyder, Karoly Kovacs, Salomon Cameo and Markie Muryawan provided valuable contribution to the inclusion of trade in services data and the improvement of production processes. However, all staff of the branch are involved in the generation of the data and the review/validation of the yearbook. Markie Muryawan, Salomon Cameo and Luis Gonzalez Morales developed the original software which is maintained by Melissa Paca and Daniel Buenavad.

Comments and feedback on the yearbook are welcome. They may be sent to comtrade@un.org / tradeserv@un.org or to United Nations Statistics Division, Trade Statistics Branch, New York, New York 10017, USA.

TABLE OF CONTENTS

Page

TABLE OF CONTENTS (continued)

Part 2 COMMODITY TRADE PROFILES

Full list of included 3-digit SITC groups (SITC, Rev.3)

Food and live animals (SITC Section 0)

Beverages and tobacco (SITC Section 1)

Crude materials, inedible, except fuels (SITC Section 2)

Mineral fuels, lubricants and related materials (SITC Section 3)

Animal and vegetable oils, fats and waxes (SITC Section 4)

Chemicals and related products, n.e.s. (SITC Section 5)

Manufactured goods classified chiefly by material (SITC Section 6)

Machinery and transport equipment (SITC Section 7)

Miscellaneous manufactured articles (SITC Section 8)

Commodities and transactions not classified elsewhere in SITC (SITC Section 9)

INTRODUCTION

1. The *International Trade Statistics Yearbook: Volume II - Trade by Product*, provides an overview of the latest trends of trade in goods and services showing international trade for 257 individual commodities (3-digit SITC groups) and for the 11 main Extended Balance of Payments Services (EBOPS) categories. The publication is aimed at both specialist trade data users and common audience at large. The presented data, charts and analyses will benefit policy makers, government agencies, non-government organizations, civil society organizations, journalists, academics, researchers, students, businesses and anyone who is interested in trade issues.

2. The main content of the yearbook is divided into three parts. Part 1 consists of 11 detailed world data tables on merchandise trade. Part 2 contains the commodity trade profiles for 257 individual commodities. Part 3 contains profiles of service trade for the 11 main EBOPS categories. The profiles offer an insight into the trends in individual commodities and service categories by means of brief descriptive text, concise data tables and charts using latest available data. For further information on data availability, please see the sources section of this Introduction.

3. The yearbook is also made available online at the publications repository of the UN Statistics Division (http://unstats.un.org/unsd/pubs). For more detailed and latest available data, please consult UN Comtrade (http://comtrade.un.org), which is the source of the information presented in the yearbook, and which is continuously updated.

Concepts and definitions of International Merchandise Trade Statistics

4. The merchandise trade data in this Yearbook have been compiled by national statistical authorities largely complying with the United Nations recommended *International Merchandise Trade Statistics, Concepts and Definitions 2010* (IMTS 2010).[1] The main elements of the concepts and definitions are:

i. Coverage: As a general guideline, it is recommended that international merchandise trade statistics record all goods which add to or subtract from the stock of material resources of a country by entering (imports) or leaving (exports) its economic territory. The general guideline is subject to the clarifications provided in IMTS 2010, in particular, to the specific guidelines in chapter 1 concerning the inclusion or exclusion of certain categories of goods.

ii. Time of recording: As a general guideline, it is recommended that goods be recorded at the time when they enter or leave the economic territory of a country.

iii. Statistical territory: The statistical territory of a country is the territory with respect to which trade data are being compiled. The definition of the statistical territory may or may not coincide with the economic territory of a country or its customs territory, depending on the availability of data sources and other considerations. It follows that when the statistical territory of a country and its economic territory differ, international merchandise trade statistics do not provide a complete record of inward and outward flows of goods.

iv. Trade systems: Depending on what parts of the economic territory are included in the statistical territory, the trade data-compilation system adopted by a country (its trade system) may be referred to as general or special.

a) The general trade system is in use when the statistical territory coincides with the economic territory. Consequently, it is recommended that the statistical territory of a country applying the general trade system comprises all applicable territorial elements. In this case, imports include goods entering the free circulation area, premises for inward processing, industrial free zones, premises for customs warehousing or commercial free zones and exports include goods leaving those territorial elements;

b) The special trade system is in use when the statistical territory comprises only a particular part of the economic territory, so that certain flows of goods which are in the scope of IMTS 2010 are not included in either import or export statistics of the compiling country. The strict definition of the special trade system is in use when the statistical territory comprises only the free circulation area, that is, the part within which goods "may be

---

[1] At its forty-first session, held from 23 to 26 February 2010, the Statistical Commission adopted the revised recommendations "International merchandise trade statistics: concepts and definitions 2010" (IMTS 2010) which provide very important amendments while retaining the existing conceptual framework contained in the previous recommendations. The publication is available under Statistical Papers, Series M No. 52, Rev.3 (United Nations publication, Sales No. E.10.XVII.13) and electronically at: http://unstats.un.org/unsd/pubs/gesgrid.asp?id=449.

disposed of without customs restriction". Consequently, in such a case, imports include only goods entering the free circulation area of a compiling country and exports include only goods leaving the free circulation area of a compiling country.

c) The relaxed definition of the special trade system is in use when (a) goods that enter a country for, or leave it after, inward processing, as well as (b) goods that enter or leave an industrial free zone, are also recorded and included in international merchandise trade statistics

v. Classification: It is recommended that countries use the *Harmonized Commodity Description and Coding System* (HS) for the collection, compilation and dissemination of international merchandise trade statistics as suggested by the Statistical Commission at its twenty-seventh session (22 February to 3 March 1993).[2] The Harmonized System was adopted by the Customs Co-operation Council in June 1983, and the International Convention on the Harmonized System (HS Convention) entered into force on 1 January 1988 (HS 1988).[3] In accordance with the preamble to the HS Convention, which recognized the importance of ensuring that the HS be kept up to date in the light of changes in technology or in patterns of international trade, the HS is regularly reviewed and revised. The fifth edition, HS 2012, came into effect 1 January 2012.[4] The *Standard International Trade Classification (SITC)*[5] which was in the past used by countries in data compilation and reporting has been recognized for its continued use in analysis.[6]

vi. Valuation: At its fifteenth session, in 1953, the Economic and Social Council, taking the view that trade statistics must reflect economic realities, recommended that the Governments of Member States of the United Nations, wherever possible, use transaction values in the compilation of their national statistics of external trade or, when national practices are based on other values, endeavour to provide supplementary statistical data based on transaction values (Economic and Social Council resolution 469 B (XV)). To promote the comparability of international merchandise trade statistics and taking into account the commercial and data reporting practices of the majority of countries, it is recommended that: (a) The statistical value of imported goods be a CIF-type value; (b) The statistical value of exported goods be an FOB-type value; however, countries are encouraged to compile FOB-type value of imported goods as supplementary information. FOB-type values include the transaction value of the goods and the value of services performed to deliver goods to the border of the exporting country. CIF-type values include the transaction value of the goods, the value of services performed to deliver goods to the border of the exporting country and the value of the

---

[2] See Official Records of the Economic and Social Council, 1993, Supplement No. 6 (E/1993/26), para. 162 (d).

[3] See Customs Co-operation Council, The Harmonized Commodity Description and Coding System, Brussels, 1989.

[4] See World Customs Organization, Harmonized Commodity Description and Coding System, Fifth Edition (2012), Brussels 2010.

[5] Standard International Trade Classification, Original, Statistical Papers, Series M No.10, Second Edition, 1951 (United Nations publication, Sales No. E.51.XVII.1); subsequent editions are published as United Nations publications under Series M No.34.

[6] See Official Records of the Economic and Social Council, 1999, Supplement No. 4 (E/1993/24), para. 24 (c).

services performed to deliver the goods from the border of the exporting country to the border of the importing country.

vii. Partner country: It is recommended that in the case of imports, the country of origin be recorded; and that in the case of exports, the country of last known destination be recorded. The country of origin of a good (for imports) is determined by rules of origin established by each country. The country of last known destination is the last country - as far as it is known at the time of exportation - to which goods are to be delivered, irrespective of where they have been initially dispatched to and whether or not, on their way to that last country, they are subject to any commercial transactions or other operations which change their legal status. Further, it is recommended that country of consignment be recorded for imports as the second partner country attribution, alongside country of origin; the compilation of export statistics on the country of consignment basis is only encouraged, depending on a country's needs and circumstances.

5. The commodity trade profiles (part 2 of this publication) are based on the detailed trade data as reported by countries (or areas) and published on UN Comtrade without any adjustments for conceptual differences such as differences in the trade system, valuation and partner attribution. The explanatory notes on UN Comtrade inform about the trade system, valuation and partner attribution of individual reporter countries (or areas). For more detailed information on national practices in the compilation and dissemination of international merchandise trade data please go to http://unstats.un.org/unsd/tradereport/introduction_MM.asp.

Concepts and definitions of Statistics of International Trade in Services

6. The trade in services data in this Yearbook have been compiled by national statistical authorities or central banks largely complying with the *Manual on Statistics of International Trade in Services 2010* (MSITS 2010).[7]

7. The main elements of the concepts and definitions of MSITS 2010 are:

i. Definitions: In general, MSITS 2010 respects the 2008 SNA use of the term services, which is defined as follows (2008 SNA, para. 6.17):

a) Services are the result of a production activity that changes the conditions of the consuming units, or facilitates the exchange of products or financial assets. These types of service may be described as change-effecting services and margin services, respectively. Change-effecting services are outputs produced to order and typically consist of changes in the conditions of the consuming units realized by the activities of producers at the demand of the consumers. They can also be referred to as

[7] At its forty-first session, held from 23 to 26 February 2010, the Statistical Commission adopted the revised "Manual on Statistics of International Trade in Services" (MSITS 2010) , which sets out an internationally agreed framework for the compilation and reporting of statistics of international trade in services and align with the revisions of well-established revised international statistical standards. The publication is available under Statistical Papers, Series M No. 86, Rev.1 (United Nations publication, Sales No.E.10.XVII.14) and electronically at http://unstats.un.org/unsd/tradeserv/TFSITS/msits2010.htm.

"transformation services". Change-effecting services are not separate entities over which ownership rights can be established. They cannot be traded separately from their production. By the time their production is completed, they must have been provided to the consumers.

b) MSITS 2010 defines "international trade in services" as trade in services between residents and non-residents of an economy, as well as the supply of services through foreign affiliates established abroad and the supply of services through the presence of foreign individuals, either as foreign service suppliers themselves or as employees of a foreign service supplier.

Importantly, the services data included in this Yearbook only reflect trade in services between residents and non-residents.

ii. Concept and definition of residence: The residence of an institutional unit is the economic territory with which it has the strongest connection, constituting its centre of predominant economic interest. Each institutional unit is a resident of one and only one economic territory, as determined by its centre of predominant economic interest. An institutional unit is resident in an economic territory when there exists, within the economic territory, some location, dwelling, place of production, or other premises on which or from which the unit engages and intends to continue engaging, either indefinitely or over a finite but long period of time, in economic activities and transactions on a significant scale. The location need not be fixed as long as it remains within the economic territory. Actual or intended location for one year or more is used as an operational criterion. While the choice of one year as a specific period is somewhat arbitrary, it is adopted to eliminate uncertainty and facilitate international consistency. More specific criteria for determining residence are given in the MSITS 2010.

iii. Valuation: The market price is used as the basis for valuation of transactions in international trade in services. Market prices for transactions are defined as amounts of money that willing buyers pay to acquire something from willing sellers. The exchanges are made between independent parties and based on commercial considerations only and are sometimes called "at arm's length" transactions. These transactions will generally be valued at the actual price agreed between the supplier and the consumer.

iv. Time of recording of transactions: The appropriate time for recording transactions in services is when they are delivered or received (the "accruals basis"). Some services, such as certain transport or hotel services are provided within a discrete period, in which case there is no problem in determining the time of recording. Other services are supplied or take place on a continuous basis, for example, construction, operating leasing and insurance services. When construction takes place with a prior contract of sale, the ownership of the structure is effectively transferred progressively as the work proceeds. When services are provided over a period of time (such as freight, insurance and construction), there may be advance payments or settlements at later dates for such services. The provision of services should be recorded on an accrual basis in each accounting period, that is to say it should be recorded when the service is rendered and not when the payment occurs.

v. Framework and scope: MSITS 2010 recommends that the Sixth Edition of the Balance of Payments and International Investment Position Manual (BPM6)[8] recommendations on the principles of recording (regarding residence, valuation, time of recording, currency of recording and conversion) should be followed. The Extended Balance of Payments Services Classification (EBOPS) is a more detailed classification than that of BPM5 for international trade in services between residents and non-residents, by breaking down a number of the BPM5 service items. The main components of the EBOPS classification are presented in paragraph 7.vii below.

vi. Partner country: It is recommended that the breakdown by partner economy for services transactions between residents and non-residents be recorded, the aim being to report partner detail, first, at the level of services trade as a whole and, second, for each of the main types of services in EBOPS and (as a longer-term goal) for the more detailed EBOPS items. Partner country data for trade in services are not included in this publication, as most countries do not currently compile these data by partner country.

vii. Classification: In 1996, OECD and Eurostat, in consultation with IMF, developed for use by their members a more detailed classification than that presented in the IMF's Balance of Payments Manual (BPM5) for international trade in services between residents and non-residents, by breaking down a number of the BPM5 service items. This more detailed classification is termed the Extended Balance of Payments Services Classification (EBOPS). The EBOPS classification was published in 2002 in the MSITS 2002 and was subsequently revised to the EBOPS 2010 classification, as published in the MSITS 2010. The services data in this Yearbook follow the EBOPS 2002 classification (which corresponds to the BPM5 recommendations) due to the fact that many countries have not yet transitioned to the EBOPS 2010 classification (which corresponds to the BPM6 recommendations).

The 11 main EBOPS 2002 standard services components (as presented in the MSITS 2002) are:[9]

a) Transportation: covers all transportation services that are performed by residents of one economy for those of another and that involve the carriage of passengers, the movement of goods (freight), rentals (charters) of carriers with crew, and related supporting and auxiliary services. Some related items that are excluded from transportation services are freight insurance (included in insurance services); goods procured in ports by non-resident carriers and repairs of transportation equipment (both are treated as goods, not

[8] International Monetary Fund. *Sixth Edition of the Balance of Payments Manual (BPM6)*. 2009. http://www.imf.org/external/pubs/ft/bop/2007/pdf/bpm6.pdf. The previous edition of this manual was the *Fifth Edition of the Balance of Payments Manual (BPM5)*, which was published in 1992. https://www.imf.org/external/pubs/ft/bopman/bopman.pdf.

[9] The full detailed EBOPS 2002 classification is available as an on-line annex to the MSITS 2002. http://unstats.un.org/unsd/tradekb/Attachment358.aspx.

services); repairs of railway facilities, harbours and airfield facilities (included in construction services); and rentals or charters of carriers without crew (included in operational leasing services).

b) Travel: covers primarily the goods and services acquired from an economy by travelers during visits of less than one year to that economy. Includes business and personal travel, which includes health-related expenditure (total expenditure by those travelling for medical reasons), education-related expenditure (i.e., total expenditure by students), and all other personal travel expenditure.

c) Communications services: covers postal and courier services (which cover the pick-up, transport and delivery of letters, newspapers, periodicals, brochures, other printed matter, parcels and packages, including post office counter and mailbox rental services) and telecommunications services (which cover the transmission of sound, images or other information by telephone, telex, telegram, radio and television cable and broadcasting, satellite, electronic mail, facsimile services etc., including business network services, teleconferencing and support services). It does not include the value of the information transported. Also included are cellular telephone services, Internet backbone services and on-line access services, including provision of access to the Internet.

d) Construction services: covers work performed on construction projects and installation by employees of an enterprise in locations outside the territory of an enterprise.

e) Insurance services: covers the provision of various types of insurance to non-residents by resident insurance enterprises, and vice versa. These services are estimated or valued by the service charges included in total premiums rather than by the total value of the premiums.

f) Financial services: covers financial intermediation and auxiliary services, except those of life insurance enterprises and pension funds (which are included in life insurance and pension funding) and other insurance services that are conducted between residents and non-residents. Such services may be provided by banks, stock exchanges, factoring enterprises, credit card enterprises and other enterprises.

g) Computer and information services: covers hardware and software-related services and data-processing services; news agency services include the provision of news, photographs, and feature articles to the media; and database services and web search portals (search engine services that find internet addresses for clients who input keyword queries).

h) Royalties and license fees: covers international payments and receipts of franchising fees and the royalties paid for the use of registered trademarks and international payments and receipts for the authorised use of intangible, non-produced, non-financial assets and proprietary rights (such as patents, copyrights and industrial processes and designs) and with the use, through licensing agreements, of produced originals or prototypes (such as manuscripts, computer programs, and cinematographic works and sound recordings).

i) Other business services: covers merchanting, other trade-related services, operational leasing services, legal services, accounting, auditing, bookkeeping and tax consulting services, business and management consulting and public relations services, advertising, market research and public opinion polling, research and development, architectural, engineering and other technical services, waste treatment and de-pollution, agricultural, mining, and other on-site processing services, other business services, and services between related enterprises, not included elsewhere (n.i.e.).

j) Personal, cultural, and recreational services: covers services and associated fees related to the production of motion pictures (on film or videotape), radio and television programmes (live or on tape) and musical recordings services, as well as those services associated with museums, libraries, archives and other cultural, sporting and recreational activities.

k) Government services, not included elsewhere (n.i.e.): covers government transactions (including those of international organizations) not contained in the other components of EBOPS as defined above. Included are all transactions (in both goods and services) by embassies, consulates, military units and defence agencies with residents of economies in which the embassies, consulates, military units and defence agencies are located and all transactions with other economies. Excluded are transactions with residents of the home economies represented by the embassies, consulates, military units and defence agencies, and transactions in the commissaries, post exchanges and these embassies and consulates.

Description of world trade tables of part 1 (Tables A to K)

8. Table A: Total merchandise trade by regions and countries or areas in U.S. dollars: It provides a breakdown of merchandise imports, exports and trade balance for world, regional groupings, selected economic and/or trade groupings and individual countries or areas.

9. Total imports and exports by countries or areas in national currency (Table B): This table contains totals of imports and exports and the trade balance of individual countries (or areas) in national currency.

10. External trade conversion factors (Table C): The conversion factors for imports and exports shown in table C are used to convert trade data expressed in terms of national currency to U.S. dollars (see paragraph 13 for details).

11. World exports by provenance and destination in U.S. dollars (Table D): This table provides a breakdown of the world exports by regions and countries (or areas) according to their provenance (origin) and destination, both for total of trade and detailed by individual SITC sections and aggregations of sections, groups, subgroups and basic headings of SITC (see below in this paragraph for details).

Aggregations of SITC, Rev. 3 codes	Description
0-9	Total trade
0 and 1	Food, beverages and tobacco
041-045	Cereals
2 and 4	Crude materials (excluding fuels), oils, fats
22	Oil seeds and, oleaginous fruit
26	Textile fibers
27	Crude fertilizers and minerals
28	Metalliferous ores and metal scrap
4	Animal and vegetable oils, fats and waxes
3	Mineral fuels and related materials
5	Chemicals
7	Machinery and transport equipment
781.2, 784.1, 785.1, 785.2 and 785.31	Passenger road vehicles and their parts
6 and 8	Other manufactured goods
65	Textile yarn and fabrics
67	Iron and steel
68	Non-ferrous metals
691-695, 699 and 812	Other manufactured metal products
84	Clothing

12. Growth of world exports by provenance and destination (Table E): This table shows the growth of world exports in recent years up to the year 2016 by provenance (origin) and destination, for total exports and for a limited set of commodity classes. The annual average rates of change in percentage terms given in this table have been uniformly calculated by the use of the compound interest formula.

13. Structure of world exports by provenance and destination (Table F): This table shows the distribution (in percent) of exports by provenance (origin) and destination for total exports and a limited set of commodity classes as well as the commodity composition (in percent) of total exports by provenance (origin) and destination.

14. Indices of total exports and imports by countries or areas: Quantum and unit value indices and terms of trade in U.S. dollars (2000 = 100) (Table G): This table shows the volume and unit value (or price) indices for total exports and imports as well as the terms of trade and purchasing power of exports for individual countries or areas in U.S. dollars and with the year 2000 as base year.

15. Indices of total exports and imports by regions: Quantum and unit value indices and terms of trade in U.S. dollars (2000 = 100) (Table H): This table shows the volume and unit value indices for total exports and imports as well as the terms of trade by regions in U.S. dollars and with the year 2000 as base year.

16. Indices and values of manufactured goods exports: Unit value and volume indices (2000 = 100) and value in thousand million U.S. dollars (Table I): This table presents the unit value and the volume indices and the value of exports of manufactured goods for most developed economies and some developing economies. Manufactured goods are defined here to comprise

sections 5 through 8 of the SITC. Unit value indices are presented both in U.S. dollars and in national currency.

17. Indices and values of fuel imports – Developed economies: Unit value and volume indices (2000 = 100) and value in thousand million U.S. dollars (Table J): This table presents the unit value and the volume indices and the value of fuels imports for most developed economies. Fuel comprises section 3 of the SITC. Unit value indices are presented both in U.S. dollars and in national currency.

18. Some indicators on fuel imports - Developed economies (Table K): This table shows fuel imports as a percentage of total imports and exports, and the ratio of unit value indices of manufactured goods exports and fuel imports.

19. For the general note and footnotes, see the end of the tables. The most recent data for tables B, C, G, I, J and K are published on a monthly or quarterly basis in the *United Nations Monthly Bulletin of Statistics* (MBS).[10] Slightly different versions of Table A containing quarterly and monthly data and table H containing quarterly data are published on a monthly or quarterly basis as table 34 and table 38 in the MBS.[11] Updated, although different versions of Table D, are published as table 40, 41 and 42 in the July, September and November editions of the MBS.

Description of tables and graphs of commodity profiles in part 2 and service trade profiles in part 3

20. Part 2 contains detailed data (commodity trade profiles) for 3-digits groups of the *Standard International Trade Classification, Revision 3* (SITC).[12] All SITC groups are covered except the following groups as these were poorly reported and contain many estimates which are not sufficiently explainable: SITC group 286, Ores and concentrates of uranium and thorium; SITC group 345, Coal, water or other producer gases; SITC group 911, Postal packages not classified according to kind; and SITC group 931, Special transactions and commodities not classified according to kind. At the global level, special transactions and commodities not classified according to kind accounted for 4.1 percent of total world exports of commodities and 3.3 percent of total world imports of commodities in 2016.

21. Part 3 contains detailed data (service trade profiles) for 11 main EBOPS sub-categories. Not all countries reported data for every service category for every year. While such data may reflect the fact that certain countries may not have trade in a particular service category in a given year, it also partially reflects the fact that not all reporters always have sufficient information to allocate all international service transactions to their appropriate service

---

[10] The MBS is available as printed publication and its database can be accessed online at: http://unstats.un.org/unsd/mbs/app/DataSearchTable.aspx. In addition, the tables are also available online at http://unstats.un.org/unsd/trade/data/tables.asp.

[11] The difference between table A in this publication and table 34 in the MBS relates to the calculation of regional aggregations (see paragraph 46). The volume indices in table H are calculated using the values of table A as input. The volume indices for some regions are therefore slightly different than the ones published in table 39 of the MBS.

[12] Standard International Trade Classification, Revision 3, Statistical Papers, Series M No.34/Rev.3, (United Nations publication, Sales No. E.86.XVII.12).

categories. However, world total service trade figures in this Yearbook are not affected by this phenomenon, because they are based on the separately reported Total EBOPS Services category (EBOPS code 200), and are therefore not based on an aggregation of the 11 main EBOPS sub-categories. At the global level, unallocated services in 2015 represented 9.6 percent of total world exports of services and 7.9 percent of total world imports of services.

22. For certain commodities or service categories users will find spikes in growth rates and significant asymmetries between the total values of imports and exports. Reasons for these spikes can often be relatively easy identified (as caused i.e. by changes in the prices or classification changes) but the reasons for the asymmetries between the reported imports and exports are often less apparent.[13] However, it was decided to retain the information on these commodities and service categories as the results shown are a reflection of the data provided by countries (the influence of any estimates contained in the data is not significant) and to leave it to the users to assess the usefulness of this information for their specific purposes.

23. The following tables and graphs appear for each SITC commodity group and EBOPS category:

24. Imports and exports in current US$ (Table 1): In part 2, this table shows the values of imports and exports from 2002 to 2016 for the commodity group, and the share of the commodity group on the SITC section to which it belongs and its share on world trade. In part 3, this table shows the values of imports and exports from 2003 to 2015 for the EBOPS category and its share of world service trade, which is based on the reported Total EBOPS Services category (EBOPS code 200).

25. Top exporting and importing countries or areas in the latest year available (Tables 2 and 3): These tables present the top 15 exporting and importing countries or areas in the order of magnitude based on exports or imports values for the latest available year. For each country (or area), the tables show the value of exports or imports in current U.S. dollars, the average growth rate over the last five years (calculated using the compound interest formula), the annual growth rate for the latest available year, the share of world trade, and the cumulative share of world trade. In part 2, in preparing these tables estimates were made for countries whose data were not yet available; the estimated values of exports and imports are shown in italic. In part 3, no estimations to reported data were made.

26. Annual growth rates of exports (Graph 1): In part 2, this graph presents the annual growth rate of exports of the commodity group, the annual growth rate of exports of the SITC section to which the commodity group belongs and the annual growth rate of total exports over the last fifteen years. The annual growth rate of total exports comprises all SITC sections. In part 3, this graph presents the annual growth rate of exports of the EBOPS category, and the annual growth rate of total service exports since 2004. The annual growth rate of total exports comprises reported Total EBOPS Services category (EBOPS code 200).

---

[13] In merchandise trade, it should be noted that most countries report their imports valued CIF and their exports valued FOB. Therefore, world trade measured in terms of exports is expected to be lower than world trade measured in terms of imports. This applies to the total of trade as well as all commodities and SITC groups.

27. Trade balance by MDG Regions (Graph 2): This graph presents, for the latest year available, exports, imports and the trade balance by regions according to the regions used in the Millennium Development Goal (MDG) Indicator Database (for further information on country grouping by MDG regions, see Country Nomenclature and Country Grouping).

Sources

28. Figures on the total imports and exports of countries (or areas) presented in world tables A and B are mainly taken from *International Financial Statistics* (IFS) published monthly by the International Monetary Fund (IMF) but also from other sources such as national publications and websites and the *United Nations Monthly Bulletin of Statistics Questionnaire* (see the general note of table B for details).

29. The external trade conversion figures in world table C are derived from *International Financial Statistics* (IFS) published monthly by the International Monetary Fund (IMF).

30. The data presented in world tables D, E and F are derived from UN Comtrade data, supplemented by estimated data for non-available countries and areas.

31. The data presented in world tables G and H on the volume and unit value indices, and terms of trade for total exports and imports by countries (or areas) and regions are mostly derived from *International Financial Statistics* (IFS) published monthly by the International Monetary Fund (IMF), but also from other sources such as national publications and websites and the *United Nations Monthly Bulletin of Statistics Questionnaire*.

32. The data presented in world tables I, J and K on unit value and volume indices and value for manufactured goods exports and fuel imports are obtained from sources such as national publications and websites and the *United Nations Monthly Bulletin of Statistics Questionnaire.*

33. The data in the commodity profiles in part 2 (commodity trade profiles) and the service trade profiles in part 3 of the publication are obtained from data directly submitted by countries to the United Nations Statistics Division (UNSD). The information on commodity trade is based on data provided by 146 countries (areas), representing 95.7% of world trade in 2016 and the information on service trade for 2015 is based on data provided by 153 countries (areas). In addition, data in part 2 is supplemented by estimated data for non-available countries and areas. All data published in the country profiles is available in UN Comtrade (http://comtrade.un.org).

34. In some cases, original countries data are received via international and regional partner organizations, such as the Organization for Economic Co-operation and Development (OECD), the Food and Agriculture Organization of the United Nations (FAO), the International Monetary Fund (IMF), the International Trade Centre (ITC), the Caribbean Community (CARICOM) Secretariat, the Common Market of Eastern and Southern Africa (COMESA), the Economic Community of West African States (ECOWAS) and the UN regional commissions such as the Economic Commission for Latin America and the Caribbean (ECLAC) and the Economic and Social Commission for Western Asia (ESCWA). Data for the European Union (EU-28) is received from the Statistical Office of the European Union (Eurostat).

35. Tables A to K show data as available by end of November 2017. Part 2 and 3 contain data available in UN Comtrade by the beginning of December 2017.

Method of Estimation

36. For table A (part 1) estimates for missing data are made in order to arrive to regional totals but are otherwise not shown. The estimation process is automated using quarterly year-on-year growth rates for the extrapolation of missing quarterly data (unless quarterly data can be estimated using available monthly data within the quarter). Regional totals containing estimated data are printed in bold.

37. For world tables D, E and F (part 1) and the commodity tables and graphs in commodity trade profile (part 2), data for missing reporters are estimated either through the extrapolation of the data of the two adjacent years, or, if this is not possible, through the use of data reported by the trading partners (so called mirror data). Mirror statistics are also used in case the partner distribution or confidential data make it necessary to adjust the reported data. In addition, modifications to the received data are made in cases where the provided data are obviously incomplete, particularly in the case of unreported petroleum oils exports in merchandise data.

38. For tables H, I and J (part 1) the missing data required for the calculation of regional totals are estimated using a variety of methods and additional data sources. All estimates are reviewed and adjusted where necessary.

39. For part 3 (the service trade profiles), only received data are shown and no estimation is undertaken for missing reporters.

Conversion of classification

40. Conversion of classification for merchandise data: All countries follow recommendation to report their detailed merchandise trade data according to the Harmonized Commodity Description and Coding System (HS) (see paragraph 4.C.v). In order to provide comparable time series data in UN Comtrade for all countries, the data reported in the latest HS classification is converted into earlier versions of the HS, and to corresponding or earlier versions of the Standard International Trade Classification (SITC).[14] The latest edition of the HS classification was its fifth and was released in 2012. The commodities in this publication are mostly presented according to the three-digit sections of SITC, Rev.3 as the SITC sections provide a limited set of economically meaningful main categories.[15] In addition, data according to SITC, Rev.3 is available for long time series.

---

14 Detailed information on the data conversions used for UN Comtrade can be found on the website of the United Nations Statistics Division at: http://unstats.un.org/unsd/trade/conversions/HS%20Correlation%20and%20Conversion%20tables.htm.

15 Standard International Trade Classification, Revision 3, Statistical Papers, Series M No.34/Rev.3, (United Nations publication, Sales No. E.86.XVII.12). SITC, Revision 4 was accepted by the United Nations Statistical Commission at its thirty-seventh session in March 2006 (see Official Records of the Economic and Social Council, 2006, Supplement No. 4, (E/CN.3/2006/32), chapter III, para. 26 (b)). Yet, it will require several years until a time series of data according to SITC, Revision 4 will be sufficiently long for publication.

41. Conversion of classification for trade in services data: For services data, many countries are still compiling data according to the EBOPS 2002 classification and, therefore, all services data presented in this Yearbook are presented according to this classification. For the cases in which a country has transitioned to the EBOPS 2010 classification (as presented in MSTIS 2010) and did not provide UNSD with data based on EBOPS 2002, and for those countries for which the IMF is the only data source,[16] the data were converted to the EBOPS 2002 classification in order to maintain consistency across countries. The conversion was based on the IMF's BPM5-to-BPM6 Conversion Matrix (available at http://www.imf.org/external/pubs/ft/bop/2008/08-10b.pdf).

Currency conversion and Period

42. Currency conversion: For both merchandise and trade in services data in this publication, conversion of values from national currencies into United States dollars is done by means of currency conversion factors based on official exchange rates. Values in currencies subject to fluctuation are converted into United States dollars using weighted average exchange rates specially calculated for this purpose. The weighted average exchange rate for a given currency for a given year is the component monthly factors, furnished by the International Monetary Fund in its IFS publication, weighted by the value of the relevant trade in each month; a monthly factor is the exchange rate (or the simple average rate) in effect during that month. These factors are applied to total imports and exports and to the trade in individual commodities with individual countries. The conversion factors applied to the data presented in table A are published quarterly in the *UN Monthly Bulletin of Statistics* (http://unstats.un.org/unsd/mbs/default.aspx) and are also available at: http://unstats.un.org/unsd/trade/data/tables.asp. For data published on UN Comtrade the applied conversion factors are available in a country's metadata on UN Comtrade.

43. Period: Generally, data refer to calendar years; however, for those countries which report according to some other reference year, the data are presented in the calendar year which covers the majority of the reference year used by the country.

Country Nomenclature and Country Grouping

44. Country nomenclature: The naming of countries (or areas) in this publication follows in general the *United Nations Standard Country or Area Codes for Statistical Use.*[17] The names and composition of countries as reporter are changing over time. Also, countries rarely follow the identical nomenclature in the recording of partner information. For example when former geographical entities commonly referred to in national statistics have changed, countries may introduce the corresponding changes in their statistics at different times. In this publication, wherever possible, areas of the world have been designated the names they currently bear.

[16] The IMF is only presenting data on a BPM6 basis (which corresponds to the EBOPS 2010 classification) for data from 2009 onwards.

[17] Standard Country or Area Codes for Statistical Use, Series M No. 49, Rev.4, (United Nations publication, Sales No. M.98.XVII.9). The latest information is available online at: http://unstats.un.org/unsd/methods/m49/m49.htm.

It should be noted that, in this publication:

i. Data published for China exclude those for Taiwan Province of China. Data representing the trade with Taiwan Province, which may have been reported by any reporting country or area, are included in the grouping Asia, nes. For statistical purposes, data for China also do not include those for Hong Kong Special Administrative Region and Macao Special Administrative Region.

ii. Beginning 1 January 2000, Botswana, Lesotho, Namibia, South Africa and Swaziland provide their international trade statistics separately.

iii. On 4 February 2003, the official name of the Federal Republic of Yugoslavia has been changed to Serbia and Montenegro.

iv. On 3 June 2006, Serbia and Montenegro formally dissolved into two independent countries: Montenegro and Serbia.

v. On 10 October 2010, the federation of the Netherlands Antilles was formally dissolved. The former Dutch Caribbean dependency ceased to exist with a change of the five islands' constitutional status. Under the new political structure, Curaçao and Sint Maarten (Dutch part) have become autonomous countries within the Kingdom of the Netherlands, joining Aruba, which gained the status in 1986. The islands of the remaining territorial grouping, alternately known as Bonaire, Sint Eustatius and Saba or the BES islands, are special municipalities and part of the country of the Netherlands and overseas territories of the European Union. For statistical purposes, the data for the Netherlands do not include the BES islands. Data referring to Netherlands Antilles (as a partner) prior to 2011 refer to the former territory which included Curaçao, Sint Maarten (Dutch part), Bonaire, Sint Eustatius and Saba.

vi. On 9 July 2011, Sudan formally dissolved into two independent countries: Sudan and South Sudan. Data provided for Sudan prior to 1 January 2012 refer to the former Sudan (including South Sudan). Data referring to Sudan (as a partner) for 2012 are attributed to Sudan excluding South Sudan.

vii. From January 2013 onwards, Saint Berthélemy is no longer part of customs territory of France, therefore it is recognised as a separate statistical area both as reporter and partner. Whereas from January 2014 onwards, Mayotte became part of statistical area of France and it is no longer shown either as a reporter or a partner.

45. Regional groupings: This publication uses the regional groupings of the Millennium Development Goal (MDG) Indicator Database which are shown below (for their composition, see table A and http://comtrade.un.org/pb/groupings.aspx). The category 'Other' applies only to the presentation of data by trading partner and consists of Antarctica, Bunkers, Free Zones, 'Special Categories' (confidential partner) and Areas nes.:

World
Developed Countries
- Asia-Pacific
- Europe
- North America
South-eastern Europe
Commonwealth of Independent States
- CIS Europe
- CIS Asia
Northern Africa
Sub-Saharan Africa
Latin America & the Caribbean
- Caribbean
- Latin America
Eastern Asia
Southern Asia
South-eastern Asia
Western Asia
Oceania
Other

46. Aggregations: All regional aggregations are calculated as the sum of their components. This also includes the regional and world totals presented in table A (in bold) which, up to the 2007 edition of this yearbook and in the tables currently published in the *United Nations Monthly Bulletin of Statistics,* are calculated by subtracting re-exports from the imports and exports.

47. Additional country groupings: The composition of the additional country groupings which are used in world table A reflects membership as of the latest year published and is as follows:

ANCOM-Andean Common Market
Bolivia (Plurinational State of), Colombia, Ecuador and Peru

APEC-Asian-Pacific Economic Co-operation
Australia, Brunei Darussalam, Canada, Chile, China, Hong Kong Special Administrative Region of China, Indonesia, Japan, Malaysia, Mexico, New Zealand, Papua New Guinea, Peru, Philippines, Republic of Korea, Russian Federation, Singapore, Taiwan Province of China, Thailand, United States of America and Viet Nam

ASEAN-Association of South-East Asian Nations
Brunei Darussalam, Cambodia, Indonesia, Lao People's Democratic Republic, Malaysia, Myanmar, Philippines, Singapore, Thailand and Viet Nam

CACM-Central American Common Market
Costa Rica, El Salvador, Guatemala, Honduras and Nicaragua

CARICOM-Caribbean Community and Common Market
Antigua and Barbuda, Bahamas (member of the Community only), Barbados, Belize, Dominica, Grenada, Guyana, Haiti, Jamaica, Montserrat, Saint Kitts and Nevis, Saint Lucia, Saint Vincent and the Grenadines, Suriname, Trinidad and Tobago

COMESA-Common Market for Eastern and Southern Africa
Burundi, Comoros, Democratic Republic of the Congo, Djibouti, Egypt, Eritrea, Ethiopia, Kenya, Libya, Madagascar, Malawi, Mauritius, Rwanda, Seychelles, Sudan, Swaziland, Uganda, Zambia and Zimbabwe

ECOWAS - Economic Community of West African States
Benin, Burkina Faso, Cabo Verde, Cote d'Ivoire, Gambia, Ghana, Guinea, Guinea-Bissau, Liberia, Mali, Niger, Nigeria, Senegal, Sierra Leone and Togo

EMCCA – Economic and Monetary Community of Central Africa
Cameroon, Central African Republic, Chad, Congo, Equatorial Guinea and Gabon

EU-28 - European Union 28
Austria, Belgium, Bulgaria, Croatia, Cyprus, Czechia, Denmark, Estonia, Finland, France, Germany, Greece, Hungary, Ireland, Italy, Latvia, Lithuania, Luxembourg, Malta, Netherlands, Poland, Portugal, Romania, Slovakia, Slovenia, Spain, Sweden and United Kingdom.

EU-27 - European Union 27
Austria, Belgium, Bulgaria, Cyprus, Czechia, Denmark, Estonia, Finland, France, Germany, Greece, Hungary, Ireland, Italy, Latvia, Lithuania, Luxembourg, Malta, Netherlands, Poland, Portugal, Romania, Slovakia, Slovenia, Spain, Sweden and United Kingdom.

EU-25 - European Union 25
Austria, Belgium, Denmark, Finland, France, Germany, Greece, Ireland, Italy, Luxembourg, Netherlands, Portugal, Spain, Sweden and United Kingdom (EU15) plus Czechia, Estonia, Hungary, Latvia, Lithuania, Malta, Poland, Slovakia, Slovenia, and Cyprus

EU-15 – European Union 15
Austria, Belgium, Denmark, Finland, France, Germany, Greece, Ireland, Italy, Luxembourg, Netherlands, Portugal, Spain, Sweden, United Kingdom.

LAIA - Latin American Integration Association (formerly Latin American Free Trade Association)
Argentina, Bolivia (Plurinational State of), Brazil, Chile, Colombia, Cuba, Ecuador, Mexico, Panama, Paraguay, Peru, Uruguay and Venezuela (Bolivarian Republic of)

LDC - Least developed countries
Afghanistan, Angola, Bangladesh, Benin, Bhutan, Burkina Faso, Burundi, Cambodia, Central African Republic, Chad, Comoros, Democratic Republic of the Congo, Djibouti, Equatorial Guinea, Eritrea, Ethiopia, Gambia, Guinea, Guinea-Bissau, Haiti, Kiribati, Lao People's Democratic Republic, Lesotho, Liberia, Madagascar, Malawi, Mali, Mauritania, Mozambique, Myanmar, Nepal, Niger, Rwanda, Sao Tome and Principe, Senegal, Sierra Leone, Solomon Islands, Somalia, South Sudan, Sudan, Timor-Leste, Togo, Tuvalu, Uganda, United Republic of Tanzania, Vanuatu, Yemen and Zambia

MERCOSUR-Mercado Comun Sud-Americano
Argentina, Bolivia (Plurinational State of), Brazil, Paraguay, Uruguay and Venezuela

NAFTA-Northern American Free Trade Area
Canada, Mexico and United States of America

OECD-Organization for Economic Cooperation and Development
Australia, Austria, Belgium, Canada, Chile, Czechia, Denmark, Estonia, Finland, France, Germany, Greece, Hungary, Iceland, Ireland, Israel, Italy, Japan, Luxembourg, Mexico, Netherlands, New Zealand, Norway, Poland, Portugal, Republic of Korea, Slovakia, Slovenia, Spain, Sweden, Switzerland, Turkey, United Kingdom and United States of America

OPEC-Organization of Petroleum Exporting Countries
Algeria, Angola, Ecuador, Indonesia, Iran (Islamic Republic of), Iraq, Kuwait, Libya, Nigeria, Qatar, Saudi Arabia, United Arab Emirates and Venezuela (Bolivarian Republic of).

Abbreviations and Explanation of symbols

Names of some countries (or areas) or groups of countries (or areas) and of some commodities or groups of commodities have been abbreviated. Exact titles of countries or commodities can be found in various editions of the following publications:

(i) Standard Country or Area Codes for Statistical Use
(ii) Standard International Trade Classification (SITC)
(iii) Harmonized Commodity Description and Coding System (HS)
(iv) Extended Balance of Payments Classification (EBOPS)

In addition, the following abbreviations and symbols are used in this publication:

Not available	(na)
Not available	blank
Not available	..
Not applicable	–
Not applicable	.
Magnitude of less than half the unit used	0 or 0.0
More than 100,000 percent	>
Thousand	thsd
Million	mln
Billion	bln
Average	Avg.
Not elsewhere specified	nes
U.S. dollar	US$
Cumulated	Cum.
Imports	Imp
Exports	Exp
Balance	Bal
General trade system	G
Special trade system	S
Cost, insurance and freight	CIF
Free on board	FOB
Not included elsewhere	n.i.e.

Disclaimer

The tables, graphs and text contained in Part 2 and 3 of this publication are provided only for illustration and despite all efforts might contain errors. When using this data users are advised to verify the latest information on UN Comtrade which is the source of this data.

Contact

This yearbook has been produced by the Trade Statistics Branch of the United Nations Statistics Division/Department of Economic and Social Affairs. For questions or comments please contact us at:

Trade Statistics Branch
United Nations Statistics Division
2 United Nations Plaza, DC2-1540
New York, New York 10017
e-mail (merchandise): comtrade@un.org
e-mail (services): tradeserv@un.org

http://unstats.un.org/unsd/trade

2016 International Trade Statistics Yearbook

Volume II
Trade by Product

Part 1 – World Trade Tables

- Total imports and exports by regions and countries or areas in U.S. dollars (Table A)
- Total imports and exports by countries or areas in national currency (Table B)
- External trade conversion factors (Table C)
- World exports by provenance and destination in U.S. dollars (Table D)
- Growth of world exports by provenance and destination (Table E)
- Structure of world exports by provenance and destination (Table F)
- Indices of total exports and imports by countries or areas (Table G)
- Indices of total exports and imports by regions (Table H)
- Indices and values of manufactured goods exports (Table I)
- Indices and values of fuel imports - Developed economies (Table J)
- Some indicators on fuel imports - Developed economies (Table K)

Total imports and exports by regions and countries or areas (Table A)

Imports CIF, exports FOB and balance: million U.S. dollars *[cont.]*

Importations et exportations totales par régions et pays ou zones (Tableau A)

Importations CIF, exportations FOB et balance : en millions de dollars E.-U. *[suite]*

Country or Area - Pays ou Zone	IMP EXP BAL	G/S	2000	2008	2009	2010	2011	2012	2013	2014	2015	2016
Slovakia	IMP	S	13413	74034	56898	66110	81505	79077	83632	83675	75161	77130
Slovaquie	EXP	S	11889	70982	55553	64012	79011	79882	85244	85975	75257	77588
	BAL		-1524	-3052	-1345	-2098	-2494	805	1612	2301	96	458
Slovenia	IMP	S	10116	33991	24085	26305	31405	28392	29380	30052	26692	26695
Slovénie	EXP	S	8732	29600	22646	24717	29242	27080	28629	30522	27625	27658
	BAL		-1384	-4391	-1439	-1588	-2163	-1312	-751	471	933	963
Spain	IMP	S	152901	416631	290230	315548	362835	325836	333932	359132	312583	310618
Espagne	EXP	S	113348	277129	220377	246274	298458	286219	311638	323849	282331	287215
	BAL		-39553	-139502	-69853	-69274	-64377	-39618	-22295	-35282	-30252	-23404
Sweden	IMP	S	73328	168993	120262	148766	176950	164556	160587	162281	138345	140763
Suède	EXP	S	87737	183907	131042	158396	186904	172445	167497	164686	140015	139408
	BAL		14409	14914	10780	9630	9954	7888	6910	2405	1670	-1355
Switzerland	IMP	S	76104	173686	147894	166924	196790	188618	191705	195148	172869	176252
Suisse	EXP	S	74867	191813	166847	185790	223225	213982	217079	227605	210882	213744
	BAL		-1237	18127	18953	18866	26435	25364	25374	32457	38013	37492
United Kingdom	IMP	G	333579	642529	486279	568393	646291	654031	663131	684069	622552	588423
Royaume-Uni	EXP	G	283206	467157	356758	417686	494082	478114	474197	482354	439589	407246
	BAL		-50373	-175372	-129521	-150707	-152209	-175917	-188934	-201715	-182963	-181176
North America	IMP		**1499277**	**2580859**	**1928924**	**2363824**	**2719866**	**2801853**	**2794280**	**2879317**	**2671835**	**2657385**
Amérique du Nord	EXP		**1058904**	**1744454**	**1370536**	**1666503**	**1933093**	**2001279**	**2038280**	**2100729**	**1915423**	**1845374**
	BAL		**-440373**	**-836404**	**-558388**	**-697321**	**-786773**	**-800574**	**-756000**	**-778588**	**-756412**	**-812011**
Bermuda	IMP	G	720	1145	1034	970	869	885	1005	962	929	971
Bermudes	EXP	G	...	24	29	15	13	17	22	12	9	8
	BAL		...	-1122	-1005	-955	-855	-868	-983	-950	-920	-963
Canada[3]	IMP	G	238811	408827	321247	392119	451246	462423	461925	463141	419817	403004
Canada[3]	EXP	G	276641	456419	314002	387481	452132	454834	458397	476344	409951	390332
	BAL		37830	47593	-7245	-4638	886	-7590	-3527	13203	-9866	-12672
Greenland	IMP	G	363	895	742	808	915	850	780	764	600	631
Groenland	EXP	G	272	487	360	380	475	480	490	537	350	551
	BAL		-92	-407	-382	-428	-441	-370	-290	-227	-250	-79
United States[4]	IMP	G	1259300	2169490	1605300	1969180	2265890	2336520	2329060	2412550	2248230	2250150
Etats-Unis[4]	EXP	G	781918	1287440	1056040	1278490	1480290	1545710	1579050	1623410	1504580	1453830
	BAL		-477382	-882050	-549260	-690690	-785600	-790810	-750010	-789140	-743650	-796320
South-Eastern Europe	IMP		29538	170987	116942	125235	154705	145630	152543	159079	138563	145351
Europe du Sud-est	EXP		19546	93954	76983	89833	115572	107537	122905	129365	111596	116824
	BAL		-9992	-77033	-39959	-35402	-39133	-38093	-29638	-29714	-26967	-28527
Albania	IMP	S	1090	5251	4526	4592	5396	4882	4902	5230	4320	4669
Albanie	EXP	S	258	1355	1104	1550	1951	1968	2332	2431	1930	1962
	BAL		-832	-3896	-3422	-3042	-3445	-2914	-2571	-2799	-2391	-2707
Bosnia and Herzegovina	IMP	S	3083	12282	8794	9204	11047	10018	10303	10988	8983	9133
Bosnie-Herzégovine	EXP	S	1067	5066	3939	4802	5850	5160	5688	5893	5096	5327
	BAL		-2017	-7217	-4856	-4402	-5196	-4858	-4615	-5095	-3887	-3806
Bulgaria	IMP	S	6505	37018	23552	25473	32579	32712	34350	34730	28776	28792
Bulgarie	EXP	S	4809	22485	16378	20571	28222	26670	29492	30930	25756	26075
	BAL		-1696	-14532	-7175	-4902	-4357	-6042	-4858	-3799	-3020	-2718
Montenegro	IMP	S	.	3748	2313	2186	2544	2309	2354	2369	2038	2283
Monténégro	EXP	S	.	617	388	437	632	471	498	447	352	361
	BAL		.	-3131	-1926	-1749	-1912	-1838	-1856	-1921	-1686	-1922

Total imports and exports by regions and countries or areas (Table A)

Imports CIF, exports FOB and balance: million U.S. dollars *[cont.]*

Importations et exportations totales par régions et pays ou zones (Tableau A)

Importations CIF, exportations FOB et balance : en millions de dollars E.-U. *[suite]*

Country or Area - Pays ou Zone	IMP EXP BAL	G/ S	2000	2008	2009	2010	2011	2012	2013	2014	2015	2016
Romania	IMP	S	13055	82965	54256	61885	76251	70260	73452	77882	69852	74491
Roumanie	EXP	S	10367	49539	40621	49357	62659	57904	65881	69891	60603	63479
	BAL		-2688	-33426	-13635	-12528	-13592	-12355	-7571	-7991	-9249	-11012
Serbia	IMP	G	.	22880	18462	16423	19862	18927	20562	20604	18195	19234
Serbie	EXP	G	.	10971	11862	9766	11779	11348	14715	14839	13371	14855
	BAL		.	-11908	-6599	-6656	-8082	-7579	-5847	-5765	-4824	-4379
Serbia and Montenegro[5]	IMP	S	3711	.	.	.	.	.	.	.	.	.
Serbie et Monténégro[5]	EXP	S	1723	.	.	.	.	.	.	.	.	.
	BAL		-1988	.	.	.	.	.	.	.	.	.
TFYR Macedonia	IMP	S	2094	6843	5038	5474	7027	6522	6620	7277	6400	6749
L'ex-Ry de Macédoine	EXP	S	1323	3920	2692	3351	4478	4015	4299	4934	4490	4765
	BAL		-771	-2923	-2346	-2123	-2549	-2507	-2321	-2343	-1910	-1984
CIS	IMP		**70777**	**470015**	**303998**	**385447**	**510004**	**530799**	**536027**	**479961**	**335842**	**335204**
CEI	EXP		**143257**	**707851**	**440378**	**575087**	**762078**	**777787**	**762333**	**720601**	**501205**	**430224**
	BAL		**72480**	**237837**	**136381**	**189640**	**252074**	**246989**	**226306**	**240640**	**165363**	**95020**
Asia	IMP		**13519**	**73098**	**59307**	**56310**	**70829**	**80314**	**95582**	**92951**	**81343**	**82164**
Asie	EXP		**17794**	**139142**	**76439**	**99189**	**133567**	**135352**	**132114**	**130330**	**90899**	**82903**
	BAL		**4275**	**66043**	**17133**	**42879**	**62738**	**55038**	**36533**	**37379**	**9556**	**739**
Armenia	IMP	G	882	4427	3303	3783	4196	4267	4386	4402	3239	3283
Arménie	EXP	G	294	1057	698	1011	1316	1428	1479	1519	1485	1781
	BAL		-588	-3370	-2605	-2771	-2881	-2839	-2907	-2882	-1754	-1502
Azerbaijan	IMP	G	1172	7170	6123	6601	9756	9653	10713	9188	9217	8532
Azerbaïdjan	EXP	G	1745	47756	14701	21360	26571	23908	23975	21829	12729	9143
	BAL		573	40586	8578	14760	16815	14255	13263	12641	3512	611
Georgia	IMP	G	710	6302	4476	5236	7038	8037	8012	8602	7730	9865
Géorgie	EXP	G	324	1495	1134	1677	2187	2376	2910	2861	2205	2114
	BAL		-386	-4806	-3342	-3558	-4852	-5661	-5102	-5740	-5525	-7751
Kazakhstan	IMP	G	5040	38452	28409	24024	30000	35307	45966	41202	30179	25175
Kazakhstan	EXP	G	8812	71971	43196	57244	83316	88575	81912	79117	45722	35776
	BAL		3772	33519	14787	33220	53316	53268	35945	37915	15543	10601
Kyrgyzstan	IMP	G	558	4072	3040	3223	4261	5576	6070	5732	4070	3963
Kirghizistan	EXP	G	511	1874	1694	1779	2267	1955	2058	1897	1441	1503
	BAL		-47	-2198	-1347	-1444	-1994	-3622	-4012	-3836	-2628	-2460
Tajikistan	IMP	G	675	3273	2570	2658	3186	3779	4121	4297	3435	3031
Tadjikistan	EXP	G	784	1409	1010	1195	1257	1360	1162	977	891	899
	BAL		109	-1864	-1560	-1463	-1929	-2419	-2959	-3320	-2544	-2132
Uzbekistan	IMP	G	2697	7076	9023	8386	9953	...	13799	...	...	...
Ouzbékistan	EXP	G	2817	10369	10735	11587	13254	...	15087	...	...	...
	BAL		120	3293	1712	3201	3301	...	1288	...	...	...
Europe	IMP		57259	396916	244691	329137	439175	450485	440445	387010	254499	253040
Europe	EXP		125463	568710	363939	475898	628511	642436	630218	590271	410306	347321
	BAL		68205	171794	119248	146761	189336	191951	189773	203261	155806	94281
Belarus	IMP	G	8646	39381	28569	34884	45771	46404	42999	40614	30292	27570
Bélarus	EXP	G	7326	32571	21304	25284	41419	46060	37232	36127	26660	23416
	BAL		-1320	-6811	-7265	-9601	-4352	-345	-5766	-4487	-3631	-4154
Republic of Moldova	IMP	G	776	4899	3278	3855	5191	5213	5493	5299	3987	4021
République de Moldova	EXP	G	472	1591	1283	1542	2217	2162	2399	2335	1968	2045
	BAL		-305	-3308	-1995	-2314	-2975	-3051	-3094	-2964	-2019	-1976

Total imports and exports by regions and countries or areas (Table A)

Imports CIF, exports FOB and balance: million U.S. dollars *[cont.]*

Importations et exportations totales par régions et pays ou zones (Tableau A)

Importations CIF, exportations FOB et balance : en millions de dollars E.-U. *[suite]*

Country or Area - Pays ou Zone	IMP EXP BAL	G/S	2000	2008	2009	2010	2011	2012	2013	2014	2015	2016
Russian Federation	IMP	G	33880	267101	167411	229655	305605	314150	314967	286669	182719	182265
Fédération de Russie	EXP	G	103093	467581	301656	397668	516481	525383	527266	497909	343543	285491
	BAL		69213	200480	134245	168013	210877	211233	212299	211240	160824	103226
Ukraine	IMP	G	13956	85535	45433	60742	82608	84718	76987	54429	37502	39184
Ukraine	EXP	G	14573	66967	39696	51405	68394	68831	63321	53902	38135	36369
	BAL		617	-18568	-5737	-9337	-14214	-15887	-13666	-527	633	-2815
Northern Africa	IMP		**46956**	**164473**	**146452**	**161273**	**182419**	**208466**	**211607**	**209267**	**187551**	**162872**
Afrique du nord	EXP		**49865**	**207537**	**134078**	**164438**	**161707**	**199678**	**177149**	**147739**	**100493**	**90051**
	BAL		**2909**	**43064**	**-12374**	**3165**	**-20712**	**-8787**	**-34458**	**-61527**	**-87058**	**-72821**
Algeria	IMP	S	9172	39578	39333	40228	47279	50352	54965	58367	51763	46734
Algérie	EXP	S	22019	79587	45240	57786	73661	72857	65555	61413	35278	29668
	BAL		12848	40010	5907	17558	26383	22505	10590	3046	-16485	-17066
Egypt[6,7]	IMP	G	13963	48775	44946	52923	58903	65774	59662	61010	65044	57318
Egypte[6,7]	EXP	G	4675	26246	23062	26438	30528	29409	28493	24736	19051	21863
	BAL		-9288	-22528	-21884	-26485	-28376	-36365	-31169	-36275	-45993	-35455
Libya	IMP	G	3703	9116	10037	10506	7999	22996	27010	18994	13000	...
Libye	EXP	G	10137	62031	37265	46016	18015	58954	43986	20994	10200	...
	BAL		6434	52915	27228	35510	10016	35959	16975	2000	-2800	...
Morocco	IMP	S	11534	42366	32881	35385	44267	44885	45641	46057	37513	...
Maroc	EXP	S	7175	20345	14054	17765	21650	21444	22049	23836	21886	...
	BAL		-4359	-22021	-18827	-17620	-22617	-23441	-23592	-22221	-15627	...
Tunisia	IMP	G	8567	24622	19241	22218	23958	24447	24317	24828	20221	19456
Tunisie	EXP	G	5850	19319	14449	16427	17847	17008	17061	16756	14073	13483
	BAL		-2717	-5303	-4791	-5791	-6111	-7439	-7256	-8072	-6148	-5973
Sub-Saharan Africa	IMP		**78692**	**299518**	**252111**	**294465**	**367823**	**358205**	**384323**	**389578**	**338462**	**298355**
Afrique subsaharienne	EXP		**93394**	**355846**	**259393**	**350730**	**443466**	**433491**	**436293**	**418219**	**348424**	**312553**
	BAL		**14702**	**56328**	**7282**	**56264**	**75643**	**75286**	**51970**	**28641**	**9963**	**14199**
Angola[3]	IMP	S	3040	20982	22660	16667	22938	23717	26344	28587	20095	...
Angola[3]	EXP	S	7703	63914	40828	50595	67310	71093	68247	59170	33165	...
	BAL		4663	42932	18168	33928	44373	47376	41903	30583	13070	...
Benin	IMP	G	567	2290	1553	1494	2701	2202	2404	3446	2378	2173
Bénin	EXP	G	392	1285	423	437	1397	1402	624	1855	624	369
	BAL		-174	-1005	-1130	-1057	-1304	-800	-1780	-1591	-1754	-1804
Botswana	IMP	G	2079	5232	4771	5666	7300	9097	8424	8078	7238	6122
Botswana	EXP	G	2661	5077	3514	4692	5893	6659	7910	8510	6317	7355
	BAL		581	-155	-1257	-975	-1407	-2439	-513	433	-921	1233
Burkina Faso	IMP	G	608	2009	2084	2157	2574	3420	4163	3351	2982	...
Burkina Faso	EXP	G	213	693	868	1319	2353	2183	2356	2487	2177	...
	BAL		-395	-1315	-1216	-837	-221	-1237	-1807	-864	-805	...
Burundi	IMP	G	148	402	402	509	752	751	811	769	724	734
Burundi	EXP	G	50	54	62	100	122	132	99	124	113	111
	BAL		-98	-348	-340	-409	-630	-619	-712	-645	-611	-623
Cabo Verde	IMP	G	237	820	708	743	947	761	726	768	603	665
Cabo Verde	EXP	G	11	35	37	47	68	53	69	80	67	60
	BAL		-227	-785	-671	-696	-879	-708	-657	-687	-537	-605
Cameroon	IMP	S	1483	5699	4442	5051	6802	6515	6657	7553	6045	5205
Cameroun	EXP	S	1823	5241	3552	3881	4523	4585	4521	5153	4058	3304
	BAL		341	-458	-890	-1170	-2280	-1930	-2136	-2400	-1987	-1901

Total imports and exports by regions and countries or areas (Table A)

Imports CIF, exports FOB and balance: million U.S. dollars *[cont.]*

Importations et exportations totales par régions et pays ou zones (Tableau A)

Importations CIF, exportations FOB et balance : en millions de dollars E.-U. *[suite]*

Country or Area - Pays ou Zone	IMP EXP BAL	G/ S	2000	2008	2009	2010	2011	2012	2013	2014	2015	2016
Cent. Afr. Rep.	IMP	G	118	298	273	244	276	276	250	...	...	...
Rép. centrafricaine	EXP	G	163	150	81	91	116	112	140	...	...	...
	BAL		45	-149	-192	-153	-161	-163	-111	...	...	...
Chad	IMP	S	483	1906	2289	2507	2700	2600	2997	3496	2200	...
Tchad	EXP	S	236	4345	2636	3411	4599	3901	4496	4194	2900	...
	BAL		-248	2439	347	903	1899	1301	1498	698	700	...
Comoros	IMP	G	43	174	171	190	277	300	285	...	...	...
Comores	EXP	G	14	9	16	18	25	25	25	...	...	...
	BAL		-29	-165	-155	-172	-251	-275	-260	...	...	...
Congo	IMP	S	479	3142	2987	2987	5200	5200	5500	6200	7747	...
Congo	EXP	S	2489	8300	6100	8200	11500	11000	9800	8614	4650	...
	BAL		2010	5159	3113	5213	6300	5800	4300	2414	-3097	...
Cote d'Ivoire	IMP	S	2485	7863	7023	7863	6714	9774	12628	10722	9877	8380
Côte d'Ivoire	EXP	S	3611	10301	10326	10285	10928	10861	13687	12634	11898	10661
	BAL		1127	2438	3303	2423	4214	1087	1060	1911	2021	2281
Dem. Rep. of the Congo	IMP	S	697	4300	3900	4500	5500	6100	6300	6500	6200	...
Rép. dém. du Congo	EXP	S	824	4400	3500	5300	6600	6300	6300	6600	5800	...
	BAL		126	100	-400	800	1100	200	0	100	-400	...
Djibouti	IMP	G	207	574	451	420	511	580	560	803	890	...
Djibouti	EXP	G	32	69	77	100	93	95	120	129	132	...
	BAL		-175	-505	-373	-320	-418	-485	-440	-674	-758	...
Equatorial Guinea	IMP	G	451	3934	5205	5680	6014	5987	6990	6492	...	...
Guinée équatoriale	EXP	G	1097	15996	9108	9964	13532	15467	13981	11587	...	...
	BAL		646	12062	3903	4285	7518	9480	6990	5094	...	...
Ethiopia	IMP	G	1261	6552	6815	7544	7867	10770	11197	13358	16077	16234
Ethiopie	EXP	G	482	1415	1295	1837	2625	3101	3044	3215	2949	2793
	BAL		-779	-5137	-5520	-5707	-5241	-7669	-8153	-10143	-13128	-13441
Gabon	IMP	S	996	2607	2514	2984	3666	3630	3886	3105	3033	...
Gabon	EXP	S	2605	9566	5451	8691	9768	7704	9514	8949	5074	...
	BAL		1610	6959	2937	5706	6102	4075	5628	5844	2040	...
Gambia	IMP	G	187	325	304	300	336	380	348	385	...	...
Gambie	EXP	G	15	14	15	15	11	18	12	16	...	...
	BAL		-172	-311	-289	-285	-325	-362	-337	-369	...	...
Ghana	IMP	G	2974	10243	8069	11032	12606	13626	13190	13517	12450	...
Ghana	EXP	G	1317	5625	5840	7960	12784	11976	13691	12548	9550	...
	BAL		-1657	-4618	-2229	-3072	179	-1649	501	-969	-2900	...
Guinea	IMP	S	612	1366	1060	1405	2106	2300	2150	2115	...	...
Guinée	EXP	S	666	1342	1050	1471	1433	1400	1300	1428	...	...
	BAL		54	-24	-10	66	-673	-900	-850	-687	...	...
Guinea-Bissau	IMP	G	60	199	202	197	260	250	240	...	...	...
Guinée-Bissau	EXP	G	62	128	120	120	230	130	210	...	...	...
	BAL		3	-71	-82	-77	-30	-120	-30	...	...	...
Kenya	IMP	G	3105	11080	10207	12074	14783	16288	16358	18397	16097	14107
Kenya	EXP	G	1734	4975	4463	5149	5756	6126	5856	6046	5908	5695
	BAL		-1371	-6105	-5743	-6925	-9027	-10162	-10503	-12351	-10189	-8412
Lesotho	IMP	G	809	1995	1973	2206	1454	1598	2284	2207	1949	...
Lesotho	EXP	G	221	883	723	801	775	676	934	924	773	...
	BAL		-589	-1113	-1250	-1404	-678	-922	-1350	-1283	-1177	...

Total imports and exports by regions and countries or areas (Table A)

Imports CIF, exports FOB and balance: million U.S. dollars *[cont.]*

Importations et exportations totales par régions et pays ou zones (Tableau A)

Importations CIF, exportations FOB et balance : en millions de dollars E.-U. *[suite]*

Country or Area - Pays ou Zone	IMP EXP BAL	G/ S	2000	2008	2009	2010	2011	2012	2013	2014	2015	2016
Liberia	IMP	G	...	813	551	710	814	1076	1210	1046	...	...
Libéria	EXP	G	...	242	149	222	367	459	540	583	...	...
	BAL		...	-571	-402	-488	-447	-617	-670	-463	...	...
Madagascar	IMP	G	999	3843	3160	2546	2628	2486	3201	3254	3164	...
Madagascar	EXP	G	828	1670	1095	1082	1249	1236	1951	2142	2251	...
	BAL		-171	-2173	-2065	-1464	-1379	-1250	-1250	-1112	-913	...
Malawi	IMP	G	532	1700	2096	2162	2426	2334	2831	2960	...	...
Malawi	EXP	G	379	860	1080	1059	1398	1183	1196	1412	1048	993
	BAL		-152	-840	-1015	-1103	-1027	-1151	-1636	-1547	...	...
Mali	IMP	G	807	3343	2487	3430	3391	2940	3699	3951	3167	...
Mali	EXP	G	552	2082	1783	1996	2392	2163	2601	2097	2532	...
	BAL		-255	-1261	-704	-1434	-999	-776	-1098	-1854	-635	...
Mauritania	IMP	G	354	1669	1337	1708	2453	2971	3975	3622	3657	2113
Mauritanie	EXP	G	343	1651	1407	1799	2458	2624	2685	2293	1630	1637
	BAL		-11	-18	70	91	6	-347	-1290	-1329	-2027	-476
Mauritius	IMP	G	2206	4655	3734	4387	5149	5355	5399	5610	4794	...
Maurice	EXP	G	1803	2386	1939	2262	2565	2649	2872	3079	2686	...
	BAL		-403	-2269	-1795	-2125	-2584	-2706	-2527	-2531	-2108	...
Mozambique	IMP	G	1162	4008	3764	3864	6312	8688	10099	11611	8293	5295
Mozambique	EXP	G	364	2653	2147	2333	3604	3856	4024	5072	4195	3355
	BAL		-798	-1355	-1617	-1530	-2708	-4832	-6075	-6539	-4098	-1940
Namibia	IMP	G	1539	5260	6465	6510	6625	7321	7568	8523	7808	6900
Namibie	EXP	G	1317	5373	5122	5290	5362	5481	5740	5983	4737	4809
	BAL		-222	114	-1343	-1219	-1263	-1840	-1828	-2540	-3070	-2091
Niger	IMP	G	390	1659	1502	2179	1814	1799	1909	2247	1990	...
Niger	EXP	G	284	902	593	642	903	1503	1613	1498	1050	...
	BAL		-107	-757	-909	-1537	-910	-296	-295	-749	-940	...
Nigeria	IMP	G	8721	42378	33838	44221	64405	35703	44598	46505	34891	35175
Nigéria	EXP	G	20975	80615	56742	84000	114500	114000	...	...	...	...
	BAL		12254	38237	22904	39779	50095	78297	...	...	...	...
Rwanda	IMP	G	211	1131	1227	1401	1775	1999	2480	2457	2314	2248
Rwanda	EXP	G	52	267	193	255	464	470	689	736	559	599
	BAL		-159	-865	-1035	-1146	-1311	-1529	-1792	-1721	-1754	-1650
Saint Helena[8]	IMP	G	10	16	16	...	...	...	...	...	...	...
Sainte-Hélène[8]	EXP	G	0	0	1	...	...	...	...	...	...	...
	BAL		-10	-16	-16	...	...	...	...	...	...	...
Sao Tome and Principe	IMP	S	30	114	103	112	132	140	140	172	150	...
Sao Tomé-et-Principe	EXP	S	3	11	8	11	11	11	12	17	15	...
	BAL		-27	-103	-95	-101	-121	-129	-128	-155	-135	...
Senegal	IMP	G	1511	5585	4464	4346	5219	5772	5896	5919	5126	5028
Sénégal	EXP	G	610	1630	1572	1678	2273	2343	2339	2380	2268	2318
	BAL		-901	-3955	-2892	-2668	-2946	-3429	-3556	-3539	-2858	-2710
Seychelles	IMP	G	343	1106	807	989	1049	1074	1098	1144	991	1040
Seychelles	EXP	G	193	437	402	400	483	497	578	539	429	...
	BAL		-150	-668	-405	-589	-566	-577	-520	-605	-562	...
Sierra Leone	IMP	G	149	534	522	776	1714	1603	1617	1568	1477	...
Sierra Leone	EXP	G	13	216	233	342	350	1122	1910	1552	731	...
	BAL		-136	-318	-288	-434	-1365	-482	292	-16	-746	...

Total imports and exports by regions and countries or areas (Table A)

Imports CIF, exports FOB and balance: million U.S. dollars *[cont.]*

Importations et exportations totales par régions et pays ou zones (Tableau A)

Importations CIF, exportations FOB et balance : en millions de dollars E.-U. *[suite]*

Country or Area - Pays ou Zone	IMP EXP BAL	G/ S	2000	2008	2009	2010	2011	2012	2013	2014	2015	2016
South Africa[3,9]	IMP	G	26795	94901	64439	82961	102693	104150	103434	99884	85713	75008
Afrique du Sud[3,9]	EXP	G	29987	84488	62627	91355	108818	99555	96164	92181	81421	75180
	BAL		3192	-10413	-1812	8394	6125	-4595	-7270	-7703	-4292	173
Sudan	IMP	G	1553	9352	9691	10045	9236	9230	9918	9211	9535	8300
Soudan	EXP	G	1807	11671	8257	11404	10193	4067	4790	4454	3169	3094
	BAL		254	2319	-1434	1360	957	-5164	-5128	-4758	-6366	-5206
Swaziland	IMP	G	1039	1665	1617	1710	1940	1946	1525	...	...	...
Swaziland	EXP	G	903	1681	1479	1557	1901	1897	1894	...	...	...
	BAL		-137	16	-138	-153	-39	-49	370	...	...	...
Togo	IMP	S	562	1181	1174	1206	1764	1669	1957	1768	1735	1825
Togo	EXP	S	362	581	648	648	852	968	1149	806	711	761
	BAL		-200	-600	-526	-557	-912	-701	-809	-962	-1024	-1064
Uganda	IMP	G	1511	4559	4265	4709	4565	5230	4927	5086	4765	...
Ouganda	EXP	G	469	2717	3004	3115	2399	2861	2847	2667	2698	...
	BAL		-1043	-1841	-1261	-1594	-2166	-2369	-2080	-2420	-2067	...
United Rep. of Tanzania	IMP	G	1523	7081	6296	7893	10772	11336	12212	11994	10208	...
Rép.-Unie de Tanzanie	EXP	G	663	2674	2367	3771	4422	5106	5035	5045	4888	...
	BAL		-860	-4407	-3929	-4122	-6349	-6229	-7178	-6950	-5320	...
Zambia	IMP	G	888	5017	3791	5319	7175	8224	10176	9545	8476	7510
Zambie	EXP	G	893	5067	4310	7197	9013	9372	10601	9694	7015	6516
	BAL		4	50	519	1879	1838	1148	425	149	-1461	-993
Zimbabwe	IMP	G	1861	2630	3213	5162	7562	6710	6809	6306	6062	5211
Zimbabwe	EXP	G	1923	1660	1613	3244	4416	3808	3694	3558	3614	2832
	BAL		62	-970	-1600	-1918	-3146	-2902	-3115	-2748	-2448	-2379
Latin America & The Caribbean	IMP		**376085**	**896804**	**673719**	**854034**	**1046478**	**1074890**	**1120671**	**1116124**	**1002748**	**907081**
Amérique latine et les Caraïbes	EXP		**355950**	**888166**	**680439**	**861241**	**1072957**	**1086576**	**1091515**	**1060765**	**907516**	**870645**
	BAL		**-20135**	**-8638**	**6720**	**7207**	**26479**	**11686**	**-29156**	**-55359**	**-95232**	**-36436**
The Caribbean	IMP		**26914**	**61394**	**48506**	**50823**	**57107**	**56311**	**53766**	**53571**	**51897**	**49875**
Les Caraïbes	EXP		**11427**	**30413**	**19622**	**23150**	**29712**	**30045**	**31547**	**32622**	**30109**	**31035**
	BAL		**-15487**	**-30981**	**-28884**	**-27673**	**-27395**	**-26266**	**-22219**	**-20950**	**-21788**	**-18840**
Anguilla	IMP	G	99	272	169	157	153	150	145	152	158	...
Anguilla	EXP	G	4	11	23	12	16	8	4	4	2	...
	BAL		-95	-260	-146	-145	-137	-142	-141	-148	-157	...
Antigua and Barbuda	IMP	G	338	806	699	501	471	532	508	552	488	494
Antigua-et-Barbuda	EXP	G	42	92	206	35	29	29	33	23	26	61
	BAL		-296	-713	-493	-466	-442	-503	-476	-529	-462	-433
Aruba	IMP	G	835	1134	1147	1069	1283	1257	1303	1262	1167	1116
Aruba	EXP	G	173	100	136	125	151	173	167	111	81	95
	BAL		-662	-1034	-1012	-945	-1131	-1085	-1136	-1151	-1087	-1021
Bahamas[10]	IMP	G	2074	2354	2699	2887	3411	3658	3366	3791	3162	...
Bahamas[10]	EXP	G	576	560	585	621	927	829	812	689	449	...
	BAL		-1498	-1794	-2114	-2265	-2484	-2829	-2554	-3101	-2713	...
Barbados	IMP	G	1156	1879	1471	1562	1805	1806	1759	1739	1618	1622
Barbade	EXP	G	272	445	369	429	465	570	463	474	483	517
	BAL		-884	-1433	-1102	-1133	-1340	-1236	-1296	-1265	-1135	-1105
Cayman Islands	IMP	G	693	1078	893	828	911	910	929	977	997	1025
Îles Caïmanes	EXP	G	4	15	19	13	22	20	30	26	99	88
	BAL		-689	-1064	-874	-815	-890	-890	-899	-951	-898	-937

Total imports and exports by regions and countries or areas (Table A)

Imports CIF, exports FOB and balance: million U.S. dollars *[cont.]*

Importations et exportations totales par régions et pays ou zones (Tableau A)

Importations CIF, exportations FOB et balance : en millions de dollars E.-U. *[suite]*

Country or Area - Pays ou Zone	IMP EXP BAL	G/S	2000	2008	2009	2010	2011	2012	2013	2014	2015	2016
Cuba	IMP	S	3363	14249	...	...	...	...	...	...	...	...
Cuba	EXP	S	1219	3680	...	...	...	...	...	...	...	...
	BAL		-2144	-10570	...	...	...	...	...	...	...	...
Dominica	IMP	S	148	247	225	224	226	208	203	230	214	214
Dominique	EXP	S	54	40	34	37	31	34	35	36	30	60
	BAL		-95	-207	-191	-187	-195	-174	-168	-194	-184	-154
Dominican Republic[3,11]	IMP	G	6416	14020	10057	12885	14522	14939	13876	13838	16865	17484
République dominicaine[3,11]	EXP	G	966	2394	1690	2711	3678	4129	4474	4677	4011	4366
	BAL		-5450	-11626	-8367	-10174	-10845	-10810	-9401	-9162	-12854	-13117
Grenada	IMP	S	246	377	293	318	336	341	368	340	344	350
Grenade	EXP	S	78	30	29	23	28	30	32	33	31	26
	BAL		-168	-347	-264	-295	-307	-311	-336	-307	-313	-324
Haiti	IMP	G	1040	2310	2121	3147	3018	3170	3400	3734	3523	...
Haïti	EXP	G	313	475	576	579	767	814	885	950	1018	...
	BAL		-727	-1835	-1546	-2568	-2251	-2356	-2516	-2785	-2505	...
Jamaica	IMP	S	3302	7734	4860	5333	6439	6319	6218	5830	4995	...
Jamaïque	EXP	S	1295	2542	1319	1335	1623	1730	1569	1455	1265	...
	BAL		-2007	-5192	-3540	-3998	-4816	-4589	-4649	-4374	-3730	...
Montserrat	IMP	S	22	38	30	29	33	37	42	41	39	36
Montserrat	EXP	S	1	4	3	1	2	2	6	3	3	4
	BAL		-21	-34	-26	-28	-31	-35	-36	-38	-36	-32
Neth. Antilles[12]	IMP	S	2862	3079	2607	2687	...	...	...	...	...	...
Antilles néer.[12]	EXP	S	2009	1088	810	811	...	...	...	...	...	...
	BAL		-853	-1991	-1797	-1876	...	...	...	...	...	...
Saint Kitts-Nevis	IMP	S	196	325	285	268	248	226	249	268	297	332
Saint-Kitts-et-Nevis	EXP	S	29	51	44	46	49	53	49	50	55	51
	BAL		-167	-273	-241	-222	-199	-172	-200	-218	-241	-280
Saint Lucia	IMP	G	355	657	520	662	697	644	620	627	570	654
Sainte-Lucie	EXP	G	43	145	253	215	160	182	174	161	180	120
	BAL		-312	-512	-268	-448	-537	-461	-446	-467	-390	-535
Saint Vincent-Grenadines	IMP	S	148	373	334	338	332	356	370	361	334	335
St.Vincent-Grenadines	EXP	S	50	52	50	41	38	43	49	48	46	47
	BAL		-97	-321	-284	-297	-293	-313	-321	-313	-288	-288
Trinidad and Tobago	IMP	S	3308	9596	6953	6390	9976	9400	8799	8750	6495	...
Trinité-et-Tobago	EXP	S	4274	18663	9140	11156	14842	13100	12700	11600	7285	...
	BAL		966	9067	2187	4766	4866	3700	3902	2850	790	...
Turks and Caicos Islands	IMP	G	149	591	375	302	318	347	345	406	410	389
Îles Turques et Caïques	EXP	G	9	25	21	16	15	15	6	6	5	4
	BAL		-140	-566	-355	-286	-303	-332	-339	-400	-405	-385
Latin America	IMP		**349171**	**835409**	**625213**	**803211**	**989372**	**1018579**	**1066905**	**1062553**	**950851**	**857206**
Amérique latine	EXP		**344523**	**857753**	**660818**	**838091**	**1043245**	**1056531**	**1059967**	**1028143**	**877407**	**839609**
	BAL		**-4649**	**22343**	**35604**	**34880**	**53873**	**37952**	**-6937**	**-34410**	**-73444**	**-17596**
Argentina	IMP	S	25154	57413	39105	48048	74319	68505	74002	65323	59789	55608
Argentine	EXP	S	26341	70588	56065	64722	84269	75219	83026	71936	59706	57732
	BAL		1187	13175	16961	16674	9950	6713	9024	6613	-83	2124
Belize	IMP	G	524	837	669	709	831	882	930	1005	1020	...
Belize	EXP	G	218	290	224	280	340	340	315	303	268	...
	BAL		-306	-547	-445	-430	-491	-541	-616	-701	-752	...

Total imports and exports by regions and countries or areas (Table A)

Imports CIF, exports FOB and balance: million U.S. dollars *[cont.]*

Importations et exportations totales par régions et pays ou zones (Tableau A)

Importations CIF, exportations FOB et balance : en millions de dollars E.-U. *[suite]*

Country or Area - Pays ou Zone	IMP EXP BAL	G/ S	2000	2008	2009	2010	2011	2012	2013	2014	2015	2016
Bolivia (Plurinational State of)	IMP	G	1830	5081	4545	5590	7927	8578	9338	10421	9480	8374
Bolivie (État plurinational de)	EXP	G	1230	7058	4918	6179	8107	10312	11189	12266	8261	6969
	BAL		-600	1977	373	589	179	1733	1851	1845	-1219	-1405
Brazil	IMP	S	58643	182377	133673	191537	236946	228377	250557	239156	178832	143632
Brésil	EXP	S	55119	197942	152995	201915	256040	242580	242179	225101	191134	185280
	BAL		-3524	15565	19322	10378	19094	14203	-8378	-14055	12302	41648
Chile	IMP	G	18507	61903	41364	57928	73545	79080	80443	72433	62797	58892
Chili	EXP	G	19210	66456	51963	68996	80027	79712	77877	74547	64087	59869
	BAL		703	4553	10599	11068	6482	632	-2566	2113	1290	977
Colombia	IMP	S	11539	39320	32898	40683	54675	58633	59397	64060	54058	44890
Colombie	EXP	S	13043	38265	32784	39710	56507	59573	58657	54788	35606	30985
	BAL		1505	-1055	-114	-973	1832	941	-740	-9272	-18451	-13905
Costa Rica	IMP	G	6389	15366	11460	11606	13966	15076	15263	15751	14914	15461
Costa Rica	EXP	G	5850	9575	8711	7223	8034	8654	8548	9038	9091	9797
	BAL		-539	-5791	-2750	-4382	-5933	-6422	-6715	-6713	-5823	-5663
Ecuador	IMP	S	3721	18852	15090	20591	24286	25304	27021	27726	21518	16324
Equateur	EXP	S	4927	18818	13863	17415	22345	23765	24751	25724	18331	16798
	BAL		1206	-34	-1227	-3176	-1941	-1539	-2270	-2002	-3187	474
El Salvador	IMP	G	4948	9754	7255	8416	10118	10270	10772	10513	10416	9855
El Salvador	EXP	G	2941	4579	3797	4499	5309	5339	5491	5273	5485	5335
	BAL		-2006	-5175	-3457	-3917	-4809	-4930	-5281	-5240	-4931	-4519
Guatemala	IMP	G	5171	12835	10066	12051	14518	14873	14368	14921	14998	16987
Guatemala	EXP	G	2711	5412	3835	5907	7201	7139	6975	7366	7176	10572
	BAL		-2460	-7423	-6232	-6145	-7317	-7734	-7392	-7555	-7822	-6415
Guyana	IMP	S	582	1312	1161	1397	1763	1997	1750	1780	1550	...
Guyana	EXP	S	502	795	763	880	1116	1415	1380	1160	1100	...
	BAL		-80	-518	-398	-517	-647	-581	-370	-620	-450	...
Honduras	IMP	S	2980	8831	6133	7079	8953	9464	9169	9311	9424	8898
Honduras	EXP	S	1297	2883	2304	2712	3892	4427	3923	4063	3911	3857
	BAL		-1682	-5948	-3829	-4367	-5060	-5037	-5246	-5247	-5513	-5041
Mexico[3,13]	IMP	G	174500	310561	234385	301482	350856	370746	381202	399977	395232	387065
Mexique[3,13]	EXP	G	166368	291827	229683	298138	349569	370889	380107	397658	380763	373904
	BAL		-8132	-18734	-4702	-3344	-1287	143	-1095	-2319	-14469	-13161
Nicaragua	IMP	G	1805	4300	3438	4229	5180	5847	5647	5874	5899	5927
Nicaragua	EXP	G	643	1473	1393	1845	2294	2644	2408	2626	2423	2225
	BAL		-1163	-2827	-2045	-2384	-2886	-3204	-3239	-3248	-3476	-3701
Panama	IMP	S	3379	9050	7801	9145	11340	12494	13024	13705	12136	11697
Panama	EXP	S	859	1247	948	832	785	822	844	818	696	636
	BAL		-2519	-7803	-6853	-8313	-10554	-11672	-12180	-12887	-11440	-11061
Paraguay	IMP	G	2193	9033	6940	10040	12317	11502	12142	12169	10215	9753
Paraguay	EXP	G	2200	6407	5080	6517	7776	7283	9456	9636	8357	8501
	BAL		7	-2626	-1860	-3524	-4540	-4219	-2686	-2533	-1858	-1251
Peru[3]	IMP	S	7358	28449	21011	28815	37152	41018	42356	41042	37331	35132
Pérou[3]	EXP	S	6955	31019	27071	35803	46376	47411	42861	39533	34414	37020
	BAL		-403	2569	6060	6988	9225	6393	504	-1510	-2916	1888
Suriname	IMP	G	243	1518	1356	1380	1667	1755	2141	1982	1981	1232
Suriname	EXP	G	395	1668	1393	2057	2440	2525	2380	2113	1617	1433
	BAL		152	149	37	677	773	769	239	131	-364	201

Total imports and exports by regions and countries or areas (Table A)

Imports CIF, exports FOB and balance: million U.S. dollars *[cont.]*

Importations et exportations totales par régions et pays ou zones (Tableau A)

Importations CIF, exportations FOB et balance : en millions de dollars E.-U. *[suite]*

Country or Area - Pays ou Zone	IMP EXP BAL	G/S	2000	2008	2009	2010	2011	2012	2013	2014	2015	2016
Uruguay	IMP	S	3466	8943	6209	8619	10623	10642	10990	10901	9095	7909
Uruguay	EXP	S	2295	6421	5417	6707	7997	8601	8844	9475	7742	7180
	BAL		-1171	-2523	-792	-1912	-2626	-2041	-2146	-1425	-1354	-728
Venezuela (Bolivarian Rep. of)	IMP	G	16213	49602	40597	33815	38346	43501	46363	44478	40146	...
Venezuela (Rép. bolivarienne du)	EXP	G	31413	95021	57603	65745	92811	97877	88753	74714	37236	...
	BAL		15200	45419	17006	31930	54465	54376	42390	30236	-2910	...
Eastern Asia	IMP		**742209**	**2206817**	**1860765**	**2521545**	**3055326**	**3137293**	**3285271**	**3333544**	**2893496**	**2795174**
Asie Orientale	EXP		**774892**	**2473784**	**2093222**	**2717456**	**3202601**	**3352347**	**3546624**	**3717587**	**3568654**	**3420048**
	BAL		**32683**	**266968**	**232457**	**195911**	**147276**	**215053**	**261352**	**384043**	**675157**	**624873**
China	IMP	G	225024	1131620	1004170	1396200	1742850	1818170	1949300	1963110	1680790	1589460
Chine	EXP	G	249203	1428660	1201790	1578270	1899180	2048940	2210250	2343190	2284480	2134520
	BAL		24179	297040	197620	182070	156330	230770	260950	380080	603690	545060
China, Hong Kong SAR	IMP	G	212805	388505	347311	433111	483633	504405	523558	544112	521984	516411
Chine, Hong Kong RAS	EXP	G	201860	362675	318510	390143	428732	442799	458959	473659	465077	462284
	BAL		-10945	-25830	-28801	-42968	-54901	-61606	-64599	-70453	-56907	-54127
China, Macao SAR	IMP	G	2255	5365	4622	5513	7769	8877	10141	11262	10603	8925
Chine, Macao RAS	EXP	G	2539	1997	961	870	869	1021	1138	1241	1339	1257
	BAL		284	-3368	-3661	-4643	-6899	-7856	-9002	-10021	-9264	-7668
Korea, Republic of	IMP	G	160479	435275	323085	425212	524413	519584	515585	525514	436499	443695
Corée, République de	EXP	G	172272	422007	363534	466384	555214	547870	559632	572665	526757	535739
	BAL		11793	-13268	40449	41172	30801	28286	44047	47151	90258	92044
Mongolia	IMP	G	615	3616	2131	3278	6527	6739	6355	5237	3797	3358
Mongolie	EXP	G	536	2539	1903	2899	4780	4385	4273	5775	4670	4917
	BAL		-79	-1077	-229	-379	-1747	-2354	-2082	538	872	1559
Southern Asia	IMP		94740	465659	379515	485393	634428	661588	629913	**635309**	**553974**	**518163**
Asie Méridionale	EXP		91012	350844	282590	369974	493429	456084	455446	**469478**	**394893**	**372690**
	BAL		-3728	-114815	-96925	-115419	-140999	-205503	-174467	**-165830**	**-159081**	**-145474**
Afghanistan	IMP	G	1176	3020	3336	5154	6390	8932	8724	7729	7723	6534
Afghanistan	EXP	G	137	540	403	388	376	414	515	570	571	596
	BAL		-1039	-2480	-2933	-4766	-6014	-8518	-8209	-7159	-7151	-5938
Bangladesh	IMP	G	8358	22473	20631	26071	33978	38411	30467	35249	39482	41250
Bangladesh	EXP	G	4787	11777	12443	14195	19807	27709	22401	21061	29925	30188
	BAL		-3572	-10695	-8188	-11877	-14171	-10703	-8066	-14188	-9556	-11062
Bhutan	IMP	G	235	543	529	854	1052	992	911	934	1062	1003
Bhoutan	EXP	G	127	520	495	641	678	535	544	584	549	525
	BAL		-108	-23	-34	-213	-374	-457	-367	-351	-512	-478
India[14]	IMP	G	51563	321025	257200	330030	459750	488541	469321	462545	392787	361644
Inde[14]	EXP	G	42378	194816	164912	222694	305089	296454	313376	321541	267369	264564
	BAL		-9185	-126210	-92288	-107336	-154662	-192088	-155945	-141004	-125418	-97081
Iran (Islamic Rep. of)[15,16]	IMP	S	14347	57401	50768	65404	61808	53451	49709	53569	42500	...
Iran (Rép. islamique d')[15,16]	EXP	S	28345	113668	78830	101316	130500	95500	82000	88800	63000	...
	BAL		13998	56267	28062	35912	68692	42049	32291	35231	20500	...
Maldives	IMP	G	389	1382	963	1091	1465	1554	1733	1993	1896	2125
Maldives	EXP	G	76	126	76	74	127	162	167	145	144	140
	BAL		-313	-1256	-886	-1017	-1338	-1393	-1567	-1848	-1752	-1986
Nepal	IMP	G	1526	3562	4392	5495	5762	6499	6428	...	...	...
Népal	EXP	G	700	937	823	950	917	960	926	...	...	...
	BAL		-826	-2625	-3569	-4545	-4845	-5539	-5502	...	...	...

Total imports and exports by regions and countries or areas (Table A)

Imports CIF, exports FOB and balance: million U.S. dollars *[cont.]*

Importations et exportations totales par régions et pays ou zones (Tableau A)

Importations CIF, exportations FOB et balance : en millions de dollars E.-U. *[suite]*

Country or Area - Pays ou Zone	IMP EXP BAL	G/ S	2000	2008	2009	2010	2011	2012	2013	2014	2015	2016
Pakistan	IMP	G	10864	42300	31647	37783	43955	44105	44647	47434	43795	46568
Pakistan	EXP	G	9028	20323	17523	21410	25383	24567	25121	24706	22089	20574
	BAL		-1836	-21977	-14124	-16373	-18572	-19537	-19526	-22729	-21706	-25995
Sri Lanka	IMP	G	6281	13953	10049	13512	20268	19102	17973	19652	19039	...
Sri Lanka	EXP	G	5433	8137	7085	8307	10553	9784	10397	11199	10464	...
	BAL		-848	-5816	-2965	-5205	-9715	-9318	-7576	-8452	-8575	...
South-eastern Asia	IMP		379470	939039	728238	955392	1152044	1226074	1244115	1235923	1093828	**1095863**
Asie du Sud-est	EXP		429841	988287	813295	1049884	1232120	1252135	1269377	1287796	1160020	**1148878**
	BAL		50371	49248	85057	94492	80076	26061	25262	51873	66192	**53016**
Brunei Darussalam	IMP	S	1107	2572	2449	3365	3602	3563	3612	3597	3235	...
Brunéi Darussalam	EXP	S	3907	10322	7200	9172	12458	12982	11447	10588	6353	...
	BAL		2801	7750	4751	5808	8855	9418	7835	6990	3118	...
Cambodia	IMP	G	1424	6508	5830	6791	9300	11000	13000	13500	14400	...
Cambodge	EXP	G	1368	4708	4196	5143	6950	8200	9100	10800	11960	...
	BAL		-56	-1800	-1634	-1648	-2350	-2800	-3900	-2700	-2440	...
Indonesia	IMP	G	43075	127538	93786	135323	176881	190992	186351	178182	142691	135549
Indonésie	EXP	G	65404	139606	119646	158074	200587	188516	182659	176341	150358	144291
	BAL		22329	12068	25860	22751	23706	-2476	-3692	-1841	7667	8742
Lao P.Dem.R.	IMP	S	535	1405	1461	2060	2404	3055	3020	3300	3860	...
Rép. dém. populaire lao	EXP	S	330	1085	1053	1746	2190	2271	2264	2650	2340	...
	BAL		-205	-320	-408	-314	-215	-784	-756	-650	-1520	...
Malaysia	IMP	G	81963	156348	123757	164622	187473	196393	205898	208851	176011	168392
Malaisie	EXP	G	98229	199414	157244	198612	228086	227538	228331	233928	199158	189414
	BAL		16266	43066	33487	33990	40613	31145	22434	25077	23147	21022
Myanmar	IMP	G	2371	4256	4348	4760	9019	9151	12043	16227	16844	...
Myanmar	EXP	G	1620	6882	6662	8661	9238	8877	11233	11299	11432	...
	BAL		-751	2626	2314	3901	219	-274	-810	-4928	-5412	...
Philippines	IMP	G	36887	60491	45856	58533	64097	65845	65740	68705	74751	89435
Philippines	EXP	G	37767	49462	38421	51541	48316	52072	56698	62102	58665	57406
	BAL		880	-11030	-7436	-6992	-15781	-13772	-9042	-6603	-16085	-32029
Singapore	IMP	G	134546	319781	245785	310791	365770	379723	373016	366247	296744	291909
Singapour	EXP	G	137806	338176	269832	351867	409503	408393	410250	405295	346638	338082
	BAL		3259	18396	24048	41076	43733	28670	37234	39048	49894	46174
Thailand	IMP	S	61923	179168	134734	185121	229137	250587	249652	227997	201890	195667
Thaïlande	EXP	S	68963	175897	151910	193366	220221	227752	224863	225190	211010	213927
	BAL		7039	-3270	17176	8245	-8916	-22835	-24789	-2807	9120	18260
Timor-Leste	IMP	G	.	258	283	246	319	664	523	547	578	...
Timor-Leste	EXP	G	.	49	35	42	53	77	53	39	45	...
	BAL		.	-209	-248	-205	-266	-587	-470	-508	-533	...
Viet Nam	IMP	G	15638	80714	69949	83779	104041	115101	131260	148770	162825	174207
Viet Nam	EXP	G	14447	62685	57096	71658	94518	115458	132478	149565	162061	176411
	BAL		-1191	-18029	-12853	-12121	-9523	357	1218	795	-764	2204
Western Asia	IMP		**198063**	757727	609870	710884	864312	915188	976582	**990090**	**896807**	**811986**
Asie Occidentale	EXP		**261901**	1054195	740948	922027	1255909	1347118	1401164	**1350629**	**929960**	**773529**
	BAL		**63838**	296468	131078	211143	391596	431929	424582	**360539**	**33153**	**-38456**
Bahrain	IMP	G	4633	10800	7300	9800	12730	14900	13000	13910	9700	...
Bahreïn	EXP	G	6194	17316	11874	15400	19650	20500	17500	20520	11200	...
	BAL		1561	6516	4574	5600	6920	5600	4500	6610	1500	...

Total imports and exports by regions and countries or areas (Table A)

Imports CIF, exports FOB and balance: million U.S. dollars *[cont.]*

Importations et exportations totales par régions et pays ou zones (Tableau A)

Importations CIF, exportations FOB et balance : en millions de dollars E.-U. *[suite]*

Country or Area - Pays ou Zone	IMP EXP BAL	G/ S	2000	2008	2009	2010	2011	2012	2013	2014	2015	2016
Cyprus	IMP	G	3846	10873	7937	8647	8791	7379	6419	6828	5667	6604
Chypre	EXP	G	951	1755	1352	1507	1956	1828	2136	1924	1931	1921
	BAL		-2895	-9118	-6585	-7139	-6835	-5551	-4283	-4904	-3736	-4683
Iraq	IMP		...	33000	37000	43915	49000	57000	61000	59000	52000	...
Iraq	EXP		...	61273	41929	52483	83300	94400	89550	88968	49320	...
	BAL		...	28273	4929	8567	34300	37400	28550	29968	-2680	...
Israel[17]	IMP	S	31404	67656	49278	61209	75830	75392	74861	75483	64990	68879
Israël[17]	EXP	S	31404	60825	47934	58392	67648	63191	66607	68553	63607	60401
	BAL		0	-6831	-1344	-2817	-8182	-12201	-8254	-6931	-1382	-8478
Jordan	IMP	S	4597	16764	14534	15085	18463	20691	21701	22952	20016	19479
Jordanie	EXP	S	1899	7788	6531	7023	7964	7926	7896	8376	7849	7509
	BAL		-2698	-8976	-8002	-8062	-10499	-12765	-13804	-14576	-12166	-11970
Kuwait	IMP	S	7157	24840	19891	22691	25144	27259	29299	31019	30960	30825
Koweït	EXP	S	19434	87538	54012	62698	102731	114513	114117	100818	54119	46238
	BAL		12278	62699	34121	40007	77587	87254	84817	69798	23159	15413
Lebanon	IMP	S	6230	16754	16574	18460	20165	21287	21236	20494	18069	18705
Liban	EXP	S	715	4454	4187	5021	4267	4485	4059	4548	2952	2977
	BAL		-5515	-12300	-12387	-13439	-15898	-16802	-17176	-15945	-15116	-15729
Oman	IMP	G	5040	22925	17865	19775	23620	29447	34333	29432	29007	...
Oman	EXP	G	11319	37719	28053	36601	47092	53174	56429	52834	34734	...
	BAL		6279	14795	10188	16827	23472	23727	22096	23402	5727	...
Qatar	IMP	S	3252	27900	24922	23240	22333	25223	27038	30471	32611	32058
Qatar	EXP	S	11594	67307	48007	74800	114448	132985	136855	131261	77290	57254
	BAL		8342	39407	23085	51560	92115	107761	109817	100789	44679	25196
Saudi Arabia	IMP	G	30197	115133	95544	106864	131587	155592	168155	173908	174785	135904
Arabie saoudite	EXP	G	77480	313427	192296	251147	364699	388371	375872	342481	203652	182329
	BAL		47283	198294	96752	144283	233112	232779	207718	168573	28868	46426
State of Palestine	IMP	G	2383	3466	3601	3959	4374	4697	4580	5055	4942	5058
État de Palestine	EXP	G	401	558	518	576	746	782	839	865	912	929
	BAL		-1982	-2908	-3082	-3383	-3628	-3915	-3740	-4190	-4030	-4128
Syrian Arab Rep.	IMP	S	4055	18105	15291	16950	16400	7800	5800	...	...	...
République arabe syrienne	EXP	S	4674	15410	10855	14000	10700	4000	3000	...	...	...
	BAL		620	-2695	-4436	-2950	-5700	-3800	-2800	...	...	...
Turkey	IMP	S	54503	201964	140928	185544	240842	236545	251661	242177	207234	198484
Turquie	EXP	S	27775	132027	102143	113883	134907	152462	151803	157614	143839	142790
	BAL		-26728	-69937	-38785	-71661	-105935	-84083	-99858	-84563	-63395	-55694
United Arab Emirates	IMP	S	35009	177000	150000	165000	205000	220000	245000	262000	230000	...
Emirats arabes unis	EXP	S	49835	239213	185000	220000	285000	300000	365000	359000	265000	...
	BAL		14827	62213	35000	55000	80000	80000	120000	97000	35000	...
Yemen	IMP	S	2327	10548	9206	9746	10034	11975	12500	...	...	...
Yémen	EXP	S	3795	7584	6256	8497	10801	8500	9500	...	...	...
	BAL		1469	-2964	-2949	-1249	766	-3475	-3000	...	...	...
Oceania	IMP		**6927**	**16869**	**14570**	**16763**	**19032**	**19497**	**21643**	**22552**	**21488**	**21311**
Océanie	EXP		**5110**	**10643**	**8545**	**10492**	**12342**	**11799**	**11208**	**14513**	**13605**	**12073**
	BAL		**-1818**	**-6226**	**-6025**	**-6270**	**-6690**	**-7698**	**-10435**	**-8039**	**-7882**	**-9238**
American Samoa[18]	IMP	S	506	655	547	434	463	514	479	611	675	675
Samoa américaines[18]	EXP	S	346	592	491	316	278	419	386	346	379	388
	BAL		-160	-63	-56	-118	-185	-96	-92	-265	-297	-288

Total imports and exports by regions and countries or areas (Table A)

Imports CIF, exports FOB and balance: million U.S. dollars *[cont.]*

Importations et exportations totales par régions et pays ou zones (Tableau A)

Importations CIF, exportations FOB et balance : en millions de dollars E.-U. *[suite]*

Country or Area - Pays ou Zone	IMP EXP BAL	G/S	2000	2008	2009	2010	2011	2012	2013	2014	2015	2016
Cook Islands	IMP	G	50	105	82	91	110	112	116	121	110	107
Iles Cook	EXP	G	9	4	3	5	3	5	11	18	14	13
	BAL		-41	-101	-79	-85	-107	-106	-105	-103	-96	-93
Fiji	IMP	G	857	2265	1551	1817	2184	2252	2823	2653	2268	2316
Fidji	EXP	G	539	922	672	841	1075	1219	1149	1219	982	926
	BAL		-318	-1343	-880	-976	-1109	-1034	-1674	-1434	-1286	-1390
French Polynesia	IMP	S	905	2187	1732	1740	1796	1706	1801	1762	1527	1491
Polynésie française	EXP	S	200	195	148	153	168	139	152	170	130	173
	BAL		-705	-1991	-1584	-1587	-1628	-1567	-1649	-1592	-1397	-1319
Guam	IMP	G	...	649	635	698	708	693	687	707	705	...
Guam	EXP	G	...	105	51	46	55	46	45	41	40	33
	BAL		...	-544	-584	-652	-653	-647	-642	-666	-666	...
Kiribati	IMP	S	39	75	67	73	92	100	112	95	100	147
Kiribati	EXP	S	4	8	6	4	9	6	8	5	9	9
	BAL		-36	-68	-61	-69	-83	-94	-105	-90	-91	-138
Marshall Islands	IMP	G	55	...	...	...	...	...	...	...	...	...
Iles Marshall	EXP	G	9	...	...	...	...	...	...	...	...	...
	BAL		-46	...	...	...	...	...	...	...	...	...
Micronesia[3]	IMP	S	...	160	171	168	188	194	188	...	...	...
Micronésie[3]	EXP	S	...	21	18	23	43	52	35	...	...	...
	BAL		...	-139	-153	-145	-145	-142	-153	...	...	...
New Caledonia	IMP	G	922	3233	2574	3312	3698	3245	3240	3323	2715	2422
Nouvelle-Calédonie	EXP	G	606	1300	993	1493	1661	1321	1196	1565	1314	1344
	BAL		-317	-1933	-1581	-1820	-2037	-1923	-2044	-1758	-1402	-1079
Niue	IMP	G	2	8	6	...	...	...	...	...	...	...
Nioué	EXP	G	0	0	...	...	...	...	...	...	...	...
	BAL		-2	-8	...	...	...	...	...	...	...	...
Palau	IMP	G	127	134	104	117	137	155	162	194	177	...
Palaos	EXP	G	10	12	8	12	13	15	14	19	15	...
	BAL		-117	-122	-95	-105	-125	-140	-148	-175	-162	...
Papua New Guinea	IMP	G	1151	3547	3198	3950	4887	5500	...	...	...	...
Papouasie-Nouvelle-Guinée	EXP	G	2068	5714	4404	5742	6908	6328	5951	8790	8433	...
	BAL		917	2167	1206	1792	2021	828	...	...	...	...
Samoa	IMP	G	90	249	204	278	319	308	326	384	334	350
Samoa	EXP	G	14	11	12	13	17	34	24	46	53	56
	BAL		-76	-238	-193	-264	-302	-274	-302	-339	-281	-294
Solomon Islands	IMP	S	92	308	261	398	473	497	537	499	467	...
Iles Salomon	EXP	S	69	212	160	217	411	488	487	458	401	...
	BAL		-23	-96	-101	-181	-63	-9	-50	-41	-66	...
Tonga	IMP	G	69	168	145	159	193	199	198	218	206	...
Tonga	EXP	G	9	10	8	8	17	17	22	23	...	...
	BAL		-60	-158	-137	-151	-176	-182	-176	-196	...	...
Tuvalu	IMP	G	5	...	...	...	...	...	...	...	...	...
Tuvalu	EXP	G	0	...	...	...	...	...	...	...	...	...
	BAL		-5	...	...	...	...	...	...	...	...	...
Vanuatu	IMP	G	87	314	294	285	305	296	313	313	367	383
Vanuatu	EXP	G	26	57	57	49	67	55	39	63	39	50
	BAL		-61	-257	-237	-237	-238	-241	-275	-250	-328	-332

Total imports and exports by regions and countries or areas (Table A)

Imports CIF, exports FOB and balance: million U.S. dollars *[cont.]*

Importations et exportations totales par régions et pays ou zones (Tableau A)

Importations CIF, exportations FOB et balance : en millions de dollars E.-U. *[suite]*

Country or Area - Pays ou Zone	IMP EXP BAL	G/ S	2000	2008	2009	2010	2011	2012	2013	2014	2015	2016
Additional Country Groupings												
ANCOM	IMP		24447	91703	73543	95679	124040	133533	138112	143250	122386	104720
ANCOM	EXP		26154	95160	78635	99108	133335	141060	137457	132311	96612	91772
	BAL		1707	3457	5092	3428	9295	7527	-655	-10939	-25774	-12948
APEC	IMP		3308311	7360553	5697123	7351743	8784701	9105548	9203269	9282072	8173044	7993103
CEAP	EXP		3110918	7050525	5635208	7232832	8473488	8701592	8865543	9063865	8288461	8013539
	BAL		-197393	-310028	-61915	-118911	-311212	-403956	-337726	-218207	115418	20436
ASEAN	IMP		379470	938781	727955	955146	1151725	1225410	1243592	1235376	1093250	1095216
ANASE	EXP		429841	988238	813260	1049842	1232067	1252058	1269324	1287757	1159975	1148784
	BAL		50371	49457	85305	94696	80342	26648	25732	52381	66725	53568
CACM	IMP		21293	51085	38353	43381	52736	55530	55219	56369	55651	57127
MCAC	EXP		13442	23921	20040	22186	26730	28202	27345	28366	28086	31787
	BAL		-7850	-27164	-18313	-21194	-26006	-27328	-27873	-28003	-27564	-25339
CARICOM	IMP		13681	30362	23675	25146	31253	31331	30724	31029	26629	23409
CARICOM	EXP		8142	25852	14987	17734	22858	21697	20882	19098	13856	10721
	BAL		-5539	-4510	-8688	-7412	-8396	-9634	-9842	-11931	-12773	-12688
COMESA	IMP		34643	117472	111528	128282	141507	169824	172535	169211	164632	145658
COMESA	EXP		27213	127626	93125	116547	97859	132197	119048	92038	69267	63582
	BAL		-7431	10154	-18404	-11735	-43648	-37627	-53487	-77173	-95365	-82076
ECOWAS	IMP		20020	80607	65541	82057	107364	83276	96735	97538	80346	77783
CEDEAO	EXP		29126	105691	80399	111184	150842	150582	153537	149233	140869	135024
	BAL		9107	25085	14858	29127	43478	67306	56801	51694	60523	57241
EMCCA	IMP		4010	17587	17709	19453	24659	24208	26281	27066	25216	24908
CEMAC	EXP		8414	43598	26928	34237	44037	42770	42451	38666	26444	18654
	BAL		4404	26011	9219	14784	19379	18562	16170	11600	1227	-6254
LAIA	IMP		329864	794835	596090	767215	941892	966750	1014162	1007806	896244	801378
ALAI	EXP		331178	834748	642704	817624	1018744	1031649	1037978	1007898	860847	823093
	BAL		1314	39913	46615	50410	76852	64899	23816	92	-35397	21715
LDCs	IMP		41556	155817	150033	165200	202524	225789	238487	253441	242004	221478
PMA	EXP		33318	164917	123348	154828	196464	205544	206818	199510	170869	154132
	BAL		-8237	9101	-26685	-10372	-6060	-20245	-31669	-53931	-71135	-67346
MERCOSUR	IMP		107498	312450	231068	297650	380478	371105	403391	382447	307557	242462
MERCOSUR	EXP		118597	383437	282077	351785	457001	441870	443446	403128	312435	285877
	BAL		11099	70987	51010	54135	76522	70765	40055	20680	4878	43415
NAFTA	IMP		1672611	2888878	2160932	2662781	3067992	3169689	3172187	3275668	3063279	3040219
ALENA	EXP		1224927	2035686	1599725	1964109	2281991	2371433	2417554	2497412	2295294	2218066
	BAL		-447684	-853191	-561207	-698672	-786001	-798257	-754632	-778256	-767985	-822153
OECD	IMP		4913774	10841751	8144329	9616932	11309257	11084617	11131371	11305854	9939139	9829732
OCDE	EXP		4537544	9801919	7643349	8973189	10449685	10236805	10389124	10571600	9374139	9317027
	BAL		-376231	-1039832	-500980	-643742	-859572	-847812	-742246	-734254	-565000	-512705
OPEC	IMP		138958	618390	542193	596128	703790	743728	810389	837729	747302	617878
OPEP	EXP		300897	1291980	857066	1092692	1479090	1572020	1575636	1471220	958142	753972
	BAL		161940	673590	314873	496564	775300	828293	765246	633491	210840	136094
EU28	IMP		2441663	6127131	4603680	5204980	6088218	5720220	5822967	5929451	5125198	5099704
UE28	EXP		2394652	5831316	4519067	5074631	5948631	5683539	5880577	6006538	5245170	5258107
	BAL		-47011	-295815	-84613	-130349	-139587	-36680	57610	77087	119972	158404

Total imports and exports by regions and countries or areas (Table A)
Imports CIF, exports FOB and balance: million U.S. dollars *[cont.]*

Importations et exportations totales par régions et pays ou zones (Tableau A)
Importations CIF, exportations FOB et balance : en millions de dollars E.-U. *[suite]*

Country or Area - Pays ou Zone	IMP EXP BAL	G/S	2000	2008	2009	2010	2011	2012	2013	2014	2015	2016
Extra-EU28[19,20] Extra-UE28[19,20]	IMP		913310	2336609	1721874	2029009	2405295	2311903	2234492	2233120	1918180	1889713
	EXP		781270	1928718	1527320	1791433	2161865	2162563	2305992	2259963	1993883	1930741
	BAL		-132040	-407891	-194554	-237576	-243430	-149340	71500	26843	75703	41028
Memorandum Items												
World excluding intra-EU28 trade Monde excl. le intra-UE28 com.	IMP		**4989190**	**12435775**	**9609480**	**11974639**	**14415368**	**14739311**	**14871697**	**14938220**	**13090417**	**12617696**
	EXP		**4743311**	**12100601**	**9417693**	**11833299**	**14276472**	**14575926**	**14904529**	**14924061**	**13024616**	**12409882**
	BAL		**-245879**	**-335175**	**-191787**	**-141340**	**-138896**	**-163384**	**32832**	**-14159**	**-65801**	**-207814**
World excluding intra-EU28 trade as percent of World Monde excl. le intra-UE28 com.comme pour cent du Monde	IMP		**77**	**77**	**77**	**79**	**80**	**81**	**81**	**80**	**80**	**80**
	EXP		**75**	**76**	**76**	**78**	**79**	**81**	**81**	**80**	**80**	**79**

Total imports and exports by regions and countries or areas (Table A)

Imports CIF, exports FOB and balance: million U.S. dollars *[cont.]*

Importations et exportations totales par régions et pays ou zones (Tableau A)

Importations CIF, exportations FOB, et balance: en millions de dollars E.-U. *[suite]*

General note:

Table A is based on data as available at the end of October 2017. An earlier version of this table has been published in Volume I of the 2016 ITSY which has been produced earlier this year. The totals of imports and exports presented in world trade table A and D are not necessarily identical as table A is mainly based on data of the IMF's International Financial Statistics (IFS) which is a different data collection system with different aims, procedures, timetable and sources for update and maintenance than UN Comtrade on which table D is based (see the introduction for details). Nevertheless, discrepancies between both tables are in general minor and usually do not affect the overall information provided. A systematic comparison of the figures from both sources (which includes the description of known and relevant conceptual differences) is available at http://unstats.un.org/unsd/trade/data/tables.asp#annual. Overall, the discrepancies in the world total or world aggregate of exports in table A and table D is around 1.0 percent for all years shown, which is minor, given the differences between the two sources.

Column "G/S" indicates the trade system: G = General Trade System; S = Special Trade System. For further information on sources and presentation of table A as well as for a brief table description please see the introduction.

1 This classification is intended for statistical convenience and does not, necessarily, express a judgement about the stage reached by a particular country in the development process.
2 Developed Economies of America, Europe, and the Asia-Pacific region.
3 Imports FOB.
4 Including the trade of the U.S. Virgin Islands and Puerto Rico but excluding shipments of merchandise between the United States and its other possessions (Guam and American Samoa). Data include imports and exports of non-monetary gold.
5 Beginning 2006, data for Serbia and Montenegro is reported separately.
6 Prior to 2008, special trade.
7 Imports exclude petroleum imported without stated value. Exports cover domestic exports.
8 Year ending 31 March of the following year.
9 Exports include gold.
10 Trade statistics exclude certain oil and chemical products.
11 Export and import values exclude trade in the processing zone.

Remarque générale:

Tableau A est basé sur les données telles que disponible fin octobre 2016. Une version antérieure de ce tableau est publiée dans le volume I de l'annuaire 2016 ITSY qui a été produit plus tôt cette année. Les importations et exportations totales présentées dans les tableaux A et D ne sont pas nécessairement identiques du fait que le tableau A est basé principalement sur les données des Statistiques Financières Internationales (IFS) du FMI qui est un différent système de collecte des données avec des objectifs, des procédures, un calendrier et des sources de mise à jour et de maintenance différents de ceux de UN Comtrade sur lequel le tableau D est basé (voir l'introduction pour les détails). Toutefois, les écarts entre les deux tableaux sont en général mineurs et n'affectent pas substantiellement l'information fournie. Une comparaison systématique des données de ces deux sources (incluant une description des différences conceptuelles pertinentes connues) est disponible à http://unstats.un.org/unsd/trade/data/tables.asp#annual. En général, la différence entre les totaux des exportations mondiales présentés dans les tableaux A et D est d'environ 1,0 pour cent pour chacune des années publiées, ce qui est mineur étant donné les différences entre les deux sources.

La colonne "G/S" indique le système commercial : G=Système du Commerce Général ; S= Système du Commerce Spécial. Pour plus d'information sur les sources et la présentation du tableau A ainsi qu'une brève description, se il vous plaît se référer à l'introduction.

1 Cette classification est utilisée pour plus de commodité dans la présentation des statistiques et n'implique pas nécessairement un jugement quant au stade de développement auquel est parvenu un pays donné.
2 Économies développées de l'Amérique, de l'Europe, et de la région Asie-Pacifique.
3 Importations FOB.
4 Y compris le commerce des Iles Vierges américaines et de Porto Rico mais non compris les échanges de marchandise, entre les Etats-Unis et leurs autres possessions (Guam et Samoa américaines). Les données comprennent les importations et exportations d'or non-monétaire.
5 Depuis début 2006, les données relatives à la Serbie et au Monténégro sont déclarées séparément.
6 Avant 2008, commerce special.
7 Non compris le pétrole brute dont la valeur des importations ne sont pas stipulée. Les exportations sont les exportations d'intérieur.
8 Année finissant le 31 mars de l'année suivante.
9 Les exportations comprennent l'or.
10 Les statistiques commerciales font exclusion de certains produits pétroliers et chimiques.
11 Les valeurs à l'exportation et à l'importation excluent le commerce de la zone de transformation.

Total imports and exports by regions and countries or areas (Table A)

Imports CIF, exports FOB and balance: million U.S. dollars *[cont.]*

Importations et exportations totales par régions et pays ou zones (Tableau A)

Importations CIF, exportations FOB, et balance: en millions de dollars E.-U. *[suite]*

12 The Netherlands Antilles was dissolved on October 10, 2010. Beginning 2011, data are reported separately for Curaçao, Sint Maarten (Dutch part), Bonaire, Saint Eustatius and Saba.

13 Trade data include maquiladoras and exclude goods from customs-bonded warehouses. Total exports include revaluation and exports of silver.

14 Excluding military goods, fissionable materials, bunkers, ships, and aircraft.

15 Data include oil and gas.The value of oil exports and total exports are rough estimates based on information published in various petroleum industry journals.

16 Year ending 20 March of the year stated.

17 Imports and exports net of returned goods. The figures also exclude Judea and Samaria and the Gaza area.

18 Year ending 30 September of the years stated.

19 Excluding intra-EU trade.

20 In the year 2000, the trade values refer to extra-EU27.

12 Les Antilles néerlandaises ont été dissoutes le 10 Octobre 2010. A partir de 2011, les données sont présentées séparément pour Curaçao, Saint-Martin (partie néerlandaise), Bonaire, Saint-Eustache et Saba.

13 Les statistiques du commerce extérieur comprennent maquiladoras et ne comprennent pas les marchandises provenant des entrepôts en douane. Les exportations comprennent la réévaluation et les données sur les exportations d'argent.

14 À l'exclusion des marchandises militaires, des matières fissibles, des soutes, des bateaux, et de l'avion.

15 Les données comprennent le pétrole et le gaz. La valeur des exportations de pétrole et des exportations totales sont des évaluations grossières basées sur l'information publiée à divers journaux d'industrie de pétrole.

16 Année finissant le 20 mars de l'année indiquée.

17 Importations et exportations nets, ne comprennant pas les marchandises retournées. Sont également exclues les données de la Judée et de Samaria et ainsi que la zone de Gaza.

18 Année finissant le 30 septembre de l'année indiquée.

19 Non compris le commerce d'intra-UE.

20 En l'année 2000, les valeurs du commerce se réfèrent à extra-UE27.

Total imports and exports by countries and areas (Table B)

Imports CIF, exports FOB and balance: million of national currency

Importations et exportations totales par pays ou zone (Tableau B)

Importations CIF, exportations FOB et balance : en millions de monnaie nationale

Country or Area - Pays ou Zone	IMP EXP BAL	G/S	2000	2008	2009	2010	2011	2012	2013	2014	2015	2016
Albania	IMP	S	157109	439894	428839	477768	544004	528490	517376	552280	544605	579248
Albanie	EXP	S	37037	112572	104515	161548	196897	213030	246397	255758	243181	243492
leks	BAL		-120072	-327322	-324324	-316220	-347107	-315460	-270979	-296522	-301424	-335756
Algeria	IMP	S	690426	2549100	2857890	2991940	3446050	3906680	4358250	4699100	5188570	5114990
Algérie	EXP	S	1657220	5108650	3286510	4297730	5371280	5631780	5198500	4920260	3530070	3251010
dinars	BAL		966794	2559550	428620	1305790	1925230	1725100	840250	221160	-1658500	-1863980
Andorra	IMP	G	1111	1314	1138	1143	1149	1086	1094	1175	1169	1226
Andorre	EXP	G	49	65	46	41	55	53	74	74	81	91
euros	BAL		-1062	-1248	-1093	-1102	-1094	-1032	-1019	-1101	-1088	-1136
Anguilla[1]	IMP	G	269	734	456	425	414	405	391	409	427	...
Anguilla[1]	EXP	G	12	31	62	34	44	22	10	11	4	...
EC dollars	BAL		-257	-703	-394	-391	-370	-382	-381	-399	-423	...
Australia[4]	IMP	G	116840	225666	200393	209892	227028	241985	241005	252298	266757	254010
Australie[4]	EXP	G	110464	222364	196091	230820	263000	248002	262308	267323	249612	256713
dollars	BAL		-6376	-3302	-4302	20928	35972	6017	21303	15025	-17145	2703
Austria	IMP	S	74935	119567	97573	113652	131008	131982	129962	128961	133529	135593
Autriche	EXP	S	69692	117527	93739	109373	121774	123544	125412	127365	131538	131218
euros	BAL		-5243	-2040	-3834	-4279	-9234	-8438	-4550	-1596	-1991	-4375
Bahamas[2]	IMP	G	2074	2354	2699	2887	3411	3658	3366	3791	3162	...
Bahamas[2]	EXP	G	576	560	585	621	927	829	812	689	449	...
dollars	BAL		-1498	-1794	-2114	-2265	-2484	-2829	-2554	-3101	-2713	...
Bangladesh	IMP	G	436450	1541410	1424360	1817430	2519300	3144270	2379400	2735996	3077970	3236890
Bangladesh	EXP	G	249860	807824	859045	989345	1468340	2268000	1749090	1635145	2332550	2368760
taka	BAL		-186590	-733586	-565315	-828085	-1050960	-876270	-630310	-1100851	-745420	-868130
Barbados	IMP	G	2312	3757	2941	3124	3610	3611	3518	3478	3236	3243
Barbade	EXP	G	545	891	737	858	929	1140	926	949	966	1034
dollars	BAL		-1767	-2866	-2204	-2266	-2680	-2472	-2592	-2529	-2270	-2209
Belgium	IMP	S	192180	316330	254370	295080	335460	341760	338300	341480	338640	339780
Belgique	EXP	S	203940	319750	266240	306990	341940	347330	351950	356160	358770	363250
euros	BAL		11760	3420	11870	11910	6480	5570	13650	14680	20130	23470
Benin[3]	IMP	G	400640	1025190	729900	739000	1274186	1123022	1182950	1716240	1406340	1290660
Bénin[3]	EXP	G	279400	574200	199300	216900	661661	716846	308745	898033	369133	218323
CFA francs	BAL		-121240	-450990	-530600	-522100	-612525	-406176	-874205	-818207	-1037207	-1072337
Bhutan	IMP	G	10556	23495	25650	39084	48698	53090	53273	56885	68037	67360
Bhoutan	EXP	G	5720	22591	23974	29324	31486	28600	31853	35585	35229	35258
ngultrum	BAL		-4835	-905	-1676	-9760	-17212	-24490	-21420	-21300	-32808	-32102
Bosnia and Herzegovina	IMP	S	6583	16287	12324	13611	15514	15253	15170	16199	15852	16139
Bosnie-Herzégovine	EXP	S	2265	6714	5510	7097	8218	7858	8380	8684	8987	9417
marka	BAL		-4318	-9573	-6815	-6514	-7296	-7395	-6790	-7516	-6865	-6723
Botswana	IMP	G	10617	35575	33830	38430	49819	62113	70725	72396	73163	66613
Botswana	EXP	G	13647	33799	24726	31884	39981	45722	66392	76208	63426	80263
pula	BAL		3031	-1777	-9104	-6546	-9838	-16391	-4333	3813	-9737	13651
Brunei Darussalam	IMP	S	1908	3647	3570	4582	4528	4455	4521	4556	4448	...
Brunéi Darussalam	EXP	S	6734	14593	10477	12477	15678	16221	14309	13398	8715	...
dollars	BAL		4826	10945	6908	7896	11150	11766	9788	8842	4267	...
Bulgaria	IMP	S	13857	49079	33006	37640	45779	49794	50594	51206	50786	50910
Bulgarie	EXP	S	10247	29736	22882	30435	39634	40623	43447	45527	45449	46100
leva	BAL		-3610	-19343	-10124	-7205	-6145	-9171	-7147	-5679	-5337	-4811

Total imports and exports by countries and areas (Table B)

Imports CIF, exports FOB and balance: million of national currency *[cont.]*

Importations et exportations totales par pays ou zone (Tableau B)

Importations CIF, exportations FOB et balance : en millions de monnaie nationale *[suite]*

Country or Area - Pays ou Zone	IMP EXP BAL	G/ S	2000	2008	2009	2010	2011	2012	2013	2014	2015	2016
Burkina Faso[3]	IMP	G	435018	903555	977000	1067200	1214100	1747100	2057000	1654200	1764500	...
Burkina Faso[3]	EXP	G	148803	310400	411500	650200	1110400	1111500	1162600	1226100	1286300	...
CFA francs	BAL		-286215	-593155	-565500	-417000	-103700	-635600	-894400	-428100	-478200	...
Burundi	IMP	G	106059	477345	494828	626742	952852	1084050	1261190	1188990	1135870	1215750
Burundi	EXP	G	35223	64301	76330	123698	154405	192156	153896	191411	178544	183814
francs	BAL		-70836	-413044	-418498	-503044	-798447	-891894	-1107294	-997579	-957326	-1031936
Cabo Verde	IMP	G	27519	62191	56214	61836	75146	65711	60201	64131	60059	66384
Cabo Verde	EXP	G	1261	2668	2946	3921	5397	4566	5740	6695	6646	5962
escudos	BAL		-26258	-59523	-53268	-57915	-69749	-61145	-54461	-57436	-53413	-60422
Cameroon[3]	IMP	S	1060100	2563720	2086750	2502960	3209780	3325170	3285080	3747280	3578990	3088449
Cameroun[3]	EXP	S	1305100	2358590	1667120	1924210	2133610	2340780	2230680	2557860	2403372	1960297
CFA francs	BAL		245000	-205130	-419630	-578750	-1076170	-984390	-1054400	-1189420	-1175618	-1128152
Canada[4]	IMP	G	354728	433999	365359	403701	446442	462026	475686	512200	536296	533357
Canada[4]	EXP	G	410994	483488	357373	398857	447502	454416	472025	526773	524049	517150
dollars	BAL		56266	49489	-7986	-4844	1060	-7610	-3661	14573	-12247	-16207
Cayman Islands	IMP	G	575	899	745	690	760	759	775	814	831	854
Îles Caïmanes	EXP	G	3	12	16	11	18	17	25	22	82	74
dollars	BAL		-572	-886	-729	-679	-741	-742	-749	-793	-749	-781
Cent. Afr. Rep.[3]	IMP	G	83301	134342	128100	120800	130500	140800	123471	...	...	...
Rép. centrafricaine[3]	EXP	G	114628	67171	38100	45000	54600	57300	69144	...	...	...
CFA francs	BAL		31327	-67171	-90000	-75800	-75900	-83500	-54327	...	...	...
Chad[3]	IMP	S	342260	850830	1086030	1238190	1274186	1325178	1481657	1723289	1299385	...
Tchad[3]	EXP	S	166725	1939000	1251290	1683940	2170835	1987768	2222486	2066929	1712673	...
CFA francs	BAL		-175535	1088170	165260	445750	896649	662589	740829	343640	413288	...
Comoros	IMP	G	22961	58775	60204	70577	98027	114855	105568	...	...	...
Comores	EXP	G	7476	3023	5666	6686	8913	9575	9260	...	...	...
francs	BAL		-15485	-55752	-54538	-63891	-89114	-105280	-96308	...	...	...
Cote d'Ivoire[3]	IMP	S	1770500	3530350	3279800	3881200	3174000	4987000	6227900	5332910	5857940	4968570
Côte d'Ivoire[3]	EXP	S	2573000	4652700	4846700	5063200	5146700	5538300	6754800	6227560	7038210	6335500
CFA francs	BAL		802500	1122350	1566900	1182000	1972700	551300	526900	894650	1180270	1366930
Cuba	IMP	S	3363	13194	...	...	...	...	...	...	...	...
Cuba	EXP	S	1219	3407	...	...	...	...	...	...	...	...
pesos	BAL		-2144	-9787	...	...	...	...	...	...	...	...
Cyprus[5]	IMP	G	2402	7367	5692	6517	6311	5742	4830	5145	5112	5960
Chypre[5]	EXP	G	590	1190	970	1137	1404	1422	1609	1443	1736	1737
euros	BAL		-1812	-6176	-4721	-5381	-4907	-4320	-3221	-3701	-3375	-4223
Czechia	IMP	S	1309570	2406490	1989040	2411560	2687560	2766890	2823480	3199630	3477000	3489410
Tchéquie	EXP	S	1121100	2473740	2138620	2532800	2878690	3072600	3174700	3628830	3883250	3975960
koruny	BAL		-188470	67250	149580	121240	191130	305710	351220	429200	406250	486550
Denmark	IMP	G	358871	553294	429697	467473	517249	528678	544438	555915	573768	572494
Danemark	EXP	G	408239	586893	490066	538321	600069	613324	620002	617867	636418	634753
kroner	BAL		49368	33599	60369	70848	82820	84646	75564	61952	62650	62259
Djibouti	IMP	G	36699	101940	80101	74643	90741	103078	99524	142710	158186	...
Djibouti	EXP	G	5616	12219	13750	17772	16475	16883	21327	22955	23423	...
francs	BAL		-31083	-89722	-66351	-56871	-74266	-86195	-78197	-119755	-134763	...
Dominica	IMP	S	401	667	608	604	610	562	548	622	578	578
Dominique	EXP	S	145	108	92	99	83	91	96	97	82	163
EC dollars	BAL		-256	-559	-516	-505	-527	-471	-452	-525	-496	-415

Total imports and exports by countries and areas (Table B)

Imports CIF, exports FOB and balance: million of national currency *[cont.]*

Importations et exportations totales par pays ou zone (Tableau B)

Importations CIF, exportations FOB et balance : en millions de monnaie nationale *[suite]*

Country or Area - Pays ou Zone	IMP EXP BAL	G/ S	2000	2008	2009	2010	2011	2012	2013	2014	2015	2016
Equatorial Guinea[3]	IMP	G	321101	1750920	2455370	2823080	2828600	3061470	3457200	3203549	...	...
Guinée équatoriale[3]	EXP	G	781038	7120100	4296900	4952770	6364350	7908810	6914400	5717102	...	...
CFA francs	BAL		459937	5369180	1841530	2129690	3535750	4847340	3457200	2513553	...	...
Estonia[6]	IMP	S	72214	170488	113780	144994	12727	13848	13665	13783	13084	13507
Estonie[6]	EXP	S	53900	132483	101412	136915	12004	12518	12269	12016	11627	11886
euros	BAL		-18314	-38005	-12368	-8079	-723	-1330	-1395	-1767	-1458	-1621
Ethiopia	IMP	G	10370	62960	80515	108956	133025	190845	208522	261559	330745	353001
Ethiopie	EXP	G	3959	13550	15089	26115	44297	54772	56691	62948	60671	60526
birr	BAL		-6411	-49410	-65426	-82841	-88728	-136073	-151831	-198611	-270074	-292475
Extra-EU28[7,8]	IMP		992695	1585231	1235636	1532089	1728314	1798553	1682566	1680541	1729207	1707748
Extra-UE28[7,8]	EXP		849740	1309147	1093962	1353195	1554252	1683051	1737052	1702669	1799154	1745479
euros	BAL		-142956	-276084	-141675	-178894	-174062	-115502	54485	22128	69948	37731
Fiji	IMP	G	1822	3601	3022	3465	3914	4031	5199	5013	4757	4839
Fidji	EXP	G	1155	1471	1310	1605	1925	2182	2120	2302	2059	1937
dollars	BAL		-667	-2130	-1712	-1859	-1989	-1849	-3079	-2710	-2698	-2903
Finland	IMP	S	36837	62402	43654	51899	60537	59519	58407	57665	54494	54965
Finlande	EXP	S	49485	65581	45064	52439	56854	56878	56047	55909	53881	51873
euros	BAL		12647	3179	1410	540	-3683	-2641	-2360	-1756	-613	-3092
France	IMP	S	337489	485613	402066	459207	512346	518837	507166	504407	509248	507677
France	EXP	S	324256	412968	341585	390002	420687	434398	428186	428312	446216	442406
euros	BAL		-13233	-72645	-60481	-69205	-91659	-84439	-78980	-76095	-63032	-65271
Gabon[3]	IMP	S	708000	1160260	1179200	1475500	1730900	1850500	1916070	1542163	1795256	...
Gabon[3]	EXP	S	1852560	4256840	2532700	4262000	4605000	3936600	4703770	4419132	3001005	...
CFA francs	BAL		1144560	3096580	1353500	2786500	2874100	2086100	2787700	2876969	1205749	...
Gambia	IMP	G	2391	7151	8098	8404	9899	12159	12549	16072	...	...
Gambie	EXP	G	192	303	400	420	334	588	413	670	...	...
dalasis	BAL		-2199	-6847	-7699	-7983	-9565	-11571	-12136	-15402	...	...
Germany	IMP	S	538311	805842	664615	797098	902524	905926	898163	910145	949243	954825
Allemagne	EXP	S	597441	984139	803312	951959	1061230	1095770	1093110	1123750	1193550	1206860
euros	BAL		59130	178297	138697	154861	158706	189844	194947	213605	244307	252035
Ghana	IMP	G	1617	10863	11336	15799	19065	24421	25777	39459	46830	...
Ghana	EXP	G	732	5947	8224	11390	19325	21501	26740	36549	35798	...
cedis	BAL		-885	-4916	-3112	-4409	260	-2920	963	-2910	-11032	...
Gibraltar	IMP		318	420	434	406	439	382	478	428	510	...
Gibraltar	EXP		84	154	170	167	154	159	178	162	193	...
pounds	BAL		-234	-266	-264	-239	-285	-223	-300	-266	-317	...
Grenada[1]	IMP	S	664	1019	790	859	906	921	995	917	928	944
Grenade[1]	EXP	S	211	82	79	61	76	82	87	89	83	70
EC dollars	BAL		-453	-937	-712	-798	-830	-839	-907	-828	-845	-874
Guyana	IMP	S	106113	267225	236700	284494	359765	408065	359423	367465	320075	...
Guyana	EXP	S	91521	161819	155511	179122	227778	289278	283431	239472	227150	...
dollars	BAL		-14593	-105406	-81189	-105372	-131987	-118787	-75992	-127993	-92925	...
Haiti	IMP	G	21936	90553	87498	125207	122361	132961	147903	168790	177836	...
Haïti	EXP	G	6725	18626	23741	23045	31077	34197	38485	43002	51761	...
gourdes	BAL		-15211	-71927	-63756	-102162	-91285	-98764	-109418	-125788	-126075	...
Hungary	IMP	S	9064050	18102100	15634900	18205700	20283900	21211900	22154000	24143600	25348600	25711100
Hongrie	EXP	S	7942790	18301700	16946100	19688600	22262900	23183300	24244000	26120500	28013500	28960500
forint	BAL		-1121260	199600	1311200	1482900	1979000	1971400	2090000	1976900	2664900	3249400

Total imports and exports by countries and areas (Table B)

Imports CIF, exports FOB and balance: million of national currency *[cont.]*

Importations et exportations totales par pays ou zone (Tableau B)

Importations CIF, exportations FOB et balance : en millions de monnaie nationale *[suite]*

Country or Area - Pays ou Zone	IMP EXP BAL	G/ S	2000	2008	2009	2010	2011	2012	2013	2014	2015	2016
Iceland	IMP	S	203847	468598	446128	477222	560692	597262	584224	611530	699961	675500
Islande	EXP	S	148516	452428	500855	561032	619682	633029	609788	582123	626022	542597
kronur	BAL		-55331	-16170	54727	83810	58990	35767	25564	-29407	-73939	-132903
India[9]	IMP	G	2316550	13939400	12398400	15080700	21476000	26088400	27363000	28217100	25195100	24300800
Inde[9]	EXP	G	1906530	8412350	7967180	10174700	14223800	15820500	18364000	19620100	17138000	17774500
rupees	BAL		-410020	-5527050	-4431220	-4906000	-7252200	-10267900	-8999000	-8597000	-8057100	-6526300
Ireland	IMP	G	55909	57585	45061	48695	53035	56179	55787	62157	70111	71279
Irlande	EXP	G	83889	86395	85804	90924	93191	93507	89181	92616	112407	118357
euros	BAL		27980	28810	40743	42229	40156	37328	33394	30458	42296	47078
Italy	IMP	S	258506	382049	297608	367390	401428	380293	361002	356937	370485	365579
Italie	EXP	S	260415	369015	291732	337344	375904	390182	390234	398871	412291	417077
euros	BAL		1909	-13034	-5876	-30046	-25524	9889	29232	41934	41806	51498
Jamaica	IMP	S	141987	559908	426608	464428	553187	561077	622776	646961	583553	...
Jamaïque	EXP	S	55621	183976	115838	116449	139369	153550	156663	161290	147684	...
dollars	BAL		-86366	-375932	-310770	-347979	-413818	-407527	-466113	-485671	-435869	...
Japan	IMP	G	40915000	78959000	51365900	60622700	68037500	70655000	81249300	85875700	78445800	65972800
Japon	EXP	G	51654200	81018100	54170600	67399600	65546500	63747600	69774200	73093000	75613900	70035800
yen	BAL		10739200	2059100	2804700	6776900	-2491000	-6907400	-11475100	-12782700	-2831900	4063000
Jordan	IMP	S	3259	11897	10319	10710	13109	14691	15407	16296	14211	13830
Jordanie	EXP	S	1347	5527	4637	4986	5654	5627	5606	5947	5573	5331
dinars	BAL		-1913	-6370	-5682	-5724	-7454	-9063	-9801	-10349	-8638	-8499
Kenya	IMP	G	236613	766743	788097	957949	1315670	1376680	1408810	1618450	1580330	1431740
Kenya	EXP	G	132183	342954	344949	408103	511036	517804	504300	531190	581001	578067
shillings	BAL		-104430	-423789	-443148	-549846	-804634	-858876	-904510	-1087260	-999329	-853673
Kuwait	IMP	S	2195	6679	5723	6499	6938	7632	8309	8829	9316	9315
Koweït	EXP	S	5963	23482	15529	17959	28340	32051	32363	28637	16280	13977
dinars	BAL		3767	16803	9807	11461	21402	24420	24054	19807	6964	4662
Latvia[10]	IMP	S	1934	7528	4710	5912	7719	8794	8880	12654	12492	12301
Lettonie[10]	EXP	S	1131	4429	3602	4695	5999	6937	7043	10249	10363	10367
euros	BAL		-803	-3099	-1108	-1217	-1721	-1856	-1837	-2406	-2129	-1934
Lesotho	IMP	G	5614	16564	16524	16107	10631	13127	22140	23968	24997	...
Lesotho	EXP	G	1527	7289	6066	5857	5596	5577	9048	10033	9891	...
maloti	BAL		-4088	-9274	-10458	-10250	-5035	-7550	-13091	-13935	-15106	...
Libya	IMP	G	1911	11195	12535	13301	9792	29016	34330	24235	17967	...
Libye	EXP	G	5222	75959	46583	58336	22031	74433	55946	26738	14092	...
dinars	BAL		3310	64764	34048	45034	12240	45417	21615	2503	-3875	...
Lithuania[11]	IMP	S	20877	73006	45311	60953	78812	85902	90490	91605	25400	24699
Lituanie[11]	EXP	S	14193	55511	40732	54039	69577	79578	84748	84252	22904	22607
euros	BAL		-6684	-17495	-4579	-6914	-9236	-6324	-5742	-7353	-2496	-2092
Luxembourg	IMP	S	11633	17516	13799	16422	18901	18936	18033	17806	17691	17636
Luxembourg	EXP	S	8498	11988	9250	10785	12065	10933	10604	11318	11730	11903
euros	BAL		-3135	-5528	-4549	-5637	-6836	-8003	-7429	-6488	-5961	-5733
Madagascar	IMP	G	1349440	6532110	6188990	5305220	5303830	5438550	7061508	7810863	9188718	...
Madagascar	EXP	G	1115280	2865560	2146110	2245580	2534440	2713360	4303130	5132734	6530618	...
ariary	BAL		-234160	-3666550	-4042880	-3059640	-2769390	-2725190	-2758378	-2678129	-2658099	...
Malawi	IMP	G	32252	238898	295947	325579	380171	594760	1029800	1254960	...	...
Malawi	EXP	G	23631	120850	152460	159436	220446	292716	435222	600922	531592	714155
kwacha	BAL		-8622	-118048	-143487	-166143	-159725	-302044	-594578	-654038	...	...

Total imports and exports by countries and areas (Table B)

Imports CIF, exports FOB and balance: million of national currency *[cont.]*

Importations et exportations totales par pays ou zone (Tableau B)

Importations CIF, exportations FOB et balance : en millions de monnaie nationale *[suite]*

Country or Area - Pays ou Zone	IMP EXP BAL	G/ S	2000	2008	2009	2010	2011	2012	2013	2014	2015	2016
Malaysia	IMP	G	311459	519804	434670	528828	573626	606677	648695	682937	685778	698662
Malaisie	EXP	G	373270	663014	552518	638822	697862	702641	719992	765417	777355	785935
ringgit	BAL		61811	143210	117848	109994	124236	95964	71297	82480	91577	87273
Mali[3]	IMP	G	573900	1495190	1174000	1693100	1597000	1500000	1827380	1952532	1872688	...
Mali[3]	EXP	G	392300	939101	841300	989200	1128300	1104600	1284100	1038576	1498191	...
CFA francs	BAL		-181600	-556089	-332700	-703900	-468700	-395400	-543280	-913956	-374497	...
Malta[12]	IMP	G	1492	3897	3475	4330	5339	6187	5641	6151	6107	6355
Malte[12]	EXP	G	1072	2456	2087	2809	3819	4439	3904	3639	3527	3536
euros	BAL		-420	-1441	-1388	-1521	-1520	-1749	-1737	-2512	-2580	-2819
Mauritania	IMP	G	84529	395103	350662	474099	689657	881753	1197925	1099881	1181388	743445
Mauritanie	EXP	G	81881	392204	368978	498120	691133	777808	807278	693949	529445	577568
ouguiyas	BAL		-2647	-2899	18317	24020	1475	-103945	-390647	-405931	-651943	-165877
Mauritius	IMP	G	57940	132165	118444	134882	147815	160996	165661	172023	168077	...
Maurice	EXP	G	47511	67970	61681	69550	73586	79658	88148	94323	94108	...
rupees	BAL		-10429	-64195	-56763	-65332	-74229	-81338	-77513	-77700	-73969	...
Montenegro	IMP	S	.	2530	1654	1657	1823	1800	1773	1784	1840	2059
Monténégro	EXP	S	.	416	277	330	454	367	376	338	317	326
euros	BAL		.	-2114	-1377	-1327	-1369	-1433	-1398	-1446	-1523	-1733
Morocco	IMP	S	122527	326042	263982	297963	357770	386949	383720	386118	366034	...
Maroc	EXP	S	76242	155740	113020	149583	174994	184885	185387	200013	213641	...
dirhams	BAL		-46286	-170302	-150962	-148380	-182776	-202064	-198333	-186105	-152393	...
Namibia	IMP	G	10755	43165	52832	47642	48218	60013	73399	92093	99609	100671
Namibie	EXP	G	9164	44163	42616	38775	38985	45019	55416	64682	59962	70854
dollars	BAL		-1591	998	-10215	-8867	-9234	-14995	-17982	-27411	-39647	-29817
Nepal	IMP	G	108505	250448	339990	402351	427616	555841	601983	...	...	...
Népal	EXP	G	49823	65490	63788	69497	67960	81723	86000	...	...	...
rupees	BAL		-58682	-184958	-276202	-332854	-359656	-474118	-515983	...	...	...
Netherlands	IMP	S	216056	335929	274026	331914	364921	389449	386353	382416	383206	380569
Pays-Bas	EXP	S	231854	370488	309369	371552	409358	429715	433106	433404	427267	432343
euros	BAL		15798	34559	35343	39638	44437	40266	46753	50988	44061	51774
New Zealand	IMP	G	31463	48037	39719	42401	46896	47219	48360	51258	52510	51621
Nouvelle-Zélande	EXP	G	30536	43353	39556	43411	47702	46060	48044	50075	48974	48487
dollars	BAL		-927	-4684	-163	1010	806	-1159	-317	-1184	-3537	-3134
Niger[3]	IMP	G	281400	759672	704900	1081200	854400	918442	938383	1125000	1179871	...
Niger[3]	EXP	G	201500	407503	278900	318700	428000	765369	790217	757193	624134	...
CFA francs	BAL		-79900	-352169	-426000	-762500	-426400	-153073	-148166	-367807	-555737	...
Niue	IMP	G	4	11	9	...	...	...	...	...	...	...
Nioué	EXP	G	1	0	...	...	...	...	...	...	...	...
NZ dollars	BAL		-4	-11	...	...	...	...	...	...	...	...
Norway	IMP	G	302840	504480	430362	467285	508628	507649	528783	553738	609693	603978
Norvège	EXP	G	529812	953153	731306	788120	898593	935720	899351	894513	832344	739310
kroner	BAL		226972	448673	300944	320835	389965	428071	370568	340775	222651	135332
Oman	IMP	G	1938	8815	6869	7603	9082	11323	13201	11317	11153	...
Oman	EXP	G	4352	14503	10787	14073	18107	20445	21697	20315	13355	...
rials Omani	BAL		2414	5689	3917	6470	9025	9123	8496	8998	2202	...
Pakistan	IMP	G	582681	2947050	2587780	3218900	3797900	4119730	4531900	4796970	4502940	4878860
Pakistan	EXP	G	484476	1423450	1433550	1824380	2188530	2293570	2553390	2498590	2268530	2155500
rupees	BAL		-98205	-1523600	-1154230	-1394520	-1609370	-1826160	-1978510	-2298380	-2234410	-2723360

Total imports and exports by countries and areas (Table B)

Imports CIF, exports FOB and balance: million of national currency *[cont.]*

Importations et exportations totales par pays ou zone (Tableau B)

Importations CIF, exportations FOB et balance : en millions de monnaie nationale *[suite]*

Country or Area - Pays ou Zone	IMP EXP BAL	G/ S	2000	2008	2009	2010	2011	2012	2013	2014	2015	2016
Panama	IMP	S	3379	9050	7801	9145	11340	12494	13024	13705	12136	11697
Panama	EXP	S	859	1247	948	832	785	822	844	818	696	636
balboas	BAL		-2519	-7803	-6853	-8313	-10554	-11672	-12180	-12887	-11440	-11061
Papua New Guinea	IMP	G	3196	9611	8816	10741	11618	11465	...	...	...	...
Papouasie-Nouvelle-Guinée	EXP	G	5742	15426	12107	15602	16376	13181	13337	21626	23302	...
kina	BAL		2546	5815	3290	4861	4758	1716	...	...	...	...
Philippines	IMP	G	1636810	2668510	2185440	2637540	2776230	2780230	2794440	3050370	3406250	4249030
Philippines	EXP	G	1682810	2182680	1830980	2322990	2092230	2200130	2408800	2754940	2669220	2727370
pesos	BAL		46000	-485830	-354460	-314550	-684000	-580100	-385640	-295430	-737030	-1521660
Poland	IMP	S	213072	485833	463383	536221	611004	638288	648195	692573	731720	777539
Pologne	EXP	S	137909	399353	423241	481058	553430	597096	638600	682360	747248	798199
zlotys	BAL		-75163	-86480	-40142	-55163	-57574	-41192	-9595	-10213	15528	20660
Portugal	IMP	S	41425	64194	51368	58647	59551	56374	57013	59032	60310	61134
Portugal	EXP	S	25241	38950	31768	37268	42828	45213	47303	48054	49826	50314
euros	BAL		-16184	-25244	-19600	-21379	-16723	-11161	-9710	-10978	-10485	-10820
Qatar	IMP	S	11838	101556	90716	84593	81293	91813	98418	110916	118705	116690
Qatar	EXP	S	42203	244998	174746	272271	416592	484065	498153	477790	281335	208403
riyals	BAL		30365	143442	84030	187678	335300	392252	399735	366874	162630	91713
Rwanda	IMP	G	82586	621619	697270	816383	1068472	1232286	1593550	1672566	1667480	1768315
Rwanda	EXP	G	20521	146375	109491	148698	279326	290123	443368	501362	403012	472821
francs	BAL		-62065	-475244	-587779	-667685	-789146	-942162	-1150182	-1171204	-1264468	-1295494
Saint Helena[13]	IMP	G	7	9	10	...	...	...	...	...	...	...
Sainte-Hélèna[13]	EXP	G	0	0	0	...	...	...	...	...	...	...
pounds	BAL		-7	-9	-10	...	...	...	...	...	...	...
Saint Kitts-Nevis[1]	IMP	S	529	877	770	724	670	609	672	725	801	896
Saint-Kitts-et-Nevis[1]	EXP	S	79	139	120	123	132	144	133	136	149	139
EC dollars	BAL		-450	-738	-650	-601	-538	-465	-539	-589	-652	-757
Saint Lucia[1]	IMP	G	959	1775	1405	1789	1882	1738	1675	1694	1539	1767
Sainte-Lucie[1]	EXP	G	117	392	683	579	432	493	471	434	487	323
EC dollars	BAL		-842	-1383	-723	-1210	-1449	-1245	-1204	-1260	-1052	-1444
Saint Vincent-Grenadines[1]	IMP	S	399	1007	901	913	896	961	999	976	901	904
St.Vincent-Grenadines[1]	EXP	S	136	141	135	111	104	115	133	130	124	126
EC dollars	BAL		-263	-866	-766	-802	-792	-846	-866	-846	-777	-778
Samoa	IMP	G	298	659	550	690	739	707	753	895	855	899
Samoa	EXP	G	47	30	31	34	39	78	55	106	136	144
talas	BAL		-251	-630	-519	-657	-700	-628	-697	-789	-719	-755
Saudi Arabia	IMP	G	113240	431750	358290	400740	493450	583470	630580	651880	655030	509590
Arabie saoudite	EXP	G	290550	1175350	721110	941800	1367620	1456390	1409520	1283620	763310	683640
riyals	BAL		177310	743600	362820	541060	874170	872920	778940	631740	108280	174050
Senegal[3]	IMP	G	1081500	2483310	2101710	2154530	2462870	2948390	2910720	2934480	3032910	2977470
Sénégal[3]	EXP	G	434050	728485	740517	831560	1071390	1196740	1157780	1174720	1342630	1371270
CFA francs	BAL		-647450	-1754825	-1361193	-1322970	-1391480	-1751650	-1752940	-1759760	-1690280	-1606200
Serbia	IMP	G	.	1260290	1243650	1280680	1455390	1663980	1750980	1820760	1980310	2140060
Serbie	EXP	G	.	603512	796525	762974	861352	1000870	1253990	1310210	1455070	1652283
dinars	BAL		.	-656778	-447125	-517706	-594038	-663110	-496990	-510550	-525240	-487778
Seychelles	IMP	G	1955	9959	10792	11956	12999	14706	13229	14604	13196	13854
Seychelles	EXP	G	1106	4070	5381	4828	5983	6803	6973	6867	5710	...
rupees	BAL		-849	-5890	-5411	-7128	-7016	-7903	-6257	-7737	-7486	...

Total imports and exports by countries and areas (Table B)

Imports CIF, exports FOB and balance: million of national currency *[cont.]*

Importations et exportations totales par pays ou zone (Tableau B)

Importations CIF, exportations FOB et balance : en millions de monnaie nationale *[suite]*

Country or Area - Pays ou Zone	IMP EXP BAL	G/ S	2000	2008	2009	2010	2011	2012	2013	2014	2015	2016
Sierra Leone	IMP	G	314639	1590340	1764300	3083670	7471820	6964740	7003120	7046330	7413991	...
Sierra Leone	EXP	G	26771	643014	780941	1357290	1521010	4871100	8276290	6921720	3678486	...
leones	BAL		-287868	-947326	-983359	-1726380	-5950810	-2093640	1273170	-124610	-3735505	...
Singapore	IMP	G	232176	450893	356299	423222	459655	474554	466762	463779	407768	403305
Singapour	EXP	G	237826	476762	391118	478841	514741	510329	513391	513248	476285	466912
dollars	BAL		5650	25869	34819	55619	55086	35775	46629	49469	68517	63607
Slovakia[14]	IMP	S	619789	1573010	40714	49868	58556	61518	62937	63020	67790	69702
Slovaquie[14]	EXP	S	548527	1509110	39721	48272	56783	62144	64172	64721	67865	70087
euros	BAL		-71262	-63900	-993	-1596	-1773	626	1235	1701	75	385
Solomon Islands	IMP	S	468	2382	2100	3212	3615	3656	3922	3684	3699	...
Iles Salomon	EXP	S	351	1641	1287	1754	3116	3591	3554	3378	3176	...
dollars	BAL		-117	-742	-813	-1459	-500	-66	-369	-306	-523	...
South Africa[4,15]	IMP	G	186382	777808	541038	606249	746285	854991	998056	1083440	1087970	1099090
Afrique du Sud[4,15]	EXP	G	208476	692359	523013	666383	789971	816990	928978	1000740	1035880	1099940
rands	BAL		22094	-85449	-18025	60134	43686	-38001	-69078	-82700	-52090	850
Spain	IMP	S	166138	281982	208088	238082	260823	253401	251354	270354	281874	280726
Espagne	EXP	S	123100	187823	157933	185799	214486	222644	234708	243741	254640	259514
euros	BAL		-43038	-94159	-50155	-52283	-46337	-30757	-16646	-26613	-27234	-21212
Sri Lanka	IMP	G	485084	1510730	1154390	1526600	2241490	2441880	2322680	2565944	2592786	...
Sri Lanka	EXP	G	420114	881320	813911	937737	1167590	1245530	1342970	1462523	1424807	...
rupees	BAL		-64970	-629410	-340479	-588863	-1073900	-1196350	-979710	-1103421	-1167979	...
Suriname	IMP	G	324	4167	3723	3788	5457	5792	7065	6540	6722	7643
Suriname	EXP	G	533	4578	3823	5648	8017	8331	7853	6972	5466	9165
dollars	BAL		209	410	101	1860	2560	2539	788	432	-1256	1522
Swaziland	IMP	G	7261	14044	13558	12446	14261	16072	14798	...	...	...
Swaziland	EXP	G	6312	14044	12287	11348	13906	15669	18445	...	...	...
emalangeni	BAL		-949	0	-1271	-1098	-355	-403	3647	...	...	...
Sweden	IMP	S	672400	1097900	912900	1069200	1147900	1114400	1045900	1111000	1166800	1205500
Suède	EXP	S	804200	1194400	996700	1138200	1212300	1168300	1090800	1127000	1180600	1193700
kronor	BAL		131800	96500	83800	69000	64400	53900	44900	16000	13800	-11800
Switzerland	IMP	S	128615	186883	160187	173685	174388	176781	177642	178605	166392	173542
Suisse	EXP	S	126549	206330	180534	193253	197907	200612	201213	208357	202919	210473
francs	BAL		-2066	19447	20347	19568	23519	23831	23571	29752	36527	36931
Syrian Arab Rep.	IMP	S	45515	203226	171644	190264	184090	87555	65105	...	...	...
République arabe syrienne	EXP	S	52471	172977	121849	157150	120108	44900	33675	...	...	...
pounds	BAL		6956	-30249	-49795	-33114	-63983	-42655	-31430	...	...	...
Thailand	IMP	S	2494140	5962480	4601980	5856590	6982720	7786130	7657350	7403900	6906080	6904720
Thaïlande	EXP	S	2773830	5851370	5194600	6113340	6707990	7078420	6909740	7313070	7227160	7548570
baht	BAL		279690	-111110	592620	256750	-274730	-707710	-747610	-90830	321080	643850
Togo[3]	IMP	S	400131	528350	551945	596176	830446	851185	968046	875535	1026033	1086999
Togo[3]	EXP	S	258447	261288	301850	322656	400451	491710	567070	396185	420214	450947
CFA francs	BAL		-141684	-267062	-250095	-273520	-429995	-359475	-400976	-479350	-605819	-636052
Tonga	IMP	G	123	324	292	302	332	343	352	404	435	...
Tonga	EXP	G	16	19	16	16	30	30	39	42	...	...
pa'anga	BAL		-107	-305	-276	-286	-302	-313	-313	-362	...	...
Trinidad and Tobago	IMP	S	20840	60325	43993	40741	63949	60458	56695	56023	41426	...
Trinité-et-Tobago	EXP	S	26925	117301	57721	71127	95097	84254	81821	74288	46414	...
dollars	BAL		6086	56977	13728	30386	31148	23795	25126	18265	4988	...

Total imports and exports by countries and areas (Table B)

Imports CIF, exports FOB and balance: million of national currency *[cont.]*

Importations et exportations totales par pays ou zone (Tableau B)

Importations CIF, exportations FOB et balance : en millions de monnaie nationale *[suite]*

Country or Area - Pays ou Zone	IMP EXP BAL	G/S	2000	2008	2009	2010	2011	2012	2013	2014	2015	2016
Tunisia	IMP	G	11738	30241	25878	31817	33702	38183	39509	42043	39655	41754
Tunisie	EXP	G	8005	23637	19469	23519	25092	26548	27701	28407	27607	28948
dinars	BAL		-3733	-6604	-6408	-8298	-8610	-11635	-11808	-13636	-12048	-12806
Tuvalu	IMP	G	9	...	...	...	...	...	...	...	...	...
Tuvalu	EXP	G	0	...	...	...	...	...	...	...	...	...
Aust. dollars	BAL		-9	...	...	...	...	...	...	...	...	...
Uganda	IMP	G	2486280	7786490	8624240	10256300	11567100	13087500	12738600	13219700	15377300	...
Ouganda	EXP	G	759273	4651150	6066440	6750430	6082240	7167850	7372070	6928950	8704340	...
shillings	BAL		-1727007	-3135340	-2557800	-3505870	-5484860	-5919650	-5366530	-6290750	-6672960	...
United Kingdom	IMP	G	220397	345826	310660	367580	403126	412528	423811	415469	407304	435472
Royaume-Uni	EXP	G	187133	251565	227727	270196	308171	301621	303147	292894	287584	301405
pounds	BAL		-33264	-94261	-82933	-97384	-94955	-110907	-120664	-122575	-119720	-134067
United Rep. of Tanzania	IMP	G	1219380	8470080	8309960	11058500	16904700	17832200	19601900	19917668	20396666	...
Rép.-Unie de Tanzanie	EXP	G	531058	3201860	3124060	5302680	6915020	8033240	8080800	8400827	9855591	...
shillings	BAL		-688322	-5268220	-5185900	-5755820	-9989680	-9798960	-11521100	-11516841	-10541074	...
United States[16]	IMP	G	1259300	2169490	1605300	1969180	2265890	2336520	2329060	2412550	2248230	2250150
Etats-Unis[16]	EXP	G	781918	1287440	1056040	1278490	1480290	1545710	1579050	1623410	1504580	1453830
dollars	BAL		-477382	-882050	-549260	-690690	-785600	-790810	-750010	-789140	-743650	-796320
Vanuatu	IMP	G	11975	31667	31086	27510	27256	27454	29652	30435	39989	41407
Vanuatu	EXP	G	3579	5721	6070	4695	6012	5072	3653	6100	4249	5447
vatu	BAL		-8396	-25946	-25016	-22815	-21244	-22382	-25999	-24335	-35740	-35960
Yemen	IMP	S	375833	2106740	1863120	2130020	2145305	2565747	2686130	...	...	...
Yémen	EXP	S	613937	1514970	1269610	1866510	2309173	1822079	2041460	...	...	...
rials	BAL		238104	-591770	-593510	-263510	163868	-743668	-644670	...	...	...
Zambia	IMP	G	2752	18480	18941	25507	34952	42265	54897	58737	73610	77222
Zambie	EXP	G	2717	18653	21365	34497	43831	48191	57177	59618	60683	67085
kwacha	BAL		-35	173	2424	8989	8879	5927	2280	881	-12928	-10136

Total imports and exports by countries or areas (Table B)

Imports CIF, exports FOB and balance: millions of national currency *[cont.]*

Importations et exportations totales par pays ou zone (Tableau B)

Importations CIF, exportations FOB, et balance : en millions de monnaie nationale *[suite]*

General note:

This table contains totals of imports and exports of countries or areas which report data in national currency. Countries that are not included in this table may report their trade in US dollars and are shown in Table A. Export and import values are as compiled by the International Monetary Fund (IMF) except for Andorra, Bermuda, Cayman Is., Cuba, Gibraltar, Montenegro, Niue, Palau, Russian Federation (beginning 1994), Serbia and Montenegro, State of Palestine, Turkmenistan, Turks and Caicos, Tuvalu and Uzbekistan.

Column "G/S" indicates the trade system: G = General Trade System; S = Special Trade System. For further information on sources and presentation as well as for a brief table description please see the introduction.

1 East Caribbean dollar.
2 Trade statistics exclude certain oil and chemical products.
3 Comptoirs Francais du Afrique franc pegged to the euro at CFAF 655.957 per euro.
4 Imports FOB.
5 Prior to January 2008, data for Cyprus are in pounds.
6 Prior to January 2011, data for Estonia are in krooni.
7 Excluding intra-EU trade.
8 In the year 2000, the trade values refer to extra-EU27.
9 Excluding military goods, fissionable materials, bunkers, ships, and aircraft.
10 Prior to January 2014, data for Latvia are in lati.
11 Prior to January 2015, data for Lithuania are in litai.
12 Prior to January 2008, data for Malta are in liri.
13 Year ending 31 March of the following year.
14 Prior to January 2009, data for Slovakia are in koruny.
15 Exports include gold.
16 Including the trade of the U.S. Virgin Islands and Puerto Rico but excluding shipments of merchandise between the United States and its other possessions (Guam and American Samoa). Data include imports and exports of non-monetary gold.

Remarque générale:

Cette table contient des totaux d'd'importations et d'd'exportations les pays ou les secteurs qui rapportent des données dans la monnaie nationale.Les pays qui ne sont pas inclus dans cette table peuvent rapporter leurs échanges des dollars d'USA et sont montrés dans le Tableau A. Export et les valeurs d'importation sont comme compilé par le Fonds monétaire international (FMI) excepté Andorre, État de Palestine, les Bermudes, Iles Caïmanes, le Cuba, la Fédération Russe (commençant 1994), Gibraltar, Montenegro, Nioué, Palaos, Serbie et Monténégro, Turkmenistan, Iles Turque Caicos, Tuvalu et Ouzbékistan.

La colonne "G/S" indique le système commercial : G=Système du Commerce Général ; S= Système du Commerce Spécial. Pour plus d'information sur les sources et la présentation ainsi qu'une brève description du tableau, se il vous plaît se référer à l'introduction.

1 Dollar des caraïbes orientales.
2 Les statistiques commerciales font exclusion de certains produits pétroliers et chimiques.
3 Comptoirs Français du Afrique franc est chevillé à l'euro à CFAF 655,957 par euro.
4 Importations FOB.
5 Avant janvier 2008, les données de Chypre étaient en livres.
6 Avant janvier 2011, les données de l'Estonie étaient en krooni.
7 Non compris le commerce d'intra-UE.
8 En l'année 2000, les valeurs du commerce se réfèrent à extra-UE27.
9 À l'exclusion des marchandises militaires, des matières fissibles, des soutes, des bateaux, et de l'avion.
10 Avant janvier 2014, les données pour la Lettonie sont en lati.
11 Avant de janvier 2015, les données pour la Lituanie sont en litai.
12 Avant janvier 2008, les données de Malte étaient en lire.
13 Année finissant le 31 mars de l'année suivante.
14 Avant janvier 2009, les données de Slovaquie étaient en couronnes.
15 Les exportations comprennent l'or.
16 Y compris le commerce des Iles Vierges américaines et de Porto Rico mais non compris les échanges de marchandise, entre les Etats-Unis et leurs autres possessions (Guam et Samoa américaines). Les données comprennent les importations et exportations d'or non-monétaire.

External trade conversion factors (Table C)

Imports, exports: US dollars per national currency

Facteurs de conversion pour le commerce extérieur (Tableau C)

Importations, exportations : monnaie nationale en dollars E.-U.

Country or Area	Unit	2000	2008	2009	2010	2011	2012	2013	2014	2015	2016
						Imports - Importations					
Albania	lek	0.00694	0.01194	0.01055	0.00961	0.00992	0.00924	0.00948	0.00947	0.00793	0.00806
Algeria	dinar	0.01328	0.01553	0.01376	0.01345	0.01372	0.01289	0.01261	0.01242	0.00998	0.00914
Andorra	euro	0.91856	1.46993	1.39638	1.32850	1.38935	1.28572	1.32989	1.32482	1.10846	1.10505
Anguilla	EC dollar	0.37037	0.37037	0.37037	0.37037	0.37037	0.37037	0.37037	0.37037	0.37037	...
Australia	dollar	0.57946	0.84776	0.79304	0.92048	1.03228	1.03544	0.96511	0.90230	0.75060	0.74423
Austria	euro[1]	0.92061	1.47342	1.39466	1.32511	1.39182	1.28546	1.32805	1.32899	1.10907	1.10657
Bahamas	dollar	1.00000	1.00000	1.00000	1.00000	1.00000	1.00000	1.00000	1.00000	1.00000	...
Bangladesh	taka	0.01915	0.01458	0.01448	0.01435	0.01349	0.01222	0.01280	0.01288	0.01283	0.01274
Barbados	dollar	0.50000	0.50000	0.50000	0.50000	0.50000	0.50000	0.50000	0.50000	0.50000	0.50000
Belgium	euro[1]	0.92097	1.47453	1.39429	1.32619	1.39162	1.28597	1.32789	1.32884	1.10915	1.10648
Benin	CFA franc[2,3]	0.00142	0.00223	0.00213	0.00202	0.00212	0.00196	0.00203	0.00201	0.00169	0.00168
Bhutan	ngultrum	0.02228	0.02311	0.02064	0.02185	0.02160	0.01868	0.01710	0.01643	0.01561	0.01489
Bosnia and Herzegovina	marka	0.46840	0.75413	0.71357	0.67617	0.71203	0.65677	0.67918	0.67829	0.56667	0.56589
Botswana	pula	0.19586	0.14708	0.14102	0.14744	0.14653	0.14646	0.11911	0.11158	0.09893	0.09190
Brunei Darussalam	dollar	0.58002	0.70507	0.68607	0.73436	0.79546	0.79981	0.79911	0.78953	0.72739	...
Bulgaria	lev	0.46942	0.75425	0.71358	0.67675	0.71166	0.65695	0.67893	0.67824	0.56661	0.56555
Burkina Faso	CFA franc[3]	0.00140	0.00222	0.00213	0.00202	0.00212	0.00196	0.00202	0.00203	0.00169	...
Burundi	franc	0.00139	0.00084	0.00081	0.00081	0.00079	0.00069	0.00064	0.00065	0.00064	0.00060
Cabo Verde	escudo	0.00863	0.01319	0.01259	0.01201	0.01260	0.01158	0.01206	0.01197	0.01005	0.01002
Cameroon	CFA franc[3]	0.00140	0.00222	0.00213	0.00202	0.00212	0.00196	0.00203	0.00202	0.00169	0.00169
Canada	dollar	0.67322	0.94200	0.87926	0.97131	1.01076	1.00086	0.97107	0.90422	0.78281	0.75560
Cent. Afr. Rep.	CFA franc[2,3]	0.00142	0.00222	0.00213	0.00202	0.00212	0.00196	0.00203	...	...	...
Chad	CFA franc[2,3]	0.00141	0.00224	0.00211	0.00202	0.00212	0.00196	0.00202	0.00203	0.00169	...
Comoros	franc	0.00187	0.00296	0.00284	0.00270	0.00282	0.00261	0.00270	...	...	...
Cote d'Ivoire	CFA franc[3]	0.00140	0.00223	0.00214	0.00203	0.00212	0.00196	0.00203	0.00201	0.00169	0.00169
Cyprus	euro[1,4]	1.60134	1.47595	1.39443	1.32668	1.39312	1.28507	1.32882	1.32715	1.10858	1.10798
Czechia	koruna	0.02591	0.05908	0.05292	0.05250	0.05660	0.05115	0.05111	0.04820	0.04066	0.04093
Denmark	krone	0.12362	0.19729	0.18704	0.17791	0.18643	0.17274	0.17813	0.17841	0.14870	0.14858
Djibouti	franc	0.00563	0.00563	0.00563	0.00563	0.00563	0.00563	0.00563	0.00563	0.00563	...
Dominica	EC dollar[5]	0.37037	0.37037	0.37037	0.37037	0.37037	0.37037	0.37037	0.37037	0.37037	0.37037
Equatorial Guinea	CFA franc[3]	0.00140	0.00225	0.00212	0.00201	0.00213	0.00196	0.00202	0.00203	...	...
Estonia	euro[1,6]	0.05866	0.09419	0.08922	0.08471	1.39311	1.28519	1.32768	1.32803	1.10878	1.10686
Ethiopia	birr	0.12160	0.10406	0.08464	0.06924	0.05914	0.05643	0.05370	0.05107	0.04861	0.04599
Extra-EU28	euro	0.92003	1.47399	1.39351	1.32434	1.39170	1.28542	1.32803	1.32881	1.10928	1.10655
Fiji	dollar	0.47029	0.62885	0.51330	0.52434	0.55797	0.55877	0.54291	0.52934	0.47684	0.47858
Finland	euro[1]	0.92026	1.47688	1.39429	1.32514	1.39146	1.28629	1.32843	1.32884	1.10907	1.10630
France	euro[1]	0.92101	1.47398	1.39401	1.32545	1.39145	1.28597	1.32801	1.32876	1.10907	1.10632
Gabon	CFA franc[2,3]	0.00141	0.00225	0.00213	0.00202	0.00212	0.00196	0.00203	0.00201	0.00169	...
Gambia	dalasi	0.07831	0.04545	0.03752	0.03570	0.03396	0.03129	0.02776	0.02396	...	...
Germany	euro[1]	0.92038	1.47260	1.39352	1.32502	1.39184	1.28556	1.32799	1.32870	1.10922	1.10648
Ghana	cedi	1.83930	0.94292	0.71183	0.69827	0.66120	0.55795	0.51168	0.34256	0.26586	...
Gibraltar	pound	1.51023	1.83115	1.56517	1.54366	1.60367	1.58595	1.56431	1.64622	1.52921	...
Grenada	EC dollar[5]	0.37037	0.37037	0.37037	0.37037	0.37037	0.37037	0.37037	0.37037	0.37037	0.37037
Guyana	dollar	0.00548	0.00491	0.00490	0.00491	0.00490	0.00489	0.00487	0.00484	0.00484	...
Haiti	gourde	0.04740	0.02550	0.02424	0.02514	0.02466	0.02384	0.02299	0.02212	0.01981	...
Hungary	forint	0.00353	0.00588	0.00499	0.00481	0.00498	0.00444	0.00447	0.00431	0.00358	0.00355
Iceland	krona	0.01271	0.01198	0.00808	0.00821	0.00862	0.00799	0.00819	0.00857	0.00758	0.00829
India	rupee	0.02226	0.02303	0.02074	0.02188	0.02141	0.01873	0.01715	0.01639	0.01559	0.01488
Ireland	euro[1]	0.92002	1.47479	1.38911	1.32620	1.39067	1.28645	1.32865	1.32728	1.10813	1.10628
Italy	euro[1]	0.92076	1.47477	1.39353	1.32548	1.39206	1.28610	1.32782	1.32890	1.10913	1.10649

2000	2008	2009	2010	2011	2012	2013	2014	2015	2016	Unité	Pays ou Zone
				Exports - Exportations							
0.00696	0.01204	0.01056	0.00960	0.00991	0.00924	0.00946	0.00950	0.00793	0.00806	lek	Albanie
0.01329	0.01558	0.01377	0.01345	0.01371	0.01294	0.01261	0.01248	0.00999	0.00913	dinar	Algérie
0.91870	1.47712	1.39441	1.32073	1.39424	1.28550	1.32866	1.32769	1.10872	1.10686	euro	Andorre
0.37037	0.37037	0.37037	0.37037	0.37037	0.37037	0.37037	0.37037	0.37037	...	dollar C.O.	Anguilla
0.57827	0.84164	0.78518	0.91992	1.03321	1.03497	0.96444	0.90242	0.75174	0.74477	dollar	Australie
0.92072	1.47538	1.39527	1.32473	1.39208	1.28554	1.32799	1.32836	1.10866	1.10689	euro[1]	Autriche
1.00000	1.00000	1.00000	1.00000	1.00000	1.00000	1.00000	1.00000	1.00000	...	dollar	Bahamas
0.01916	0.01458	0.01448	0.01435	0.01349	0.01222	0.01281	0.01288	0.01283	0.01274	taka	Bangladesh
0.50000	0.50000	0.50000	0.50000	0.50000	0.50000	0.50000	0.50000	0.50000	0.50000	dollar	Barbade
0.92123	1.47594	1.39497	1.32595	1.39200	1.28592	1.32775	1.32905	1.10920	1.10658	euro[1]	Belgique
0.00140	0.00224	0.00212	0.00202	0.00211	0.00196	0.00202	0.00207	0.00169	0.00169	franc CFA[2,3]	Bénin
0.02225	0.02301	0.02066	0.02186	0.02152	0.01869	0.01707	0.01641	0.01560	0.01489	ngultrum	Bhoutan
0.47100	0.75446	0.71484	0.67656	0.71189	0.65663	0.67873	0.67866	0.56701	0.56570	marka	Bosnie-Herzégovine
0.19495	0.15022	0.14212	0.14714	0.14739	0.14563	0.11915	0.11167	0.09960	0.09163	pula	Botswana
0.58029	0.70734	0.68722	0.73513	0.79456	0.80031	0.80000	0.79022	0.72900	...	dollar	Brunéi Darussalam
0.46931	0.75617	0.71575	0.67589	0.71206	0.65652	0.67881	0.67939	0.56670	0.56562	lev	Bulgarie
0.00143	0.00223	0.00211	0.00203	0.00212	0.00196	0.00203	0.00203	0.00169	...	franc CFA[3]	Burkina Faso
0.00142	0.00084	0.00081	0.00081	0.00079	0.00069	0.00064	0.00065	0.00063	0.00060	franc	Burundi
0.00859	0.01321	0.01252	0.01206	0.01258	0.01161	0.01206	0.01200	0.01006	0.01001	escudo	Cabo Verde
0.00140	0.00222	0.00213	0.00202	0.00212	0.00196	0.00203	0.00201	0.00169	0.00169	franc CFA[3]	Cameroun
0.67310	0.94401	0.87864	0.97148	1.01035	1.00092	0.97113	0.90427	0.78228	0.75477	dollar	Canada
0.00142	0.00223	0.00212	0.00202	0.00212	0.00196	0.00202	...	...	...	franc CFA[2,3]	Rép. centrafricaine
0.00141	0.00224	0.00211	0.00203	0.00212	0.00196	0.00202	0.00203	0.00169	...	franc CFA[2,3]	Tchad
0.00187	0.00296	0.00284	0.00269	0.00282	0.00261	0.00270	...	...	...	franc	Comores
0.00140	0.00221	0.00213	0.00203	0.00212	0.00196	0.00203	0.00203	0.00169	0.00168	franc CFA[3]	Côte d'Ivoire
1.61099	1.47432	1.39337	1.32577	1.39342	1.28545	1.32704	1.33305	1.11221	1.10623	euro[1,4]	Chypre
0.02592	0.05918	0.05292	0.05252	0.05659	0.05115	0.05112	0.04823	0.04066	0.04094	couronne	Tchéquie
0.12343	0.19753	0.18736	0.17788	0.18648	0.17265	0.17810	0.17848	0.14865	0.14863	couronne	Danemark
0.00563	0.00563	0.00563	0.00563	0.00563	0.00563	0.00563	0.00563	0.00563	...	franc	Djibouti
0.37037	0.37037	0.37037	0.37037	0.37037	0.37037	0.37037	0.37037	0.37037	0.37037	dollar C.O.[5]	Dominique
0.00140	0.00225	0.00212	0.00201	0.00213	0.00196	0.00202	0.00203	...	...	franc CFA[3]	Guinée équatoriale
0.05874	0.09411	0.08932	0.08477	1.39329	1.28481	1.32777	1.32851	1.10892	1.10704	euro[1,6]	Estonie
0.12182	0.10442	0.08581	0.07035	0.05927	0.05662	0.05370	0.05107	0.04861	0.04614	birr	Ethiopie
0.91942	1.47326	1.39614	1.32385	1.39094	1.28491	1.32753	1.32731	1.10823	1.10614	euro	Extra-UE28
0.46700	0.62687	0.51264	0.52376	0.55841	0.55861	0.54191	0.52959	0.47693	0.47800	dollar	Fidji
0.91911	1.47741	1.39517	1.32520	1.39175	1.28546	1.32828	1.32802	1.10874	1.10680	euro[1]	Finlande
0.92139	1.47455	1.39379	1.32552	1.39134	1.28582	1.32783	1.32808	1.10897	1.10621	euro[1]	France
0.00141	0.00225	0.00215	0.00204	0.00212	0.00196	0.00202	0.00202	0.00169	...	franc CFA[2,3]	Gabon
0.07833	0.04514	0.03747	0.03561	0.03424	0.03131	0.02810	0.02428	...	...	dalasi	Gambie
0.92097	1.47478	1.39506	1.32524	1.39174	1.28528	1.32798	1.32818	1.10903	1.10689	euro[1]	Allemagne
1.79936	0.94582	0.71012	0.69889	0.66155	0.55701	0.51202	0.34332	0.26678	...	cedi	Ghana
1.50704	1.82327	1.56954	1.54645	1.60246	1.58625	1.56579	1.64458	1.52964	...	livre	Gibraltar
0.37037	0.37037	0.37037	0.37037	0.37037	0.37037	0.37037	0.37037	0.37037	0.37037	dollar C.O.[5]	Grenade
0.00548	0.00491	0.00490	0.00491	0.00490	0.00489	0.00487	0.00484	0.00484	...	dollar	Guyana
0.04649	0.02548	0.02424	0.02513	0.02468	0.02381	0.02299	0.02208	0.01966	...	gourde	Haïti
0.00353	0.00587	0.00499	0.00481	0.00498	0.00444	0.00447	0.00430	0.00358	0.00356	forint	Hongrie
0.01273	0.01147	0.00810	0.00821	0.00862	0.00800	0.00818	0.00855	0.00757	0.00829	couronne	Islande
0.02223	0.02316	0.02070	0.02189	0.02145	0.01874	0.01706	0.01639	0.01560	0.01488	roupie	Inde
0.91899	1.47061	1.38996	1.32605	1.39224	1.28447	1.32741	1.32775	1.10870	1.10649	euro[1]	Irlande
0.92123	1.47680	1.39403	1.32462	1.39206	1.28538	1.32773	1.32816	1.10840	1.10654	euro[1]	Italie

External trade conversion factors (Table C)

Imports, exports: US dollars per national currency *[cont.]*

Facteurs de conversion pour le commerce extérieur (Tableau C)

Importations, exportations : monnaie nationale en dollars É.-U. *[suite]*

Country or Area	Unit	2000	2008	2009	2010	2011	2012	2013	2014	2015	2016
						Imports - Importations *[cont.]*					
Jamaica	dollar	0.02325	0.01381	0.01139	0.01148	0.01164	0.01126	0.00998	0.00901	0.00856	...
Japan	yen	0.00928	0.00966	0.01072	0.01142	0.01255	0.01253	0.01025	0.00945	0.00826	0.00920
Jordan	dinar	1.41044	1.40908	1.40845	1.40845	1.40845	1.40845	1.40845	1.40845	1.40845	1.40845
Kenya	shilling	0.01312	0.01445	0.01295	0.01260	0.01124	0.01183	0.01161	0.01137	0.01019	0.00985
Kuwait	dinar	3.25974	3.71925	3.47591	3.49173	3.62404	3.57183	3.52625	3.51323	3.32325	3.30921
Latvia	euro[1,7]	1.64778	2.09557	1.98447	1.88479	2.00044	1.82835	1.88976	1.32682	1.10902	1.10624
Lesotho	loti	0.14414	0.12047	0.11943	0.13694	0.13674	0.12172	0.10315	0.09209	0.07799	...
Libya	dinar	1.93754	0.81428	0.80068	0.78987	0.81692	0.79251	0.78678	0.78375	0.72355	...
Lithuania	euro[1,8]	0.25000	0.42866	0.40478	0.38365	0.40363	0.37237	0.38473	0.38472	1.10847	1.10664
Luxembourg	euro[1]	0.92046	1.47456	1.39473	1.32369	1.39215	1.28647	1.32746	1.32701	1.10840	1.10667
Madagascar	ariary	0.00074	0.00059	0.00051	0.00048	0.00050	0.00046	0.00045	0.00042	0.00034	...
Malawi	kwacha	0.01649	0.00712	0.00708	0.00664	0.00638	0.00392	0.00275	0.00236	...	...
Malaysia	ringgit	0.26316	0.30078	0.28471	0.31130	0.32682	0.32372	0.31740	0.30581	0.25666	0.24102
Mali	CFA franc[2,3]	0.00141	0.00224	0.00212	0.00203	0.00212	0.00196	0.00202	0.00202	0.00169	...
Malta	euro[1,9]	2.27827	1.47390	1.39408	1.32442	1.38875	1.28058	1.32580	1.32612	1.11010	1.10885
Mauritania	ouguiya	0.00419	0.00422	0.00381	0.00360	0.00356	0.00337	0.00332	0.00329	0.00310	0.00284
Mauritius	rupee	0.03807	0.03522	0.03152	0.03252	0.03484	0.03326	0.03259	0.03261	0.02852	...
Montenegro	euro	.	1.48173	1.39845	1.31872	1.39522	1.28304	1.32759	1.32796	1.10747	1.10858
Morocco	dirham	0.09413	0.12994	0.12456	0.11875	0.12373	0.11600	0.11894	0.11928	0.10249	...
Namibia	dollar	0.14310	0.12185	0.12236	0.13664	0.13739	0.12199	0.10311	0.09255	0.07838	0.06854
Nepal	rupee	0.01407	0.01422	0.01292	0.01366	0.01347	0.01169	0.01068	...	...	...
Netherlands	euro[1]	0.92071	1.47369	1.39504	1.32572	1.39142	1.28552	1.32808	1.32894	1.10876	1.10642
New Zealand	dollar	0.45242	0.70854	0.63595	0.72277	0.79122	0.81014	0.81970	0.82950	0.69614	0.69860
Niger	CFA franc[3]	0.00139	0.00218	0.00213	0.00202	0.00212	0.00196	0.00203	0.00200	0.00169	...
Niue	NZ dollar	0.45360	0.70944	0.65079	...	...	...	...	...	...	...
Norway	krone	0.11357	0.17898	0.16026	0.16548	0.17849	0.17200	0.17018	0.15902	0.12412	0.11923
Oman	rial Omani	2.60078	2.60078	2.60078	2.60078	2.60078	2.60078	2.60078	2.60078	2.60078	...
Pakistan	rupee	0.01865	0.01435	0.01223	0.01174	0.01157	0.01071	0.00985	0.00989	0.00973	0.00954
Panama	balboa	1.00000	1.00000	1.00000	1.00000	1.00000	1.00000	1.00000	1.00000	1.00000	1.00000
Papua New Guinea	kina	0.36017	0.36908	0.36271	0.36772	0.42064	0.47970	...	...	...	...
Philippines	peso	0.02254	0.02267	0.02098	0.02219	0.02309	0.02368	0.02353	0.02252	0.02195	0.02105
Poland	zloty	0.22983	0.42169	0.32311	0.33223	0.33853	0.30738	0.31653	0.31745	0.26531	0.25387
Portugal	euro[1]	0.92205	1.47562	1.39664	1.32466	1.39257	1.28580	1.32826	1.32792	1.10881	1.10629
Qatar	riyal	0.27473	0.27473	0.27473	0.27473	0.27473	0.27473	0.27473	0.27473	0.27473	0.27473
Rwanda	franc	0.00255	0.00182	0.00176	0.00172	0.00166	0.00162	0.00156	0.00147	0.00139	0.00127
Saint Helena	pound	1.51611	1.85324	1.56448	...	...	...	...	...	...	...
Saint Kitts-Nevis	EC dollar[5]	0.37037	0.37037	0.37037	0.37037	0.37037	0.37037	0.37037	0.37037	0.37037	0.37037
Saint Lucia	EC dollar[5]	0.37037	0.37037	0.37037	0.37037	0.37037	0.37037	0.37037	0.37037	0.37037	0.37037
Saint Vincent-Grenadines	EC dollar[5]	0.37037	0.37037	0.37037	0.37037	0.37037	0.37037	0.37037	0.37037	0.37037	0.37037
Samoa	tala	0.30374	0.37763	0.37144	0.40273	0.43132	0.43616	0.43270	0.42894	0.39023	0.38986
Saudi Arabia	riyal	0.26667	0.26667	0.26667	0.26667	0.26667	0.26667	0.26667	0.26678	0.26683	0.26669
Senegal	CFA franc[3]	0.00140	0.00225	0.00212	0.00202	0.00212	0.00196	0.00203	0.00202	0.00169	0.00169
Serbia	dinar	.	0.01815	0.01484	0.01282	0.01365	0.01137	0.01174	0.01132	0.00919	0.00899
Seychelles	rupee	0.17549	0.11101	0.07475	0.08270	0.08071	0.07303	0.08299	0.07834	0.07508	0.07507
Sierra Leone	leone	0.00047	0.00034	0.00030	0.00025	0.00023	0.00023	0.00023	0.00022	0.00020	...
Singapore	dollar	0.57950	0.70922	0.68983	0.73435	0.79575	0.80017	0.79916	0.78970	0.72773	0.72379
Slovakia	euro[1,10]	0.02164	0.04707	1.39751	1.32569	1.39191	1.28544	1.32883	1.32775	1.10873	1.10657
Solomon Islands	dollar	0.19652	0.12915	0.12414	0.12400	0.13096	0.13596	0.13694	0.13553	0.12628	...
South Africa	rand	0.14376	0.12201	0.11910	0.13684	0.13761	0.12181	0.10364	0.09219	0.07878	0.06825
Spain	euro[1]	0.92032	1.47751	1.39475	1.32537	1.39111	1.28585	1.32853	1.32838	1.10895	1.10648

2000	2008	2009	2010	2011	2012	2013	2014	2015	2016	Unité	Pays ou Zone
					Exports - Exportations *[suite]*						
0.02328	0.01382	0.01139	0.01147	0.01164	0.01127	0.01002	0.00902	0.00857	...	dollar	Jamaïque
0.00928	0.00965	0.01072	0.01142	0.01255	0.01253	0.01024	0.00944	0.00826	0.00921	yen	Japon
1.41044	1.40903	1.40845	1.40845	1.40845	1.40845	1.40845	1.40845	1.40845	1.40845	dinar	Jordanie
0.01312	0.01451	0.01294	0.01262	0.01126	0.01183	0.01161	0.01138	0.01017	0.00985	shilling	Kenya
3.25932	3.72796	3.47802	3.49114	3.62497	3.57281	3.52611	3.52060	3.32420	3.30820	dinar	Koweït
1.65011	2.09490	1.99146	1.88513	1.99970	1.82816	1.89083	1.32704	1.10904	1.10649	euro[1,7]	Lettonie
0.14443	0.12109	0.11918	0.13680	0.13859	0.12127	0.10323	0.09214	0.07814	...	loti	Lesotho
1.94149	0.81664	0.79997	0.78882	0.81772	0.79205	0.78623	0.78519	0.72383	...	dinar	Libye
0.25000	0.42820	0.40500	0.38355	0.40354	0.37227	0.38472	0.38455	1.10866	1.10627	euro[1,8]	Lituanie
0.92175	1.47938	1.39507	1.32523	1.39232	1.28586	1.32830	1.33005	1.10924	1.10724	euro[1]	Luxembourg
0.00074	0.00058	0.00051	0.00048	0.00049	0.00046	0.00045	0.00042	0.00034	...	ariary	Madagascar
0.01606	0.00712	0.00708	0.00665	0.00634	0.00404	0.00275	0.00235	0.00197	0.00139	kwacha	Malawi
0.26316	0.30077	0.28460	0.31090	0.32684	0.32383	0.31713	0.30562	0.25620	0.24101	ringgit	Malaisie
0.00141	0.00222	0.00212	0.00202	0.00212	0.00196	0.00203	0.00202	0.00169	...	franc CFA[2,3]	Mali
2.27775	1.46977	1.39917	1.32455	1.38361	1.28351	1.32724	1.33126	1.10982	1.10773	euro[1,9]	Malte
0.00419	0.00421	0.00381	0.00361	0.00356	0.00337	0.00333	0.00330	0.00308	0.00283	ouguiya	Mauritanie
0.03794	0.03510	0.03144	0.03253	0.03486	0.03326	0.03258	0.03265	0.02854	...	rupee	Maurice
.	1.48263	1.39897	1.32172	1.39043	1.28472	1.32688	1.32286	1.10912	1.10647	euro	Monténégro
0.09411	0.13063	0.12435	0.11876	0.12372	0.11599	0.11893	0.11917	0.10244	...	dirham	Maroc
0.14370	0.12167	0.12018	0.13643	0.13753	0.12174	0.10357	0.09250	0.07900	0.06787	dollar	Namibie
0.01405	0.01431	0.01290	0.01366	0.01350	0.01174	0.01076	...	...	...	rupee	Népal
0.92051	1.47345	1.39541	1.32617	1.39124	1.28590	1.32803	1.32837	1.10911	1.10629	euro[1]	Pays-Bas
0.45450	0.71287	0.62844	0.72123	0.78967	0.80985	0.82102	0.83120	0.70159	0.69586	dollar	Nouvelle-Zélande
0.00141	0.00221	0.00213	0.00201	0.00211	0.00196	0.00204	0.00198	0.00168	...	franc CFA[3]	Niger
0.45625	0.71697	...	...	...	...	...	...	...	...	dollar NZ	Nioué
0.11337	0.18021	0.15968	0.16580	0.17840	0.17209	0.17033	0.15908	0.12424	0.11907	couronne	Norvège
2.60078	2.60078	2.60078	2.60078	2.60078	2.60078	2.60078	2.60078	2.60078	...	rial omani	Oman
0.01864	0.01428	0.01222	0.01174	0.01160	0.01071	0.00984	0.00989	0.00974	0.00954	rupee	Pakistan
1.00000	1.00000	1.00000	1.00000	1.00000	1.00000	1.00000	1.00000	1.00000	1.00000	balboa	Panama
0.36016	0.37042	0.36377	0.36801	0.42186	0.48004	0.44619	0.40647	0.36187	...	kina	Papouasie-Nouvelle-Guinée
0.02244	0.02266	0.02098	0.02219	0.02309	0.02367	0.02354	0.02254	0.02198	0.02105	peso	Philippines
0.22975	0.42237	0.32319	0.33224	0.33817	0.30736	0.31649	0.31752	0.26528	0.25386	zloty	Pologne
0.92232	1.47773	1.39603	1.32576	1.39181	1.28533	1.32756	1.32838	1.10907	1.10660	euro[1]	Portugal
0.27473	0.27473	0.27473	0.27473	0.27473	0.27473	0.27473	0.27473	0.27473	0.27473	riyal	Qatar
0.00255	0.00182	0.00176	0.00171	0.00166	0.00162	0.00155	0.00147	0.00139	0.00127	franc	Rwanda
1.51611	1.85324	1.56448	...	...	...	...	...	...	...	livre	Sainte-Hélèna
0.37037	0.37037	0.37037	0.37037	0.37037	0.37037	0.37037	0.37037	0.37037	0.37037	dollar C.O.[5]	Saint-Kitts-et-Nevis
0.37037	0.37037	0.37037	0.37037	0.37037	0.37037	0.37037	0.37037	0.37037	0.37037	dollar C.O.[5]	Sainte-Lucie
0.37037	0.37037	0.37037	0.37037	0.37037	0.37037	0.37037	0.37037	0.37037	0.37037	dollar C.O.[5]	St.Vincent-Grenadines
0.30446	0.37987	0.37169	0.40204	0.43183	0.43625	0.43228	0.42913	0.38816	0.39077	tala	Samoa
0.26667	0.26667	0.26667	0.26667	0.26667	0.26667	0.26667	0.26681	0.26680	0.26670	riyal	Arabie saoudite
0.00141	0.00224	0.00212	0.00202	0.00212	0.00196	0.00202	0.00203	0.00169	0.00169	franc CFA.[3]	Sénégal
.	0.01818	0.01489	0.01280	0.01368	0.01134	0.01173	0.01133	0.00919	0.00899	dinar	Serbie
0.17468	0.10742	0.07472	0.08289	0.08074	0.07301	0.08292	0.07849	0.07507	...	rupee	Seychelles
0.00049	0.00034	0.00030	0.00025	0.00023	0.00023	0.00023	0.00022	0.00020	...	leone	Sierra Leone
0.57944	0.70932	0.68990	0.73483	0.79555	0.80025	0.79910	0.78967	0.72779	0.72408	dollar	Singapour
0.02167	0.04704	1.39858	1.32606	1.39145	1.28543	1.32836	1.32840	1.10891	1.10703	euro[1,10]	Slovaquie
0.19654	0.12915	0.12413	0.12400	0.13187	0.13596	0.13695	0.13562	0.12616	...	dollar	Iles Salomon
0.14384	0.12203	0.11974	0.13709	0.13775	0.12186	0.10352	0.09211	0.07860	0.06835	rand	Afrique du Sud
0.92078	1.47548	1.39538	1.32548	1.39150	1.28554	1.32777	1.32866	1.10875	1.10674	euro[1]	Espagne

External trade conversion factors (Table C)

Imports, exports: US dollars per national currency *[cont.]*

Facteurs de conversion pour le commerce extérieur (Tableau C)

Importations, exportations : monnaie nationale en dollars É.-U. *[suite]*

Country or Area	Unit	2000	2008	2009	2010	2011	2012	2013	2014	2015	2016
						Imports - Importations *[cont.]*					
Sri Lanka	rupee	0.01295	0.00924	0.00871	0.00885	0.00904	0.00782	0.00774	0.00766	0.00734	...
Suriname	dollar	0.75087	0.36430	0.36430	0.36424	0.30557	0.30303	0.30303	0.30303	0.29475	0.16122
Swaziland	lilangeni	0.14311	0.11858	0.11926	0.13741	0.13605	0.12111	0.10305	...	...	...
Sweden	krona	0.10905	0.15392	0.13174	0.13914	0.15415	0.14766	0.15354	0.14607	0.11857	0.11677
Switzerland	franc	0.59172	0.92938	0.92326	0.96108	1.12846	1.06696	1.07917	1.09262	1.03893	1.01561
Syrian Arab Rep.	pound	0.08909	0.08909	0.08909	0.08909	0.08909	0.08909	0.08909	...	...	...
Thailand	baht	0.02483	0.03005	0.02928	0.03161	0.03281	0.03218	0.03260	0.03079	0.02923	0.02834
Togo	CFA franc[2,3]	0.00141	0.00223	0.00213	0.00202	0.00212	0.00196	0.00202	0.00202	0.00169	0.00168
Tonga	pa'anga	0.56409	0.51709	0.49573	0.52617	0.58081	0.58111	0.56317	0.54013	0.47342	...
Trinidad and Tobago	dollar	0.15874	0.15907	0.15805	0.15685	0.15601	0.15548	0.15519	0.15618	0.15678	...
Tunisia	dinar	0.72984	0.81420	0.74352	0.69829	0.71089	0.64026	0.61547	0.59054	0.50992	0.46596
Tuvalu	Aust. dollar	0.58059	...	...	...	...	...	...	...	...	...
Uganda	shilling	0.00061	0.00059	0.00049	0.00046	0.00039	0.00040	0.00039	0.00038	0.00031	...
United Kingdom	pound	1.51354	1.85795	1.56531	1.54631	1.60320	1.58542	1.56469	1.64650	1.52847	1.35123
United Rep. of Tanzania	shilling	0.00125	0.00084	0.00076	0.00071	0.00064	0.00064	0.00062	0.00060	0.00050	...
Vanuatu	vatu	0.00725	0.00991	0.00945	0.01038	0.01118	0.01079	0.01057	0.01029	0.00917	0.00924
Yemen	rial	0.00619	0.00501	0.00494	0.00458	0.00468	0.00467	0.00465	...	...	...
Zambia	kwacha	0.32281	0.27149	0.20012	0.20851	0.20529	0.19459	0.18536	0.16251	0.11515	0.09725

2000	2008	2009	2010	2011	2012	2013	2014	2015	2016	Unité	Pays ou Zone
				Exports - Exportations *[suite]*							
0.01293	0.00923	0.00870	0.00886	0.00904	0.00786	0.00774	0.00766	0.00734	...	rupee	Sri Lanka
0.74176	0.36430	0.36430	0.36426	0.30437	0.30303	0.30303	0.30303	0.29584	0.15632	dollar	Suriname
0.14300	0.11969	0.12040	0.13721	0.13672	0.12107	0.10271	...	...	...	lilangeni	Swaziland
0.10910	0.15397	0.13148	0.13916	0.15417	0.14760	0.15355	0.14613	0.11860	0.11679	couronne	Suède
0.59161	0.92964	0.92418	0.96138	1.12793	1.06665	1.07885	1.09238	1.03924	1.01554	franc	Suisse
0.08909	0.08909	0.08909	0.08909	0.08909	0.08909	0.08909	...	...	...	livre	République arabe syrienne
0.02486	0.03006	0.02924	0.03163	0.03283	0.03218	0.03254	0.03079	0.02920	0.02834	baht	Thaïlande
0.00140	0.00222	0.00215	0.00201	0.00213	0.00197	0.00203	0.00204	0.00169	0.00169	franc CFA[2,3]	Togo
0.55465	0.51314	0.50336	0.52832	0.58368	0.58282	0.56202	0.53987	...	...	pa'anga	Tonga
0.15873	0.15910	0.15834	0.15685	0.15607	0.15548	0.15522	0.15614	0.15695	...	dollar	Trinité-et-Tobago
0.73083	0.81733	0.74217	0.69844	0.71126	0.64064	0.61588	0.58985	0.50978	0.46577	dinar	Tunisie
0.57480	...	...	...	...	...	...	...	...	...	dollar aust.	Tuvalu
0.00062	0.00058	0.00050	0.00046	0.00039	0.00040	0.00039	0.00038	0.00031	...	shilling	Ouganda
1.51340	1.85700	1.56660	1.54586	1.60327	1.58515	1.56425	1.64685	1.52856	1.35116	livre	Royaume-Uni
0.00125	0.00084	0.00076	0.00071	0.00064	0.00064	0.00062	0.00060	0.00050	...	shilling	Rép.-Unie de Tanzanie
0.00726	0.00992	0.00934	0.01034	0.01119	0.01078	0.01055	0.01031	0.00913	0.00924	vatu	Vanuatu
0.00618	0.00501	0.00493	0.00455	0.00468	0.00466	0.00465	...	...	...	rial	Yémen
0.32860	0.27162	0.20172	0.20863	0.20563	0.19448	0.18540	0.16260	0.11560	0.09713	kwacha	Zambie

External trade conversion factors (Table C)

Imports, exports: US dollars per national currency *[cont.]*

Facteurs de conversion pour le commerce extérieur (Tableau C)

Importations, exportations : monnaie nationale en dollars É.-U. *[suite]*

General note:

Trade conversion factors are weighted averages of monthly or quarterly exchange rates, the weights being the corresponding monthly or quarterly values of imports and exports. The exchange rates are as compiled by the IMF or provided by the country concerned. The conversion factors shown in this table are used to obtain trade data in terms of US dollars.

For further information on sources and presentation, as well as a brief table description, please see the introduction.

1 The conversion factors are calculated for each country of euro zone separately and may vary due to differences in relative weights of monthly or quarterly values of imports and exports.

2 The conversion factors are not trade weighted.

3 Comptoirs Francais du Afrique franc pegged to the euro at CFAF 655.957 per euro.

4 Prior to January 2008, data for Cyprus are in pounds.

5 East Caribbean dollar.

6 Prior to January 2011, data for Estonia are in krooni.

7 Prior to January 2014, data for Latvia are in lati.

8 Prior to January 2015, data for Lithuania are in litai.

9 Prior to January 2008, data for Malta are in liri.

10 Prior to January 2009, data for Slovakia are in koruny.

Note generale:

Les facteurs de conversion pour le commerce extérieur sont les moyennes pondérées des taux de change mensuelles ou trimestrielles. Les coefficients de pondération sont les valeurs mensuelles ou trimestrielles correspondantes des importations ou des exportations. Les taux de change sont les taux calculés par le secretariat du FMI ou fournis par le pays. Les facteurs de conversion montrés dans cette table sont employés pour obtenir les données commerciales en termes de dollars de E.U..

Pour plus d'information sur les sources et la présentation ainsi qu'une brève description du tableau, se il vous plaît se référer à l'introduction.

1 Les facteurs de conversion sont calculés pour chaque pays d'euro zone séparément et peuvent varier en raison des différences dans les ponderation relatifs de valeurs mensuelles ou trimestrielles des importations et des exportations.

2 Les facteurs de conversion ne sont pas pondérés.

3 Comptoirs Français du Afrique franc est chevillé à l'euro à CFAF 655,957 par euro.

4 Avant janvier 2008, les données de Chypre étaient en livres.

5 Dollar des caraïbes orientales.

6 Avant janvier 2011, les données de l'Estonie étaient en krooni.

7 Avant de Janvier 2014, les données pour la Lettonie sont en lati.

8 Avant de janvier 2015, les données pour la Lituanie sont en litai.

9 Avant janvier 2008, les données de Malte étaient en lire.

10 Avant janvier 2009, les données de Slovaquie étaient en couronnes.

World exports by provenance and destination (Table D)

In million U.S. dollars f.o.b.

Exports to ⟶ / ↓ Exports from	Year	World 1/ Monde 1/	Developed economies 2/ Economies développées 2/ Total	Asia-Pacific Asie-Pacifique Total	Asia-Pacific Japan Japon	Europe Total	Europe Germany Allemagne	North America Amérique du Nord Total	North America U.S.A. É.-U.	Commonwealth of Independent States Communauté d'Etats Indépendants Total	Commonwealth of Independent States Europe
Total trade (SITC, Rev. 3, 0-9) 3/											
World 1/	2000	6367105	4393134	404964	327768	2572892	476513	1415279	1161462	77180	64962
	2013	18834659	9841630	949878	699300	6227140	1123501	2664612	2123129	574396	457486
	2014	18824368	9937946	929931	679789	6260438	1146200	2747577	2216767	509273	396726
	2015	16472189	8789898	786308	561018	5434466	1002343	2569124	2117509	334276	252086
	2016	15832640	8635639	758800	546008	5386023	1001415	2490817	2087764	314604	241343
Developed Economies - Asia-Pacific 2/	2000	556339	283777	30765	14422	93424	21063	159588	150830	1004	824
	2013	1006696	328637	80527	47092	91811	21049	156299	146034	14226	12588
	2014	972298	321560	76593	45578	90725	20833	154242	144629	12123	10415
	2015	847023	291568	58972	31898	82741	17835	149854	140405	6815	5945
	2016	868432	306253	56960	28423	96045	19459	153248	143049	7105	5975
Japan	2000	479276	243818	9835	.	83786	19997	150197	142480	793	624
	2013	715097	238107	19161	.	75694	18959	143252	134540	13036	11583
	2014	690217	230734	16545	.	75397	19055	138792	130773	11161	9622
	2015	624874	218311	14961	.	69151	16237	134199	126387	6103	5339
	2016	644932	232713	16293	.	77373	17653	139047	130586	6494	5439
Developed Economies - Europe 2/	2000	2526900	2122748	63492	46070	1802286	345321	256969	232372	31181	28101
	2013	6414745	4723374	130831	79678	4119887	819891	472656	423640	230820	207745
	2014	6382186	4772338	127116	78904	4147082	834954	498140	450405	195456	173724
	2015	5579943	4200422	113006	70035	3596155	716612	491262	446724	122984	106117
	2016	5552682	4220162	115629	72043	3621983	711307	482550	438523	120080	105776
France	2000	295345	239365	6445	4983	204528	44461	28392	25937	2392	1952
	2013	567988	406238	13292	9026	353231	93525	39714	35765	13666	11799
	2014	566656	408722	13132	9056	355259	93804	40331	36382	12084	10293
	2015	493941	354728	10365	6974	304541	79146	39823	36216	7543	5878
	2016	488885	355439	9977	6916	305946	78851	39516	36127	7446	6371
Germany	2000	549607	458641	15684	12137	382583	.	60374	56393	8923	8069
	2013	1450951	1045764	35759	22873	879257	.	130748	118864	65874	59901
	2014	1498158	1090773	34610	22778	916753	.	139409	127771	53090	47763
	2015	1328549	983287	29521	18940	815611	.	138155	126566	33736	30038
	2016	1340752	985281	32043	20691	823982	.	129256	118605	32754	29525
Developed Economies - North America 2/	2000	1059595	701883	86433	71053	194292	31570	421158	241761	3298	2495
	2013	2035018	1088478	106858	75539	334120	50053	647500	346045	18050	14770
	2014	2095899	1131150	109266	76551	343604	51715	678280	364970	17041	13409
	2015	1911586	1027909	100575	70087	332188	52349	595146	313627	10480	8667
	2016	1840742	994416	98861	71323	331224	52125	564331	296635	10235	7743
United States	2000	781831	438752	79374	64922	180027	29446	179351	.	3118	2342
	2013	1577587	693458	94545	65214	297671	46863	301242	.	16210	13210
	2014	1619743	715439	97575	66826	304833	49028	313031	.	15533	12121
	2015	1501846	672146	91090	62441	299864	49641	281192	.	9673	8025
	2016	1450457	654767	88949	63234	298421	49165	267397	.	9457	7079
South-Eastern Europe	2000	19514	13492	50	37	12587	2634	855	763	814	674
	2013	122815	80861	451	359	78057	20172	2353	2072	8107	7070
	2014	127834	85758	451	334	82897	21798	2411	2120	7482	6461
	2015	111635	76844	455	332	74251	20015	2138	1969	4747	4052
	2016	116949	82089	454	342	79669	22737	1966	1770	4610	3934
Commonwealth of Independent States	2000	143026	80405	2954	2938	70174	11061	7277	5787	29043	24078
	2013	764753	418021	25792	25279	374989	28439	17240	13858	149977	106529
	2014	720732	394232	27798	27173	352698	31250	13736	11941	124637	85966
	2015	500388	259236	19423	18866	228827	20411	10987	10047	86515	57368
	2016	397975	196919	10157	9983	175229	23671	11533	10536	68854	44806
Russian Federation	2000	103093	65496	2771	2764	57875	9232	4850	4648	13824	10807
	2013	527266	319303	24351	23948	283303	22962	11649	11177	82694	53358
	2014	497834	297983	26673	26124	261094	25071	10216	9611	66094	41058
	2015	343908	192709	18236	17730	165423	16012	9051	8598	47569	28278
	2016	285491	149687	9526	9384	130315	21258	9845	9426	38198	21243

For general note and footnotes see end of table

Exportations mondiales par provenance et destination (Tableau D)

En millions de dollars E.-U. f.o.b.

← Exportations vers

South-Eastern Europe Europe du Sud-est	Northern Africa Afrique du Nord	Sub-Saharan Africa Afrique subsahari-enne	Latin America and the Caribbean Amérique latine et Caraïbes	Eastern Asia Asie orientale	Southern Asia Asie méridionale	South-eastern Asia Asie du Sud-est	Western Asia Asie occidentale	Oceania Océanie	Others 4/ Autre 4/	Année	Exportations en provenance de ↓
			Commerce total (CTCI, Rev. 3, 0-9) 3/								
27653	53288	75174	364238	703058	82265	358523	191494	6993	34104	2000	Monde 1/
144041	225126	421562	1137897	3473270	567707	1254148	959565	31850	203467	2013	
153570	228701	427505	1118036	3369060	581417	1265926	975778	33070	224088	2014	
136088	188242	360667	985732	2865222	519008	1140186	858721	31152	262996	2015	
140749	178930	311414	892312	2684250	515247	1125728	784218	30126	219424	2016	
153	1694	4909	22054	140231	6988	78409	13638	2260	1223	2000	Economies Développées - Asie-Pacifique 2/
546	3659	12465	37490	401067	23127	138235	37566	6133	3545	2013	
670	3881	11124	34842	375972	22751	135524	40364	6013	7474	2014	
556	3151	9140	30334	315846	22933	117866	36456	5612	6746	2015	
640	3033	7903	29383	327854	23421	117642	33645	5456	6099	2016	
108	1196	3721	20779	124536	4751	68494	10619	460	0	2000	Japon
411	2418	8968	34412	265544	11749	110974	27839	1638	...	2013	
465	2319	8097	31727	256625	12158	104638	30346	1948	0	2014	
431	1935	6593	27241	225846	12718	94999	28314	2382	0	2015	
512	1812	5875	26757	233566	13139	95590	26267	2208	...	2016	
19337	29952	31466	57255	78361	22285	40579	83772	1260	8703	2000	Economies Développées - Europe 2/
97767	98561	111081	166271	402570	93174	135396	305324	3789	46619	2013	
104284	99124	107779	157373	396960	88498	122406	291180	4215	42574	2014	
92804	82784	89471	140098	355911	82552	107793	266898	3369	34858	2015	
98566	80814	77583	131730	350028	77026	107802	251114	3598	34179	2016	
1282	9180	7741	7237	9366	2416	4752	10136	822	658	2000	France
5975	20739	16237	17563	33997	5160	19032	26597	2077	706	2013	
6199	20113	16373	15468	36237	5427	17704	25903	1779	646	2014	
5253	18157	13534	14550	32535	5933	14716	24431	1671	889	2015	
5586	15831	12443	13948	30410	6119	16322	22870	1697	774	2016	
4185	4001	5607	13858	21330	4087	9799	17506	132	1537	2000	Allemagne
20644	11179	18360	43204	124265	17064	29456	69800	361	4982	2013	
23412	12171	18116	41175	137348	17483	29891	69086	916	4697	2014	
21919	10535	16383	36853	114540	15722	25662	66029	795	3088	2015	
24207	11767	14995	35906	121005	16954	26706	63341	303	7533	2016	
563	5657	6359	174241	88736	5624	48689	23401	387	756	2000	Economies Développées - Amérique du Nord 2/
1638	12736	26408	421401	261421	30042	84248	89619	769	207	2013	
1893	13903	28428	435492	262942	29872	83917	90437	802	22	2014	
1475	10265	20441	397954	246305	30427	79874	85642	784	29	2015	
1621	9327	15410	375199	241637	30946	78761	82298	853	38	2016	
510	5026	5936	170031	83092	4640	47139	22458	373	756	2000	États-Unis
1400	11243	23993	408200	231836	26259	78930	85191	689	180	2013	
1637	12555	25497	422568	236263	25630	78554	85345	721	0	2014	
1289	9099	18023	386343	223119	25428	74836	81229	659	...	2015	
1269	8334	13491	364039	219507	26192	74493	78135	773	2	2016	
2212	359	156	160	218	139	76	1700	1	188	2000	Europe du Sud-est
13255	3103	1182	1319	2795	866	922	10082	46	277	2013	
13752	3392	1080	1129	2527	904	1245	10096	15	454	2014	
12467	2913	847	825	2281	855	846	8528	307	175	2015	
13148	2906	810	778	2028	1002	860	7854	590	274	2016	
2773	1375	555	5985	9137	2995	1717	9020	4	17	2000	Communauté d'Etats Indépendants
12896	9966	3301	10258	86324	16586	15424	40893	19	1089	2013	
12857	11300	3426	8411	87008	14371	16394	47006	17	1074	2014	
10676	8735	2919	6459	65967	14141	8065	36142	36	1499	2015	
7338	9662	2718	5950	57918	14025	6680	27075	39	798	2016	
1822	746	344	4307	6980	1896	1120	6556	2	0	2000	Fédération de Russie
7804	5559	1664	8216	60125	9571	8491	23771	16	50	2013	
7106	6464	2020	6690	63717	6644	11864	29199	13	39	2014	
6890	5450	1958	5346	47825	6478	5356	23837	34	456	2015	
5125	8903	2517	5252	42413	8364	5567	19384	37	43	2016	

Voir la fin du tableau pour la remarque générale et les notes.

World exports by provenance and destination (Table D)

In million U.S. dollars f.o.b.

Exports to ⟶ / ↓ Exports from	Year	World 1/ Monde 1/	Developed economies 2/ Economies développées 2/ Total	Asia-Pacific Asie-Pacifique Total	Japan Japon	Europe Total	Germany Allemagne	North America Amérique du Nord Total	U.S.A. É.-U.	Commonwealth of Independent States Communauté d'Etats Indépendants Total	Europe
Total trade (SITC, Rev. 3, 0-9) 3/ [cont.]											
Northern Africa	2000	50201	41036	490	424	35513	3926	5033	4205	101	81
	2013	177789	127695	3196	2258	110187	9182	14311	10543	847	697
	2014	148770	103143	2102	1928	91764	5774	9277	7242	790	741
	2015	102590	67529	1035	917	60413	3834	6081	4714	676	625
	2016	93834	59384	781	440	51002	2977	7601	6045	554	535
Sub-Saharan Africa	2000	95660	60389	2656	2083	35119	3108	22614	21638	237	189
	2013	409981	170660	16625	11764	118470	8289	35565	28826	1179	1031
	2014	407901	162739	16354	11883	119944	8303	26440	21591	1052	922
	2015	338432	137239	12553	9185	105300	8457	19386	16632	920	781
	2016	242172	96109	7034	5209	70373	8225	18702	15747	1107	982
South Africa	2000	26298	15846	1873	1362	10968	1902	3004	2783	79	33
	2013	95112	33845	6525	5611	20064	3841	7256	6888	526	460
	2014	90612	34365	5826	4869	21276	4234	7263	6550	499	461
	2015	69631	26834	4319	3648	16734	4265	5781	5349	391	350
	2016	74111	29524	4279	3455	19238	5318	6007	5557	406	352
Latin America and the Caribbean	2000	354156	265394	8573	7732	43693	6862	213127	206810	1330	1280
	2013	1112043	632389	27484	23602	135683	17317	469222	415484	9242	8301
	2014	1085914	634938	25263	21207	129024	16968	480651	431042	9984	9087
	2015	927732	566520	20385	16943	109215	14724	436920	401307	7200	6485
	2016	884567	548273	20612	17400	108798	14945	418864	396180	7297	6665
Brazil	2000	55119	33690	2853	2481	16230	2520	14607	14041	522	487
	2013	242033	88583	8496	7973	50899	6821	29189	26482	4119	3504
	2014	225098	83778	7228	6740	44978	6918	31572	29219	4538	4106
	2015	191127	69868	5311	4848	36589	5327	27968	25616	2830	2562
	2016	185235	67380	5124	4609	35577	5005	26679	24322	2726	2412
Eastern Asia	2000	776276	411019	101783	90092	125367	27229	183869	173206	4993	3848
	2013	3613890	1296680	283874	221402	464466	90393	548340	506633	104291	74913
	2014	3760975	1374558	283662	218660	501584	95806	589311	546790	104593	74654
	2015	3597769	1346974	262650	196425	484094	90402	600230	558721	68484	47103
	2016	3397304	1286855	247931	188291	472517	86290	566407	528060	72410	51045
China	2000	249203	142806	45499	41654	41976	9278	55331	52156	3183	2411
	2013	2209007	931031	191818	150133	340740	67343	398473	369064	83517	58425
	2014	2342293	992251	193275	149391	371683	72703	427294	397099	85739	60009
	2015	2273468	978375	180842	135616	357766	69155	439767	409979	58005	39121
	2016	2097637	924839	171313	129268	340305	65214	413221	385678	61894	42723
Southern Asia	2000	91623	55021	8445	7708	29131	3854	17446	16367	1848	1204
	2013	480250	161374	20555	16891	82808	14101	58011	54371	6253	4499
	2014	456859	145155	18138	14562	72842	11811	54175	51150	5765	3946
	2015	393456	148607	15593	10844	76392	13810	56622	53028	4567	3116
	2016	369188	151258	12734	8225	80840	13611	57684	54258	4222	3132
South-Eastern Asia	2000	426829	218831	69524	57855	65451	12035	83855	80843	606	556
	2013	1270966	428497	174553	123486	130732	25807	123212	115613	7683	6802
	2014	1290957	443173	172526	120531	138777	26773	131870	124081	7468	6379
	2015	1158886	410232	142781	101872	133443	26727	134008	126729	5898	5003
	2016	1148139	415457	134406	96616	143481	27848	137570	130123	6157	5444
Western Asia	2000	261988	136094	28010	26461	64849	7665	43235	26629	2711	1622
	2013	1414987	379176	75473	70971	184164	18385	119539	59653	23712	12532
	2014	1359787	361259	65554	61059	187136	19591	108569	60343	22868	11011
	2015	989784	250596	33996	30942	150432	16889	66168	43299	14988	6820
	2016	908981	272956	49004	45820	153936	18068	70016	66501	11970	5304
Oceania	2000	4996	3047	1789	892	1006	185	252	250	14	10
	2013	10725	5788	3659	978	1766	423	363	358	10	8
	2014	14257	7942	5108	1418	2360	625	474	464	15	12
	2015	12963	6222	4885	2671	1016	277	321	305	5	5
	2016	11674	5509	4239	1890	926	152	345	336	3	3

For general note and footnotes see end of table

Exportations mondiales par provenance et destination (Tableau D)

En millions de dollars E.-U. f.o.b.

South-Eastern Europe / Europe du Sud-est	Northern Africa / Afrique septentrionale	Sub-Saharan Africa / Afrique du Nord	Latin America and the Caribbean / Amérique latine et Caraïbes	Eastern Asia / Asie orientale	Southern Asia / Asie méridionale	South-eastern Asia / Asie du Sud-est	Western Asia / Asie occidentale	Oceania / Océanie	Others 4/ / Autre 4/	Année	← Exportations vers / Exportations en provence de ↓
											Commerce total (CTCI, Rev. 3, 0-9) 3/ [suite]
92	1178	336	2058	315	793	277	3165	1	849	2000	Afrique du Nord
651	8832	3911	5323	7422	5571	2091	13503	3	1942	2013	
688	7661	3979	4743	5635	4657	1951	13554	6	1963	2014	
673	5691	3893	2903	3434	2910	1399	12191	74	1217	2015	
609	5096	3948	3136	1921	2720	1929	13672	4	861	2016	
66	417	12505	2551	9564	5265	1958	1861	40	806	2000	Afrique subsaharienne
482	1361	81914	15936	77629	29260	11781	16685	729	2365	2013	
508	1315	79888	17574	73817	32609	16011	18943	534	2909	2014	
451	1534	66808	14471	51465	31131	14351	16074	404	3584	2015	
207	1429	54867	4165	39334	21057	9856	12363	246	1433	2016	
30	91	4147	576	2657	531	739	1012	6	587	2000	Afrique du sud
84	535	26829	1700	18905	4981	3548	3628	32	500	2013	
68	401	27210	1370	14381	4898	2792	4024	48	556	2014	
39	591	21209	1056	10093	3813	1868	2524	44	1168	2015	
70	406	21005	1069	12080	4044	1966	2903	47	589	2016	
324	1359	1675	63198	8850	2276	2794	2816	18	4123	2000	Amérique latine et Caraïbes
2161	9874	10055	228452	151257	19077	24359	19969	41	5167	2013	
2020	9817	9590	207708	139119	20447	25946	19904	51	6390	2014	
1751	7804	7896	165377	111682	16827	21676	17640	65	3295	2015	
1481	8219	7645	142330	102533	20217	24295	18968	46	3263	2016	
129	506	888	13886	2603	621	926	1345	4	...	2000	Brésil
766	5020	6516	54494	56918	6065	9215	10318	18	0	2013	
636	4820	5603	47081	49457	7440	11446	10282	17	0	2014	
473	4019	4448	39748	42397	6871	10716	9733	24	0	2015	
443	3661	4307	37419	41708	7106	10622	9846	15	0	2016	
688	3065	8346	25195	220136	13063	68294	18699	1258	1519	2000	Asie orientale
6244	27541	86818	182689	1198808	127286	419757	147808	11886	4081	2013	
7368	31412	96255	184614	1177400	151593	451796	164704	12898	3785	2014	
6904	31565	95535	175103	1102729	151483	443164	158825	14300	2702	2015	
7505	29757	81798	150647	1036976	153486	422032	138576	14366	2896	2016	
356	1410	3602	7125	62121	4510	17341	6683	65	2	2000	Chine
4937	21765	70897	133232	525547	89284	244087	101780	2929	...	2013	
5722	24223	81626	135107	519016	110168	272106	113646	2688	...	2014	
5331	25579	82748	131246	485747	112014	277395	111764	5263	...	2015	
5704	23696	68348	113229	428157	112258	256165	96765	5452	1131	2016	
48	2665	2171	1904	13213	3396	3788	7528	32	8	2000	Asie méridionale
727	5611	31241	16954	81852	42166	39806	88034	167	6065	2013	
966	5481	31745	16521	81183	47455	33336	86344	144	2764	2014	
702	4260	23761	12212	60289	39181	28817	68493	238	2329	2015	
862	4014	20544	11595	50287	34667	29128	60596	125	1890	2016	
156	1009	4130	6783	75807	11390	98157	8580	996	385	2000	Asie Sud-est
809	6004	25468	36944	323347	60418	330675	41967	7347	1809	2013	
911	6123	26407	35100	325600	62677	329564	44231	7362	2343	2014	
853	5214	21512	30639	298313	56594	281965	40244	5162	2260	2015	
880	4840	17453	29769	296347	54886	278105	37748	4353	2145	2016	
1239	4560	2529	2577	57987	8037	13500	17312	654	14789	2000	Asie occidentale
6864	37876	27619	14695	477378	119825	50606	148106	514	128617	2013	
7652	35290	27721	14285	438779	105158	46642	148993	510	150629	2014	
6762	24325	18425	9345	247398	69701	33564	111575	460	202647	2015	
7893	19831	20698	7616	174324	81634	47768	100301	157	163835	2016	
2	0	37	277	502	15	285	2	81	736	2000	Océanie
1	2	100	164	1399	310	850	10	406	1683	2013	
2	2	83	244	2118	427	1193	21	503	1707	2014	
12	0	20	14	3602	273	806	13	341	1654	2015	
0	1	38	14	3064	159	871	8	293	1713	2016	

Voir la fin du tableau pour la remarque générale et les notes.

World exports by provenance and destination (Table D)

In million U.S. dollars f.o.b.

Exports to ⟶ / ↓ Exports from	Year	World 1/ Monde 1/	Developed economies 2/ Economies développées 2/ Total	Asia-Pacific Asie-Pacifique Total	Asia-Pacific Japan Japon	Europe Total	Europe Germany Allemagne	North America Amérique du Nord Total	North America U.S.A. É.-U.	Commonwealth of Independent States Communauté d'Etats Indépendants Total	Commonwealth of Independent States Europe
Food, beverages and tobacco (SITC, Rev. 3, 0 and 1)											
World 1/	2000	387522	271587	40604	36935	175512	32486	55471	43989	9637	8437
	2013	1260642	725940	73159	57073	511823	87076	140958	106792	59159	47820
	2014	1301004	746223	74229	56679	520143	89036	151851	116307	54288	42329
	2015	1178240	676525	66066	50315	460245	77780	150215	115867	37012	27506
	2016	1188161	688568	66731	50811	468527	79602	153310	118866	34693	26759
Developed Economies - Asia-Pacific 2/	2000	19827	9696	4287	3291	2443	277	2966	2615	52	44
	2013	54669	17948	8455	4668	4121	505	5371	4695	744	613
	2014	58666	20123	8439	4580	4315	458	7369	6572	552	413
	2015	53337	19018	7333	3974	4028	437	7657	6810	255	173
	2016	51544	17873	7718	4046	3814	432	6341	5645	280	223
Japan	2000	2088	612	72	.	107	14	432	395	9	9
	2013	4447	1025	104	.	199	42	722	671	37	36
	2014	4530	1097	106	.	218	32	773	715	45	41
	2015	4933	1146	116	.	244	37	786	728	30	26
	2016	5575	1279	124	.	283	41	873	807	28	27
Developed Economies - Europe 2/	2000	178437	151894	5172	4319	136289	26443	10433	8969	3784	3519
	2013	537332	435470	10767	7116	400612	71681	24091	20070	21060	19677
	2014	545495	441360	11565	7666	404443	71821	25352	21295	16852	15308
	2015	476209	387030	9935	6345	352042	62037	25053	21299	9306	8138
	2016	488805	398958	10614	6845	361825	64377	26518	22652	9038	8089
France	2000	31410	26548	981	902	23387	4572	2180	1853	351	335
	2013	71698	54041	1798	1404	47933	7682	4310	3498	1128	1031
	2014	69131	52259	1813	1403	46031	7417	4415	3668	926	813
	2015	60107	44899	1600	1210	38804	6105	4494	3816	499	415
	2016	58215	44244	1590	1190	37799	5947	4855	4167	466	391
Germany	2000	21712	18446	290	250	17384	.	772	696	643	595
	2013	80143	67110	903	515	63885	.	2323	1955	2915	2630
	2014	81732	68275	1122	699	64839	.	2314	1967	2226	1949
	2015	69707	57413	815	434	54586	.	2012	1716	1466	1247
	2016	70447	58057	839	453	55116	.	2102	1790	1416	1255
Developed Economies - North America 2/	2000	63030	38838	13344	12808	6706	911	18788	10626	758	660
	2013	151832	75222	16218	14122	12885	1715	46120	22061	2237	1888
	2014	160333	79795	17281	14985	14195	1837	48320	23541	1582	1305
	2015	147951	75180	14922	12822	13238	1705	47019	22952	503	322
	2016	145134	73712	14629	12714	12421	1458	46663	22915	472	328
United States	2000	46652	25718	11964	11506	5597	832	8157	.	727	631
	2013	114236	48372	13812	11962	10651	1590	23909	.	1697	1410
	2014	119839	50588	14848	12800	11169	1683	24571	.	1096	862
	2015	109308	47460	12874	11012	10794	1575	23792	.	425	270
	2016	107641	45970	12475	10774	9947	1321	23549	.	383	253
South-Eastern Europe	2000	1232	651	17	12	588	125	45	39	75	57
	2013	12941	6190	69	44	5944	639	177	147	575	532
	2014	13388	6434	73	40	6182	670	180	148	787	726
	2015	11939	5812	112	76	5510	565	189	160	579	539
	2016	12464	5960	109	82	5683	599	169	143	587	554
Commonwealth of Independent States	2000	3260	709	150	145	524	90	35	32	2116	1720
	2013	37045	5642	575	547	4928	447	139	120	17964	10797
	2014	39738	6256	348	324	5759	542	148	131	17170	9617
	2015	33979	5578	451	444	4978	466	149	130	13235	7125
	2016	25949	3229	350	345	2761	334	117	100	11739	6770
Russian Federation	2000	1016	394	140	137	231	34	23	21	379	91
	2013	13709	1774	224	218	1485	138	65	52	4732	1656
	2014	16338	2265	251	246	1957	167	57	49	4983	1593
	2015	13891	1899	291	287	1557	98	51	42	4026	1258
	2016	14279	2133	342	338	1739	126	52	43	3853	1319

For general note and footnotes see end of table

Exportations mondiales par provenance et destination (Tableau D)

En millions de dollars E.-U. f.o.b.

South-Eastern Europe Europe du Sud-est	Northern Africa Afrique septentrio-nale	Sub-Saharan Africa Afrique du Nord	Latin America and the Caribbean Amérique latine et Caraïbes	Eastern Asia Asie orientale	Southern Asia Asie méridionale	South-eastern Asia Asie du Sud-est	Western Asia Asie occidentale	Oceania Océanie	Others 4/ Autre 4/	← Exportations vers Année	Exportations en provence de ↓
			Produits alimentaires, boisson et tabac (CTCI, Rev. 3, 0 et 1)								
2504	7330	8338	22145	23654	5235	16040	18516	773	1762	2000	Monde 1/
13999	29221	49070	75253	108360	27833	83954	81363	2559	3929	2013	
14598	31730	48021	77415	117311	30162	90410	84120	2640	4086	2014	
13251	26229	41151	68414	115348	28821	87251	77641	2459	4138	2015	
13767	23592	38570	67691	123299	28350	91380	71902	2419	3930	2016	
5	396	398	490	3381	863	3022	988	438	98	2000	Economies Développées - Asie-Pacifique 2/
6	990	1504	1080	14982	1551	9379	4514	1167	804	2013	
6	1357	1311	882	16191	1645	10553	4811	1134	100	2014	
6	1090	963	931	14699	1911	9070	3555	909	929	2015	
7	1031	748	733	15374	2102	8739	3111	899	647	2016	
0	0	18	23	1135	6	205	26	56	0	2000	Japon
0	31	45	24	2338	14	825	76	33	...	2013	
1	27	44	16	2367	15	797	88	33	...	2014	
1	35	52	15	2695	13	816	98	29	...	2015	
1	28	78	21	3148	18	858	89	26	...	2016	
1688	2963	3064	3113	2851	484	2053	5467	136	940	2000	Economies Développées - Europe 2/
9182	8850	12143	7034	14822	1923	7787	17776	390	897	2013	
9470	10197	12394	7352	17707	2588	8203	18113	409	850	2014	
8617	8335	10371	6714	17528	1849	7427	18008	348	678	2015	
9193	7345	9169	6709	19560	1965	7878	17942	358	689	2016	
79	984	883	429	542	106	406	968	112	2	2000	France
389	3537	2921	896	3458	156	2038	2794	296	43	2013	
394	3699	2764	749	3425	167	2086	2309	312	39	2014	
322	2721	2314	723	3951	275	1965	2163	260	15	2015	
319	2445	2087	695	3545	287	1834	2009	261	21	2016	
193	367	112	203	255	126	188	974	1	204	2000	Allemagne
1455	737	942	463	1770	477	801	3280	4	189	2013	
1554	848	888	531	2239	939	917	3108	4	204	2014	
1371	894	1065	522	2275	451	748	3329	4	171	2015	
1488	517	834	532	2860	420	827	3284	4	208	2016	
73	1934	802	9212	5434	817	2246	2744	78	93	2000	Economies Développées - Amérique du Nord 2/
166	2733	3201	29848	21841	2618	8187	5598	166	17	2013	
136	2664	2998	32523	22729	2896	8822	5994	178	16	2014	
117	1948	2301	28900	22078	3532	7876	5302	192	22	2015	
118	1933	2069	29191	21093	3083	7857	5419	159	26	2016	
71	1498	658	8172	4897	267	1950	2525	77	93	2000	États-Unis
133	1982	2438	27075	19384	1215	7052	4725	155	7	2013	
116	1882	2158	29562	20347	1282	7818	4826	164	...	2014	
99	1204	1633	26371	19484	1507	6649	4299	179	...	2015	
99	1279	1497	27074	18154	1457	7032	4547	150	...	2016	
284	44	6	3	4	34	5	114	1	13	2000	Europe du Sud-est
2662	1176	66	16	360	109	100	1671	0	16	2013	
2876	1138	123	23	228	70	138	1546	0	24	2014	
2547	760	115	23	211	166	117	1588	0	21	2015	
2626	840	264	22	172	88	322	1564	0	17	2016	
27	17	15	6	160	30	2	162	...	14	2000	Communauté d'Etats Indépendants
209	2455	1018	234	3000	1457	422	4550	0	93	2013	
233	3218	1398	238	3368	1944	377	5422	3	112	2014	
235	2617	1079	155	3741	1956	722	4530	0	131	2015	
260	1497	944	148	3151	1831	249	2817	0	84	2016	
6	6	0	1	155	7	1	67	...	0	2000	Fédération de Russie
105	877	621	197	2514	472	141	2262	0	14	2013	
110	1401	1060	195	2415	677	94	3127	0	11	2014	
96	1106	830	83	2475	739	84	2545	0	8	2015	
121	1297	931	138	2755	780	147	2115	0	9	2016	

Voir la fin du tableau pour la remarque générale et les notes.

World exports by provenance and destination (Table D)

In million U.S. dollars f.o.b.

Exports to ⟶ / ↓ Exports from	Year	World 1/ Monde 1/	Developed economies 2/ Economies développées 2/ Total	Asia-Pacific Asie-Pacifique Total	Japan Japon	Europe Total	Germany Allemagne	North America Amérique du Nord Total	U.S.A. É.-U.	Commonwealth of Independent States Communauté d'Etats Indépendants Total	Europe
Food, beverages and tobacco (SITC, Rev. 3, 0 and 1) [cont.]											
Northern Africa	2000	2277	1661	281	279	1299	71	81	58	63	63
	2013	9724	4258	174	162	3813	214	271	209	584	574
	2014	9825	4373	165	156	3956	277	251	201	568	558
	2015	9565	4136	152	141	3711	225	273	209	495	486
	2016	9923	4500	180	167	4058	238	262	197	455	449
Sub-Saharan Africa	2000	10611	6635	527	453	5477	622	632	556	112	111
	2013	37805	16528	948	741	13878	1192	1703	1422	517	449
	2014	38761	16276	790	618	13460	1276	2026	1723	513	441
	2015	38414	16632	676	512	13761	1549	2196	1829	498	424
	2016	36065	15989	723	559	12978	1437	2288	1943	565	506
South Africa	2000	2168	1261	176	144	923	69	161	110	8	7
	2013	9003	3247	482	349	2412	248	353	216	209	205
	2014	9172	3082	314	208	2392	232	376	236	190	184
	2015	7718	2720	172	85	2213	251	334	201	189	178
	2016	8159	2911	202	113	2327	264	382	235	156	149
Latin America and the Caribbean	2000	46799	31044	2601	2312	13423	2179	15020	14343	1095	1082
	2013	175182	84694	8014	7012	37007	5119	39672	37327	6859	6343
	2014	176236	86760	7052	5829	37421	6084	42287	39750	7526	6982
	2015	164772	84294	6514	5356	34658	5298	43121	40692	5277	4853
	2016	174381	88800	6518	5367	37075	5479	45208	42488	5337	4890
Brazil	2000	10142	6609	710	514	4599	667	1300	1179	471	460
	2013	57396	21110	2822	2693	14609	2106	3679	3036	3402	3038
	2014	53971	19611	2265	2121	13724	2701	3622	3019	3789	3436
	2015	48285	17454	2137	1990	11702	2171	3614	3102	2278	2049
	2016	47292	16381	2074	1899	10860	1943	3447	2942	1952	1684
Eastern Asia	2000	21062	11179	7892	7697	1446	308	1841	1605	297	254
	2013	75457	29137	13895	12564	6743	1458	8499	7441	2977	2435
	2014	80818	29811	13923	12494	7009	1551	8878	7743	3160	2571
	2015	80748	28562	12846	11452	6906	1520	8810	7751	2475	1918
	2016	86026	29032	12802	11399	7113	1437	9116	7938	2527	2069
China	2000	13027	7217	4960	4877	1214	296	1044	910	189	162
	2013	58335	24830	11208	10172	6351	1423	7272	6393	2657	2171
	2014	61797	25091	11097	10029	6562	1504	7432	6515	2828	2287
	2015	61464	24040	10263	9254	6440	1480	7337	6478	2260	1752
	2016	64616	24231	10147	9104	6550	1390	7534	6566	2340	1924
Southern Asia	2000	8344	3486	828	754	1715	288	944	857	581	432
	2013	46130	9918	1337	1021	5642	740	2939	2596	1761	1342
	2014	44634	9896	1121	779	5494	685	3282	2899	1669	1239
	2015	39094	9380	1055	739	5017	645	3308	2947	1447	1079
	2016	36283	9365	1005	694	4846	610	3514	3167	1274	954
South-Eastern Asia	2000	23694	12540	5245	4706	3056	465	4239	3873	168	159
	2013	85035	32352	12039	8728	9635	1723	10678	9592	1170	1042
	2014	92961	35291	12657	8778	10474	1948	12160	10942	1174	1055
	2015	87397	31813	11445	8124	9431	1634	10937	9854	905	823
	2016	90490	32605	11513	8294	9548	1677	11544	10358	910	816
Western Asia	2000	8472	2869	147	100	2350	630	372	343	535	335
	2013	36057	7676	418	227	6181	1423	1076	894	2702	2121
	2014	38208	8599	488	263	6819	1560	1291	1060	2720	2103
	2015	33720	8460	455	246	6732	1618	1273	1020	2030	1621
	2016	29908	7893	418	228	6135	1439	1341	1096	1506	1109
Oceania	2000	475	385	113	58	197	76	74	73	0	0
	2013	1434	904	249	121	434	222	221	218	10	8
	2014	1942	1250	326	166	615	327	309	303	14	11
	2015	1114	631	169	84	233	82	228	215	5	5
	2016	1190	651	152	73	270	85	229	224	2	2

For general note and footnotes see end of table

Exportations mondiales par provenance et destination (Tableau D)

En millions de dollars E.-U. f.o.b.

South-Eastern Europe Europe du Sud-est	Northern Africa Afrique septentrio-nale	Sub-Saharan Africa Afrique du Nord	Latin America and the Caribbean Amérique latine et Caraïbes	Eastern Asia Asie orientale	Southern Asia Asie méridionale	South-eastern Asia Asie du Sud-est	Western Asia Asie occidentale	Oceania Océanie	Others 4/ Autre 4/	Année	← Exportations vers Exportations en provence de ↓
			Produits alimentaires, boisson et tabac (CTCI, Rev. 3, 0 et 1) [suite]								
10	168	84	5	11	2	10	238	1	24	2000	Afrique du Nord
50	1014	1048	56	77	82	116	2326	2	110	2013	
58	1038	993	44	89	108	128	2320	2	103	2014	
56	855	984	43	101	84	141	2543	2	124	2015	
50	904	969	89	114	98	135	2472	2	133	2016	
23	203	2076	81	234	457	189	563	6	31	2000	Afrique subsaharienne
149	580	12151	349	1034	1906	1568	2946	18	60	2013	
240	617	11883	322	1336	2663	1924	2919	9	58	2014	
186	608	10748	398	1013	2768	2180	3335	9	39	2015	
86	551	9687	406	1198	2793	2521	2222	9	38	2016	
4	8	536	11	103	65	36	130	0	7	2000	Afrique du sud
2	24	4078	137	479	56	280	476	5	11	2013	
8	29	4096	53	698	85	352	553	5	21	2014	
7	41	3321	30	476	63	333	526	5	8	2015	
12	34	3483	33	536	78	301	586	7	22	2016	
167	811	566	8728	1523	396	735	1497	11	227	2000	Amérique latine et Caraïbes
737	7010	4775	32693	14296	3476	9367	10837	20	418	2013	
721	7101	3985	31895	13492	4034	10283	9954	28	457	2014	
744	5812	3529	27541	13986	3834	10138	9151	26	441	2015	
661	5800	4061	26289	16218	4488	11901	10392	24	408	2016	
85	185	264	1061	372	139	250	705	0	...	2000	Brésil
436	3603	3180	5851	6935	2751	3667	6455	7	...	2013	
376	3268	2629	5885	5608	2892	4200	5706	6	...	2014	
280	2994	2141	4991	5422	3024	4339	5354	7	...	2015	
251	2837	2324	3779	6129	3607	4320	5705	6	...	2016	
26	145	344	185	6267	195	2052	310	34	28	2000	Asie orientale
97	687	2083	2192	19507	1046	15642	1820	256	11	2013	
94	671	2190	2039	22271	1203	17085	2029	256	9	2014	
83	678	2039	1936	22600	1392	18647	2038	291	6	2015	
83	635	2031	2262	26617	1659	18735	2142	281	24	2016	
26	142	295	145	3365	152	1242	247	5	...	2000	Chine
93	645	1880	2076	12956	954	10712	1428	104	...	2013	
87	623	1984	1849	14650	1074	11971	1506	134	...	2014	
77	631	1851	1785	14692	1288	13209	1481	150	...	2015	
75	603	1843	2072	16213	1538	14062	1500	138	...	2016	
11	216	182	102	413	819	622	1907	2	1	2000	Asie méridionale
74	1089	4476	341	2089	8561	8054	9724	13	30	2013	
55	1166	3824	384	2128	7389	7636	10418	12	56	2014	
70	899	3501	339	1888	5870	6310	9362	11	16	2015	
51	855	3319	364	1441	4683	6816	8097	12	6	2016	
36	127	650	150	3276	656	5000	975	46	70	2000	Asie Sud-est
157	1023	4080	1185	15906	2219	22164	3692	377	709	2013	
147	1103	4574	1429	17239	2679	23890	3746	457	1231	2014	
138	970	3551	1211	17035	2887	23698	3497	558	1134	2015	
140	1024	3323	1258	17909	2980	25171	3374	570	1226	2016	
153	305	144	71	79	482	70	3551	0	213	2000	Asie occidentale
510	1614	2520	226	370	2881	891	15907	5	755	2013	
560	1458	2344	281	403	2938	990	16847	7	1061	2014	
441	1657	1968	222	385	2569	664	14727	5	590	2015	
491	1177	1975	215	355	2574	746	12344	5	626	2016	
0	...	6	0	21	0	33	0	21	10	2000	Océanie
1	0	4	2	75	3	278	2	146	9	2013	
2	1	3	2	129	5	380	2	146	8	2014	
12	0	1	1	84	2	261	4	106	7	2015	
0	0	10	5	98	3	309	5	100	5	2016	

Voir la fin du tableau pour la remarque générale et les notes.

World exports by provenance and destination (Table D)

In million U.S. dollars f.o.b.

Exports to ⟶ / ↓ Exports from	Year	World 1/ Monde 1/	Developed economies 2/ Economies développées 2/ Total	Asia-Pacific Asie-Pacifique Total	Japan Japon	Europe Total	Germany Allemagne	North America Amérique du Nord Total	U.S.A. É.-U.	Commonwealth of Independent States Communauté d'Etats Indépendants Total	Europe
		Cereals (SITC, Rev. 3, 041-045)									
World 1/	2000	33065	11142	3022	2941	6974	796	1145	847	615	515
	2013	122556	35889	7280	6878	23803	3351	4806	4096	2398	1078
	2014	119846	33211	6275	5796	22663	3335	4272	3388	2125	877
	2015	103703	27613	5194	4828	19067	2745	3352	2544	1673	543
	2016	91622	24434	4873	4577	16849	2448	2711	2050	1432	519
Developed Economies - Asia-Pacific 2/	2000	2868	500	431	393	69	0	1	0	0	0
	2013	8089	871	749	574	107	12	15	14	0	0
	2014	7496	785	682	488	86	1	17	16	1	1
	2015	6478	495	429	283	61	1	5	3	1	1
	2016	5150	507	427	307	75	1	5	4	1	1
Japan	2000	14	0	0	.	0	...	0	0	0	0
	2013	18	2	1	.	1	0	0	0	0	0
	2014	25	2	1	.	1	0	0	0	0	0
	2015	36	3	1	.	1	0	1	1	0	0
	2016	33	5	1	.	2	0	2	2	0	0
Developed Economies - Europe 2/	2000	8358	5731	32	30	5632	749	67	63	229	210
	2013	25454	16951	58	48	16778	3070	115	98	377	369
	2014	23809	15383	48	32	15144	2983	191	162	335	328
	2015	21687	13091	90	82	12851	2502	150	99	197	191
	2016	18659	12334	46	36	12172	2288	117	93	194	189
France	2000	3913	2939	2	2	2928	409	9	9	11	10
	2013	10862	6581	38	36	6526	813	17	16	71	70
	2014	8971	5236	16	7	5206	632	14	13	71	70
	2015	7991	4266	9	8	4252	468	5	4	46	45
	2016	6206	3644	9	8	3603	430	32	32	35	34
Germany	2000	1594	700	28	28	672	.	0	0	45	37
	2013	4251	2424	11	11	2388	.	25	25	25	25
	2014	3770	1939	23	23	1899	.	17	17	12	12
	2015	3338	1453	36	36	1407	.	11	10	9	9
	2016	2766	1384	4	4	1366	.	14	13	9	9
Developed Economies - North America 2/	2000	12707	3731	2363	2355	605	26	763	508	127	107
	2013	28373	7596	3863	3843	1146	23	2587	2069	22	22
	2014	31605	8922	4609	4563	1837	42	2476	1829	23	23
	2015	26136	6737	3585	3547	1205	29	1948	1372	9	9
	2016	24624	6023	3476	3452	1019	33	1527	1037	6	5
United States	2000	9737	2788	2109	2106	424	26	255	.	127	106
	2013	20301	4273	3199	3180	555	16	518	.	21	21
	2014	22851	5297	3998	3952	652	11	647	.	22	22
	2015	18800	4181	3148	3111	458	9	575	.	9	8
	2016	19000	3885	3011	2987	385	12	489	.	5	5
South-Eastern Europe	2000	149	20	...	...	20	3	0	0	24	18
	2013	4686	1467	29	29	1432	48	7	5	149	147
	2014	4467	1472	30	23	1432	66	11	6	175	171
	2015	3664	1246	37	26	1191	30	18	11	100	100
	2016	3928	1299	11	11	1279	27	9	6	84	83
Commonwealth of Independent States	2000	281	34	...	...	31	0	3	3	118	81
	2013	12651	2417	357	338	2059	77	1	0	1595	395
	2014	14974	2434	107	90	2327	145	0	0	1341	188
	2015	12674	2083	108	108	1973	93	2	2	1157	119
	2016	7170	695	51	51	639	23	5	5	934	131
Russian Federation	2000	96	5	...	...	5	0	0	0	35	5
	2013	4752	259	10	10	248	13	0	0	449	15
	2014	7087	420	13	13	406	40	0	0	560	13
	2015	5653	280	12	12	267	11	2	2	525	10
	2016	5606	449	51	51	398	17	0	0	381	13

For general note and footnotes see end of table

Exportations mondiales par provenance et destination (Tableau D)

En millions de dollars E.-U. f.o.b.

← Exportations vers

South-Eastern Europe Europe du Sud-est	Northern Africa Afrique septentrionale	Sub-Saharan Africa Afrique du Nord	Latin America and the Caribbean Amérique latine et Caraïbes	Eastern Asia Asie orientale	Southern Asia Asie méridionale	South-eastern Asia Asie du Sud-est	Western Asia Asie occidentale	Oceania Océanie	Others 4/ Autre 4/	Année	Exportations en provence de ↓
					Céréales (CTCI, Rev. 3, 041-045)						
176	3106	1997	5100	2824	1784	2540	3586	97	98	2000	Monde 1/
1214	10191	11754	16094	11790	7024	8884	15956	376	986	2013	
1265	11263	11508	15161	11949	7512	9859	15413	398	182	2014	
1247	8947	9598	12808	13009	5370	10091	12097	401	850	2015	
1140	7410	9647	13450	9245	4504	9203	10031	365	762	2016	
...	117	230	7	430	498	694	298	82	11	2000	Economies Développées - Asie-Pacifique 2/
...	151	754	11	1207	236	2195	1652	302	710	2013	
0	119	538	1	1963	325	2297	1173	295	0	2014	
...	134	341	0	1799	224	2017	650	184	633	2015	
0	37	160	0	1189	266	1709	603	142	536	2016	
...	...	7	...	4	0	0	2	0	...	2000	Japon
...	0	8	0	5	0	3	0	0	...	2013	
...	...	11	0	7	0	4	0	0	...	2014	
...	...	17	0	10	0	5	0	0	...	2015	
...	...	8	0	13	0	7	0	0	...	2016	
91	822	224	136	108	172	8	830	0	6	2000	Economies Développées - Europe 2/
512	3007	1220	284	168	764	9	2160	0	2	2013	
452	3348	1196	237	286	1199	35	1334	0	2	2014	
544	2914	1297	299	988	433	265	1655	0	3	2015	
400	2299	1030	195	150	266	167	1622	0	2	2016	
11	463	171	84	54	70	0	110	0	...	2000	France
82	2272	742	207	161	19	3	726	0	0	2013	
46	2278	689	113	262	1	21	254	0	0	2014	
41	1657	530	142	911	73	176	150	0	0	2015	
38	1449	413	125	139	45	96	223	0	...	2016	
1	193	14	0	26	85	1	529	...	0	2000	Allemagne
6	309	358	1	4	320	2	801	0	2	2013	
4	340	268	48	2	758	2	395	0	1	2014	
3	398	472	54	2	282	2	661	0	1	2015	
2	184	288	41	2	181	11	662	0	2	2016	
15	1599	524	3216	1224	502	734	956	4	74	2000	Economies Développées - Amérique du Nord 2/
5	1241	1922	9773	4178	587	1850	1182	9	7	2013	
2	1511	1735	10793	4549	550	1964	1541	15	...	2014	
1	997	1310	8664	4820	612	1855	1086	46	...	2015	
3	1162	1170	9192	3723	484	1693	1152	18	...	2016	
15	1227	410	2629	1041	95	501	825	4	74	2000	États-Unis
2	671	1321	8087	3708	228	1207	765	9	7	2013	
1	892	1017	8964	4105	107	1458	971	15	...	2014	
1	463	765	7115	4262	159	1058	742	46	...	2015	
2	680	705	8018	3331	143	1286	927	18	...	2016	
28	14	2	0	0	22	0	41	...	0	2000	Europe du Sud-est
608	992	54	0	287	93	43	992	...	...	2013	
717	954	112	0	115	36	71	814	...	0	2014	
602	630	99	0	113	90	67	718	...	...	2015	
633	650	230	0	57	22	276	677	...	0	2016	
2	8	0	3	2	12	...	102	...	0	2000	Communauté d'Etats Indépendants
55	2262	951	191	425	1084	369	3302	0	0	2013	
65	2986	1325	210	914	1417	296	3985	0	0	2014	
60	2352	1008	131	1203	1050	628	3002	0	...	2015	
73	1399	917	135	408	884	148	1578	0	0	2016	
0	4	...	...	1	7	...	45	...	...	2000	Fédération de Russie
45	783	591	181	86	412	118	1828	...	0	2013	
48	1341	1032	189	157	636	71	2632	0	0	2014	
34	1060	804	77	185	628	50	2012	...	...	2015	
47	1249	915	130	226	647	71	1490	...	0	2016	

Voir la fin du tableau pour la remarque générale et les notes.

World exports by provenance and destination (Table D)

In million U.S. dollars f.o.b.

Exports to ⟶ / ↓ Exports from	Year	World 1/ Monde 1/	Developed economies 2/ Economies développées 2/ Total	Asia-Pacific Asie-Pacifique Total	Japan Japon	Europe Total	Germany Allemagne	North America Amérique du Nord Total	U.S.A. É.-U.	Commonwealth of Independent States Communauté d'Etats Indépendants Total	Europe
Cereals (SITC, Rev. 3, 041-045) [cont.]											
Northern Africa	2000	111	2	0	0	1	0	0	0	0	0
	2013	217	39	0	0	39	0	1	0	2	0
	2014	40	27	0	0	27	0	0	0	0	0
	2015	92	35	0	...	35	0	0	0	0	0
	2016	33	15	...	...	15	0	0	0	...	...
Sub-Saharan Africa	2000	152	32	26	26	6	0	0	0	...	...
	2013	1611	282	197	197	84	0	2	2	0	0
	2014	1295	91	43	43	45	0	3	2	0	0
	2015	865	10	0	0	8	0	2	2	...	...
	2016	1000	9	0	0	6	0	3	2	0	0
South Africa	2000	92	25	25	25	1	...	0	0	...	...
	2013	940	249	196	196	52	0	0	0	0	0
	2014	804	86	43	43	42	0	1	1	0	0
	2015	370	6	0	0	4	0	1	1	...	...
	2016	442	7	0	0	5	0	2	1	0	0
Latin America and the Caribbean	2000	2915	435	48	46	288	3	100	99	2	0
	2013	18627	3891	1659	1644	1015	61	1217	1196	4	3
	2014	12866	1540	371	350	522	38	646	609	1	1
	2015	13134	1622	605	593	592	25	425	399	1	1
	2016	13777	1536	542	536	666	22	327	309	2	1
Brazil	2000	17	1	1	0	0	0	0	0	...	...
	2013	7068	1923	902	902	698	35	322	322	0	0
	2014	4438	378	235	235	126	...	16	16	...	...
	2015	5725	773	463	462	246	0	65	64	0	0
	2016	4110	708	457	457	195	0	57	56	0	0
Eastern Asia	2000	1666	63	56	56	5	1	2	1	63	59
	2013	542	65	52	50	7	1	5	4	9	7
	2014	472	64	51	48	7	1	6	5	7	6
	2015	382	74	58	55	7	2	9	7	3	2
	2016	504	61	48	46	6	1	7	5	3	3
China	2000	1643	61	56	55	5	0	1	1	63	59
	2013	514	58	50	50	6	1	2	2	6	4
	2014	445	58	48	48	6	1	4	3	7	6
	2015	322	67	56	55	6	2	5	4	3	2
	2016	429	54	46	45	5	1	3	2	2	2
Southern Asia	2000	1181	174	7	1	120	6	46	36	8	8
	2013	13058	938	74	5	602	25	262	208	141	48
	2014	12282	1107	85	6	718	31	304	240	157	85
	2015	8846	879	73	6	553	26	254	195	149	75
	2016	7317	724	65	5	446	25	214	168	159	63
South-Eastern Asia	2000	2357	370	60	33	149	6	161	135	20	19
	2013	8750	1287	242	150	458	30	587	492	95	85
	2014	10102	1298	249	154	465	24	583	490	79	73
	2015	8993	1241	207	127	513	30	521	439	50	44
	2016	8771	1182	206	132	491	23	485	409	47	42
Western Asia	2000	319	50	0	0	49	3	1	1	23	13
	2013	494	84	0	0	75	3	9	9	5	1
	2014	437	87	0	0	52	4	35	30	5	1
	2015	751	98	0	0	80	8	18	16	4	1
	2016	688	47	0	0	34	5	13	12	5	1
Oceania	2000	0	0	0	...	...	...	0	0	...	...
	2013	3	0	0	...	...	...	...	...	...	...
	2014	1	0	0	0	0	0	0	0	...	...
	2015	1	0	0	...	0	...	0	...	...	...
	2016	1	0	0	...	0	...	...	...	...	...

For general note and footnotes see end of table

Exportations mondiales par provenance et destination (Tableau D)

En millions de dollars E.-U. f.o.b.

← Exportations vers

Céréales (CTCI, Rev. 3, 041-045) [suite]

South-Eastern Europe Europe du Sud-est	Northern Africa Afrique septentrionale	Sub-Saharan Africa Afrique du Nord	Latin America and the Caribbean Amérique latine et Caraïbes	Eastern Asia Asie orientale	Southern Asia Asie méridionale	South-eastern Asia Asie du Sud-est	Western Asia Asie occidentale	Oceania Océanie	Others 4/ Autre 4/	Année	Exportations en provence de ↓
9	30	12	...	...	0	...	57	...	0	2000	Afrique du Nord
5	75	5	...	2	0	0	89	...	...	2013	
1	6	1	...	0	0	0	4	...	...	2014	
2	15	4	...	...	0	0	35	...	0	2015	
1	7	2	...	0	0	...	8	...	0	2016	
0	2	95	0	4	7	1	11	0	0	2000	Afrique subsaharienne
1	0	882	101	122	25	179	18	0	0	2013	
1	0	916	2	202	23	25	24	0	12	2014	
1	0	770	0	8	18	38	18	0	1	2015	
0	0	825	1	10	21	117	15	0	1	2016	
...	0	49	0	4	6	0	7	0	0	2000	Afrique du sud
...	0	454	97	115	1	18	5	...	0	2013	
...	0	473	0	202	1	18	13	0	12	2014	
...	0	328	0	3	0	29	3	0	1	2015	
0	...	418	1	3	1	8	3	0	1	2016	
0	313	118	1662	5	137	31	207	...	5	2000	Amérique latine et Caraïbes
15	2342	439	5639	2344	618	1255	1952	0	128	2013	
5	2215	327	3762	775	890	1798	1553	0	0	2014	
2	1789	479	3649	1076	893	2655	967	0	0	2015	
1	1708	945	3864	881	1042	2694	1104	0	1	2016	
...	...	1	14	...	...	...	0	...	...	2000	Brésil
0	853	228	826	1447	515	768	509	0	...	2013	
0	543	150	425	627	877	1165	273	...	...	2014	
0	652	170	529	933	823	1570	274	...	...	2015	
0	362	138	328	511	917	971	175	...	...	2016	
12	21	182	41	687	43	504	51	0	...	2000	Asie orientale
...	0	2	3	391	23	48	1	0	0	2013	
0	0	9	2	314	29	45	1	1	...	2014	
0	0	1	1	202	22	44	1	33	...	2015	
0	1	77	6	225	34	53	4	40	0	2016	
12	21	166	41	682	42	504	51	0	...	2000	Chine
...	0	2	3	375	23	46	1	...	...	2013	
...	0	9	2	297	29	43	1	1	...	2014	
0	0	1	1	185	22	42	1	0	...	2015	
0	1	76	1	208	34	50	2	0	...	2016	
0	72	96	0	2	154	36	639	0	0	2000	Asie méridionale
2	51	2912	24	496	3404	1378	3710	2	0	2013	
4	75	2321	16	238	2880	1053	4427	2	2	2014	
4	68	2098	13	188	1611	355	3476	1	3	2015	
4	85	1956	8	232	1038	225	2886	1	0	2016	
3	18	504	34	362	164	533	338	11	0	2000	Asie Sud-est
10	48	2589	61	2156	112	1549	648	62	133	2013	
16	42	3014	132	2592	68	2275	352	84	150	2014	
30	25	2178	43	2610	18	2167	309	136	186	2015	
25	35	2324	46	2369	24	2119	236	163	201	2016	
15	90	10	0	0	75	0	55	...	1	2000	Asie occidentale
1	21	22	6	14	77	9	250	...	5	2013	
2	7	14	6	1	95	0	205	0	14	2014	
2	24	12	8	2	398	1	179	0	22	2015	
0	27	13	2	2	423	2	148	0	20	2016	
...	...	...	...	...	...	...	...	0	0	2000	Océanie
...	...	2	...	...	0	0	...	1	...	2013	
...	...	0	0	...	...	0	...	1	0	2014	
...	0	...	...	0	...	0	...	1	0	2015	
...	0	0	...	...	...	0	...	1	0	2016	

Voir la fin du tableau pour la remarque générale et les notes.

World exports by provenance and destination (Table D)

In million U.S. dollars f.o.b.

Exports from ↓ / Exports to →	Year	World 1/ Monde 1/	Developed economies 2/ Economies développées 2/ Total	Asia-Pacific Asie-Pacifique Total	Asia-Pacific Asie-Pacifique Japan Japon	Europe Total	Europe Germany Allemagne	North America Amérique du Nord Total	North America Amérique du Nord U.S.A. É.-U.	Commonwealth of Independent States Communauté d'Etats Indépendants Total	Commonwealth of Independent States Communauté d'Etats Indépendants Europe
Crude materials (excluding fuels), oils, fats (SITC, Rev. 3, 2 and 4)											
World 1/	2000	213763	135493	21328	19784	84301	15266	29863	23121	3270	2921
	2013	843263	332669	53820	49710	224694	43354	54155	41430	17131	13995
	2014	804440	325276	50755	46817	218898	40442	55623	42405	15716	12281
	2015	657369	265687	38149	34818	179640	33062	47897	36369	12213	9493
	2016	635742	254869	37317	33840	171290	31988	46263	35400	11221	8656
Developed Economies - Asia-Pacific 2/	2000	17277	6945	3046	2578	2419	328	1480	1121	171	169
	2013	114849	18065	12596	11980	3656	775	1812	1377	415	387
	2014	104439	15931	11026	10376	3308	755	1597	1348	381	369
	2015	73930	11195	6979	6398	2701	564	1515	1266	490	478
	2016	74092	10529	6241	5664	2757	821	1531	1029	335	334
Japan	2000	3369	747	30	.	437	96	280	268	5	4
	2013	12528	1635	34	.	898	238	703	686	76	67
	2014	11444	1521	29	.	731	220	761	739	84	73
	2015	9551	1331	25	.	640	170	667	636	106	95
	2016	8879	1267	22	.	676	163	569	552	36	35
Developed Economies - Europe 2/	2000	61182	51586	1529	1332	47688	9926	2369	2050	811	783
	2013	186619	139927	2623	2140	132116	29310	5188	4316	4163	3888
	2014	182428	139017	2450	1911	130856	27896	5711	4682	3287	2987
	2015	149588	113691	2139	1686	106548	22314	5004	4063	2337	2102
	2016	147518	112509	2391	1851	104886	22098	5232	4340	2501	2316
France	2000	6036	5195	62	54	4960	957	173	159	43	39
	2013	14614	11859	84	64	11420	2313	355	324	271	257
	2014	14339	11768	96	71	11299	2128	373	335	171	161
	2015	11467	9301	92	61	8866	1716	343	319	116	108
	2016	11266	9046	91	63	8605	1710	350	330	172	163
Germany	2000	9272	7481	98	75	7114	.	269	236	175	169
	2013	28377	22684	208	150	21456	.	1020	941	638	608
	2014	28058	22873	189	132	21635	.	1049	957	491	447
	2015	22659	18744	159	109	17696	.	889	812	331	293
	2016	21747	17797	193	144	16754	.	850	791	367	336
Developed Economies - North America 2/	2000	52948	35073	6991	6669	10354	1671	17728	12780	59	49
	2013	134151	49107	9086	8567	17418	3000	22603	14769	568	512
	2014	134335	51556	9046	8471	18094	2617	24416	16060	507	466
	2015	114088	44890	7608	7112	16419	2592	20863	13750	379	369
	2016	112903	43178	7451	7022	15230	2121	20498	14071	259	247
United States	2000	30374	15490	4048	3897	6497	965	4946	.	53	43
	2013	90192	23164	4293	3992	11040	2340	7831	.	547	493
	2014	90214	24484	4611	4272	11519	2042	8354	.	477	437
	2015	76195	21724	3937	3647	10679	2018	7108	.	368	359
	2016	75573	20253	3819	3552	10017	1612	6417	.	232	222
South-Eastern Europe	2000	1743	850	9	8	827	121	15	5	105	105
	2013	8901	4558	227	227	4235	520	97	30	66	62
	2014	7992	4087	159	156	3871	678	56	40	75	70
	2015	6269	3442	94	89	3288	643	61	56	61	58
	2016	6469	3753	90	85	3603	753	60	56	93	90
Commonwealth of Independent States	2000	9232	4909	597	597	4224	457	88	78	1628	1361
	2013	38558	11390	658	642	10520	736	212	196	7741	5396
	2014	37726	10597	654	644	9682	746	260	209	7411	4878
	2015	30067	7763	519	516	7035	575	209	177	5375	3428
	2016	22106	5145	484	482	4513	422	147	122	4630	2665
Russian Federation	2000	4752	2850	588	587	2214	173	48	40	338	229
	2013	18172	6158	552	551	5411	348	194	180	2973	1208
	2014	17990	5562	555	551	4788	352	220	170	2999	1164
	2015	13916	3964	451	450	3346	291	166	136	2062	752
	2016	14379	4052	475	473	3443	298	135	110	2056	743

For general note and footnotes see end of table

Exportations mondiales par provenance et destination (Tableau D)

En millions de dollars E.-U. f.o.b.

South-Eastern Europe Europe du Sud-est	Northern Africa Afrique septentrio-nale	Sub-Saharan Africa Afrique du Nord	Latin America and the Caribbean Amérique latine et Caraïbes	Eastern Asia Asie orientale	Southern Asia Asie méridionale	South-eastern Asia Asie du Sud-est	Western Asia Asie occidentale	Oceania Océanie	Others 4/ Autre 4/	Année	← Exportations vers Exportations en provence de ↓
Matières brutes (sauf combustibles), huiles et graisses (CTCI, Rev. 3, 2 et 4)											
1159	2799	3078	10197	32663	6995	9200	6671	86	2152	2000	Monde 1/
7933	12048	14030	30998	309379	41455	38612	36394	278	2336	2013	
7617	12090	14087	31196	277352	43736	39042	36551	302	1473	2014	
6344	9176	11271	26486	218163	40818	34499	30093	271	2347	2015	
5942	8486	10533	24559	217890	38994	35510	25624	271	1842	2016	
55	113	343	117	6146	678	1503	457	29	721	2000	Economies Développées - Asie-Pacifique 2/
110	72	809	271	85088	2769	4859	2168	99	125	2013	
163	99	756	214	76186	2583	5445	2483	99	98	2014	
82	85	565	324	51967	2163	4057	2192	82	728	2015	
84	66	531	161	53217	2280	4531	1828	93	437	2016	
1	3	41	33	1879	111	525	22	1	...	2000	Japon
19	7	210	111	8509	222	1635	101	2	...	2013	
16	4	222	100	7386	248	1737	124	2	...	2014	
14	3	209	93	5793	266	1622	113	2	...	2015	
15	4	180	84	5361	262	1579	91	1	...	2016	
397	1141	627	613	2814	636	651	1535	11	360	2000	Economies Développées - Europe 2/
3712	4120	1865	2090	17475	3189	2314	7500	29	236	2013	
3649	4358	1679	1910	15069	3644	2086	7533	22	174	2014	
2987	3359	1451	1650	13467	3070	1940	5380	16	241	2015	
2912	3133	1472	1620	12317	3061	2129	5651	19	195	2016	
16	118	62	61	280	115	29	109	7	0	2000	France
110	318	117	179	1085	133	203	315	13	9	2013	
106	302	123	123	1096	138	226	264	12	10	2014	
91	267	111	115	897	145	184	220	9	10	2015	
122	238	122	106	891	116	160	277	11	5	2016	
95	91	101	110	601	125	140	206	1	146	2000	Allemagne
337	438	267	335	2166	407	353	749	0	1	2013	
352	509	228	324	1755	453	329	737	0	5	2014	
294	421	191	271	1264	369	266	504	1	3	2015	
370	274	162	270	1361	366	260	518	1	1	2016	
26	189	314	5377	8242	520	1916	976	21	234	2000	Economies Développées - Amérique du Nord 2/
97	1771	647	13624	53986	2602	6699	4837	40	172	2013	
112	1716	591	14483	50397	3182	7136	4598	56	0	2014	
108	1146	504	13514	40024	3556	6307	3601	58	...	2015	
162	827	450	12183	41462	3923	7154	3245	59	2	2016	
21	163	248	5018	6392	357	1465	912	19	234	2000	États-Unis
36	1511	523	12229	39797	2085	5800	4294	33	172	2013	
44	1530	461	13113	37601	2320	6022	4108	54	0	2014	
62	1080	407	12364	29119	2516	5450	3069	37	...	2015	
57	773	356	11133	31199	2706	6163	2659	41	2	2016	
231	122	2	8	102	6	3	310	0	3	2000	Europe du Sud-est
1175	186	252	14	702	110	32	1769	0	36	2013	
1139	197	208	8	532	178	29	1502	0	37	2014	
965	186	176	16	386	35	9	968	1	24	2015	
967	124	144	11	415	97	10	830	2	23	2016	
127	270	6	47	1256	178	63	749	0	0	2000	Communauté d'Etats Indépendants
807	1369	72	190	10744	2559	358	3328	0	0	2013	
748	1566	136	229	9974	3142	274	3649	0	0	2014	
825	1051	159	265	8131	3029	358	3113	0	0	2015	
639	790	63	181	6947	1688	209	1814	0	0	2016	
23	190	1	12	973	45	21	300	0	0	2000	Fédération de Russie
213	748	21	117	5671	497	183	1591	0	0	2013	
185	1103	48	153	5269	630	136	1904	0	0	2014	
149	799	65	179	4609	496	156	1436	0	0	2015	
138	697	51	149	5114	575	155	1390	0	0	2016	

Voir la fin du tableau pour la remarque générale et les notes.

World exports by provenance and destination (Table D)

In million U.S. dollars f.o.b.

Exports from ↓ / Exports to →	Year	World 1/ Monde 1/	Developed economies 2/ Economies développées 2/ Total	Asia-Pacific Asie-Pacifique Total	Japan Japon	Europe Total	Germany Allemagne	North America Amérique du Nord Total	U.S.A. É.-U.	Commonwealth of Independent States Communauté d'Etats Indépendants Total	Europe
Crude materials (excluding fuels), oils, fats (SITC, Rev. 3, 2 and 4) [cont.]											
Northern Africa	2000	1415	946	61	24	773	42	111	102	12	12
	2013	4666	2343	92	26	1682	116	568	537	33	29
	2014	4115	1965	96	23	1446	120	423	324	39	29
	2015	4656	2445	116	36	1836	102	494	380	59	50
	2016	3608	1726	125	28	1275	115	326	226	20	18
Sub-Saharan Africa	2000	7533	4522	521	506	3463	539	537	476	14	14
	2013	42421	14611	1703	1618	10841	1230	2068	1571	366	342
	2014	37125	12284	1802	1733	8653	1057	1828	1304	238	205
	2015	28097	9340	981	922	6977	1017	1383	1153	221	177
	2016	25175	8097	904	840	6145	845	1048	861	296	275
South Africa	2000	2693	1932	411	400	1205	338	315	306	8	8
	2013	17538	4975	1237	1198	3041	284	697	678	86	78
	2014	15297	4609	1251	1211	2559	364	799	574	114	99
	2015	9607	2964	494	478	1917	464	553	543	87	75
	2016	10509	2714	641	604	1656	387	418	399	103	100
Latin America and the Caribbean	2000	25154	15250	2683	2608	7737	1255	4830	4008	149	149
	2013	147427	47772	12361	11895	25098	4418	10314	8135	1217	1080
	2014	140233	45481	11356	10816	23292	3669	10833	8691	1647	1446
	2015	118023	37099	7954	7337	19103	2790	10042	7850	1458	1236
	2016	115279	35062	7928	7221	17774	2639	9360	7228	1470	1322
Brazil	2000	9140	6169	900	881	4222	771	1047	980	12	12
	2013	71528	20962	3813	3778	14234	2146	2915	2195	127	100
	2014	65951	19141	3104	3073	12445	1758	3592	2802	374	373
	2015	52067	14322	1706	1675	9584	1078	3032	2169	402	376
	2016	48701	12847	1598	1552	8397	978	2853	1974	595	556
Eastern Asia	2000	11347	4318	1979	1894	1470	229	869	814	91	88
	2013	31576	10448	3538	3257	4021	955	2889	2588	411	367
	2014	33607	10884	3572	3285	4243	998	3070	2783	402	362
	2015	28863	9365	3056	2756	3587	818	2722	2465	335	294
	2016	27090	8954	3051	2768	3417	809	2485	2261	305	271
China	2000	4575	2767	1241	1205	1051	169	475	454	56	53
	2013	15192	6975	2102	1931	2811	695	2062	1891	244	213
	2014	16504	7359	2143	1965	3038	729	2177	2011	268	235
	2015	14609	6511	1932	1727	2624	603	1956	1785	222	186
	2016	13715	6156	1853	1676	2523	595	1781	1640	208	178
Southern Asia	2000	2589	1252	296	277	664	105	292	279	92	72
	2013	23784	5692	711	618	2077	453	2903	2783	211	162
	2014	19485	5118	674	574	1971	413	2473	2325	198	163
	2015	14935	3626	475	381	1794	340	1358	1226	152	119
	2016	13725	3212	427	309	1643	280	1141	1045	149	118
South-Eastern Asia	2000	18175	7768	3106	2833	3214	376	1447	1323	71	69
	2013	90559	24361	9324	8009	9904	1399	5133	4790	1575	1505
	2014	83019	23196	8609	7760	9938	968	4649	4360	1205	1082
	2015	73232	19676	7714	7132	8017	867	3944	3712	1079	995
	2016	72966	19318	7524	6958	7793	795	4001	3791	966	876
Western Asia	2000	3400	1386	156	150	1141	145	90	79	65	51
	2013	16438	2704	219	179	2136	281	349	319	366	264
	2014	15601	2768	280	199	2205	287	283	256	324	225
	2015	13067	2299	210	164	1806	249	283	252	268	186
	2016	12297	2507	266	196	1824	228	417	354	198	126
Oceania	2000	1768	688	353	308	328	71	7	7	3	0
	2013	3315	1692	682	551	990	161	20	20	0	0
	2014	4336	2392	1031	869	1339	238	22	22	0	0
	2015	2553	856	306	288	531	192	19	19	0	0
	2016	2514	880	435	416	429	63	16	16	0	0

For general note and footnotes see end of table

Exportations mondiales par provenance et destination (Tableau D)

En millions de dollars E.-U. f.o.b.

South-Eastern Europe / Europe du Sud-est	Northern Africa / Afrique septentrionale	Sub-Saharan Africa / Afrique du Nord	Latin America and the Caribbean / Amérique latine et Caraïbes	Eastern Asia / Asie orientale	Southern Asia / Asie méridionale	South-eastern Asia / Asie du Sud-est	Western Asia / Asie occidentale	Oceania / Océanie	Others 4/ / Autre 4/	Année	← Exportations vers / Exportations en provence de ↓
Matières brutes (sauf combustibles), huiles et graisses (CTCI, Rev. 3, 2 et 4) [suite]											
35	45	13	89	63	63	32	107	0	9	2000	Afrique du Nord
61	224	197	209	359	430	215	576	0	19	2013	
69	242	177	235	335	432	111	494	0	16	2014	
102	195	206	254	317	489	116	455	0	18	2015	
98	231	181	211	284	384	87	354	0	32	2016	
18	109	1046	116	757	328	373	223	1	27	2000	Afrique subsaharienne
130	169	4945	265	14850	1816	2704	2482	9	74	2013	
37	213	4432	253	12697	2410	1971	2489	13	90	2014	
39	202	3059	151	8964	2055	1638	2213	3	211	2015	
13	165	3048	171	8333	2161	1565	1184	2	139	2016	
10	6	112	23	358	62	154	29	0	0	2000	Afrique du sud
8	28	680	89	9718	837	884	228	1	3	2013	
4	30	708	128	7598	1346	496	250	12	1	2014	
3	12	661	57	4815	567	299	140	2	1	2015	
5	31	903	102	5273	890	378	101	2	6	2016	
145	361	222	3341	3249	1370	669	389	1	8	2000	Amérique latine et Caraïbes
1237	2120	556	11426	68601	5611	4125	3577	3	1184	2013	
1049	1560	631	11013	63676	6549	4345	3822	2	459	2014	
792	1172	637	8054	53675	6979	4331	3228	4	595	2015	
627	1432	619	7931	54527	6909	3687	2439	3	571	2016	
41	196	50	682	1211	328	210	241	1	...	2000	Brésil
274	956	184	2458	40350	941	2692	2584	1	...	2013	
196	827	205	2369	35874	1174	2936	2854	1	...	2014	
146	571	192	1423	27787	1672	3181	2370	1	...	2015	
126	453	216	1366	27091	1923	2520	1563	1	...	2016	
7	33	46	98	5248	440	948	116	1	1	2000	Asie orientale
119	224	407	825	11362	1967	4779	1029	5	0	2013	
121	192	490	870	12160	2053	5240	1188	6	0	2014	
107	215	527	810	9770	1858	4748	1122	6	0	2015	
123	169	452	690	8861	1832	4718	977	9	0	2016	
6	18	23	42	1000	251	360	52	0	...	2000	Chine
106	189	200	486	3394	984	1950	664	1	...	2013	
104	158	288	563	3487	1128	2306	842	2	...	2014	
90	183	358	572	2691	1111	2046	821	2	...	2015	
103	144	310	494	2446	1092	2046	712	4	...	2016	
6	31	39	56	495	215	223	179	0	0	2000	Asie méridionale
27	145	230	219	11049	2545	1804	1839	7	16	2013	
31	155	230	187	7783	2324	1662	1763	5	29	2014	
24	119	205	158	5048	2496	1491	1610	2	4	2015	
22	149	168	142	4996	2134	1458	1289	2	5	2016	
41	202	375	281	4017	2231	2376	794	15	4	2000	Asie Sud-est
144	1338	3672	1590	30137	14993	10045	2601	74	27	2013	
148	1469	4326	1451	24605	14142	9866	2505	81	25	2014	
103	1195	3409	1133	22576	12632	9028	2316	74	10	2015	
111	1092	3099	1165	22938	12248	9418	2532	68	11	2016	
69	182	38	55	164	319	214	836	0	72	2000	Asie occidentale
313	308	378	124	4206	2593	309	4689	0	447	2013	
353	324	432	128	3151	2700	354	4525	0	544	2014	
210	252	372	153	2465	2293	335	3895	11	515	2015	
183	308	304	88	2188	2187	422	3480	4	427	2016	
1	...	7	1	111	10	229	...	5	714	2000	Océanie
0	2	0	149	820	270	370	0	11	0	2013	
0	1	0	217	788	397	524	0	16	0	2014	
0	...	2	6	1371	164	141	0	13	0	2015	
...	...	1	5	1404	91	122	1	10	0	2016	

Voir la fin du tableau pour la remarque générale et les notes.

World exports by provenance and destination (Table D)

In million U.S. dollars f.o.b.

Exports to ⟶ / ↓ Exports from	Year	World 1/ Monde 1/	Developed economies 2/ Economies développées 2/ Total	Asia-Pacific Asie-Pacifique Total	Japan Japon	Europe Total	Germany Allemagne	North America Amérique du Nord Total	U.S.A. É.-U.	Commonwealth of Independent States Communauté d'Etats Indépendants Total	Europe
					Oil seeds and, oleaginous fruit (SITC, Rev. 3, 22)						
World 1/	2000	14361	7330	1656	1630	5096	979	578	313	95	80
	2013	85268	25773	3793	3708	19906	5889	2074	1586	1452	1340
	2014	85171	23697	3532	3457	17535	4560	2630	2094	1656	1545
	2015	73082	19600	3061	2999	14985	4264	1554	1104	1387	1254
	2016	72482	18554	2732	2681	14384	4324	1438	981	1574	1453
Developed Economies - Asia-Pacific 2/	2000	419	154	110	106	7	1	38	36	...	...
	2013	2471	1298	142	135	1097	174	59	55	0	0
	2014	1483	864	121	115	685	185	57	54	0	0
	2015	1218	826	155	150	660	111	11	8	...	...
	2016	1026	891	78	70	792	344	20	18	0	0
Japan	2000	1	0	...	.	0	0	0	0	...	...
	2013	3	2	0	.	1	0	0	0	0	0
	2014	5	3	0	.	3	0	1	1	0	0
	2015	6	3	0	.	2	0	1	1	...	...
	2016	10	2	0	.	1	1	1	1	...	...
Developed Economies - Europe 2/	2000	1531	1331	2	1	1317	564	12	11	13	13
	2013	8059	7346	6	3	7310	3803	31	19	365	350
	2014	6846	6220	4	3	6186	2994	29	26	277	263
	2015	5882	5317	7	4	5274	2562	36	29	226	215
	2016	5737	5114	8	3	5081	2590	25	22	327	318
France	2000	558	429	0	0	428	178	1	1	5	5
	2013	1319	1066	1	1	1061	596	4	4	127	126
	2014	1174	1000	1	0	995	494	4	4	85	85
	2015	1037	887	2	0	880	423	5	5	62	62
	2016	1109	899	2	0	892	496	4	4	112	111
Germany	2000	159	125	0	0	125	.	0	0	0	0
	2013	379	298	1	0	296	.	2	1	62	59
	2014	439	357	1	0	355	.	1	1	54	50
	2015	342	298	2	1	293	.	3	3	26	23
	2016	339	286	1	1	280	.	5	4	33	30
Developed Economies - North America 2/	2000	6969	3034	1242	1232	1446	147	345	141	2	1
	2013	31002	6982	2808	2788	2948	909	1226	856	232	231
	2014	33333	7005	2504	2490	3097	651	1404	978	231	230
	2015	27128	6176	2223	2212	2928	913	1024	669	213	211
	2016	31500	6168	2211	2205	3067	584	891	518	79	78
United States	2000	5831	2349	822	812	1323	139	204	.	2	1
	2013	24178	3555	1096	1077	2089	781	371	.	230	228
	2014	26234	3831	1112	1103	2293	624	426	.	225	225
	2015	20853	3744	1130	1123	2258	840	356	.	209	207
	2016	24801	3636	1059	1054	2205	483	373	.	61	61
South-Eastern Europe	2000	60	34	...	...	34	6	0	0	0	0
	2013	2092	1536	0	0	1512	124	24	11	28	27
	2014	1896	1291	3	0	1259	115	30	16	34	33
	2015	1573	1156	3	0	1132	114	22	18	21	20
	2016	2033	1501	3	0	1469	230	28	25	58	57
Commonwealth of Independent States	2000	413	231	0	...	228	18	3	3	49	34
	2013	2698	1675	15	1	1660	118	1	0	223	145
	2014	2432	1204	4	1	1189	104	11	11	164	88
	2015	2265	951	0	0	949	43	1	1	157	56
	2016	1037	322	0	0	318	22	3	3	145	60
Russian Federation	2000	191	105	...	...	105	14	0	0	6	1
	2013	325	188	...	...	188	10	0	0	26	11
	2014	354	147	0	...	136	10	11	11	32	18
	2015	374	138	0	0	138	12	0	0	34	20
	2016	500	143	0	0	140	8	3	3	49	25

For general note and footnotes see end of table

Exportations mondiales par provenance et destination (Tableau D)

En millions de dollars E.-U. f.o.b.

South-Eastern Europe Europe du Sud-est	Northern Africa Afrique septentrio-nale	Sub-Saharan Africa Afrique du Nord	Latin America and the Caribbean Amérique latine et Caraïbes	Eastern Asia Asie orientale	Southern Asia Asie méridionale	South-eastern Asia Asie du Sud-est	Western Asia Asie occidentale	Oceania Océanie	Others 4/ Autre 4/	Année	← Exportations vers Exportations en provence de ↓
											Graines et fruits oléagineux (CTCI, Rev. 3, 22)
33	167	107	1658	3205	264	793	467	4	240	2000	Monde 1/
445	1439	348	4617	40600	1149	5008	3318	17	1101	2013	
462	1636	375	4567	42066	1799	5173	3713	15	12	2014	
508	1252	328	3478	36359	2463	4532	3144	15	15	2015	
494	918	306	3853	37247	2548	4803	2156	12	16	2016	
...	0	1	13	193	41	8	7	1	...	2000	Economies Développées - Asie-Pacifique 2/
...	0	1	1	696	153	37	283	2	...	2013	
...	...	2	1	298	124	60	132	1	...	2014	
0	...	5	1	198	85	27	75	1	0	2015	
...	...	1	0	79	28	19	5	2	...	2016	
...	...	0	0	0	...	0	0	...	...	2000	Japon
...	...	0	0	1	...	0	0	0	...	2013	
...	...	...	0	1	0	0	0	0	...	2014	
...	...	0	0	1	0	2	0	0	...	2015	
...	...	0	0	6	...	1	0	0	...	2016	
9	12	2	7	47	90	0	19	0	0	2000	Economies Développées - Europe 2/
184	15	9	67	6	4	3	51	0	9	2013	
216	19	8	13	4	7	2	72	0	8	2014	
205	14	5	13	12	8	1	70	0	10	2015	
178	17	7	12	6	8	3	60	0	5	2016	
2	10	0	5	31	73	0	3	0	...	2000	France
65	2	1	39	1	0	0	8	0	9	2013	
59	3	1	1	0	2	0	16	0	7	2014	
48	3	1	1	0	2	0	23	0	10	2015	
68	3	1	1	1	1	1	17	0	5	2016	
0	0	0	1	15	17	0	0	...	0	2000	Allemagne
12	0	1	2	1	0	1	2	0	0	2013	
19	0	1	2	1	0	1	4	...	0	2014	
14	0	0	2	1	1	0	1	...	0	2015	
14	0	0	1	0	1	0	2	...	0	2016	
3	51	3	1080	1899	32	457	173	2	233	2000	Economies Développées - Amérique du Nord 2/
24	525	22	3266	16576	114	2545	529	13	172	2013	
21	530	25	3375	18216	421	2732	767	12	0	2014	
40	300	27	2829	13681	963	2296	591	13	...	2015	
23	289	8	2903	17624	1145	2742	508	9	2	2016	
3	43	3	918	1680	0	428	171	2	233	2000	Etats-Unis
18	457	19	2513	14247	87	2415	453	13	172	2013	
20	497	14	2701	15658	191	2505	580	12	0	2014	
40	273	21	2228	11396	485	2103	342	13	...	2015	
23	287	4	2300	15183	475	2576	244	9	2	2016	
4	...	0	5	6	0	0	10	...	0	2000	Europe du Sud-est
112	11	39	4	2	75	3	283	...	0	2013	
109	10	25	3	1	136	5	282	...	...	2014	
135	7	13	4	1	5	1	230	...	...	2015	
146	2	29	5	1	62	1	228	...	0	2016	
10	11	...	1	9	5	...	98	...	0	2000	Communauté d'Etats Indépendants
50	127	0	1	23	137	90	373	0	0	2013	
55	105	0	0	60	295	41	508	0	0	2014	
80	51	0	1	165	256	8	596	0	0	2015	
94	40	0	0	183	47	5	201	...	0	2016	
...	1	...	...	9	3	...	68	...	...	2000	Fédération de Russie
1	4	...	1	17	8	6	75	...	...	2013	
0	4	0	...	30	17	2	122	...	...	2014	
3	2	0	...	126	3	1	67	0	0	2015	
5	4	0	...	148	18	4	129	...	0	2016	

Voir la fin du tableau pour la remarque générale et les notes.

World exports by provenance and destination (Table D)

In million U.S. dollars f.o.b.

Exports to ⟶ / ↓ Exports from	Year	World 1/ Monde 1/	Developed economies 2/ Economies développées 2/ Total	Asia-Pacific Asie-Pacifique Total	Japan Japon	Europe Total	Germany Allemagne	North America Amérique du Nord Total	U.S.A. É.-U.	Commonwealth of Independent States Communauté d'Etats Indépendants Total	Europe
		Oil seeds and, oleaginous fruit (SITC, Rev. 3, 22) [cont.]									
Northern Africa	2000	12	4	0	...	4	1	0	0	0	0
	2013	86	43	2	2	40	5	1	0	0	0
	2014	75	23	5	5	17	2	1	0	0	0
	2015	50	12	2	1	10	4	0	0	0	0
	2016	56	13	3	3	9	3	0	0	0	0
Sub-Saharan Africa	2000	329	104	38	37	58	2	9	8	1	0
	2013	2572	604	217	217	350	140	37	34	1	1
	2014	3067	473	274	272	177	26	22	18	0	0
	2015	2649	435	249	248	154	29	33	30	0	0
	2016	1240	176	74	73	94	9	8	6	0	0
South Africa	2000	26	17	7	6	9	1	1	1	0	...
	2013	44	13	6	5	8	0	0	0	...	...
	2014	35	12	5	5	6	0	1	1	0	0
	2015	32	9	5	5	3	0	0	0	...	...
	2016	35	6	3	3	3	0	0	0	0	...
Latin America and the Caribbean	2000	3743	2029	121	117	1786	218	123	71	0	0
	2013	32699	5429	432	417	4534	539	462	421	466	466
	2014	32172	5682	423	406	4480	407	778	749	797	796
	2015	29035	3985	291	274	3523	434	171	154	677	676
	2016	26363	3618	239	227	3206	490	173	151	856	856
Brazil	2000	2190	1612	103	103	1508	201	1	1	...	...
	2013	22923	3436	331	329	2931	168	175	175	15	15
	2014	23390	4169	308	307	3322	328	538	538	311	311
	2015	21128	2532	195	193	2336	177	1	1	249	249
	2016	19480	2278	180	179	2097	272	0	0	446	446
Eastern Asia	2000	428	251	119	113	128	11	5	2	20	20
	2013	1044	339	83	75	163	26	93	79	10	7
	2014	1065	304	81	74	138	21	85	73	13	7
	2015	1063	262	73	67	130	12	60	44	7	3
	2016	1035	259	65	60	144	10	50	34	11	4
China	2000	417	251	118	113	128	11	5	2	20	20
	2013	1018	335	82	74	163	26	91	78	10	7
	2014	1020	302	81	73	138	21	83	72	13	7
	2015	1017	260	72	67	130	12	58	43	7	3
	2016	975	257	64	60	144	10	49	33	11	4
Southern Asia	2000	244	85	8	8	47	7	30	29	7	7
	2013	1540	392	60	44	201	35	131	102	55	50
	2014	1951	489	66	47	218	40	206	162	68	62
	2015	1506	384	35	22	158	31	191	145	47	39
	2016	1452	281	25	14	125	23	131	100	51	37
South-Eastern Asia	2000	130	26	13	13	2	1	11	10	0	0
	2013	602	30	19	18	10	1	1	1	0	0
	2014	480	54	36	36	16	1	1	1	0	0
	2015	422	22	14	14	6	1	1	1	0	0
	2016	546	23	16	16	5	1	2	2	0	0
Western Asia	2000	68	39	2	2	36	4	1	1	3	3
	2013	361	97	8	7	80	15	9	8	72	62
	2014	308	88	11	10	72	15	5	5	71	64
	2015	246	72	8	7	60	11	4	4	39	33
	2016	397	187	9	9	73	17	105	103	48	42
Oceania	2000	16	7	1	1	6	0	0	0	...	...
	2013	42	0	0	...	0	...	0	0	...	...
	2014	63	0	0	...	0	0	0	0	...	...
	2015	43	2	1	0	0	...	0	0	...	...
	2016	62	1	0	...	0	0	0	0	...	...

For general note and footnotes see end of table

Exportations mondiales par provenance et destination (Tableau D)

En millions de dollars E.-U. f.o.b.

South-Eastern Europe Europe du Sud-est	Northern Africa Afrique septentrio-nale	Sub-Saharan Africa Afrique du Nord	Latin America and the Caribbean Amérique latine et Caraïbes	Eastern Asia Asie orientale	Southern Asia Asie méridionale	South-eastern Asia Asie du Sud-est	Western Asia Asie occidentale	Oceania Océanie	Others 4/ Autre 4/	Année	← Exportations vers Exportations en provence de ↓
					Graines et fruits oléagineux (CTCI, Rev. 3, 22) [suite]						
0	6	0	...	...	...	...	1	...	0	2000	Afrique du Nord
2	8	0	0	0	0	0	32	...	0	2013	
0	11	0	0	0	0	0	39	...	0	2014	
0	14	0	0	0	0	0	24	...	...	2015	
0	16	0	0	0	0	0	26	...	...	2016	
1	35	81	7	22	0	1	71	...	6	2000	Afrique subsaharienne
0	65	248	9	550	120	222	696	0	58	2013	
1	114	256	1	1070	266	130	754	0	1	2014	
2	129	169	1	785	268	110	750	0	0	2015	
0	84	129	1	329	156	83	282	0	0	2016	
0	...	8	1	0	0	0	0	...	0	2000	Afrique du sud
...	0	18	1	1	1	9	0	...	0	2013	
...	1	21	0	0	1	1	0	...	0	2014	
...	0	22	...	0	1	0	0	...	...	2015	
...	...	29	0	0	0	0	0	0	0	2016	
0	24	15	527	920	62	142	24	...	0	2000	Amérique latine et Caraïbes
45	519	6	1246	21839	262	1228	804	0	855	2013	
27	713	34	1142	21537	231	1144	867	0	0	2014	
23	588	86	606	20824	560	1146	540	...	0	2015	
25	335	106	912	18353	714	830	612	...	0	2016	
...	19	0	87	379	62	20	10	...	...	2000	Brésil
40	26	1	172	17865	94	964	312	...	...	2013	
9	235	10	50	17225	57	880	444	...	...	2014	
18	293	35	15	16454	261	982	289	...	...	2015	
20	46	5	64	14930	672	740	280	...	...	2016	
3	11	2	4	73	1	43	20	0	...	2000	Asie orientale
13	106	1	3	270	31	155	116	0	...	2013	
9	61	2	5	331	65	163	112	0	...	2014	
6	87	1	3	245	133	183	135	0	0	2015	
4	65	1	2	215	172	188	118	0	0	2016	
3	11	2	4	65	1	41	20	0	...	2000	Chine
13	106	1	3	255	31	150	114	0	...	2013	
9	61	2	5	300	64	152	112	0	...	2014	
6	87	1	3	213	133	172	135	0	...	2015	
4	65	1	2	187	172	159	118	0	...	2016	
0	15	2	12	12	14	67	27	0	0	2000	Asie méridionale
8	38	9	19	200	135	562	122	1	0	2013	
11	55	7	23	286	142	719	147	2	1	2014	
8	34	5	13	187	96	623	107	0	1	2015	
8	27	13	11	182	118	679	83	0	0	2016	
0	0	1	1	22	5	74	0	0	...	2000	Asie Sud-est
...	1	6	0	431	6	120	6	0	0	2013	
0	3	12	1	262	26	115	7	0	0	2014	
0	2	6	0	258	28	99	6	0	1	2015	
...	2	6	0	274	37	196	6	0	1	2016	
2	1	0	0	0	6	1	16	...	0	2000	Asie occidentale
7	25	6	1	7	112	4	24	...	5	2013	
12	16	4	2	1	84	1	26	0	3	2014	
9	25	11	7	1	57	1	21	0	3	2015	
16	39	7	6	1	57	2	27	...	8	2016	
...	...	...	0	0	8	0	...	0	0	2000	Océanie
...	...	0	1	0	0	41	...	0	0	2013	
...	...	0	1	...	1	61	...	0	0	2014	
...	...	...	0	0	5	36	...	0	0	2015	
...	...	...	0	...	4	57	...	0	0	2016	

Voir la fin du tableau pour la remarque générale et les notes.

World exports by provenance and destination (Table D)

In million U.S. dollars f.o.b.

Exports from ↓ / Exports to →	Year	World 1/ Monde 1/	Developed economies 2/ Economies développées 2/ Total	Asia-Pacific Asie-Pacifique Total	Asia-Pacific Asie-Pacifique Japan Japon	Europe Total	Europe Germany Allemagne	North America Amérique du Nord Total	North America Amérique du Nord U.S.A. É.-U.	Commonwealth of Independent States Communauté d'Etats Indépendants Total	Commonwealth of Independent States Communauté d'Etats Indépendants Europe
Textile fibres (SITC, Rev. 3, 26)											
World 1/	2000	22374	9266	966	868	7253	967	1047	674	624	611
	2013	48008	9891	762	625	7616	1457	1513	1180	1115	1049
	2014	43751	9976	757	620	7628	1322	1592	1262	1023	952
	2015	37752	8875	682	558	6606	1130	1587	1287	836	775
	2016	35683	8562	650	536	6498	1015	1415	1154	829	779
Developed Economies - Asia-Pacific 2/	2000	4239	1397	272	234	1018	140	108	100	6	4
	2013	7362	735	75	61	540	82	120	117	68	57
	2014	6384	767	66	51	561	84	140	134	76	64
	2015	5227	727	55	39	526	93	147	128	92	81
	2016	5035	662	57	44	484	63	122	118	29	29
Japan	2000	1008	169	9	.	117	27	43	40	2	1
	2013	1663	237	3	.	133	42	101	100	67	57
	2014	1682	267	2	.	142	42	123	119	73	63
	2015	1575	276	2	.	143	54	130	113	92	81
	2016	1035	213	0	.	104	26	108	106	29	29
Developed Economies - Europe 2/	2000	4662	3239	67	49	3060	393	112	101	94	90
	2013	7373	3757	49	39	3497	668	211	188	390	366
	2014	7416	3837	56	45	3521	639	260	231	329	307
	2015	6353	3315	64	49	2966	547	284	254	251	234
	2016	6127	3047	44	29	2815	496	188	162	299	283
France	2000	594	455	16	16	427	40	11	10	5	4
	2013	583	274	6	6	254	40	13	12	1	1
	2014	710	321	7	7	291	47	23	22	1	1
	2015	591	264	6	6	246	39	13	12	0	0
	2016	603	229	4	4	215	33	10	8	1	1
Germany	2000	1394	967	12	6	915	.	40	37	42	40
	2013	1275	747	4	2	661	.	83	77	71	64
	2014	1236	739	3	2	624	.	112	106	61	54
	2015	1084	677	3	1	577	.	98	93	46	41
	2016	1003	620	2	1	561	.	57	55	45	41
Developed Economies - North America 2/	2000	3410	949	200	191	379	76	370	44	8	7
	2013	8477	714	127	123	314	38	273	31	105	104
	2014	7202	725	120	116	343	33	262	31	82	81
	2015	6372	701	96	92	395	36	210	33	76	75
	2016	6094	676	94	91	393	30	189	28	82	79
United States	2000	3227	897	198	191	373	76	326	.	6	5
	2013	8262	674	126	121	306	37	241	.	104	102
	2014	6988	687	118	115	338	33	231	.	81	80
	2015	6183	661	94	90	389	35	177	.	75	74
	2016	5934	642	92	89	388	30	161	.	81	79
South-Eastern Europe	2000	43	18	0	0	17	5	1	0	1	1
	2013	215	155	0	0	155	39	0	0	7	6
	2014	211	149	0	0	149	31	0	0	5	3
	2015	180	122	0	0	122	24	1	1	5	4
	2016	178	116	0	...	115	21	1	1	4	4
Commonwealth of Independent States	2000	1719	766	7	7	752	70	7	7	488	483
	2013	2535	152	1	1	149	18	2	2	343	328
	2014	2264	124	2	1	122	20	1	1	354	335
	2015	2708	99	1	1	97	11	0	0	289	270
	2016	2243	94	1	1	92	7	0	0	298	278
Russian Federation	2000	37	9	0	0	9	4	0	0	3	1
	2013	52	8	...	...	8	1	...	...	31	22
	2014	58	9	0	0	9	2	0	0	34	23
	2015	50	5	...	...	5	2	0	0	23	14
	2016	46	4	0	0	4	1	...	...	25	16

For general note and footnotes see end of table

Exportations mondiales par provenance et destination (Tableau D)

En millions de dollars E.-U. f.o.b.

South-Eastern Europe Europe du Sud-est	Northern Africa Afrique septentrionale	Sub-Saharan Africa Afrique du Nord	Latin America and the Caribbean Amérique latine et Caraïbes	Eastern Asia Asie orientale	Southern Asia Asie méridionale	South-eastern Asia Asie du Sud-est	Western Asia Asie occidentale	Oceania Océanie	Others 4/ Autre 4/	Année	← Exportations vers Exportations en provence de ↓
				Fibres textiles (CTCI, Rev. 3, 26)							
179	369	755	1623	4596	1375	2208	1326	11	40	2000	Monde 1/
527	729	2201	2319	16622	5224	6024	3271	34	50	2013	
555	756	2234	2319	12133	5023	6297	3364	27	43	2014	
524	625	1963	2126	9287	5394	5471	2607	25	20	2015	
552	544	1776	1933	7794	5613	5435	2587	28	29	2016	
3	8	49	41	1595	348	718	63	10	2	2000	Economies Développées - Asie-Pacifique 2/
1	42	221	22	4808	449	925	65	25	0	2013	
1	35	228	18	3670	490	984	91	25	...	2014	
1	35	216	20	3037	358	646	71	23	...	2015	
8	36	183	18	2662	686	669	58	23	...	2016	
1	1	35	9	498	51	227	13	0	...	2000	Japon
0	5	197	17	696	55	361	28	0	...	2013	
...	2	209	12	605	85	387	43	0	...	2014	
0	0	200	13	522	95	336	41	0	...	2015	
0	2	169	13	328	49	223	10	0	...	2016	
116	147	280	87	233	77	36	350	0	2	2000	Economies Développées - Europe 2/
380	324	838	102	612	227	70	673	0	0	2013	
399	342	810	98	673	251	110	567	0	0	2014	
373	275	741	79	573	190	63	492	0	0	2015	
376	258	685	91	568	226	146	431	0	0	2016	
2	10	22	2	74	8	1	15	0	...	2000	France
2	27	39	2	201	14	0	22	0	...	2013	
2	33	40	3	271	19	0	20	0	0	2014	
1	31	40	2	224	16	0	13	0	0	2015	
1	40	36	4	262	16	0	14	0	...	2016	
59	36	59	41	33	28	23	105	0	2	2000	Allemagne
63	50	136	35	35	20	2	115	0	0	2013	
65	58	131	28	34	21	1	98	0	0	2014	
65	54	105	17	27	17	2	74	...	0	2015	
74	42	84	21	21	20	4	72	...	0	2016	
3	16	107	984	594	133	359	257	0	0	2000	Economies Développées - Amérique du Nord 2/
4	161	299	1406	3167	542	1165	913	1	...	2013	
4	161	298	1384	2028	413	1170	938	0	...	2014	
4	127	236	1312	1569	423	1351	572	0	...	2015	
8	81	192	1176	1088	649	1515	627	1	...	2016	
3	15	82	978	514	129	347	256	0	0	2000	États-Unis
3	154	191	1394	3165	518	1160	900	1	...	2013	
2	155	189	1370	2023	388	1165	926	0	...	2014	
2	121	151	1298	1563	403	1346	562	0	...	2015	
6	74	124	1161	1086	630	1510	620	1	...	2016	
9	1	0	0	0	1	0	11	...	1	2000	Europe du Sud-est
14	1	11	0	3	3	0	22	0	0	2013	
15	1	9	0	3	3	1	27	0	...	2014	
18	1	8	0	2	2	0	22	...	0	2015	
23	1	7	0	2	4	0	20	...	0	2016	
27	4	4	28	149	89	34	129	...	0	2000	Communauté d'Etats Indépendants
8	10	0	0	1093	630	6	293	...	...	2013	
8	8	1	0	980	555	10	224	...	0	2014	
6	3	1	1	1110	972	41	187	0	...	2015	
4	1	0	0	711	904	20	212	0	...	2016	
1	0	0	0	2	2	0	20	...	...	2000	Fédération de Russie
2	0	...	0	3	6	0	1	...	...	2013	
2	0	0	0	4	8	0	2	...	...	2014	
2	0	0	0	13	5	0	2	...	...	2015	
1	...	0	0	5	7	2	1	...	...	2016	

Voir la fin du tableau pour la remarque générale et les notes.

World exports by provenance and destination (Table D)

In million U.S. dollars f.o.b.

Exports to ⟶ / ↓ Exports from	Year	World 1/ Monde 1/	Developed economies 2/ Economies développées 2/ Total	Asia-Pacific Asie-Pacifique Total	Japan Japon	Europe Total	Germany Allemagne	North America Amérique du Nord Total	U.S.A. É.-U.	Commonwealth of Independent States Communauté d'Etats Indépendants Total	Europe
Textile fibres (SITC, Rev. 3, 26) [cont.]											
Northern Africa	2000	224	117	10	10	91	6	16	15	0	0
	2013	312	97	3	3	87	5	7	6	2	2
	2014	269	116	2	2	106	4	8	7	2	1
	2015	224	97	2	2	91	3	4	4	1	0
	2016	236	86	1	1	82	5	3	1	1	1
Sub-Saharan Africa	2000	1449	603	22	21	563	78	18	13	0	0
	2013	2979	468	8	7	446	79	14	14	0	0
	2014	2895	518	7	6	496	31	15	14	0	0
	2015	2336	389	6	5	364	23	19	19	0	0
	2016	2232	508	3	3	487	20	18	18	6	6
South Africa	2000	190	119	10	10	100	13	9	4	0	0
	2013	420	131	5	5	124	11	2	2	0	…
	2014	397	119	4	4	113	12	1	1	0	0
	2015	313	112	4	4	105	6	2	2	0	…
	2016	402	119	2	2	115	9	1	1	0	…
Latin America and the Caribbean	2000	1002	428	21	20	241	58	167	165	1	1
	2013	2361	448	47	41	316	87	86	85	0	0
	2014	2606	394	45	40	263	69	86	84	0	0
	2015	2343	355	33	32	253	62	68	67	0	0
	2016	2252	384	31	30	300	89	53	52	0	0
Brazil	2000	92	35	0	0	32	15	2	2	…	…
	2013	1307	104	27	26	76	9	1	1	0	0
	2014	1543	76	19	19	43	7	13	13	0	0
	2015	1439	69	16	16	48	6	5	5	0	0
	2016	1346	67	15	15	42	3	10	10	0	0
Eastern Asia	2000	3414	1010	263	244	550	60	197	182	5	5
	2013	6631	2170	279	212	1327	307	564	522	151	143
	2014	6793	2192	297	230	1307	298	589	548	133	125
	2015	5949	1945	265	208	1100	221	579	538	87	80
	2016	5683	1837	277	225	1011	186	549	510	75	69
China	2000	1085	495	159	158	320	27	16	16	2	1
	2013	3158	1203	155	135	751	172	297	280	73	68
	2014	3440	1178	156	136	723	167	298	281	74	70
	2015	3169	1093	143	124	625	126	325	304	48	44
	2016	3086	1026	149	131	573	104	305	286	43	39
Southern Asia	2000	462	148	19	16	111	17	18	16	16	16
	2013	6522	548	37	28	377	73	133	125	19	16
	2014	4463	498	35	26	342	50	120	111	19	16
	2015	3397	489	39	29	319	42	131	120	17	15
	2016	2886	548	41	30	343	41	163	153	19	17
South-Eastern Asia	2000	589	91	38	28	34	7	19	17	0	0
	2013	2350	386	132	110	178	26	76	72	9	9
	2014	2232	392	124	103	188	28	80	76	7	7
	2015	2061	367	118	100	168	27	82	77	3	3
	2016	2008	361	97	81	182	21	81	76	4	3
Western Asia	2000	1160	499	48	48	436	58	15	14	4	4
	2013	891	261	4	1	230	35	26	18	21	18
	2014	1015	264	4	1	230	34	30	23	15	13
	2015	603	269	2	1	205	41	62	47	14	13
	2016	709	243	3	1	194	36	46	34	10	9
Oceania	2000	0	0	0	…	0	…	0	0	…	…
	2013	0	0	0	…	0	…	0	0	…	…
	2014	0	0	0	0	0	0	0	0	…	…
	2015	0	0	0	0	0	0	0	0	…	…
	2016	0	0	0	…	0	0	0	0	…	…

For general note and footnotes see end of table

Exportations mondiales par provenance et destination (Tableau D)

En millions de dollars E.-U. f.o.b.

South-Eastern Europe Europe du Sud-est	Northern Africa Afrique septentrionale	Sub-Saharan Africa Afrique du Nord	Latin America and the Caribbean Amérique latine et Caraïbes	Eastern Asia Asie orientale	Southern Asia Asie méridionale	South-eastern Asia Asie du Sud-est	Western Asia Asie occidentale	Oceania Océanie	Others 4/ Autre 4/	Année	← Exportations vers Exportations en provence de ↓
											Fibres textiles (CTCI, Rev. 3, 26) [suite]
1	1	5	6	29	29	13	24	0	0	2000	Afrique du Nord
2	6	15	4	33	97	13	44	...	0	2013	
2	2	16	5	18	64	4	39	...	0	2014	
1	3	16	2	16	55	2	31	...	0	2015	
2	3	18	3	10	82	1	29	...	0	2016	
0	40	262	63	116	151	174	22	0	16	2000	Afrique subsaharienne
5	54	350	2	972	276	799	45	6	0	2013	
4	64	312	11	637	328	967	54	0	0	2014	
9	47	221	2	344	422	816	84	0	0	2015	
4	35	217	4	374	425	584	75	0	0	2016	
0	4	19	1	33	7	2	4	0	0	2000	Afrique du sud
4	10	25	1	219	25	2	2	...	0	2013	
4	7	30	1	218	15	1	2	...	0	2014	
2	4	21	0	148	16	7	2	...	0	2015	
3	3	27	1	222	23	2	3	0	0	2016	
0	2	1	345	156	22	17	30	0	0	2000	Amérique latine et Caraïbes
10	10	7	345	863	112	485	81	0	0	2013	
14	14	4	353	891	127	683	124	0	0	2014	
13	14	6	287	686	147	661	175	0	0	2015	
19	18	11	241	544	250	609	176	0	0	2016	
0	0	1	39	2	3	3	9	...	...	2000	Brésil
...	5	4	108	532	75	433	47	...	...	2013	
0	7	1	101	597	92	586	84	...	...	2014	
0	9	2	79	405	113	616	147	...	...	2015	
0	8	4	58	324	205	534	145	...	...	2016	
1	16	15	50	1452	310	493	60	0	1	2000	Asie orientale
79	70	257	357	1113	807	1193	434	0	0	2013	
79	75	324	368	1029	886	1191	516	0	0	2014	
73	67	360	324	855	804	991	442	0	0	2015	
85	45	312	296	794	776	1029	430	3	0	2016	
0	1	2	12	224	171	163	15	0	...	2000	Chine
69	44	79	193	293	500	426	278	0	...	2013	
64	55	151	225	280	573	476	364	0	...	2014	
60	48	212	213	233	535	433	293	0	...	2015	
70	31	195	194	212	513	481	319	3	...	2016	
2	8	19	8	62	67	86	46	0	0	2000	Asie méridionale
4	29	106	58	3355	1545	604	252	0	2	2013	
5	21	100	56	1662	1309	540	251	0	3	2014	
5	20	93	55	594	1551	384	187	0	3	2015	
5	25	68	53	558	1125	323	158	1	3	2016	
0	4	5	8	183	88	179	31	0	...	2000	Asie Sud-est
3	6	40	20	497	359	745	282	1	0	2013	
6	11	42	25	466	363	624	296	1	0	2014	
5	17	33	37	431	374	510	283	1	0	2015	
5	22	36	44	412	354	503	268	0	0	2016	
17	122	7	4	26	60	100	303	0	17	2000	Asie occidentale
18	17	58	4	104	177	17	166	0	48	2013	
19	22	90	3	76	237	13	236	0	38	2014	
15	17	34	6	70	96	6	61	0	16	2015	
14	20	49	6	71	132	36	102	0	26	2016	
0	...	0	...	...	0	0	...	0	0	2000	Océanie
...	...	0	...	0	0	0	...	0	0	2013	
...	...	...	0	0	...	0	...	0	0	2014	
...	...	0	...	0	0	0	0	0	0	2015	
...	...	0	...	0	0	0	...	0	0	2016	

Voir la fin du tableau pour la remarque générale et les notes.

World exports by provenance and destination (Table D)

In million U.S. dollars f.o.b.

Exports to ⟶ / ↓ Exports from	Year	World 1/ Monde 1/	Developed economies 2/ Economies développées 2/							Commonwealth of Independent States Communauté d'Etats Indépendants	
				Asia-Pacific Asie-Pacifique		Europe		North America Amérique du Nord			
			Total	Total	Japan Japon	Total	Germany Allemagne	Total	U.S.A. É.-U.	Total	Europe
		Crude fertilizers and minerals (SITC, Rev. 3, 27)									
World 1/	2000	13459	8935	1120	968	6125	845	1690	1246	271	236
	2013	38280	17490	1610	1215	12014	1840	3866	2980	1787	1556
	2014	38991	17940	1692	1274	12263	1978	3985	2974	1550	1312
	2015	35303	15819	1550	1154	10540	1648	3729	2832	1202	993
	2016	30686	14363	1394	1064	9947	1549	3022	2250	879	720
Developed Economies - Asia-Pacific 2/	2000	463	199	112	95	49	6	39	37	1	1
	2013	808	168	41	10	66	17	61	60	0	0
	2014	936	180	38	11	78	14	64	62	0	0
	2015	957	203	53	27	73	16	77	76	1	0
	2016	986	201	54	26	81	16	66	64	1	1
Japan	2000	184	46	6	.	19	4	21	21	1	1
	2013	460	57	13	.	18	8	26	25	0	0
	2014	508	59	10	.	18	9	30	29	0	0
	2015	476	59	10	.	19	7	30	30	0	0
	2016	452	60	10	.	21	8	29	29	1	1
Developed Economies - Europe 2/	2000	5217	4321	76	64	4028	726	217	192	61	59
	2013	11185	8122	71	48	7835	1534	216	186	259	250
	2014	11342	8341	72	48	8037	1625	231	201	226	218
	2015	9702	7188	68	44	6880	1365	240	209	193	186
	2016	9370	7094	63	42	6802	1286	229	196	149	143
France	2000	508	445	6	6	426	99	12	11	5	4
	2013	819	651	7	5	619	126	26	22	16	16
	2014	829	662	6	5	632	128	24	21	7	7
	2015	696	564	5	4	541	110	19	14	2	2
	2016	718	585	5	3	560	109	20	17	4	4
Germany	2000	836	730	9	7	712	.	9	8	6	5
	2013	1882	1579	13	9	1544	.	22	19	27	26
	2014	1882	1596	11	7	1557	.	28	24	25	23
	2015	1580	1347	9	6	1310	.	28	25	20	19
	2016	1557	1334	9	5	1302	.	23	20	21	20
Developed Economies - North America 2/	2000	2533	1660	376	324	514	64	771	397	4	3
	2013	3710	2358	341	216	507	98	1510	765	11	9
	2014	4121	2593	389	246	520	96	1684	879	15	13
	2015	3816	2349	357	227	485	87	1508	825	9	6
	2016	3226	1900	282	207	447	82	1171	605	9	6
United States	2000	1797	1196	330	297	492	60	373	.	4	3
	2013	2648	1458	240	212	473	86	745	.	11	9
	2014	2929	1555	269	241	482	88	805	.	15	12
	2015	2692	1387	253	223	454	77	680	.	8	6
	2016	2393	1215	226	204	423	76	566	.	9	6
South-Eastern Europe	2000	61	33	0	0	32	3	1	1	4	4
	2013	205	102	0	0	101	6	0	0	7	6
	2014	226	114	0	0	113	9	0	0	8	6
	2015	204	100	0	0	98	7	1	1	12	11
	2016	194	93	0	0	90	2	3	3	7	6
Commonwealth of Independent States	2000	461	219	2	2	210	2	7	0	122	98
	2013	2770	688	1	1	677	20	10	10	1181	1014
	2014	2829	736	2	2	713	18	21	21	1013	840
	2015	2226	648	2	2	613	14	33	33	678	527
	2016	1578	469	3	3	454	9	12	12	520	399
Russian Federation	2000	298	155	2	2	146	1	7	0	46	35
	2013	1373	512	1	1	501	14	10	10	278	219
	2014	1492	534	2	2	517	14	15	15	223	171
	2015	1127	460	2	2	434	9	24	24	137	89
	2016	1014	414	3	3	405	9	7	6	188	145

For general note and footnotes see end of table

Exportations mondiales par provenance et destination (Tableau D)

En millions de dollars E.-U. f.o.b.

⟵ Exportations vers

South-Eastern Europe / Europe du Sud-est	Northern Africa / Afrique septentrionale	Sub-Saharan Africa / Afrique du Nord	Latin America and the Caribbean / Amérique latine et Caraïbes	Eastern Asia / Asie orientale	Southern Asia / Asie méridionale	South-eastern Asia / Asie du Sud-est	Western Asia / Asie occidentale	Oceania / Océanie	Others 4/ / Autre 4/	Année	Exportations en provenance de ↓
			Engrais et minéraux bruts (CTCI, Rev. 3, 27)								
118	210	231	679	1255	339	684	621	9	107	2000	Monde 1/
346	797	966	1897	6698	2258	2415	3352	49	223	2013	
383	909	1034	1985	6366	2337	2485	3660	83	261	2014	
331	669	925	1934	5709	2272	2198	3787	71	385	2015	
292	557	788	1492	5166	2073	1994	2782	68	232	2016	
0	0	2	2	171	8	72	3	3	0	2000	Economies Développées - Asie-Pacifique 2/
0	0	5	7	432	19	133	29	8	5	2013	
0	0	9	7	482	25	186	38	7	1	2014	
0	0	6	8	491	28	176	36	7	1	2015	
0	0	8	7	507	26	169	60	7	0	2016	
...	0	1	0	100	7	28	1	0	...	2000	Japon
...	0	3	4	291	16	76	12	1	...	2013	
...	0	5	3	321	22	81	16	1	...	2014	
0	0	2	4	293	24	71	22	1	...	2015	
0	0	3	3	265	21	69	28	0	...	2016	
40	114	45	81	197	38	87	139	2	93	2000	Economies Développées - Europe 2/
104	338	118	248	941	221	286	450	3	96	2013	
118	351	117	247	858	216	289	471	3	103	2014	
98	284	102	224	657	220	241	402	1	91	2015	
101	261	86	193	660	224	227	330	2	41	2016	
2	15	12	7	6	2	5	9	1	...	2000	France
3	42	19	18	35	5	12	15	2	0	2013	
4	35	19	18	42	5	19	15	3	0	2014	
3	27	13	15	29	5	22	15	1	0	2015	
3	24	11	13	40	5	14	17	2	0	2016	
6	11	6	10	7	5	32	13	1	10	2000	Allemagne
17	15	10	44	62	14	68	46	0	0	2013	
19	13	8	37	63	12	63	42	0	4	2014	
17	21	9	34	37	11	51	32	0	2	2015	
17	11	9	35	43	12	44	31	0	0	2016	
0	18	37	327	296	38	118	34	0	0	2000	Economies Développées - Amérique du Nord 2/
2	29	47	631	395	44	104	80	8	...	2013	
2	56	57	725	414	49	108	70	32	...	2014	
3	39	45	711	405	48	109	71	28	...	2015	
2	45	39	560	405	55	113	63	36	...	2016	
0	8	14	232	227	11	80	25	0	0	2000	États-Unis
2	29	44	573	340	42	97	48	4	...	2013	
2	52	56	626	390	47	97	59	32	...	2014	
3	38	44	625	354	46	106	63	18	...	2015	
2	41	38	511	343	53	109	51	22	...	2016	
21	0	0	0	0	0	0	2	0	0	2000	Europe du Sud-est
52	10	0	0	4	2	2	19	...	9	2013	
59	16	0	0	5	1	1	23	...	0	2014	
49	13	0	...	4	1	2	23	...	0	2015	
51	9	1	0	6	1	2	23	...	1	2016	
11	52	0	3	14	12	15	14	...	0	2000	Communauté d'Etats Indépendants
31	223	19	85	251	156	66	71	0	0	2013	
29	318	9	139	220	213	64	88	0	0	2014	
26	195	26	121	201	152	72	106	0	0	2015	
27	119	12	55	141	138	51	46	0	0	2016	
8	50	0	3	13	8	12	5	...	...	2000	Fédération de Russie
20	182	4	49	129	119	62	20	...	0	2013	
17	251	4	72	120	176	58	36	0	0	2014	
16	165	7	57	80	104	62	40	...	0	2015	
22	89	0	27	87	107	47	32	...	0	2016	

Voir la fin du tableau pour la remarque générale et les notes.

World exports by provenance and destination (Table D)

In million U.S. dollars f.o.b.

Exports to ⟶ / ↓ Exports from	Year	Developed economies 2/ Economies développées 2/								Commonwealth of Independent States Communauté d'Etats Indépendants	
				Asia-Pacific Asie-Pacifique		Europe		North America Amérique du Nord			
		World 1/ Monde 1/	Total	Total	Japan Japon	Total	Germany Allemagne	Total	U.S.A. É.-U.	Total	Europe
Crude fertilizers and minerals (SITC, Rev. 3, 27) [cont.]											
Northern Africa	2000	540	331	43	6	218	4	70	64	5	5
	2013	2024	968	70	7	526	3	371	355	16	16
	2014	1700	735	74	5	422	3	238	170	17	15
	2015	1747	662	84	10	396	2	182	106	41	39
	2016	1278	501	96	4	281	1	124	58	6	6
Sub-Saharan Africa	2000	517	251	22	21	188	5	42	38	0	0
	2013	2777	946	43	23	629	18	275	274	1	1
	2014	2616	820	28	24	581	35	211	208	1	1
	2015	2410	700	29	15	405	8	265	242	1	1
	2016	1783	494	30	17	279	9	185	163	1	1
South Africa	2000	208	154	13	12	111	1	30	28	0	...
	2013	791	477	25	23	182	5	269	268	0	0
	2014	712	416	28	24	198	16	190	189	1	1
	2015	592	412	19	14	162	6	231	230	1	1
	2016	469	278	23	17	101	4	155	152	0	0
Latin America and the Caribbean	2000	720	538	49	48	194	6	295	283	0	0
	2013	2439	1235	130	109	378	36	726	670	9	9
	2014	2368	1313	123	111	383	57	807	742	6	6
	2015	2290	1313	114	95	339	21	860	812	4	4
	2016	2021	1139	97	88	346	25	696	648	2	2
Brazil	2000	281	212	31	31	148	1	33	33	0	0
	2013	796	393	10	9	245	27	137	101	0	0
	2014	776	412	14	11	259	47	140	107	0	0
	2015	694	396	10	8	252	12	134	103	0	0
	2016	641	363	8	7	236	15	119	86	0	0
Eastern Asia	2000	1379	820	361	338	255	12	204	192	47	47
	2013	3596	1536	677	636	441	35	419	399	113	98
	2014	3978	1689	685	650	506	33	498	481	99	91
	2015	3608	1393	618	576	438	39	337	328	99	92
	2016	3035	1231	550	520	392	38	289	281	85	81
China	2000	1103	704	296	275	215	11	192	180	27	27
	2013	2966	1371	560	521	407	29	404	386	62	55
	2014	3370	1524	579	546	462	29	483	468	59	53
	2015	3057	1255	540	501	395	34	320	312	62	57
	2016	2575	1108	479	450	360	35	269	262	46	42
Southern Asia	2000	400	188	26	22	133	6	29	27	9	7
	2013	2971	570	74	53	340	25	156	142	30	15
	2014	2846	561	77	60	355	22	129	114	30	15
	2015	2755	504	62	48	325	20	117	99	30	14
	2016	2297	490	55	42	304	19	130	113	28	19
South-Eastern Asia	2000	492	83	40	37	39	2	4	3	0	0
	2013	1487	172	106	83	14	3	53	53	1	1
	2014	1288	153	112	90	17	2	23	20	2	2
	2015	1142	154	100	83	19	2	35	28	1	1
	2016	1170	164	104	88	14	1	46	39	1	1
Western Asia	2000	676	292	14	11	266	9	12	11	18	12
	2013	4118	619	50	28	500	45	69	67	160	136
	2014	4466	705	90	27	537	64	78	75	133	104
	2015	4436	606	63	28	469	68	74	72	134	112
	2016	3742	589	60	26	458	61	71	69	68	54
Oceania	2000	2	0	0	0	0	...	0	0	...	...
	2013	189	6	6	...	0	...	0	0	...	...
	2014	273	1	0	0	0	0	0	0	...	...
	2015	8	0	0	0	0	...	0	0	...	...
	2016	6	0	0	0	0	...	0	0	...	...

For general note and footnotes see end of table

Exportations mondiales par provenance et destination (Tableau D)

En millions de dollars E.-U. f.o.b.

South-Eastern Europe / Europe du Sud-est	Northern Africa / Afrique septentrionale	Sub-Saharan Africa / Afrique du Nord	Latin America and the Caribbean / Amérique latine et Caraïbes	Eastern Asia / Asie orientale	Southern Asia / Asie méridionale	South-eastern Asia / Asie du Sud-est	Western Asia / Asie occidentale	Oceania / Océanie	Others 4/ / Autre 4/	Année	⟵ Exportations vers / Exportations en provence de ↓
			Engrais et minéraux bruts (CTCI, Rev. 3, 27) [suite]								
19	5	7	79	24	26	18	26	0	0	2000	Afrique du Nord
35	52	80	192	94	237	191	155	0	3	2013	
58	66	53	205	62	244	90	168	0	1	2014	
80	43	72	218	47	336	104	142	0	3	2015	
68	35	48	170	43	229	74	102	...	2	2016	
2	1	107	20	19	46	33	36	0	2	2000	Afrique subsaharienne
1	4	422	4	211	100	42	1043	1	0	2013	
1	6	417	8	126	132	27	986	4	89	2014	
1	7	346	8	131	89	11	909	1	208	2015	
2	2	371	6	97	82	6	590	0	133	2016	
0	0	24	2	18	3	4	2	0	0	2000	Afrique du sud
1	3	161	1	53	17	40	38	1	0	2013	
0	6	155	1	57	19	21	31	4	0	2014	
0	7	103	2	52	6	2	7	0	0	2015	
2	2	127	5	34	9	4	7	0	1	2016	
...	1	9	121	26	12	11	2	0	1	2000	Amérique latine et Caraïbes
1	12	19	571	370	145	65	11	1	2	2013	
1	13	36	515	295	129	47	12	1	2	2014	
1	12	50	522	224	111	41	10	0	3	2015	
1	7	25	408	283	92	48	12	0	3	2016	
...	...	7	19	23	10	8	2	...	...	2000	Brésil
0	0	16	73	235	39	36	4	0	...	2013	
0	0	24	76	188	48	26	2	...	...	2014	
0	0	22	74	136	38	24	3	0	...	2015	
1	0	20	55	152	24	20	5	0	...	2016	
3	5	10	14	313	72	83	13	1	0	2000	Asie orientale
3	9	40	76	1021	207	461	126	3	0	2013	
6	13	42	74	1156	194	487	215	4	0	2014	
4	9	49	65	1084	143	497	262	3	0	2015	
3	11	30	53	857	165	444	152	3	0	2016	
2	5	9	14	201	65	64	11	0	...	2000	Chine
3	9	35	76	758	148	384	120	1	...	2013	
6	13	36	72	860	176	418	207	1	...	2014	
4	9	46	61	826	134	400	259	1	...	2015	
3	11	28	50	663	150	367	148	1	...	2016	
0	3	4	2	96	27	26	44	0	0	2000	Asie méridionale
2	18	66	27	1387	225	183	456	5	3	2013	
2	8	80	20	1315	248	155	422	3	2	2014	
2	7	71	9	1206	260	184	482	1	0	2015	
3	12	55	10	883	289	161	366	1	0	2016	
0	0	2	0	56	13	179	157	2	0	2000	Asie Sud-est
0	0	11	1	265	299	594	130	14	0	2013	
0	1	11	1	277	147	638	39	18	0	2014	
0	1	14	2	228	122	578	30	12	0	2015	
0	1	11	2	278	131	526	46	11	0	2016	
23	11	8	28	43	48	44	150	...	12	2000	Asie occidentale
115	102	139	54	1327	602	112	783	0	106	2013	
107	61	201	44	1155	738	132	1129	0	62	2014	
69	59	143	46	1029	761	183	1315	11	80	2015	
34	53	103	27	1005	641	173	993	3	52	2016	
...	...	0	...	...	...	...	...	1	0	2000	Océanie
...	0	0	0	0	...	177	...	6	0	2013	
...	...	0	0	0	...	262	0	11	0	2014	
...	...	0	0	0	0	0		7	0	2015	
...	...	0	0	0	...	0	...	5	0	2016	

Voir la fin du tableau pour la remarque générale et les notes.

World exports by provenance and destination (Table D)

In million U.S. dollars f.o.b.

Exports to ⟶ / ↓ Exports from	Year	World 1/ Monde 1/	Developed economies 2/ Economies développées 2/ Total	Asia-Pacific Asie-Pacifique Total	Japan Japon	Europe Total	Germany Allemagne	North America Amérique du Nord Total	U.S.A. É.-U.	Commonwealth of Independent States Communauté d'Etats Indépendants Total	Europe
		Metalliferous ores and metal scrap (SITC, Rev. 3, 28)									
World 1/	2000	49128	31492	6559	6283	18934	3745	5999	3492	1210	1072
	2013	345489	118261	32422	31014	71645	14156	14194	8137	5284	4556
	2014	321241	115534	30239	29287	70496	13489	14799	8555	5207	4175
	2015	234347	85736	20199	19450	53593	10525	11943	6550	4080	3200
	2016	225321	78627	20064	19134	47664	9302	10898	5761	3519	2535
Developed Economies - Asia-Pacific 2/	2000	8135	3514	1682	1556	964	111	867	535	159	159
	2013	92187	13386	11301	11113	1155	377	930	529	299	283
	2014	83949	11693	9765	9574	1228	343	700	492	285	284
	2015	56299	7308	5817	5615	810	248	680	476	379	379
	2016	56492	6700	5226	5035	723	283	751	280	297	297
Japan	2000	879	105	1	.	78	10	26	24	...	...
	2013	5718	526	1	.	304	88	220	219	3	3
	2014	4863	399	1	.	134	69	265	261	6	6
	2015	3673	297	0	.	95	31	201	200	10	10
	2016	3486	269	1	.	125	38	144	142	2	2
Developed Economies - Europe 2/	2000	10941	9207	185	182	8557	1823	465	357	90	89
	2013	54051	38422	355	329	36364	7865	1703	1418	533	501
	2014	54259	39311	464	427	37052	7788	1796	1498	331	293
	2015	40392	29636	399	375	27873	5874	1364	1044	162	136
	2016	37311	26983	434	408	25138	5315	1411	1105	174	172
France	2000	1300	1258	7	6	1203	262	48	46	1	0
	2013	5310	4648	20	19	4542	711	86	81	10	6
	2014	5314	4742	23	21	4637	702	82	75	3	3
	2015	3705	3255	24	19	3157	523	73	68	3	3
	2016	3356	2895	22	21	2802	457	72	69	2	1
Germany	2000	2336	2053	12	12	1948	.	93	72	2	2
	2013	10547	9001	27	26	8402	.	572	519	32	32
	2014	10684	9314	28	28	8750	.	536	466	26	26
	2015	8003	7118	31	30	6666	.	420	362	17	16
	2016	7099	6223	22	21	5816	.	386	346	27	27
Developed Economies - North America 2/	2000	7458	5423	648	611	2357	355	2418	1142	8	6
	2013	40258	16982	2433	2331	8569	1181	5980	2994	116	68
	2014	39192	18386	2691	2568	8976	1071	6719	3321	75	42
	2015	30634	14788	2080	1989	7771	969	4937	2199	13	12
	2016	26339	12855	2120	2033	6451	839	4284	1971	25	23
United States	2000	4355	2591	379	365	938	197	1274	.	8	6
	2013	26031	8128	1112	1026	4030	806	2986	.	115	68
	2014	24711	8822	1275	1159	4148	677	3398	.	75	42
	2015	19440	7028	861	771	3429	566	2739	.	12	12
	2016	16312	6117	923	839	2887	530	2307	.	23	22
South-Eastern Europe	2000	589	252	7	7	235	45	9	1	87	87
	2013	3189	890	0	0	837	187	53	1	2	2
	2014	2532	882	1	1	880	357	1	1	6	6
	2015	1722	717	...	...	716	344	0	0	8	8
	2016	1657	762	0	0	762	351	0	0	3	3
Commonwealth of Independent States	2000	2714	1223	29	29	1161	203	33	33	686	558
	2013	13731	3087	204	204	2873	186	10	9	3706	3233
	2014	13200	3124	255	255	2843	218	25	24	3830	3104
	2015	8719	1952	165	165	1752	184	35	34	2780	2173
	2016	6563	1235	136	136	1094	109	5	4	2410	1580
Russian Federation	2000	985	495	27	27	457	46	11	11	170	155
	2013	4934	1105	117	117	980	50	8	7	856	559
	2014	4938	1366	167	167	1181	71	18	17	1059	646
	2015	3251	842	105	105	721	66	15	15	765	396
	2016	3398	1036	130	130	903	80	3	2	717	316

For general note and footnotes see end of table

Exportations mondiales par provenance et destination (Tableau D)

En millions de dollars E.-U. f.o.b.

South-Eastern Europe Europe du Sud-est	Northern Africa Afrique septentrionale	Sub-Saharan Africa Afrique du Nord	Latin America and the Caribbean Amérique latine et Caraïbes	Eastern Asia Asie orientale	Southern Asia Asie méridionale	South-eastern Asia Asie du Sud-est	Western Asia Asie occidentale	Oceania Océanie	Others 4/ Autre 4/	Année	← Exportations vers Exportations en provence de ↓
											Minerais métallifères et dechets de metaux (CTCI, Rev. 3, 28)
462	337	614	1385	8561	1153	1399	1400	1	1114	2000	Monde 1/
4373	2227	3635	7796	170123	10998	7444	14918	30	399	2013	
4122	2099	2836	8281	148783	12217	7102	14511	22	526	2014	
3111	803	1729	6495	104901	10237	5771	10388	19	1076	2015	
2602	796	1968	5207	107507	9242	6230	8866	11	744	2016	
50	98	264	14	2892	177	264	329	1	375	2000	Economies Développées - Asie-Pacifique 2/
85	5	510	120	72313	1768	1942	1632	8	120	2013	
136	0	415	70	65157	1525	2467	2091	12	97	2014	
60	0	248	184	42429	1334	1762	1894	9	691	2015	
57	0	279	33	43871	1148	2079	1585	8	436	2016	
...	0	1	0	723	8	42	1	...	...	2000	Japon
...	0	0	1	4941	15	226	5	0	...	2013	
...	0	...	1	4129	13	311	4	0	...	2014	
...	0	0	1	2918	31	414	2	0	...	2015	
0	0	0	0	2691	62	458	3	...	...	2016	
50	65	30	62	743	243	176	258	0	18	2000	Economies Développées - Europe 2/
1751	809	65	190	6071	1754	580	3869	7	0	2013	
1661	843	35	88	5592	2179	292	3926	1	0	2014	
1239	359	22	80	4649	1714	222	2310	0	0	2015	
975	328	11	55	4215	1675	267	2627	0	0	2016	
2	1	1	4	15	10	1	7	0	...	2000	France
0	50	2	17	353	69	16	144	0	...	2013	
0	43	5	7	311	67	22	113	0	0	2014	
1	22	2	4	272	50	18	79	0	...	2015	
1	9	3	5	241	44	18	138	0	...	2016	
1	0	8	5	160	40	20	33	0	13	2000	Allemagne
17	35	9	22	942	239	30	219	0	...	2013	
25	31	19	14	745	259	24	225	...	...	2014	
22	7	11	16	536	186	20	72	...	...	2015	
43	5	4	14	503	167	13	100	...	...	2016	
4	1	17	344	1454	71	109	27	0	...	2000	Economies Développées - Amérique du Nord 2/
51	640	33	2976	15462	930	887	2176	3	...	2013	
67	553	11	3611	12768	1102	870	1750	0	...	2014	
45	215	10	3586	9164	1148	427	1230	7	...	2015	
106	64	38	2673	7901	1063	491	1122	0	...	2016	
0	1	17	338	1249	57	75	19	0	...	2000	États-Unis
0	465	31	2698	11242	661	753	1935	3	...	2013	
4	434	8	3364	9006	720	702	1577	0	...	2014	
2	196	6	3432	6508	800	351	1104	0	...	2015	
6	46	19	2540	5505	773	374	908	0	...	2016	
76	0	0	2	52	4	3	112	0	1	2000	Europe du Sud-est
633	0	180	9	535	13	19	908	...	...	2013	
611	0	94	3	356	14	13	553	...	0	2014	
426	0	94	9	243	10	0	214	1	0	2015	
380	...	53	5	282	7	0	162	2	0	2016	
56	38	0	5	340	31	8	328	0	0	2000	Communauté d'Etats Indépendants
496	0	0	11	5386	32	7	1005	...	0	2013	
418	12	1	8	4519	42	14	1231	...	...	2014	
476	4	2	13	2548	25	30	889	...	...	2015	
378	3	1	1	1898	28	28	582	...	...	2016	
1	7	0	2	211	3	4	92	...	...	2000	Fédération de Russie
76	...	0	1	2159	15	4	717	...	0	2013	
61	12	1	2	1519	21	14	883	...	...	2014	
45	3	2	1	981	7	26	580	...	...	2015	
17	3	1	0	1032	11	22	558	...	...	2016	

Voir la fin du tableau pour la remarque générale et les notes.

World exports by provenance and destination (Table D)

In million U.S. dollars f.o.b.

Exports to ⟶ / ↓ Exports from	Year	World 1/ Monde 1/	Developed economies 2/ Economies développées 2/ Total	Asia-Pacific Asie-Pacifique Total	Japan Japon	Europe Total	Germany Allemagne	North America Amérique du Nord Total	U.S.A. É.-U.	Commonwealth of Independent States Communauté d'Etats Indépendants Total	Europe
		Metalliferous ores and metal scrap (SITC, Rev. 3, 28) [cont.]									
Northern Africa	2000	174	136	0	0	132	13	3	1	6	6
	2013	692	345	0	0	333	59	12	12	4	1
	2014	704	330	0	0	299	47	31	17	8	0
	2015	577	248	2	2	221	36	26	8	6	0
	2016	541	223	0	0	212	49	11	3	2	1
Sub-Saharan Africa	2000	2503	1977	223	217	1413	314	341	292	12	12
	2013	24241	7503	1206	1172	5091	548	1205	749	182	160
	2014	20763	7062	1254	1225	4568	660	1240	759	198	166
	2015	13235	4835	524	513	3520	707	791	628	184	142
	2016	13488	4487	568	543	3313	575	607	475	210	191
South Africa	2000	1383	1094	194	188	702	264	199	196	8	8
	2013	14613	3869	1032	1001	2469	237	368	352	85	77
	2014	12382	3554	1046	1018	1969	271	539	316	113	97
	2015	7161	2044	348	341	1423	400	273	264	86	74
	2016	7921	1870	428	404	1235	339	208	192	102	99
Latin America and the Caribbean	2000	10259	6747	1800	1766	3181	739	1766	1061	92	92
	2013	81770	29152	10568	10346	14590	3385	3995	2133	322	215
	2014	75023	26251	9567	9294	12711	2650	3973	2149	438	257
	2015	56892	20052	6456	6091	9695	1878	3901	1963	510	315
	2016	57150	19049	6532	6046	8942	1604	3575	1714	379	252
Brazil	2000	3536	2135	465	461	1396	435	273	221	12	12
	2013	37437	12438	3118	3118	8347	1819	972	314	52	30
	2014	31231	9879	2473	2473	6197	1200	1208	475	24	24
	2015	19669	6768	1213	1213	4312	748	1243	435	125	100
	2016	18437	6055	1106	1101	3766	569	1184	361	120	82
Eastern Asia	2000	897	269	170	157	72	8	28	24	11	10
	2013	4626	819	552	532	181	39	85	77	2	2
	2014	6239	956	596	574	220	67	140	130	8	7
	2015	5118	687	452	425	143	46	92	86	17	16
	2016	5313	746	528	506	143	61	75	71	7	6
China	2000	114	61	32	30	23	2	7	6	2	1
	2013	402	99	46	44	24	5	29	29	2	1
	2014	455	190	47	45	67	9	76	75	4	3
	2015	338	109	45	35	24	2	40	40	2	1
	2016	280	142	65	58	32	1	45	44	4	4
Southern Asia	2000	556	217	157	153	37	1	22	21	30	27
	2013	6825	468	344	342	116	27	8	7	26	4
	2014	5337	410	285	283	113	29	12	11	15	7
	2015	3514	246	114	112	127	17	6	5	9	8
	2016	3830	227	124	90	95	12	7	6	1	0
South-Eastern Asia	2000	2772	1837	1277	1257	533	67	28	12	0	0
	2013	14872	5369	4693	3990	500	115	177	177	78	78
	2014	11395	4781	4236	4105	428	41	117	117	1	0
	2015	11331	4157	3818	3797	252	109	87	87	2	2
	2016	11022	4096	3830	3800	162	40	103	103	2	2
Western Asia	2000	670	228	79	79	136	12	14	11	27	26
	2013	7443	925	113	113	777	94	36	31	15	10
	2014	6469	1086	141	141	899	81	45	38	14	9
	2015	4881	786	107	107	654	54	24	20	10	9
	2016	4532	853	166	140	621	53	67	29	10	9
Oceania	2000	1459	462	301	269	157	54	3	3	3	...
	2013	1603	912	653	542	260	93	0	0	...	...
	2014	2179	1264	984	840	280	137	0	0	0	0
	2015	1034	325	264	259	60	59	0	0	...	...
	2016	1083	409	399	395	10	10	0	0	...	...

For general note and footnotes see end of table

Exportations mondiales par provenance et destination (Tableau D)

En millions de dollars E.-U. f.o.b.

South-Eastern Europe Europe du Sud-est	Northern Africa Afrique septentrio-nale	Sub-Saharan Africa Afrique du Nord	Latin America and the Caribbean Amérique latine et Caraïbes	Eastern Asia Asie orientale	Southern Asia Asie méridionale	South-eastern Asia Asie du Sud-est	Western Asia Asie occidentale	Oceania Océanie	Others 4/ Autre 4/	Année	← Exportations vers Exportations en provenance de ↓
				Minerais métallifères et dechets de metaux (CTCI, Rev. 3, 28) [suite]							
16	0	0	...	9	2	0	6	...	0	2000	Afrique du Nord
17	1	10	3	209	56	5	38	...	3	2013	
5	7	4	4	231	43	9	60	...	4	2014	
17	1	8	0	228	33	3	33	...	1	2015	
25	1	9	0	210	25	4	38	...	1	2016	
13	0	180	14	237	24	36	10	...	0	2000	Afrique subsaharienne
13	25	2598	85	12004	986	643	200	2	0	2013	
3	15	1910	148	9461	1417	306	234	8	0	2014	
2	0	1040	58	6100	688	169	155	1	1	2015	
2	25	1319	103	6212	785	242	98	1	4	2016	
9	0	6	13	206	13	29	4	...	0	2000	Afrique du sud
0	13	94	73	9099	692	556	131	0	0	2013	
0	15	80	111	6868	1215	229	189	8	0	2014	
...	0	163	44	4189	450	67	116	1	0	2015	
...	25	375	77	4642	628	127	71	1	3	2016	
144	125	83	911	1422	262	238	233	...	0	2000	Amérique latine et Caraïbes
1174	669	214	4276	39285	2546	1781	2352	...	0	2013	
1000	472	342	4210	34930	3149	1798	2434	...	2	2014	
745	147	257	2491	26340	2511	1823	2015	0	0	2015	
574	267	231	2312	29475	2173	1543	1145	0	2	2016	
41	111	30	335	556	34	78	205	...	...	2000	Brésil
232	650	94	1584	18852	290	1120	2125	...	...	2013	
183	456	118	1631	15036	422	1262	2220	...	...	2014	
126	132	79	728	8126	422	1365	1798	...	...	2015	
103	266	99	653	8661	442	1021	1015	...	...	2016	
0	0	10	1	576	7	24	1	0	...	2000	Asie orientale
0	1	7	32	3337	118	277	34	0	...	2013	
0	1	7	24	4614	154	444	31	...	0	2014	
1	0	5	9	3750	221	411	15	0	0	2015	
0	0	9	3	3981	162	392	12	0	...	2016	
0	0	5	0	36	2	7	0	0	...	2000	Chine
0	1	1	6	176	49	35	34	0	...	2013	
0	1	2	8	115	62	44	28	...	...	2014	
...	0	2	3	54	94	60	14	0	...	2015	
0	0	2	3	59	32	27	11	0	...	2016	
2	0	2	18	238	28	4	18	...	0	2000	Asie méridionale
0	20	5	7	5208	187	185	713	0	7	2013	
1	37	2	2	3886	208	28	725	0	23	2014	
0	38	1	2	2448	140	37	592	...	...	2015	
0	67	2	1	2856	131	70	475	0	...	2016	
28	0	19	16	457	151	262	1	0	0	2000	Asie Sud-est
0	0	1	8	7343	1073	956	35	10	0	2013	
25	0	3	0	5154	781	636	12	0	1	2014	
0	1	4	8	5108	1261	778	12	0	0	2015	
0	0	8	9	4919	934	1037	17	0	0	2016	
24	10	4	0	79	154	60	78	...	7	2000	Asie occidentale
151	56	13	18	2650	1315	75	1955	0	268	2013	
194	160	12	22	1731	1278	109	1464	...	400	2014	
100	38	37	53	1266	1108	71	1028	...	383	2015	
104	40	7	12	1030	1097	74	1002	...	302	2016	
1	...	5	...	61	...	215	...	0	713	2000	Océanie
...	...	0	62	321	220	87	...	0	...	2013	
...	...	...	92	384	325	114	...	0	0	2014	
...	...	...	...	628	46	35	...	0	0	2015	
...	...	0	...	655	16	3	...	0	0	2016	

Voir la fin du tableau pour la remarque générale et les notes.

World exports by provenance and destination (Table D)

In million U.S. dollars f.o.b.

Exports to ⟶ / ↓ Exports from	Year	World 1/ Monde 1/	Developed economies 2/ Economies développées 2/ Total	Asia-Pacific Asie-Pacifique Total	Japan Japon	Europe Total	Germany Allemagne	North America Amérique du Nord Total	U.S.A. É.-U.	Commonwealth of Independent States Communauté d'Etats Indépendants Total	Europe
		Animal and vegetable oils, fats and waxes (SITC, Rev. 3, 4)									
World 1/	2000	19188	9130	727	528	6721	802	1682	1403	537	455
	2013	98465	41471	2134	1470	32494	4536	6844	5910	2865	2224
	2014	96757	40963	2341	1579	31530	3989	7092	6154	2330	1647
	2015	85274	35477	2063	1458	26831	3186	6582	5770	2002	1350
	2016	83317	35991	2040	1385	26893	3316	7058	6223	1855	1218
Developed Economies - Asia-Pacific 2/	2000	326	115	59	48	26	3	30	29	0	0
	2013	927	212	70	17	63	14	80	73	0	0
	2014	903	194	65	16	52	14	77	69	0	0
	2015	740	167	52	21	49	9	66	62	0	0
	2016	786	200	74	14	59	12	68	61	0	0
Japan	2000	81	37	1	.	11	2	25	24	0	0
	2013	167	81	4	.	27	12	50	45	0	0
	2014	183	83	2	.	28	12	53	47	0	0
	2015	147	76	2	.	24	8	51	46	0	0
	2016	168	101	1	.	45	10	54	48	0	0
Developed Economies - Europe 2/	2000	6475	5137	188	105	4456	624	493	438	268	257
	2013	26993	22484	478	304	20798	3651	1208	1071	770	733
	2014	24461	21005	501	338	19127	3166	1377	1217	496	441
	2015	21255	17991	452	319	16297	2421	1242	1109	287	235
	2016	22978	19453	509	329	17427	2636	1517	1346	314	273
France	2000	436	332	3	3	324	34	6	5	10	10
	2013	1681	1494	12	10	1449	140	33	30	44	43
	2014	1483	1356	13	12	1302	128	40	35	7	6
	2015	1313	1146	9	7	1093	118	44	40	1	1
	2016	1454	1297	11	9	1246	123	39	34	2	2
Germany	2000	1012	827	8	3	811	.	8	8	58	57
	2013	3903	3106	17	13	3058	.	32	30	157	151
	2014	3238	2755	19	16	2698	.	38	37	77	57
	2015	2928	2474	16	13	2425	.	34	33	51	32
	2016	3029	2651	15	11	2605	.	31	30	42	29
Developed Economies - North America 2/	2000	1868	753	79	74	159	10	515	313	24	19
	2013	6841	3068	151	135	437	86	2480	1860	5	5
	2014	5965	2892	157	124	366	101	2370	1808	19	18
	2015	5566	2689	118	102	364	53	2207	1724	5	4
	2016	5885	2993	123	101	450	47	2420	1944	7	6
United States	2000	1437	404	59	55	143	9	202	.	24	18
	2013	3568	1099	66	54	412	82	620	.	1	1
	2014	3211	975	69	51	345	87	561	.	7	6
	2015	2983	882	58	45	342	49	482	.	5	4
	2016	3014	963	60	41	428	42	475	.	7	6
South-Eastern Europe	2000	50	18	...	...	17	2	1	0	5	5
	2013	809	543	0	...	543	23	1	1	1	1
	2014	772	438	0	0	433	28	5	5	6	6
	2015	724	387	0	0	386	33	1	1	1	0
	2016	747	366	0	0	366	21	0	0	1	1
Commonwealth of Independent States	2000	337	102	0	0	98	3	3	3	126	80
	2013	5899	1349	2	1	1340	18	6	6	706	191
	2014	6306	1370	7	1	1356	22	7	6	659	168
	2015	5348	1075	1	0	1068	29	5	5	655	149
	2016	2588	424	0	0	423	17	1	1	598	102
Russian Federation	2000	79	3	0	0	3	0	0	0	29	1
	2013	2011	665	1	0	663	11	1	1	428	53
	2014	2102	365	4	0	360	11	1	1	467	70
	2015	1731	237	0	0	237	13	0	0	445	74
	2016	2065	236	0	0	236	8	0	0	546	86

For general note and footnotes see end of table

Exportations mondiales par provenance et destination (Tableau D)

En millions de dollars E.-U. f.o.b.

South-Eastern Europe Europe du Sud-est	Northern Africa Afrique septentrio-nale	Sub-Saharan Africa Afrique du Nord	Latin America and the Caribbean Amérique latine et Caraïbes	Eastern Asia Asie orientale	Southern Asia Asie méridionale	South-eastern Asia Asie du Sud-est	Western Asia Asie occidentale	Oceania Océanie	Others 4/ Autre 4/	Année	← Exportations vers Exportations en provence de ↓
			Hulies et graisses d'origine animale ou vegetale (CTCI, Rev. 3, 4)								
118	778	749	1484	1622	2767	873	1057	20	53	2000	Monde 1/
654	3828	5243	6280	12272	15006	5563	5056	69	156	2013	
581	3296	6014	6166	10522	15379	6283	5058	80	86	2014	
540	2981	4940	5146	9620	14048	5749	4496	75	200	2015	
613	3206	4478	5080	8688	12887	6082	4218	73	145	2016	
...	0	14	0	126	36	32	0	2	0	2000	Economies Développées - Asie-Pacifique 2/
0	0	2	4	239	19	430	13	8	0	2013	
0	1	18	6	288	19	363	6	7	0	2014	
0	0	17	10	208	21	272	3	4	36	2015	
0	2	2	5	186	6	378	2	5	0	2016	
...	0	0	0	27	1	16	0	0	...	2000	Japon
0	0	0	2	60	1	21	1	0	...	2013	
0	...	1	5	70	1	22	1	0	...	2014	
0	0	0	4	44	3	17	1	0	...	2015	
0	0	1	3	41	2	19	1	0	...	2016	
80	279	165	147	92	55	27	189	6	31	2000	Economies Développées - Europe 2/
346	613	493	589	884	150	216	353	15	80	2013	
325	514	376	574	500	92	189	369	12	10	2014	
273	629	285	487	523	176	183	306	11	104	2015	
361	578	393	499	587	115	178	380	13	106	2016	
3	34	12	2	2	6	2	28	5	...	2000	France
4	16	12	14	39	4	25	21	8	0	2013	
6	9	13	13	19	4	30	19	6	0	2014	
9	30	13	14	24	30	24	17	5	0	2015	
13	19	22	9	38	4	22	21	7	0	2016	
13	26	10	5	33	19	4	16	0	1	2000	Allemagne
41	216	40	18	217	7	57	44	0	1	2013	
38	248	13	17	22	7	29	31	0	1	2014	
30	262	15	16	26	7	22	23	0	1	2015	
34	144	12	22	56	7	26	34	0	1	2016	
9	41	78	535	200	41	25	161	0	0	2000	Economies Développées - Amérique du Nord 2/
2	171	143	1557	1409	59	103	322	1	...	2013	
1	176	86	1511	847	30	90	314	1	...	2014	
3	229	83	1410	735	35	96	281	0	...	2015	
5	133	84	1285	879	68	202	228	0	...	2016	
9	40	77	526	139	38	20	161	0	0	2000	États-Unis
2	171	139	1422	291	56	69	316	1	...	2013	
1	160	82	1327	262	27	59	309	1	...	2014	
3	222	82	1271	157	29	54	277	0	...	2015	
5	117	83	1175	289	43	108	224	0	...	2016	
16	1	0	0	0	0	0	10	...	0	2000	Europe du Sud-est
204	10	17	...	1	...	0	33	...	2	2013	
172	3	77	0	1	3	0	69	...	3	2014	
180	18	54	0	3	7	0	73	...	0	2015	
195	23	51	0	2	12	2	94	...	0	2016	
5	69	0	3	1	10	0	21	...	0	2000	Communauté d'Etats Indépendants
50	753	38	26	469	1296	66	1144	0	0	2013	
25	785	110	9	409	1725	69	1144	0	0	2014	
27	461	114	12	662	1275	124	943	0	0	2015	
14	404	40	30	266	231	16	565	0	0	2016	
2	36	...	0	1	0	0	8	...	...	2000	Fédération de Russie
23	310	3	0	26	59	0	495	0	0	2013	
2	503	30	6	28	120	2	579	0	0	2014	
1	298	41	5	104	63	3	533	0	0	2015	
9	380	39	28	185	129	11	502	0	0	2016	

Voir la fin du tableau pour la remarque générale et les notes.

World exports by provenance and destination (Table D)

In million U.S. dollars f.o.b.

Exports to ⟶ / ↓ Exports from	Year	World 1/ Monde 1/	Developed economies 2/ Economies développées 2/ Total	Asia-Pacific Asie-Pacifique Total	Japan Japon	Europe Total	Germany Allemagne	North America Amérique du Nord Total	U.S.A. É.-U.	Commonwealth of Independent States Communauté d'Etats Indépendants Total	Europe
Animal and vegetable oils, fats and waxes (SITC, Rev. 3, 4) [cont.]											
Northern Africa	2000	245	188	0	0	178	0	10	10	...	...
	2013	992	575	1	1	448	4	126	116	3	3
	2014	738	405	2	1	316	6	86	74	2	2
	2015	1409	1076	12	10	840	6	224	209	1	1
	2016	883	531	8	7	396	4	127	108	1	1
Sub-Saharan Africa	2000	229	105	2	2	101	6	2	2	0	0
	2013	1150	285	6	5	273	12	6	5	0	0
	2014	1422	341	11	10	324	6	6	5	0	0
	2015	1358	179	10	9	162	6	7	6	0	0
	2016	1008	174	10	6	153	10	11	10	0	0
South Africa	2000	38	5	0	...	5	0	1	0	...	...
	2013	247	16	0	0	15	2	1	1	0	0
	2014	248	19	1	1	16	1	1	1	0	0
	2015	226	16	6	6	10	1	1	0	...	...
	2016	232	22	4	2	17	1	1	0	0	0
Latin America and the Caribbean	2000	2599	341	44	32	207	25	89	84	40	40
	2013	10092	1590	160	79	1024	90	405	333	6	6
	2014	9142	1693	155	71	1134	182	404	325	14	14
	2015	9321	1732	153	75	1148	164	431	382	19	18
	2016	9459	1700	130	63	1169	202	400	331	13	13
Brazil	2000	476	83	24	20	41	5	18	18	1	1
	2013	1788	307	46	33	210	27	51	51	0	0
	2014	1484	246	37	27	148	63	61	61	1	1
	2015	1569	247	41	35	151	57	55	55	5	5
	2016	1225	185	38	31	101	27	46	46	4	4
Eastern Asia	2000	304	54	21	17	19	4	14	12	2	2
	2013	878	391	110	87	133	35	148	128	9	7
	2014	896	367	82	59	150	36	136	116	10	8
	2015	907	425	108	77	165	38	153	110	6	5
	2016	822	370	80	57	164	29	126	99	7	5
China	2000	116	33	12	10	15	3	7	6	0	0
	2013	630	320	78	60	116	33	126	109	6	4
	2014	678	300	52	34	134	35	113	96	7	5
	2015	692	346	66	40	147	38	133	93	5	3
	2016	614	290	53	34	132	28	106	82	5	4
Southern Asia	2000	284	164	21	20	107	5	36	36	25	12
	2013	1321	519	44	37	339	19	136	131	9	7
	2014	1214	544	67	52	321	21	156	140	8	7
	2015	1291	592	97	77	318	19	176	150	10	9
	2016	1131	521	75	55	298	18	148	136	14	11
South-Eastern Asia	2000	6010	1948	307	229	1173	103	468	459	38	36
	2013	39507	9406	1076	783	6206	507	2124	2075	1334	1266
	2014	41675	10521	1260	892	6838	299	2423	2351	1096	977
	2015	35037	8550	1036	755	5484	267	2030	1978	1006	925
	2016	34711	8622	1006	740	5424	257	2191	2145	892	805
Western Asia	2000	298	43	1	0	21	2	20	17	9	3
	2013	2237	325	31	21	171	11	124	113	21	5
	2014	2066	136	24	15	67	11	45	37	19	7
	2015	1815	144	19	12	87	11	38	32	12	4
	2016	1869	216	19	13	151	10	46	40	8	1
Oceania	2000	163	162	3	...	159	14	0	0	...	...
	2013	819	726	6	0	720	66	0	0	...	...
	2014	1197	1056	9	0	1047	98	0	0	...	...
	2015	502	469	5	0	463	132	2	2	...	...
	2016	451	420	5	0	414	53	2	2	0	...

For general note and footnotes see end of table

Exportations mondiales par provenance et destination (Tableau D)

En millions de dollars E.-U. f.o.b.

← Exportations vers

South-Eastern Europe Europe du Sud-est	Northern Africa Afrique septentrio-nale	Sub-Saharan Africa Afrique du Nord	Latin America and the Caribbean Amérique latine et Caraïbes	Eastern Asia Asie orientale	Southern Asia Asie méridionale	South-eastern Asia Asie du Sud-est	Western Asia Asie occidentale	Oceania Océanie	Others 4/ Autre 4/	Année	Exportations en provenance de ↓
Hulies et graisses d'origine animale ou vegetale (CTCI, Rev. 3, 4) [suite]											
...	15	1	3	0	0	...	30	...	7	2000	Afrique du Nord
3	94	68	2	8	1	2	223	...	13	2013	
1	83	69	13	14	26	4	111	...	10	2014	
2	70	72	27	18	0	2	128	...	14	2015	
1	137	68	31	11	1	3	89	...	10	2016	
0	0	116	0	5	0	2	0	0	0	2000	Afrique subsaharienne
19	5	774	1	17	11	33	5	0	1	2013	
20	1	987	3	34	5	25	6	0	0	2014	
20	3	855	8	253	2	32	7	0	0	2015	
0	3	648	4	23	4	141	10	0	1	2016	
0	0	26	0	5	0	1	0	...	0	2000	Afrique du sud
...	...	227	0	1	0	2	0	0	1	2013	
0	...	225	1	2	0	1	1	0	0	2014	
0	0	204	2	2	1	0	1	0	0	2015	
...	0	201	2	1	0	1	5	0	1	2016	
0	175	89	720	114	995	78	43	1	4	2000	Amérique latine et Caraïbes
0	886	218	3289	1520	2344	162	38	1	38	2013	
0	328	127	3084	932	2683	210	37	0	33	2014	
0	386	160	2512	811	3402	201	66	0	32	2015	
0	774	175	2515	624	3385	223	41	0	9	2016	
...	48	7	47	47	213	24	5	1	...	2000	Brésil
0	262	18	206	585	391	16	2	0	...	2013	
0	117	9	203	384	500	21	3	...	...	2014	
0	122	15	176	217	747	32	8	...	...	2015	
0	112	43	144	232	478	24	5	...	...	2016	
0	0	0	1	215	2	28	1	0	...	2000	Asie orientale
2	3	8	29	282	13	128	12	1	...	2013	
2	5	9	37	298	19	135	13	1	0	2014	
3	6	7	64	251	11	120	14	1	0	2015	
2	8	6	45	226	12	121	25	1	0	2016	
0	0	0	1	74	1	7	0	0	...	2000	Chine
2	2	7	27	171	9	76	10	0	...	2013	
2	3	8	35	213	11	88	12	0	...	2014	
3	2	6	61	181	8	71	9	0	...	2015	
2	3	5	40	175	9	76	9	0	...	2016	
0	1	3	1	29	34	19	7	0	0	2000	Asie méridionale
1	5	12	34	410	181	80	72	0	0	2013	
1	3	14	28	308	161	87	59	0	0	2014	
0	4	14	23	319	127	136	67	0	0	2015	
1	5	10	20	305	130	74	50	0	0	2016	
5	175	270	68	839	1569	663	421	10	4	2000	Asie Sud-est
25	1223	3398	649	6979	10790	4277	1364	43	20	2013	
31	1368	4086	748	6753	10498	5043	1461	57	11	2014	
29	1099	3209	574	5768	8904	4520	1319	58	1	2015	
31	1001	2921	636	5532	8828	4653	1541	53	1	2016	
1	22	12	5	1	24	0	173	0	7	2000	Asie occidentale
4	64	74	21	51	141	56	1477	0	2	2013	
3	29	55	35	129	119	55	1469	0	17	2014	
2	75	71	18	69	87	35	1289	0	13	2015	
3	137	82	9	43	92	67	1194	0	17	2016	
0	...	...	...	...	0	0	...	0	0	2000	Océanie
...	2	0	79	2	0	10	0	0	...	2013	
...	1	0	117	7	0	14	...	1	0	2014	
...	...	...	...	3	1	28	0	0	0	2015	
...	...	0	1	2	3	25	...	0	0	2016	

Voir la fin du tableau pour la remarque générale et les notes.

World exports by provenance and destination (Table D)

In million U.S. dollars f.o.b.

Exports to ⟶ / Exports from	Year	World 1/ Monde 1/	Developed economies 2/ Economies développées 2/ Total	Asia-Pacific Asie-Pacifique Total	Japan Japon	Europe Total	Germany Allemagne	North America Amérique du Nord Total	U.S.A. É.-U.	Commonwealth of Independent States Communauté d'Etats Indépendants Total	Europe
Mineral fuels and related materials (SITC, Rev. 3, 3)											
World 1/	2000	665632	441344	62918	56939	230352	28721	148073	121796	11137	9696
	2013	3243243	1648755	223710	188063	1012626	116689	412420	282110	61342	50072
	2014	3012289	1488145	206410	171486	904344	102986	377391	262393	47450	39335
	2015	1857675	913101	127339	104061	577621	67415	208141	147587	33028	26149
	2016	1451042	698985	112737	94421	410236	41925	176011	150736	17040	12861
Developed Economies - Asia-Pacific 2/	2000	15224	7843	5805	5125	901	85	1137	1136	7	7
	2013	83321	36401	32428	27684	3174	108	799	750	70	65
	2014	81097	33818	31045	27154	2241	94	532	529	142	140
	2015	59500	24967	22085	19032	2170	123	713	712	152	149
	2016	58395	22291	19498	16814	2294	83	499	499	83	80
Japan	2000	1520	518	83	.	40	4	395	394	7	7
	2013	16682	4809	3385	.	660	10	764	715	67	64
	2014	15824	3212	2562	.	180	11	470	467	68	66
	2015	11380	3005	2355	.	125	8	525	525	53	50
	2016	9372	2438	1919	.	136	10	383	382	55	52
Developed Economies - Europe 2/	2000	131109	119059	136	102	101983	20560	16940	13149	384	367
	2013	550181	447837	1118	1001	414814	84521	31905	27643	4862	4292
	2014	489931	398076	1580	1483	368757	74022	27738	24454	4786	4346
	2015	323988	261639	564	487	243671	49598	17404	14764	4037	3780
	2016	253316	200749	481	405	184546	28397	15721	12540	2168	1875
France	2000	8183	7258	28	13	6660	1009	570	561	16	15
	2013	22236	17650	107	71	16091	1420	1452	1389	30	26
	2014	21984	17477	20	16	16209	1453	1248	1193	37	30
	2015	14597	11775	50	47	10910	1024	814	758	26	20
	2016	11282	9203	192	188	8322	727	689	658	30	28
Germany	2000	7757	5384	13	9	4961	.	410	406	35	33
	2013	35042	33109	45	22	32878	.	186	149	694	617
	2014	33726	31135	40	19	30880	.	216	143	1459	1388
	2015	28347	25611	32	15	25454	.	125	94	1899	1850
	2016	21863	20709	37	16	20542	.	130	103	251	210
Developed Economies - North America 2/	2000	49973	41778	1515	1356	2000	104	38263	35442	8	7
	2013	269090	173704	4660	4226	31682	876	137362	112367	509	497
	2014	284028	186962	4162	3717	29330	745	153470	120629	445	431
	2015	181422	116449	2828	2538	18698	599	94924	73630	428	420
	2016	155900	93973	3585	3262	16037	425	74351	57532	355	349
United States	2000	13382	5589	1003	844	1767	80	2819	.	8	7
	2013	148724	57405	3138	2708	29277	795	24991	.	459	448
	2014	155416	61820	3143	2703	25849	667	32828	.	408	396
	2015	103972	40869	2039	1752	17543	510	21286	.	313	306
	2016	93614	34190	2722	2414	14685	354	16783	.	232	226
South-Eastern Europe	2000	1442	243	...	...	231	6	12	12	225	152
	2013	10104	3297	0	0	3264	242	33	33	2031	1482
	2014	9199	2224	0	0	2222	189	2	2	1483	1008
	2015	6453	1741	0	0	1719	82	21	21	790	482
	2016	5767	1629	0	0	1627	48	2	2	627	332
Commonwealth of Independent States	2000	62916	41908	302	302	40073	3736	1534	215	10328	9053
	2013	479744	329612	21758	21429	300177	19995	7678	5162	52558	43049
	2014	447779	305988	24138	23663	276315	21385	5535	4559	39231	32637
	2015	271405	180833	15998	15566	161539	12696	3295	3083	26538	20712
	2016	176304	110271	7231	7155	99322	10137	3718	3472	13215	9868
Russian Federation	2000	52166	36681	302	302	36076	3554	303	189	6979	6287
	2013	372036	261566	21626	21298	235749	17369	4191	4135	42715	34922
	2014	346119	240769	23928	23454	212863	18238	3978	3811	29749	24913
	2015	216101	145046	15636	15206	126234	10865	3176	3056	20125	16076
	2016	134703	85070	7019	6944	74628	8999	3423	3392	8718	6482

For general note and footnotes see end of table

Exportations mondiales par provenance et destination (Tableau D)

En millions de dollars E.-U. f.o.b.

← Exportations vers

South-Eastern Europe Europe du Sud-est	Northern Africa Afrique septentrionale	Sub-Saharan Africa Afrique du Nord	Latin America and the Caribbean Amérique latine et Caraïbes	Eastern Asia Asie orientale	Southern Asia Asie méridionale	South-eastern Asia Asie du Sud-est	Western Asia Asie occidentale	Oceania Océanie	Others 4/ Autre 4/	Année	Exportations en provenance de ↓
				Combustibles minéraux et produits assimiles (CTCI, Rev. 3, 3)							
3281	5870	6037	34956	92717	11794	28096	11783	1760	16859	2000	Monde 1/
17243	40742	64544	169110	751061	130035	212189	84489	4968	58763	2013	
16602	35736	66582	169634	705101	127022	211181	88723	4884	51228	2014	
12909	21693	47006	109953	419952	83876	130518	51953	3201	30485	2015	
8897	17941	36125	83830	308775	86447	132150	45070	2359	13423	2016	
0	8	65	320	3610	499	1633	112	421	706	2000	Economies Développées - Asie-Pacifique 2/
1	1	246	872	28438	5072	9282	160	705	2073	2013	
1	1	157	1455	29225	5044	10009	168	702	375	2014	
13	29	104	1627	20356	4694	6670	320	436	132	2015	
6	48	137	1478	22346	4911	6336	240	510	10	2016	
...	0	2	42	701	27	220	4	0	...	2000	Japon
0	1	84	103	7351	231	3961	62	13	...	2013	
0	1	51	351	7969	210	3695	78	189	...	2014	
0	1	6	431	4893	66	2647	86	192	...	2015	
0	1	4	361	4349	95	1867	58	142	...	2016	
784	1350	1171	767	506	436	286	1985	6	4375	2000	Economies Développées - Europe 2/
5676	13750	17555	10018	7857	527	4615	16313	18	21152	2013	
5284	11692	17253	7159	7842	551	4198	15979	12	17099	2014	
3819	8415	11940	4341	5998	567	3897	9968	47	9320	2015	
3172	6971	9255	4202	5765	626	5101	7810	65	7431	2016	
8	212	257	130	23	21	19	204	3	34	2000	France
32	742	1397	265	153	26	121	1642	5	172	2013	
26	643	1939	224	254	27	108	1210	4	36	2014	
18	683	1209	68	56	21	57	631	4	50	2015	
18	373	688	88	58	33	40	402	4	345	2016	
22	10	35	117	35	12	13	38	0	2056	2000	Allemagne
94	45	198	121	259	46	78	257	0	140	2013	
129	37	101	189	290	44	73	178	0	89	2014	
115	36	79	108	210	40	52	153	0	44	2015	
103	48	69	86	263	49	59	167	0	59	2016	
73	105	141	6231	822	95	433	272	2	13	2000	Economies Développées - Amérique du Nord 2/
177	2411	3463	70139	8322	1471	5138	3730	28	...	2013	
302	2562	3885	74959	6287	1493	4328	2797	8	0	2014	
134	1305	1432	51315	4886	1243	2539	1690	1	0	2015	
83	930	827	48403	5720	1549	2434	1601	25	0	2016	
61	97	131	6145	583	85	433	235	2	13	2000	États-Unis
154	2409	3460	69436	5406	1249	5071	3648	28	...	2013	
256	2555	3883	74025	4404	1251	4232	2574	8	...	2014	
103	1285	1430	51057	3676	1096	2527	1614	1	...	2015	
77	907	826	47978	4285	1192	2404	1498	25	...	2016	
661	13	65	17	0	1	12	186	...	19	2000	Europe du Sud-est
1864	326	342	2	2	40	431	1722	1	45	2013	
1861	463	153	2	1	31	737	2182	1	61	2014	
1459	567	18	1	4	14	347	1472	0	41	2015	
1415	594	10	1	2	20	153	1197	0	118	2016	
1626	28	22	4633	697	251	464	2956	1	2	2000	Communauté d'Etats Indépendants
9314	2282	212	2290	55881	2433	9596	15344	0	222	2013	
8908	2945	175	1176	59266	2718	13083	14113	0	175	2014	
7178	824	315	737	40579	1892	4463	7608	17	421	2015	
3793	1020	264	1436	34613	1474	3347	6829	36	5	2016	
1407	24	15	3416	590	15	428	2611	0	0	2000	Fédération de Russie
6386	1669	189	1748	41732	621	4665	10726	...	19	2013	
5354	2283	159	1003	47731	555	9977	8529	0	11	2014	
5583	807	309	732	33584	403	3263	5891	17	341	2015	
2873	799	251	1416	27334	520	3065	4620	36	2	2016	

Voir la fin du tableau pour la remarque générale et les notes.

World exports by provenance and destination (Table D)

In million U.S. dollars f.o.b.

Exports from ↓ / Exports to →	Year	World 1/ Monde 1/	Developed economies 2/ Economies développées 2/ Total	Asia-Pacific Asie-Pacifique Total	Japan Japon	Europe Total	Germany Allemagne	North America Amérique du Nord Total	U.S.A. É.-U.	Commonwealth of Independent States Communauté d'Etats Indépendants Total	Europe
Mineral fuels and related materials (SITC, Rev. 3, 3) [cont.]											
Northern Africa	2000	34248	28440	95	95	24060	2700	4285	3508	10	0
	2013	119360	94260	2815	1984	80187	6476	11258	8132	115	1
	2014	87901	67392	1676	1676	59437	2775	6279	4958	50	49
	2015	46787	35166	682	682	31575	1277	2909	2279	43	21
	2016	35972	26712	350	175	21203	381	5158	3885	0	0
Sub-Saharan Africa	2000	45298	27624	229	193	9472	281	17923	17266	3	3
	2013	204770	91191	8861	5097	58890	2100	23440	17929	1	1
	2014	207809	82690	8719	5737	59977	2012	13994	10748	93	93
	2015	169797	68112	6685	4350	52957	2054	8470	7138	88	87
	2016	81209	30522	1464	793	21072	976	7985	6303	10	10
South Africa	2000	2664	1005	72	36	902	32	31	29	0	0
	2013	10108	1425	63	54	1237	53	126	123	0	0
	2014	9507	1798	29	21	1517	72	251	239	42	42
	2015	8161	882	24	15	740	84	118	95	36	36
	2016	7087	769	15	9	670	85	84	81	9	9
Latin America and the Caribbean	2000	63577	43894	434	371	3985	406	39475	38637	2	1
	2013	238347	127708	1042	1032	23976	581	102691	71174	9	9
	2014	213826	108919	836	836	21706	395	86377	59730	10	10
	2015	115624	55477	1199	1198	12089	117	42189	29232	14	12
	2016	78246	38170	1536	1531	8673	164	27961	27818	6	4
Brazil	2000	908	600	0	0	66	6	533	529	...	...
	2013	17822	7720	11	1	3425	111	4284	3704	0	0
	2014	20650	6571	0	0	2816	72	3755	3608	0	...
	2015	13748	3450	0	0	1141	13	2309	2196	0	0
	2016	11581	2595	7	1	1127	17	1461	1443	0	0
Eastern Asia	2000	19504	7958	5952	5704	452	46	1553	1477	97	78
	2013	113941	26581	16067	10621	5456	426	5059	4853	615	433
	2014	109828	24718	14855	8354	5072	382	4792	4602	602	368
	2015	74631	18581	11267	5192	3196	245	4118	3992	471	336
	2016	66441	15012	8468	3735	2609	198	3935	3725	307	262
China	2000	7855	3226	2080	1973	436	46	711	689	70	51
	2013	33786	5479	2105	1829	1879	423	1496	1307	443	286
	2014	34446	5125	2161	1432	1520	374	1444	1294	429	221
	2015	27902	5089	2645	1523	1366	241	1078	960	332	218
	2016	26871	5005	2379	1129	1166	192	1460	1267	195	172
Southern Asia	2000	26842	16067	5335	5321	10595	184	137	136	11	3
	2013	121779	24972	11594	11530	9569	37	3810	3747	193	13
	2014	120628	20836	10435	10068	5883	30	4518	4517	213	12
	2015	66475	12711	6998	5877	3570	7	2143	2142	235	7
	2016	57605	14744	4541	3703	8245	35	1958	1958	124	8
South-Eastern Asia	2000	45414	18800	16753	13540	405	19	1643	1637	2	2
	2013	220676	59265	53719	35160	2296	39	3250	3069	67	64
	2014	208908	54199	49344	30762	2360	74	2494	2326	63	50
	2015	136222	31730	27851	18837	1703	36	2176	2078	38	34
	2016	111906	23794	20398	12734	1721	38	1676	1600	41	38
Western Asia	2000	169386	87133	25766	24830	36194	593	25173	9180	58	22
	2013	831412	233869	69592	68242	79140	1288	85137	27252	311	166
	2014	750746	202239	59536	57955	71043	881	71659	25338	332	190
	2015	400878	103258	28745	28113	44735	582	29779	8517	193	108
	2016	366876	119487	43555	42834	42885	1044	33047	31402	102	36
Oceania	2000	699	597	597	0	0	.	0	0	...	...
	2013	516	57	57	55	0	0	0	0	...	...
	2014	609	83	83	81	0	0	0	0	...	...
	2015	4493	2438	2437	2189	0	0	0	0	...	...
	2016	3105	1631	1631	1280	0	0	0	0	...	...

For general note and footnotes see end of table

Exportations mondiales par provenance et destination (Tableau D)

En millions de dollars E.-U. f.o.b.

South-Eastern Europe Europe du Sud-est	Northern Africa Afrique septentrionale	Sub-Saharan Africa Afrique du Nord	Latin America and the Caribbean Amérique latine et Caraïbes	Eastern Asia Asie orientale	Southern Asia Asie méridionale	South-eastern Asia Asie du Sud-est	Western Asia Asie occidentale	Oceania Océanie	Others 4/ Autre 4/	Année	← Exportations vers Exportations en provence de ↓
			Combustibles minéraux et produits assimiles (CTCI, Rev. 3, 3) [suite]								
35	471	59	1830	167	173	172	2234	...	656	2000	Afrique du Nord
96	4166	297	3493	6648	3627	1366	3962	0	1330	2013	
131	3193	475	3349	4855	2389	1258	3494	0	1313	2014	
101	2040	231	1829	2765	860	755	2329	72	596	2015	
2	1399	191	1946	1292	815	1310	2130	0	176	2016	
9	37	3582	1797	6404	4023	788	293	28	710	2000	Afrique subsaharienne
34	46	19965	13974	50019	21706	4949	1639	231	1016	2013	
52	145	21750	15450	48986	23420	8792	4205	42	2183	2014	
71	489	19164	12733	32569	22388	7757	3429	49	2948	2015	
43	509	11293	2611	19631	11771	3046	1100	43	630	2016	
2	35	580	45	129	83	42	168	1	573	2000	Afrique du sud
27	23	3435	300	1437	1815	505	716	2	422	2013	
6	110	3290	187	350	2168	404	663	22	468	2014	
3	413	2416	139	191	2456	163	322	27	1116	2015	
14	216	2537	135	329	2171	138	322	24	424	2016	
3	1	92	16904	438	209	176	105	0	1751	2000	Amérique latine et Caraïbes
0	16	414	53088	41116	7929	6003	1023	1	1039	2013	
0	93	1019	51335	36047	7802	5158	1633	4	1806	2014	
5	102	436	31015	21368	3060	2369	1130	6	642	2015	
4	129	374	19276	10940	5900	1905	1147	3	392	2016	
...	...	25	238	36	1	8	0	...	...	2000	Brésil
...	0	54	3638	4051	1587	736	35	0	...	2013	
...	0	60	7075	3485	2348	1062	49	1	...	2014	
0	0	47	4464	4147	1109	491	40	...	...	2015	
0	33	32	3812	4087	679	310	34	0	0	2016	
10	7	77	363	6606	489	2581	66	133	1116	2000	Asie orientale
0	145	2388	4020	31436	2080	40870	1712	971	3123	2013	
8	259	1578	3157	28746	2875	41403	1763	1473	3245	2014	
13	31	1045	2270	20988	2132	24726	1404	960	2010	2015	
10	160	1880	1808	19763	2182	22713	1279	617	711	2016	
10	6	59	209	2528	334	1360	53	0	...	2000	Chine
0	11	763	3230	11246	1000	10465	856	293	...	2013	
8	4	952	2748	11000	1806	11197	916	262	...	2014	
12	23	590	1875	9432	1485	7955	865	244	...	2015	
10	70	675	1438	8077	1560	8865	804	173	...	2016	
0	2008	8	680	7175	177	504	211	0	0	2000	Asie méridionale
4	539	9391	3845	32910	12453	11184	21146	5	5137	2013	
3	662	10867	4446	37952	15933	7586	21140	2	987	2014	
2	116	5223	808	22067	10077	4430	9578	17	1211	2015	
85	46	3754	139	15674	8713	5138	8169	1	1018	2016	
3	9	28	78	13054	1725	11079	110	523	3	2000	Asie Sud-est
0	223	2773	532	52175	12800	87961	1637	2525	717	2013	
2	2	3101	518	46057	13942	87436	830	2248	509	2014	
0	42	3026	110	31938	9974	57201	513	1151	500	2015	
0	41	788	292	27848	8094	49133	510	984	381	2016	
78	1832	726	1336	53138	3716	9966	3251	645	7507	2000	Asie occidentale
77	16838	7495	6834	436175	59897	30759	16100	368	22688	2013	
50	13719	6169	6621	399716	50824	27133	20419	253	23271	2014	
116	7734	4073	3165	214943	26950	15026	12511	353	12556	2015	
284	6095	7349	2238	144184	40390	31233	13059	20	2436	2016	
0	...	0	...	99	...	2	...	1	0	2000	Océanie
...	...	1	3	82	1	37	0	115	221	2013	
...	...	1	7	119	0	59	...	136	204	2014	
...	...	0	1	1490	25	337	0	92	109	2015	
0	1	3	0	998	0	301	0	55	116	2016	

Voir la fin du tableau pour la remarque générale et les notes.

World exports by provenance and destination (Table D)

In million U.S. dollars f.o.b.

Exports to ⟶ / ↓ Exports from	Year	World 1/ Monde 1/	Developed economies 2/ Economies développées 2/ Total	Asia-Pacific Asie-Pacifique Total	Japan Japon	Europe Total	Germany Allemagne	North America Amérique du Nord Total	U.S.A. É.-U.	Commonwealth of Independent States Communauté d'Etats Indépendants Total	Europe
						Chemicals (SITC, Rev. 3, 5)					
World 1/	2000	565720	375846	29372	21422	260879	42895	85596	66214	7297	6113
	2013	1973305	1135618	83862	58420	815695	142709	236060	188403	63931	53858
	2014	2003957	1160318	81867	56945	833507	144539	244944	196934	59411	49378
	2015	1812781	1064293	76288	53043	741245	128874	246759	202173	44079	35947
	2016	1763348	1047220	75985	53375	729557	128982	241678	198959	42375	34831
Developed Economies - Asia-Pacific 2/	2000	39061	14664	1393	353	6096	976	7176	6972	23	19
	2013	85259	20662	2354	549	8202	1748	10107	9764	200	192
	2014	80828	20113	2237	567	7871	1707	10006	9738	201	191
	2015	70285	18137	1989	477	7267	1486	8882	8572	146	139
	2016	72260	18618	2028	482	7396	1557	9195	8931	151	142
Japan	2000	35160	12405	386	.	5500	899	6520	6354	22	18
	2013	75823	16498	424	.	7236	1522	8838	8610	180	173
	2014	72120	16090	364	.	6989	1511	8737	8557	180	171
	2015	62847	14384	376	.	6382	1304	7625	7408	134	128
	2016	64317	14627	389	.	6555	1388	7683	7487	139	130
Developed Economies - Europe 2/	2000	317313	260844	11710	8572	212447	36797	36687	33952	4360	4031
	2013	1023759	797198	30910	21025	661819	122861	104469	93711	39551	36008
	2014	1039826	811248	28184	18760	673010	123828	110053	99854	36156	32720
	2015	935172	732869	27815	19044	586094	109388	118960	109400	25583	22757
	2016	927631	728073	27873	18823	581701	109280	118499	109232	25533	22923
France	2000	40440	32870	1270	908	27982	5990	3618	3362	530	469
	2013	101349	72277	3209	2400	62603	13895	6465	5633	3698	3350
	2014	100776	71878	2785	2015	62524	13746	6569	5844	3418	3051
	2015	86160	60719	2368	1743	51692	11485	6659	6024	2280	1991
	2016	85133	60278	2436	1771	50880	11063	6961	6362	2178	1906
Germany	2000	69666	53574	3003	2398	43607	.	6964	6327	1211	1124
	2013	217212	163425	6543	4809	135933	.	20948	19298	10417	9643
	2014	225383	171076	6711	4926	140798	.	23567	21829	9460	8736
	2015	199449	151932	6062	4394	122074	.	23797	22179	6659	6077
	2016	200602	152474	6305	4675	122899	.	23270	21606	6849	6312
Developed Economies - North America 2/	2000	94663	61241	8463	6535	24789	2860	27989	12116	311	267
	2013	246579	137651	15429	11383	61165	7617	61056	27828	1548	1337
	2014	249797	141291	16017	12089	62995	7820	62279	28217	1264	1085
	2015	242947	140891	15150	11176	66800	8036	58941	27507	1179	1066
	2016	231616	134878	15254	11698	63426	8202	56197	26081	960	854
United States	2000	79847	48118	8141	6324	24106	2734	15872	.	301	260
	2013	208859	105871	14935	11128	57714	7199	33222	.	1478	1274
	2014	211822	108977	15014	11323	59906	7559	34057	.	1205	1033
	2015	206276	110077	14546	10798	64103	7791	31428	.	1140	1037
	2016	197399	105775	14521	11155	61143	7850	30111	.	929	831
South-Eastern Europe	2000	1337	540	2	2	513	46	25	25	148	138
	2013	8402	4392	25	15	4190	1420	177	173	1219	1098
	2014	8789	4696	21	13	4487	1553	188	180	1198	1064
	2015	7838	4420	24	11	4269	1503	127	115	843	739
	2016	8101	4807	21	12	4683	1599	103	88	796	707
Commonwealth of Independent States	2000	8549	4575	35	33	3216	282	1324	1292	1361	839
	2013	36824	11993	157	70	9975	842	1862	1504	10660	7622
	2014	36499	12385	148	76	10756	722	1481	1237	10085	7011
	2015	32766	10810	121	61	8842	561	1847	1595	8632	6088
	2016	25466	7136	75	37	5959	404	1102	914	7489	4975
Russian Federation	2000	6181	3740	23	21	2535	218	1183	1165	607	189
	2013	23533	8703	75	27	7508	569	1120	1004	6383	4272
	2014	23517	9009	70	31	7906	441	1033	959	6078	3971
	2015	19950	7328	60	34	5936	336	1331	1244	5199	3471
	2016	15716	5103	41	28	4431	286	630	573	4865	3015

For general note and footnotes see end of table

Exportations mondiales par provenance et destination (Tableau D)

En millions de dollars E.-U. f.o.b.

South-Eastern Europe Europe du Sud-est	Northern Africa Afrique septentrio-nale	Sub-Saharan Africa Afrique du Nord	Latin America and the Caribbean Amérique latine et Caraïbes	Eastern Asia Asie orientale	Southern Asia Asie méridionale	South-eastern Asia Asie du Sud-est	Western Asia Asie occidentale	Oceania Océanie	Others 4/ Autre 4/	Année	← Exportations vers Exportations en provence de ↓
				Produits chimiques (CTCI, Rev. 3, 5)							
2699	4632	7735	38899	67237	9470	27955	16827	324	6800	2000	Monde 1/
19106	22485	40972	149392	273617	60734	116259	85680	1126	4386	2013	
19504	23203	41690	149737	271161	65604	120276	87818	1137	4098	2014	
17300	20574	37716	136186	239519	62547	108941	76992	983	3652	2015	
18181	19617	34678	124005	234039	59449	108397	71381	977	3029	2016	
2	52	161	1390	16114	491	5662	301	95	107	2000	Economies Développées - Asie-Pacifique 2/
31	81	310	1352	49480	1403	10571	885	273	11	2013	
37	89	293	1399	45433	1533	10572	890	251	16	2014	
34	86	225	1266	38294	1700	9249	894	221	32	2015	
35	99	286	1179	39389	1841	9556	846	225	33	2016	
2	45	105	1298	15458	446	5143	230	6	...	2000	Japon
26	67	220	1029	46953	1084	9041	719	6	...	2013	
30	70	216	1095	43388	1203	9133	711	6	...	2014	
31	76	162	1026	36805	1382	8152	691	4	...	2015	
32	82	238	979	37584	1515	8474	643	4	...	2016	
2196	3328	3858	9213	8702	2805	4847	10665	146	6351	2000	Economies Développées - Europe 2/
14964	13053	13193	33565	42462	9941	16453	40456	382	2540	2013	
15179	13442	13508	34023	45374	10415	16703	40948	435	2395	2014	
13380	11848	12349	31130	42871	9498	15483	37701	318	2142	2015	
14277	11539	11477	28035	44588	10167	15938	36082	327	1596	2016	
193	1065	1052	1207	1065	286	690	1358	122	2	2000	France
1058	3367	3530	4282	4435	991	2699	4676	312	24	2013	
1098	3398	3154	4534	4598	1045	2662	4664	308	18	2014	
998	2883	3168	3886	4129	1051	2440	4333	262	11	2015	
1084	2738	3141	3094	4526	1097	2527	4186	271	14	2016	
423	372	616	2378	2718	681	1316	2344	6	4026	2000	Allemagne
2723	1618	2059	7829	13591	2779	3740	8855	7	170	2013	
2930	1644	2334	7772	14353	2918	3986	8755	6	148	2014	
2683	1434	2094	7132	13340	2548	3492	7986	6	144	2015	
2844	1512	1933	6671	13801	2721	3692	7969	5	132	2016	
19	215	667	17043	9172	676	3841	1455	13	10	2000	Economies Développées - Amérique du Nord 2/
91	959	2106	55199	29113	3853	10608	5417	35	0	2013	
112	963	2089	55304	29479	3749	9980	5533	32	0	2014	
103	855	1948	50914	28083	3989	9767	5175	43	0	2015	
126	829	1615	47297	27544	4135	9246	4946	39	0	2016	
17	207	649	16607	8291	619	3601	1415	12	10	2000	Etats-Unis
87	940	1964	53283	27082	3445	9445	5235	29	...	2013	
103	949	1933	53588	27451	3326	8949	5318	23	...	2014	
96	833	1838	48918	26017	3557	8830	4950	21	...	2015	
95	788	1516	45525	25794	3740	8510	4704	23	...	2016	
224	21	21	18	9	19	19	262	0	57	2000	Europe du Sud-est
1714	120	70	55	93	82	43	611	0	5	2013	
1767	85	57	64	107	132	57	611	0	13	2014	
1597	90	49	47	92	138	72	479	0	10	2015	
1690	81	34	48	72	75	59	426	0	12	2016	
65	78	40	548	1031	245	118	487	1	1	2000	Communauté d'Etats Indépendants
444	276	782	3462	4793	1277	981	2105	0	51	2013	
438	206	562	3728	4811	1172	1149	1904	10	48	2014	
438	223	380	2905	4967	1771	1104	1489	1	45	2015	
412	145	297	2343	4090	1358	852	1311	1	33	2016	
38	48	16	378	889	159	62	243	1	0	2000	Fédération de Russie
335	111	449	2595	2280	682	577	1410	...	8	2013	
338	142	341	2812	2152	757	614	1257	9	8	2014	
318	112	252	2244	1822	1030	638	1001	0	6	2015	
350	112	233	1788	1368	690	464	730	0	13	2016	

Voir la fin du tableau pour la remarque générale et les notes.

World exports by provenance and destination (Table D)

In million U.S. dollars f.o.b.

Exports to ⟶ ↓ Exports from	Year	World 1/ Monde 1/	Developed economies 2/ Economies développées 2/ Total	Asia-Pacific Asie-Pacifique Total	Japan Japon	Europe Total	Germany Allemagne	North America Amérique du Nord Total	U.S.A. É.-U.	Commonwealth of Independent States Communauté d'Etats Indépendants Total	Europe
Chemicals (SITC, Rev. 3, 5) [cont.]											
Northern Africa	2000	2362	1094	25	2	1014	49	55	54	3	3
	2013	10658	3938	18	10	3636	42	284	274	25	18
	2014	11124	4667	71	5	4194	99	402	373	32	23
	2015	9211	3618	5	1	3198	90	415	391	23	18
	2016	9085	3351	31	3	2732	97	588	556	29	25
Sub-Saharan Africa	2000	2856	948	141	79	446	64	361	330	38	38
	2013	11948	2547	284	103	1404	152	858	811	46	45
	2014	11887	2848	224	89	1679	331	946	924	38	37
	2015	9801	2075	165	61	1185	202	725	696	26	24
	2016	10130	2377	195	107	1496	244	686	653	19	15
South Africa	2000	2055	874	137	79	382	57	355	324	1	0
	2013	6857	1757	281	103	795	87	681	660	7	6
	2014	7042	2074	217	84	1100	281	757	735	6	5
	2015	5564	1495	162	60	761	169	572	555	18	17
	2016	5523	1596	161	74	911	215	525	511	10	7
Latin America and the Caribbean	2000	16636	7478	325	259	2088	315	5065	4946	12	11
	2013	62172	27069	1169	877	7480	721	18419	17776	79	74
	2014	60045	25866	845	580	7813	773	17208	16561	92	83
	2015	53887	22887	796	564	6537	701	15553	14906	75	67
	2016	49246	21431	861	666	5569	730	15002	14365	118	112
Brazil	2000	3565	1471	157	141	649	152	665	641	3	3
	2013	14268	6153	328	281	2840	313	2984	2898	26	24
	2014	13221	5290	327	278	2587	304	2376	2287	43	41
	2015	11440	4530	287	232	2310	261	1934	1859	26	23
	2016	10991	4584	302	253	2053	266	2229	2143	31	30
Eastern Asia	2000	45641	11728	4104	3441	4184	868	3439	3221	444	368
	2013	243655	62881	19570	15133	23236	4201	20075	18696	5794	4414
	2014	259059	69035	20194	15464	26095	4703	22746	21228	5810	4500
	2015	237428	65645	18848	14144	25068	4279	21729	20265	4330	3269
	2016	227333	63998	18082	13564	25176	4157	20740	19389	4424	3447
China	2000	12098	6060	1714	1493	2570	645	1775	1661	131	93
	2013	119566	43841	11424	8422	17573	3319	14844	13836	4278	3238
	2014	134482	47730	12338	8917	19129	3538	16263	15160	4473	3473
	2015	129526	46076	11946	8413	18421	3335	15709	14677	3443	2578
	2016	121846	43955	11313	7913	17881	3178	14761	13791	3536	2750
Southern Asia	2000	5011	1852	170	101	1149	223	533	481	233	152
	2013	50024	16801	1160	696	8240	1552	7401	6943	1429	1093
	2014	47305	16174	1083	641	7741	1379	7351	6977	1215	880
	2015	46925	16550	1116	642	7383	1268	8051	7662	995	675
	2016	43150	16915	1189	691	7254	1210	8472	8071	960	697
South-Eastern Asia	2000	21083	6188	2395	1681	2423	199	1369	1309	43	41
	2013	106949	26858	11026	7769	10737	560	5094	4900	334	292
	2014	111763	28676	11087	7826	11414	613	6175	5729	367	336
	2015	96681	25921	9030	6290	11495	594	5397	5147	269	242
	2016	95949	26389	9232	6748	11956	715	5201	4938	223	195
Western Asia	2000	11191	4690	608	363	2512	216	1570	1514	319	205
	2013	86618	23381	1558	676	15567	962	6256	6021	3045	1666
	2014	86410	22981	1477	674	15398	964	6106	5913	2951	1448
	2015	69691	20440	1210	560	13098	767	6132	5916	1978	863
	2016	63202	19214	1125	530	12199	785	5890	5739	1672	738
Oceania	2000	17	3	1	0	2	0	0	0	0	0
	2013	457	247	202	113	43	32	2	2	0	0
	2014	626	336	279	160	55	47	2	2	0	0
	2015	149	29	18	11	9	1	2	1	0	0
	2016	178	34	20	13	10	1	3	3	0	0

For general note and footnotes see end of table

Exportations mondiales par provenance et destination (Tableau D)

En millions de dollars E.-U. f.o.b.

South-Eastern Europe / Europe du Sud-est	Northern Africa / Afrique septentrionale	Sub-Saharan Africa / Afrique du Nord	Latin America and the Caribbean / Amérique latine et Caraïbes	Eastern Asia / Asie orientale	Southern Asia / Asie méridionale	South-eastern Asia / Asie du Sud-est	Western Asia / Asie occidentale	Oceania / Océanie	Others 4/ / Autre 4/	Année	← Exportations vers / Exportations en provence de ↓
											Produits chimiques (CTCI, Rev. 3, 5) [suite]
9	172	44	118	32	545	42	268	0	34	2000	Afrique du Nord
237	813	760	1414	87	1274	69	1931	0	109	2013	
173	757	871	981	94	1502	104	1822	0	122	2014	
164	635	1018	664	45	1319	48	1569	0	108	2015	
205	554	1095	792	45	1259	34	1589	0	132	2016	
5	9	1255	105	116	233	72	66	0	6	2000	Afrique subsaharienne
18	50	7090	390	430	567	379	410	2	21	2013	
21	37	6743	340	531	505	439	365	3	17	2014	
19	45	6153	162	322	398	341	239	2	19	2015	
6	36	5579	235	403	816	380	207	3	69	2016	
5	9	658	101	114	160	70	62	0	1	2000	Afrique du sud
1	22	3489	366	352	289	316	247	1	11	2013	
2	21	3442	277	378	214	363	258	2	7	2014	
1	19	2978	150	283	149	286	172	2	10	2015	
6	14	2688	156	305	177	315	190	2	64	2016	
2	19	147	8280	362	66	162	83	0	24	2000	Amérique latine et Caraïbes
27	107	493	30215	2031	399	611	617	0	521	2013	
22	133	592	29320	2114	416	553	454	0	482	2014	
30	121	536	26709	1804	433	529	382	1	381	2015	
22	144	467	23245	1969	564	545	433	1	307	2016	
1	10	88	1693	156	21	80	40	0	...	2000	Brésil
3	46	310	6202	821	176	261	270	0	...	2013	
2	50	260	6021	894	204	219	237	0	...	2014	
7	50	229	5115	810	258	193	222	0	...	2015	
5	56	203	4554	815	286	204	251	0	0	2016	
42	205	627	1318	23685	1634	5179	759	17	3	2000	Asie orientale
451	1985	6278	14764	90164	20253	31636	9306	137	5	2013	
480	2265	6966	15993	88849	23363	35135	10992	156	14	2014	
450	1951	6364	15027	77333	22780	33747	9600	187	14	2015	
436	1834	5578	13651	74509	20424	33810	8449	174	46	2016	
23	91	219	511	2632	779	1356	290	6	...	2000	Chine
295	1200	4625	10708	17610	14005	17493	5424	87	...	2013	
325	1386	5395	11947	19271	17015	20390	6438	112	...	2014	
299	1345	5106	11612	18123	17424	20253	5706	140	...	2015	
299	1294	4549	10686	16960	14989	20258	5197	123	0	2016	
8	65	352	280	647	492	517	560	4	0	2000	Asie méridionale
202	704	4481	2817	8918	5206	4405	4863	28	169	2013	
210	648	4407	2798	8051	5036	3917	4807	27	16	2014	
193	766	4364	2656	8027	5577	3339	4383	25	49	2015	
205	752	4301	2676	5539	4488	3399	3785	26	104	2016	
14	55	275	232	6051	1229	6582	369	43	1	2000	Asie Sud-est
41	294	1655	4051	31621	7476	32268	2088	232	32	2013	
55	325	1731	3376	33397	8164	33135	2315	180	42	2014	
50	317	1531	2840	27471	7163	28920	2008	150	40	2015	
40	255	1440	2788	27131	6931	28547	2009	154	42	2016	
113	414	282	354	1315	1035	911	1551	0	206	2000	Asie occidentale
886	4042	3735	2108	14305	9004	8193	16990	8	921	2013	
1011	4253	3865	2409	12734	9617	8470	17176	9	933	2014	
841	3637	2797	1865	10146	7783	6316	13072	7	809	2015	
727	3349	2507	1715	8690	7390	5979	11299	5	654	2016	
0	0	7	0	0	0	3	...	4	0	2000	Océanie
0	...	20	0	119	1	43	0	27	0	2013	
0	...	5	2	185	0	63	0	34	1	2014	
0	0	4	1	62	0	26	0	27	1	2015	
0	0	1	1	68	0	52	0	22	1	2016	

Voir la fin du tableau pour la remarque générale et les notes.

World exports by provenance and destination (Table D)

In million U.S. dollars f.o.b.

Exports to ⟶ / ↓ Exports from	Year	World 1/ Monde 1/	Developed economies 2/ Economies développées 2/ Total	Asia-Pacific Asie-Pacifique Total	Asia-Pacific Asie-Pacifique Japan Japon	Europe Total	Europe Germany Allemagne	North America Amérique du Nord Total	North America Amérique du Nord U.S.A. É.-U.	Commonwealth of Independent States Communauté d'Etats Indépendants Total	Commonwealth of Independent States Communauté d'Etats Indépendants Europe
Machinery and transport equipment (SITC, Rev. 3, 7)											
World 1/	2000	2620383	1800629	136856	102298	986163	188989	677610	554497	19746	15832
	2013	6072867	3089045	269203	173984	1759054	383580	1060788	881241	204404	167363
	2014	6266317	3265428	270939	178422	1866789	412058	1127700	944968	176340	140128
	2015	5895782	3118922	253997	165591	1740158	377683	1124767	952883	104282	80610
	2016	5834598	3148307	246184	162239	1796027	391828	1106096	940159	106618	85885
Developed Economies - Asia-Pacific 2/	2000	338298	189906	9501	291	63126	14800	117279	110881	536	422
	2013	430090	172130	15489	204	47968	12058	108673	101536	10662	9553
	2014	415926	167670	14257	193	48809	12144	104605	97944	9074	7848
	2015	381298	159036	12572	209	45072	10364	101391	95050	4702	4131
	2016	399484	170126	13046	228	50107	11064	106973	100273	5225	4330
Japan	2000	329680	185109	7675	.	61931	14533	115503	109214	526	414
	2013	414378	164643	12381	.	46456	11812	105806	98909	10583	9501
	2014	400127	159755	11059	.	47084	11900	101612	95220	9011	7806
	2015	366772	151813	9721	.	43647	10123	98444	92307	4657	4106
	2016	385518	163053	10271	.	48702	10844	104080	97641	5191	4309
Developed Economies - Europe 2/	2000	1019028	835583	24276	16826	697329	127649	113979	104689	11248	9772
	2013	2148825	1486395	51517	27015	1247529	267707	187349	169906	101905	91591
	2014	2234006	1576794	50160	27638	1322182	287818	204452	185779	84320	74542
	2015	2021409	1460641	43209	23632	1210779	258820	206654	188550	49302	42384
	2016	2061319	1508993	44794	24846	1263509	267945	200689	183268	49475	43295
France	2000	132952	103387	1699	1089	86545	19223	15143	14101	962	653
	2013	216670	142086	4757	2583	120385	45840	16944	15750	6247	5113
	2014	217571	145586	5133	3043	123041	46581	17412	16134	5484	4488
	2015	196548	131321	3509	1840	110300	39767	17512	16305	2774	2251
	2016	198784	135827	3181	1909	115412	40776	17234	16141	3294	2807
Germany	2000	272345	223326	8768	6855	175308	.	39250	37072	4105	3664
	2013	685120	451478	20960	12898	350066	.	80452	72889	35772	32333
	2014	711427	476324	19523	12376	372205	.	84596	77505	26929	24038
	2015	643659	444743	16216	9986	342659	.	85868	78417	15746	13919
	2016	648994	448395	17974	11063	352619	.	77802	71352	15964	14420
Developed Economies - North America 2/	2000	524958	336727	36627	28068	99653	18534	200447	101673	1554	1085
	2013	649387	326321	28689	14735	76668	18351	220964	95424	8201	6623
	2014	671447	337866	29187	15124	82832	19076	225848	98658	7588	5990
	2015	644796	327623	29178	15206	82765	19730	215680	98171	4148	3265
	2016	623184	320898	26942	15218	82246	20681	211710	97662	4608	3224
United States	2000	413516	229213	35823	27681	94626	17750	98764	.	1477	1017
	2013	533880	222984	27345	14238	70117	17235	125521	.	7306	5897
	2014	552090	230615	27865	14610	75582	18105	127168	.	6890	5435
	2015	527207	221269	27907	14693	75863	18698	117499	.	3696	2918
	2016	505668	214365	25620	14657	74714	19524	114031	.	4208	2899
South-Eastern Europe	2000	2785	2115	3	0	2009	521	103	93	83	72
	2013	38264	29053	60	29	28002	9704	991	944	2278	2086
	2014	41061	32001	71	32	31017	11345	913	862	2289	2085
	2015	37628	29755	73	36	28853	10398	829	781	1419	1273
	2016	41376	33003	66	29	32207	12409	729	669	1462	1286
Commonwealth of Independent States	2000	10405	3201	38	34	2870	479	293	271	4444	3311
	2013	42231	7296	267	247	6524	1229	505	481	26735	17815
	2014	36999	8585	92	82	8010	3337	483	448	20915	12462
	2015	28293	8666	417	406	7380	2505	868	836	12001	7077
	2016	20776	3761	211	202	3020	756	531	514	10057	6316
Russian Federation	2000	6422	2634	35	34	2410	387	189	179	1573	749
	2013	21365	4413	249	246	3787	709	376	360	11096	5168
	2014	20107	5607	84	81	5153	2769	370	344	9082	3465
	2015	18509	6176	408	404	5035	1995	733	716	6351	2610
	2016	14466	2955	208	202	2303	600	445	432	5544	2655

For general note and footnotes see end of table

Exportations mondiales par provenance et destination (Tableau D)

En millions de dollars E.-U. f.o.b.

South-Eastern Europe Europe du Sud-est	Northern Africa Afrique septentrio-nale	Sub-Saharan Africa Afrique du Nord	Latin America and the Caribbean Amérique latine et Caraïbes	Eastern Asia Asie orientale	Southern Asia Asie méridionale	South-eastern Asia Asie du Sud-est	Western Asia Asie occidentale	Oceania Océanie	Others 4/ Autre 4/	Année	← Exportations vers / Exportations en provence de ↓
			Machines et matériel de transport (CTCI, Rev. 3, 7)								
7389	17502	28924	158768	287551	22801	198553	71033	2015	5472	2000	Monde 1/
41693	62320	132224	428317	1203556	119113	453731	311246	16168	11051	2013	
46168	66486	129435	408157	1227384	129867	459150	326697	17241	13963	2014	
42690	56393	109194	380407	1181694	127592	445263	301252	18729	9365	2015	
45972	56045	93604	356378	1154806	134280	439520	272608	18890	7569	2016	
76	919	3093	17123	67403	2899	46357	8977	622	389	2000	Economies Développées - Asie-Pacifique 2/
319	1710	7391	27500	118546	6092	59601	23283	2822	36	2013	
378	1727	6641	24552	115595	6565	55462	25431	2762	69	2014	
332	1351	5343	20634	104659	6904	50629	24529	3044	136	2015	
407	1320	4692	20698	112774	7737	50951	22557	2893	107	2016	
74	909	2942	16949	66606	2790	45359	8114	304	0	2000	Japon
293	1667	6830	27085	116889	5913	57656	21356	1462	...	2013	
338	1688	6197	24121	113966	6403	53474	23543	1630	...	2014	
303	1313	4947	20343	103270	6732	48684	22637	2073	0	2015	
372	1288	4324	20417	111310	7527	49152	20959	1926	...	2016	
6113	11744	15238	29111	38549	8198	22947	36130	553	3614	2000	Economies Développées - Europe 2/
32947	33198	41727	76719	170049	24761	56488	119736	2232	2667	2013	
36250	33656	40664	71306	185158	25234	55196	120176	2617	2636	2014	
33505	29571	34520	63692	152144	24781	47316	118993	2035	4910	2015	
35790	30519	29964	61093	154002	25399	47988	113541	2215	2342	2016	
536	4200	4160	4149	5250	1384	2817	5172	337	600	2000	France
2817	8173	5428	8814	16874	2528	11573	11029	977	124	2013	
2935	7430	5399	6985	18600	2669	10244	11410	647	182	2014	
2421	7621	4265	7234	16441	3144	7902	12154	725	546	2015	
2562	5939	4224	7668	14345	3280	9265	11501	723	154	2016	
1738	1857	3307	7626	12322	1917	5981	9509	102	555	2000	Allemagne
9232	5842	10790	24217	81504	8924	17118	39737	304	203	2013	
10701	6321	10645	22635	91845	8660	17362	39079	854	72	2014	
10468	5504	9607	20025	74352	8056	14982	39175	733	268	2015	
11273	6800	8755	19437	78092	8416	14727	36758	239	139	2016	
266	2440	3062	84913	48839	2261	32212	12205	172	307	2000	Economies Développées - Amérique du Nord 2/
698	3449	10635	153822	74177	6961	29817	35070	234	1	2013	
791	4686	10484	155315	80898	6783	30427	36394	215	1	2014	
649	3445	7924	152180	77628	5899	29265	35787	248	1	2015	
712	2666	5842	143712	78582	5194	29961	30714	292	3	2016	
244	2347	2938	83480	47440	2167	31896	11840	166	307	2000	États-Unis
613	3120	9786	149945	71269	6539	28479	33642	197	...	2013	
715	4470	9559	151985	77818	6416	29007	34434	181	...	2014	
592	3248	7129	148900	74790	5438	27923	34011	211	...	2015	
553	2513	5223	140263	75342	4866	28841	29221	273	...	2016	
193	70	20	25	35	42	17	154	0	30	2000	Europe du Sud-est
1649	823	321	983	709	352	187	1864	42	3	2013	
1777	940	368	758	778	302	177	1658	11	2	2014	
1658	841	318	470	676	363	168	1654	305	1	2015	
1776	856	211	483	700	546	164	1564	587	24	2016	
197	155	103	138	841	677	146	496	1	6	2000	Communauté d'Etats Indépendants
800	496	223	982	2283	1867	881	657	11	1	2013	
690	689	258	641	2534	1668	339	675	3	1	2014	
726	906	247	473	2432	1406	664	754	16	1	2015	
628	861	217	455	2063	1765	402	565	1	2	2016	
165	100	84	117	765	568	115	294	1	6	2000	Fédération de Russie
394	389	92	747	1720	1448	717	338	10	0	2013	
305	543	118	425	2103	1296	239	388	2	0	2014	
331	823	147	365	2189	1073	572	466	16	0	2015	
324	813	180	427	1911	1616	358	336	0	2	2016	

Voir la fin du tableau pour la remarque générale et les notes.

World exports by provenance and destination (Table D)

In million U.S. dollars f.o.b.

Exports to ⟶			Developed economies 2/ Economies développées 2/							Commonwealth of Independent States Communauté d'Etats Indépendants	
				Asia-Pacific Asie-Pacifique		Europe		North America Amérique du Nord			
↓ Exports from	Year	World 1/ Monde 1/	Total	Total	Japan Japon	Total	Germany Allemagne	Total	U.S.A. É.-U.	Total	Europe
Machinery and transport equipment (SITC, Rev. 3, 7) [cont.]											
Northern Africa	2000	1753	1566	1	1	1559	277	6	5	1	1
	2013	12560	9746	52	49	9441	1183	253	251	33	28
	2014	15140	11387	46	42	11062	1399	278	266	44	33
	2015	13751	10432	34	32	10131	1218	268	244	32	29
	2016	14690	11377	46	41	11073	1235	257	243	25	23
Sub-Saharan Africa	2000	5348	3401	403	155	2353	970	644	610	15	14
	2013	29201	9264	998	553	5525	2068	2741	2631	176	146
	2014	29708	11907	1132	626	8455	2169	2320	2116	114	102
	2015	24141	11113	887	555	8447	2194	1779	1596	41	32
	2016	21044	10435	899	432	7319	3272	2217	2002	51	33
South Africa	2000	4570	3150	390	143	2156	950	604	577	14	14
	2013	17873	7690	940	539	4362	1999	2387	2311	159	129
	2014	18693	8368	1106	610	5170	2122	2093	1904	100	90
	2015	15598	7917	851	540	5476	2151	1591	1419	26	17
	2016	16892	9466	859	408	6530	3222	2077	1875	37	20
Latin America and the Caribbean	2000	122172	108700	764	615	6608	1776	101327	98449	19	18
	2013	283780	214024	2291	1090	16872	4523	194861	188052	819	586
	2014	289595	232164	2293	1283	13499	3808	216372	208840	482	423
	2015	286675	238544	1951	993	13609	3913	222984	214771	214	201
	2016	282520	235876	2066	1289	15232	4128	218577	210798	242	230
Brazil	2000	15416	8675	358	290	3065	497	5252	5157	3	3
	2013	44072	14275	436	249	8054	1173	5785	5528	441	226
	2014	33089	12818	403	262	5130	880	7286	7031	237	191
	2015	31266	12155	315	198	4053	829	7787	7499	39	33
	2016	34792	14239	447	302	5463	869	8329	8140	77	73
Eastern Asia	2000	347615	188126	37112	32788	64658	14462	86355	82182	1051	698
	2013	1784498	623865	118253	94235	223738	45126	281874	262763	42453	32497
	2014	1856454	667352	120385	96305	239775	48147	307192	287576	40670	30839
	2015	1836742	654987	114631	89381	235509	45725	304848	286400	25608	18456
	2016	1756403	629504	108788	86058	227596	45965	293121	276766	28691	22841
China	2000	82600	46255	10601	9716	16464	3921	19191	18323	325	217
	2013	1039527	431488	81346	65041	155907	30957	194236	183018	27873	21045
	2014	1071813	463610	83311	66584	168761	33903	211538	199910	27514	20703
	2015	1060769	443767	77099	60254	159563	32285	207106	196282	18803	13313
	2016	985554	426580	72793	57659	154888	32190	198898	189036	21871	17397
Southern Asia	2000	3620	1639	150	103	956	203	532	511	71	33
	2013	47573	15393	1122	611	9277	1666	4995	4777	861	701
	2014	50230	15219	1049	571	8745	1558	5425	5220	763	617
	2015	45187	15256	1291	917	8475	1543	5490	5206	533	419
	2016	44940	15630	1073	645	9193	1751	5364	5094	605	504
South-Eastern Asia	2000	225568	118401	27610	23208	38165	7455	52626	51240	145	131
	2013	470241	154459	49396	34807	55388	13709	49676	46963	3081	2620
	2014	482783	160647	51240	36201	57474	14107	51933	49723	3147	2524
	2015	475455	162181	48910	33839	58040	15021	55231	52887	2601	2005
	2016	474126	164385	47281	32821	60270	15680	56834	54390	2915	2496
Western Asia	2000	18679	11160	342	204	6816	1836	4002	3875	569	265
	2013	135853	40888	919	407	32096	6254	7873	7482	7200	3117
	2014	142438	43596	836	326	34908	7151	7851	7508	6932	2662
	2015	100227	40594	789	380	31067	6254	8737	8385	3681	1338
	2016	94484	44188	909	428	34215	6940	9064	8452	3262	1307
Oceania	2000	153	105	29	4	59	28	18	17	10	10
	2013	362	211	152	1	27	1	33	33	0	0
	2014	530	240	191	1	19	0	30	27	0	0
	2015	183	95	55	5	32	0	8	8	0	0
	2016	252	133	64	2	41	0	28	27	0	0

For general note and footnotes see end of table

Exportations mondiales par provenance et destination (Tableau D)

En millions de dollars E.-U. f.o.b.

South-Eastern Europe Europe du Sud-est	Northern Africa Afrique septentrionale	Sub-Saharan Africa Afrique du Nord	Latin America and the Caribbean Amérique latine et Caraïbes	Eastern Asia Asie orientale	Southern Asia Asie méridionale	South-eastern Asia Asie du Sud-est	Western Asia Asie occidentale	Oceania Océanie	Others 4/ Autre 4/	Année	← Exportations vers Exportations en provence de ↓
				Machines et matériel de transport (CTCI, Rev. 3, 7) [suite]							
0	62	28	0	1	3	1	65	0	26	2000	Afrique du Nord
160	710	357	23	24	27	294	998	1	186	2013	
185	723	459	22	38	67	303	1701	3	207	2014	
187	654	393	31	30	29	262	1516	0	183	2015	
207	787	384	34	41	29	270	1357	0	178	2016	
4	26	1406	92	140	40	118	97	3	7	2000	Afrique subsaharienne
42	425	16361	497	645	217	428	627	442	78	2013	
43	213	12858	818	1100	221	897	1035	462	40	2014	
33	103	9566	610	405	191	764	956	331	28	2015	
16	74	7873	383	681	265	492	539	180	55	2016	
4	21	967	88	136	25	96	65	2	2	2000	Afrique du sud
21	408	7809	417	523	164	277	376	3	25	2013	
19	187	8066	385	366	186	428	560	3	25	2014	
12	83	5970	411	217	140	338	463	2	18	2015	
14	64	5650	317	412	219	286	374	4	50	2016	
3	47	287	11654	632	99	526	174	1	30	2000	Amérique latine et Caraïbes
76	220	1883	56758	5600	612	1897	1338	11	543	2013	
111	533	1585	43548	5564	554	2968	1685	9	392	2014	
96	252	1350	36835	4809	564	2262	1387	18	343	2015	
68	235	1151	34760	4610	552	3476	1160	7	383	2016	
1	41	254	6013	131	70	97	130	1	...	2000	Brésil
22	182	1477	25513	988	233	588	346	6	0	2013	
17	392	1101	15466	676	247	1580	552	3	...	2014	
13	198	889	14504	1417	234	1411	393	12	0	2015	
19	168	884	15280	1210	231	2163	520	2	0	2016	
234	1157	3444	11505	92413	4160	37352	7455	528	188	2000	Asie orientale
2948	11301	35158	91473	682508	48021	174525	62643	9567	35	2013	
3676	13426	37163	92361	678224	55162	188141	70221	10015	43	2014	
3518	12789	36240	85753	685640	60083	194129	66238	11709	46	2015	
3955	13505	32307	74736	649592	66498	186429	58964	12145	78	2016	
39	283	1034	2120	21483	1303	7934	1814	10	...	2000	Chine
2155	7574	25174	59245	317400	34170	96227	36382	1838	...	2013	
2654	8734	27596	59661	294613	39930	104648	41345	1509	...	2014	
2497	8851	27456	56822	304798	43090	110746	40073	3866	...	2015	
2736	9060	22835	49338	264980	49051	99486	35448	4170	...	2016	
3	69	318	125	154	336	455	448	1	1	2000	Asie méridionale
129	1568	5388	3324	2031	4270	6366	8034	28	182	2013	
275	1306	5710	3455	2170	6246	5797	9254	33	3	2014	
126	1073	4541	3562	1757	5252	5454	7451	129	53	2015	
217	1060	3536	4168	1774	5204	5626	6924	24	170	2016	
31	254	1346	3706	37735	3155	57989	2659	114	32	2000	Asie Sud-est
326	1938	5459	13426	139866	13433	118743	18748	641	121	2013	
379	2067	4766	13005	148994	13468	115219	20035	830	226	2014	
406	1615	4713	14400	145336	13471	109627	19997	805	302	2015	
421	1470	4219	14483	143670	13966	110114	17838	420	225	2016	
269	559	579	375	806	931	420	2171	7	832	2000	Asie occidentale
1598	6482	7309	2802	7099	12499	4430	38245	105	7197	2013	
1612	6520	8453	2364	6280	13592	4109	38428	209	10342	2014	
1454	3793	4028	1763	6172	8637	4703	21984	60	3358	2015	
1776	2693	3188	1371	6311	7123	3594	16884	96	3999	2016	
0	...	1	1	2	0	13	0	13	10	2000	Océanie
0	0	12	8	20	1	73	3	32	1	2013	
0	0	27	12	52	6	117	3	72	1	2014	
0	0	11	2	7	12	21	6	28	1	2015	
0	0	21	2	6	2	53	2	31	1	2016	

Voir la fin du tableau pour la remarque générale et les notes.

World exports by provenance and destination (Table D)

In million U.S. dollars f.o.b.

Exports to ⟶ ↓ Exports from	Year	World 1/ Monde 1/	Developed economies 2/ Economies développées 2/ Total	Asia-Pacific Asie-Pacifique Total	Japan Japon	Europe Total	Germany Allemagne	North America Amérique du Nord Total	U.S.A. É.-U.	Commonwealth of Independent States Communauté d'Etats Indépendants Total	Europe
		Passenger road vehicles and their parts (SITC, Rev. 3, 781.2, 784.1, 785.1, 785.2 and 785.31)									
World 1/	2000	318997	280554	12909	6833	143925	24202	123721	108466	1650	1442
	2013	712586	473967	33065	12408	255720	47931	185182	159746	33159	27850
	2014	743848	502854	31230	11638	285181	53563	186443	159823	25862	20435
	2015	710743	508964	29369	10304	282434	51466	197161	171034	11534	9715
	2016	734573	540461	31439	11141	309152	58222	199870	173408	10998	9594
Developed Economies - Asia-Pacific 2/	2000	63560	52590	3693	30	12486	2479	36412	33920	154	148
	2013	97646	59703	7819	4	9648	1665	42236	38998	7023	6189
	2014	93676	56000	6910	5	11639	1927	37451	34944	5737	4984
	2015	90590	56896	6174	4	11857	1640	38865	36259	2695	2484
	2016	96302	63253	6509	6	13293	1993	43451	40591	2874	2582
Japan	2000	62192	52147	3482	.	12472	2478	36193	33701	154	148
	2013	95667	59101	7515	.	9588	1661	41999	38761	7023	6189
	2014	92027	55555	6623	.	11581	1923	37351	34845	5737	4983
	2015	88927	56457	5949	.	11788	1637	38719	36114	2695	2484
	2016	94845	62897	6286	.	13245	1989	43366	40508	2874	2582
Developed Economies - Europe 2/	2000	162532	149044	6302	5066	122455	18702	20287	19464	1177	1103
	2013	353238	268472	14759	8715	212115	34488	41598	37715	13700	12747
	2014	381861	294760	13853	8124	236551	39937	44356	40256	9804	8917
	2015	367011	295294	13196	7259	232366	37442	49732	45593	5213	4859
	2016	382749	312992	14353	8237	251942	41590	46698	42258	4543	4292
France	2000	19406	17382	163	131	17193	2757	26	15	28	28
	2013	19147	16591	299	181	16127	3080	165	94	218	207
	2014	19789	17587	263	146	16916	2873	408	279	173	166
	2015	18171	16329	243	129	15647	2534	439	324	46	43
	2016	18987	17410	218	185	16881	3139	311	229	44	42
Germany	2000	61492	55191	4192	3688	37221	.	13778	13357	786	726
	2013	150926	109489	8985	6103	71199	.	29305	26403	5628	5199
	2014	162990	119143	8718	5932	80306	.	30119	27290	3860	3420
	2015	155717	118693	7484	4773	80364	.	30845	28142	2687	2453
	2016	154651	118565	8111	5065	84244	.	26209	23358	2264	2124
Developed Economies - North America 2/	2000	53039	48261	1258	953	2615	1277	44388	34581	21	17
	2013	103611	70148	2752	939	9285	5055	58111	43917	1830	1439
	2014	107654	72831	3183	826	10808	5679	58841	43497	1928	1569
	2015	101297	71876	2793	704	10945	6218	58138	43279	392	288
	2016	103770	75752	2416	664	12256	6725	61080	46341	319	214
United States	2000	18084	13460	1153	850	2500	1261	9807	.	18	15
	2013	58399	26097	2728	924	9176	5030	14193	.	1812	1425
	2014	62783	29172	3155	808	10674	5652	15344	.	1918	1563
	2015	56417	28411	2769	693	10784	6165	14858	.	389	287
	2016	54966	29185	2376	647	12070	6673	14738	.	316	213
South-Eastern Europe	2000	62	19	...	...	19	0	0	0	1	1
	2013	6627	5256	0	0	4901	884	354	354	129	112
	2014	6253	4998	0	0	4814	823	184	183	66	54
	2015	5070	3944	0	0	3855	697	90	89	46	40
	2016	4981	4068	0	0	4041	767	27	26	60	57
Commonwealth of Independent States	2000	478	135	0	0	134	7	1	1	247	135
	2013	3606	93	0	0	84	3	8	8	3399	1592
	2014	3461	68	1	1	56	2	11	11	3289	1043
	2015	1676	161	1	0	138	65	22	22	1328	524
	2016	1796	377	1	1	334	175	41	41	1054	627
Russian Federation	2000	360	132	0	0	131	6	1	1	142	34
	2013	1518	34	0	0	27	1	7	6	1455	441
	2014	1514	26	1	1	20	1	5	4	1443	277
	2015	1130	111	1	0	92	49	19	19	875	248
	2016	1112	258	1	1	220	131	37	36	561	322

For general note and footnotes see end of table

Exportations mondiales par provenance et destination (Tableau D)

En millions de dollars E.-U. f.o.b.

South-Eastern Europe Europe du Sud-est	Northern Africa Afrique septentrionale	Sub-Saharan Africa Afrique du Nord	Latin America and the Caribbean Amérique latine et Caraïbes	Eastern Asia Asie orientale	Southern Asia Asie méridionale	South-eastern Asia Asie du Sud-est	Western Asia Asie occidentale	Oceania Océanie	Others 4/ Autre 4/	Année	← Exportations vers / Exportations en provenance de ↓
Véhicules routiers et pièces detachées pour transports passagères (CTCI, Rev. 3, 781.2, 784.1, 785.1, 785.2 et 785.31)											
650	1381	2319	11672	3858	859	4280	11423	194	157	2000	Monde 1/
3291	9350	16304	43127	57159	5511	15211	54820	348	339	2013	
3928	8663	15503	36235	69947	6689	14840	56555	380	2391	2014	
3835	6602	11777	33932	55178	6505	14278	56994	402	741	2015	
4841	6179	9073	33809	55970	7001	15759	49161	425	896	2016	
21	95	453	2729	1350	381	1826	3888	73	...	2000	Economies Développées - Asie-Pacifique 2/
50	317	1581	4632	7462	789	3721	12236	132	0	2013	
58	283	1608	3952	8397	1193	3018	13279	152	0	2014	
45	315	1501	4102	6830	1588	3111	13317	168	20	2015	
53	342	1262	3884	7813	1358	3222	12029	212	0	2016	
21	94	451	2696	1346	380	1712	3123	67	...	2000	Japon
50	316	1574	4630	7455	785	3703	10915	114	...	2013	
58	282	1602	3950	8387	1189	2993	12142	134	...	2014	
45	314	1492	4101	6817	1584	3079	12189	154	...	2015	
53	341	1247	3882	7796	1346	3198	11018	193	...	2016	
496	953	1338	1614	1198	180	793	5576	101	61	2000	Economies Développées - Europe 2/
2846	4714	4968	6084	33502	339	2860	15658	95	1	2013	
3425	4511	4110	4979	41203	381	2625	15962	99	3	2014	
3310	3311	3642	5106	31129	412	2051	17441	101	1	2015	
4175	3305	2836	4406	31325	528	2182	16382	73	2	2016	
52	490	275	347	30	101	44	591	67	0	2000	France
127	767	181	351	276	3	111	480	41	0	2013	
174	774	112	175	276	2	137	331	46	2	2014	
117	526	112	197	327	4	54	410	50	0	2015	
143	434	91	143	227	9	31	425	30	0	2016	
224	175	520	601	871	53	425	2578	17	51	2000	Allemagne
895	1219	2050	3311	19415	179	1224	7492	23	0	2013	
1064	1193	1815	2688	24204	207	1135	7657	25	0	2014	
1036	955	1561	2157	19539	201	988	7876	23	0	2015	
1249	1111	1268	1960	19912	265	1126	6912	19	1	2016	
13	22	76	3562	289	2	85	692	4	12	2000	Economies Développées - Amérique du Nord 2/
28	292	2413	6785	10142	58	524	11384	8	...	2013	
34	171	2156	6563	13310	58	632	9961	10	...	2014	
28	84	1425	5825	11458	55	638	9506	8	...	2015	
58	71	926	6365	12116	84	537	7530	11	...	2016	
12	22	73	3472	268	2	85	656	4	12	2000	États-Unis
26	224	2284	6358	9982	58	520	11030	8	...	2013	
31	133	2031	6225	12991	58	627	9588	10	...	2014	
26	70	1304	5439	11027	54	624	9065	8	...	2015	
53	58	803	5772	11071	78	516	7104	10	...	2016	
9	4	0	3	17	0	0	8	...	0	2000	Europe du Sud-est
151	404	43	3	2	0	0	630	9	0	2013	
122	471	100	15	1	0	0	470	9	0	2014	
161	298	102	23	2	3	0	484	7	0	2015	
186	152	67	32	5	15	1	387	9	0	2016	
9	3	1	15	14	1	9	45	...	0	2000	Communauté d'Etats Indépendants
2	15	1	12	8	5	1	71	...	...	2013	
2	11	17	8	16	13	1	36	...	...	2014	
7	20	5	2	91	15	5	42	...	...	2015	
14	22	3	10	214	28	12	64	...	0	2016	
8	2	1	15	14	1	1	44	...	...	2000	Fédération de Russie
2	14	0	9	2	0	1	2	...	...	2013	
2	7	16	5	13	0	1	2	...	...	2014	
7	19	4	1	87	4	5	17	...	...	2015	
8	21	1	7	201	15	12	28	...	...	2016	

Voir la fin du tableau pour la remarque générale et les notes.

World exports by provenance and destination (Table D)

In million U.S. dollars f.o.b.

Exports to → / ↓ Exports from	Year	World 1/ Monde 1/	Developed economies 2/ Economies développées 2/ Total	Asia-Pacific Asie-Pacifique Total	Japan Japon	Europe Total	Germany Allemagne	North America Amérique du Nord Total	U.S.A. É.-U.	Commonwealth of Independent States Communauté d'Etats Indépendants Total	Europe
Passenger road vehicles and their parts (SITC, Rev. 3, 781.2, 784.1, 785.1, 785.2 and 785.31) [cont.]											
Northern Africa	2000	6	4	0	0	4	0	0	0	...	...
	2013	1596	1125	2	0	1123	109	0	0	17	16
	2014	2360	1897	0	0	1896	225	0	0	15	13
	2015	2467	1851	0	0	1850	210	0	0	14	14
	2016	3003	2252	0	...	2251	243	1	0	14	14
Sub-Saharan Africa	2000	1119	895	269	136	534	395	93	93	0	0
	2013	4041	2917	740	498	626	545	1551	1551	0	0
	2014	4637	3407	942	586	1233	659	1232	1135	0	0
	2015	4932	3940	742	523	2431	1097	766	665	0	0
	2016	5494	4485	749	409	2556	1828	1181	1112	0	0
South Africa	2000	1048	874	262	130	520	394	92	92	0	0
	2013	3701	2873	738	496	587	537	1549	1549	0	0
	2014	4409	3373	938	581	1206	655	1229	1132	0	0
	2015	4754	3915	740	522	2411	1094	764	663	0	...
	2016	5304	4444	733	394	2533	1822	1179	1110	0	...
Latin America and the Caribbean	2000	19792	16933	185	165	947	715	15801	14263	0	0
	2013	44026	26486	327	165	2532	2077	23627	22249	196	196
	2014	40289	27003	320	171	2097	1572	24586	22496	27	27
	2015	39528	29242	172	49	2761	1517	26309	24171	8	8
	2016	39149	28885	108	62	3301	1800	25476	23361	6	5
Brazil	2000	2025	526	1	0	224	7	302	301	...	...
	2013	6429	47	20	4	4	1	23	20	...	...
	2014	4015	53	21	4	6	2	26	19	...	...
	2015	4077	53	17	1	7	2	29	23	...	...
	2016	5435	294	16	3	13	5	264	261	0	0
Eastern Asia	2000	16144	11584	1081	456	3790	407	6713	6129	25	23
	2013	62616	28477	3836	1244	7935	2269	16706	14067	5902	4852
	2014	63701	30682	3628	1236	7908	1706	19146	16752	4406	3447
	2015	60240	33241	3354	1098	7559	1477	22328	20124	1603	1307
	2016	55461	32729	3443	965	8167	1513	21120	18971	1693	1437
China	2000	1855	772	232	197	62	6	478	467	3	3
	2013	13656	3662	1164	944	962	200	1535	1205	1380	1274
	2014	13887	3634	1157	965	1007	110	1470	1324	1106	943
	2015	13822	4020	1036	834	1141	159	1843	1719	416	320
	2016	14121	4992	921	744	1365	186	2706	2543	528	457
Southern Asia	2000	265	104	3	1	99	5	2	2	3	0
	2013	7702	1843	243	14	1544	111	56	54	43	26
	2014	8165	1525	242	31	1245	97	38	35	42	15
	2015	7762	1469	132	19	1272	105	65	63	13	7
	2016	8711	2073	142	67	1888	221	43	40	17	6
South-Eastern Asia	2000	839	374	118	25	235	40	20	11	0	0
	2013	12203	4176	2534	797	1190	189	453	367	112	109
	2014	12321	3632	2102	639	1010	152	519	440	22	13
	2015	15232	4827	2740	606	1612	306	476	402	88	81
	2016	17888	5862	3614	644	1614	341	634	549	130	113
Western Asia	2000	1160	611	1	1	607	176	3	2	21	15
	2013	15670	5270	53	33	4735	537	482	466	807	571
	2014	19443	6050	47	21	5924	783	79	74	525	353
	2015	14929	6221	65	41	5786	691	370	365	134	103
	2016	15262	7731	102	85	7509	1027	120	116	287	247
Oceania	2000	1	1	0	0	0	...	0	0	...	...
	2013	4	2	1	0	1	...	0	0	...	...
	2014	25	2	1	0	1	...	0	0	0	0
	2015	9	2	1	0	1	...	0	0	...	...
	2016	7	2	0	0	1	0	0	0	...	...

For general note and footnotes see end of table

Exportations mondiales par provenance et destination (Tableau D)

En millions de dollars E.-U. f.o.b.

South-Eastern Europe Europe du Sud-est	Northern Africa Afrique septentrionale	Sub-Saharan Africa Afrique du Nord	Latin America and the Caribbean Amérique latine et Caraïbes	Eastern Asia Asie orientale	Southern Asia Asie méridionale	South-eastern Asia Asie du Sud-est	Western Asia Asie occidentale	Oceania Océanie	Others 4/ Autre 4/	Année	← Exportations vers Exportations en provence de ↓
éhicules routiers et pièces detachées pour transports passagères (CTCI, Rev. 3, 781.2, 784.1, 785.1, 785.2 et 785.31) [suit											
...	1	0	...	...	...	0	0	...	0	2000	Afrique du Nord
49	164	7	0	0	0	...	229	0	5	2013	
73	134	22	3	0	1	0	210	1	6	2014	
69	246	6	7	0	0	0	270	0	3	2015	
85	257	10	9	0	0	0	373	...	3	2016	
0	1	133	0	57	0	31	2	0	0	2000	Afrique subsaharienne
1	19	871	2	188	1	37	1	...	4	2013	
1	2	855	80	69	2	188	34	0	1	2014	
1	1	599	170	82	4	32	104	0	0	2015	
0	0	582	44	238	9	69	65	0	0	2016	
0	0	86	0	56	0	30	0	0	0	2000	Afrique du sud
0	18	580	1	187	0	37	0	...	4	2013	
0	1	669	80	69	0	187	30	0	1	2014	
0	0	451	170	81	4	31	102	0	0	2015	
0	0	440	44	235	8	69	63	0	0	2016	
0	10	52	2758	10	19	5	5	0	0	2000	Amérique latine et Caraïbes
1	28	84	15552	1507	0	97	54	0	21	2013	
1	44	81	11219	1786	1	95	24	0	7	2014	
4	31	56	8857	1025	1	243	43	0	16	2015	
0	18	54	9071	651	65	84	292	0	24	2016	
...	10	51	1409	2	19	3	4	0	...	2000	Brésil
...	25	58	6271	1	0	27	1	...	...	2013	
0	43	65	3806	2	1	42	4	...	...	2014	
0	25	44	3712	2	0	224	17	0	...	2015	
0	18	52	4718	6	65	73	210	0	...	2016	
61	211	220	916	884	182	1183	811	14	54	2000	Asie orientale
59	1811	2690	7765	3001	781	2688	9351	79	11	2013	
72	1555	2607	6634	3077	1289	2885	10393	83	19	2014	
70	1192	1912	6207	2327	1854	2858	8871	79	28	2015	
82	1142	1435	5333	1291	2247	2978	6432	71	28	2016	
4	12	62	80	180	31	651	60	1	...	2000	Chine
32	588	1592	3296	326	684	1235	852	11	...	2013	
25	516	1700	2659	367	1210	1469	1187	13	...	2014	
16	437	1260	2843	550	1422	1611	1234	14	...	2015	
18	456	1026	2187	502	1813	1600	987	12	...	2016	
0	8	22	21	0	80	11	15	0	0	2000	Asie méridionale
8	661	1833	1555	23	676	354	704	3	0	2013	
7	570	1792	1879	73	980	420	874	3	...	2014	
4	436	1403	2050	35	1172	468	708	3	0	2015	
7	355	1062	2753	19	1244	441	732	8	0	2016	
0	6	7	52	25	7	329	37	2	1	2000	Asie Sud-est
1	75	433	576	145	223	4811	1620	18	12	2013	
1	175	360	860	269	100	4875	1995	19	14	2014	
0	126	338	1522	423	118	4745	3002	29	14	2015	
1	52	240	1789	739	188	6067	2776	34	12	2016	
41	68	18	1	12	7	7	346	0	29	2000	Asie occidentale
95	851	1379	162	1180	2638	117	2883	2	286	2013	
131	736	1796	43	1726	2672	103	3318	1	2342	2014	
135	542	787	59	1772	1284	127	3207	2	658	2015	
180	463	597	113	1560	1235	167	2100	2	826	2016	
...	...	0	...	...	...	...	...	0	0	2000	Océanie
...	...	0	0	0	...	0	0	1	...	2013	
...	0	0	0	21	0	0	0	2	0	2014	
...	...	0	...	4	...	0	0	3	0	2015	
...	...	0	...	0	...	0	...	5	0	2016	

Voir la fin du tableau pour la remarque générale et les notes.

World exports by provenance and destination (Table D)

In million U.S. dollars f.o.b.

Exports from ↓ / Exports to →	Year	World 1/ Monde 1/	Developed economies 2/ Economies développées 2/ Total	Asia-Pacific Asie-Pacifique Total	Asia-Pacific Asie-Pacifique Japan Japon	Europe Total	Europe Germany Allemagne	North America Amérique du Nord Total	North America Amérique du Nord U.S.A. É.-U.	Commonwealth of Independent States Communauté d'Etats Indépendants Total	Commonwealth of Independent States Communauté d'Etats Indépendants Europe
Other manufactured goods (SITC, Rev. 3, 6 and 8)											
World 1/	2000	1643616	1161297	104723	84772	683970	138358	372604	313750	20448	16971
	2013	4351052	2466445	225505	159884	1567980	304848	672959	564355	156501	116368
	2014	4499262	2562607	225458	157647	1629461	315440	707689	597976	146735	106640
	2015	4108580	2384629	205441	142436	1468716	283213	710472	607607	97950	67722
	2016	3956553	2348821	199342	140012	1466924	285119	682556	584282	93305	65202
Developed Economies - Asia-Pacific 2/	2000	102599	42208	5325	1931	13669	3644	23214	22046	218	166
	2013	173628	47225	7925	1912	16830	4196	22470	21191	1958	1691
	2014	168923	47617	8227	2570	16703	4138	22686	21451	1648	1400
	2015	146769	42731	6715	1642	14774	3532	21242	20060	1058	896
	2016	143043	42556	7331	1433	14711	3965	20513	19219	945	816
Japan	2000	89968	35395	1375	.	12381	3478	21639	20559	215	164
	2013	150188	36108	2206	.	13763	3882	20139	19011	1917	1655
	2014	145678	36007	1886	.	14071	3889	20050	18990	1622	1381
	2015	126955	32871	1827	.	12272	3306	18772	17724	1039	883
	2016	124470	33320	2651	.	12383	3740	18286	17132	925	801
Developed Economies - Europe 2/	2000	677647	571131	17790	13205	487170	100929	66171	60940	9402	8646
	2013	1537428	1177055	30753	19614	1043385	210835	102917	93978	53169	48014
	2014	1576217	1220311	30864	20024	1077446	219968	112002	102700	46510	41468
	2015	1384215	1081926	27259	17537	948020	191850	106647	97986	30667	25700
	2016	1389209	1095945	27299	17840	965069	197690	103578	94982	29470	25776
France	2000	69667	58683	2212	1860	50245	11675	6226	5461	431	384
	2013	125822	96240	3012	2257	83922	19434	9305	8381	2032	1774
	2014	127610	98235	2989	2283	85960	19706	9286	8292	1796	1508
	2015	111966	86864	2489	1874	75229	16759	9147	8224	1647	901
	2016	111087	86793	2229	1603	76078	16365	8486	7612	1104	894
Germany	2000	127887	107652	3018	2157	93680	.	10954	10094	2264	2096
	2013	331733	255752	6344	3966	226166	.	23242	21323	13011	11914
	2014	340106	265230	6202	4042	234897	.	24130	22200	11180	10122
	2015	295219	232760	5484	3469	204981	.	22295	20507	7059	6292
	2016	296080	232843	5625	3557	205112	.	22106	20362	7057	6372
Developed Economies - North America 2/	2000	223195	151466	16780	14023	39616	6268	95071	51873	400	325
	2013	372413	217023	21036	14669	68766	10567	127221	57118	1984	1688
	2014	384782	222498	20388	14013	73600	11308	128509	58492	2012	1680
	2015	366916	210819	19331	13530	70558	11264	120930	57544	1571	1238
	2016	357640	206132	19075	13254	70479	11423	116578	56240	1351	1122
United States	2000	165379	95754	15802	13162	36766	5962	43186	.	355	285
	2013	301225	153140	19967	13967	63099	10150	70074	.	1730	1472
	2014	311915	157326	19354	13331	67982	10859	69990	.	1823	1518
	2015	297057	147759	18421	12945	65972	10849	63366	.	1470	1160
	2016	289425	144666	18074	12636	66280	10976	60312	.	1253	1040
South-Eastern Europe	2000	10591	8971	17	13	8306	1808	648	581	177	149
	2013	40779	30643	67	42	29765	7081	811	681	1912	1791
	2014	42634	32854	124	91	31748	6834	982	800	1632	1495
	2015	37683	28999	146	113	28073	6093	781	708	1003	913
	2016	38798	30090	166	134	29168	6520	756	672	1035	962
Commonwealth of Independent States	2000	31234	16350	1249	1245	12213	2077	2888	2790	5106	3958
	2013	104328	41140	2186	2153	33879	4852	5074	4851	32270	20808
	2014	100336	39563	2330	2297	31599	4377	5634	5285	28124	17764
	2015	81386	33632	1906	1861	27610	3488	4116	3882	19300	11646
	2016	67997	28453	1729	1685	22305	2641	4418	4135	17006	10541
Russian Federation	2000	20412	12932	1181	1179	9588	1460	2163	2115	1350	486
	2013	59661	30260	1623	1608	24529	3517	4108	3933	13818	6067
	2014	58990	28884	1768	1743	22616	2983	4500	4221	12303	5086
	2015	49231	24252	1379	1338	19486	2322	3387	3199	9036	3407
	2016	45773	22922	1365	1324	17736	1984	3820	3600	8872	3753

For general note and footnotes see end of table

Exportations mondiales par provenance et destination (Tableau D)

En millions de dollars E.-U. f.o.b.

South-Eastern Europe Europe du Sud-est	Northern Africa Afrique septentrio-nale	Sub-Saharan Africa Afrique du Nord	Latin America and the Caribbean Amérique latine et Caraïbes	Eastern Asia Asie orientale	Southern Asia Asie méridionale	South-eastern Asia Asie du Sud-est	Western Asia Asie occidentale	Oceania Océanie	Others 4/ Autre 4/	Année	⟵ Exportations vers Exportations en provence de ↓
				Articles manufacturés divers (CTCI, Rev. 3, 6 et 8)							
9882	13833	18040	86946	180587	22634	66754	56689	1632	4873	2000	Monde 1/
40585	52625	99288	238079	595445	135966	284943	267693	3335	10148	2013	
44877	55618	107766	239199	607671	145762	298231	276394	3218	11184	2014	
39843	51793	99609	224503	528863	134568	281736	253300	3030	8754	2015	
42871	46073	83979	201460	495280	134447	268014	231131	3093	8079	2016	
20	205	719	2343	37315	1498	15120	2101	435	418	2000	Economies Développées - Asie-Pacifique 2/
58	505	1720	5794	71537	4131	34392	5311	934	63	2013	
70	574	1408	5824	68597	4163	32544	5612	790	75	2014	
74	492	1231	5117	59366	4304	27157	4474	704	62	2015	
84	395	1041	4578	57979	3768	26803	4161	693	40	2016	
18	201	563	2211	34439	1304	13567	1972	83	...	2000	Japon
53	458	1427	5536	65841	3675	30103	4968	103	...	2013	
64	499	1193	5551	63664	3693	28056	5260	70	0	2014	
68	474	1035	4839	54474	3806	24110	4174	65	...	2015	
74	375	870	4351	53421	3309	23841	3912	71	...	2016	
7705	8472	6123	12084	19793	7926	7754	23563	367	3327	2000	Economies Développées - Europe 2/
28358	23390	19831	32066	80259	25800	23833	69413	631	3622	2013	
31162	23721	19449	31168	83112	23661	23022	69856	663	3581	2014	
27677	19968	16282	27583	73942	20120	20732	62195	549	2574	2015	
29992	20021	14366	25630	73099	19936	19824	58341	555	2032	2016	
431	2476	1193	1051	1971	424	652	2111	235	8	2000	France
1467	4301	2526	2708	7285	1120	2048	5537	438	122	2013	
1543	4330	2673	2415	7486	1124	2040	5373	463	131	2014	
1302	3726	2204	2098	6395	1060	1903	4332	385	50	2015	
1393	3761	1911	1944	6408	1081	2256	4008	398	31	2016	
1524	1044	1070	2787	3817	904	1667	3434	15	1709	2000	Allemagne
5653	2074	3103	8242	20594	3484	5643	13413	36	728	2013	
6545	2194	3191	7635	21743	3385	5091	13350	35	526	2014	
5792	1794	2759	6604	18977	3154	4513	11469	29	308	2015	
6297	1987	2474	6347	20121	3495	4700	10439	32	288	2016	
60	697	1044	43183	13777	987	6691	4784	56	49	2000	Economies Développées - Amérique du Nord 2/
268	907	3235	72948	37907	8441	10878	18699	123	0	2013	
306	1001	3888	76088	40926	7944	10820	19195	106	0	2014	
257	973	3107	73799	40430	8231	10411	17228	92	0	2015	
256	928	2271	70023	38384	9516	11681	16983	115	0	2016	
53	641	1000	42418	13107	888	6474	4586	54	49	2000	États-Unis
237	790	2752	70636	35839	7733	10371	17882	113	...	2013	
273	874	3058	73700	38756	7302	10396	18309	97	...	2014	
231	875	2408	71653	38403	7523	10024	16629	82	...	2015	
227	869	1795	67880	36296	8844	11289	16201	105	...	2016	
587	85	31	84	67	31	17	523	0	19	2000	Europe du Sud-est
3921	464	101	242	928	136	119	2286	1	26	2013	
3836	508	115	267	851	133	94	2335	1	10	2014	
3595	436	113	263	908	98	111	2147	0	9	2015	
4003	384	113	210	663	140	129	2016	1	12	2016	
568	688	262	560	3651	1049	876	2122	1	0	2000	Communauté d'Etats Indépendants
1311	1894	892	1250	7100	3348	1678	13423	7	17	2013	
1774	2669	815	2017	6928	3704	998	13726	0	18	2014	
1260	3111	666	1462	5962	3433	661	11787	0	113	2015	
729	1402	253	1246	6031	3455	825	8572	0	25	2016	
171	319	145	381	2710	817	484	1103	0	0	2000	Fédération de Russie
364	578	251	974	3694	2459	1028	6220	6	9	2013	
756	994	255	1734	3930	2716	651	6758	0	9	2014	
401	1803	295	1300	3000	2645	600	5799	0	100	2015	
444	1237	195	1192	2909	2252	616	5117	0	18	2016	

Voir la fin du tableau pour la remarque générale et les notes.

World exports by provenance and destination (Table D)

In million U.S. dollars f.o.b.

Exports to ⟶ ↓ Exports from	Year	World 1/ Monde 1/	Developed economies 2/ Economies développées 2/ Total	Asia-Pacific Asie-Pacifique Total	Japan Japon	Europe Total	Germany Allemagne	North America Amérique du Nord Total	U.S.A. É.-U.	Commonwealth of Independent States Communauté d'Etats Indépendants Total	Europe
Other manufactured goods (SITC, Rev. 3, 6 and 8) [cont.]											
Northern Africa	2000	8012	7227	27	23	6791	787	409	394	9	1
	2013	19159	12527	44	28	11305	1148	1178	1134	56	48
	2014	18759	12804	46	27	11586	1097	1172	1110	55	48
	2015	16440	11184	45	25	9865	916	1275	1202	22	19
	2016	16071	11198	47	26	10148	900	1004	933	24	20
Sub-Saharan Africa	2000	18775	13621	825	687	10679	619	2117	2001	8	8
	2013	59190	29824	3786	3610	21533	1506	4505	4390	53	48
	2014	62724	29981	3604	3075	21325	1440	5051	4565	54	44
	2015	52001	24413	3147	2779	16646	1377	4620	4041	44	36
	2016	48364	20976	2838	2470	13895	1335	4243	3786	93	71
South Africa	2000	8588	5284	678	552	3444	452	1162	1062	2	2
	2013	26681	13641	3481	3328	7209	1154	2952	2895	46	41
	2014	25712	12375	2894	2735	6671	1157	2810	2730	47	40
	2015	20471	10115	2608	2468	5005	1117	2502	2433	35	28
	2016	21685	10331	2396	2242	5524	1082	2411	2366	88	67
Latin America and the Caribbean	2000	73210	54766	1743	1546	7992	869	45031	44224	21	19
	2013	165129	97241	2537	1634	15181	1547	79523	77236	247	198
	2014	169033	104382	2837	1823	16488	1815	85057	82713	225	142
	2015	155625	99128	1929	1457	14133	1545	83067	80783	159	115
	2016	148220	96341	1656	1282	12673	1470	82012	80063	117	103
Brazil	2000	14499	8863	718	645	3358	408	4787	4533	8	8
	2013	29425	13887	1075	959	5460	688	7352	7132	123	115
	2014	31079	15680	1106	982	6424	905	8151	7887	94	65
	2015	28979	14256	861	748	6160	800	7235	6960	84	80
	2016	26857	12697	691	595	5638	778	6368	6106	71	69
Eastern Asia	2000	327647	186361	44289	38458	52386	11301	89686	83791	3012	2361
	2013	1279478	540772	111528	84861	200264	38111	228981	209512	51991	34731
	2014	1363773	570203	110098	82305	217907	39953	242198	222453	53929	36004
	2015	1286320	567150	101392	73073	208254	37734	257503	237375	35247	22820
	2016	1168426	525675	95550	70011	194251	33562	235875	216909	36066	22073
China	2000	128535	77216	24867	22355	20229	4200	32120	30105	2412	1835
	2013	940873	418387	83632	62737	156205	30521	178549	162603	48012	31473
	2014	1020983	443304	82222	60461	172657	32650	188426	172195	50220	33090
	2015	976818	452868	76954	54442	169340	31207	206574	189790	32938	21074
	2016	879236	417852	72581	51585	156966	27618	188305	172930	33665	20229
Southern Asia	2000	44120	30005	1628	1130	13744	2800	14634	13743	844	507
	2013	171757	85998	4524	2312	47034	9390	34439	32015	1797	1188
	2014	158768	77532	3655	1810	42839	7711	31039	29124	1698	1028
	2015	164885	90439	4563	2194	49760	9922	36117	33693	1198	813
	2016	164418	91083	4465	2152	49468	9697	37150	34852	1083	827
South-Eastern Asia	2000	84386	51730	13530	11297	16411	3164	21789	20766	149	129
	2013	253987	121750	37001	27943	36294	7711	48455	45735	1371	1220
	2014	270358	131465	38072	28194	39744	8494	53650	50528	1488	1316
	2015	260583	131702	36587	26830	39254	8307	55861	52733	978	889
	2016	263877	136816	36632	28186	42338	8729	57845	54668	1082	1007
Western Asia	2000	40404	26263	863	704	14577	4083	10823	10477	1103	703
	2013	169776	62817	1973	971	43531	7902	17314	16445	9691	4944
	2014	177616	69974	2154	1284	48208	8304	19612	18659	9359	4250
	2015	153455	62005	2076	1306	41669	7184	18260	17544	6703	2637
	2016	148060	63011	2178	1433	42303	7186	18530	17770	5031	1884
Oceania	2000	1795	1198	657	511	417	10	124	123	0	0
	2013	3999	2430	2145	136	214	1	70	70	0	0
	2014	5341	3423	3059	136	268	1	96	96	0	0
	2015	2300	502	346	91	101	1	55	54	0	0
	2016	2429	543	375	106	114	1	54	53	0	0

For general note and footnotes see end of table

Exportations mondiales par provenance et destination (Tableau D)

En millions de dollars E.-U. f.o.b.

South-Eastern Europe Europe du Sud-est	Northern Africa Afrique septentrio-nale	Sub-Saharan Africa Afrique du Nord	Latin America and the Caribbean Amérique latine et Caraïbes	Eastern Asia Asie orientale	Southern Asia Asie méridionale	South-eastern Asia Asie du Sud-est	Western Asia Asie occidentale	Oceania Océanie	Others 4/ Autre 4/	Année	← Exportations vers Exportations en provence de ↓
											Articles manufacturés divers (CTCI, Rev. 3, 6 et 8) [suite]
3	260	107	17	41	7	19	221	0	101	2000	Afrique du Nord
47	1871	963	127	225	105	28	3023	0	186	2013	
51	1681	927	109	223	133	46	2526	1	202	2014	
60	1287	975	81	175	122	73	2273	0	186	2015	
40	1194	906	63	144	131	92	2066	1	211	2016	
4	27	2580	356	1025	165	407	559	2	20	2000	Afrique subsaharienne
108	88	15384	457	7446	998	1077	3425	23	307	2013	
108	78	16219	388	7383	1902	1778	4422	6	405	2014	
95	75	13999	324	6709	1504	1584	3034	9	211	2015	
29	85	12775	348	7027	1617	1743	3297	9	365	2016	
3	13	1049	305	958	119	333	516	2	3	2000	Afrique du sud
25	29	7335	391	3232	292	626	1018	20	28	2013	
28	26	7605	340	3260	299	540	1154	4	34	2014	
13	24	5793	257	2692	295	420	805	7	14	2015	
18	46	5682	321	3241	299	492	1138	8	22	2016	
3	120	281	14153	2642	131	503	509	3	76	2000	Amérique latine et Caraïbes
78	240	1195	42909	18202	456	2050	1573	6	932	2013	
89	234	1146	39369	17958	516	2482	1704	8	919	2014	
50	317	984	34198	15870	475	1985	1558	10	892	2015	
61	364	729	30498	14216	523	2735	1780	8	848	2016	
2	74	154	4157	696	61	275	209	1	...	2000	Brésil
28	94	729	9891	2964	169	1044	493	4	...	2013	
27	121	765	9220	2782	253	1355	777	6	0	2014	
23	177	696	8578	2779	287	1090	1005	4	0	2015	
39	112	500	8516	2347	290	1102	1176	6	0	2016	
368	1509	3787	11712	84945	5973	19780	9555	543	103	2000	Asie orientale
2611	13172	40454	69123	289873	53425	146252	70846	939	19	2013	
2984	14595	47847	70141	296824	66009	162098	78125	987	30	2014	
2721	15894	49219	69233	243845	63024	161072	77744	1142	30	2015	
2888	13439	39451	57400	217793	60442	147586	66499	1136	50	2016	
252	860	1960	4095	31066	1530	5081	4019	44	...	2000	Chine
2289	12145	38256	57486	161532	38170	106964	57025	605	...	2013	
2545	13317	45411	58335	173917	49215	121451	62598	671	...	2014	
2356	14545	47315	58577	134193	47607	122743	62815	862	...	2015	
2478	12515	38058	49150	117839	43996	109779	53062	842	0	2016	
19	274	1257	647	4309	1173	1428	4134	24	4	2000	Asie méridionale
274	1469	6867	5048	24687	8271	7788	29062	65	431	2013	
391	1536	6696	5232	23059	8948	6676	25810	65	1124	2014	
285	1273	5915	4658	21426	8755	6730	23612	54	541	2015	
281	1145	5460	4101	20807	8976	6582	24562	61	277	2016	
27	349	1149	1281	10611	2213	13342	3351	176	8	2000	Asie Sud-est
136	1115	3458	6033	45188	8841	53724	11649	522	201	2013	
164	1111	3754	6468	47944	9579	54364	13220	492	309	2014	
154	1040	2737	6016	48615	9823	47745	11104	396	273	2015	
165	935	2679	5879	48351	9764	46817	10695	434	259	2016	
517	1147	683	251	2142	1477	812	5265	0	744	2000	Asie occidentale
3413	7510	5127	2080	11838	21981	3099	38979	17	3223	2013	
3940	7911	5454	2125	13305	19050	3280	39849	15	3354	2014	
3616	6926	4381	1767	11150	14621	3464	36144	8	2671	2015	
4343	5779	3935	1483	10299	16116	3164	32160	8	2729	2016	
1	...	15	275	268	5	5	2	24	2	2000	Océanie
0	0	62	3	255	34	24	5	67	1121	2013	
0	0	47	4	562	19	30	14	85	1157	2014	
0	0	1	3	465	58	11	3	66	1191	2015	
0	0	1	0	487	63	32	0	72	1230	2016	

Voir la fin du tableau pour la remarque générale et les notes.

World exports by provenance and destination (Table D)

In million U.S. dollars f.o.b.

Exports from ↓ / Exports to ⟶	Year	World 1/ Monde 1/	Developed economies 2/ Economies développées 2/ Total	Asia-Pacific Asie-Pacifique Total	Japan Japon	Europe Total	Germany Allemagne	North America Amérique du Nord Total	U.S.A. É.-U.	Commonwealth of Independent States Communauté d'Etats Indépendants Total	Europe
Textile yarn and fabrics (SITC, Rev. 3, 65)											
World 1/	2000	166424	81791	6532	4738	55754	10728	19504	15323	2423	2083
	2013	312281	123742	12006	8586	79600	15799	32135	27242	13890	10215
	2014	319540	128911	12051	8596	83909	16114	32951	28151	13008	9514
	2015	298589	119275	11255	7813	74227	13844	33793	29143	9281	6617
	2016	288148	118272	11042	7781	74191	13894	33039	28490	9656	6664
Developed Economies - Asia-Pacific 2/	2000	7516	1628	247	9	697	153	685	637	10	10
	2013	7326	1465	291	5	632	150	542	510	25	25
	2014	7152	1488	276	4	621	138	591	559	25	25
	2015	6599	1361	240	3	554	124	567	543	24	23
	2016	6835	1385	235	3	606	120	544	516	26	25
Japan	2000	7023	1334	56	.	656	151	621	582	10	10
	2013	6843	1124	23	.	613	148	488	463	25	25
	2014	6680	1150	23	.	598	135	529	504	24	23
	2015	6166	1065	27	.	531	123	507	487	22	21
	2016	6420	1099	28	.	582	118	489	466	23	23
Developed Economies - Europe 2/	2000	57174	45325	1016	712	41096	7960	3213	2889	930	910
	2013	71622	51847	1095	690	47678	9567	3074	2719	2747	2626
	2014	73870	53880	1073	672	49519	9681	3288	2954	2430	2302
	2015	63496	46616	919	564	42563	8129	3134	2831	1629	1535
	2016	63842	47041	923	579	43025	8314	3094	2785	1684	1580
France	2000	6607	4840	95	69	4436	911	309	284	43	42
	2013	5453	3490	69	45	3193	613	228	213	78	67
	2014	5563	3583	64	38	3291	619	228	213	60	51
	2015	4721	3107	62	36	2819	526	226	203	40	35
	2016	4688	3115	71	40	2818	525	226	200	42	38
Germany	2000	11037	8356	127	72	7783	.	446	409	308	302
	2013	14460	10479	180	104	9685	.	613	562	560	527
	2014	14878	10883	188	111	10038	.	658	616	487	455
	2015	12735	9374	147	80	8617	.	609	573	323	300
	2016	12816	9442	140	79	8656	.	646	599	346	322
Developed Economies - North America 2/	2000	13152	6749	439	283	1454	196	4856	2013	27	23
	2013	15823	6332	554	310	1388	252	4390	1706	72	67
	2014	16205	6319	524	281	1467	248	4328	1640	123	116
	2015	15717	6031	472	251	1421	246	4138	1610	51	46
	2016	14907	5875	450	246	1369	223	4055	1585	24	21
United States	2000	10947	4633	423	278	1367	185	2843	.	24	21
	2013	13924	4569	542	307	1344	248	2683	.	70	65
	2014	14373	4627	514	277	1425	244	2687	.	121	114
	2015	13935	4379	465	249	1387	242	2527	.	50	45
	2016	13118	4246	444	244	1332	218	2470	.	24	20
South-Eastern Europe	2000	410	299	3	2	270	57	27	23	27	26
	2013	2043	1634	2	1	1615	283	17	15	122	120
	2014	2184	1721	2	1	1699	299	20	18	117	115
	2015	1968	1525	2	0	1500	268	23	21	93	92
	2016	2143	1668	2	1	1642	281	24	21	112	110
Commonwealth of Independent States	2000	1282	501	15	15	424	67	62	60	542	499
	2013	2767	443	6	4	423	97	14	13	1679	1374
	2014	3326	521	8	6	500	118	14	13	1782	1457
	2015	3599	531	6	4	501	105	24	22	1746	1461
	2016	3730	433	9	6	392	75	33	31	2064	1765
Russian Federation	2000	394	237	0	0	208	21	29	28	97	65
	2013	453	89	2	2	83	28	4	4	314	178
	2014	470	107	3	2	99	33	5	5	307	161
	2015	387	104	2	1	90	25	12	11	238	126
	2016	418	125	2	1	101	25	21	20	253	145

For general note and footnotes see end of table

Exportations mondiales par provenance et destination (Tableau D)

En millions de dollars E.-U. f.o.b.

South-Eastern Europe Europe du Sud-est	Northern Africa Afrique septentrionale	Sub-Saharan Africa Afrique du Nord	Latin America and the Caribbean Amérique latine et Caraïbes	Eastern Asia Asie orientale	Southern Asia Asie méridionale	South-eastern Asia Asie du Sud-est	Western Asia Asie occidentale	Oceania Océanie	Others 4/ Autre 4/	Année	← Exportations vers Exportations en provence de ↓
				Fils et tissus de matières textiles (CTCI, Rev. 3, 65)							
2519	3758	3452	11563	34979	5158	10761	8769	473	779	2000	Monde 1/
6031	9025	12231	24735	43365	20581	37164	20589	193	736	2013	
6441	9019	13106	25132	40358	22115	39667	20919	215	651	2014	
5779	8126	12415	23205	37349	22764	40770	18782	217	627	2015	
6325	7605	10461	21397	33351	22518	40885	16953	209	515	2016	
1	5	32	64	4333	137	933	291	81	0	2000	Economies Développées - Asie-Pacifique 2/
10	15	37	49	3513	200	1555	412	43	1	2013	
9	18	27	55	3309	210	1604	369	38	0	2014	
6	14	29	60	2952	215	1509	393	35	0	2015	
9	14	30	67	2968	214	1692	396	35	0	2016	
1	4	27	60	4271	122	877	287	31	...	2000	Japon
10	14	33	44	3485	191	1507	407	2	...	2013	
9	17	25	48	3281	201	1558	365	2	...	2014	
6	14	27	51	2916	210	1464	387	4	...	2015	
9	14	28	61	2929	210	1652	392	4	...	2016	
2155	2673	551	760	1587	277	585	1925	20	387	2000	Economies Développées - Europe 2/
4322	3359	1150	1192	2728	576	810	2738	18	134	2013	
4615	3455	1207	1174	2805	584	840	2721	20	140	2014	
4058	2881	945	1086	2500	500	766	2385	18	110	2015	
4197	3021	858	1053	2497	518	798	2139	14	21	2016	
169	943	98	69	148	19	56	214	8	0	2000	France
308	865	184	78	157	30	82	170	12	0	2013	
300	897	177	75	170	29	81	175	13	2	2014	
231	732	136	68	148	24	67	157	11	0	2015	
211	738	134	64	143	24	70	135	10	0	2016	
800	355	69	100	180	58	132	386	3	290	2000	Allemagne
1089	284	162	246	617	140	235	644	1	4	2013	
1151	299	173	252	629	140	251	607	2	3	2014	
1007	262	138	217	513	118	214	566	2	2	2015	
1016	275	127	221	558	113	219	497	1	4	2016	
8	18	57	5226	625	65	180	191	4	2	2000	Economies Développées - Amérique du Nord 2/
6	15	67	7453	1252	124	290	208	5	0	2013	
5	16	65	7838	1159	146	308	224	1	0	2014	
6	31	68	7783	1055	159	294	236	4	...	2015	
7	45	54	7238	968	181	317	197	3	0	2016	
6	16	50	5191	606	64	173	180	4	2	2000	Etats-Unis
5	13	62	7381	1219	120	281	200	5	...	2013	
5	13	61	7763	1123	143	299	218	1	...	2014	
5	27	65	7712	1024	155	285	230	3	...	2015	
6	43	51	7128	941	177	308	191	3	...	2016	
49	3	3	2	4	2	0	19	...	3	2000	Europe du Sud-est
141	13	1	10	10	6	3	103	0	0	2013	
187	11	2	13	11	5	5	111	0	0	2014	
202	18	1	12	11	5	7	94	0	0	2015	
218	8	2	11	12	8	9	96	0	0	2016	
10	1	3	4	78	32	4	106	0	0	2000	Communauté d'Etats Indépendants
30	7	4	7	305	27	9	256	0	0	2013	
35	16	4	17	579	29	16	329	0	0	2014	
39	17	2	20	978	29	9	225	0	1	2015	
40	11	2	21	772	29	8	349	0	1	2016	
3	1	3	3	30	10	1	8	...	...	2000	Fédération de Russie
3	0	2	2	6	21	3	12	...	0	2013	
3	1	2	3	7	20	4	16	...	0	2014	
5	1	1	3	7	14	2	11	...	1	2015	
4	1	1	4	9	13	2	7	0	0	2016	

Voir la fin du tableau pour la remarque générale et les notes.

World exports by provenance and destination (Table D)

In million U.S. dollars f.o.b.

Exports from ↓ / Exports to →	Year	World 1/ Monde 1/	Developed economies 2/ Economies développées 2/ Total	Asia-Pacific Asie-Pacifique Total	Japan Japon	Europe Total	Germany Allemagne	North America Amérique du Nord Total	U.S.A. É.-U.	Commonwealth of Independent States Communauté d'Etats Indépendants Total	Europe
Textile yarn and fabrics (SITC, Rev. 3, 65) [cont.]											
Northern Africa	2000	688	592	2	0	502	41	87	84	0	0
	2013	2267	1575	17	8	1273	104	285	262	11	11
	2014	2359	1658	16	7	1379	118	262	239	12	12
	2015	2232	1544	14	5	1244	86	286	265	7	7
	2016	2028	1427	12	5	1206	90	209	186	6	6
Sub-Saharan Africa	2000	675	316	18	3	238	31	59	56	1	1
	2013	1371	280	24	3	234	53	21	19	2	1
	2014	2003	838	23	3	766	33	50	48	0	0
	2015	1891	818	21	2	753	24	44	43	0	0
	2016	913	137	22	2	95	21	21	19	0	0
South Africa	2000	237	122	15	1	71	10	36	33	1	1
	2013	424	93	22	2	54	14	17	15	1	0
	2014	407	99	22	2	58	24	19	17	0	0
	2015	326	81	20	1	48	16	14	13	0	0
	2016	330	85	20	0	47	15	18	16	0	0
Latin America and the Caribbean	2000	4614	2829	69	52	233	52	2526	2419	1	1
	2013	6607	2549	31	19	212	23	2307	2241	3	3
	2014	6460	2692	30	19	214	25	2448	2382	9	9
	2015	6102	2733	26	15	212	21	2496	2428	4	4
	2016	5583	2696	18	11	208	18	2470	2388	3	3
Brazil	2000	895	373	46	41	122	26	205	182	0	0
	2013	949	167	15	13	53	7	98	93	2	2
	2014	883	175	13	11	53	7	109	104	2	2
	2015	875	175	8	7	50	4	117	109	2	2
	2016	793	174	8	7	54	4	112	106	2	2
Eastern Asia	2000	54515	10743	3254	2639	3564	615	3925	3460	429	318
	2013	139568	33586	7120	5579	13023	2638	13443	12239	6679	3923
	2014	143642	35446	7202	5538	14157	2830	14087	12897	6349	3790
	2015	138382	34595	6735	5009	13160	2463	14700	13545	4322	2377
	2016	131531	33917	6572	4922	13125	2420	14219	13123	4704	2456
China	2000	16135	5077	2059	1786	1618	349	1400	1233	208	115
	2013	106578	29289	6159	4769	11498	2359	11632	10576	6377	3748
	2014	111664	31054	6225	4727	12572	2532	12257	11204	6066	3618
	2015	108934	30557	5858	4283	11786	2210	12913	11891	4150	2263
	2016	104605	29993	5686	4174	11773	2170	12534	11569	4551	2345
Southern Asia	2000	11712	6651	579	351	3506	843	2565	2305	167	112
	2013	30750	13006	876	374	6448	1200	5681	5311	334	275
	2014	28962	12538	739	352	6467	1146	5332	5042	256	199
	2015	27951	12667	811	347	6086	1125	5770	5420	187	149
	2016	26103	12687	750	319	6224	1091	5713	5383	183	153
South-Eastern Asia	2000	8304	2841	843	650	1157	142	842	759	8	7
	2013	16175	4446	1820	1520	1416	276	1210	1115	52	49
	2014	17061	4786	1993	1649	1537	288	1256	1147	45	43
	2015	16326	4490	1866	1570	1267	252	1357	1223	49	47
	2016	16447	4603	1907	1639	1286	268	1410	1274	64	63
Western Asia	2000	6306	3302	34	21	2613	572	655	616	282	177
	2013	15949	6575	167	72	5257	1155	1150	1092	2164	1740
	2014	16303	7018	158	64	5584	1192	1276	1212	1861	1447
	2015	14314	6360	139	41	4967	1001	1255	1191	1169	877
	2016	14076	6399	139	48	5014	974	1247	1177	786	482
Oceania	2000	76	15	13	0	1	0	1	1	...	...
	2013	12	5	4	0	0	0	0	0	...	...
	2014	15	6	6	0	0	0	0	0	0	0
	2015	12	5	4	0	0	0	0	0	0	0
	2016	10	4	3	0	0	0	0	0	0	0

For general note and footnotes see end of table

Exportations mondiales par provenance et destination (Tableau D)

En millions de dollars E.-U. f.o.b.

Fils et tissus de matières textiles (CTCI, Rev. 3, 65) [suite]

South-Eastern Europe Europe du Sud-est	Northern Africa Afrique septentrionale	Sub-Saharan Africa Afrique du Nord	Latin America and the Caribbean Amérique latine et Caraïbes	Eastern Asia Asie orientale	Southern Asia Asie méridionale	South-eastern Asia Asie du Sud-est	Western Asia Asie occidentale	Oceania Océanie	Others 4/ Autre 4/	Année	← Exportations vers Exportations en provence de ↓
2	9	7	3	10	1	1	35	0	28	2000	Afrique du Nord
3	95	55	32	14	33	7	392	0	49	2013	
4	102	50	35	16	28	5	406	0	40	2014	
4	94	57	37	14	22	6	419	0	29	2015	
4	95	48	22	11	19	4	365	0	28	2016	
0	1	279	24	19	7	12	9	0	7	2000	Afrique subsaharienne
9	2	949	10	21	19	8	45	1	26	2013	
7	2	1022	9	12	19	6	44	1	42	2014	
8	3	923	8	19	21	7	46	0	37	2015	
2	2	628	7	49	20	9	27	0	30	2016	
0	0	61	22	11	4	8	9	0	0	2000	Afrique du sud
0	0	305	9	1	1	2	10	0	2	2013	
0	1	288	8	1	1	1	7	0	1	2014	
1	0	222	7	2	2	2	8	0	1	2015	
1	1	225	6	1	2	1	7	0	1	2016	
0	5	8	1544	188	4	10	16	0	9	2000	Amérique latine et Caraïbes
6	4	20	3839	61	13	28	14	0	68	2013	
6	4	18	3543	67	11	26	26	0	56	2014	
6	5	17	3133	82	25	27	18	1	51	2015	
7	4	11	2713	36	22	36	12	0	42	2016	
0	2	5	497	7	1	1	8	0	...	2000	Brésil
6	2	17	725	13	5	10	2	...	...	2013	
6	2	13	655	11	4	8	6	0	...	2014	
6	1	10	612	45	8	13	5	...	...	2015	
7	2	7	562	6	10	18	5	0	...	2016	
69	396	1405	3285	24872	3212	6889	2825	309	80	2000	Asie orientale
465	2987	7473	9336	26486	13437	29597	9444	79	0	2013	
498	3010	8190	9767	24068	14664	32094	9458	91	8	2014	
437	2949	8050	8842	21547	15334	33483	8715	97	10	2015	
498	2572	6736	8121	18812	14917	33401	7747	95	11	2016	
30	152	702	739	6310	865	1228	807	17	...	2000	Chine
410	2771	7107	8071	13088	11480	19991	7941	53	...	2013	
437	2805	7846	8554	12106	12674	22167	7896	59	...	2014	
373	2790	7746	7836	11149	13350	23610	7303	68	...	2015	
424	2447	6473	7257	10020	13008	23816	6548	68	...	2016	
9	188	649	303	1483	537	361	1356	7	1	2000	Asie méridionale
69	791	1695	1700	5090	3659	1216	3011	13	167	2013	
67	791	1760	1574	4033	3643	1138	3101	16	45	2014	
51	661	1643	1281	3880	3723	987	2723	12	136	2015	
58	559	1489	1224	2790	3625	906	2439	13	129	2016	
3	62	323	298	1675	576	1744	724	48	0	2000	Asie Sud-est
25	310	462	875	3549	1156	3471	1781	30	17	2013	
31	319	407	865	3971	1271	3465	1838	43	21	2014	
41	285	342	743	4031	1301	3506	1487	45	7	2015	
35	272	341	712	4155	1229	3535	1447	46	8	2016	
212	396	134	49	49	306	42	1271	0	261	2000	Asie occidentale
944	1427	317	229	336	1331	170	2184	0	272	2013	
976	1273	354	238	327	1504	160	2293	0	298	2014	
922	1169	337	198	279	1428	167	2040	0	246	2015	
1250	1002	261	207	281	1735	170	1740	0	245	2016	
1	...	0	1	57	0	0	...	3	0	2000	Océanie
0	...	1	2	0	0	0	0	4	0	2013	
0	...	0	3	0	0	0	0	5	1	2014	
...	0	0	2	1	0	0	0	4	0	2015	
0	...	0	0	1	1	0	0	3	0	2016	

Voir la fin du tableau pour la remarque générale et les notes.

World exports by provenance and destination (Table D)

In million U.S. dollars f.o.b.

Exports to ⟶		Developed economies 2/ Economies développées 2/								Commonwealth of Independent States Communauté d'Etats Indépendants	
				Asia-Pacific Asie-Pacifique		Europe		North America Amérique du Nord			
↓ Exports from	Year	World 1/ Monde 1/	Total	Total	Japan Japon	Total	Germany Allemagne	Total	U.S.A. É.-U.	Total	Europe
					Iron and steel (SITC, Rev. 3, 67)						
World 1/	2000	140111	88414	4447	3399	61355	12136	22613	17450	2287	1693
	2013	451165	216635	12294	7971	155949	32728	48393	36446	20408	12453
	2014	467167	230863	13247	8775	157300	33051	60315	47085	16521	9916
	2015	375797	183965	10548	6531	129853	27541	43564	34033	11218	5732
	2016	333905	165534	8798	6310	121867	26006	34870	26795	8607	4878
Developed Economies - Asia-Pacific 2/	2000	15647	2932	406	32	693	64	1833	1594	46	28
	2013	39901	4839	770	10	1039	125	3030	2785	473	335
	2014	38260	5032	639	9	1012	147	3382	3108	350	207
	2015	31050	4364	463	4	1081	136	2820	2558	184	99
	2016	26771	3398	422	4	930	125	2046	1875	88	40
Japan	2000	14833	2510	259	.	609	63	1642	1415	46	28
	2013	38868	4304	477	.	998	124	2829	2604	471	334
	2014	37379	4461	388	.	988	146	3085	2834	347	205
	2015	30314	3921	266	.	1045	135	2609	2356	184	99
	2016	26182	3084	260	.	896	124	1928	1761	87	40
Developed Economies - Europe 2/	2000	65518	57583	425	200	51826	11073	5332	4610	512	433
	2013	169821	133028	1098	404	123244	28891	8686	7679	3043	2699
	2014	167950	134706	827	402	122833	29365	11046	9817	2701	2167
	2015	136222	110035	730	336	100907	24406	8398	7361	2553	1414
	2016	126899	104236	625	314	97230	23332	6381	5628	1948	1317
France	2000	8850	7853	52	22	6883	1841	919	756	12	7
	2013	16090	12473	53	31	11764	3663	656	593	111	104
	2014	16341	12930	63	40	11985	3791	882	815	101	91
	2015	13449	10457	62	42	9608	3051	787	723	679	78
	2016	11702	9595	38	24	8970	2799	587	539	115	53
Germany	2000	13445	11343	64	32	10039	.	1240	1071	122	109
	2013	33081	26138	317	51	23757	.	2064	1787	527	441
	2014	32065	26078	123	52	23613	.	2342	2070	557	459
	2015	26514	21843	104	44	19700	.	2038	1811	366	314
	2016	24359	19851	98	46	18242	.	1511	1355	271	229
Developed Economies - North America 2/	2000	9531	7211	205	169	752	146	6253	3068	36	28
	2013	26797	16677	276	137	1668	277	14733	6004	93	75
	2014	27466	17338	264	133	1656	290	15418	6652	110	93
	2015	22420	13784	253	131	1526	241	12005	5593	123	86
	2016	19077	11869	214	121	1244	206	10412	4788	85	69
United States	2000	6317	4083	194	161	704	142	3185	.	36	27
	2013	19910	10473	242	128	1502	271	8729	.	86	71
	2014	19993	10509	231	125	1513	281	8765	.	89	74
	2015	16058	8035	227	125	1396	236	6411	.	106	70
	2016	13564	6946	196	117	1126	204	5624	.	70	53
South-Eastern Europe	2000	1634	1069	0	0	864	148	205	174	24	16
	2013	4860	2445	4	2	2202	478	239	162	156	142
	2014	4816	2719	3	1	2331	422	385	265	125	110
	2015	4066	2162	2	0	2013	376	147	143	61	56
	2016	3712	2006	5	3	1905	393	97	81	67	64
Commonwealth of Independent States	2000	11626	3308	60	58	2128	356	1120	1045	1614	1176
	2013	42149	14564	714	707	11928	1533	1923	1796	11755	6755
	2014	40047	13469	779	770	9691	1143	2999	2793	9183	5248
	2015	27453	9871	655	645	7514	905	1701	1574	5478	2775
	2016	18729	6743	519	516	5005	596	1219	1049	3932	1976
Russian Federation	2000	6146	2251	40	40	1537	288	674	639	379	91
	2013	21017	8641	217	213	7207	929	1217	1102	5584	2131
	2014	20906	7651	265	260	5209	639	2178	1993	4358	1574
	2015	15166	5789	183	174	4340	503	1266	1150	3014	946
	2016	14195	5270	190	188	4086	403	993	872	2658	1031

For general note and footnotes see end of table

Exportations mondiales par provenance et destination (Tableau D)

En millions de dollars E.-U. f.o.b.

South-Eastern Europe Europe du Sud-est	Northern Africa Afrique septentrio-nale	Sub-Saharan Africa Afrique du Nord	Latin America and the Caribbean Amérique latine et Caraïbes	Eastern Asia Asie orientale	Southern Asia Asie méridionale	South-eastern Asia Asie du Sud-est	Western Asia Asie occidentale	Oceania Océanie	Others 4/ Autre 4/	Année	⟵ Exportations vers Exportations en provence de ↓
				Fer et acier (CTCI, Rev. 3, 67)							
994	1780	1601	6606	20615	2617	9021	5826	107	243	2000	Monde 1/
5792	9814	13234	30254	51209	15627	48112	39248	337	494	2013	
6498	10774	12830	31393	53009	18715	47687	37990	330	557	2014	
4880	9449	10592	25835	40439	17248	39707	31773	303	388	2015	
5043	7712	7666	21044	38657	15004	38507	25446	308	376	2016	
1	57	172	704	7099	468	3634	479	54	0	2000	Economies Développées - Asie-Pacifique 2/
9	178	815	2169	15349	1966	11875	2103	118	7	2013	
14	210	656	2294	14493	2041	10682	2386	92	10	2014	
15	235	533	2166	11023	2048	8633	1753	94	1	2015	
9	146	431	2019	9717	1538	7863	1475	86	1	2016	
1	57	159	651	6971	456	3517	460	6	...	2000	Japon
8	178	804	2129	15289	1958	11639	2076	11	...	2013	
14	207	650	2281	14472	2014	10548	2376	9	...	2014	
14	235	522	2162	10992	2042	8507	1726	10	...	2015	
9	143	426	2014	9690	1532	7742	1446	8	...	2016	
341	776	525	1186	1286	685	658	1760	20	185	2000	Economies Développées - Europe 2/
3022	5035	2037	4020	5577	1883	3331	8698	38	108	2013	
3304	4898	2107	3521	5477	1600	2316	7172	35	114	2014	
2603	3673	1634	2757	4008	1408	1463	5963	25	100	2015	
2894	3462	1036	2045	3622	1427	1112	5011	21	85	2016	
11	180	92	150	146	82	80	230	13	0	2000	France
139	411	229	308	703	236	109	1356	15	0	2013	
140	403	274	307	696	190	129	1154	16	1	2014	
120	338	237	247	458	145	76	675	13	4	2015	
127	325	118	169	391	207	62	579	13	...	2016	
50	111	101	317	441	233	141	422	0	163	2000	Allemagne
301	215	296	909	1772	517	924	1387	0	94	2013	
581	203	343	717	1774	356	359	992	2	102	2014	
368	169	228	632	1324	344	257	907	0	76	2015	
525	280	155	520	1264	319	244	861	0	70	2016	
1	23	41	1664	254	80	139	81	2	1	2000	Economies Développées - Amérique du Nord 2/
21	86	365	7125	1062	353	401	611	4	...	2013	
38	79	395	7276	1082	295	362	489	2	...	2014	
17	79	275	6244	898	280	294	425	3	0	2015	
12	69	98	5331	811	268	197	316	19	...	2016	
1	22	40	1625	239	62	132	76	2	1	2000	États-Unis
19	72	351	6737	972	234	372	589	4	...	2013	
36	67	381	6846	1005	229	351	477	2	...	2014	
16	72	264	5810	817	234	285	416	3	...	2015	
12	63	90	4920	734	214	191	306	19	...	2016	
101	19	1	58	47	19	12	279	0	3	2000	Europe du Sud-est
1208	92	18	75	146	53	18	633	...	16	2013	
1012	113	13	99	164	47	16	508	0	1	2014	
898	79	18	85	210	23	11	516	0	2	2015	
958	66	13	53	87	32	15	407	0	8	2016	
472	586	207	428	2221	552	787	1448	1	0	2000	Communauté d'Etats Indépendants
695	1604	699	837	2626	1469	1119	6775	6	...	2013	
1152	2272	636	1776	2680	1605	564	6710	0	...	2014	
659	2057	402	1102	1684	1136	185	4880	0	0	2015	
206	918	68	893	1880	1035	303	2751	0	0	2016	
122	235	103	271	1360	377	403	644	...	0	2000	Fédération de Russie
73	327	88	633	1911	711	507	2536	6	...	2013	
476	667	113	1545	2026	700	281	3086	...	...	2014	
131	820	66	985	1078	523	172	2588	0	0	2015	
139	777	47	873	1159	541	265	2467	0	0	2016	

Voir la fin du tableau pour la remarque générale et les notes.

World exports by provenance and destination (Table D)

In million U.S. dollars f.o.b.

Exports to ⟶ ↓ Exports from	Year	World 1/ Monde 1/	Developed economies 2/ Economies développées 2/ Total	Asia-Pacific Asie-Pacifique Total	Japan Japon	Europe Total	Germany Allemagne	North America Amérique du Nord Total	U.S.A. É.-U.	Commonwealth of Independent States Communauté d'Etats Indépendants Total	Europe
Iron and steel (SITC, Rev. 3, 67) [cont.]											
Northern Africa	2000	332	201	8	8	185	5	8	5	7	0
	2013	1357	293	0	0	288	1	4	4	9	9
	2014	947	252	0	...	229	3	22	22	9	8
	2015	518	102	0	...	96	2	6	5	0	0
	2016	644	183	0	0	163	2	19	18	0	0
Sub-Saharan Africa	2000	3002	1847	314	283	949	101	583	513	1	1
	2013	7324	2501	382	353	1374	274	745	720	28	27
	2014	7967	2929	445	412	1505	265	979	927	32	31
	2015	5359	2007	282	264	1151	172	574	529	21	20
	2016	5943	1844	279	260	970	120	595	578	54	53
South Africa	2000	2758	1709	275	245	877	81	557	486	1	1
	2013	6204	2471	381	353	1353	274	736	711	27	27
	2014	6796	2880	443	410	1465	264	972	919	31	31
	2015	4521	1973	275	257	1132	169	566	521	20	20
	2016	5333	1813	275	257	944	117	594	576	52	52
Latin America and the Caribbean	2000	8145	5014	176	162	1351	109	3487	3183	3	1
	2013	20369	9909	429	420	2039	147	7440	7118	106	75
	2014	21240	12531	436	416	2928	315	9168	8785	107	40
	2015	16583	9133	286	277	2540	327	6307	6060	90	54
	2016	14212	7483	330	321	2121	348	5032	4797	57	47
Brazil	2000	3633	2261	145	137	716	89	1400	1273	0	0
	2013	9025	5093	350	348	1342	104	3401	3332	44	43
	2014	10714	6798	327	310	2289	287	4182	4073	36	14
	2015	9728	5724	245	240	2135	298	3344	3211	48	47
	2016	8230	4435	250	246	1810	327	2375	2262	38	38
Eastern Asia	2000	17592	6217	2503	2249	1136	38	2577	2213	29	6
	2013	93934	21831	6611	5144	6818	561	8402	7320	3735	1867
	2014	114529	29382	7414	5764	9454	629	12514	10893	2947	1653
	2015	97248	22188	5419	4148	8323	543	8446	7251	1952	1080
	2016	86109	19086	5139	3968	7551	473	6397	5480	1869	1159
China	2000	4391	1673	627	597	385	12	661	566	17	3
	2013	54689	9653	2191	1546	4017	378	3445	2820	3135	1438
	2014	72260	13987	2725	1900	6117	420	5145	4141	2392	1260
	2015	63829	11125	1988	1333	5529	395	3609	2919	1577	811
	2016	55321	8264	1682	1120	4364	313	2218	1731	1498	886
Southern Asia	2000	1591	787	51	44	308	25	428	361	3	0
	2013	13835	4439	408	318	2768	229	1263	1166	222	186
	2014	13196	4815	380	266	2773	206	1662	1450	182	149
	2015	10297	3854	247	178	2547	212	1060	978	80	58
	2016	9852	3495	206	149	2558	154	732	654	81	65
South-Eastern Asia	2000	2644	947	227	127	284	22	435	385	1	1
	2013	12605	2758	1444	375	566	29	748	642	78	54
	2014	13305	3400	1883	500	907	38	609	521	75	41
	2015	11155	3269	2071	486	609	35	589	530	36	30
	2016	10219	2066	957	580	502	40	607	563	39	36
Western Asia	2000	2478	1072	6	4	748	49	319	267	9	3
	2013	17654	3065	62	9	1886	183	1117	988	711	229
	2014	16577	3959	84	13	1832	228	2043	1767	703	168
	2015	12810	3011	82	5	1457	185	1472	1411	641	59
	2016	11077	2925	41	12	1593	217	1291	1243	388	51
Oceania	2000	371	227	65	63	130	1	32	32	...	...
	2013	558	287	95	93	129	0	62	62	...	...
	2014	867	330	94	91	149	0	87	87	...	...
	2015	616	186	58	57	88	...	39	39	0	0
	2016	662	200	62	62	95	...	43	43	0	0

For general note and footnotes see end of table

Exportations mondiales par provenance et destination (Tableau D)

En millions de dollars E.-U. f.o.b.

South-Eastern Europe Europe du Sud-est	Northern Africa Afrique septentrio-nale	Sub-Saharan Africa Afrique du Nord	Latin America and the Caribbean Amérique latine et Caraïbes	Eastern Asia Asie orientale	Southern Asia Asie méridionale	South-eastern Asia Asie du Sud-est	Western Asia Asie occidentale	Oceania Océanie	Others 4/ Autre 4/	Année	← Exportations vers Exportations en provence de ↓
				Fer et acier (CTCI, Rev. 3, 67) [suite]							
0	72	12	0	5	0	5	29	...	1	2000	Afrique du Nord
7	215	99	12	3	1	0	711	0	7	2013	
2	178	69	14	11	1	13	389	0	9	2014	
11	113	67	2	0	1	31	185	0	7	2015	
3	127	71	2	0	0	49	201	0	7	2016	
0	2	291	164	410	75	131	80	0	1	2000	Afrique subsaharienne
9	15	2403	181	1671	124	216	172	0	5	2013	
9	8	2544	179	1707	172	187	179	1	20	2014	
9	4	1759	87	1115	102	173	78	0	5	2015	
1	5	1541	149	1800	120	194	225	0	10	2016	
0	2	190	164	408	74	131	79	0	1	2000	Afrique du sud
1	10	1386	153	1663	111	211	168	0	4	2013	
1	7	1453	178	1701	170	183	175	1	15	2014	
1	2	980	87	1108	99	171	77	0	3	2015	
1	4	987	149	1787	118	190	224	0	8	2016	
0	65	94	1927	646	50	199	147	0	1	2000	Amérique latine et Caraïbes
39	146	481	6697	1536	120	596	735	0	3	2013	
47	135	339	5147	1184	170	727	849	1	3	2014	
18	199	263	4255	1216	175	572	657	3	2	2015	
14	242	155	3722	898	208	541	890	0	1	2016	
...	39	21	666	383	21	160	81	0	...	2000	Brésil
4	18	133	2117	918	46	495	158	...	...	2013	
0	44	107	1725	845	117	649	393	0	...	2014	
0	109	107	1680	856	149	530	524	0	...	2015	
0	37	66	1763	644	112	485	651	0	...	2016	
51	40	81	341	7803	343	2191	481	14	0	2000	Asie orientale
266	786	3742	7483	20154	6487	21837	7505	108	1	2013	
343	1414	4154	9228	23053	9145	25443	9295	124	0	2014	
229	1513	4271	7890	17594	9350	22955	9167	137	0	2015	
220	1482	3240	5768	16411	7680	22754	7460	139	0	2016	
15	12	35	62	1717	81	581	196	0	...	2000	Chine
179	648	3354	5150	11491	3640	12623	4748	67	...	2013	
183	1188	3847	6726	14299	6013	16974	6573	79	...	2014	
143	1316	4036	5604	10845	6501	16307	6287	88	...	2015	
117	1323	3067	3866	10042	5260	16485	5312	86	0	2016	
1	6	114	27	136	136	167	213	0	0	2000	Asie méridionale
68	151	1273	650	1249	1599	1702	2468	0	14	2013	
62	117	845	727	956	2087	985	2413	1	7	2014	
34	99	604	516	652	1560	719	2170	1	8	2015	
33	72	492	448	783	1616	965	1855	1	9	2016	
0	14	10	30	423	126	1012	68	14	0	2000	Asie Sud-est
4	58	295	98	1449	609	6663	533	58	2	2013	
10	36	279	203	1588	714	6183	746	68	3	2014	
2	36	191	148	1604	767	4579	479	34	10	2015	
4	30	132	168	2156	728	4389	463	34	11	2016	
26	121	51	78	146	77	88	760	...	50	2000	Asie occidentale
445	1446	976	908	184	935	349	8304	1	331	2013	
503	1315	751	930	147	821	204	6853	1	389	2014	
387	1362	576	582	62	344	90	5500	2	252	2015	
689	1094	391	446	89	297	124	4391	1	243	2016	
0	...	0	...	138	5	0	...	1	0	2000	Océanie
...	...	33	0	202	28	4	...	4	0	2013	
...	...	42	0	467	18	4	0	5	0	2014	
...	...	0	0	372	53	1	0	4	0	2015	
...	...	0	0	402	55	0	0	4	0	2016	

Voir la fin du tableau pour la remarque générale et les notes.

World exports by provenance and destination (Table D)

In million U.S. dollars f.o.b.

Exports to ⟶ ↓ Exports from	Year	World 1/ Monde 1/	Developed economies 2/ Economies développées 2/ Total	Asia-Pacific Asie-Pacifique Total	Japan Japon	Europe Total	Germany Allemagne	North America Amérique du Nord Total	U.S.A. É.-U.	Commonwealth of Independent States Communauté d'Etats Indépendants Total	Europe
Non-ferrous metals (SITC, Rev. 3, 68)											
World 1/	2000	112759	79555	8873	8236	50049	9560	20633	17599	801	711
	2013	353612	194787	19108	14479	132298	26916	43380	37678	3727	3054
	2014	350640	195005	21018	14951	130645	26173	43341	37661	3134	2487
	2015	304765	165478	15269	12700	110939	22226	39270	33637	2419	1866
	2016	283082	157501	14062	11602	104613	21195	38826	33539	2178	1728
Developed Economies - Asia-Pacific 2/	2000	10460	3591	1685	1488	878	175	1028	983	18	3
	2013	24702	4865	1758	1425	1909	158	1199	1159	5	5
	2014	23824	5161	2453	2110	1330	152	1378	1314	7	6
	2015	19677	3731	1555	1244	1167	156	1009	978	3	2
	2016	18246	3123	1303	1001	925	141	894	870	2	1
Japan	2000	4854	990	31	.	348	105	612	588	18	3
	2013	13893	1751	28	.	836	143	887	857	3	2
	2014	13084	1709	47	.	733	149	930	891	4	3
	2015	11315	1240	81	.	511	151	648	627	3	2
	2016	10978	1115	76	.	396	139	643	621	2	1
Developed Economies - Europe 2/	2000	45180	40166	1547	1395	34149	8196	4470	4288	307	296
	2013	116570	91982	1443	1052	84575	21148	5965	5453	929	859
	2014	114532	92517	1647	1203	83798	20988	7072	6674	804	721
	2015	97548	78608	1342	979	71490	17426	5776	5241	681	618
	2016	91341	76242	1099	764	69648	16858	5495	4783	621	560
France	2000	3859	3505	50	43	3256	922	198	183	7	6
	2013	6706	5449	67	51	5001	1475	381	352	19	15
	2014	6512	5366	42	32	4876	1561	448	418	14	11
	2015	5783	4721	44	32	4222	1308	454	423	9	8
	2016	5372	4448	42	29	4014	1183	392	370	8	7
Germany	2000	10368	8668	320	266	7380	.	968	911	122	119
	2013	27675	21676	295	213	19035	.	2346	2200	322	292
	2014	27571	21745	322	240	19347	.	2076	1941	280	250
	2015	23132	18632	325	237	16542	.	1764	1612	184	164
	2016	22005	17942	302	199	15879	.	1762	1608	191	167
Developed Economies - North America 2/	2000	16479	12924	1073	1012	2338	301	9513	6829	8	8
	2013	34517	23034	1372	1202	4357	778	17305	13340	40	19
	2014	34996	23087	1197	1064	4670	740	17220	13274	28	14
	2015	31244	20900	1154	1048	3756	772	15991	12201	24	12
	2016	30694	19666	1042	947	3358	738	15266	11662	21	10
United States	2000	8270	5159	735	691	1741	292	2683	.	8	8
	2013	17908	7889	1013	865	2912	735	3964	.	38	17
	2014	18602	8091	849	741	3296	696	3946	.	27	13
	2015	16507	7483	860	777	2832	724	3790	.	23	11
	2016	16612	6966	704	628	2658	674	3604	.	21	10
South-Eastern Europe	2000	1376	1093	3	3	1069	73	21	13	9	8
	2013	5701	3933	4	0	3866	1113	63	53	115	115
	2014	5374	3678	3	0	3611	573	63	49	79	78
	2015	4750	3268	3	1	3210	557	54	38	60	58
	2016	4048	2746	1	0	2715	584	31	21	47	46
Commonwealth of Independent States	2000	9320	7842	1129	1128	5567	411	1146	1142	423	372
	2013	25502	16015	1176	1174	12679	1701	2159	2152	1880	1528
	2014	23301	14383	1176	1175	11713	1562	1493	1466	1474	1173
	2015	23036	14143	991	989	11515	1139	1637	1627	1067	790
	2016	20661	12672	1043	1040	9271	880	2359	2336	1051	812
Russian Federation	2000	8137	7079	1096	1095	4927	283	1056	1053	76	32
	2013	17818	14075	1134	1131	10930	1605	2011	2009	924	673
	2014	16582	12948	1141	1139	10484	1417	1324	1317	674	483
	2015	15916	12086	947	945	9694	988	1445	1444	500	322
	2016	14129	10839	1018	1015	7541	758	2281	2260	529	368

For general note and footnotes see end of table

Exportations mondiales par provenance et destination (Tableau D)

En millions de dollars E.-U. f.o.b.

South-Eastern Europe Europe du Sud-est	Northern Africa Afrique septentrionale	Sub-Saharan Africa Afrique du Nord	Latin America and the Caribbean Amérique latine et Caraïbes	Eastern Asia Asie orientale	Southern Asia Asie méridionale	South-eastern Asia Asie du Sud-est	Western Asia Asie occidentale	Oceania Océanie	Others 4/ Autre 4/	Année	← Exportations vers / Exportations en provence de ↓
				Metaux non ferreux (CTCI, Rev. 3, 68)							
318	431	760	4395	16497	1307	5752	2506	19	419	2000	Monde 1/
2840	3173	3286	14453	73763	11021	27423	17373	68	1699	2013	
3610	3451	3688	14173	67737	11917	28392	18061	63	1410	2014	
3320	3229	3193	12641	60412	10492	25951	16504	56	1071	2015	
3370	2815	2854	11459	54590	8316	25949	13571	48	431	2016	
0	2	81	51	4509	135	1964	99	8	0	2000	Economies Développées - Asie-Pacifique 2/
1	35	52	88	12508	301	6630	204	13	0	2013	
3	53	27	109	11241	394	6467	347	14	0	2014	
2	5	30	126	10105	510	4922	210	13	20	2015	
2	4	32	120	9803	397	4533	221	11	0	2016	
0	2	14	32	2576	49	1118	53	0	...	2000	Japon
1	6	11	50	8037	142	3785	107	0	...	2013	
1	4	9	47	7495	204	3370	241	0	...	2014	
1	4	8	46	6502	254	3108	150	0	...	2015	
0	3	7	46	6627	187	2815	176	0	...	2016	
187	297	223	563	1498	423	395	759	6	356	2000	Economies Développées - Europe 2/
2017	1805	573	1291	8237	3367	1876	3414	11	1068	2013	
2645	1883	753	1328	5862	2651	1451	3648	11	979	2014	
2459	1704	547	1155	4707	2658	1221	3091	10	708	2015	
2513	1605	492	1101	4013	1172	921	2393	10	259	2016	
3	74	32	24	88	9	35	77	3	3	2000	France
40	263	95	80	301	53	92	292	7	14	2013	
59	258	106	72	249	46	61	257	7	16	2014	
61	239	105	75	270	45	38	202	7	10	2015	
68	224	88	60	207	33	34	186	7	7	2016	
35	55	73	308	433	57	152	207	0	259	2000	Allemagne
499	137	162	633	1678	273	814	945	2	534	2013	
588	157	168	578	1581	267	632	1179	3	393	2014	
538	121	129	475	1127	216	430	1076	2	203	2015	
536	107	134	499	1000	272	373	824	1	125	2016	
2	6	186	1727	1151	21	261	192	1	0	2000	Economies Développées - Amérique du Nord 2/
11	18	41	6087	3839	242	510	691	4	...	2013	
11	15	82	6236	4135	234	606	561	2	0	2014	
9	10	26	5909	3068	403	529	365	2	0	2015	
7	13	22	5564	3020	266	1769	341	4	0	2016	
2	5	184	1667	868	17	179	179	1	0	2000	Etats-Unis
10	18	34	5783	2949	146	402	636	2	...	2013	
11	14	81	5926	3230	181	539	501	1	...	2014	
9	10	24	5660	2160	315	473	349	1	...	2015	
7	13	16	5268	2091	213	1691	325	2	...	2016	
94	19	2	20	7	4	2	125	...	3	2000	Europe du Sud-est
332	104	4	3	552	3	57	598	0	0	2013	
319	98	3	3	398	3	22	771	0	0	2014	
326	87	2	3	389	5	39	570	0	0	2015	
390	38	1	2	257	3	47	517	...	0	2016	
11	0	6	79	696	25	19	217	...	0	2000	Communauté d'Etats Indépendants
159	51	9	150	2840	193	55	4150	0	...	2013	
135	69	29	46	2300	442	71	4351	0	...	2014	
149	95	26	125	2049	467	109	4720	0	86	2015	
123	155	47	102	2221	249	257	3785	0	0	2016	
4	0	6	73	678	21	18	181	...	...	2000	Fédération de Russie
134	41	8	131	612	185	47	1660	0	...	2013	
126	33	21	38	683	430	62	1567	...	...	2014	
120	64	19	118	822	418	89	1595	...	86	2015	
106	155	20	98	811	194	111	1265	...	0	2016	

Voir la fin du tableau pour la remarque générale et les notes.

World exports by provenance and destination (Table D)

In million U.S. dollars f.o.b.

Exports from ↓ / Exports to ⟶	Year	World 1/ Monde 1/	Developed economies 2/ Economies développées 2/ Total	Asia-Pacific Asie-Pacifique Total	Japan Japon	Europe Total	Germany Allemagne	North America Amérique du Nord Total	U.S.A. É.-U.	Commonwealth of Independent States Communauté d'Etats Indépendants Total	Europe
		Non-ferrous metals (SITC, Rev. 3, 68) [cont.]									
Northern Africa	2000	266	214	8	8	202	4	4	4	0	0
	2013	1182	710	8	8	688	70	14	14	0	0
	2014	1086	630	10	10	593	59	27	13	1	1
	2015	887	548	7	7	501	43	40	11	...	...
	2016	825	524	7	7	483	53	34	10	...	...
Sub-Saharan Africa	2000	2281	1372	314	310	917	32	141	132	0	0
	2013	23857	15689	3225	3214	10711	744	1754	1744	4	4
	2014	23528	15324	2971	2611	10748	717	1604	1581	4	4
	2015	20380	12588	2647	2427	8089	823	1852	1800	4	4
	2016	18522	11497	2304	2085	7693	837	1500	1476	4	4
South Africa	2000	1209	526	246	242	169	7	110	102	0	0
	2013	10958	8718	2955	2945	4106	601	1657	1647	4	4
	2014	9065	7107	2314	2302	3396	618	1398	1392	4	4
	2015	8437	6473	2158	2137	2739	757	1576	1573	4	4
	2016	8185	6245	1914	1880	3006	746	1326	1323	4	4
Latin America and the Caribbean	2000	11203	7837	1142	1135	3436	170	3259	3238	2	2
	2013	38242	18049	1471	869	6067	166	10511	9876	2	2
	2014	35428	16141	1701	1007	5881	237	8558	7954	0	0
	2015	28927	12332	923	744	4095	172	7313	6641	2	2
	2016	26558	10861	653	545	3048	149	7160	6818	3	3
Brazil	2000	1757	1477	391	388	735	11	350	348	1	1
	2013	2598	1247	483	482	461	33	302	299	0	0
	2014	2228	1225	534	531	403	57	289	286	0	0
	2015	2340	1021	408	405	396	43	217	216	1	1
	2016	2099	759	263	260	292	44	204	203	0	0
Eastern Asia	2000	9406	2290	965	854	672	75	653	593	9	8
	2013	44181	10880	4119	3534	3919	439	2841	2406	530	434
	2014	47721	11834	4297	3599	3818	520	3718	3236	505	392
	2015	41878	10120	3659	2920	3069	620	3392	2981	396	318
	2016	39307	10088	3686	2946	3264	478	3138	2690	299	248
China	2000	3363	1340	563	498	500	29	278	252	6	5
	2013	22655	6419	1992	1561	2384	307	2042	1724	512	421
	2014	25432	7289	2058	1576	2739	386	2493	2153	481	384
	2015	23225	6663	1760	1271	2580	448	2323	1987	380	309
	2016	20799	6161	1716	1235	2198	358	2247	1914	288	242
Southern Asia	2000	499	100	4	2	64	18	32	29	4	3
	2013	6411	373	47	31	178	37	148	139	13	0
	2014	6979	427	56	35	195	24	176	163	2	0
	2015	6658	442	98	55	116	16	228	219	5	1
	2016	5386	574	103	67	236	17	235	229	5	3
South-Eastern Asia	2000	3876	1079	770	683	160	9	150	140	3	2
	2013	18187	3670	1846	1524	986	63	837	788	14	14
	2014	16874	4037	1852	1384	1118	117	1066	990	30	28
	2015	16195	3525	1868	1466	864	53	793	735	7	5
	2016	14825	3662	1817	1406	860	27	986	931	3	2
Western Asia	2000	2413	1046	234	217	596	97	216	209	18	9
	2013	12586	3622	744	447	2294	499	584	554	193	74
	2014	14079	4884	852	752	3067	486	964	948	199	70
	2015	13403	5095	842	820	3069	449	1184	1167	169	56
	2016	12475	5655	816	796	3111	432	1728	1714	124	38
Oceania	2000	1	1	0	...	0	...	0	0	...	...
	2013	1974	1965	1896	0	70	0	0	.	...	...
	2014	2918	2903	2800	0	103	0	0	0	...	...
	2015	182	179	179	...	0	0	0	0	...	...
	2016	191	190	190	0	0	0	0	0	...	...

For general note and footnotes see end of table

Exportations mondiales par provenance et destination (Tableau D)

En millions de dollars E.-U. f.o.b.

South-Eastern Europe Europe du Sud-est	Northern Africa Afrique septentrio-nale	Sub-Saharan Africa Afrique du Nord	Latin America and the Caribbean Amérique latine et Caraïbes	Eastern Asia Asie orientale	Southern Asia Asie méridionale	South-eastern Asia Asie du Sud-est	Western Asia Asie occidentale	Oceania Océanie	Others 4/ Autre 4/	Année	← Exportations vers Exportations en provence de ↓
											Metaux non ferreux (CTCI, Rev. 3, 68) [suite]
0	18	2	0	2	0	11	19	...	0	2000	Afrique du Nord
2	138	42	3	36	13	4	230	...	4	2013	
11	133	56	3	27	17	9	200	...	0	2014	
8	105	31	1	24	8	2	157	...	3	2015	
5	88	29	1	27	3	2	143	...	2	2016	
0	1	174	82	425	10	145	71	0	0	2000	Afrique subsaharienne
0	27	899	98	4979	377	515	1253	14	1	2013	
0	29	992	47	4704	213	768	1446	0	0	2014	
3	28	826	103	4864	255	800	905	4	0	2015	
2	16	721	66	4572	121	793	727	3	0	2016	
0	0	40	48	394	9	143	49	0	0	2000	Afrique du sud
0	4	133	93	1386	100	338	166	14	1	2013	
0	5	102	43	1316	52	262	173	...	0	2014	
...	7	76	71	1413	113	177	99	4	0	2015	
0	9	85	61	1320	86	184	186	2	0	2016	
0	7	17	1792	1242	13	58	210	...	23	2000	Amérique latine et Caraïbes
3	11	88	5007	14123	117	452	387	0	3	2013	
6	10	154	4234	13968	102	500	308	0	4	2014	
1	48	222	3358	12279	60	377	247	0	1	2015	
9	34	170	2943	11125	75	1100	237	0	1	2016	
...	3	10	207	17	6	13	23	...	...	2000	Brésil
0	8	78	615	622	7	3	19	...	...	2013	
0	8	123	532	287	11	20	22	0	...	2014	
0	14	187	488	587	6	11	26	...	...	2015	
9	0	123	568	468	50	42	79	0	...	2016	
2	6	25	68	5432	289	1123	160	1	0	2000	Asie orientale
50	259	1115	1245	16310	2892	9280	1604	15	1	2013	
72	258	1141	1174	16193	4354	10652	1521	17	0	2014	
62	267	1125	1179	13803	3125	10075	1707	19	0	2015	
73	258	933	1105	12777	2909	9515	1333	17	0	2016	
2	2	15	21	1541	32	352	52	0	...	2000	Chine
48	229	1009	1139	5460	1078	5407	1348	7	...	2013	
69	236	1044	1092	6211	1450	6316	1232	10	...	2014	
54	249	1013	1100	4959	1443	5993	1359	11	...	2015	
53	236	857	1024	4412	1258	5450	1050	11	...	2016	
0	3	10	1	97	55	126	104	0	0	2000	Asie méridionale
33	32	207	330	3177	240	957	1048	0	1	2013	
137	24	137	728	3099	268	931	1225	0	0	2014	
53	10	125	380	2640	293	1548	1161	0	0	2015	
31	9	113	260	1922	293	1187	991	0	1	2016	
1	5	17	5	1015	259	1430	61	1	0	2000	Asie Sud-est
6	45	81	87	5630	1910	6340	395	7	1	2013	
2	35	73	151	4092	1923	6089	428	7	9	2014	
1	37	66	129	5203	1963	4821	437	5	3	2015	
0	37	66	88	3786	1802	4694	680	4	3	2016	
20	68	17	6	424	72	218	488	0	35	2000	Asie occidentale
226	646	175	64	1527	1367	747	3399	0	620	2013	
267	846	239	114	1710	1315	826	3256	6	416	2014	
249	831	167	173	1283	745	1507	2934	0	250	2015	
214	558	228	106	1068	1025	1130	2203	0	164	2016	
...	...	0	...	0	...	...	...	0	0	2000	Océanie
...	...	0	0	4	0	0	0	4	0	2013	
0	...	0	0	8	...	0	0	6	0	2014	
...	...	0	0	0	0	0	...	3	0	2015	
...	...	0	0	0	0	0	0	0	0	2016	

Voir la fin du tableau pour la remarque générale et les notes.

World exports by provenance and destination (Table D)

In million U.S. dollars f.o.b.

Exports to ⟶ ↓ Exports from	Year	Developed economies 2/ Economies développées 2/ World 1/ Monde 1/	 Total	Asia-Pacific Asie-Pacifique Total	 Japan Japon	Europe Total	 Germany Allemagne	North America Amérique du Nord Total	 U.S.A. É.-U.	Commonwealth of Independent States Communauté d'Etats Indépendants Total	 Europe
Other manufactured metal products (SITC, Rev. 3, 691-695, 699 and 812)											
World 1/	2000	117693	88670	4453	3151	57076	12703	27141	19379	1308	992
	2013	356347	221278	18676	10748	150155	33251	52447	40015	15245	11711
	2014	373092	230575	18957	11366	156198	34752	55420	42992	14717	10980
	2015	343728	212175	18391	10669	137836	30005	55948	44303	10260	6875
	2016	332517	211206	16900	10613	140630	30906	53675	42334	9488	6763
Developed Economies - Asia-Pacific 2/	2000	6630	2982	252	23	861	168	1870	1762	8	6
	2013	12824	3927	446	31	1206	260	2275	2159	147	133
	2014	12317	3812	455	31	1165	273	2193	2102	97	87
	2015	10855	3499	387	25	1041	234	2071	1960	100	90
	2016	11165	3666	384	32	1089	251	2194	2102	63	53
Japan	2000	6114	2675	70	.	820	162	1785	1692	8	5
	2013	11524	3359	78	.	1115	244	2166	2062	139	128
	2014	11063	3243	76	.	1076	255	2091	2010	92	84
	2015	9824	3020	73	.	976	221	1971	1868	96	88
	2016	10120	3171	54	.	1018	240	2099	2015	60	52
Developed Economies - Europe 2/	2000	59895	52072	900	547	47121	10410	4051	3602	740	634
	2013	165914	129516	2283	1056	118293	26304	8940	7964	6479	5901
	2014	170857	133989	2332	1218	121918	27290	9739	8663	5872	5276
	2015	145962	115621	1987	1006	104940	23039	8695	7765	3583	3079
	2016	147684	118226	2093	1090	107546	24036	8586	7624	3440	3012
France	2000	6147	5280	64	44	4751	1283	464	384	32	25
	2013	10798	7704	130	61	6896	1774	678	572	171	137
	2014	10965	7851	126	79	6974	1837	751	619	141	111
	2015	9301	6715	114	69	5972	1534	629	534	79	66
	2016	9222	6644	118	78	6013	1538	513	417	84	66
Germany	2000	15167	13206	266	161	11808	.	1132	1036	217	190
	2013	46294	34975	702	354	31232	.	3041	2785	2009	1874
	2014	48087	36657	755	419	32551	.	3351	3063	1793	1658
	2015	41239	32170	607	324	28424	.	3138	2888	1054	957
	2016	41114	32099	613	307	28515	.	2970	2726	1064	979
Developed Economies - North America 2/	2000	20453	13784	580	410	2215	425	10990	4352	32	24
	2013	34242	19254	1312	798	4550	786	13391	4520	275	217
	2014	35660	19819	1471	921	4758	930	13590	4808	302	235
	2015	34341	19125	1539	1053	4568	883	13018	5100	234	182
	2016	33037	18541	1391	974	4563	903	12587	5225	223	182
United States	2000	15763	9224	550	392	2040	402	6635	.	25	18
	2013	28717	14326	1250	770	4209	722	8866	.	231	181
	2014	29825	14590	1403	889	4409	851	8778	.	271	208
	2015	28211	13562	1466	1022	4181	805	7915	.	216	166
	2016	26866	12914	1332	949	4223	830	7359	.	210	171
South-Eastern Europe	2000	356	269	0	0	255	58	14	14	8	5
	2013	3239	2428	7	4	2374	582	48	41	203	185
	2014	3437	2588	7	2	2526	639	56	50	194	166
	2015	3091	2312	4	2	2246	582	62	56	140	122
	2016	3313	2518	4	2	2445	637	69	63	132	121
Commonwealth of Independent States	2000	2115	1624	24	24	1505	639	95	92	360	244
	2013	4276	980	8	4	801	235	171	160	2666	1817
	2014	3938	1024	6	3	863	276	155	151	2431	1554
	2015	3370	851	4	3	687	221	160	157	1846	1030
	2016	2936	816	8	6	658	208	149	147	1541	819
Russian Federation	2000	1780	1527	24	24	1416	626	87	85	147	52
	2013	2265	675	3	2	531	178	141	138	1118	504
	2014	2132	646	3	2	498	146	144	142	1110	433
	2015	1986	551	3	2	398	158	149	148	994	301
	2016	1997	626	8	5	478	165	140	138	965	315

For general note and footnotes see end of table

Exportations mondiales par provenance et destination (Tableau D)

En millions de dollars E.-U. f.o.b.

South-Eastern Europe Europe du Sud-est	Northern Africa Afrique septentrionale	Sub-Saharan Africa Afrique du Nord	Latin America and the Caribbean Amérique latine et Caraïbes	Eastern Asia Asie orientale	Southern Asia Asie méridionale	South-eastern Asia Asie du Sud-est	Western Asia Asie occidentale	Oceania Océanie	Others 4/ Autre 4/	Année	← Exportations vers Exportations en provence de ↓
			Autres produits en metal manufacturés (CTCI, Rev. 3, 691-695, 699 et 812)								
670	936	1609	8330	6598	1048	5166	3042	159	158	2000	Monde 1/
4720	4331	10603	24484	24700	7555	23424	18622	560	826	2013	
5044	4696	12185	24826	26636	8514	25429	19043	531	894	2014	
4532	4725	11226	24220	25303	8010	25094	17120	506	556	2015	
4790	4782	9172	22103	24044	7881	22617	14849	562	1023	2016	
1	14	51	222	1615	165	1420	83	68	0	2000	Economies Développées - Asie-Pacifique 2/
10	18	157	651	3995	346	3188	198	168	19	2013	
9	13	124	694	3970	295	2920	187	170	26	2014	
8	14	119	561	3447	314	2452	189	135	17	2015	
8	20	80	514	3471	305	2637	242	142	16	2016	
1	13	45	218	1585	158	1336	71	5	...	2000	Japon
8	17	61	629	3864	334	2932	172	8	...	2013	
8	11	50	675	3837	285	2697	157	7	...	2014	
6	12	63	545	3326	301	2287	162	4	...	2015	
7	16	31	498	3378	295	2439	215	8	...	2016	
553	663	750	1371	980	321	727	1569	48	101	2000	Economies Développées - Europe 2/
3639	2230	3012	4895	5608	1416	2122	6449	106	442	2013	
3859	2270	3201	4758	6387	1387	2202	6395	105	433	2014	
3401	2022	2883	3954	5463	1295	1978	5522	82	156	2015	
3597	2186	2439	3685	5403	1409	1765	4959	87	490	2016	
15	165	161	120	79	47	52	157	37	0	2000	France
236	513	449	503	449	134	145	420	74	1	2013	
260	508	582	375	479	160	120	407	75	8	2014	
230	477	482	265	395	105	130	358	62	1	2015	
242	485	407	276	347	115	172	383	67	1	2016	
99	77	126	425	362	76	186	378	1	15	2000	Allemagne
909	211	461	1366	2818	437	649	2445	4	9	2013	
1002	225	471	1242	3135	471	638	2443	4	8	2014	
899	179	417	1034	2724	447	555	1753	2	5	2015	
960	201	347	1015	2929	482	519	1473	3	23	2016	
8	52	89	5145	618	52	405	256	9	3	2000	Economies Développées - Amérique du Nord 2/
40	115	469	9562	2022	258	1071	1155	22	0	2013	
49	137	580	10124	2165	261	1032	1180	12	0	2014	
46	93	406	9933	2135	262	919	1175	13	0	2015	
38	98	271	9813	1865	243	917	1001	28	0	2016	
7	50	80	5089	592	51	392	241	8	3	2000	États-Unis
28	97	429	9319	1914	236	1024	1092	21	...	2013	
36	119	535	9869	2068	247	978	1102	11	...	2014	
37	84	378	9657	2043	243	860	1118	12	...	2015	
28	90	240	9534	1770	232	866	955	26	...	2016	
51	4	1	0	1	1	0	17	...	4	2000	Europe du Sud-est
297	83	13	36	10	18	5	143	0	3	2013	
331	89	23	34	19	16	8	134	0	0	2014	
309	87	22	29	21	14	9	148	0	0	2015	
335	77	19	26	23	22	9	151	1	1	2016	
9	4	3	10	47	40	2	17	0	0	2000	Communauté d'Etats Indépendants
61	7	24	30	154	245	28	79	0	0	2013	
57	12	13	24	160	136	19	62	0	0	2014	
41	14	14	49	210	130	12	196	0	6	2015	
36	19	12	45	162	115	19	168	0	5	2016	
3	1	1	8	46	37	2	8	...	0	2000	Fédération de Russie
24	5	16	16	138	199	27	48	0	0	2013	
18	9	4	17	147	125	17	38	0	0	2014	
11	12	4	43	200	113	10	43	0	6	2015	
12	15	12	40	150	109	18	46	0	5	2016	

Voir la fin du tableau pour la remarque générale et les notes.

World exports by provenance and destination (Table D)

In million U.S. dollars f.o.b.

Exports to ⟶ / ↓ Exports from	Year	World 1/ Monde 1/	Developed economies 2/ Economies développées 2/ Total	Asia-Pacific Asie-Pacifique Total	Japan Japon	Europe Total	Germany Allemagne	North America Amérique du Nord Total	U.S.A. É.-U.	Commonwealth of Independent States Communauté d'Etats Indépendants Total	Europe
Other manufactured metal products (SITC, Rev. 3, 691-695, 699 and 812) [cont.]											
Northern Africa	2000	465	411	1	1	408	4	2	1	0	0
	2013	1162	375	0	0	365	15	10	9	8	4
	2014	1050	447	0	0	427	17	20	19	9	8
	2015	982	416	0	0	398	13	17	17	2	1
	2016	897	436	0	0	410	17	26	21	4	2
Sub-Saharan Africa	2000	636	264	49	30	174	15	42	32	0	0
	2013	2210	278	43	19	144	20	91	80	1	0
	2014	2328	356	27	7	214	23	115	106	3	2
	2015	1837	339	77	58	185	18	77	71	2	0
	2016	1752	277	117	94	111	18	48	38	10	9
South Africa	2000	442	172	30	12	104	13	38	29	0	0
	2013	1604	210	40	18	94	17	76	66	1	0
	2014	1607	185	26	6	97	20	62	53	2	2
	2015	1262	182	71	57	78	17	33	28	1	0
	2016	1228	229	114	94	73	16	42	34	10	9
Latin America and the Caribbean	2000	4874	3807	17	7	156	23	3634	3579	0	0
	2013	11455	7860	86	73	1266	106	6508	6352	11	7
	2014	12037	8562	81	68	1355	98	7127	6967	13	10
	2015	12221	9114	89	79	1609	94	7416	7257	9	8
	2016	12074	9152	81	68	1710	102	7361	7196	7	7
Brazil	2000	531	200	12	4	63	9	126	120	0	0
	2013	2436	1373	42	37	1006	50	324	313	4	1
	2014	2483	1485	37	33	1097	37	351	345	3	1
	2015	2579	1697	31	28	1367	37	299	290	1	1
	2016	2610	1743	30	27	1424	39	289	281	1	1
Eastern Asia	2000	16394	10611	1974	1604	3085	668	5553	5130	62	44
	2013	85771	41949	9945	6129	14455	3083	17550	15662	4001	2817
	2014	95219	45367	10339	6635	16169	3383	18859	16862	4169	3013
	2015	98276	47185	10169	6229	16103	3313	20913	18684	3066	1987
	2016	88418	43811	8826	6050	15844	3175	19141	16678	3073	2216
China	2000	5952	3677	780	653	1193	248	1704	1585	33	18
	2013	61571	29054	6599	3960	10357	2085	12099	10710	3397	2314
	2014	68978	31237	6729	4399	11653	2289	12855	11340	3500	2489
	2015	72417	32997	6610	4227	11791	2334	14596	12989	2630	1677
	2016	62899	29486	6211	3998	10609	2143	12667	11338	2479	1782
Southern Asia	2000	894	515	34	9	236	40	245	233	14	3
	2013	6861	3616	189	70	2015	547	1413	1229	112	97
	2014	7200	3543	174	60	2002	545	1368	1232	133	98
	2015	6537	3426	161	54	1824	454	1441	1311	74	50
	2016	6019	3185	161	55	1719	413	1304	1199	69	39
South-Eastern Asia	2000	3185	1309	578	468	382	96	349	317	6	2
	2013	16350	6900	4199	2503	1507	454	1195	1116	63	53
	2014	16341	6682	3884	2342	1428	331	1371	1266	79	63
	2015	15481	6477	3817	2076	1298	308	1361	1261	47	32
	2016	14914	6397	3618	2108	1375	321	1403	1313	79	66
Western Asia	2000	1787	1015	43	28	676	156	296	262	76	29
	2013	12002	4170	135	62	3180	859	856	723	1278	481
	2014	12650	4356	156	79	3373	945	828	765	1414	467
	2015	10756	3800	146	84	2937	845	717	663	1158	293
	2016	10274	4160	199	134	3154	825	807	727	848	239
Oceania	2000	9	7	2	0	3	2	2	2	0	...
	2013	42	24	23	0	1	0	0	0	0	0
	2014	57	30	27	0	2	0	1	1	0	0
	2015	19	11	10	0	1	0	0	0	0	0
	2016	34	22	18	0	4	0	0	0	0	0

For general note and footnotes see end of table

Exportations mondiales par provenance et destination (Tableau D)

En millions de dollars E.-U. f.o.b.

South-Eastern Europe Europe du Sud-est	Northern Africa Afrique septentrio-nale	Sub-Saharan Africa Afrique du Nord	Latin America and the Caribbean Amérique latine et Caraïbes	Eastern Asia Asie orientale	Southern Asia Asie méridionale	South-eastern Asia Asie du Sud-est	Western Asia Asie occidentale	Oceania Océanie	Others 4/ Autre 4/	Année	← Exportations vers Exportations en provence de ↓
											Autres produits en metal manufacturés (CTCI, Rev. 3, 691-695, 699 et 812) [suite]
0	18	11	7	1	0	0	13	0	3	2000	Afrique du Nord
6	256	166	3	1	2	1	330	0	14	2013	
6	250	137	2	2	2	2	183	0	10	2014	
7	190	138	1	2	4	2	213	0	8	2015	
6	183	124	2	2	1	3	125	0	11	2016	
0	1	306	17	14	5	13	14	0	1	2000	Afrique subsaharienne
5	2	1672	43	80	10	36	72	0	10	2013	
7	3	1629	33	71	39	27	153	0	7	2014	
7	4	1264	25	54	47	37	49	1	9	2015	
2	2	1287	27	42	16	44	34	1	10	2016	
0	1	211	16	11	5	12	11	0	1	2000	Afrique du sud
0	1	1262	41	16	7	30	30	0	4	2013	
1	2	1287	28	44	6	24	24	0	5	2014	
2	1	950	24	35	6	36	25	0	2	2015	
2	1	844	25	32	8	42	30	1	4	2016	
0	4	18	1000	7	10	12	12	1	2	2000	Amérique latine et Caraïbes
6	6	96	3143	122	20	131	29	2	29	2013	
6	6	104	3017	127	23	112	37	2	28	2014	
6	5	76	2718	126	26	87	29	2	23	2015	
11	3	70	2504	165	22	84	28	2	25	2016	
0	2	14	294	4	2	4	10	1	...	2000	Brésil
3	5	65	811	47	11	102	13	2	...	2013	
4	4	67	750	55	16	81	15	2	...	2014	
5	2	60	657	65	14	62	13	2	...	2015	
10	2	54	608	101	14	60	15	2	...	2016	
11	89	243	482	2909	269	1232	467	18	0	2000	Asie orientale
252	933	3434	5207	10724	3726	10331	5043	164	6	2013	
289	1226	4537	5212	11517	4631	12584	5524	160	3	2014	
272	1531	4750	5980	11868	4312	13551	5561	195	4	2015	
264	1533	3476	4725	10937	4154	11646	4573	222	4	2016	
7	57	146	195	1095	108	387	242	4	...	2000	Chine
204	802	3209	4044	6136	3041	7724	3819	140	...	2013	
227	1056	3993	4124	6579	3935	9857	4328	141	...	2014	
211	1280	4509	4933	7067	3620	10612	4383	175	...	2015	
210	1325	3346	3727	6350	3496	8877	3422	182	...	2016	
1	17	51	20	27	41	57	149	0	0	2000	Asie méridionale
17	94	639	257	128	295	368	1318	6	9	2013	
25	100	778	299	137	341	380	1452	10	3	2014	
21	121	634	402	123	285	365	1078	5	3	2015	
20	75	605	295	122	330	322	985	9	4	2016	
2	13	37	26	346	81	1284	68	13	0	2000	Asie Sud-est
10	38	342	432	1648	512	5974	344	81	6	2013	
16	47	343	443	1748	604	5962	348	62	7	2014	
16	72	280	388	1608	597	5522	358	65	52	2015	
17	82	233	334	1606	628	5046	419	63	11	2016	
34	56	49	28	34	64	14	375	...	42	2000	Asie occidentale
377	550	579	224	208	707	159	3461	3	286	2013	
390	545	717	186	333	780	169	3382	1	377	2014	
399	572	640	179	246	724	159	2601	2	277	2015	
457	506	556	133	243	636	125	2165	0	445	2016	
...	...	0	0	0	0	0	...	2	0	2000	Océanie
0	...	0	0	1	0	9	0	7	0	2013	
0	0	0	0	1	0	13	5	8	0	2014	
0	...	0	0	1	0	0	0	6	1	2015	
0	0	0	0	3	0	2	0	7	0	2016	

Voir la fin du tableau pour la remarque générale et les notes.

World exports by provenance and destination (Table D)

In million U.S. dollars f.o.b.

Exports to ⟶ / ↓ Exports from	Year	World 1/ Monde 1/	Developed economies 2/ Economies développées 2/ Total	Asia-Pacific Asie-Pacifique Total	Japan Japon	Europe Total	Germany Allemagne	North America Amérique du Nord Total	U.S.A. É.-U.	Commonwealth of Independent States Communauté d'Etats Indépendants Total	Europe
Clothing (SITC, Rev. 3, 84)											
World 1/	2000	202158	161951	20949	18560	83556	20003	57446	53890	3217	2847
	2013	471327	335412	39678	32192	196871	40012	98863	89306	26397	19214
	2014	485709	344590	37131	29257	207358	40738	100101	90862	25671	18511
	2015	470371	338160	35222	26962	195829	38266	107110	97522	16970	12647
	2016	454199	330930	33930	26214	195624	38728	101376	92152	18041	12370
Developed Economies - Asia-Pacific 2/	2000	846	450	169	7	138	26	142	136	1	1
	2013	944	563	343	5	127	22	93	85	4	4
	2014	985	607	370	3	135	22	102	93	4	3
	2015	941	564	313	3	131	20	120	110	3	3
	2016	1033	591	286	3	183	25	122	110	7	7
Japan	2000	534	222	5	.	119	21	98	92	1	0
	2013	487	178	9	.	100	19	69	63	3	3
	2014	502	189	9	.	109	19	71	64	3	3
	2015	498	191	8	.	104	17	79	72	2	2
	2016	602	229	11	.	134	22	85	75	7	7
Developed Economies - Europe 2/	2000	53018	47098	1561	1442	42397	9608	3139	2881	993	955
	2013	116867	96118	2437	1926	89573	15940	4107	3549	6679	6100
	2014	124790	103457	2437	1890	96476	17341	4544	3937	5868	5281
	2015	110680	92687	2242	1661	85818	15510	4626	4020	3530	3084
	2016	115149	97302	2216	1672	90556	17375	4530	3881	3371	3014
France	2000	5303	4353	329	318	3698	610	325	291	66	63
	2013	11181	8683	414	370	7610	1227	658	589	347	293
	2014	11699	9135	407	367	8016	1208	712	636	288	238
	2015	10756	8467	354	306	7395	1097	718	640	162	128
	2016	10978	8841	320	271	7825	1132	696	615	148	125
Germany	2000	6852	6348	96	80	6043	.	209	166	165	156
	2013	19178	16642	158	72	16210	.	274	185	1465	1360
	2014	20349	17919	142	62	17462	.	314	224	1299	1192
	2015	17382	15646	117	50	15228	.	301	221	755	678
	2016	17634	15993	121	50	15588	.	283	205	699	641
Developed Economies - North America 2/	2000	10724	3688	507	475	428	55	2753	1996	7	5
	2013	7149	4636	488	349	999	129	3149	1008	49	36
	2014	7481	4786	471	324	958	123	3357	1106	49	36
	2015	7544	4706	420	272	959	107	3328	1159	28	17
	2016	7025	4528	392	242	970	98	3166	1054	27	20
United States	2000	8646	1632	493	463	382	50	757	.	5	3
	2013	5858	3421	451	327	832	106	2137	.	39	25
	2014	6108	3489	430	299	810	101	2249	.	42	29
	2015	6128	3365	379	245	820	89	2166	.	24	13
	2016	5708	3283	353	219	820	78	2110	.	24	17
South-Eastern Europe	2000	3689	3635	1	1	3394	1091	240	233	7	6
	2013	6980	6547	9	8	6465	1809	73	64	171	169
	2014	7329	6922	12	10	6836	1854	73	65	146	143
	2015	6145	5826	14	11	5743	1534	69	60	88	86
	2016	6391	6009	12	9	5929	1585	68	58	108	106
Commonwealth of Independent States	2000	1068	887	0	0	700	318	187	183	131	123
	2013	2453	855	0	0	849	245	5	4	1459	1151
	2014	2620	907	0	0	902	255	5	3	1557	1179
	2015	2156	767	1	0	761	206	5	3	1243	958
	2016	2008	415	0	0	410	64	5	3	1471	1194
Russian Federation	2000	234	208	0	0	140	53	68	68	10	4
	2013	337	78	0	0	76	5	2	2	243	106
	2014	406	77	0	0	75	1	2	1	316	136
	2015	321	70	0	0	68	1	2	1	240	97
	2016	310	48	0	0	46	1	2	1	250	127

For general note and footnotes see end of table

Exportations mondiales par provenance et destination (Tableau D)

En millions de dollars E.-U. f.o.b.

South-Eastern Europe Europe du Sud-est	Northern Africa Afrique septentrionale	Sub-Saharan Africa Afrique du Nord	Latin America and the Caribbean Amérique latine et Caraïbes	Eastern Asia Asie orientale	Southern Asia Asie méridionale	South-eastern Asia Asie du Sud-est	Western Asia Asie occidentale	Oceania Océanie	Others 4/ Autre 4/	Année	⟵ Exportations vers Exportations en provence de ↓
				Vêtements (CTCI, Rev. 3, 84)							
1098	1531	1302	11355	13959	310	2317	4813	105	201	2000	Monde 1/
2899	4095	6916	18267	29058	4143	18406	23782	181	1772	2013	
3388	4026	9291	18565	30114	4569	18296	25280	175	1744	2014	
3081	3933	9952	18104	29969	4235	16695	27317	173	1781	2015	
3248	3284	9036	14875	30385	4138	13301	24966	173	1824	2016	
0	1	2	2	336	2	35	6	12	0	2000	Economies Développées - Asie-Pacifique 2/
0	0	7	4	259	1	68	14	23	0	2013	
0	0	6	5	261	1	66	14	20	0	2014	
0	0	4	7	268	3	61	12	19	1	2015	
0	0	5	5	323	2	72	9	18	0	2016	
0	1	1	2	280	1	23	4	0	...	2000	Japon
0	0	1	2	241	0	52	8	0	...	2013	
0	0	2	3	246	0	50	9	0	...	2014	
0	0	1	2	251	0	44	6	0	...	2015	
0	0	1	2	304	1	55	4	0	...	2016	
924	842	128	436	1050	45	143	1296	32	32	2000	Economies Développées - Europe 2/
1945	810	409	1203	4587	155	687	4209	46	20	2013	
2167	898	454	1224	5308	166	736	4442	47	21	2014	
1918	805	350	1204	5320	161	701	3948	41	15	2015	
2251	799	286	1230	5241	187	738	3685	37	21	2016	
101	194	41	48	235	2	29	214	21	0	2000	France
75	237	111	70	963	13	129	509	43	2	2013	
69	243	115	66	1056	13	138	526	44	4	2014	
57	224	84	59	1043	12	149	460	38	1	2015	
61	208	86	61	931	11	187	409	34	0	2016	
64	35	9	20	83	4	15	96	0	12	2000	Allemagne
212	43	43	75	322	15	52	306	1	3	2013	
239	46	43	72	334	14	51	328	1	3	2014	
203	37	32	65	310	12	39	279	1	2	2015	
224	39	27	63	283	14	36	249	1	4	2016	
2	6	10	6800	89	6	46	65	3	1	2000	Economies Développées - Amérique du Nord 2/
4	7	45	1674	332	18	86	293	5	...	2013	
4	11	48	1828	338	19	76	315	6	...	2014	
3	10	37	1952	358	26	66	352	6	...	2015	
3	7	28	1668	327	31	62	337	6	0	2016	
2	6	9	6794	84	5	45	58	3	1	2000	États-Unis
3	6	44	1658	311	17	81	274	5	...	2013	
4	11	45	1814	315	18	71	293	6	...	2014	
2	8	35	1938	337	25	59	329	5	...	2015	
3	7	26	1656	301	29	57	317	6	...	2016	
33	0	0	1	1	0	0	13	...	1	2000	Europe du Sud-est
164	11	1	2	15	1	3	63	0	0	2013	
173	3	3	3	22	1	3	52	0	0	2014	
153	5	2	3	23	1	3	42	0	0	2015	
193	0	1	3	20	1	2	53	0	0	2016	
1	0	0	5	14	0	1	29	0	0	2000	Communauté d'Etats Indépendants
47	2	0	9	2	3	1	72	0	2	2013	
51	1	0	1	2	1	3	92	...	5	2014	
45	0	1	1	3	5	1	89	0	3	2015	
27	1	0	1	4	4	1	81	0	2	2016	
0	0	0	0	14	0	1	1	...	0	2000	Fédération de Russie
0	1	0	8	1	1	0	3	...	1	2013	
0	0	0	0	1	1	2	5	...	3	2014	
0	0	0	0	1	4	0	4	...	1	2015	
0	1	0	0	3	4	1	2	0	1	2016	

Voir la fin du tableau pour la remarque générale et les notes.

World exports by provenance and destination (Table D)

In million U.S. dollars f.o.b.

Exports to ⟶ / ↓ Exports from	Year	World 1/ Monde 1/	Developed economies 2/ Economies développées 2/ Total	Asia-Pacific Asie-Pacifique Total	Japan Japon	Europe Total	Germany Allemagne	North America Amérique du Nord Total	U.S.A. É.-U.	Commonwealth of Independent States Communauté d'Etats Indépendants Total	Europe
						Clothing (SITC, Rev. 3, 84) [cont.]					
Northern Africa	2000	4942	4857	4	4	4579	640	274	268	0	0
	2013	7322	7006	8	5	6235	646	762	747	7	6
	2014	7372	7091	8	5	6339	558	743	726	7	7
	2015	6322	6051	7	4	5224	433	820	802	2	2
	2016	6332	6062	7	3	5449	426	606	593	4	4
Sub-Saharan Africa	2000	2004	1815	6	4	945	73	864	851	0	0
	2013	2692	1719	17	3	731	103	971	951	1	1
	2014	2885	1902	20	4	842	110	1040	1016	4	1
	2015	2502	1623	22	1	745	138	856	834	0	0
	2016	2535	1649	23	2	712	126	914	894	1	1
South Africa	2000	218	181	2	1	62	2	117	117	0	0
	2013	503	23	3	0	14	1	7	6	0	0
	2014	496	24	3	0	15	1	7	7	1	0
	2015	411	29	4	0	12	3	12	10	0	0
	2016	414	26	4	0	12	1	9	9	0	0
Latin America and the Caribbean	2000	11261	10396	49	11	203	56	10144	10088	1	1
	2013	15390	11202	65	36	315	62	10822	10643	4	3
	2014	15478	11654	61	32	337	63	11257	11080	4	2
	2015	14555	11385	56	32	316	56	11013	10865	3	1
	2016	13140	10343	59	31	303	59	9982	9843	2	1
Brazil	2000	282	140	4	4	35	12	101	99	...	...
	2013	163	47	9	5	13	1	25	24	1	1
	2014	159	51	8	3	17	1	25	24	0	0
	2015	140	46	6	3	17	1	23	22	0	0
	2016	132	45	5	2	16	1	24	23	1	0
Eastern Asia	2000	70341	50636	16462	14772	13827	2997	20347	18846	1325	1171
	2013	202658	120665	29544	24343	47366	9920	43756	39777	16081	10343
	2014	210577	125402	27242	21690	52764	10380	45396	41598	16144	10609
	2015	196286	118368	24438	18990	46956	8666	46974	43341	10524	7414
	2016	176939	107181	22554	17667	41821	7272	42806	39547	11487	6923
China	2000	36071	22838	12571	11513	4943	923	5324	4780	1230	1087
	2013	177435	101429	26549	22107	40700	8292	34180	30989	15856	10133
	2014	186613	107610	24522	19705	46505	8886	36582	33471	15951	10431
	2015	174573	102626	22069	17297	41777	7463	38781	35773	10417	7320
	2016	158180	93699	20346	16044	37505	6301	35847	33095	11410	6856
Southern Asia	2000	15372	13550	264	167	6094	1367	7192	6746	417	283
	2013	45667	38170	1426	773	23554	5591	13190	11874	480	294
	2014	37463	30060	945	500	18950	3955	10165	9330	541	267
	2015	54759	44651	1896	953	27914	6393	14842	13420	462	351
	2016	53363	43524	1860	930	27245	6226	14420	13060	384	349
South-Eastern Asia	2000	18848	16435	1456	1312	5126	1191	9853	9428	63	60
	2013	42576	34552	5222	4710	8959	2332	20371	19135	378	350
	2014	46492	37366	5439	4766	10215	2651	21713	20303	350	340
	2015	47952	38681	5702	5009	10334	2450	22645	21200	254	243
	2016	50257	40622	6410	5626	11269	2724	22942	21408	296	286
Western Asia	2000	8975	7728	15	10	5471	2581	2242	2168	272	242
	2013	19446	13324	64	33	11695	3213	1565	1469	1083	758
	2014	21016	14380	72	34	12601	3424	1706	1604	998	643
	2015	19279	12801	63	26	10926	2753	1812	1707	834	489
	2016	18749	12657	66	29	10775	2747	1815	1702	883	467
Oceania	2000	1071	777	456	354	254	1	67	67	0	0
	2013	1186	56	54	0	2	0	0	0	0	0
	2014	1222	56	53	0	3	1	0	0	0	0
	2015	1248	51	49	0	2	0	0	0	0	0
	2016	1279	46	43	0	3	0	0	0	0	0

For general note and footnotes see end of table

Exportations mondiales par provenance et destination (Tableau D)

En millions de dollars E.-U. f.o.b.

South-Eastern Europe Europe du Sud-est	Northern Africa Afrique septentrio-nale	Sub-Saharan Africa Afrique du Nord	Latin America and the Caribbean Amérique latine et Caraïbes	Eastern Asia Asie orientale	Southern Asia Asie méridionale	South-eastern Asia Asie du Sud-est	Western Asia Asie occidentale	Oceania Océanie	Others 4/ Autre 4/	Année	⟵ Exportations vers Exportations en provenance de ↓
				Vêtements (CTCI, Rev. 3, 84) [suite]							
0	10	19	1	1	0	0	13	0	40	2000	Afrique du Nord
1	27	21	11	17	0	2	216	0	15	2013	
6	23	18	8	15	1	2	187	0	14	2014	
11	25	17	11	16	1	3	180	0	6	2015	
1	41	14	9	14	2	2	172	1	10	2016	
0	0	167	6	4	1	1	8	0	3	2000	Afrique subsaharienne
2	0	925	11	7	3	2	21	0	1	2013	
2	2	925	15	9	3	2	20	0	1	2014	
2	0	824	12	10	3	4	23	0	1	2015	
0	1	833	15	12	2	6	14	0	1	2016	
0	0	26	3	1	0	0	7	0	0	2000	Afrique du sud
0	0	462	1	1	0	1	14	0	0	2013	
0	2	457	0	2	1	0	8	0	1	2014	
0	0	367	0	2	0	0	12	0	0	2015	
0	1	376	5	1	0	0	5	0	0	2016	
0	0	2	830	6	0	1	8	0	18	2000	Amérique latine et Caraïbes
0	0	17	3750	40	1	10	21	0	344	2013	
0	1	14	3392	44	1	13	23	0	331	2014	
0	0	9	2748	47	1	14	25	0	324	2015	
1	0	5	2391	40	10	17	18	0	311	2016	
0	0	1	139	0	0	0	1	0	...	2000	Brésil
0	0	14	96	0	0	1	3	0	...	2013	
0	0	11	92	1	0	1	3	0	...	2014	
0	0	7	82	1	0	1	4	0	...	2015	
0	0	3	78	1	0	0	4	0	...	2016	
83	388	530	2581	11821	126	1385	1431	27	8	2000	Asie orientale
239	2466	4307	9313	19255	3240	15658	11373	61	1	2013	
251	2195	6503	9856	18886	3613	15453	12218	54	1	2014	
199	2311	7371	9802	17897	2993	13724	13034	64	0	2015	
175	1744	6583	7414	17902	2529	10345	11512	65	2	2016	
81	277	287	1316	8384	52	611	991	5	...	2000	Chine
233	2444	4189	8882	16201	3090	14206	10869	35	...	2013	
242	2172	6394	9471	15667	3465	13932	11676	32	...	2014	
193	2300	7286	9442	14675	2823	12227	12534	49	...	2015	
172	1732	6516	7139	15066	2370	8950	11074	51	...	2016	
3	9	129	157	84	48	85	882	6	1	2000	Asie méridionale
26	60	738	1152	712	355	416	3536	10	13	2013	
21	50	812	976	590	323	411	3650	10	20	2014	
50	43	859	1162	1074	527	587	5262	11	70	2015	
36	33	811	1023	1052	565	528	5340	10	57	2016	
8	51	241	262	515	45	611	593	22	4	2000	Asie Sud-est
17	80	233	1097	3714	162	1445	841	28	30	2013	
19	82	256	1216	4496	187	1491	974	29	27	2014	
16	76	250	1142	4844	180	1496	964	26	23	2015	
17	62	228	1067	5288	201	1482	935	27	32	2016	
43	225	74	8	19	37	7	470	0	93	2000	Asie occidentale
454	633	214	41	117	204	30	3124	0	223	2013	
693	759	252	38	142	253	39	3293	0	169	2014	
686	656	227	60	110	335	37	3386	0	148	2015	
542	596	242	47	162	603	46	2809	0	163	2016	
...	...	0	266	21	0	3	0	3	1	2000	Océanie
0	0	0	0	0	0	0	0	8	1121	2013	
0	...	0	0	1	0	0	0	9	1155	2014	
0	0	0	0	0	0	0	0	7	1189	2015	
0	0	0	0	0	0	0	0	8	1225	2016	

Voir la fin du tableau pour la remarque générale et les notes.

World exports by provenance and destination (Table D)

General Note

Table D is based on data of UN Comtrade as of mid November 2017. An earlier version of this table has been published in Volume I of the 2016 ITSY which has been produced earlier this year. The totals of imports and exports presented in table A and D are not necessarily identical as table A is mainly based on the data of the IMF's International Financial Statistics (IFS) which is a different data collection system with different aims, procedures, timetable and sources for update and maintenance than UN Comtrade (see the introduction for details). Nevertheless, discrepancies between both tables are in general minor and usually do not affect the overall information provided. A systematic comparison of the figures from both sources (which includes the description of known and relevant conceptual differences) is available at http://unstats.un.org/unsd/trade/data/tables.asp#annual.

Overall, the discrepancies in the world total or world aggregate of exports in table A and table D is around 1.0 percent for all years shown, which is minor, given the differences between the two sources. For further information on sources and presentation of table D as well as for a brief table description please see the introduction.

1/ Exports for which country of destination is not available are included in the totals for the 'World' and in region “Others” (see footnote number 4 for further explanation).

2/ This classification is intended for statistical convenience and does not, necessarily, express a judgment about the stage reached by a particular country in the development process.

3/ Section 9 of the SITC, which comprises commodities and transactions not classified elsewhere, is included in the total trade but is not shown.

4/ The region "Others" as destination for exports contains the following trading partners: Antarctica, bunkers, free zones, confidential and not elsewhere specified countries

Exportations mondiales par provenance et destination (Tableau D)

Remarque générale

Tableau D est basée sur les données de UN Comtrade telles que disponible mi-novembre 2017. Une version antérieure de cette table est publiée dans le volume I de l'annuaire 2016 ITSY qui a été produit plus tôt cette année. Les importations et exportations totales présentées dans les tableaux A et D ne sont pas nécessairement identiques du fait que le tableau A est basé principalement sur les données des Statistiques Financières Internationales (IFS) du FMI qui est un différent système de collecte des données avec des objectifs, des procédures, un calendrier et des sources de mise à jour et de maintenance différents de ceux de UN Comtrade sur lequel le tableau D est basé (voir l'introduction pour les détails). Toutefois, les écarts entre les deux tableaux sont en général mineurs et n'affectent pas substantiellement l'information fournie. Une comparaison systématique des données de ces deux sources (incluant une description des différences conceptuelles pertinentes connues) est disponible à http://unstats.un.org/unsd/trade/data/tables.asp#annual.

En général, la différence entre les totaux des exportations mondiales présentés dans les tableaux A et D est d'environ 1.0 pour cent pur chacune des années publiées, ce qui est mineur étant donné les différences entre les deux sources. Pour plus d'information sur les sources et la présentation du tableau D ainsi qu'une brève description, se il vous plaît se référer à l'introduction.

1/ Exportations dont les pays de destination n'est pas disponible sont incluses dansles totaux pour le 'Monde' et dans la région "les autres " (voir note n ° 4 pour plus d'explications)
2/ Cette classification est utilisée pour plus de commodité dans la présentation des statistiques et n'implique pas nécessairement un jugement quant au stade de développement auquel est parvenu un pays donné.
3/ Section 9 de la CTCI, qui représente les articles et transactions non classes ailleurs est comprise dans le commerce total mais n'est pas présentée séparément dans ce tableau.
4/ La région "Autres" comme destination des exportations comprend les partenaires commerciaux suivants: Antarctique, combustibles de soute, zones franches, partenaires confidentiels ou non specifiés ailleurs

Growth of world exports by provenance and destination (Table E)

Annual average rate: in per cent

SITC	Commodity classes	Year	World 1/ Monde 1/	Developed economies 2/ Economies développées 2/ Total	Asia-Pacific Asie-Pacifique Total	Japan Japon	Europe Total	Germany Allemagne	North America Amérique du Nord Total	U.S.A. É.-U.	Commonwealth of Independent States Communauté d'Etats Indépendants Total	Europe
	Origin of exports of major commodity classes											
0-9	All commodities 3/	2000/2016	5.9	4.4	2.8	1.9	5.0	5.7	3.5	3.9	6.6	5.9
		2012/2013	2.8	3.2	-7.8	-10.5	5.6	2.9	1.8	2.1	-2.0	-1.8
		2013/2014	-0.1	-0.1	-3.4	-3.5	-0.5	3.3	3.0	2.7	-5.8	-6.4
		2014/2015	-12.5	-11.8	-12.9	-9.5	-12.6	-11.3	-8.8	-7.3	-30.6	-30.4
		2015/2016	-3.9	-0.9	2.5	3.2	-0.5	0.9	-3.7	-3.4	-20.5	-23.5
0&1	Food, live animals, beverages and tobacco	2000/2016	7.3	6.2	6.2	6.3	6.5	7.6	5.4	5.4	13.8	13.3
		2012/2013	6.9	8.4	3.8	0.3	9.3	7.8	6.9	6.8	0.5	0.1
		2013/2014	3.2	2.8	7.3	1.9	1.5	2.0	5.6	4.9	7.3	7.3
		2014/2015	-9.4	-11.4	-9.1	8.9	-12.7	-14.7	-7.7	-8.8	-14.5	-15.3
		2015/2016	0.8	1.2	-3.4	13.0	2.6	1.1	-1.9	-1.5	-23.6	-30.4
2&4	Crude materials, oils and fats, (fuels excluded)	2000/2016	7.0	6.0	9.5	6.2	5.7	5.5	4.8	5.9	5.6	5.2
		2012/2013	-0.5	0.6	9.0	-6.9	0.0	-5.1	-4.8	-6.3	-5.3	-0.5
		2013/2014	-4.6	-3.3	-9.1	-8.7	-2.2	-1.1	0.1	0.0	-2.2	-1.8
		2014/2015	-18.3	-19.8	-29.2	-16.5	-18.0	-19.2	-15.1	-15.5	-20.3	-21.7
		2015/2016	-3.3	-0.9	0.2	-7.0	1.4	-4.0	-1.0	-0.8	-26.5	-32.0
3	Mineral fuels, lubricants and related material	2000/2016	5.0	5.6	8.8	12.0	4.2	6.7	7.4	12.9	6.7	6.1
		2012/2013	-1.7	3.9	-5.4	24.2	4.4	2.1	6.2	8.4	0.0	-0.5
		2013/2014	-7.1	-5.3	-2.7	-5.1	-11.0	-3.8	5.6	4.5	-6.7	-6.9
		2014/2015	-38.3	-33.9	-26.6	-28.1	-33.9	-15.9	-36.1	-33.1	-39.4	-37.7
		2015/2016	-21.9	-17.2	-1.9	-17.6	-21.8	-22.9	-14.1	10.0	-35.0	-37.8
5	Chemicals	2000/2016	7.4	6.5	3.9	3.8	6.9	6.8	5.8	5.8	7.1	5.5
		2012/2013	3.0	4.0	-4.7	-3.9	5.5	4.7	1.1	0.9	-15.5	-16.4
		2013/2014	1.6	1.1	-5.2	-4.9	1.6	3.8	1.3	1.4	-0.9	-1.2
		2014/2015	-9.5	-8.9	-13.0	-12.9	-10.1	-11.5	-2.7	-2.6	-10.2	-15.0
		2015/2016	-2.7	-1.4	2.8	2.3	-0.8	0.6	-4.7	-4.3	-22.3	-26.3
7	Machinery and transport equipment	2000/2016	5.1	3.1	1.0	1.0	4.5	5.6	1.1	1.3	4.4	4.1
		2012/2013	3.5	0.7	-12.7	-13.0	4.3	2.4	-0.4	0.3	-1.9	-1.7
		2013/2014	3.2	2.9	-3.3	-3.4	4.0	3.8	3.4	3.4	-12.4	-14.8
		2014/2015	-5.9	-8.2	-8.3	-8.3	-9.5	-9.5	-4.0	-4.5	-23.5	-17.8
		2015/2016	-1.0	1.2	4.8	5.1	2.0	0.8	-3.4	-4.1	-26.6	-28.5
6&8	Other manufactured goods	2000/2016	5.6	4.0	2.1	2.0	4.6	5.4	3.0	3.6	5.0	3.6
		2012/2013	3.3	2.4	-10.3	-11.4	4.2	2.6	1.8	2.6	-7.5	-3.5
		2013/2014	3.4	2.2	-2.7	-3.0	2.5	2.5	3.3	3.5	-3.8	-4.6
		2014/2015	-8.7	-10.9	-13.1	-12.9	-12.2	-13.2	-4.6	-4.8	-18.9	-21.9
		2015/2016	-3.7	-0.4	-2.5	-2.0	0.4	0.3	-2.5	-2.6	-16.5	-21.6
	Destination of exports of major commodity classes											
0-9	All commodities 3/	2000/2016	5.9	4.3	4.0	3.2	4.7	4.8	3.6	3.7	9.2	8.5
		2012/2013	2.8	1.3	-2.8	-2.4	2.2	2.9	0.7	0.4	1.9	0.1
		2013/2014	-0.1	1.0	-2.1	-2.8	0.5	2.0	3.1	4.4	-11.3	-13.3
		2014/2015	-12.5	-11.6	-15.4	-17.5	-13.2	-12.6	-6.5	-4.5	-34.4	-36.5
		2015/2016	-3.9	-1.8	-3.5	-2.7	-0.9	-0.1	-3.0	-1.4	-5.9	-4.3
0&1	Food, live animals, beverages and tobacco	2000/2016	7.3	6.0	3.2	2.0	6.3	5.8	6.6	6.4	8.3	7.5
		2012/2013	6.9	6.5	-2.5	-5.1	8.3	8.0	5.1	5.5	7.9	7.0
		2013/2014	3.2	2.8	1.5	-0.7	1.6	2.3	7.7	8.9	-8.2	-11.5
		2014/2015	-9.4	-9.3	-11.0	-11.2	-11.5	-12.6	-1.1	-0.4	-31.8	-35.0
		2015/2016	0.8	1.8	1.0	1.0	1.8	2.3	2.1	2.6	-6.3	-2.7
2&4	Crude materials, oils and fats, (fuels excluded)	2000/2016	7.0	4.0	3.6	3.4	4.5	4.7	2.8	2.7	8.0	7.0
		2012/2013	-0.5	-2.9	-1.7	-2.0	-2.3	-2.0	-6.3	-6.4	1.7	3.6
		2013/2014	-4.6	-2.2	-5.7	-5.8	-2.6	-6.7	2.7	2.4	-8.3	-12.2
		2014/2015	-18.3	-18.3	-24.8	-25.6	-17.9	-18.2	-13.9	-14.2	-22.3	-22.7
		2015/2016	-3.3	-4.1	-2.2	-2.8	-4.6	-3.2	-3.4	-2.7	-8.1	-8.8
3	Mineral fuels, lubricants and related material	2000/2016	5.0	2.9	3.7	3.2	3.7	2.4	1.1	1.3	2.7	1.8
		2012/2013	-1.7	-1.6	-2.3	-2.2	0.8	17.0	-6.8	-11.7	-11.1	-15.0
		2013/2014	-7.1	-9.7	-7.7	-8.8	-10.7	-11.7	-8.5	-7.0	-22.6	-21.4
		2014/2015	-38.3	-38.6	-38.3	-39.3	-36.1	-34.5	-44.8	-43.8	-30.4	-33.5
		2015/2016	-21.9	-23.4	-11.5	-9.3	-29.0	-37.8	-15.4	2.1	-48.4	-50.8
5	Chemicals	2000/2016	7.4	6.6	6.1	5.9	6.6	7.1	6.7	7.1	11.6	11.5
		2012/2013	3.0	2.3	-5.4	-5.5	3.8	4.0	0.4	-0.5	7.5	6.7
		2013/2014	1.6	2.2	-2.4	-2.5	2.2	1.3	3.8	4.5	-7.1	-8.3
		2014/2015	-9.5	-8.3	-6.8	-6.9	-11.1	-10.8	0.7	2.7	-25.8	-27.2
		2015/2016	-2.7	-1.6	-0.4	0.6	-1.6	0.1	-2.1	-1.6	-3.9	-3.1
7	Machinery and transport equipment	2000/2016	5.1	3.6	3.7	2.9	3.8	4.7	3.1	3.4	11.1	11.1
		2012/2013	3.5	2.6	-2.5	0.8	3.4	2.0	2.5	3.0	-1.7	-3.6
		2013/2014	3.2	5.7	0.6	2.6	6.1	7.4	6.3	7.2	-13.7	-16.3
		2014/2015	-5.9	-4.5	-6.3	-7.2	-6.8	-8.3	-0.3	0.8	-40.9	-42.5
		2015/2016	-1.0	0.9	-3.1	-2.0	3.2	3.7	-1.7	-1.3	2.2	6.5
6&8	Other manufactured goods	2000/2016	5.6	4.5	4.1	3.2	4.9	4.6	3.9	4.0	10.0	8.8
		2012/2013	3.3	2.6	-1.6	-3.3	3.1	3.1	2.8	3.5	8.0	7.5
		2013/2014	3.4	3.9	0.0	-1.4	3.9	3.5	5.2	6.0	-6.2	-8.4
		2014/2015	-8.7	-6.9	-8.9	-9.6	-9.9	-10.2	0.4	1.6	-33.2	-36.5
		2015/2016	-3.7	-1.5	-3.0	-1.7	-0.1	0.7	-3.9	-3.8	-4.7	-3.7

For general note and footnotes see end of Special Table F.

Croissance des exportations mondiales par provenance et destination (Tableau E)

Taux annuel moyen: en pourcentage

← En provenance ou vers

South-Eastern Europe Europe du Sud-est	Northern Africa Afrique du Nord	Sub-Saharai Africa Afrique subsahari-enne	Latin America and the Caribbean Amérique latine et Caraïbes	Eastern Asia Asie orientale	Southern Asia Asie méridionale	outh-easter Asia Asie du Sud-est	Western Asia Asie occidentale	Oceania Océanie	Others 4/ Autre 4/	Année	CTCI: Classes de marchandises ↓	
Provenance des exportations de grandes catégories de marchandises												
11.8	4.0	6.0	5.9	9.7	9.1	6.4	8.1	5.4	0.0	2000/2016	0-9	Tous produits 3/
14.3	-10.5	-10.6	0.0	6.4	7.8	1.6	1.8	14.0	0.0	2012/2013		
4.1	-16.3	-0.5	-2.3	4.1	-4.9	1.6	-3.9	32.9	0.0	2013/2014		
-12.7	-31.0	-17.0	-14.6	-4.3	-13.9	-10.2	-27.2	-9.1	0.0	2014/2015		
4.8	-8.5	-28.4	-4.7	-5.6	-6.2	-0.9	-8.2	-9.9	0.0	2015/2016		
15.6	9.6	7.9	8.6	9.2	9.6	8.7	8.2	5.9	0.0	2000/2016	0&1	Produits alimentaires, boissons et tabacs
19.3	13.8	-6.2	3.2	5.0	23.0	1.3	11.9	2.6	0.0	2012/2013		
3.5	1.0	2.5	0.6	7.1	-3.2	9.3	6.0	35.4	0.0	2013/2014		
-10.8	-2.6	-0.9	-6.5	-0.1	-12.4	-6.0	-11.7	-42.6	0.0	2014/2015		
4.4	3.7	-6.1	5.8	6.5	-7.2	3.5	-11.3	6.8	0.0	2015/2016		
8.5	6.0	7.8	10.0	5.6	11.0	9.1	8.4	2.2	0.0	2000/2016	2&4	Matières premières huiles & graisses (combust. exclu.)
12.1	-13.2	-9.5	3.5	-1.9	-10.3	-4.0	7.3	22.2	0.0	2012/2013		
-10.2	-11.8	-12.5	-4.9	6.4	-18.1	-8.3	-5.1	30.8	0.0	2013/2014		
-21.6	13.2	-24.3	-15.8	-14.1	-23.4	-11.8	-16.2	-41.1	0.0	2014/2015		
3.2	-22.5	-10.4	-2.3	-6.1	-8.1	-0.4	-5.9	-1.5	0.0	2015/2016		
9.1	0.3	3.7	1.3	8.0	4.9	5.8	4.9	9.8	0.0	2000/2016	3	Combustibles minéraux et produits
9.5	-15.5	-17.1	-6.2	0.6	1.6	-3.0	-0.9	7.2	0.0	2012/2013		
-9.0	-26.4	1.5	-10.3	-3.6	-0.9	-5.3	-9.7	18.0	0.0	2013/2014		
-29.8	-46.8	-18.3	-45.9	-32.0	-44.9	-34.8	-46.6	637.4	0.0	2014/2015		
-10.6	-23.1	-52.2	-32.3	-11.0	-13.3	-17.9	-8.5	-30.9	0.0	2015/2016		
11.9	8.8	8.2	7.0	10.6	14.4	9.9	11.4	15.9	0.0	2000/2016	5	Produits chimiques
7.4	-1.9	-0.6	-1.0	4.9	13.2	-1.5	-2.1	28.0	0.0	2012/2013		
4.6	4.4	-0.5	-3.4	6.3	-5.4	4.5	-0.2	36.9	0.0	2013/2014		
-10.8	-17.2	-17.6	-10.3	-8.3	-0.8	-13.5	-19.3	-76.2	0.0	2014/2015		
3.3	-1.4	3.4	-8.6	-4.3	-8.0	-0.8	-9.3	19.8	0.0	2015/2016		
18.4	14.2	8.9	5.4	10.7	17.0	4.8	10.7	3.2	0.0	2000/2016	7	Machines et matériels de transports
22.9	12.6	8.1	6.0	6.8	15.0	4.6	15.8	11.1	0.0	2012/2013		
7.3	20.5	1.7	2.0	4.0	5.6	2.7	4.8	46.1	0.0	2013/2014		
-8.4	-9.2	-18.7	-1.0	-1.1	-10.0	-1.5	-29.6	-65.5	0.0	2014/2015		
10.0	6.8	-12.8	-1.4	-4.4	-0.5	-0.3	-5.7	38.1	0.0	2015/2016		
8.5	4.4	6.1	4.5	8.3	8.6	7.4	8.5	1.9	0.0	2000/2016	6&8	Articles manufacturés divers
7.7	1.1	4.0	-1.6	5.1	7.5	5.9	5.0	12.0	0.0	2012/2013		
4.6	-2.1	6.0	2.4	6.6	-7.6	6.4	4.6	33.6	0.0	2013/2014		
-11.6	-12.4	-17.1	-7.9	-5.7	3.9	-3.6	-13.6	-56.9	0.0	2014/2015		
3.0	-2.2	-7.0	-4.8	-9.2	-0.3	1.3	-3.5	5.6	0.0	2015/2016		
Destination des exportations de grandes catégories de marchandises												
10.7	7.9	9.3	5.8	8.7	12.2	7.4	9.2	9.6	12.3	2000/2016	0-9	Tous produits 3/
2.6	2.6	4.7	-1.3	7.2	-4.5	4.9	8.6	2.9	13.7	2012/2013		
6.6	1.6	1.4	-1.7	-3.0	2.4	0.9	1.7	3.8	10.1	2013/2014		
-11.4	-17.7	-15.6	-11.8	-15.0	-10.7	-9.9	-12.0	-5.8	17.4	2014/2015		
3.4	-4.9	-13.7	-9.5	-6.3	-0.7	-1.3	-8.7	-3.3	-16.6	2015/2016		
11.2	7.6	10.0	7.2	10.9	11.1	11.5	8.8	7.4	5.1	2000/2016	0&1	Produits alimentaires, boissons et tabacs
6.0	-2.2	5.1	1.4	12.7	5.2	10.0	10.0	-1.5	8.5	2012/2013		
4.3	8.6	-2.1	2.9	8.3	8.4	7.7	3.4	3.1	4.0	2013/2014		
-9.2	-17.3	-14.3	-11.6	-1.7	-4.4	-3.5	-7.7	-6.8	1.3	2014/2015		
3.9	-10.1	-6.3	-1.1	6.9	-1.6	4.7	-7.4	-1.6	-5.0	2015/2016		
10.8	7.2	8.0	5.6	12.6	11.3	8.8	8.8	7.5	-1.0	2000/2016	2&4	Matières premières huiles & graisses (combust. exclu.)
3.6	-6.1	-0.9	-6.8	5.8	-12.8	-5.6	-2.6	-4.4	53.9	2012/2013		
-4.0	0.4	0.4	0.6	-10.4	5.5	1.1	0.4	8.7	-36.9	2013/2014		
-16.7	-24.1	-20.0	-15.1	-21.3	-6.7	-11.6	-17.7	-10.3	59.3	2014/2015		
-6.3	-7.5	-6.6	-7.3	-0.1	-4.5	2.9	-14.8	0.1	-21.5	2015/2016		
6.4	7.2	11.8	5.6	7.8	13.3	10.2	8.7	1.8	-1.4	2000/2016	3	Combustibles minéraux et produits
-24.4	-0.5	1.6	-11.5	-0.1	-5.4	2.4	1.4	-19.9	15.9	2012/2013		
-3.7	-12.3	3.2	0.3	-6.1	-2.3	-0.5	5.0	-1.7	-12.8	2013/2014		
-22.2	-39.3	-29.4	-35.2	-40.4	-34.0	-38.2	-41.4	-34.5	-40.5	2014/2015		
-31.1	-17.3	-23.1	-23.8	-26.5	3.1	1.3	-13.2	-26.3	-56.0	2015/2016		
12.7	9.4	9.8	7.5	8.1	12.2	8.8	9.5	7.1	-4.9	2000/2016	5	Produits chimiques
9.4	7.8	9.9	2.3	2.7	-1.6	3.7	8.8	0.4	6.6	2012/2013		
2.1	3.2	1.8	0.2	-0.9	8.0	3.5	2.5	0.9	-6.6	2013/2014		
-11.3	-11.3	-9.5	-9.0	-11.7	-4.7	-9.4	-12.3	-13.5	-10.9	2014/2015		
5.1	-4.7	-8.1	-8.9	-2.3	-5.0	-0.5	-7.3	-0.7	-17.1	2015/2016		
12.1	7.5	7.6	5.2	9.1	11.7	5.1	8.8	15.0	2.0	2000/2016	7	Machines et matériels de transports
9.9	3.6	7.9	2.9	7.5	-3.7	0.5	7.1	18.2	25.9	2012/2013		
10.7	6.7	-2.1	-4.7	2.0	9.0	1.2	5.0	6.6	26.4	2013/2014		
-7.5	-15.2	-15.6	-6.8	-3.7	-1.8	-3.0	-7.8	8.6	-32.9	2014/2015		
7.7	-0.6	-14.3	-6.3	-2.3	5.2	-1.3	-9.5	0.9	-19.2	2015/2016		
9.6	7.8	10.1	5.4	6.5	11.8	9.1	9.2	4.1	3.2	2000/2016	6&8	Articles manufacturés divers
6.5	5.4	6.1	-1.1	2.9	5.0	9.2	4.3	-13.2	14.7	2012/2013		
10.6	5.7	8.5	0.5	2.1	7.2	4.7	3.3	-3.5	10.2	2013/2014		
-11.2	-6.9	-7.6	-6.1	-13.0	-7.7	-5.5	-8.4	-5.8	-21.7	2014/2015		
7.6	-11.0	-15.7	-10.3	-6.3	-0.1	-4.9	-8.8	2.1	-7.7	2015/2016		

Voir la fin du Tableau Spécial F pour la remarque générale et les notes.

Structure of world exports by provenance and destination (Table F)

in per cent

Origin or destination ⟶				Developed economies 2/ Economies développées 2/							Commonwealth of Independent States Communauté d'Etats Indépendants	
					Asia-Pacific Asie-Pacifique		Europe		North America Amérique du Nord			
↓ SITC Commodity classes		Year	World 1/ Monde 1/	Total	Total	Japan Japon	Total	Germany Allemagne	Total	U.S.A. É.-U.	Total	Europe
Origin of exports of major commodity classes												
0-9	All commodities 3/	2000	100.0	65.1	8.7	7.5	39.7	8.6	16.6	12.3	2.2	2.0
		2013	100.0	50.2	5.3	3.8	34.1	7.7	10.8	8.4	4.1	3.3
		2014	100.0	50.2	5.2	3.7	33.9	8.0	11.1	8.6	3.8	3.1
		2015	100.0	50.6	5.1	3.8	33.9	8.1	11.6	9.1	3.0	2.5
		2016	100.0	52.2	5.5	4.1	35.1	8.5	11.6	9.2	2.5	2.0
0&1	Food, live animals, beverages and tobacco	2000	100.0	67.4	5.1	0.5	46.0	5.6	16.3	12.0	0.8	0.7
		2013	100.0	59.0	4.3	0.4	42.6	6.4	12.0	9.1	2.9	2.5
		2014	100.0	58.8	4.5	0.3	41.9	6.3	12.3	9.2	3.1	2.6
		2015	100.0	57.5	4.5	0.4	40.4	5.9	12.6	9.3	2.9	2.4
		2016	100.0	57.7	4.3	0.5	41.1	5.9	12.2	9.1	2.2	1.7
2&4	Crude materials, oils and fats, (fuels excluded)	2000	100.0	61.5	8.1	1.6	28.6	4.3	24.8	14.2	4.3	3.4
		2013	100.0	51.7	13.6	1.5	22.1	3.4	15.9	10.7	4.6	3.7
		2014	100.0	52.4	13.0	1.4	22.7	3.5	16.7	11.2	4.7	3.8
		2015	100.0	51.4	11.2	1.5	22.8	3.4	17.4	11.6	4.6	3.6
		2016	100.0	52.6	11.7	1.4	23.2	3.4	17.8	11.9	3.5	2.5
3	Mineral fuels, lubricants and related material	2000	100.0	29.5	2.3	0.2	19.7	1.2	7.5	2.0	9.5	8.2
		2013	100.0	27.8	2.6	0.5	17.0	1.1	8.3	4.6	14.8	11.9
		2014	100.0	28.4	2.7	0.5	16.3	1.1	9.4	5.2	14.9	12.0
		2015	100.0	30.4	3.2	0.6	17.4	1.5	9.8	5.6	14.6	12.1
		2016	100.0	32.2	4.0	0.6	17.5	1.5	10.7	6.5	12.2	9.6
5	Chemicals	2000	100.0	79.7	6.9	6.2	56.1	12.3	16.7	14.1	1.5	1.5
		2013	100.0	68.7	4.3	3.8	51.9	11.0	12.5	10.6	1.9	1.6
		2014	100.0	68.4	4.0	3.6	51.9	11.2	12.5	10.6	1.8	1.6
		2015	100.0	68.9	3.9	3.5	51.6	11.0	13.4	11.4	1.8	1.5
		2016	100.0	69.8	4.1	3.6	52.6	11.4	13.1	11.2	1.4	1.1
7	Machinery and transport equipment	2000	100.0	71.8	12.9	12.6	38.9	10.4	20.0	15.8	0.4	0.4
		2013	100.0	53.2	7.1	6.8	35.4	11.3	10.7	8.8	0.7	0.6
		2014	100.0	53.0	6.6	6.4	35.7	11.4	10.7	8.8	0.6	0.5
		2015	100.0	51.7	6.5	6.2	34.3	10.9	10.9	8.9	0.5	0.5
		2016	100.0	52.9	6.8	6.6	35.3	11.1	10.7	8.7	0.4	0.3
6&8	Other manufactured goods	2000	100.0	61.1	6.2	5.5	41.2	7.8	13.6	10.1	1.9	1.8
		2013	100.0	47.9	4.0	3.5	35.3	7.6	8.6	6.9	2.4	2.1
		2014	100.0	47.3	3.8	3.2	35.0	7.6	8.6	6.9	2.2	1.9
		2015	100.0	46.2	3.6	3.1	33.7	7.2	8.9	7.2	2.0	1.6
		2016	100.0	47.8	3.6	3.1	35.1	7.5	9.0	7.3	1.7	1.3
Destination of exports of major commodity classes												
0-9	All commodities 3/	2000	100.0	69.0	6.4	5.1	40.4	7.5	22.2	18.2	1.2	1.0
		2013	100.0	52.3	5.0	3.7	33.1	6.0	14.1	11.3	3.0	2.4
		2014	100.0	52.8	4.9	3.6	33.3	6.1	14.6	11.8	2.7	2.1
		2015	100.0	53.4	4.8	3.4	33.0	6.1	15.6	12.9	2.0	1.5
		2016	100.0	54.5	4.8	3.4	34.0	6.3	15.7	13.2	2.0	1.5
0&1	Food, live animals, beverages and tobacco	2000	100.0	70.1	10.5	9.5	45.3	8.4	14.3	11.4	2.5	2.2
		2013	100.0	57.6	5.8	4.5	40.6	6.9	11.2	8.5	4.7	3.8
		2014	100.0	57.4	5.7	4.4	40.0	6.8	11.7	8.9	4.2	3.3
		2015	100.0	57.4	5.6	4.3	39.1	6.6	12.7	9.8	3.1	2.3
		2016	100.0	58.0	5.6	4.3	39.4	6.7	12.9	10.0	2.9	2.3
2&4	Crude materials, oils and fats, (fuels excluded)	2000	100.0	63.4	10.0	9.3	39.4	7.1	14.0	10.8	1.5	1.4
		2013	100.0	39.5	6.4	5.9	26.6	5.1	6.4	4.9	2.0	1.7
		2014	100.0	40.4	6.3	5.8	27.2	5.0	6.9	5.3	2.0	1.5
		2015	100.0	40.4	5.8	5.3	27.3	5.0	7.3	5.5	1.9	1.4
		2016	100.0	40.1	5.9	5.3	26.9	5.0	7.3	5.6	1.8	1.4
3	Mineral fuels, lubricants and related material	2000	100.0	66.3	9.5	8.6	34.6	4.3	22.2	18.3	1.7	1.5
		2013	100.0	50.8	6.9	5.8	31.2	3.6	12.7	8.7	1.9	1.5
		2014	100.0	49.4	6.9	5.7	30.0	3.4	12.5	8.7	1.6	1.3
		2015	100.0	49.2	6.9	5.6	31.1	3.6	11.2	7.9	1.8	1.4
		2016	100.0	48.2	7.8	6.5	28.3	2.9	12.1	10.4	1.2	0.9
5	Chemicals	2000	100.0	66.4	5.2	3.8	46.1	7.6	15.1	11.7	1.3	1.1
		2013	100.0	57.5	4.2	3.0	41.3	7.2	12.0	9.5	3.2	2.7
		2014	100.0	57.9	4.1	2.8	41.6	7.2	12.2	9.8	3.0	2.5
		2015	100.0	58.7	4.2	2.9	40.9	7.1	13.6	11.2	2.4	2.0
		2016	100.0	59.4	4.3	3.0	41.4	7.3	13.7	11.3	2.4	2.0
7	Machinery and transport equipment	2000	100.0	68.7	5.2	3.9	37.6	7.2	25.9	21.2	0.8	0.6
		2013	100.0	50.9	4.4	2.9	29.0	6.3	17.5	14.5	3.4	2.8
		2014	100.0	52.1	4.3	2.8	29.8	6.6	18.0	15.1	2.8	2.2
		2015	100.0	52.9	4.3	2.8	29.5	6.4	19.1	16.2	1.8	1.4
		2016	100.0	54.0	4.2	2.8	30.8	6.7	19.0	16.1	1.8	1.5
6&8	Other manufactured goods	2000	100.0	70.7	6.4	5.2	41.6	8.4	22.7	19.1	1.2	1.0
		2013	100.0	56.7	5.2	3.7	36.0	7.0	15.5	13.0	3.6	2.7
		2014	100.0	57.0	5.0	3.5	36.2	7.0	15.7	13.3	3.3	2.4
		2015	100.0	58.0	5.0	3.5	35.7	6.9	17.3	14.8	2.4	1.6
		2016	100.0	59.4	5.0	3.5	37.1	7.2	17.3	14.8	2.4	1.6

For general note and footnotes see end of Special Table F.

Structure des exportations mondiales par provenance et destination (Tableau F)

en pourcentage

South-Eastern Europe / Europe du Sud-est	Northern Africa / Afrique du Nord	Sub-Saharan Africa / Afrique subsaharienne	Latin America and the Caribbean / Amérique latine et Caraïbes	Eastern Asia / Asie orientale	Southern Asia / Asie méridionale	South-eastern Asia / Asie du Sud-est	Western Asia / Asie occidentale	Oceania / Océanie	Others 4/ / Autre 4/	Année ← En provenance ou vers	CTCI: Classes de marchandises ↓	
Provenance des exportations de grandes catégories de marchandises												
0.3	0.8	1.5	5.6	12.2	1.4	6.7	4.1	0.1	0.0	2000	0-9	Tous produits 3/
0.7	0.9	2.2	5.9	19.2	2.5	6.7	7.5	0.1	0.0	2013		
0.7	0.8	2.2	5.8	20.0	2.4	6.9	7.2	0.1	0.0	2014		
0.7	0.6	2.1	5.6	21.8	2.4	7.0	6.0	0.1	0.0	2015		
0.7	0.6	1.5	5.6	21.5	2.3	7.3	5.7	0.1	0.0	2016		
0.3	0.6	2.7	12.1	5.4	2.2	6.1	2.2	0.1	0.0	2000	0&1	Produits alimentaires, boissons et tabacs
1.0	0.8	3.0	13.9	6.0	3.7	6.7	2.9	0.1	0.0	2013		
1.0	0.8	3.0	13.5	6.2	3.4	7.1	2.9	0.1	0.0	2014		
1.0	0.8	3.3	14.0	6.9	3.3	7.4	2.9	0.1	0.0	2015		
1.0	0.8	3.0	14.7	7.2	3.1	7.6	2.5	0.1	0.0	2016		
0.8	0.7	3.5	11.8	5.3	1.2	8.5	1.6	0.8	0.0	2000	2&4	Matières premières huiles & graisses (combust. exclu.)
1.1	0.6	5.0	17.5	3.7	2.8	10.7	1.9	0.4	0.0	2013		
1.0	0.5	4.6	17.4	4.2	2.4	10.3	1.9	0.5	0.0	2014		
1.0	0.7	4.3	18.0	4.4	2.3	11.1	2.0	0.4	0.0	2015		
1.0	0.6	4.0	18.1	4.3	2.2	11.5	1.9	0.4	0.0	2016		
0.2	5.1	6.8	9.6	2.9	4.0	6.8	25.4	0.1	0.0	2000	3	Combustibles minéraux et produits
0.3	3.7	6.3	7.3	3.5	3.8	6.8	25.6	0.0	0.0	2013		
0.3	2.9	6.9	7.1	3.6	4.0	6.9	24.9	0.0	0.0	2014		
0.3	2.5	9.1	6.2	4.0	3.6	7.3	21.6	0.2	0.0	2015		
0.4	2.5	5.6	5.4	4.6	4.0	7.7	25.3	0.2	0.0	2016		
0.2	0.4	0.5	2.9	8.1	0.9	3.7	2.0	0.0	0.0	2000	5	Produits chimiques
0.4	0.5	0.6	3.2	12.3	2.5	5.4	4.4	0.0	0.0	2013		
0.4	0.6	0.6	3.0	12.9	2.4	5.6	4.3	0.0	0.0	2014		
0.4	0.5	0.5	3.0	13.1	2.6	5.3	3.8	0.0	0.0	2015		
0.5	0.5	0.6	2.8	12.9	2.4	5.4	3.6	0.0	0.0	2016		
0.1	0.1	0.2	4.7	13.3	0.1	8.6	0.7	0.0	0.0	2000	7	Machines et matériels de transports
0.6	0.2	0.5	4.7	29.4	0.8	7.7	2.2	0.0	0.0	2013		
0.7	0.2	0.5	4.6	29.6	0.8	7.7	2.3	0.0	0.0	2014		
0.6	0.2	0.4	4.9	31.2	0.8	8.1	1.7	0.0	0.0	2015		
0.7	0.3	0.4	4.8	30.1	0.8	8.1	1.6	0.0	0.0	2016		
0.6	0.5	1.1	4.5	19.9	2.7	5.1	2.5	0.1	0.0	2000	6&8	Articles manufacturés divers
0.9	0.4	1.4	3.8	29.4	3.9	5.8	3.9	0.1	0.0	2013		
0.9	0.4	1.4	3.8	30.3	3.5	6.0	3.9	0.1	0.0	2014		
0.9	0.4	1.3	3.8	31.3	4.0	6.3	3.7	0.1	0.0	2015		
1.0	0.4	1.2	3.7	29.5	4.2	6.7	3.7	0.1	0.0	2016		
Destination des exportations de grandes catégories de marchandises												
0.4	0.8	1.2	5.7	11.0	1.3	5.6	3.0	0.1	0.5	2000	0-9	Tous produits 3/
0.8	1.2	2.2	6.0	18.4	3.0	6.7	5.1	0.2	1.1	2013		
0.8	1.2	2.3	5.9	17.9	3.1	6.7	5.2	0.2	1.2	2014		
0.8	1.1	2.2	6.0	17.4	3.2	6.9	5.2	0.2	1.6	2015		
0.9	1.1	2.0	5.6	17.0	3.3	7.1	5.0	0.2	1.4	2016		
0.6	1.9	2.2	5.7	6.1	1.4	4.1	4.8	0.2	0.5	2000	0&1	Produits alimentaires, boissons et tabacs
1.1	2.3	3.9	6.0	8.6	2.2	6.7	6.5	0.2	0.3	2013		
1.1	2.4	3.7	6.0	9.0	2.3	6.9	6.5	0.2	0.3	2014		
1.1	2.2	3.5	5.8	9.8	2.4	7.4	6.6	0.2	0.4	2015		
1.2	2.0	3.2	5.7	10.4	2.4	7.7	6.1	0.2	0.3	2016		
0.5	1.3	1.4	4.8	15.3	3.3	4.3	3.1	0.0	1.0	2000	2&4	Matières premières huiles & graisses (combust. exclu.)
0.9	1.4	1.7	3.7	36.7	4.9	4.6	4.3	0.0	0.3	2013		
0.9	1.5	1.8	3.9	34.5	5.4	4.9	4.5	0.0	0.2	2014		
1.0	1.4	1.7	4.0	33.2	6.2	5.2	4.6	0.0	0.4	2015		
0.9	1.3	1.7	3.9	34.3	6.1	5.6	4.0	0.0	0.3	2016		
0.5	0.9	0.9	5.3	13.9	1.8	4.2	1.8	0.3	2.5	2000	3	Combustibles minéraux et produits
0.5	1.3	2.0	5.2	23.2	4.0	6.5	2.6	0.2	1.8	2013		
0.6	1.2	2.2	5.6	23.4	4.2	7.0	2.9	0.2	1.7	2014		
0.7	1.2	2.5	5.9	22.6	4.5	7.0	2.8	0.2	1.6	2015		
0.6	1.2	2.5	5.8	21.3	6.0	9.1	3.1	0.2	0.9	2016		
0.5	0.8	1.4	6.9	11.9	1.7	4.9	3.0	0.1	1.2	2000	5	Produits chimiques
1.0	1.1	2.1	7.6	13.9	3.1	5.9	4.3	0.1	0.2	2013		
1.0	1.2	2.1	7.5	13.5	3.3	6.0	4.4	0.1	0.2	2014		
1.0	1.1	2.1	7.5	13.2	3.5	6.0	4.2	0.1	0.2	2015		
1.0	1.1	2.0	7.0	13.3	3.4	6.1	4.0	0.1	0.2	2016		
0.3	0.7	1.1	6.1	11.0	0.9	7.6	2.7	0.1	0.2	2000	7	Machines et matériels de transports
0.7	1.0	2.2	7.1	19.8	2.0	7.5	5.1	0.3	0.2	2013		
0.7	1.1	2.1	6.5	19.6	2.1	7.3	5.2	0.3	0.2	2014		
0.7	1.0	1.9	6.5	20.0	2.2	7.6	5.1	0.3	0.2	2015		
0.8	1.0	1.6	6.1	19.8	2.3	7.5	4.7	0.3	0.1	2016		
0.6	0.8	1.1	5.3	11.0	1.4	4.1	3.4	0.1	0.3	2000	6&8	Articles manufacturés divers
0.9	1.2	2.3	5.5	13.7	3.1	6.5	6.2	0.1	0.2	2013		
1.0	1.2	2.4	5.3	13.5	3.2	6.6	6.1	0.1	0.2	2014		
1.0	1.3	2.4	5.5	12.9	3.3	6.9	6.2	0.1	0.2	2015		
1.1	1.2	2.1	5.1	12.5	3.4	6.8	5.8	0.1	0.2	2016		

Voir la fin du Tableau Spécial F pour la remarque générale et les notes.

Structure of world exports by provenance and destination (Table F)

in per cent

Origin or destination → ↓ SITC Commodity classes		Year	World 1/ Monde 1/	Developed economies 2/ Economies développées 2/ Total	Asia-Pacific Asie-Pacifique Total	Japan Japon	Europe Total	Germany Allemagne	North America Amérique du Nord Total	U.S.A. É.-U.	Commonwealth of Independent States Communauté d'Etats Indépendants Total	Europe
	Commodity composition of the total exports of selected regions											
0-9	All commodities 3/	2000	100.0	100.0	100.0	100.0	100.0	100.0	100.0	100.0	100.0	100.0
		2013	100.0	100.0	100.0	100.0	100.0	100.0	100.0	100.0	100.0	100.0
		2014	100.0	100.0	100.0	100.0	100.0	100.0	100.0	100.0	100.0	100.0
		2015	100.0	100.0	100.0	100.0	100.0	100.0	100.0	100.0	100.0	100.0
		2016	100.0	100.0	100.0	100.0	100.0	100.0	100.0	100.0	100.0	100.0
0&1	Food, live animals, beverages and tobacco	2000	6.1	6.3	3.6	0.4	7.1	4.0	5.9	6.0	2.3	2.1
		2013	6.7	7.9	5.4	0.6	8.4	5.5	7.5	7.2	4.8	5.0
		2014	6.9	8.1	6.0	0.7	8.5	5.5	7.6	7.4	5.5	5.7
		2015	7.2	8.1	6.3	0.8	8.5	5.2	7.7	7.3	6.8	6.9
		2016	7.5	8.3	5.9	0.9	8.8	5.3	7.9	7.4	6.5	6.3
2&4	Crude materials, oils and fats, (fuels excluded)	2000	3.4	3.2	3.1	0.7	2.4	1.7	5.0	3.9	6.5	5.7
		2013	4.5	4.6	11.4	1.8	2.9	2.0	6.6	5.7	5.0	4.9
		2014	4.3	4.5	10.7	1.7	2.9	1.9	6.4	5.6	5.2	5.2
		2015	4.0	4.0	8.7	1.5	2.7	1.7	6.0	5.1	6.0	5.8
		2016	4.0	4.0	8.5	1.4	2.7	1.6	6.1	5.2	5.6	5.2
3	Mineral fuels, lubricants and related material	2000	10.5	4.7	2.7	0.3	5.2	1.4	4.7	1.7	44.0	43.4
		2013	17.2	9.5	8.3	2.3	8.6	2.4	13.2	9.4	62.7	61.4
		2014	16.0	9.0	8.3	2.3	7.7	2.3	13.6	9.6	62.1	61.0
		2015	11.3	6.8	7.0	1.8	5.8	2.1	9.5	6.9	54.2	54.6
		2016	9.2	5.7	6.7	1.5	4.6	1.6	8.5	6.5	44.3	44.4
5	Chemicals	2000	8.9	10.9	7.0	7.3	12.6	12.7	8.9	10.2	6.0	6.7
		2013	10.5	14.3	8.5	10.6	16.0	15.0	12.1	13.2	4.8	5.1
		2014	10.6	14.5	8.3	10.4	16.3	15.0	11.9	13.1	5.1	5.3
		2015	11.0	15.0	8.3	10.1	16.8	15.0	12.7	13.7	6.5	6.5
		2016	11.1	14.9	8.3	10.0	16.7	15.0	12.6	13.6	6.4	6.3
7	Machinery and transport equipment	2000	41.2	45.4	60.8	68.8	40.3	49.6	49.5	52.9	7.3	8.0
		2013	32.2	34.1	42.7	57.9	33.5	47.2	31.9	33.8	5.5	6.1
		2014	33.3	35.1	42.8	58.0	35.0	47.5	32.0	34.1	5.1	5.5
		2015	35.8	36.5	45.0	58.7	36.2	48.4	33.7	35.1	5.7	6.5
		2016	36.9	37.3	46.0	59.8	37.1	48.4	33.9	34.9	5.2	6.1
6&8	Other manufactured goods	2000	25.8	24.2	18.4	18.8	26.8	23.3	21.1	21.2	21.8	23.9
		2013	23.1	22.0	17.2	21.0	24.0	22.9	18.3	19.1	13.6	14.3
		2014	23.9	22.5	17.4	21.1	24.7	22.7	18.4	19.3	13.9	14.6
		2015	24.9	22.8	17.3	20.3	24.8	22.2	19.2	19.8	16.3	16.3
		2016	25.0	22.9	16.5	19.3	25.0	22.1	19.4	20.0	17.1	16.8
	Commodity composition of the world exports to selected regions											
0-9	All commodities 3/	2000	100.0	100.0	100.0	100.0	100.0	100.0	100.0	100.0	100.0	100.0
		2013	100.0	100.0	100.0	100.0	100.0	100.0	100.0	100.0	100.0	100.0
		2014	100.0	100.0	100.0	100.0	100.0	100.0	100.0	100.0	100.0	100.0
		2015	100.0	100.0	100.0	100.0	100.0	100.0	100.0	100.0	100.0	100.0
		2016	100.0	100.0	100.0	100.0	100.0	100.0	100.0	100.0	100.0	100.0
0&1	Food, live animals, beverages and tobacco	2000	6.1	6.2	10.0	11.3	6.8	6.8	3.9	3.8	12.5	13.0
		2013	6.7	7.4	7.7	8.2	8.2	7.8	5.3	5.0	10.3	10.5
		2014	6.9	7.5	8.0	8.3	8.3	7.8	5.5	5.2	10.7	10.7
		2015	7.2	7.7	8.4	9.0	8.5	7.8	5.8	5.5	11.1	10.9
		2016	7.5	8.0	8.8	9.3	8.7	7.9	6.2	5.7	11.0	11.1
2&4	Crude materials, oils and fats, (fuels excluded)	2000	3.4	3.1	5.3	6.0	3.3	3.2	2.1	2.0	4.2	4.5
		2013	4.5	3.4	5.7	7.1	3.6	3.9	2.0	2.0	3.0	3.1
		2014	4.3	3.3	5.5	6.9	3.5	3.5	2.0	1.9	3.1	3.1
		2015	4.0	3.0	4.9	6.2	3.3	3.3	1.9	1.7	3.7	3.8
		2016	4.0	3.0	4.9	6.2	3.2	3.2	1.9	1.7	3.6	3.6
3	Mineral fuels, lubricants and related material	2000	10.5	10.0	15.5	17.4	9.0	6.0	10.5	10.5	14.4	14.9
		2013	17.2	16.8	23.6	26.9	16.3	10.4	15.5	13.3	10.7	10.9
		2014	16.0	15.0	22.2	25.2	14.4	9.0	13.7	11.8	9.3	9.9
		2015	11.3	10.4	16.2	18.5	10.6	6.7	8.1	7.0	9.9	10.4
		2016	9.2	8.1	14.9	17.3	7.6	4.2	7.1	7.2	5.4	5.3
5	Chemicals	2000	8.9	8.6	7.3	6.5	10.1	9.0	6.0	5.7	9.5	9.4
		2013	10.5	11.5	8.8	8.4	13.1	12.7	8.9	8.9	11.1	11.8
		2014	10.6	11.7	8.8	8.4	13.3	12.6	8.9	8.9	11.7	12.4
		2015	11.0	12.1	9.7	9.5	13.6	12.9	9.6	9.5	13.2	14.3
		2016	11.1	12.1	10.0	9.8	13.5	12.9	9.7	9.5	13.5	14.4
7	Machinery and transport equipment	2000	41.2	41.0	33.8	31.2	38.3	39.7	47.9	47.7	25.6	24.4
		2013	32.2	31.4	28.3	24.9	28.2	34.1	39.8	41.5	35.6	36.6
		2014	33.3	32.9	29.1	26.2	29.8	35.9	41.0	42.6	34.6	35.3
		2015	35.8	35.5	32.3	29.5	32.0	37.7	43.8	45.0	31.2	32.0
		2016	36.9	36.5	32.4	29.7	33.3	39.1	44.4	45.0	33.9	35.6
6&8	Other manufactured goods	2000	25.8	26.4	25.9	25.9	26.6	29.0	26.3	27.0	26.5	26.1
		2013	23.1	25.1	23.7	22.9	25.2	27.1	25.3	26.6	27.2	25.4
		2014	23.9	25.8	24.2	23.2	26.0	27.5	25.8	27.0	28.8	26.9
		2015	24.9	27.1	26.1	25.4	27.0	28.3	27.7	28.7	29.3	26.9
		2016	25.0	27.2	26.3	25.6	27.2	28.5	27.4	28.0	29.7	27.0

For general note and footnotes see end of Special Table F.

Structure des exportations mondiales par provenance et destination (Tableau F)

en pourcentage

South-Eastern Europe Europe du Sud-est	Northern Africa Afrique du Nord	Sub-Saharan Africa Afrique subsahari-enne	Latin America and the Caribbean Amérique latine et Caraïbes	Eastern Asia Asie orientale	Southern Asia Asie méridionale	South-eastern Asia Asie du Sud-est	Western Asia Asie occidentale	Oceania Océanie	Others 4/ Autre 4/	⟵ En provenance ou vers Année		CTCI: Classes de marchandises ↓
Composition par marchandises des exportations mondiales des régions selectionnées												
100.0	100.0	100.0	100.0	100.0	100.0	100.0	100.0	100.0	0.0	2000	0-9	Tous produits 3/
100.0	100.0	100.0	100.0	100.0	100.0	100.0	100.0	100.0	0.0	2013		
100.0	100.0	100.0	100.0	100.0	100.0	100.0	100.0	100.0	0.0	2014		
100.0	100.0	100.0	100.0	100.0	100.0	100.0	100.0	100.0	0.0	2015		
100.0	100.0	100.0	100.0	100.0	100.0	100.0	100.0	100.0	0.0	2016		
6.3	4.5	11.1	13.2	2.7	9.1	5.6	3.2	9.5	0.0	2000	0&1	Produits alimentaires,
10.5	5.5	9.2	15.8	2.1	9.6	6.7	2.5	13.4	0.0	2013		boissons et tabacs
10.5	6.6	9.5	16.2	2.1	9.8	7.2	2.8	13.6	0.0	2014		
10.7	9.3	11.4	17.8	2.2	9.9	7.5	3.4	8.6	0.0	2015		
10.7	10.6	14.9	19.7	2.5	9.8	7.9	3.3	10.2	0.0	2016		
8.9	2.8	7.9	7.1	1.5	2.8	4.3	1.3	35.4	0.0	2000	2&4	Matières premières
7.2	2.6	10.3	13.3	0.9	5.0	7.1	1.2	30.9	0.0	2013		huiles & graisses
6.3	2.8	9.1	12.9	0.9	4.3	6.4	1.1	30.4	0.0	2014		(combust. exclu.)
5.6	4.5	8.3	12.7	0.8	3.8	6.3	1.3	19.7	0.0	2015		
5.5	3.8	10.4	13.0	0.8	3.7	6.4	1.4	21.5	0.0	2016		
7.4	68.2	47.4	18.0	2.5	29.3	10.6	64.7	14.0	0.0	2000	3	Combustibles
8.2	67.1	49.9	21.4	3.2	25.4	17.4	58.8	4.8	0.0	2013		minéraux et produits
7.2	59.1	50.9	19.7	2.9	26.4	16.2	55.2	4.3	0.0	2014		
5.8	45.6	50.2	12.5	2.1	16.9	11.8	40.5	34.7	0.0	2015		
4.9	38.3	33.5	8.8	2.0	15.6	9.7	40.4	26.6	0.0	2016		
6.9	4.7	3.0	4.7	5.9	5.5	4.9	4.3	0.3	0.0	2000	5	Produits chimiques
6.8	6.0	2.9	5.6	6.7	10.4	8.4	6.1	4.3	0.0	2013		
6.9	7.5	2.9	5.5	6.9	10.4	8.7	6.4	4.4	0.0	2014		
7.0	9.0	2.9	5.8	6.6	11.9	8.3	7.0	1.1	0.0	2015		
6.9	9.7	4.2	5.6	6.7	11.7	8.4	7.0	1.5	0.0	2016		
14.3	3.5	5.6	34.5	44.8	4.0	52.8	7.1	3.1	0.0	2000	7	Machines et matèriels
31.2	7.1	7.1	25.5	49.4	9.9	37.0	9.6	3.4	0.0	2013		de transports
32.1	10.2	7.3	26.7	49.4	11.0	37.4	10.5	3.7	0.0	2014		
33.7	13.4	7.1	30.9	51.1	11.5	41.0	10.1	1.4	0.0	2015		
35.4	15.7	8.7	31.9	51.7	12.2	41.3	10.4	2.2	0.0	2016		
54.3	16.0	19.6	20.7	42.2	48.2	19.8	15.4	35.9	0.0	2000	6&8	Articles manufacturés
33.2	10.8	14.4	14.8	35.4	35.8	20.0	12.0	37.3	0.0	2013		divers
33.4	12.6	15.4	15.6	36.3	34.8	20.9	13.1	37.5	0.0	2014		
33.8	16.0	15.4	16.8	35.8	41.9	22.5	15.5	17.7	0.0	2015		
33.2	17.1	20.0	16.8	34.4	44.5	23.0	16.3	20.8	0.0	2016		
Composition par marchandises des exportations mondiales vers régions selectionnées												
100.0	100.0	100.0	100.0	100.0	100.0	100.0	100.0	100.0	100.0	2000	0-9	Tous produits 3/
100.0	100.0	100.0	100.0	100.0	100.0	100.0	100.0	100.0	100.0	2013		
100.0	100.0	100.0	100.0	100.0	100.0	100.0	100.0	100.0	100.0	2014		
100.0	100.0	100.0	100.0	100.0	100.0	100.0	100.0	100.0	100.0	2015		
100.0	100.0	100.0	100.0	100.0	100.0	100.0	100.0	100.0	100.0	2016		
9.1	13.8	11.1	6.1	3.4	6.4	4.5	9.7	11.1	5.2	2000	0&1	Produits alimentaires,
9.7	13.0	11.6	6.6	3.1	4.9	6.7	8.5	8.0	1.9	2013		boissons et tabacs
9.5	13.9	11.2	6.9	3.5	5.2	7.1	8.6	8.0	1.8	2014		
9.7	13.9	11.4	6.9	4.0	5.6	7.7	9.0	7.9	1.6	2015		
9.8	13.2	12.4	7.6	4.6	5.5	8.1	9.2	8.0	1.8	2016		
4.2	5.3	4.1	2.8	4.6	8.5	2.6	3.5	1.2	6.3	2000	2&4	Matières premières
5.5	5.4	3.3	2.7	8.9	7.3	3.1	3.8	0.9	1.1	2013		huiles & graisses
5.0	5.3	3.3	2.8	8.2	7.5	3.1	3.7	0.9	0.7	2014		(combust. exclu.)
4.7	4.9	3.1	2.7	7.6	7.9	3.0	3.5	0.9	0.9	2015		
4.2	4.7	3.4	2.8	8.1	7.6	3.2	3.3	0.9	0.8	2016		
11.9	11.0	8.0	9.6	13.2	14.3	7.8	6.2	25.2	49.4	2000	3	Combustibles
12.0	18.1	15.3	14.9	21.6	22.9	16.9	8.8	15.6	28.9	2013		minéraux et produits
10.8	15.6	15.6	15.2	20.9	21.8	16.7	9.1	14.8	22.9	2014		
9.5	11.5	13.0	11.2	14.7	16.2	11.4	6.1	10.3	11.6	2015		
6.3	10.0	11.6	9.4	11.5	16.8	11.7	5.7	7.8	6.1	2016		
9.8	8.7	10.3	10.7	9.6	11.5	7.8	8.8	4.6	19.9	2000	5	Produits chimiques
13.3	10.0	9.7	13.1	7.9	10.7	9.3	8.9	3.5	2.2	2013		
12.7	10.1	9.8	13.4	8.0	11.3	9.5	9.0	3.4	1.8	2014		
12.7	10.9	10.5	13.8	8.4	12.1	9.6	9.0	3.2	1.4	2015		
12.9	11.0	11.1	13.9	8.7	11.5	9.6	9.1	3.2	1.4	2016		
26.7	32.8	38.5	43.6	40.9	27.7	55.4	37.1	28.8	16.0	2000	7	Machines et matèriels
28.9	27.7	31.4	37.6	34.7	21.0	36.2	32.4	50.8	5.4	2013		de transports
30.1	29.1	30.3	36.5	36.4	22.3	36.3	33.5	52.1	6.2	2014		
31.4	30.0	30.3	38.6	41.2	24.6	39.1	35.1	60.1	3.6	2015		
32.7	31.3	30.1	39.9	43.0	26.1	39.0	34.8	62.7	3.4	2016		
35.7	26.0	24.0	23.9	25.7	27.5	18.6	29.6	23.3	14.3	2000	6&8	Articles manufacturés
28.2	23.4	23.6	20.9	17.1	23.9	22.7	27.9	10.5	5.0	2013		divers
29.2	24.3	25.2	21.4	18.0	25.1	23.6	28.3	9.7	5.0	2014		
29.3	27.5	27.6	22.8	18.5	25.9	24.7	29.5	9.7	3.3	2015		
30.5	25.7	27.0	22.6	18.5	26.1	23.8	29.5	10.3	3.7	2016		

Voir la fin du Tableau Spécial F pour la remarque générale et les notes.

Growth and structure of world exports by provenance and destination (Tables E and F)
Croissance et structure des exportations mondiales par provenance et destination (Tableaux E et F)

General note

The figures in tables E and F are derived from the data in Special Table D.

The commodity classification is in accordance with the United Nations' Standard International Trade Classification (SITC), Revision 3, except for countries which report trade data only in terms of the SITC, Revision 2, or the SITC, Revised.

The data approximate total exports of all countries and areas of the world. They are based on official export figures converted, where necessary, to U.S. dollars according to conversion factors published in Table C for each country in this volume. Where official figures are not available, estimates based on the imports reported by partner countries and on other subsidiary data are used. Some official national data have been adjusted
(a) to approximate the commodity groupings of the SITC and
(b) to approximate calendar years.

The data include special category (confidential) exports, ships' stores and bunkers and exports of minor importance, the destination of which cannot be determined. These data are included in the world totals for each commodity group and in total exports, and are available separately in region "Others"

1/ Exports for which country of destination is not available are included in the totals for the 'World' and in region "Others" (see footnote number 4 for further explanation).
2/ This classification is intended for statistical convenience and does not, necessarily, express a judgment about the stage reached by a particular country in the development process.
3/ Section 9 of the SITC, which comprises commodities and transactions not classified elsewhere, is included in the total trade but is not shown separately in this table.
4/ The region "Others" as destination for exports contains the following trading partners: Antarctica, bunkers, free zones, confidential and not elsewhere specified countries

Remarque générale

Les données des tables E et F sont derivées de celles publiées dans le Tableau Spécial D.

La classification par marchandise utilisée est la Classification Type pour le Commerce International (CTCI), Revision 3,) en dehors des pays qui rapportent exclusivement les données du commerce en accord avec la CTCI, Revision 2, ou la CTCI, Revisée.

Les données sont une estimation des exportations totales de tous les pays et régions du monde. Elles sont basées sur les chiffres des exportations officielles nationales convertis en dollars E.-U. selon les facteurs de conversion pour chaque pays publiés dans le Tableau C de ce volume. Quand les chiffres officiels ne sont pas disponibles, des estimations basées sur les importations rapportées par les pays partenaires ou sur d'autres données subsidiaries sont utilisées. Quelques données officielles nationales ont été ajustées afin
(a) qu'elles correspondent aux groupes des marchandises de la CTCI et
(b) qu'elles correspondent aux années civiles.

Les données comprennent les exportations de 'special category' (confidentielles), les approvisionnments des navires et combustible de soute et autres exportations de moindre importance dont la destination n'a pu être déterminée. Ces donnés sont comprises dans le total pour chaque groupe de marchandise et dans les exportations totales, et sont disponibles separemment dans la région "Autres".

1/ Exportations dont les pays de destination n'est pas disponible sont incluses dansles totaux pour le 'Monde' et dans la région "les autres " (voir note n ° 4 pour plus d'explications)
2/ Cette classification est utilisée pour plus de commodité dans la présentation des statistiques et n'implique pas nécessairement un jugement quant au stade de développement auquel est parvenu un pays donné.
3/ Section 9 de la CTCI, qui représente les articles et transactions non ailleurs est comprise dans le commerce total mais n'est pas présentée séparément dans ce tableau.
4/ La région "Autres" comme destination des exportations comprend les partenaires commerciaux suivants: Antarctique, combustibles de soute, zones franches, partenaires confidentiels ou non specifiés ailleurs.

Indices of total exports and imports by countries or areas (Table G)

Quantum and unit value indices and terms of trade in US dollars (2000 = 100)

Indices des exportations et importations totales par pays ou zones (Tableau G)

Indices du quantum et de la valeur unitaire et termes de l'échange en dollars É.-U. (2000 = 100)

Countries	2007	2008	2009	2010	2011	2012	2013	2014	2015	2016	Pays
Argentina											Argentine
Imp: Quantum	154	176	135	188	230	214	220	194	...	...	Imp: quantum
Imp: Unit Value	114	128	113	119	127	125	131	132	...	...	Imp: valeur unitaire
Exp: Quantum	164	162	145	165	170	159	165	148	...	...	Exp: quantum
Exp: Unit Value	130	164	146	157	187	192	188	184	...	...	Exp: valeur unitaire
Terms of Trade	*114*	*128*	*129*	*133*	*148*	*154*	*143*	*140*	...	...	*Termes de l'échange*
Purchasing Power of Exports	*187*	*207*	*187*	*218*	*251*	*244*	*236*	*207*	...	...	*Pouvoir d'achat des export.*
Australia											Australie
Imp: Quantum	155	186	164	173	192	208	211	209	217	...	Imp: quantum
Imp: Unit Value[1]	128	141	132	145	164	167	159	153	129	124	Imp: valeur unitaire[1]
Exp: Quantum	145	191	168	198	229	212	225	228	214	...	Exp: quantum
Exp: Unit Value[1]	196	245	214	260	329	304	282	254	192	182	Exp: valeur unitaire[1]
Terms of Trade	*153*	*174*	*162*	*179*	*201*	*182*	*177*	*165*	*149*	*147*	*Termes de l'échange*
Purchasing Power of Exports	*220*	*331*	*272*	*354*	*461*	*386*	*398*	*378*	*318*	...	*Pouvoir d'achat des export.*
Austria											Autriche
Imp: Quantum	118	124	128	137	143	146	151	151	158	163	Imp: quantum
Imp: Unit Value[1]	163	184	164	164	183	172	176	173	141	137	Imp: valeur unitaire[1]
Exp: Quantum	123	129	134	145	151	160	164	165	170	173	Exp: quantum
Exp: Unit Value[1]	157	173	159	156	170	158	162	160	133	131	Exp: valeur unitaire[1]
Terms of Trade	*96*	*94*	*97*	*95*	*93*	*92*	*92*	*93*	*94*	*95*	*Termes de l'échange*
Purchasing Power of Exports	*118*	*122*	*131*	*138*	*140*	*147*	*151*	*153*	*160*	*164*	*Pouvoir d'achat des export.*
Belgium											Belgique
Imp: Quantum	138	139	123	130	136	133	133	137	136	138	Imp: quantum
Imp: Unit Value	171	192	165	172	196	188	193	189	158	154	Imp: valeur unitaire
Exp: Quantum	135	132	117	126	130	129	131	132	133	138	Exp: quantum
Exp: Unit Value	171	191	169	174	196	186	192	192	161	156	Exp: valeur unitaire
Terms of Trade	*100*	*99*	*103*	*101*	*100*	*99*	*99*	*101*	*102*	*101*	*Termes de l'échange*
Purchasing Power of Exports	*135*	*132*	*120*	*126*	*130*	*127*	*129*	*134*	*135*	*139*	*Pouvoir d'achat des export.*
Bolivia (Plurinational State of)											Bolivie (État plurinational de)
Imp: Quantum	...	...	...	...	...	...	...	...	...	...	Imp: quantum
Imp: Unit Value	...	...	...	...	...	...	...	...	...	...	Imp: valeur unitaire
Exp: Quantum	315	358	325	394	373	415	470	490	482	457	Exp: quantum
Exp: Unit Value	289	321	259	298	432	456	425	407	338	292	Exp: valeur unitaire
Terms of Trade	...	...	...	...	...	...	...	...	...	...	*Termes de l'échange*
Purchasing Power of Exports	...	...	...	...	...	...	...	...	...	...	*Pouvoir d'achat des export.*
Brazil											Brésil
Imp: Quantum	128	134	112	149	160	153	172	178	158	151	Imp: quantum
Imp: Unit Value	167	230	204	217	251	262	249	231	198	166	Imp: valeur unitaire
Exp: Quantum	189	192	186	213	222	223	228	236	261	264	Exp: quantum
Exp: Unit Value	154	188	149	171	208	198	192	173	133	128	Exp: valeur unitaire
Terms of Trade	*92*	*82*	*73*	*79*	*83*	*76*	*77*	*75*	*67*	*77*	*Termes de l'échange*
Purchasing Power of Exports	*174*	*157*	*136*	*167*	*184*	*169*	*176*	*177*	*176*	*203*	*Pouvoir d'achat des export.*
Bulgaria											Bulgarie
Imp: Quantum	...	...	...	...	...	...	...	...	...	...	Imp: quantum
Imp: Unit Value[1]	182	208	178	177	199	188	189	181	149	140	Imp: valeur unitaire[1]
Exp: Quantum	...	...	...	...	...	...	...	...	...	...	Exp: quantum
Exp: Unit Value[1]	194	227	188	197	232	225	227	217	177	171	Exp: valeur unitaire[1]
Terms of Trade	*107*	*109*	*106*	*112*	*117*	*120*	*120*	*120*	*119*	*122*	*Termes de l'échange*
Purchasing Power of Exports	...	...	...	...	...	...	...	...	...	...	*Pouvoir d'achat des export.*

Indices of total exports and imports by countries or areas (Table G)

Quantum and unit value indices and terms of trade in US dollars (2000 = 100)

Indices des exportations et importations totales par pays ou zones (Tableau G)

Indices du quantum et de la valeur unitaire et termes de l'échange en dollars É.-U. (2000 = 100)

Countries	2007	2008	2009	2010	2011	2012	2013	2014	2015	2016	Pays
Canada											Canada
Imp: Quantum	130	130	110	127	135	138	142	146	146	146	Imp: quantum
Imp: Unit Value	125	134	125	132	143	145	142	140	128	128	Imp: valeur unitaire
Exp: Quantum	105	100	85	91	96	100	102	108	113	114	Exp: quantum
Exp: Unit Value	154	175	145	163	178	174	172	169	144	137	Exp: valeur unitaire
Terms of Trade	*123*	*130*	*116*	*123*	*124*	*121*	*121*	*121*	*112*	*107*	*Termes de l'échange*
Purchasing Power of Exports	*129*	*130*	*99*	*113*	*120*	*120*	*123*	*130*	*126*	*122*	*Pouvoir d'achat des export.*
China, Hong Kong SAR											China, Hong Kong RAS
Imp: Quantum	183	186	167	198	206	208	215	220	213	215	Imp: quantum
Imp: Unit Value	102	107	107	114	123	128	129	131	131	128	Imp: valeur unitaire
Exp: Quantum	189	192	167	196	201	201	206	209	206	208	Exp: quantum
Exp: Unit Value	99	103	105	109	118	122	124	126	127	124	Exp: valeur unitaire
Terms of Trade	*97*	*96*	*98*	*96*	*96*	*96*	*96*	*97*	*97*	*97*	*Termes de l'échange*
Purchasing Power of Exports	*183*	*185*	*163*	*188*	*192*	*192*	*198*	*202*	*199*	*202*	*Pouvoir d'achat des export.*
Colombia											Colombie
Imp: Quantum	...	...	...	...	...	...	...	...	...	...	Imp: quantum
Imp: Unit Value[1]	117	125	116	...	...	...	...	...	...	...	Imp: valeur unitaire[1]
Exp: Quantum	...	...	...	...	...	...	...	...	...	...	Exp: quantum
Exp: Unit Value[1]	130	159	151	...	...	...	...	...	...	...	Exp: valeur unitaire[1]
Terms of Trade	*111*	*128*	*130*	...	...	...	...	...	...	...	*Termes de l'échange*
Purchasing Power of Exports	...	...	...	...	...	...	...	...	...	...	*Pouvoir d'achat des export.*
Czechia											Tchéquie
Imp: Quantum	...	...	...	...	...	...	...	...	...	...	Imp: quantum
Imp: Unit Value[1]	175	201	173	175	197	186	185	178	147	142	Imp: valeur unitaire[1]
Exp: Quantum	...	...	...	...	...	...	...	...	...	...	Exp: quantum
Exp: Unit Value[1]	185	210	189	185	203	189	191	187	155	151	Exp: valeur unitaire[1]
Terms of Trade	*106*	*105*	*109*	*106*	*103*	*102*	*103*	*105*	*105*	*106*	*Termes de l'échange*
Purchasing Power of Exports	...	...	...	...	...	...	...	...	...	...	*Pouvoir d'achat des export.*
Denmark											Danemark
Imp: Quantum	147	141	114	123	134	136	142	145	153	161	Imp: quantum
Imp: Unit Value	160	173	154	150	163	152	154	153	125	120	Imp: valeur unitaire
Exp: Quantum	131	130	114	120	128	128	132	136	141	148	Exp: quantum
Exp: Unit Value	160	178	160	159	173	166	167	163	134	127	Exp: valeur unitaire
Terms of Trade	*100*	*103*	*103*	*106*	*106*	*109*	*109*	*106*	*107*	*106*	*Termes de l'échange*
Purchasing Power of Exports	*132*	*133*	*118*	*127*	*135*	*139*	*144*	*144*	*151*	*158*	*Pouvoir d'achat des export.*
Ecuador											Equateur
Imp: Quantum	262	280	274	331	350	345	377	416	375	330	Imp: quantum
Imp: Unit Value	...	...	...	...	...	...	...	...	...	...	Imp: valeur unitaire
Exp: Quantum	139	141	137	133	138	140	146	157	159	160	Exp: quantum
Exp: Unit Value	212	289	202	267	369	346	342	308	183	162	Exp: valeur unitaire
Terms of Trade	...	...	...	...	...	...	...	...	...	...	*Termes de l'échange*
Purchasing Power of Exports	...	...	...	...	...	...	...	...	...	...	*Pouvoir d'achat des export.*
Estonia											Estonie
Imp: Quantum	...	...	...	...	...	...	...	...	...	...	Imp: quantum
Imp: Unit Value[1]	166	189	170	176	205	197	200	196	160	159	Imp: valeur unitaire[1]
Exp: Quantum	...	...	...	...	...	...	...	...	...	...	Exp: quantum
Exp: Unit Value[1]	247	276	252	254	292	275	281	273	219	218	Exp: valeur unitaire[1]
Terms of Trade	*148*	*146*	*149*	*144*	*142*	*139*	*140*	*139*	*137*	*137*	*Termes de l'échange*
Purchasing Power of Exports	...	...	...	...	...	...	...	...	...	...	*Pouvoir d'achat des export.*

Indices of total exports and imports by countries or areas (Table G)

Quantum and unit value indices and terms of trade in US dollars (2000 = 100)

Indices des exportations et importations totales par pays ou zones (Tableau G)

Indices du quantum et de la valeur unitaire et termes de l'échange en dollars É.-U. (2000 = 100)

Countries	2007	2008	2009	2010	2011	2012	2013	2014	2015	2016	Pays
Finland											Finlande
Imp: Quantum	128	130	100	109	118	108	98	99	98	98	Imp: quantum
Imp: Unit Value[1]	166	184	159	160	182	173	175	171	134	129	Imp: valeur unitaire[1]
Exp: Quantum	120	121	88	94	94	94	97	99	95	91	Exp: quantum
Exp: Unit Value[1]	134	145	126	124	137	127	129	128	105	102	Exp: valeur unitaire[1]
Terms of Trade	*81*	*79*	*79*	*78*	*75*	*73*	*74*	*75*	*78*	*79*	*Termes de l'échange*
Purchasing Power of Exports	*98*	*96*	*70*	*73*	*71*	*69*	*72*	*74*	*74*	*72*	*Pouvoir d'achat des export.*
France											France
Imp: Quantum	121	121	109	120	122	121	121	126	136	146	Imp: quantum
Imp: Unit Value[1]	165	187	161	163	185	176	178	168	133	125	Imp: valeur unitaire[1]
Exp: Quantum	114	114	99	110	114	116	115	106	110	113	Exp: quantum
Exp: Unit Value[1]	161	179	161	156	171	160	165	180	150	144	Exp: valeur unitaire[1]
Terms of Trade	*97*	*96*	*100*	*96*	*92*	*91*	*93*	*107*	*112*	*115*	*Termes de l'échange*
Purchasing Power of Exports	*111*	*109*	*99*	*105*	*105*	*106*	*107*	*113*	*124*	*131*	*Pouvoir d'achat des export.*
Germany											Allemagne
Imp: Quantum	148	150	131	148	158	155	156	161	166	162	Imp: quantum
Imp: Unit Value[1]	157	177	153	156	174	164	165	169	142	139	Imp: valeur unitaire[1]
Exp: Quantum	164	166	136	155	168	169	170	174	179	177	Exp: quantum
Exp: Unit Value[1]	156	171	158	155	168	158	162	166	143	141	Exp: valeur unitaire[1]
Terms of Trade	*99*	*97*	*104*	*100*	*97*	*96*	*98*	*98*	*100*	*102*	*Termes de l'échange*
Purchasing Power of Exports	*163*	*161*	*140*	*154*	*162*	*162*	*166*	*171*	*180*	*181*	*Pouvoir d'achat des export.*
Greece											Grèce
Imp: Quantum	...	...	...	...	...	...	...	...	...	...	Imp: quantum
Imp: Unit Value[1]	185	213	198	201	227	219	220	212	159	154	Imp: valeur unitaire[1]
Exp: Quantum	...	...	...	...	...	...	...	...	...	...	Exp: quantum
Exp: Unit Value[1]	177	202	180	187	213	205	208	202	150	139	Exp: valeur unitaire[1]
Terms of Trade	*96*	*95*	*91*	*93*	*94*	*93*	*94*	*95*	*94*	*91*	*Termes de l'échange*
Purchasing Power of Exports	...	...	...	...	...	...	...	...	...	...	*Pouvoir d'achat des export.*
Guyana											Guyana
Imp: Quantum	...	...	...	...	...	...	...	...	...	...	Imp: quantum
Imp: Unit Value	...	...	...	...	...	...	...	...	...	...	Imp: valeur unitaire
Exp: Quantum	99	86	77	78	90	100	...	...	...	...	Exp: quantum
Exp: Unit Value	...	...	...	...	...	...	...	...	...	...	Exp: valeur unitaire
Terms of Trade	...	...	...	...	...	...	...	...	...	...	*Termes de l'échange*
Purchasing Power of Exports	...	...	...	...	...	...	...	...	...	...	*Pouvoir d'achat des export.*
Honduras											Honduras
Imp: Quantum	...	...	...	...	...	...	...	...	...	...	Imp: quantum
Imp: Unit Value	...	...	...	...	...	...	...	...	...	...	Imp: valeur unitaire
Exp: Quantum	119	123	113	116	131	165	144	145	163	...	Exp: quantum
Exp: Unit Value	135	162	152	183	263	224	174	183	184	...	Exp: valeur unitaire
Terms of Trade	...	...	...	...	...	...	...	...	...	...	*Termes de l'échange*
Purchasing Power of Exports	...	...	...	...	...	...	...	...	...	...	*Pouvoir d'achat des export.*
Hungary											Hongrie
Imp: Quantum	189	198	165	185	198	198	208	226	240	252	Imp: quantum
Imp: Unit Value[1]	156	171	147	144	157	146	146	140	116	112	Imp: valeur unitaire[1]
Exp: Quantum	225	235	206	235	258	260	271	290	312	326	Exp: quantum
Exp: Unit Value[1]	149	160	140	138	147	135	136	132	110	108	Exp: valeur unitaire[1]
Terms of Trade	*95*	*94*	*96*	*95*	*94*	*93*	*93*	*94*	*95*	*96*	*Termes de l'échange*
Purchasing Power of Exports	*215*	*220*	*197*	*224*	*242*	*241*	*253*	*273*	*296*	*314*	*Pouvoir d'achat des export.*

Indices of total exports and imports by countries or areas (Table G)

Quantum and unit value indices and terms of trade in US dollars (2000 = 100)

Indices des exportations et importations totales par pays ou zones (Tableau G)

Indices du quantum et de la valeur unitaire et termes de l'échange en dollars É.-U. (2000 = 100)

Countries	2007	2008	2009	2010	2011	2012	2013	2014	2015	2016	Pays
Iceland											Islande
Imp: Quantum	154	132	96	101	...	...	...	...	...	...	Imp: quantum
Imp: Unit Value	166	185	148	157	...	...	...	...	...	...	Imp: valeur unitaire
Exp: Quantum	129	161	166	170	...	...	...	...	...	...	Exp: quantum
Exp: Unit Value	167	167	125	144	...	...	...	...	...	...	Exp: valeur unitaire
Terms of Trade	*101*	*91*	*84*	*92*	...	...	...	...	...	...	*Termes de l'échange*
Purchasing Power of Exports	*130*	*146*	*140*	*156*	...	...	...	...	...	...	*Pouvoir d'achat des export.*
India											Inde
Imp: Quantum	290	241	236	282	247	231	240	234	224	211	Imp: quantum
Imp: Unit Value	139	150	121	145	248	234	242	243	220	224	Imp: valeur unitaire
Exp: Quantum	212	206	193	230	274	264	271	292	270	240	Exp: quantum
Exp: Unit Value	159	177	160	192	226	210	224	212	229	216	Exp: valeur unitaire
Terms of Trade	*114*	*118*	*132*	*133*	*91*	*90*	*93*	*87*	*104*	*96*	*Termes de l'échange*
Purchasing Power of Exports	*242*	*243*	*254*	*305*	*250*	*236*	*251*	*255*	*281*	*230*	*Pouvoir d'achat des export.*
Ireland											Irlande
Imp: Quantum	122	110	90	89	88	85	82	87	88	86	Imp: quantum
Imp: Unit Value	137	150	134	134	155	156	166	176	164	170	Imp: valeur unitaire
Exp: Quantum	120	121	116	122	118	124	118	120	129	121	Exp: quantum
Exp: Unit Value	132	137	130	127	142	123	129	132	123	138	Exp: valeur unitaire
Terms of Trade	*96*	*91*	*97*	*94*	*91*	*79*	*77*	*75*	*75*	*81*	*Termes de l'échange*
Purchasing Power of Exports	*116*	*110*	*112*	*115*	*107*	*98*	*91*	*89*	*97*	*98*	*Pouvoir d'achat des export.*
Israel											Israël
Imp: Quantum	114	116	99	115	126	128	127	130	130	143	Imp: quantum
Imp: Unit Value	138	158	134	144	165	160	159	156	135	129	Imp: valeur unitaire
Exp: Quantum	136	134	112	132	144	128	114	140	136	132	Exp: quantum
Exp: Unit Value	127	147	136	141	151	157	160	158	150	147	Exp: valeur unitaire
Terms of Trade	*92*	*93*	*102*	*98*	*91*	*98*	*101*	*101*	*112*	*114*	*Termes de l'échange*
Purchasing Power of Exports	*125*	*124*	*114*	*130*	*132*	*125*	*114*	*142*	*152*	*150*	*Pouvoir d'achat des export.*
Italy											Italie
Imp: Quantum	116	109	94	105	104	94	91	92	99	103	Imp: quantum
Imp: Unit Value	185	218	185	194	226	218	221	215	173	165	Imp: valeur unitaire
Exp: Quantum	115	110	89	97	100	100	99	99	101	103	Exp: quantum
Exp: Unit Value	181	206	191	192	217	209	219	221	188	187	Exp: valeur unitaire
Terms of Trade	*98*	*95*	*103*	*99*	*96*	*96*	*99*	*103*	*109*	*114*	*Termes de l'échange*
Purchasing Power of Exports	*112*	*104*	*92*	*96*	*96*	*96*	*97*	*102*	*110*	*117*	*Pouvoir d'achat des export.*
Jamaica											Jamaïque
Imp: Quantum	...	...	...	...	...	...	...	...	...	...	Imp: quantum
Imp: Unit Value	...	...	...	...	...	...	...	...	...	...	Imp: valeur unitaire
Exp: Quantum	107	116	60	54	67	60	61	60	61	...	Exp: quantum
Exp: Unit Value	139	140	119	136	138	144	138	141	146	...	Exp: valeur unitaire
Terms of Trade	...	...	...	...	...	...	...	...	...	...	*Termes de l'échange*
Purchasing Power of Exports	...	...	...	...	...	...	...	...	...	...	*Pouvoir d'achat des export.*
Japan											Japon
Imp: Quantum	119	119	102	116	119	121	122	123	119	119	Imp: quantum
Imp: Unit Value[1]	133	163	135	154	183	182	170	164	127	118	Imp: valeur unitaire[1]
Exp: Quantum	130	128	94	117	112	107	105	106	105	105	Exp: quantum
Exp: Unit Value[1]	95	101	101	105	112	110	100	95	85	85	Exp: valeur unitaire[1]
Terms of Trade	*72*	*62*	*74*	*68*	*62*	*60*	*59*	*58*	*67*	*72*	*Termes de l'échange*
Purchasing Power of Exports	*93*	*79*	*70*	*79*	*69*	*65*	*62*	*62*	*70*	*76*	*Pouvoir d'achat des export.*

Indices of total exports and imports by countries or areas (Table G)

Quantum and unit value indices and terms of trade in US dollars (2000 = 100)

Indices des exportations et importations totales par pays ou zones (Tableau G)

Indices du quantum et de la valeur unitaire et termes de l'échange en dollars É.-U. (2000 = 100)

Countries	2007	2008	2009	2010	2011	2012	2013	2014	2015	2016	Pays
Jordan											Jordanie
Imp: Quantum	162	166	155	138	132	151	155	155	153	144	Imp: quantum
Imp: Unit Value	184	221	197	243	305	300	303	321	284	297	Imp: valeur unitaire
Exp: Quantum	173	158	142	188	190	175	195	204	197	189	Exp: quantum
Exp: Unit Value	170	261	237	207	233	252	230	230	227	212	Exp: valeur unitaire
Terms of Trade	*92*	*118*	*120*	*85*	*77*	*84*	*76*	*72*	*80*	*72*	*Termes de l'échange*
Purchasing Power of Exports	*160*	*186*	*171*	*160*	*145*	*146*	*148*	*146*	*158*	*135*	*Pouvoir d'achat des export.*
Korea, Republic of											Corée, République de
Imp: Quantum	160	172	152	177	186	187	195	204	211	213	Imp: quantum
Imp: Unit Value[1]	144	168	137	159	185	181	172	166	131	122	Imp: valeur unitaire[1]
Exp: Quantum	221	232	232	283	322	340	356	371	381	384	Exp: quantum
Exp: Unit Value[1]	95	99	84	90	94	91	89	87	77	73	Exp: valeur unitaire[1]
Terms of Trade	*66*	*59*	*61*	*57*	*51*	*50*	*52*	*53*	*59*	*60*	*Termes de l'échange*
Purchasing Power of Exports	*146*	*137*	*142*	*161*	*164*	*171*	*185*	*196*	*225*	*229*	*Pouvoir d'achat des export.*
Latvia											Lettonie
Imp: Quantum	...	...	...	...	...	...	...	...	...	...	Imp: quantum
Imp: Unit Value	...	...	...	...	...	...	...	...	...	...	Imp: valeur unitaire
Exp: Quantum	...	...	...	...	...	...	...	...	...	...	Exp: quantum
Exp: Unit Value	209	242	207	212	253	240	252	245	205	199	Exp: valeur unitaire
Terms of Trade	...	...	...	...	...	...	...	...	...	...	*Termes de l'échange*
Purchasing Power of Exports	...	...	...	...	...	...	...	...	...	...	*Pouvoir d'achat des export.*
Lithuania											Lituanie
Imp: Quantum	257	280	197	239	271	285	310	321	344	353	Imp: quantum
Imp: Unit Value	174	211	169	178	214	207	209	201	154	146	Imp: valeur unitaire
Exp: Quantum	250	284	251	296	336	373	405	414	413	422	Exp: quantum
Exp: Unit Value	185	216	179	191	227	218	221	213	169	163	Exp: valeur unitaire
Terms of Trade	*106*	*102*	*106*	*107*	*106*	*105*	*105*	*106*	*110*	*112*	*Termes de l'échange*
Purchasing Power of Exports	*266*	*289*	*265*	*316*	*357*	*392*	*427*	*439*	*453*	*472*	*Pouvoir d'achat des export.*
Mauritius											Maurice
Imp: Quantum	114	114	108	115	119	122	114	123	135	...	Imp: quantum
Imp: Unit Value[1]	111	133	112	124	141	143	112	108	84	...	Imp: valeur unitaire[1]
Exp: Quantum	95	96	87	101	104	106	96	108	105	...	Exp: quantum
Exp: Unit Value[1]	96	102	91	91	101	103	97	93	83	...	Exp: valeur unitaire[1]
Terms of Trade	*87*	*77*	*81*	*73*	*72*	*72*	*87*	*86*	*98*	...	*Termes de l'échange*
Purchasing Power of Exports	*83*	*73*	*71*	*74*	*75*	*77*	*83*	*93*	*103*	...	*Pouvoir d'achat des export.*
Mexico											Mexique
Imp: Quantum	...	...	...	...	...	...	...	...	...	...	Imp: quantum
Imp: Unit Value[1]	109	117	92	102	112	106	109	106	...	...	Imp: valeur unitaire[1]
Exp: Quantum	...	...	...	...	...	...	...	...	...	...	Exp: quantum
Exp: Unit Value[1]	124	135	94	113	132	121	125	114	...	...	Exp: valeur unitaire[1]
Terms of Trade	*114*	*116*	*103*	*111*	*118*	*114*	*114*	*108*	...	...	*Termes de l'échange*
Purchasing Power of Exports	...	...	...	...	...	...	...	...	...	...	*Pouvoir d'achat des export.*
Morocco											Maroc
Imp: Quantum	176	...	...	...	...	228	...	...	...	...	Imp: quantum
Imp: Unit Value	152	...	...	...	...	164	...	...	...	...	Imp: valeur unitaire
Exp: Quantum	131	...	...	...	...	148	...	...	...	...	Exp: quantum
Exp: Unit Value	150	...	...	...	...	186	...	...	...	...	Exp: valeur unitaire
Terms of Trade	*98*	...	...	...	...	*114*	...	...	...	...	*Termes de l'échange*
Purchasing Power of Exports	*129*	...	...	...	...	*168*	...	...	...	...	*Pouvoir d'achat des export.*

Indices of total exports and imports by countries or areas (Table G)

Quantum and unit value indices and terms of trade in US dollars (2000 = 100)

Indices des exportations et importations totales par pays ou zones (Tableau G)

Indices du quantum et de la valeur unitaire et termes de l'échange en dollars É.-U. (2000 = 100)

Countries	2007	2008	2009	2010	2011	2012	2013	2014	2015	2016	Pays
Netherlands											Pays-Bas
Imp: Quantum	141	146	130	147	151	155	157	163	170	178	Imp: quantum
Imp: Unit Value	150	169	147	150	170	162	164	160	126	120	Imp: valeur unitaire
Exp: Quantum	144	147	134	151	157	163	166	171	177	184	Exp: quantum
Exp: Unit Value	155	175	151	153	171	163	166	162	130	125	Exp: valeur unitaire
Terms of Trade	*103*	*103*	*103*	*103*	*101*	*101*	*101*	*101*	*103*	*104*	*Termes de l'échange*
Purchasing Power of Exports	*149*	*151*	*138*	*155*	*158*	*164*	*167*	*173*	*182*	*191*	*Pouvoir d'achat des export.*
New Zealand											Nouvelle-Zélande
Imp: Quantum	166	164	148	164	174	176	195	214	221	231	Imp: quantum
Imp: Unit Value[1]	134	147	121	138	153	153	147	142	118	113	Imp: valeur unitaire[1]
Exp: Quantum	129	124	134	136	139	150	150	153	157	161	Exp: quantum
Exp: Unit Value[1]	157	178	133	170	193	180	198	191	155	148	Exp: valeur unitaire[1]
Terms of Trade	*117*	*122*	*109*	*124*	*127*	*118*	*135*	*135*	*131*	*131*	*Termes de l'échange*
Purchasing Power of Exports	*151*	*150*	*146*	*168*	*176*	*176*	*201*	*206*	*206*	*211*	*Pouvoir d'achat des export.*
Norway											Norvège
Imp: Quantum[2]	157	158	139	149	157	159	161	162	164	162	Imp: quantum[2]
Imp: Unit Value[2]	158	172	152	156	175	169	171	169	140	136	Imp: valeur unitaire[2]
Exp: Quantum[2]	106	107	103	101	98	99	94	96	100	99	Exp: quantum[2]
Exp: Unit Value[2]	214	270	189	217	276	274	277	251	175	150	Exp: valeur unitaire[2]
Terms of Trade	*136*	*157*	*124*	*139*	*158*	*162*	*161*	*149*	*125*	*110*	*Termes de l'échange*
Purchasing Power of Exports	*144*	*168*	*128*	*140*	*154*	*160*	*152*	*143*	*125*	*109*	*Pouvoir d'achat des export.*
Oman											Oman
Imp: Quantum	...	...	...	...	...	...	...	...	...	...	Imp: quantum
Imp: Unit Value	...	...	...	...	...	...	...	...	...	...	Imp: valeur unitaire
Exp: Quantum	...	...	...	...	...	...	...	...	...	...	Exp: quantum
Exp: Unit Value	244	378	212	287	385	410	395	386	212	150	Exp: valeur unitaire
Terms of Trade	...	...	...	...	...	...	...	...	...	...	*Termes de l'échange*
Purchasing Power of Exports	...	...	...	...	...	...	...	...	...	...	*Pouvoir d'achat des export.*
Pakistan											Pakistan
Imp: Quantum	169	184	178	173	161	157	153	178	198	215	Imp: quantum
Imp: Unit Value	167	216	178	203	251	263	269	267	248	223	Imp: valeur unitaire
Exp: Quantum	124	133	126	131	126	132	155	150	131	146	Exp: quantum
Exp: Unit Value	110	124	115	131	156	156	152	157	150	140	Exp: valeur unitaire
Terms of Trade	*66*	*57*	*65*	*65*	*62*	*59*	*57*	*59*	*60*	*63*	*Termes de l'échange*
Purchasing Power of Exports	*81*	*76*	*82*	*85*	*78*	*78*	*88*	*88*	*79*	*92*	*Pouvoir d'achat des export.*
Panama											Panama
Imp: Quantum	...	...	...	...	...	...	...	...	...	...	Imp: quantum
Imp: Unit Value	...	...	...	...	...	...	...	...	...	...	Imp: valeur unitaire
Exp: Quantum	96	75	62	60	...	...	...	...	...	...	Exp: quantum
Exp: Unit Value	...	...	...	...	...	...	...	...	...	...	Exp: valeur unitaire
Terms of Trade	...	...	...	...	...	...	...	...	...	...	*Termes de l'échange*
Purchasing Power of Exports	...	...	...	...	...	...	...	...	...	...	*Pouvoir d'achat des export.*
Papua New Guinea											Papouasie-Nouvelle-Guinée
Imp: Quantum	...	...	...	...	...	...	...	...	...	...	Imp: quantum
Imp: Unit Value	...	...	...	...	...	...	...	...	...	...	Imp: valeur unitaire
Exp: Quantum	94	100	102	102	103	88	91	99	97	...	Exp: quantum
Exp: Unit Value	271	329	222	291	380	373	344	306	227	...	Exp: valeur unitaire
Terms of Trade	...	...	...	...	...	...	...	...	...	...	*Termes de l'échange*
Purchasing Power of Exports	...	...	...	...	...	...	...	...	...	...	*Pouvoir d'achat des export.*

Indices of total exports and imports by countries or areas (Table G)

Quantum and unit value indices and terms of trade in US dollars (2000 = 100)

Indices des exportations et importations totales par pays ou zones (Tableau G)

Indices du quantum et de la valeur unitaire et termes de l'échange en dollars É.-U. (2000 = 100)

Countries	2007	2008	2009	2010	2011	2012	2013	2014	2015	2016	Pays
Peru											Pérou
Imp: Quantum	...	...	...	...	...	...	...	...	...	...	Imp: quantum
Imp: Unit Value	...	...	...	...	...	...	...	...	...	...	Imp: valeur unitaire
Exp: Quantum	150	163	162	159	159	173	169	172	...	...	Exp: quantum
Exp: Unit Value	316	297	231	336	404	368	303	325	...	...	Exp: valeur unitaire
Terms of Trade	...	...	...	...	...	...	...	...	...	...	*Termes de l'échange*
Purchasing Power of Exports	...	...	...	...	...	...	...	...	...	...	*Pouvoir d'achat des export.*
Poland											Pologne
Imp: Quantum	200	218	186	211	223	207	225	245	258	276	Imp: quantum
Imp: Unit Value[1]	171	199	166	174	193	185	186	183	152	145	Imp: valeur unitaire[1]
Exp: Quantum	243	260	238	270	291	278	321	338	366	392	Exp: quantum
Exp: Unit Value[1]	186	213	185	190	207	197	204	205	173	165	Exp: valeur unitaire[1]
Terms of Trade	*109*	*107*	*111*	*110*	*107*	*107*	*110*	*112*	*113*	*114*	*Termes de l'échange*
Purchasing Power of Exports	*264*	*278*	*265*	*296*	*313*	*297*	*351*	*379*	*415*	*446*	*Pouvoir d'achat des export.*
Portugal											Portugal
Imp: Quantum	99	92	80	96	...	...	...	...	...	...	Imp: quantum
Imp: Unit Value[1]	137	153	125	138	...	...	...	...	...	...	Imp: valeur unitaire[1]
Exp: Quantum	93	88	76	87	...	...	...	...	...	...	Exp: quantum
Exp: Unit Value[1]	144	155	136	143	...	...	...	...	...	...	Exp: valeur unitaire[1]
Terms of Trade	*105*	*101*	*109*	*104*	...	...	...	...	...	...	*Termes de l'échange*
Purchasing Power of Exports	*97*	*89*	*83*	*90*	...	...	...	...	...	...	*Pouvoir d'achat des export.*
Republic of Moldova											République de Moldova
Imp: Quantum	317	364	271	311	383	393	419	420	402	436	Imp: quantum
Imp: Unit Value	152	208	176	161	187	179	171	148	87	76	Imp: valeur unitaire
Exp: Quantum	244	268	248	290	399	406	462	482	489	530	Exp: quantum
Exp: Unit Value	124	159	131	121	138	129	121	101	63	57	Exp: valeur unitaire
Terms of Trade	*81*	*77*	*74*	*75*	*74*	*72*	*71*	*68*	*72*	*75*	*Termes de l'échange*
Purchasing Power of Exports	*199*	*205*	*184*	*218*	*294*	*293*	*329*	*330*	*354*	*399*	*Pouvoir d'achat des export.*
Romania											Roumanie
Imp: Quantum	369	394	299	345	381	376	387	421	463	508	Imp: quantum
Imp: Unit Value	100	103	92	96	102	102	100	98	96	93	Imp: valeur unitaire
Exp: Quantum	204	225	216	259	291	279	316	340	354	379	Exp: quantum
Exp: Unit Value	107	111	100	107	115	120	116	115	115	113	Exp: valeur unitaire
Terms of Trade	*108*	*108*	*109*	*112*	*113*	*117*	*116*	*117*	*120*	*121*	*Termes de l'échange*
Purchasing Power of Exports	*221*	*243*	*235*	*289*	*330*	*326*	*366*	*398*	*424*	*457*	*Pouvoir d'achat des export.*
Russian Federation											Fédération de Russie
Imp: Quantum	...	470	492	672	902	934	947	844	539	538	Imp: quantum
Imp: Unit Value	...	...	...	...	...	...	...	...	...	...	Imp: valeur unitaire
Exp: Quantum	...	261	291	387	501	509	513	483	333	277	Exp: quantum
Exp: Unit Value	...	...	...	...	...	...	...	...	...	...	Exp: valeur unitaire
Terms of Trade	...	...	...	...	...	...	...	...	...	...	*Termes de l'échange*
Purchasing Power of Exports	...	...	...	...	...	...	...	...	...	...	*Pouvoir d'achat des export.*
Saudi Arabia											Arabie saoudite
Imp: Quantum	...	...	...	...	...	...	...	...	...	...	Imp: quantum
Imp: Unit Value	...	...	...	...	...	...	...	...	...	...	Imp: valeur unitaire
Exp: Quantum	...	...	...	...	...	...	...	...	...	...	Exp: quantum
Exp: Unit Value	284	397	252	331	460	438	445	412	210	172	Exp: valeur unitaire
Terms of Trade	...	...	...	...	...	...	...	...	...	...	*Termes de l'échange*
Purchasing Power of Exports	...	...	...	...	...	...	...	...	...	...	*Pouvoir d'achat des export.*

Indices of total exports and imports by countries or areas (Table G)

Quantum and unit value indices and terms of trade in US dollars (2000 = 100)

Indices des exportations et importations totales par pays ou zones (Tableau G)

Indices du quantum et de la valeur unitaire et termes de l'échange en dollars É.-U. (2000 = 100)

Countries	2007	2008	2009	2010	2011	2012	2013	2014	2015	2016	Pays
Serbia											Serbie
Imp: Quantum	129	109	85	108	178	299	349	383	477	588	Imp: quantum
Imp: Unit Value	106	113	79	96	138	145	134	120	88	75	Imp: valeur unitaire
Exp: Quantum	126	112	90	122	168	236	306	336	375	436	Exp: quantum
Exp: Unit Value	110	110	83	97	155	187	185	175	139	132	Exp: valeur unitaire
Terms of Trade	*104*	*97*	*104*	*102*	*112*	*129*	*139*	*146*	*159*	*175*	*Termes de l'échange*
Purchasing Power of Exports	*131*	*109*	*94*	*125*	*188*	*304*	*425*	*491*	*595*	*762*	*Pouvoir d'achat des export.*
Singapore											Singapour
Imp: Quantum	158	175	150	177	183	190	192	196	198	206	Imp: quantum
Imp: Unit Value[1]	124	136	122	131	148	149	144	139	112	105	Imp: valeur unitaire[1]
Exp: Quantum	208	217	195	235	247	248	256	262	261	271	Exp: quantum
Exp: Unit Value[1]	104	113	101	109	120	120	116	112	96	91	Exp: valeur unitaire[1]
Terms of Trade	*84*	*83*	*83*	*83*	*81*	*81*	*81*	*81*	*86*	*86*	*Termes de l'échange*
Purchasing Power of Exports	*176*	*181*	*161*	*196*	*201*	*200*	*206*	*212*	*226*	*233*	*Pouvoir d'achat des export.*
Slovakia											Slovaquie
Imp: Quantum	...	...	...	...	...	...	...	...	...	...	Imp: quantum
Imp: Unit Value[1]	196	235	197	194	219	197	202	193	153	147	Imp: valeur unitaire[1]
Exp: Quantum	...	...	...	...	...	...	...	...	...	...	Exp: quantum
Exp: Unit Value[1]	221	248	220	243	270	243	245	236	193	187	Exp: valeur unitaire[1]
Terms of Trade	*112*	*106*	*111*	*125*	*123*	*123*	*121*	*122*	*126*	*127*	*Termes de l'échange*
Purchasing Power of Exports	...	...	...	...	...	...	...	...	...	...	*Pouvoir d'achat des export.*
Slovenia											Slovénie
Imp: Quantum	...	...	...	...	...	...	...	...	...	...	Imp: quantum
Imp: Unit Value	175	183	166	179	194	198	194	192	190	185	Imp: valeur unitaire
Exp: Quantum	...	...	...	...	...	...	...	...	...	...	Exp: quantum
Exp: Unit Value	168	171	163	172	184	186	184	182	183	180	Exp: valeur unitaire
Terms of Trade	*96*	*94*	*98*	*96*	*94*	*94*	*95*	*95*	*96*	*97*	*Termes de l'échange*
Purchasing Power of Exports	...	...	...	...	...	...	...	...	...	...	*Pouvoir d'achat des export.*
Spain											Espagne
Imp: Quantum	158	153	128	140	141	131	135	146	156	...	Imp: quantum
Imp: Unit Value	159	179	148	148	168	162	161	157	128	124	Imp: valeur unitaire
Exp: Quantum	133	136	122	142	157	157	166	174	180	...	Exp: quantum
Exp: Unit Value	166	181	160	154	169	160	165	163	137	135	Exp: valeur unitaire
Terms of Trade	*104*	*101*	*107*	*104*	*101*	*98*	*102*	*104*	*107*	*109*	*Termes de l'échange*
Purchasing Power of Exports	*139*	*138*	*132*	*148*	*158*	*155*	*170*	*180*	*192*	...	*Pouvoir d'achat des export.*
Sri Lanka											Sri Lanka
Imp: Quantum	140	147	131	149	...	...	...	...	...	...	Imp: quantum
Imp: Unit Value	53	48	56	...	...	...	...	...	...	...	Imp: valeur unitaire
Exp: Quantum	126	126	111	130	...	...	...	...	...	...	Exp: quantum
Exp: Unit Value	113	119	118	132	...	...	...	...	...	...	Exp: valeur unitaire
Terms of Trade	*213*	*250*	*211*	...	...	...	...	...	...	...	*Termes de l'échange*
Purchasing Power of Exports	*268*	*315*	*234*	...	...	...	...	...	...	...	*Pouvoir d'achat des export.*
Sweden											Suède
Imp: Quantum	140	142	119	140	152	150	146	154	162	171	Imp: quantum
Imp: Unit Value[1]	166	183	155	164	185	175	175	169	135	129	Imp: valeur unitaire[1]
Exp: Quantum	136	138	114	131	142	140	135	137	143	147	Exp: quantum
Exp: Unit Value[1]	148	158	139	145	161	152	151	148	122	117	Exp: valeur unitaire[1]
Terms of Trade	*89*	*87*	*89*	*89*	*87*	*87*	*86*	*88*	*90*	*90*	*Termes de l'échange*
Purchasing Power of Exports	*122*	*120*	*102*	*116*	*124*	*122*	*117*	*120*	*128*	*133*	*Pouvoir d'achat des export.*

Indices of total exports and imports by countries or areas (Table G)

Quantum and unit value indices and terms of trade in US dollars (2000 = 100)

Indices des exportations et importations totales par pays ou zones (Tableau G)

Indices du quantum et de la valeur unitaire et termes de l'échange en dollars É.-U. (2000 = 100)

Countries	2007	2008	2009	2010	2011	2012	2013	2014	2015	2016	Pays
Switzerland											Suisse
Imp: Quantum	124	126	113	123	127	127	126	125	125	127	Imp: quantum
Imp: Unit Value	161	179	171	179	204	195	200	205	182	183	Imp: valeur unitaire
Exp: Quantum	141	143	122	131	141	142	142	145	143	142	Exp: quantum
Exp: Unit Value	156	178	182	190	210	201	203	210	196	201	Exp: valeur unitaire
Terms of Trade	*96*	*99*	*107*	*106*	*103*	*103*	*102*	*102*	*108*	*110*	*Termes de l'échange*
Purchasing Power of Exports	*136*	*142*	*130*	*139*	*146*	*147*	*145*	*148*	*155*	*156*	*Pouvoir d'achat des export.*
Thailand											Thaïlande
Imp: Quantum	170	193	146	186	213	228	233	218	219	213	Imp: quantum
Imp: Unit Value	128	142	144	155	171	173	173	170	163	163	Imp: valeur unitaire
Exp: Quantum	178	186	160	186	203	207	208	210	207	207	Exp: quantum
Exp: Unit Value	128	144	139	152	160	161	158	155	138	135	Exp: valeur unitaire
Terms of Trade	*100*	*102*	*97*	*98*	*94*	*93*	*91*	*91*	*84*	*83*	*Termes de l'échange*
Purchasing Power of Exports	*178*	*190*	*155*	*183*	*190*	*193*	*190*	*191*	*175*	*171*	*Pouvoir d'achat des export.*
Turkey											Turquie
Imp: Quantum	179	177	154	181	204	206	223	221	224	236	Imp: quantum
Imp: Unit Value	162	195	157	170	195	190	187	181	153	139	Imp: valeur unitaire
Exp: Quantum	250	266	246	274	291	338	336	354	358	371	Exp: quantum
Exp: Unit Value	155	180	151	156	174	169	169	167	151	144	Exp: valeur unitaire
Terms of Trade	*96*	*92*	*96*	*92*	*89*	*89*	*90*	*92*	*98*	*103*	*Termes de l'échange*
Purchasing Power of Exports	*240*	*246*	*236*	*251*	*259*	*301*	*304*	*325*	*352*	*384*	*Pouvoir d'achat des export.*
United Kingdom											Royaume-Uni
Imp: Quantum	139	137	121	134	136	140	142	147	154	159	Imp: quantum
Imp: Unit Value[1]	135	143	123	129	145	143	141	143	125	114	Imp: valeur unitaire[1]
Exp: Quantum	115	117	105	115	123	121	119	121	130	129	Exp: quantum
Exp: Unit Value[1]	137	145	124	131	146	144	144	145	125	117	Exp: valeur unitaire[1]
Terms of Trade	*102*	*101*	*101*	*102*	*101*	*101*	*102*	*102*	*100*	*102*	*Termes de l'échange*
Purchasing Power of Exports	*117*	*118*	*105*	*117*	*124*	*122*	*122*	*123*	*130*	*131*	*Pouvoir d'achat des export.*
United States											Etats-Unis
Imp: Quantum	133	129	107	123	128	132	133	139	144	149	Imp: quantum
Imp: Unit Value[1]	120	134	119	127	141	141	139	138	124	120	Imp: valeur unitaire[1]
Exp: Quantum[3]	126	134	115	133	142	148	152	157	155	155	Exp: quantum[3]
Exp: Unit Value[1,3]	116	123	117	123	133	134	133	132	124	120	Exp: valeur unitaire[1,3]
Terms of Trade	*97*	*92*	*99*	*97*	*95*	*95*	*95*	*96*	*100*	*100*	*Termes de l'échange*
Purchasing Power of Exports	*122*	*123*	*114*	*129*	*135*	*140*	*145*	*150*	*155*	*155*	*Pouvoir d'achat des export.*
Venezuela (Bolivarian Rep. of)											Venezuela (Rép. bolivarienne du)
Imp: Quantum	...	...	...	...	...	...	...	...	...	...	Imp: quantum
Imp: Unit Value[1]	150	179	227	236	171	185	185	243	...	...	Imp: valeur unitaire[1]
Exp: Quantum	...	...	...	...	...	...	...	...	...	...	Exp: quantum
Exp: Unit Value	...	...	...	...	...	...	...	...	...	...	Exp: valeur unitaire
Terms of Trade	...	...	...	...	...	...	...	...	...	...	*Termes de l'échange*
Purchasing Power of Exports	...	...	...	...	...	...	...	...	...	...	*Pouvoir d'achat des export.*

Indices of total exports and imports by countries or areas (Table G)

Quantum and unit value indices and terms of trade in US dollars (2000 = 100)

Indices des exportations et importations totales par pays ou zones (Tableau G)

Indices du quantum et de la valeur unitaire et termes de l'échange en dollars É.-U. (2000 = 100)

General Note:

The volume and unit value/price indices are as compiled by countries. They show the changes in the volume (volume index) and the average price (unit value/price index) of total imports and exports. Using these indices UNSD calculates the terms of trade indices (export unit value/price indices divided by the corresponding import unit value/price indices), and the index of the purchasing power of exports (the terms of trade multiplied by the volume index of exports). Country footnotes which appear in Special Table B of this volume also apply to the country indices published in this table.

For further information on sources and presentation as well as for a brief table description please see the introduction.

1 Price indices.
2 Index numbers exclude ships.
3 Excluding military goods.

Remarque générale :

Les indices du volume et les indices de la valeur unitaire/prix sont comme compilées par les pays. Ils indiquent les variations des quantitées (indice du volume) et des prix moyens (indice de la valeur unitaire/prix) des importations ou exportations totales. Utilisant ces indices la Division de Statistique des Nations Unies calcule les indices des termes de l'échange (sont obtenus en divisant les indices de la valeur unitaire à l'exportation par ceux à l'importation), et l'indice du pouvoir d'achat des exportations (sont obtenu en multipliant l'indice des termes de l'échange du volume des exportations). Les notes se rapportant aux pays qui apparaissent dans le Tableau Spécial B de ce tome s'appliquent aussi aux indices de ce tableau.

Pour plus d'information sur les sources et la présentation ainsi qu'une brève description du tableau, se il vous plaît se référer à l'introduction.

1 Les indices des prix.
2 Les indices ne comprennent pas de navires.
3 Non compris les importations des economats militaires.

Indices of total exports and imports by regions (Table H)

Quantum and unit value indices and terms of trade in US dollars (2000 = 100)

Indices des exportations et importations totales par région (Tableau H)

Indices du quantum et de la valeur unitaire et termes de l'échange en dollars É.-U. (2000 = 100)

Regions - Régions	2005	2006	2007	2008	2009	2010	2011	2012	2013	2014	2015	2016
Exports - Unit value index / Exportations - Indice de la valeur unitaire[1]												
Total - Totaux	121	125	135	147	133	138	150	144	143	142	124	120
Developed economies - Economies développées[2]	127	131	143	157	143	146	161	155	156	155	134	131
North America - Amérique du Nord	113	118	124	133	123	131	141	141	140	139	128	123
Europe	138	143	159	176	158	158	175	166	170	171	144	141
Asia-Pacific - Asie-Pacifique	102	102	105	115	114	121	136	131	122	116	99	99
Africa - Afrique	123	123	127	122	119	128	137	122	111	105	91	81
Northern Africa - Afrique du Nord	100	102	110	116	114	112	127	117	116	126	120	126
Sub-Saharan Africa - Afrique subsaharienne	149	148	146	128	124	140	141	126	108	97	84	73
Latin America & The Caribbean - Amérique latine et	111	119	126	139	114	127	124	117	107	103	90	82
Latin America - Amérique latine	111	119	126	139	114	127	124	117	107	103	90	82
Western Asia - Asie Occidentale[3]	126	131	145	170	148	152	167	167	168	166	152	146
Other Asia - Autres Pays d'Asie	102	105	109	116	106	115	125	124	124	122	112	105
Eastern Asia - Asie Orientale	101	101	102	107	97	104	111	110	111	110	102	95
Southern Asia - Asie Méridionale	126	133	151	170	154	185	219	204	216	207	220	207
South-eastern Asia - Asie du Sud-est	99	106	111	121	111	120	130	131	127	123	109	104
Imports - Unit value index / Importations - Indice de la valeur unitaire[1]												
Total - Totaux	123	130	141	160	144	148	168	165	164	160	139	135
Developed economies - Economies développées[2]	125	132	144	162	141	147	166	161	160	158	133	128
North America - Amérique du Nord	110	116	121	134	120	128	141	142	140	138	125	121
Europe	136	144	159	178	154	158	178	170	171	169	140	134
Asia-Pacific - Asie-Pacifique	116	124	132	158	134	152	177	177	167	160	127	119
Africa - Afrique	137	...	...	...	...	...	...	...	...	...	...	...
Northern Africa - Afrique du Nord	95	101	117	123	111	108	123	100	97	107	100	103
Latin America & The Caribbean - Amérique latine et	121	134	148	184	175	184	193	202	206	192	209	341
Western Asia - Asie Occidentale	132	143	157	186	153	166	191	186	184	180	153	142
Other Asia - Autres Pays d'Asie	110	116	124	...	...	138	166	166	164	161	142	135
Eastern Asia - Asie Orientale	111	118	123	137	122	135	153	153	151	149	133	125
Southern Asia - Asie Méridionale	126	127	142	155	126	149	248	236	244	245	222	224
South-eastern Asia - Asie du Sud-est	110	119	124	136	127	137	153	154	152	146	127	121
Terms of trade / Termes de l'échange[4]												
Developed economies - Economies développées[2]	102	99	99	97	102	99	97	96	97	98	100	102
North America - Amérique du Nord	103	102	103	99	103	102	100	100	100	101	103	102
Europe	101	100	100	99	103	100	98	98	99	101	103	105
Asia-Pacific - Asie-Pacifique	88	83	80	73	85	80	77	74	73	72	78	83
Africa - Afrique	90	...	...	...	...	...	...	...	...	...	...	...
Northern Africa - Afrique du Nord	105	101	94	94	103	104	103	117	120	119	121	122
Latin America & The Caribbean - Amérique latine et	91	89	85	75	65	69	64	58	52	54	43	24
Western Asia - Asie Occidentale	95	92	93	92	97	92	87	90	91	92	99	103
Other Asia - Autres Pays d'Asie	93	90	87	...	...	83	75	75	76	76	79	78
Eastern Asia - Asie Orientale	90	86	83	78	80	77	72	72	73	74	77	76
Southern Asia - Asie Méridionale	100	104	107	109	122	124	88	86	89	84	99	93
South-eastern Asia - Asie du Sud-est	90	89	89	89	87	88	85	85	84	84	86	86

Indices of total exports and imports by regions (Table H)

Quantum and unit value indices and terms of trade in US dollars (2000 = 100)

Indices des exportations et importations totales par région (Tableau H)

Indices du quantum et de la valeur unitaire et termes de l'échange en dollars É.-U. (2000 = 100)

Regions - Régions	2005	2006	2007	2008	2009	2010	2011	2012	2013	2014	2015	2016
Exports - Volume index / Exportations - Indice du volume[5]												
Total - Totaux	133	148	158	167	145	170	185	193	198	202	203	205
Developed economies - Economies développées[2]	117	128	135	137	116	133	140	142	143	146	149	152
North America - Amérique du Nord	105	113	119	123	105	121	129	134	137	143	142	141
Europe	120	132	137	138	120	134	142	143	144	146	151	154
Asia-Pacific - Asie-Pacifique	127	139	151	155	120	150	150	149	148	151	154	159
Africa - Afrique	178	206	237	323	230	282	309	362	383	375	343	344
Northern Africa - Afrique du Nord	221	257	280	360	236	296	256	343	306	234	168	144
Sub-Saharan Africa - Afrique subsaharienne	147	168	204	297	225	267	338	368	428	456	443	452
Latin America & The Caribbean - Amérique latine et	143	159	171	180	169	191	245	262	288	290	285	301
Latin America - Amérique latine	143	158	170	179	169	192	244	262	288	289	284	299
Western Asia - Asie Occidentale	168	191	196	237	191	231	287	308	319	311	233	202
Other Asia - Autres Pays d'Asie	180	209	236	253	232	278	304	315	328	347	353	364
Eastern Asia - Asie Orientale	197	235	275	298	277	337	373	393	414	437	452	465
Southern Asia - Asie Méridionale	163	194	197	227	202	220	248	245	231	249	198	197
South-eastern Asia - Asie du Sud-est	154	170	182	190	170	204	220	223	232	243	248	257
Imports - Volume index / Importations - Indice du volume[5]												
Total - Totaux	131	142	150	152	131	154	162	165	169	175	178	177
Developed economies - Economies développées[2]	123	132	136	135	117	130	136	136	137	142	147	152
North America - Amérique du Nord	124	131	133	128	108	124	129	132	133	139	143	147
Europe	122	133	139	139	122	134	139	137	139	143	149	155
Asia-Pacific - Asie-Pacifique	124	129	133	135	119	131	138	144	144	146	151	151
Africa - Afrique	143	...	...	...	...	...	...	...	...	...	...	...
Northern Africa - Afrique du Nord	180	182	206	285	282	319	316	446	465	418	401	335
Latin America & The Caribbean - Amérique latine et	113	122	132	130	103	124	145	142	145	156	128	71
Western Asia - Asie Occidentale	157	171	195	206	202	217	229	248	268	277	295	290
Other Asia - Autres Pays d'Asie	168	185	200	...	...	236	240	249	259	266	262	268
Eastern Asia - Asie Orientale	171	189	209	216	206	251	269	276	293	301	294	301
Southern Asia - Asie Méridionale	198	233	255	316	318	343	270	296	272	274	263	244
South-eastern Asia - Asie du Sud-est	144	152	164	181	151	184	199	209	216	223	227	238

Indices of total exports and imports by regions (Table H)

Quantum and unit value indices and terms of trade in US dollars (2000 = 100)

Indices des exportations et importations totales par région (Tableau H)

Indices du quantum et de la valeur unitaire et termes de l'échange en dollars É.-U. (2000 = 100)

Source:

Compiled by the United Nations Statistics Division from international and national publications.For the composition of the regions, see Special Table A of this issue.

For further information on sources and presentation as well as for brief table description, please see the introduction.

1 Regional aggregates are current period weighted.

2 This classification is intended for statistical convenience and does not, necessarily, express a judgement about the stage reached by a particular country in the development process.

3 Index does not include data of the major oil producing countries.

4 Unit value index of exports divided by unit value index of imports.

5 Volume indices are derived from value data and unit value indices. They are base period weighted.

Source:

Compilé par la Division de statistique des Nations Unies à partir de publications internationales et nationales. Pour la composition des régions, voir tableau special A du présent numéro.

Pour plus d'informaton sur les sources et présentation ainsi qu'une brève description de la table, se il vous plaît se référer à l'introduction.

1 Les totaux généraux ont été pondérés selon la période en cours.

2 Cette classification est utilisée pour plus de commodité dans la présentation des statistiques et n'implique pas nécessairement un jugement quant au stade de développement auquel est parvenu un pays donné.

3 L'indice ne comprend pas les données des principaux pays producteurs de pétrole.

4 Indice de la valeur unitaire des exportations divisé par l'indice de la valeur unitaire des importations.

5 Les indices de volume proviennent des données sur la valeur et des indices de la valeur unitaire. Ils sont pondérés selon la période de base.

Indices and values of manufactured goods exports (Table I)

Unit value and volume indices (2000=100) and value in thousand million U.S. dollars

Indices et valeurs des exportations des produits manufacturés (Tableau I)

Indices de valeur unitaire et de volume (2000=100), et valeur en milliards de dollars E.-U.

Region, country or area	2005	2006	2007	2008	2009	2010	2011	2012	2013	2014	2015	2016
Unit value indices in U.S. dollars - Indices de valeur unitaire en dollars des E.-U. 2000 = 100												
Total 1/	**112**	**115**	**126**	**133**	**124**	**126**	**137**	**124**	**131**	**131**	**121**	**118**
Developed economies	**121**	**125**	**135**	**143**	**136**	**138**	**150**	**146**	**149**	**148**	**133**	**132**
America	108	111	115	120	115	121	129	126	131	127	120	116
Canada	119	128	135	142	128	142	152	149	143	139	127	121
United States 2/	104	107	110	116	113	117	124	122	128	124	119	115
Europe	128	132	146	154	145	144	156	152	157	159	140	140
Austria	...	...	...	173	164	163	178	164	161	160	140	139
Belgium	148	156	179	186	173	173	195	185	189	194	...	...
Denmark	138	141	145	157	155	147	156	144	148	143	122	116
Finland	130	141	166	178	158	163	185	186	204	213	188	194
France	111	109	118	124	125	121	132	123	127	127	106	104
Germany	128	132	144	155	145	140	149	144	150	152	131	131
Greece	...	...	...	...	...	...	...	...	...	...	...	...
Iceland	...	...	...	...	...	...	...	...	...	...	...	...
Ireland	...	...	...	...	...	...	...	...	...	...	...	...
Italy	143	150	174	195	184	183	202	191	198	200	174	175
Netherlands	139	144	176	...	...	...	...	...	...	...	...	...
Norway	131	145	169	176	148	155	174	164	161	160	137	128
Portugal	...	...	...	...	...	...	...	...	...	...	...	...
Spain	...	...	...	...	...	...	...	...	...	...	...	...
Sweden	...	...	...	...	...	...	...	...	...	...	...	...
Switzerland	...	...	...	...	...	...	...	...	...	...	...	...
United Kingdom	120	123	133	136	124	125	132	132	130	133	124	116
Other developed economies	112	114	119	128	129	138	151	153	139	133	121	123
Australia	151	203	245	223	155	205	235	225	213	...	...	...
Israel	109	118	124	126	120	121	129	131	133	125	117	114
Japan	111	112	117	129	133	141	155	158	144	139	128	133
New Zealand	136	140	155	163	131	152	171	166	164	164	140	132
South Africa	...	...	...	...	...	...	...	...	...	...	...	...
Developing economies	**98**	**102**	**110**	**117**	**103**	**108**	**117**	**96**	**108**	**107**	**103**	**98**
China, Hong Kong SAR	96	93	94	99	100	105	110	116	119	117	113	116
India	143	...	...	144	132	166	...	188	...	...	159	157
Korea, Republic of 3/	96	101	106	99	84	90	98	90	89	87	77	...
Pakistan	106	108	108	108	101	118	150	149	147	142	131	...
Singapore	77	79	79	80	77	79	82	81	80	78	74	71
Turkey 4/	130	127	137	171	...	153	170	163	165	162	148	142
Unit value indices in 'SDR' - Indices de valeur unitaire en 'DTS' 2000 = 100												
Total	**99**	**103**	**108**	**111**	**105**	**109**	**114**	**106**	**114**	**113**	**114**	**112**
Developed economies	**108**	**112**	**116**	**119**	**116**	**119**	**125**	**126**	**129**	**128**	**125**	**125**
Developing economies	**87**	**91**	**94**	**97**	**88**	**93**	**97**	**82**	**93**	**93**	**97**	**93**

For general note and footnotes see end of Table K.

Indices and values of manufactured goods exports (Table I)

Unit value and volume indices (2000=100) and value in thousand million U.S. dollars

Indices et valeurs des exportations des produits manufacturés (Tableau I)

Indices de valeur unitaire et de volume (2000=100), et valeur en milliards de dollars E.-U.

Unit value indices in national currency - Indices de valeur unitaire en monnaie nationale

2000 = 100

2005	2006	2007	2008	2009	2010	2011	2012	2013	2014	2015	2016	Région, pays ou zones
...	...	...	...	...	...	...	...	...	...	...	...	**Totaux 1/**
...	...	...	...	...	...	...	...	...	...	...	...	**Economies dévelopeées**
...	...	...	...	...	...	...	...	...	...	...	...	Amérique
97	98	97	101	98	98	101	100	99	103	109	108	Canada
104	107	110	116	113	117	124	122	128	124	119	115	Etats-Unis 2/
...	...	...	...	...	...	...	...	...	...	...	...	Europe
...	...	...	109	109	113	118	118	112	112	117	116	Autriche
110	115	120	116	114	121	130	133	131	135	...	...	Belgique
102	103	97	98	102	102	104	103	103	99	102	97	Danemark
97	104	112	111	105	114	123	134	142	148	157	162	Finlande
82	81	80	78	83	84	88	89	88	89	88	87	France
95	97	97	97	96	97	99	104	104	105	109	109	Allemagne
...	...	...	...	...	...	...	...	...	...	...	...	Grèce
...	...	...	...	...	...	...	...	...	...	...	...	Islande
...	...	...	...	...	...	...	...	...	...	...	...	Irlande
107	111	118	123	123	128	135	138	139	140	146	147	Italie
103	106	118	...	...	...	...	...	...	...	...	...	Pays-Bas
96	106	112	111	105	106	110	108	107	114	125	122	Norvège
...	...	...	...	...	...	...	...	...	...	...	...	Portugal
...	...	...	...	...	...	...	...	...	...	...	...	Espagne
...	...	...	...	...	...	...	...	...	...	...	...	Suède
...	...	...	...	...	...	...	...	...	...	...	...	Suisse
100	101	101	111	120	122	125	126	126	122	122	129	Royaume-Uni
...	...	...	...	...	...	...	...	...	...	...	...	Autres économies dévelopées
114	156	169	153	114	129	131	125	127	...	...	...	Australie
...	...	...	...	...	...	...	...	...	...	...	...	Israël
114	121	127	124	115	115	115	117	131	136	144	134	Japon
88	98	96	104	95	95	98	93	91	90	90	86	Nouvelle-Zélande
...	...	...	...	...	...	...	...	...	...	...	...	Afrique du Sud
...	...	...	...	...	...	...	...	...	...	...	...	**Economies en voie de développement**
96	93	94	99	99	104	110	115	119	116	112	116	Chine, Hong-Kong RAS
140	...	...	138	141	169	...	224	...	...	227	235	Inde
87	85	87	94	95	92	96	90	86	81	77	...	Corée, République de 3/
119	123	124	143	156	191	244	264	282	273	254	...	Pakistan
75	73	69	65	64	63	60	59	58	57	59	57	Singapour
...	...	...	...	...	...	...	...	...	...	...	...	Turquie 4/

Voir à la fin du Tableau K pour la remarque générale et les notes.

Indices and values of manufactured goods exports (Table I)

Unit value and volume indices (2000=100) and value in thousand million U.S. dollars

Indices et valeurs des exportations des produits manufacturés (Tableau I)

Indices de valeur unitaire et de volume (2000=100), et valeur en milliards de dollars E.-U.

Region, country or area	2005	2006	2007	2008	2009	2010	2011	2012	2013	2014	2015	2016
						Volume indices - Indices de volume 2000 = 100						
Total	138	152	144	144	124	142	147	160	156	158	159	163
Developed economies	118	128	134	133	109	124	130	129	127	132	135	136
America	104	113	120	118	97	108	112	119	115	122	125	122
Canada	100	99	100	90	72	78	80	83	85	90	96	98
United States	105	118	126	126	104	117	121	130	124	132	133	129
Europe	126	136	141	141	119	134	142	138	137	141	147	148
Austria	...	...	...	174	137	149	163	165	179	184	182	185
Belgium	107	107	109	111	83	92	94	91	92	94	...	...
Denmark	129	137	148	153	125	135	149	151	153	165	170	183
Finland	108	116	116	115	84	85	83	75	67	66	63	57
France	133	149	152	159	124	139	143	148	152	167	175	178
Germany	138	152	165	153	138	165	180	176	174	178	183	186
Greece	...	...	...	...	...	...	...	...	...	...	...	...
Iceland	...	...	...	...	...	...	...	...	...	...	...	...
Ireland	...	...	...	...	...	...	...	...	...	...	...	...
Italy	106	112	116	110	87	95	100	100	101	104	104	104
Netherlands	135	147	147	...	...	...	...	...	...	...	...	...
Norway	119	129	141	149	134	139	133	132	136	137	141	133
Portugal	...	...	...	...	...	...	...	...	...	...	...	...
Spain	...	...	...	...	...	...	...	...	...	...	...	...
Sweden	...	...	...	...	...	...	...	...	...	...	...	...
Switzerland	...	...	...	...	...	...	...	...	...	...	...	...
United Kingdom	111	124	112	113	96	107	116	116	119	119	122	121
Other developed economies	112	120	127	128	94	115	113	109	109	112	110	111
Australia	88	73	73	85	93	86	86	88	88	...	...	...
Israel	125	123	134	135	123	145	151	146	148	165	169	165
Japan	110	117	123	121	86	108	105	101	98	98	96	95
New Zealand	115	117	119	113	112	113	117	118	117	119	127	126
South Africa	...	...	...	...	...	...	...	...	...	...	...	...
Developing economies	185	208	167	169	156	181	187	231	220	217	213	226
China, Hong Kong SAR	75	77	60	45	27	31	26	22	19	20	17	14
India	148	...	...	233	263	249	...	...	...	...	337	347
Korea, Republic of	175	188	203	241	249	297	315	333	351	370	398	...
Pakistan	155	160	163	176	163	165	151	148	150	156	151	...
Singapore	191	230	250	253	223	274	289	296	307	316	312	310
Turkey	204	240	279	268	...	259	277	301	314	335	327	336

For general note and footnotes see end of Table K.

Indices and values of manufactured goods exports (Table I)

Unit value and volume indices (2000=100) and value in thousand million U.S. dollars

Indices et valeurs des exportations des produits manufacturés (Tableau I)

Indices de valeur unitaire et de volume (2000=100), et valeur en milliards de dollars E.-U.

In thousand million U.S. dollars — En milliards de dollars E.-U.

Value - Valeur
In thousand million U.S. dollars - En milliards de dollars E.-U.

2005	2006	2007	2008	2009	2010	2011	2012	2013	2014	2015	2016	Région, pays ou zones
7143.91	8110.93	8385.88	8879.06	7057.63	8273.09	9301.19	9151.33	9427.95	9547.27	8907.39	8883.91	**Totaux**
4593.91	5130.93	5795.88	6099.06	4777.63	5523.09	6231.19	6041.33	6097.95	6275.74	5799.48	5766.58	**Economies dévelopées**
872	983	1071	1105	870	1017	1123	1169	1174.69	1206.37	1165.96	1104.49	Amérique
219	235	248	235	170	203	225	228	224.69	229.24	223.78	219.72	Canada
653	748	823	870	700	814	898	941	950	977.13	942.18	884.77	Etats-Unis
3058.41	3429.65	3929.33	4135.75	3273.29	3668.95	4206.11	3994.22	4124	4290.77	3930.05	3946.01	Europe
100	114	134	150	112	121	145	135	143.57	146.75	126.86	127.43	Autriche
210	222	258	275	191	213	243	223	231	242.35	305.06	308.99	Belgique
56.59	61.09	68.42	76.18	61.4	63.34	73.81	68.99	72.12	75.41	66.32	67.7	Danemark
56.06	65.09	76.79	81.29	52.6	55.4	61.02	55.38	54.69	56.11	46.94	43.6	Finlande
365	405	449	490	384	419	470	454	479.7	530.54	463.97	461.85	France
849	970	1140	1140	962	1110	1290	1220	1256.82	1294.01	1156.64	1167.07	Allemagne
10.72	11.98	14	15.43	11.68	...	...	...	...	...	12.4	12.19	Grèce
1.06	1.25	1.85	2.9	1.97	2.55	2.88	2.6	2.42	2.54	2.43	2.15	Islande
94	96.45	102	108	98.19	98.63	110	100	97.19	97.4	106.43	113.07	Irlande
324	362	433	462	343	376	435	410	432.26	447.22	390.18	393.86	Italie
240	271	331	351	286	324	357	337	344	358.99	309.37	321.21	Pays-Bas
25.9	31.11	39.53	43.61	33.11	35.61	38.46	36.02	36.22	36.32	32.09	28.21	Norvège
28.83	32.14	32.93	39.73	30.34	35.05	44.18	42.83	45.73	47.89	41.68	42.68	Portugal
150	167	197	209	166	182	212	197	218.37	224.36	203.78	208.19	Espagne
111	124	143	151	107	128	151	134	128	128.01	112.3	112.37	Suède
123	138	158	182	...	...	...	202	208	217.13	201.12	205.99	Suisse
311	355	348	356	278	311	359	358	360.8	369.34	350.41	326.8	Royaume-Uni
663.51	718.29	795.55	858.31	634.34	837.14	902.08	878.11	799.25	778.6	703.47	716.07	Autres économies dévelopées
28.17	31.61	38.06	40.31	30.57	37.16	43.01	41.88	39.59	37.47	33.35	32.52	Australie
40.47	43.33	49.36	50.67	44.06	52.12	57.88	56.74	58.26	61.04	58.62	55.72	Israël
554	597	654	708	519	695	741	725	640.97	619.47	557.71	575.93	Japon
7.32	7.68	8.64	8.65	6.88	8.04	9.38	9.22	9	9.17	8.34	7.81	Nouvelle-Zélande
33.54	38.67	45.49	50.68	33.83	44.81	50.8	45.27	51.44	51.46	45.45	44.1	Afrique du Sud
2550	2980	2590	2780	2280	2750	3070	3110	3330	3271.52	3107.91	3117.34	**Economies en voie de développement**
16.3	16.01	12.52	10.03	6.14	7.21	6.38	5.66	5.15	5.22	4.21	3.74	Chine, Hong-Kong RAS
74.07	86.12	96.89	117	121.24	145.12	188.89	184.56	207.5	204.83	187.54	190.67	Inde
263	297	339	373	329	420	485	473	491.22	506.29	480.78	454.54	Corée, République de
12.69	13.37	13.61	14.66	12.68	15.06	17.49	17.12	16.94	17.19	15.21	14.81	Pakistan
176	217	234	240	203	259	284	286	293	294.5	274.41	263.68	Singapour
61.13	70.89	88.65	106	80.3	91.65	109	113	120	125.92	111.7	110.03	Turquie

Voir à la fin du Tableau K pour la remarque générale et les notes.

Indices and values of fuel imports - Developed economies (Table J)

Unit value and volume indices (2000=100) and value in thousand million U.S. dollars

Indices et valeurs des importations de produits énergétiques - Pays à économies développées (Tableau J)

Indices de valeur unitaire et de volume (2000=100), et valeur en milliards de dollars E.-U.

Region, country or area	2005	2006	2007	2008	2009	2010	2011	2012	2013	2014	2015	2016
Unit Value Indices in U.S. dollars - Indices de valeur unitaire en dollars des E.-U. 2000 = 100												
Developed economies	175	192	207	293	197	244	318	321	312	296	191	161
America	187	220	243	331	207	262	348	343	337	323	180	145
Canada	215	255	279	374	236	291	362	354	345	325	189	160
United States 1/..............	185	217	240	328	204	259	346	342	336	323	178	143
Europe 2/	175	203	217	296	195	232	296	302	297	279	196	174
Austria	190	227	244	347	231	268	348	339	330	298	191	151
Belgium............................	188	210	217	316	194	248	344	323	320	286	...	...
Denmark	188	220	241	333	211	249	327	316	300	285	181	145
Finland	167	205	224	317	212	261	362	483	670	814	545	436
France	198	240	263	370	208	251	344	402	391	358	217	173
Germany	189	228	234	341	227	255	347	402	397	356	221	173
Greece	...	...	...	...	...	...	...	...	...	...	...	...
Iceland	...	...	...	...	...	...	...	...	...	...	...	...
Ireland	...	...	...	...	...	...	...	...	...	...	...	...
Italy	178	218	249	340	225	296	398	403	385	357	213	176
Netherlands	...	...	...	...	...	...	...	...	...	...	...	...
Norway	182	221	242	331	221	276	362	359	348	315	201	173
Portugal	...	...	...	...	...	...	...	...	...	...	...	...
Spain	135	161	174	231	150	179	236	240	227	210	131	...
Sweden	...	...	...	...	...	...	...	...	...	...	...	...
Switzerland	...	...	...	...	...	...	...	...	...	...	...	...
United Kingdom	222	275	300	402	267	338	451	458	465	409	247	225
Other developed economies ..	158	138	150	242	190	252	337	347	325	307	193	153
Australia	214	265	285	405	250	327	454	452	431	...	...	...
Israel	190	205	228	349	227	285	397	379	367	338	196	164
Japan	153	128	138	234	186	249	338	353	331	318	186	141
New Zealand	196	244	266	364	211	277	377	397	381	359	204	160
South Africa	...	...	...	...	...	...	...	...	...	...	...	...

For general note and footnotes see end of Table K.

Indices and values of fuel imports - Developed economies (Table J)

Unit value and volume indices (2000=100) and value in thousand million U.S. dollars

Indices et valeurs des importations de produits énergétiques - Pays à économies développées (Tableau J)

Indices de valeur unitaire et de volume (2000=100), et valeur en milliards de dollars E.-U.

In thousand million U.S. dollars — En milliards de dollars E.-U.

Unit value indices in national currency - Indices de valeur unitaire en monnaie nationale
2000 = 100

2005	2006	2007	2008	2009	2010	2011	2012	2013	2014	2015	2016	Région, pays ou zones
...	...	...	...	...	...	...	...	...	...	...	...	**Economies dévelopeées**
...	...	...	...	...	...	...	...	...	...	...	...	Amérique
176	195	201	267	181	202	241	238	239	242	162	142	Canada
185	217	240	328	204	259	346	342	336	323	178	143	Etats-Unis 1/
...	...	...	...	...	...	...	...	...	...	...	...	Europe 2/
141	167	165	218	153	187	231	244	229	207	159	126	Autriche
139	154	146	198	129	173	228	232	223	199	...	...	Belgique
139	161	162	209	140	173	217	227	208	197	151	121	Danemark
124	151	151	198	140	182	240	347	466	566	454	364	Finlande
147	176	177	232	138	175	228	289	272	249	180	145	France
140	167	158	214	151	178	231	289	276	248	184	144	Allemagne
...	...	...	...	...	...	...	...	...	...	...	...	Grece
...	...	...	...	...	...	...	...	...	...	...	...	Islande
...	...	...	...	...	...	...	...	...	...	...	...	Irlande
133	162	169	214	150	207	266	292	270	250	179	148	Italie
...	...	...	...	...	...	...	...	...	...	...	...	Pays-Bas
133	161	160	210	156	189	230	237	232	225	183	164	Norvège
...	...	...	...	...	...	...	...	...	...	...	...	Portugal
100	119	117	145	100	125	157	172	158	146	109	...	Espagne
...	...	...	...	...	...	...	...	...	...	...	...	Suède
...	...	...	...	...	...	...	...	...	...	...	...	Suisse
185	226	227	327	258	331	426	437	450	376	245	252	Royaume-Uni
...	...	...	...	...	...	...	...	...	...	...	...	Autres économies dévelopées
163	204	197	277	183	207	255	253	259	...	...	...	Australie
...	...	...	...	...	...	...	...	...	...	...	...	Israël
157	138	151	225	161	202	250	261	300	312	209	142	Japon
126	170	163	232	150	173	215	222	210	196	132	104	Nouvelle-Zélande
...	...	...	...	...	...	...	...	...	...	...	...	Afrique du Sud

Voir à la fin du Tableau K pour la remarque générale et les notes.

Indices and values of fuel imports - Developed economies (Table J)

Unit value and volume indices (2000=100) and value in thousand million U.S. dollars

Indices et valeurs des importations de produits énergétiques - Pays à économies développées (Tableau J)

Indices de valeur unitaire et de volume (2000=100), et valeur en milliards de dollars E.-U.

Region, country or area	2005	2006	2007	2008	2009	2010	2011	2012	2013	2014	2015	2016
Volume indices - indices de volume 2000 = 100												
Developed economies	121	134	133	134	119	121	124	127	123	117	110	103
America	110	109	107	107	95	99	96	91	84	80	80	81
Canada	107	100	102	108	102	107	118	116	117	116	125	127
United States	111	110	108	106	95	98	94	89	81	76	76	77
Europe	133	142	140	148	139	144	151	156	154	144	132	120
Austria	205	218	172	163	166	160	168	177	160	157	163	173
Belgium	132	132	131	145	126	128	127	131	145	139	...	...
Denmark	106	100	91	109	110	110	121	125	152	121	125	123
Finland	118	129	126	127	120	120	125	87	66	49	38	44
France	109	110	106	108	120	115	115	98	97	92	97	94
Germany	110	114	111	111	107	112	111	100	102	102	102	102
Greece	...	...	...	...	...	...	...	...	...	...	...	...
Iceland	...	...	...	...	...	...	...	...	...	...	...	...
Ireland	...	...	...	...	...	...	...	...	...	...	...	...
Italy	148	153	145	144	140	132	120	117	107	94	104	101
Netherlands	...	...	...	...	...	...	...	...	...	...	...	...
Norway	92	97	105	97	116	139	122	115	138	115	126	116
Portugal	...	...	...	...	...	...	...	...	...	...	...	...
Spain	163	173	181	189	170	175	177	179	180	188	177	...
Sweden	...	...	...	...	...	...	...	...	...	...	...	...
Switzerland	...	...	...	...	...	...	...	...	...	...	...	...
United Kingdom	130	133	134	139	126	127	136	154	141	142	159	137
Other developed economies	111	159	161	151	113	110	114	123	123	120	112	105
Australia	113	120	130	135	144	143	155	167	169	...	...	...
Israel	99	90	105	100	85	96	96	118	110	105	105	99
Japan	110	162	162	147	106	103	104	110	110	106	105	102
New Zealand	105	105	111	110	120	110	111	113	116	118	120	127
South Africa	...	...	...	...	...	...	...	...	...	...	...	...

For general note and footnotes see end of Table K.

Indices and values of fuel imports - Developed economies (Table J)

Unit value and volume indices (2000=100) and value in thousand million U.S. dollars

Indices et valeurs des importations de produits énergétiques - Pays à économies développées (Tableau J)

Indices de valeur unitaire et de volume (2000=100), et valeur en milliards de dollars E.-U.

In thousand million U.S. dollars — En milliards de dollars E.-U.

Value - Valeur

In thousand million U.S. dollars - En milliards de dollars E.-U.

2005	2006	2007	2008	2009	2010	2011	2012	2013	2014	2015	2016	Région, pays ou zones
937.04	1136.83	1218.46	1736.72	1033.34	1308.77	1745.64	1797.71	1700.09	1530.09	930.14	738.55	**Economies dévelopeées**
314.86	365.39	396.39	538.47	300.13	393.06	508.15	476.37	430.21	392.95	220.32	179.31	Amérique
28.86	31.9	35.39	50.47	30.13	39.06	53.15	51.37	50.21	47.14	29.48	25.27	Canada
286	333.49	361	488	270	354	455	425	380	345.8	190.85	154.04	Etats-Unis
459.51	569.86	599.76	862.12	535.75	660.56	882.65	930.12	902.85	796	511.28	411.4	Europe
14.44	18.33	15.57	21.05	14.29	15.92	21.77	22.3	19.61	17.34	11.57	9.7	Autriche
38.21	42.6	43.79	70.49	37.63	48.98	67.06	64.85	71.18	61.16	45.66	37.89	Belgique
5.01	5.56	5.54	9.19	5.86	6.9	10	9.99	11.53	8.68	5.74	4.51	Danemark
7.87	10.52	11.24	16.08	10.13	12.54	17.98	16.7	17.73	15.87	8.31	7.56	Finlande
65.94	80.29	84.83	122	76.07	88.5	121	121	116.45	100.93	63.85	49.99	France
89.55	112	112	164	105	123	166	173	174.45	155.97	97.41	75.85	Allemagne
9.82	12.21	11.51	20.38	12.29	16.29	20.61	23.5	22.82	21.36	12.67	10.58	Grèce
0.48	0.5	0.55	0.71	0.42	0.51	0.72	0.72	0.72	0.8	0.63	0.6	Islande
4.77	5.59	6.47	10.24	6.44	7.41	9.39	9.02	9.14	8.63	5.7	4.14	Irlande
61.09	77.26	83.18	113	72.75	89.93	110	109	95.15	77.05	51.38	41.12	Italie
45.25	59	66.27	90.4	59.89	80.1	110	127	128	111.62	70.47	60.44	Pays-Bas
2.29	2.95	3.5	4.42	3.53	5.28	6.07	5.68	6.59	4.96	3.48	2.75	Norvège
8.97	9.95	9.16	14.99	9.02	11.01	14.17	14.77	14.67	13.5	8.86	6.77	Portugal
40.76	51.8	58.4	81.33	47.36	58.23	77.65	79.66	75.91	73.5	42.82	32.73	Espagne
13.04	15.74	16.89	24.38	13.97	20.02	25.1	26.42	22.94	22.26	13.53	12.5	Suède
9.05	11.24	11.15	16.21	11.15	...	...	18.95	16.51	13.55	9.37	6.82	Suisse
42.56	53.94	59.13	82.38	49.52	63.33	90.68	104	96.48	85.43	57.95	45.59	Royaume-Uni
162.67	201.58	222.31	336.12	197.46	255.15	354.84	391.23	367.03	341.14	198.54	147.84	Autres économies dévelopées
13.94	18.45	21.39	31.57	20.88	27.05	40.66	43.51	41.94	36.46	22.84	18.14	Australie
6.76	6.6	8.58	12.5	6.9	9.78	13.63	16.08	14.55	12.76	7.38	5.81	Israël
131	160	173	266	152	198	273	302	281.58	262.25	150.68	110.77	Japon
3.12	3.86	4.46	6.06	3.84	4.61	6.36	6.78	6.67	6.42	3.71	3.08	Nouvelle-Zélande
7.85	12.68	14.88	20	13.84	15.71	21.19	22.86	22.28	23.26	13.92	10.04	Afrique du Sud

Voir à la fin du Tableau K pour la remarque générale et les notes.

Some indicators on fuel imports - Developed economies (Table K)

Fuel imports as a percentage of total imports and exports, and ratio of unit value indices of manufactured goods exports and fuel imports

Quelques indicateurs sur les importations de produits énergétiques - Pays à économies développées (Tableau K)

Importation des produits énergétiques en pourcentage des importations et des exportations totales,
et quotient des indices de la valeur unitaire des exportations des produits manufacturés et des importations des produits énergétiques

Region, country or area	2005	2006	2007	2008	2009	2010	2011	2012	2013	2014	2015	2016
Fuel Imports as percent of total imports / Importation des produits énergétiques en pourcentage des importations totales												
Developed economies	14.2	15.2	14.6	18.6	14.7	16.0	18.3	19.2	18.1	16.1	11.1	9.0
America	15.3	16.1	16.5	20.9	15.6	16.6	18.7	17.0	15.4	13.7	8.1	6.9
Canada	8.9	9.1	9.3	12.4	9.4	10.0	11.8	10.9	10.9	10.1	7.0	6.2
United States	16.4	17.4	17.9	22.5	16.8	18.0	20.0	18.2	16.3	14.3	8.3	7.0
Europe	12.1	13.2	12.0	15.5	12.7	13.9	16.0	17.9	17.1	14.9	11.0	8.9
Austria	12.0	14.0	9.9	12.0	10.5	10.6	12.1	13.2	11.3	10.1	7.8	6.5
Belgium	11.9	12.1	10.6	15.1	10.7	12.6	14.5	14.9	15.7	13.6	12.0	10.2
Denmark	6.7	6.5	5.7	8.4	7.3	8.3	10.4	10.8	11.7	8.8	6.8	5.3
Finland	13.5	15.2	13.8	17.4	16.6	18.4	21.5	22.2	23.0	20.8	13.9	12.5
France	13.4	14.7	13.4	17.0	13.6	14.8	17.2	18.3	17.4	15.3	11.3	8.9
Germany	11.5	12.1	10.6	13.8	11.3	11.6	13.2	14.8	14.7	12.8	9.3	7.2
Greece	18.0	19.2	15.1	22.7	18.1	25.5	35.9	44.0	36.8	33.7	26.3	21.9
Iceland	10.5	9.9	8.7	12.7	11.7	13.1	15.3	15.4	15.0	15.3	12.0	10.7
Ireland	6.9	6.7	7.6	12.4	10.3	12.3	14.1	14.3	13.9	12.2	8.0	5.8
Italy	15.9	17.5	16.3	20.1	17.5	18.5	19.7	22.4	19.9	16.4	12.6	10.2
Netherlands	14.5	16.4	15.7	18.3	15.7	18.2	21.8	25.5	25.2	21.9	16.8	14.3
Norway	4.1	4.6	4.4	4.9	5.1	6.9	6.7	6.6	7.3	5.6	4.6	3.8
Portugal	16.8	15.2	12.0	15.8	12.6	14.6	17.8	20.5	19.5	17.4	13.3	10.0
Spain	14.2	15.9	15.2	19.5	16.3	18.4	21.4	24.4	22.7	20.9	14.1	10.5
Sweden	11.8	12.4	11.0	14.4	11.6	13.5	14.3	16.4	14.4	14.0	9.9	8.9
Switzerland	7.5	8.5	7.3	9.3	7.5	...	...	10.0	8.6	6.9	5.4	3.9
United Kingdom	8.8	9.8	9.5	12.9	10.2	11.3	14.2	16.1	14.9	12.9	9.2	7.7
Other developed economies	21.2	23.3	23.3	29.0	23.1	24.0	27.1	28.7	28.5	27.1	19.2	15.1
Australia	11.2	13.3	13.0	15.7	12.7	13.4	16.7	16.7	17.3	16.0	11.4	9.6
Israel	14.3	13.1	14.5	18.5	14.0	16.0	18.1	21.3	19.9	16.9	11.4	8.4
Japan	25.4	27.6	27.9	34.9	27.6	28.6	32.0	34.1	33.8	32.3	23.2	18.3
New Zealand	11.9	14.6	14.4	17.6	15.0	15.6	17.1	17.7	16.8	15.1	10.1	8.5
South Africa	14.3	18.7	18.6	21.1	21.5	19.6	21.3	22.6	22.0	23.3	16.2	13.4
Fuel imports as percent of total exports / Importations des produits énergétiques en pourcentage des exportations totales												
Developed economies	15.8	17.1	16.1	20.6	15.8	17.3	19.9	20.9	19.6	17.4	12.0	9.6
America	24.9	25.6	25.2	30.7	21.8	23.6	26.3	23.7	21.1	18.8	11.5	9.7
Canada	8.0	8.2	8.5	11.2	9.6	10.1	11.8	11.1	11.0	10.0	7.2	6.5
United States	31.5	32.1	31.1	37.5	25.5	27.7	30.7	27.4	24.1	21.3	12.7	10.6
Europe	12.0	13.2	12.0	15.6	12.5	13.9	15.9	17.4	16.5	14.3	10.6	8.5
Austria	12.2	14.1	9.9	12.2	10.9	11.1	12.8	14.0	11.7	10.2	7.9	6.7
Belgium	11.4	11.6	10.2	14.9	10.2	11.9	14.1	14.5	15.1	13.0	11.4	9.5
Denmark	6.0	6.1	5.4	7.9	6.4	7.2	8.9	9.4	10.4	7.9	6.1	4.8
Finland	12.1	13.6	12.5	16.6	16.1	18.1	22.8	23.0	23.9	21.5	14.0	13.2
France	14.9	16.4	15.4	20.0	16.0	17.3	20.8	21.8	20.6	17.7	12.9	10.2
Germany	9.2	10.0	8.5	11.3	9.4	9.8	11.2	12.3	12.0	10.4	7.3	5.7
Greece	56.8	58.8	48.8	79.5	60.0	75.5	67.4	70.4	62.9	59.6	44.5	37.7
Iceland	16.2	15.6	12.2	13.7	10.4	11.2	13.4	14.3	14.3	16.1	13.4	13.4
Ireland	4.3	5.3	5.3	8.1	5.5	6.2	7.3	7.6	7.9	7.3	4.7	3.3
Italy	16.4	18.6	16.6	20.7	17.9	20.1	21.0	21.8	18.4	14.6	11.2	9.0
Netherlands	12.9	14.7	13.9	16.7	13.9	16.3	19.5	22.8	22.5	19.4	15.0	11.8
Norway	2.2	2.4	2.6	2.6	2.9	4.1	3.8	3.6	4.3	3.5	3.4	3.1
Portugal	27.9	23.2	18.2	26.0	20.4	22.6	24.1	25.3	23.3	21.1	16.0	12.2
Spain	21.3	24.3	23.6	29.3	21.4	23.7	26.1	27.9	24.4	23.0	15.4	11.4
Sweden	10.0	10.7	10.0	13.3	10.7	12.6	13.4	15.4	13.7	13.7	9.7	9.0
Switzerland	7.2	7.9	6.8	8.4	6.7	...	...	8.7	7.6	5.9	4.4	3.2
United Kingdom	11.5	12.6	13.6	17.6	13.9	15.4	18.9	21.8	20.2	17.9	13.3	11.2
Other developed economies	19.9	22.5	22.1	29.4	22.7	22.1	27.4	31.5	31.7	30.1	20.0	14.7
Australia	13.2	15.0	15.2	16.9	13.6	12.8	14.9	16.9	16.6	15.1	12.1	9.5
Israel	15.8	14.1	15.9	20.5	14.4	16.8	21.1	25.4	21.9	18.6	11.6	9.7
Japan	22.0	24.7	24.2	34.0	26.2	25.7	33.2	37.8	39.4	38.0	24.1	17.2
New Zealand	14.4	17.2	16.5	19.8	15.4	15.3	16.9	18.2	16.9	15.4	10.8	9.1
South Africa	15.2	21.8	21.3	23.7	22.1	19.2	21.9	26.2	26.7	25.5	17.0	13.1

For general note and footnotes see end of table.

Some indicators on fuel imports - Developed economies (Table K)

Fuel imports as a percentage of total imports and exports, and ratio of unit value indices of manufactured goods exports and fuel imports

Quelques indicateurs sur les importations de produits énergétiques - Pays à économies développées (Tableau K)

Importation des produits énergétiques en pourcentage des importations et des exportations totales,
et quotient des indices de la valeur unitaire des exportations des produits manufacturés et des importations des produits énergétiques

2005	2006	2007	2008	2009	2010	2011	2012	2013	2014	2015	2016	Région, pays ou zones
Ratio of unit value indices of manufactured goods exports and fuel imports Quotient des indices de la valeur unitaire des exportations des produits manufacturés et des importations des produits énergétiques 2000 = 100												
69.0	65.0	65.0	49.0	69.0	57.0	47.0	46.0	48.0	50.0	70.0	82.0	**Economies dévelopeées**
58.0	50.0	47.0	36.0	56.0	46.0	37.0	37.0	39.0	39.0	67.0	80.0	Amérique
55.0	50.0	48.0	38.0	54.0	49.0	42.0	42.0	41.0	43.0	67.0	76.0	Canada
57.0	49.0	46.0	35.0	55.0	45.0	36.0	36.0	38.0	38.0	66.0	81.0	Etats-Unis
73.0	65.0	67.0	52.0	74.0	62.0	53.0	50.0	53.0	57.0	72.0	80.0	Europe
...	...	...	50.0	71.0	61.0	51.0	48.0	49.0	54.0	73.0	92.0	Autriche
79.0	75.0	82.0	59.0	89.0	70.0	57.0	57.0	59.0	68.0	...	...	Belgique
74.0	64.0	60.0	47.0	73.0	59.0	48.0	45.0	49.0	50.0	67.0	80.0	Danemark
78.0	69.0	74.0	56.0	75.0	63.0	51.0	39.0	30.0	26.0	35.0	45.0	Finlande
56.0	46.0	45.0	33.0	60.0	48.0	38.0	31.0	32.0	36.0	49.0	60.0	France
68.0	58.0	61.0	45.0	64.0	55.0	43.0	36.0	38.0	43.0	59.0	76.0	Allemagne
...	...	...	...	...	...	...	...	...	...	...	...	Grèce
...	...	...	...	...	...	...	...	...	...	...	...	Islande
...	...	...	...	...	...	...	...	...	...	...	...	Irlande
80.0	69.0	70.0	57.0	82.0	62.0	51.0	47.0	52.0	56.0	82.0	99.0	Italie
												Pays-Bas
72.0	66.0	70.0	53.0	67.0	56.0	48.0	46.0	46.0	51.0	68.0	74.0	Norvège
...	...	...	...	...	...	...	...	...	...	...	...	Portugal
...	...	...	...	...	...	...	...	...	...	...	...	Espagne
...	...	...	...	...	...	...	...	...	...	...	...	Suède
...	...	...	...	...	...	...	...	...	...	...	...	Suisse
54.0	45.0	44.0	34.0	47.0	37.0	29.0	29.0	28.0	33.0	50.0	52.0	Royaume-Uni
71.0	83.0	80.0	53.0	68.0	55.0	45.0	44.0	43.0	43.0	63.0	80.0	Autres économies dévelopées
71.0	77.0	86.0	55.0	62.0	63.0	52.0	50.0	49.0	...	...	...	Australie
57.0	58.0	54.0	36.0	53.0	42.0	33.0	35.0	36.0	37.0	59.0	70.0	Israël
72.0	88.0	84.0	55.0	71.0	57.0	46.0	45.0	44.0	44.0	69.0	94.0	Japon
70.0	58.0	58.0	45.0	62.0	55.0	45.0	42.0	43.0	46.0	69.0	83.0	Nouvelle-Zélande
...	...	...	...	...	...	...	...	...	...	...	...	Afrique du Sud

Voir la fin du tableau pour la remarque générale et les notes.

Tables I, J and K

General note:

Manufactured goods are here defined to comprise sections 5 through 8 of the Standard International Trade Classification (SITC). These sections are: chemicals and related products, manufactured goods classified chiefly by material, machinery and transport equipment and miscellaneous manufactured articles. Fuels are here defined to comprise all the products in section 3 of the SITC. These products are: coal, coke and briquettes, petroleum, petroleum products and related materials gas and electric current. The unit value indices are obtained from national sources, except those of a few countries which the United Nations Statistics Division compiles using their quantity and value figures. For countries that do not compile indices for manufactured goods exports and fuel imports conforming to the above definition, sub-indices are aggregated to approximate an index of SITC sections 5-8 and SITC section 3 respectively. Unit value indices obtained from national indices are rebased, where necessary, so that 2000=100. Indices in national currency are converted into U.S. dollars using conversion factors obtained by dividing the weighted average exchange rate of a given currency in the current period by the weighted average exchange rate in the base period. All aggregate unit value indices are current period weighted. The indices in SDRs are calculated by multiplying the equivalent aggregate indices in U.S. dollars by conversion factors obtained by dividing the SDR/$US exchange rate in the current period by the rate in the base period. The quantum indices are derived from the value data and the unit value indices. All aggregate quantum indices are base period weighted. The figures in Table K are calculated from those prepared for Tables I and J. Total imports and exports used in the calculations are, in general, those published in Table A.

Table I:

1/ Excludes trade of the countries of Eastern Europe and Commonwealth of Independent States.
2/ Beginning 1989, derived from price indices; national unit value index is discontinued.
3/ Average price indexes of manufacturing industry products.
4/ Industrial product.

Table J:

1/ Beginning 1989, derived from price indices; national unit value index is discontinued.
2/ In December 2011, estimates of 2010 unit value indices for certain European economies were revised.

Remarque générale:

Les produits manufacturéscomprennent les sections 5 à 8 de la Classificationtype pour le commerce international (CTCI). Ces sections sont produits chimiques et produits connexes, articles manufacturés classés principalement d'après la matière primière, machines et matérial de transport et articles manufacturés divers. Les produits énergétiques comprennent tous les produits appartenant à la section 3 de la CTCI. Ces produits sont huilles, cokes et briquettes, pétrole, produits dérives du pétrole et produits connexes, gaz et énergie électrique. Les indices de la valeur unitaire sont obtenus de sources nationales, á l'exception de quelque pays pour lesquels la Division de Statistique des Nations Unies calcule ces indices en utilisant le chiffres de la valeur et du volume fournis par ces pays. Pour les pays ne calculant pas leurs indices des exportations des produits manufacturés et importations des produits énergétiques selon la definition décrite ci-dessus les sous-indices sont agrégés en un indice qui se rapproche les sections 5 à 8 de la CTCI et la section 3 de la CTCI respectivement. Les indices en monnaie nationale son convertis en dollars des E.-U. en les multipliant par un facteur de conversion obtenu en divisant le taux de change courant, moyenne pondérés, d'une monnaie donnée par celui de la période de base. Tous les agrégés des indices de la valeur unitaire, sont à coéfficients de pondération correspondant à la période indiquée. Les indices indices en DTS son calculés en multipliant les indices totaux equivlents en dollars E.-U. par un facteur de conversion obtenu en divisant le taux de change cournat du DTS/$E-U d'une monnaie donnée par celui de la période de base. Les indices du quantum sont calculés à partir de chiffres de la valeur et lés indices de la valeur unitaire. Tous les agrégés des indices du quantum sont à coéfficients de pondération correspondant à la période en base. Les chiffres dans le tableau K sont calculés selon des données preparées pour les tableaux I et J. Les totaux des importations et exportations utilisées dans les calculs sont, en général, celles publiées dans le Tableau A.

Tableau I:

1/ Non compris le commerce des pays de l'Europe de l'Est et Communauté des États indépendants.
2/ A partir de 1989, calculés à partir des indices des prix; l'indice de valeur unitaire national est discontinué.
3/ Les indices moyens de prix des produits de l'industrie manufacturiere.
4/ Produit industriel.

Tableau J:

1/ A partir de 1989, calculés à partir des indices des prix; l'indice de valeur unitaire national est discontinué.
2/ En décembre 2011, les estimations des indices de valeur unitaire 2010 pour certaines économies européennes ont été mises à jour.

2016
International Trade Statistics Yearbook

Volume II
Trade by Product

Part 2 – Commodity Trade Profiles

- Food and live animals (SITC Section 0)
- Beverages and tobacco (SITC Section 1)
- Crude materials, inedible, except fuels (SITC Section 2)
- Mineral fuels, lubricants and related materials (SITC Section 3)
- Animal and vegetable oils, fats and waxes (SITC Section 4)
- Chemicals and related products, n.e.s. (SITC Section 5)
- Manufactured goods classified chiefly by material (SITC Section 6)
- Machinery and transport equipment (SITC Section 7)
- Miscellaneous manufactured articles (SITC Section 8)
- Commodities and transactions not classified elsewhere in SITC (SITC Section 9)

Food and live animals

(SITC Section 0)

001 Live animals other than animals of division 03

In 2016, the value (in current US$) of exports of "live animals other than animals of division 03" (SITC group 001) decreased by 9.0 percent (compared to -3.5 percent average growth rate from 2012-2016) to reach 19.3 bln US$ (see table 2), while imports decreased by 11.7 percent to reach 18.8 bln US$ (see table 3). Exports of this commodity accounted for 1.6 percent of world exports of SITC sections 0+1, and 0.1 percent of total world merchandise exports (see table 1). France, Netherlands and Canada were the top exporters in 2016 (see table 2). They accounted for 11.2, 9.6 and 8.4 percent of world exports, respectively. USA, Germany and Italy were the top destinations, with respectively 15.0, 9.5 and 7.9 percent of world imports (see table 3).

The top 15 countries/areas accounted for 75.7 and 67.6 percent of total world exports and imports, respectively (see tables 2 and 3). In 2016, France was the country/area with the highest value of net exports (+1.9 bln US$), followed by Canada (+1.4 bln US$). By MDG regions (see graph 2), the largest surpluses in this product group were recorded by Developed Europe (+2.4 bln US$), Developed Asia-Pacific (+1.3 bln US$) and Latin America and the Caribbean (+930.0 mln US$). The largest trade deficits were recorded by Western Asia (-2.0 bln US$), South-eastern Asia (-1.0 bln US$) and Developed North America (-630.1 mln US$).

Table 1: Imports (Imp.) and exports (Exp.), 2002-2016, in current US$

		2002	2003	2004	2005	2006	2007	2008	2009	2010	2011	2012	2013	2014	2015	2016
Values in Bln US$	Imp.	9.5	9.5	10.6	12.7	14.3	15.6	17.2	16.4	18.7	20.5	21.8	21.8	23.3	21.3	18.8
	Exp.	10.9	10.9	12.1	13.1	14.5	15.9	17.6	17.3	18.2	20.9	22.3	23.2	24.1	21.2	19.3
As a percentage of SITC section (%)	Imp.	2.1	1.8	1.8	2.0	2.1	1.9	1.7	1.8	1.9	1.7	1.8	1.8	1.8	1.8	1.6
	Exp.	2.6	2.2	2.2	2.2	2.2	2.0	1.8	2.0	1.9	1.8	1.9	1.8	1.9	1.8	1.6
As a percentage of world trade (%)	Imp.	0.1	0.1	0.1	0.1	0.1	0.1	0.1	0.1	0.1	0.1	0.1	0.1	0.1	0.1	0.1
	Exp.	0.2	0.1	0.1	0.1	0.1	0.1	0.1	0.1	0.1	0.1	0.1	0.1	0.1	0.1	0.1

Graph 1: Annual growth rates of exports, 2002–2016
(In percentage by year)

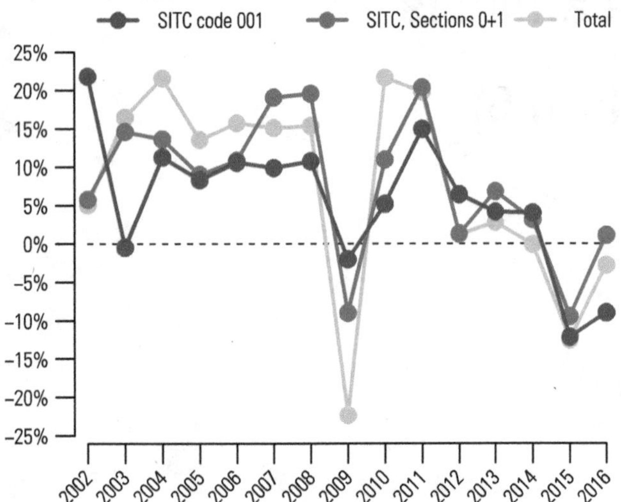

Graph 2: Trade Balance by MDG regions 2016
(Bln US$)

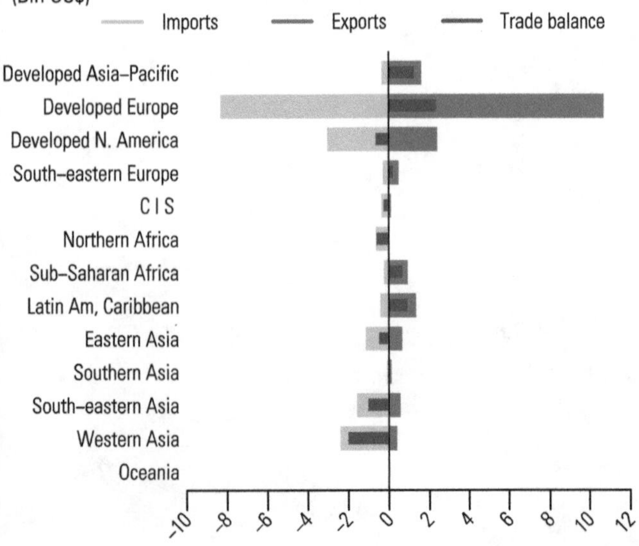

Table 2: Top exporting countries or areas in 2016

Country or area	Value (million US$)	Avg. Growth (%) 12-16	Growth (%) 15-16	World share %	Cum.
World	19302.1	-3.5	-9.0	100.0	
France	2152.6	-3.6	-2.9	11.2	11.2
Netherlands	1846.0	-8.5	-13.0	9.6	20.7
Canada	1613.7	-0.1	-15.8	8.4	29.1
Australia	1398.8	6.6	-1.8	7.2	36.3
Germany	1297.6	-7.2	-11.7	6.7	43.0
Denmark	1148.4	-0.6	13.0	5.9	49.0
USA	783.9	-9.9	3.5	4.1	53.1
Spain	693.4	4.5	6.8	3.6	56.6
United Kingdom	680.0	4.1	0.8	3.5	60.2
Mexico	669.0	-3.0	-25.3	3.5	63.6
China	646.7	2.6	8.2	3.4	67.0
Belgium	527.0	0.6	9.2	2.7	69.7
Romania	393.1	0.9	14.1	2.0	71.8
Czechia	377.7	1.4	3.5	2.0	73.7
Ireland	375.9	-2.9	-21.3	1.9	75.7

Table 3: Top importing countries or areas in 2016

Country or area	Value (million US$)	Avg. Growth (%) 12-16	Growth (%) 15-16	World share %	Cum.
World	18767.6	-3.7	-11.7	100.0	
USA	2823.1	1.7	-15.1	15.0	15.0
Germany	1779.9	-4.9	11.9	9.5	24.5
Italy	1487.0	-5.4	3.0	7.9	32.4
Netherlands	956.7	-8.6	-20.9	5.1	37.5
Belgium	651.0	-3.7	12.3	3.5	41.0
Indonesia	616.1	21.1	11.4	3.3	44.3
United Kingdom	608.4	-1.1	-21.4	3.2	47.5
Poland	606.1	2.9	9.6	3.2	50.8
Turkey	603.8	-8.2	87.1	3.2	54.0
China, Hong Kong SAR	596.9	-1.2	-5.9	3.2	57.2
Viet Nam	*494.5*	91.7	5.1	2.6	59.8
Spain	445.4	3.1	-3.1	2.4	62.2
China	394.5	-5.7	-28.2	2.1	64.3
Lebanon	310.7	2.0	-4.2	1.7	65.9
Ireland	304.5	5.7	-13.8	1.6	67.6

In 2016, the value (in current US$) of exports of "meat of bovine animals, fresh, chilled or frozen" (SITC group 011) decreased by 5.4 percent (compared to 1.2 percent average growth rate from 2012-2016) to reach 41.2 bln US$ (see table 2), while imports decreased by 8.0 percent to reach 38.2 bln US$ (see table 3). Exports of this commodity accounted for 3.5 percent of world exports of SITC sections 0+1, and 0.3 percent of total world merchandise exports (see table 1). Australia, USA and Brazil were the top exporters in 2016 (see table 2). They accounted for 13.4, 12.7 and 10.5 percent of world exports, respectively. USA, Japan and China were the top destinations, with respectively 13.0, 6.9 and 6.6 percent of world imports (see table 3).

The top 15 countries/areas accounted for 86.2 and 71.6 percent of total world exports and imports, respectively (see tables 2 and 3). In 2016, Australia was the country/area with the highest value of net exports (+5.5 bln US$), followed by Brazil (+4.1 bln US$). By MDG regions (see graph 2), the largest surpluses in this product group were recorded by Latin America and the Caribbean (+6.9 bln US$), Developed Asia-Pacific (+4.9 bln US$) and Southern Asia (+3.6 bln US$). The largest trade deficits were recorded by Eastern Asia (-6.8 bln US$), Western Asia (-1.7 bln US$) and South-eastern Asia (-1.6 bln US$).

Table 1: Imports (Imp.) and exports (Exp.), 2002-2016, in current US$

		2002	2003	2004	2005	2006	2007	2008	2009	2010	2011	2012	2013	2014	2015	2016
Values in Bln US$	Imp.	14.2	16.6	18.3	20.6	23.3	26.3	31.4	28.4	30.4	36.0	36.6	39.3	43.1	41.5	38.2
	Exp.	14.3	16.6	18.7	21.5	24.2	26.7	32.5	28.9	32.5	39.0	39.3	43.3	47.5	43.6	41.2
As a percentage of SITC section (%)	Imp.	3.1	3.2	3.1	3.2	3.3	3.2	3.2	3.2	3.1	3.0	3.1	3.2	3.3	3.5	3.2
	Exp.	3.3	3.4	3.4	3.6	3.6	3.3	3.4	3.3	3.4	3.4	3.3	3.4	3.7	3.7	3.5
As a percentage of world trade (%)	Imp.	0.2	0.2	0.2	0.2	0.2	0.2	0.2	0.2	0.2	0.2	0.2	0.2	0.2	0.3	0.2
	Exp.	0.2	0.2	0.2	0.2	0.2	0.2	0.2	0.2	0.2	0.2	0.2	0.2	0.3	0.3	0.3

Graph 1: Annual growth rates of exports, 2002–2016
(In percentage by year)

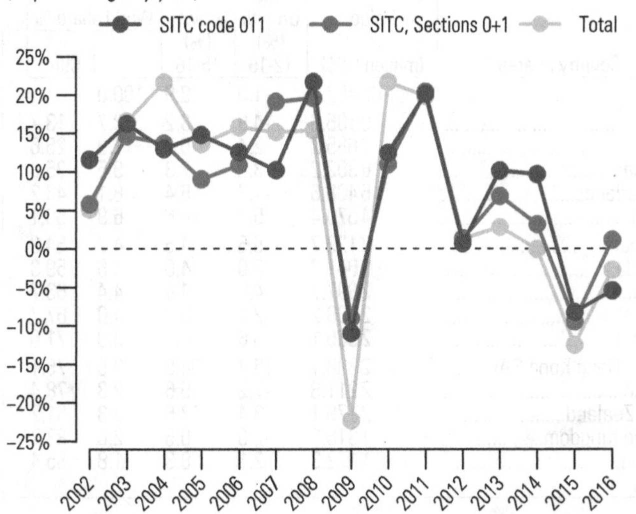

Table 2: Top exporting countries or areas in 2016

Country or area	Value (million US$)	Avg. Growth (%) 12-16	Growth (%) 15-16	World share %	Cum.
World	41224.8	1.2	-5.4	100.0	
Australia	5524.7	2.9	-21.0	13.4	13.4
USA	5249.1	3.0	1.4	12.7	26.1
Brazil	4344.8	-0.8	-6.8	10.5	36.7
India	3735.8	5.7	-8.9	9.1	45.7
Netherlands	2969.1	-0.2	18.5	7.2	52.9
Ireland	2015.0	0.1	3.3	4.9	57.8
New Zealand	1946.9	3.7	-15.1	4.7	62.5
Canada	1493.9	9.1	-2.4	3.6	66.2
Uruguay	1437.0	0.6	1.0	3.5	69.7
Germany	1372.5	-9.1	-7.3	3.3	73.0
Poland	1249.7	3.6	-4.4	3.0	76.0
Paraguay	1100.7	9.9	-1.9	2.7	78.7
Mexico	1093.4	10.0	0.2	2.7	81.3
Argentina	1027.8	0.9	19.0	2.5	83.8
France	995.5	-7.6	-1.9	2.4	86.2

Graph 2: Trade Balance by MDG regions 2016
(Bln US$)

Imports — Exports — Trade balance

Developed Asia-Pacific
Developed Europe
Developed N. America
South-eastern Europe
CIS
Northern Africa
Sub-Saharan Africa
Latin Am, Caribbean
Eastern Asia
Southern Asia
South-eastern Asia
Western Asia
Oceania

-15 -10 -5 0 5 10 15

Table 3: Top importing countries or areas in 2016

Country or area	Value (million US$)	Avg. Growth (%) 12-16	Growth (%) 15-16	World share %	Cum.
World	38170.8	1.0	-8.0	100.0	
USA	4972.7	9.3	-22.4	13.0	13.0
Japan	2649.7	-1.0	-4.8	6.9	20.0
China	2515.9	77.3	8.4	6.6	26.6
Italy	2093.7	-6.0	-5.8	5.5	32.0
Rep. of Korea	2091.5	13.5	15.2	5.5	37.5
Germany	2015.5	-2.1	-3.9	5.3	42.8
Netherlands	1991.4	0.1	6.7	5.2	48.0
China, Hong Kong SAR	1720.9	21.8	13.0	4.5	52.5
United Kingdom	1373.3	0.8	-12.9	3.6	56.1
France	1285.9	-8.0	-8.8	3.4	59.5
Russian Federation	1121.5	-21.5	-25.1	2.9	62.4
Egypt	1008.4	2.5	-30.7	2.6	65.1
Chile	895.6	1.6	8.7	2.3	67.4
Canada	835.2	-8.0	-18.3	2.2	69.6
Other Asia, nes	755.7	11.4	8.7	2.0	71.6

012 Other meat, meat offal, fresh, chilled, frozen (for human)

In 2016, the value (in current US$) of exports of "other meat, meat offal, fresh, chilled, frozen (for human)" (SITC group 012) increased by 2.9 percent (compared to -1.9 percent average growth rate from 2012-2016) to reach 66.5 bln US$ (see table 2), while imports increased by 0.1 percent to reach 63.1 bln US$ (see table 3). Exports of this commodity accounted for 5.6 percent of world exports of SITC sections 0+1, and 0.4 percent of total world merchandise exports (see table 1). USA, Brazil and Germany were the top exporters in 2016 (see table 2). They accounted for 13.7, 11.9 and 9.5 percent of world exports, respectively. China, Japan and China, Hong Kong SAR were the top destinations, with respectively 12.1, 10.1 and 6.4 percent of world imports (see table 3).

The top 15 countries/areas accounted for 85.4 and 69.3 percent of total world exports and imports, respectively (see tables 2 and 3). In 2016, Brazil was the country/area with the highest value of net exports (+7.8 bln US$), followed by USA (+6.4 bln US$). By MDG regions (see graph 2), the largest surpluses in this product group were recorded by Developed Europe (+9.9 bln US$), Developed North America (+8.3 bln US$) and Latin America and the Caribbean (+5.3 bln US$). The largest trade deficits were recorded by Eastern Asia (-10.7 bln US$), Western Asia (-2.2 bln US$) and Developed Asia-Pacific (-2.0 bln US$).

Table 1: Imports (Imp.) and exports (Exp.), 2002-2016, in current US$

		2002	2003	2004	2005	2006	2007	2008	2009	2010	2011	2012	2013	2014	2015	2016
Values in Bln US$	Imp.	26.1	29.6	34.6	38.9	39.9	46.4	58.3	52.9	56.9	68.8	69.1	70.5	73.2	63.0	63.1
	Exp.	24.7	28.6	34.1	39.3	40.0	47.4	59.7	53.9	58.8	71.1	71.7	74.2	77.1	64.6	66.5
As a percentage of SITC section (%)	Imp.	5.8	5.7	5.9	6.1	5.7	5.6	5.9	5.9	5.8	5.8	5.8	5.7	5.7	5.3	5.4
	Exp.	5.8	5.8	6.1	6.5	6.0	5.9	6.2	6.2	6.1	6.1	6.1	5.9	5.9	5.5	5.6
As a percentage of world trade (%)	Imp.	0.4	0.4	0.4	0.4	0.3	0.3	0.4	0.4	0.4	0.4	0.4	0.4	0.4	0.4	0.4
	Exp.	0.4	0.4	0.4	0.4	0.3	0.3	0.4	0.4	0.4	0.4	0.4	0.4	0.4	0.4	0.4

Graph 1: Annual growth rates of exports, 2002–2016
(In percentage by year)

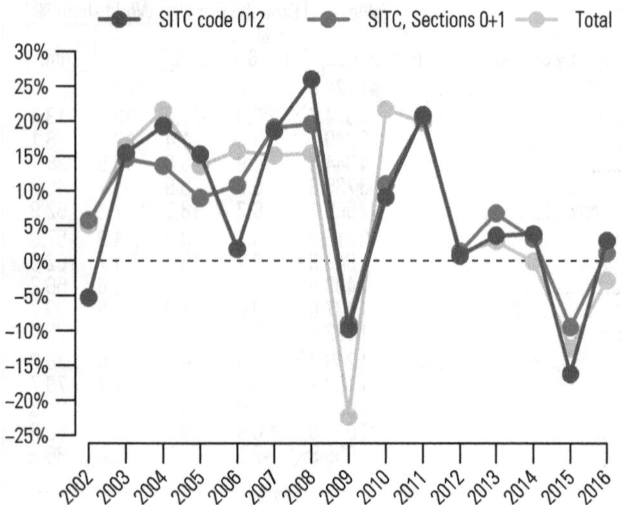

Table 2: Top exporting countries or areas in 2016

Country or area	Value (million US$)	Avg. Growth (%) 12-16	Growth (%) 15-16	World share %	Cum.
World	66467.8	-1.9	2.9	100.0	
USA	9105.6	-4.9	3.2	13.7	13.7
Brazil	7885.2	-2.4	-0.7	11.9	25.6
Germany	6302.2	-3.2	7.3	9.5	35.0
Netherlands	5408.6	-1.7	6.4	8.1	43.2
Spain	4570.4	5.0	16.6	6.9	50.1
Denmark	3122.7	-5.5	4.5	4.7	54.8
Canada	3041.7	-2.6	4.6	4.6	59.3
Poland	2897.7	4.0	4.4	4.4	63.7
Australia	2668.2	2.1	-5.3	4.0	67.7
Belgium	2565.1	-5.6	0.8	3.9	71.6
China, Hong Kong SAR	2338.1	15.7	34.6	3.5	75.1
France	2211.8	-7.2	-5.6	3.3	78.4
New Zealand	2179.1	-3.4	-12.6	3.3	81.7
United Kingdom	1315.3	-2.0	-0.5	2.0	83.7
Ireland	1172.3	2.1	8.3	1.8	85.4

Graph 2: Trade Balance by MDG regions 2016
(Bln US$)

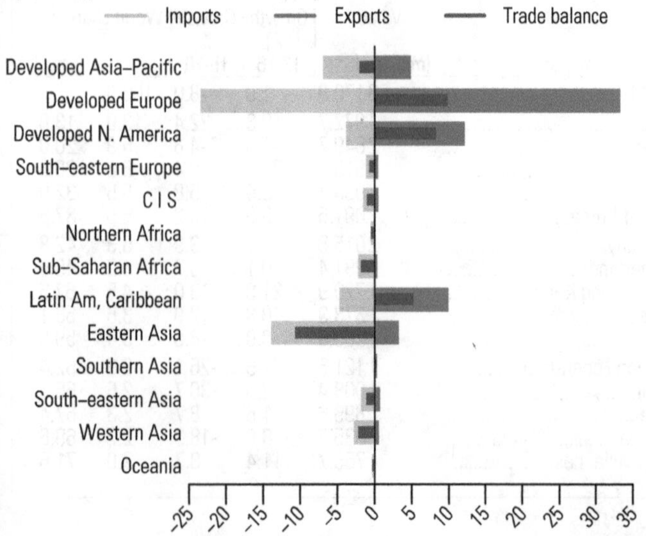

Table 3: Top importing countries or areas in 2016

Country or area	Value (million US$)	Avg. Growth (%) 12-16	Growth (%) 15-16	World share %	Cum.
World	63073.5	-2.3	0.1	100.0	
China	7600.9	18.6	71.0	12.1	12.1
Japan	6354.7	-2.5	11.2	10.1	22.1
China, Hong Kong SAR	4043.6	2.8	9.0	6.4	28.5
Germany	3745.0	-5.2	0.5	5.9	34.5
United Kingdom	3174.8	-0.3	-2.8	5.0	39.5
France	2754.1	-5.8	-6.9	4.4	43.9
USA	2752.7	6.6	-1.1	4.4	48.2
Mexico	2709.1	1.3	-3.3	4.3	52.5
Italy	2443.9	-5.0	-3.0	3.9	56.4
Rep. of Korea	1759.6	2.5	-4.0	2.8	59.2
Netherlands	1641.7	-5.3	-8.6	2.6	61.8
Poland	1419.8	-2.7	-0.8	2.3	64.1
United Arab Emirates	1154.5	1.3	-2.1	1.8	65.9
Russian Federation	1133.6	-26.7	-27.8	1.8	67.7
Canada	1041.6	-2.8	-5.4	1.7	69.3

In 2016, the value (in current US$) of exports of "meat, edible offal, salted, in brine, dried, etc; flours, meals" (SITC group 016) decreased by 4.4 percent (compared to -1.3 percent average growth rate from 2012-2016) to reach 4.5 bln US$ (see table 2), while imports decreased by 1.8 percent to reach 4.1 bln US$ (see table 3). Exports of this commodity accounted for 0.4 percent of world exports of SITC sections 0+1, and less than 0.1 percent of total world merchandise exports (see table 1). Italy, Netherlands and Spain were the top exporters in 2016 (see table 2). They accounted for 21.3, 18.0 and 11.3 percent of world exports, respectively. United Kingdom, Netherlands and France were the top destinations, with respectively 22.2, 12.5 and 10.6 percent of world imports (see table 3).

The top 15 countries/areas accounted for 95.9 and 84.7 percent of total world exports and imports, respectively (see tables 2 and 3). In 2016, Italy was the country/area with the highest value of net exports (+828.1 mln US$), followed by Spain (+435.0 mln US$). By MDG regions (see graph 2), the largest surpluses in this product group were recorded by Latin America and the Caribbean (+278.6 mln US$), South-eastern Asia (+162.8 mln US$) and Developed Europe (+100.0 mln US$). The largest trade deficits were recorded by Developed Asia-Pacific (-88.7 mln US$), Eastern Asia (-58.9 mln US$) and South-eastern Europe (-20.1 mln US$).

Table 1: Imports (Imp.) and exports (Exp.), 2002-2016, in current US$

		2002	2003	2004	2005	2006	2007	2008	2009	2010	2011	2012	2013	2014	2015	2016
Values in Bln US$	Imp.	2.2	2.6	2.6	2.5	2.9	3.7	4.2	3.9	4.0	4.4	4.3	4.6	4.8	4.1	4.1
	Exp.	1.9	2.4	2.7	2.6	3.0	3.9	4.7	4.1	4.3	4.9	4.7	5.2	5.5	4.7	4.5
As a percentage of SITC section (%)	Imp.	0.5	0.5	0.4	0.4	0.4	0.4	0.4	0.4	0.4	0.4	0.4	0.4	0.4	0.4	0.3
	Exp.	0.5	0.5	0.5	0.4	0.4	0.5	0.5	0.5	0.4	0.4	0.4	0.4	0.4	0.4	0.4
As a percentage of world trade (%)	Imp.	0.0	0.0	0.0	0.0	0.0	0.0	0.0	0.0	0.0	0.0	0.0	0.0	0.0	0.0	0.0
	Exp.	0.0	0.0	0.0	0.0	0.0	0.0	0.0	0.0	0.0	0.0	0.0	0.0	0.0	0.0	0.0

Graph 1: Annual growth rates of exports, 2002–2016
(In percentage by year)

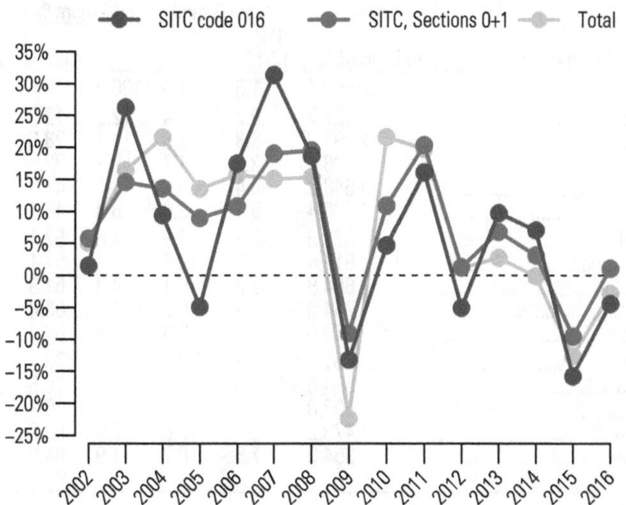

Table 2: Top exporting countries or areas in 2016

Country or area	Value (million US$)	Avg. Growth (%) 12-16	Growth (%) 15-16	World share %	Cum.
World	4451.5	-1.3	-4.4	100.0	
Italy	949.2	2.2	2.5	21.3	21.3
Netherlands	801.9	1.7	-4.2	18.0	39.3
Spain	504.1	6.7	2.3	11.3	50.7
Brazil	420.5	-5.3	-9.3	9.4	60.1
Germany	388.3	-4.9	-7.4	8.7	68.8
USA	257.5	0.4	0.9	5.8	74.6
Thailand	186.2	22.1	-13.6	4.2	78.8
Denmark	183.4	-16.7	-25.5	4.1	82.9
Belgium	115.1	-4.6	13.0	2.6	85.5
Canada	107.7	0.3	-1.1	2.4	87.9
Poland	101.2	-2.0	-17.7	2.3	90.2
France	77.5	-7.0	-11.5	1.7	91.9
United Kingdom	71.7	-5.4	-10.4	1.6	93.5
Austria	56.1	3.5	11.8	1.3	94.8
Switzerland	48.6	-2.3	16.1	1.1	95.9

Graph 2: Trade Balance by MDG regions 2016
(Bln US$)

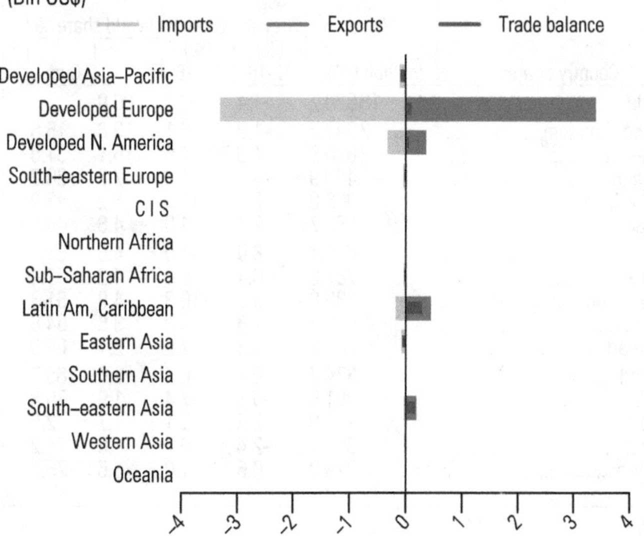

Table 3: Top importing countries or areas in 2016

Country or area	Value (million US$)	Avg. Growth (%) 12-16	Growth (%) 15-16	World share %	Cum.
World	4069.6	-1.1	-1.8	100.0	
United Kingdom	904.5	-6.0	-10.2	22.2	22.2
Netherlands	510.3	3.4	9.0	12.5	34.8
France	430.4	-1.4	4.5	10.6	45.3
Germany	397.6	-3.4	-4.3	9.8	55.1
USA	182.3	3.1	6.7	4.5	59.6
Belgium	174.5	0.4	3.9	4.3	63.9
Denmark	129.4	0.9	-1.4	3.2	67.1
Canada	128.1	2.2	6.8	3.1	70.2
Italy	121.1	-0.2	-7.3	3.0	73.2
Mexico	99.2	3.1	-4.1	2.4	75.6
Ireland	98.6	8.4	5.4	2.4	78.0
Austria	77.7	8.1	14.9	1.9	80.0
Spain	69.1	13.6	20.8	1.7	81.7
Japan	63.7	5.5	4.0	1.6	83.2
Switzerland	60.5	0.5	9.9	1.5	84.7

017 Meat and edible meat offal, prepared or preserved, nes

In 2016, the value (in current US$) of exports of "meat and edible meat offal, prepared or preserved, nes" (SITC group 017) decreased by 1.0 percent (compared to -1.3 percent average growth rate from 2012-2016) to reach 18.9 bln US$ (see table 2), while imports decreased by 2.7 percent to reach 18.6 bln US$ (see table 3). Exports of this commodity accounted for 1.6 percent of world exports of SITC sections 0+1, and 0.1 percent of total world merchandise exports (see table 1). Thailand, Germany and USA were the top exporters in 2016 (see table 2). They accounted for 12.3, 11.1 and 9.1 percent of world exports, respectively. United Kingdom, Japan and Germany were the top destinations, with respectively 15.8, 15.1 and 7.7 percent of world imports (see table 3).

The top 15 countries/areas accounted for 84.0 and 75.7 percent of total world exports and imports, respectively (see tables 2 and 3). In 2016, Thailand was the country/area with the highest value of net exports (+2.3 bln US$), followed by China (+1.6 bln US$). By MDG regions (see graph 2), the largest surpluses in this product group were recorded by South-eastern Asia (+2.2 bln US$), Latin America and the Caribbean (+828.0 mln US$) and Eastern Asia (+761.9 mln US$). The largest trade deficits were recorded by Developed Asia-Pacific (-2.7 bln US$), Developed Europe (-420.4 mln US$) and Western Asia (-311.3 mln US$).

Table 1: Imports (Imp.) and exports (Exp.), 2002-2016, in current US$

		2002	2003	2004	2005	2006	2007	2008	2009	2010	2011	2012	2013	2014	2015	2016
Values in Bln US$	Imp.	6.4	7.5	8.9	10.4	11.6	13.5	16.1	15.3	15.7	19.3	19.7	20.6	21.2	19.1	18.6
	Exp.	6.5	7.5	8.9	10.7	11.7	13.9	16.8	15.6	16.3	19.3	19.9	21.3	21.5	19.1	18.9
As a percentage of SITC section (%)	Imp.	1.4	1.4	1.5	1.6	1.7	1.6	1.6	1.7	1.6	1.6	1.7	1.7	1.6	1.6	1.6
	Exp.	1.5	1.5	1.6	1.8	1.7	1.7	1.8	1.8	1.7	1.7	1.7	1.7	1.7	1.6	1.6
As a percentage of world trade (%)	Imp.	0.1	0.1	0.1	0.1	0.1	0.1	0.1	0.1	0.1	0.1	0.1	0.1	0.1	0.1	0.1
	Exp.	0.1	0.1	0.1	0.1	0.1	0.1	0.1	0.1	0.1	0.1	0.1	0.1	0.1	0.1	0.1

Graph 1: Annual growth rates of exports, 2002–2016

(In percentage by year)

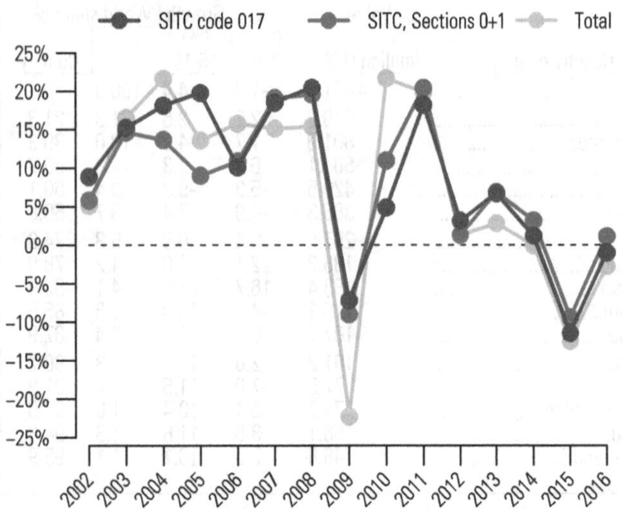

Table 2: Top exporting countries or areas in 2016

Country or area	Value (million US$)	Avg. Growth (%) 12-16	Growth (%) 15-16	World share %	Cum.
World	18862.4	-1.3	-1.0	100.0	
Thailand	2327.7	0.2	3.4	12.3	12.3
Germany	2097.9	-3.3	-2.5	11.1	23.5
USA	1708.1	3.8	-4.7	9.1	32.5
China	1648.3	-6.4	-6.3	8.7	41.3
Brazil	1290.4	-5.1	-3.6	6.8	48.1
Poland	872.3	8.9	4.8	4.6	52.7
Netherlands	817.4	-2.5	-13.5	4.3	57.1
Italy	804.8	2.2	8.1	4.3	61.3
Ireland	764.6	1.6	-8.9	4.1	65.4
Belgium	754.5	-3.6	2.6	4.0	69.4
France	751.1	-1.5	4.6	4.0	73.4
Denmark	594.8	-3.8	-3.2	3.2	76.5
Spain	593.0	0.0	2.8	3.1	79.7
Austria	473.2	2.1	17.6	2.5	82.2
Canada	354.5	7.5	6.7	1.9	84.0

Graph 2: Trade Balance by MDG regions 2016

(Bln US$)

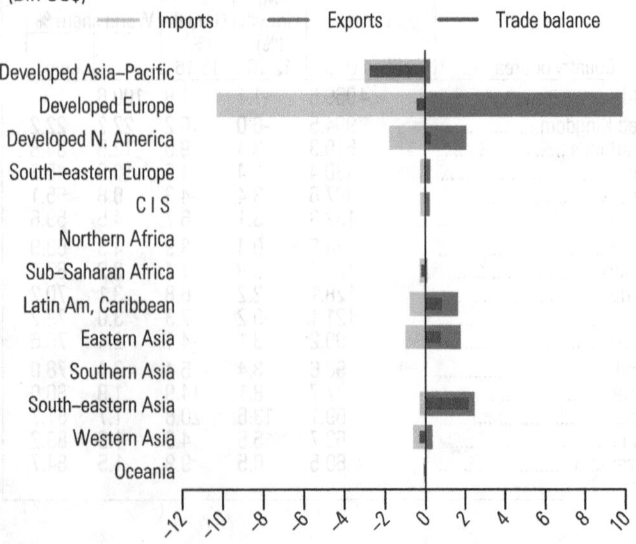

Table 3: Top importing countries or areas in 2016

Country or area	Value (million US$)	Avg. Growth (%) 12-16	Growth (%) 15-16	World share %	Cum.
World	18620.2	-1.4	-2.7	100.0	
United Kingdom	2943.7	-1.9	-6.1	15.8	15.8
Japan	2820.8	-4.9	-1.6	15.1	31.0
Germany	1440.9	-4.1	1.3	7.7	38.7
Netherlands	966.0	-2.8	-11.8	5.2	43.9
Canada	860.7	2.7	-4.0	4.6	48.5
USA	859.1	8.0	-1.0	4.6	53.1
France	787.6	-0.4	0.0	4.2	57.4
China, Hong Kong SAR	735.8	-3.3	-16.3	4.0	61.3
Belgium	653.2	-1.8	6.8	3.5	64.8
Denmark	389.2	0.3	-2.9	2.1	66.9
Ireland	374.7	-0.4	-0.4	2.0	68.9
Spain	351.6	-0.3	-7.4	1.9	70.8
Sweden	324.9	-2.5	2.1	1.7	72.5
Italy	301.4	-2.4	-0.7	1.6	74.2
Austria	279.3	0.5	11.0	1.5	75.7

In 2016, the value (in current US$) of exports of "milk and cream and milk products other than butter or cheese" (SITC group 022) decreased by 8.3 percent (compared to -5.1 percent average growth rate from 2012-2016) to reach 33.7 bln US$ (see table 2), while imports decreased by 8.2 percent to reach 35.0 bln US$ (see table 3). Exports of this commodity accounted for 2.8 percent of world exports of SITC sections 0+1, and 0.2 percent of total world merchandise exports (see table 1). New Zealand, Germany and France were the top exporters in 2016 (see table 2). They accounted for 14.6, 12.8 and 9.0 percent of world exports, respectively. China, Germany and Netherlands were the top destinations, with respectively 7.7, 6.0 and 5.0 percent of world imports (see table 3).

The top 15 countries/areas accounted for 76.2 and 55.3 percent of total world exports and imports, respectively (see tables 2 and 3). In 2016, New Zealand was the country/area with the highest value of net exports (+4.8 bln US$), followed by Germany (+2.2 bln US$). By MDG regions (see graph 2), the largest surpluses in this product group were recorded by Developed Asia-Pacific (+5.4 bln US$), Developed Europe (+5.2 bln US$) and Developed North America (+1.7 bln US$). The largest trade deficits were recorded by Eastern Asia (-4.3 bln US$), South-eastern Asia (-2.4 bln US$) and Western Asia (-1.8 bln US$).

Table 1: Imports (Imp.) and exports (Exp.), 2002-2016, in current US$

		2002	2003	2004	2005	2006	2007	2008	2009	2010	2011	2012	2013	2014	2015	2016
Values in Bln US$	Imp.	14.7	17.3	20.4	22.3	23.4	31.9	35.6	28.1	33.3	42.6	41.4	47.2	52.2	38.1	35.0
	Exp.	14.3	17.0	20.5	22.3	23.8	32.1	36.7	27.9	34.1	42.1	41.5	48.1	50.6	36.7	33.7
As a percentage of SITC section (%)	Imp.	3.2	3.3	3.5	3.5	3.4	3.8	3.6	3.2	3.4	3.6	3.5	3.8	4.0	3.2	3.0
	Exp.	3.3	3.5	3.7	3.7	3.5	4.0	3.8	3.2	3.5	3.6	3.5	3.8	3.9	3.1	2.8
As a percentage of world trade (%)	Imp.	0.2	0.2	0.2	0.2	0.2	0.2	0.2	0.2	0.2	0.2	0.2	0.3	0.3	0.2	0.2
	Exp.	0.2	0.2	0.2	0.2	0.2	0.2	0.2	0.2	0.2	0.2	0.2	0.3	0.3	0.2	0.2

Graph 1: Annual growth rates of exports, 2002–2016
(In percentage by year)

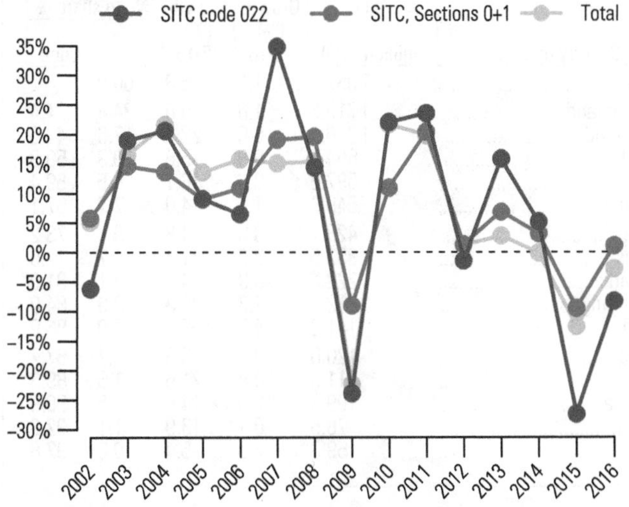

Graph 2: Trade Balance by MDG regions 2016
(Bln US$)

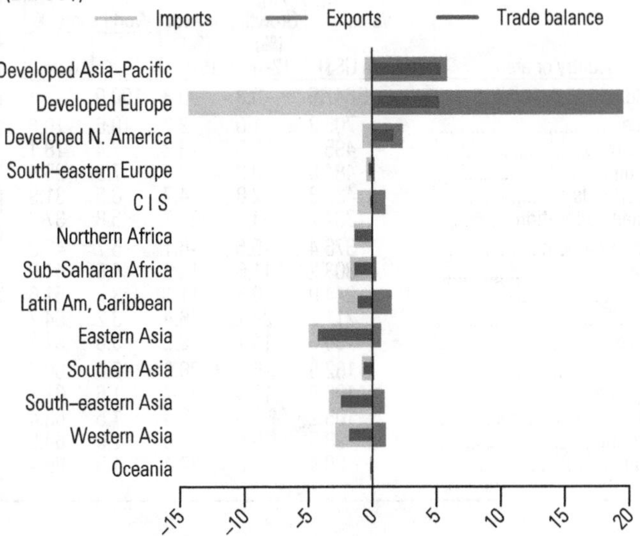

Table 2: Top exporting countries or areas in 2016

Country or area	Value (million US$)	Avg. Growth (%) 12-16	Growth (%) 15-16	World share %	Cum.
World	33709.9	-5.1	-8.3	100.0	
New Zealand	4921.8	-6.7	-7.2	14.6	14.6
Germany	4314.0	-3.5	-4.9	12.8	27.4
France	3037.4	-5.4	-6.9	9.0	36.4
Netherlands	2751.2	-1.7	2.4	8.2	44.6
USA	2236.8	-3.5	-11.9	6.6	51.2
Belgium	1925.2	-4.7	-4.2	5.7	56.9
Australia	927.6	-7.7	-8.7	2.8	59.7
United Kingdom	888.4	-1.4	-6.5	2.6	62.3
Poland	868.0	-3.1	-12.8	2.6	64.9
Belarus	802.1	-3.2	-3.4	2.4	67.3
Austria	706.1	-1.4	5.6	2.1	69.4
Spain	661.9	-3.5	1.0	2.0	71.3
Denmark	631.3	-5.5	-0.4	1.9	73.2
China, Hong Kong SAR	514.1	38.5	17.9	1.5	74.7
Italy	510.7	-1.8	1.8	1.5	76.2

Table 3: Top importing countries or areas in 2016

Country or area	Value (million US$)	Avg. Growth (%) 12-16	Growth (%) 15-16	World share %	Cum.
World	35033.5	-4.1	-8.2	100.0	
China	2709.5	-1.5	3.0	7.7	7.7
Germany	2105.8	-2.1	-0.6	6.0	13.7
Netherlands	1748.0	-6.4	-4.7	5.0	18.7
China, Hong Kong SAR	1689.9	8.9	3.9	4.8	23.6
Italy	1664.7	-7.1	-8.2	4.8	28.3
Belgium	1519.4	-2.8	7.9	4.3	32.6
United Kingdom	1287.0	-1.3	-3.8	3.7	36.3
France	1265.8	-5.3	-3.8	3.6	39.9
United Arab Emirates	914.7	0.3	-12.4	2.6	42.5
Mexico	828.7	-6.1	-3.6	2.4	44.9
Russian Federation	815.2	-0.6	12.0	2.3	47.2
Algeria	807.3	-7.4	-19.8	2.3	49.5
Spain	753.6	-10.0	-13.4	2.2	51.7
Indonesia	650.0	-9.2	-11.9	1.9	53.5
Philippines	628.0	-0.6	13.9	1.8	55.3

023 Butter and other fats and oils derived from milk

In 2016, the value (in current US$) of exports of "butter and other fats and oils derived from milk" (SITC group 023) increased by 5.3 percent (compared to 1.1 percent average growth rate from 2012-2016) to reach 7.1 bln US$ (see table 2), while imports decreased by 0.3 percent to reach 6.6 bln US$ (see table 3). Exports of this commodity accounted for 0.6 percent of world exports of SITC sections 0+1, and less than 0.1 percent of total world merchandise exports (see table 1). New Zealand, Netherlands and Ireland were the top exporters in 2016 (see table 2). They accounted for 24.4, 17.3 and 9.3 percent of world exports, respectively. France, Germany and Belgium were the top destinations, with respectively 10.6, 7.4 and 7.3 percent of world imports (see table 3).

The top 15 countries/areas accounted for 92.8 and 66.4 percent of total world exports and imports, respectively (see tables 2 and 3). In 2016, New Zealand was the country/area with the highest value of net exports (+1.7 bln US$), followed by Netherlands (+785.9 mln US$). By MDG regions (see graph 2), the largest surpluses in this product group were recorded by Developed Asia-Pacific (+1.7 bln US$) and Developed Europe (+1.1 bln US$). The largest trade deficits were recorded by Eastern Asia (-480.3 mln US$), South-eastern Asia (-431.7 mln US$) and Western Asia (-310.2 mln US$).

Table 1: Imports (Imp.) and exports (Exp.), 2002-2016, in current US$

		2002	2003	2004	2005	2006	2007	2008	2009	2010	2011	2012	2013	2014	2015	2016
Values in Bln US$	Imp.	2.9	4.0	4.3	4.4	4.5	5.4	5.9	4.7	6.4	7.8	6.7	8.0	8.7	6.7	6.6
	Exp.	2.6	3.4	4.1	4.2	4.0	5.3	6.0	4.7	6.7	8.2	6.8	8.3	8.6	6.7	7.1
As a percentage of SITC section (%)	Imp.	0.6	0.8	0.7	0.7	0.6	0.6	0.6	0.5	0.7	0.7	0.6	0.6	0.7	0.6	0.6
	Exp.	0.6	0.7	0.7	0.7	0.6	0.7	0.6	0.5	0.7	0.7	0.6	0.7	0.7	0.6	0.6
As a percentage of world trade (%)	Imp.	0.0	0.1	0.0	0.0	0.0	0.0	0.0	0.0	0.0	0.0	0.0	0.0	0.0	0.0	0.0
	Exp.	0.0	0.0	0.0	0.0	0.0	0.0	0.0	0.0	0.0	0.0	0.0	0.0	0.0	0.0	0.0

Graph 1: Annual growth rates of exports, 2002–2016
(In percentage by year)

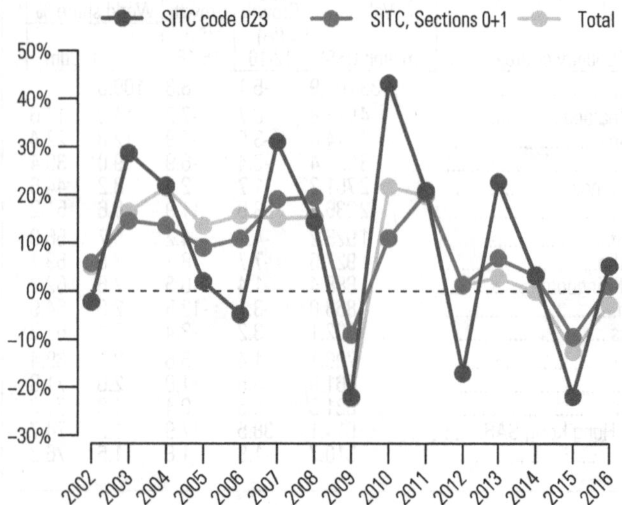

Graph 2: Trade Balance by MDG regions 2016
(Bln US$)

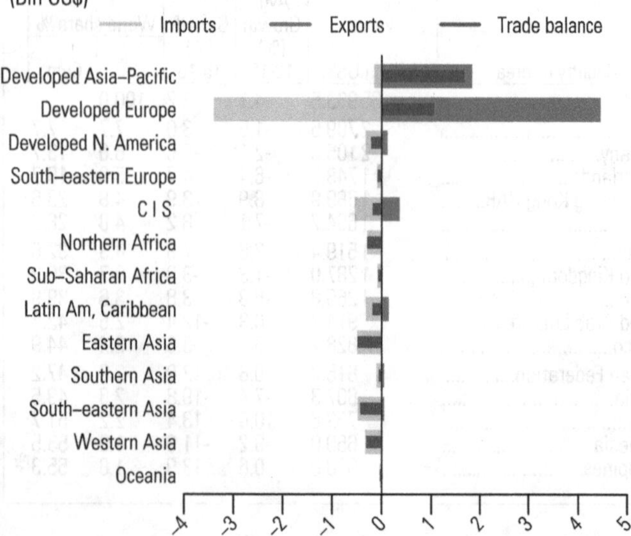

Table 2: Top exporting countries or areas in 2016

Country or area	Value (million US$)	Avg. Growth (%) 12-16	Growth (%) 15-16	World share %	Cum.
World	7057.9	1.1	5.3	100.0	
New Zealand	1719.5	1.6	5.0	24.4	24.4
Netherlands	1218.2	6.6	22.3	17.3	41.6
Ireland	654.1	0.9	-5.6	9.3	50.9
Belgium	597.2	3.6	18.1	8.5	59.4
Germany	546.6	1.1	-4.0	7.7	67.1
France	428.1	0.8	-4.8	6.1	73.2
Belarus	332.5	2.2	21.4	4.7	77.9
Denmark	222.0	-6.3	4.3	3.1	81.0
United Kingdom	212.2	7.2	20.3	3.0	84.0
Poland	141.2	4.7	7.3	2.0	86.0
Finland	120.0	0.8	-6.9	1.7	87.7
USA	111.5	-10.8	21.6	1.6	89.3
Australia	109.3	-13.9	-14.6	1.5	90.9
Spain	78.5	-0.1	13.9	1.1	92.0
Portugal	59.3	-2.9	-5.4	0.8	92.8

Table 3: Top importing countries or areas in 2016

Country or area	Value (million US$)	Avg. Growth (%) 12-16	Growth (%) 15-16	World share %	Cum.
World	6647.9	-0.3	-0.3	100.0	
France	705.3	1.0	2.2	10.6	10.6
Germany	495.2	-3.3	-9.2	7.4	18.1
Belgium	484.8	0.3	-7.4	7.3	25.4
Netherlands	432.3	2.8	-4.7	6.5	31.9
Russian Federation	387.2	-4.3	26.3	5.8	37.7
United Kingdom	376.4	-5.5	-6.1	5.7	43.3
China	303.2	11.6	14.2	4.6	47.9
Italy	244.0	-0.5	-11.1	3.7	51.6
USA	211.2	29.2	16.4	3.2	54.7
Mexico	198.6	14.1	49.2	3.0	57.7
Egypt	162.8	-5.4	-28.6	2.4	60.2
Philippines	106.9	13.4	29.7	1.6	61.8
United Arab Emirates	106.2	2.8	-8.4	1.6	63.4
Australia	99.5	5.5	37.5	1.5	64.9
Canada	99.4	41.8	72.4	1.5	66.4

In 2016, the value (in current US$) of exports of "cheese and curd" (SITC group 024) decreased by 1.3 percent (compared to -2.1 percent average growth rate from 2012-2016) to reach 26.5 bln US$ (see table 2), while imports decreased by 4.7 percent to reach 25.8 bln US$ (see table 3). Exports of this commodity accounted for 2.2 percent of world exports of SITC sections 0+1, and 0.2 percent of total world merchandise exports (see table 1). Germany, Netherlands and France were the top exporters in 2016 (see table 2). They accounted for 13.9, 13.8 and 12.4 percent of world exports, respectively. Germany, United Kingdom and Italy were the top destinations, with respectively 14.4, 7.1 and 6.7 percent of world imports (see table 3).

The top 15 countries/areas accounted for 85.5 and 68.3 percent of total world exports and imports, respectively (see tables 2 and 3). In 2016, Netherlands was the country/area with the highest value of net exports (+2.5 bln US$), followed by France (+1.8 bln US$). By MDG regions (see graph 2), the largest surpluses in this product group were recorded by Developed Europe (+4.4 bln US$) and Developed Asia-Pacific (+345.7 mln US$). The largest trade deficits were recorded by Eastern Asia (-1.1 bln US$), Western Asia (-840.1 mln US$) and Latin America and the Caribbean (-779.3 mln US$).

Table 1: Imports (Imp.) and exports (Exp.), 2002-2016, in current US$

		2002	2003	2004	2005	2006	2007	2008	2009	2010	2011	2012	2013	2014	2015	2016
Values in Bln US$	Imp.	11.2	13.3	15.7	16.6	17.9	21.3	25.8	22.4	24.3	28.2	28.1	31.5	32.6	27.0	25.8
	Exp.	11.2	13.7	16.1	17.2	18.5	22.2	27.1	23.0	25.6	29.7	28.8	32.2	33.3	26.8	26.5
As a percentage of SITC section (%)	Imp.	2.5	2.6	2.7	2.6	2.6	2.6	2.6	2.5	2.5	2.4	2.4	2.5	2.5	2.3	2.2
	Exp.	2.6	2.8	2.9	2.8	2.8	2.8	2.8	2.6	2.6	2.6	2.4	2.6	2.6	2.3	2.2
As a percentage of world trade (%)	Imp.	0.2	0.2	0.2	0.2	0.1	0.2	0.2	0.2	0.2	0.2	0.2	0.2	0.2	0.2	0.2
	Exp.	0.2	0.2	0.2	0.2	0.2	0.2	0.2	0.2	0.2	0.2	0.2	0.2	0.2	0.2	0.2

Graph 1: Annual growth rates of exports, 2002–2016

(In percentage by year)

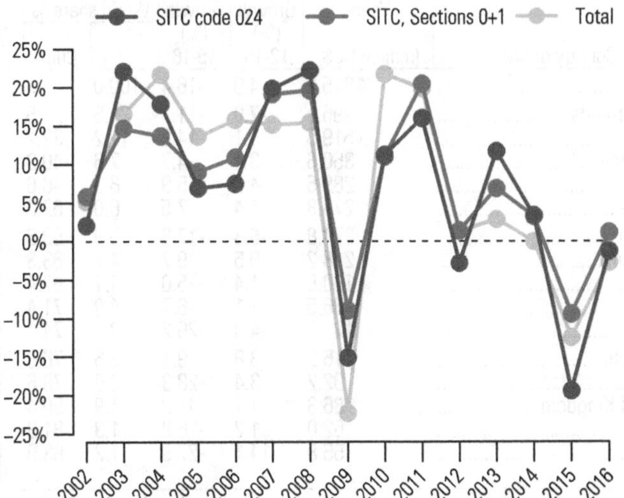

Table 2: Top exporting countries or areas in 2016

Country or area	Value (million US$)	Avg. Growth (%) 12-16	Growth (%) 15-16	World share %	Cum.
World	26463.6	-2.1	-1.3	100.0	
Germany	3673.1	-5.1	-2.4	13.9	13.9
Netherlands	3649.1	-0.6	5.9	13.8	27.7
France	3283.7	-3.0	-1.7	12.4	40.1
Italy	2675.6	1.3	6.8	10.1	50.2
Denmark	1444.2	0.3	4.7	5.5	55.6
USA	1208.7	1.9	-13.2	4.6	60.2
New Zealand	1206.8	0.6	3.6	4.6	64.8
Belgium	870.6	0.4	6.5	3.3	68.1
Ireland	767.6	-3.1	-1.7	2.9	71.0
Belarus	690.0	4.4	8.0	2.6	73.6
United Kingdom	675.0	1.5	-1.6	2.6	76.1
Poland	672.7	-1.1	3.4	2.5	78.7
Australia	610.4	-5.6	-6.9	2.3	81.0
Austria	601.3	2.5	5.2	2.3	83.2
Switzerland	590.6	0.4	-1.5	2.2	85.5

Graph 2: Trade Balance by MDG regions 2016

(Bln US$)

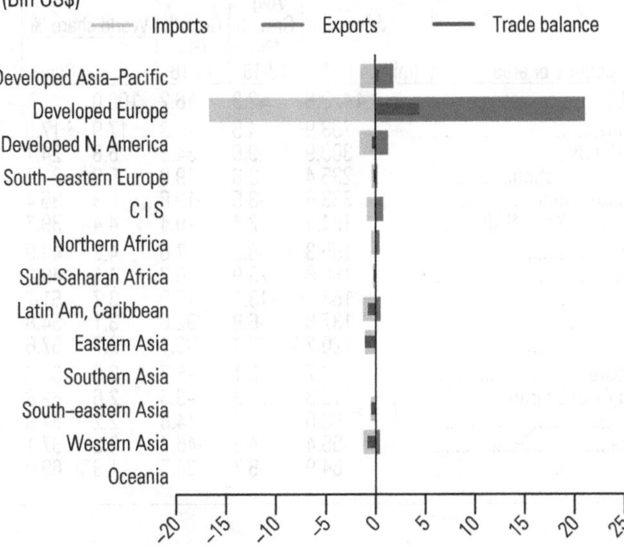

Table 3: Top importing countries or areas in 2016

Country or area	Value (million US$)	Avg. Growth (%) 12-16	Growth (%) 15-16	World share %	Cum.
World	25759.9	-2.2	-4.7	100.0	
Germany	3713.0	-1.6	-1.3	14.4	14.4
United Kingdom	1831.6	-2.3	-7.9	7.1	21.5
Italy	1715.9	-4.8	-3.8	6.7	28.2
France	1498.6	0.0	1.0	5.8	34.0
USA	1308.2	3.6	-3.1	5.1	39.1
Belgium	1299.7	-1.6	9.0	5.0	44.1
Netherlands	1100.3	-0.7	-10.5	4.3	48.4
Japan	978.4	-4.2	-6.9	3.8	52.2
Spain	964.1	-3.3	0.1	3.7	55.9
Russian Federation	732.5	-20.3	1.7	2.8	58.8
Sweden	565.7	1.1	3.4	2.2	61.0
Austria	515.7	1.0	12.3	2.0	63.0
Mexico	495.8	5.0	-1.3	1.9	64.9
Australia	446.5	2.8	1.4	1.7	66.6
Greece	436.9	-3.5	1.4	1.7	68.3

025 Eggs, birds', egg yolks, fresh, dried or preserved; egg albumin

In 2016, the value (in current US$) of exports of "eggs, birds', egg yolks, fresh, dried or preserved; egg albumin" (SITC group 025) decreased by 16.4 percent (compared to -4.0 percent average growth rate from 2012-2016) to reach 4.6 bln US$ (see table 2), while imports decreased by 16.2 percent to reach 4.4 bln US$ (see table 3). Exports of this commodity accounted for 0.4 percent of world exports of SITC sections 0+1, and less than 0.1 percent of total world merchandise exports (see table 1). Netherlands, USA and Germany were the top exporters in 2016 (see table 2). They accounted for 21.5, 11.2 and 7.6 percent of world exports, respectively. Germany, Netherlands and Russian Federation were the top destinations, with respectively 17.9, 6.8 and 5.3 percent of world imports (see table 3).

The top 15 countries/areas accounted for 83.0 and 69.0 percent of total world exports and imports, respectively (see tables 2 and 3). In 2016, Netherlands was the country/area with the highest value of net exports (+694.2 mln US$), followed by USA (+399.3 mln US$). By MDG regions (see graph 2), the largest surpluses in this product group were recorded by Developed Europe (+462.8 mln US$), Developed North America (+362.4 mln US$) and Southern Asia (+59.9 mln US$). The largest trade deficits were recorded by Latin America and the Caribbean (-224.4 mln US$), Commonwealth of Independent States (-155.0 mln US$) and Developed Asia-Pacific (-133.0 mln US$).

Table 1: Imports (Imp.) and exports (Exp.), 2002-2016, in current US$

		2002	2003	2004	2005	2006	2007	2008	2009	2010	2011	2012	2013	2014	2015	2016
Values in Bln US$	Imp.	1.6	1.9	2.2	2.4	2.5	3.1	3.8	3.9	4.0	4.4	4.9	5.2	5.4	5.3	4.4
	Exp.	1.6	2.0	2.1	2.2	2.4	3.2	4.1	4.5	4.5	4.8	5.4	5.8	6.0	5.5	4.6
As a percentage of SITC section (%)	Imp.	0.4	0.4	0.4	0.4	0.4	0.4	0.4	0.4	0.4	0.4	0.4	0.4	0.4	0.4	0.4
	Exp.	0.4	0.4	0.4	0.4	0.4	0.4	0.4	0.5	0.5	0.4	0.5	0.5	0.5	0.5	0.4
As a percentage of world trade (%)	Imp.	0.0	0.0	0.0	0.0	0.0	0.0	0.0	0.0	0.0	0.0	0.0	0.0	0.0	0.0	0.0
	Exp.	0.0	0.0	0.0	0.0	0.0	0.0	0.0	0.0	0.0	0.0	0.0	0.0	0.0	0.0	0.0

Graph 1: Annual growth rates of exports, 2002–2016
(In percentage by year)

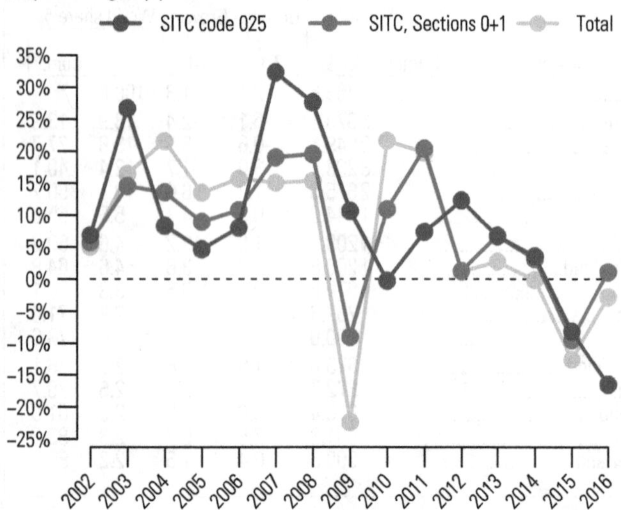

Table 2: Top exporting countries or areas in 2016

Country or area	Value (million US$)	Avg. Growth (%) 12-16	Growth (%) 15-16	World share %	Cum.
World	4625.6	-4.0	-16.4	100.0	
Netherlands	995.1	-7.0	-11.7	21.5	21.5
USA	519.5	1.1	-14.8	11.2	32.7
Germany	350.6	-3.4	-4.7	7.6	40.3
Turkey	289.5	-4.7	5.9	6.3	46.6
France	278.8	-1.4	-7.5	6.0	52.6
Poland	274.8	-6.3	-17.6	5.9	58.6
Belgium	218.2	0.5	-9.7	4.7	63.3
Spain	190.9	-1.4	-25.0	4.1	67.4
China	186.5	1.1	-6.7	4.0	71.4
Italy	123.0	-4.3	-26.2	2.7	74.1
Malaysia	115.2	-3.8	-9.1	2.5	76.6
India	92.2	-3.4	-28.3	2.0	78.6
United Kingdom	86.3	-1.1	-41.8	1.9	80.4
Canada	62.0	1.2	-16.8	1.3	81.8
Brazil	55.8	-14.1	-27.8	1.2	83.0

Graph 2: Trade Balance by MDG regions 2016
(Bln US$)

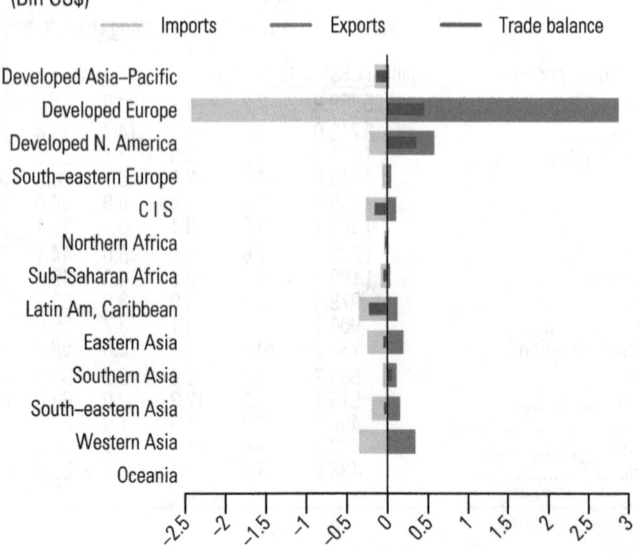

Table 3: Top importing countries or areas in 2016

Country or area	Value (million US$)	Avg. Growth (%) 12-16	Growth (%) 15-16	World share %	Cum.
World	4423.8	-2.3	-16.2	100.0	
Germany	793.9	-4.5	-0.3	17.9	17.9
Netherlands	300.9	-9.6	-34.2	6.8	24.7
Russian Federation	235.4	3.8	-19.0	5.3	30.1
United Kingdom	233.6	-3.5	-19.8	5.3	35.4
China, Hong Kong SAR	194.4	2.4	-9.4	4.4	39.7
Belgium	185.3	-0.2	7.0	4.2	43.9
Mexico	180.8	23.9	-10.2	4.1	48.0
France	163.9	-13.1	-15.8	3.7	51.7
Japan	137.8	-6.8	-32.0	3.1	54.8
USA	120.2	28.4	-39.1	2.7	57.6
Singapore	116.7	0.1	-5.7	2.6	60.2
United Arab Emirates	113.3	24.3	-3.3	2.6	62.8
Spain	96.5	-1.2	14.8	2.2	64.9
Canada	95.4	4.3	-46.7	2.2	67.1
Italy	84.9	-8.7	-34.5	1.9	69.0

In 2016, the value (in current US$) of exports of "fish, fresh (live or dead), chilled or frozen" (SITC group 034) increased by 9.4 percent (compared to 2.4 percent average growth rate from 2012-2016) to reach 64.2 bln US$ (see table 2), while imports increased by 7.4 percent to reach 64.5 bln US$ (see table 3). Exports of this commodity accounted for 5.4 percent of world exports of SITC sections 0+1, and 0.4 percent of total world merchandise exports (see table 1). Norway, China and Chile were the top exporters in 2016 (see table 2). They accounted for 15.0, 12.1 and 6.4 percent of world exports, respectively. USA, Japan and Sweden were the top destinations, with respectively 12.9, 10.6 and 6.7 percent of world imports (see table 3).

The top 15 countries/areas accounted for 72.1 and 73.0 percent of total world exports and imports, respectively (see tables 2 and 3). In 2016, Norway was the country/area with the highest value of net exports (+9.3 bln US$), followed by Chile (+4.1 bln US$). By MDG regions (see graph 2), the largest surpluses in this product group were recorded by Latin America and the Caribbean (+3.9 bln US$), Eastern Asia (+2.5 bln US$) and Developed Europe (+1.5 bln US$). The largest trade deficits were recorded by Developed Asia-Pacific (-5.7 bln US$), Developed North America (-4.3 bln US$) and Sub-Saharan Africa (-985.9 mln US$).

Table 1: Imports (Imp.) and exports (Exp.), 2002-2016, in current US$

		2002	2003	2004	2005	2006	2007	2008	2009	2010	2011	2012	2013	2014	2015	2016
Values in Bln US$	Imp.	27.2	29.6	33.3	37.9	42.3	47.0	51.0	46.7	53.0	62.6	61.1	63.2	66.1	60.1	64.5
	Exp.	23.2	25.8	29.6	33.8	37.3	40.1	44.0	43.2	50.4	58.9	58.3	62.5	65.2	58.6	64.2
As a percentage of SITC section (%)	Imp.	6.0	5.7	5.7	5.9	6.1	5.6	5.2	5.2	5.4	5.3	5.2	5.1	5.1	5.1	5.5
	Exp.	5.5	5.3	5.3	5.6	5.6	5.0	4.6	5.0	5.2	5.1	4.9	5.0	5.0	5.0	5.4
As a percentage of world trade (%)	Imp.	0.4	0.4	0.4	0.4	0.3	0.3	0.3	0.4	0.3	0.3	0.3	0.3	0.4	0.4	0.4
	Exp.	0.4	0.3	0.3	0.3	0.3	0.3	0.3	0.3	0.3	0.3	0.3	0.3	0.3	0.4	0.4

Graph 1: Annual growth rates of exports, 2002–2016

(In percentage by year)

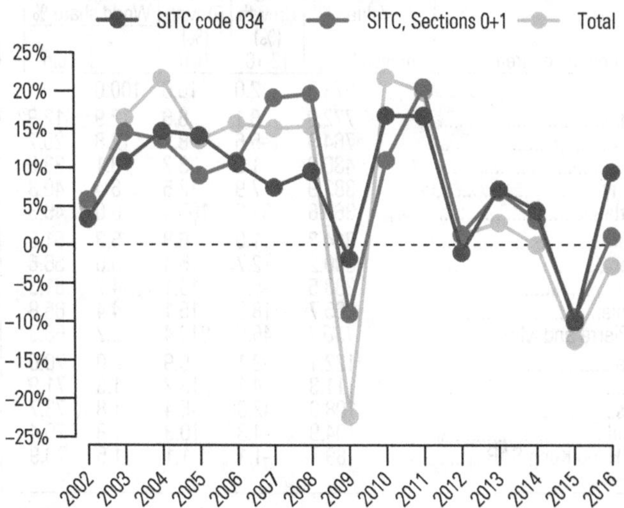

Graph 2: Trade Balance by MDG regions 2016

(Bln US$)

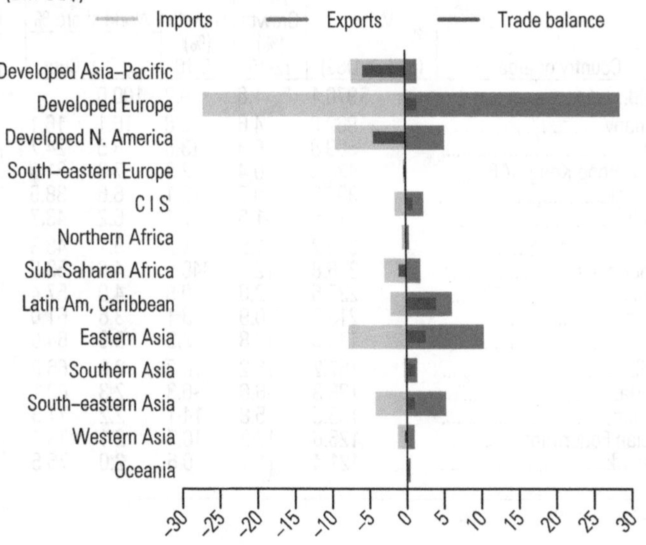

Table 2: Top exporting countries or areas in 2016

Country or area	Value (million US$)	Avg. Growth (%) 12-16	Growth (%) 15-16	World share %	Cum.
World	64175.0	2.4	9.4	100.0	
Norway	9596.7	6.2	20.7	15.0	15.0
China	7742.9	1.9	2.8	12.1	27.0
Chile	4099.0	7.0	10.3	6.4	33.4
Sweden	3972.4	14.1	23.0	6.2	39.6
USA	3285.0	-1.4	-4.0	5.1	44.7
Viet Nam	*2798.9*	0.9	8.9	4.4	49.1
Netherlands	2314.2	5.2	31.0	3.6	52.7
Russian Federation	2244.5	1.4	4.4	3.5	56.2
Denmark	1819.7	7.9	18.3	2.8	59.0
Spain	1773.9	-1.5	4.9	2.8	61.8
Canada	1522.3	4.8	20.5	2.4	64.2
Other Asia, nes	1374.0	-6.9	1.0	2.1	66.3
Iceland	1366.8	-0.4	9.1	2.1	68.4
United Kingdom	1294.5	2.7	9.4	2.0	70.4
Germany	1057.9	1.7	6.8	1.6	72.1

Table 3: Top importing countries or areas in 2016

Country or area	Value (million US$)	Avg. Growth (%) 12-16	Growth (%) 15-16	World share %	Cum.
World	64490.0	1.3	7.4	100.0	
USA	8350.0	4.6	6.6	12.9	12.9
Japan	6818.0	-6.2	4.3	10.6	23.5
Sweden	4348.2	12.1	20.4	6.7	30.3
China	3835.2	1.3	6.2	5.9	36.2
France	3107.2	2.1	12.8	4.8	41.0
Spain	2883.9	3.3	12.8	4.5	45.5
Germany	2728.4	1.9	7.1	4.2	49.7
Rep. of Korea	2273.8	3.0	7.2	3.5	53.3
Italy	2206.9	3.6	15.0	3.4	56.7
Thailand	2161.1	-4.0	19.2	3.4	60.0
United Kingdom	1969.7	0.9	6.0	3.1	63.1
Poland	1900.7	9.5	20.8	2.9	66.0
Netherlands	1853.2	4.7	35.8	2.9	68.9
Denmark	1525.3	9.9	23.4	2.4	71.3
China, Hong Kong SAR	1125.3	6.5	4.3	1.7	73.0

035 Fish, dried, salted or in brine; smoked fish; flours, meals, etc

In 2016, the value (in current US$) of exports of "fish, dried, salted or in brine; smoked fish; flours, meals, etc" (SITC group 035) increased by 10.0 percent (compared to 2.0 percent average growth rate from 2012-2016) to reach 6.0 bln US$ (see table 2), while imports increased by 9.7 percent to reach 6.0 bln US$ (see table 3). Exports of this commodity accounted for 0.5 percent of world exports of SITC sections 0+1, and less than 0.1 percent of total world merchandise exports (see table 1). Poland, Norway and China were the top exporters in 2016 (see table 2). They accounted for 12.9, 12.8 and 8.1 percent of world exports, respectively. Germany, Italy and China, Hong Kong SAR were the top destinations, with respectively 16.1, 8.5 and 7.3 percent of world imports (see table 3).

The top 15 countries/areas accounted for 76.9 and 75.5 percent of total world exports and imports, respectively (see tables 2 and 3). In 2016, Poland was the country/area with the highest value of net exports (+755.4 mln US$), followed by Norway (+750.7 mln US$). By MDG regions (see graph 2), the largest surpluses in this product group were recorded by Developed Europe (+468.6 mln US$), South-eastern Asia (+241.5 mln US$) and Western Asia (+31.3 mln US$). The largest trade deficits were recorded by Sub-Saharan Africa (-241.8 mln US$), Developed Asia-Pacific (-230.0 mln US$) and Latin America and the Caribbean (-161.5 mln US$).

Table 1: Imports (Imp.) and exports (Exp.), 2002-2016, in current US$

		2002	2003	2004	2005	2006	2007	2008	2009	2010	2011	2012	2013	2014	2015	2016
Values in Bln US$	Imp.	2.7	2.9	3.2	3.6	3.9	4.6	4.9	4.6	5.0	5.8	5.6	5.6	6.0	5.4	6.0
	Exp.	2.8	2.9	3.5	3.7	4.0	4.5	4.8	4.3	4.8	5.7	5.5	5.6	5.9	5.4	6.0
As a percentage of SITC section (%)	Imp.	0.6	0.6	0.6	0.6	0.6	0.5	0.5	0.5	0.5	0.5	0.5	0.5	0.5	0.5	0.5
	Exp.	0.6	0.6	0.6	0.6	0.6	0.6	0.5	0.5	0.5	0.5	0.5	0.4	0.5	0.5	0.5
As a percentage of world trade (%)	Imp.	0.0	0.0	0.0	0.0	0.0	0.0	0.0	0.0	0.0	0.0	0.0	0.0	0.0	0.0	0.0
	Exp.	0.0	0.0	0.0	0.0	0.0	0.0	0.0	0.0	0.0	0.0	0.0	0.0	0.0	0.0	0.0

Graph 1: Annual growth rates of exports, 2002–2016

(In percentage by year)

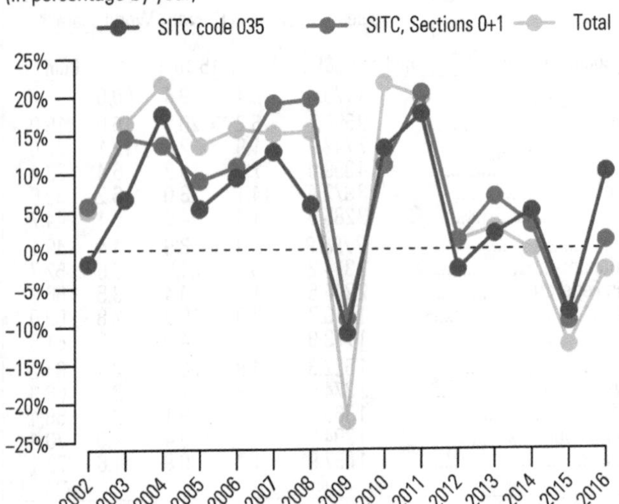

Graph 2: Trade Balance by MDG regions 2016

(Bln US$)

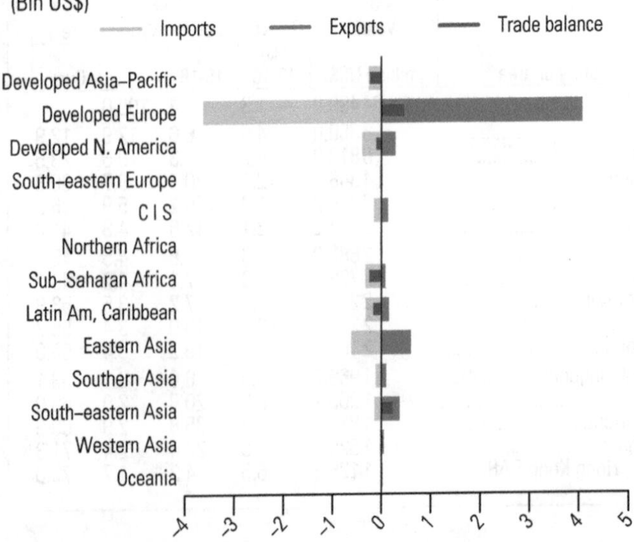

Table 2: Top exporting countries or areas in 2016

Country or area	Value (million US$)	Avg. Growth (%) 12-16	Growth (%) 15-16	World share %	Cum.
World	5973.5	2.0	10.0	100.0	
Poland	772.0	8.1	8.6	12.9	12.9
Norway	764.9	-5.6	-8.2	12.8	25.7
China	486.0	1.9	3.2	8.1	33.9
Germany	382.9	7.9	12.5	6.4	40.3
Netherlands	360.6	32.0	165.4	6.0	46.3
Denmark	314.2	1.0	6.8	5.3	51.6
Sweden	300.2	-2.7	5.4	5.0	56.6
Iceland	283.5	-6.1	-13.1	4.7	61.3
Lithuania	265.7	18.2	15.1	4.4	65.8
Saint Pierre and Miquelon	*130.1*	46.6	810.4	2.2	68.0
Canada	122.1	-3.1	9.9	2.0	70.0
Spain	111.3	4.1	13.2	1.9	71.9
Belarus	108.0	42.3	-5.4	1.8	73.7
Thailand	104.9	-4.3	10.3	1.8	75.4
China, Hong Kong SAR	89.7	-1.1	1.1	1.5	76.9

Table 3: Top importing countries or areas in 2016

Country or area	Value (million US$)	Avg. Growth (%) 12-16	Growth (%) 15-16	World share %	Cum.
World	5970.1	1.6	9.7	100.0	
Germany	962.0	4.6	9.8	16.1	16.1
Italy	509.8	6.3	13.8	8.5	24.7
China, Hong Kong SAR	433.5	-0.4	2.9	7.3	31.9
Portugal	392.2	-0.7	12.1	6.6	38.5
Sweden	311.5	-1.5	7.1	5.2	43.7
USA	305.2	1.6	-1.2	5.1	48.8
Netherlands	276.8	12.8	346.5	4.6	53.5
Spain	237.5	2.6	-0.9	4.0	57.4
France	213.2	0.9	3.1	3.6	61.0
Japan	178.0	-12.8	2.2	3.0	64.0
Brazil	167.2	-15.2	-18.3	2.8	66.8
Nigeria	138.3	-6.6	-6.3	2.3	69.1
Belgium	133.5	5.8	14.1	2.2	71.3
Russian Federation	125.6	17.2	10.7	2.1	73.4
Denmark	121.4	11.1	-0.5	2.0	75.5

Source: UN Comtrade

In 2016, the value (in current US$) of exports of "crustaceans, molluscs, aquatic invertebrates; flours and pellets" (SITC group 036) increased by 9.7 percent (compared to 6.7 percent average growth rate from 2012-2016) to reach 39.4 bln US$ (see table 2), while imports increased by 7.8 percent to reach 34.8 bln US$ (see table 3). Exports of this commodity accounted for 3.3 percent of world exports of SITC sections 0+1, and 0.2 percent of total world merchandise exports (see table 1). China, India and Canada were the top exporters in 2016 (see table 2). They accounted for 13.9, 10.8 and 7.0 percent of world exports, respectively. USA, Japan and Spain were the top destinations, with respectively 22.2, 10.9 and 9.0 percent of world imports (see table 3).

The top 15 countries/areas accounted for 73.6 and 85.1 percent of total world exports and imports, respectively (see tables 2 and 3). In 2016, India was the country/area with the highest value of net exports (+4.3 bln US$), followed by Ecuador (+2.6 bln US$). By MDG regions (see graph 2), the largest surpluses in this product group were recorded by Latin America and the Caribbean (+6.4 bln US$), Southern Asia (+4.8 bln US$) and South-eastern Asia (+4.6 bln US$). The largest trade deficits were recorded by Developed Europe (-6.0 bln US$), Developed North America (-4.0 bln US$) and Developed Asia-Pacific (-2.3 bln US$).

Table 1: Imports (Imp.) and exports (Exp.), 2002-2016, in current US$

		2002	2003	2004	2005	2006	2007	2008	2009	2010	2011	2012	2013	2014	2015	2016
Values in Bln US$	Imp.	18.4	20.1	21.1	21.8	23.4	24.5	25.3	22.7	26.0	31.4	30.1	31.7	36.0	32.3	34.8
	Exp.	16.6	18.1	18.8	19.3	20.7	21.9	22.5	21.6	25.5	30.9	30.4	34.4	39.4	35.9	39.4
As a percentage of SITC section (%)	Imp.	4.1	3.9	3.6	3.4	3.4	2.9	2.6	2.6	2.7	2.7	2.5	2.6	2.8	2.7	3.0
	Exp.	3.9	3.7	3.4	3.2	3.1	2.7	2.3	2.5	2.6	2.7	2.6	2.7	3.0	3.0	3.3
As a percentage of world trade (%)	Imp.	0.3	0.3	0.2	0.2	0.2	0.2	0.2	0.2	0.2	0.2	0.2	0.2	0.2	0.2	0.2
	Exp.	0.3	0.2	0.2	0.2	0.2	0.2	0.1	0.2	0.2	0.2	0.2	0.2	0.2	0.2	0.2

Graph 1: Annual growth rates of exports, 2002–2016

(In percentage by year)

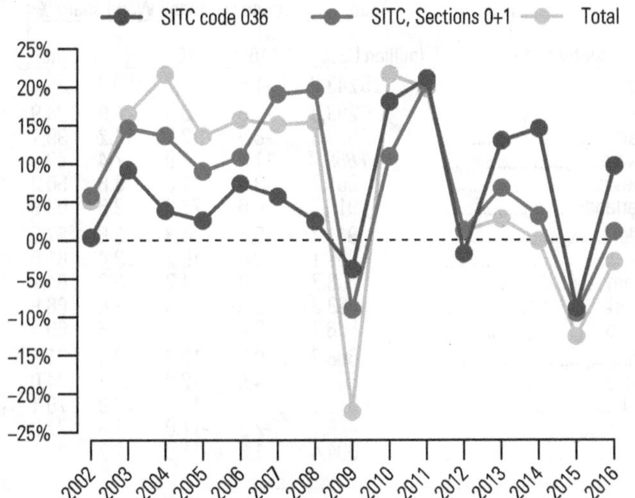

Table 2: Top exporting countries or areas in 2016

Country or area	Value (million US$)	Avg. Growth (%) 12-16	Growth (%) 15-16	World share %	Cum.
World	39351.8	6.7	9.7	100.0	
China	5476.5	10.5	3.0	13.9	13.9
India	4268.7	16.3	14.7	10.8	24.8
Canada	2767.2	4.7	-1.4	7.0	31.8
Ecuador	2592.9	19.3	13.1	6.6	38.4
Viet Nam	*2385.6*	3.5	8.9	6.1	44.4
Indonesia	1816.0	6.5	13.5	4.6	49.1
USA	1652.2	2.7	1.2	4.2	53.3
Thailand	1446.2	-8.0	25.4	3.7	56.9
Spain	1193.3	7.3	15.6	3.0	60.0
Argentina	1168.9	13.5	25.2	3.0	62.9
Cuba	*915.2*	58.9	129.4	2.3	65.3
Morocco	899.2	7.8	17.4	2.3	67.5
Netherlands	851.5	1.0	17.5	2.2	69.7
Australia	769.1	4.0	-0.5	2.0	71.7
Russian Federation	742.4	21.1	21.5	1.9	73.6

Graph 2: Trade Balance by MDG regions 2016

(Bln US$)

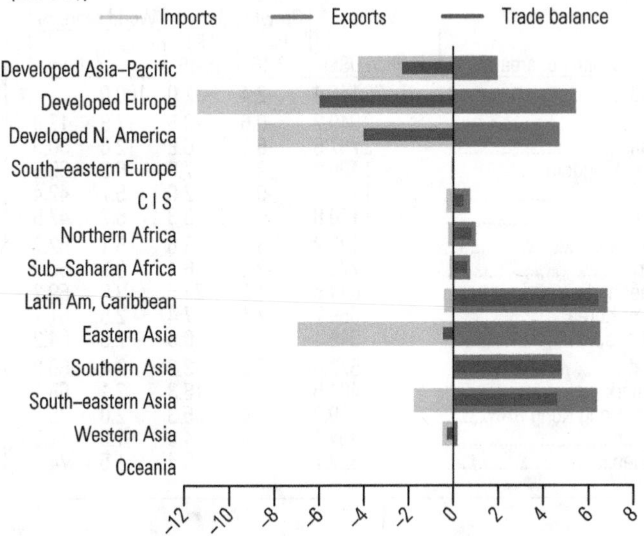

Table 3: Top importing countries or areas in 2016

Country or area	Value (million US$)	Avg. Growth (%) 12-16	Growth (%) 15-16	World share %	Cum.
World	34776.2	3.7	7.8	100.0	
USA	7713.5	6.1	4.8	22.2	22.2
Japan	3799.7	-5.8	7.6	10.9	33.1
Spain	3112.9	5.3	14.8	9.0	42.1
China	3055.2	13.6	13.3	8.8	50.8
Italy	2085.2	3.5	13.3	6.0	56.8
China, Hong Kong SAR	1757.5	-0.6	7.3	5.1	61.9
France	1643.8	0.0	5.1	4.7	66.6
Rep. of Korea	1567.1	8.7	3.9	4.5	71.1
Canada	997.9	3.4	2.5	2.9	74.0
Belgium	753.1	-1.2	9.0	2.2	76.2
Netherlands	726.1	8.2	32.2	2.1	78.2
United Kingdom	676.4	7.3	7.9	1.9	80.2
Germany	600.7	2.0	1.9	1.7	81.9
Thailand	566.1	15.2	17.8	1.6	83.5
Portugal	545.2	5.9	10.9	1.6	85.1

037 Fish, crustaceans, molluscs, aquatic invertebrates, prepared, nes

In 2016, the value (in current US$) of exports of "fish, crustaceans, molluscs, aquatic invertebrates, prepared, nes" (SITC group 037) increased by 2.7 percent (compared to -1.5 percent average growth rate from 2012-2016) to reach 25.2 bln US$ (see table 2), while imports decreased by 2.0 percent to reach 22.1 bln US$ (see table 3). Exports of this commodity accounted for 2.1 percent of world exports of SITC sections 0+1, and 0.2 percent of total world merchandise exports (see table 1). China, Thailand and Viet Nam were the top exporters in 2016 (see table 2). They accounted for 24.9, 14.2 and 7.4 percent of world exports, respectively. USA, Japan and United Kingdom were the top destinations, with respectively 17.8, 12.6 and 6.3 percent of world imports (see table 3).

The top 15 countries/areas accounted for 79.1 and 74.0 percent of total world exports and imports, respectively (see tables 2 and 3). In 2016, China was the country/area with the highest value of net exports (+6.1 bln US$), followed by Thailand (+3.4 bln US$). By MDG regions (see graph 2), the largest surpluses in this product group were recorded by South-eastern Asia (+6.1 bln US$), Eastern Asia (+5.3 bln US$) and Sub-Saharan Africa (+621.2 mln US$). The largest trade deficits were recorded by Developed Europe (-3.4 bln US$), Developed North America (-3.4 bln US$) and Developed Asia-Pacific (-2.7 bln US$).

Table 1: Imports (Imp.) and exports (Exp.), 2002-2016, in current US$

		2002	2003	2004	2005	2006	2007	2008	2009	2010	2011	2012	2013	2014	2015	2016
Values in Bln US$	Imp.	10.7	11.6	13.2	14.1	15.6	17.2	19.8	18.1	19.1	23.0	24.4	25.1	25.0	22.6	22.1
	Exp.	10.1	11.4	13.1	14.6	17.1	18.9	21.7	18.6	20.6	25.1	26.8	28.1	27.8	24.6	25.2
As a percentage of SITC section (%)	Imp.	2.4	2.2	2.2	2.2	2.2	2.1	2.0	2.0	2.0	1.9	2.1	2.0	1.9	1.9	1.9
	Exp.	2.4	2.3	2.4	2.4	2.5	2.4	2.3	2.1	2.1	2.2	2.3	2.2	2.1	2.1	2.1
As a percentage of world trade (%)	Imp.	0.2	0.2	0.1	0.1	0.1	0.1	0.1	0.1	0.1	0.1	0.1	0.1	0.1	0.1	0.1
	Exp.	0.2	0.2	0.1	0.1	0.1	0.1	0.1	0.2	0.1	0.1	0.1	0.1	0.1	0.1	0.2

Graph 1: Annual growth rates of exports, 2002–2016

(In percentage by year)

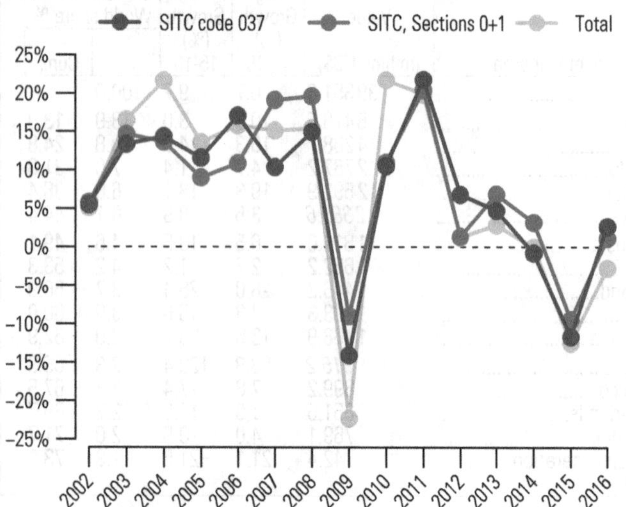

Table 2: Top exporting countries or areas in 2016

Country or area	Value (million US$)	Avg. Growth (%) 12-16	Growth (%) 15-16	World share %	Cum.
World	25243.9	-1.5	2.7	100.0	
China	6293.3	-1.9	0.8	24.9	24.9
Thailand	3579.8	-8.9	-2.3	14.2	39.1
Viet Nam	*1859.7*	11.1	8.9	7.4	46.5
Indonesia	961.7	3.4	1.8	3.8	50.3
Netherlands	915.7	16.6	27.3	3.6	53.9
Ecuador	911.7	-5.1	-4.3	3.6	57.5
Spain	865.1	-0.6	10.2	3.4	61.0
Germany	808.7	-1.3	-4.2	3.2	64.2
Denmark	663.3	-2.5	-2.5	2.6	66.8
Morocco	656.1	-0.4	0.9	2.6	69.4
Japan	608.2	-0.2	12.7	2.4	71.8
Canada	569.4	4.5	12.0	2.3	74.0
Poland	513.3	1.1	11.7	2.0	76.1
USA	448.1	-2.2	-11.0	1.8	77.9
Chile	304.4	-1.8	-11.0	1.2	79.1

Graph 2: Trade Balance by MDG regions 2016

(Bln US$)

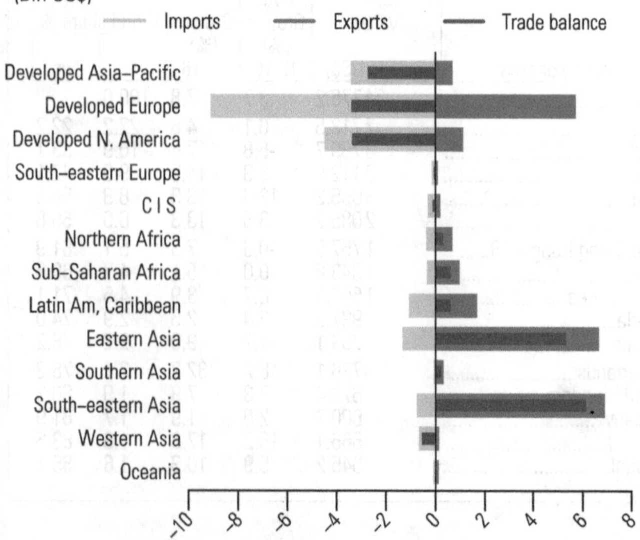

Table 3: Top importing countries or areas in 2016

Country or area	Value (million US$)	Avg. Growth (%) 12-16	Growth (%) 15-16	World share %	Cum.
World	22146.4	-2.4	-2.0	100.0	
USA	3949.2	-0.6	-3.5	17.8	17.8
Japan	2797.5	-6.1	0.8	12.6	30.5
United Kingdom	1400.0	-2.3	-7.6	6.3	36.8
Italy	1254.2	-0.7	2.0	5.7	42.4
Germany	1140.8	0.2	3.3	5.2	47.6
France	1126.2	-3.1	-3.6	5.1	52.7
Spain	775.1	-3.9	-6.4	3.5	56.2
Netherlands	664.5	1.9	24.5	3.0	59.2
Rep. of Korea	559.7	7.1	7.4	2.5	61.7
Australia	549.1	-3.8	0.6	2.5	64.2
Canada	523.6	-3.2	-3.2	2.4	66.6
Denmark	464.5	-2.5	-18.3	2.1	68.7
China, Hong Kong SAR	449.3	-4.4	5.3	2.0	70.7
Belgium	404.1	-0.4	4.6	1.8	72.5
Sweden	327.7	-0.2	6.4	1.5	74.0

In 2016, the value (in current US$) of exports of "wheat (including spelt) and meslin, unmilled" (SITC group 041) decreased by 12.5 percent (compared to -8.7 percent average growth rate from 2012-2016) to reach 33.9 bln US$ (see table 2), while imports decreased by 8.8 percent to reach 37.9 bln US$ (see table 3). Exports of this commodity accounted for 2.8 percent of world exports of SITC sections 0+1, and 0.2 percent of total world merchandise exports (see table 1). USA, Canada and Russian Federation were the top exporters in 2016 (see table 2). They accounted for 15.9, 13.3 and 12.4 percent of world exports, respectively. Indonesia, Algeria and Italy were the top destinations, with respectively 6.4, 4.7 and 4.7 percent of world imports (see table 3).

The top 15 countries/areas accounted for 89.8 and 52.2 percent of total world exports and imports, respectively (see tables 2 and 3). In 2016, USA was the country/area with the highest value of net exports (+4.9 bln US$), followed by Canada (+4.5 bln US$). By MDG regions (see graph 2), the largest surpluses in this product group were recorded by Developed North America (+9.4 bln US$), Commonwealth of Independent States (+3.9 bln US$) and Developed Europe (+2.5 bln US$). The largest trade deficits were recorded by South-eastern Asia (-5.4 bln US$), Northern Africa (-5.3 bln US$) and Western Asia (-3.5 bln US$).

Table 1: Imports (Imp.) and exports (Exp.), 2002-2016, in current US$

		2002	2003	2004	2005	2006	2007	2008	2009	2010	2011	2012	2013	2014	2015	2016
Values in Bln US$	Imp.	16.6	17.5	21.1	20.8	21.4	33.1	48.1	33.5	35.5	52.0	47.6	47.5	49.2	41.5	37.9
	Exp.	15.8	16.1	19.7	17.8	20.6	30.5	45.0	32.0	32.7	47.5	48.8	49.0	47.8	38.7	33.9
As a percentage of SITC section (%)	Imp.	3.7	3.4	3.6	3.3	3.1	4.0	4.9	3.8	3.6	4.4	4.0	3.8	3.8	3.5	3.2
	Exp.	3.7	3.3	3.6	2.9	3.1	3.8	4.7	3.7	3.4	4.1	4.1	3.9	3.7	3.3	2.8
As a percentage of world trade (%)	Imp.	0.3	0.2	0.2	0.2	0.2	0.2	0.3	0.3	0.2	0.3	0.3	0.3	0.3	0.3	0.2
	Exp.	0.2	0.2	0.2	0.2	0.2	0.2	0.3	0.3	0.2	0.3	0.3	0.3	0.3	0.2	0.2

Graph 1: Annual growth rates of exports, 2002–2016
(In percentage by year)

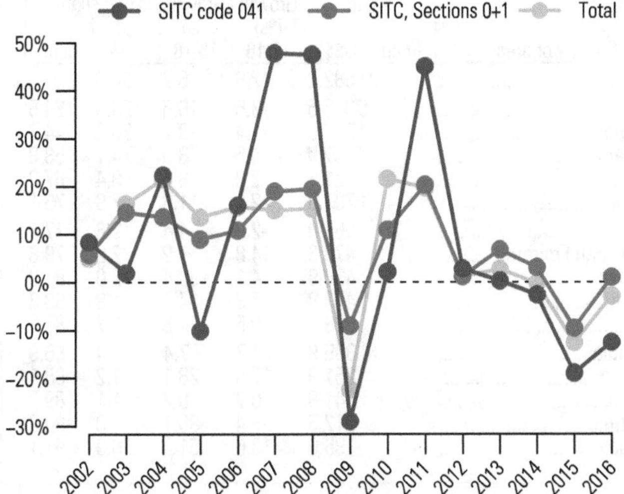

Table 2: Top exporting countries or areas in 2016

Country or area	Value (million US$)	Avg. Growth (%) 12-16	Growth (%) 15-16	World share %	Cum.
World	33918.4	-8.7	-12.5	100.0	
USA	5387.3	-9.9	-4.4	15.9	15.9
Canada	4504.1	-7.5	-27.6	13.3	29.2
Russian Federation	4215.8	-1.7	6.8	12.4	41.6
Australia	3621.3	-14.4	-17.2	10.7	52.3
France	3371.8	-9.6	-21.0	9.9	62.2
Germany	1933.1	-3.4	-20.4	5.7	67.9
Argentina	1867.7	-10.8	80.8	5.5	73.4
Romania	1264.1	16.2	64.3	3.7	77.1
Poland	806.9	26.7	-5.4	2.4	79.5
Bulgaria	767.7	1.7	17.6	2.3	81.8
Kazakhstan	685.1	-19.1	-0.5	2.0	83.8
Lithuania	595.1	1.4	18.1	1.8	85.6
United Kingdom	516.9	4.8	27.5	1.5	87.1
Czechia	497.2	3.9	1.2	1.5	88.5
Hungary	440.7	3.5	18.3	1.3	89.8

Graph 2: Trade Balance by MDG regions 2016
(Bln US$)

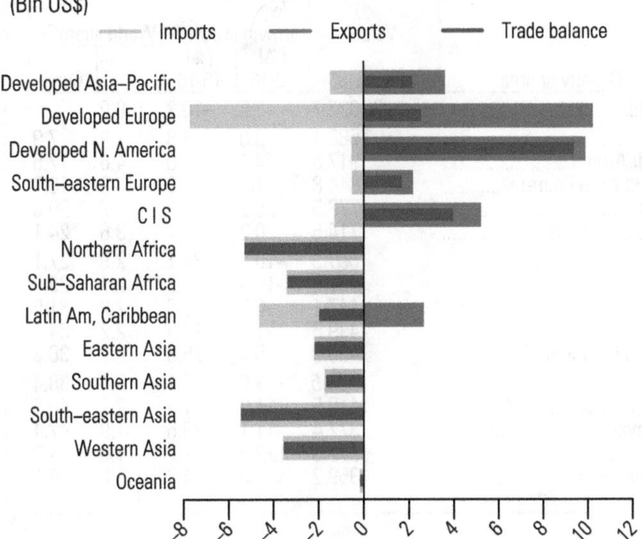

Table 3: Top importing countries or areas in 2016

Country or area	Value (million US$)	Avg. Growth (%) 12-16	Growth (%) 15-16	World share %	Cum.
World	37871.9	-5.5	-8.8	100.0	
Indonesia	2408.2	1.7	15.6	6.4	6.4
Algeria	1790.5	-4.2	-25.4	4.7	11.1
Italy	1786.9	-3.3	-12.7	4.7	15.8
Egypt	1537.6	-16.7	-39.4	4.1	19.9
Japan	1361.7	-10.8	-17.6	3.6	23.5
Brazil	1335.4	-6.1	9.8	3.5	27.0
Morocco	1304.3	-1.7	48.8	3.4	30.4
Spain	1296.4	-6.5	7.9	3.4	33.9
Nigeria	1088.3	-7.6	-16.6	2.9	36.7
Philippines	1040.8	1.7	6.0	2.7	39.5
Rep. of Korea	1007.6	-13.2	-8.9	2.7	42.1
Mexico	986.6	7.4	-4.0	2.6	44.7
Thailand	971.6	4.2	-14.2	2.6	47.3
Netherlands	942.0	-5.8	-19.8	2.5	49.8
Germany	906.7	-4.1	-9.5	2.4	52.2

Source: UN Comtrade

042 Rice

In 2016, the value (in current US$) of exports of "rice" (SITC group 042) decreased by 6.7 percent (compared to -2.6 percent average growth rate from 2012-2016) to reach 21.7 bln US$ (see table 2), while imports decreased by 10.3 percent to reach 20.0 bln US$ (see table 3). Exports of this commodity accounted for 1.8 percent of world exports of SITC sections 0+1, and 0.1 percent of total world merchandise exports (see table 1). India, Thailand and Viet Nam were the top exporters in 2016 (see table 2). They accounted for 24.5, 20.2 and 14.1 percent of world exports, respectively. China, Saudi Arabia and United Arab Emirates were the top destinations, with respectively 7.9, 4.6 and 4.2 percent of world imports (see table 3).

The top 15 countries/areas accounted for 91.1 and 46.1 percent of total world exports and imports, respectively (see tables 2 and 3). In 2016, India was the country/area with the highest value of net exports (+5.3 bln US$), followed by Thailand (+4.4 bln US$). By MDG regions (see graph 2), the largest surpluses in this product group were recorded by South-eastern Asia (+6.8 bln US$), Southern Asia (+5.9 bln US$) and Developed North America (+819.2 mln US$). The largest trade deficits were recorded by Sub-Saharan Africa (-4.3 bln US$), Western Asia (-2.8 bln US$) and Eastern Asia (-1.8 bln US$).

Table 1: Imports (Imp.) and exports (Exp.), 2002-2016, in current US$

		2002	2003	2004	2005	2006	2007	2008	2009	2010	2011	2012	2013	2014	2015	2016
Values in Bln US$	Imp.	6.7	7.8	9.3	10.1	10.6	13.7	22.2	19.1	19.9	23.1	23.1	22.5	24.0	22.3	20.0
	Exp.	6.7	7.3	8.7	10.1	10.5	13.2	21.3	19.1	20.3	24.1	24.1	25.7	26.4	23.2	21.7
As a percentage of SITC section (%)	Imp.	1.5	1.5	1.6	1.6	1.5	1.6	2.2	2.1	2.0	1.9	2.0	1.8	1.9	1.9	1.7
	Exp.	1.6	1.5	1.6	1.7	1.6	1.7	2.2	2.2	2.1	2.1	2.0	2.0	2.0	2.0	1.8
As a percentage of world trade (%)	Imp.	0.1	0.1	0.1	0.1	0.1	0.1	0.1	0.2	0.1	0.1	0.1	0.1	0.1	0.1	0.1
	Exp.	0.1	0.1	0.1	0.1	0.1	0.1	0.1	0.2	0.1	0.1	0.1	0.1	0.1	0.1	0.1

Graph 1: Annual growth rates of exports, 2002–2016

(In percentage by year)

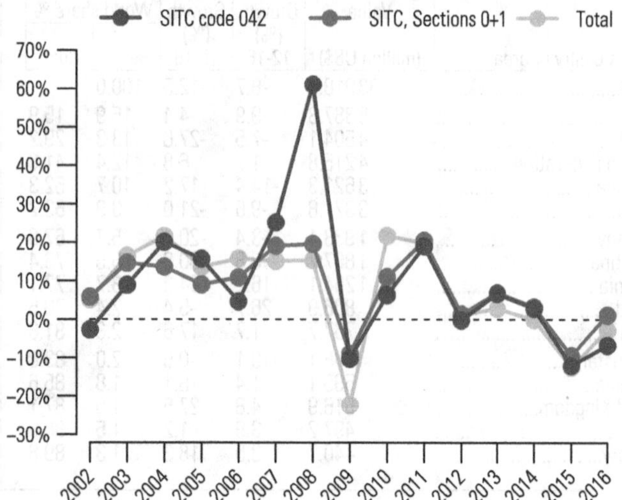

Graph 2: Trade Balance by MDG regions 2016

(Bln US$)

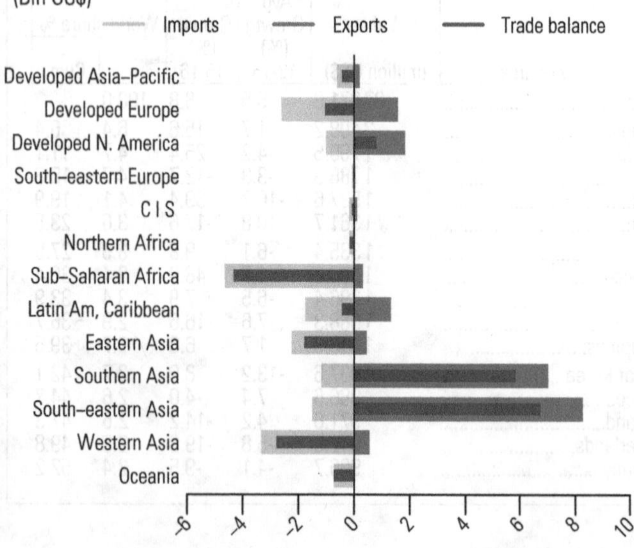

Table 2: Top exporting countries or areas in 2016

Country or area	Value (million US$)	Avg. Growth (%) 12-16	Growth (%) 15-16	World share %	Cum.
World	21682.2	-2.6	-6.7	100.0	
India	5315.5	-3.5	-16.7	24.5	24.5
Thailand	4377.9	-1.4	-3.7	20.2	44.7
Viet Nam	*3057.4*	-4.5	8.9	14.1	58.8
USA	1821.5	-2.9	-8.6	8.4	67.2
Pakistan	1703.0	-2.5	-11.6	7.9	75.1
Italy	565.0	-2.6	-4.4	2.6	77.7
United Arab Emirates	470.3	14.8	1.9	2.2	79.8
Myanmar	438.9	4.1	-30.4	2.0	81.9
Uruguay	413.8	-7.3	14.5	1.9	83.8
China	378.8	8.6	41.8	1.7	85.5
Cambodia	305.9	21.7	7.4	1.4	86.9
Brazil	251.9	-17.6	-28.1	1.2	88.1
Belgium	241.8	0.7	-0.2	1.1	89.2
Argentina	212.5	-8.4	36.1	1.0	90.2
Paraguay	196.0	13.6	51.0	0.9	91.1

Table 3: Top importing countries or areas in 2016

Country or area	Value (million US$)	Avg. Growth (%) 12-16	Growth (%) 15-16	World share %	Cum.
World	20027.7	-3.5	-10.3	100.0	
China	1586.1	9.0	7.8	7.9	7.9
Saudi Arabia	917.3	-4.1	-39.0	4.6	12.5
United Arab Emirates	844.8	1.9	-11.0	4.2	16.7
Benin	773.5	25.2	69.2	3.9	20.6
USA	714.5	-0.2	-9.7	3.6	24.1
Iran	*581.3*	-10.5	-34.1	2.9	27.1
Indonesia	531.8	-13.4	51.3	2.7	29.7
France	447.1	-0.7	-3.6	2.2	31.9
Japan	439.6	-1.6	-13.3	2.2	34.1
United Kingdom	430.9	-5.4	-25.8	2.2	36.3
Côte d'Ivoire	*429.5*	-11.0	-12.1	2.1	38.4
South Africa	419.5	-11.6	31.5	2.1	40.5
Malaysia	377.4	-11.1	-29.5	1.9	42.4
N. Mariana Isds	*372.9*	122.6	1.2	1.9	44.3
Germany	359.2	1.0	-4.2	1.8	46.1

In 2016, the value (in current US$) of exports of "barley, unmilled" (SITC group 043) decreased by 29.4 percent (compared to -8.5 percent average growth rate from 2012-2016) to reach 5.5 bln US$ (see table 2), while imports decreased by 32.8 percent to reach 5.6 bln US$ (see table 3). Exports of this commodity accounted for 0.5 percent of world exports of SITC sections 0+1, and less than 0.1 percent of total world merchandise exports (see table 1). Australia, France and Argentina were the top exporters in 2016 (see table 2). They accounted for 20.4, 19.3 and 10.8 percent of world exports, respectively. China, Saudi Arabia and Netherlands were the top destinations, with respectively 20.3, 12.6 and 6.1 percent of world imports (see table 3).

The top 15 countries/areas accounted for 93.9 and 78.7 percent of total world exports and imports, respectively (see tables 2 and 3). In 2016, Australia was the country/area with the highest value of net exports (+1.1 bln US$), followed by France (+1.1 bln US$). By MDG regions (see graph 2), the largest surpluses in this product group were recorded by Developed Europe (+1.0 bln US$), Developed Asia-Pacific (+867.3 mln US$) and Commonwealth of Independent States (+536.2 mln US$). The largest trade deficits were recorded by Western Asia (-1.3 bln US$), Eastern Asia (-1.2 bln US$) and Northern Africa (-541.6 mln US$).

Table 1: Imports (Imp.) and exports (Exp.), 2002-2016, in current US$

		2002	2003	2004	2005	2006	2007	2008	2009	2010	2011	2012	2013	2014	2015	2016
Values in Bln US$	Imp.	2.7	3.3	3.9	4.0	4.0	6.0	8.9	5.0	5.6	7.5	8.2	9.4	8.3	8.4	5.6
	Exp.	2.6	3.1	3.3	3.6	3.5	5.4	7.7	4.5	4.9	7.4	7.9	8.7	7.8	7.8	5.5
As a percentage of SITC section (%)	Imp.	0.6	0.6	0.7	0.6	0.6	0.7	0.9	0.6	0.6	0.6	0.7	0.8	0.6	0.7	0.5
	Exp.	0.6	0.6	0.6	0.6	0.5	0.7	0.8	0.5	0.5	0.6	0.7	0.7	0.6	0.7	0.5
As a percentage of world trade (%)	Imp.	0.0	0.0	0.0	0.0	0.0	0.0	0.1	0.0	0.0	0.0	0.0	0.1	0.0	0.1	0.0
	Exp.	0.0	0.0	0.0	0.0	0.0	0.0	0.0	0.0	0.0	0.0	0.0	0.0	0.0	0.0	0.0

Graph 1: Annual growth rates of exports, 2002–2016

(In percentage by year)

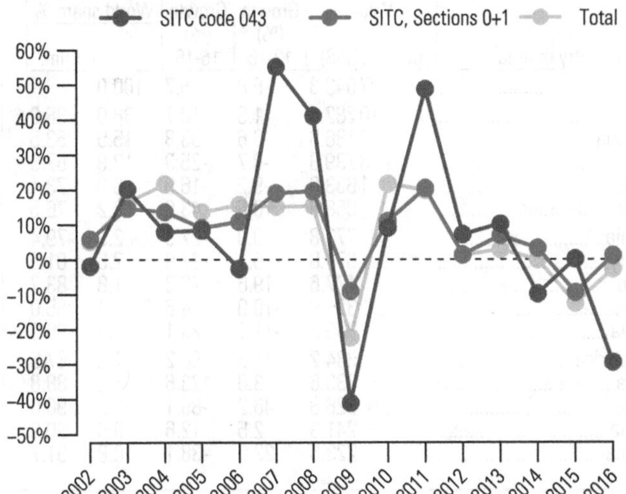

Graph 2: Trade Balance by MDG regions 2016

(Bln US$)

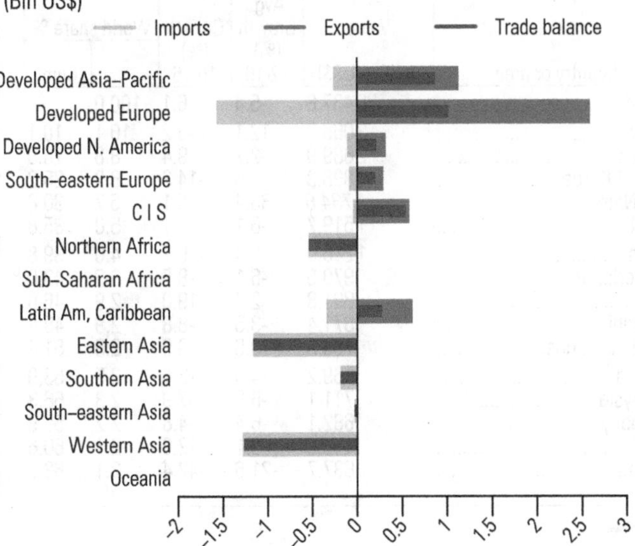

Table 2: Top exporting countries or areas in 2016

Country or area	Value (million US$)	Avg. Growth (%) 12-16	Growth (%) 15-16	World share %	Cum.
World	5532.7	-8.5	-29.4	100.0	
Australia	1131.1	-4.6	-13.6	20.4	20.4
France	1067.8	-5.4	-31.9	19.3	39.7
Argentina	599.7	-8.2	71.9	10.8	50.6
Germany	499.4	2.8	-11.7	9.0	59.6
Russian Federation	424.4	-17.1	-55.1	7.7	67.3
United Kingdom	313.0	15.6	-0.5	5.7	72.9
Canada	293.4	-11.8	-17.3	5.3	78.2
Romania	215.0	2.9	-35.6	3.9	82.1
Denmark	142.8	-18.8	-38.8	2.6	84.7
Kazakhstan	109.1	9.3	4.5	2.0	86.7
Hungary	100.5	4.0	-30.0	1.8	88.5
Sweden	96.9	-9.0	-2.8	1.8	90.2
Czechia	85.9	-6.3	-10.6	1.6	91.8
Bulgaria	70.0	-6.5	-6.0	1.3	93.1
Estonia	46.0	14.8	-11.2	0.8	93.9

Table 3: Top importing countries or areas in 2016

Country or area	Value (million US$)	Avg. Growth (%) 12-16	Growth (%) 15-16	World share %	Cum.
World	5637.0	-8.8	-32.8	100.0	
China	1141.9	10.0	-60.1	20.3	20.3
Saudi Arabia	713.1	-27.0	-51.5	12.6	32.9
Netherlands	345.8	-6.6	16.5	6.1	39.0
Belgium	324.5	-11.3	-2.2	5.8	44.8
Japan	261.2	-10.8	-10.8	4.6	49.4
Germany	253.2	-12.0	-15.7	4.5	53.9
Spain	200.3	24.1	22.6	3.6	57.5
Jordan	190.1	-5.4	21.9	3.4	60.9
Morocco	179.1	2.0	123.5	3.2	64.0
Brazil	169.3	21.8	22.8	3.0	67.0
Algeria	153.4	7.7	-7.7	2.7	69.8
Iran	*145.9*	-18.9	-35.2	2.6	72.3
Italy	135.4	-1.3	2.0	2.4	74.7
Tunisia	121.6	21.7	7.6	2.2	76.9
United Arab Emirates	103.4	25.9	-21.0	1.8	78.7

044 Maize (not including sweet corn), unmilled

In 2016, the value (in current US$) of exports of "maize (not including sweet corn), unmilled" (SITC group 044) decreased by 5.7 percent (compared to -6.8 percent average growth rate from 2012-2016) to reach 27.0 bln US$ (see table 2), while imports decreased by 6.1 percent to reach 30.4 bln US$ (see table 3). Exports of this commodity accounted for 2.3 percent of world exports of SITC sections 0+1, and 0.2 percent of total world merchandise exports (see table 1). USA, Argentina and Brazil were the top exporters in 2016 (see table 2). They accounted for 38.0, 15.5 and 13.8 percent of world exports, respectively. Japan, Mexico and Rep. of Korea were the top destinations, with respectively 10.1, 8.8 and 6.2 percent of world imports (see table 3).

The top 15 countries/areas accounted for 91.7 and 62.7 percent of total world exports and imports, respectively (see tables 2 and 3). In 2016, USA was the country/area with the highest value of net exports (+9.7 bln US$), followed by Argentina (+4.2 bln US$). By MDG regions (see graph 2), the largest surpluses in this product group were recorded by Developed North America (+9.8 bln US$), Latin America and the Caribbean (+2.2 bln US$) and South-eastern Europe (+1.1 bln US$). The largest trade deficits were recorded by Eastern Asia (-3.3 bln US$), Developed Asia-Pacific (-3.0 bln US$) and Northern Africa (-2.9 bln US$).

Table 1: Imports (Imp.) and exports (Exp.), 2002-2016, in current US$

		2002	2003	2004	2005	2006	2007	2008	2009	2010	2011	2012	2013	2014	2015	2016
Values in Bln US$	Imp.	11.4	13.0	15.0	13.7	15.2	24.5	32.2	22.7	25.7	36.5	38.1	38.1	36.4	32.4	30.4
	Exp.	9.9	11.1	11.7	11.2	13.2	20.6	27.2	19.9	23.3	33.9	35.8	35.4	33.1	28.7	27.0
As a percentage of SITC section (%)	Imp.	2.5	2.5	2.6	2.1	2.2	2.9	3.3	2.6	2.6	3.1	3.2	3.1	2.8	2.7	2.6
	Exp.	2.3	2.3	2.1	1.9	2.0	2.6	2.8	2.3	2.4	2.9	3.0	2.8	2.5	2.4	2.3
As a percentage of world trade (%)	Imp.	0.2	0.2	0.2	0.1	0.1	0.2	0.2	0.2	0.2	0.2	0.2	0.2	0.2	0.2	0.2
	Exp.	0.2	0.1	0.1	0.1	0.1	0.1	0.2	0.2	0.2	0.2	0.2	0.2	0.2	0.2	0.2

Graph 1: Annual growth rates of exports, 2002–2016
(In percentage by year)

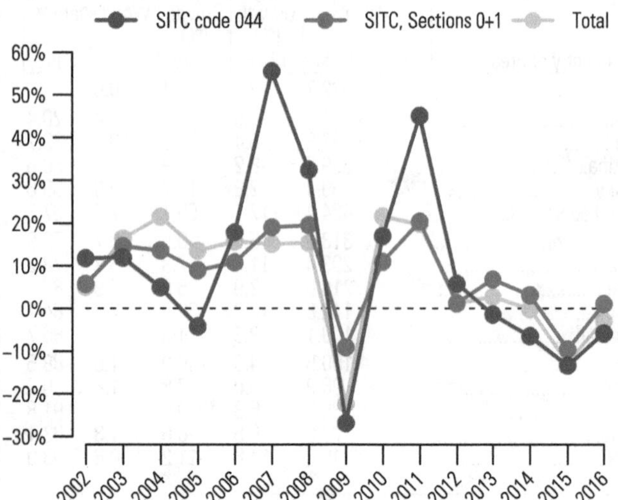

Table 2: Top exporting countries or areas in 2016

Country or area	Value (million US$)	Avg. Growth (%) 12-16	Growth (%) 15-16	World share %	Cum.
World	27 043.3	-6.8	-5.7	100.0	
USA	10 282.4	1.5	18.7	38.0	38.0
Argentina	4 186.6	-3.6	33.8	15.5	53.5
Brazil	3 739.9	-8.7	-25.3	13.8	67.3
France	1 633.6	-9.2	-16.9	6.0	73.4
Russian Federation	858.9	10.6	43.0	3.2	76.5
Romania	773.8	0.0	-27.5	2.9	79.4
Hungary	671.8	-15.1	-27.9	2.5	81.9
Mexico	477.6	19.6	73.3	1.8	83.7
Serbia	371.8	-10.0	-4.6	1.4	85.0
Paraguay	339.2	-11.5	-23.1	1.3	86.3
South Africa	334.2	-11.5	60.2	1.2	87.5
Canada	333.6	3.0	123.6	1.2	88.8
Ukraine	326.8	-46.2	-89.1	1.2	90.0
Bulgaria	241.3	2.5	12.6	0.9	90.9
Myanmar	223.5	23.0	-38.1	0.8	91.7

Graph 2: Trade Balance by MDG regions 2016
(Bln US$)

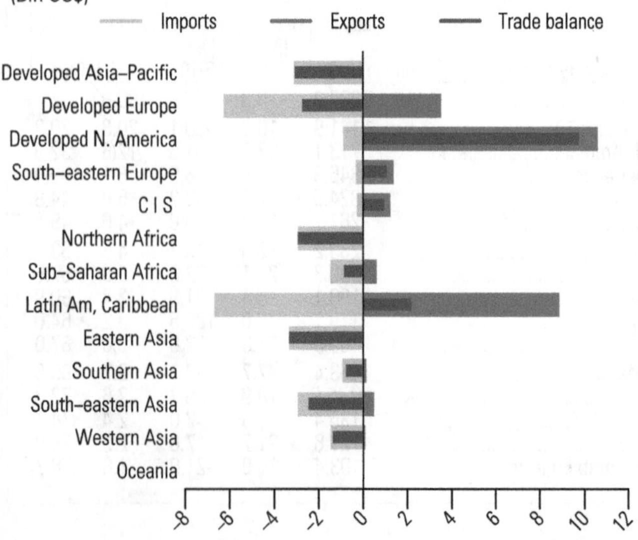

Table 3: Top importing countries or areas in 2016

Country or area	Value (million US$)	Avg. Growth (%) 12-16	Growth (%) 15-16	World share %	Cum.
World	30 437.6	-5.4	-6.1	100.0	
Japan	3 066.8	-12.1	-5.2	10.1	10.1
Mexico	2 689.9	-2.7	9.4	8.8	18.9
Rep. of Korea	1 898.3	-7.6	-14.3	6.2	25.2
Viet Nam	*1 734.8*	36.4	5.1	5.7	30.8
Egypt	1 519.7	-6.1	-15.1	5.0	35.8
Spain	1 215.0	-9.4	-15.7	4.0	39.8
Netherlands	970.5	-6.1	-8.5	3.2	43.0
Italy	891.8	2.0	19.0	2.9	46.0
Colombia	871.4	-3.5	-8.8	2.9	48.8
Other Asia, nes	786.5	-13.6	-9.9	2.6	51.4
Algeria	769.2	-4.9	-12.0	2.5	53.9
Malaysia	711.1	-6.5	-7.9	2.3	56.3
Germany	682.1	-6.4	-4.8	2.2	58.5
Iran	*642.0*	-9.1	-12.0	2.1	60.6
China	637.7	-21.6	-42.4	2.1	62.7

In 2016, the value (in current US$) of exports of "cereals, unmilled (other than wheat, rice, barley and maize)" (SITC group 045) decreased by 33.7 percent (compared to 0.6 percent average growth rate from 2012-2016) to reach 3.4 bln US$ (see table 2), while imports decreased by 33.5 percent to reach 3.9 bln US$ (see table 3). Exports of this commodity accounted for 0.3 percent of world exports of SITC sections 0+1, and less than 0.1 percent of total world merchandise exports (see table 1). USA, Canada and Australia were the top exporters in 2016 (see table 2). They accounted for 43.3, 14.1 and 4.9 percent of world exports, respectively. China, USA and Germany were the top destinations, with respectively 38.5, 12.1 and 6.4 percent of world imports (see table 3).

The top 15 countries/areas accounted for 88.9 and 83.0 percent of total world exports and imports, respectively (see tables 2 and 3). In 2016, USA was the country/area with the highest value of net exports (+1.0 bln US$), followed by Canada (+440.5 mln US$). By MDG regions (see graph 2), the largest surpluses in this product group were recorded by Developed North America (+1.5 bln US$), Commonwealth of Independent States (+21.2 mln US$) and Latin America and the Caribbean (+20.8 mln US$). The largest trade deficits were recorded by Eastern Asia (-1.5 bln US$), Western Asia (-149.8 mln US$) and Developed Europe (-136.6 mln US$).

Table 1: Imports (Imp.) and exports (Exp.), 2002-2016, in current US$

		2002	2003	2004	2005	2006	2007	2008	2009	2010	2011	2012	2013	2014	2015	2016
Values in Bln US$	Imp.	1.7	1.8	1.9	1.8	2.0	3.0	4.3	2.6	2.9	3.8	3.7	4.3	4.9	5.8	3.9
	Exp.	1.5	1.5	1.6	1.6	1.8	2.8	3.5	2.3	2.6	3.5	3.3	3.8	4.7	5.2	3.4
As a percentage of SITC section (%)	Imp.	0.4	0.3	0.3	0.3	0.3	0.4	0.4	0.3	0.3	0.3	0.3	0.3	0.4	0.5	0.3
	Exp.	0.3	0.3	0.3	0.3	0.3	0.3	0.4	0.3	0.3	0.3	0.3	0.3	0.4	0.4	0.3
As a percentage of world trade (%)	Imp.	0.0	0.0	0.0	0.0	0.0	0.0	0.0	0.0	0.0	0.0	0.0	0.0	0.0	0.0	0.0
	Exp.	0.0	0.0	0.0	0.0	0.0	0.0	0.0	0.0	0.0	0.0	0.0	0.0	0.0	0.0	0.0

Graph 1: Annual growth rates of exports, 2002–2016

(In percentage by year)

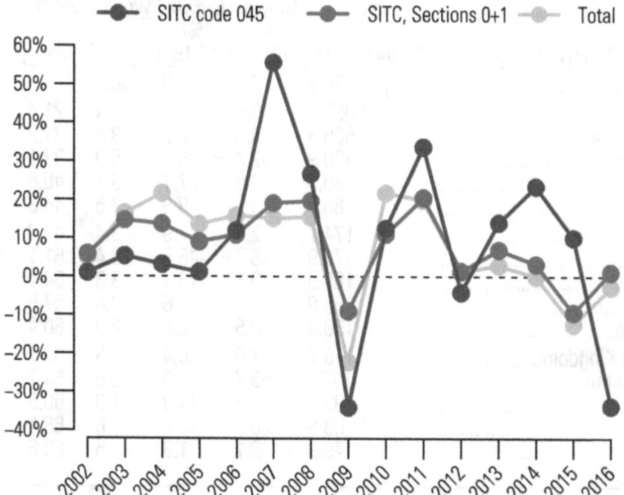

Graph 2: Trade Balance by MDG regions 2016

(Bln US$)

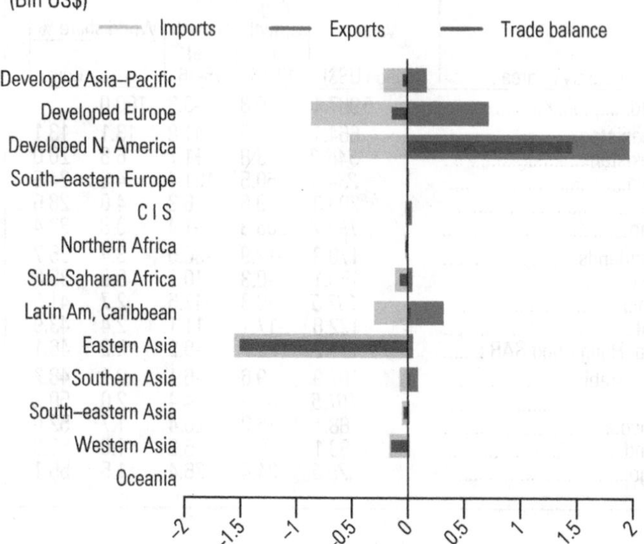

Table 2: Top exporting countries or areas in 2016

Country or area	Value (million US$)	Avg. Growth (%) 12-16	Growth (%) 15-16	World share %	Cum.
World	3430.9	0.6	-33.7	100.0	
USA	1484.9	24.5	-39.0	43.3	43.3
Canada	485.2	-4.6	-19.8	14.1	57.4
Australia	168.6	12.0	-60.1	4.9	62.3
Poland	149.2	5.6	-30.1	4.3	66.7
Argentina	108.5	-34.5	-37.7	3.2	69.8
Peru	106.7	31.6	-27.0	3.1	73.0
Germany	85.8	-10.8	-9.5	2.5	75.5
Bolivia	82.3	-1.0	-26.3	2.4	77.9
France	77.2	-7.3	-36.8	2.2	80.1
Sweden	62.7	-5.0	-3.0	1.8	81.9
Finland	60.5	-12.7	-12.4	1.8	83.7
India	56.0	-9.3	-22.8	1.6	85.3
China	44.2	-10.2	-8.8	1.3	86.6
Lithuania	40.9	-10.3	-36.9	1.2	87.8
Spain	37.0	17.3	8.4	1.1	88.9

Table 3: Top importing countries or areas in 2016

Country or area	Value (million US$)	Avg. Growth (%) 12-16	Growth (%) 15-16	World share %	Cum.
World	3879.0	1.0	-33.5	100.0	
China	1494.3	129.7	-50.6	38.5	38.5
USA	468.7	-3.8	-25.8	12.1	50.6
Germany	246.9	-2.8	-17.9	6.4	57.0
Japan	197.3	-23.0	-24.4	5.1	62.1
Mexico	194.6	-19.1	41.9	5.0	67.1
Spain	107.9	-7.3	-18.1	2.8	69.9
Netherlands	84.8	-12.4	-15.6	2.2	72.0
Italy	72.0	0.0	-33.8	1.9	73.9
Belgium	68.3	-4.7	-9.0	1.8	75.7
Qatar	57.3	149.7	44.0	1.5	77.1
Pakistan	53.0	102.9	125.9	1.4	78.5
France	49.1	5.4	-11.1	1.3	79.8
United Kingdom	46.5	1.4	-24.7	1.2	81.0
Canada	44.7	8.3	-17.3	1.2	82.1
State of Palestine	34.9	-0.7	11.1	0.9	83.0

Source: UN Comtrade

046 Meal and flour of wheat and flour of meslin

In 2016, the value (in current US$) of exports of "meal and flour of wheat and flour of meslin" (SITC group 046) decreased by 4.8 percent (compared to -2.5 percent average growth rate from 2012-2016) to reach 5.1 bln US$ (see table 2), while imports decreased by 3.3 percent to reach 5.1 bln US$ (see table 3). Exports of this commodity accounted for 0.4 percent of world exports of SITC sections 0+1, and less than 0.1 percent of total world merchandise exports (see table 1). Turkey, Kazakhstan and Germany were the top exporters in 2016 (see table 2). They accounted for 21.4, 9.9 and 5.9 percent of world exports, respectively. Afghanistan, Uzbekistan and Eritrea were the top destinations, with respectively 13.1, 6.8 and 4.6 percent of world imports (see table 3).

The top 15 countries/areas accounted for 69.6 and 55.1 percent of total world exports and imports, respectively (see tables 2 and 3). In 2016, Turkey was the country/area with the highest value of net exports (+1.1 bln US$), followed by Kazakhstan (+504.1 mln US$). By MDG regions (see graph 2), the largest surpluses in this product group were recorded by Western Asia (+792.6 mln US$), Developed Europe (+444.4 mln US$) and Commonwealth of Independent States (+293.7 mln US$). The largest trade deficits were recorded by Sub-Saharan Africa (-989.0 mln US$), Southern Asia (-383.2 mln US$) and South-eastern Asia (-126.4 mln US$).

Table 1: Imports (Imp.) and exports (Exp.), 2002-2016, in current US$

		2002	2003	2004	2005	2006	2007	2008	2009	2010	2011	2012	2013	2014	2015	2016
Values in Bln US$	Imp.	1.7	1.8	2.2	2.4	2.6	3.8	5.1	4.2	4.0	5.5	5.2	5.4	5.5	5.2	5.1
	Exp.	1.9	2.1	2.3	2.5	2.7	3.8	5.8	4.3	4.2	6.0	5.7	5.9	5.6	5.4	5.1
As a percentage of SITC section (%)	Imp.	0.4	0.4	0.4	0.4	0.4	0.5	0.5	0.5	0.4	0.5	0.4	0.4	0.4	0.4	0.4
	Exp.	0.4	0.4	0.4	0.4	0.4	0.5	0.6	0.5	0.4	0.5	0.5	0.5	0.4	0.5	0.4
As a percentage of world trade (%)	Imp.	0.0	0.0	0.0	0.0	0.0	0.0	0.0	0.0	0.0	0.0	0.0	0.0	0.0	0.0	0.0
	Exp.	0.0	0.0	0.0	0.0	0.0	0.0	0.0	0.0	0.0	0.0	0.0	0.0	0.0	0.0	0.0

Graph 1: Annual growth rates of exports, 2002–2016

(In percentage by year)

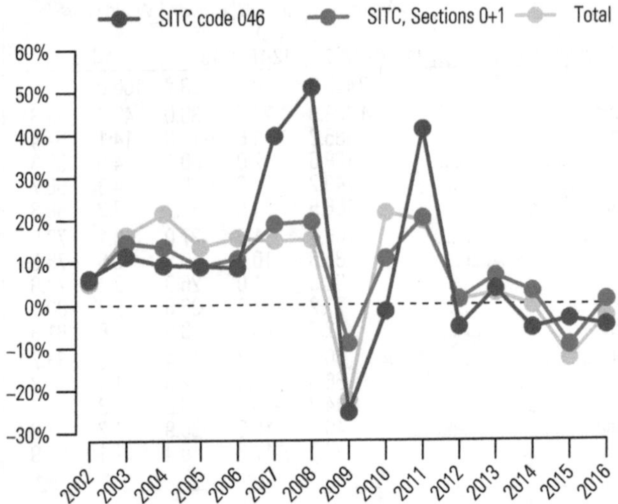

Table 2: Top exporting countries or areas in 2016

Country or area	Value (million US$)	Avg. Growth (%) 12-16	Growth (%) 15-16	World share %	Cum.
World	5126.8	-2.5	-4.8	100.0	
Turkey	1095.8	5.9	9.3	21.4	21.4
Kazakhstan	505.3	-4.5	2.2	9.9	31.2
Germany	300.9	-2.4	-5.4	5.9	37.1
Argentina	189.9	-14.5	27.1	3.7	40.8
France	180.7	-13.2	-9.9	3.5	44.3
USA	174.7	2.4	7.9	3.4	47.7
Pakistan	172.9	-8.7	-46.5	3.4	51.1
Belgium	169.9	-9.1	-13.4	3.3	54.4
Italy	155.9	8.1	3.6	3.0	57.5
Canada	150.9	8.5	-8.6	2.9	60.4
United Kingdom	115.7	-7.6	-6.4	2.3	62.7
Uzbekistan	*102.3*	253.7	15.9	2.0	64.7
India	93.1	3.9	-24.9	1.8	66.5
Egypt	83.5	20.2	-10.9	1.6	68.1
Spain	79.2	-6.1	1.8	1.5	69.6

Graph 2: Trade Balance by MDG regions 2016

(Bln US$)

Imports — Exports — Trade balance

Developed Asia-Pacific
Developed Europe
Developed N. America
South-eastern Europe
CIS
Northern Africa
Sub-Saharan Africa
Latin Am, Caribbean
Eastern Asia
Southern Asia
South-eastern Asia
Western Asia
Oceania

-1.5 -1 -0.5 0 0.5 1 1.5

Table 3: Top importing countries or areas in 2016

Country or area	Value (million US$)	Avg. Growth (%) 12-16	Growth (%) 15-16	World share %	Cum.
World	5067.1	-0.8	-3.3	100.0	
Afghanistan	664.1	39.5	41.8	13.1	13.1
Uzbekistan	*346.9*	3.8	-11.7	6.8	20.0
Eritrea	*234.9*	50.5	131.4	4.6	24.6
USA	203.3	9.6	-6.3	4.0	28.6
Sudan	*191.7*	206.3	-1.4	3.8	32.4
Netherlands	170.3	-12.9	-30.5	3.4	35.7
France	153.1	-0.3	-10.1	3.0	38.8
Angola	*137.5*	-20.3	-47.5	2.7	41.5
Brazil	122.8	-17.1	11.1	2.4	43.9
China, Hong Kong SAR	111.2	-2.7	-9.2	2.2	46.1
Saudi Arabia	107.9	9.6	-6.1	2.1	48.2
Yemen	*101.5*	63.3	4.4	2.0	50.2
Mexico	88.1	16.2	26.4	1.7	52.0
Ireland	83.1	0.2	5.2	1.6	53.6
Congo	*75.6*	34.4	26.4	1.5	55.1

Source: UN Comtrade

In 2016, the value (in current US$) of exports of "other cereal meals and flours" (SITC group 047) increased by 7.4 percent (compared to 1.3 percent average growth rate from 2012-2016) to reach 1.4 bln US$ (see table 2), while imports decreased by 1.0 percent to reach 1.4 bln US$ (see table 3). Exports of this commodity accounted for 0.1 percent of world exports of SITC sections 0+1, and less than 0.1 percent of total world merchandise exports (see table 1). USA, Thailand and South Africa were the top exporters in 2016 (see table 2). They accounted for 11.9, 9.4 and 9.0 percent of world exports, respectively. USA, Spain and Angola were the top destinations, with respectively 15.4, 6.1 and 4.5 percent of world imports (see table 3).

The top 15 countries/areas accounted for 79.2 and 59.1 percent of total world exports and imports, respectively (see tables 2 and 3). In 2016, Thailand was the country/area with the highest value of net exports (+128.1 mln US$), followed by South Africa (+121.0 mln US$). By MDG regions (see graph 2), the largest surpluses in this product group were recorded by Latin America and the Caribbean (+48.8 mln US$), South-eastern Asia (+46.5 mln US$) and Southern Asia (+33.1 mln US$). The largest trade deficits were recorded by Sub-Saharan Africa (-107.8 mln US$), Eastern Asia (-42.3 mln US$) and Northern Africa (-14.7 mln US$).

Table 1: Imports (Imp.) and exports (Exp.), 2002-2016, in current US$

		2002	2003	2004	2005	2006	2007	2008	2009	2010	2011	2012	2013	2014	2015	2016
Values in Bln US$	Imp.	0.6	0.6	0.8	0.7	0.7	1.1	1.5	1.4	1.2	1.6	1.6	1.7	1.6	1.5	1.4
	Exp.	0.5	0.5	0.6	0.7	0.7	0.9	1.2	1.1	1.1	1.4	1.3	1.5	1.6	1.3	1.4
As a percentage of SITC section (%)	Imp.	0.1	0.1	0.1	0.1	0.1	0.1	0.2	0.2	0.1	0.1	0.1	0.1	0.1	0.1	0.1
	Exp.	0.1	0.1	0.1	0.1	0.1	0.1	0.1	0.1	0.1	0.1	0.1	0.1	0.1	0.1	0.1
As a percentage of world trade (%)	Imp.	0.0	0.0	0.0	0.0	0.0	0.0	0.0	0.0	0.0	0.0	0.0	0.0	0.0	0.0	0.0
	Exp.	0.0	0.0	0.0	0.0	0.0	0.0	0.0	0.0	0.0	0.0	0.0	0.0	0.0	0.0	0.0

Graph 1: Annual growth rates of exports, 2002–2016
(In percentage by year)

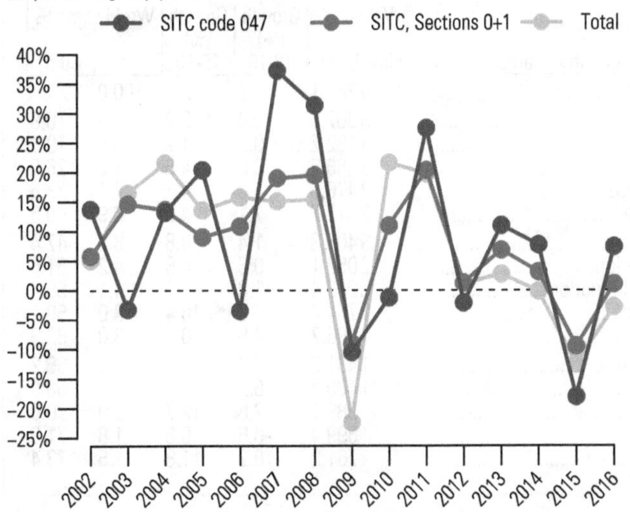

Graph 2: Trade Balance by MDG regions 2016
(Mln US$)

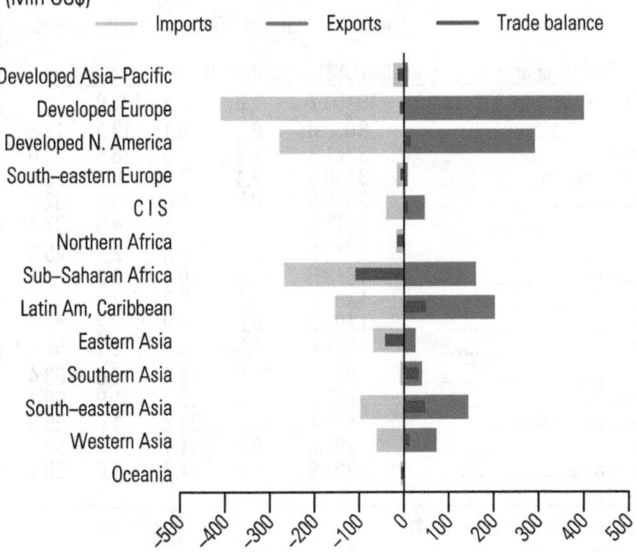

Table 2: Top exporting countries or areas in 2016

Country or area	Value (million US$)	Avg. Growth (%) 12-16	Growth (%) 15-16	World share %	Cum.
World	1404.4	1.3	7.4	100.0	
USA	167.6	-1.0	11.1	11.9	11.9
Thailand	131.8	-1.4	6.9	9.4	21.3
South Africa	126.7	3.0	22.3	9.0	30.3
Canada	124.3	3.9	-8.9	8.8	39.2
Mexico	74.5	17.6	44.5	5.3	44.5
France	70.5	-6.8	1.8	5.0	49.5
Italy	68.1	-8.7	10.0	4.8	54.4
Turkey	66.0	34.5	24.2	4.7	59.1
Germany	63.2	1.7	-10.1	4.5	63.6
Belgium	61.1	31.4	18.0	4.3	67.9
Brazil	39.2	0.8	1.1	2.8	70.7
India	32.7	4.8	-6.8	2.3	73.0
El Salvador	31.0	-8.0	18.5	2.2	75.2
Poland	27.8	8.5	16.0	2.0	77.2
Belarus	27.6	18.4	213.0	2.0	79.2

Table 3: Top importing countries or areas in 2016

Country or area	Value (million US$)	Avg. Growth (%) 12-16	Growth (%) 15-16	World share %	Cum.
World	1443.5	-2.3	-1.0	100.0	
USA	222.3	7.8	7.3	15.4	15.4
Spain	87.9	0.2	-1.4	6.1	21.5
Angola	*64.3*	-23.0	-47.5	4.5	25.9
Malaysia	56.8	-12.0	12.9	3.9	29.9
Canada	55.3	0.2	6.1	3.8	33.7
Mexico	52.2	2.4	4.6	3.6	37.3
Germany	51.6	0.7	-2.1	3.6	40.9
Lesotho	*44.0*	6.4	-18.9	3.0	43.9
France	39.0	1.8	8.0	2.7	46.6
Netherlands	36.6	-7.1	-18.1	2.5	49.2
Belgium	35.6	3.4	29.3	2.5	51.6
United Kingdom	33.5	5.5	4.9	2.3	54.0
China	29.3	0.4	2.1	2.0	56.0
Honduras	24.1	0.5	20.3	1.7	57.7
China, Hong Kong SAR	21.1	-4.7	12.3	1.5	59.1

Source: UN Comtrade

048 Cereal, flour or starch preparations of fruits or vegetables

In 2016, the value (in current US$) of exports of "cereal, flour or starch preparations of fruits or vegetables" (SITC group 048) increased by 2.6 percent (compared to 1.7 percent average growth rate from 2012-2016) to reach 49.3 bln US$ (see table 2), while imports increased by 2.9 percent to reach 49.4 bln US$ (see table 3). Exports of this commodity accounted for 4.1 percent of world exports of SITC sections 0+1, and 0.3 percent of total world merchandise exports (see table 1). Germany, Italy and USA were the top exporters in 2016 (see table 2). They accounted for 10.8, 8.5 and 7.2 percent of world exports, respectively. USA, Germany and United Kingdom were the top destinations, with respectively 13.5, 6.5 and 6.4 percent of world imports (see table 3).

The top 15 countries/areas accounted for 73.4 and 60.1 percent of total world exports and imports, respectively (see tables 2 and 3). In 2016, Italy was the country/area with the highest value of net exports (+2.8 bln US$), followed by Germany (+2.1 bln US$). By MDG regions (see graph 2), the largest surpluses in this product group were recorded by Developed Europe (+5.7 bln US$), South-eastern Asia (+580.6 mln US$) and Southern Asia (+355.2 mln US$). The largest trade deficits were recorded by Developed North America (-2.1 bln US$), Sub-Saharan Africa (-1.3 bln US$) and Developed Asia-Pacific (-915.4 mln US$).

Table 1: Imports (Imp.) and exports (Exp.), 2002-2016, in current US$

		2002	2003	2004	2005	2006	2007	2008	2009	2010	2011	2012	2013	2014	2015	2016
Values in Bln US$	Imp.	16.7	20.0	23.2	25.0	27.4	33.0	40.0	37.7	38.3	44.7	46.0	49.4	51.0	48.0	49.4
	Exp.	16.6	19.9	23.1	25.0	27.5	32.5	39.9	37.3	38.1	44.8	46.2	50.2	51.7	48.0	49.3
As a percentage of SITC section (%)	Imp.	3.7	3.9	4.0	3.9	3.9	4.0	4.0	4.2	3.9	3.8	3.9	4.0	4.0	4.1	4.2
	Exp.	3.9	4.1	4.2	4.1	4.1	4.1	4.2	4.3	3.9	3.8	3.9	4.0	4.0	4.1	4.1
As a percentage of world trade (%)	Imp.	0.3	0.3	0.2	0.2	0.2	0.2	0.2	0.3	0.3	0.2	0.3	0.3	0.3	0.3	0.3
	Exp.	0.3	0.3	0.3	0.2	0.2	0.2	0.2	0.3	0.3	0.2	0.3	0.3	0.3	0.3	0.3

Graph 1: Annual growth rates of exports, 2002–2016
(In percentage by year)

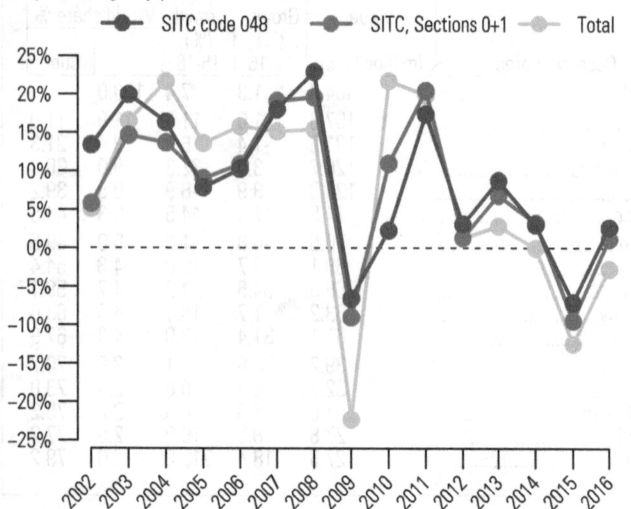

Graph 2: Trade Balance by MDG regions 2016
(Bln US$)

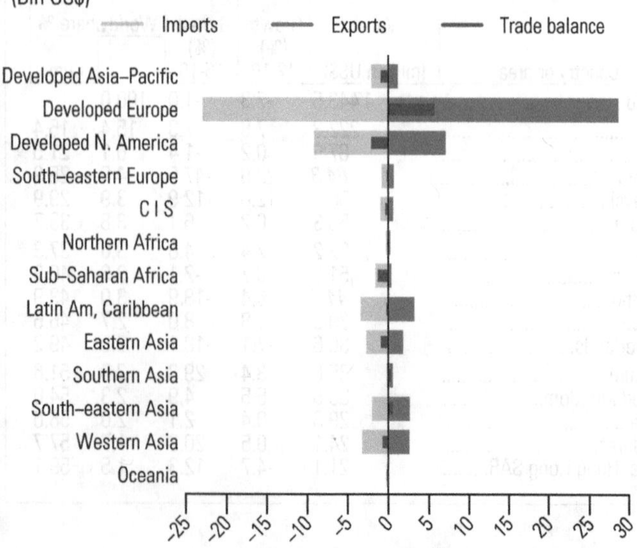

Table 2: Top exporting countries or areas in 2016

Country or area	Value (million US$)	Avg. Growth (%) 12-16	Growth (%) 15-16	World share %	Cum.
World	49287.1	1.7	2.6	100.0	
Germany	5307.1	0.0	2.9	10.8	10.8
Italy	4192.2	0.3	1.2	8.5	19.3
USA	3566.2	0.6	-4.6	7.2	26.5
Canada	3476.5	4.3	4.7	7.1	33.6
France	3412.7	-1.1	4.3	6.9	40.5
Belgium	3406.3	1.4	8.8	6.9	47.4
Netherlands	2052.1	0.6	-0.6	4.2	51.6
United Kingdom	2019.4	-1.8	-8.9	4.1	55.7
Poland	1764.4	13.7	16.4	3.6	59.2
Turkey	1496.7	4.5	-0.2	3.0	62.3
Mexico	1431.2	8.3	17.0	2.9	65.2
Spain	1400.4	6.2	8.0	2.8	68.0
Austria	989.1	2.8	12.7	2.0	70.0
China	899.4	-0.6	0.6	1.8	71.9
Malaysia	761.2	10.2	11.8	1.5	73.4

Table 3: Top importing countries or areas in 2016

Country or area	Value (million US$)	Avg. Growth (%) 12-16	Growth (%) 15-16	World share %	Cum.
World	49404.7	1.8	2.9	100.0	
USA	6658.8	6.2	8.1	13.5	13.5
Germany	3221.3	1.7	2.9	6.5	20.0
United Kingdom	3140.3	2.4	-2.4	6.4	26.4
France	3048.8	0.5	5.0	6.2	32.5
Canada	2417.8	1.9	-3.1	4.9	37.4
Belgium	1713.9	-1.3	9.6	3.5	40.9
Netherlands	1613.5	-1.4	-6.0	3.3	44.2
Italy	1401.1	-0.1	5.3	2.8	47.0
Spain	1102.3	0.8	8.9	2.2	49.2
Japan	1061.4	-4.6	0.2	2.1	51.4
China	978.2	24.9	13.3	2.0	53.4
Austria	957.2	2.5	13.7	1.9	55.3
United Arab Emirates	810.1	14.2	32.2	1.6	56.9
Ireland	792.2	0.4	-1.1	1.6	58.5
Saudi Arabia	791.9	7.4	-1.7	1.6	60.1

In 2016, the value (in current US$) of exports of "vegetables, fresh, chilled , frozen, simply preserved; roots" (SITC group 054) increased by 3.8 percent (compared to 3.7 percent average growth rate from 2012-2016) to reach 65.9 bln US$ (see table 2), while imports increased by 2.9 percent to reach 66.7 bln US$ (see table 3). Exports of this commodity accounted for 5.5 percent of world exports of SITC sections 0+1, and 0.4 percent of total world merchandise exports (see table 1). China, Netherlands and Mexico were the top exporters in 2016 (see table 2). They accounted for 11.8, 10.2 and 10.0 percent of world exports, respectively. USA, Germany and United Kingdom were the top destinations, with respectively 15.3, 8.8 and 6.2 percent of world imports (see table 3).

The top 15 countries/areas accounted for 77.2 and 67.7 percent of total world exports and imports, respectively (see tables 2 and 3). In 2016, Mexico was the country/area with the highest value of net exports (+6.2 bln US$), followed by China (+5.8 bln US$). By MDG regions (see graph 2), the largest surpluses in this product group were recorded by Latin America and the Caribbean (+6.6 bln US$), Eastern Asia (+4.5 bln US$) and Northern Africa (+825.3 mln US$). The largest trade deficits were recorded by Southern Asia (-4.7 bln US$), Developed North America (-3.8 bln US$) and Developed Europe (-2.8 bln US$).

Table 1: Imports (Imp.) and exports (Exp.), 2002-2016, in current US$

		2002	2003	2004	2005	2006	2007	2008	2009	2010	2011	2012	2013	2014	2015	2016
Values in Bln US$	Imp.	24.7	28.2	31.3	34.2	38.5	45.4	50.2	47.6	54.3	59.9	59.4	66.0	65.5	64.8	66.7
	Exp.	23.1	27.4	29.9	32.4	37.3	43.8	49.4	48.0	54.3	60.0	56.9	63.7	64.2	63.4	65.9
As a percentage of SITC section (%)	Imp.	5.5	5.5	5.3	5.4	5.5	5.4	5.1	5.3	5.6	5.0	5.0	5.3	5.1	5.5	5.7
	Exp.	5.4	5.6	5.4	5.4	5.6	5.5	5.2	5.5	5.6	5.2	4.8	5.0	4.9	5.4	5.5
As a percentage of world trade (%)	Imp.	0.4	0.4	0.3	0.3	0.3	0.3	0.3	0.4	0.4	0.3	0.3	0.4	0.3	0.4	0.4
	Exp.	0.4	0.4	0.3	0.3	0.3	0.3	0.3	0.4	0.4	0.3	0.3	0.3	0.3	0.4	0.4

Graph 1: Annual growth rates of exports, 2002–2016
(In percentage by year)

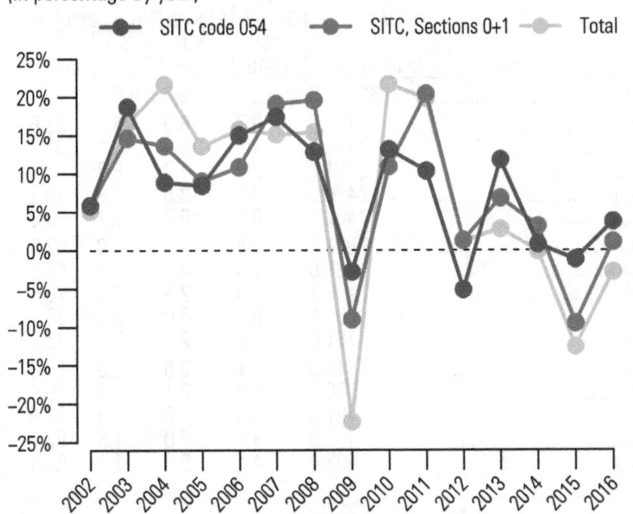

Graph 2: Trade Balance by MDG regions 2016
(Bln US$)

Imports
Exports
Trade balance

Developed Asia-Pacific
Developed Europe
Developed N. America
South-eastern Europe
C I S
Northern Africa
Sub-Saharan Africa
Latin Am, Caribbean
Eastern Asia
Southern Asia
South-eastern Asia
Western Asia
Oceania

-30 -25 -20 -15 -10 -5 0 5 10 15 20 25

Table 2: Top exporting countries or areas in 2016

Country or area	Value (million US$)	Avg. Growth (%) 12-16	Growth (%) 15-16	World share %	Cum.
World	65850.3	3.7	3.8	100.0	
China	7797.6	8.0	14.5	11.8	11.8
Netherlands	6705.8	-0.8	-3.3	10.2	22.0
Mexico	6588.7	9.0	13.9	10.0	32.0
Spain	6511.2	4.0	8.9	9.9	41.9
Canada	4838.5	10.9	-0.9	7.3	49.3
USA	4604.7	4.2	8.5	7.0	56.3
Belgium	2407.8	1.0	2.7	3.7	59.9
France	2226.9	-0.8	10.8	3.4	63.3
Australia	1667.8	6.6	13.9	2.5	65.8
Italy	1606.0	1.6	7.5	2.4	68.3
Myanmar	1419.9	-1.7	6.8	2.2	70.4
Thailand	1372.3	0.1	-24.0	2.1	72.5
Germany	1145.4	0.5	6.9	1.7	74.2
India	1007.7	7.5	-0.2	1.5	75.8
Morocco	940.0	7.6	12.5	1.4	77.2

Table 3: Top importing countries or areas in 2016

Country or area	Value (million US$)	Avg. Growth (%) 12-16	Growth (%) 15-16	World share %	Cum.
World	66682.2	3.0	2.9	100.0	
USA	10173.3	6.7	10.7	15.3	15.3
Germany	5868.8	0.6	1.8	8.8	24.1
United Kingdom	4143.3	2.2	-2.1	6.2	30.3
India	4025.0	15.3	9.5	6.0	36.3
France	3185.9	1.2	5.9	4.8	41.1
Canada	2984.5	5.4	4.8	4.5	45.6
Japan	2219.7	-2.3	4.8	3.3	48.9
Netherlands	2066.4	-4.3	-8.7	3.1	52.0
Belgium	2052.9	3.5	19.9	3.1	55.1
China	1950.2	-5.8	-28.2	2.9	58.0
Italy	1580.6	-0.1	-1.5	2.4	60.4
Russian Federation	1384.1	-13.4	-26.1	2.1	62.4
Spain	1303.5	1.0	16.3	2.0	64.4
United Arab Emirates	1265.0	12.3	1.8	1.9	66.3
Malaysia	957.3	9.1	12.1	1.4	67.7

Source: UN Comtrade

056 Vegetables, roots and tubers, prepared or preserved, nes

In 2016, the value (in current US$) of exports of "vegetables, roots and tubers, prepared or preserved, nes" (SITC group 056) increased by 5.0 percent (compared to 3.5 percent average growth rate from 2012-2016) to reach 31.4 bln US$ (see table 2), while imports increased by 1.5 percent to reach 27.5 bln US$ (see table 3). Exports of this commodity accounted for 2.6 percent of world exports of SITC sections 0+1, and 0.2 percent of total world merchandise exports (see table 1). China, Netherlands and USA were the top exporters in 2016 (see table 2). They accounted for 22.6, 10.1 and 8.7 percent of world exports, respectively. USA, Germany and Japan were the top destinations, with respectively 11.9, 8.1 and 7.5 percent of world imports (see table 3).

The top 15 countries/areas accounted for 84.0 and 66.5 percent of total world exports and imports, respectively (see tables 2 and 3). In 2016, China was the country/area with the highest value of net exports (+6.8 bln US$), followed by Netherlands (+2.2 bln US$). By MDG regions (see graph 2), the largest surpluses in this product group were recorded by Eastern Asia (+5.9 bln US$), Developed Europe (+2.7 bln US$) and Southern Asia (+362.3 mln US$). The largest trade deficits were recorded by Developed Asia-Pacific (-2.5 bln US$), Commonwealth of Independent States (-593.3 mln US$) and Western Asia (-473.7 mln US$).

Table 1: Imports (Imp.) and exports (Exp.), 2002-2016, in current US$

		2002	2003	2004	2005	2006	2007	2008	2009	2010	2011	2012	2013	2014	2015	2016
Values in Bln US$	Imp.	11.1	12.7	14.6	15.5	17.0	20.2	22.8	21.9	22.9	26.2	25.9	27.8	29.2	27.1	27.5
	Exp.	11.3	13.3	15.1	15.9	17.9	21.4	24.2	23.3	24.8	28.8	27.4	30.9	32.1	29.9	31.4
As a percentage of SITC section (%)	Imp.	2.5	2.5	2.5	2.4	2.4	2.4	2.3	2.5	2.3	2.2	2.2	2.2	2.3	2.3	2.3
	Exp.	2.7	2.7	2.7	2.6	2.7	2.7	2.5	2.7	2.6	2.5	2.3	2.5	2.5	2.5	2.6
As a percentage of world trade (%)	Imp.	0.2	0.2	0.2	0.1	0.1	0.1	0.1	0.2	0.1	0.1	0.1	0.1	0.2	0.2	0.2
	Exp.	0.2	0.2	0.2	0.2	0.1	0.2	0.2	0.2	0.2	0.2	0.1	0.2	0.2	0.2	0.2

Graph 1: Annual growth rates of exports, 2002–2016
(In percentage by year)

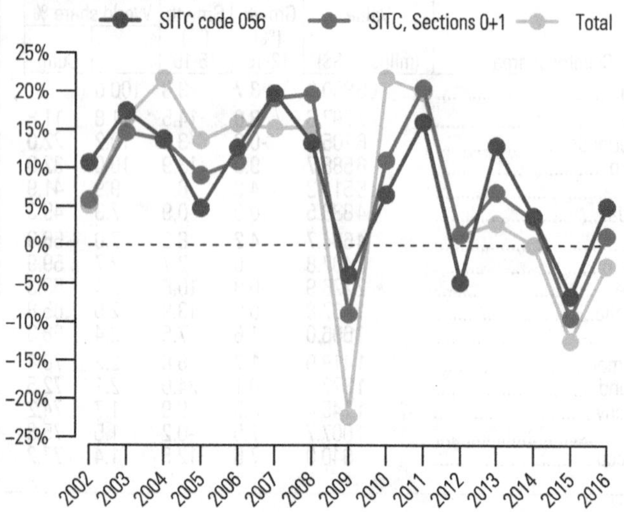

Table 2: Top exporting countries or areas in 2016

Country or area	Value (million US$)	Avg. Growth (%) 12-16	Growth (%) 15-16	World share %	Cum.
World	31 427.8	3.5	5.0	100.0	
China	7 103.5	9.7	6.9	22.6	22.6
Netherlands	3 174.4	4.3	16.3	10.1	32.7
USA	2 721.1	2.5	-1.3	8.7	41.4
Belgium	2 470.5	3.5	13.5	7.9	49.2
Italy	2 407.1	0.4	0.7	7.7	56.9
Spain	1 871.2	2.4	2.7	6.0	62.8
Germany	1 285.6	1.3	4.7	4.1	66.9
Canada	1 138.2	2.5	2.5	3.6	70.5
France	981.1	-5.5	-3.0	3.1	73.7
Turkey	751.0	3.8	2.9	2.4	76.1
Greece	618.5	2.1	2.5	2.0	78.0
Poland	569.3	5.9	10.1	1.8	79.8
Peru	491.8	0.5	-2.6	1.6	81.4
India	406.9	3.1	-2.0	1.3	82.7
Mexico	403.4	4.4	5.3	1.3	84.0

Graph 2: Trade Balance by MDG regions 2016
(Bln US$)

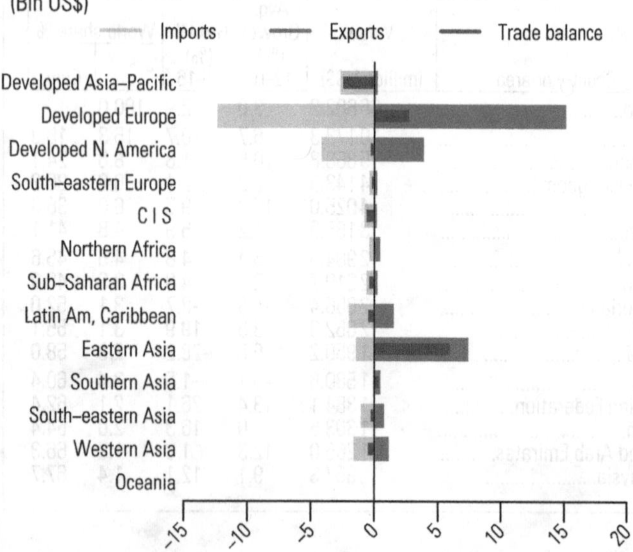

Table 3: Top importing countries or areas in 2016

Country or area	Value (million US$)	Avg. Growth (%) 12-16	Growth (%) 15-16	World share %	Cum.
World	27 507.3	1.6	1.5	100.0	
USA	3 271.3	3.0	6.9	11.9	11.9
Germany	2 222.7	-0.2	-0.4	8.1	20.0
Japan	2 071.6	-4.1	-1.4	7.5	27.5
France	1 918.7	0.3	4.3	7.0	34.5
United Kingdom	1 778.9	0.8	-6.5	6.5	40.9
Netherlands	1 008.0	0.4	-2.2	3.7	44.6
Italy	920.9	2.7	6.1	3.3	48.0
Canada	856.7	0.9	-1.5	3.1	51.1
Belgium	725.4	0.3	3.3	2.6	53.7
Spain	706.4	3.7	7.3	2.6	56.3
Rep. of Korea	613.7	7.8	6.3	2.2	58.5
Russian Federation	573.0	-6.5	1.8	2.1	60.6
Brazil	558.4	5.7	7.8	2.0	62.6
Saudi Arabia	556.3	6.2	-5.1	2.0	64.6
Australia	503.2	1.0	5.2	1.8	66.5

In 2016, the value (in current US$) of exports of "fruit and nuts (not including oil nuts), fresh or dried" (SITC group 057) increased by 5.3 percent (compared to 5.4 percent average growth rate from 2012-2016) to reach 105.4 bln US$ (see table 2), while imports increased by 1.8 percent to reach 109.1 bln US$ (see table 3). Exports of this commodity accounted for 8.8 percent of world exports of SITC sections 0+1, and 0.7 percent of total world merchandise exports (see table 1). USA, Spain and Netherlands were the top exporters in 2016 (see table 2). They accounted for 13.1, 8.5 and 6.0 percent of world exports, respectively. USA, Germany and Netherlands were the top destinations, with respectively 14.5, 8.4 and 6.4 percent of world imports (see table 3).

The top 15 countries/areas accounted for 67.0 and 71.8 percent of total world exports and imports, respectively (see tables 2 and 3). In 2016, Spain was the country/area with the highest value of net exports (+6.0 bln US$), followed by Chile (+5.3 bln US$). By MDG regions (see graph 2), the largest surpluses in this product group were recorded by Latin America and the Caribbean (+19.5 bln US$), Sub-Saharan Africa (+6.0 bln US$) and South-eastern Asia (+2.5 bln US$). The largest trade deficits were recorded by Developed Europe (-18.5 bln US$), Developed North America (-6.0 bln US$) and Eastern Asia (-4.5 bln US$).

Table 1: Imports (Imp.) and exports (Exp.), 2002-2016, in current US$

		2002	2003	2004	2005	2006	2007	2008	2009	2010	2011	2012	2013	2014	2015	2016
Values in Bln US$	Imp.	34.9	41.3	46.9	52.6	57.1	65.6	76.1	72.0	78.4	89.9	91.9	101.1	106.5	107.2	109.1
	Exp.	30.1	36.0	40.5	46.9	50.7	58.0	68.9	65.9	72.8	83.6	85.4	94.5	100.9	100.1	105.4
As a percentage of SITC section (%)	Imp.	7.7	8.0	8.0	8.2	8.2	7.9	7.7	8.1	8.0	7.6	7.8	8.1	8.3	9.1	9.3
	Exp.	7.1	7.4	7.3	7.8	7.6	7.2	7.2	7.6	7.5	7.2	7.2	7.5	7.8	8.5	8.8
As a percentage of world trade (%)	Imp.	0.5	0.5	0.5	0.5	0.5	0.5	0.5	0.6	0.5	0.5	0.5	0.5	0.6	0.6	0.7
	Exp.	0.5	0.5	0.4	0.5	0.4	0.4	0.4	0.5	0.5	0.5	0.5	0.5	0.5	0.6	0.7

Graph 1: Annual growth rates of exports, 2002–2016
(In percentage by year)

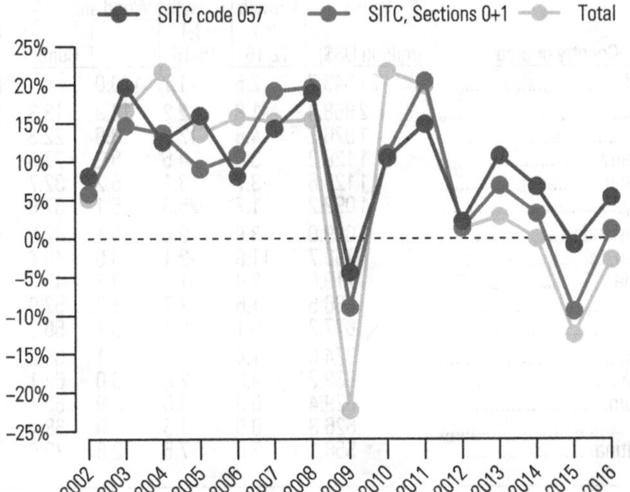

Table 2: Top exporting countries or areas in 2016

Country or area	Value (million US$)	Avg. Growth (%) 12-16	Growth (%) 15-16	World share %	Cum.
World	105433.1	5.4	5.3	100.0	
USA	13817.2	1.5	-2.8	13.1	13.1
Spain	8930.2	2.9	0.3	8.5	21.6
Netherlands	6302.5	9.6	37.4	6.0	27.6
Chile	5472.4	4.9	10.0	5.2	32.7
Mexico	5248.7	16.9	23.4	5.0	37.7
China	5209.0	11.2	6.7	4.9	42.7
Turkey	3803.1	0.4	-11.2	3.6	46.3
Italy	3802.1	0.6	3.4	3.6	49.9
Viet Nam	*3520.1*	15.7	8.9	3.3	53.2
South Africa	2880.4	5.2	2.4	2.7	55.9
Ecuador	2841.3	7.1	-2.1	2.7	58.6
Belgium	2511.2	-2.9	0.2	2.4	61.0
China, Hong Kong SAR	2413.2	7.1	27.4	2.3	63.3
Costa Rica	2002.0	5.7	14.2	1.9	65.2
New Zealand	1890.8	10.8	18.1	1.8	67.0

Graph 2: Trade Balance by MDG regions 2016
(Bln US$)

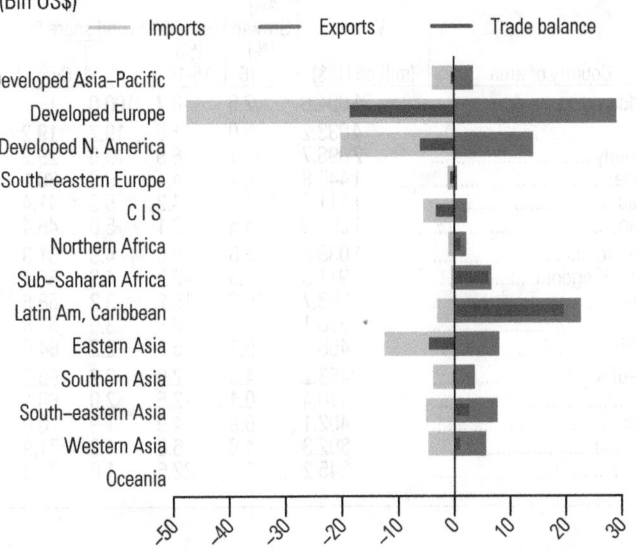

Table 3: Top importing countries or areas in 2016

Country or area	Value (million US$)	Avg. Growth (%) 12-16	Growth (%) 15-16	World share %	Cum.
World	109076.0	4.4	1.8	100.0	
USA	15836.5	10.3	9.5	14.5	14.5
Germany	9112.1	3.7	-0.7	8.4	22.9
Netherlands	6936.2	8.3	33.6	6.4	29.2
United Kingdom	6100.9	4.0	2.0	5.6	34.8
China	5719.3	11.7	-2.6	5.2	40.1
France	5012.4	3.3	6.1	4.6	44.7
Canada	4274.1	1.2	0.0	3.9	48.6
China, Hong Kong SAR	4271.6	5.3	13.8	3.9	52.5
Russian Federation	3779.3	-11.7	-2.7	3.5	56.0
Belgium	3372.8	0.6	7.2	3.1	59.1
Italy	3240.2	5.3	-2.6	3.0	62.0
Spain	2922.5	10.4	7.0	2.7	64.7
Japan	2916.6	-0.1	6.3	2.7	67.4
India	2801.9	10.8	-7.9	2.6	69.9
United Arab Emirates	2049.0	9.1	-6.3	1.9	71.8

Source: UN Comtrade

058 Fruits, preserved, and fruit preparations (excluding fruit juices)

In 2016, the value (in current US$) of exports of "fruits, preserved, and fruit preparations (excluding fruit juices)" (SITC group 058) decreased by 1.7 percent (compared to 2.5 percent average growth rate from 2012-2016) to reach 21.5 bln US$ (see table 2), while imports decreased by 0.7 percent to reach 21.0 bln US$ (see table 3). Exports of this commodity accounted for 1.8 percent of world exports of SITC sections 0+1, and 0.1 percent of total world merchandise exports (see table 1). China, USA and Germany were the top exporters in 2016 (see table 2). They accounted for 13.3, 8.9 and 5.2 percent of world exports, respectively. USA, Germany and France were the top destinations, with respectively 19.2, 10.0 and 6.9 percent of world imports (see table 3).

The top 15 countries/areas accounted for 70.6 and 73.5 percent of total world exports and imports, respectively (see tables 2 and 3). In 2016, China was the country/area with the highest value of net exports (+2.2 bln US$), followed by Turkey (+1.0 bln US$). By MDG regions (see graph 2), the largest surpluses in this product group were recorded by Latin America and the Caribbean (+2.0 bln US$), South-eastern Asia (+1.6 bln US$) and Eastern Asia (+1.6 bln US$). The largest trade deficits were recorded by Developed North America (-2.5 bln US$), Developed Europe (-2.2 bln US$) and Developed Asia-Pacific (-1.4 bln US$).

Table 1: Imports (Imp.) and exports (Exp.), 2002-2016, in current US$

		2002	2003	2004	2005	2006	2007	2008	2009	2010	2011	2012	2013	2014	2015	2016
Values in Bln US$	Imp.	6.8	8.3	9.5	10.6	11.7	13.7	15.8	13.9	14.9	18.4	19.0	20.2	21.0	21.1	21.0
	Exp.	6.6	7.9	9.0	10.0	11.6	13.8	16.2	13.9	15.2	18.7	19.5	20.8	21.5	21.9	21.5
As a percentage of SITC section (%)	Imp.	1.5	1.6	1.6	1.7	1.7	1.6	1.6	1.6	1.5	1.5	1.6	1.6	1.6	1.8	1.8
	Exp.	1.6	1.6	1.6	1.7	1.7	1.7	1.7	1.6	1.6	1.6	1.7	1.6	1.7	1.9	1.8
As a percentage of world trade (%)	Imp.	0.1	0.1	0.1	0.1	0.1	0.1	0.1	0.1	0.1	0.1	0.1	0.1	0.1	0.1	0.1
	Exp.	0.1	0.1	0.1	0.1	0.1	0.1	0.1	0.1	0.1	0.1	0.1	0.1	0.1	0.1	0.1

Graph 1: Annual growth rates of exports, 2002–2016
(In percentage by year)

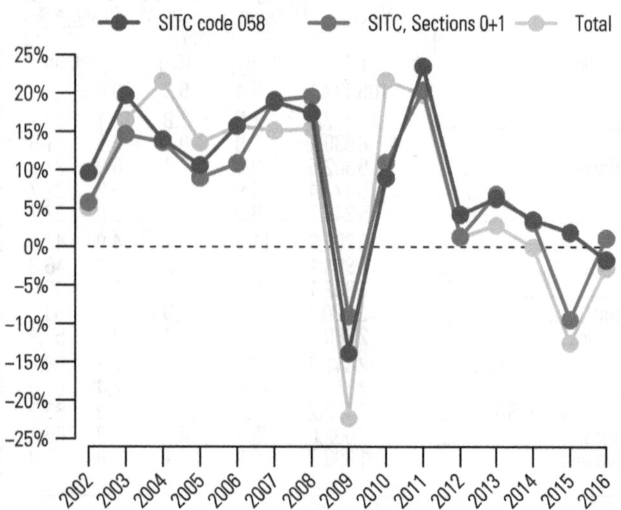

Table 2: Top exporting countries or areas in 2016

Country or area	Value (million US$)	Avg. Growth (%) 12-16	Growth (%) 15-16	World share %	Cum.
World	21 543.7	2.5	-1.7	100.0	
China	2 868.4	-1.8	-2.2	13.3	13.3
USA	1 926.2	4.8	-12.5	8.9	22.3
Germany	1 128.2	3.3	4.5	5.2	27.5
Thailand	1 126.6	3.7	3.1	5.2	32.7
Turkey	1 092.2	1.7	-25.3	5.1	37.8
Netherlands	1 089.0	3.0	9.0	5.1	42.8
Mexico	760.7	11.6	-2.1	3.5	46.4
Canada	719.6	2.4	-1.0	3.3	49.7
Chile	686.5	1.6	2.7	3.2	52.9
Spain	677.2	6.1	0.1	3.1	56.0
Poland	674.0	-1.4	1.3	3.1	59.2
France	639.2	4.0	2.8	3.0	62.1
Belgium	629.4	0.3	3.8	2.9	65.1
Italy	626.3	0.0	-1.3	2.9	68.0
Argentina	558.1	-3.0	7.5	2.6	70.6

Graph 2: Trade Balance by MDG regions 2016
(Bln US$)

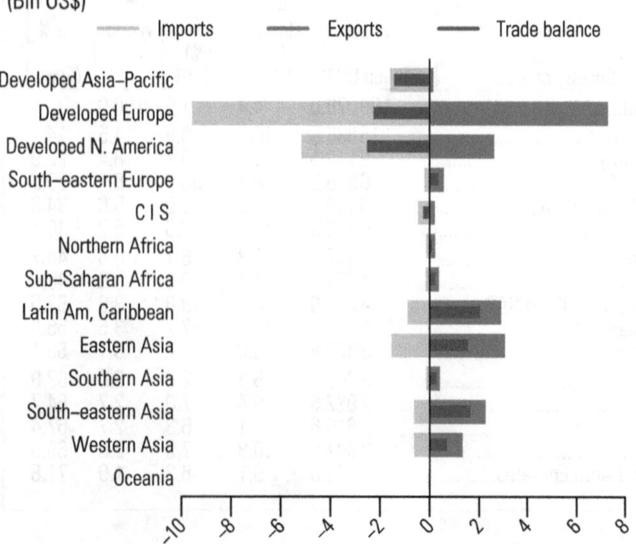

Table 3: Top importing countries or areas in 2016

Country or area	Value (million US$)	Avg. Growth (%) 12-16	Growth (%) 15-16	World share %	Cum.
World	21 004.6	2.5	-0.7	100.0	
USA	4 033.2	5.0	-1.5	19.2	19.2
Germany	2 096.7	-1.1	-6.9	10.0	29.2
France	1 445.8	0.7	4.4	6.9	36.1
Canada	1 111.4	4.6	-4.2	5.3	41.4
Japan	1 059.3	-4.5	-2.1	5.0	46.4
Netherlands	1 033.6	6.6	8.6	4.9	51.3
United Kingdom	911.3	1.3	-0.7	4.3	55.7
China	663.7	16.9	15.2	3.2	58.8
Belgium	630.1	1.3	0.8	3.0	61.8
Austria	458.8	5.1	5.3	2.2	64.0
Rep. of Korea	453.2	4.3	-2.0	2.2	66.2
Italy	410.4	-0.4	-2.5	2.0	68.1
Spain	402.1	6.9	4.9	1.9	70.0
Australia	392.3	4.9	6.8	1.9	71.9
Poland	345.2	1.6	-22.6	1.6	73.5

In 2016, the value (in current US$) of exports of "fruit and vegetable juices, unfermented and without added spirit" (SITC group 059) increased by 3.6 percent (compared to -2.0 percent average growth rate from 2012-2016) to reach 15.5 bln US$ (see table 2), while imports increased by 2.2 percent to reach 15.3 bln US$ (see table 3). Exports of this commodity accounted for 1.3 percent of world exports of SITC sections 0+1, and 0.1 percent of total world merchandise exports (see table 1). Brazil, Netherlands and Belgium were the top exporters in 2016 (see table 2). They accounted for 13.6, 10.9 and 6.5 percent of world exports, respectively. USA, Netherlands and Germany were the top destinations, with respectively 12.5, 11.7 and 8.9 percent of world imports (see table 3).

The top 15 countries/areas accounted for 76.3 and 73.5 percent of total world exports and imports, respectively (see tables 2 and 3). In 2016, Brazil was the country/area with the highest value of net exports (+2.1 bln US$), followed by Thailand (+664.1 mln US$). By MDG regions (see graph 2), the largest surpluses in this product group were recorded by Latin America and the Caribbean (+3.3 bln US$), South-eastern Asia (+1.2 bln US$) and Eastern Asia (+226.1 mln US$). The largest trade deficits were recorded by Developed Europe (-2.1 bln US$), Developed North America (-1.5 bln US$) and Developed Asia-Pacific (-701.3 mln US$).

Table 1: Imports (Imp.) and exports (Exp.), 2002-2016, in current US$

		2002	2003	2004	2005	2006	2007	2008	2009	2010	2011	2012	2013	2014	2015	2016
Values in Bln US$	Imp.	6.9	8.2	8.6	9.5	11.4	14.6	16.5	13.3	13.7	17.4	17.0	17.0	16.8	14.9	15.3
	Exp.	6.4	7.7	7.9	8.9	10.8	14.3	15.4	12.7	13.5	17.2	16.8	17.0	16.0	15.0	15.5
As a percentage of SITC section (%)	Imp.	1.5	1.6	1.5	1.5	1.6	1.8	1.7	1.5	1.4	1.5	1.4	1.4	1.3	1.3	1.3
	Exp.	1.5	1.6	1.4	1.5	1.6	1.8	1.6	1.5	1.4	1.5	1.4	1.4	1.2	1.3	1.3
As a percentage of world trade (%)	Imp.	0.1	0.1	0.1	0.1	0.1	0.1	0.1	0.1	0.1	0.1	0.1	0.1	0.1	0.1	0.1
	Exp.	0.1	0.1	0.1	0.1	0.1	0.1	0.1	0.1	0.1	0.1	0.1	0.1	0.1	0.1	0.1

Graph 1: Annual growth rates of exports, 2002–2016

(In percentage by year)

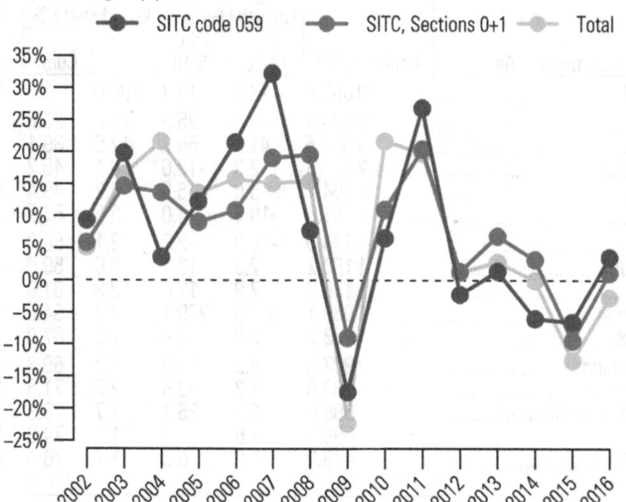

Table 2: Top exporting countries or areas in 2016

Country or area	Value (million US$)	Avg. Growth (%) 12-16	Growth (%) 15-16	World share %	Cum.
World	15488.0	-2.0	3.6	100.0	
Brazil	2105.2	-3.7	2.7	13.6	13.6
Netherlands	1692.0	3.9	26.8	10.9	24.5
Belgium	1007.5	-5.4	6.5	6.5	31.0
USA	998.9	-5.5	-7.3	6.4	37.5
Germany	802.5	-4.2	1.4	5.2	42.7
Thailand	738.2	14.6	19.1	4.8	47.4
China	668.6	-15.4	-3.9	4.3	51.7
Spain	667.9	-5.8	1.5	4.3	56.0
Poland	600.9	-4.1	12.9	3.9	59.9
Viet Nam	*531.7*	137.8	8.9	3.4	63.4
Italy	516.0	-7.8	4.6	3.3	66.7
Mexico	468.3	10.8	-0.3	3.0	69.7
Saudi Arabia	368.7	2.5	-17.3	2.4	72.1
Argentina	331.8	-9.3	-9.8	2.1	74.2
Austria	313.7	-3.5	16.6	2.0	76.3

Graph 2: Trade Balance by MDG regions 2016

(Bln US$)

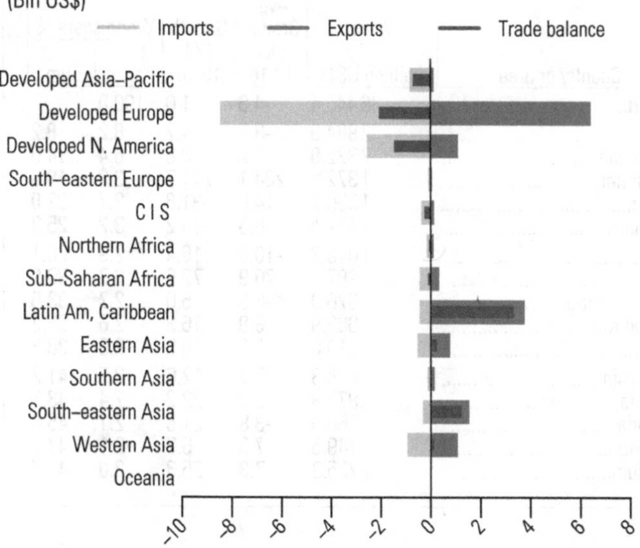

Table 3: Top importing countries or areas in 2016

Country or area	Value (million US$)	Avg. Growth (%) 12-16	Growth (%) 15-16	World share %	Cum.
World	15272.2	-2.6	2.2	100.0	
USA	1905.9	-1.8	0.1	12.5	12.5
Netherlands	1785.0	3.7	29.0	11.7	24.2
Germany	1354.8	-6.9	-0.6	8.9	33.0
France	1181.0	-2.4	12.1	7.7	40.8
United Kingdom	1007.9	-2.1	9.4	6.6	47.4
Belgium	884.6	-0.7	-23.4	5.8	53.2
Canada	629.3	-4.6	-5.7	4.1	57.3
Japan	616.6	-10.0	-5.8	4.0	61.3
Austria	323.5	-5.8	13.7	2.1	63.4
Spain	312.7	3.2	19.0	2.0	65.5
Russian Federation	286.4	-13.3	6.2	1.9	67.4
Saudi Arabia	282.3	1.9	-16.1	1.8	69.2
China	226.2	0.9	8.9	1.5	70.7
Italy	221.1	-7.4	-13.0	1.4	72.1
Poland	201.2	-2.5	0.5	1.3	73.5

Source: UN Comtrade

061 Sugars, molasses and honey

In 2016, the value (in current US$) of exports of "sugars, molasses and honey" (SITC group 061) increased by 18.7 percent (compared to -2.2 percent average growth rate from 2012-2016) to reach 39.7 bln US$ (see table 2), while imports increased by 11.0 percent to reach 36.4 bln US$ (see table 3). Exports of this commodity accounted for 3.3 percent of world exports of SITC sections 0+1, and 0.2 percent of total world merchandise exports (see table 1). Brazil, Cuba and Thailand were the top exporters in 2016 (see table 2). They accounted for 26.6, 12.5 and 6.1 percent of world exports, respectively. USA, Indonesia and Myanmar were the top destinations, with respectively 8.2, 6.4 and 3.8 percent of world imports (see table 3).

The top 15 countries/areas accounted for 76.0 and 49.7 percent of total world exports and imports, respectively (see tables 2 and 3). In 2016, Brazil was the country/area with the highest value of net exports (+10.5 bln US$), followed by Cuba (+5.0 bln US$). By MDG regions (see graph 2), the largest surplus in this product group was recorded solely by Latin America and the Caribbean (+17.1 bln US$). The largest trade deficits were recorded by Sub-Saharan Africa (-2.4 bln US$), Developed Europe (-1.9 bln US$) and Developed North America (-1.9 bln US$).

Table 1: Imports (Imp.) and exports (Exp.), 2002-2016, in current US$

		2002	2003	2004	2005	2006	2007	2008	2009	2010	2011	2012	2013	2014	2015	2016
Values in Bln US$	Imp.	13.9	15.5	16.8	19.9	24.2	25.2	28.0	28.5	37.1	48.8	44.0	42.0	38.9	32.8	36.4
	Exp.	12.0	13.2	14.1	17.4	22.6	22.4	24.6	27.0	36.2	44.7	43.4	42.3	37.5	33.4	39.7
As a percentage of SITC section (%)	Imp.	3.1	3.0	2.9	3.1	3.5	3.0	2.8	3.2	3.8	4.1	3.7	3.4	3.0	2.8	3.1
	Exp.	2.8	2.7	2.5	2.9	3.4	2.8	2.6	3.1	3.7	3.8	3.7	3.4	2.9	2.8	3.3
As a percentage of world trade (%)	Imp.	0.2	0.2	0.2	0.2	0.2	0.2	0.2	0.2	0.2	0.3	0.2	0.2	0.2	0.2	0.2
	Exp.	0.2	0.2	0.2	0.2	0.2	0.2	0.2	0.2	0.2	0.2	0.2	0.2	0.2	0.2	0.2

Graph 1: Annual growth rates of exports, 2002–2016
(In percentage by year)

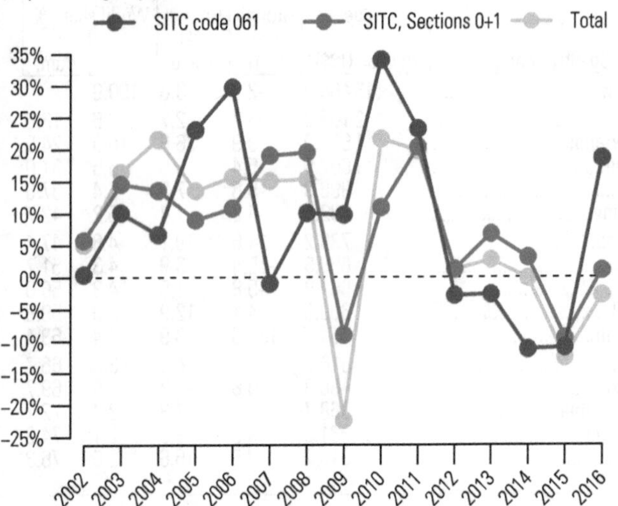

Graph 2: Trade Balance by MDG regions 2016
(Bln US$)

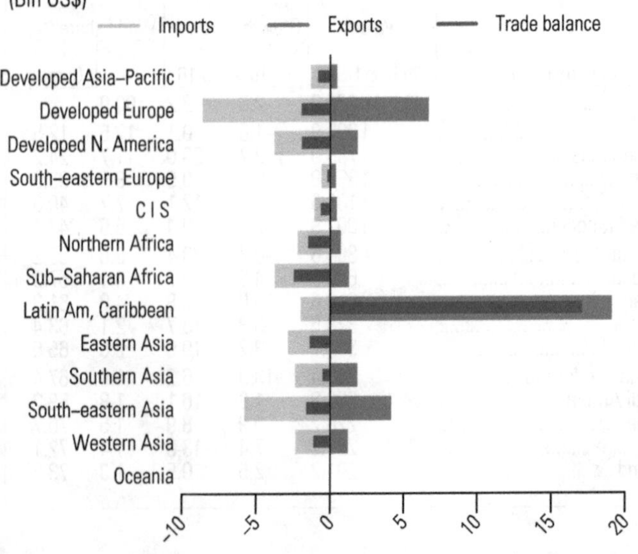

Table 2: Top exporting countries or areas in 2016

Country or area	Value (million US$)	Avg. Growth (%) 12-16	Growth (%) 15-16	World share %	Cum.
World	39662.4	-2.2	18.7	100.0	
Brazil	10539.4	-4.6	36.3	26.6	26.6
Cuba	*4961.5*	41.2	69.2	12.5	39.1
Thailand	2425.6	-12.3	-12.6	6.1	45.2
India	1664.7	-6.6	15.0	4.2	49.4
USA	1381.6	-10.1	-4.0	3.5	52.9
France	1238.0	-10.9	-2.7	3.1	56.0
Germany	1193.2	-7.3	13.1	3.0	59.0
China	1136.6	7.9	12.6	2.9	61.9
Myanmar	1069.1	205.6	279.1	2.7	64.6
Mexico	973.2	0.9	-12.4	2.5	67.0
Netherlands	907.3	4.2	11.5	2.3	69.3
Guatemala	883.6	1.2	-3.6	2.2	71.5
United Arab Emirates	686.6	5.3	25.1	1.7	73.3
Belgium	599.9	-7.6	7.8	1.5	74.8
Canada	478.3	-0.9	0.3	1.2	76.0

Table 3: Top importing countries or areas in 2016

Country or area	Value (million US$)	Avg. Growth (%) 12-16	Growth (%) 15-16	World share %	Cum.
World	36445.4	-4.6	11.0	100.0	
USA	2984.9	-3.5	-4.7	8.2	8.2
Indonesia	2322.9	5.8	58.8	6.4	14.6
Myanmar	1372.5	204.1	241.7	3.8	18.3
China	1350.7	-14.0	-31.6	3.7	22.0
Germany	1177.4	-8.3	-10.2	3.2	25.3
Italy	1048.2	-10.6	16.4	2.9	28.1
India	987.4	20.9	72.5	2.7	30.9
Rep. of Korea	976.0	-6.6	5.0	2.7	33.5
United Kingdom	963.9	-8.8	-16.3	2.6	36.2
Japan	919.0	-6.5	19.9	2.5	38.7
Malaysia	895.3	-5.7	12.6	2.5	41.2
Algeria	877.8	-2.8	22.2	2.4	43.6
Canada	760.9	-3.8	21.6	2.1	45.6
Nigeria	749.5	-7.3	5.7	2.1	47.7
Belgium	735.3	-7.3	25.3	2.0	49.7

In 2016, the value (in current US$) of exports of "sugar confectionery" (SITC group 062) increased by 2.4 percent (compared to 1.8 percent average growth rate from 2012-2016) to reach 11.5 bln US$ (see table 2), while imports increased by 1.8 percent to reach 10.5 bln US$ (see table 3). Exports of this commodity accounted for 1.0 percent of world exports of SITC sections 0+1, and 0.1 percent of total world merchandise exports (see table 1). China, Germany and Belgium were the top exporters in 2016 (see table 2). They accounted for 9.5, 9.5 and 6.2 percent of world exports, respectively. USA, Germany and United Kingdom were the top destinations, with respectively 17.6, 6.8 and 5.7 percent of world imports (see table 3).

The top 15 countries/areas accounted for 69.9 and 58.6 percent of total world exports and imports, respectively (see tables 2 and 3). In 2016, China was the country/area with the highest value of net exports (+896.6 mln US$), followed by Mexico (+549.2 mln US$). By MDG regions (see graph 2), the largest surpluses in this product group were recorded by Developed Europe (+1.1 bln US$), Eastern Asia (+659.6 mln US$) and Latin America and the Caribbean (+495.3 mln US$). The largest trade deficits were recorded by Developed North America (-1.2 bln US$), Commonwealth of Independent States (-164.3 mln US$) and Developed Asia-Pacific (-163.1 mln US$).

Table 1: Imports (Imp.) and exports (Exp.), 2002-2016, in current US$

		2002	2003	2004	2005	2006	2007	2008	2009	2010	2011	2012	2013	2014	2015	2016
Values in Bln US$	Imp.	4.6	5.4	6.1	6.5	6.8	7.6	8.4	7.9	8.5	9.7	9.8	10.7	11.2	10.4	10.5
	Exp.	4.6	5.5	6.2	6.5	7.0	8.1	9.2	8.6	9.3	10.6	10.7	11.9	12.5	11.2	11.5
As a percentage of SITC section (%)	Imp.	1.0	1.0	1.0	1.0	1.0	0.9	0.8	0.9	0.9	0.8	0.8	0.9	0.9	0.9	0.9
	Exp.	1.1	1.1	1.1	1.1	1.0	1.0	1.0	1.0	1.0	0.9	0.9	0.9	1.0	1.0	1.0
As a percentage of world trade (%)	Imp.	0.1	0.1	0.1	0.1	0.1	0.1	0.1	0.1	0.1	0.1	0.1	0.1	0.1	0.1	0.1
	Exp.	0.1	0.1	0.1	0.1	0.1	0.1	0.1	0.1	0.1	0.1	0.1	0.1	0.1	0.1	0.1

Graph 1: Annual growth rates of exports, 2002–2016
(In percentage by year)

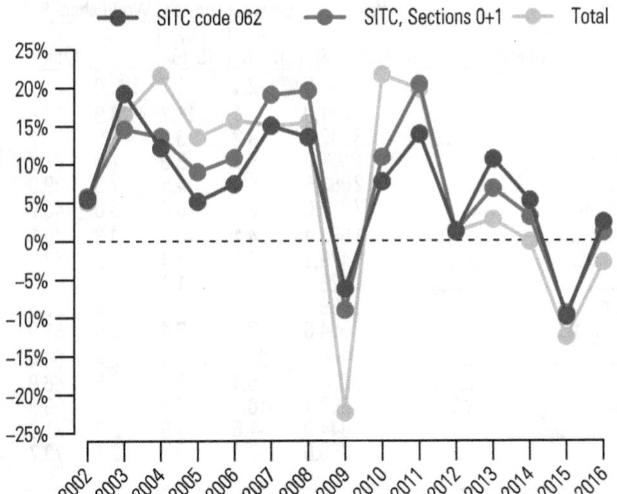

Graph 2: Trade Balance by MDG regions 2016
(Bln US$)

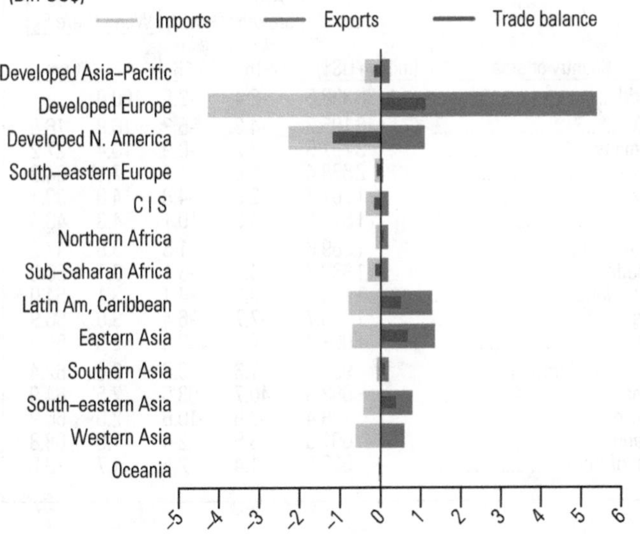

Table 2: Top exporting countries or areas in 2016

Country or area	Value (million US$)	Avg. Growth (%) 12-16	Growth (%) 15-16	World share %	Cum.
World	11516.3	1.8	2.4	100.0	
China	1094.8	6.0	1.7	9.5	9.5
Germany	1091.8	2.6	3.7	9.5	19.0
Belgium	714.6	3.9	7.6	6.2	25.2
Netherlands	683.6	3.0	7.6	5.9	31.1
Mexico	660.9	5.6	7.2	5.7	36.9
USA	571.5	4.4	-0.1	5.0	41.8
Spain	524.7	1.2	10.4	4.6	46.4
Canada	522.4	1.3	1.5	4.5	50.9
Turkey	414.5	0.6	-6.3	3.6	54.5
Thailand	401.5	1.2	8.1	3.5	58.0
Poland	348.9	9.9	5.7	3.0	61.0
United Kingdom	271.8	0.8	-7.5	2.4	63.4
Italy	258.7	4.5	-1.4	2.2	65.6
Colombia	251.2	-2.7	1.9	2.2	67.8
France	239.0	-3.2	-1.0	2.1	69.9

Table 3: Top importing countries or areas in 2016

Country or area	Value (million US$)	Avg. Growth (%) 12-16	Growth (%) 15-16	World share %	Cum.
World	10538.9	1.8	1.8	100.0	
USA	1855.4	4.4	7.3	17.6	17.6
Germany	720.3	1.4	-4.0	6.8	24.4
United Kingdom	600.5	0.4	-7.6	5.7	30.1
France	450.3	2.0	9.4	4.3	34.4
Canada	408.2	2.1	3.1	3.9	38.3
Netherlands	319.7	1.5	-7.3	3.0	41.3
Belgium	302.6	2.4	11.7	2.9	44.2
Sweden	216.8	1.7	2.5	2.1	46.2
China, Hong Kong SAR	201.6	1.1	-3.3	1.9	48.2
China	198.2	17.1	1.0	1.9	50.0
Rep. of Korea	196.5	18.9	16.2	1.9	51.9
Australia	194.2	-0.1	-0.4	1.8	53.7
Italy	177.8	1.6	4.1	1.7	55.4
Poland	174.0	2.4	-4.1	1.7	57.1
Spain	161.3	0.5	11.9	1.5	58.6

071 Coffee and coffee substitutes

In 2016, the value (in current US$) of exports of "coffee and coffee substitutes" (SITC group 071) decreased by 1.7 percent (compared to -2.1 percent average growth rate from 2012-2016) to reach 36.7 bln US$ (see table 2), while imports decreased by 2.5 percent to reach 36.4 bln US$ (see table 3). Exports of this commodity accounted for 3.1 percent of world exports of SITC sections 0+1, and 0.2 percent of total world merchandise exports (see table 1). Brazil, Germany and Viet Nam were the top exporters in 2016 (see table 2). They accounted for 14.9, 8.8 and 7.9 percent of world exports, respectively. USA, Germany and France were the top destinations, with respectively 16.8, 10.4 and 7.1 percent of world imports (see table 3).

The top 15 countries/areas accounted for 73.7 and 70.5 percent of total world exports and imports, respectively (see tables 2 and 3). In 2016, Brazil was the country/area with the highest value of net exports (+5.4 bln US$), followed by Viet Nam (+2.8 bln US$). By MDG regions (see graph 2), the largest surpluses in this product group were recorded by Latin America and the Caribbean (+11.0 bln US$), South-eastern Asia (+3.7 bln US$) and Sub-Saharan Africa (+1.5 bln US$). The largest trade deficits were recorded by Developed North America (-5.8 bln US$), Developed Europe (-5.0 bln US$) and Developed Asia-Pacific (-2.1 bln US$).

Table 1: Imports (Imp.) and exports (Exp.), 2002-2016, in current US$

		2002	2003	2004	2005	2006	2007	2008	2009	2010	2011	2012	2013	2014	2015	2016
Values in Bln US$	Imp.	9.2	11.0	12.7	16.2	19.0	22.3	27.2	25.0	29.3	42.8	40.2	35.9	38.1	37.3	36.4
	Exp.	8.5	9.9	11.7	15.5	18.3	22.0	26.9	24.6	29.5	42.6	40.0	35.8	39.5	37.3	36.7
As a percentage of SITC section (%)	Imp.	2.0	2.1	2.2	2.5	2.7	2.7	2.7	2.8	3.0	3.6	3.4	2.9	3.0	3.2	3.1
	Exp.	2.0	2.0	2.1	2.6	2.7	2.8	2.8	2.8	3.1	3.7	3.4	2.8	3.0	3.2	3.1
As a percentage of world trade (%)	Imp.	0.1	0.1	0.1	0.2	0.2	0.2	0.2	0.2	0.2	0.2	0.2	0.2	0.2	0.2	0.2
	Exp.	0.1	0.1	0.1	0.1	0.2	0.2	0.2	0.2	0.2	0.2	0.2	0.2	0.2	0.2	0.2

Graph 1: Annual growth rates of exports, 2002–2016
(In percentage by year)

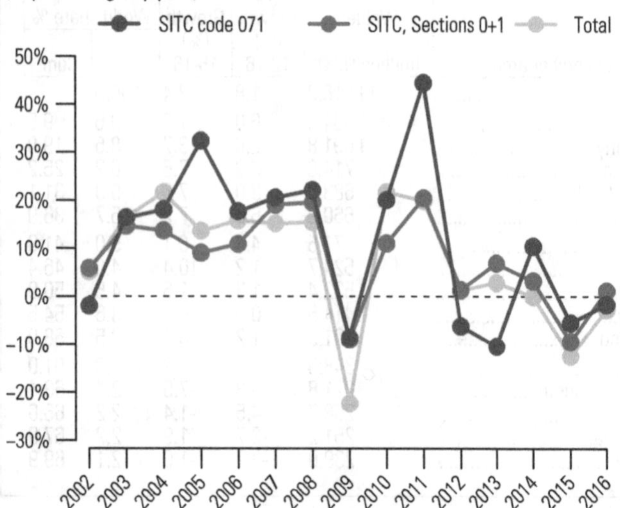

Table 2: Top exporting countries or areas in 2016

Country or area	Value (million US$)	Avg. Growth (%) 12-16	Growth (%) 15-16	World share %	Cum.
World	36715.8	-2.1	-1.7	100.0	
Brazil	5471.9	-4.1	-11.2	14.9	14.9
Germany	3242.4	-3.2	3.0	8.8	23.7
Viet Nam	*2908.3*	-5.7	8.9	7.9	31.7
Colombia	2682.5	5.0	-4.5	7.3	39.0
Switzerland	2212.0	2.1	0.6	6.0	45.0
Italy	1583.4	4.1	10.3	4.3	49.3
Indonesia	1429.1	-2.3	-7.4	3.9	53.2
USA	1126.2	-3.1	1.1	3.1	56.3
Belgium	1099.2	-5.3	-7.2	3.0	59.3
Netherlands	954.6	12.1	9.4	2.6	61.9
China	946.6	34.8	111.9	2.6	64.4
France	924.7	8.4	2.7	2.5	66.9
Honduras	859.1	-10.5	-7.9	2.3	69.3
India	844.0	-1.6	3.9	2.3	71.6
Peru	758.6	-7.3	29.7	2.1	73.7

Graph 2: Trade Balance by MDG regions 2016
(Bln US$)

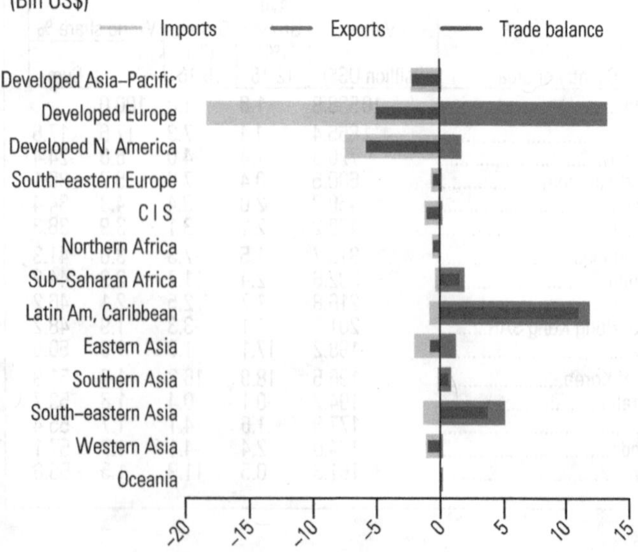

Table 3: Top importing countries or areas in 2016

Country or area	Value (million US$)	Avg. Growth (%) 12-16	Growth (%) 15-16	World share %	Cum.
World	36398.6	-2.4	-2.5	100.0	
USA	6105.2	-4.2	-5.3	16.8	16.8
Germany	3797.5	-7.2	-0.9	10.4	27.2
France	2568.4	-0.6	-1.7	7.1	34.3
Italy	1761.7	-2.9	-4.8	4.8	39.1
Japan	1573.8	-4.3	-10.1	4.3	43.4
United Kingdom	1369.6	2.0	1.6	3.8	47.2
Canada	1338.7	-4.0	-3.1	3.7	50.9
Netherlands	1126.5	3.8	-4.1	3.1	54.0
Belgium	1080.7	-7.7	-6.4	3.0	56.9
Spain	1063.4	-4.1	-2.8	2.9	59.9
Russian Federation	931.4	-1.3	3.6	2.6	62.4
China	903.9	40.7	98.5	2.5	64.9
Switzerland	728.4	-3.8	-10.6	2.0	66.9
Poland	691.9	-3.5	-2.4	1.9	68.8
Rep. of Korea	635.6	1.4	2.5	1.7	70.5

In 2016, the value (in current US$) of exports of "cocoa" (SITC group 072) decreased by 3.1 percent (compared to 0.8 percent average growth rate from 2012-2016) to reach 20.1 bln US$ (see table 2), while imports increased by 10.0 percent to reach 22.1 bln US$ (see table 3). Exports of this commodity accounted for 1.7 percent of world exports of SITC sections 0+1, and 0.1 percent of total world merchandise exports (see table 1). Côte d'Ivoire, Netherlands and Ghana were the top exporters in 2016 (see table 2). They accounted for 22.5, 16.0 and 9.4 percent of world exports, respectively. Netherlands, USA and Germany were the top destinations, with respectively 17.9, 11.5 and 11.0 percent of world imports (see table 3).

The top 15 countries/areas accounted for 89.6 and 81.3 percent of total world exports and imports, respectively (see tables 2 and 3). In 2016, Côte d'Ivoire was the country/area with the highest value of net exports (+4.5 bln US$), followed by Ghana (+1.9 bln US$). By MDG regions (see graph 2), the largest surpluses in this product group were recorded by Sub-Saharan Africa (+7.7 bln US$), South-eastern Asia (+1.2 bln US$) and Latin America and the Caribbean (+941.9 mln US$). The largest trade deficits were recorded by Developed Europe (-6.5 bln US$), Developed North America (-2.6 bln US$) and Developed Asia-Pacific (-754.3 mln US$).

Table 1: Imports (Imp.) and exports (Exp.), 2002-2016, in current US$

		2002	2003	2004	2005	2006	2007	2008	2009	2010	2011	2012	2013	2014	2015	2016
Values in Bln US$	Imp.	6.8	9.8	9.3	9.9	10.1	12.2	15.5	16.1	19.2	23.4	17.6	17.3	21.1	20.1	22.1
	Exp.	7.0	8.0	8.5	8.4	9.0	10.5	13.1	15.7	18.0	19.8	19.5	17.2	20.0	20.7	20.1
As a percentage of SITC section (%)	Imp.	1.5	1.9	1.6	1.6	1.5	1.5	1.6	1.8	2.0	2.0	1.5	1.4	1.6	1.7	1.9
	Exp.	1.6	1.6	1.5	1.4	1.3	1.3	1.4	1.8	1.9	1.7	1.6	1.4	1.5	1.8	1.7
As a percentage of world trade (%)	Imp.	0.1	0.1	0.1	0.1	0.1	0.1	0.1	0.1	0.1	0.1	0.1	0.1	0.1	0.1	0.1
	Exp.	0.1	0.1	0.1	0.1	0.1	0.1	0.1	0.1	0.1	0.1	0.1	0.1	0.1	0.1	0.1

Graph 1: Annual growth rates of exports, 2002–2016
(In percentage by year)

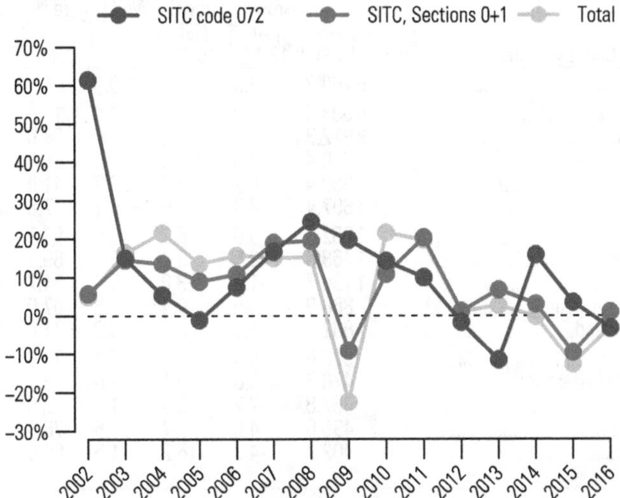

Graph 2: Trade Balance by MDG regions 2016
(Bln US$)

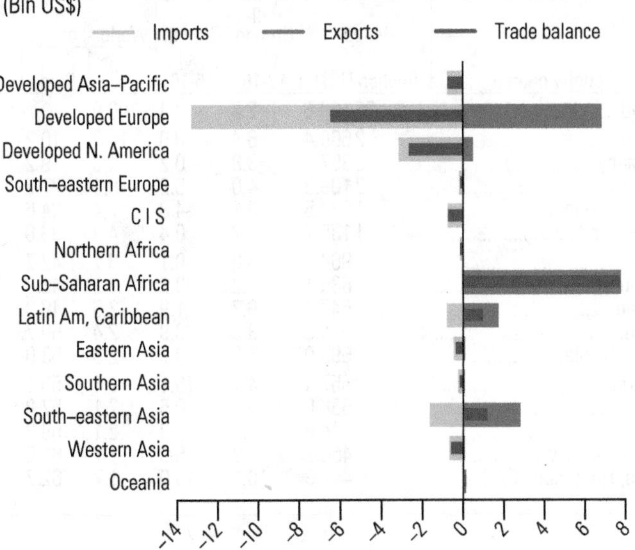

Table 2: Top exporting countries or areas in 2016

Country or area	Value (million US$)	Avg. Growth (%) 12-16	Growth (%) 15-16	World share %	Cum.
World	20062.6	0.8	-3.1	100.0	
Côte d'Ivoire	*4521.2*	8.3	-10.0	22.5	22.5
Netherlands	3206.9	3.8	-1.6	16.0	38.5
Ghana	1893.8	-1.7	11.6	9.4	48.0
Germany	1237.5	12.1	18.0	6.2	54.1
Malaysia	1222.2	3.8	6.1	6.1	60.2
Indonesia	1193.0	4.6	-6.2	5.9	66.2
Belgium	820.3	16.9	26.4	4.1	70.3
Cameroon	765.0	12.5	-10.4	3.8	74.1
France	743.9	1.1	-6.6	3.7	77.8
Ecuador	726.2	14.2	-8.3	3.6	81.4
USA	425.3	5.7	34.6	2.1	83.5
Singapore	355.5	1.9	16.8	1.8	85.3
Brazil	297.1	4.4	4.6	1.5	86.8
Nigeria	292.6	-47.3	-66.7	1.5	88.2
Peru	278.7	27.0	11.0	1.4	89.6

Table 3: Top importing countries or areas in 2016

Country or area	Value (million US$)	Avg. Growth (%) 12-16	Growth (%) 15-16	World share %	Cum.
World	22106.6	5.8	10.0	100.0	
Netherlands	3947.1	13.5	27.7	17.9	17.9
USA	2548.3	4.4	1.1	11.5	29.4
Germany	2434.7	3.8	12.3	11.0	40.4
Belgium	2021.6	16.6	20.0	9.1	49.5
France	1258.0	2.8	7.0	5.7	55.2
Malaysia	881.9	-3.9	-6.7	4.0	59.2
Italy	704.1	6.0	5.0	3.2	62.4
Russian Federation	627.3	2.5	-2.6	2.8	65.2
Canada	582.9	8.3	8.3	2.6	67.9
United Kingdom	579.9	1.7	-3.9	2.6	70.5
Spain	578.1	5.5	10.3	2.6	73.1
Japan	491.3	6.5	23.9	2.2	75.3
Poland	486.1	9.9	9.9	2.2	77.5
Turkey	458.7	5.9	-1.6	2.1	79.6
Singapore	375.5	3.8	1.2	1.7	81.3

Source: UN Comtrade

073 Chocolate and other food preparations containing cocoa, nes

In 2016, the value (in current US$) of exports of "chocolate and other food preparations containing cocoa, nes" (SITC group 073) increased by 2.8 percent (compared to 2.3 percent average growth rate from 2012-2016) to reach 26.5 bln US$ (see table 2), while imports increased by 2.4 percent to reach 26.2 bln US$ (see table 3). Exports of this commodity accounted for 2.2 percent of world exports of SITC sections 0+1, and 0.2 percent of total world merchandise exports (see table 1). Germany, Belgium and Netherlands were the top exporters in 2016 (see table 2). They accounted for 17.0, 11.0 and 7.5 percent of world exports, respectively. USA, Germany and France were the top destinations, with respectively 10.2, 9.0 and 8.1 percent of world imports (see table 3).

The top 15 countries/areas accounted for 80.0 and 62.7 percent of total world exports and imports, respectively (see tables 2 and 3). In 2016, Germany was the country/area with the highest value of net exports (+2.1 bln US$), followed by Belgium (+2.1 bln US$). By MDG regions (see graph 2), the largest surpluses in this product group were recorded by Developed Europe (+4.5 bln US$) and Latin America and the Caribbean (+75.2 mln US$). The largest trade deficits were recorded by Western Asia (-1.1 bln US$), Developed Asia-Pacific (-793.7 mln US$) and Eastern Asia (-711.3 mln US$).

Table 1: Imports (Imp.) and exports (Exp.), 2002-2016, in current US$

		2002	2003	2004	2005	2006	2007	2008	2009	2010	2011	2012	2013	2014	2015	2016
Values in Bln US$	Imp.	8.0	9.7	11.3	12.3	13.6	16.3	18.8	17.5	19.2	22.9	23.5	25.6	27.5	25.6	26.2
	Exp.	8.2	10.0	11.7	12.6	14.0	16.9	19.4	18.3	20.0	23.6	24.2	26.4	28.0	25.7	26.5
As a percentage of SITC section (%)	Imp.	1.8	1.9	1.9	1.9	2.0	2.0	1.9	2.0	2.0	1.9	2.0	2.1	2.1	2.2	2.2
	Exp.	1.9	2.0	2.1	2.1	2.1	2.1	2.0	2.1	2.1	2.0	2.1	2.1	2.1	2.2	2.2
As a percentage of world trade (%)	Imp.	0.1	0.1	0.1	0.1	0.1	0.1	0.1	0.1	0.1	0.1	0.1	0.1	0.1	0.2	0.2
	Exp.	0.1	0.1	0.1	0.1	0.1	0.1	0.1	0.1	0.1	0.1	0.1	0.1	0.1	0.2	0.2

Graph 1: Annual growth rates of exports, 2002–2016
(In percentage by year)

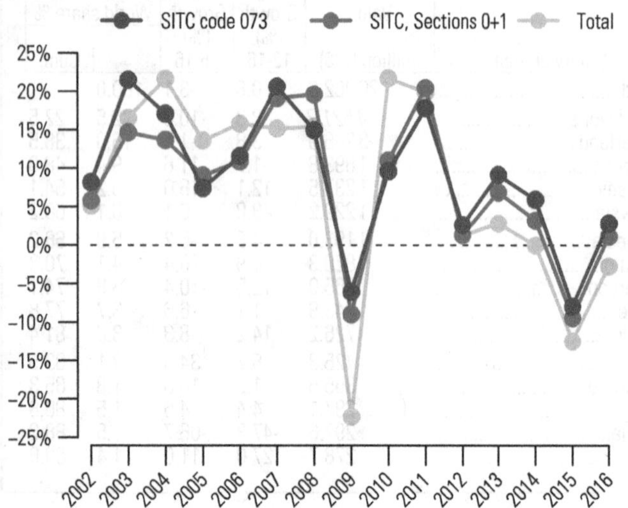

Graph 2: Trade Balance by MDG regions 2016
(Bln US$)

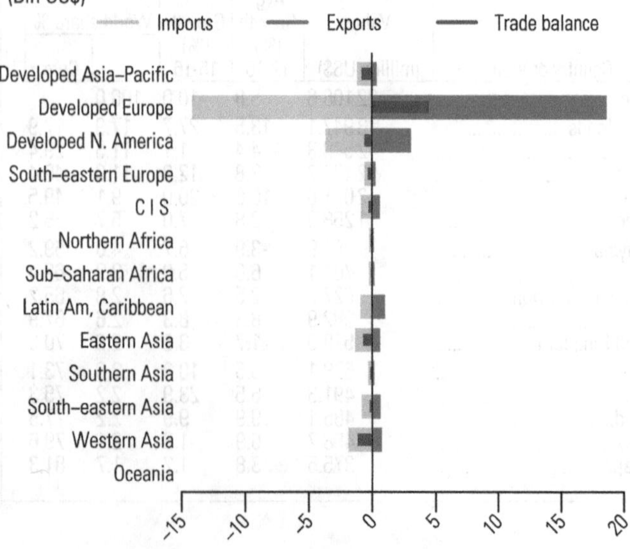

Table 2: Top exporting countries or areas in 2016

Country or area	Value (million US$)	Avg. Growth (%) 12-16	Growth (%) 15-16	World share %	Cum.
World	26469.3	2.3	2.8	100.0	
Germany	4503.3	2.9	2.8	17.0	17.0
Belgium	2912.3	4.0	8.0	11.0	28.0
Netherlands	1990.4	4.0	12.8	7.5	35.5
Italy	1650.4	0.7	3.7	6.2	41.8
USA	1607.4	4.0	-1.6	6.1	47.8
Poland	1552.3	9.0	6.2	5.9	53.7
Canada	1468.3	9.5	8.4	5.5	59.3
France	1430.7	-1.5	3.6	5.4	64.7
United Kingdom	868.9	1.5	0.4	3.3	67.9
Switzerland	802.2	1.3	-2.5	3.0	71.0
Mexico	628.6	0.9	5.1	2.4	73.3
Russian Federation	476.7	-3.8	9.1	1.8	75.1
Austria	457.8	2.2	3.9	1.7	76.9
Spain	435.6	4.8	-2.7	1.6	78.5
Turkey	402.7	-4.2	-15.2	1.5	80.0

Table 3: Top importing countries or areas in 2016

Country or area	Value (million US$)	Avg. Growth (%) 12-16	Growth (%) 15-16	World share %	Cum.
World	26169.6	2.8	2.4	100.0	
USA	2660.4	6.4	8.0	10.2	10.2
Germany	2357.4	3.8	0.2	9.0	19.2
France	2109.8	4.0	5.2	8.1	27.2
United Kingdom	1937.5	3.1	-4.8	7.4	34.6
Netherlands	1135.7	5.2	0.4	4.3	39.0
Canada	964.3	3.0	-0.1	3.7	42.7
Belgium	836.1	7.2	23.2	3.2	45.9
Poland	647.9	9.2	1.9	2.5	48.3
Spain	615.3	3.8	9.9	2.4	50.7
Saudi Arabia	593.0	3.5	8.7	2.3	53.0
Austria	557.4	4.1	15.1	2.1	55.1
Italy	556.0	-0.9	0.5	2.1	57.2
Japan	544.6	-3.4	-2.3	2.1	59.3
Australia	456.7	2.8	-5.9	1.7	61.0
China, Hong Kong SAR	447.3	10.1	15.0	1.7	62.7

In 2016, the value (in current US$) of exports of "tea and mate" (SITC group 074) increased by 0.7 percent (compared to 0.4 percent average growth rate from 2012-2016) to reach 8.4 bln US$ (see table 2), while imports decreased by 2.5 percent to reach 7.7 bln US$ (see table 3). Exports of this commodity accounted for 0.7 percent of world exports of SITC sections 0+1, and 0.1 percent of total world merchandise exports (see table 1). China, Sri Lanka and Kenya were the top exporters in 2016 (see table 2). They accounted for 19.0, 15.1 and 14.9 percent of world exports, respectively. USA, Russian Federation and United Arab Emirates were the top destinations, with respectively 8.7, 7.3 and 6.4 percent of world imports (see table 3).

The top 15 countries/areas accounted for 83.6 and 60.2 percent of total world exports and imports, respectively (see tables 2 and 3). In 2016, China was the country/area with the highest value of net exports (+1.5 bln US$), followed by Sri Lanka (+1.3 bln US$). By MDG regions (see graph 2), the largest surpluses in this product group were recorded by Eastern Asia (+1.4 bln US$), Southern Asia (+1.2 bln US$) and Sub-Saharan Africa (+1.2 bln US$). The largest trade deficits were recorded by Commonwealth of Independent States (-826.0 mln US$), Western Asia (-728.0 mln US$) and Northern Africa (-527.1 mln US$).

Table 1: Imports (Imp.) and exports (Exp.), 2002-2016, in current US$

		2002	2003	2004	2005	2006	2007	2008	2009	2010	2011	2012	2013	2014	2015	2016
Values in Bln US$	Imp.	3.3	3.5	3.9	4.0	4.3	5.0	6.1	5.8	6.7	7.6	8.0	8.5	8.4	7.9	7.7
	Exp.	2.8	3.4	3.8	4.2	4.7	5.3	6.5	6.3	7.2	8.1	8.3	9.2	9.2	8.4	8.4
As a percentage of SITC section (%)	Imp.	0.7	0.7	0.7	0.6	0.6	0.6	0.6	0.6	0.7	0.6	0.7	0.7	0.7	0.7	0.7
	Exp.	0.7	0.7	0.7	0.7	0.7	0.7	0.7	0.7	0.7	0.7	0.7	0.7	0.7	0.7	0.7
As a percentage of world trade (%)	Imp.	0.1	0.0	0.0	0.0	0.0	0.0	0.0	0.0	0.0	0.0	0.0	0.0	0.0	0.0	0.0
	Exp.	0.0	0.0	0.0	0.0	0.0	0.0	0.0	0.1	0.0	0.0	0.0	0.0	0.0	0.1	0.1

Graph 1: Annual growth rates of exports, 2002–2016

(In percentage by year)

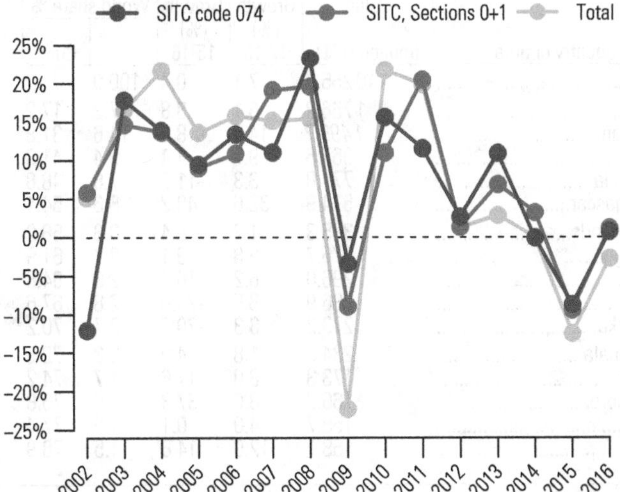

Graph 2: Trade Balance by MDG regions 2016

(Bln US$)

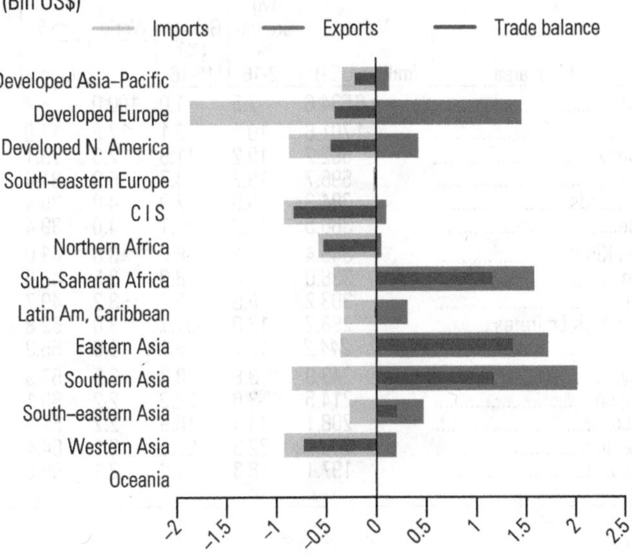

Table 2: Top exporting countries or areas in 2016

Country or area	Value (million US$)	Avg. Growth (%) 12-16	Growth (%) 15-16	World share %	Cum.
World	8427.9	0.4	0.7	100.0	
China	1602.2	9.3	7.7	19.0	19.0
Sri Lanka	1268.5	-2.7	-5.2	15.1	34.1
Kenya	*1252.6*	-1.9	-3.9	14.9	48.9
India	705.2	-0.6	-1.1	8.4	57.3
Netherlands	328.5	5.9	20.1	3.9	61.2
USA	317.6	1.2	5.2	3.8	65.0
Germany	307.2	1.8	4.6	3.6	68.6
Viet Nam	*236.5*	1.2	8.9	2.8	71.4
Poland	218.0	5.0	10.7	2.6	74.0
United Kingdom	179.1	-3.8	-9.5	2.1	76.1
Argentina	172.9	-0.7	-18.8	2.1	78.2
United Arab Emirates	118.1	-9.8	0.7	1.4	79.6
Japan	117.4	13.0	25.2	1.4	81.0
Indonesia	116.8	-7.6	-10.3	1.4	82.4
Canada	101.6	-2.2	4.2	1.2	83.6

Table 3: Top importing countries or areas in 2016

Country or area	Value (million US$)	Avg. Growth (%) 12-16	Growth (%) 15-16	World share %	Cum.
World	7744.8	-0.7	-2.5	100.0	
USA	675.0	2.3	4.7	8.7	8.7
Russian Federation	566.9	-4.3	-13.9	7.3	16.0
United Arab Emirates	498.0	-5.5	3.0	6.4	22.5
Pakistan	490.4	7.9	7.0	6.3	28.8
United Kingdom	387.8	-3.7	-8.0	5.0	33.8
Egypt	282.9	-3.8	-2.6	3.7	37.5
Germany	265.1	0.8	0.8	3.4	40.9
France	224.7	1.4	1.9	2.9	43.8
Netherlands	219.5	3.7	25.8	2.8	46.6
Morocco	199.5	4.5	1.2	2.6	49.2
Iran	*195.0*	-6.2	-22.1	2.5	51.7
Canada	194.1	-4.4	3.7	2.5	54.2
Japan	192.1	-5.8	-8.6	2.5	56.7
Kenya	*149.4*	65.1	652.6	1.9	58.6
China	123.8	12.5	3.1	1.6	60.2

075 Spices

In 2016, the value (in current US$) of exports of "spices" (SITC group 075) decreased by 0.4 percent (compared to 7.1 percent average growth rate from 2012-2016) to reach 10.3 bln US$ (see table 2), while imports decreased by 1.0 percent to reach 9.5 bln US$ (see table 3). Exports of this commodity accounted for 0.9 percent of world exports of SITC sections 0+1, and 0.1 percent of total world merchandise exports (see table 1). India, Viet Nam and China were the top exporters in 2016 (see table 2). They accounted for 17.2, 14.6 and 9.4 percent of world exports, respectively. USA, Germany and India were the top destinations, with respectively 17.8, 7.3 and 6.3 percent of world imports (see table 3).

The top 15 countries/areas accounted for 78.9 and 66.5 percent of total world exports and imports, respectively (see tables 2 and 3). In 2016, Viet Nam was the country/area with the highest value of net exports (+1.3 bln US$), followed by India (+1.2 bln US$). By MDG regions (see graph 2), the largest surpluses in this product group were recorded by South-eastern Asia (+1.6 bln US$), Southern Asia (+1.2 bln US$) and Eastern Asia (+757.8 mln US$). The largest trade deficits were recorded by Developed North America (-1.7 bln US$), Developed Europe (-1.4 bln US$) and Developed Asia-Pacific (-428.0 mln US$).

Table 1: Imports (Imp.) and exports (Exp.), 2002-2016, in current US$

		2002	2003	2004	2005	2006	2007	2008	2009	2010	2011	2012	2013	2014	2015	2016
Values in Bln US$	Imp.	2.7	3.0	3.2	3.1	3.3	4.1	4.9	4.7	5.8	7.7	7.1	7.6	8.8	9.6	9.5
	Exp.	2.9	2.9	3.1	2.9	3.4	4.3	5.5	5.1	6.0	8.1	7.8	8.2	9.7	10.3	10.3
As a percentage of SITC section (%)	Imp.	0.6	0.6	0.6	0.5	0.5	0.5	0.5	0.5	0.6	0.6	0.6	0.6	0.7	0.8	0.8
	Exp.	0.7	0.6	0.6	0.5	0.5	0.5	0.6	0.6	0.6	0.7	0.7	0.7	0.7	0.9	0.9
As a percentage of world trade (%)	Imp.	0.0	0.0	0.0	0.0	0.0	0.0	0.0	0.0	0.0	0.0	0.0	0.0	0.0	0.1	0.1
	Exp.	0.0	0.0	0.0	0.0	0.0	0.0	0.0	0.0	0.0	0.0	0.0	0.0	0.1	0.1	0.1

Graph 1: Annual growth rates of exports, 2002–2016
(In percentage by year)

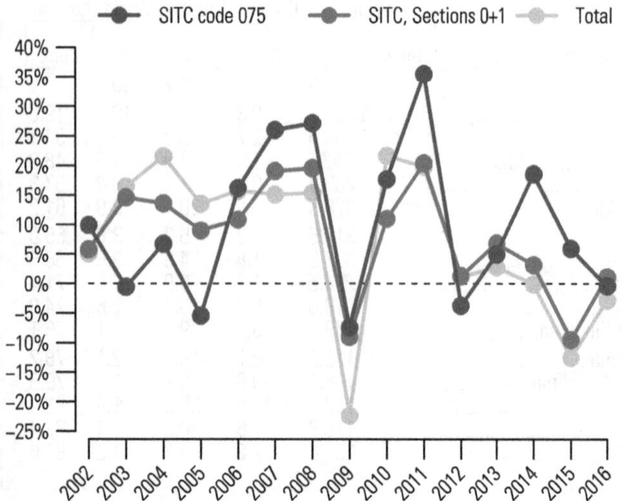

Table 2: Top exporting countries or areas in 2016

Country or area	Value (million US$)	Avg. Growth (%) 12-16	Growth (%) 15-16	World share %	Cum.
World	10255.6	7.1	-0.4	100.0	
India	1766.2	6.1	3.8	17.2	17.2
Viet Nam	*1499.7*	14.6	8.9	14.6	31.8
China	967.5	9.7	4.4	9.4	41.3
Indonesia	774.8	3.3	-11.2	7.6	48.8
Madagascar	574.9	32.6	48.2	5.6	54.4
Netherlands	385.3	1.7	5.4	3.8	58.2
Germany	376.7	9.8	9.1	3.7	61.9
Spain	296.0	6.2	16.2	2.9	64.8
Brazil	286.9	8.5	-23.6	2.8	67.6
Sri Lanka	273.2	3.3	-20.7	2.7	70.2
Guatemala	234.3	-1.8	-4.9	2.3	72.5
France	173.3	8.0	11.6	1.7	74.2
Singapore	166.2	-8.0	-37.3	1.6	75.8
USA	158.7	4.0	0.1	1.5	77.4
Turkey	158.1	12.0	14.8	1.5	78.9

Graph 2: Trade Balance by MDG regions 2016
(Bln US$)

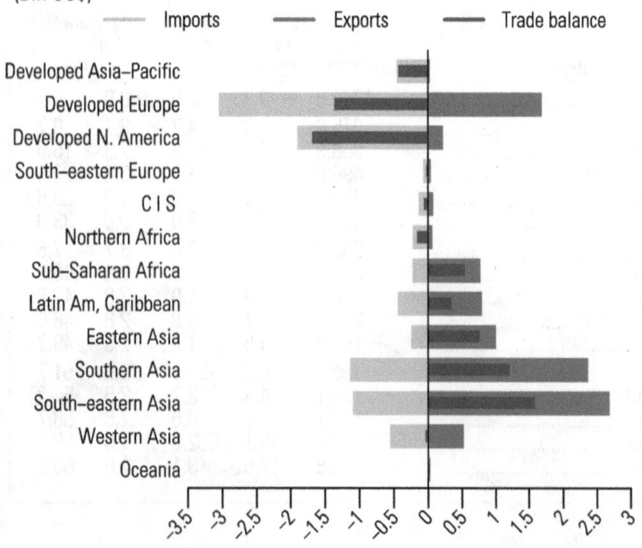

Table 3: Top importing countries or areas in 2016

Country or area	Value (million US$)	Avg. Growth (%) 12-16	Growth (%) 15-16	World share %	Cum.
World	9534.6	7.5	-1.0	100.0	
USA	1701.8	10.1	2.1	17.8	17.8
Germany	692.2	10.2	11.9	7.3	25.1
India	596.7	19.7	4.7	6.3	31.4
Netherlands	384.3	5.9	7.9	4.0	35.4
France	380.5	17.2	27.1	4.0	39.4
United Kingdom	345.4	6.1	-6.2	3.6	43.0
Japan	338.0	1.6	-8.9	3.5	46.6
Spain	303.2	6.6	5.2	3.2	49.7
United Arab Emirates	288.2	13.0	-31.1	3.0	52.8
Viet Nam	*244.2*	17.7	5.1	2.6	55.3
Malaysia	243.0	3.8	8.3	2.5	57.9
Singapore	214.5	-3.6	-32.9	2.2	60.1
Mexico	208.1	14.4	10.9	2.2	62.3
Thailand	203.3	32.3	62.5	2.1	64.4
Canada	197.1	8.3	1.8	2.1	66.5

In 2016, the value (in current US$) of exports of "feeding stuff for animals (not including unmilled cereals)" (SITC group 081) decreased by 5.1 percent (compared to -1.7 percent average growth rate from 2012-2016) to reach 70.1 bln US$ (see table 2), while imports decreased by 7.0 percent to reach 72.8 bln US$ (see table 3). Exports of this commodity accounted for 5.9 percent of world exports of SITC sections 0+1, and 0.4 percent of total world merchandise exports (see table 1). USA, Argentina and Brazil were the top exporters in 2016 (see table 2). They accounted for 16.2, 15.4 and 7.9 percent of world exports, respectively. China, Germany and Viet Nam were the top destinations, with respectively 4.9, 4.9 and 4.9 percent of world imports (see table 3).

The top 15 countries/areas accounted for 77.7 and 54.8 percent of total world exports and imports, respectively (see tables 2 and 3). In 2016, Argentina was the country/area with the highest value of net exports (+10.7 bln US$), followed by USA (+8.4 bln US$). By MDG regions (see graph 2), the largest surpluses in this product group were recorded by Latin America and the Caribbean (+13.6 bln US$) and Developed North America (+9.1 bln US$). The largest trade deficits were recorded by South-eastern Asia (-7.4 bln US$), Developed Europe (-3.9 bln US$) and Eastern Asia (-3.5 bln US$).

Table 1: Imports (Imp.) and exports (Exp.), 2002-2016, in current US$

		2002	2003	2004	2005	2006	2007	2008	2009	2010	2011	2012	2013	2014	2015	2016
Values in Bln US$	Imp.	25.2	28.2	33.7	33.6	36.3	45.7	61.9	56.3	61.8	71.4	78.9	86.2	88.7	78.3	72.8
	Exp.	23.0	25.5	29.6	30.1	33.1	41.4	54.6	52.8	57.6	67.0	75.0	83.3	84.8	73.9	70.1
As a percentage of SITC section (%)	Imp.	5.6	5.4	5.7	5.3	5.2	5.5	6.3	6.3	6.3	6.0	6.7	6.9	6.9	6.6	6.2
	Exp.	5.4	5.2	5.3	5.0	4.9	5.2	5.7	6.1	6.0	5.8	6.4	6.6	6.5	6.3	5.9
As a percentage of world trade (%)	Imp.	0.4	0.4	0.4	0.3	0.3	0.3	0.4	0.4	0.4	0.4	0.4	0.5	0.5	0.5	0.5
	Exp.	0.4	0.3	0.3	0.3	0.3	0.3	0.3	0.4	0.4	0.4	0.4	0.4	0.5	0.4	0.4

Graph 1: Annual growth rates of exports, 2002–2016

(In percentage by year)

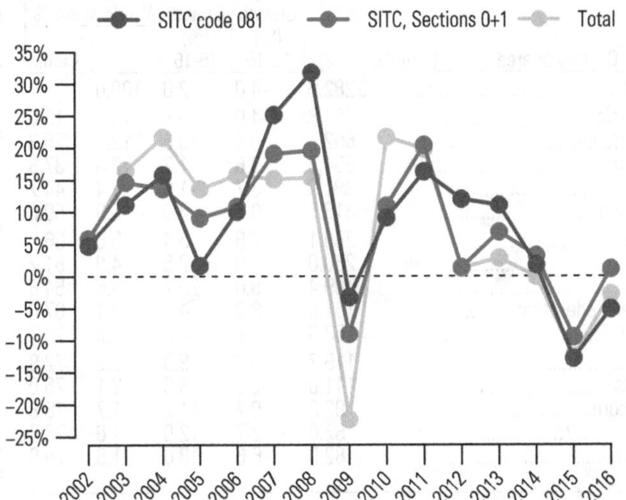

Table 2: Top exporting countries or areas in 2016

Country or area	Value (million US$)	Avg. Growth (%) 12-16	Growth (%) 15-16	World share %	Cum.
World	70145.7	-1.7	-5.1	100.0	
USA	11336.2	0.1	-10.3	16.2	16.2
Argentina	10791.3	-0.4	1.3	15.4	31.5
Brazil	5539.0	-5.4	-10.3	7.9	39.4
Netherlands	4719.2	-5.3	-9.0	6.7	46.2
Germany	4327.6	-0.7	-3.4	6.2	52.3
France	2984.0	-1.7	-7.7	4.3	56.6
China	2770.5	-1.7	3.4	3.9	60.5
Belgium	2294.3	0.5	1.7	3.3	63.8
Canada	2241.9	1.2	-0.8	3.2	67.0
United Kingdom	1513.8	4.6	9.1	2.2	69.2
Thailand	1503.8	4.2	0.0	2.1	71.3
Spain	1319.1	-1.3	-0.5	1.9	73.2
Peru	1207.0	-11.2	-9.6	1.7	74.9
Italy	975.6	6.8	-1.8	1.4	76.3
Russian Federation	946.9	3.4	-2.7	1.3	77.7

Graph 2: Trade Balance by MDG regions 2016

(Bln US$)

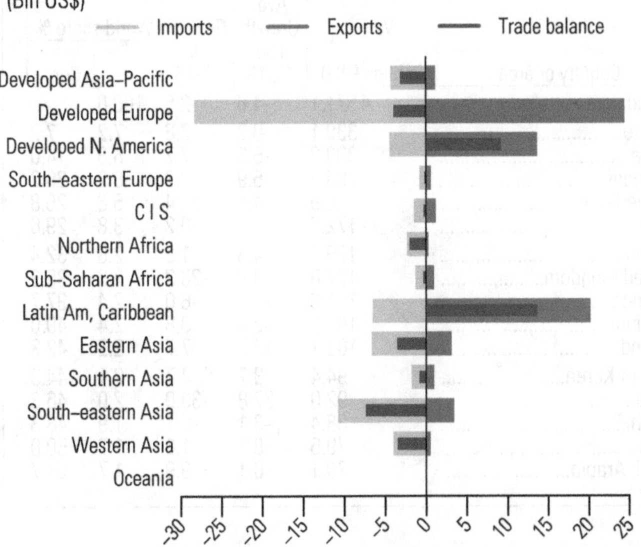

Table 3: Top importing countries or areas in 2016

Country or area	Value (million US$)	Avg. Growth (%) 12-16	Growth (%) 15-16	World share %	Cum.
World	72776.0	-2.0	-7.0	100.0	
China	3601.5	2.7	-27.5	4.9	4.9
Germany	3571.7	-5.5	-7.4	4.9	9.9
Viet Nam	*3570.3*	9.7	5.1	4.9	14.8
Netherlands	3295.7	-9.4	-16.6	4.5	19.3
Japan	3112.8	-8.1	-9.9	4.3	23.6
USA	2890.0	1.1	-5.6	4.0	27.5
France	2883.8	-3.6	-9.5	4.0	31.5
United Kingdom	2692.2	-0.6	-7.9	3.7	35.2
Indonesia	2481.4	-3.0	-9.3	3.4	38.6
Rep. of Korea	2239.3	-1.5	-7.1	3.1	41.7
Italy	2087.6	-3.1	-10.9	2.9	44.6
Thailand	1975.8	-0.9	-4.8	2.7	47.3
Belgium	1939.1	-1.4	2.1	2.7	49.9
Spain	1924.9	-2.0	-4.8	2.6	52.6
Mexico	1618.2	1.0	-0.3	2.2	54.8

091 Margarine and shortening

In 2016, the value (in current US$) of exports of "margarine and shortening" (SITC group 091) increased by 2.0 percent (compared to -4.0 percent average growth rate from 2012-2016) to reach 5.3 bln US$ (see table 2), while imports decreased by 2.5 percent to reach 4.6 bln US$ (see table 3). Exports of this commodity accounted for 0.4 percent of world exports of SITC sections 0+1, and less than 0.1 percent of total world merchandise exports (see table 1). Indonesia, Netherlands and Belgium were the top exporters in 2016 (see table 2). They accounted for 13.0, 12.4 and 12.0 percent of world exports, respectively. France, China and Germany were the top destinations, with respectively 7.2, 6.8 and 6.2 percent of world imports (see table 3).

The top 15 countries/areas accounted for 79.9 and 51.7 percent of total world exports and imports, respectively (see tables 2 and 3). In 2016, Indonesia was the country/area with the highest value of net exports (+650.0 mln US$), followed by Belgium (+526.4 mln US$). By MDG regions (see graph 2), the largest surpluses in this product group were recorded by South-eastern Asia (+909.9 mln US$), Developed Europe (+571.3 mln US$) and Developed North America (+196.4 mln US$). The largest trade deficits were recorded by Eastern Asia (-415.8 mln US$), Latin America and the Caribbean (-157.0 mln US$) and Commonwealth of Independent States (-130.6 mln US$).

Table 1: Imports (Imp.) and exports (Exp.), 2002-2016, in current US$

		2002	2003	2004	2005	2006	2007	2008	2009	2010	2011	2012	2013	2014	2015	2016
Values in Bln US$	Imp.	1.6	1.8	2.2	2.3	2.6	3.4	4.7	3.9	4.2	5.6	5.5	5.3	5.4	4.7	4.6
	Exp.	1.6	2.0	2.4	2.6	3.0	4.0	6.0	4.8	4.9	6.7	6.2	6.2	6.2	5.2	5.3
As a percentage of SITC section (%)	Imp.	0.4	0.3	0.4	0.4	0.4	0.4	0.5	0.4	0.4	0.5	0.5	0.4	0.4	0.4	0.4
	Exp.	0.4	0.4	0.4	0.4	0.4	0.5	0.6	0.6	0.5	0.6	0.5	0.5	0.5	0.4	0.4
As a percentage of world trade (%)	Imp.	0.0	0.0	0.0	0.0	0.0	0.0	0.0	0.0	0.0	0.0	0.0	0.0	0.0	0.0	0.0
	Exp.	0.0	0.0	0.0	0.0	0.0	0.0	0.0	0.0	0.0	0.0	0.0	0.0	0.0	0.0	0.0

Graph 1: Annual growth rates of exports, 2002–2016
(In percentage by year)

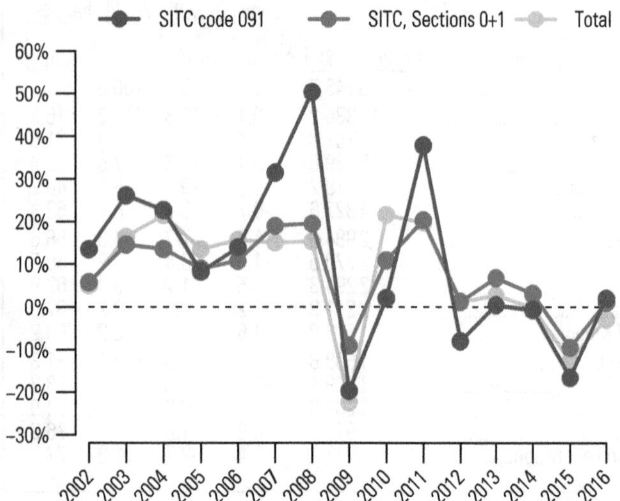

Graph 2: Trade Balance by MDG regions 2016
(Bln US$)

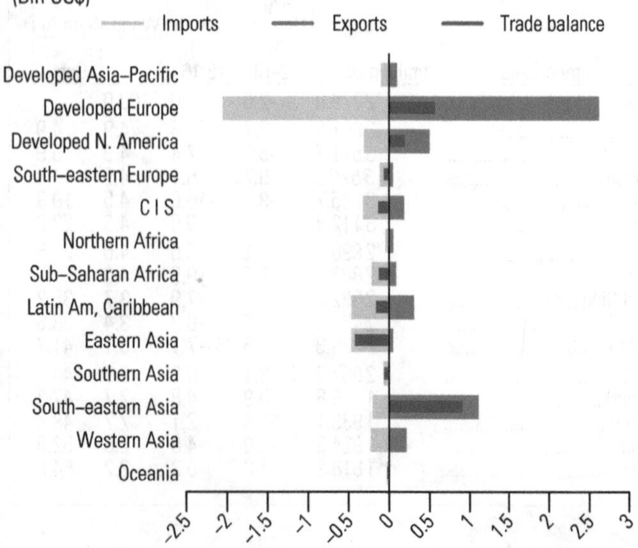

Table 2: Top exporting countries or areas in 2016

Country or area	Value (million US$)	Avg. Growth (%) 12-16	Growth (%) 15-16	World share %	Cum.
World	5282.6	-4.0	2.0	100.0	
Indonesia	684.6	-4.0	10.8	13.0	13.0
Netherlands	652.6	0.4	13.6	12.4	25.3
Belgium	634.3	-3.6	-1.2	12.0	37.3
USA	391.9	-3.7	-1.0	7.4	44.7
Malaysia	318.5	0.7	8.9	6.0	50.8
Germany	290.1	-7.8	5.4	5.5	56.3
Sweden	260.0	0.8	-2.5	4.9	61.2
Turkey	189.4	5.6	20.7	3.6	64.8
Russian Federation	161.6	-3.3	4.1	3.1	67.8
Poland	153.3	-4.8	4.3	2.9	70.7
Spain	115.7	0.9	9.3	2.2	72.9
Canada	111.0	-2.1	13.6	2.1	75.0
Singapore	92.3	-0.7	-11.2	1.7	76.8
Italy	82.6	2.7	12.0	1.6	78.3
Australia	82.0	-6.6	18.6	1.6	79.9

Table 3: Top importing countries or areas in 2016

Country or area	Value (million US$)	Avg. Growth (%) 12-16	Growth (%) 15-16	World share %	Cum.
World	4571.1	-4.6	-2.5	100.0	
France	330.1	-8.2	-2.8	7.2	7.2
China	309.3	-5.3	7.7	6.8	14.0
Germany	283.3	-5.9	-9.7	6.2	20.2
Netherlands	256.9	4.5	28.4	5.6	25.8
USA	172.9	-2.0	10.2	3.8	29.6
Canada	129.7	-4.8	1.2	2.8	32.4
United Kingdom	127.8	-3.8	-28.3	2.8	35.2
Poland	111.8	-11.1	-6.0	2.4	37.7
Belgium	107.9	-2.4	3.8	2.4	40.0
Ireland	102.1	13.3	-7.7	2.2	42.3
Rep. of Korea	94.4	3.7	4.7	2.1	44.3
Chile	92.0	-27.8	-33.0	2.0	46.3
Spain	88.4	-3.1	-0.1	1.9	48.3
Italy	79.5	-6.7	-1.0	1.7	50.0
Saudi Arabia	79.1	0.1	9.9	1.7	51.7

In 2016, the value (in current US$) of exports of "edible products and preparations, nes" (SITC group 098) increased by 4.8 percent (compared to 4.4 percent average growth rate from 2012-2016) to reach 75.3 bln US$ (see table 2), while imports increased by 2.4 percent to reach 74.3 bln US$ (see table 3). Exports of this commodity accounted for 6.3 percent of world exports of SITC sections 0+1, and 0.5 percent of total world merchandise exports (see table 1). USA, Netherlands and Germany were the top exporters in 2016 (see table 2). They accounted for 11.8, 9.2 and 7.6 percent of world exports, respectively. China, USA and United Kingdom were the top destinations, with respectively 7.2, 6.4 and 5.7 percent of world imports (see table 3).

The top 15 countries/areas accounted for 67.6 and 52.6 percent of total world exports and imports, respectively (see tables 2 and 3). In 2016, Netherlands was the country/area with the highest value of net exports (+4.6 bln US$), followed by USA (+4.2 bln US$). By MDG regions (see graph 2), the largest surpluses in this product group were recorded by Developed Europe (+11.8 bln US$), Developed North America (+2.6 bln US$) and South-eastern Asia (+2.1 bln US$). The largest trade deficits were recorded by Eastern Asia (-3.8 bln US$), Western Asia (-3.6 bln US$) and Latin America and the Caribbean (-2.6 bln US$).

Table 1: Imports (Imp.) and exports (Exp.), 2002-2016, in current US$

		2002	2003	2004	2005	2006	2007	2008	2009	2010	2011	2012	2013	2014	2015	2016
Values in Bln US$	Imp.	22.3	26.3	31.0	34.3	37.5	44.4	52.6	50.9	54.5	67.3	65.2	72.5	75.4	72.6	74.3
	Exp.	20.8	24.7	29.2	32.5	35.7	41.9	49.4	47.5	52.2	61.2	63.4	71.9	77.1	71.8	75.3
As a percentage of SITC section (%)	Imp.	4.9	5.1	5.3	5.4	5.4	5.3	5.3	5.7	5.6	5.7	5.5	5.8	5.8	6.1	6.3
	Exp.	4.9	5.1	5.3	5.4	5.3	5.2	5.2	5.5	5.4	5.3	5.4	5.7	5.9	6.1	6.3
As a percentage of world trade (%)	Imp.	0.3	0.3	0.3	0.3	0.3	0.3	0.3	0.4	0.4	0.4	0.4	0.4	0.4	0.4	0.5
	Exp.	0.3	0.3	0.3	0.3	0.3	0.3	0.3	0.4	0.3	0.3	0.3	0.4	0.4	0.4	0.5

Graph 1: Annual growth rates of exports, 2002–2016

(In percentage by year)

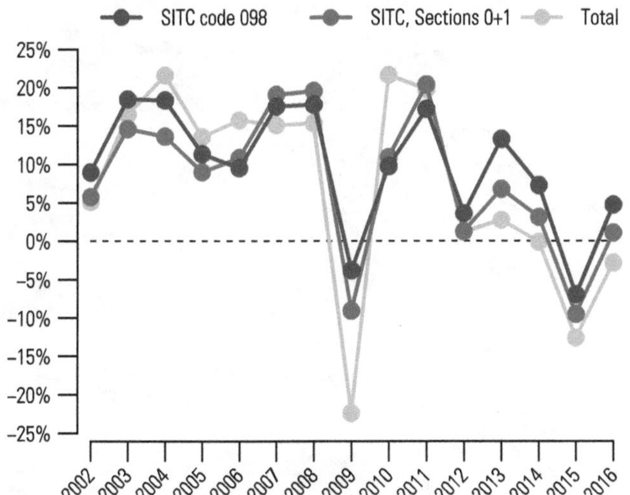

Table 2: Top exporting countries or areas in 2016

Country or area	Value (million US$)	Avg. Growth (%) 12-16	Growth (%) 15-16	World share %	Cum.
World	75250.9	4.4	4.8	100.0	
USA	8911.4	4.9	4.0	11.8	11.8
Netherlands	6888.4	4.7	5.4	9.2	21.0
Germany	5701.1	2.3	6.0	7.6	28.6
China	3610.1	5.6	1.3	4.8	33.4
France	3402.0	-1.0	1.8	4.5	37.9
Italy	2946.5	3.9	6.4	3.9	41.8
Singapore	2914.0	10.9	-3.2	3.9	45.7
Ireland	2552.5	8.6	11.2	3.4	49.1
United Kingdom	2387.7	7.5	-1.3	3.2	52.2
Thailand	2385.7	4.8	4.6	3.2	55.4
Belgium	2128.9	1.1	10.5	2.8	58.2
Denmark	1851.7	1.0	2.3	2.5	60.7
Poland	1766.1	7.8	2.7	2.3	63.1
Australia	1766.1	20.4	38.9	2.3	65.4
Canada	1654.6	0.1	-0.5	2.2	67.6

Graph 2: Trade Balance by MDG regions 2016

(Bln US$)

Imports — Exports — Trade balance

Developed Asia-Pacific
Developed Europe
Developed N. America
South-eastern Europe
C I S
Northern Africa
Sub-Saharan Africa
Latin Am, Caribbean
Eastern Asia
Southern Asia
South-eastern Asia
Western Asia
Oceania

-30 -25 -20 -15 -10 -5 0 5 10 15 20 25 30 35 40

Table 3: Top importing countries or areas in 2016

Country or area	Value (million US$)	Avg. Growth (%) 12-16	Growth (%) 15-16	World share %	Cum.
World	74314.7	3.3	2.4	100.0	
China	5357.6	22.0	18.2	7.2	7.2
USA	4756.5	4.0	5.5	6.4	13.6
United Kingdom	4209.5	2.9	-4.1	5.7	19.3
Germany	3436.3	4.0	2.4	4.6	23.9
Canada	3016.0	3.5	3.6	4.1	28.0
France	2557.9	1.0	4.1	3.4	31.4
Netherlands	2333.6	3.8	-4.0	3.1	34.5
Australia	2128.1	3.7	9.5	2.9	37.4
Saudi Arabia	2004.2	1.9	-7.4	2.7	40.1
China, Hong Kong SAR	1880.1	12.8	20.1	2.5	42.6
Japan	1804.0	-5.3	-0.7	2.4	45.1
Rep. of Korea	1498.8	9.0	12.8	2.0	47.1
Mexico	1398.5	4.1	4.1	1.9	49.0
Belgium	1352.6	-0.8	9.2	1.8	50.8
Spain	1344.3	-3.9	4.9	1.8	52.6

Source: UN Comtrade

In 2016, the value (in current US$) of exports of "edible products and preparations, nes" (SITC group 098) increased by 4.8 percent (compared to 4.4 percent average growth rate from 2012-2016) to reach 75.3 bln US$ (see table 2), while imports increased by 2.4 percent to reach 74.3 bln US$ (see table 3). Exports of this commodity accounted for 6.3 percent of world exports of SITC sections 0+1, and 0.5 percent of total world merchandise exports (see table 1). USA, Netherlands and Germany were the top exporters in 2016 (see table 2). They accounted for 11.8, 9.2 and 7.6 percent of world exports, respectively. China, USA and United Kingdom were the top destinations, with respectively 7.2, 6.4 and 5.7 percent of world imports (see table 3).

The top 15 countries/areas accounted for 67.6 and 52.6 percent of total world exports and imports, respectively (see tables 2 and 3). In 2016, Netherlands was the country/area with the highest value of net exports (+4.6 bln US$), followed by USA (+4.2 bln US$). By MDG regions (see graph 2), the largest surpluses in this product group were recorded by Developed Europe (+11.8 bln US$), Developed North America (+2.6 bln US$) and South-eastern Asia (+2.1 bln US$). The largest trade deficits were recorded by Eastern Asia (-3.8 bln US$), Western Asia (-3.6 bln US$) and Latin America and the Caribbean (-2.6 bln US$).

Table 1: Imports (Imp.) and exports (Exp.), 2002-2016, in current US$

		2002	2003	2004	2005	2006	2007	2008	2009	2010	2011	2012	2013	2014	2015	2016
Values in Bln US$	Imp.	22.3	26.8	31.0	33.3	37.5	44.4	52.6	50.9	54.5	67.3	65.2	72.5	75.4	72.6	74.3
	Exp.	20.8	24.7	29.2	32.5	35.7	41.9	49.4	47.5	52.2	61.2	63.4	71.0	77.1	71.6	75.3
As a percentage of SITC section (%)	Imp.	4.9	5.1	5.3	5.4	5.4	5.3	5.3	5.7	5.6	5.7	5.5	5.8	5.8	6.1	6.3
	Exp.	4.9	5.1	5.3	5.4	5.3	5.2	5.2	5.5	5.4	5.3	5.4	5.7	5.9	6.1	6.3
As a percentage of world trade (%)	Imp.	0.3	0.3	0.3	0.3	0.3	0.3	0.3	0.4	0.4	0.4	0.4	0.4	0.4	0.4	0.5
	Exp.	0.3	0.3	0.3	0.3	0.3	0.3	0.3	0.4	0.3	0.3	0.3	0.4	0.4	0.4	0.5

Table 2: Top exporting countries or areas in 2016

Country or area	Value (million US$)	Avg. Growth (%) 12-16	Growth (%) 15-16	World share %	Cum.
World	75270.9	4.4	4.8	100.0	
USA	8911.4	4.9	4.0	11.8	11.8
Netherlands	6938.4	4.7	5.4	9.2	21.0
Germany	5701.4	2.3	6.0	7.6	28.6
China	3610.1	5.6	1.3	4.8	33.4
France	3402.0	-1.0	1.8	4.5	37.9
Italy	2946.5	3.9	6.4	3.9	41.8
Singapore	2514.0	10.9	3.2	3.3	45.1
Ireland	2552.5	8.8	11.2	3.4	49.1
United Kingdom	2387.7	7.5	1.3	3.2	52.2
Thailand	2385.7	4.8	4.6	3.2	55.4
Belgium	2128.9	1.1	10.5	2.8	58.2
Denmark	1851.7	1.0	2.3	2.5	60.7
Poland	1755.4	7.8	7.7	2.3	63.1
Australia	1756.1	20.4	20.6	2.3	65.4
Canada	1654.5	0.1	-0.5	2.2	67.6

Table 3: Top importing countries or areas in 2016

Country or area	Value (million US$)	Avg. Growth (%) 12-16	Growth (%) 15-16	World share %	Cum.
World	74314.7	3.3	2.4	100.0	
China	5357.6	12.0	16.2	7.2	7.2
USA	4756.5	4.0	6.5	6.4	13.6
United Kingdom	4209.5	2.9	-4.1	5.7	19.3
Germany	3455.3	4.0	7.4	4.6	23.8
Canada	3016.0	3.5	3.6	4.1	28.0
France	2567.9	1.0	4.1	3.4	31.4
Netherlands	2333.6	3.8	4.0	3.1	34.5
Australia	2178.1	3.7	9.5	2.9	37.4
Saudi Arabia	2004.2	1.9	-7.4	2.7	40.1
China, Hong Kong SAR	1880.1	12.8	20.1	2.5	42.6
Japan	1804.0	-5.3	-0.7	2.4	45.1
Rep. of Korea	1496.8	9.0	12.8	2.0	47.1
Mexico	1396.5	4.1	4.1	1.9	49.0
Belgium	1352.6	-0.8	9.2	1.8	50.8
Spain	1344.3	3.3	4.9	1.8	52.6

Graph 1: Annual growth rates of exports, 2002-2016

(in percentage by year)

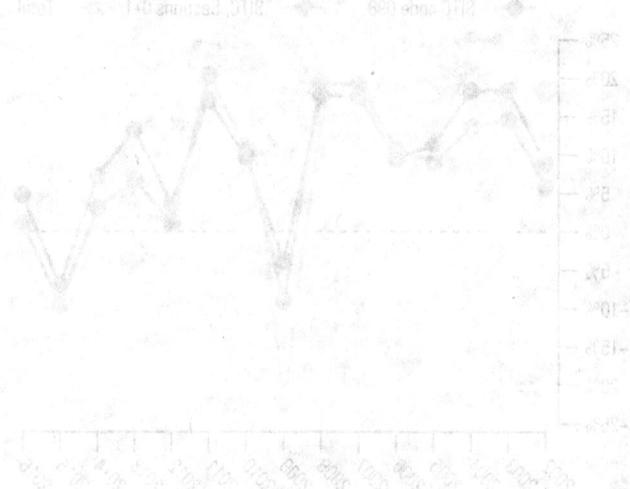

Graph 2: Trade Balance by MDG regions 2016

(Bln US$)

Imports
Exports
Trade balance

Developed Asia-Pacific
Developed Europe
Developed N. America
South-eastern Europe
CIS
Northern Africa
Sub-Saharan Africa
Latin Am, Caribbean
Eastern Asia
Southern Asia
South-eastern Asia
Western Asia
Oceania

Beverages and tobacco
(SITC Section 1)

111 Non-alcoholic beverages, nes

In 2016, the value (in current US$) of exports of "non-alcoholic beverages, nes" (SITC group 111) increased by 4.8 percent (compared to 3.7 percent average growth rate from 2012-2016) to reach 22.4 bln US$ (see table 2), while imports increased by 6.9 percent to reach 22.1 bln US$ (see table 3). Exports of this commodity accounted for 1.9 percent of world exports of SITC sections 0+1, and 0.1 percent of total world merchandise exports (see table 1). Austria, Switzerland and Germany were the top exporters in 2016 (see table 2). They accounted for 12.1, 8.5 and 7.9 percent of world exports, respectively. USA, United Kingdom and Germany were the top destinations, with respectively 16.6, 6.4 and 5.6 percent of world imports (see table 3).

The top 15 countries/areas accounted for 75.7 and 62.2 percent of total world exports and imports, respectively (see tables 2 and 3). In 2016, Austria was the country/area with the highest value of net exports (+1.9 bln US$), followed by Switzerland (+1.6 bln US$). By MDG regions (see graph 2), the largest surpluses in this product group were recorded by Developed Europe (+5.0 bln US$) and South-eastern Asia (+963.1 mln US$). The largest trade deficits were recorded by Developed North America (-3.1 bln US$), Western Asia (-734.5 mln US$) and Latin America and the Caribbean (-403.1 mln US$).

Table 1: Imports (Imp.) and exports (Exp.), 2002-2016, in current US$

		2002	2003	2004	2005	2006	2007	2008	2009	2010	2011	2012	2013	2014	2015	2016
Values in Bln US$	Imp.	6.6	7.9	9.1	10.4	12.0	14.7	16.2	14.9	15.4	18.1	18.5	19.7	21.0	20.7	22.1
	Exp.	6.6	8.4	9.9	10.8	12.8	14.9	17.8	15.4	16.0	18.8	19.4	21.3	22.5	21.4	22.4
As a percentage of SITC section (%)	Imp.	1.5	1.5	1.6	1.6	1.7	1.8	1.6	1.7	1.6	1.5	1.6	1.6	1.6	1.7	1.9
	Exp.	1.5	1.7	1.8	1.8	1.9	1.9	1.9	1.8	1.7	1.6	1.6	1.7	1.7	1.8	1.9
As a percentage of world trade (%)	Imp.	0.1	0.1	0.1	0.1	0.1	0.1	0.1	0.1	0.1	0.1	0.1	0.1	0.1	0.1	0.1
	Exp.	0.1	0.1	0.1	0.1	0.1	0.1	0.1	0.1	0.1	0.1	0.1	0.1	0.1	0.1	0.1

Graph 1: Annual growth rates of exports, 2002–2016

(In percentage by year)

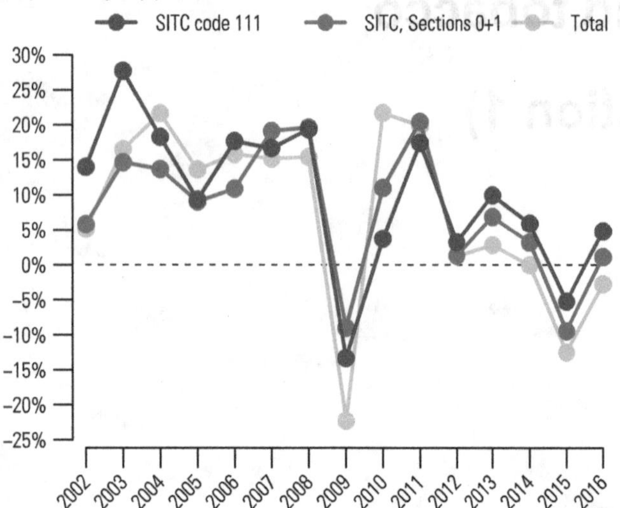

Table 2: Top exporting countries or areas in 2016

Country or area	Value (million US$)	Avg. Growth (%) 12-16	Growth (%) 15-16	World share %	Cum.
World	22395.6	3.7	4.8	100.0	
Austria	2703.1	8.2	46.0	12.1	12.1
Switzerland	1896.3	3.6	-0.6	8.5	20.5
Germany	1772.8	1.4	6.3	7.9	28.5
France	1700.1	0.8	3.9	7.6	36.0
USA	1410.5	4.5	-5.3	6.3	42.3
Netherlands	1359.8	-3.7	-6.3	6.1	48.4
Thailand	1145.8	14.8	15.0	5.1	53.5
Italy	989.1	7.6	1.9	4.4	57.9
Belgium	986.9	-0.3	-10.2	4.4	62.4
China	848.2	7.0	4.8	3.8	66.1
United Kingdom	651.0	3.2	2.4	2.9	69.0
Rep. of Korea	409.0	8.2	12.4	1.8	70.9
Poland	374.9	12.3	-1.3	1.7	72.5
Malaysia	361.9	3.9	3.3	1.6	74.2
Mexico	348.8	6.5	10.2	1.6	75.7

Graph 2: Trade Balance by MDG regions 2016

(Bln US$)

Imports — Exports — Trade balance

Developed Asia-Pacific
Developed Europe
Developed N. America
South-eastern Europe
C I S
Northern Africa
Sub-Saharan Africa
Latin Am, Caribbean
Eastern Asia
Southern Asia
South-eastern Asia
Western Asia
Oceania

-10 -8 -6 -4 -2 0 2 4 6 8 10 12 14 16

Table 3: Top importing countries or areas in 2016

Country or area	Value (million US$)	Avg. Growth (%) 12-16	Growth (%) 15-16	World share %	Cum.
World	22105.0	4.6	6.9	100.0	
USA	3678.7	8.9	7.3	16.6	16.6
United Kingdom	1403.7	6.1	5.3	6.4	23.0
Germany	1232.4	3.4	7.4	5.6	28.6
Belgium	1091.3	3.2	5.0	4.9	33.5
Canada	924.7	3.4	-1.7	4.2	37.7
China, Hong Kong SAR	874.8	6.4	3.9	4.0	41.6
France	838.7	-2.2	3.1	3.8	45.4
Austria	829.7	45.7	280.6	3.8	49.2
Netherlands	707.2	-3.8	-6.9	3.2	52.4
China	422.0	36.1	1.9	1.9	54.3
Japan	414.9	-6.7	-7.1	1.9	56.2
Spain	403.8	-0.3	1.3	1.8	58.0
Switzerland	335.4	1.4	-1.8	1.5	59.5
Ireland	309.5	0.6	-0.9	1.4	60.9
Singapore	279.8	5.4	10.4	1.3	62.2

In 2016, the value (in current US$) of exports of "alcoholic beverages" (SITC group 112) increased by 2.3 percent (compared to -0.3 percent average growth rate from 2012-2016) to reach 77.2 bln US$ (see table 2), while imports increased by 1.6 percent to reach 76.5 bln US$ (see table 3). Exports of this commodity accounted for 6.5 percent of world exports of SITC sections 0+1, and 0.5 percent of total world merchandise exports (see table 1). France, United Kingdom and Italy were the top exporters in 2016 (see table 2). They accounted for 18.4, 11.1 and 9.6 percent of world exports, respectively. USA, United Kingdom and Germany were the top destinations, with respectively 24.8, 7.8 and 6.6 percent of world imports (see table 3).

The top 15 countries/areas accounted for 80.1 and 73.9 percent of total world exports and imports, respectively (see tables 2 and 3). In 2016, France was the country/area with the highest value of net exports (+11.3 bln US$), followed by Italy (+6.1 bln US$). By MDG regions (see graph 2), the largest surpluses in this product group were recorded by Developed Europe (+20.6 bln US$), Latin America and the Caribbean (+6.0 bln US$) and South-eastern Asia (+360.4 mln US$). The largest trade deficits were recorded by Developed North America (-17.4 bln US$), Eastern Asia (-4.9 bln US$) and Commonwealth of Independent States (-1.1 bln US$).

Table 1: Imports (Imp.) and exports (Exp.), 2002-2016, in current US$

		2002	2003	2004	2005	2006	2007	2008	2009	2010	2011	2012	2013	2014	2015	2016
Values in Bln US$	Imp.	34.4	39.6	44.9	48.4	53.0	62.5	67.8	59.5	64.3	74.9	76.9	80.9	81.6	75.3	76.5
	Exp.	33.0	38.9	43.4	45.9	51.0	61.2	66.0	58.1	64.1	75.1	78.1	82.3	82.2	75.5	77.2
As a percentage of SITC section (%)	Imp.	7.6	7.7	7.6	7.6	7.6	7.5	6.8	6.7	6.6	6.3	6.5	6.5	6.3	6.4	6.5
	Exp.	7.7	8.0	7.8	7.6	7.6	7.6	6.9	6.7	6.6	6.5	6.6	6.5	6.3	6.4	6.5
As a percentage of world trade (%)	Imp.	0.5	0.5	0.5	0.5	0.4	0.4	0.4	0.5	0.4	0.4	0.4	0.4	0.4	0.5	0.5
	Exp.	0.5	0.5	0.5	0.4	0.4	0.4	0.4	0.5	0.4	0.4	0.4	0.4	0.4	0.5	0.5

Graph 1: Annual growth rates of exports, 2002–2016
(In percentage by year)

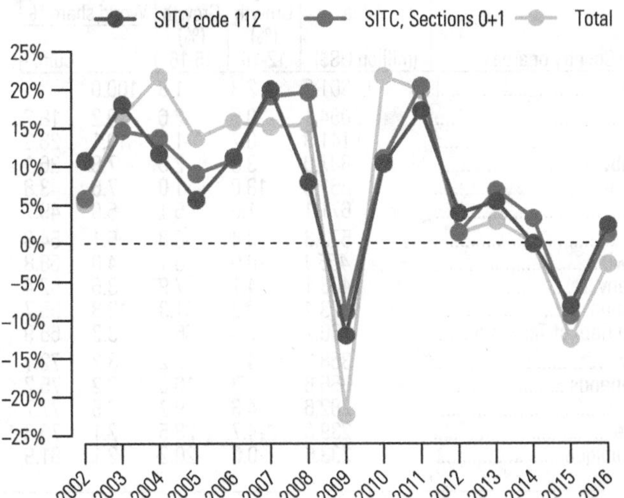

Table 2: Top exporting countries or areas in 2016

Country or area	Value (million US$)	Avg. Growth (%) 12-16	Growth (%) 15-16	World share %	Cum.
World	77230.0	-0.3	2.3	100.0	
France	14223.0	-2.0	1.4	18.4	18.4
United Kingdom	8573.7	-4.2	-4.9	11.1	29.5
Italy	7407.3	0.5	3.9	9.6	39.1
Mexico	4146.5	7.1	7.0	5.4	44.5
USA	4135.4	2.7	-2.3	5.4	49.8
Germany	3971.7	-1.9	2.3	5.1	55.0
Spain	3931.8	-1.9	0.5	5.1	60.1
Netherlands	3349.9	2.1	11.1	4.3	64.4
Singapore	2582.8	0.5	-1.1	3.3	67.7
Belgium	1955.7	3.2	10.7	2.5	70.3
Chile	1884.0	0.6	0.7	2.4	72.7
Australia	1881.3	-2.5	4.6	2.4	75.2
China	1313.0	17.8	14.4	1.7	76.9
Ireland	1272.8	-1.0	4.0	1.6	78.5
Cuba	*1243.7*	43.9	86.3	1.6	80.1

Graph 2: Trade Balance by MDG regions 2016
(Bln US$)

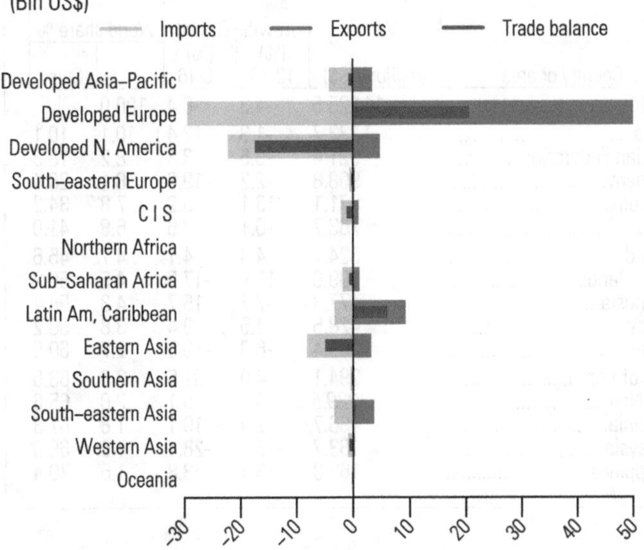

Table 3: Top importing countries or areas in 2016

Country or area	Value (million US$)	Avg. Growth (%) 12-16	Growth (%) 15-16	World share %	Cum.
World	76535.7	-0.1	1.6	100.0	
USA	18954.2	4.3	5.2	24.8	24.8
United Kingdom	5995.7	-3.3	-8.0	7.8	32.6
Germany	5036.4	-2.5	1.7	6.6	39.2
China	3946.4	7.4	12.9	5.2	44.3
Canada	3137.2	-1.9	-1.0	4.1	48.4
France	2878.2	0.1	7.3	3.8	52.2
Japan	2453.1	-2.0	2.1	3.2	55.4
China, Hong Kong SAR	2291.3	7.5	12.3	3.0	58.4
Netherlands	2173.1	-2.1	-9.6	2.8	61.2
Singapore	2050.2	-2.1	-2.4	2.7	63.9
Russian Federation	1613.1	-13.5	1.1	2.1	66.0
Belgium	1605.4	-5.1	-0.6	2.1	68.1
Spain	1585.5	-2.5	3.3	2.1	70.2
Australia	1411.1	-1.2	-1.0	1.8	72.0
Switzerland	1404.8	-2.0	-0.2	1.8	73.9

Source: UN Comtrade

121 Tobacco, unmanufactured; tobacco refuse

In 2016, the value (in current US$) of exports of "tobacco, unmanufactured; tobacco refuse" (SITC group 121) increased by 1.8 percent (compared to -2.3 percent average growth rate from 2012-2016) to reach 11.3 bln US$ (see table 2), while imports decreased by 8.4 percent to reach 11.2 bln US$ (see table 3). Exports of this commodity accounted for 0.9 percent of world exports of SITC sections 0+1, and 0.1 percent of total world merchandise exports (see table 1). Brazil, USA and Zimbabwe were the top exporters in 2016 (see table 2). They accounted for 18.2, 10.1 and 7.8 percent of world exports, respectively. China, Russian Federation and Germany were the top destinations, with respectively 10.1, 8.2 and 8.1 percent of world imports (see table 3).

The top 15 countries/areas accounted for 81.9 and 70.4 percent of total world exports and imports, respectively (see tables 2 and 3). In 2016, Brazil was the country/area with the highest value of net exports (+2.0 bln US$), followed by Zimbabwe (+872.1 mln US$). By MDG regions (see graph 2), the largest surpluses in this product group were recorded by Latin America and the Caribbean (+2.3 bln US$), Sub-Saharan Africa (+1.6 bln US$) and Southern Asia (+627.9 mln US$). The largest trade deficits were recorded by Developed Europe (-1.2 bln US$), Eastern Asia (-994.8 mln US$) and Commonwealth of Independent States (-989.2 mln US$).

Table 1: Imports (Imp.) and exports (Exp.), 2002-2016, in current US$

		2002	2003	2004	2005	2006	2007	2008	2009	2010	2011	2012	2013	2014	2015	2016
Values in Bln US$	Imp.	7.5	7.6	7.9	7.9	8.0	9.4	10.7	11.8	11.8	13.1	13.4	13.6	13.4	12.3	11.2
	Exp.	5.3	5.7	6.8	7.0	7.5	8.6	10.2	11.3	10.8	11.4	12.4	12.9	12.0	11.1	11.3
As a percentage of SITC section (%)	Imp.	1.7	1.5	1.3	1.2	1.1	1.1	1.1	1.3	1.2	1.1	1.1	1.1	1.0	1.0	1.0
	Exp.	1.3	1.2	1.2	1.2	1.1	1.1	1.1	1.3	1.1	1.0	1.1	1.0	0.9	0.9	0.9
As a percentage of world trade (%)	Imp.	0.1	0.1	0.1	0.1	0.1	0.1	0.1	0.1	0.1	0.1	0.1	0.1	0.1	0.1	0.1
	Exp.	0.1	0.1	0.1	0.1	0.1	0.1	0.1	0.1	0.1	0.1	0.1	0.1	0.1	0.1	0.1

Graph 1: Annual growth rates of exports, 2002–2016

(In percentage by year)

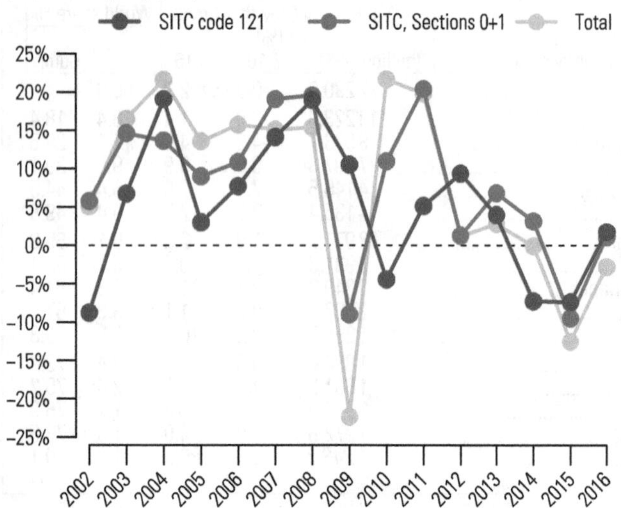

Table 2: Top exporting countries or areas in 2016

Country or area	Value (million US$)	Avg. Growth (%) 12-16	Growth (%) 15-16	World share %	Cum.
World	11 301.2	-2.3	1.8	100.0	
Brazil	2 054.1	-10.5	-2.6	18.2	18.2
USA	1 141.9	0.2	-1.1	10.1	28.3
Zimbabwe	887.0	3.3	2.6	7.8	36.1
Belgium	861.9	18.0	-1.0	7.6	43.8
India	671.1	-1.0	5.1	5.9	49.7
China	573.3	-3.4	-0.8	5.1	54.8
Malawi	*455.1*	-8.0	-8.1	4.0	58.8
Germany	408.1	4.1	7.9	3.6	62.4
Argentina	373.4	0.2	91.3	3.3	65.7
United Rep. of Tanzania	360.2	17.6	66.3	3.2	68.9
Turkey	358.2	-4.3	-7.2	3.2	72.1
Netherlands	356.6	2.3	10.8	3.2	75.2
Italy	282.6	-4.8	9.7	2.5	77.7
Greece	239.6	-4.7	28.5	2.1	79.8
Mozambique	233.6	0.6	-20.2	2.1	81.9

Graph 2: Trade Balance by MDG regions 2016

(Bln US$)

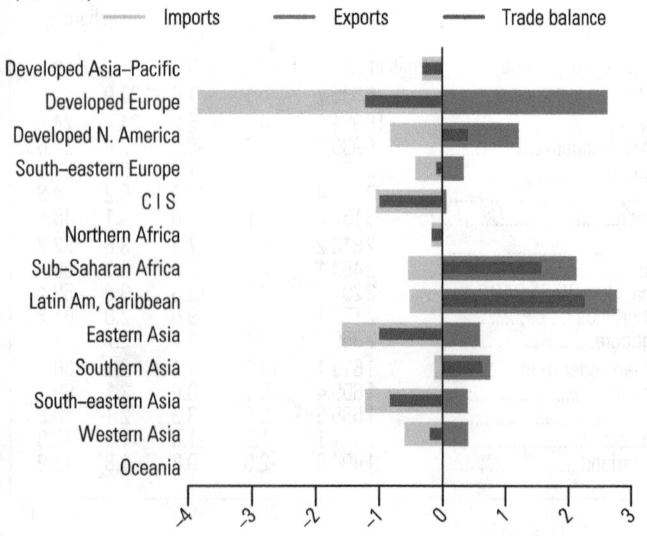

Table 3: Top importing countries or areas in 2016

Country or area	Value (million US$)	Avg. Growth (%) 12-16	Growth (%) 15-16	World share %	Cum.
World	11 225.5	-4.3	-8.4	100.0	
China	1 133.7	-1.3	-12.4	10.1	10.1
Russian Federation	921.4	-5.5	-3.3	8.2	18.3
Germany	908.8	-2.2	-19.6	8.1	26.4
Belgium	871.1	13.1	0.2	7.8	34.2
USA	763.7	-6.1	2.6	6.8	41.0
Poland	524.7	4.4	-4.1	4.7	45.6
Netherlands	509.0	-11.9	-17.5	4.5	50.2
Indonesia	477.3	-7.7	15.7	4.3	54.4
Turkey	428.5	4.5	9.4	3.8	58.2
Japan	299.4	-6.3	-19.0	2.7	60.9
Rep. of Korea	294.1	4.0	31.6	2.6	63.5
Viet Nam	*229.5*	3.5	5.1	2.0	65.6
Romania	196.7	2.4	-19.1	1.8	67.3
Malaysia	183.7	-15.1	-28.4	1.6	69.0
Philippines	163.3	3.1	43.8	1.5	70.4

In 2016, the value (in current US$) of exports of "tobacco, manufactured (whether or not containing tobacco substitutes)" (SITC group 122) increased by 9.1 percent (compared to 1.6 percent average growth rate from 2012-2016) to reach 32.8 bln US$ (see table 2), while imports increased by 5.1 percent to reach 30.2 bln US$ (see table 3). Exports of this commodity accounted for 2.8 percent of world exports of SITC sections 0+1, and 0.2 percent of total world merchandise exports (see table 1). Germany, Cuba and Netherlands were the top exporters in 2016 (see table 2). They accounted for 13.7, 9.4 and 9.3 percent of world exports, respectively. Japan, Italy and France were the top destinations, with respectively 12.4, 7.5 and 6.5 percent of world imports (see table 3).

The top 15 countries/areas accounted for 70.2 and 64.3 percent of total world exports and imports, respectively (see tables 2 and 3). In 2016, Germany was the country/area with the highest value of net exports (+3.3 bln US$), followed by Cuba (+3.1 bln US$). By MDG regions (see graph 2), the largest surpluses in this product group were recorded by Latin America and the Caribbean (+3.8 bln US$), Developed Europe (+2.7 bln US$) and South-eastern Asia (+1.3 bln US$). The largest trade deficits were recorded by Developed Asia-Pacific (-4.4 bln US$), Western Asia (-1.6 bln US$) and Northern Africa (-584.7 mln US$).

Table 1: Imports (Imp.) and exports (Exp.), 2002-2016, in current US$

		2002	2003	2004	2005	2006	2007	2008	2009	2010	2011	2012	2013	2014	2015	2016
Values in Bln US$	Imp.	15.4	16.8	19.5	20.9	21.0	23.7	24.5	24.5	25.7	32.4	32.6	33.4	32.4	28.7	30.2
	Exp.	15.8	16.0	16.8	18.1	19.2	21.5	23.7	23.4	24.4	29.1	30.8	32.6	33.8	30.1	32.8
As a percentage of SITC section (%)	Imp.	3.4	3.3	3.3	3.3	3.0	2.8	2.5	2.7	2.6	2.7	2.8	2.7	2.5	2.4	2.6
	Exp.	3.7	3.3	3.0	3.0	2.9	2.7	2.5	2.7	2.5	2.5	2.6	2.6	2.6	2.6	2.8
As a percentage of world trade (%)	Imp.	0.2	0.2	0.2	0.2	0.2	0.2	0.2	0.2	0.2	0.2	0.2	0.2	0.2	0.2	0.2
	Exp.	0.2	0.2	0.2	0.2	0.2	0.2	0.1	0.2	0.2	0.2	0.2	0.2	0.2	0.2	0.2

Graph 1: Annual growth rates of exports, 2002–2016

(In percentage by year)

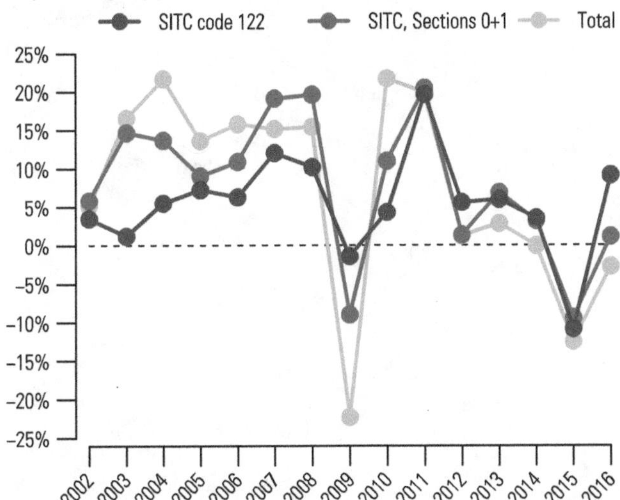

Table 2: Top exporting countries or areas in 2016

Country or area	Value (million US$)	Avg. Growth (%) 12-16	Growth (%) 15-16	World share %	Cum.
World	32847.4	1.6	9.1	100.0	
Germany	4511.6	-2.6	3.1	13.7	13.7
Cuba	*3090.5*	47.0	116.1	9.4	23.1
Netherlands	3067.0	-7.6	58.2	9.3	32.5
Poland	2101.4	3.9	-10.8	6.4	38.9
China, Hong Kong SAR	1193.5	5.2	-0.7	3.6	42.5
Singapore	1161.5	9.6	-2.3	3.5	46.0
USA	1155.9	21.7	25.2	3.5	49.6
United Arab Emirates	1019.9	-19.9	18.9	3.1	52.7
Rep. of Korea	1003.3	13.0	11.4	3.1	55.7
Indonesia	881.0	8.5	6.8	2.7	58.4
Czechia	870.5	14.8	16.9	2.7	61.1
Romania	828.7	8.8	-19.1	2.5	63.6
China	804.2	7.4	4.0	2.4	66.0
Dominican Rep.	689.5	12.2	6.1	2.1	68.1
Portugal	686.1	12.6	-4.2	2.1	70.2

Graph 2: Trade Balance by MDG regions 2016

(Bln US$)

Imports — Exports — Trade balance

Developed Asia-Pacific
Developed Europe
Developed N. America
South-eastern Europe
CIS
Northern Africa
Sub-Saharan Africa
Latin Am, Caribbean
Eastern Asia
Southern Asia
South-eastern Asia
Western Asia
Oceania

-15 -10 -5 0 5 10 15 20

Table 3: Top importing countries or areas in 2016

Country or area	Value (million US$)	Avg. Growth (%) 12-16	Growth (%) 15-16	World share %	Cum.
World	30159.9	-1.9	5.1	100.0	
Japan	3744.9	-8.8	19.6	12.4	12.4
Italy	2253.4	-5.1	9.6	7.5	19.9
France	1964.6	-4.4	4.6	6.5	26.4
Spain	1584.1	0.2	19.1	5.3	31.7
USA	1437.0	12.8	6.2	4.8	36.4
Saudi Arabia	1225.4	7.5	3.1	4.1	40.5
Germany	1195.7	-4.1	15.6	4.0	44.4
Netherlands	1003.4	-0.5	21.7	3.3	47.8
China, Hong Kong SAR	864.1	5.0	-2.2	2.9	50.6
Singapore	788.9	4.5	7.5	2.6	53.3
Australia	739.9	25.9	4.7	2.5	55.7
Belgium	719.3	-0.6	2.2	2.4	58.1
United Arab Emirates	702.3	-16.5	-6.1	2.3	60.4
China	594.0	49.3	4.2	2.0	62.4
Other Asia, nes	567.6	1.1	5.9	1.9	64.3

Crude materials, inedible, except fuels

(SITC Section 2)

211 Hides and skins (except furskins), raw

In 2016, the value (in current US$) of exports of "hides and skins (except furskins), raw" (SITC group 211) decreased by 17.0 percent (compared to -7.5 percent average growth rate from 2012-2016) to reach 5.8 bln US$ (see table 2), while imports decreased by 17.9 percent to reach 6.1 bln US$ (see table 3). Exports of this commodity accounted for 0.9 percent of world exports of SITC sections 2+4, and less than 0.1 percent of total world merchandise exports (see table 1). USA, Australia and France were the top exporters in 2016 (see table 2). They accounted for 28.0, 10.6 and 6.3 percent of world exports, respectively. China, Italy and Rep. of Korea were the top destinations, with respectively 36.3, 18.0 and 5.0 percent of world imports (see table 3).

The top 15 countries/areas accounted for 80.9 and 88.2 percent of total world exports and imports, respectively (see tables 2 and 3). In 2016, USA was the country/area with the highest value of net exports (+1.6 bln US$), followed by Australia (+615.5 mln US$). By MDG regions (see graph 2), the largest surpluses in this product group were recorded by Developed North America (+1.8 bln US$), Developed Asia-Pacific (+736.8 mln US$) and Sub-Saharan Africa (+138.8 mln US$). The largest trade deficits were recorded by Eastern Asia (-2.6 bln US$), South-eastern Asia (-383.1 mln US$) and Latin America and the Caribbean (-61.9 mln US$).

Table 1: Imports (Imp.) and exports (Exp.), 2002-2016, in current US$

		2002	2003	2004	2005	2006	2007	2008	2009	2010	2011	2012	2013	2014	2015	2016
Values in Bln US$	Imp.	5.5	5.5	5.6	5.6	5.9	6.3	6.2	4.2	6.3	8.0	8.0	9.1	9.0	7.4	6.1
	Exp.	5.4	5.6	5.7	5.7	6.1	6.4	5.9	4.1	6.4	8.1	7.9	9.3	8.8	7.0	5.8
As a percentage of SITC section (%)	Imp.	2.3	1.9	1.5	1.3	1.2	1.0	0.8	0.8	0.8	0.8	0.9	1.0	1.0	1.0	0.9
	Exp.	2.5	2.2	1.8	1.6	1.4	1.2	0.9	0.8	0.9	0.9	0.9	1.1	1.1	1.1	0.9
As a percentage of world trade (%)	Imp.	0.1	0.1	0.1	0.1	0.0	0.0	0.0	0.0	0.0	0.0	0.0	0.0	0.0	0.0	0.0
	Exp.	0.1	0.1	0.1	0.1	0.1	0.0	0.0	0.0	0.0	0.0	0.0	0.0	0.0	0.0	0.0

Graph 1: Annual growth rates of exports, 2002–2016
(In percentage by year)

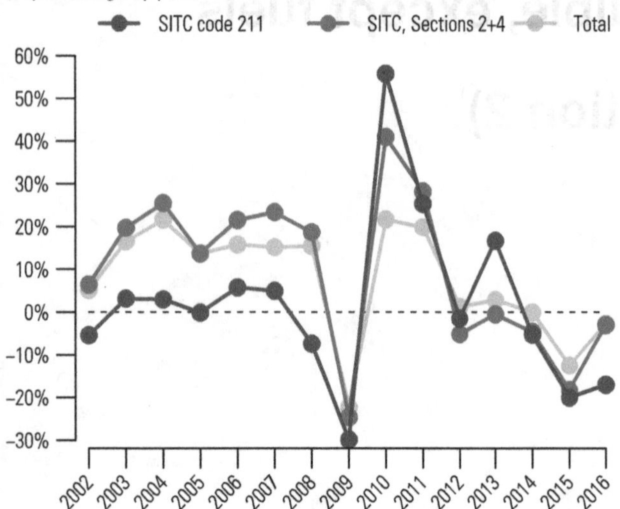

Table 2: Top exporting countries or areas in 2016

Country or area	Value (million US$)	Avg. Growth (%) 12-16	Growth (%) 15-16	World share %	Cum.
World	5829.3	-7.5	-17.0	100.0	
USA	1634.3	-7.7	-16.7	28.0	28.0
Australia	618.4	-7.6	-19.9	10.6	38.6
France	366.0	-5.1	-12.2	6.3	44.9
Germany	313.8	-4.4	-14.9	5.4	50.3
Netherlands	289.0	-6.0	-17.2	5.0	55.3
Canada	242.4	-4.9	-10.9	4.2	59.4
United Kingdom	227.3	-7.9	-22.7	3.9	63.3
Spain	209.4	-11.8	-11.9	3.6	66.9
Italy	166.3	-11.8	-17.3	2.9	69.8
Ireland	138.3	0.7	-13.7	2.4	72.1
New Zealand	125.0	-18.5	-29.7	2.1	74.3
Austria	105.8	7.0	4.2	1.8	76.1
Japan	101.9	-9.4	6.4	1.7	77.8
South Africa	92.2	-4.9	-32.6	1.6	79.4
Belgium	84.6	-1.9	-14.6	1.5	80.9

Graph 2: Trade Balance by MDG regions 2016
(Bln US$)

Imports — Exports — Trade balance

Developed Asia-Pacific
Developed Europe
Developed N. America
South-eastern Europe
C I S
Northern Africa
Sub-Saharan Africa
Latin Am, Caribbean
Eastern Asia
Southern Asia
South-eastern Asia
Western Asia
Oceania

-3 -2.5 -2 -1.5 -1 -0.5 0 0.5 1 1.5 2 2.5

Table 3: Top importing countries or areas in 2016

Country or area	Value (million US$)	Avg. Growth (%) 12-16	Growth (%) 15-16	World share %	Cum.
World	6078.7	-6.5	-17.9	100.0	
China	2208.7	-7.5	-27.7	36.3	36.3
Italy	1095.6	-3.2	-9.8	18.0	54.4
Rep. of Korea	306.8	-11.2	-32.1	5.0	59.4
Germany	234.9	5.4	8.2	3.9	63.3
Mexico	202.0	4.6	-2.4	3.3	66.6
Thailand	200.7	-2.6	-5.2	3.3	69.9
Austria	166.9	-1.4	-12.1	2.7	72.6
France	155.2	0.0	-9.3	2.6	75.2
Netherlands	148.6	-1.4	-16.5	2.4	77.6
Viet Nam	*144.9*	18.6	5.1	2.4	80.0
China, Hong Kong SAR	119.6	-18.5	6.8	2.0	82.0
Spain	107.3	-1.3	20.7	1.8	83.8
Japan	103.4	-9.8	-18.5	1.7	85.5
Other Asia, nes	91.0	-17.5	-32.6	1.5	87.0
Turkey	77.6	-33.7	-21.2	1.3	88.2

Furskins, raw (including heads, tails, paws, etc), other than those of 211 212

In 2016, the value (in current US$) of exports of "furskins, raw (including heads, tails, paws, etc), other than those of 211" (SITC group 212) decreased by 47.8 percent (compared to -17.9 percent average growth rate from 2012-2016) to reach 2.6 bln US$ (see table 2), while imports decreased by 33.1 percent to reach 2.7 bln US$ (see table 3). Exports of this commodity accounted for 0.4 percent of world exports of SITC sections 2+4, and less than 0.1 percent of total world merchandise exports (see table 1). Denmark, Canada and Finland were the top exporters in 2016 (see table 2). They accounted for 34.9, 14.1 and 13.1 percent of world exports, respectively. China, Denmark and Canada were the top destinations, with respectively 29.9, 14.9 and 12.2 percent of world imports (see table 3).

The top 15 countries/areas accounted for 98.1 and 98.0 percent of total world exports and imports, respectively (see tables 2 and 3). In 2016, Denmark was the country/area with the highest value of net exports (+501.9 mln US$), followed by Poland (+237.6 mln US$). By MDG regions (see graph 2), the largest surpluses in this product group were recorded by Developed Europe (+976.7 mln US$), Developed North America (+244.7 mln US$) and Commonwealth of Independent States (+49.0 mln US$). The largest trade deficits were recorded by Eastern Asia (-1.0 bln US$), South-eastern Asia (-344.8 mln US$) and Developed Asia-Pacific (-6.5 mln US$).

Table 1: Imports (Imp.) and exports (Exp.), 2002-2016, in current US$

		2002	2003	2004	2005	2006	2007	2008	2009	2010	2011	2012	2013	2014	2015	2016
Values in Bln US$	Imp.	1.2	1.3	1.6	1.7	2.1	1.9	2.1	1.7	2.5	3.2	3.6	4.9	4.3	4.0	2.7
	Exp.	1.6	1.8	2.2	2.3	3.0	2.5	3.1	2.4	3.8	4.7	5.7	7.4	5.0	5.0	2.6
As a percentage of SITC section (%)	Imp.	0.5	0.5	0.4	0.4	0.4	0.3	0.3	0.3	0.3	0.3	0.4	0.5	0.5	0.6	0.4
	Exp.	0.7	0.7	0.7	0.6	0.7	0.5	0.5	0.5	0.5	0.5	0.7	0.9	0.6	0.8	0.4
As a percentage of world trade (%)	Imp.	0.0	0.0	0.0	0.0	0.0	0.0	0.0	0.0	0.0	0.0	0.0	0.0	0.0	0.0	0.0
	Exp.	0.0	0.0	0.0	0.0	0.0	0.0	0.0	0.0	0.0	0.0	0.0	0.0	0.0	0.0	0.0

Graph 1: Annual growth rates of exports, 2002–2016

(In percentage by year)

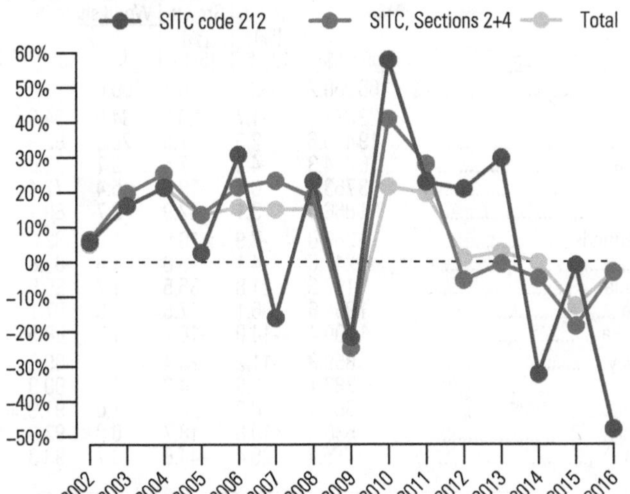

Graph 2: Trade Balance by MDG regions 2016

(Bln US$)

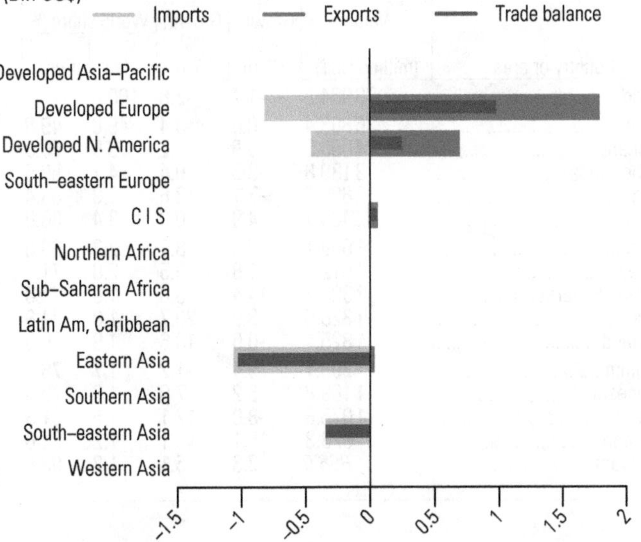

Table 2: Top exporting countries or areas in 2016

Country or area	Value (million US$)	Avg. Growth (%) 12-16	Growth (%) 15-16	World share %	Cum.
World	2590.8	-17.9	-47.8	100.0	
Denmark	903.1	-16.8	-43.9	34.9	34.9
Canada	364.9	-14.1	-39.1	14.1	48.9
Finland	338.7	-20.2	-50.6	13.1	62.0
USA	332.9	-11.3	-30.8	12.8	74.9
Poland	289.5	24.4	-24.7	11.2	86.0
Greece	58.4	10.3	-3.9	2.3	88.3
Norway	53.2	-2.6	-19.9	2.1	90.3
Russian Federation	49.6	-23.6	-19.7	1.9	92.3
Lithuania	32.9	-2.2	-27.5	1.3	93.5
China, Hong Kong SAR	31.4	-56.5	-95.5	1.2	94.7
Netherlands	29.1	-33.7	-72.6	1.1	95.9
Germany	23.9	-10.6	-6.3	0.9	96.8
Spain	11.4	-27.1	-35.1	0.4	97.2
Sweden	11.4	-26.2	-51.4	0.4	97.7
Belarus	10.9	-30.3	-26.7	0.4	98.1

Table 3: Top importing countries or areas in 2016

Country or area	Value (million US$)	Avg. Growth (%) 12-16	Growth (%) 15-16	World share %	Cum.
World	2698.3	-6.8	-33.1	100.0	
China	806.8	6.1	-14.6	29.9	29.9
Denmark	401.3	19.1	-34.2	14.9	44.8
Canada	329.4	15.2	-17.5	12.2	57.0
Finland	181.1	-9.5	-26.6	6.7	63.7
Cambodia	166.4	...	47.8	6.2	69.9
China, Hong Kong SAR	156.1	-41.8	-84.1	5.8	75.6
USA	123.6	-8.7	-34.7	4.6	80.2
Rep. of Korea	99.1	-9.6	-20.2	3.7	83.9
Viet Nam	*98.4*	578.8	5.1	3.6	87.5
Italy	84.5	-16.0	-17.0	3.1	90.7
Thailand	66.3	342.8	>	2.5	93.1
Poland	51.9	-1.7	12.5	1.9	95.1
Greece	47.0	-28.9	-20.1	1.7	96.8
Germany	18.8	-16.8	32.6	0.7	97.5
Malaysia	12.7	-12.7	-31.9	0.5	98.0

222 Oil-seeds and oleaginous fruits used for extraction of 'soft' fixed oils

In 2016, the value (in current US$) of exports of "oil-seeds and oleaginous fruits used for extraction of 'soft' fixed oils" (SITC group 222) decreased by 0.7 percent (compared to -2.1 percent average growth rate from 2012-2016) to reach 69.0 bln US$ (see table 2), while imports decreased by 2.8 percent to reach 74.0 bln US$ (see table 3). Exports of this commodity accounted for 10.8 percent of world exports of SITC sections 2+4, and 0.4 percent of total world merchandise exports (see table 1). USA, Brazil and Canada were the top exporters in 2016 (see table 2). They accounted for 34.6, 28.3 and 9.1 percent of world exports, respectively. China, Germany and Netherlands were the top destinations, with respectively 49.8, 5.5 and 4.2 percent of world imports (see table 3).

The top 15 countries/areas accounted for 93.3 and 83.8 percent of total world exports and imports, respectively (see tables 2 and 3). In 2016, USA was the country/area with the highest value of net exports (+23.0 bln US$), followed by Brazil (+19.3 bln US$). By MDG regions (see graph 2), the largest surpluses in this product group were recorded by Developed North America (+28.9 bln US$), Latin America and the Caribbean (+22.5 bln US$) and South-eastern Europe (+1.5 bln US$). The largest trade deficits were recorded by Eastern Asia (-37.9 bln US$), Developed Europe (-10.4 bln US$) and South-eastern Asia (-3.6 bln US$).

Table 1: Imports (Imp.) and exports (Exp.), 2002-2016, in current US$

		2002	2003	2004	2005	2006	2007	2008	2009	2010	2011	2012	2013	2014	2015	2016
Values in Bln US$	Imp.	16.8	22.6	26.5	25.4	25.1	35.9	60.7	50.7	58.8	73.4	79.4	84.2	88.8	76.1	74.0
	Exp.	14.8	20.4	21.4	21.4	22.7	32.3	50.3	45.9	54.3	65.5	75.1	80.9	80.8	69.5	69.0
As a percentage of SITC section (%)	Imp.	6.9	7.8	7.0	6.1	5.1	5.8	7.9	9.3	7.7	7.4	8.6	9.2	10.0	10.4	10.6
	Exp.	6.9	7.9	6.6	5.8	5.1	5.8	7.7	9.3	7.8	7.3	8.9	9.6	10.0	10.6	10.8
As a percentage of world trade (%)	Imp.	0.3	0.3	0.3	0.2	0.2	0.3	0.4	0.4	0.4	0.4	0.4	0.4	0.5	0.5	0.5
	Exp.	0.2	0.3	0.2	0.2	0.2	0.2	0.3	0.4	0.4	0.4	0.4	0.4	0.4	0.4	0.4

Graph 1: Annual growth rates of exports, 2002–2016
(In percentage by year)

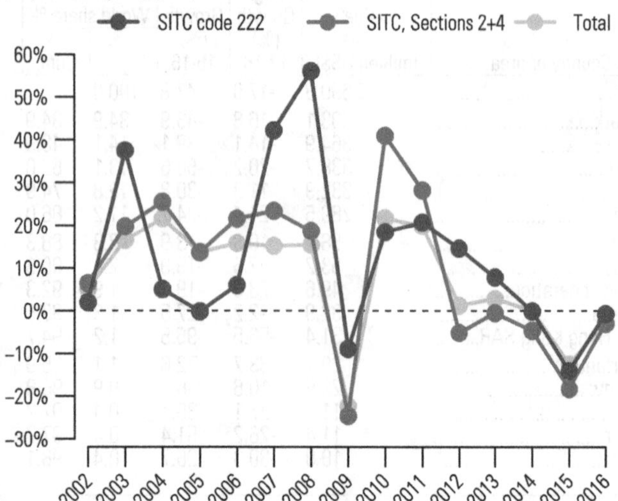

Graph 2: Trade Balance by MDG regions 2016
(Bln US$)

Imports — Exports — Trade balance

Developed Asia-Pacific
Developed Europe
Developed N. America
South-eastern Europe
CIS
Northern Africa
Sub-Saharan Africa
Latin Am, Caribbean
Eastern Asia
Southern Asia
South-eastern Asia
Western Asia
Oceania

-40 -30 -20 -10 0 10 20 30 40

Table 2: Top exporting countries or areas in 2016

Country or area	Value (million US$)	Avg. Growth (%) 12-16	Growth (%) 15-16	World share %	Cum.
World	68950.2	-2.1	-0.7	100.0	
USA	23878.6	-1.7	20.5	34.6	34.6
Brazil	19479.6	2.9	-7.8	28.3	62.9
Canada	6284.3	-4.4	7.5	9.1	72.0
Argentina	3753.3	0.3	-19.5	5.4	77.4
Paraguay	1866.0	3.1	12.9	2.7	80.1
Netherlands	1269.0	-7.9	10.5	1.8	82.0
India	1242.6	-4.1	-3.0	1.8	83.8
Romania	1197.5	21.8	35.5	1.7	85.5
France	1064.6	-6.1	7.5	1.5	87.1
Australia	1000.4	-14.0	-16.1	1.5	88.5
Uruguay	859.3	-11.2	-23.4	1.2	89.8
China	782.1	-3.6	-4.3	1.1	90.9
Bulgaria	657.4	0.3	28.1	1.0	91.9
Hungary	530.5	-10.8	18.7	0.8	92.6
Sudan	*466.1*	25.4	-44.6	0.7	93.3

Table 3: Top importing countries or areas in 2016

Country or area	Value (million US$)	Avg. Growth (%) 12-16	Growth (%) 15-16	World share %	Cum.
World	73964.3	-1.7	-2.8	100.0	
China	36803.4	-0.6	-3.4	49.8	49.8
Germany	4098.8	-5.9	-1.2	5.5	55.3
Netherlands	3139.8	-3.5	0.4	4.2	59.5
Japan	2880.2	-7.1	-13.6	3.9	63.4
Mexico	2489.7	4.9	0.3	3.4	66.8
Spain	1658.1	-8.8	-8.1	2.2	69.0
Turkey	1512.6	1.8	-5.5	2.0	71.1
Russian Federation	1391.7	14.4	8.8	1.9	73.0
France	1326.5	8.9	20.7	1.8	74.8
Thailand	1325.4	-0.5	10.6	1.8	76.6
Belgium	1293.1	-9.4	-1.2	1.7	78.3
Indonesia	1169.8	-5.2	-7.0	1.6	79.9
Other Asia, nes	1075.8	-8.0	-12.1	1.5	81.3
Pakistan	923.3	15.1	40.1	1.2	82.6
Viet Nam	*866.9*	2.3	5.1	1.2	83.8

In 2016, the value (in current US$) of exports of "oil seeds and oleaginous fruits used for the extraction of other fixed oils" (SITC group 223) decreased by 1.7 percent (compared to -2.6 percent average growth rate from 2012-2016) to reach 3.6 bln US$ (see table 2), while imports decreased by 5.4 percent to reach 3.1 bln US$ (see table 3). Exports of this commodity accounted for 0.6 percent of world exports of SITC sections 2+4, and less than 0.1 percent of total world merchandise exports (see table 1). USA, Canada and Russian Federation were the top exporters in 2016 (see table 2). They accounted for 26.0, 11.6 and 6.9 percent of world exports, respectively. Belgium, USA and Germany were the top destinations, with respectively 10.5, 9.4 and 8.0 percent of world imports (see table 3).

The top 15 countries/areas accounted for 77.1 and 71.2 percent of total world exports and imports, respectively (see tables 2 and 3). In 2016, USA was the country/area with the highest value of net exports (+634.1 mln US$), followed by Canada (+360.9 mln US$). By MDG regions (see graph 2), the largest surpluses in this product group were recorded by Developed North America (+994.9 mln US$), Commonwealth of Independent States (+298.0 mln US$) and Sub-Saharan Africa (+88.5 mln US$). The largest trade deficits were recorded by Developed Europe (-580.9 mln US$), Eastern Asia (-194.2 mln US$) and Western Asia (-111.3 mln US$).

Table 1: Imports (Imp.) and exports (Exp.), 2002-2016, in current US$

		2002	2003	2004	2005	2006	2007	2008	2009	2010	2011	2012	2013	2014	2015	2016
Values in Bln US$	Imp.	0.9	1.0	1.2	1.3	1.4	1.8	2.6	2.1	2.3	2.4	2.6	2.9	3.3	3.2	3.1
	Exp.	0.8	0.9	1.2	1.5	1.5	1.9	2.8	2.2	2.2	2.6	4.0	4.3	4.3	3.6	3.6
As a percentage of SITC section (%)	Imp.	0.4	0.4	0.3	0.3	0.3	0.3	0.3	0.4	0.3	0.2	0.3	0.3	0.4	0.4	0.4
	Exp.	0.4	0.3	0.4	0.4	0.3	0.4	0.4	0.4	0.3	0.3	0.5	0.5	0.5	0.6	0.6
As a percentage of world trade (%)	Imp.	0.0	0.0	0.0	0.0	0.0	0.0	0.0	0.0	0.0	0.0	0.0	0.0	0.0	0.0	0.0
	Exp.	0.0	0.0	0.0	0.0	0.0	0.0	0.0	0.0	0.0	0.0	0.0	0.0	0.0	0.0	0.0

Graph 1: Annual growth rates of exports, 2002–2016

(In percentage by year)

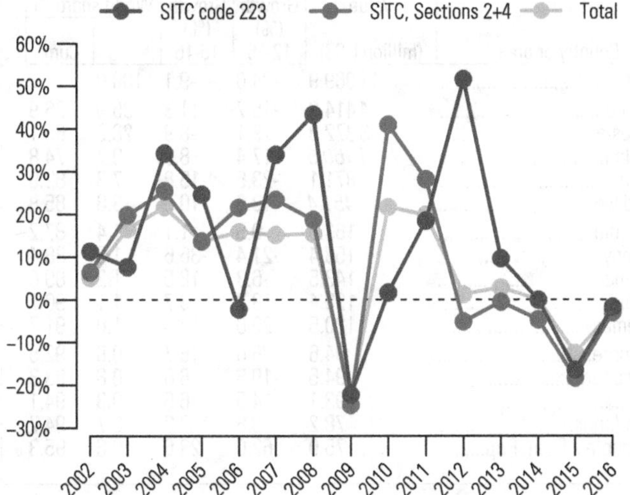

Graph 2: Trade Balance by MDG regions 2016

(Bln US$)

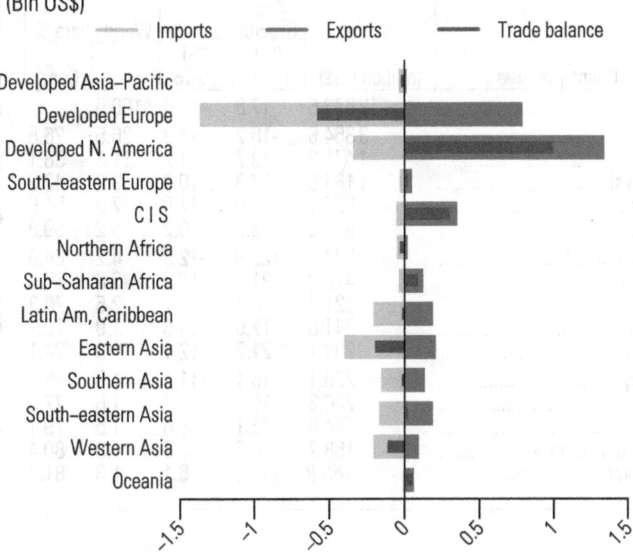

Table 2: Top exporting countries or areas in 2016

Country or area	Value (million US$)	Avg. Growth (%) 12-16	Growth (%) 15-16	World share %	Cum.
World	3553.7	-2.6	-1.7	100.0	
USA	922.6	-10.5	-11.4	26.0	26.0
Canada	414.0	3.9	-3.7	11.6	37.6
Russian Federation	245.2	4.7	32.5	6.9	44.5
China	193.1	4.4	-3.5	5.4	49.9
Netherlands	135.2	-21.6	1.3	3.8	53.8
India	108.9	18.0	-14.4	3.1	56.8
Belgium	106.6	-1.0	-18.0	3.0	59.8
Indonesia	102.5	24.6	145.2	2.9	62.7
Kazakhstan	101.1	-13.5	-20.7	2.8	65.5
Italy	97.2	10.5	-6.4	2.7	68.3
Austria	86.3	9.5	25.0	2.4	70.7
Turkey	61.8	4.0	47.1	1.7	72.4
Czechia	56.3	-7.3	-11.0	1.6	74.0
Spain	54.6	9.4	36.1	1.5	75.6
Germany	53.6	8.0	-18.8	1.5	77.1

Table 3: Top importing countries or areas in 2016

Country or area	Value (million US$)	Avg. Growth (%) 12-16	Growth (%) 15-16	World share %	Cum.
World	3056.6	4.4	-5.4	100.0	
Belgium	320.5	-1.4	-10.7	10.5	10.5
USA	288.5	4.0	-22.6	9.4	19.9
Germany	244.8	4.4	-12.0	8.0	27.9
China	244.1	22.7	-0.7	8.0	35.9
Turkey	155.2	15.5	25.2	5.1	41.0
Netherlands	152.4	7.3	-3.1	5.0	46.0
Rep. of Korea	123.5	16.0	37.3	4.0	50.0
Spain	106.3	4.6	-11.7	3.5	53.5
India	95.8	18.3	-8.8	3.1	56.6
Dominican Rep.	81.7	7.0	-6.9	2.7	59.3
United Kingdom	81.5	4.3	-29.2	2.7	62.0
Philippines	78.7	10.8	55.3	2.6	64.6
Austria	76.9	10.1	-13.6	2.5	67.1
France	71.1	1.5	13.8	2.3	69.4
Malaysia	54.5	-0.6	53.5	1.8	71.2

Source: UN Comtrade

231 Natural rubber, balata, gutta-percha, chicle, etc, in primary forms

In 2016, the value (in current US$) of exports of "natural rubber, balata, gutta-percha, chicle, etc, in primary forms" (SITC group 231) decreased by 9.1 percent (compared to -24.0 percent average growth rate from 2012-2016) to reach 12.0 bln US$ (see table 2), while imports decreased by 11.6 percent to reach 12.7 bln US$ (see table 3). Exports of this commodity accounted for 1.9 percent of world exports of SITC sections 2+4, and 0.1 percent of total world merchandise exports (see table 1). Thailand, Indonesia and Viet Nam were the top exporters in 2016 (see table 2). They accounted for 36.9, 28.2 and 9.7 percent of world exports, respectively. China, USA and Malaysia were the top destinations, with respectively 26.5, 11.6 and 9.2 percent of world imports (see table 3).

The top 15 countries/areas accounted for 95.3 and 81.7 percent of total world exports and imports, respectively (see tables 2 and 3). In 2016, Thailand was the country/area with the highest value of net exports (+4.4 bln US$), followed by Indonesia (+3.3 bln US$). By MDG regions (see graph 2), the largest surpluses in this product group were recorded by South-eastern Asia (+8.9 bln US$), Sub-Saharan Africa (+621.4 mln US$) and Oceania (+5.8 mln US$). The largest trade deficits were recorded by Eastern Asia (-4.0 bln US$), Developed Europe (-1.7 bln US$) and Developed North America (-1.6 bln US$).

Table 1: Imports (Imp.) and exports (Exp.), 2002-2016, in current US$

		2002	2003	2004	2005	2006	2007	2008	2009	2010	2011	2012	2013	2014	2015	2016
Values in Bln US$	Imp.	4.7	6.8	9.0	9.9	14.5	15.9	20.0	11.8	23.8	39.4	27.8	24.8	18.4	14.3	12.7
	Exp.	4.3	6.5	8.6	9.8	14.9	16.3	19.8	11.9	24.5	45.7	35.8	25.8	16.8	13.2	12.0
As a percentage of SITC section (%)	Imp.	1.9	2.4	2.4	2.4	2.9	2.6	2.6	2.2	3.1	4.0	3.0	2.7	2.1	2.0	1.8
	Exp.	2.0	2.5	2.7	2.7	3.3	2.9	3.0	2.4	3.5	5.1	4.2	3.1	2.1	2.0	1.9
As a percentage of world trade (%)	Imp.	0.1	0.1	0.1	0.1	0.1	0.1	0.1	0.1	0.2	0.2	0.2	0.1	0.1	0.1	0.1
	Exp.	0.1	0.1	0.1	0.1	0.1	0.1	0.1	0.1	0.2	0.3	0.2	0.1	0.1	0.1	0.1

Graph 1: Annual growth rates of exports, 2002–2016

(In percentage by year)

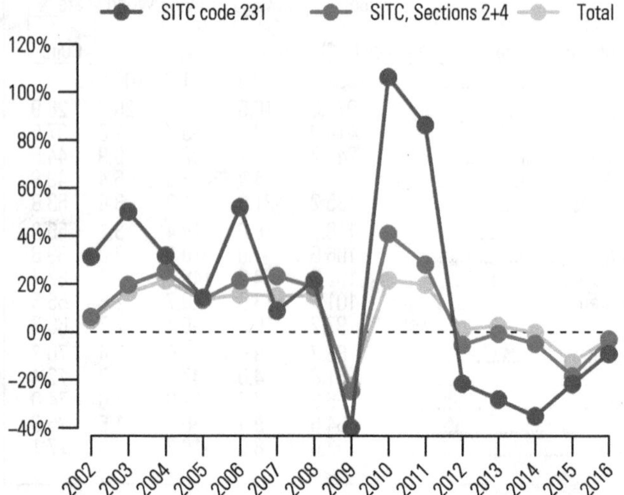

Table 2: Top exporting countries or areas in 2016

Country or area	Value (million US$)	Avg. Growth (%) 12-16	Growth (%) 15-16	World share %	Cum.
World	11 969.9	-24.0	-9.1	100.0	
Thailand	4 414.9	-15.7	-11.3	36.9	36.9
Indonesia	3 372.3	-19.1	-8.9	28.2	65.1
Viet Nam	*1 160.5*	-17.4	8.9	9.7	74.8
Malaysia	871.1	-23.5	-15.8	7.3	82.0
Côte d'Ivoire	*451.4*	-13.6	-10.0	3.8	85.8
Cambodia	163.3	-0.5	1.1	1.4	87.2
Germany	153.4	-21.4	-36.6	1.3	88.4
Myanmar	143.5	-6.3	18.5	1.2	89.6
Belgium	126.4	-13.7	3.7	1.1	90.7
Guatemala	120.5	-20.0	-12.8	1.0	91.7
Singapore	94.6	-26.0	-16.7	0.8	92.5
Luxembourg	94.5	-19.5	6.6	0.8	93.3
USA	93.1	-14.5	-16.5	0.8	94.1
Netherlands	78.2	-8.8	153.3	0.7	94.7
Lao People's Dem. Rep.	75.0	62.0	23.6	0.6	95.3

Graph 2: Trade Balance by MDG regions 2016

(Bln US$)

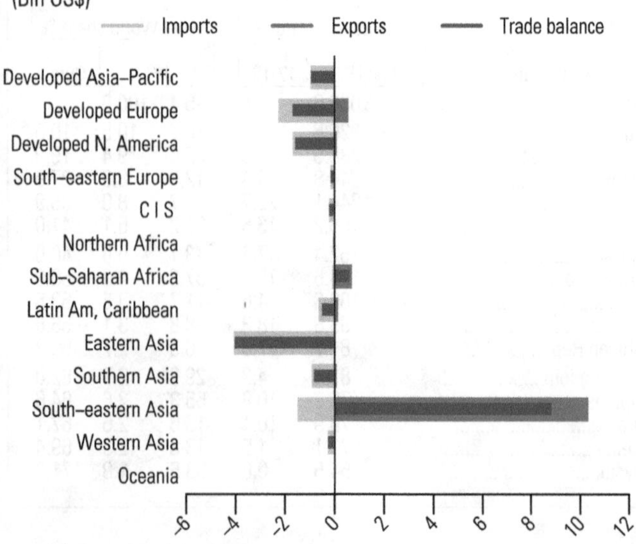

Table 3: Top importing countries or areas in 2016

Country or area	Value (million US$)	Avg. Growth (%) 12-16	Growth (%) 15-16	World share %	Cum.
World	12 673.6	-17.8	-11.6	100.0	
China	3 354.6	-16.2	-14.3	26.5	26.5
USA	1 471.6	-19.7	-11.2	11.6	38.1
Malaysia	1 163.9	-17.3	-10.9	9.2	47.3
Japan	927.2	-22.0	-14.8	7.3	54.6
India	656.0	-9.2	-9.2	5.2	59.8
Rep. of Korea	537.1	-20.9	-12.3	4.2	64.0
Germany	478.9	-21.7	-18.8	3.8	67.8
Brazil	321.7	-16.5	-5.7	2.5	70.3
Spain	241.8	-17.6	-14.6	1.9	72.2
France	239.1	-21.2	-12.1	1.9	74.1
Turkey	228.1	-16.1	-11.1	1.8	75.9
Italy	206.3	-15.2	-7.6	1.6	77.5
Canada	194.5	-22.1	-18.6	1.5	79.1
Russian Federation	168.7	-5.2	3.2	1.3	80.4
Viet Nam	*165.8*	-11.5	5.1	1.3	81.7

In 2016, the value (in current US$) of exports of "synthetic and reclaimed rubber; waste, scrap of unhardened rubber" (SITC group 232) increased by 3.5 percent (compared to -8.0 percent average growth rate from 2012-2016) to reach 19.1 bln US$ (see table 2), while imports increased by 2.9 percent to reach 21.3 bln US$ (see table 3). Exports of this commodity accounted for 3.0 percent of world exports of SITC sections 2+4, and 0.1 percent of total world merchandise exports (see table 1). USA, Japan and Rep. of Korea were the top exporters in 2016 (see table 2). They accounted for 12.9, 11.6 and 11.3 percent of world exports, respectively. China, USA and Germany were the top destinations, with respectively 25.4, 7.0 and 5.4 percent of world imports (see table 3).

The top 15 countries/areas accounted for 88.2 and 72.4 percent of total world exports and imports, respectively (see tables 2 and 3). In 2016, Japan was the country/area with the highest value of net exports (+1.8 bln US$), followed by Rep. of Korea (+1.7 bln US$). By MDG regions (see graph 2), the largest surpluses in this product group were recorded by Developed Asia-Pacific (+1.7 bln US$), Commonwealth of Independent States (+1.0 bln US$) and Developed North America (+835.0 mln US$). The largest trade deficits were recorded by Eastern Asia (-2.6 bln US$), Southern Asia (-924.5 mln US$) and Latin America and the Caribbean (-755.9 mln US$).

Table 1: Imports (Imp.) and exports (Exp.), 2002-2016, in current US$

		2002	2003	2004	2005	2006	2007	2008	2009	2010	2011	2012	2013	2014	2015	2016
Values in Bln US$	Imp.	7.9	9.1	11.0	13.4	15.3	17.6	21.6	15.3	22.6	31.8	30.0	26.1	24.4	20.7	21.3
	Exp.	6.5	7.5	9.4	11.7	13.7	15.8	18.7	13.8	20.3	28.5	26.7	23.5	21.7	18.5	19.1
As a percentage of SITC section (%)	Imp.	3.2	3.2	2.9	3.2	3.1	2.8	2.8	2.8	3.0	3.2	3.2	2.8	2.7	2.8	3.1
	Exp.	3.0	2.9	2.9	3.2	3.1	2.9	2.9	2.8	2.9	3.2	3.1	2.8	2.7	2.8	3.0
As a percentage of world trade (%)	Imp.	0.1	0.1	0.1	0.1	0.1	0.1	0.1	0.1	0.1	0.2	0.2	0.1	0.1	0.1	0.1
	Exp.	0.1	0.1	0.1	0.1	0.1	0.1	0.1	0.1	0.1	0.2	0.1	0.1	0.1	0.1	0.1

Graph 1: Annual growth rates of exports, 2002–2016

(In percentage by year)

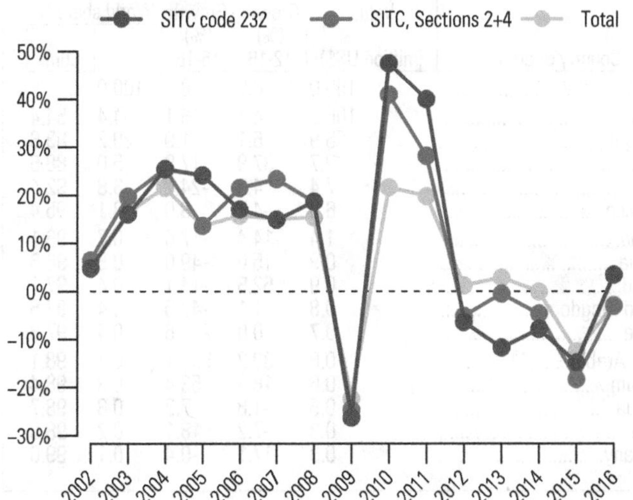

Table 2: Top exporting countries or areas in 2016

Country or area	Value (million US$)	Avg. Growth (%) 12-16	Growth (%) 15-16	World share %	Cum.
World	19127.3	-8.0	3.5	100.0	
USA	2476.9	-11.4	-7.3	12.9	12.9
Japan	2212.7	-7.2	2.2	11.6	24.5
Rep. of Korea	2159.3	-12.9	-3.6	11.3	35.8
Germany	1403.5	-9.6	-1.9	7.3	43.1
Russian Federation	1294.0	-16.6	-6.1	6.8	49.9
Belgium	1218.0	-9.0	-2.1	6.4	56.3
Thailand	1211.2	43.9	121.4	6.3	62.6
Singapore	902.2	53.3	23.9	4.7	67.3
Other Asia, nes	898.6	-9.3	-2.4	4.7	72.0
Netherlands	684.3	11.3	12.4	3.6	75.6
Malaysia	677.3	32.8	74.3	3.5	79.1
France	521.2	-17.2	-15.8	2.7	81.9
China	520.3	-10.8	-5.9	2.7	84.6
Poland	361.5	-12.1	7.6	1.9	86.5
Italy	325.6	-6.5	3.4	1.7	88.2

Graph 2: Trade Balance by MDG regions 2016

(Bln US$)

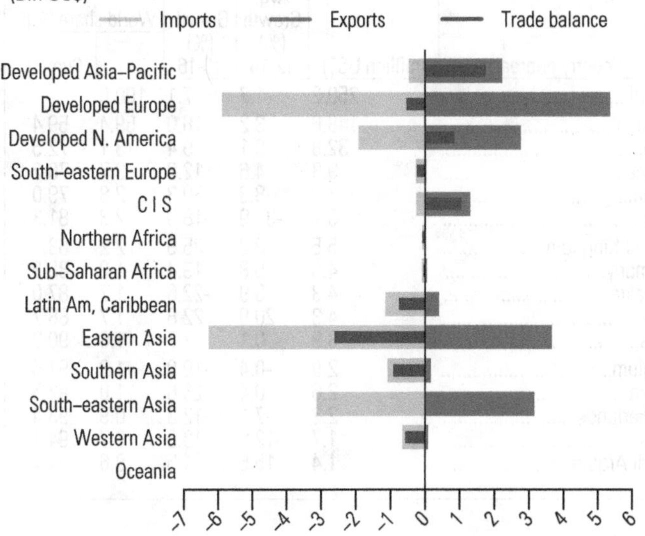

Table 3: Top importing countries or areas in 2016

Country or area	Value (million US$)	Avg. Growth (%) 12-16	Growth (%) 15-16	World share %	Cum.
World	21292.1	-8.2	2.9	100.0	
China	5397.9	1.3	37.7	25.4	25.4
USA	1480.4	-9.0	-6.2	7.0	32.3
Germany	1139.7	-10.4	-6.1	5.4	37.7
Belgium	937.8	-7.2	1.9	4.4	42.1
Thailand	908.5	-9.6	-0.2	4.3	46.3
India	811.7	-14.4	-6.2	3.8	50.1
Malaysia	773.1	-3.5	-0.3	3.6	53.8
Indonesia	583.9	-10.9	1.4	2.7	56.5
Italy	528.1	-10.8	-3.6	2.5	59.0
France	519.9	-12.4	-3.5	2.4	61.4
Rep. of Korea	487.9	-9.0	-10.2	2.3	63.7
Turkey	483.2	-11.6	-9.4	2.3	66.0
Poland	480.0	-10.1	-1.8	2.3	68.3
Brazil	450.2	-12.8	2.7	2.1	70.4
Canada	438.4	-12.6	-8.7	2.1	72.4

244 Cork, natural, raw, and waste (including natural cork in blocks or sheets)

In 2016, the value (in current US$) of exports of "cork, natural, raw, and waste (including natural cork in blocks or sheets)" (SITC group 244) increased by 8.0 percent (compared to 0.5 percent average growth rate from 2012-2016) to reach 195.0 mln US$ (see table 2), while imports increased by 7.1 percent to reach 250.2 mln US$ (see table 3). Exports of this commodity accounted for less than 0.1 percent of world exports of SITC sections 2+4, and less than 0.1 percent of total world merchandise exports (see table 1). Spain, Portugal and USA were the top exporters in 2016 (see table 2). They accounted for 54.4, 29.2 and 5.0 percent of world exports, respectively. Portugal, Spain and France were the top destinations, with respectively 59.4, 13.1 and 3.7 percent of world imports (see table 3).

The top 15 countries/areas accounted for 99.0 and 94.7 percent of total world exports and imports, respectively (see tables 2 and 3). In 2016, Spain was the country/area with the highest value of net exports (+73.4 mln US$), followed by Morocco (+5.8 mln US$). By MDG regions (see graph 2), the largest surpluses in this product group were recorded by Northern Africa (+8.0 mln US$) and Developed North America (+5.4 mln US$). The largest trade deficits were recorded by Developed Europe (-46.0 mln US$), Eastern Asia (-7.9 mln US$) and Southern Asia (-3.9 mln US$).

Table 1: Imports (Imp.) and exports (Exp.), 2002-2016, in current US$

		2002	2003	2004	2005	2006	2007	2008	2009	2010	2011	2012	2013	2014	2015	2016
Values in Mln US$	Imp.	202.0	264.2	245.2	242.1	243.5	273.9	275.5	194.2	210.9	286.1	268.0	267.3	266.9	233.6	250.2
	Exp.	192.2	254.2	235.6	236.2	242.6	252.3	254.3	149.2	153.4	193.9	191.0	174.8	217.1	180.6	195.0
As a percentage of SITC section (%)	Imp.	0.1	0.1	0.1	0.1	0.0	0.0	0.0	0.0	0.0	0.0	0.0	0.0	0.0	0.0	0.0
	Exp.	0.1	0.1	0.1	0.1	0.1	0.0	0.0	0.0	0.0	0.0	0.0	0.0	0.0	0.0	0.0
As a percentage of world trade (%)	Imp.	0.0	0.0	0.0	0.0	0.0	0.0	0.0	0.0	0.0	0.0	0.0	0.0	0.0	0.0	0.0
	Exp.	0.0	0.0	0.0	0.0	0.0	0.0	0.0	0.0	0.0	0.0	0.0	0.0	0.0	0.0	0.0

Graph 1: Annual growth rates of exports, 2002–2016
(In percentage by year)

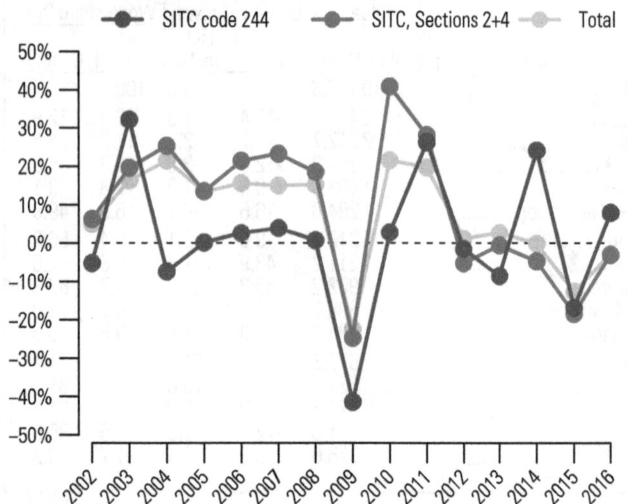

Graph 2: Trade Balance by MDG regions 2016
(Mln US$)

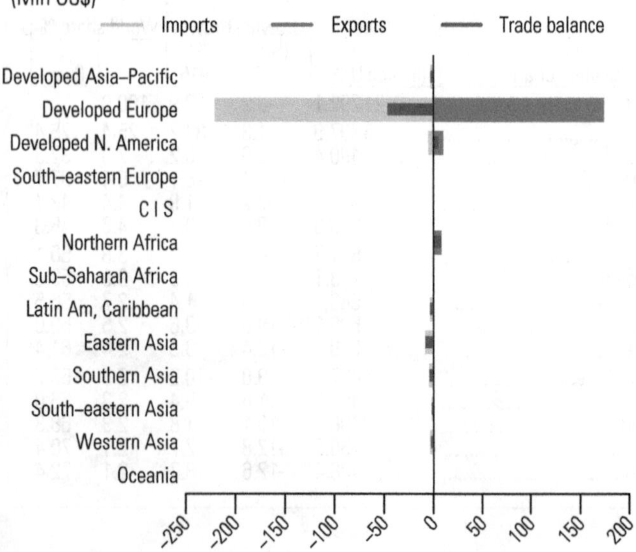

Table 2: Top exporting countries or areas in 2016

Country or area	Value (million US$)	Avg. Growth (%) 12-16	Growth (%) 15-16	World share %	Cum.
World	195.0	0.5	8.0	100.0	
Spain	106.2	4.1	18.1	54.4	54.4
Portugal	56.9	-6.1	1.9	29.2	83.6
USA	9.7	37.9	17.8	5.0	88.6
Italy	7.4	4.3	-24.7	3.8	92.4
Morocco	6.0	-4.7	-8.0	3.1	95.4
Tunisia	1.4	-14.4	-17.0	0.7	96.1
Algeria	0.9	-15.0	-49.0	0.5	96.6
Poland	0.9	52.5	-14.1	0.4	97.1
United Kingdom	0.8	-1.1	-47.5	0.4	97.5
France	0.7	0.0	227.6	0.4	97.8
Saudi Arabia	0.6	39.2	580.1	0.3	98.1
Belgium	0.6	18.3	53.4	0.3	98.4
Canada	0.5	-1.8	7.2	0.3	98.7
China	0.3	-7.2	-8.1	0.2	98.8
Germany	0.3	-17.1	-0.4	0.1	99.0

Table 3: Top importing countries or areas in 2016

Country or area	Value (million US$)	Avg. Growth (%) 12-16	Growth (%) 15-16	World share %	Cum.
World	250.2	-1.7	7.1	100.0	
Portugal	148.6	3.2	18.0	59.4	59.4
Spain	32.8	-0.1	9.4	13.1	72.5
France	9.3	4.6	12.8	3.7	76.2
China	7.0	-8.3	-30.3	2.8	79.0
Italy	5.7	-31.9	-18.0	2.3	81.3
United Kingdom	5.5	9.2	35.5	2.2	83.5
Germany	4.5	5.8	-19.4	1.8	85.3
Slovakia	4.3	-3.9	-22.6	1.7	87.0
USA	4.3	20.9	-22.8	1.7	88.7
India	3.9	-0.1	7.7	1.6	90.3
Belgium	2.9	-0.4	-10.9	1.2	91.5
Japan	2.6	0.4	26.6	1.0	92.5
Netherlands	2.2	-7.1	-12.3	0.9	93.4
Brazil	1.7	-12.8	13.0	0.7	94.1
Saudi Arabia	1.4	15.5	24.5	0.6	94.7

In 2016, the value (in current US$) of exports of "fuel wood (excluding wood waste) and wood charcoal" (SITC group 245) increased by 5.3 percent (compared to 11.1 percent average growth rate from 2012-2016) to reach 1.9 bln US$ (see table 2), while imports decreased by 1.8 percent to reach 1.6 bln US$ (see table 3). Exports of this commodity accounted for 0.3 percent of world exports of SITC sections 2+4, and less than 0.1 percent of total world merchandise exports (see table 1). Cuba, Indonesia and Poland were the top exporters in 2016 (see table 2). They accounted for 26.9, 10.1 and 5.5 percent of world exports, respectively. Germany, Japan and Rep. of Korea were the top destinations, with respectively 8.4, 8.0 and 7.0 percent of world imports (see table 3).

The top 15 countries/areas accounted for 73.5 and 66.8 percent of total world exports and imports, respectively (see tables 2 and 3). In 2016, Cuba was the country/area with the highest value of net exports (+510.7 mln US$), followed by Indonesia (+190.9 mln US$). By MDG regions (see graph 2), the largest surpluses in this product group were recorded by Latin America and the Caribbean (+588.7 mln US$), South-eastern Asia (+259.9 mln US$) and Sub-Saharan Africa (+137.9 mln US$). The largest trade deficits were recorded by Developed Europe (-285.4 mln US$), Western Asia (-233.2 mln US$) and Developed Asia-Pacific (-129.4 mln US$).

Table 1: Imports (Imp.) and exports (Exp.), 2002-2016, in current US$

		2002	2003	2004	2005	2006	2007	2008	2009	2010	2011	2012	2013	2014	2015	2016
Values in Bln US$	Imp.	0.4	0.5	0.6	0.7	0.8	0.9	1.0	1.1	1.2	1.5	1.5	1.7	1.7	1.6	1.6
	Exp.	0.3	0.5	0.5	0.6	0.6	0.8	0.9	1.0	1.0	1.3	1.2	1.5	1.6	1.8	1.9
As a percentage of SITC section (%)	Imp.	0.2	0.2	0.2	0.2	0.2	0.1	0.1	0.2	0.2	0.2	0.2	0.2	0.2	0.2	0.2
	Exp.	0.2	0.2	0.2	0.1	0.1	0.1	0.1	0.2	0.2	0.1	0.1	0.2	0.2	0.3	0.3
As a percentage of world trade (%)	Imp.	0.0	0.0	0.0	0.0	0.0	0.0	0.0	0.0	0.0	0.0	0.0	0.0	0.0	0.0	0.0
	Exp.	0.0	0.0	0.0	0.0	0.0	0.0	0.0	0.0	0.0	0.0	0.0	0.0	0.0	0.0	0.0

Graph 1: Annual growth rates of exports, 2002–2016
(In percentage by year)

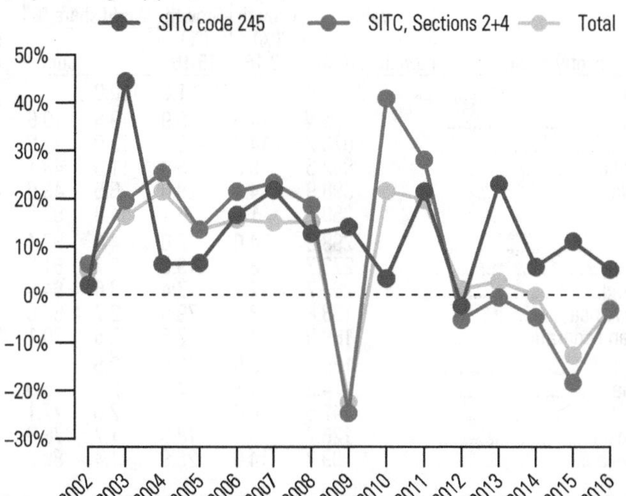

Table 2: Top exporting countries or areas in 2016

Country or area	Value (million US$)	Avg. Growth (%) 12-16	Growth (%) 15-16	World share %	Cum.
World	1895.5	11.1	5.3	100.0	
Cuba	*510.7*	72.4	68.6	26.9	26.9
Indonesia	191.1	15.9	2.8	10.1	37.0
Poland	103.5	7.3	15.8	5.5	42.5
China	102.5	23.2	-6.7	5.4	47.9
Ghana	90.9	179.4	11.6	4.8	52.7
Bosnia Herzegovina	58.6	5.7	12.8	3.1	55.8
Croatia	55.2	12.6	10.0	2.9	58.7
Belgium	41.0	6.0	12.2	2.2	60.9
Mexico	38.2	14.9	12.7	2.0	62.9
Viet Nam	*35.6*	60.1	8.9	1.9	64.8
Latvia	34.7	6.3	26.9	1.8	66.6
Slovenia	34.4	7.2	35.3	1.8	68.4
France	33.5	-1.3	-10.9	1.8	70.2
USA	33.4	8.2	-15.4	1.8	71.9
Paraguay	30.1	-3.5	-4.3	1.6	73.5

Graph 2: Trade Balance by MDG regions 2016
(Mln US$)

Imports — Exports — Trade balance

Developed Asia-Pacific
Developed Europe
Developed N. America
South-eastern Europe
CIS
Northern Africa
Sub-Saharan Africa
Latin Am, Caribbean
Eastern Asia
Southern Asia
South-eastern Asia
Western Asia
Oceania

-800 -600 -400 -200 0 200 400 600 800

Table 3: Top importing countries or areas in 2016

Country or area	Value (million US$)	Avg. Growth (%) 12-16	Growth (%) 15-16	World share %	Cum.
World	1605.3	1.3	-1.8	100.0	
Germany	135.0	-2.4	-9.8	8.4	8.4
Japan	127.9	-0.6	-4.7	8.0	16.4
Rep. of Korea	112.1	4.0	-1.2	7.0	23.4
Italy	106.5	-0.5	0.2	6.6	30.0
USA	80.7	12.3	-0.8	5.0	35.0
France	66.5	3.8	-9.8	4.1	39.2
Saudi Arabia	60.6	30.0	19.1	3.8	42.9
United Kingdom	60.4	7.6	-16.1	3.8	46.7
Belgium	57.7	-2.6	-1.9	3.6	50.3
Austria	54.9	-7.0	-6.9	3.4	53.7
China	46.1	-5.7	-8.2	2.9	56.6
Poland	42.4	8.2	24.3	2.6	59.2
Turkey	41.6	8.4	5.4	2.6	61.8
Greece	41.1	-9.6	-2.8	2.6	64.4
United Arab Emirates	38.5	7.7	-16.2	2.4	66.8

246 Wood in chips or particles and wood waste

In 2016, the value (in current US$) of exports of "wood in chips or particles and wood waste" (SITC group 246) increased by 1.8 percent (compared to 4.6 percent average growth rate from 2012-2016) to reach 7.3 bln US$ (see table 2), while imports increased by 0.3 percent to reach 8.6 bln US$ (see table 3). Exports of this commodity accounted for 1.1 percent of world exports of SITC sections 2+4, and less than 0.1 percent of total world merchandise exports (see table 1). Viet Nam, USA and Australia were the top exporters in 2016 (see table 2). They accounted for 19.6, 12.0 and 11.5 percent of world exports, respectively. Japan, China and United Kingdom were the top destinations, with respectively 25.5, 22.4 and 14.5 percent of world imports (see table 3).

The top 15 countries/areas accounted for 80.2 and 90.9 percent of total world exports and imports, respectively (see tables 2 and 3). In 2016, Viet Nam was the country/area with the highest value of net exports (+1.4 bln US$), followed by Australia (+837.9 mln US$). By MDG regions (see graph 2), the largest surpluses in this product group were recorded by South-eastern Asia (+1.9 bln US$), Developed North America (+1.1 bln US$) and Latin America and the Caribbean (+575.0 mln US$). The largest trade deficits were recorded by Eastern Asia (-2.3 bln US$), Developed Europe (-1.5 bln US$) and Developed Asia-Pacific (-1.3 bln US$).

Table 1: Imports (Imp.) and exports (Exp.), 2002-2016, in current US$

		2002	2003	2004	2005	2006	2007	2008	2009	2010	2011	2012	2013	2014	2015	2016
Values in Bln US$	Imp.	2.4	2.8	3.3	3.7	4.1	5.0	6.0	5.1	6.5	7.8	7.7	8.4	8.9	8.6	8.6
	Exp.	1.8	2.1	2.5	2.9	3.3	3.9	4.8	4.1	5.3	6.2	6.1	7.0	7.5	7.2	7.3
As a percentage of SITC section (%)	Imp.	1.0	1.0	0.9	0.9	0.8	0.8	0.8	0.9	0.8	0.8	0.8	0.9	1.0	1.2	1.2
	Exp.	0.8	0.8	0.8	0.8	0.7	0.7	0.7	0.8	0.8	0.7	0.7	0.8	0.9	1.1	1.1
As a percentage of world trade (%)	Imp.	0.0	0.0	0.0	0.0	0.0	0.0	0.0	0.0	0.0	0.0	0.0	0.0	0.0	0.1	0.1
	Exp.	0.0	0.0	0.0	0.0	0.0	0.0	0.0	0.0	0.0	0.0	0.0	0.0	0.0	0.0	0.0

Graph 1: Annual growth rates of exports, 2002–2016

(In percentage by year)

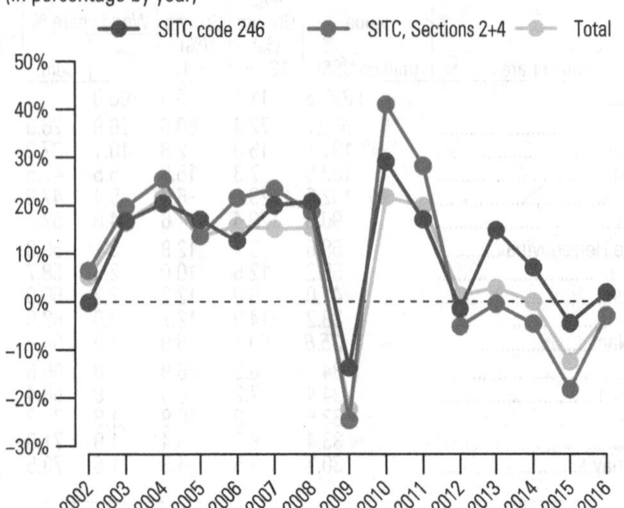

Table 2: Top exporting countries or areas in 2016

Country or area	Value (million US$)	Avg. Growth (%) 12-16	Growth (%) 15-16	World share %	Cum.
World	7304.0	4.6	1.8	100.0	
Viet Nam	1428.4	14.5	8.9	19.6	19.6
USA	876.2	14.2	-12.5	12.0	31.6
Australia	842.5	5.0	6.9	11.5	43.1
Canada	398.9	4.4	28.8	5.5	48.5
Chile	350.1	-1.4	26.1	4.8	53.3
Latvia	298.0	4.0	2.0	4.1	57.4
Germany	273.7	-8.1	-13.0	3.7	61.2
Thailand	263.7	-7.1	-7.4	3.6	64.8
South Africa	198.8	3.6	79.8	2.7	67.5
Russian Federation	189.9	-4.1	2.5	2.6	70.1
Austria	186.3	2.9	11.9	2.6	72.7
Estonia	174.3	11.9	7.7	2.4	75.0
Brazil	147.6	6.0	5.1	2.0	77.1
Indonesia	126.7	0.4	-18.8	1.7	78.8
Malaysia	99.3	14.0	25.9	1.4	80.2

Graph 2: Trade Balance by MDG regions 2016

(Bln US$)

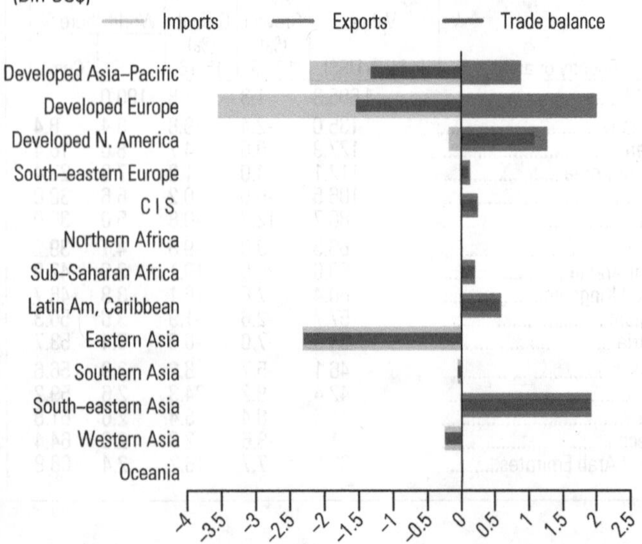

Table 3: Top importing countries or areas in 2016

Country or area	Value (million US$)	Avg. Growth (%) 12-16	Growth (%) 15-16	World share %	Cum.
World	8624.0	2.8	0.3	100.0	
Japan	2201.3	-3.7	-3.1	25.5	25.5
China	1934.6	9.8	13.7	22.4	48.0
United Kingdom	1252.0	42.9	3.7	14.5	62.5
Italy	369.6	0.7	-4.5	4.3	66.8
Denmark	329.0	-5.8	-9.3	3.8	70.6
Rep. of Korea	284.2	22.5	0.1	3.3	73.9
Belgium	234.5	-6.0	-1.9	2.7	76.6
Turkey	232.6	-6.4	-25.9	2.7	79.3
Germany	203.8	-0.7	-17.1	2.4	81.7
Austria	196.9	1.7	7.9	2.3	83.9
Sweden	133.4	-13.1	11.5	1.5	85.5
France	130.7	14.2	26.2	1.5	87.0
Portugal	125.3	20.4	17.5	1.5	88.5
Finland	113.7	-13.9	-9.0	1.3	89.8
Canada	93.6	-3.0	-21.7	1.1	90.9

In 2016, the value (in current US$) of exports of "wood in the rough or roughly squared" (SITC group 247) increased by 1.7 percent (compared to -1.5 percent average growth rate from 2012-2016) to reach 12.8 bln US$ (see table 2), while imports decreased by 3.0 percent to reach 16.3 bln US$ (see table 3). Exports of this commodity accounted for 2.0 percent of world exports of SITC sections 2+4, and 0.1 percent of total world merchandise exports (see table 1). USA, New Zealand and Russian Federation were the top exporters in 2016 (see table 2). They accounted for 16.4, 14.0 and 10.6 percent of world exports, respectively. China, India and Japan were the top destinations, with respectively 49.7, 7.8 and 5.1 percent of world imports (see table 3).

The top 15 countries/areas accounted for 78.9 and 89.7 percent of total world exports and imports, respectively (see tables 2 and 3). In 2016, USA was the country/area with the highest value of net exports (+2.0 bln US$), followed by New Zealand (+1.8 bln US$). By MDG regions (see graph 2), the largest surpluses in this product group were recorded by Developed North America (+2.3 bln US$), Developed Asia-Pacific (+1.4 bln US$) and Commonwealth of Independent States (+1.4 bln US$). The largest trade deficits were recorded by Eastern Asia (-8.7 bln US$), Southern Asia (-1.4 bln US$) and Developed Europe (-505.5 mln US$).

Table 1: Imports (Imp.) and exports (Exp.), 2002-2016, in current US$

		2002	2003	2004	2005	2006	2007	2008	2009	2010	2011	2012	2013	2014	2015	2016
Values in Bln US$	Imp.	9.6	10.6	12.4	13.2	14.3	17.6	16.6	11.5	15.1	18.8	17.1	20.1	22.7	16.8	16.3
	Exp.	7.5	7.6	9.1	10.6	11.3	14.5	13.2	9.4	12.0	14.6	13.6	14.8	15.2	12.6	12.8
As a percentage of SITC section (%)	Imp.	4.0	3.7	3.3	3.2	2.9	2.8	2.2	2.1	2.0	1.9	1.8	2.2	2.5	2.3	2.3
	Exp.	3.5	3.0	2.8	2.9	2.5	2.6	2.0	1.9	1.7	1.6	1.6	1.8	1.9	1.9	2.0
As a percentage of world trade (%)	Imp.	0.1	0.1	0.1	0.1	0.1	0.1	0.1	0.1	0.1	0.1	0.1	0.1	0.1	0.1	0.1
	Exp.	0.1	0.1	0.1	0.1	0.1	0.1	0.1	0.1	0.1	0.1	0.1	0.1	0.1	0.1	0.1

Graph 1: Annual growth rates of exports, 2002–2016
(In percentage by year)

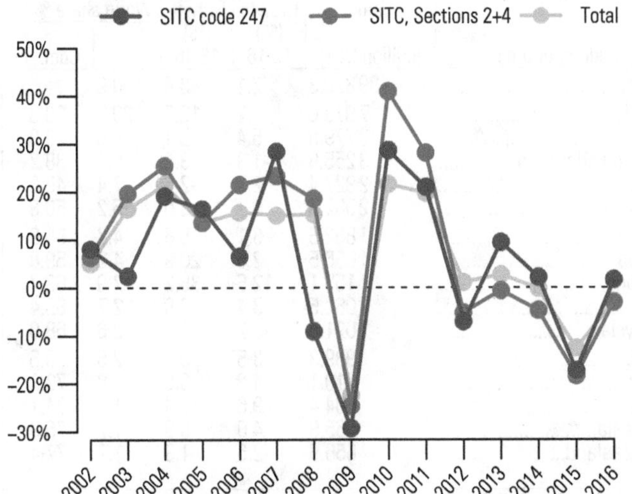

Table 2: Top exporting countries or areas in 2016

Country or area	Value (million US$)	Avg. Growth (%) 12-16	Growth (%) 15-16	World share %	Cum.
World	12772.1	-1.5	1.7	100.0	
USA	2097.8	1.2	2.5	16.4	16.4
New Zealand	1786.6	8.8	28.0	14.0	30.4
Russian Federation	1351.4	-3.1	0.9	10.6	41.0
Canada	679.0	-0.3	9.2	5.3	46.3
Uruguay	566.3	20.4	-0.8	4.4	50.7
Papua New Guinea	*541.1*	22.5	-24.8	4.2	55.0
Czechia	481.2	4.8	18.5	3.8	58.7
Equatorial Guinea	*440.3*	35.1	71.7	3.4	62.2
Australia	394.0	29.8	33.6	3.1	65.3
Malaysia	388.5	-8.2	-25.2	3.0	68.3
Germany	365.8	0.2	0.3	2.9	71.2
France	293.9	-2.7	-7.9	2.3	73.5
Solomon Isds	289.6	10.4	93.6	2.3	75.8
Slovenia	201.8	21.7	25.3	1.6	77.3
Norway	200.4	10.1	-15.7	1.6	78.9

Graph 2: Trade Balance by MDG regions 2016
(Bln US$)

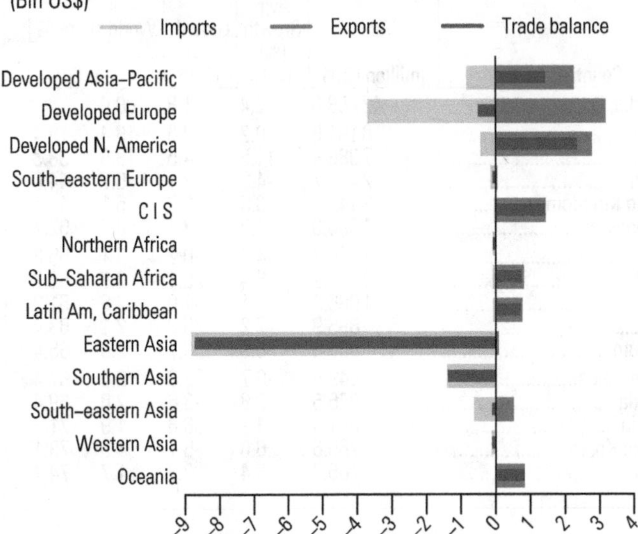

Table 3: Top importing countries or areas in 2016

Country or area	Value (million US$)	Avg. Growth (%) 12-16	Growth (%) 15-16	World share %	Cum.
World	16280.2	-1.2	-3.0	100.0	
China	8085.2	2.8	0.3	49.7	49.7
India	1277.7	-10.7	-18.3	7.8	57.5
Japan	824.3	-5.4	3.3	5.1	62.6
Austria	810.5	2.2	23.6	5.0	67.6
Germany	621.6	0.8	-6.7	3.8	71.4
Rep. of Korea	578.0	-3.1	-2.7	3.6	74.9
Viet Nam	*539.4*	13.6	5.1	3.3	78.2
Sweden	373.9	-7.6	-9.4	2.3	80.5
Canada	291.6	-0.4	-12.4	1.8	82.3
Finland	263.7	-9.0	-4.0	1.6	83.9
Italy	262.6	-3.0	2.4	1.6	85.6
Belgium	230.6	-1.1	4.2	1.4	87.0
Portugal	161.1	-1.1	5.2	1.0	88.0
Czechia	149.4	-7.0	-17.0	0.9	88.9
USA	137.2	-4.4	-12.3	0.8	89.7

Source: UN Comtrade

248 Wood, simply worked, and railway sleepers of wood

In 2016, the value (in current US$) of exports of "wood, simply worked, and railway sleepers of wood" (SITC group 248) increased by 3.4 percent (compared to 2.1 percent average growth rate from 2012-2016) to reach 39.3 bln US$ (see table 2), while imports increased by 1.8 percent to reach 42.3 bln US$ (see table 3). Exports of this commodity accounted for 6.2 percent of world exports of SITC sections 2+4, and 0.2 percent of total world merchandise exports (see table 1). Canada, USA and Russian Federation were the top exporters in 2016 (see table 2). They accounted for 20.3, 9.6 and 8.3 percent of world exports, respectively. China, USA and Japan were the top destinations, with respectively 19.4, 18.9 and 5.7 percent of world imports (see table 3).

The top 15 countries/areas accounted for 77.4 and 74.7 percent of total world exports and imports, respectively (see tables 2 and 3). In 2016, Canada was the country/area with the highest value of net exports (+7.1 bln US$), followed by Russian Federation (+3.2 bln US$). By MDG regions (see graph 2), the largest surpluses in this product group were recorded by Developed North America (+2.9 bln US$), Commonwealth of Independent States (+2.8 bln US$) and Developed Europe (+1.8 bln US$). The largest trade deficits were recorded by Eastern Asia (-8.6 bln US$), Developed Asia-Pacific (-2.3 bln US$) and Northern Africa (-1.8 bln US$).

Table 1: Imports (Imp.) and exports (Exp.), 2002-2016, in current US$

		2002	2003	2004	2005	2006	2007	2008	2009	2010	2011	2012	2013	2014	2015	2016
Values in Bln US$	Imp.	28.1	30.4	37.0	38.5	40.5	43.9	38.4	28.8	35.1	39.3	38.4	42.2	46.1	41.5	42.3
	Exp.	25.4	27.5	33.6	35.4	38.3	41.8	36.2	27.9	33.6	36.8	36.1	40.2	43.4	38.1	39.3
As a percentage of SITC section (%)	Imp.	11.6	10.5	9.8	9.2	8.2	7.1	5.0	5.3	4.6	4.0	4.2	4.6	5.2	5.7	6.1
	Exp.	11.8	10.7	10.4	9.6	8.6	7.6	5.5	5.6	4.8	4.1	4.3	4.8	5.4	5.8	6.2
As a percentage of world trade (%)	Imp.	0.4	0.4	0.4	0.4	0.3	0.3	0.2	0.2	0.2	0.2	0.2	0.2	0.2	0.3	0.3
	Exp.	0.4	0.4	0.4	0.3	0.3	0.3	0.2	0.2	0.2	0.2	0.2	0.2	0.2	0.2	0.2

Graph 1: Annual growth rates of exports, 2002–2016
(In percentage by year)

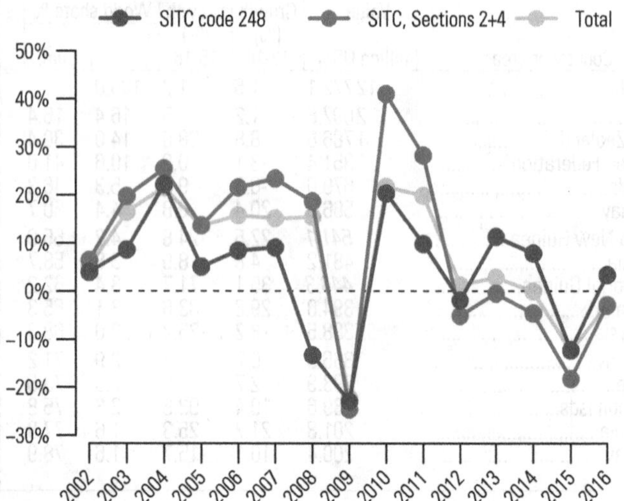

Table 2: Top exporting countries or areas in 2016

Country or area	Value (million US$)	Avg. Growth (%) 12-16	Growth (%) 15-16	World share %	Cum.
World	39329.3	2.1	3.4	100.0	
Canada	7973.0	7.2	12.5	20.3	20.3
USA	3779.8	5.4	5.1	9.6	29.9
Russian Federation	3255.6	-1.3	3.5	8.3	38.2
Sweden	2927.4	-2.7	-2.6	7.4	45.6
Germany	2062.5	0.1	6.0	5.2	50.8
Finland	1852.5	3.1	5.6	4.7	55.6
Austria	1655.5	2.5	20.9	4.2	59.8
Thailand	1155.1	12.5	35.2	2.9	62.7
Chile	1062.5	3.4	-2.9	2.7	65.4
Malaysia	1021.5	-0.2	-1.4	2.6	68.0
Brazil	989.3	3.5	5.3	2.5	70.5
Latvia	710.1	4.8	3.5	1.8	72.3
China	684.4	-9.6	-10.4	1.7	74.1
Indonesia	665.9	4.0	0.9	1.7	75.8
New Zealand	656.9	-2.5	1.3	1.7	77.4

Graph 2: Trade Balance by MDG regions 2016
(Bln US$)

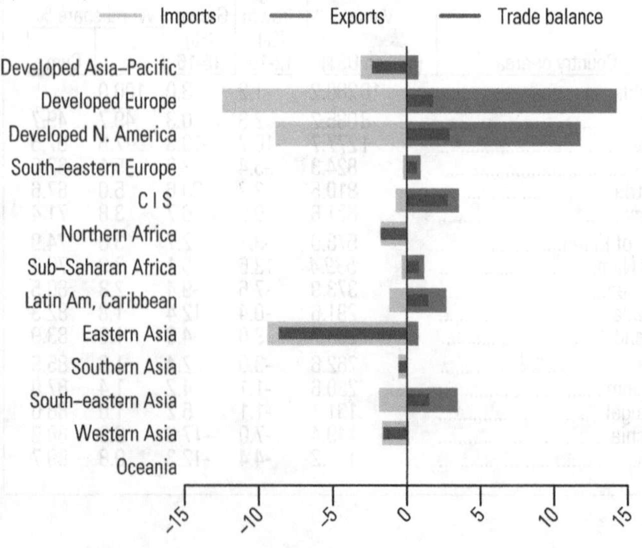

Table 3: Top importing countries or areas in 2016

Country or area	Value (million US$)	Avg. Growth (%) 12-16	Growth (%) 15-16	World share %	Cum.
World	42258.0	2.4	1.8	100.0	
China	8191.6	10.2	8.5	19.4	19.4
USA	7988.4	11.5	14.5	18.9	38.3
Japan	2404.7	-4.3	2.1	5.7	44.0
United Kingdom	2143.7	3.3	-5.2	5.1	49.1
Germany	1560.0	-1.3	2.4	3.7	52.7
Italy	1296.7	-4.3	-0.2	3.1	55.8
Viet Nam	*1205.7*	18.4	5.1	2.9	58.7
France	1085.2	-5.1	-1.0	2.6	61.2
Egypt	895.9	-7.2	-25.8	2.1	63.4
Belgium	863.8	-0.9	3.7	2.0	65.4
Netherlands	849.5	-6.7	-22.0	2.0	67.4
Canada	826.5	-2.8	-3.6	2.0	69.4
Austria	801.4	4.2	36.6	1.9	71.3
Rep. of Korea	765.6	6.0	-5.1	1.8	73.1
Mexico	705.7	5.4	-0.3	1.7	74.7

In 2016, the value (in current US$) of exports of "pulp and waste paper" (SITC group 251) decreased by less than 0.1 percent (compared to -1.0 percent average growth rate from 2012-2016) to reach 42.7 bln US$ (see table 2), while imports decreased by 3.2 percent to reach 47.7 bln US$ (see table 3). Exports of this commodity accounted for 6.7 percent of world exports of SITC sections 2+4, and 0.3 percent of total world merchandise exports (see table 1). USA, Canada and Brazil were the top exporters in 2016 (see table 2). They accounted for 19.8, 13.5 and 13.1 percent of world exports, respectively. China, Germany and USA were the top destinations, with respectively 36.1, 7.9 and 6.6 percent of world imports (see table 3).

The top 15 countries/areas accounted for 84.7 and 82.6 percent of total world exports and imports, respectively (see tables 2 and 3). In 2016, Canada was the country/area with the highest value of net exports (+5.4 bln US$), followed by USA (+5.3 bln US$). By MDG regions (see graph 2), the largest surpluses in this product group were recorded by Developed North America (+10.7 bln US$), Latin America and the Caribbean (+6.4 bln US$) and Commonwealth of Independent States (+991.4 mln US$). The largest trade deficits were recorded by Eastern Asia (-19.0 bln US$), Southern Asia (-1.9 bln US$) and Developed Europe (-1.4 bln US$).

Table 1: Imports (Imp.) and exports (Exp.), 2002-2016, in current US$

		2002	2003	2004	2005	2006	2007	2008	2009	2010	2011	2012	2013	2014	2015	2016
Values in Bln US$	Imp.	21.3	24.2	28.5	30.3	33.3	40.6	46.8	34.1	49.3	57.2	49.6	50.5	50.6	49.3	47.7
	Exp.	18.8	21.9	24.8	26.2	30.1	37.1	41.1	30.9	43.9	49.7	44.3	45.4	45.4	42.7	42.7
As a percentage of SITC section (%)	Imp.	8.8	8.4	7.6	7.3	6.7	6.6	6.1	6.3	6.5	5.8	5.4	5.5	5.7	6.7	6.8
	Exp.	8.8	8.5	7.7	7.1	6.7	6.7	6.3	6.2	6.3	5.6	5.2	5.4	5.6	6.5	6.7
As a percentage of world trade (%)	Imp.	0.3	0.3	0.3	0.3	0.3	0.3	0.3	0.3	0.3	0.3	0.3	0.3	0.3	0.3	0.3
	Exp.	0.3	0.3	0.3	0.3	0.3	0.3	0.3	0.2	0.3	0.3	0.2	0.2	0.2	0.3	0.3

Graph 1: Annual growth rates of exports, 2002–2016
(In percentage by year)

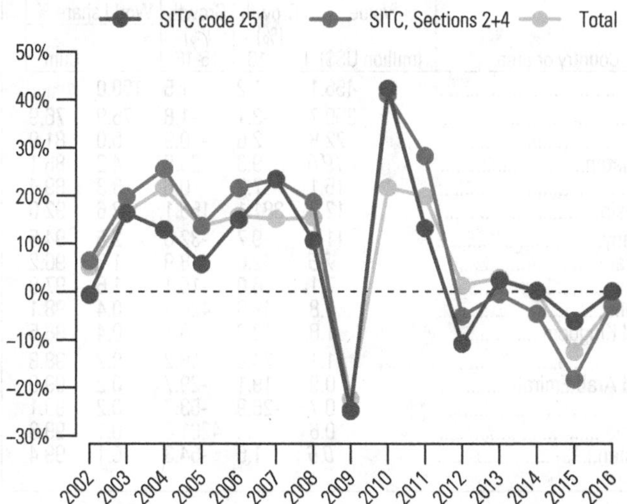

Table 2: Top exporting countries or areas in 2016

Country or area	Value (million US$)	Avg. Growth (%) 12-16	Growth (%) 15-16	World share %	Cum.
World	42668.8	-0.9	0.0	100.0	
USA	8442.6	-2.4	-3.0	19.8	19.8
Canada	5747.3	-4.0	-8.7	13.5	33.3
Brazil	5575.3	4.3	-0.5	13.1	46.3
Chile	2390.6	-1.3	-7.2	5.6	51.9
Sweden	2117.5	-4.7	-8.2	5.0	56.9
Finland	1956.9	2.8	-2.3	4.6	61.5
Netherlands	1918.9	7.1	112.2	4.5	66.0
Indonesia	1562.3	0.2	-9.6	3.7	69.6
Germany	1256.5	-2.9	-2.8	2.9	72.6
Russian Federation	1084.7	-2.8	-5.7	2.5	75.1
Japan	946.0	-4.6	-3.6	2.2	77.3
France	849.6	-4.1	1.3	2.0	79.3
South Africa	835.0	5.0	9.9	2.0	81.3
United Kingdom	750.3	-3.1	-2.0	1.8	83.0
Belgium	714.2	-7.0	-4.9	1.7	84.7

Graph 2: Trade Balance by MDG regions 2016
(Bln US$)

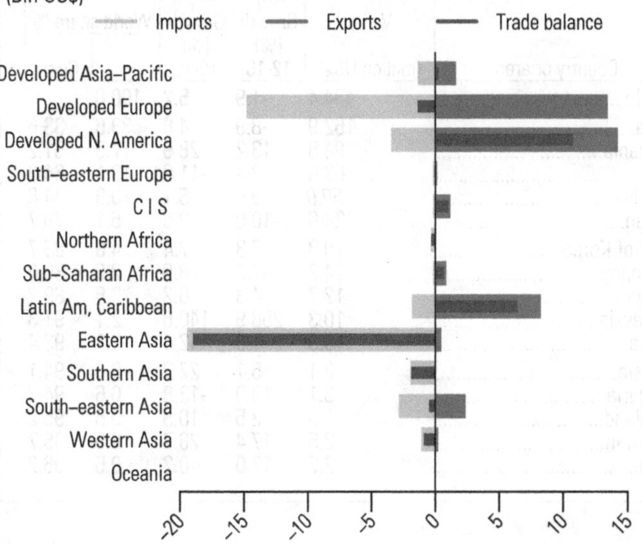

Table 3: Top importing countries or areas in 2016

Country or area	Value (million US$)	Avg. Growth (%) 12-16	Growth (%) 15-16	World share %	Cum.
World	47731.1	-1.0	-3.2	100.0	
China	17229.6	0.0	-4.5	36.1	36.1
Germany	3787.1	-3.9	-4.0	7.9	44.0
USA	3140.8	-2.7	-8.5	6.6	50.6
Italy	2011.1	-2.3	-11.7	4.2	54.8
Netherlands	2003.4	4.3	79.5	4.2	59.0
India	1622.3	6.0	0.8	3.4	62.4
Rep. of Korea	1575.9	-4.2	-13.1	3.3	65.7
Indonesia	1346.8	-3.5	5.0	2.8	68.5
France	1328.0	-2.9	-11.0	2.8	71.3
Japan	1196.2	-4.7	-10.3	2.5	73.8
Mexico	979.5	0.7	1.5	2.1	75.9
Spain	918.1	0.8	-5.3	1.9	77.8
Austria	852.1	0.8	2.9	1.8	79.6
Turkey	742.9	7.3	0.7	1.6	81.2
United Kingdom	701.6	-4.6	-18.1	1.5	82.6

In 2016, the value (in current US$) of exports of "silk" (SITC group 261) decreased by 1.5 percent (compared to -1.2 percent average growth rate from 2012-2016) to reach 456.1 mln US$ (see table 2), while imports increased by 5.2 percent to reach 484.4 mln US$ (see table 3). Exports of this commodity accounted for 0.1 percent of world exports of SITC sections 2+4, and less than 0.1 percent of total world merchandise exports (see table 1). China, Italy and Uzbekistan were the top exporters in 2016 (see table 2). They accounted for 76.9, 5.0 and 4.2 percent of world exports, respectively. India, Romania and Italy were the top destinations, with respectively 33.6, 17.5 and 13.1 percent of world imports (see table 3).

The top 15 countries/areas accounted for 99.4 and 96.2 percent of total world exports and imports, respectively (see tables 2 and 3). In 2016, China was the country/area with the highest value of net exports (+340.7 mln US$), followed by Uzbekistan (+19.0 mln US$). By MDG regions (see graph 2), the largest surpluses in this product group were recorded by Eastern Asia (+322.0 mln US$), Commonwealth of Independent States (+19.8 mln US$) and Oceania (less than 0.1 mln US$). The largest trade deficits were recorded by Southern Asia (-152.6 mln US$), South-eastern Europe (-80.6 mln US$) and Developed Europe (-59.1 mln US$).

Table 1: Imports (Imp.) and exports (Exp.), 2002-2016, in current US$

		2002	2003	2004	2005	2006	2007	2008	2009	2010	2011	2012	2013	2014	2015	2016
Values in Mln US$	Imp.	399.4	360.2	370.2	453.8	490.7	463.0	477.3	374.2	455.7	537.3	523.6	536.0	475.6	460.5	484.4
	Exp.	334.4	301.6	314.6	349.9	340.4	453.4	437.5	318.0	476.0	491.1	478.5	516.4	487.4	463.2	456.1
As a percentage of SITC section (%)	Imp.	0.2	0.1	0.1	0.1	0.1	0.1	0.1	0.1	0.1	0.1	0.1	0.1	0.1	0.1	0.1
	Exp.	0.2	0.1	0.1	0.1	0.1	0.1	0.1	0.1	0.1	0.1	0.1	0.1	0.1	0.1	0.1
As a percentage of world trade (%)	Imp.	0.0	0.0	0.0	0.0	0.0	0.0	0.0	0.0	0.0	0.0	0.0	0.0	0.0	0.0	0.0
	Exp.	0.0	0.0	0.0	0.0	0.0	0.0	0.0	0.0	0.0	0.0	0.0	0.0	0.0	0.0	0.0

Graph 1: Annual growth rates of exports, 2002–2016

(In percentage by year)

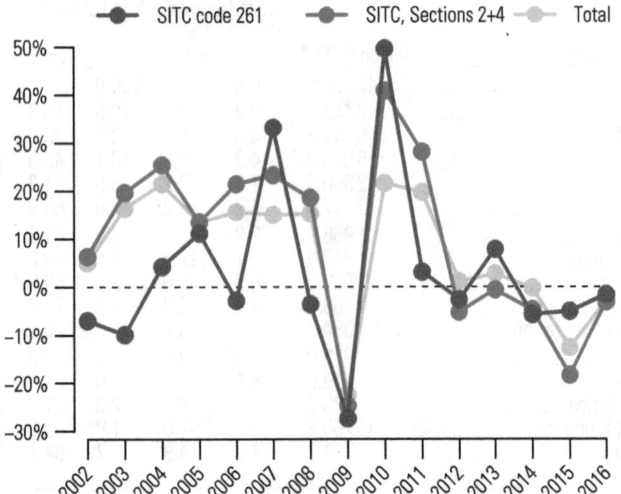

Table 2: Top exporting countries or areas in 2016

Country or area	Value (million US$)	Avg. Growth (%) 12-16	Growth (%) 15-16	World share %	Cum.
World	456.1	-1.2	-1.5	100.0	
China	350.7	-3.1	-1.8	76.9	76.9
Italy	22.8	2.6	-10.9	5.0	81.9
Uzbekistan	*19.0*	9.3	23.8	4.2	86.1
India	15.1	7.2	0.6	3.3	89.4
Malaysia	12.0	381.1	155.1	2.6	92.0
Germany	11.4	-9.7	-32.6	2.5	94.5
Viet Nam	*7.6*	42.6	8.9	1.7	96.2
Romania	7.1	6.0	-15.1	1.6	97.8
Belgium	1.8	49.9	428.4	0.4	98.1
United Kingdom	1.8	10.2	16.1	0.4	98.5
Brazil	1.1	24.8	46.2	0.2	98.8
United Arab Emirates	0.9	19.1	-29.7	0.2	99.0
USA	0.7	-26.9	-53.7	0.2	99.1
Slovenia	0.6	...	4201.8	0.1	99.3
Tajikistan	*0.6*	1.6	-54.3	0.1	99.4

Graph 2: Trade Balance by MDG regions 2016

(Mln US$)

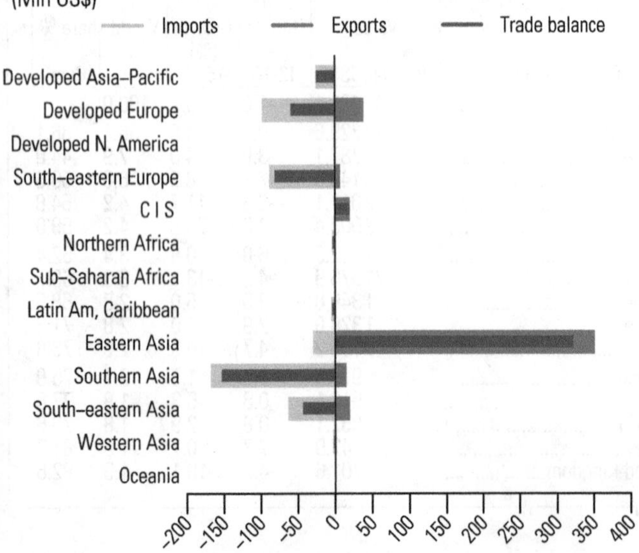

Table 3: Top importing countries or areas in 2016

Country or area	Value (million US$)	Avg. Growth (%) 12-16	Growth (%) 15-16	World share %	Cum.
World	484.4	-1.9	5.2	100.0	
India	162.9	-8.9	4.6	33.6	33.6
Romania	84.8	13.2	28.9	17.5	51.2
Italy	63.6	2.4	-11.8	13.1	64.3
Viet Nam	*50.0*	0.6	5.1	10.3	74.6
Japan	24.6	-10.0	-9.6	5.1	79.7
Rep. of Korea	19.3	-7.3	7.4	4.0	83.7
Germany	14.2	-3.2	-8.9	2.9	86.6
France	12.7	4.3	-6.2	2.6	89.2
Malaysia	10.3	268.9	140.6	2.1	91.3
China	10.0	-1.3	42.4	2.1	93.4
Tunisia	3.1	5.1	22.2	0.6	94.1
Bulgaria	3.1	13.9	-13.8	0.6	94.7
Thailand	2.6	2.5	10.8	0.5	95.2
Pakistan	2.5	17.4	28.7	0.5	95.7
Peru	2.2	17.0	-0.2	0.5	96.2

In 2016, the value (in current US$) of exports of "cotton" (SITC group 263) decreased by 5.1 percent (compared to -13.5 percent average growth rate from 2012-2016) to reach 13.0 bln US$ (see table 2), while imports decreased by 7.9 percent to reach 12.3 bln US$ (see table 3). Exports of this commodity accounted for 2.0 percent of world exports of SITC sections 2+4, and 0.1 percent of total world merchandise exports (see table 1). USA, Uzbekistan and India were the top exporters in 2016 (see table 2). They accounted for 31.0, 12.5 and 11.2 percent of world exports, respectively. Bangladesh, China and Viet Nam were the top destinations, with respectively 15.7, 14.4 and 13.8 percent of world imports (see table 3).

The top 15 countries/areas accounted for 89.9 and 90.9 percent of total world exports and imports, respectively (see tables 2 and 3). In 2016, USA was the country/area with the highest value of net exports (+4.0 bln US$), followed by Uzbekistan (+1.6 bln US$). By MDG regions (see graph 2), the largest surpluses in this product group were recorded by Developed North America (+4.0 bln US$), Commonwealth of Independent States (+1.8 bln US$) and Sub-Saharan Africa (+1.5 bln US$). The largest trade deficits were recorded by South-eastern Asia (-3.3 bln US$), Eastern Asia (-2.4 bln US$) and Southern Asia (-1.9 bln US$).

Table 1: Imports (Imp.) and exports (Exp.), 2002-2016, in current US$

		2002	2003	2004	2005	2006	2007	2008	2009	2010	2011	2012	2013	2014	2015	2016
Values in Bln US$	Imp.	6.9	8.7	12.0	10.8	12.7	12.5	14.1	9.8	17.2	25.8	24.1	21.3	16.5	13.4	12.3
	Exp.	7.1	9.9	12.2	10.4	11.8	12.3	12.7	10.1	17.3	23.3	23.2	21.1	16.9	13.7	13.0
As a percentage of SITC section (%)	Imp.	2.8	3.0	3.2	2.6	2.6	2.0	1.8	1.8	2.3	2.6	2.6	2.3	1.9	1.8	1.8
	Exp.	3.3	3.9	3.8	2.8	2.6	2.2	1.9	2.0	2.5	2.6	2.7	2.5	2.1	2.1	2.0
As a percentage of world trade (%)	Imp.	0.1	0.1	0.1	0.1	0.1	0.1	0.1	0.1	0.1	0.1	0.1	0.1	0.1	0.1	0.1
	Exp.	0.1	0.1	0.1	0.1	0.1	0.1	0.1	0.1	0.1	0.1	0.1	0.1	0.1	0.1	0.1

Graph 1: Annual growth rates of exports, 2002–2016

(In percentage by year)

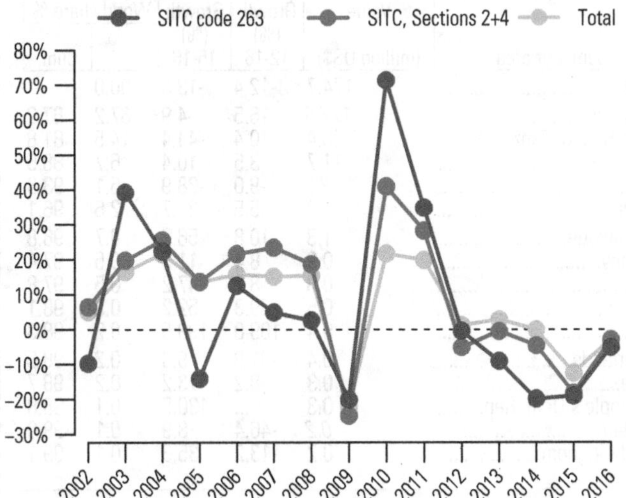

Table 2: Top exporting countries or areas in 2016

Country or area	Value (million US$)	Avg. Growth (%) 12-16	Growth (%) 15-16	World share %	Cum.
World	12992.6	-13.5	-5.1	100.0	
USA	4031.0	-10.7	0.9	31.0	31.0
Uzbekistan	*1624.9*	-8.1	-23.3	12.5	43.5
India	1451.4	-21.2	-25.2	11.2	54.7
Brazil	1228.5	-12.8	-5.3	9.5	64.2
Australia	1207.6	-18.4	48.4	9.3	73.5
Burkina Faso	424.4	9.6	42.8	3.3	76.7
Greece	349.7	-11.4	5.4	2.7	79.4
Mali	264.7	-9.0	12.5	2.0	81.4
Côte d'Ivoire	*212.2*	-1.3	-10.0	1.6	83.1
Turkey	197.1	-2.8	29.1	1.5	84.6
Benin	176.5	4.4	-32.8	1.4	86.0
Turkmenistan	*152.1*	19.5	21.8	1.2	87.1
Cameroon	148.1	0.7	-10.7	1.1	88.3
Spain	123.4	-0.1	64.6	0.9	89.2
Egypt	93.7	-17.0	4.4	0.7	89.9

Graph 2: Trade Balance by MDG regions 2016

(Bln US$)

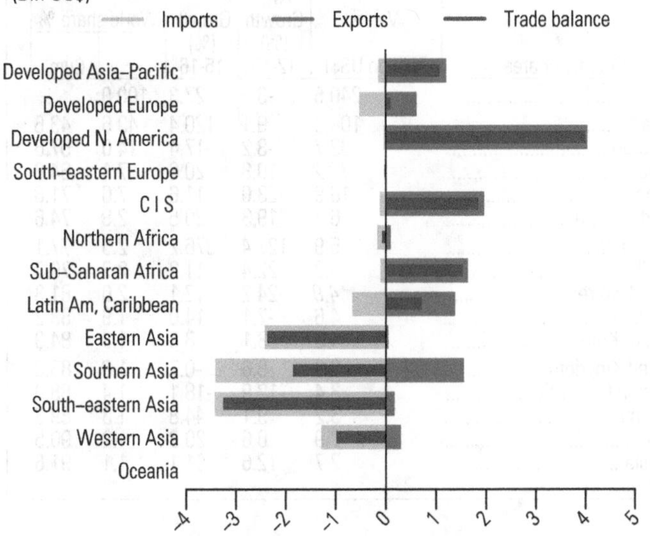

Table 3: Top importing countries or areas in 2016

Country or area	Value (million US$)	Avg. Growth (%) 12-16	Growth (%) 15-16	World share %	Cum.
World	12312.6	-15.5	-7.9	100.0	
Bangladesh	*1935.1*	-2.9	-14.2	15.7	15.7
China	1778.3	-38.0	-34.6	14.4	30.2
Viet Nam	*1701.3*	17.9	5.1	13.8	44.0
Turkey	1247.1	-0.6	0.3	10.1	54.1
Indonesia	1087.9	-5.0	-0.1	8.8	62.9
India	885.3	17.0	126.7	7.2	70.1
Pakistan	582.8	0.8	6.7	4.7	74.9
Thailand	444.5	-14.4	-19.4	3.6	78.5
Rep. of Korea	380.5	-13.8	-21.6	3.1	81.6
Mexico	356.7	-6.2	3.8	2.9	84.5
Other Asia, nes	239.2	-13.0	-22.1	1.9	86.4
Malaysia	160.2	-28.9	-0.6	1.3	87.7
Egypt	140.8	33.0	-3.3	1.1	88.8
Japan	139.7	-9.5	-8.9	1.1	90.0
Germany	110.3	-9.4	-7.9	0.9	90.9

264 Jute, other textile bast fibres, nes, not spun; tow and waste

In 2016, the value (in current US$) of exports of "jute, other textile bast fibres, nes, not spun; tow and waste" (SITC group 264) decreased by 13.8 percent (compared to -12.4 percent average growth rate from 2012-2016) to reach 174.7 mln US$ (see table 2), while imports increased by 27.3 percent to reach 240.5 mln US$ (see table 3). Exports of this commodity accounted for less than 0.1 percent of world exports of SITC sections 2+4, and less than 0.1 percent of total world merchandise exports (see table 1). Bangladesh, United Rep. of Tanzania and India were the top exporters in 2016 (see table 2). They accounted for 67.2, 14.5 and 6.7 percent of world exports, respectively. India, Pakistan and Nepal were the top destinations, with respectively 43.6, 14.0 and 7.1 percent of world imports (see table 3).

The top 15 countries/areas accounted for 99.1 and 91.6 percent of total world exports and imports, respectively (see tables 2 and 3). In 2016, Bangladesh was the country/area with the highest value of net exports (+117.4 mln US$), followed by United Rep. of Tanzania (+25.2 mln US$). By MDG regions (see graph 2), the largest surplus in this product group was recorded solely by Sub-Saharan Africa (+20.4 mln US$). The largest trade deficits were recorded by Southern Asia (-26.8 mln US$), Eastern Asia (-20.8 mln US$) and Developed Europe (-10.5 mln US$).

Table 1: Imports (Imp.) and exports (Exp.), 2002-2016, in current US$

		2002	2003	2004	2005	2006	2007	2008	2009	2010	2011	2012	2013	2014	2015	2016
Values in Mln US$	Imp.	115.0	101.6	100.9	121.0	160.9	186.7	211.7	207.4	299.3	351.5	277.3	200.8	171.8	188.9	240.5
	Exp.	62.4	61.5	103.2	139.2	155.3	228.2	206.7	204.4	351.9	361.8	296.5	203.7	128.4	202.7	174.7
As a percentage of SITC section (%)	Imp.	0.0	0.0	0.0	0.0	0.0	0.0	0.0	0.0	0.0	0.0	0.0	0.0	0.0	0.0	0.0
	Exp.	0.0	0.0	0.0	0.0	0.0	0.0	0.0	0.0	0.1	0.0	0.0	0.0	0.0	0.0	0.0
As a percentage of world trade (%)	Imp.	0.0	0.0	0.0	0.0	0.0	0.0	0.0	0.0	0.0	0.0	0.0	0.0	0.0	0.0	0.0
	Exp.	0.0	0.0	0.0	0.0	0.0	0.0	0.0	0.0	0.0	0.0	0.0	0.0	0.0	0.0	0.0

Graph 1: Annual growth rates of exports, 2002–2016
(In percentage by year)

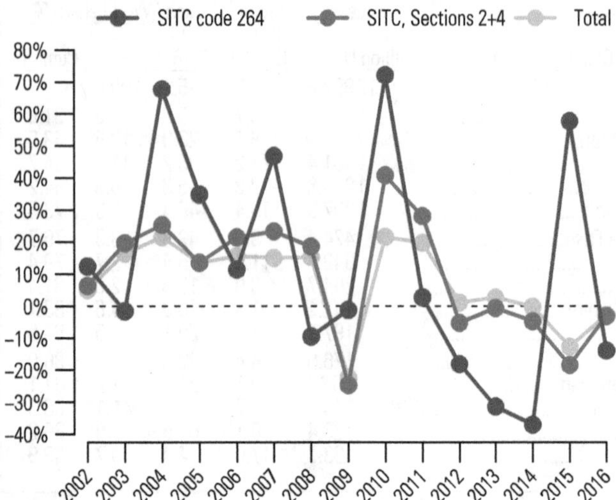

Table 2: Top exporting countries or areas in 2016

Country or area	Value (million US$)	Avg. Growth (%) 12-16	Growth (%) 15-16	World share %	Cum.
World	174.7	-12.4	-13.8	100.0	
Bangladesh	*117.5*	-16.5	-4.9	67.2	67.2
United Rep. of Tanzania	25.4	10.4	-44.4	14.5	81.8
India	11.7	3.5	10.4	6.7	88.5
Kenya	*9.0*	-9.0	-28.9	5.1	93.6
Belgium	4.3	5.5	23.7	2.5	96.1
Mozambique	1.3	10.8	56.2	0.7	96.8
Germany	0.9	8.4	11.3	0.5	97.4
USA	0.8	-8.2	47.2	0.5	97.8
Spain	0.5	39.3	-52.2	0.3	98.1
China	0.4	109.0	199.5	0.2	98.3
Netherlands	0.4	-31.9	9.3	0.2	98.5
France	0.3	-8.2	-13.2	0.2	98.7
Lao People's Dem. Rep.	0.3	...	130.5	0.1	98.8
Viet Nam	*0.2*	-46.4	8.9	0.1	99.0
United Kingdom	0.2	-13.2	35.3	0.1	99.1

Graph 2: Trade Balance by MDG regions 2016
(Mln US$)

Imports
Exports
Trade balance

Developed Asia-Pacific
Developed Europe
Developed N. America
South-eastern Europe
C I S
Northern Africa
Sub-Saharan Africa
Latin Am, Caribbean
Eastern Asia
Southern Asia
South-eastern Asia
Western Asia
Oceania

-200 -150 -100 -50 0 50 100 150

Table 3: Top importing countries or areas in 2016

Country or area	Value (million US$)	Avg. Growth (%) 12-16	Growth (%) 15-16	World share %	Cum.
World	240.5	-3.5	27.3	100.0	
India	104.9	9.1	120.4	43.6	43.6
Pakistan	33.7	-8.2	-17.4	14.0	57.6
Nepal	*17.2*	-10.8	-20.6	7.1	64.8
China	16.9	-23.0	11.6	7.0	71.8
Saudi Arabia	6.7	19.3	30.5	2.8	74.6
Nigeria	5.9	127.4	376.2	2.5	77.1
Brazil	5.2	22.4	-11.2	2.2	79.3
Côte d'Ivoire	*4.9*	-24.2	-12.1	2.0	81.3
Germany	4.6	-2.1	14.0	1.9	83.2
Rep. of Korea	4.3	-3.1	8.8	1.8	84.9
United Kingdom	3.9	8.6	-0.7	1.6	86.6
Russian Federation	3.4	-12.9	-18.1	1.4	88.0
Ethiopia	3.2	9.1	44.8	1.3	89.3
USA	2.9	0.6	20.3	1.2	90.5
Tunisia	2.7	12.6	61.1	1.1	91.6

In 2016, the value (in current US$) of exports of "vegetable textile fibres (other than cotton or jute) not spun; waste" (SITC group 265) increased by 5.5 percent (compared to 9.5 percent average growth rate from 2012-2016) to reach 1.3 bln US$ (see table 2), while imports decreased by 2.1 percent to reach 1.2 bln US$ (see table 3). Exports of this commodity accounted for 0.2 percent of world exports of SITC sections 2+4, and less than 0.1 percent of total world merchandise exports (see table 1). France, India and Belgium were the top exporters in 2016 (see table 2). They accounted for 30.4, 17.6 and 15.6 percent of world exports, respectively. China, Belgium and USA were the top destinations, with respectively 50.7, 8.0 and 5.0 percent of world imports (see table 3).

The top 15 countries/areas accounted for 94.7 and 87.8 percent of total world exports and imports, respectively (see tables 2 and 3). In 2016, France was the country/area with the highest value of net exports (+371.2 mln US$), followed by India (+191.0 mln US$). By MDG regions (see graph 2), the largest surpluses in this product group were recorded by Developed Europe (+335.2 mln US$), Southern Asia (+318.5 mln US$) and South-eastern Asia (+67.8 mln US$). The largest trade deficits were recorded by Eastern Asia (-615.6 mln US$), Developed North America (-54.5 mln US$) and Developed Asia-Pacific (-26.8 mln US$).

Table 1: Imports (Imp.) and exports (Exp.), 2002-2016, in current US$

		2002	2003	2004	2005	2006	2007	2008	2009	2010	2011	2012	2013	2014	2015	2016
Values in Bln US$	Imp.	0.5	0.7	0.8	0.7	0.7	0.8	0.7	0.6	0.8	1.0	0.9	1.0	1.3	1.3	1.2
	Exp.	0.5	0.7	0.8	0.7	0.7	0.7	0.6	0.6	0.8	0.9	0.9	1.0	1.3	1.2	1.3
As a percentage of SITC section (%)	Imp.	0.2	0.3	0.2	0.2	0.1	0.1	0.1	0.1	0.1	0.1	0.1	0.1	0.1	0.2	0.2
	Exp.	0.2	0.3	0.2	0.2	0.2	0.1	0.1	0.1	0.1	0.1	0.1	0.1	0.2	0.2	0.2
As a percentage of world trade (%)	Imp.	0.0	0.0	0.0	0.0	0.0	0.0	0.0	0.0	0.0	0.0	0.0	0.0	0.0	0.0	0.0
	Exp.	0.0	0.0	0.0	0.0	0.0	0.0	0.0	0.0	0.0	0.0	0.0	0.0	0.0	0.0	0.0

Graph 1: Annual growth rates of exports, 2002–2016
(In percentage by year)

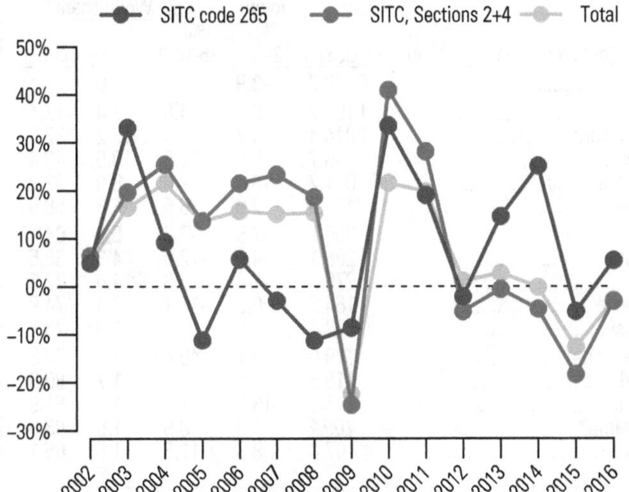

Table 2: Top exporting countries or areas in 2016

Country or area	Value (million US$)	Avg. Growth (%) 12-16	Growth (%) 15-16	World share %	Cum.
World	1293.4	9.5	5.5	100.0	
France	393.3	12.2	9.4	30.4	30.4
India	228.2	18.7	37.7	17.6	48.1
Belgium	201.6	6.7	-15.1	15.6	63.6
Sri Lanka	135.5	4.8	14.6	10.5	74.1
Brazil	45.9	8.8	-14.6	3.5	77.7
Viet Nam	*37.2*	5.9	8.9	2.9	80.5
Philippines	33.0	27.9	30.2	2.6	83.1
Kenya	*26.4*	1.9	11.6	2.0	85.1
Belarus	25.4	10.4	-32.9	2.0	87.1
Ecuador	25.1	10.3	70.2	1.9	89.1
Lithuania	17.9	7.6	-5.5	1.4	90.4
Italy	14.9	41.0	-7.6	1.2	91.6
Egypt	14.1	8.5	19.8	1.1	92.7
Netherlands	12.9	-14.8	6.9	1.0	93.7
Thailand	12.6	-5.0	-29.9	1.0	94.7

Graph 2: Trade Balance by MDG regions 2016
(Mln US$)

Imports — Exports — Trade balance

Developed Asia-Pacific
Developed Europe
Developed N. America
South-eastern Europe
C I S
Northern Africa
Sub-Saharan Africa
Latin Am, Caribbean
Eastern Asia
Southern Asia
South-eastern Asia
Western Asia
Oceania

-800 -600 -400 -200 0 200 400 600 800

Table 3: Top importing countries or areas in 2016

Country or area	Value (million US$)	Avg. Growth (%) 12-16	Growth (%) 15-16	World share %	Cum.
World	1224.3	8.3	-2.1	100.0	
China	621.1	9.6	-8.5	50.7	50.7
Belgium	98.1	11.0	-10.9	8.0	58.7
USA	61.4	7.9	-3.1	5.0	63.8
India	37.3	13.6	20.7	3.0	66.8
Spain	36.6	5.0	19.7	3.0	69.8
United Kingdom	32.4	8.1	6.8	2.6	72.4
Netherlands	24.9	-6.3	97.6	2.0	74.5
Poland	24.4	35.1	10.1	2.0	76.5
France	22.1	-0.1	-20.9	1.8	78.3
Japan	21.4	6.7	-3.9	1.7	80.0
Lithuania	21.3	10.7	1.3	1.7	81.7
Philippines	20.7	174.2	686.3	1.7	83.4
Mexico	19.9	11.4	19.1	1.6	85.1
Germany	18.1	-0.8	8.9	1.5	86.5
Tunisia	15.6	-3.3	15.3	1.3	87.8

266 Synthetic fibres suitable for spinning

In 2016, the value (in current US$) of exports of "synthetic fibres suitable for spinning" (SITC group 266) decreased by 6.8 percent (compared to -3.9 percent average growth rate from 2012-2016) to reach 6.9 bln US$ (see table 2), while imports decreased by 10.5 percent to reach 8.0 bln US$ (see table 3). Exports of this commodity accounted for 1.1 percent of world exports of SITC sections 2+4, and less than 0.1 percent of total world merchandise exports (see table 1). China, Rep. of Korea and Japan were the top exporters in 2016 (see table 2). They accounted for 17.4, 15.2 and 10.9 percent of world exports, respectively. USA, China and Germany were the top destinations, with respectively 11.7, 9.0 and 7.6 percent of world imports (see table 3).

The top 15 countries/areas accounted for 85.1 and 67.2 percent of total world exports and imports, respectively (see tables 2 and 3). In 2016, Rep. of Korea was the country/area with the highest value of net exports (+992.6 mln US$), followed by Japan (+603.0 mln US$). By MDG regions (see graph 2), the largest surpluses in this product group were recorded by Eastern Asia (+2.0 bln US$) and Developed Asia-Pacific (+539.2 mln US$). The largest trade deficits were recorded by Developed Europe (-1.3 bln US$), Developed North America (-705.0 mln US$) and Western Asia (-468.8 mln US$).

Table 1: Imports (Imp.) and exports (Exp.), 2002-2016, in current US$

		2002	2003	2004	2005	2006	2007	2008	2009	2010	2011	2012	2013	2014	2015	2016
Values in Bln US$	Imp.	5.6	6.5	7.6	7.8	7.4	8.2	8.6	6.6	8.7	11.0	9.4	10.0	10.1	8.9	8.0
	Exp.	4.3	4.8	5.4	5.9	5.9	6.7	6.8	5.2	7.2	9.1	8.1	8.5	8.5	7.4	6.9
As a percentage of SITC section (%)	Imp.	2.3	2.2	2.0	1.9	1.5	1.3	1.1	1.2	1.1	1.1	1.0	1.1	1.1	1.2	1.1
	Exp.	2.0	1.9	1.7	1.6	1.3	1.2	1.0	1.1	1.0	1.0	1.0	1.0	1.1	1.1	1.1
As a percentage of world trade (%)	Imp.	0.1	0.1	0.1	0.1	0.1	0.1	0.1	0.1	0.1	0.1	0.1	0.1	0.1	0.1	0.0
	Exp.	0.1	0.1	0.1	0.1	0.0	0.0	0.0	0.0	0.0	0.1	0.0	0.0	0.0	0.0	0.0

Graph 1: Annual growth rates of exports, 2002–2016

(In percentage by year)

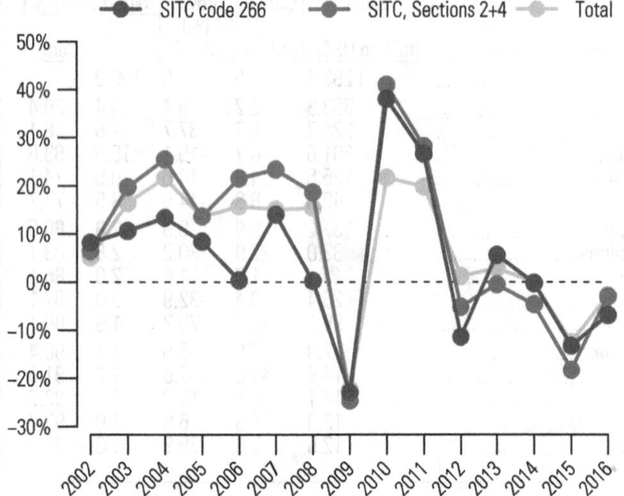

Table 2: Top exporting countries or areas in 2016

Country or area	Value (million US$)	Avg. Growth (%) 12-16	Growth (%) 15-16	World share %	Cum.
World	6879.7	-3.9	-6.8	100.0	
China	1197.2	0.0	-4.8	17.4	17.4
Rep. of Korea	1044.4	-4.7	-5.4	15.2	32.6
Japan	746.7	-5.5	-12.8	10.9	43.4
Other Asia, nes	611.2	-10.6	-7.8	8.9	52.3
Thailand	454.0	-2.9	-8.5	6.6	58.9
USA	359.7	-7.5	-7.2	5.2	64.1
Belgium	298.1	-4.0	-12.0	4.3	68.5
India	276.8	-1.2	6.3	4.0	72.5
Indonesia	164.2	5.2	-12.1	2.4	74.9
Malaysia	132.4	-1.6	0.3	1.9	76.8
Netherlands	119.0	10.1	49.6	1.7	78.5
Ireland	118.5	-5.5	-7.6	1.7	80.3
Belarus	115.6	-13.9	-1.3	1.7	81.9
Viet Nam	*109.2*	1.0	8.9	1.6	83.5
Turkey	107.0	8.3	-11.2	1.6	85.1

Graph 2: Trade Balance by MDG regions 2016

(Bln US$)

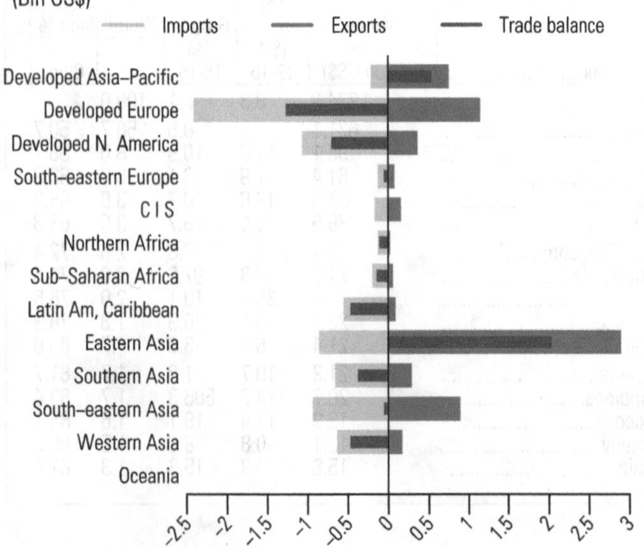

Table 3: Top importing countries or areas in 2016

Country or area	Value (million US$)	Avg. Growth (%) 12-16	Growth (%) 15-16	World share %	Cum.
World	7957.5	-4.2	-10.5	100.0	
USA	929.2	-2.0	-16.3	11.7	11.7
China	716.3	-8.2	-18.6	9.0	20.7
Germany	601.7	-5.0	-8.4	7.6	28.2
Turkey	466.6	-1.4	-5.1	5.9	34.1
Italy	368.4	-4.9	-7.3	4.6	38.7
Indonesia	366.4	-2.9	-6.5	4.6	43.3
Viet Nam	*342.4*	-5.7	5.1	4.3	47.6
Spain	241.7	9.3	0.5	3.0	50.7
United Kingdom	239.4	-3.4	-15.0	3.0	53.7
Bangladesh	*206.8*	8.4	-14.2	2.6	56.3
Mexico	201.9	-5.9	-8.6	2.5	58.8
France	193.5	-5.5	-3.8	2.4	61.3
India	190.6	7.3	-18.6	2.4	63.7
Japan	143.7	5.8	7.0	1.8	65.5
Canada	138.4	-4.2	-9.6	1.7	67.2

In 2016, the value (in current US$) of exports of "other man-made fibres suitable for spinning; waste of man-made fibres" (SITC group 267) decreased by 8.8 percent (compared to -5.8 percent average growth rate from 2012-2016) to reach 3.6 bln US$ (see table 2), while imports decreased by 3.9 percent to reach 5.1 bln US$ (see table 3). Exports of this commodity accounted for 0.6 percent of world exports of SITC sections 2+4, and less than 0.1 percent of total world merchandise exports (see table 1). USA, China and Belgium were the top exporters in 2016 (see table 2). They accounted for 24.2, 15.8 and 9.4 percent of world exports, respectively. Turkey, China and Indonesia were the top destinations, with respectively 12.7, 9.4 and 8.1 percent of world imports (see table 3).

The top 15 countries/areas accounted for 95.0 and 69.9 percent of total world exports and imports, respectively (see tables 2 and 3). In 2016, USA was the country/area with the highest value of net exports (+639.5 mln US$), followed by Belgium (+195.6 mln US$). By MDG regions (see graph 2), the largest surpluses in this product group were recorded by Developed North America (+608.1 mln US$), Developed Asia-Pacific (+129.4 mln US$) and Eastern Asia (+111.1 mln US$). The largest trade deficits were recorded by Western Asia (-727.6 mln US$), Southern Asia (-404.0 mln US$) and Developed Europe (-352.8 mln US$).

Table 1: Imports (Imp.) and exports (Exp.), 2002-2016, in current US$

		2002	2003	2004	2005	2006	2007	2008	2009	2010	2011	2012	2013	2014	2015	2016
Values in Bln US$	Imp.	2.3	2.6	3.0	3.0	3.1	4.2	4.7	4.4	5.1	6.1	6.0	5.7	5.7	5.3	5.1
	Exp.	2.6	2.7	3.3	3.2	3.5	4.4	4.4	3.6	4.3	5.0	4.6	4.6	4.5	3.9	3.6
As a percentage of SITC section (%)	Imp.	1.0	0.9	0.8	0.7	0.6	0.7	0.6	0.8	0.7	0.6	0.6	0.6	0.6	0.7	0.7
	Exp.	1.2	1.1	1.0	0.9	0.8	0.8	0.7	0.7	0.6	0.6	0.5	0.5	0.6	0.6	0.6
As a percentage of world trade (%)	Imp.	0.0	0.0	0.0	0.0	0.0	0.0	0.0	0.0	0.0	0.0	0.0	0.0	0.0	0.0	0.0
	Exp.	0.0	0.0	0.0	0.0	0.0	0.0	0.0	0.0	0.0	0.0	0.0	0.0	0.0	0.0	0.0

Graph 1: Annual growth rates of exports, 2002–2016

(In percentage by year)

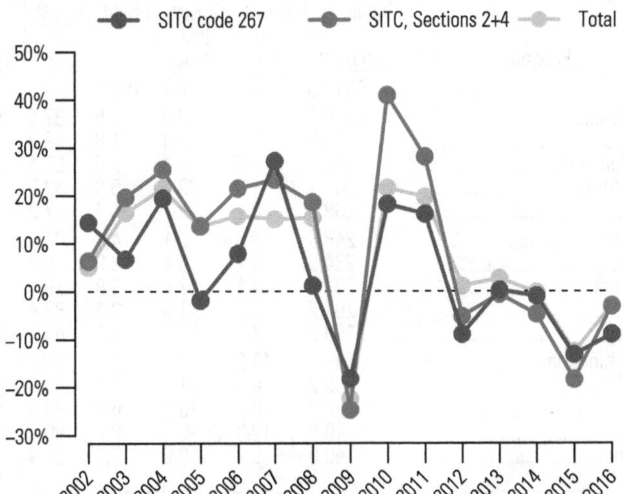

Graph 2: Trade Balance by MDG regions 2016

(Bln US$)

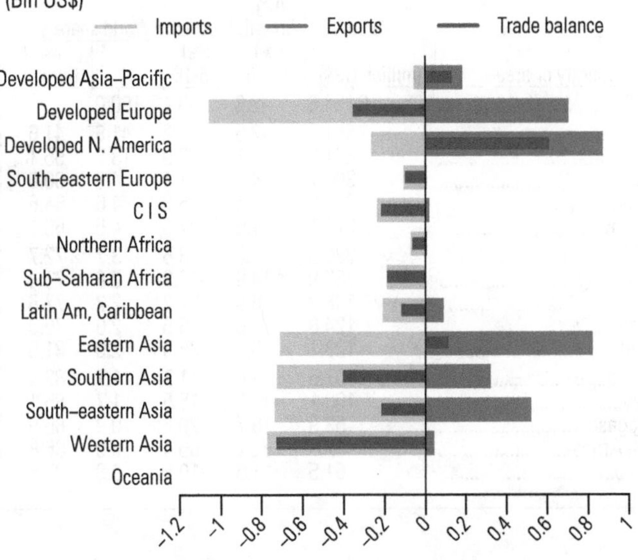

Table 2: Top exporting countries or areas in 2016

Country or area	Value (million US$)	Avg. Growth (%) 12-16	Growth (%) 15-16	World share %	Cum.
World	3589.9	-5.8	-8.8	100.0	
USA	867.2	-6.1	-10.2	24.2	24.2
China	566.2	-1.4	31.5	15.8	39.9
Belgium	336.6	-1.8	-15.2	9.4	49.3
India	299.9	6.9	9.4	8.4	57.7
Indonesia	257.1	-10.6	-10.5	7.2	64.8
Thailand	208.5	-4.9	10.8	5.8	70.6
Japan	184.8	-23.3	-68.8	5.1	75.8
Germany	180.4	-5.8	4.1	5.0	80.8
Other Asia, nes	171.6	1.1	-4.7	4.8	85.6
Netherlands	96.5	74.2	668.0	2.7	88.3
Rep. of Korea	80.2	-7.8	-4.4	2.2	90.5
Mexico	64.7	-11.7	-4.2	1.8	92.3
Singapore	46.9	21.5	34.8	1.3	93.6
United Arab Emirates	26.9	36.4	40.2	0.8	94.4
Brazil	24.3	-9.7	-3.6	0.7	95.0

Table 3: Top importing countries or areas in 2016

Country or area	Value (million US$)	Avg. Growth (%) 12-16	Growth (%) 15-16	World share %	Cum.
World	5122.6	-3.8	-3.9	100.0	
Turkey	651.4	-3.0	9.1	12.7	12.7
China	480.2	-20.3	-39.2	9.4	22.1
Indonesia	416.7	-1.5	7.2	8.1	30.2
Pakistan	308.9	11.2	11.6	6.0	36.3
Germany	236.3	-3.3	-3.9	4.6	40.9
USA	227.7	-0.3	1.3	4.4	45.3
India	177.0	10.2	3.9	3.5	48.8
Russian Federation	155.9	-4.7	0.1	3.0	51.8
Rep. of Korea	151.2	-9.2	9.3	3.0	54.8
Viet Nam	*146.4*	4.4	5.1	2.9	57.6
Bangladesh	*141.4*	6.8	-14.2	2.8	60.4
Belgium	141.0	4.2	9.4	2.8	63.1
Nigeria	130.0	4.8	112.9	2.5	65.7
Poland	119.4	3.4	5.9	2.3	68.0
Italy	96.3	-6.6	1.6	1.9	69.9

Source: UN Comtrade

268 Wool and other animal hair (including wool tops)

In 2016, the value (in current US$) of exports of "wool and other animal hair (including wool tops)" (SITC group 268) decreased by 2.7 percent (compared to -3.0 percent average growth rate from 2012-2016) to reach 6.0 bln US$ (see table 2), while imports decreased by 3.1 percent to reach 6.2 bln US$ (see table 3). Exports of this commodity accounted for 0.9 percent of world exports of SITC sections 2+4, and less than 0.1 percent of total world merchandise exports (see table 1). Australia, China and New Zealand were the top exporters in 2016 (see table 2). They accounted for 37.5, 11.8 and 7.8 percent of world exports, respectively. China, Italy and India were the top destinations, with respectively 41.6, 13.5 and 4.9 percent of world imports (see table 3).

The top 15 countries/areas accounted for 91.4 and 87.6 percent of total world exports and imports, respectively (see tables 2 and 3). In 2016, Australia was the country/area with the highest value of net exports (+2.2 bln US$), followed by New Zealand (+462.1 mln US$). By MDG regions (see graph 2), the largest surpluses in this product group were recorded by Developed Asia-Pacific (+2.6 bln US$), Latin America and the Caribbean (+414.0 mln US$) and Sub-Saharan Africa (+250.0 mln US$). The largest trade deficits were recorded by Eastern Asia (-1.8 bln US$), Developed Europe (-909.9 mln US$) and Southern Asia (-283.3 mln US$).

Table 1: Imports (Imp.) and exports (Exp.), 2002-2016, in current US$

		2002	2003	2004	2005	2006	2007	2008	2009	2010	2011	2012	2013	2014	2015	2016
Values in Bln US$	Imp.	4.8	5.0	5.3	5.1	5.2	6.0	5.7	4.0	5.6	7.9	6.8	7.0	6.7	6.4	6.2
	Exp.	4.7	4.7	5.0	4.9	5.2	6.1	5.4	4.0	5.5	7.7	6.8	6.9	6.6	6.2	6.0
As a percentage of SITC section (%)	Imp.	2.0	1.7	1.4	1.2	1.1	1.0	0.7	0.7	0.7	0.8	0.7	0.8	0.8	0.9	0.9
	Exp.	2.2	1.8	1.6	1.3	1.2	1.1	0.8	0.8	0.8	0.9	0.8	0.8	0.8	0.9	0.9
As a percentage of world trade (%)	Imp.	0.1	0.1	0.1	0.0	0.0	0.0	0.0	0.0	0.0	0.0	0.0	0.0	0.0	0.0	0.0
	Exp.	0.1	0.1	0.1	0.0	0.0	0.0	0.0	0.0	0.0	0.0	0.0	0.0	0.0	0.0	0.0

Graph 1: Annual growth rates of exports, 2002–2016
(In percentage by year)

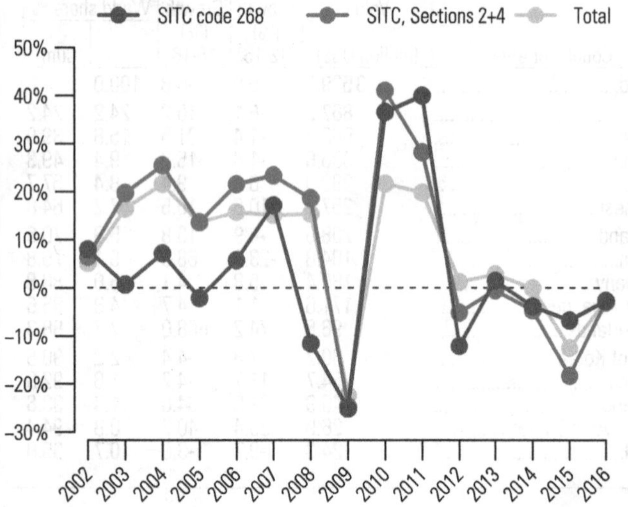

Table 2: Top exporting countries or areas in 2016

Country or area	Value (million US$)	Avg. Growth (%) 12-16	Growth (%) 15-16	World share %	Cum.
World	6014.3	-3.0	-2.7	100.0	
Australia	2256.0	-3.6	2.8	37.5	37.5
China	710.5	-5.9	-6.4	11.8	49.3
New Zealand	468.2	-5.5	-18.4	7.8	57.1
South Africa	347.1	-1.3	28.1	5.8	62.9
Mongolia	263.0	0.1	-2.7	4.4	67.3
Germany	243.8	-8.8	0.1	4.1	71.3
Czechia	234.5	1.7	6.4	3.9	75.2
Argentina	233.0	4.1	42.8	3.9	79.1
Italy	202.2	3.0	1.5	3.4	82.4
Uruguay	198.6	-4.0	-17.7	3.3	85.7
United Kingdom	149.2	12.2	-14.5	2.5	88.2
Peru	65.2	6.9	-21.5	1.1	89.3
Spain	44.6	-0.9	-10.1	0.7	90.0
Egypt	40.5	12.3	-6.9	0.7	90.7
Belgium	40.5	-0.7	-10.0	0.7	91.4

Graph 2: Trade Balance by MDG regions 2016
(Bln US$)

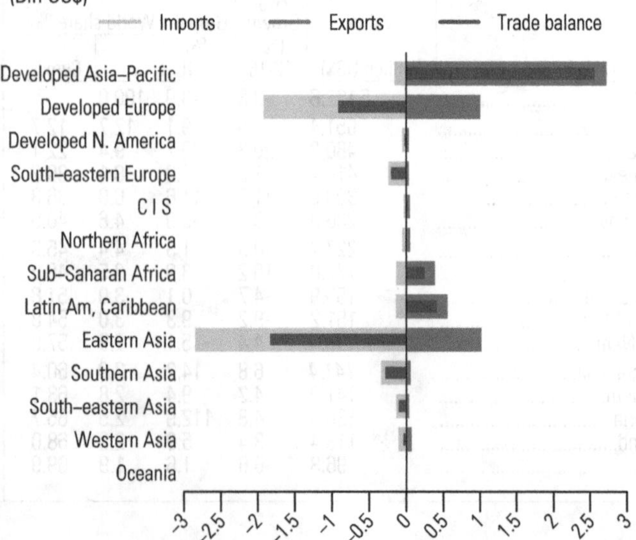

Table 3: Top importing countries or areas in 2016

Country or area	Value (million US$)	Avg. Growth (%) 12-16	Growth (%) 15-16	World share %	Cum.
World	6154.6	-2.6	-3.1	100.0	
China	2561.5	-2.5	-7.2	41.6	41.6
Italy	831.6	-3.1	-2.9	13.5	55.1
India	300.7	-4.3	-7.1	4.9	60.0
Czechia	282.2	1.6	5.8	4.6	64.6
Germany	274.1	-11.9	27.5	4.5	69.1
Rep. of Korea	225.6	0.6	-3.6	3.7	72.7
United Kingdom	162.9	14.8	-18.2	2.6	75.4
Japan	138.3	-8.0	-12.2	2.2	77.6
Romania	124.8	2.0	15.5	2.0	79.6
Poland	123.1	-0.8	35.9	2.0	81.6
Bulgaria	107.6	4.0	11.7	1.7	83.4
Turkey	103.1	-11.6	-15.5	1.7	85.1
Madagascar	53.9	18.7	-20.5	0.9	85.9
South Africa	52.7	32.2	65.4	0.9	86.8
Mexico	51.5	-11.6	-10.5	0.8	87.6

In 2016, the value (in current US$) of exports of "worn clothing and other worn textile articles; rags" (SITC group 269) decreased by 6.5 percent (compared to -2.9 percent average growth rate from 2012-2016) to reach 4.4 bln US$ (see table 2), while imports decreased by 3.9 percent to reach 3.8 bln US$ (see table 3). Exports of this commodity accounted for 0.7 percent of world exports of SITC sections 2+4, and less than 0.1 percent of total world merchandise exports (see table 1). USA, United Kingdom and Germany were the top exporters in 2016 (see table 2). They accounted for 14.6, 11.1 and 9.5 percent of world exports, respectively. Pakistan, India and Malaysia were the top destinations, with respectively 6.4, 4.6 and 4.1 percent of world imports (see table 3).

The top 15 countries/areas accounted for 75.6 and 44.6 percent of total world exports and imports, respectively (see tables 2 and 3). In 2016, USA was the country/area with the highest value of net exports (+540.3 mln US$), followed by United Kingdom (+462.6 mln US$). By MDG regions (see graph 2), the largest surpluses in this product group were recorded by Developed Europe (+1.3 bln US$), Developed North America (+634.2 mln US$) and Eastern Asia (+399.5 mln US$). The largest trade deficits were recorded by Sub-Saharan Africa (-908.4 mln US$), Latin America and the Caribbean (-369.1 mln US$) and Southern Asia (-262.2 mln US$).

Table 1: Imports (Imp.) and exports (Exp.), 2002-2016, in current US$

		2002	2003	2004	2005	2006	2007	2008	2009	2010	2011	2012	2013	2014	2015	2016
Values in Bln US$	Imp.	1.6	1.6	1.7	1.9	2.1	2.3	2.7	2.8	2.9	3.6	4.1	4.2	4.8	3.9	3.8
	Exp.	1.7	1.7	1.9	2.1	2.4	2.9	3.1	3.1	3.4	4.5	4.9	5.1	5.2	4.7	4.4
As a percentage of SITC section (%)	Imp.	0.7	0.5	0.5	0.4	0.4	0.4	0.4	0.5	0.4	0.4	0.4	0.5	0.5	0.5	0.5
	Exp.	0.8	0.7	0.6	0.6	0.5	0.5	0.5	0.6	0.5	0.5	0.6	0.6	0.7	0.7	0.7
As a percentage of world trade (%)	Imp.	0.0	0.0	0.0	0.0	0.0	0.0	0.0	0.0	0.0	0.0	0.0	0.0	0.0	0.0	0.0
	Exp.	0.0	0.0	0.0	0.0	0.0	0.0	0.0	0.0	0.0	0.0	0.0	0.0	0.0	0.0	0.0

Graph 1: Annual growth rates of exports, 2002–2016
(In percentage by year)

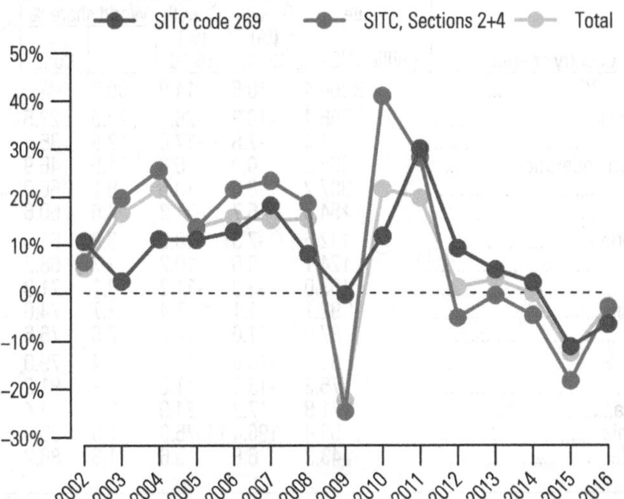

Table 2: Top exporting countries or areas in 2016

Country or area	Value (million US$)	Avg. Growth (%) 12-16	Growth (%) 15-16	World share %	Cum.
World	4360.2	-2.9	-6.5	100.0	
USA	638.7	-3.4	-18.5	14.6	14.6
United Kingdom	483.3	-4.4	-0.6	11.1	25.7
Germany	413.9	-2.6	-7.5	9.5	35.2
Rep. of Korea	271.4	-6.4	-14.8	6.2	41.5
China	237.4	35.4	-21.7	5.4	46.9
Netherlands	178.7	-7.5	-19.9	4.1	51.0
Poland	174.9	8.3	18.5	4.0	55.0
Italy	152.8	-2.4	-6.5	3.5	58.5
Belgium	149.7	-2.2	-3.3	3.4	61.9
Canada	140.9	-9.8	-13.0	3.2	65.2
Malaysia	113.4	0.3	-2.5	2.6	67.8
Japan	99.9	-7.2	-17.8	2.3	70.1
France	85.8	1.2	-1.9	2.0	72.0
India	85.7	1.6	-25.8	2.0	74.0
Indonesia	69.7	-14.5	-3.8	1.6	75.6

Graph 2: Trade Balance by MDG regions 2016
(Bln US$)

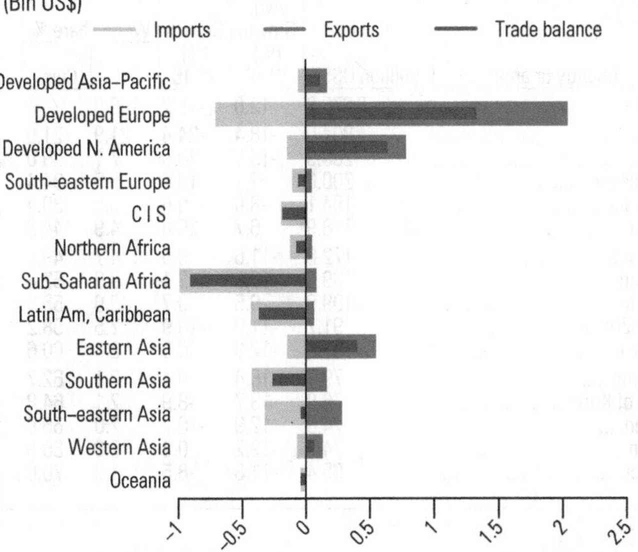

Table 3: Top importing countries or areas in 2016

Country or area	Value (million US$)	Avg. Growth (%) 12-16	Growth (%) 15-16	World share %	Cum.
World	3773.3	-1.8	-3.9	100.0	
Pakistan	240.1	11.7	14.3	6.4	6.4
India	173.4	0.0	-8.0	4.6	11.0
Malaysia	153.0	2.6	2.3	4.1	15.0
Russian Federation	120.5	-6.3	-0.8	3.2	18.2
Kenya	*115.3*	4.6	21.1	3.1	21.3
Tunisia	105.9	3.1	9.8	2.8	24.1
USA	98.4	-5.2	-8.3	2.6	26.7
Guatemala	97.7	10.9	8.4	2.6	29.3
Poland	92.1	-1.4	-7.9	2.4	31.7
Germany	88.9	-3.5	-5.8	2.4	34.1
China	87.9	-8.2	-10.8	2.3	36.4
Ghana	81.9	1.6	-8.7	2.2	38.6
Italy	80.9	5.6	10.8	2.1	40.7
Hungary	75.8	-4.0	12.8	2.0	42.7
Uganda	72.4	8.8	8.1	1.9	44.6

Source: UN Comtrade

272 Fertilizers crude, other than those of division 56

In 2016, the value (in current US$) of exports of "fertilizers crude, other than those of division 56" (SITC group 272) decreased by 14.9 percent (compared to -10.5 percent average growth rate from 2012-2016) to reach 3.4 bln US$ (see table 2), while imports decreased by 15.2 percent to reach 3.7 bln US$ (see table 3). Exports of this commodity accounted for 0.5 percent of world exports of SITC sections 2+4, and less than 0.1 percent of total world merchandise exports (see table 1). Morocco, Jordan and Russian Federation were the top exporters in 2016 (see table 2). They accounted for 22.5, 12.9 and 11.5 percent of world exports, respectively. India, USA and Indonesia were the top destinations, with respectively 21.9, 7.1 and 5.5 percent of world imports (see table 3).

The top 15 countries/areas accounted for 86.2 and 70.6 percent of total world exports and imports, respectively (see tables 2 and 3). In 2016, Morocco was the country/area with the highest value of net exports (+745.8 mln US$), followed by Jordan (+434.3 mln US$). By MDG regions (see graph 2), the largest surpluses in this product group were recorded by Northern Africa (+966.6 mln US$), Western Asia (+370.9 mln US$) and Commonwealth of Independent States (+295.9 mln US$). The largest trade deficits were recorded by Southern Asia (-872.0 mln US$), Developed Europe (-366.0 mln US$) and South-eastern Asia (-267.0 mln US$).

Table 1: Imports (Imp.) and exports (Exp.), 2002-2016, in current US$

		2002	2003	2004	2005	2006	2007	2008	2009	2010	2011	2012	2013	2014	2015	2016
Values in Bln US$	Imp.	1.6	1.6	1.9	2.2	2.3	2.8	7.3	3.2	3.8	5.6	6.1	4.6	4.2	4.3	3.7
	Exp.	1.5	1.5	1.8	1.8	1.8	1.9	5.7	2.8	3.5	4.7	5.2	4.4	3.9	4.0	3.4
As a percentage of SITC section (%)	Imp.	0.6	0.6	0.5	0.5	0.5	0.4	1.0	0.6	0.5	0.6	0.7	0.5	0.5	0.6	0.5
	Exp.	0.7	0.6	0.6	0.5	0.4	0.3	0.9	0.6	0.5	0.5	0.6	0.5	0.5	0.6	0.5
As a percentage of world trade (%)	Imp.	0.0	0.0	0.0	0.0	0.0	0.0	0.0	0.0	0.0	0.0	0.0	0.0	0.0	0.0	0.0
	Exp.	0.0	0.0	0.0	0.0	0.0	0.0	0.0	0.0	0.0	0.0	0.0	0.0	0.0	0.0	0.0

Graph 1: Annual growth rates of exports, 2002–2016
(In percentage by year)

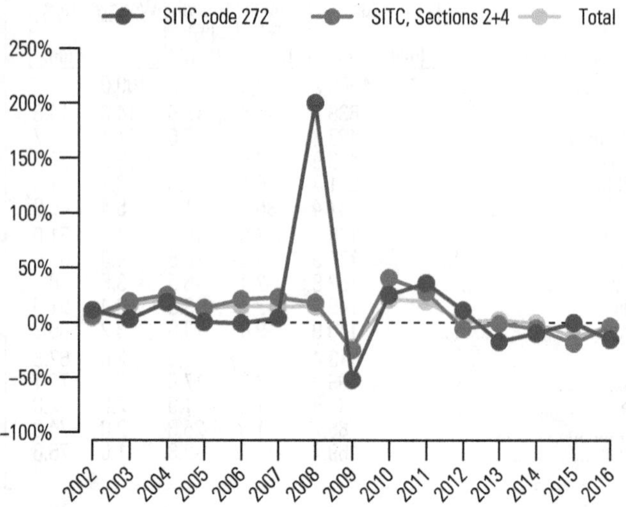

Table 2: Top exporting countries or areas in 2016

Country or area	Value (million US$)	Avg. Growth (%) 12-16	Growth (%) 15-16	World share %	Cum.
World	3364.4	-10.5	-14.9	100.0	
Morocco	756.4	-16.3	-26.1	22.5	22.5
Jordan	434.4	-7.8	-17.0	12.9	35.4
Russian Federation	385.9	0.0	16.3	11.5	46.9
Peru	307.2	-8.5	-13.5	9.1	56.0
Egypt	154.0	-15.7	-27.2	4.6	60.6
Netherlands	132.5	-7.3	-28.0	3.9	64.5
Italy	124.1	-8.0	-10.2	3.7	68.2
Israel	103.0	-3.3	-11.2	3.1	71.3
Belgium	92.1	1.1	7.4	2.7	74.0
Chile	87.0	-11.0	12.3	2.6	76.6
Togo	81.2	-10.6	-18.9	2.4	79.0
China	75.3	-13.3	11.8	2.2	81.2
Algeria	71.8	-17.2	-24.9	2.1	83.4
Slovenia	53.4	196.4	14075.6	1.6	85.0
Canada	43.3	6.8	5.6	1.3	86.2

Graph 2: Trade Balance by MDG regions 2016
(Mln US$)

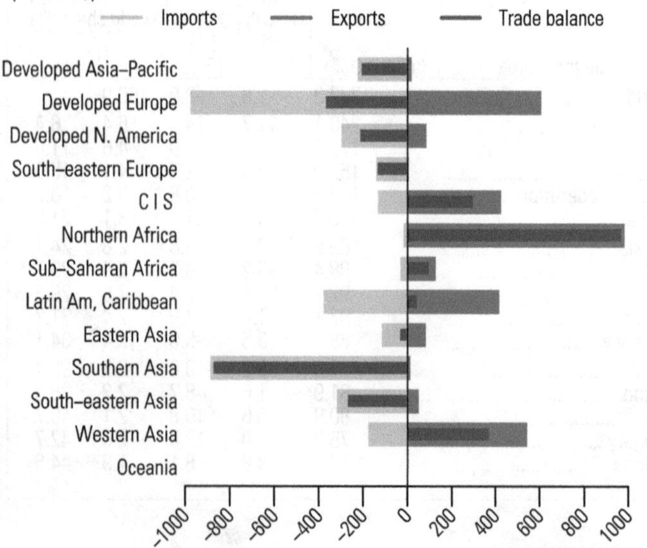

Table 3: Top importing countries or areas in 2016

Country or area	Value (million US$)	Avg. Growth (%) 12-16	Growth (%) 15-16	World share %	Cum.
World	3678.3	-12.0	-15.2	100.0	
India	804.0	-18.4	-24.4	21.9	21.9
USA	260.9	-15.5	-20.9	7.1	29.0
Indonesia	200.6	2.2	19.6	5.5	34.4
Lithuania	184.1	-8.0	-19.6	5.0	39.4
Brazil	178.9	-6.7	-25.8	4.9	44.3
Belgium	172.8	-11.6	0.5	4.7	49.0
Poland	139.8	-10.8	3.1	3.8	52.8
Turkey	109.9	-0.5	3.7	3.0	55.8
New Zealand	91.2	-11.0	-18.9	2.5	58.2
Mexico	85.1	-12.9	-30.0	2.3	60.6
Belarus	79.1	-16.4	0.4	2.1	62.7
Rep. of Korea	76.9	-13.7	-8.9	2.1	64.8
Japan	74.8	-12.9	-16.7	2.0	66.8
Spain	74.5	-12.2	0.3	2.0	68.9
France	65.4	-11.8	-8.5	1.8	70.6

In 2016, the value (in current US$) of exports of "stone, sand and gravel" (SITC group 273) decreased by 8.0 percent (compared to -2.6 percent average growth rate from 2012-2016) to reach 9.0 bln US$ (see table 2), while imports decreased by 7.3 percent to reach 11.2 bln US$ (see table 3). Exports of this commodity accounted for 1.4 percent of world exports of SITC sections 2+4, and 0.1 percent of total world merchandise exports (see table 1). Turkey, India and United Arab Emirates were the top exporters in 2016 (see table 2). They accounted for 10.6, 9.3 and 7.9 percent of world exports, respectively. China, India and Qatar were the top destinations, with respectively 19.4, 5.6 and 4.2 percent of world imports (see table 3).

The top 15 countries/areas accounted for 70.3 and 65.7 percent of total world exports and imports, respectively (see tables 2 and 3). In 2016, Turkey was the country/area with the highest value of net exports (+904.3 mln US$), followed by United Arab Emirates (+512.2 mln US$). By MDG regions (see graph 2), the largest surpluses in this product group were recorded by Western Asia (+643.1 mln US$), Southern Asia (+285.8 mln US$) and Latin America and the Caribbean (+126.1 mln US$). The largest trade deficits were recorded by Eastern Asia (-2.6 bln US$), South-eastern Asia (-333.4 mln US$) and Sub-Saharan Africa (-129.8 mln US$).

Table 1: Imports (Imp.) and exports (Exp.), 2002-2016, in current US$

		2002	2003	2004	2005	2006	2007	2008	2009	2010	2011	2012	2013	2014	2015	2016
Values in Bln US$	Imp.	5.1	6.1	7.1	7.8	8.9	10.8	12.5	10.5	10.9	12.2	12.5	13.7	14.3	12.1	11.2
	Exp.	4.2	4.7	5.5	5.9	7.3	8.5	9.7	8.1	8.4	9.7	10.0	10.8	10.8	9.7	9.0
As a percentage of SITC section (%)	Imp.	2.1	2.1	1.9	1.9	1.8	1.7	1.6	1.9	1.4	1.2	1.4	1.5	1.6	1.7	1.6
	Exp.	1.9	1.8	1.7	1.6	1.6	1.5	1.5	1.6	1.2	1.1	1.2	1.3	1.3	1.5	1.4
As a percentage of world trade (%)	Imp.	0.1	0.1	0.1	0.1	0.1	0.1	0.1	0.1	0.1	0.1	0.1	0.1	0.1	0.1	0.1
	Exp.	0.1	0.1	0.1	0.1	0.1	0.1	0.1	0.1	0.1	0.1	0.1	0.1	0.1	0.1	0.1

Graph 1: Annual growth rates of exports, 2002–2016
(In percentage by year)

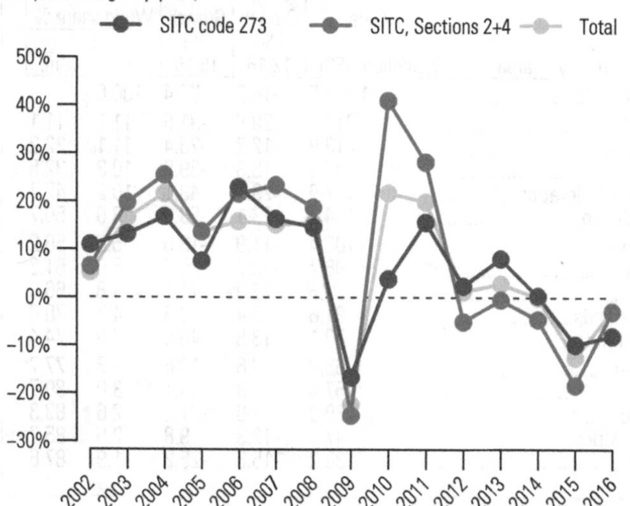

Graph 2: Trade Balance by MDG regions 2016
(Bln US$)

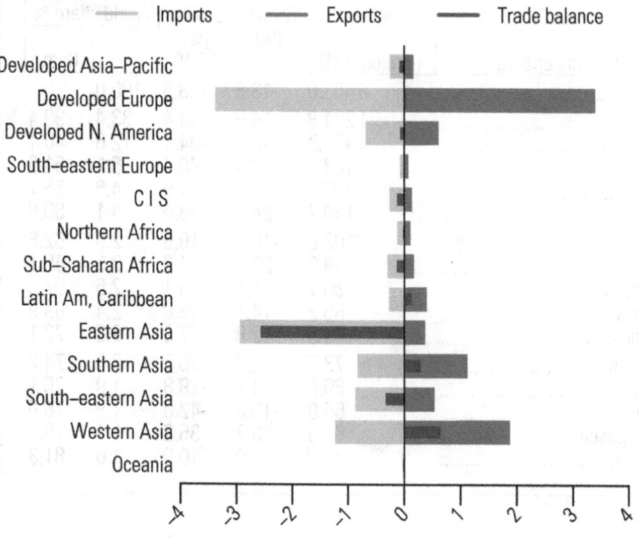

Table 2: Top exporting countries or areas in 2016

Country or area	Value (million US$)	Avg. Growth (%) 12-16	Growth (%) 15-16	World share %	Cum.
World	8958.8	-2.6	-8.0	100.0	
Turkey	949.3	-3.1	-2.3	10.6	10.6
India	835.6	-2.0	-6.5	9.3	19.9
United Arab Emirates	707.7	9.2	-17.9	7.9	27.8
Germany	502.0	-5.6	-0.6	5.6	33.4
Italy	477.7	-3.5	-7.0	5.3	38.8
USA	472.2	-1.9	-17.1	5.3	44.0
Belgium	365.3	-1.4	5.5	4.1	48.1
Spain	328.2	-8.5	-11.1	3.7	51.8
Norway	325.1	-0.3	-5.7	3.6	55.4
China	316.1	14.6	-29.4	3.5	58.9
France	248.5	0.3	6.6	2.8	61.7
Thailand	202.6	1.4	-9.5	2.3	64.0
Brazil	199.6	-4.7	-1.4	2.2	66.2
Iran	*186.2*	-1.6	-29.5	2.1	68.3
Greece	183.5	4.2	16.9	2.0	70.3

Table 3: Top importing countries or areas in 2016

Country or area	Value (million US$)	Avg. Growth (%) 12-16	Growth (%) 15-16	World share %	Cum.
World	11209.8	-2.7	-7.3	100.0	
China	2179.0	-5.4	-6.5	19.4	19.4
India	629.2	2.4	-13.1	5.6	25.1
Qatar	465.4	8.5	-4.3	4.2	29.2
Other Asia, nes	438.2	-4.3	-22.6	3.9	33.1
USA	434.7	3.7	-6.0	3.9	37.0
Germany	420.5	-5.7	0.0	3.8	40.7
Singapore	405.4	-6.7	-2.0	3.6	44.4
Italy	374.4	-4.3	-9.1	3.3	47.7
United Kingdom	368.1	6.3	0.3	3.3	51.0
Netherlands	332.2	-12.1	-27.5	3.0	53.9
Belgium	305.8	-8.4	0.6	2.7	56.7
France	275.8	-5.2	13.0	2.5	59.1
Switzerland	254.9	-1.2	1.2	2.3	61.4
Kuwait	243.3	8.5	-15.5	2.2	63.6
Canada	241.9	3.3	-14.4	2.2	65.7

Source: UN Comtrade

274 Sulphur and unroasted iron pyrites

In 2016, the value (in current US$) of exports of "sulphur and unroasted iron pyrites" (SITC group 274) decreased by 37.4 percent (compared to -16.2 percent average growth rate from 2012-2016) to reach 1.9 bln US$ (see table 2), while imports decreased by 29.5 percent to reach 3.6 bln US$ (see table 3). Exports of this commodity accounted for 0.3 percent of world exports of SITC sections 2+4, and less than 0.1 percent of total world merchandise exports (see table 1). Canada, USA and Qatar were the top exporters in 2016 (see table 2). They accounted for 11.1, 11.1 and 10.3 percent of world exports, respectively. China, Morocco and Brazil were the top destinations, with respectively 33.4, 12.6 and 5.1 percent of world imports (see table 3).

The top 15 countries/areas accounted for 87.6 and 81.3 percent of total world exports and imports, respectively (see tables 2 and 3). In 2016, Canada was the country/area with the highest value of net exports (+204.6 mln US$), followed by Qatar (+199.1 mln US$). By MDG regions (see graph 2), the largest surpluses in this product group were recorded by Commonwealth of Independent States (+339.5 mln US$), Developed North America (+329.3 mln US$) and Developed Europe (+131.9 mln US$). The largest trade deficits were recorded by Eastern Asia (-1.1 bln US$), Northern Africa (-574.6 mln US$) and Latin America and the Caribbean (-304.4 mln US$).

Table 1: Imports (Imp.) and exports (Exp.), 2002-2016, in current US$

		2002	2003	2004	2005	2006	2007	2008	2009	2010	2011	2012	2013	2014	2015	2016
Values in Bln US$	Imp.	0.9	1.5	2.0	2.3	2.0	3.0	12.5	2.0	3.5	6.0	6.4	4.4	5.2	5.1	3.6
	Exp.	0.5	0.7	0.9	1.1	1.1	1.5	6.5	1.0	1.9	3.8	3.9	2.7	3.1	3.1	1.9
As a percentage of SITC section (%)	Imp.	0.4	0.5	0.5	0.5	0.4	0.5	1.6	0.4	0.5	0.6	0.7	0.5	0.6	0.7	0.5
	Exp.	0.2	0.3	0.3	0.3	0.2	0.3	1.0	0.2	0.3	0.4	0.5	0.3	0.4	0.5	0.3
As a percentage of world trade (%)	Imp.	0.0	0.0	0.0	0.0	0.0	0.0	0.1	0.0	0.0	0.0	0.0	0.0	0.0	0.0	0.0
	Exp.	0.0	0.0	0.0	0.0	0.0	0.0	0.0	0.0	0.0	0.0	0.0	0.0	0.0	0.0	0.0

Graph 1: Annual growth rates of exports, 2002–2016

(In percentage by year)

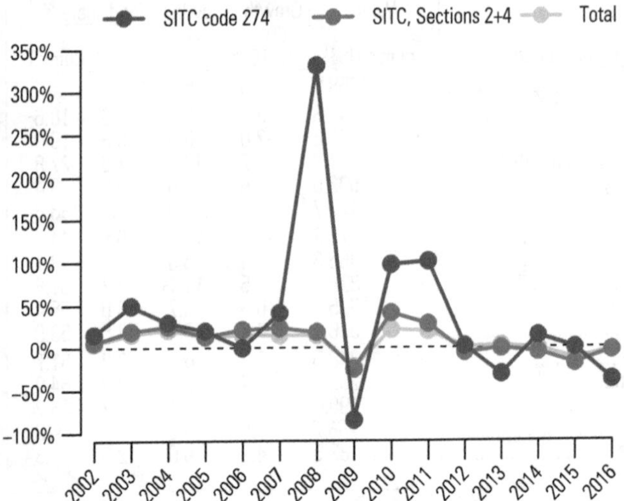

Table 2: Top exporting countries or areas in 2016

Country or area	Value (million US$)	Avg. Growth (%) 12-16	Growth (%) 15-16	World share %	Cum.
World	1931.5	-16.2	-37.4	100.0	
Canada	214.1	-20.9	-31.5	11.1	11.1
USA	213.8	-12.3	-23.4	11.1	22.2
Qatar	199.2	-15.3	-39.9	10.3	32.5
Russian Federation	197.9	-23.2	-43.1	10.2	42.7
Kazakhstan	154.4	-23.1	-53.0	8.0	50.7
Germany	106.4	-11.9	-18.5	5.5	56.2
Japan	96.7	-10.7	-25.4	5.0	61.2
Iran	*92.8*	-22.3	-71.1	4.8	66.0
Netherlands	91.6	0.4	-0.3	4.7	70.8
Rep. of Korea	70.1	-13.5	-40.8	3.6	74.4
Sweden	63.9	113.6	10.6	3.3	77.7
India	57.4	12.3	-33.1	3.0	80.7
Poland	50.3	-11.8	-21.2	2.6	83.3
South Africa	47.4	-12.3	9.8	2.5	85.7
Spain	36.2	-15.8	-25.2	1.9	87.6

Graph 2: Trade Balance by MDG regions 2016

(Bln US$)

Imports — Exports — Trade balance

Developed Asia-Pacific
Developed Europe
Developed N. America
South-eastern Europe
CIS
Northern Africa
Sub-Saharan Africa
Latin Am, Caribbean
Eastern Asia
Southern Asia
South-eastern Asia
Western Asia
Oceania

-1.4 -1.2 -1 -0.8 -0.6 -0.4 -0.2 0 0.2 0.4 0.6

Table 3: Top importing countries or areas in 2016

Country or area	Value (million US$)	Avg. Growth (%) 12-16	Growth (%) 15-16	World share %	Cum.
World	3603.0	-13.5	-29.5	100.0	
China	1204.8	-14.9	-34.4	33.4	33.4
Morocco	455.3	-13.9	-34.1	12.6	46.1
Brazil	183.9	-18.4	-40.4	5.1	51.2
Iraq	*163.9*	-5.3	-11.9	4.6	55.7
India	146.7	-24.0	-38.6	4.1	59.8
Tunisia	102.0	-16.0	10.8	2.8	62.6
USA	89.0	-23.7	-44.8	2.5	65.1
Viet Nam	*88.7*	11.6	5.1	2.5	67.6
Australia	85.2	-14.1	-25.8	2.4	69.9
Indonesia	79.8	2.8	-27.0	2.2	72.1
Belgium	73.7	-9.3	-20.5	2.0	74.2
Mexico	69.6	-4.7	-29.8	1.9	76.1
Israel	68.0	-15.6	-42.0	1.9	78.0
Madagascar	61.5	25.7	-35.8	1.7	79.7
Zambia	*56.9*	-6.0	-10.8	1.6	81.3

In 2016, the value (in current US$) of exports of "natural abrasives, nes (including industrial diamonds)" (SITC group 277) decreased by 17.2 percent (compared to -11.1 percent average growth rate from 2012-2016) to reach 2.0 bln US$ (see table 2), while imports decreased by 20.2 percent to reach 1.1 bln US$ (see table 3). Exports of this commodity accounted for 0.3 percent of world exports of SITC sections 2+4, and less than 0.1 percent of total world merchandise exports (see table 1). Angola, Singapore and China were the top exporters in 2016 (see table 2). They accounted for 35.4, 8.5 and 7.8 percent of world exports, respectively. USA, Singapore and United Arab Emirates were the top destinations, with respectively 11.3, 10.4 and 9.6 percent of world imports (see table 3).

The top 15 countries/areas accounted for 90.1 and 74.2 percent of total world exports and imports, respectively (see tables 2 and 3). In 2016, Angola was the country/area with the highest value of net exports (+691.3 mln US$), followed by China (+118.9 mln US$). By MDG regions (see graph 2), the largest surpluses in this product group were recorded by Sub-Saharan Africa (+862.2 mln US$), Eastern Asia (+85.9 mln US$) and Commonwealth of Independent States (+76.5 mln US$). The largest trade deficits were recorded by Western Asia (-129.6 mln US$), Developed Europe (-94.6 mln US$) and Developed North America (-23.2 mln US$).

Table 1: Imports (Imp.) and exports (Exp.), 2002-2016, in current US$

		2002	2003	2004	2005	2006	2007	2008	2009	2010	2011	2012	2013	2014	2015	2016
Values in Bln US$	Imp.	1.0	1.2	1.2	1.2	1.4	1.3	1.3	1.0	1.2	1.4	1.6	1.8	1.4	1.4	1.1
	Exp.	1.0	1.2	1.1	1.2	1.1	2.4	2.9	2.0	2.5	2.9	3.1	3.0	2.6	2.4	2.0
As a percentage of SITC section (%)	Imp.	0.4	0.4	0.3	0.3	0.3	0.2	0.2	0.2	0.2	0.1	0.2	0.2	0.2	0.2	0.2
	Exp.	0.4	0.5	0.3	0.3	0.2	0.4	0.4	0.4	0.4	0.3	0.4	0.4	0.3	0.4	0.3
As a percentage of world trade (%)	Imp.	0.0	0.0	0.0	0.0	0.0	0.0	0.0	0.0	0.0	0.0	0.0	0.0	0.0	0.0	0.0
	Exp.	0.0	0.0	0.0	0.0	0.0	0.0	0.0	0.0	0.0	0.0	0.0	0.0	0.0	0.0	0.0

Graph 1: Annual growth rates of exports, 2002–2016

(In percentage by year)

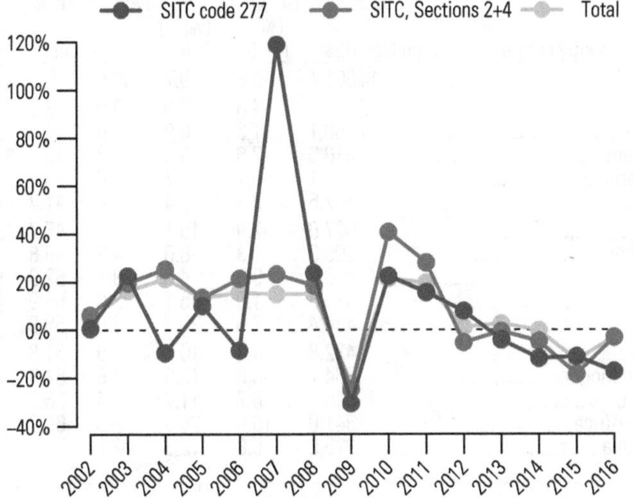

Table 2: Top exporting countries or areas in 2016

Country or area	Value (million US$)	Avg. Growth (%) 12-16	Growth (%) 15-16	World share %	Cum.
World	1952.7	-11.1	-17.2	100.0	
Angola	*691.4*	-11.2	-36.4	35.4	35.4
Singapore	166.0	-2.8	40.6	8.5	43.9
China	152.8	0.2	0.2	7.8	51.7
USA	114.7	-6.6	-11.3	5.9	57.6
Zimbabwe	106.4	-36.6	-32.1	5.4	63.1
India	101.9	-3.4	-2.0	5.2	68.3
Russian Federation	91.2	-5.4	-16.2	4.7	72.9
Australia	75.3	2.9	19.3	3.9	76.8
Dem.Rep. of the Congo	*42.3*	6.6	14.6	2.2	79.0
Ireland	40.6	184.5	-27.3	2.1	81.0
China, Hong Kong SAR	40.3	-9.3	-5.0	2.1	83.1
Malaysia	40.1	55.0	574.3	2.1	85.2
Belgium	34.7	-7.6	-3.1	1.8	86.9
United Arab Emirates	33.9	9.1	36.6	1.7	88.7
United Kingdom	27.8	-17.5	-11.4	1.4	90.1

Graph 2: Trade Balance by MDG regions 2016

(Mln US$)

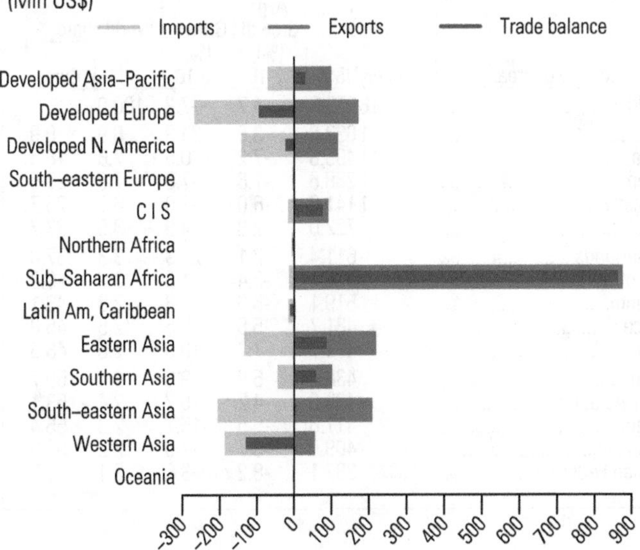

Table 3: Top importing countries or areas in 2016

Country or area	Value (million US$)	Avg. Growth (%) 12-16	Growth (%) 15-16	World share %	Cum.
World	1102.5	-9.1	-20.2	100.0	
USA	124.3	-9.9	-26.8	11.3	11.3
Singapore	115.1	-16.2	-17.9	10.4	21.7
United Arab Emirates	105.7	-10.1	-8.8	9.6	31.3
Japan	62.6	0.1	3.9	5.7	37.0
Malaysia	56.2	7.0	180.9	5.1	42.1
Rep. of Korea	55.3	0.3	6.7	5.0	47.1
Italy	45.7	0.2	-11.4	4.1	51.2
India	37.5	7.3	28.7	3.4	54.6
Belgium	34.0	-19.0	-30.4	3.1	57.7
Germany	34.0	2.5	17.5	3.1	60.8
China	33.9	-3.3	-15.5	3.1	63.9
Ireland	30.4	-4.0	4.1	2.8	66.6
China, Hong Kong SAR	29.2	-13.0	0.1	2.7	69.3
United Kingdom	28.9	-35.9	-17.0	2.6	71.9
Saudi Arabia	24.9	11.7	38.0	2.3	74.2

278 Other crude minerals

In 2016, the value (in current US$) of exports of "other crude minerals" (SITC group 278) decreased by 9.7 percent (compared to -3.8 percent average growth rate from 2012-2016) to reach 14.6 bln US$ (see table 2), while imports decreased by 7.2 percent to reach 18.4 bln US$ (see table 3). Exports of this commodity accounted for 2.3 percent of world exports of SITC sections 2+4, and 0.1 percent of total world merchandise exports (see table 1). China, USA and Germany were the top exporters in 2016 (see table 2). They accounted for 13.9, 10.6 and 6.2 percent of world exports, respectively. USA, China and Japan were the top destinations, with respectively 8.9, 7.6 and 7.0 percent of world imports (see table 3).

The top 15 countries/areas accounted for 71.2 and 59.7 percent of total world exports and imports, respectively (see tables 2 and 3). In 2016, China was the country/area with the highest value of net exports (+621.5 mln US$), followed by Turkey (+519.4 mln US$). By MDG regions (see graph 2), the largest surpluses in this product group were recorded by Latin America and the Caribbean (+274.2 mln US$) and Southern Asia (+101.6 mln US$). The largest trade deficits were recorded by Developed Europe (-1.4 bln US$), South-eastern Asia (-1.1 bln US$) and Developed Asia-Pacific (-790.3 mln US$).

Table 1: Imports (Imp.) and exports (Exp.), 2002-2016, in current US$

		2002	2003	2004	2005	2006	2007	2008	2009	2010	2011	2012	2013	2014	2015	2016
Values in Bln US$	Imp.	9.5	10.5	13.3	13.7	15.0	16.5	20.8	15.9	19.5	23.6	22.3	22.4	22.6	19.8	18.4
	Exp.	7.1	8.2	9.6	10.1	11.2	12.1	14.6	11.4	14.9	16.8	17.0	17.5	18.5	16.2	14.6
As a percentage of SITC section (%)	Imp.	3.9	3.6	3.5	3.3	3.0	2.7	2.7	2.9	2.6	2.4	2.4	2.4	2.5	2.7	2.6
	Exp.	3.3	3.2	3.0	2.7	2.5	2.2	2.2	2.3	2.1	1.9	2.0	2.1	2.3	2.5	2.3
As a percentage of world trade (%)	Imp.	0.1	0.1	0.1	0.1	0.1	0.1	0.1	0.1	0.1	0.1	0.1	0.1	0.1	0.1	0.1
	Exp.	0.1	0.1	0.1	0.1	0.1	0.1	0.1	0.1	0.1	0.1	0.1	0.1	0.1	0.1	0.1

Graph 1: Annual growth rates of exports, 2002–2016
(In percentage by year)

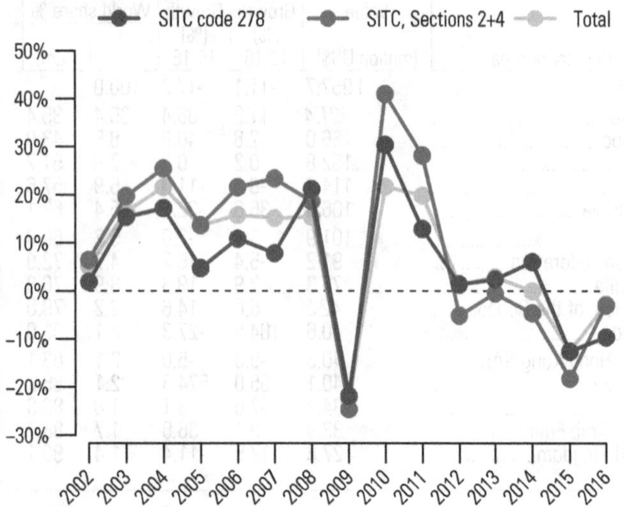

Table 2: Top exporting countries or areas in 2016

Country or area	Value (million US$)	Avg. Growth (%) 12-16	Growth (%) 15-16	World share %	Cum.
World	14601.4	-3.8	-9.7	100.0	
China	2025.1	-4.8	-15.0	13.9	13.9
USA	1550.1	-1.3	-6.9	10.6	24.5
Germany	910.6	-2.6	0.9	6.2	30.7
Netherlands	847.1	0.1	7.7	5.8	36.5
Turkey	707.5	3.9	2.4	4.8	41.4
India	627.0	-2.9	15.1	4.3	45.7
Belgium	609.2	1.3	-6.0	4.2	49.8
Spain	445.4	-3.9	4.5	3.1	52.9
France	435.3	-1.9	5.1	3.0	55.9
Canada	434.4	-2.5	-28.1	3.0	58.8
Brazil	432.8	-4.2	-10.3	3.0	61.8
United Kingdom	364.7	-3.6	-10.9	2.5	64.3
Mexico	346.7	-6.7	-11.7	2.4	66.7
South Africa	341.0	-16.6	-26.9	2.3	69.0
Australia	325.6	5.8	12.5	2.2	71.2

Graph 2: Trade Balance by MDG regions 2016
(Bln US$)

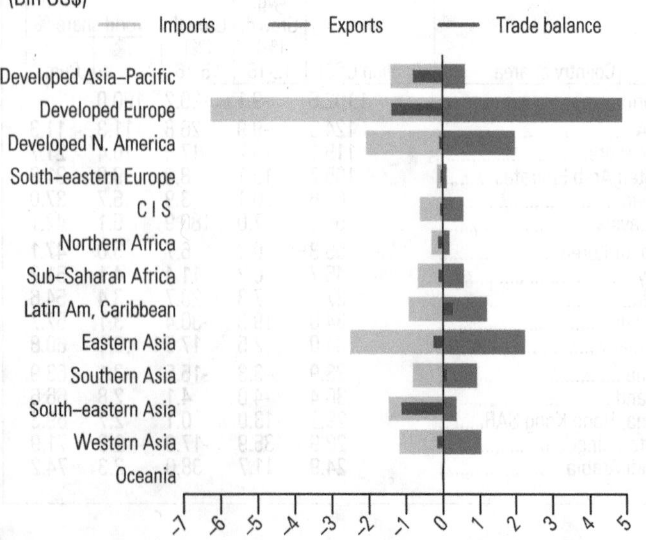

Table 3: Top importing countries or areas in 2016

Country or area	Value (million US$)	Avg. Growth (%) 12-16	Growth (%) 15-16	World share %	Cum.
World	18378.6	-4.7	-7.2	100.0	
USA	1633.8	-3.8	-24.3	8.9	8.9
China	1403.6	-7.2	0.5	7.6	16.5
Japan	1288.6	-7.6	-7.3	7.0	23.5
Germany	1141.0	-6.0	-1.0	6.2	29.7
Italy	722.0	-2.8	4.9	3.9	33.7
Netherlands	611.4	-2.1	21.3	3.3	37.0
Rep. of Korea	610.1	-3.4	-1.8	3.3	40.3
Belgium	519.1	-5.9	-7.8	2.8	43.1
France	481.7	-5.8	-5.5	2.6	45.8
India	472.7	-7.7	-10.8	2.6	48.3
Spain	438.8	5.9	9.3	2.4	50.7
Other Asia, nes	438.5	-4.2	-15.2	2.4	53.1
Canada	417.6	-5.5	-15.7	2.3	55.4
Indonesia	409.6	-5.7	-7.0	2.2	57.6
Russian Federation	387.1	-8.2	-3.6	2.1	59.7

In 2016, the value (in current US$) of exports of "iron ore and concentrates" (SITC group 281) increased by 4.3 percent (compared to -13.5 percent average growth rate from 2012-2016) to reach 70.4 bln US$ (see table 2), while imports decreased by 4.5 percent to reach 85.9 bln US$ (see table 3). Exports of this commodity accounted for 11.0 percent of world exports of SITC sections 2+4, and 0.4 percent of total world merchandise exports (see table 1). Australia, Brazil and South Africa were the top exporters in 2016 (see table 2). They accounted for 56.4, 18.9 and 5.1 percent of world exports, respectively. China, Japan and Rep. of Korea were the top destinations, with respectively 67.6, 8.6 and 4.7 percent of world imports (see table 3).

The top 15 countries/areas accounted for 97.6 and 93.6 percent of total world exports and imports, respectively (see tables 2 and 3). In 2016, Australia was the country/area with the highest value of net exports (+39.7 bln US$), followed by Brazil (+13.3 bln US$). By MDG regions (see graph 2), the largest surpluses in this product group were recorded by Developed Asia-Pacific (+32.3 bln US$), Latin America and the Caribbean (+14.1 bln US$) and Sub-Saharan Africa (+4.1 bln US$). The largest trade deficits were recorded by Eastern Asia (-63.1 bln US$), Developed Europe (-5.5 bln US$) and Western Asia (-1.9 bln US$).

Table 1: Imports (Imp.) and exports (Exp.), 2002-2016, in current US$

		2002	2003	2004	2005	2006	2007	2008	2009	2010	2011	2012	2013	2014	2015	2016
Values in Bln US$	Imp.	13.1	16.9	29.6	40.7	47.4	65.8	108.5	77.4	132.1	184.6	156.7	162.9	146.4	89.9	85.9
	Exp.	9.9	11.3	16.5	28.1	33.2	41.2	67.3	56.2	105.2	149.7	125.5	138.4	116.9	67.5	70.4
As a percentage of SITC section (%)	Imp.	5.4	5.8	7.9	9.8	9.6	10.6	14.2	14.2	17.4	18.7	17.0	17.7	16.4	12.3	12.3
	Exp.	4.6	4.4	5.1	7.6	7.4	7.5	10.3	11.4	15.1	16.8	14.8	16.4	14.5	10.3	11.0
As a percentage of world trade (%)	Imp.	0.2	0.2	0.3	0.4	0.4	0.5	0.7	0.6	0.9	1.0	0.9	0.9	0.8	0.5	0.5
	Exp.	0.2	0.2	0.2	0.3	0.3	0.3	0.4	0.5	0.7	0.8	0.7	0.7	0.6	0.4	0.4

Graph 1: Annual growth rates of exports, 2002–2016

(In percentage by year)

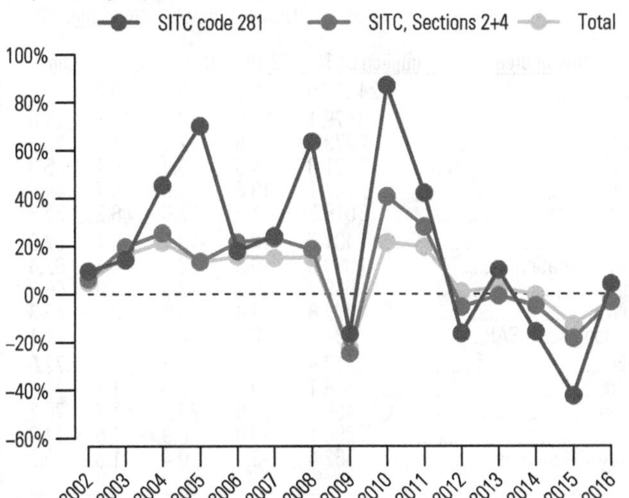

Table 2: Top exporting countries or areas in 2016

Country or area	Value (million US$)	Avg. Growth (%) 12-16	Growth (%) 15-16	World share %	Cum.
World	70407.0	-13.5	4.3	100.0	
Australia	39691.5	-8.5	8.0	56.4	56.4
Brazil	13289.3	-19.1	-5.6	18.9	75.2
South Africa	3582.3	-17.5	35.1	5.1	80.3
Canada	2882.2	-8.8	2.6	4.1	84.4
Sweden	1608.8	-16.8	2.6	2.3	86.7
Netherlands	1227.2	235.0	4068.3	1.7	88.5
India	1005.3	-19.8	377.2	1.4	89.9
Chile	828.6	-11.3	15.5	1.2	91.1
Malaysia	814.4	23.5	58.4	1.2	92.2
Russian Federation	802.3	-24.7	-20.9	1.1	93.4
Iran	*787.3*	-20.4	-25.1	1.1	94.5
Bahrain	777.0	-13.2	96.5	1.1	95.6
USA	580.8	-20.3	-11.1	0.8	96.4
Mauritania	487.7	-16.7	-25.1	0.7	97.1
Kazakhstan	386.7	-36.7	-4.5	0.5	97.6

Graph 2: Trade Balance by MDG regions 2016

(Bln US$)

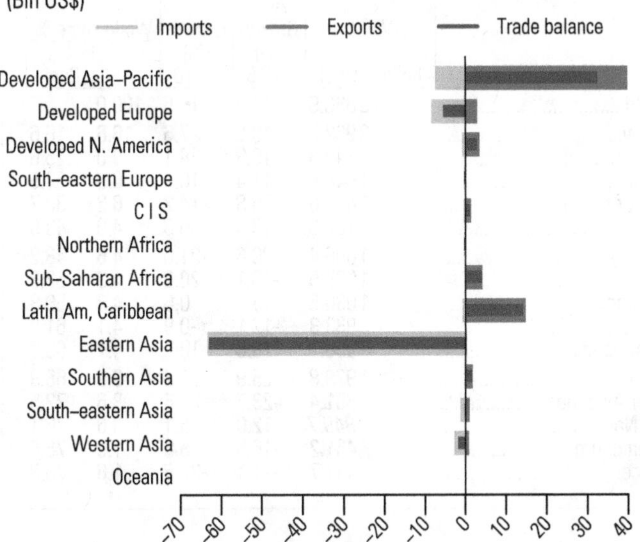

Table 3: Top importing countries or areas in 2016

Country or area	Value (million US$)	Avg. Growth (%) 12-16	Growth (%) 15-16	World share %	Cum.
World	85876.7	-14.0	-4.5	100.0	
China	58032.6	-11.7	1.1	67.6	67.6
Japan	7348.6	-21.3	-20.9	8.6	76.1
Rep. of Korea	4052.7	-19.2	-17.3	4.7	80.9
Germany	2441.2	-18.1	-12.3	2.8	83.7
Netherlands	1938.8	14.4	252.1	2.3	86.0
Other Asia, nes	1325.4	-15.7	-15.0	1.5	87.5
France	765.6	-19.2	-9.9	0.9	88.4
Malaysia	756.1	6.3	31.3	0.9	89.3
Turkey	697.8	-11.7	-12.8	0.8	90.1
United Kingdom	571.7	-18.8	-24.6	0.7	90.7
Saudi Arabia	558.3	-21.1	-20.9	0.7	91.4
Italy	513.1	-27.1	-6.2	0.6	92.0
United Arab Emirates	496.6	-6.2	-7.0	0.6	92.6
Canada	470.4	-15.0	-13.1	0.5	93.1
Belgium	444.1	-14.8	-0.8	0.5	93.6

Source: UN Comtrade

282 Ferrous waste and scrap; remelting scrap ingots of iron or steel

In 2016, the value (in current US$) of exports of "ferrous waste and scrap; remelting scrap ingots of iron or steel" (SITC group 282) decreased by 9.5 percent (compared to -15.9 percent average growth rate from 2012-2016) to reach 24.6 bln US$ (see table 2), while imports decreased by 15.5 percent to reach 23.8 bln US$ (see table 3). Exports of this commodity accounted for 3.9 percent of world exports of SITC sections 2+4, and 0.2 percent of total world merchandise exports (see table 1). USA, Germany and Japan were the top exporters in 2016 (see table 2). They accounted for 14.6, 11.3 and 9.4 percent of world exports, respectively. Turkey, India and Belgium were the top destinations, with respectively 16.6, 9.0 and 6.9 percent of world imports (see table 3).

The top 15 countries/areas accounted for 79.2 and 79.8 percent of total world exports and imports, respectively (see tables 2 and 3). In 2016, USA was the country/area with the highest value of net exports (+2.6 bln US$), followed by Japan (+2.2 bln US$). By MDG regions (see graph 2), the largest surpluses in this product group were recorded by Developed Europe (+4.0 bln US$), Developed North America (+3.5 bln US$) and Developed Asia-Pacific (+2.7 bln US$). The largest trade deficits were recorded by Western Asia (-3.5 bln US$), Southern Asia (-3.4 bln US$) and Eastern Asia (-2.6 bln US$).

Table 1: Imports (Imp.) and exports (Exp.), 2002-2016, in current US$

		2002	2003	2004	2005	2006	2007	2008	2009	2010	2011	2012	2013	2014	2015	2016
Values in Bln US$	Imp.	9.8	14.9	27.1	27.0	32.7	45.0	58.2	31.3	45.3	58.5	52.8	44.4	43.0	28.2	23.8
	Exp.	8.7	12.8	23.1	23.9	30.8	41.6	51.2	30.2	43.9	55.2	49.2	42.4	41.3	27.1	24.6
As a percentage of SITC section (%)	Imp.	4.0	5.1	7.2	6.5	6.6	7.3	7.6	5.8	6.0	5.9	5.7	4.8	4.8	3.8	3.4
	Exp.	4.1	5.0	7.1	6.5	6.9	7.5	7.8	6.1	6.3	6.2	5.8	5.0	5.1	4.1	3.9
As a percentage of world trade (%)	Imp.	0.1	0.2	0.3	0.3	0.3	0.3	0.4	0.2	0.3	0.3	0.3	0.2	0.2	0.2	0.1
	Exp.	0.1	0.2	0.3	0.2	0.3	0.3	0.3	0.2	0.3	0.3	0.3	0.2	0.2	0.2	0.2

Graph 1: Annual growth rates of exports, 2002–2016

(In percentage by year)

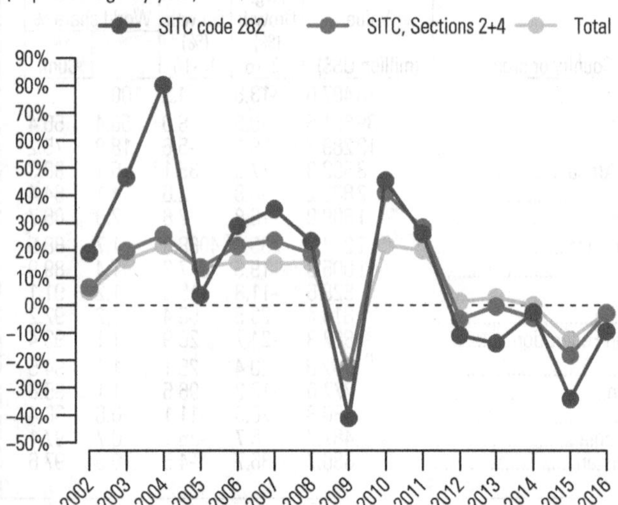

Graph 2: Trade Balance by MDG regions 2016

(Bln US$)

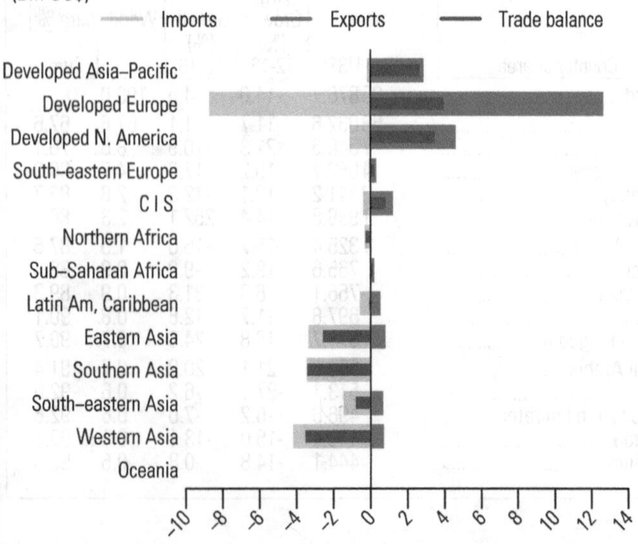

Table 2: Top exporting countries or areas in 2016

Country or area	Value (million US$)	Avg. Growth (%) 12-16	Growth (%) 15-16	World share %	Cum.
World	24577.9	-15.9	-9.5	100.0	
USA	3579.1	-21.5	-10.8	14.6	14.6
Germany	2773.9	-15.5	-12.5	11.3	25.8
Japan	2321.8	-14.3	-3.4	9.4	35.3
Netherlands	2147.1	-13.6	-2.8	8.7	44.0
United Kingdom	2018.3	-11.9	-7.6	8.2	52.2
France	1401.7	-16.0	-12.7	5.7	57.9
Russian Federation	1089.8	-6.3	-12.2	4.4	62.4
Canada	939.2	-16.2	-3.0	3.8	66.2
Belgium	773.8	-14.4	-0.9	3.1	69.3
China, Hong Kong SAR	437.5	-2.0	2.7	1.8	71.1
Czechia	417.4	-14.9	-7.8	1.7	72.8
Denmark	416.1	-9.5	7.3	1.7	74.5
Australia	408.3	-20.0	-23.2	1.7	76.2
Poland	386.1	-19.0	-20.9	1.6	77.8
United Arab Emirates	362.4	-3.1	0.4	1.5	79.2

Table 3: Top importing countries or areas in 2016

Country or area	Value (million US$)	Avg. Growth (%) 12-16	Growth (%) 15-16	World share %	Cum.
World	23836.9	-18.0	-15.5	100.0	
Turkey	3962.2	-19.5	-7.6	16.6	16.6
India	2143.8	-16.8	-28.1	9.0	25.6
Belgium	1648.6	-11.4	-10.7	6.9	32.5
Rep. of Korea	1473.0	-25.8	-14.2	6.2	38.7
Spain	1160.8	-13.9	-30.3	4.9	43.6
Germany	1096.4	-20.6	-21.0	4.6	48.2
Italy	1035.0	-18.1	-20.2	4.3	52.5
Pakistan	1030.5	13.7	0.6	4.3	56.8
USA	983.3	-12.1	-0.9	4.1	61.0
Netherlands	966.1	-16.8	-18.7	4.1	65.0
China	929.8	-25.9	-21.8	3.9	68.9
Other Asia, nes	851.4	-23.7	-21.8	3.6	72.5
Viet Nam	*849.7*	-12.0	5.1	3.6	76.1
Luxembourg	451.2	-16.5	-8.8	1.9	78.0
France	431.7	-21.1	-32.6	1.8	79.8

In 2016, the value (in current US$) of exports of "copper ores and concentrates; copper mattes, cement copper" (SITC group 283) increased by 1.5 percent (compared to -2.3 percent average growth rate from 2012-2016) to reach 47.3 bln US$ (see table 2), while imports decreased by 4.0 percent to reach 43.9 bln US$ (see table 3). Exports of this commodity accounted for 7.4 percent of world exports of SITC sections 2+4, and 0.3 percent of total world merchandise exports (see table 1). Chile, Peru and Australia were the top exporters in 2016 (see table 2). They accounted for 26.5, 18.5 and 7.4 percent of world exports, respectively. China, Japan and Rep. of Korea were the top destinations, with respectively 47.8, 17.0 and 6.7 percent of world imports (see table 3).

The top 15 countries/areas accounted for 90.8 and 96.4 percent of total world exports and imports, respectively (see tables 2 and 3). In 2016, Chile was the country/area with the highest value of net exports (+12.3 bln US$), followed by Peru (+8.7 bln US$). By MDG regions (see graph 2), the largest surpluses in this product group were recorded by Latin America and the Caribbean (+24.4 bln US$), Developed North America (+4.8 bln US$) and South-eastern Asia (+4.5 bln US$). The largest trade deficits were recorded by Eastern Asia (-22.2 bln US$), Developed Asia-Pacific (-4.1 bln US$) and Developed Europe (-3.5 bln US$).

Table 1: Imports (Imp.) and exports (Exp.), 2002-2016, in current US$

		2002	2003	2004	2005	2006	2007	2008	2009	2010	2011	2012	2013	2014	2015	2016
Values in Bln US$	Imp.	6.0	7.3	12.2	16.4	32.9	37.9	38.0	30.9	46.6	53.8	52.7	57.3	54.1	45.7	43.9
	Exp.	6.2	8.2	13.3	19.4	32.3	37.9	34.5	31.4	44.6	51.7	51.9	53.1	53.3	46.6	47.3
As a percentage of SITC section (%)	Imp.	2.5	2.5	3.2	3.9	6.6	6.1	5.0	5.7	6.1	5.4	5.7	6.2	6.1	6.2	6.3
	Exp.	2.9	3.2	4.1	5.3	7.2	6.9	5.3	6.3	6.4	5.8	6.1	6.3	6.6	7.1	7.4
As a percentage of world trade (%)	Imp.	0.1	0.1	0.1	0.2	0.3	0.3	0.2	0.2	0.3	0.3	0.3	0.3	0.3	0.3	0.3
	Exp.	0.1	0.1	0.1	0.2	0.3	0.3	0.2	0.3	0.3	0.3	0.3	0.3	0.3	0.3	0.3

Graph 1: Annual growth rates of exports, 2002–2016
(In percentage by year)

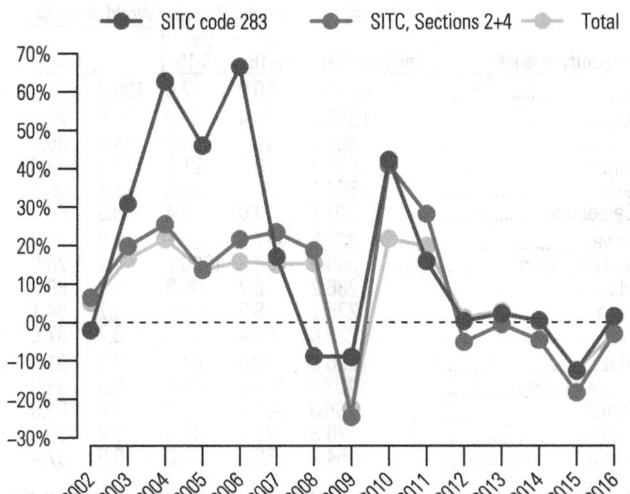

Graph 2: Trade Balance by MDG regions 2016
(Bln US$)

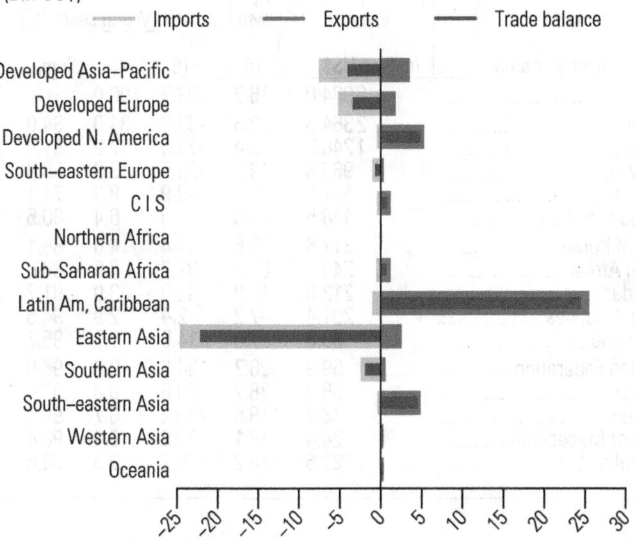

Table 2: Top exporting countries or areas in 2016

Country or area	Value (million US$)	Avg. Growth (%) 12-16	Growth (%) 15-16	World share %	Cum.
World	47309.8	-2.3	1.5	100.0	
Chile	12519.5	-6.2	-10.0	26.5	26.5
Peru	8734.7	0.9	32.9	18.5	44.9
Australia	3489.0	-10.6	-4.7	7.4	52.3
Indonesia	3482.0	7.6	6.2	7.4	59.7
Canada	2821.7	-3.5	-9.1	6.0	65.6
USA	2447.4	0.5	-20.6	5.2	70.8
Brazil	1928.8	5.1	-4.3	4.1	74.9
Mongolia	1607.8	13.3	-29.5	3.4	78.3
Mexico	1477.7	0.7	21.6	3.1	81.4
Spain	1182.2	0.7	4.5	2.5	83.9
Other Asia, nes	813.9	182.3	18958.4	1.7	85.6
Lao People's Dem. Rep.	728.0	35.4	17.1	1.5	87.2
Argentina	640.9	-19.3	39.2	1.4	88.5
Namibia	544.5	31.7	610.7	1.2	89.7
Philippines	527.1	23.2	-24.7	1.1	90.8

Table 3: Top importing countries or areas in 2016

Country or area	Value (million US$)	Avg. Growth (%) 12-16	Growth (%) 15-16	World share %	Cum.
World	43874.9	-4.5	-4.0	100.0	
China	20976.8	5.0	10.9	47.8	47.8
Japan	7452.9	-10.3	-4.9	17.0	64.8
Rep. of Korea	2935.4	-10.7	-19.9	6.7	71.5
India	2458.5	-15.8	-39.9	5.6	77.1
Spain	2286.1	-8.1	-11.9	5.2	82.3
Germany	1643.6	-14.2	-21.5	3.7	86.0
Bulgaria	922.2	-12.6	-31.1	2.1	88.1
Other Asia, nes	765.6	603.5	>	1.7	89.9
Brazil	688.8	5.1	-29.2	1.6	91.5
Finland	516.2	-13.3	-19.7	1.2	92.6
Sweden	414.7	-13.1	-11.0	0.9	93.6
Zambia	*337.1*	-20.6	-10.8	0.8	94.4
Poland	326.2	34.1	-21.3	0.7	95.1
Canada	316.6	-12.0	-5.7	0.7	95.8
Georgia	248.5	1224.6	19.6	0.6	96.4

284 Nickel ores and concentrates; nickel mattes, nickel oxide sinters

In 2016, the value (in current US$) of exports of "nickel ores and concentrates; nickel mattes, nickel oxide sinters" (SITC group 284) decreased by 17.0 percent (compared to -10.9 percent average growth rate from 2012-2016) to reach 6.3 bln US$ (see table 2), while imports decreased by 23.7 percent to reach 7.0 bln US$ (see table 3). Exports of this commodity accounted for 1.0 percent of world exports of SITC sections 2+4, and less than 0.1 percent of total world merchandise exports (see table 1). Canada, Cuba and Philippines were the top exporters in 2016 (see table 2). They accounted for 22.0, 14.4 and 13.3 percent of world exports, respectively. China, Japan and Norway were the top destinations, with respectively 34.0, 17.9 and 13.9 percent of world imports (see table 3).

The top 15 countries/areas accounted for 97.4 and 98.8 percent of total world exports and imports, respectively (see tables 2 and 3). In 2016, Canada was the country/area with the highest value of net exports (+1.2 bln US$), followed by Cuba (+905.2 mln US$). By MDG regions (see graph 2), the largest surpluses in this product group were recorded by South-eastern Asia (+1.5 bln US$), Developed North America (+1.4 bln US$) and Latin America and the Caribbean (+980.7 mln US$). The largest trade deficits were recorded by Eastern Asia (-2.9 bln US$), Developed Europe (-1.8 bln US$) and Developed Asia-Pacific (-1.0 bln US$).

Table 1: Imports (Imp.) and exports (Exp.), 2002-2016, in current US$

		2002	2003	2004	2005	2006	2007	2008	2009	2010	2011	2012	2013	2014	2015	2016
Values in Bln US$	Imp.	2.2	3.2	5.1	6.0	8.9	18.5	13.3	6.7	11.5	16.8	14.1	13.2	12.9	9.1	7.0
	Exp.	2.0	2.7	5.0	5.4	6.0	13.1	10.1	5.3	9.1	11.3	9.9	9.8	9.0	7.6	6.3
As a percentage of SITC section (%)	Imp.	0.9	1.1	1.4	1.4	1.8	3.0	1.7	1.2	1.5	1.7	1.5	1.4	1.4	1.2	1.0
	Exp.	0.9	1.1	1.6	1.5	1.4	2.4	1.5	1.1	1.3	1.3	1.2	1.2	1.1	1.1	1.0
As a percentage of world trade (%)	Imp.	0.0	0.0	0.1	0.1	0.1	0.1	0.1	0.1	0.1	0.1	0.1	0.1	0.1	0.1	0.0
	Exp.	0.0	0.0	0.1	0.1	0.1	0.1	0.1	0.0	0.1	0.1	0.1	0.1	0.0	0.0	0.0

Graph 1: Annual growth rates of exports, 2002–2016

(In percentage by year)

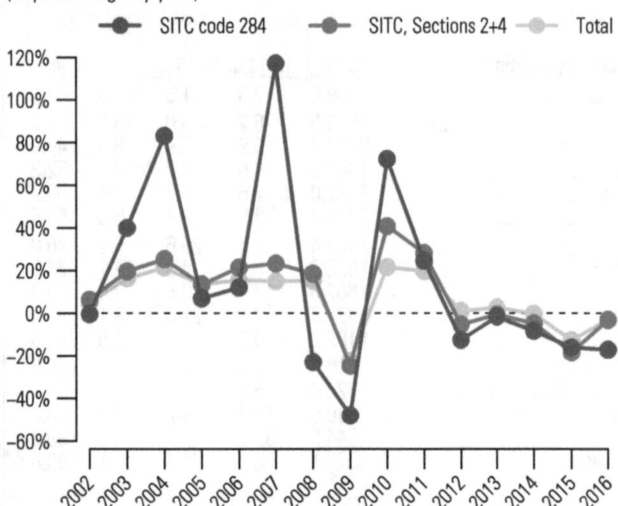

Table 2: Top exporting countries or areas in 2016

Country or area	Value (million US$)	Avg. Growth (%) 12-16	Growth (%) 15-16	World share %	Cum.
World	6273.9	-10.9	-17.0	100.0	
Canada	1380.2	-13.4	-36.2	22.0	22.0
Cuba	*906.1*	10.7	54.9	14.4	36.4
Philippines	837.3	6.1	-21.7	13.3	49.8
Indonesia	584.1	-30.3	-26.0	9.3	59.1
New Caledonia	*501.6*	3.0	8.4	8.0	67.1
Zimbabwe	328.5	-17.5	36.6	5.2	72.3
Russian Federation	266.0	94.3	1390.2	4.2	76.6
Finland	236.2	6.7	95.6	3.8	80.3
Botswana	235.2	-8.3	-26.6	3.7	84.1
USA	230.6	66.4	-38.9	3.7	87.8
Australia	226.0	-38.0	-61.3	3.6	91.4
Papua New Guinea	*157.8*	164.0	-18.4	2.5	93.9
Viet Nam	*86.3*	369.1	8.9	1.4	95.3
South Africa	78.3	46.7	-43.3	1.2	96.5
Guatemala	54.2	59.0	-37.6	0.9	97.4

Graph 2: Trade Balance by MDG regions 2016

(Bln US$)

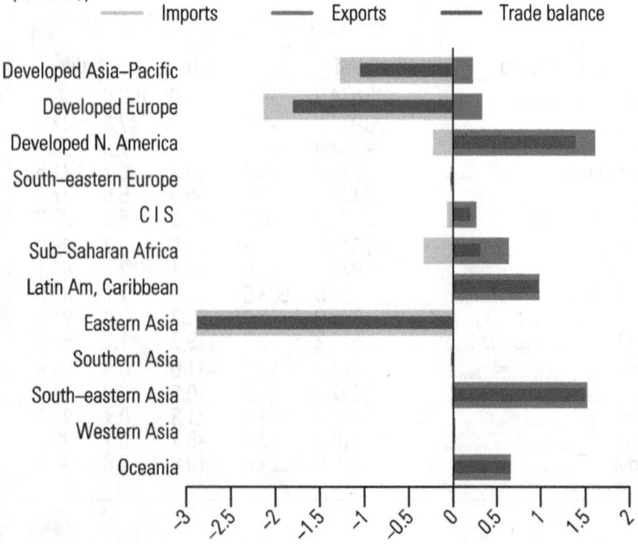

Table 3: Top importing countries or areas in 2016

Country or area	Value (million US$)	Avg. Growth (%) 12-16	Growth (%) 15-16	World share %	Cum.
World	6964.0	-16.2	-23.7	100.0	
China	2364.3	-22.3	-33.6	34.0	34.0
Japan	1248.5	-9.4	-23.6	17.9	51.9
Norway	969.8	-19.2	-26.9	13.9	65.8
Finland	577.5	-3.6	18.9	8.3	74.1
United Kingdom	448.5	-11.0	-17.9	6.4	80.5
Rep. of Korea	317.6	-8.6	14.4	4.6	85.1
South Africa	244.7	66.5	87.7	3.5	88.6
Canada	212.0	-16.9	-32.0	3.0	91.7
Other Asia, nes	201.4	-7.2	-2.4	2.9	94.5
Botswana	83.0	57.0	-14.8	1.2	95.7
Russian Federation	59.9	-26.7	54.6	0.9	96.6
France	55.3	-28.7	-39.6	0.8	97.4
Belgium	48.3	19.6	799.2	0.7	98.1
TFYR of Macedonia	24.4	-36.1	-72.6	0.4	98.4
Australia	22.6	-16.2	-75.2	0.3	98.8

In 2016, the value (in current US$) of exports of "aluminium ores and concentrates (including alumina)" (SITC group 285) decreased by 18.4 percent (compared to -2.0 percent average growth rate from 2012-2016) to reach 12.5 bln US$ (see table 2), while imports decreased by 15.7 percent to reach 14.8 bln US$ (see table 3). Exports of this commodity accounted for 2.0 percent of world exports of SITC sections 2+4, and 0.1 percent of total world merchandise exports (see table 1). Australia, Brazil and Guinea were the top exporters in 2016 (see table 2). They accounted for 38.7, 19.9 and 5.1 percent of world exports, respectively. China, United Arab Emirates and Canada were the top destinations, with respectively 22.7, 9.3 and 8.7 percent of world imports (see table 3).

The top 15 countries/areas accounted for 92.7 and 81.3 percent of total world exports and imports, respectively (see tables 2 and 3). In 2016, Australia was the country/area with the highest value of net exports (+4.8 bln US$), followed by Brazil (+2.5 bln US$). By MDG regions (see graph 2), the largest surpluses in this product group were recorded by Developed Asia-Pacific (+4.7 bln US$), Latin America and the Caribbean (+2.8 bln US$) and Sub-Saharan Africa (+319.3 mln US$). The largest trade deficits were recorded by Eastern Asia (-3.5 bln US$), Western Asia (-2.4 bln US$) and Developed Europe (-1.6 bln US$).

Table 1: Imports (Imp.) and exports (Exp.), 2002-2016, in current US$

		2002	2003	2004	2005	2006	2007	2008	2009	2010	2011	2012	2013	2014	2015	2016
Values in Bln US$	Imp.	6.6	7.6	9.8	12.4	15.0	16.7	19.0	10.9	13.6	15.1	16.5	18.2	17.9	17.6	14.8
	Exp.	5.2	6.3	8.1	9.9	12.5	13.9	15.0	9.6	13.7	14.8	13.6	15.3	14.9	15.3	12.5
As a percentage of SITC section (%)	Imp.	2.7	2.6	2.6	3.0	3.0	2.7	2.5	2.0	1.8	1.5	1.8	2.0	2.0	2.4	2.1
	Exp.	2.4	2.4	2.5	2.7	2.8	2.5	2.3	1.9	2.0	1.7	1.6	1.8	1.8	2.3	2.0
As a percentage of world trade (%)	Imp.	0.1	0.1	0.1	0.1	0.1	0.1	0.1	0.1	0.1	0.1	0.1	0.1	0.1	0.1	0.1
	Exp.	0.1	0.1	0.1	0.1	0.1	0.1	0.1	0.1	0.1	0.1	0.1	0.1	0.1	0.1	0.1

Graph 1: Annual growth rates of exports, 2002–2016
(In percentage by year)

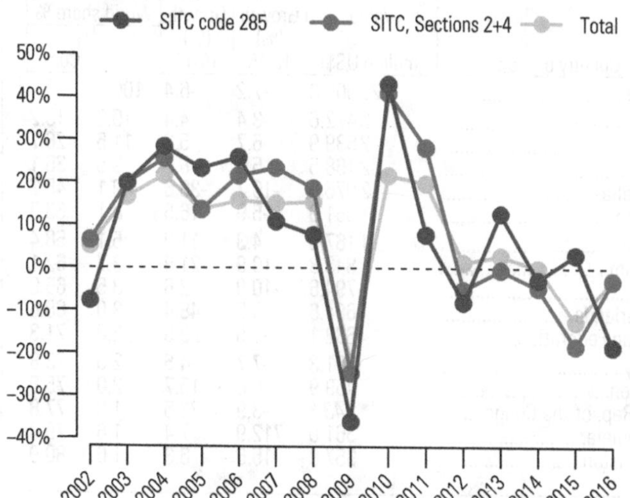

Graph 2: Trade Balance by MDG regions 2016
(Bln US$)

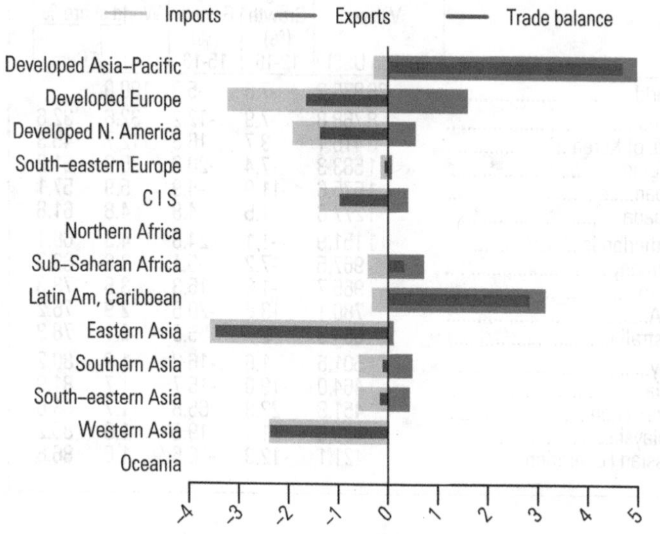

Table 2: Top exporting countries or areas in 2016

Country or area	Value (million US$)	Avg. Growth (%) 12-16	Growth (%) 15-16	World share %	Cum.
World	12508.5	-2.0	-18.4	100.0	
Australia	4836.4	-3.0	-14.1	38.7	38.7
Brazil	2484.3	2.6	-10.4	19.9	58.5
Guinea	*642.0*	17.2	11.4	5.1	63.7
Jamaica	538.9	-4.2	-19.8	4.3	68.0
USA	511.6	-9.8	-40.0	4.1	72.1
India	480.0	4.6	-31.2	3.8	75.9
Ireland	464.0	-0.7	-21.7	3.7	79.6
Kazakhstan	311.1	0.5	-7.1	2.5	82.1
Germany	306.6	-2.7	5.8	2.5	84.5
France	249.6	-2.1	6.7	2.0	86.5
Spain	181.2	4.9	-21.6	1.4	88.0
Viet Nam	*159.8*	657.7	8.9	1.3	89.3
Malaysia	151.2	92.0	-78.6	1.2	90.5
Netherlands	140.1	47.2	-12.4	1.1	91.6
Japan	138.4	-3.2	-4.9	1.1	92.7

Table 3: Top importing countries or areas in 2016

Country or area	Value (million US$)	Avg. Growth (%) 12-16	Growth (%) 15-16	World share %	Cum.
World	14822.5	-2.7	-15.7	100.0	
China	3369.2	-2.3	-25.6	22.7	22.7
United Arab Emirates	1371.9	3.9	-10.2	9.3	32.0
Canada	1290.5	-2.1	-4.3	8.7	40.7
Russian Federation	1282.1	-6.4	-11.6	8.6	49.3
Norway	646.5	-2.5	-16.4	4.4	53.7
USA	619.8	-16.1	-43.1	4.2	57.9
India	514.9	9.3	11.7	3.5	61.4
Bahrain	433.8	18.1	-18.0	2.9	64.3
Iceland	428.2	-4.2	-17.4	2.9	67.2
Germany	401.9	-2.0	-1.2	2.7	69.9
Malaysia	385.0	34.5	37.3	2.6	72.5
Netherlands	349.6	4.7	61.4	2.4	74.8
South Africa	348.7	-5.3	33.9	2.4	77.2
Qatar	303.8	-7.9	-21.3	2.0	79.2
France	298.3	-5.7	-23.6	2.0	81.3

Source: UN Comtrade

287 Ores and concentrates of base metals, nes

In 2016, the value (in current US$) of exports of "ores and concentrates of base metals, nes" (SITC group 287) decreased by 6.4 percent (compared to -7.2 percent average growth rate from 2012-2016) to reach 22.9 bln US$ (see table 2), while imports decreased by 5.3 percent to reach 26.9 bln US$ (see table 3). Exports of this commodity accounted for 3.6 percent of world exports of SITC sections 2+4, and 0.1 percent of total world merchandise exports (see table 1). South Africa, Peru and USA were the top exporters in 2016 (see table 2). They accounted for 15.2, 11.5 and 9.5 percent of world exports, respectively. China, Rep. of Korea and Belgium were the top destinations, with respectively 32.6, 12.7 and 5.9 percent of world imports (see table 3).

The top 15 countries/areas accounted for 80.9 and 86.8 percent of total world exports and imports, respectively (see tables 2 and 3). In 2016, South Africa was the country/area with the highest value of net exports (+3.5 bln US$), followed by Peru (+2.6 bln US$). By MDG regions (see graph 2), the largest surpluses in this product group were recorded by Latin America and the Caribbean (+6.7 bln US$), Sub-Saharan Africa (+4.8 bln US$) and Western Asia (+460.9 mln US$). The largest trade deficits were recorded by Eastern Asia (-11.9 bln US$), Developed Europe (-3.9 bln US$) and South-eastern Asia (-499.7 mln US$).

Table 1: Imports (Imp.) and exports (Exp.), 2002-2016, in current US$

		2002	2003	2004	2005	2006	2007	2008	2009	2010	2011	2012	2013	2014	2015	2016
Values in Bln US$	Imp.	6.1	7.5	13.3	20.8	25.1	33.7	36.8	21.0	31.8	38.8	36.9	33.6	33.9	28.4	26.9
	Exp.	5.0	5.7	10.7	17.8	22.8	29.4	29.3	17.8	27.7	33.2	30.9	29.3	30.6	24.5	22.9
As a percentage of SITC section (%)	Imp.	2.5	2.6	3.5	5.0	5.1	5.4	4.8	3.9	4.2	3.9	4.0	3.7	3.8	3.9	3.9
	Exp.	2.3	2.2	3.3	4.8	5.1	5.3	4.5	3.6	4.0	3.7	3.6	3.5	3.8	3.7	3.6
As a percentage of world trade (%)	Imp.	0.1	0.1	0.1	0.2	0.2	0.2	0.2	0.2	0.2	0.2	0.2	0.2	0.2	0.2	0.2
	Exp.	0.1	0.1	0.1	0.2	0.2	0.2	0.2	0.1	0.2	0.2	0.2	0.2	0.2	0.1	0.1

Graph 1: Annual growth rates of exports, 2002–2016

(In percentage by year)

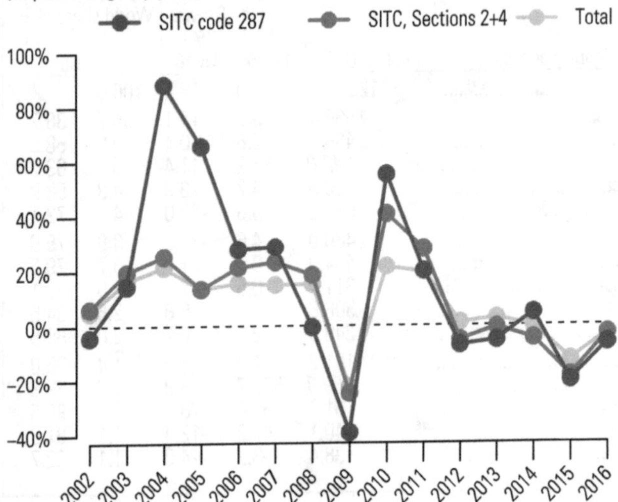

Graph 2: Trade Balance by MDG regions 2016

(Bln US$)

Imports — Exports — Trade balance

Developed Asia-Pacific
Developed Europe
Developed N. America
South-eastern Europe
CIS
Northern Africa
Sub-Saharan Africa
Latin Am, Caribbean
Eastern Asia
Southern Asia
South-eastern Asia
Western Asia
Oceania

-14 -12 -10 -8 -6 -4 -2 0 2 4 6 8

Table 2: Top exporting countries or areas in 2016

Country or area	Value (million US$)	Avg. Growth (%) 12-16	Growth (%) 15-16	World share %	Cum.
World	22909.6	-7.2	-6.4	100.0	
South Africa	3472.6	-3.4	4.4	15.2	15.2
Peru	2639.9	-6.7	5.3	11.5	26.7
USA	2168.5	-5.1	-8.7	9.5	36.1
Australia	2075.5	-16.7	-38.6	9.1	45.2
Mexico	1861.9	-5.9	-16.5	8.1	53.3
Bolivia	1167.8	4.3	11.9	5.1	58.4
Belgium	843.3	-10.9	-21.8	3.7	62.1
Chile	794.6	-10.9	-2.6	3.5	65.6
Netherlands	684.6	-0.5	48.4	3.0	68.6
Russian Federation	632.1	-2.8	29.5	2.8	71.3
Turkey	571.3	-7.7	-4.5	2.5	73.8
Sweden	459.9	6.6	15.7	2.0	75.8
Dem.Rep. of the Congo	*443.8*	-3.9	-32.5	1.9	77.8
Guatemala	361.0	712.9	7.4	1.6	79.3
Kazakhstan	357.8	-15.6	6.3	1.6	80.9

Table 3: Top importing countries or areas in 2016

Country or area	Value (million US$)	Avg. Growth (%) 12-16	Growth (%) 15-16	World share %	Cum.
World	26876.2	-7.6	-5.3	100.0	
China	8768.8	-7.9	-12.2	32.6	32.6
Rep. of Korea	3416.1	-3.7	16.3	12.7	45.3
Belgium	1583.3	-7.4	-20.8	5.9	51.2
Japan	1575.6	-11.9	-4.9	5.9	57.1
Canada	1277.6	-1.5	-4.8	4.8	61.8
Netherlands	1151.9	-1.1	24.8	4.3	66.1
Germany	967.5	-7.2	-5.1	3.6	69.7
Spain	965.7	-1.8	15.3	3.6	73.3
USA	780.1	-13.6	-20.5	2.9	76.2
Australia	564.9	2.7	55.5	2.1	78.3
Italy	501.5	1.6	-16.3	1.9	80.2
India	464.0	-19.0	-15.7	1.7	81.9
Kazakhstan	451.8	22.3	65.8	1.7	83.6
Malaysia	439.5	1.4	19.5	1.6	85.2
Russian Federation	421.1	-12.9	-16.6	1.6	86.8

Source: UN Comtrade

In 2016, the value (in current US$) of exports of "non-ferrous base metal waste and scrap, nes" (SITC group 288) decreased by 9.3 percent (compared to -9.9 percent average growth rate from 2012-2016) to reach 28.6 bln US$ (see table 2), while imports decreased by 16.0 percent to reach 33.1 bln US$ (see table 3). Exports of this commodity accounted for 4.5 percent of world exports of SITC sections 2+4, and 0.2 percent of total world merchandise exports (see table 1). USA, Germany and United Kingdom were the top exporters in 2016 (see table 2). They accounted for 15.3, 10.2 and 6.5 percent of world exports, respectively. China, Germany and India were the top destinations, with respectively 25.3, 11.2 and 6.9 percent of world imports (see table 3).

The top 15 countries/areas accounted for 71.2 and 85.0 percent of total world exports and imports, respectively (see tables 2 and 3). In 2016, USA was the country/area with the highest value of net exports (+2.6 bln US$), followed by Canada (+981.6 mln US$). By MDG regions (see graph 2), the largest surpluses in this product group were recorded by Developed North America (+3.6 bln US$), Latin America and the Caribbean (+2.1 bln US$) and Western Asia (+1.2 bln US$). The largest trade deficits were recorded by Eastern Asia (-10.7 bln US$), Southern Asia (-2.2 bln US$) and South-eastern Europe (-109.6 mln US$).

Table 1: Imports (Imp.) and exports (Exp.), 2002-2016, in current US$

		2002	2003	2004	2005	2006	2007	2008	2009	2010	2011	2012	2013	2014	2015	2016
Values in Bln US$	Imp.	9.6	11.0	16.2	19.2	32.0	40.4	38.4	26.2	46.2	59.5	54.8	50.4	47.9	39.4	33.1
	Exp.	8.0	9.4	12.9	17.0	30.0	35.8	34.6	23.7	37.5	46.3	43.4	40.0	38.5	31.5	28.6
As a percentage of SITC section (%)	Imp.	4.0	3.8	4.3	4.6	6.5	6.5	5.0	4.8	6.1	6.0	5.9	5.5	5.4	5.4	4.8
	Exp.	3.7	3.7	4.0	4.6	6.7	6.5	5.3	4.8	5.4	5.2	5.1	4.7	4.8	4.8	4.5
As a percentage of world trade (%)	Imp.	0.1	0.1	0.2	0.2	0.3	0.3	0.2	0.2	0.3	0.3	0.3	0.3	0.3	0.2	0.2
	Exp.	0.1	0.1	0.1	0.2	0.2	0.3	0.2	0.2	0.2	0.3	0.2	0.2	0.2	0.2	0.2

Graph 1: Annual growth rates of exports, 2002–2016
(In percentage by year)

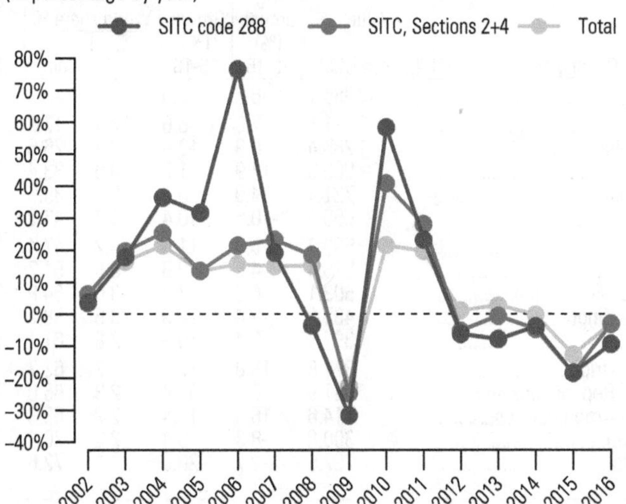

Table 2: Top exporting countries or areas in 2016

Country or area	Value (million US$)	Avg. Growth (%) 12-16	Growth (%) 15-16	World share %	Cum.
World	28550.4	-9.9	-9.3	100.0	
USA	4372.9	-14.6	-20.4	15.3	15.3
Germany	2917.6	-10.6	-14.7	10.2	25.5
United Kingdom	1849.8	-10.9	-4.1	6.5	32.0
Netherlands	1585.1	-6.3	-12.9	5.6	37.6
Canada	1536.9	-9.6	-8.2	5.4	42.9
France	1511.4	-11.0	-9.8	5.3	48.2
Belgium	844.5	-10.4	-5.3	3.0	51.2
Spain	810.4	-5.9	-7.9	2.8	54.0
Japan	797.6	-11.7	-9.0	2.8	56.8
Italy	787.1	-5.9	0.1	2.8	59.6
Australia	763.0	-8.0	-2.0	2.7	62.3
Mexico	698.8	-13.5	-1.4	2.4	64.7
Chile	685.4	11.6	-1.9	2.4	67.1
Saudi Arabia	663.7	21.9	-4.7	2.3	69.4
Poland	498.6	-0.9	-6.8	1.7	71.2

Graph 2: Trade Balance by MDG regions 2016
(Bln US$)

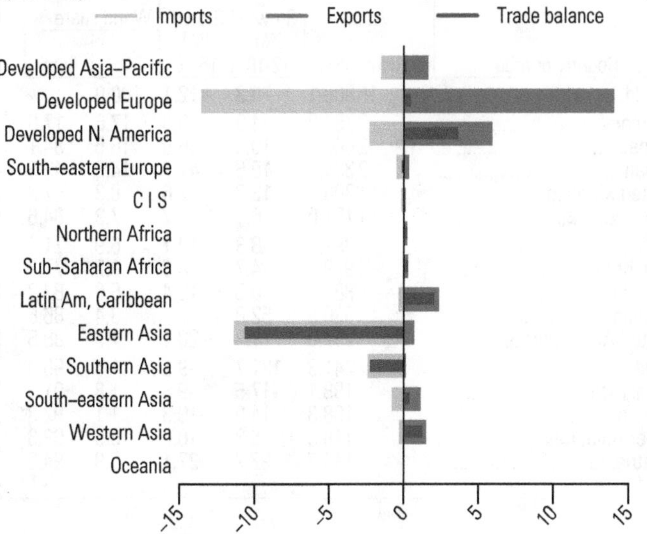

Table 3: Top importing countries or areas in 2016

Country or area	Value (million US$)	Avg. Growth (%) 12-16	Growth (%) 15-16	World share %	Cum.
World	33124.8	-11.8	-16.0	100.0	
China	8392.0	-18.5	-25.7	25.3	25.3
Germany	3694.6	-8.8	-9.6	11.2	36.5
India	2272.5	-4.4	-8.4	6.9	43.3
Rep. of Korea	2136.0	-10.4	-21.0	6.4	49.8
Belgium	1732.6	-12.3	4.9	5.2	55.0
USA	1728.7	-6.4	-3.9	5.2	60.2
Japan	1477.5	-13.6	-28.8	4.5	64.7
Italy	1412.3	-5.4	-14.0	4.3	69.0
United Kingdom	910.4	-11.4	-27.7	2.7	71.7
Austria	861.2	-12.4	1.0	2.6	74.3
Spain	786.2	-5.3	-8.2	2.4	76.7
Netherlands	767.3	-12.8	-11.6	2.3	79.0
Poland	687.3	3.2	-9.4	2.1	81.1
France	671.1	-8.5	-31.5	2.0	83.1
Other Asia, nes	640.3	-7.9	-4.0	1.9	85.0

289 Ores, concentrates of precious metals; waste, scrap and sweepings (no gold)

In 2016, the value (in current US$) of exports of "ores, concentrates of precious metals; waste, scrap and sweepings (no gold)" (SITC group 289) increased by 2.9 percent (compared to -6.2 percent average growth rate from 2012-2016) to reach 14.0 bln US$ (see table 2), while imports increased by 12.1 percent to reach 15.8 bln US$ (see table 3). Exports of this commodity accounted for 2.2 percent of world exports of SITC sections 2+4, and 0.1 percent of total world merchandise exports (see table 1). USA, Australia and Germany were the top exporters in 2016 (see table 2). They accounted for 17.3, 9.2 and 6.9 percent of world exports, respectively. Germany, China and Japan were the top destinations, with respectively 17.6, 16.5 and 14.9 percent of world imports (see table 3).

The top 15 countries/areas accounted for 72.6 and 94.2 percent of total world exports and imports, respectively (see tables 2 and 3). In 2016, USA was the country/area with the highest value of net exports (+1.3 bln US$), followed by Australia (+1.3 bln US$). By MDG regions (see graph 2), the largest surpluses in this product group were recorded by Latin America and the Caribbean (+2.5 bln US$), South-eastern Asia (+808.2 mln US$) and Sub-Saharan Africa (+746.5 mln US$). The largest trade deficits were recorded by Developed Europe (-3.6 bln US$), Eastern Asia (-3.3 bln US$) and Developed Asia-Pacific (-846.0 mln US$).

Table 1: Imports (Imp.) and exports (Exp.), 2002-2016, in current US$

		2002	2003	2004	2005	2006	2007	2008	2009	2010	2011	2012	2013	2014	2015	2016
Values in Bln US$	Imp.	3.4	3.5	3.5	4.6	7.2	10.1	13.1	8.4	11.1	15.7	16.0	16.1	16.6	14.1	15.8
	Exp.	2.7	2.9	3.2	3.8	6.4	9.6	14.3	11.6	16.9	18.8	18.1	15.8	15.8	13.6	14.0
As a percentage of SITC section (%)	Imp.	1.4	1.2	0.9	1.1	1.5	1.6	1.7	1.5	1.5	1.6	1.7	1.8	1.9	1.9	2.3
	Exp.	1.2	1.1	1.0	1.0	1.4	1.7	2.2	2.3	2.4	2.1	2.1	1.9	2.0	2.1	2.2
As a percentage of world trade (%)	Imp.	0.1	0.0	0.0	0.0	0.1	0.1	0.1	0.1	0.1	0.1	0.1	0.1	0.1	0.1	0.1
	Exp.	0.0	0.0	0.0	0.0	0.1	0.1	0.1	0.1	0.1	0.1	0.1	0.1	0.1	0.1	0.1

Graph 1: Annual growth rates of exports, 2002–2016

(In percentage by year)

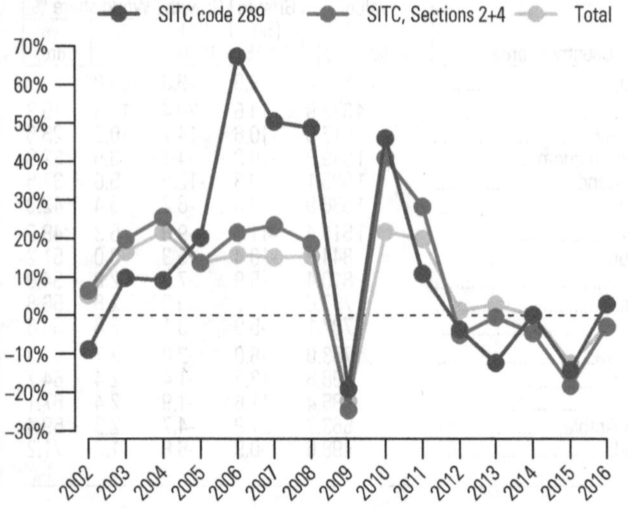

Table 2: Top exporting countries or areas in 2016

Country or area	Value (million US$)	Avg. Growth (%) 12-16	Growth (%) 15-16	World share %	Cum.
World	13 985.1	-6.2	2.9	100.0	
USA	2 421.6	-7.0	-6.6	17.3	17.3
Australia	1 285.4	0.9	13.8	9.2	26.5
Germany	960.5	-14.9	1.2	6.9	33.4
Indonesia	721.4	4.9	9.8	5.2	38.5
Bolivia	650.9	-10.5	10.4	4.7	43.2
Mexico	590.7	15.8	11.6	4.2	47.4
Peru	525.4	-4.6	9.8	3.8	51.2
Russian Federation	503.1	-0.3	37.2	3.6	54.8
United Kingdom	485.8	-9.4	12.9	3.5	58.2
India	397.5	-5.4	-10.9	2.8	61.1
South Africa	371.6	15.8	-17.8	2.7	63.7
United Rep. of Tanzania	321.9	-6.5	-31.4	2.3	66.0
United Arab Emirates	314.6	16.8	-17.4	2.2	68.3
Bulgaria	300.8	-8.3	5.4	2.2	70.4
Canada	297.5	-2.7	20.0	2.1	72.6

Graph 2: Trade Balance by MDG regions 2016

(Bln US$)

Imports — Exports — Trade balance

Developed Asia-Pacific
Developed Europe
Developed N. America
South-eastern Europe
CIS
Northern Africa
Sub-Saharan Africa
Latin Am, Caribbean
Eastern Asia
Southern Asia
South-eastern Asia
Western Asia
Oceania

-7 -6 -5 -4 -3 -2 -1 0 1 2 3

Table 3: Top importing countries or areas in 2016

Country or area	Value (million US$)	Avg. Growth (%) 12-16	Growth (%) 15-16	World share %	Cum.
World	15 809.1	-0.3	12.1	100.0	
Germany	2 784.2	-4.9	-9.0	17.6	17.6
China	2 608.1	19.5	36.9	16.5	34.1
Japan	2 354.5	15.6	47.7	14.9	49.0
United Kingdom	1 308.5	-13.2	2.6	8.3	57.3
Italy	1 151.0	-6.1	2.2	7.3	64.6
USA	1 097.9	-8.3	-10.1	6.9	71.5
Rep. of Korea	978.2	-4.7	-8.6	6.2	77.7
Canada	880.0	0.5	12.4	5.6	83.3
Belgium	530.5	52.8		3.4	86.6
United Arab Emirates	297.0	1.3	-20.1	1.9	88.5
India	241.3	131.7	-9.2	1.5	90.0
Kazakhstan	198.1	-17.5	-9.8	1.3	91.3
Singapore	168.3	-14.0	-19.3	1.1	92.3
Other Asia, nes	148.8	-6.3	16.6	0.9	93.3
Austria	143.7	92.7	27.1	0.9	94.2

In 2016, the value (in current US$) of exports of "crude animal materials, nes" (SITC group 291) decreased by 4.9 percent (compared to -2.9 percent average growth rate from 2012-2016) to reach 8.4 bln US$ (see table 2), while imports decreased by 4.7 percent to reach 8.2 bln US$ (see table 3). Exports of this commodity accounted for 1.3 percent of world exports of SITC sections 2+4, and 0.1 percent of total world merchandise exports (see table 1). China, USA and Germany were the top exporters in 2016 (see table 2). They accounted for 21.0, 12.0 and 9.6 percent of world exports, respectively. USA, Germany and Japan were the top destinations, with respectively 12.2, 10.5 and 7.5 percent of world imports (see table 3).

The top 15 countries/areas accounted for 78.5 and 70.2 percent of total world exports and imports, respectively (see tables 2 and 3). In 2016, China was the country/area with the highest value of net exports (+1.3 bln US$), followed by Brazil (+267.6 mln US$). By MDG regions (see graph 2), the largest surpluses in this product group were recorded by Eastern Asia (+1.1 bln US$), Latin America and the Caribbean (+141.4 mln US$) and Developed North America (+138.1 mln US$). The largest trade deficits were recorded by Developed Europe (-403.6 mln US$), South-eastern Asia (-390.7 mln US$) and Developed Asia-Pacific (-164.2 mln US$).

Table 1: Imports (Imp.) and exports (Exp.), 2002-2016, in current US$

		2002	2003	2004	2005	2006	2007	2008	2009	2010	2011	2012	2013	2014	2015	2016
Values in Bln US$	Imp.	3.9	4.3	5.0	5.3	5.5	6.0	7.1	6.6	7.1	8.6	9.2	9.8	10.0	8.6	8.2
	Exp.	3.6	4.0	4.7	5.1	5.3	5.9	7.3	6.5	7.0	8.8	9.5	10.4	10.7	8.9	8.4
As a percentage of SITC section (%)	Imp.	1.6	1.5	1.3	1.3	1.1	1.0	0.9	1.2	0.9	0.9	1.0	1.1	1.1	1.2	1.2
	Exp.	1.7	1.5	1.5	1.4	1.2	1.1	1.1	1.3	1.0	1.0	1.1	1.2	1.3	1.4	1.3
As a percentage of world trade (%)	Imp.	0.1	0.1	0.1	0.0	0.0	0.0	0.0	0.1	0.0	0.0	0.0	0.1	0.1	0.1	0.1
	Exp.	0.1	0.1	0.1	0.0	0.0	0.0	0.0	0.1	0.0	0.0	0.1	0.1	0.1	0.1	0.1

Graph 1: Annual growth rates of exports, 2002–2016
(In percentage by year)

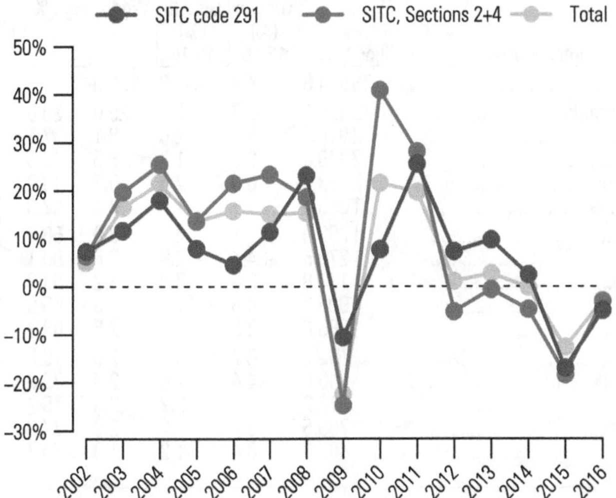

Graph 2: Trade Balance by MDG regions 2016
(Bln US$)

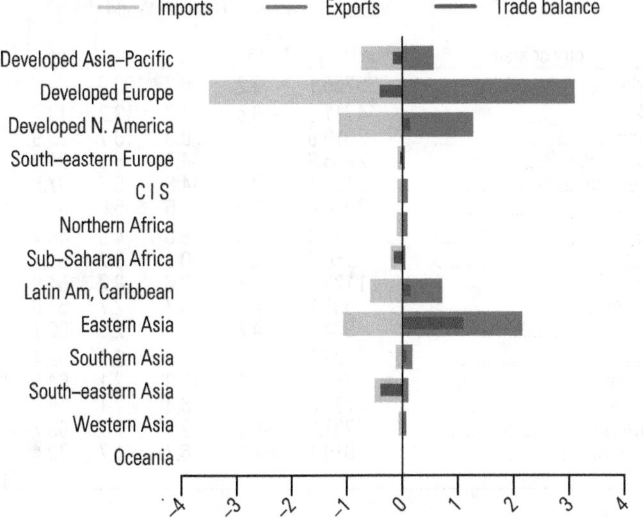

Table 2: Top exporting countries or areas in 2016

Country or area	Value (million US$)	Avg. Growth (%) 12-16	Growth (%) 15-16	World share %	Cum.
World	8446.7	-2.9	-4.9	100.0	
China	1772.4	-3.7	0.0	21.0	21.0
USA	1013.5	3.2	-10.4	12.0	33.0
Germany	812.2	-4.2	-0.9	9.6	42.6
Netherlands	532.8	-2.9	-3.7	6.3	48.9
Brazil	417.6	-7.7	-6.5	4.9	53.8
New Zealand	287.2	-5.1	-21.2	3.4	57.2
Poland	260.2	3.3	14.9	3.1	60.3
Spain	259.6	-1.5	3.5	3.1	63.4
Canada	258.7	3.1	-1.5	3.1	66.5
France	220.4	-6.0	-12.4	2.6	69.1
Australia	208.0	11.0	-2.8	2.5	71.5
Other Asia, nes	180.7	-8.7	-12.0	2.1	73.7
Denmark	149.6	-3.9	1.3	1.8	75.4
Belgium	128.4	-2.1	-1.6	1.5	77.0
Rep. of Korea	127.2	-6.1	4.8	1.5	78.5

Table 3: Top importing countries or areas in 2016

Country or area	Value (million US$)	Avg. Growth (%) 12-16	Growth (%) 15-16	World share %	Cum.
World	8162.8	-2.8	-4.7	100.0	
USA	992.3	1.8	-7.6	12.2	12.2
Germany	853.1	-6.1	-3.0	10.5	22.6
Japan	611.5	-8.1	0.1	7.5	30.1
China	522.2	4.0	11.9	6.4	36.5
Netherlands	388.1	-7.8	-13.6	4.8	41.3
France	373.8	-7.5	-11.5	4.6	45.8
Denmark	298.6	4.2	13.5	3.7	49.5
Mexico	241.7	3.6	-11.8	3.0	52.5
Other Asia, nes	237.3	-6.2	-6.9	2.9	55.4
Viet Nam	*234.2*	11.0	5.1	2.9	58.2
Italy	215.0	-6.8	-8.8	2.6	60.9
Spain	211.8	-1.9	1.3	2.6	63.5
Rep. of Korea	193.6	-9.3	-12.6	2.4	65.8
Poland	189.9	-6.6	-6.7	2.3	68.2
Belgium	170.3	-3.5	3.5	2.1	70.2

292 Crude vegetable materials, nes

In 2016, the value (in current US$) of exports of "crude vegetable materials, nes" (SITC group 292) decreased by 1.8 percent (compared to -4.4 percent average growth rate from 2012-2016) to reach 36.0 bln US$ (see table 2), while imports decreased by 0.2 percent to reach 35.8 bln US$ (see table 3). Exports of this commodity accounted for 5.6 percent of world exports of SITC sections 2+4, and 0.2 percent of total world merchandise exports (see table 1). Netherlands, China and USA were the top exporters in 2016 (see table 2). They accounted for 29.0, 8.1 and 6.5 percent of world exports, respectively. USA, Germany and Netherlands were the top destinations, with respectively 13.2, 10.7 and 8.1 percent of world imports (see table 3).

The top 15 countries/areas accounted for 78.7 and 70.4 percent of total world exports and imports, respectively (see tables 2 and 3). In 2016, Netherlands was the country/area with the highest value of net exports (+7.5 bln US$), followed by China (+1.8 bln US$). By MDG regions (see graph 2), the largest surpluses in this product group were recorded by Latin America and the Caribbean (+2.1 bln US$), Eastern Asia (+1.2 bln US$) and Sub-Saharan Africa (+924.6 mln US$). The largest trade deficits were recorded by Developed North America (-2.4 bln US$), Developed Asia-Pacific (-1.6 bln US$) and Commonwealth of Independent States (-1.2 bln US$).

Table 1: Imports (Imp.) and exports (Exp.), 2002-2016, in current US$

		2002	2003	2004	2005	2006	2007	2008	2009	2010	2011	2012	2013	2014	2015	2016
Values in Bln US$	Imp.	17.0	19.5	22.1	23.4	24.8	28.1	31.4	28.1	31.0	37.2	39.1	39.0	39.5	35.8	35.8
	Exp.	16.1	19.2	21.1	22.6	24.9	28.1	31.5	29.7	31.6	39.3	43.1	42.2	42.2	36.7	36.0
As a percentage of SITC section (%)	Imp.	7.0	6.7	5.9	5.6	5.0	4.5	4.1	5.2	4.1	3.8	4.2	4.2	4.4	4.9	5.1
	Exp.	7.5	7.4	6.5	6.1	5.6	5.1	4.8	6.0	4.5	4.4	5.1	5.0	5.3	5.6	5.6
As a percentage of world trade (%)	Imp.	0.3	0.3	0.2	0.2	0.2	0.2	0.2	0.2	0.2	0.2	0.2	0.2	0.2	0.2	0.2
	Exp.	0.3	0.3	0.2	0.2	0.2	0.2	0.2	0.2	0.2	0.2	0.2	0.2	0.2	0.2	0.2

Graph 1: Annual growth rates of exports, 2002–2016
(In percentage by year)

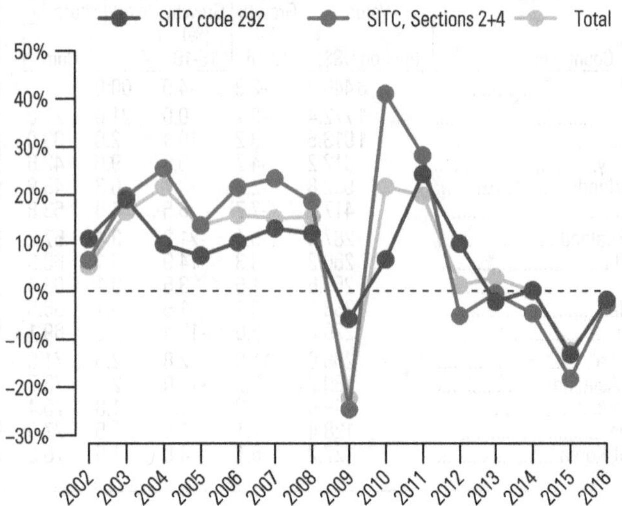

Table 2: Top exporting countries or areas in 2016

Country or area	Value (million US$)	Avg. Growth (%) 12-16	Growth (%) 15-16	World share %	Cum.
World	35984.8	-4.4	-1.8	100.0	
Netherlands	10425.1	-3.7	-3.2	29.0	29.0
China	2910.9	3.9	-2.0	8.1	37.1
USA	2328.0	-0.7	1.7	6.5	43.5
Germany	2033.2	0.0	7.3	5.7	49.2
Colombia	1356.4	1.1	1.7	3.8	52.9
Italy	1293.9	-1.1	8.8	3.6	56.5
India	1279.5	-34.4	-12.8	3.6	60.1
France	1133.8	0.8	7.8	3.2	63.3
Spain	905.2	4.6	11.9	2.5	65.8
Belgium	886.0	-8.3	3.0	2.5	68.2
Kenya	*842.5*	6.7	34.6	2.3	70.6
Denmark	840.5	-4.4	1.6	2.3	72.9
Ecuador	812.2	1.0	-2.2	2.3	75.2
Canada	786.5	3.7	0.0	2.2	77.3
Chile	485.0	-0.4	-1.2	1.3	78.7

Graph 2: Trade Balance by MDG regions 2016
(Bln US$)

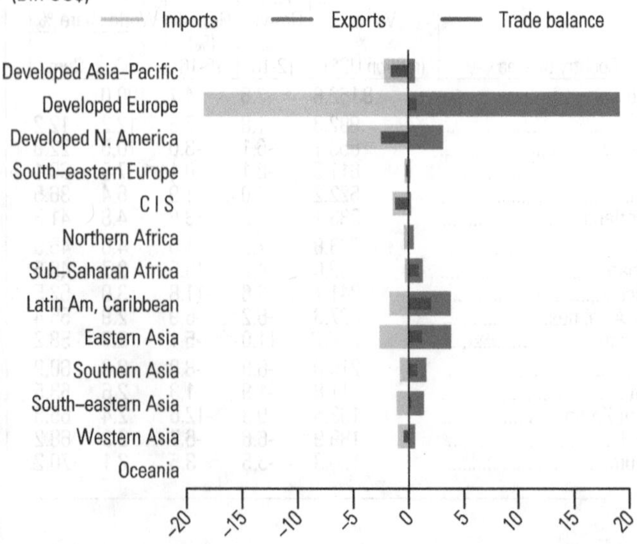

Table 3: Top importing countries or areas in 2016

Country or area	Value (million US$)	Avg. Growth (%) 12-16	Growth (%) 15-16	World share %	Cum.
World	35765.1	-2.2	-0.2	100.0	
USA	4711.5	-10.6	-4.2	13.2	13.2
Germany	3819.5	-2.9	0.3	10.7	23.9
Netherlands	2885.6	1.4	-4.7	8.1	31.9
United Kingdom	2101.1	0.1	-4.8	5.9	37.8
France	2076.4	-1.0	5.6	5.8	43.6
Japan	1733.8	-2.0	8.6	4.8	48.4
China	1150.2	2.8	-10.1	3.2	51.7
Italy	1129.9	-1.8	2.6	3.2	54.8
Russian Federation	981.1	-8.7	-8.7	2.7	57.6
Spain	904.1	4.2	14.8	2.5	60.1
Canada	828.7	-1.8	0.2	2.3	62.4
Belgium	755.9	-6.4	11.3	2.1	64.5
Mexico	738.8	3.4	6.4	2.1	66.6
Switzerland	737.6	-1.8	2.7	2.1	68.7
Rep. of Korea	619.1	2.1	6.7	1.7	70.4

Mineral fuels, lubricants and related materials

(SITC Section 3)

321 Coal, whether or not pulverized, but not agglomerated

In 2016, the value (in current US$) of exports of "coal, whether or not pulverized, but not agglomerated" (SITC group 321) increased by 0.1 percent (compared to -12.3 percent average growth rate from 2012-2016) to reach 74.3 bln US$ (see table 2), while imports decreased by 6.0 percent to reach 85.0 bln US$ (see table 3). Exports of this commodity accounted for 5.1 percent of world exports of SITC section 3, and 0.5 percent of total world merchandise exports (see table 1). Australia, Indonesia and Russian Federation were the top exporters in 2016 (see table 2). They accounted for 39.8, 17.3 and 12.0 percent of world exports, respectively. Japan, India and China were the top destinations, with respectively 17.9, 15.0 and 13.5 percent of world imports (see table 3).

The top 15 countries/areas accounted for 98.9 and 85.3 percent of total world exports and imports, respectively (see tables 2 and 3). In 2016, Australia was the country/area with the highest value of net exports (+29.6 bln US$), followed by Indonesia (+12.6 bln US$). By MDG regions (see graph 2), the largest surpluses in this product group were recorded by Developed Asia-Pacific (+14.3 bln US$), South-eastern Asia (+8.8 bln US$) and Commonwealth of Independent States (+8.7 bln US$). The largest trade deficits were recorded by Eastern Asia (-23.8 bln US$), Southern Asia (-13.7 bln US$) and Developed Europe (-11.5 bln US$).

Table 1: Imports (Imp.) and exports (Exp.), 2002-2016, in current US$

		2002	2003	2004	2005	2006	2007	2008	2009	2010	2011	2012	2013	2014	2015	2016
Values in Bln US$	Imp.	25.5	28.1	43.8	58.3	60.4	70.1	121.5	94.6	113.1	151.9	145.3	127.9	113.2	90.4	85.0
	Exp.	20.4	21.9	31.7	46.1	49.6	52.7	94.4	80.7	104.2	139.4	125.9	110.9	95.7	74.3	74.3
As a percentage of SITC section (%)	Imp.	4.1	3.6	4.2	4.1	3.4	3.6	4.3	5.3	4.9	4.8	4.4	3.9	3.7	4.9	5.6
	Exp.	3.3	2.9	3.1	3.2	2.8	2.7	3.4	4.7	4.6	4.4	3.8	3.4	3.2	4.0	5.1
As a percentage of world trade (%)	Imp.	0.4	0.4	0.5	0.6	0.5	0.5	0.7	0.8	0.7	0.8	0.8	0.7	0.6	0.5	0.5
	Exp.	0.3	0.3	0.3	0.4	0.4	0.4	0.6	0.7	0.7	0.8	0.7	0.6	0.5	0.5	0.5

Graph 1: Annual growth rates of exports, 2002–2016

(In percentage by year)

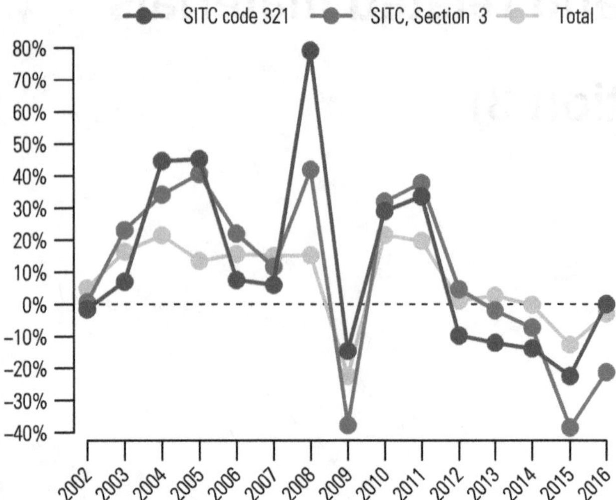

Table 2: Top exporting countries or areas in 2016

Country or area	Value (million US$)	Avg. Growth (%) 12-16	Growth (%) 15-16	World share %	Cum.
World	74341.9	-12.3	0.1	100.0	
Australia	29579.6	-8.8	4.1	39.8	39.8
Indonesia	12898.1	-14.6	-12.4	17.3	57.1
Russian Federation	8907.2	-9.0	-6.0	12.0	69.1
Colombia	4392.7	-11.9	3.2	5.9	75.0
USA	4336.1	-26.5	-23.5	5.8	80.9
South Africa	3829.4	-13.1	-9.5	5.2	86.0
Canada	3351.9	-14.7	23.6	4.5	90.5
Netherlands	2594.1	14.3	287.0	3.5	94.0
Mongolia	971.8	-4.0	75.1	1.3	95.3
China	675.6	-18.7	43.1	0.9	96.2
Poland	657.5	-9.0	-10.0	0.9	97.1
DPR Korea	*405.0*	3.1	21.7	0.5	97.7
Philippines	319.6	18.2	116.2	0.4	98.1
Kazakhstan	302.0	-25.2	-31.2	0.4	98.5
Czechia	289.5	-23.1	-11.1	0.4	98.9

Graph 2: Trade Balance by MDG regions 2016

(Bln US$)

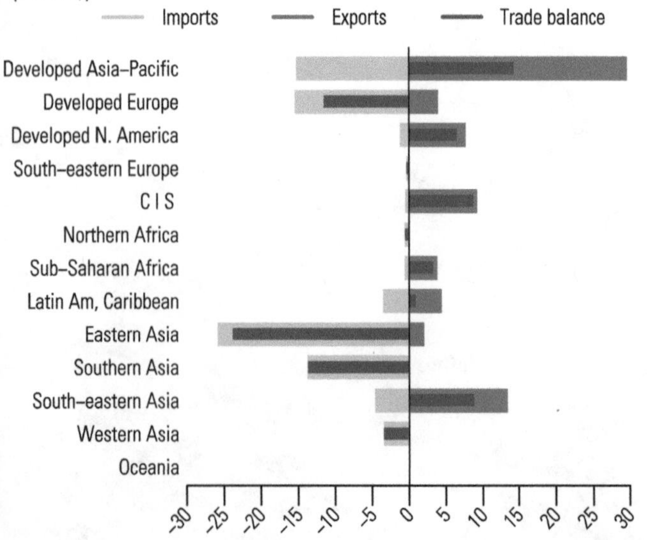

Table 3: Top importing countries or areas in 2016

Country or area	Value (million US$)	Avg. Growth (%) 12-16	Growth (%) 15-16	World share %	Cum.
World	84986.0	-12.5	-6.0	100.0	
Japan	15223.6	-14.9	-6.7	17.9	17.9
India	12707.3	-4.3	-10.0	15.0	32.9
China	11506.5	-17.9	13.6	13.5	46.4
Rep. of Korea	9226.3	-12.7	-6.4	10.9	57.3
Other Asia, nes	4516.0	-13.2	-7.6	5.3	62.6
Netherlands	4005.9	13.4	93.3	4.7	67.3
Germany	3789.9	-10.6	-12.4	4.5	71.7
Turkey	2627.9	23.4	-11.1	3.1	74.8
Brazil	1758.9	-12.5	-14.0	2.1	76.9
Malaysia	1432.4	-9.7	9.1	1.7	78.6
Italy	1342.6	-22.2	-11.7	1.6	80.2
France	1189.8	-20.0	-9.4	1.4	81.6
Thailand	1180.8	-5.3	-10.0	1.4	83.0
Philippines	1026.5	7.1	53.1	1.2	84.2
Spain	935.1	-21.0	-28.6	1.1	85.3

In 2016, the value (in current US$) of exports of "briquettes, lignite and peat" (SITC group 322) decreased by 11.8 percent (compared to 0.4 percent average growth rate from 2012-2016) to reach 3.9 bln US$ (see table 2), while imports increased by 3.0 percent to reach 5.5 bln US$ (see table 3). Exports of this commodity accounted for 0.3 percent of world exports of SITC section 3, and less than 0.1 percent of total world merchandise exports (see table 1). Indonesia, Iran and Canada were the top exporters in 2016 (see table 2). They accounted for 41.3, 12.2 and 9.1 percent of world exports, respectively. China, Afghanistan and Netherlands were the top destinations, with respectively 48.7, 10.9 and 9.3 percent of world imports (see table 3).

The top 15 countries/areas accounted for 94.7 and 89.5 percent of total world exports and imports, respectively (see tables 2 and 3). In 2016, Indonesia was the country/area with the highest value of net exports (+1.6 bln US$), followed by Iran (+477.3 mln US$). By MDG regions (see graph 2), the largest surpluses in this product group were recorded by South-eastern Asia (+1.6 bln US$), Commonwealth of Independent States (+152.7 mln US$) and Sub-Saharan Africa (+21.4 mln US$). The largest trade deficits were recorded by Eastern Asia (-2.7 bln US$), Developed Europe (-218.3 mln US$) and Latin America and the Caribbean (-195.5 mln US$).

Table 1: Imports (Imp.) and exports (Exp.), 2002-2016, in current US$

		2002	2003	2004	2005	2006	2007	2008	2009	2010	2011	2012	2013	2014	2015	2016
Values in Bln US$	Imp.	0.8	0.9	1.0	1.1	1.2	1.4	1.9	1.8	2.9	5.1	7.3	6.9	7.2	5.3	5.5
	Exp.	0.7	0.8	0.8	0.9	1.0	1.2	1.5	1.5	1.9	3.7	3.8	4.1	4.8	4.4	3.9
As a percentage of SITC section (%)	Imp.	0.1	0.1	0.1	0.1	0.1	0.1	0.1	0.1	0.1	0.2	0.2	0.2	0.2	0.3	0.4
	Exp.	0.1	0.1	0.1	0.1	0.1	0.1	0.1	0.1	0.1	0.1	0.1	0.1	0.2	0.2	0.3
As a percentage of world trade (%)	Imp.	0.0	0.0	0.0	0.0	0.0	0.0	0.0	0.0	0.0	0.0	0.0	0.0	0.0	0.0	0.0
	Exp.	0.0	0.0	0.0	0.0	0.0	0.0	0.0	0.0	0.0	0.0	0.0	0.0	0.0	0.0	0.0

Graph 1: Annual growth rates of exports, 2002–2016

(In percentage by year)

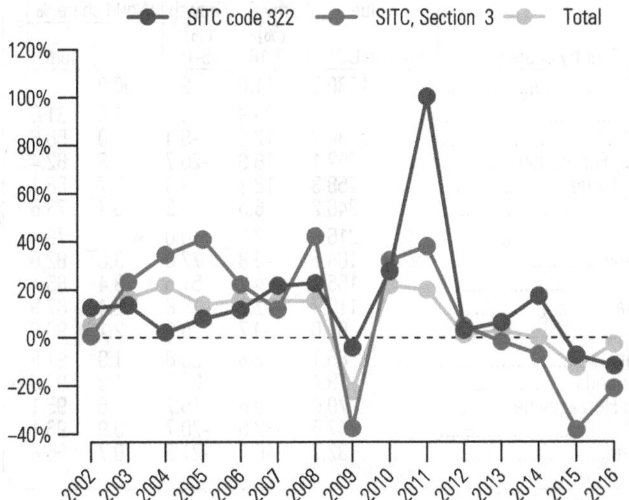

Graph 2: Trade Balance by MDG regions 2016

(Bln US$)

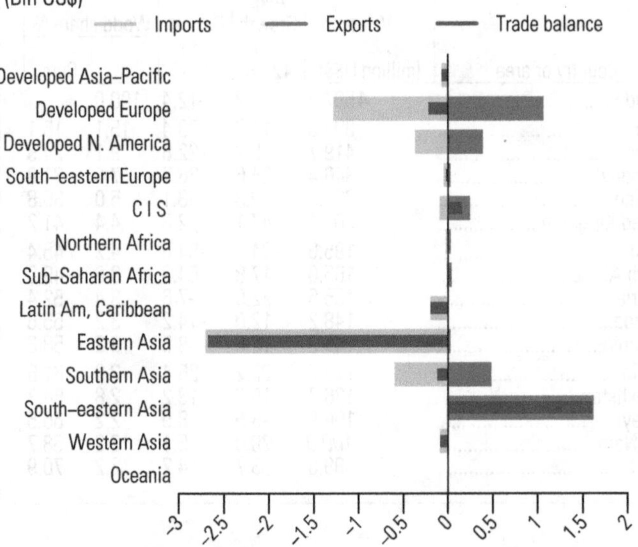

Table 2: Top exporting countries or areas in 2016

Country or area	Value (million US$)	Avg. Growth (%) 12-16	Growth (%) 15-16	World share %	Cum.
World	3911.2	0.4	-11.8	100.0	
Indonesia	1613.7	-3.8	25.9	41.3	41.3
Iran	*478.5*	71.2	-59.5	12.2	53.5
Canada	355.3	5.0	0.8	9.1	62.6
Germany	338.0	-2.9	-4.4	8.6	71.2
Russian Federation	176.0	20.9	27.7	4.5	75.7
Latvia	162.3	4.7	12.3	4.1	79.9
Netherlands	122.7	-3.9	-14.9	3.1	83.0
Ireland	95.0	3.6	-1.9	2.4	85.4
Estonia	71.1	-1.6	4.4	1.8	87.3
Czechia	70.9	-11.4	-3.9	1.8	89.1
Lithuania	62.8	1.0	4.2	1.6	90.7
Belgium	57.7	-1.4	-4.8	1.5	92.1
Kazakhstan	34.0	-13.1	-28.1	0.9	93.0
South Africa	33.0	-16.7	92.0	0.8	93.9
USA	32.4	-0.1	1.4	0.8	94.7

Table 3: Top importing countries or areas in 2016

Country or area	Value (million US$)	Avg. Growth (%) 12-16	Growth (%) 15-16	World share %	Cum.
World	5503.6	-6.7	3.0	100.0	
China	2678.5	-6.0	33.3	48.7	48.7
Afghanistan	598.2	-20.8	-51.6	10.9	59.5
Netherlands	512.8	7.2	28.7	9.3	68.9
USA	353.1	6.4	0.2	6.4	75.3
Cayman Isds	*139.4*	-7.5	85.8	2.5	77.8
France	97.8	-7.3	-6.3	1.8	79.6
Germany	87.1	-3.9	-16.8	1.6	81.2
Belgium	80.3	-3.1	-2.9	1.5	82.6
Italy	66.7	-3.9	-1.1	1.2	83.8
Uzbekistan	*59.5*	110.1	6.1	1.1	84.9
United Kingdom	58.7	1.7	1.8	1.1	86.0
Japan	54.8	-7.5	-6.3	1.0	87.0
Slovakia	50.4	-8.4	14.8	0.9	87.9
Czechia	46.7	-0.1	-0.9	0.8	88.7
Poland	44.4	6.3	19.3	0.8	89.5

Source: UN Comtrade

325 Coke, semi-coke of coal, lignite or peat, agglomerated or not; retort carbon

In 2016, the value (in current US$) of exports of "coke, semi-coke of coal, lignite or peat, agglomerated or not; retort carbon" (SITC group 325) decreased by 9.8 percent (compared to -11.6 percent average growth rate from 2012-2016) to reach 4.5 bln US$ (see table 2), while imports decreased by 12.4 percent to reach 4.6 bln US$ (see table 3). Exports of this commodity accounted for 0.3 percent of world exports of SITC section 3, and less than 0.1 percent of total world merchandise exports (see table 1). China, Poland and Russian Federation were the top exporters in 2016 (see table 2). They accounted for 31.6, 25.0 and 5.8 percent of world exports, respectively. India, Japan and Germany were the top destinations, with respectively 15.1, 9.1 and 7.5 percent of world imports (see table 3).

The top 15 countries/areas accounted for 96.8 and 70.9 percent of total world exports and imports, respectively (see tables 2 and 3). In 2016, China was the country/area with the highest value of net exports (+1.4 bln US$), followed by Poland (+1.1 bln US$). By MDG regions (see graph 2), the largest surpluses in this product group were recorded by Eastern Asia (+1.3 bln US$), Developed Europe (+460.7 mln US$) and Sub-Saharan Africa (+70.9 mln US$). The largest trade deficits were recorded by Southern Asia (-826.0 mln US$), Developed Asia-Pacific (-286.1 mln US$) and South-eastern Asia (-280.6 mln US$).

Table 1: Imports (Imp.) and exports (Exp.), 2002-2016, in current US$

		2002	2003	2004	2005	2006	2007	2008	2009	2010	2011	2012	2013	2014	2015	2016
Values in Bln US$	Imp.	2.9	4.1	9.8	7.4	6.8	8.2	15.2	4.8	9.1	11.0	7.7	6.2	6.3	5.2	4.6
	Exp.	2.4	3.7	8.4	6.1	7.5	7.4	13.5	3.9	8.0	9.2	7.4	6.5	6.4	5.0	4.5
As a percentage of SITC section (%)	Imp.	0.5	0.5	0.9	0.5	0.4	0.4	0.5	0.3	0.4	0.3	0.2	0.2	0.2	0.3	0.3
	Exp.	0.4	0.5	0.8	0.4	0.4	0.4	0.5	0.2	0.4	0.3	0.2	0.2	0.2	0.3	0.3
As a percentage of world trade (%)	Imp.	0.0	0.1	0.1	0.1	0.1	0.1	0.1	0.0	0.1	0.1	0.0	0.0	0.0	0.0	0.0
	Exp.	0.0	0.0	0.1	0.1	0.1	0.1	0.1	0.0	0.1	0.1	0.0	0.0	0.0	0.0	0.0

Graph 1: Annual growth rates of exports, 2002–2016

(In percentage by year)

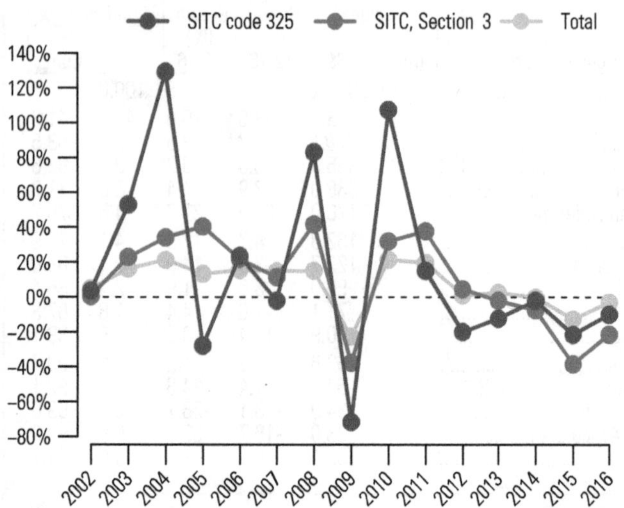

Table 2: Top exporting countries or areas in 2016

Country or area	Value (million US$)	Avg. Growth (%) 12-16	Growth (%) 15-16	World share %	Cum.
World	4530.5	-11.6	-9.8	100.0	
China	1432.1	33.9	-5.0	31.6	31.6
Poland	1134.2	-12.5	-5.4	25.0	56.6
Russian Federation	262.1	-18.0	-26.7	5.8	62.4
Mozambique	258.3	-12.2	-33.3	5.7	68.1
Colombia	246.2	-16.5	-18.6	5.4	73.6
USA	216.9	2.6	10.0	4.8	78.4
Germany	164.5	9.8	72.0	3.6	82.0
Japan	155.2	-24.2	51.5	3.4	85.4
Czechia	110.7	-12.2	-18.8	2.4	87.9
Italy	95.0	-9.7	5.2	2.1	90.0
Hungary	85.1	-2.8	29.8	1.9	91.8
Netherlands	79.4	-2.1	69.7	1.8	93.6
Bosnia Herzegovina	70.0	0.6	15.7	1.5	95.1
Spain	42.6	-32.8	-20.7	0.9	96.1
Belgium	32.7	-46.3	-21.5	0.7	96.8

Graph 2: Trade Balance by MDG regions 2016

(Bln US$)

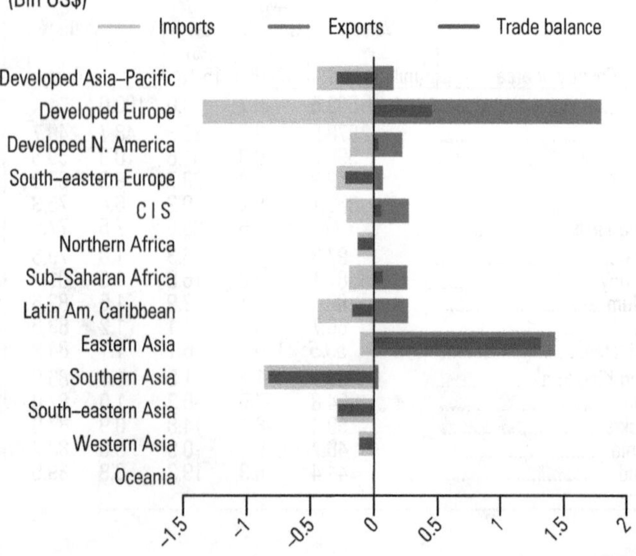

Table 3: Top importing countries or areas in 2016

Country or area	Value (million US$)	Avg. Growth (%) 12-16	Growth (%) 15-16	World share %	Cum.
World	4597.4	-12.2	-12.4	100.0	
India	695.6	-11.7	33.4	15.1	15.1
Japan	419.7	5.2	-22.6	9.1	24.3
Germany	346.4	-24.6	-26.5	7.5	31.8
Mexico	228.7	9.3	48.1	5.0	36.8
United Kingdom	202.1	47.1	2.8	4.4	41.2
Brazil	195.0	-24.3	-54.0	4.2	45.4
South Africa	165.0	-17.8	64.3	3.6	49.0
Austria	155.5	-22.0	-7.6	3.4	52.4
Canada	148.2	12.0	-14.2	3.2	55.6
Romania	145.2	-12.0	-8.5	3.2	58.8
Serbia	129.2	22.2	25.4	2.8	61.6
Kazakhstan	126.7	-15.9	-13.2	2.8	64.3
Turkey	100.6	-3.5	-8.9	2.2	66.5
Viet Nam	*100.0*	28.0	5.1	2.2	68.7
Egypt	99.6	53.7	14.2	2.2	70.9

"Petroleum oils and oils obtained from bituminous minerals, crude" (SITC group 333) is amongst the top exported commodities in 2016 with 4.0 percent of total exports (see table 1). The value (in current US$) of exports of this commodity decreased by 20.0 percent (compared to -20.9 percent average growth rate from 2012-2016) to reach 647.2 bln US$ (see table 2), while imports decreased by 15.9 percent to reach 681.5 bln US$ (see table 3). Exports of this commodity accounted for 44.2 percent of world exports of SITC section 3 (see table 1). Saudi Arabia, Russian Federation and Iraq were the top exporters in 2016 (see table 2). They accounted for 21.0, 11.4 and 6.7 percent of world exports, respectively. China, USA and India were the top destinations, with respectively 17.1, 15.9 and 8.9 percent of world imports (see table 3).

The top 15 countries/areas accounted for 81.6 and 83.1 percent of total world exports and imports, respectively (see tables 2 and 3). In 2016, Saudi Arabia was the country/area with the highest value of net exports (+136.0 bln US$), followed by Russian Federation (+73.6 bln US$). By MDG regions (see graph 2), the largest surpluses in this product group were recorded by Western Asia (+259.9 bln US$), Commonwealth of Independent States (+96.1 bln US$) and Sub-Saharan Africa (+54.5 bln US$). The largest trade deficits were recorded by Eastern Asia (-172.6 bln US$), Developed Europe (-139.4 bln US$) and Developed North America (-70.0 bln US$).

Table 1: Imports (Imp.) and exports (Exp.), 2002-2016, in current US$

		2002	2003	2004	2005	2006	2007	2008	2009	2010	2011	2012	2013	2014	2015	2016
Values in Bln US$	Imp.	340.8	427.6	577.1	800.2	993.2	1 086.3	1 551.8	914.9	1 213.9	1 638.8	1 727.5	1 635.3	1 516.1	810.6	681.5
	Exp.	337.4	411.0	545.6	768.6	948.9	1 050.3	1 443.1	854.7	1 129.6	1 577.6	1 652.5	1 559.7	1 424.0	808.5	647.2
As a percentage of SITC section (%)	Imp.	55.2	54.6	55.1	55.6	55.9	55.2	55.1	51.4	52.1	51.5	52.0	50.4	50.2	43.9	44.7
	Exp.	55.1	54.5	53.8	53.9	54.4	53.9	52.1	49.5	49.5	50.1	50.1	48.1	47.3	43.5	44.2
As a percentage of world trade (%)	Imp.	5.2	5.6	6.2	7.6	8.1	7.7	9.5	7.3	8.0	9.0	9.4	8.7	8.1	4.9	4.2
	Exp.	5.2	5.5	6.0	7.4	7.9	7.6	9.0	6.9	7.5	8.7	9.0	8.3	7.6	4.9	4.0

Graph 1: Annual growth rates of exports, 2002–2016
(In percentage by year)

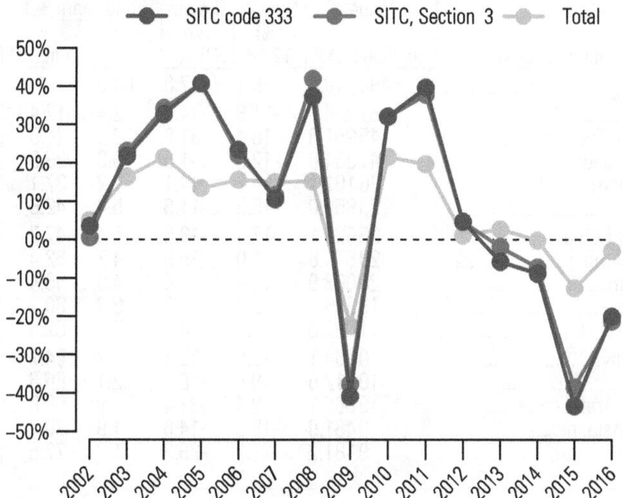

Table 2: Top exporting countries or areas in 2016

Country or area	Value (million US$)	Avg. Growth (%) 12-16	Growth (%) 15-16	World share %	Cum.
World	647 205.4	-20.9	-20.0	100.0	
Saudi Arabia	136 000.0	-18.3	4.8	21.0	21.0
Russian Federation	73 676.3	-20.1	-17.8	11.4	32.4
Iraq	43 622.9	-17.5	-11.1	6.7	39.1
Canada	39 523.6	-14.7	-21.3	6.1	45.2
United Arab Emirates	32 999.4	-23.5	-2.3	5.1	50.3
Kuwait	30 694.7	-21.1	-10.1	4.7	55.1
Nigeria	26 979.8	-27.8	-65.3	4.2	59.3
Iran	*26 926.4*	-17.0	-13.4	4.2	63.4
Norway	22 832.1	-19.6	-9.9	3.5	66.9
Angola	*19 959.4*	-26.6	-36.4	3.1	70.0
Kazakhstan	19 378.0	-23.5	-27.6	3.0	73.0
Mexico	15 574.8	-24.1	-16.1	2.4	75.4
Venezuela	*14 080.8*	-32.8	-55.6	2.2	77.6
United Kingdom	13 187.3	-19.0	-18.6	2.0	79.6
Oman	12 868.0	-19.5	-26.2	2.0	81.6

Graph 2: Trade Balance by MDG regions 2016
(Bln US$)

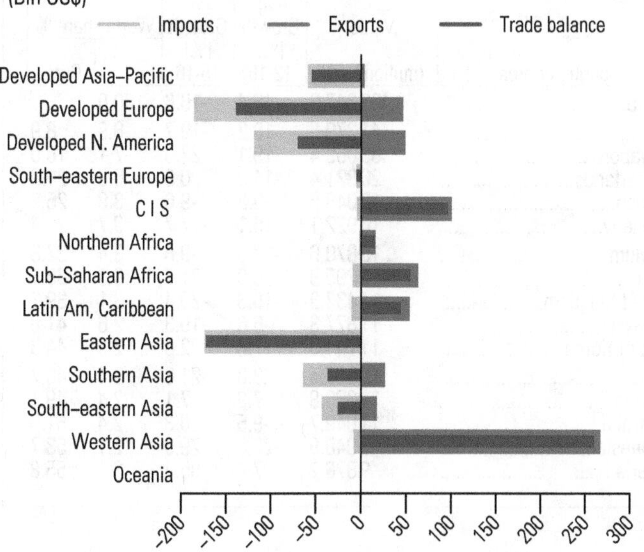

Table 3: Top importing countries or areas in 2016

Country or area	Value (million US$)	Avg. Growth (%) 12-16	Growth (%) 15-16	World share %	Cum.
World	681 534.9	-20.7	-15.9	100.0	
China	116 660.7	-14.7	-13.2	17.1	17.1
USA	108 066.5	-23.9	-18.5	15.9	33.0
India	60 869.1	-20.0	-15.8	8.9	41.9
Japan	50 767.5	-24.1	12.8	7.4	49.4
Rep. of Korea	44 294.8	-20.0	-19.6	6.5	55.9
Netherlands	32 390.6	-11.7	28.5	4.8	60.6
Germany	28 718.5	-21.8	-21.3	4.2	64.8
Italy	18 893.1	-24.1	-20.6	2.8	67.6
Spain	18 732.8	-20.2	-24.4	2.7	70.3
France	17 912.8	-21.7	-21.5	2.6	73.0
Thailand	15 236.4	-19.3	-21.7	2.2	75.2
Singapore	15 047.4	-21.6	-17.3	2.2	77.4
United Kingdom	14 305.6	-26.1	-22.3	2.1	79.5
Other Asia, nes	12 890.1	-22.5	-20.0	1.9	81.4
Belgium	11 543.7	-20.6	-20.5	1.7	83.1

334 Petroleum oils and oils obtained from bituminous minerals, (not crude)

"Petroleum oils and oils obtained from bituminous minerals, (not crude)" (SITC group 334) is amongst the top exported commodities in 2016 with 3.1 percent of total exports (see table 1). The value (in current US$) of exports of this commodity decreased by 17.0 percent (compared to -16.1 percent average growth rate from 2012-2016) to reach 498.9 bln US$ (see table 2), while imports decreased by 16.6 percent to reach 463.2 bln US$ (see table 3). Exports of this commodity accounted for 34.0 percent of world exports of SITC section 3 (see table 1). USA, Russian Federation and Netherlands were the top exporters in 2016 (see table 2). They accounted for 12.4, 9.2 and 8.3 percent of world exports, respectively. USA, Singapore and Netherlands were the top destinations, with respectively 8.9, 7.1 and 5.8 percent of world imports (see table 3).

The top 15 countries/areas accounted for 72.5 and 55.8 percent of total world exports and imports, respectively (see tables 2 and 3). In 2016, Russian Federation was the country/area with the highest value of net exports (+45.2 bln US$), followed by India (+23.3 bln US$). By MDG regions (see graph 2), the largest surpluses in this product group were recorded by Commonwealth of Independent States (+46.2 bln US$), Western Asia (+34.0 bln US$) and Developed North America (+17.2 bln US$). The largest trade deficits were recorded by Latin America and the Caribbean (-38.9 bln US$), Sub-Saharan Africa (-23.9 bln US$) and South-eastern Asia (-18.5 bln US$).

Table 1: Imports (Imp.) and exports (Exp.), 2002-2016, in current US$

		2002	2003	2004	2005	2006	2007	2008	2009	2010	2011	2012	2013	2014	2015	2016
Values in Bln US$	Imp.	136.9	172.4	239.6	342.4	429.5	503.1	704.5	451.8	614.7	876.4	906.3	921.4	849.4	555.3	463.2
	Exp.	145.2	179.6	262.1	383.1	462.7	549.3	793.6	505.8	682.7	929.9	1008.3	1028.7	964.4	601.3	498.9
As a percentage of SITC section (%)	Imp.	22.2	22.0	22.9	23.8	24.2	25.6	25.0	25.4	26.4	27.5	27.3	28.4	28.1	30.1	30.4
	Exp.	23.7	23.8	25.9	26.8	26.5	28.2	28.7	29.3	29.9	29.5	30.5	31.7	32.0	32.4	34.0
As a percentage of world trade (%)	Imp.	2.1	2.2	2.6	3.2	3.5	3.6	4.3	3.6	4.0	4.8	4.9	4.9	4.5	3.4	2.9
	Exp.	2.3	2.4	2.9	3.7	3.9	4.0	5.0	4.1	4.5	5.1	5.5	5.5	5.1	3.7	3.1

Graph 1: Annual growth rates of exports, 2002–2016
(In percentage by year)

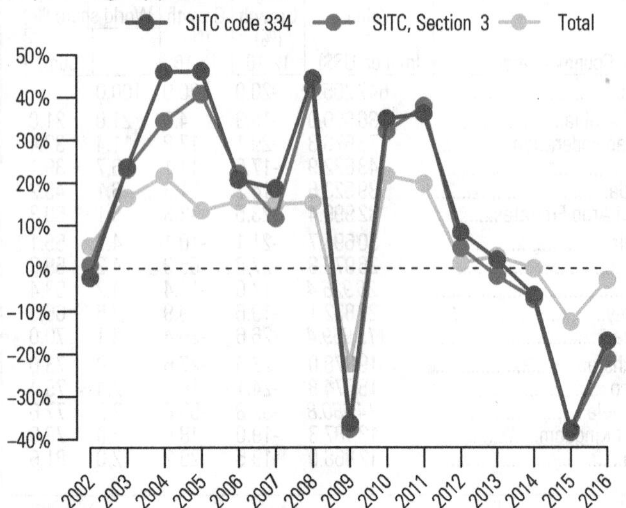

Table 2: Top exporting countries or areas in 2016

Country or area	Value (million US$)	Avg. Growth (%) 12-16	Growth (%) 15-16	World share %	Cum.
World	498949.4	-16.1	-17.0	100.0	
USA	61966.1	-11.8	-14.8	12.4	12.4
Russian Federation	45951.8	-18.4	-31.8	9.2	21.6
Netherlands	41334.0	-12.8	-1.5	8.3	29.9
Singapore	36101.1	-16.2	-14.1	7.2	37.1
India	26951.0	-15.5	-11.5	5.4	42.6
Rep. of Korea	25528.1	-17.4	-16.6	5.1	47.7
Saudi Arabia	23674.6	1.0	35.9	4.7	52.4
Belgium	20003.9	-14.4	-17.6	4.0	56.4
China	19395.5	-2.3	1.6	3.9	60.3
Malaysia	11099.9	-7.9	4.3	2.2	62.5
Germany	10964.1	-12.0	-12.1	2.2	64.7
Italy	10517.6	-19.4	-19.1	2.1	66.8
United Arab Emirates	9668.1	-8.4	-31.4	1.9	68.8
Other Asia, nes	9481.9	-18.0	-14.6	1.9	70.7
Kuwait	9181.2	-22.2	-29.3	1.8	72.5

Graph 2: Trade Balance by MDG regions 2016
(Bln US$)

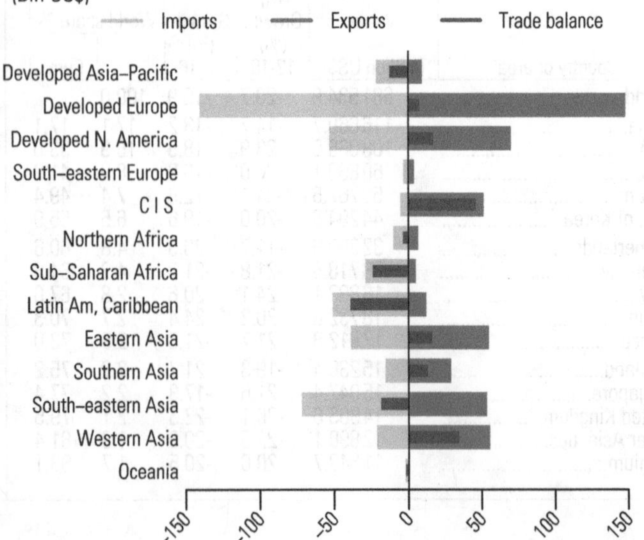

Table 3: Top importing countries or areas in 2016

Country or area	Value (million US$)	Avg. Growth (%) 12-16	Growth (%) 15-16	World share %	Cum.
World	463247.8	-15.4	-16.6	100.0	
USA	41279.5	-18.2	-19.7	8.9	8.9
Singapore	33069.4	-19.1	-22.3	7.1	16.0
Netherlands	26821.4	-14.3	0.8	5.8	21.8
Mexico	18048.8	-9.8	-9.6	3.9	25.7
Germany	16922.1	-16.1	-17.7	3.7	29.4
Belgium	15870.6	-12.8	-9.8	3.4	32.8
France	15295.9	-20.0	-21.7	3.3	36.1
United Kingdom	14432.3	-15.3	-20.4	3.1	39.2
Malaysia	11877.3	-6.6	-19.3	2.6	41.8
Rep. of Korea	11744.0	-17.8	-22.0	2.5	44.3
China	11157.4	-23.8	-21.6	2.4	46.7
Canada	11063.8	-7.9	-7.1	2.4	49.1
Australia	11049.7	-9.5	-20.3	2.4	51.5
Indonesia	9940.9	-22.8	-29.0	2.1	53.7
Nigeria	9876.2	107.4	85.4	2.1	55.8

In 2016, the value (in current US$) of exports of "residual petroleum products, nes, and related materials" (SITC group 335) decreased by 17.6 percent (compared to -11.1 percent average growth rate from 2012-2016) to reach 30.9 bln US$ (see table 2), while imports decreased by 16.6 percent to reach 36.6 bln US$ (see table 3). Exports of this commodity accounted for 2.1 percent of world exports of SITC section 3, and 0.2 percent of total world merchandise exports (see table 1). USA, Netherlands and Rep. of Korea were the top exporters in 2016 (see table 2). They accounted for 13.5, 12.7 and 5.3 percent of world exports, respectively. China, Netherlands and USA were the top destinations, with respectively 30.6, 7.1 and 5.0 percent of world imports (see table 3).

The top 15 countries/areas accounted for 77.9 and 73.2 percent of total world exports and imports, respectively (see tables 2 and 3). In 2016, USA was the country/area with the highest value of net exports (+2.3 bln US$), followed by Netherlands (+1.3 bln US$). By MDG regions (see graph 2), the largest surpluses in this product group were recorded by Developed Europe (+2.8 bln US$), Developed North America (+2.7 bln US$) and South-eastern Asia (+2.0 bln US$). The largest trade deficits were recorded by Eastern Asia (-10.1 bln US$), Latin America and the Caribbean (-1.9 bln US$) and Southern Asia (-1.3 bln US$).

Table 1: Imports (Imp.) and exports (Exp.), 2002-2016, in current US$

		2002	2003	2004	2005	2006	2007	2008	2009	2010	2011	2012	2013	2014	2015	2016
Values in Bln US$	Imp.	10.5	13.0	18.2	21.4	27.0	39.5	43.5	28.3	38.5	50.7	53.8	53.0	55.3	43.9	36.6
	Exp.	9.2	11.7	15.0	17.6	22.4	27.5	40.1	27.6	37.6	52.4	49.5	51.5	52.6	37.5	30.9
As a percentage of SITC section (%)	Imp.	1.7	1.7	1.7	1.5	1.5	2.0	1.5	1.6	1.7	1.6	1.6	1.6	1.8	2.4	2.4
	Exp.	1.5	1.5	1.5	1.2	1.3	1.4	1.4	1.6	1.6	1.7	1.5	1.6	1.7	2.0	2.1
As a percentage of world trade (%)	Imp.	0.2	0.2	0.2	0.2	0.2	0.3	0.3	0.2	0.3	0.3	0.3	0.3	0.3	0.3	0.2
	Exp.	0.1	0.2	0.2	0.2	0.2	0.2	0.3	0.2	0.2	0.3	0.3	0.3	0.3	0.2	0.2

Graph 1: Annual growth rates of exports, 2002–2016
(In percentage by year)

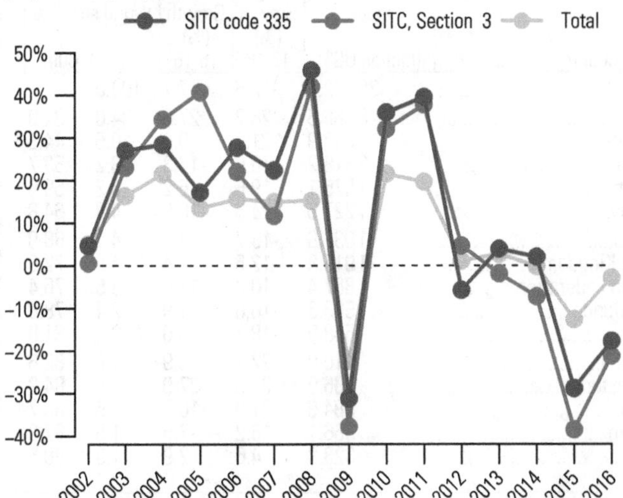

Table 2: Top exporting countries or areas in 2016

Country or area	Value (million US$)	Avg. Growth (%) 12-16	Growth (%) 15-16	World share %	Cum.
World	30856.9	-11.1	-17.6	100.0	
USA	4174.0	-14.7	-12.8	13.5	13.5
Netherlands	3909.0	1.1	54.5	12.7	26.2
Rep. of Korea	1624.9	-9.4	-26.9	5.3	31.5
Germany	1614.0	-14.0	-12.9	5.2	36.7
Belgium	1612.7	-5.7	29.8	5.2	41.9
Spain	1597.7	-2.5	-16.2	5.2	47.1
Japan	1527.3	6.6	-2.6	4.9	52.0
Malaysia	1458.5	19.2	-46.7	4.7	56.8
China	1436.3	-9.8	-20.5	4.7	61.4
Singapore	1089.2	-13.4	-19.2	3.5	65.0
Russian Federation	1005.6	7.0	13.8	3.3	68.2
Canada	905.1	-15.6	-15.9	2.9	71.1
Thailand	758.2	-16.8	-36.2	2.5	73.6
Indonesia	725.1	-27.4	-43.2	2.3	76.0
France	590.5	-14.6	-5.7	1.9	77.9

Graph 2: Trade Balance by MDG regions 2016
(Bln US$)

Imports — Exports — Trade balance

Developed Asia-Pacific
Developed Europe
Developed N. America
South-eastern Europe
C I S
Northern Africa
Sub-Saharan Africa
Latin Am, Caribbean
Eastern Asia
Southern Asia
South-eastern Asia
Western Asia
Oceania

-15 -10 -5 0 5 10 15

Table 3: Top importing countries or areas in 2016

Country or area	Value (million US$)	Avg. Growth (%) 12-16	Growth (%) 15-16	World share %	Cum.
World	36601.4	-9.2	-16.6	100.0	
China	11200.4	3.1	-11.3	30.6	30.6
Netherlands	2613.8	-17.8	10.2	7.1	37.7
USA	1843.0	-10.2	-17.7	5.0	42.8
India	1757.6	5.0	-0.4	4.8	47.6
Rep. of Korea	1523.6	-9.7	-10.3	4.2	51.7
Germany	1256.5	-9.8	-36.4	3.4	55.2
Belgium	1139.6	-3.6	9.8	3.1	58.3
Ecuador	997.8	-16.9	-39.1	2.7	61.0
France	821.6	-17.1	-21.3	2.2	63.3
Other Asia, nes	722.6	-15.4	14.7	2.0	65.2
Japan	692.5	-21.5	-26.2	1.9	67.1
Mexico	584.5	-13.1	-13.9	1.6	68.7
Viet Nam	*572.5*	7.9	5.1	1.6	70.3
Canada	560.4	-16.7	-22.0	1.5	71.8
Indonesia	492.5	-9.8	-20.1	1.3	73.2

342 Liquefied propane and butane

In 2016, the value (in current US$) of exports of "liquefied propane and butane" (SITC group 342) decreased by 7.7 percent (compared to -12.6 percent average growth rate from 2012-2016) to reach 25.2 bln US$ (see table 2), while imports decreased by 11.1 percent to reach 34.5 bln US$ (see table 3). Exports of this commodity accounted for 1.7 percent of world exports of SITC section 3, and 0.2 percent of total world merchandise exports (see table 1). USA, Saudi Arabia and Algeria were the top exporters in 2016 (see table 2). They accounted for 34.0, 10.5 and 9.2 percent of world exports, respectively. China, Japan and India were the top destinations, with respectively 17.6, 11.9 and 9.9 percent of world imports (see table 3).

The top 15 countries/areas accounted for 88.5 and 78.6 percent of total world exports and imports, respectively (see tables 2 and 3). In 2016, USA was the country/area with the highest value of net exports (+7.4 bln US$), followed by Saudi Arabia (+2.6 bln US$). By MDG regions (see graph 2), the largest surpluses in this product group were recorded by Developed North America (+8.3 bln US$), Western Asia (+4.1 bln US$) and Commonwealth of Independent States (+1.3 bln US$). The largest trade deficits were recorded by Eastern Asia (-8.7 bln US$), Developed Asia-Pacific (-3.9 bln US$) and Southern Asia (-3.4 bln US$).

Table 1: Imports (Imp.) and exports (Exp.), 2002-2016, in current US$

		2002	2003	2004	2005	2006	2007	2008	2009	2010	2011	2012	2013	2014	2015	2016
Values in Bln US$	Imp.	12.8	17.5	21.6	27.3	33.9	37.6	47.9	30.7	43.4	58.3	60.2	60.3	63.0	38.8	34.5
	Exp.	11.2	15.1	19.0	24.7	28.4	33.0	40.8	28.5	36.6	47.3	43.1	41.5	44.4	27.3	25.2
As a percentage of SITC section (%)	Imp.	2.1	2.2	2.1	1.9	1.9	1.9	1.7	1.7	1.9	1.8	1.8	1.9	2.1	2.1	2.3
	Exp.	1.8	2.0	1.9	1.7	1.6	1.7	1.5	1.6	1.6	1.5	1.3	1.3	1.5	1.5	1.7
As a percentage of world trade (%)	Imp.	0.2	0.2	0.2	0.3	0.3	0.3	0.3	0.2	0.3	0.3	0.3	0.3	0.3	0.2	0.2
	Exp.	0.2	0.2	0.2	0.2	0.2	0.2	0.3	0.2	0.2	0.3	0.2	0.2	0.2	0.2	0.2

Graph 1: Annual growth rates of exports, 2002–2016

(In percentage by year)

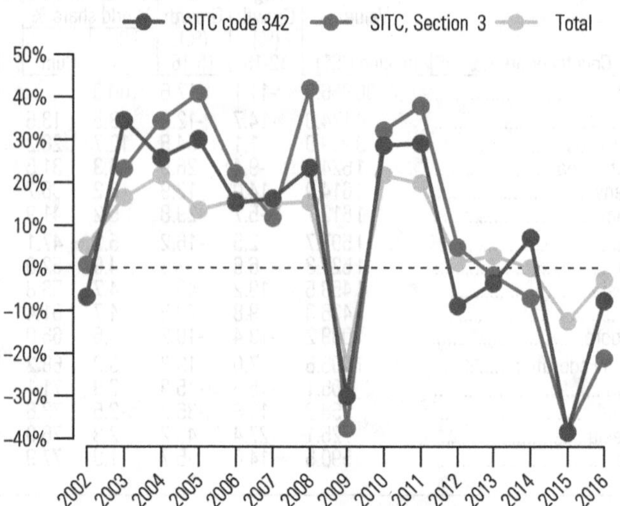

Table 2: Top exporting countries or areas in 2016

Country or area	Value (million US$)	Avg. Growth (%) 12-16	Growth (%) 15-16	World share %	Cum.
World	25 202.4	-12.6	-7.7	100.0	
USA	8 566.5	26.2	27.0	34.0	34.0
Saudi Arabia	2 643.9	-21.3	-9.0	10.5	44.5
Algeria	2 318.2	-16.6	-17.3	9.2	53.7
Kuwait	1 575.1	-19.6	-15.2	6.2	59.9
Norway	1 227.5	-24.5	-18.0	4.9	64.8
Canada	1 031.6	-13.7	-3.9	4.1	68.9
United Kingdom	1 015.8	-12.5	17.4	4.0	72.9
Russian Federation	887.4	-10.0	13.6	3.5	76.4
Netherlands	593.3	-16.0	1.9	2.4	78.8
China	548.5	-18.2	-28.0	2.2	81.0
Australia	410.0	-22.1	-9.9	1.6	82.6
Kazakhstan	406.0	-24.3	-27.9	1.6	84.2
France	384.9	-21.9	-10.7	1.5	85.7
Belgium	366.1	-16.2	-7.5	1.5	87.2
Spain	323.3	4.6	2.9	1.3	88.5

Graph 2: Trade Balance by MDG regions 2016

(Bln US$)

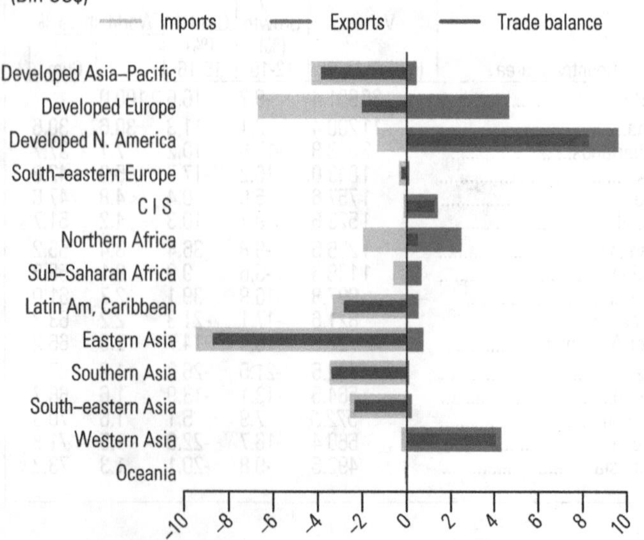

Table 3: Top importing countries or areas in 2016

Country or area	Value (million US$)	Avg. Growth (%) 12-16	Growth (%) 15-16	World share %	Cum.
World	34 525.7	-13.0	-11.1	100.0	
China	6 085.9	18.9	-0.3	17.6	17.6
Japan	4 101.0	-24.7	-23.7	11.9	29.5
India	3 412.8	-9.6	-20.3	9.9	39.4
Rep. of Korea	2 575.8	-17.6	-2.4	7.5	46.9
Indonesia	1 665.0	-13.9	-17.0	4.8	51.7
Netherlands	1 391.9	-5.8	-4.8	4.0	55.7
Mexico	1 239.7	6.1	22.4	3.6	59.3
USA	1 134.3	-14.7	-6.9	3.3	62.6
France	1 085.9	-17.9	-15.1	3.1	65.7
Morocco	925.0	-17.1	-11.8	2.7	68.4
Egypt	898.3	-20.3	-16.7	2.6	71.0
Italy	762.5	-19.8	-6.4	2.2	73.2
Brazil	625.7	-10.3	5.1	1.8	75.0
Other Asia, nes	620.8	-2.6	-2.9	1.8	76.8
Belgium	611.5	-18.1	-18.0	1.8	78.6

In 2016, the value (in current US$) of exports of "natural gas, whether or not liquefied" (SITC group 343) decreased by 43.2 percent (compared to -19.5 percent average growth rate from 2012-2016) to reach 150.9 bln US$ (see table 2), while imports decreased by 30.5 percent to reach 181.7 bln US$ (see table 3). Exports of this commodity accounted for 10.3 percent of world exports of SITC section 3, and 0.9 percent of total world merchandise exports (see table 1). Qatar, Norway and Australia were the top exporters in 2016 (see table 2). They accounted for 23.3, 12.7 and 8.9 percent of world exports, respectively. Japan, Germany and China were the top destinations, with respectively 16.6, 12.4 and 9.1 percent of world imports (see table 3).

The top 15 countries/areas accounted for 85.1 and 83.2 percent of total world exports and imports, respectively (see tables 2 and 3). In 2016, Qatar was the country/area with the highest value of net exports (+35.2 bln US$), followed by Norway (+19.2 bln US$). By MDG regions (see graph 2), the largest surpluses in this product group were recorded by Western Asia (+35.6 bln US$), South-eastern Asia (+14.3 bln US$) and Northern Africa (+7.5 bln US$). The largest trade deficits were recorded by Developed Europe (-41.5 bln US$), Eastern Asia (-33.8 bln US$) and Developed Asia-Pacific (-16.8 bln US$).

Table 1: Imports (Imp.) and exports (Exp.), 2002-2016, in current US$

		2002	2003	2004	2005	2006	2007	2008	2009	2010	2011	2012	2013	2014	2015	2016
Values in Bln US$	Imp.	71.5	99.6	112.7	148.8	186.1	186.4	280.0	216.0	250.9	340.9	365.3	389.4	367.1	261.6	181.7
	Exp.	66.6	85.7	101.5	145.0	179.2	181.5	286.9	187.5	240.3	338.6	359.4	397.5	379.0	265.8	150.9
As a percentage of SITC section (%)	Imp.	11.6	12.7	10.8	10.3	10.5	9.5	9.9	12.1	10.8	10.7	11.0	12.0	12.1	14.2	11.9
	Exp.	10.9	11.4	10.0	10.2	10.3	9.3	10.4	10.8	10.5	10.7	10.9	12.3	12.6	14.3	10.3
As a percentage of world trade (%)	Imp.	1.1	1.3	1.2	1.4	1.5	1.3	1.7	1.7	1.6	1.9	2.0	2.1	2.0	1.6	1.1
	Exp.	1.0	1.1	1.1	1.4	1.5	1.3	1.8	1.5	1.6	1.9	2.0	2.1	2.0	1.6	0.9

Graph 1: Annual growth rates of exports, 2002–2016
(In percentage by year)

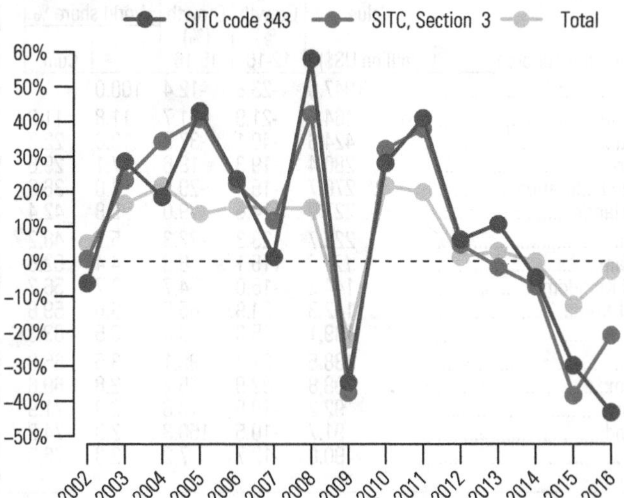

Table 2: Top exporting countries or areas in 2016

Country or area	Value (million US$)	Avg. Growth (%) 12-16	Growth (%) 15-16	World share %	Cum.
World	150880.0	-19.5	-43.2	100.0	
Qatar	35157.1	-19.2	-30.4	23.3	23.3
Norway	19179.0	-18.5	-30.7	12.7	36.0
Australia	13368.7	-1.2	7.6	8.9	44.9
Algeria	9444.0	-19.3	-20.7	6.3	51.1
Malaysia	7716.3	-19.3	-36.1	5.1	56.2
Indonesia	6992.4	-23.6	-32.3	4.6	60.9
Canada	6538.8	-7.3	-16.7	4.3	65.2
Germany	5491.6	-6.7	-41.1	3.6	68.9
USA	4566.9	-1.8	-4.3	3.0	71.9
Belgium	4085.8	-14.1	-27.7	2.7	74.6
Nigeria	3846.7	-8.8	-60.0	2.5	77.1
Myanmar	3170.2	9.5	-35.5	2.1	79.2
Uzbekistan	*3002.8*	54.4	29.8	2.0	81.2
Russian Federation	2899.8	-54.4	-93.7	1.9	83.2
United Arab Emirates	2882.4	-21.8	-35.6	1.9	85.1

Graph 2: Trade Balance by MDG regions 2016
(Bln US$)

Imports
Exports
Trade balance

Developed Asia-Pacific
Developed Europe
Developed N. America
South-eastern Europe
CIS
Northern Africa
Sub-Saharan Africa
Latin Am, Caribbean
Eastern Asia
Southern Asia
South-eastern Asia
Western Asia
Oceania

-80 -70 -60 -50 -40 -30 -20 -10 0 10 20 30 40

Table 3: Top importing countries or areas in 2016

Country or area	Value (million US$)	Avg. Growth (%) 12-16	Growth (%) 15-16	World share %	Cum.
World	181656.1	-16.0	-30.5	100.0	
Japan	30212.3	-20.4	-33.7	16.6	16.6
Germany	22472.5	-13.6	-28.3	12.4	29.0
China	16489.0	-0.5	-10.8	9.1	38.1
Rep. of Korea	12170.1	-18.3	-35.2	6.7	44.8
Italy	11562.6	-22.0	-28.7	6.4	51.1
France	9546.8	-18.7	-26.1	5.3	56.4
United Kingdom	8130.3	-9.7	-19.4	4.5	60.9
USA	7216.0	-4.6	-19.2	4.0	64.8
Belgium	6976.3	-15.7	-26.5	3.8	68.7
Spain	6222.0	-17.9	-23.8	3.4	72.1
India	5425.5	-8.7	-23.9	3.0	75.1
Other Asia, nes	5027.2	-15.2	-20.8	2.8	77.9
Mexico	4058.9	17.2	5.4	2.2	80.1
Thailand	2920.7	-8.7	-37.3	1.6	81.7
Singapore	2618.2	-19.1	-26.6	1.4	83.2

344 Petroleum gases and other gaseous hydrocarbons, nes

In 2016, the value (in current US$) of exports of "petroleum gases and other gaseous hydrocarbons, nes" (SITC group 344) decreased by 12.4 percent (compared to -23.8 percent average growth rate from 2012-2016) to reach 3.9 bln US$ (see table 2), while imports decreased by 0.4 percent to reach 7.1 bln US$ (see table 3). Exports of this commodity accounted for 0.3 percent of world exports of SITC section 3, and less than 0.1 percent of total world merchandise exports (see table 1). Malaysia, Nigeria and Norway were the top exporters in 2016 (see table 2). They accounted for 11.8, 10.8 and 7.1 percent of world exports, respectively. Turkey, India and Tunisia were the top destinations, with respectively 16.5, 10.5 and 8.9 percent of world imports (see table 3).

The top 15 countries/areas accounted for 76.5 and 80.7 percent of total world exports and imports, respectively (see tables 2 and 3). In 2016, Nigeria was the country/area with the highest value of net exports (+423.6 mln US$), followed by Norway (+263.3 mln US$). By MDG regions (see graph 2), the largest surpluses in this product group were recorded by Sub-Saharan Africa (+320.9 mln US$), Commonwealth of Independent States (+232.7 mln US$) and South-eastern Asia (+90.6 mln US$). The largest trade deficits were recorded by Western Asia (-1.2 bln US$), Southern Asia (-1.1 bln US$) and Northern Africa (-611.0 mln US$).

Table 1: Imports (Imp.) and exports (Exp.), 2002-2016, in current US$

		2002	2003	2004	2005	2006	2007	2008	2009	2010	2011	2012	2013	2014	2015	2016
Values in Bln US$	Imp.	3.8	4.8	5.5	7.3	9.4	9.9	13.3	7.8	11.3	13.9	14.6	14.1	13.3	7.2	7.1
	Exp.	5.5	7.6	9.1	9.3	11.2	16.4	14.4	5.6	10.0	11.8	11.7	8.5	7.7	4.5	3.9
As a percentage of SITC section (%)	Imp.	0.6	0.6	0.5	0.5	0.5	0.5	0.5	0.4	0.5	0.4	0.4	0.4	0.4	0.4	0.5
	Exp.	0.9	1.0	0.9	0.6	0.6	0.8	0.5	0.3	0.4	0.4	0.4	0.3	0.3	0.2	0.3
As a percentage of world trade (%)	Imp.	0.1	0.1	0.1	0.1	0.1	0.1	0.1	0.1	0.1	0.1	0.1	0.1	0.1	0.0	0.0
	Exp.	0.1	0.1	0.1	0.1	0.1	0.1	0.1	0.0	0.1	0.1	0.1	0.0	0.0	0.0	0.0

Graph 1: Annual growth rates of exports, 2002–2016

(In percentage by year)

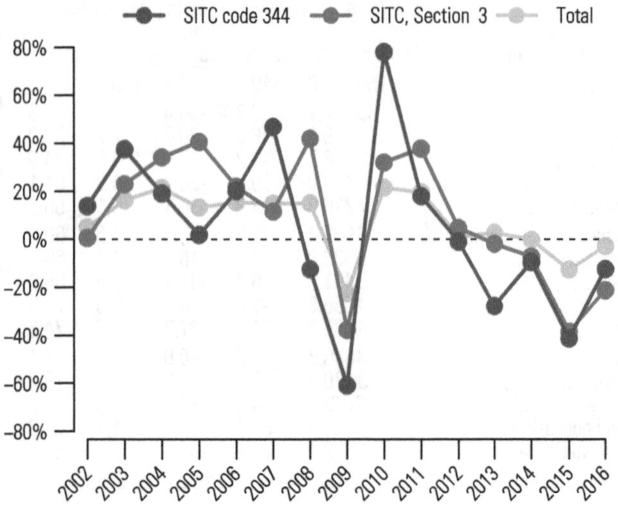

Graph 2: Trade Balance by MDG regions 2016

(Bln US$)

Imports | Exports | Trade balance

Developed Asia-Pacific
Developed Europe
Developed N. America
South-eastern Europe
CIS
Northern Africa
Sub-Saharan Africa
Latin Am, Caribbean
Eastern Asia
Southern Asia
South-eastern Asia
Western Asia
Oceania

-2 -1.5 -1 -0.5 0 0.5 1 1.5

Table 2: Top exporting countries or areas in 2016

Country or area	Value (million US$)	Avg. Growth (%) 12-16	Growth (%) 15-16	World share %	Cum.
World	3947.0	-23.8	-12.4	100.0	
Malaysia	464.5	-21.9	-11.7	11.8	11.8
Nigeria	424.6	-40.1	-37.3	10.8	22.5
Norway	280.4	-19.3	18.6	7.1	29.6
Russian Federation	276.7	-15.7	-20.1	7.0	36.6
Netherlands	227.9	-14.6	-9.0	5.8	42.4
Canada	226.7	-23.3	-22.3	5.7	48.2
Viet Nam	*171.7*	115.1	8.9	4.4	52.5
United Kingdom	144.2	-16.0	-4.7	3.7	56.2
Rep. of Korea	142.3	24.9	65.5	3.6	59.8
India	139.1	-5.3	3.8	3.5	63.3
USA	138.5	-27.7	98.1	3.5	66.8
Belgium	108.8	-32.9	-35.2	2.8	69.6
Germany	92.2	-19.5	-18.6	2.3	71.9
Thailand	91.7	-10.5	150.3	2.3	74.2
Italy	90.8	-12.7	7.2	2.3	76.5

Table 3: Top importing countries or areas in 2016

Country or area	Value (million US$)	Avg. Growth (%) 12-16	Growth (%) 15-16	World share %	Cum.
World	7136.4	-16.4	-0.4	100.0	
Turkey	1180.9	-19.7	-16.5	16.5	16.5
India	747.9	-9.4	63.6	10.5	27.0
Tunisia	634.4	-9.0	-8.3	8.9	35.9
Belgium	506.2	-18.4	4.1	7.1	43.0
China	427.2	7.8	40.7	6.0	49.0
Germany	370.0	-22.7	-28.3	5.2	54.2
Mexico	304.9	-19.3	164.6	4.3	58.5
USA	271.6	-31.7	-23.0	3.8	62.3
Philippines	242.1	-15.4	-12.3	3.4	65.7
Pakistan	210.8	40.3	40.7	3.0	68.6
Viet Nam	*210.5*	-7.7	5.1	2.9	71.6
Malaysia	208.2	-0.1	-38.2	2.9	74.5
Sri Lanka	156.8	-8.0	-1.1	2.2	76.7
Netherlands	148.9	-21.1	-36.2	2.1	78.8
Rep. of Korea	138.5	-37.2	0.0	1.9	80.7

In 2016, the value (in current US$) of exports of "electric current" (SITC group 351) decreased by 11.2 percent (compared to -9.8 percent average growth rate from 2012-2016) to reach 25.7 bln US$ (see table 2), while imports decreased by 9.0 percent to reach 25.0 bln US$ (see table 3). Exports of this commodity accounted for 1.8 percent of world exports of SITC section 3, and 0.2 percent of total world merchandise exports (see table 1). Germany, Canada and France were the top exporters in 2016 (see table 2). They accounted for 11.8, 8.6 and 8.4 percent of world exports, respectively. USA, Italy and Switzerland were the top destinations, with respectively 8.8, 7.5 and 6.0 percent of world imports (see table 3).

The top 15 countries/areas accounted for 75.6 and 66.3 percent of total world exports and imports, respectively (see tables 2 and 3). In 2016, Paraguay was the country/area with the highest value of net exports (+2.1 bln US$), followed by Canada (+2.0 bln US$). By MDG regions (see graph 2), the largest surpluses in this product group were recorded by Latin America and the Caribbean (+1.8 bln US$), South-eastern Europe (+579.2 mln US$) and Commonwealth of Independent States (+556.6 mln US$). The largest trade deficits were recorded by South-eastern Asia (-1.0 bln US$), Western Asia (-795.1 mln US$) and Developed Europe (-537.5 mln US$).

Table 1: Imports (Imp.) and exports (Exp.), 2002-2016, in current US$

		2002	2003	2004	2005	2006	2007	2008	2009	2010	2011	2012	2013	2014	2015	2016
Values in Bln US$	Imp.	11.9	15.4	17.8	24.5	30.4	25.3	35.2	28.9	31.0	38.1	37.0	33.0	31.2	27.5	25.0
	Exp.	13.3	17.0	20.1	25.6	32.2	29.3	40.6	32.7	33.2	40.2	38.9	34.4	33.3	29.0	25.7
As a percentage of SITC section (%)	Imp.	1.9	2.0	1.7	1.7	1.7	1.3	1.2	1.6	1.3	1.2	1.1	1.0	1.0	1.5	1.6
	Exp.	2.2	2.3	2.0	1.8	1.8	1.5	1.5	1.9	1.5	1.3	1.2	1.1	1.1	1.6	1.8
As a percentage of world trade (%)	Imp.	0.2	0.2	0.2	0.2	0.2	0.2	0.2	0.2	0.2	0.2	0.2	0.2	0.2	0.2	0.2
	Exp.	0.2	0.2	0.2	0.2	0.3	0.2	0.3	0.3	0.2	0.2	0.2	0.2	0.2	0.2	0.2

Graph 1: Annual growth rates of exports, 2002–2016
(In percentage by year)

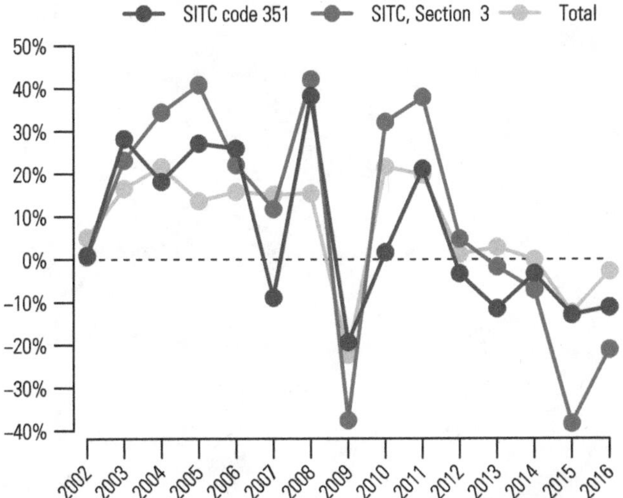

Graph 2: Trade Balance by MDG regions 2016
(Bln US$)

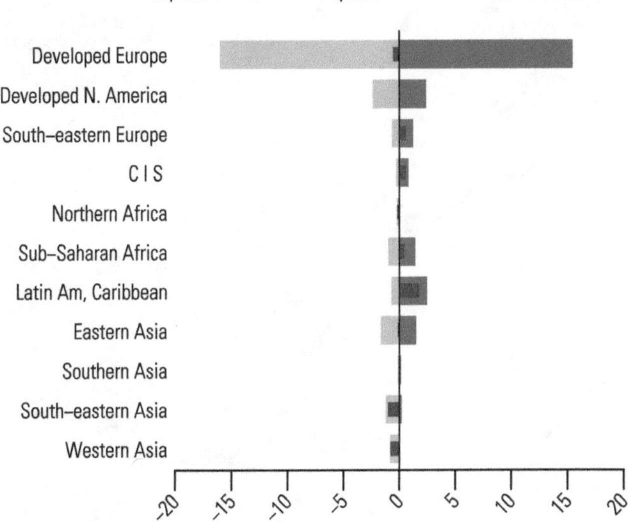

Table 2: Top exporting countries or areas in 2016

Country or area	Value (million US$)	Avg. Growth (%) 12-16	Growth (%) 15-16	World share %	Cum.
World	25725.0	-9.8	-11.2	100.0	
Germany	3044.6	-10.4	-23.2	11.8	11.8
Canada	2199.9	3.3	-10.4	8.6	20.4
France	2149.2	-9.2	-28.4	8.4	28.7
Paraguay	2130.5	-1.0	4.7	8.3	37.0
Switzerland	1626.8	-29.1	-25.8	6.3	43.3
China	1402.3	3.3	-0.5	5.5	48.8
Czechia	1067.4	-17.7	-15.2	4.1	52.9
Austria	962.5	-15.7	1.3	3.7	56.7
Netherlands	866.4	-3.4	-20.2	3.4	60.1
Sweden	840.9	-9.5	7.3	3.3	63.3
South Africa	695.3	7.5	42.9	2.7	66.0
Russian Federation	660.0	-10.3	-11.3	2.6	68.6
Norway	649.9	-7.1	26.5	2.5	71.1
Hungary	615.9	-12.6	-16.6	2.4	73.5
Slovenia	532.5	-9.4	21.3	2.1	75.6

Table 3: Top importing countries or areas in 2016

Country or area	Value (million US$)	Avg. Growth (%) 12-16	Growth (%) 15-16	World share %	Cum.
World	25026.5	-9.3	-9.0	100.0	
USA	2192.1	3.5	-10.9	8.8	8.8
Italy	1866.7	-13.7	-24.8	7.5	16.2
Switzerland	1490.5	-28.2	-19.7	6.0	22.2
Hungary	1127.6	-7.7	-15.8	4.5	26.7
Austria	1114.4	-7.6	-8.9	4.5	31.1
Germany	1107.8	-21.8	-33.9	4.4	35.6
Netherlands	1069.1	-9.4	1890.6	4.3	39.8
United Kingdom	1057.4	-0.3	-27.2	4.2	44.1
Thailand	1014.5	19.3	76.4	4.1	48.1
France	981.5	1.2	117.6	3.9	52.0
Czechia	780.4	-15.8	-27.3	3.1	55.1
China, Hong Kong SAR	775.9	5.5	0.4	3.1	58.3
Finland	763.7	-6.0	8.3	3.1	61.3
Croatia	670.2	1.1	-10.3	2.7	64.0
Poland	582.6	-0.4	-8.7	2.3	66.3

Animal and vegetable oils, fats and waxes

(SITC Section 4)

411 Animal oils and fats

In 2016, the value (in current US$) of exports of "animal oils and fats" (SITC group 411) increased by 6.0 percent (compared to -7.7 percent average growth rate from 2012-2016) to reach 4.5 bln US$ (see table 2), while imports increased by 2.0 percent to reach 4.2 bln US$ (see table 3). Exports of this commodity accounted for 0.7 percent of world exports of SITC sections 2+4, and less than 0.1 percent of total world merchandise exports (see table 1). USA, Germany and Denmark were the top exporters in 2016 (see table 2). They accounted for 14.6, 8.2 and 7.1 percent of world exports, respectively. Norway, China and Mexico were the top destinations, with respectively 9.6, 7.4 and 6.9 percent of world imports (see table 3).

The top 15 countries/areas accounted for 79.4 and 70.7 percent of total world exports and imports, respectively (see tables 2 and 3). In 2016, USA was the country/area with the highest value of net exports (+410.8 mln US$), followed by Australia (+270.0 mln US$). By MDG regions (see graph 2), the largest surpluses in this product group were recorded by Developed North America (+475.3 mln US$), Developed Asia-Pacific (+240.4 mln US$) and Developed Europe (+128.7 mln US$). The largest trade deficits were recorded by Eastern Asia (-206.4 mln US$), South-eastern Asia (-125.4 mln US$) and Commonwealth of Independent States (-59.4 mln US$).

Table 1: Imports (Imp.) and exports (Exp.), 2002-2016, in current US$

		2002	2003	2004	2005	2006	2007	2008	2009	2010	2011	2012	2013	2014	2015	2016
Values in Bln US$	Imp.	1.8	2.2	2.7	2.6	2.8	3.6	5.5	4.0	4.5	6.3	5.9	5.2	4.8	4.1	4.2
	Exp.	1.7	2.0	2.7	2.5	2.7	3.6	5.5	3.9	4.6	6.3	6.2	5.9	5.4	4.3	4.5
As a percentage of SITC section (%)	Imp.	0.7	0.8	0.7	0.6	0.6	0.6	0.7	0.7	0.6	0.6	0.6	0.6	0.5	0.6	0.6
	Exp.	0.8	0.8	0.8	0.7	0.6	0.7	0.8	0.8	0.7	0.7	0.7	0.7	0.7	0.6	0.7
As a percentage of world trade (%)	Imp.	0.0	0.0	0.0	0.0	0.0	0.0	0.0	0.0	0.0	0.0	0.0	0.0	0.0	0.0	0.0
	Exp.	0.0	0.0	0.0	0.0	0.0	0.0	0.0	0.0	0.0	0.0	0.0	0.0	0.0	0.0	0.0

Graph 1: Annual growth rates of exports, 2002–2016

(In percentage by year)

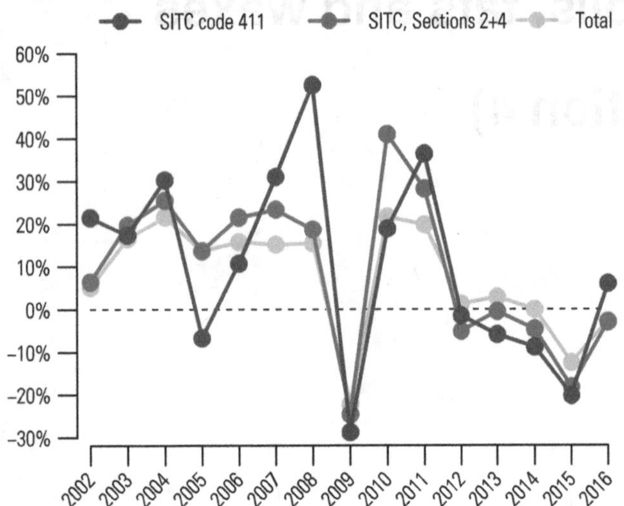

Table 2: Top exporting countries or areas in 2016

Country or area	Value (million US$)	Avg. Growth (%) 12-16	Growth (%) 15-16	World share %	Cum.
World	4526.4	-7.7	6.0	100.0	
USA	659.6	-7.7	18.0	14.6	14.6
Germany	372.2	-9.0	15.8	8.2	22.8
Denmark	320.2	-3.4	12.2	7.1	29.9
Australia	314.8	-2.8	6.4	7.0	36.8
France	292.2	-8.6	7.4	6.5	43.3
Peru	268.6	-16.1	-8.5	5.9	49.2
Netherlands	214.6	-12.7	17.7	4.7	54.0
Canada	205.7	-8.3	21.7	4.5	58.5
China	174.6	-0.7	-23.9	3.9	62.4
United Kingdom	171.8	-3.8	2.3	3.8	66.2
Spain	142.4	-12.2	-0.1	3.1	69.3
Norway	126.8	-2.8	-8.7	2.8	72.1
Belgium	120.9	-9.8	11.9	2.7	74.8
Chile	108.6	-4.5	-15.9	2.4	77.2
New Zealand	102.8	-8.3	16.3	2.3	79.4

Graph 2: Trade Balance by MDG regions 2016

(Bln US$)

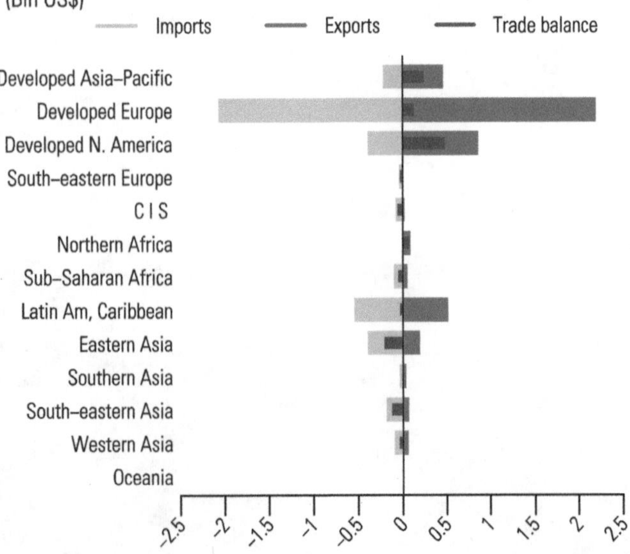

Table 3: Top importing countries or areas in 2016

Country or area	Value (million US$)	Avg. Growth (%) 12-16	Growth (%) 15-16	World share %	Cum.
World	4155.4	-8.3	2.0	100.0	
Norway	397.8	3.6	-2.4	9.6	9.6
China	305.7	0.0	29.0	7.4	16.9
Mexico	288.0	2.2	-6.9	6.9	23.9
USA	248.8	0.2	1.1	6.0	29.8
Denmark	211.8	-10.4	6.3	5.1	34.9
Netherlands	193.5	-15.1	9.4	4.7	39.6
France	183.9	6.9	43.7	4.4	44.0
Belgium	182.8	-7.9	11.9	4.4	48.4
Spain	160.1	-3.3	18.0	3.9	52.3
Japan	153.5	-9.6	-5.9	3.7	56.0
Germany	153.3	-3.8	10.0	3.7	59.7
Canada	140.9	-2.6	12.7	3.4	63.1
United Kingdom	128.5	-9.8	-14.0	3.1	66.1
Italy	95.9	-5.9	7.9	2.3	68.5
Chile	92.3	-6.0	-29.9	2.2	70.7

In 2016, the value (in current US$) of exports of "fixed vegetable fats and oils, 'soft', crude, refined or fractionated" (SITC group 421) decreased by 6.0 percent (compared to -5.6 percent average growth rate from 2012-2016) to reach 31.4 bln US$ (see table 2), while imports increased by 2.4 percent to reach 35.0 bln US$ (see table 3). Exports of this commodity accounted for 4.9 percent of world exports of SITC sections 2+4, and 0.2 percent of total world merchandise exports (see table 1). Argentina, Spain and Canada were the top exporters in 2016 (see table 2). They accounted for 15.3, 13.5 and 8.0 percent of world exports, respectively. India, USA and Italy were the top destinations, with respectively 13.5, 9.6 and 7.3 percent of world imports (see table 3).

The top 15 countries/areas accounted for 79.0 and 63.5 percent of total world exports and imports, respectively (see tables 2 and 3). In 2016, Argentina was the country/area with the highest value of net exports (+4.8 bln US$), followed by Spain (+3.2 bln US$). By MDG regions (see graph 2), the largest surpluses in this product group were recorded by Latin America and the Caribbean (+4.2 bln US$), Developed Europe (+2.2 bln US$) and Commonwealth of Independent States (+1.5 bln US$). The largest trade deficits were recorded by Southern Asia (-5.9 bln US$), Eastern Asia (-2.6 bln US$) and Northern Africa (-1.1 bln US$).

Table 1: Imports (Imp.) and exports (Exp.), 2002-2016, in current US$

		2002	2003	2004	2005	2006	2007	2008	2009	2010	2011	2012	2013	2014	2015	2016
Values in Bln US$	Imp.	10.9	13.9	16.4	17.0	20.1	25.4	35.6	25.8	28.0	38.3	39.4	38.5	35.5	34.1	35.0
	Exp.	10.7	13.5	15.7	16.6	19.9	24.7	34.5	24.7	28.5	38.3	39.6	38.1	35.0	33.4	31.4
As a percentage of SITC section (%)	Imp.	4.5	4.8	4.4	4.1	4.0	4.1	4.6	4.8	3.7	3.9	4.3	4.2	4.0	4.7	5.0
	Exp.	5.0	5.2	4.9	4.5	4.5	4.5	5.3	5.0	4.1	4.3	4.7	4.5	4.4	5.1	4.9
As a percentage of world trade (%)	Imp.	0.2	0.2	0.2	0.2	0.2	0.2	0.2	0.2	0.2	0.2	0.2	0.2	0.2	0.2	0.2
	Exp.	0.2	0.2	0.2	0.2	0.2	0.2	0.2	0.2	0.2	0.2	0.2	0.2	0.2	0.2	0.2

Graph 1: Annual growth rates of exports, 2002–2016
(In percentage by year)

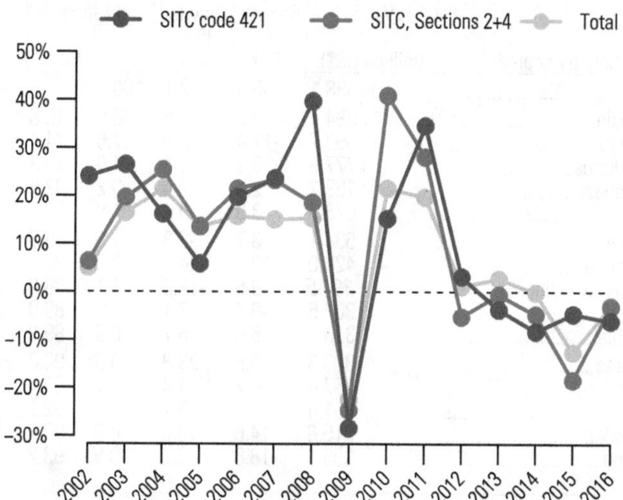

Table 2: Top exporting countries or areas in 2016

Country or area	Value (million US$)	Avg. Growth (%) 12-16	Growth (%) 15-16	World share %	Cum.
World	31 443.4	-5.6	-6.0	100.0	
Argentina	4 803.2	-3.2	7.7	15.3	15.3
Spain	4 252.4	4.4	17.5	13.5	28.8
Canada	2 521.1	-7.9	11.6	8.0	36.8
Russian Federation	1 978.5	-1.0	16.7	6.3	43.1
Italy	1 935.9	1.8	6.4	6.2	49.3
USA	1 519.7	-10.5	-1.3	4.8	54.1
Germany	1 441.7	-5.5	4.0	4.6	58.7
Netherlands	1 311.6	-5.8	12.9	4.2	62.9
Brazil	1 007.1	-17.8	-19.9	3.2	66.1
France	886.9	-7.9	12.2	2.8	68.9
Turkey	806.6	10.1	1.3	2.6	71.4
Greece	710.2	11.3	-6.9	2.3	73.7
Portugal	576.6	4.4	-0.8	1.8	75.5
Belgium	573.9	-7.9	17.3	1.8	77.4
Czechia	518.2	4.4	9.1	1.6	79.0

Graph 2: Trade Balance by MDG regions 2016
(Bln US$)

Imports — Exports — Trade balance

Developed Asia-Pacific
Developed Europe
Developed N. America
South-eastern Europe
C I S
Northern Africa
Sub-Saharan Africa
Latin Am, Caribbean
Eastern Asia
Southern Asia
South-eastern Asia
Western Asia
Oceania

-15 -10 -5 0 5 10 15

Table 3: Top importing countries or areas in 2016

Country or area	Value (million US$)	Avg. Growth (%) 12-16	Growth (%) 15-16	World share %	Cum.
World	34 958.8	-3.0	2.4	100.0	
India	4 715.0	13.3	8.8	13.5	13.5
USA	3 360.1	1.1	8.8	9.6	23.1
Italy	2 563.5	4.8	-1.3	7.3	30.4
China	2 153.4	-15.6	-4.1	6.2	36.6
Netherlands	1 248.7	-6.6	4.3	3.6	40.2
Germany	1 078.7	0.5	4.9	3.1	43.2
Turkey	1 070.9	0.9	-6.2	3.1	46.3
Spain	1 044.5	9.6	-11.1	3.0	49.3
France	1 023.1	-6.0	17.3	2.9	52.2
Belgium	871.1	-7.2	8.7	2.5	54.7
Bangladesh	*814.5*	-3.6	-14.2	2.3	57.0
United Kingdom	757.6	-5.9	-6.1	2.2	59.2
Algeria	582.7	-7.6	11.0	1.7	60.9
Mexico	453.3	1.6	2.6	1.3	62.2
Morocco	451.5	-3.8	17.0	1.3	63.5

Source: UN Comtrade

422 Fixed vegetable fats and oils, crude, refined or fractionated, not 'soft'

In 2016, the value (in current US$) of exports of "fixed vegetable fats and oils, crude, refined or fractionated, not 'soft'" (SITC group 422) decreased by 2.1 percent (compared to -5.8 percent average growth rate from 2012-2016) to reach 36.5 bln US$ (see table 2), while imports decreased by 4.6 percent to reach 37.6 bln US$ (see table 3). Exports of this commodity accounted for 5.7 percent of world exports of SITC sections 2+4, and 0.2 percent of total world merchandise exports (see table 1). Indonesia, Malaysia and Netherlands were the top exporters in 2016 (see table 2). They accounted for 46.8, 27.6 and 4.9 percent of world exports, respectively. India, China and Netherlands were the top destinations, with respectively 15.3, 10.8 and 7.1 percent of world imports (see table 3).

The top 15 countries/areas accounted for 93.2 and 71.0 percent of total world exports and imports, respectively (see tables 2 and 3). In 2016, Indonesia was the country/area with the highest value of net exports (+17.1 bln US$), followed by Malaysia (+9.2 bln US$). By MDG regions (see graph 2), the largest surpluses in this product group were recorded by South-eastern Asia (+26.8 bln US$), Oceania (+399.7 mln US$) and Latin America and the Caribbean (+131.9 mln US$). The largest trade deficits were recorded by Southern Asia (-8.5 bln US$), Developed Europe (-6.6 bln US$) and Eastern Asia (-4.7 bln US$).

Table 1: Imports (Imp.) and exports (Exp.), 2002-2016, in current US$

		2002	2003	2004	2005	2006	2007	2008	2009	2010	2011	2012	2013	2014	2015	2016
Values in Bln US$	Imp.	9.0	12.1	15.0	15.2	16.9	23.7	37.3	30.0	37.9	53.1	50.4	45.3	43.1	39.4	37.6
	Exp.	8.3	10.7	13.1	13.4	15.4	24.1	37.1	28.2	37.1	50.3	46.3	41.0	43.9	37.3	36.5
As a percentage of SITC section (%)	Imp.	3.7	4.2	4.0	3.6	3.4	3.8	4.9	5.5	5.0	5.4	5.5	4.9	4.8	5.4	5.4
	Exp.	3.8	4.1	4.1	3.6	3.4	4.4	5.7	5.7	5.3	5.6	5.5	4.9	5.5	5.7	5.7
As a percentage of world trade (%)	Imp.	0.1	0.2	0.2	0.1	0.1	0.2	0.2	0.2	0.2	0.3	0.3	0.2	0.2	0.2	0.2
	Exp.	0.1	0.1	0.1	0.1	0.1	0.2	0.2	0.2	0.2	0.3	0.3	0.2	0.2	0.2	0.2

Graph 1: Annual growth rates of exports, 2002–2016
(In percentage by year)

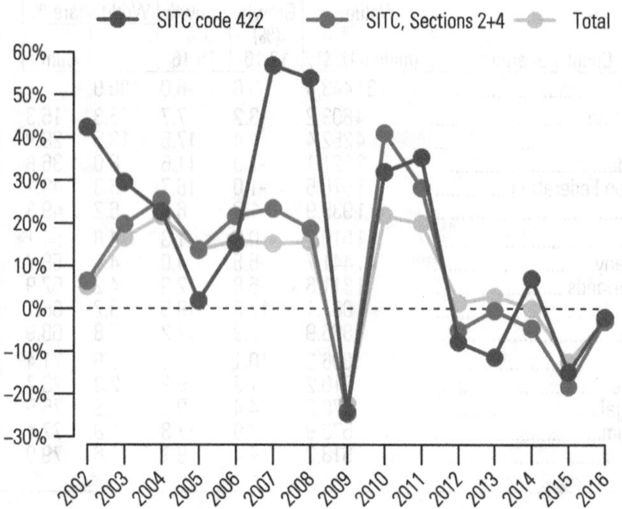

Table 2: Top exporting countries or areas in 2016

Country or area	Value (million US$)	Avg. Growth (%) 12-16	Growth (%) 15-16	World share %	Cum.
World	36538.1	-5.8	-2.1	100.0	
Indonesia	17094.7	-3.9	-3.8	46.8	46.8
Malaysia	10093.7	-11.4	-2.9	27.6	74.4
Netherlands	1777.9	-3.3	11.4	4.9	79.3
Philippines	1163.2	2.4	2.4	3.2	82.5
India	673.3	-3.0	-9.4	1.8	84.3
Germany	534.1	3.7	-2.3	1.5	85.8
Guatemala	421.0	10.3	34.7	1.2	86.9
Papua New Guinea	*394.5*	-9.5	-12.6	1.1	88.0
USA	362.6	-0.4	7.1	1.0	89.0
Colombia	316.7	6.6	-6.7	0.9	89.9
Honduras	306.3	-0.8	23.8	0.8	90.7
Ecuador	257.4	-4.7	4.4	0.7	91.4
Italy	251.4	1.9	3.7	0.7	92.1
Denmark	215.6	14.6	10.0	0.6	92.7
Thailand	195.1	-18.8	-2.7	0.5	93.2

Graph 2: Trade Balance by MDG regions 2016
(Bln US$)

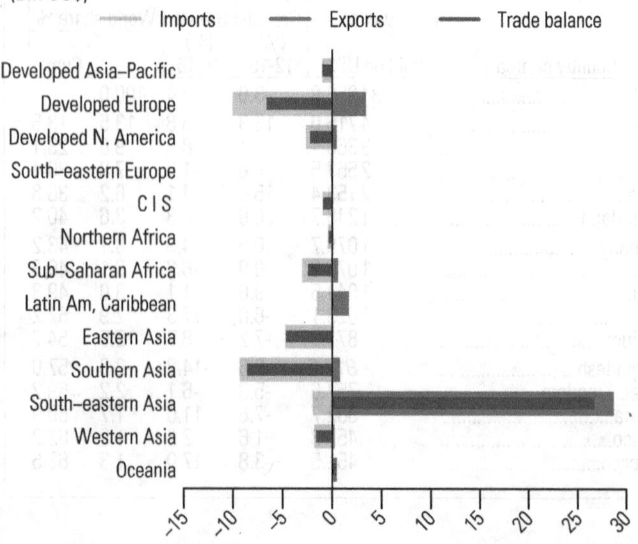

Table 3: Top importing countries or areas in 2016

Country or area	Value (million US$)	Avg. Growth (%) 12-16	Growth (%) 15-16	World share %	Cum.
World	37615.2	-7.1	-4.6	100.0	
India	5737.5	-8.3	-6.3	15.3	15.3
China	4075.1	-14.8	-15.4	10.8	26.1
Netherlands	2686.3	-6.9	7.9	7.1	33.2
USA	2424.1	0.3	3.7	6.4	39.7
Germany	1938.6	-3.5	3.7	5.2	44.8
Pakistan	1725.5	-5.4	3.3	4.6	49.4
Bangladesh	*1547.4*	-6.4	-14.2	4.1	53.5
Italy	1252.9	-0.8	-10.0	3.3	56.9
Spain	1153.3	12.6	18.0	3.1	59.9
Malaysia	857.2	-23.3	-35.0	2.3	62.2
Russian Federation	814.4	-2.1	4.2	2.2	64.4
Japan	750.0	-5.3	-7.0	2.0	66.4
France	665.8	-5.1	-1.6	1.8	68.1
Belgium	532.2	-2.4	6.6	1.4	69.5
Ethiopia	531.1	9.2	-48.0	1.4	71.0

In 2016, the value (in current US$) of exports of "animal or vegetable fats and oils, processed; waxes of; inedible" (SITC group 431) increased by 8.1 percent (compared to -6.0 percent average growth rate from 2012-2016) to reach 11.1 bln US$ (see table 2), while imports increased by 9.4 percent to reach 12.7 bln US$ (see table 3). Exports of this commodity accounted for 1.7 percent of world exports of SITC sections 2+4, and 0.1 percent of total world merchandise exports (see table 1). Malaysia, Indonesia and Netherlands were the top exporters in 2016 (see table 2). They accounted for 26.8, 19.9 and 12.8 percent of world exports, respectively. Netherlands, Germany and China were the top destinations, with respectively 10.4, 7.7 and 6.4 percent of world imports (see table 3).

The top 15 countries/areas accounted for 86.4 and 64.3 percent of total world exports and imports, respectively (see tables 2 and 3). In 2016, Malaysia was the country/area with the highest value of net exports (+2.3 bln US$), followed by Indonesia (+2.1 bln US$). By MDG regions (see graph 2), the largest surplus in this product group was recorded solely by South-eastern Asia (+2.8 bln US$). The largest trade deficits were recorded by Developed Europe (-1.5 bln US$), Eastern Asia (-954.0 mln US$) and Southern Asia (-595.8 mln US$).

Table 1: Imports (Imp.) and exports (Exp.), 2002-2016, in current US$

		2002	2003	2004	2005	2006	2007	2008	2009	2010	2011	2012	2013	2014	2015	2016
Values in Bln US$	Imp.	3.3	4.1	4.7	5.1	5.6	7.3	10.1	7.2	8.9	13.4	12.6	12.2	13.8	11.6	12.7
	Exp.	3.8	4.5	5.6	5.6	6.1	8.1	11.2	7.8	9.8	14.3	14.2	13.4	12.5	10.2	11.1
As a percentage of SITC section (%)	Imp.	1.4	1.4	1.3	1.2	1.1	1.2	1.3	1.3	1.2	1.4	1.4	1.3	1.5	1.6	1.8
	Exp.	1.7	1.8	1.7	1.5	1.4	1.5	1.7	1.6	1.4	1.6	1.7	1.6	1.6	1.6	1.7
As a percentage of world trade (%)	Imp.	0.1	0.1	0.1	0.0	0.0	0.1	0.1	0.1	0.1	0.1	0.1	0.1	0.1	0.1	0.1
	Exp.	0.1	0.1	0.1	0.1	0.1	0.1	0.1	0.1	0.1	0.1	0.1	0.1	0.1	0.1	0.1

Graph 1: Annual growth rates of exports, 2002–2016

(In percentage by year)

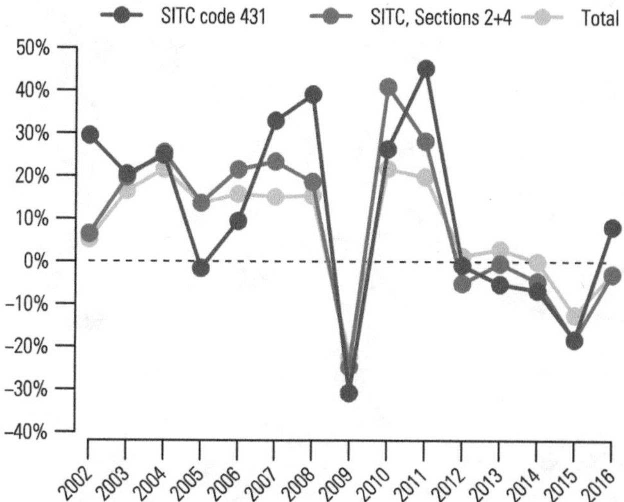

Table 2: Top exporting countries or areas in 2016

Country or area	Value (million US$)	Avg. Growth (%) 12-16	Growth (%) 15-16	World share %	Cum.
World	11 072.6	-6.0	8.1	100.0	
Malaysia	2 964.2	-5.8	7.4	26.8	26.8
Indonesia	2 200.2	3.0	25.2	19.9	46.6
Netherlands	1 415.5	-7.8	19.5	12.8	59.4
Germany	680.9	-10.4	1.0	6.1	65.6
USA	472.1	-11.8	-13.5	4.3	69.8
Belgium	433.2	-4.3	11.0	3.9	73.8
China	206.3	7.0	14.1	1.9	75.6
India	198.4	3.4	-15.6	1.8	77.4
Sweden	178.0	-3.6	8.7	1.6	79.0
Spain	174.3	11.4	23.4	1.6	80.6
Brazil	151.4	-8.0	-16.0	1.4	82.0
United Kingdom	141.4	-8.7	5.3	1.3	83.2
Argentina	133.9	-13.5	5.6	1.2	84.4
France	132.2	-3.5	13.3	1.2	85.6
Italy	84.3	-15.6	15.0	0.8	86.4

Graph 2: Trade Balance by MDG regions 2016

(Bln US$)

Imports — Exports — Trade balance

Developed Asia-Pacific
Developed Europe
Developed N. America
South-eastern Europe
C I S
Northern Africa
Sub-Saharan Africa
Latin Am, Caribbean
Eastern Asia
Southern Asia
South-eastern Asia
Western Asia
Oceania

-6 -5 -4 -3 -2 -1 0 1 2 3 4 5 6

Table 3: Top importing countries or areas in 2016

Country or area	Value (million US$)	Avg. Growth (%) 12-16	Growth (%) 15-16	World share %	Cum.
World	12 724.6	0.3	9.4	100.0	
Netherlands	1 320.5	1.3	32.0	10.4	10.4
Germany	983.6	-2.9	11.8	7.7	18.1
China	817.6	-3.6	11.6	6.4	24.5
Philippines	676.6	28.2	79.5	5.3	29.8
Malaysia	639.2	9.5	16.4	5.0	34.9
Myanmar	530.9	18.4	-5.8	4.2	39.0
USA	526.2	6.5	0.6	4.1	43.2
Singapore	437.1	18.1	10.4	3.4	46.6
India	356.6	12.6	62.8	2.8	49.4
Spain	339.5	-1.2	5.9	2.7	52.1
Rep. of Korea	335.4	-2.2	9.7	2.6	54.7
United Kingdom	323.6	-11.3	8.2	2.5	57.3
Afghanistan	316.5	...	-8.7	2.5	59.8
France	293.3	-0.9	3.8	2.3	62.1
Italy	280.4	-5.5	8.1	2.2	64.3

Source: UN Comtrade

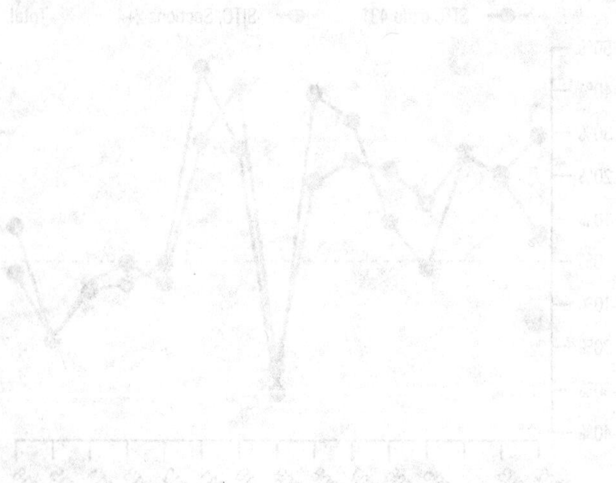

Chemicals and related products, n.e.s.

(SITC Section 5)

511 Hydrocarbons, nes, and their derivatives

In 2016, the value (in current US$) of exports of "hydrocarbons, nes, and their derivatives" (SITC group 511) decreased by 7.3 percent (compared to -9.8 percent average growth rate from 2012-2016) to reach 61.9 bln US$ (see table 2), while imports decreased by 7.0 percent to reach 67.2 bln US$ (see table 3). Exports of this commodity accounted for 3.5 percent of world exports of SITC section 5, and 0.4 percent of total world merchandise exports (see table 1). Rep. of Korea, USA and Japan were the top exporters in 2016 (see table 2). They accounted for 16.9, 12.0 and 11.1 percent of world exports, respectively. China, Belgium and USA were the top destinations, with respectively 31.3, 8.1 and 6.6 percent of world imports (see table 3).

The top 15 countries/areas accounted for 86.3 and 82.7 percent of total world exports and imports, respectively (see tables 2 and 3). In 2016, Rep. of Korea was the country/area with the highest value of net exports (+7.7 bln US$), followed by Japan (+5.8 bln US$). By MDG regions (see graph 2), the largest surpluses in this product group were recorded by Developed Asia-Pacific (+5.7 bln US$), Developed North America (+3.3 bln US$) and Western Asia (+2.4 bln US$). The largest trade deficits were recorded by Eastern Asia (-11.1 bln US$), Latin America and the Caribbean (-3.1 bln US$) and Developed Europe (-2.3 bln US$).

Table 1: Imports (Imp.) and exports (Exp.), 2002-2016, in current US$

		2002	2003	2004	2005	2006	2007	2008	2009	2010	2011	2012	2013	2014	2015	2016
Values in Bln US$	Imp.	23.5	31.6	46.4	53.2	61.4	72.8	77.5	54.2	75.6	98.1	96.4	106.1	100.3	72.2	67.2
	Exp.	21.9	29.3	43.6	48.3	56.9	68.8	71.2	52.1	71.4	92.9	93.5	99.7	94.7	66.8	61.9
As a percentage of SITC section (%)	Imp.	3.3	3.8	4.6	4.6	4.8	4.8	4.5	3.7	4.3	4.8	4.8	5.1	4.7	3.7	3.5
	Exp.	3.3	3.7	4.6	4.5	4.7	4.8	4.3	3.7	4.3	4.8	4.9	5.1	4.7	3.7	3.5
As a percentage of world trade (%)	Imp.	0.4	0.4	0.5	0.5	0.5	0.5	0.5	0.4	0.5	0.5	0.5	0.6	0.5	0.4	0.4
	Exp.	0.3	0.4	0.5	0.5	0.5	0.5	0.4	0.4	0.5	0.5	0.5	0.5	0.5	0.4	0.4

Graph 1: Annual growth rates of exports, 2002–2016
(In percentage by year)

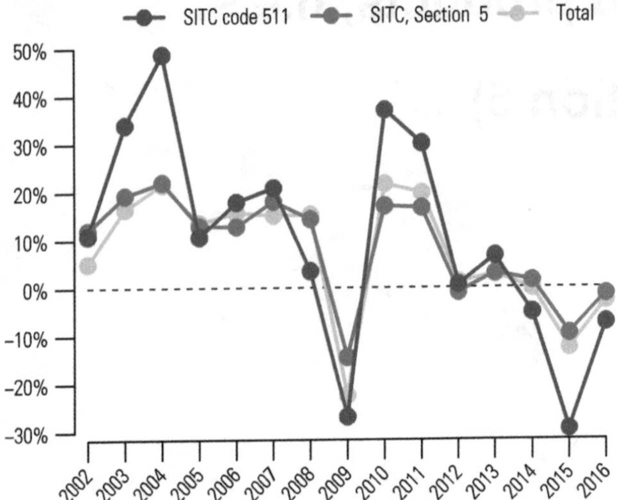

Graph 2: Trade Balance by MDG regions 2016
(Bln US$)

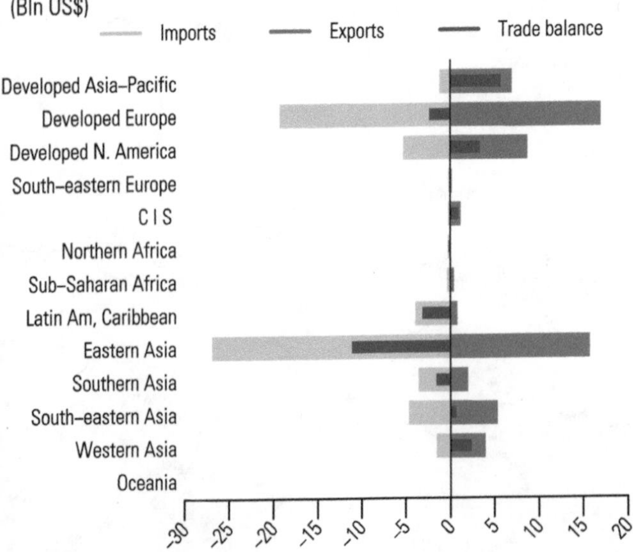

Table 2: Top exporting countries or areas in 2016

Country or area	Value (million US$)	Avg. Growth (%) 12-16	Growth (%) 15-16	World share %	Cum.
World	61923.2	-9.8	-7.3	100.0	
Rep. of Korea	10471.2	-5.3	-1.1	16.9	16.9
USA	7437.9	-6.7	2.9	12.0	28.9
Japan	6867.8	-9.6	-16.7	11.1	40.0
Netherlands	6051.7	-12.9	10.2	9.8	49.8
Germany	3387.2	-10.0	-7.9	5.5	55.3
Other Asia, nes	2971.5	-2.9	-9.0	4.8	60.1
Singapore	2584.5	-5.3	-18.2	4.2	64.2
China	2262.7	-7.8	-9.4	3.7	67.9
Saudi Arabia	2199.9	-10.2	-7.8	3.6	71.4
Belgium	2175.3	-10.4	-2.3	3.5	74.9
United Kingdom	1830.2	-14.0	-10.4	3.0	77.9
India	1571.7	-14.8	-10.0	2.5	80.4
Thailand	1300.1	-14.0	-11.5	2.1	82.5
Canada	1228.4	-15.4	-17.8	2.0	84.5
Russian Federation	1096.1	-14.0	-20.6	1.8	86.3

Table 3: Top importing countries or areas in 2016

Country or area	Value (million US$)	Avg. Growth (%) 12-16	Growth (%) 15-16	World share %	Cum.
World	67157.7	-8.6	-7.0	100.0	
China	20998.7	-3.0	-3.8	31.3	31.3
Belgium	5447.1	-11.8	-11.7	8.1	39.4
USA	4407.8	-9.7	-17.5	6.6	45.9
India	3006.7	-1.7	8.8	4.5	50.4
Germany	2983.2	-11.9	-17.1	4.4	54.9
Netherlands	2935.9	-12.8	-4.7	4.4	59.2
Other Asia, nes	2820.0	-15.9	-3.6	4.2	63.4
Rep. of Korea	2762.4	-14.3	-17.7	4.1	67.5
Mexico	2481.4	-10.3	-2.1	3.7	71.2
France	2048.9	-9.1	-2.9	3.1	74.3
Indonesia	1691.8	-14.2	-28.9	2.5	76.8
Japan	1108.4	-5.1	-3.1	1.7	78.5
Spain	980.3	-6.7	-6.4	1.5	79.9
Singapore	922.4	7.4	12.6	1.4	81.3
Canada	920.7	-7.0	-8.3	1.4	82.7

Source: UN Comtrade

In 2016, the value (in current US$) of exports of "alcohols, phenols, phenol-alcohols and their derivatives" (SITC group 512) decreased by 11.7 percent (compared to -9.7 percent average growth rate from 2012-2016) to reach 37.4 bln US$ (see table 2), while imports decreased by 11.3 percent to reach 45.5 bln US$ (see table 3). Exports of this commodity accounted for 2.1 percent of world exports of SITC section 5, and 0.2 percent of total world merchandise exports (see table 1). USA, Netherlands and Germany were the top exporters in 2016 (see table 2). They accounted for 13.5, 8.0 and 7.2 percent of world exports, respectively. China, USA and Netherlands were the top destinations, with respectively 23.3, 6.8 and 6.6 percent of world imports (see table 3).

The top 15 countries/areas accounted for 73.1 and 76.1 percent of total world exports and imports, respectively (see tables 2 and 3). In 2016, USA was the country/area with the highest value of net exports (+1.9 bln US$), followed by Malaysia (+1.4 bln US$). By MDG regions (see graph 2), the largest surpluses in this product group were recorded by Developed North America (+2.1 bln US$), South-eastern Asia (+1.9 bln US$) and Western Asia (+1.3 bln US$). The largest trade deficits were recorded by Eastern Asia (-9.3 bln US$), Developed Europe (-3.1 bln US$) and Southern Asia (-667.8 mln US$).

Table 1: Imports (Imp.) and exports (Exp.), 2002-2016, in current US$

		2002	2003	2004	2005	2006	2007	2008	2009	2010	2011	2012	2013	2014	2015	2016
Values in Bln US$	Imp.	16.9	22.1	28.5	33.6	38.1	46.2	53.0	35.8	51.2	68.4	65.6	67.1	63.4	51.3	45.5
	Exp.	15.0	18.8	25.0	29.2	32.6	39.8	46.3	31.1	43.4	58.8	56.3	55.1	53.4	42.3	37.4
As a percentage of SITC section (%)	Imp.	2.4	2.6	2.8	2.9	3.0	3.1	3.1	2.4	2.9	3.3	3.3	3.2	3.0	2.7	2.4
	Exp.	2.3	2.4	2.6	2.7	2.7	2.8	2.8	2.2	2.6	3.0	2.9	2.8	2.7	2.3	2.1
As a percentage of world trade (%)	Imp.	0.3	0.3	0.3	0.3	0.3	0.3	0.3	0.3	0.3	0.4	0.4	0.4	0.3	0.3	0.3
	Exp.	0.2	0.3	0.3	0.3	0.3	0.3	0.3	0.3	0.3	0.3	0.3	0.3	0.3	0.3	0.2

Graph 1: Annual growth rates of exports, 2002–2016
(In percentage by year)

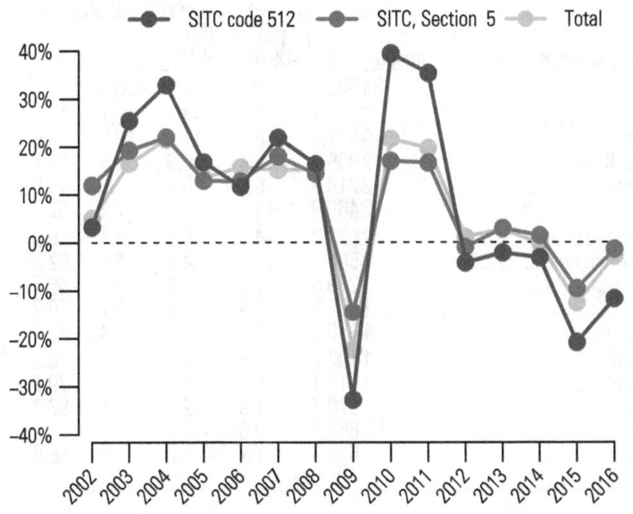

Graph 2: Trade Balance by MDG regions 2016
(Bln US$)

Imports — Exports — Trade balance

Developed Asia-Pacific
Developed Europe
Developed N. America
South-eastern Europe
C I S
Northern Africa
Sub-Saharan Africa
Latin Am, Caribbean
Eastern Asia
Southern Asia
South-eastern Asia
Western Asia
Oceania

-15 -10 -5 0 5 10 15

Table 2: Top exporting countries or areas in 2016

Country or area	Value (million US$)	Avg. Growth (%) 12-16	Growth (%) 15-16	World share %	Cum.
World	37 368.4	-9.7	-11.7	100.0	
USA	5 034.6	-4.2	3.6	13.5	13.5
Netherlands	2 972.3	-5.7	-0.3	8.0	21.4
Germany	2 706.3	-6.1	-5.3	7.2	28.7
Belgium	2 052.1	-10.5	-10.2	5.5	34.2
Malaysia	1 752.9	-3.7	16.3	4.7	38.9
Other Asia, nes	1 664.4	-11.6	-17.8	4.5	43.3
China	1 504.4	-0.2	-0.1	4.0	47.3
Saudi Arabia	1 432.2	-27.6	-44.0	3.8	51.2
Singapore	1 330.8	-15.0	-33.9	3.6	54.7
Rep. of Korea	1 200.5	-4.6	-12.9	3.2	57.9
Japan	1 199.0	-10.8	-10.8	3.2	61.1
Iran	*1 194.0*	-9.5	-43.8	3.2	64.3
Canada	1 114.8	-6.8	-12.6	3.0	67.3
Brazil	1 094.3	-18.1	0.4	2.9	70.3
Indonesia	1 056.6	-0.7	19.4	2.8	73.1

Table 3: Top importing countries or areas in 2016

Country or area	Value (million US$)	Avg. Growth (%) 12-16	Growth (%) 15-16	World share %	Cum.
World	45 489.4	-8.8	-11.3	100.0	
China	10 597.1	-9.8	-14.7	23.3	23.3
USA	3 092.9	-16.6	-23.9	6.8	30.1
Netherlands	3 002.3	-5.8	6.4	6.6	36.7
Germany	2 675.4	-10.4	-8.0	5.9	42.6
India	2 607.5	1.4	-4.6	5.7	48.3
Rep. of Korea	1 943.9	-7.4	-9.7	4.3	52.6
Belgium	1 843.5	-6.0	-5.1	4.1	56.6
Japan	1 722.0	-7.5	-4.8	3.8	60.4
United Kingdom	1 213.6	-6.1	-9.5	2.7	63.1
Italy	1 108.1	-11.7	-14.1	2.4	65.5
Other Asia, nes	1 086.5	-8.6	-8.1	2.4	67.9
Brazil	1 001.7	-3.3	1.2	2.2	70.1
Canada	967.3	-6.4	-10.8	2.1	72.2
France	933.5	-9.1	-14.2	2.1	74.3
Thailand	825.1	-12.7	-18.8	1.8	76.1

513 Carboxylic acids, and their derivatives

In 2016, the value (in current US$) of exports of "carboxylic acids, and their derivatives" (SITC group 513) decreased by 6.5 percent (compared to -8.1 percent average growth rate from 2012-2016) to reach 34.3 bln US$ (see table 2), while imports decreased by 8.9 percent to reach 38.4 bln US$ (see table 3). Exports of this commodity accounted for 1.9 percent of world exports of SITC section 5, and 0.2 percent of total world merchandise exports (see table 1). China, USA and Rep. of Korea were the top exporters in 2016 (see table 2). They accounted for 18.1, 10.5 and 8.5 percent of world exports, respectively. USA, Germany and China were the top destinations, with respectively 9.7, 7.8 and 6.2 percent of world imports (see table 3).

The top 15 countries/areas accounted for 86.6 and 69.1 percent of total world exports and imports, respectively (see tables 2 and 3). In 2016, China was the country/area with the highest value of net exports (+3.8 bln US$), followed by Rep. of Korea (+1.7 bln US$). By MDG regions (see graph 2), the largest surpluses in this product group were recorded by Eastern Asia (+6.4 bln US$) and South-eastern Asia (+684.2 mln US$). The largest trade deficits were recorded by Developed Europe (-4.4 bln US$), Latin America and the Caribbean (-1.7 bln US$) and Southern Asia (-1.5 bln US$).

Table 1: Imports (Imp.) and exports (Exp.), 2002-2016, in current US$

		2002	2003	2004	2005	2006	2007	2008	2009	2010	2011	2012	2013	2014	2015	2016
Values in Bln US$	Imp.	22.1	25.8	32.3	36.7	40.2	43.8	45.8	36.7	47.4	57.2	52.8	52.2	51.0	42.2	38.4
	Exp.	17.9	22.2	28.5	33.1	37.1	40.3	41.2	33.0	42.3	52.5	48.2	46.8	44.9	36.7	34.3
As a percentage of SITC section (%)	Imp.	3.1	3.1	3.2	3.2	3.1	2.9	2.6	2.5	2.7	2.8	2.6	2.5	2.4	2.2	2.0
	Exp.	2.7	2.8	3.0	3.1	3.0	2.8	2.5	2.3	2.6	2.7	2.5	2.4	2.2	2.0	1.9
As a percentage of world trade (%)	Imp.	0.3	0.3	0.3	0.3	0.3	0.3	0.3	0.3	0.3	0.3	0.3	0.3	0.3	0.3	0.2
	Exp.	0.3	0.3	0.3	0.3	0.3	0.3	0.3	0.3	0.3	0.3	0.3	0.2	0.2	0.2	0.2

Graph 1: Annual growth rates of exports, 2002–2016
(In percentage by year)

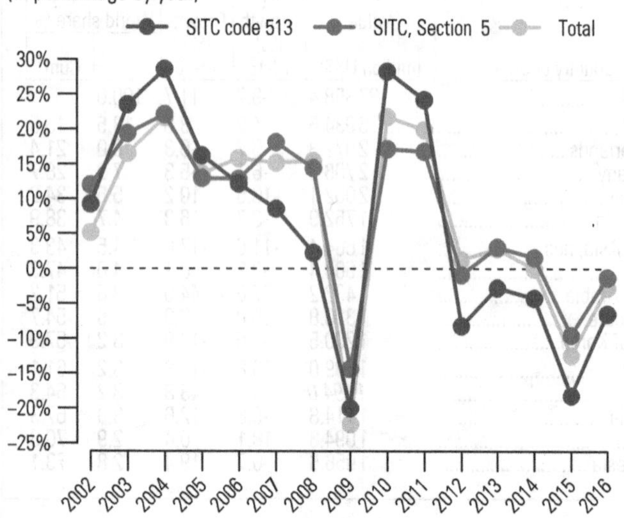

Table 2: Top exporting countries or areas in 2016

Country or area	Value (million US$)	Avg. Growth (%) 12-16	Growth (%) 15-16	World share %	Cum.
World	34 302.8	-8.1	-6.5	100.0	
China	6 214.1	0.7	-4.1	18.1	18.1
USA	3 602.8	-8.5	-17.9	10.5	28.6
Rep. of Korea	2 905.2	-15.4	-9.9	8.5	37.1
Germany	2 719.9	-6.8	-10.2	7.9	45.0
Belgium	2 466.9	-13.9	-12.5	7.2	52.2
Netherlands	2 077.7	-4.3	8.7	6.1	58.3
Other Asia, nes	1 565.7	-18.9	-4.6	4.6	62.8
Japan	1 269.5	-7.1	-1.4	3.7	66.5
India	1 257.5	5.4	4.8	3.7	70.2
Singapore	1 150.0	-3.3	-5.8	3.4	73.5
Malaysia	1 102.7	-5.5	-0.7	3.2	76.8
Thailand	1 017.7	-15.1	-3.1	3.0	79.7
Italy	870.7	-1.9	2.1	2.5	82.3
Mexico	851.5	-9.6	-12.7	2.5	84.8
Indonesia	639.8	7.7	8.2	1.9	86.6

Graph 2: Trade Balance by MDG regions 2016
(Bln US$)

Imports | Exports | Trade balance

Developed Asia-Pacific
Developed Europe
Developed N. America
South-eastern Europe
CIS
Northern Africa
Sub-Saharan Africa
Latin Am, Caribbean
Eastern Asia
Southern Asia
South-eastern Asia
Western Asia
Oceania

-20 -15 -10 -5 0 5 10 15

Table 3: Top importing countries or areas in 2016

Country or area	Value (million US$)	Avg. Growth (%) 12-16	Growth (%) 15-16	World share %	Cum.
World	38 449.4	-7.6	-8.9	100.0	
USA	3 735.7	-0.6	-3.5	9.7	9.7
Germany	3 003.7	-3.8	-7.9	7.8	17.5
China	2 391.4	-27.1	-9.7	6.2	23.7
Belgium	2 381.0	-4.4	-12.5	6.2	29.9
India	2 341.3	-3.4	-17.2	6.1	36.0
Netherlands	1 881.3	1.0	2.0	4.9	40.9
Italy	1 700.8	-7.3	-5.8	4.4	45.3
Japan	1 492.8	-4.3	0.8	3.9	49.2
France	1 303.1	-6.9	-8.0	3.4	52.6
Spain	1 199.8	2.0	-12.4	3.1	55.7
Rep. of Korea	1 162.5	-2.1	-1.6	3.0	58.8
Turkey	1 074.0	-3.7	-12.7	2.8	61.6
Mexico	994.6	-2.9	-6.3	2.6	64.1
United Kingdom	981.8	-9.0	-14.0	2.6	66.7
Brazil	921.5	-13.5	-14.9	2.4	69.1

In 2016, the value (in current US$) of exports of "nitrogen-function compounds" (SITC group 514) decreased by 2.5 percent (compared to -3.6 percent average growth rate from 2012-2016) to reach 46.3 bln US$ (see table 2), while imports decreased by 5.2 percent to reach 47.9 bln US$ (see table 3). Exports of this commodity accounted for 2.6 percent of world exports of SITC section 5, and 0.3 percent of total world merchandise exports (see table 1). China, Belgium and USA were the top exporters in 2016 (see table 2). They accounted for 17.6, 11.7 and 9.4 percent of world exports, respectively. Germany, USA and Belgium were the top destinations, with respectively 13.1, 10.8 and 9.4 percent of world imports (see table 3).

The top 15 countries/areas accounted for 87.3 and 72.5 percent of total world exports and imports, respectively (see tables 2 and 3). In 2016, China was the country/area with the highest value of net exports (+5.0 bln US$), followed by Singapore (+3.3 bln US$). By MDG regions (see graph 2), the largest surpluses in this product group were recorded by Eastern Asia (+4.6 bln US$) and South-eastern Asia (+2.1 bln US$). The largest trade deficits were recorded by Latin America and the Caribbean (-2.5 bln US$), Developed North America (-1.5 bln US$) and Southern Asia (-886.2 mln US$).

Table 1: Imports (Imp.) and exports (Exp.), 2002-2016, in current US$

		2002	2003	2004	2005	2006	2007	2008	2009	2010	2011	2012	2013	2014	2015	2016
Values in Bln US$	Imp.	22.5	26.8	31.6	35.0	37.1	45.5	49.3	40.8	48.3	56.0	57.3	55.0	55.5	50.6	47.9
	Exp.	21.1	26.1	31.0	33.7	34.7	41.9	44.6	38.1	45.5	52.6	53.6	53.5	52.7	47.5	46.3
As a percentage of SITC section (%)	Imp.	3.2	3.2	3.1	3.0	2.9	3.0	2.8	2.8	2.8	2.7	2.8	2.7	2.6	2.6	2.5
	Exp.	3.2	3.3	3.2	3.1	2.8	2.9	2.7	2.7	2.8	2.7	2.8	2.7	2.6	2.6	2.6
As a percentage of world trade (%)	Imp.	0.3	0.3	0.3	0.3	0.3	0.3	0.3	0.3	0.3	0.3	0.3	0.3	0.3	0.3	0.3
	Exp.	0.3	0.3	0.3	0.3	0.3	0.3	0.3	0.3	0.3	0.3	0.3	0.3	0.3	0.3	0.3

Graph 1: Annual growth rates of exports, 2002–2016
(In percentage by year)

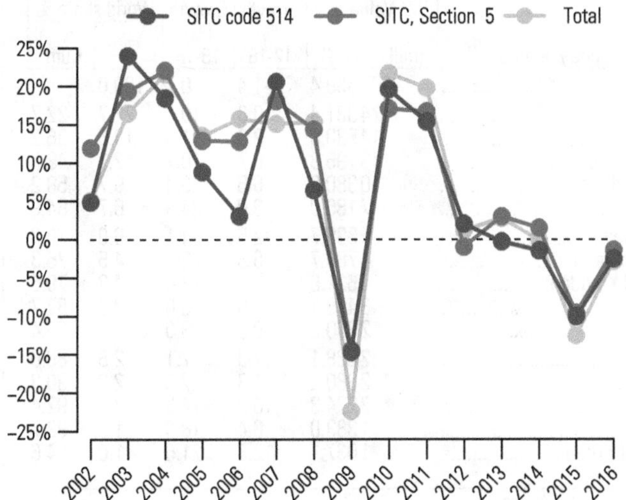

Table 2: Top exporting countries or areas in 2016

Country or area	Value (million US$)	Avg. Growth (%) 12-16	Growth (%) 15-16	World share %	Cum.
World	46 293.6	-3.6	-2.5	100.0	
China	8 144.7	2.4	-0.8	17.6	17.6
Belgium	5 394.4	0.1	-3.0	11.7	29.2
USA	4 357.9	-9.5	-15.2	9.4	38.7
Singapore	3 796.1	-8.2	-1.0	8.2	46.9
Germany	3 593.9	-1.3	5.0	7.8	54.6
Switzerland	2 813.1	-10.0	-15.9	6.1	60.7
Netherlands	1 714.5	0.3	5.5	3.7	64.4
Ireland	1 673.2	2.3	4.3	3.6	68.0
Japan	1 639.5	-8.7	-6.3	3.5	71.6
United Kingdom	1 549.4	-8.9	0.9	3.3	74.9
India	1 535.8	9.2	3.3	3.3	78.2
Rep. of Korea	1 456.5	-4.6	10.9	3.1	81.4
Norway	977.8	10.9	9.6	2.1	83.5
Italy	945.9	-2.0	-3.1	2.0	85.5
Panama	826.9	0.7	51.2	1.8	87.3

Graph 2: Trade Balance by MDG regions 2016
(Bln US$)

Imports — Exports — Trade balance

Developed Asia-Pacific
Developed Europe
Developed N. America
South-eastern Europe
C I S
Northern Africa
Sub-Saharan Africa
Latin Am, Caribbean
Eastern Asia
Southern Asia
South-eastern Asia
Western Asia
Oceania

-25 -20 -15 -10 -5 0 5 10 15 20 25

Table 3: Top importing countries or areas in 2016

Country or area	Value (million US$)	Avg. Growth (%) 12-16	Growth (%) 15-16	World share %	Cum.
World	47 934.1	-4.4	-5.2	100.0	
Germany	6 285.0	-5.3	-9.5	13.1	13.1
USA	5 187.5	-2.1	0.1	10.8	23.9
Belgium	4 486.7	0.5	-3.9	9.4	33.3
China	3 116.1	-3.8	-4.5	6.5	39.8
Japan	1 934.5	-6.1	-7.3	4.0	43.8
India	1 899.4	-0.4	-9.9	4.0	47.8
Italy	1 611.6	-5.5	-8.7	3.4	51.2
Netherlands	1 586.6	-5.6	-1.2	3.3	54.5
Rep. of Korea	1 551.2	-0.5	-0.8	3.2	57.7
France	1 421.6	-13.2	-2.5	3.0	60.7
Brazil	1 342.7	-3.8	-14.3	2.8	63.5
United Kingdom	1 245.4	-17.6	-13.8	2.6	66.1
Spain	1 190.7	-3.3	-6.6	2.5	68.5
Switzerland	1 106.9	-6.0	-10.2	2.3	70.9
Panama	776.7	-2.9	30.8	1.6	72.5

515 Organo-inorganic and heterocyclic compounds, nucleic acids; salts

In 2016, the value (in current US$) of exports of "organo-inorganic and heterocyclic compounds, nucleic acids; salts" (SITC group 515) increased by 0.7 percent (compared to -1.4 percent average growth rate from 2012-2016) to reach 107.3 bln US$ (see table 2), while imports increased by 0.3 percent to reach 123.1 bln US$ (see table 3). Exports of this commodity accounted for 6.0 percent of world exports of SITC section 5, and 0.7 percent of total world merchandise exports (see table 1). Ireland, China and Belgium were the top exporters in 2016 (see table 2). They accounted for 22.7, 13.5 and 12.3 percent of world exports, respectively. USA, Belgium and Germany were the top destinations, with respectively 23.0, 10.6 and 9.1 percent of world imports (see table 3).

The top 15 countries/areas accounted for 94.6 and 82.6 percent of total world exports and imports, respectively (see tables 2 and 3). In 2016, Ireland was the country/area with the highest value of net exports (+20.9 bln US$), followed by China (+10.3 bln US$). By MDG regions (see graph 2), the largest surpluses in this product group were recorded by Developed Europe (+10.1 bln US$), Eastern Asia (+8.4 bln US$) and South-eastern Asia (+1.6 bln US$). The largest trade deficits were recorded by Developed North America (-22.3 bln US$), Latin America and the Caribbean (-7.1 bln US$) and Developed Asia-Pacific (-3.1 bln US$).

Table 1: Imports (Imp.) and exports (Exp.), 2002-2016, in current US$

		2002	2003	2004	2005	2006	2007	2008	2009	2010	2011	2012	2013	2014	2015	2016
Values in Bln US$	Imp.	61.3	68.3	81.3	88.7	94.5	108.5	113.4	110.6	112.3	129.5	131.7	128.9	123.3	122.7	123.1
	Exp.	54.8	61.2	68.8	77.5	83.4	96.0	99.8	93.3	98.9	110.9	113.8	115.4	106.4	106.6	107.3
As a percentage of SITC section (%)	Imp.	8.7	8.2	8.0	7.7	7.4	7.2	6.5	7.5	6.5	6.3	6.5	6.2	5.8	6.4	6.5
	Exp.	8.3	7.8	7.2	7.2	6.8	6.7	6.0	6.6	6.0	5.7	5.9	5.8	5.3	5.9	6.0
As a percentage of world trade (%)	Imp.	0.9	0.9	0.9	0.8	0.8	0.8	0.7	0.9	0.7	0.7	0.7	0.7	0.7	0.7	0.8
	Exp.	0.9	0.8	0.8	0.7	0.7	0.7	0.6	0.8	0.7	0.6	0.6	0.6	0.6	0.6	0.7

Graph 1: Annual growth rates of exports, 2002–2016
(In percentage by year)

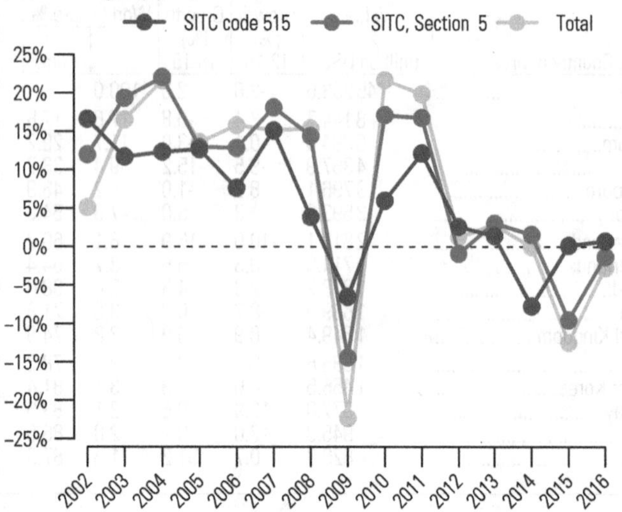

Table 2: Top exporting countries or areas in 2016

Country or area	Value (million US$)	Avg. Growth (%) 12-16	Growth (%) 15-16	World share %	Cum.
World	107339.4	-1.4	0.7	100.0	
Ireland	24331.4	0.3	10.3	22.7	22.7
China	14530.8	2.3	1.5	13.5	36.2
Belgium	13195.3	0.7	10.7	12.3	48.5
Switzerland	10380.9	6.5	20.4	9.7	58.2
USA	7186.0	-9.0	-24.3	6.7	64.9
Germany	6388.7	-2.5	-4.1	6.0	70.8
Singapore	4786.7	-6.8	23.2	4.5	75.3
United Kingdom	4521.6	-3.7	-37.6	4.2	79.5
Japan	3469.1	-9.6	-5.6	3.2	82.7
Netherlands	2890.5	-0.3	28.0	2.7	85.4
India	2828.1	17.3	7.1	2.6	88.0
Italy	2380.2	1.3	7.5	2.2	90.3
France	2274.3	-10.8	-14.3	2.1	92.4
Spain	1383.0	8.4	18.0	1.3	93.7
Rep. of Korea	1037.1	12.3	21.5	1.0	94.6

Graph 2: Trade Balance by MDG regions 2016
(Bln US$)

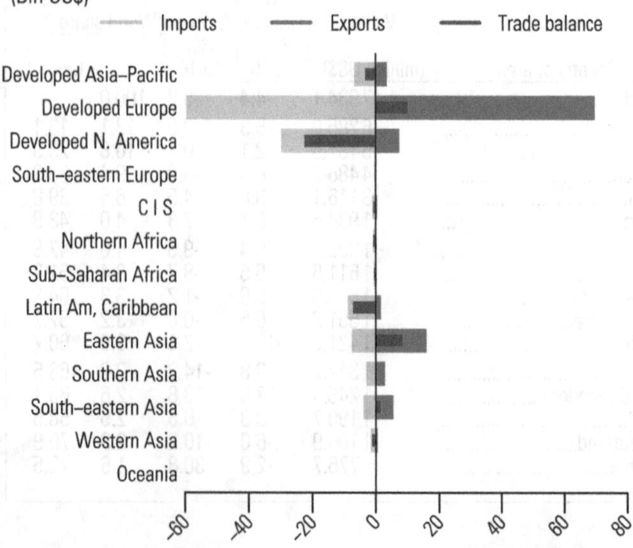

Table 3: Top importing countries or areas in 2016

Country or area	Value (million US$)	Avg. Growth (%) 12-16	Growth (%) 15-16	World share %	Cum.
World	123081.5	-1.7	0.3	100.0	
USA	28281.6	0.6	0.9	23.0	23.0
Belgium	13068.8	2.3	1.1	10.6	33.6
Germany	11178.8	8.6	7.7	9.1	42.7
Switzerland	8106.1	-0.1	22.7	6.6	49.3
Japan	5744.0	-7.8	2.0	4.7	53.9
Italy	4749.0	-2.9	8.0	3.9	57.8
France	4532.9	-12.1	-0.2	3.7	61.5
China	4193.4	-5.6	-14.6	3.4	64.9
Brazil	4027.3	-0.6	-5.4	3.3	68.2
Spain	3599.4	-0.3	4.4	2.9	71.1
Ireland	3470.6	12.1	18.2	2.8	73.9
United Kingdom	3346.7	-16.9	-0.7	2.7	76.6
Netherlands	2940.0	2.1	12.2	2.4	79.0
Rep. of Korea	2233.9	1.7	-2.0	1.8	80.8
India	2153.3	6.4	0.0	1.7	82.6

In 2016, the value (in current US$) of exports of "other organic chemicals" (SITC group 516) decreased by 9.7 percent (compared to -6.7 percent average growth rate from 2012-2016) to reach 32.2 bln US$ (see table 2), while imports decreased by 9.5 percent to reach 31.1 bln US$ (see table 3). Exports of this commodity accounted for 1.8 percent of world exports of SITC section 5, and 0.2 percent of total world merchandise exports (see table 1). USA, Germany and Saudi Arabia were the top exporters in 2016 (see table 2). They accounted for 14.8, 11.4 and 10.3 percent of world exports, respectively. USA, China and Germany were the top destinations, with respectively 9.9, 8.3 and 6.7 percent of world imports (see table 3).

The top 15 countries/areas accounted for 88.2 and 73.4 percent of total world exports and imports, respectively (see tables 2 and 3). In 2016, Saudi Arabia was the country/area with the highest value of net exports (+3.2 bln US$), followed by USA (+1.7 bln US$). By MDG regions (see graph 2), the largest surpluses in this product group were recorded by Western Asia (+2.6 bln US$), Developed North America (+1.5 bln US$) and Developed Europe (+1.2 bln US$). The largest trade deficits were recorded by Latin America and the Caribbean (-1.9 bln US$), South-eastern Asia (-817.7 mln US$) and Developed Asia-Pacific (-809.7 mln US$).

Table 1: Imports (Imp.) and exports (Exp.), 2002-2016, in current US$

		2002	2003	2004	2005	2006	2007	2008	2009	2010	2011	2012	2013	2014	2015	2016
Values in Bln US$	Imp.	14.4	16.5	20.1	24.6	26.6	29.9	33.0	26.7	33.0	39.5	38.9	39.4	41.2	34.3	31.1
	Exp.	14.3	16.5	19.4	23.3	26.0	29.0	32.1	26.9	33.1	38.8	42.5	42.7	43.5	35.6	32.2
As a percentage of SITC section (%)	Imp.	2.0	2.0	2.0	2.1	2.1	2.0	1.9	1.8	1.9	1.9	1.9	1.9	2.0	1.8	1.6
	Exp.	2.2	2.1	2.0	2.2	2.1	2.0	1.9	1.9	2.0	2.0	2.2	2.2	2.2	2.0	1.8
As a percentage of world trade (%)	Imp.	0.2	0.2	0.2	0.2	0.2	0.2	0.2	0.2	0.2	0.2	0.2	0.2	0.2	0.2	0.2
	Exp.	0.2	0.2	0.2	0.2	0.2	0.2	0.2	0.2	0.2	0.2	0.2	0.2	0.2	0.2	0.2

Graph 1: Annual growth rates of exports, 2002–2016

(In percentage by year)

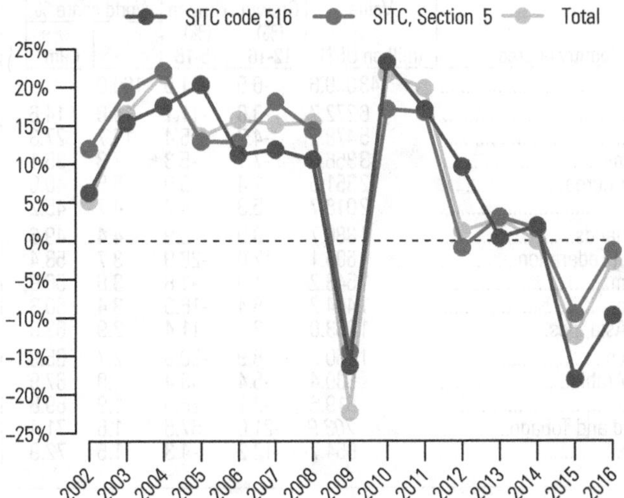

Graph 2: Trade Balance by MDG regions 2016

(Bln US$)

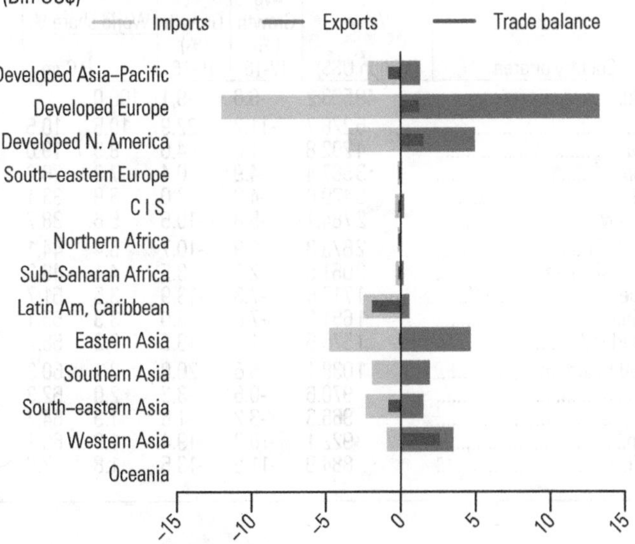

Table 2: Top exporting countries or areas in 2016

Country or area	Value (million US$)	Avg. Growth (%) 12-16	Growth (%) 15-16	World share %	Cum.
World	32172.4	-6.7	-9.7	100.0	
USA	4758.0	-6.4	-6.5	14.8	14.8
Germany	3661.7	-5.1	-11.9	11.4	26.2
Saudi Arabia	3300.3	-2.7	-27.0	10.3	36.4
China	3287.2	-0.6	-5.4	10.2	46.6
Netherlands	2958.8	-7.5	-1.1	9.2	55.8
India	1917.9	-14.0	-11.3	6.0	61.8
Belgium	1765.3	-5.9	-17.5	5.5	67.3
Japan	1299.4	-5.2	-8.3	4.0	71.3
France	1220.1	-9.8	-11.1	3.8	75.1
Denmark	1192.1	1.7	3.1	3.7	78.8
Other Asia, nes	809.0	-9.9	-2.4	2.5	81.3
Singapore	740.5	-11.0	-12.8	2.3	83.6
Rep. of Korea	539.4	5.7	-5.2	1.7	85.3
Switzerland	466.3	3.9	10.9	1.4	86.8
Thailand	447.0	-15.9	-11.2	1.4	88.2

Table 3: Top importing countries or areas in 2016

Country or area	Value (million US$)	Avg. Growth (%) 12-16	Growth (%) 15-16	World share %	Cum.
World	31054.8	-5.5	-9.5	100.0	
USA	3086.5	0.0	-9.0	9.9	9.9
China	2567.1	-8.1	-4.4	8.3	18.2
Germany	2071.2	-6.4	-10.9	6.7	24.9
Netherlands	2038.6	-5.2	-15.8	6.6	31.4
Japan	1973.1	2.1	18.0	6.4	37.8
India	1659.1	-6.2	-21.4	5.3	43.1
Belgium	1556.8	-4.6	-8.4	5.0	48.1
Rep. of Korea	1153.4	-7.1	-16.7	3.7	51.9
Italy	1107.0	-8.9	-9.1	3.6	55.4
France	1068.8	-6.6	-14.2	3.4	58.9
Other Asia, nes	1013.4	-0.7	-10.3	3.3	62.1
Singapore	945.6	-13.6	-21.1	3.0	65.2
United Kingdom	901.7	-3.4	-1.0	2.9	68.1
Mexico	892.5	-5.8	-11.1	2.9	71.0
Spain	774.5	-11.6	-19.0	2.5	73.4

522 Inorganic chemical elements, oxides and halogen salts

In 2016, the value (in current US$) of exports of "inorganic chemical elements, oxides and halogen salts" (SITC group 522) decreased by 11.0 percent (compared to -6.5 percent average growth rate from 2012-2016) to reach 43.1 bln US$ (see table 2), while imports decreased by 9.1 percent to reach 49.6 bln US$ (see table 3). Exports of this commodity accounted for 2.4 percent of world exports of SITC section 5, and 0.3 percent of total world merchandise exports (see table 1). China, USA and Germany were the top exporters in 2016 (see table 2). They accounted for 14.6, 12.7 and 7.8 percent of world exports, respectively. USA, China and Japan were the top destinations, with respectively 10.5, 8.5 and 7.2 percent of world imports (see table 3).

The top 15 countries/areas accounted for 72.9 and 67.9 percent of total world exports and imports, respectively (see tables 2 and 3). In 2016, China was the country/area with the highest value of net exports (+2.1 bln US$), followed by Russian Federation (+1.2 bln US$). By MDG regions (see graph 2), the largest surpluses in this product group were recorded by Commonwealth of Independent States (+1.3 bln US$), Northern Africa (+1.3 bln US$) and Eastern Asia (+891.6 mln US$). The largest trade deficits were recorded by Developed Europe (-3.8 bln US$), Southern Asia (-3.4 bln US$) and Developed Asia-Pacific (-2.0 bln US$).

Table 1: Imports (Imp.) and exports (Exp.), 2002-2016, in current US$

		2002	2003	2004	2005	2006	2007	2008	2009	2010	2011	2012	2013	2014	2015	2016
Values in Bln US$	Imp.	18.4	22.0	27.1	32.8	37.3	44.6	66.6	42.3	54.5	71.4	65.2	60.6	61.3	54.5	49.6
	Exp.	16.2	18.8	24.0	28.6	32.3	38.8	58.3	35.1	47.3	61.9	56.4	54.9	55.8	48.4	43.1
As a percentage of SITC section (%)	Imp.	2.6	2.6	2.7	2.9	2.9	2.9	3.8	2.9	3.1	3.5	3.2	2.9	2.9	2.8	2.6
	Exp.	2.5	2.4	2.5	2.6	2.6	2.7	3.5	2.5	2.9	3.2	2.9	2.8	2.8	2.7	2.4
As a percentage of world trade (%)	Imp.	0.3	0.3	0.3	0.3	0.3	0.3	0.4	0.3	0.4	0.4	0.4	0.3	0.3	0.3	0.3
	Exp.	0.3	0.3	0.3	0.3	0.3	0.3	0.4	0.3	0.3	0.3	0.3	0.3	0.3	0.3	0.3

Graph 1: Annual growth rates of exports, 2002–2016

(In percentage by year)

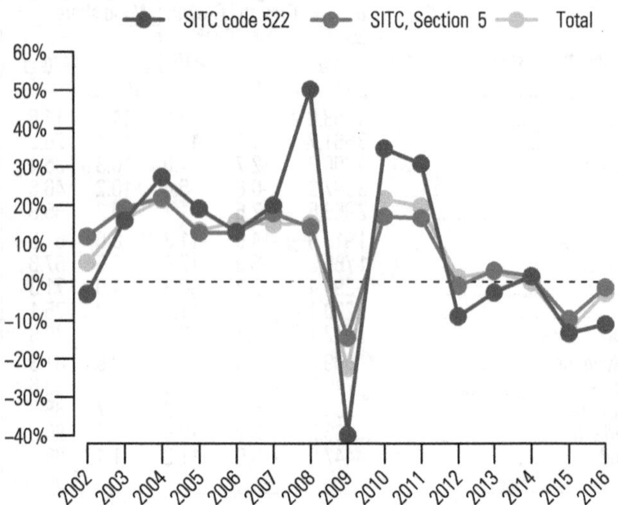

Table 2: Top exporting countries or areas in 2016

Country or area	Value (million US$)	Avg. Growth (%) 12-16	Growth (%) 15-16	World share %	Cum.
World	43 050.6	-6.5	-11.0	100.0	
China	6 272.7	-3.6	-11.1	14.6	14.6
USA	5 478.2	-4.2	5.4	12.7	27.3
Germany	3 356.0	-7.1	-5.3	7.8	35.1
Rep. of Korea	2 351.6	1.4	-5.0	5.5	40.6
Japan	2 018.7	-5.3	4.2	4.7	45.2
Netherlands	1 886.7	0.9	5.9	4.4	49.6
Russian Federation	1 606.1	-12.0	-26.9	3.7	53.4
Belgium	1 543.2	-1.9	-1.8	3.6	56.9
Canada	1 464.2	-8.4	-16.9	3.4	60.3
Other Asia, nes	1 253.0	2.1	11.4	2.9	63.3
Morocco	1 150.2	-8.9	-30.9	2.7	65.9
Saudi Arabia	830.4	-5.4	-43.4	1.9	67.9
Brazil	819.6	-2.1	25.0	1.9	69.8
Trinidad and Tobago	*703.9*	-21.0	-57.5	1.6	71.4
Chile	654.7	-12.2	-4.3	1.5	72.9

Graph 2: Trade Balance by MDG regions 2016

(Bln US$)

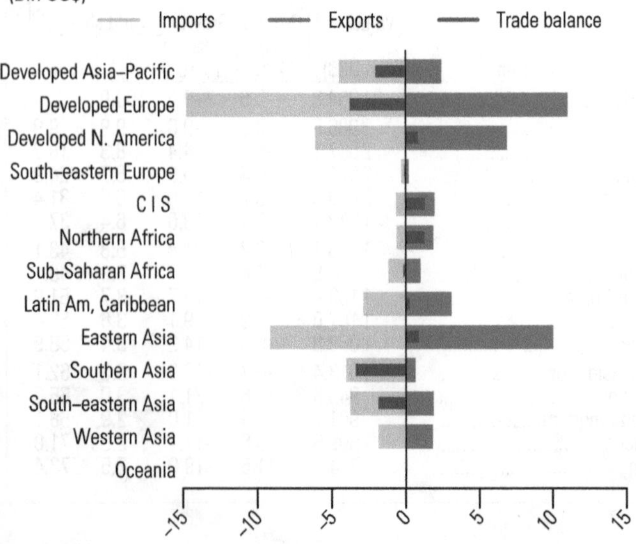

Table 3: Top importing countries or areas in 2016

Country or area	Value (million US$)	Avg. Growth (%) 12-16	Growth (%) 15-16	World share %	Cum.
World	49 593.2	-6.6	-9.1	100.0	
USA	5 228.7	-11.2	-22.9	10.5	10.5
China	4 202.8	-1.0	4.0	8.5	19.0
Japan	3 567.4	-4.9	0.4	7.2	26.2
India	3 429.6	-4.9	-7.0	6.9	33.1
Germany	2 784.1	-5.8	-10.5	5.6	38.7
Rep. of Korea	2 673.3	-5.9	-10.7	5.4	44.1
Other Asia, nes	2 051.5	-2.1	-3.5	4.1	48.3
France	1 717.6	-7.3	-13.9	3.5	51.7
Belgium	1 651.2	-7.0	-3.0	3.3	55.1
Netherlands	1 575.5	1.6	19.5	3.2	58.2
United Kingdom	1 038.1	-6.6	-20.0	2.1	60.3
Thailand	970.6	-0.6	-3.3	2.0	62.3
Italy	966.3	-3.2	-1.6	1.9	64.2
Spain	922.1	-10.3	-19.4	1.9	66.1
Brazil	884.9	-11.5	-13.5	1.8	67.9

In 2016, the value (in current US$) of exports of "metal salts and peroxysalts, of inorganic acids" (SITC group 523) decreased by 1.8 percent (compared to -1.5 percent average growth rate from 2012-2016) to reach 20.1 bln US$ (see table 2), while imports decreased by 2.9 percent to reach 24.4 bln US$ (see table 3). Exports of this commodity accounted for 1.1 percent of world exports of SITC section 5, and 0.1 percent of total world merchandise exports (see table 1). China, USA and Germany were the top exporters in 2016 (see table 2). They accounted for 20.6, 16.7 and 7.9 percent of world exports, respectively. USA, China and Japan were the top destinations, with respectively 8.2, 4.5 and 4.3 percent of world imports (see table 3).

The top 15 countries/areas accounted for 76.6 and 53.3 percent of total world exports and imports, respectively (see tables 2 and 3). In 2016, China was the country/area with the highest value of net exports (+3.0 bln US$), followed by USA (+1.3 bln US$). By MDG regions (see graph 2), the largest surpluses in this product group were recorded by Eastern Asia (+2.4 bln US$), Developed North America (+1.3 bln US$) and South-eastern Europe (+260.0 mln US$). The largest trade deficits were recorded by South-eastern Asia (-1.8 bln US$), Developed Europe (-1.7 bln US$) and Latin America and the Caribbean (-1.4 bln US$).

Table 1: Imports (Imp.) and exports (Exp.), 2002-2016, in current US$

		2002	2003	2004	2005	2006	2007	2008	2009	2010	2011	2012	2013	2014	2015	2016
Values in Bln US$	Imp.	10.1	10.9	12.6	14.2	15.7	18.7	24.7	19.4	22.0	25.8	26.1	26.0	26.6	25.1	24.4
	Exp.	8.2	9.0	10.5	12.1	13.9	16.2	21.0	15.3	18.2	21.4	21.4	21.6	22.0	20.5	20.1
As a percentage of SITC section (%)	Imp.	1.4	1.3	1.2	1.2	1.2	1.2	1.4	1.3	1.3	1.3	1.3	1.3	1.3	1.3	1.3
	Exp.	1.2	1.1	1.1	1.1	1.1	1.1	1.3	1.1	1.1	1.1	1.1	1.1	1.1	1.1	1.1
As a percentage of world trade (%)	Imp.	0.2	0.1	0.1	0.1	0.1	0.1	0.2	0.2	0.1	0.1	0.1	0.1	0.1	0.2	0.2
	Exp.	0.1	0.1	0.1	0.1	0.1	0.1	0.1	0.1	0.1	0.1	0.1	0.1	0.1	0.1	0.1

Graph 1: Annual growth rates of exports, 2002–2016

(In percentage by year)

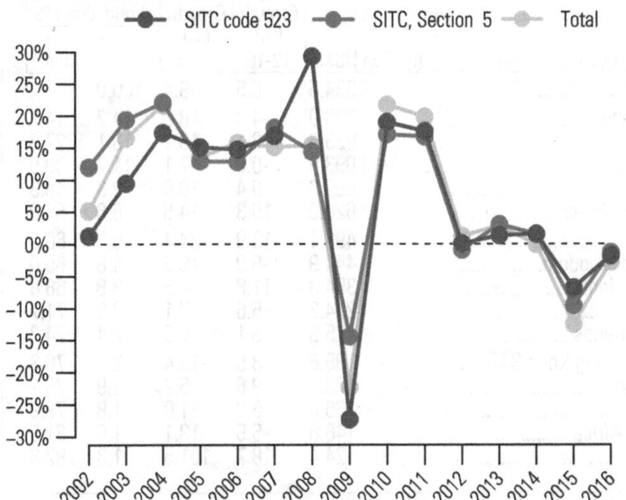

Graph 2: Trade Balance by MDG regions 2016

(Bln US$)

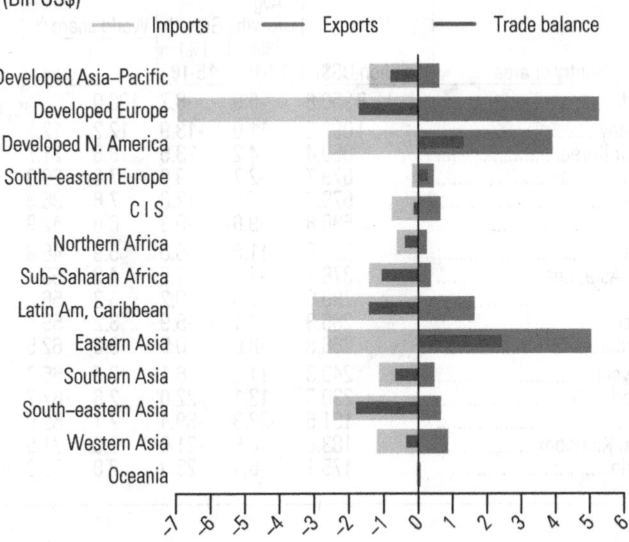

Table 2: Top exporting countries or areas in 2016

Country or area	Value (million US$)	Avg. Growth (%) 12-16	Growth (%) 15-16	World share %	Cum.
World	20101.3	-1.5	-1.8	100.0	
China	4142.5	-1.9	-7.1	20.6	20.6
USA	3358.2	0.4	-2.7	16.7	37.3
Germany	1583.9	-1.8	2.4	7.9	45.2
Chile	784.6	3.2	44.9	3.9	49.1
Netherlands	713.5	14.2	7.3	3.5	52.6
Belgium	616.0	-9.8	-10.6	3.1	55.7
Japan	562.9	-0.8	8.5	2.8	58.5
Canada	537.9	-4.9	-8.9	2.7	61.2
Russian Federation	519.4	-2.8	-7.2	2.6	63.8
Spain	518.4	5.1	-7.9	2.6	66.4
Rep. of Korea	505.3	0.6	3.7	2.5	68.9
India	416.8	0.2	7.2	2.1	70.9
Turkey	409.1	40.5	-1.7	2.0	73.0
France	389.7	-2.2	-3.0	1.9	74.9
Mexico	334.9	-3.4	-7.3	1.7	76.6

Table 3: Top importing countries or areas in 2016

Country or area	Value (million US$)	Avg. Growth (%) 12-16	Growth (%) 15-16	World share %	Cum.
World	24421.9	-1.7	-2.9	100.0	
USA	2013.5	-1.7	-6.3	8.2	8.2
China	1101.3	5.3	25.1	4.5	12.8
Japan	1057.1	1.6	5.1	4.3	17.1
Rep. of Korea	1048.8	2.1	0.6	4.3	21.4
Germany	1019.3	-3.0	-3.5	4.2	25.6
Mexico	837.1	4.0	2.5	3.4	29.0
Netherlands	753.5	0.2	1.9	3.1	32.1
France	717.2	-3.1	1.0	2.9	35.0
Brazil	695.6	-4.3	-4.9	2.8	37.8
Indonesia	680.2	-1.2	1.3	2.8	40.6
India	678.3	-0.5	-6.8	2.8	43.4
Belgium	661.8	-3.0	0.0	2.7	46.1
United Kingdom	616.0	3.4	4.8	2.5	48.6
Canada	572.5	-2.7	-9.3	2.3	51.0
Spain	557.7	1.3	-3.6	2.3	53.3

Source: UN Comtrade

In 2016, the value (in current US$) of exports of "other inorganic chemicals; organic, inorganic compounds precious metals" (SITC group 524) decreased by 9.4 percent (compared to -6.5 percent average growth rate from 2012-2016) to reach 9.3 bln US$ (see table 2), while imports decreased by 8.7 percent to reach 9.0 bln US$ (see table 3). Exports of this commodity accounted for 0.5 percent of world exports of SITC section 5, and 0.1 percent of total world merchandise exports (see table 1). Germany, China and USA were the top exporters in 2016 (see table 2). They accounted for 14.2, 13.1 and 11.7 percent of world exports, respectively. Germany, Rep. of Korea and Japan were the top destinations, with respectively 12.2, 9.5 and 7.6 percent of world imports (see table 3).

The top 15 countries/areas accounted for 82.8 and 73.9 percent of total world exports and imports, respectively (see tables 2 and 3). In 2016, USA was the country/area with the highest value of net exports (+557.0 mln US$), followed by China (+544.3 mln US$). By MDG regions (see graph 2), the largest surpluses in this product group were recorded by Developed North America (+497.5 mln US$), Developed Europe (+233.5 mln US$) and Western Asia (+163.9 mln US$). The largest trade deficits were recorded by South-eastern Asia (-381.5 mln US$), Latin America and the Caribbean (-252.7 mln US$) and Southern Asia (-213.7 mln US$).

Table 1: Imports (Imp.) and exports (Exp.), 2002-2016, in current US$

		2002	2003	2004	2005	2006	2007	2008	2009	2010	2011	2012	2013	2014	2015	2016
Values in Bln US$	Imp.	3.9	4.1	5.5	6.7	7.9	9.7	10.8	7.0	11.1	13.7	11.9	11.5	12.2	9.8	9.0
	Exp.	3.6	3.9	5.3	6.7	8.1	10.3	12.1	7.4	11.9	14.1	12.2	12.4	13.0	10.3	9.3
As a percentage of SITC section (%)	Imp.	0.6	0.5	0.5	0.6	0.6	0.6	0.6	0.5	0.6	0.7	0.6	0.6	0.6	0.5	0.5
	Exp.	0.6	0.5	0.6	0.6	0.7	0.7	0.7	0.5	0.7	0.7	0.6	0.6	0.7	0.6	0.5
As a percentage of world trade (%)	Imp.	0.1	0.1	0.1	0.1	0.1	0.1	0.1	0.1	0.1	0.1	0.1	0.1	0.1	0.1	0.1
	Exp.	0.1	0.1	0.1	0.1	0.1	0.1	0.1	0.1	0.1	0.1	0.1	0.1	0.1	0.1	0.1

Graph 1: Annual growth rates of exports, 2002–2016

(In percentage by year)

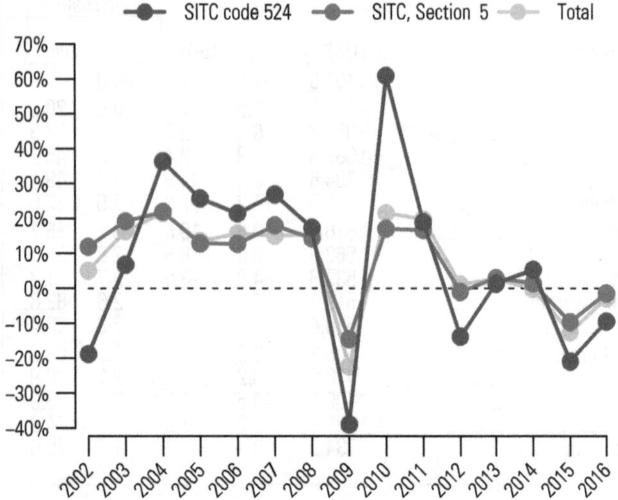

Graph 2: Trade Balance by MDG regions 2016

(Bln US$)

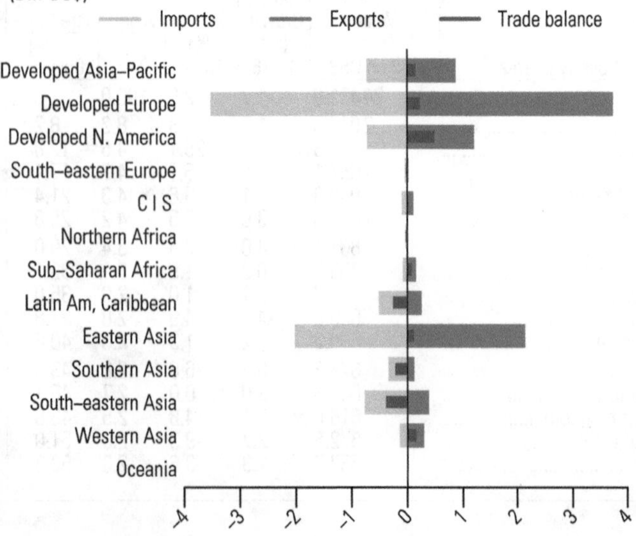

Table 2: Top exporting countries or areas in 2016

Country or area	Value (million US$)	Avg. Growth (%) 12-16	Growth (%) 15-16	World share %	Cum.
World	9334.5	-6.5	-9.4	100.0	
Germany	1323.9	-4.3	-18.9	14.2	14.2
China	1223.6	-2.1	-10.1	13.1	27.3
USA	1093.8	-0.6	-7.1	11.7	39.0
Japan	869.0	-0.4	18.6	9.3	48.3
Rep. of Korea	620.0	10.3	14.5	6.6	55.0
Italy	493.1	-13.9	-34.4	5.3	60.2
United Kingdom	444.9	-9.9	19.3	4.8	65.0
Switzerland	354.8	-11.8	-4.5	3.8	68.8
Israel	274.3	-5.6	7.1	2.9	71.7
Netherlands	225.9	-5.1	-6.5	2.4	74.2
China, Hong Kong SAR	195.6	-8.5	-13.4	2.1	76.3
Belgium	173.6	-9.6	5.7	1.9	78.1
Brazil	166.6	-6.9	21.0	1.8	79.9
South Africa	146.8	-5.5	13.1	1.6	81.5
Spain	124.4	18.7	101.5	1.3	82.8

Table 3: Top importing countries or areas in 2016

Country or area	Value (million US$)	Avg. Growth (%) 12-16	Growth (%) 15-16	World share %	Cum.
World	8950.8	-6.9	-8.7	100.0	
Germany	1092.2	-11.0	-13.9	12.2	12.2
Rep. of Korea	850.4	4.2	23.5	9.5	21.7
Japan	679.7	-2.7	-9.6	7.6	29.3
China	679.3	5.5	12.8	7.6	36.9
USA	536.8	-9.6	-9.3	6.0	42.9
France	531.6	-11.8	-5.0	5.9	48.8
Other Asia, nes	378.7	-4.4	-2.5	4.2	53.1
India	290.6	-1.5	-0.2	3.2	56.3
Mexico	285.3	3.1	-5.9	3.2	59.5
Singapore	268.8	-8.0	0.6	3.0	62.5
Malaysia	240.3	11.0	6.1	2.7	65.2
Netherlands	230.5	13.1	22.0	2.6	67.7
Italy	191.5	-32.3	-69.4	2.1	69.9
United Kingdom	183.0	-10.5	-21.0	2.0	71.9
Canada	175.1	-6.4	-23.3	2.0	73.9

In 2016, the value (in current US$) of exports of "radioactive and associated materials" (SITC group 525) decreased by 16.1 percent (compared to -10.2 percent average growth rate from 2012-2016) to reach 9.9 bln US$ (see table 2), while imports decreased by 11.9 percent to reach 13.3 bln US$ (see table 3). Exports of this commodity accounted for 0.6 percent of world exports of SITC section 5, and 0.1 percent of total world merchandise exports (see table 1). Kazakhstan, Canada and Uzbekistan were the top exporters in 2016 (see table 2). They accounted for 17.9, 16.0 and 10.8 percent of world exports, respectively. USA, China and France were the top destinations, with respectively 27.0, 16.3 and 10.8 percent of world imports (see table 3).

The top 15 countries/areas accounted for 95.1 and 94.2 percent of total world exports and imports, respectively (see tables 2 and 3). In 2016, Kazakhstan was the country/area with the highest value of net exports (+1.7 bln US$), followed by Canada (+1.1 bln US$). By MDG regions (see graph 2), the largest surpluses in this product group were recorded by Commonwealth of Independent States (+2.4 bln US$), Sub-Saharan Africa (+57.1 mln US$) and Southern Asia (+3.8 mln US$). The largest trade deficits were recorded by Eastern Asia (-2.6 bln US$), Developed North America (-1.6 bln US$) and Developed Europe (-1.3 bln US$).

Table 1: Imports (Imp.) and exports (Exp.), 2002-2016, in current US$

		2002	2003	2004	2005	2006	2007	2008	2009	2010	2011	2012	2013	2014	2015	2016
Values in Bln US$	Imp.	7.4	9.3	10.1	11.2	13.6	17.8	18.5	18.2	21.0	25.0	20.4	19.5	16.1	15.1	13.3
	Exp.	5.0	5.8	6.3	7.4	9.4	14.8	14.5	13.3	14.8	19.2	15.2	12.8	11.0	11.8	9.9
As a percentage of SITC section (%)	Imp.	1.1	1.1	1.0	1.0	1.1	1.2	1.1	1.2	1.2	1.2	1.0	0.9	0.8	0.8	0.7
	Exp.	0.8	0.7	0.7	0.7	0.8	1.0	0.9	0.9	0.9	1.0	0.8	0.6	0.5	0.7	0.6
As a percentage of world trade (%)	Imp.	0.1	0.1	0.1	0.1	0.1	0.1	0.1	0.1	0.1	0.1	0.1	0.1	0.1	0.1	0.1
	Exp.	0.1	0.1	0.1	0.1	0.1	0.1	0.1	0.1	0.1	0.1	0.1	0.1	0.1	0.1	0.1

Graph 1: Annual growth rates of exports, 2002–2016
(In percentage by year)

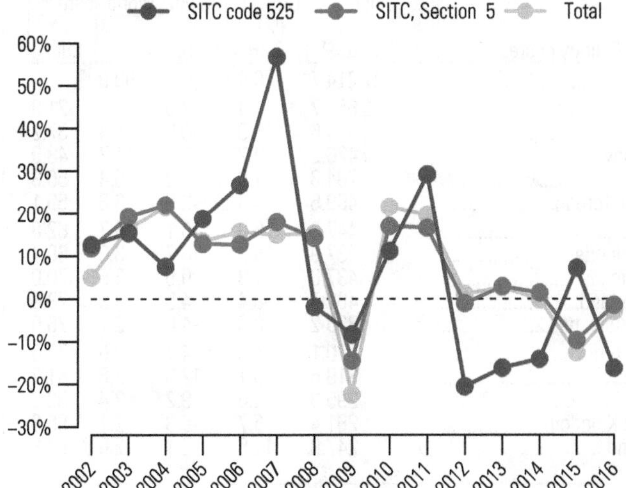

Table 2: Top exporting countries or areas in 2016

Country or area	Value (million US$)	Avg. Growth (%) 12-16	Growth (%) 15-16	World share %	Cum.
World	9892.2	-10.2	-16.1	100.0	
Kazakhstan	1772.4	-10.5	-24.7	17.9	17.9
Canada	1586.2	-6.5	2.7	16.0	34.0
Uzbekistan	*1065.9*	14.3	-31.9	10.8	44.7
Netherlands	1059.8	-13.4	-0.1	10.7	55.4
France	1021.7	-15.3	34.6	10.3	65.8
USA	898.4	-17.7	-46.9	9.1	74.8
Germany	730.2	-16.6	-15.7	7.4	82.2
China	430.7	-14.7	-0.7	4.4	86.6
Japan	186.6	-10.1	5.7	1.9	88.5
Malaysia	163.9	167.1	25.8	1.7	90.1
Russian Federation	132.7	-11.6	-60.0	1.3	91.5
Belgium	109.1	-8.7	15.3	1.1	92.6
China, Hong Kong SAR	91.7	9.8	281.4	0.9	93.5
South Africa	83.8	-5.9	21.8	0.8	94.3
United Kingdom	79.1	-6.7	-38.6	0.8	95.1

Graph 2: Trade Balance by MDG regions 2016
(Bln US$)

Imports — Exports — Trade balance

Developed Asia-Pacific
Developed Europe
Developed N. America
South-eastern Europe
CIS
Northern Africa
Sub-Saharan Africa
Latin Am, Caribbean
Eastern Asia
Southern Asia
South-eastern Asia
Western Asia
Oceania

-5 -4 -3 -2 -1 0 1 2 3 4

Table 3: Top importing countries or areas in 2016

Country or area	Value (million US$)	Avg. Growth (%) 12-16	Growth (%) 15-16	World share %	Cum.
World	13307.9	-10.1	-11.9	100.0	
USA	3593.5	-6.5	19.2	27.0	27.0
China	2169.1	0.4	-21.6	16.3	43.3
France	1439.3	-15.5	-18.8	10.8	54.1
Germany	824.5	-14.1	-9.0	6.2	60.3
Rep. of Korea	702.7	-4.0	-26.9	5.3	65.6
Netherlands	667.9	-5.8	-8.2	5.0	70.6
Sweden	546.5	-16.2	-32.3	4.1	74.7
Russian Federation	490.3	-0.9	-51.1	3.7	78.4
Japan	448.0	-26.9	-20.5	3.4	81.8
Canada	441.7	-17.6	-4.4	3.3	85.1
United Kingdom	353.9	-26.4	-30.5	2.7	87.7
Spain	287.8	-18.5	-30.6	2.2	89.9
Other Asia, nes	255.6	38.8	393.1	1.9	91.8
Belgium	211.4	-11.9	42.5	1.6	93.4
Viet Nam	*109.8*	17.6	5.1	0.8	94.2

Source: UN Comtrade

531 Synthetic organic colouring matter and preparations based thereon

In 2016, the value (in current US$) of exports of "synthetic organic colouring matter and preparations based thereon" (SITC group 531) increased by 0.1 percent (compared to 0.4 percent average growth rate from 2012-2016) to reach 12.2 bln US$ (see table 2), while imports decreased by 0.4 percent to reach 13.2 bln US$ (see table 3). Exports of this commodity accounted for 0.7 percent of world exports of SITC section 5, and 0.1 percent of total world merchandise exports (see table 1). China, India and Germany were the top exporters in 2016 (see table 2). They accounted for 21.8, 15.4 and 11.7 percent of world exports, respectively. Germany, USA and Rep. of Korea were the top destinations, with respectively 7.5, 6.9 and 6.4 percent of world imports (see table 3).

The top 15 countries/areas accounted for 87.8 and 62.1 percent of total world exports and imports, respectively (see tables 2 and 3). In 2016, China was the country/area with the highest value of net exports (+1.9 bln US$), followed by India (+1.6 bln US$). By MDG regions (see graph 2), the largest surpluses in this product group were recorded by Eastern Asia (+1.4 bln US$) and Southern Asia (+905.4 mln US$). The largest trade deficits were recorded by Latin America and the Caribbean (-887.1 mln US$), South-eastern Asia (-776.6 mln US$) and Western Asia (-599.8 mln US$).

Table 1: Imports (Imp.) and exports (Exp.), 2002-2016, in current US$

		2002	2003	2004	2005	2006	2007	2008	2009	2010	2011	2012	2013	2014	2015	2016
Values in Bln US$	Imp.	9.2	9.9	10.6	10.3	11.2	12.1	12.7	10.1	12.5	13.2	12.7	13.4	14.3	13.2	13.2
	Exp.	9.1	9.8	10.4	10.4	11.1	12.0	12.4	9.9	12.2	12.5	12.0	12.8	13.7	12.2	12.2
As a percentage of SITC section (%)	Imp.	1.3	1.2	1.0	0.9	0.9	0.8	0.7	0.7	0.7	0.6	0.6	0.6	0.7	0.7	0.7
	Exp.	1.4	1.3	1.1	1.0	0.9	0.8	0.8	0.7	0.7	0.6	0.6	0.6	0.7	0.7	0.7
As a percentage of world trade (%)	Imp.	0.1	0.1	0.1	0.1	0.1	0.1	0.1	0.1	0.1	0.1	0.1	0.1	0.1	0.1	0.1
	Exp.	0.1	0.1	0.1	0.1	0.1	0.1	0.1	0.1	0.1	0.1	0.1	0.1	0.1	0.1	0.1

Graph 1: Annual growth rates of exports, 2002–2016

(In percentage by year)

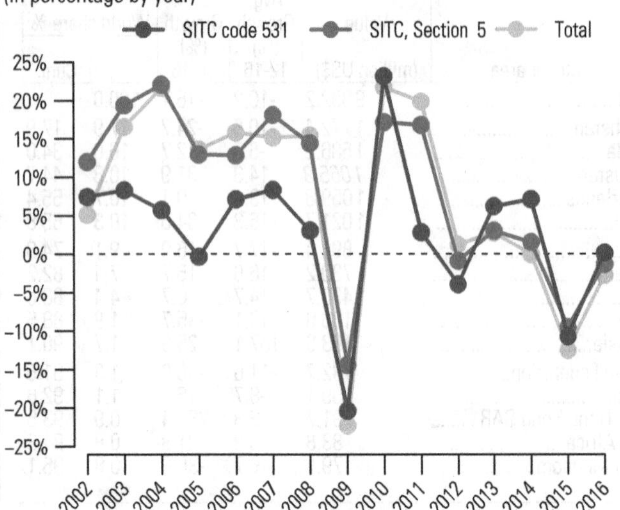

Table 2: Top exporting countries or areas in 2016

Country or area	Value (million US$)	Avg. Growth (%) 12-16	Growth (%) 15-16	World share %	Cum.
World	12214.7	0.4	0.1	100.0	
China	2658.7	1.4	-7.0	21.8	21.8
India	1884.6	6.0	-0.9	15.4	37.2
Germany	1426.2	-3.2	-0.2	11.7	48.9
USA	784.3	1.6	-2.9	6.4	55.3
Rep. of Korea	469.5	4.3	2.9	3.8	59.1
Japan	447.3	-5.6	16.1	3.7	62.8
Netherlands	437.9	15.2	76.7	3.6	66.4
Belgium	437.6	-1.8	0.9	3.6	70.0
Switzerland	402.7	-8.4	-4.5	3.3	73.3
Other Asia, nes	330.2	0.5	-4.6	2.7	76.0
Singapore	320.1	4.8	4.1	2.6	78.6
France	319.6	0.1	12.8	2.6	81.2
Spain	295.8	2.0	9.2	2.4	83.6
United Kingdom	261.4	-5.7	-6.3	2.1	85.8
Thailand	247.8	11.5	6.1	2.0	87.8

Graph 2: Trade Balance by MDG regions 2016

(Bln US$)

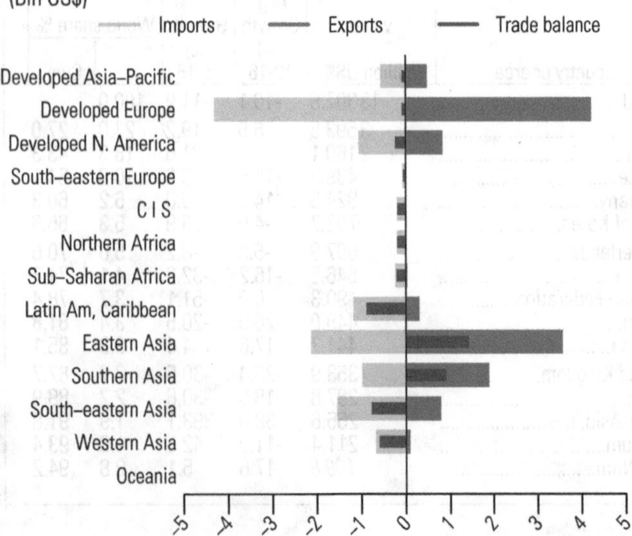

Table 3: Top importing countries or areas in 2016

Country or area	Value (million US$)	Avg. Growth (%) 12-16	Growth (%) 15-16	World share %	Cum.
World	13185.5	0.9	-0.4	100.0	
Germany	989.9	0.2	0.1	7.5	7.5
USA	907.1	-1.9	-9.3	6.9	14.4
Rep. of Korea	840.4	5.4	4.4	6.4	20.8
China	758.2	3.5	3.9	5.8	26.5
Italy	505.5	1.3	1.9	3.8	30.3
Turkey	502.1	1.1	-8.8	3.8	34.2
Japan	490.8	-3.2	0.3	3.7	37.9
Indonesia	453.8	4.3	3.8	3.4	41.3
Netherlands	445.5	9.0	51.6	3.4	44.7
Other Asia, nes	433.6	3.1	-3.8	3.3	48.0
France	414.1	-0.8	10.5	3.1	51.1
Belgium	391.7	0.9	13.8	3.0	54.1
Mexico	386.3	2.5	-2.9	2.9	57.0
Bangladesh	*337.2*	9.3	-14.2	2.6	59.6
Viet Nam	*325.9*	14.4	5.1	2.5	62.1

In 2016, the value (in current US$) of exports of "dyeing and tanning extracts, and synthetic tanning materials" (SITC group 532) increased by 11.3 percent (compared to 2.2 percent average growth rate from 2012-2016) to reach 2.3 bln US$ (see table 2), while imports increased by 6.6 percent to reach 2.6 bln US$ (see table 3). Exports of this commodity accounted for 0.1 percent of world exports of SITC section 5, and less than 0.1 percent of total world merchandise exports (see table 1). Italy, Netherlands and Germany were the top exporters in 2016 (see table 2). They accounted for 10.5, 9.7 and 8.6 percent of world exports, respectively. China, USA and Japan were the top destinations, with respectively 9.7, 7.8 and 5.8 percent of world imports (see table 3).

The top 15 countries/areas accounted for 80.9 and 65.2 percent of total world exports and imports, respectively (see tables 2 and 3). In 2016, Netherlands was the country/area with the highest value of net exports (+124.8 mln US$), followed by Italy (+89.9 mln US$). By MDG regions (see graph 2), the largest surpluses in this product group were recorded by Developed Europe (+300.3 mln US$), Western Asia (+36.2 mln US$) and Sub-Saharan Africa (+36.1 mln US$). The largest trade deficits were recorded by Southern Asia (-142.9 mln US$), Developed Asia-Pacific (-135.0 mln US$) and Developed North America (-126.8 mln US$).

Table 1: Imports (Imp.) and exports (Exp.), 2002-2016, in current US$

		2002	2003	2004	2005	2006	2007	2008	2009	2010	2011	2012	2013	2014	2015	2016
Values in Bln US$	Imp.	1.1	1.3	1.4	1.5	1.6	1.8	1.9	1.8	2.3	2.9	2.7	2.6	2.5	2.5	2.6
	Exp.	1.0	1.1	1.3	1.4	1.5	1.6	1.6	1.5	1.9	2.2	2.1	2.1	2.2	2.0	2.3
As a percentage of SITC section (%)	Imp.	0.2	0.2	0.1	0.1	0.1	0.1	0.1	0.1	0.1	0.1	0.1	0.1	0.1	0.1	0.1
	Exp.	0.1	0.1	0.1	0.1	0.1	0.1	0.1	0.1	0.1	0.1	0.1	0.1	0.1	0.1	0.1
As a percentage of world trade (%)	Imp.	0.0	0.0	0.0	0.0	0.0	0.0	0.0	0.0	0.0	0.0	0.0	0.0	0.0	0.0	0.0
	Exp.	0.0	0.0	0.0	0.0	0.0	0.0	0.0	0.0	0.0	0.0	0.0	0.0	0.0	0.0	0.0

Graph 1: Annual growth rates of exports, 2002–2016
(In percentage by year)

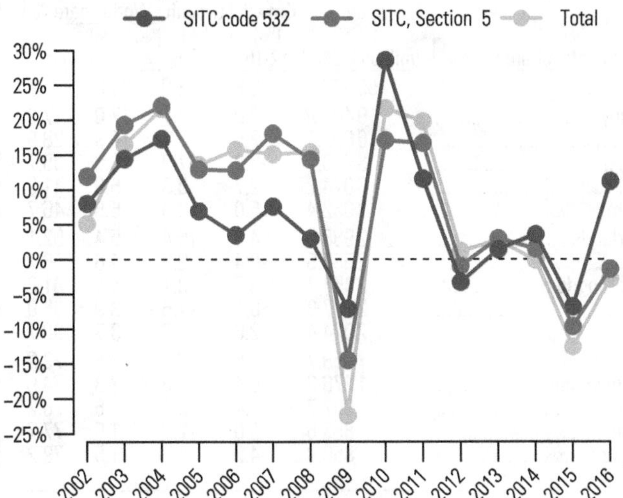

Table 2: Top exporting countries or areas in 2016

Country or area	Value (million US$)	Avg. Growth (%) 12-16	Growth (%) 15-16	World share %	Cum.
World	2276.9	2.2	11.3	100.0	
Italy	238.8	0.4	11.2	10.5	10.5
Netherlands	221.8	10.6	40.8	9.7	20.2
Germany	196.5	-1.4	5.9	8.6	28.9
China	183.7	42.4	37.3	8.1	36.9
Spain	147.1	-2.6	15.8	6.5	43.4
France	126.8	-2.2	-2.7	5.6	49.0
USA	107.5	-2.8	-1.1	4.7	53.7
Denmark	101.3	2.8	9.6	4.4	58.1
South Africa	93.0	0.8	28.7	4.1	62.2
Peru	86.7	5.9	37.8	3.8	66.0
Brazil	75.5	1.0	17.3	3.3	69.3
Turkey	73.3	-0.3	-13.4	3.2	72.6
Argentina	72.2	-5.2	9.4	3.2	75.7
India	60.9	-2.6	-2.2	2.7	78.4
Ireland	56.1	2.2	12.6	2.5	80.9

Graph 2: Trade Balance by MDG regions 2016
(Bln US$)

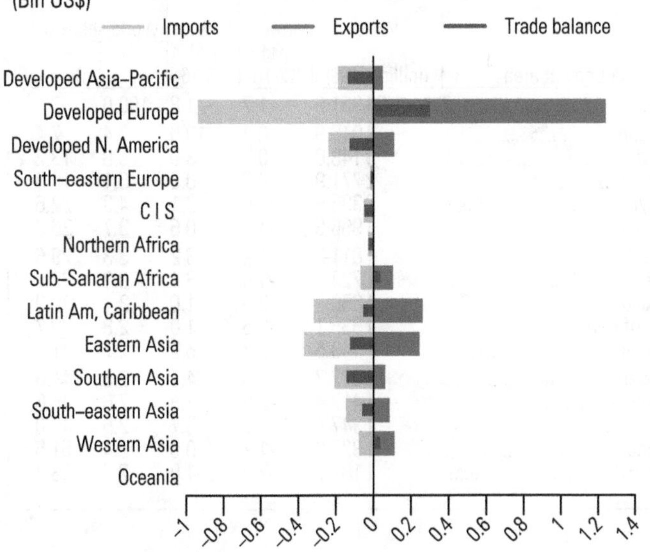

Table 3: Top importing countries or areas in 2016

Country or area	Value (million US$)	Avg. Growth (%) 12-16	Growth (%) 15-16	World share %	Cum.
World	2636.3	-0.4	6.6	100.0	
China	255.7	0.5	7.5	9.7	9.7
USA	206.6	0.9	14.3	7.8	17.5
Japan	152.8	-3.5	1.2	5.8	23.3
Italy	148.9	1.3	16.5	5.6	29.0
Germany	121.2	-1.8	11.4	4.6	33.6
Spain	115.0	1.6	18.8	4.4	37.9
Mexico	113.9	-2.5	-9.9	4.3	42.3
India	111.5	7.8	9.9	4.2	46.5
Netherlands	97.1	1.2	62.6	3.7	50.2
United Kingdom	85.1	-0.5	-0.3	3.2	53.4
France	80.1	-3.3	-6.2	3.0	56.4
Denmark	63.8	3.3	11.6	2.4	58.9
Brazil	58.1	-4.7	10.9	2.2	61.1
Rep. of Korea	57.3	-1.3	-0.7	2.2	63.2
Viet Nam	*50.7*	8.3	5.1	1.9	65.2

533 Pigments, paints, varnishes and related materials

In 2016, the value (in current US$) of exports of "pigments, paints, varnishes and related materials" (SITC group 533) increased by 2.8 percent (compared to -2.8 percent average growth rate from 2012-2016) to reach 55.4 bln US$ (see table 2), while imports increased by 1.8 percent to reach 54.4 bln US$ (see table 3). Exports of this commodity accounted for 3.1 percent of world exports of SITC section 5, and 0.3 percent of total world merchandise exports (see table 1). Germany, USA and Japan were the top exporters in 2016 (see table 2). They accounted for 17.0, 11.9 and 6.8 percent of world exports, respectively. Germany, China and USA were the top destinations, with respectively 7.4, 5.8 and 5.1 percent of world imports (see table 3).

The top 15 countries/areas accounted for 79.2 and 53.7 percent of total world exports and imports, respectively (see tables 2 and 3). In 2016, Germany was the country/area with the highest value of net exports (+5.4 bln US$), followed by USA (+3.8 bln US$). By MDG regions (see graph 2), the largest surpluses in this product group were recorded by Developed Europe (+8.1 bln US$), Developed Asia-Pacific (+2.7 bln US$) and Developed North America (+2.7 bln US$). The largest trade deficits were recorded by Latin America and the Caribbean (-3.1 bln US$), South-eastern Asia (-2.4 bln US$) and Western Asia (-1.9 bln US$).

Table 1: Imports (Imp.) and exports (Exp.), 2002-2016, in current US$

		2002	2003	2004	2005	2006	2007	2008	2009	2010	2011	2012	2013	2014	2015	2016
Values in Bln US$	Imp.	26.1	30.1	35.1	38.0	42.3	48.1	52.3	44.1	51.0	60.5	58.3	59.6	60.2	53.4	54.4
	Exp.	25.9	30.2	35.4	38.6	43.1	48.7	52.4	44.3	52.2	63.4	62.0	60.2	61.0	53.9	55.4
As a percentage of SITC section (%)	Imp.	3.7	3.6	3.5	3.3	3.3	3.2	3.0	3.0	2.9	2.9	2.9	2.9	2.9	2.8	2.9
	Exp.	3.9	3.9	3.7	3.6	3.5	3.4	3.2	3.1	3.2	3.3	3.2	3.0	3.0	3.0	3.1
As a percentage of world trade (%)	Imp.	0.4	0.4	0.4	0.4	0.3	0.3	0.3	0.4	0.3	0.3	0.3	0.3	0.3	0.3	0.3
	Exp.	0.4	0.4	0.4	0.4	0.4	0.4	0.3	0.4	0.3	0.4	0.3	0.3	0.3	0.3	0.3

Graph 1: Annual growth rates of exports, 2002–2016
(In percentage by year)

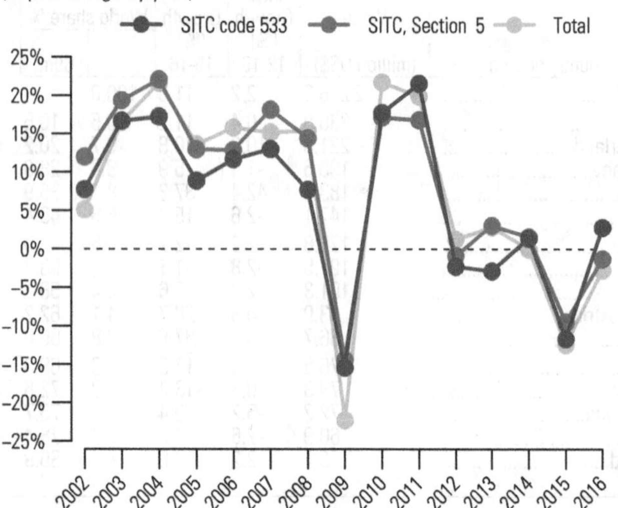

Table 2: Top exporting countries or areas in 2016

Country or area	Value (million US$)	Avg. Growth (%) 12-16	Growth (%) 15-16	World share %	Cum.
World	55377.1	-2.8	2.8	100.0	
Germany	9405.9	-0.8	9.1	17.0	17.0
USA	6602.1	-2.5	-1.7	11.9	28.9
Japan	3743.7	-3.9	7.9	6.8	35.7
China	3074.2	2.7	-3.3	5.6	41.2
Belgium	3052.4	-5.0	2.3	5.5	46.7
Netherlands	2988.0	4.1	16.4	5.4	52.1
Italy	2555.5	-0.4	2.9	4.6	56.7
United Kingdom	2453.7	-2.5	-3.1	4.4	61.2
Spain	2137.0	0.1	-1.6	3.9	65.0
France	2024.4	-2.6	-1.3	3.7	68.7
Rep. of Korea	1958.7	4.5	6.5	3.5	72.2
Other Asia, nes	1276.3	-0.4	2.8	2.3	74.5
Canada	907.7	-1.4	3.4	1.6	76.2
Sweden	853.6	-5.0	-2.3	1.5	77.7
Singapore	850.9	-4.2	-6.7	1.5	79.2

Graph 2: Trade Balance by MDG regions 2016
(Bln US$)

Imports — Exports — Trade balance

Developed Asia-Pacific
Developed Europe
Developed N. America
South-eastern Europe
C I S
Northern Africa
Sub-Saharan Africa
Latin Am, Caribbean
Eastern Asia
Southern Asia
South-eastern Asia
Western Asia
Oceania

-25 -20 -15 -10 -5 0 5 10 15 20 25 30 35

Table 3: Top importing countries or areas in 2016

Country or area	Value (million US$)	Avg. Growth (%) 12-16	Growth (%) 15-16	World share %	Cum.
World	54351.6	-1.7	1.8	100.0	
Germany	4045.9	0.4	19.0	7.4	7.4
China	3148.0	-0.5	3.0	5.8	13.2
USA	2771.9	0.7	-0.5	5.1	18.3
France	2335.6	-3.0	3.1	4.3	22.6
Canada	1996.8	-1.1	0.6	3.7	26.3
United Kingdom	1811.8	1.2	3.2	3.3	29.6
Italy	1723.1	-1.6	3.1	3.2	32.8
Mexico	1659.7	2.0	-1.0	3.1	35.9
Rep. of Korea	1535.1	-2.5	-1.0	2.8	38.7
Belgium	1443.5	-2.3	6.2	2.7	41.3
Russian Federation	1422.7	-12.3	-4.7	2.6	44.0
Netherlands	1417.4	-2.9	4.8	2.6	46.6
Spain	1347.4	2.7	5.7	2.5	49.0
Poland	1323.9	-1.7	0.9	2.4	51.5
Turkey	1187.7	-2.2	-1.9	2.2	53.7

"Medicinal and pharmaceutical products, other than medicament of 542" (SITC group 541) is amongst the top exported commodities in 2016 with 1.2 percent of total exports (see table 1). The value (in current US$) of exports of this commodity increased by 6.2 percent (compared to 4.7 percent average growth rate from 2012-2016) to reach 198.3 bln US$ (see table 2), while imports increased by 6.2 percent to reach 197.6 bln US$ (see table 3). Exports of this commodity accounted for 11.1 percent of world exports of SITC section 5 (see table 1). Switzerland, Germany and USA were the top exporters in 2016 (see table 2). They accounted for 15.9, 14.0 and 13.8 percent of world exports, respectively. USA, Germany and Belgium were the top destinations, with respectively 14.0, 11.7 and 7.7 percent of world imports (see table 3).

The top 15 countries/areas accounted for 91.5 and 77.7 percent of total world exports and imports, respectively (see tables 2 and 3). In 2016, Switzerland was the country/area with the highest value of net exports (+22.3 bln US$), followed by Ireland (+10.2 bln US$). By MDG regions (see graph 2), the largest surpluses in this product group were recorded by Developed Europe (+33.3 bln US$) and Eastern Asia (+1.1 bln US$). The largest trade deficits were recorded by Developed Asia-Pacific (-8.3 bln US$), Latin America and the Caribbean (-7.5 bln US$) and Western Asia (-4.5 bln US$).

Table 1: Imports (Imp.) and exports (Exp.), 2002-2016, in current US$

		2002	2003	2004	2005	2006	2007	2008	2009	2010	2011	2012	2013	2014	2015	2016
Values in Bln US$	Imp.	44.1	52.3	60.7	66.7	75.6	96.0	109.0	116.9	133.1	159.6	163.6	177.1	191.8	186.0	197.6
	Exp.	40.7	49.9	59.3	65.5	73.6	93.5	111.7	123.5	134.8	152.0	164.8	177.9	189.8	186.7	198.3
As a percentage of SITC section (%)	Imp.	6.3	6.3	6.0	5.8	5.9	6.3	6.3	7.9	7.7	7.8	8.1	8.5	9.1	9.6	10.4
	Exp.	6.2	6.4	6.2	6.0	6.0	6.5	6.8	8.7	8.1	7.9	8.6	9.0	9.5	10.3	11.1
As a percentage of world trade (%)	Imp.	0.7	0.7	0.6	0.6	0.6	0.7	0.7	0.9	0.9	0.9	0.9	0.9	1.0	1.1	1.2
	Exp.	0.6	0.7	0.6	0.6	0.6	0.7	0.7	1.0	0.9	0.8	0.9	0.9	1.0	1.1	1.2

Graph 1: Annual growth rates of exports, 2002–2016
(In percentage by year)

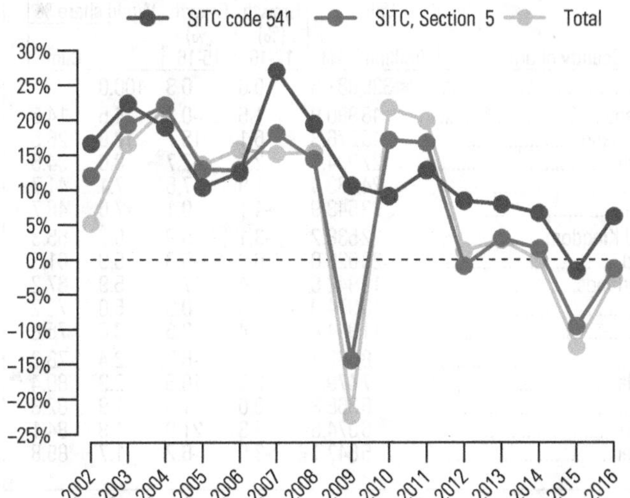

Table 2: Top exporting countries or areas in 2016

Country or area	Value (million US$)	Avg. Growth (%) 12-16	Growth (%) 15-16	World share %	Cum.
World	198277.8	4.7	6.2	100.0	
Switzerland	31478.2	3.8	4.6	15.9	15.9
Germany	27816.1	2.2	3.6	14.0	29.9
USA	27268.4	10.0	3.5	13.8	43.7
Belgium	18040.3	1.8	-1.1	9.1	52.8
Netherlands	13431.1	29.7	41.6	6.8	59.5
Ireland	13219.0	2.9	16.7	6.7	66.2
United Kingdom	10799.4	0.1	-7.9	5.4	71.6
China	10199.2	2.9	1.5	5.1	76.8
France	7313.2	-2.1	1.5	3.7	80.5
Italy	5643.1	14.1	31.8	2.8	83.3
Austria	4089.6	2.4	-6.0	2.1	85.4
Denmark	3564.4	5.8	-3.6	1.8	87.2
Spain	3418.6	1.3	0.8	1.7	88.9
Singapore	2668.6	-9.3	10.9	1.3	90.3
Sweden	2428.1	4.0	1.4	1.2	91.5

Graph 2: Trade Balance by MDG regions 2016
(Bln US$)

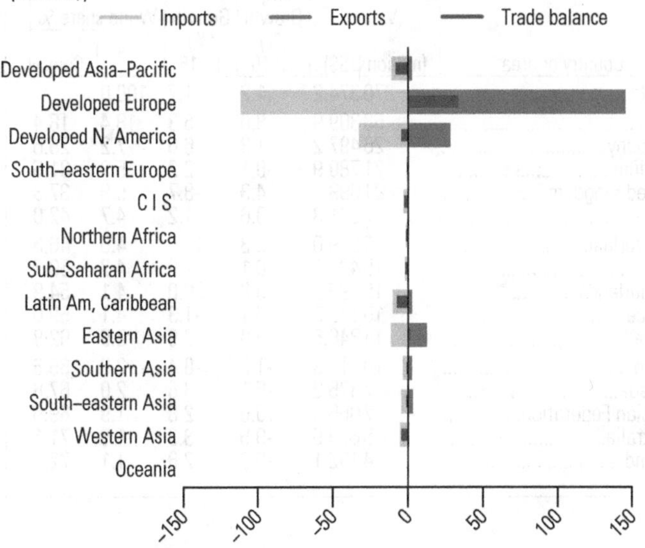

Table 3: Top importing countries or areas in 2016

Country or area	Value (million US$)	Avg. Growth (%) 12-16	Growth (%) 15-16	World share %	Cum.
World	197551.8	4.8	6.2	100.0	
USA	27622.3	9.7	11.2	14.0	14.0
Germany	23064.2	2.0	3.9	11.7	25.7
Belgium	15282.0	-1.4	-6.0	7.7	33.4
United Kingdom	11681.9	4.9	7.8	5.9	39.3
France	10250.2	-0.5	-5.6	5.2	44.5
Netherlands	9707.8	42.8	58.9	4.9	49.4
Switzerland	9156.0	6.6	3.0	4.6	54.0
Italy	8919.7	1.3	3.2	4.5	58.6
Japan	8018.8	2.3	22.7	4.1	62.6
China	7705.0	20.1	9.9	3.9	66.5
Austria	6199.1	7.1	10.6	3.1	69.7
Canada	5063.0	7.4	2.8	2.6	72.2
Spain	4127.3	3.0	3.2	2.1	74.3
Brazil	3706.1	-1.7	-3.1	1.9	76.2
Ireland	3061.6	15.7	49.3	1.5	77.7

542 Medicaments (including veterinary medicaments)

"Medicaments (including veterinary medicaments)" (SITC group 542) is amongst the top exported commodities in 2016 with 2.1 percent of total exports (see table 1). The value (in current US$) of exports of this commodity increased by 0.3 percent (compared to 0.6 percent average growth rate from 2012-2016) to reach 336.9 bln US$ (see table 2), while imports increased by 1.7 percent to reach 370.4 bln US$ (see table 3). Exports of this commodity accounted for 18.8 percent of world exports of SITC section 5 (see table 1). Germany, Switzerland and Belgium were the top exporters in 2016 (see table 2). They accounted for 14.5, 12.0 and 8.0 percent of world exports, respectively. USA, Germany and Belgium were the top destinations, with respectively 18.4, 7.2 and 5.9 percent of world imports (see table 3).

The top 15 countries/areas accounted for 85.8 and 72.2 percent of total world exports and imports, respectively (see tables 2 and 3). In 2016, Switzerland was the country/area with the highest value of net exports (+23.4 bln US$), followed by Germany (+22.5 bln US$). By MDG regions (see graph 2), the largest surpluses in this product group were recorded by Developed Europe (+79.4 bln US$) and Southern Asia (+9.6 bln US$). The largest trade deficits were recorded by Developed North America (-44.2 bln US$), Developed Asia-Pacific (-18.9 bln US$) and Eastern Asia (-16.8 bln US$).

Table 1: Imports (Imp.) and exports (Exp.), 2002-2016, in current US$

		2002	2003	2004	2005	2006	2007	2008	2009	2010	2011	2012	2013	2014	2015	2016
Values in Bln US$	Imp.	132.4	161.3	191.3	216.0	245.6	283.9	320.0	322.7	335.7	357.6	352.8	360.5	372.4	364.1	370.4
	Exp.	125.8	151.7	186.3	206.1	237.4	274.2	303.9	309.4	320.1	337.4	329.2	339.6	351.7	335.9	336.9
As a percentage of SITC section (%)	Imp.	18.8	19.3	18.9	18.8	19.1	18.7	18.4	21.8	19.3	17.4	17.5	17.4	17.6	18.8	19.5
	Exp.	19.1	19.3	19.5	19.0	19.4	19.0	18.4	21.9	19.3	17.5	17.2	17.2	17.6	18.5	18.8
As a percentage of world trade (%)	Imp.	2.0	2.1	2.0	2.0	2.0	2.0	2.0	2.6	2.2	2.0	1.9	1.9	2.0	2.2	2.3
	Exp.	2.0	2.0	2.0	2.0	2.0	2.0	1.9	2.5	2.1	1.9	1.8	1.8	1.9	2.0	2.1

Graph 1: Annual growth rates of exports, 2002–2016
(In percentage by year)

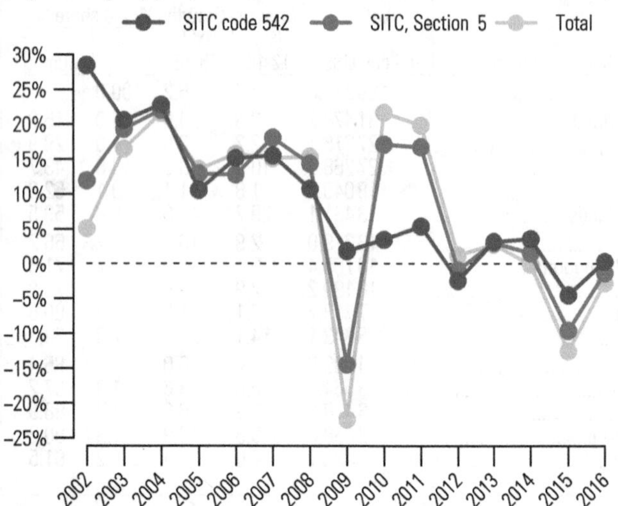

Table 2: Top exporting countries or areas in 2016

Country or area	Value (million US$)	Avg. Growth (%) 12-16	Growth (%) 15-16	World share %	Cum.
World	336 887.8	0.6	0.3	100.0	
Germany	48 980.9	1.5	-0.3	14.5	14.5
Switzerland	40 276.3	6.1	15.7	12.0	26.5
Belgium	27 034.1	-2.7	-2.7	8.0	34.5
USA	24 083.4	-1.9	-7.5	7.1	41.7
France	23 543.9	-4.1	0.1	7.0	48.7
United Kingdom	22 538.2	-3.1	-9.9	6.7	55.3
Ireland	20 026.0	0.6	-9.3	5.9	61.3
Netherlands	19 942.8	10.4	17.3	5.9	67.2
Italy	16 974.9	-1.4	0.9	5.0	72.2
India	11 964.4	7.4	3.5	3.6	75.8
Spain	8 062.7	-3.9	-6.7	2.4	78.2
Canada	7 479.3	16.3	10.5	2.2	80.4
Israel	6 368.3	0.0	1.0	1.9	82.3
Austria	6 074.6	2.3	21.9	1.8	84.1
Sweden	5 643.1	-3.0	-6.2	1.7	85.8

Graph 2: Trade Balance by MDG regions 2016
(Bln US$)

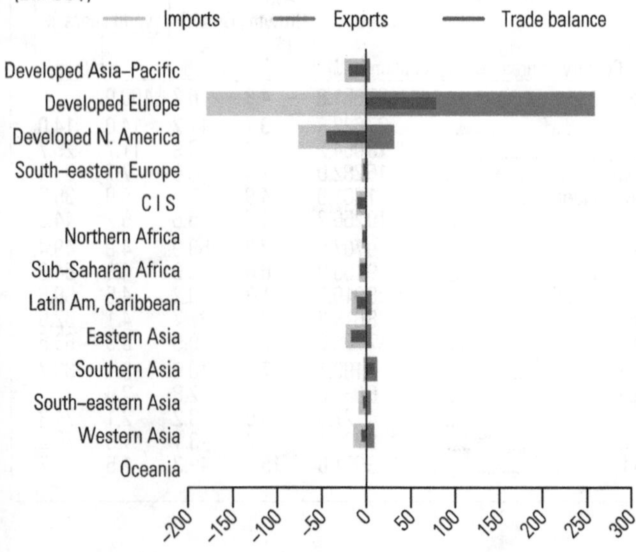

Table 3: Top importing countries or areas in 2016

Country or area	Value (million US$)	Avg. Growth (%) 12-16	Growth (%) 15-16	World share %	Cum.
World	370 374.2	1.2	1.7	100.0	
USA	68 309.9	8.0	5.3	18.4	18.4
Germany	26 497.2	1.3	6.0	7.2	25.6
Belgium	21 780.9	-0.1	-2.2	5.9	31.5
United Kingdom	21 699.3	4.3	-8.7	5.9	37.3
Japan	17 361.3	0.6	-1.2	4.7	42.0
Switzerland	16 829.0	3.3	18.5	4.5	46.6
Italy	15 426.0	-0.1	2.9	4.2	50.7
Netherlands	15 299.9	5.8	30.0	4.1	54.9
France	15 140.6	-6.1	-1.3	4.1	59.0
China	14 346.5	9.0	7.9	3.9	62.8
Spain	10 418.3	-1.8	-8.4	2.8	65.6
Canada	7 375.2	-5.1	-3.8	2.0	67.6
Russian Federation	7 065.0	-10.0	2.8	1.9	69.5
Australia	5 679.5	-9.5	3.3	1.5	71.1
Poland	4 132.1	-0.3	2.8	1.1	72.2

In 2016, the value (in current US$) of exports of "essential oils, perfume and flavour materials" (SITC group 551) increased by 1.4 percent (compared to 1.8 percent average growth rate from 2012-2016) to reach 27.4 bln US$ (see table 2), while imports increased by 1.4 percent to reach 26.7 bln US$ (see table 3). Exports of this commodity accounted for 1.5 percent of world exports of SITC section 5, and 0.2 percent of total world merchandise exports (see table 1). Ireland, USA and France were the top exporters in 2016 (see table 2). They accounted for 29.4, 9.6 and 8.7 percent of world exports, respectively. USA, France and Mexico were the top destinations, with respectively 13.2, 9.5 and 6.2 percent of world imports (see table 3).

The top 15 countries/areas accounted for 87.8 and 62.1 percent of total world exports and imports, respectively (see tables 2 and 3). In 2016, Ireland was the country/area with the highest value of net exports (+7.6 bln US$), followed by Switzerland (+1.3 bln US$). By MDG regions (see graph 2), the largest surpluses in this product group were recorded by Developed Europe (+7.6 bln US$) and Southern Asia (+296.5 mln US$). The largest trade deficits were recorded by Latin America and the Caribbean (-1.7 bln US$), Developed North America (-1.4 bln US$) and Sub-Saharan Africa (-1.0 bln US$).

Table 1: Imports (Imp.) and exports (Exp.), 2002-2016, in current US$

		2002	2003	2004	2005	2006	2007	2008	2009	2010	2011	2012	2013	2014	2015	2016
Values in Bln US$	Imp.	9.2	11.7	13.8	14.9	15.6	17.7	19.5	18.3	20.4	22.6	23.4	25.2	26.5	26.3	26.7
	Exp.	10.0	12.9	14.9	15.6	16.6	18.7	20.9	19.3	21.2	24.8	25.5	26.3	27.9	27.0	27.4
As a percentage of	Imp.	1.3	1.4	1.4	1.3	1.2	1.2	1.1	1.2	1.2	1.1	1.2	1.2	1.3	1.4	1.4
SITC section (%)	Exp.	1.5	1.6	1.6	1.4	1.4	1.3	1.3	1.4	1.3	1.3	1.3	1.3	1.4	1.5	1.5
As a percentage of	Imp.	0.1	0.2	0.1	0.1	0.1	0.1	0.1	0.1	0.1	0.1	0.1	0.1	0.1	0.2	0.2
world trade (%)	Exp.	0.2	0.2	0.2	0.2	0.1	0.1	0.1	0.2	0.1	0.1	0.1	0.1	0.1	0.2	0.2

Graph 1: Annual growth rates of exports, 2002–2016

(In percentage by year)

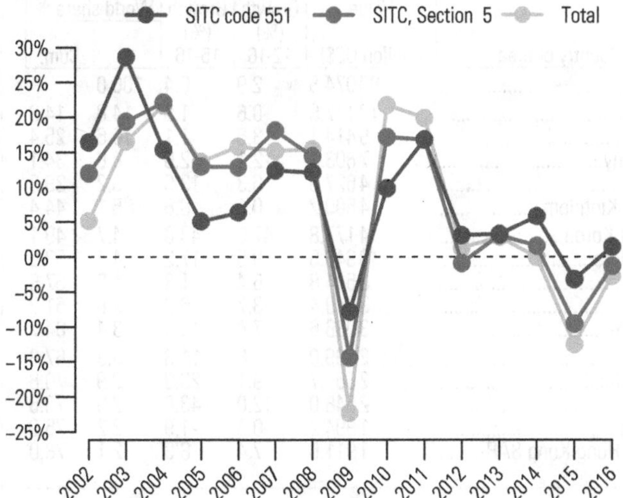

Table 2: Top exporting countries or areas in 2016

Country or area	Value (million US$)	Avg. Growth (%) 12-16	Growth (%) 15-16	World share %	Cum.
World	27 363.7	1.8	1.4	100.0	
Ireland	8 055.8	2.5	-1.4	29.4	29.4
USA	2 634.6	4.2	5.5	9.6	39.1
France	2 381.1	1.0	8.8	8.7	47.8
Germany	2 031.9	1.1	3.1	7.4	55.2
Switzerland	1 680.3	-3.7	-2.1	6.1	61.3
Netherlands	1 267.8	7.6	22.0	4.6	66.0
Singapore	1 226.7	-10.5	3.2	4.5	70.5
United Kingdom	991.9	-1.3	-2.9	3.6	74.1
India	860.1	-2.6	5.6	3.1	77.2
China	742.4	8.8	-32.6	2.7	79.9
Spain	672.5	4.9	1.1	2.5	82.4
Swaziland	*430.9*	-1.6	-15.3	1.6	84.0
Brazil	395.3	6.5	23.2	1.4	85.4
Mexico	335.9	6.3	3.6	1.2	86.6
Indonesia	318.4	9.3	8.0	1.2	87.8

Graph 2: Trade Balance by MDG regions 2016

(Bln US$)

Imports — Exports — Trade balance

Developed Asia-Pacific
Developed Europe
Developed N. America
South-eastern Europe
CIS
Northern Africa
Sub-Saharan Africa
Latin Am, Caribbean
Eastern Asia
Southern Asia
South-eastern Asia
Western Asia
Oceania

-15 -10 -5 0 5 10 15 20

Table 3: Top importing countries or areas in 2016

Country or area	Value (million US$)	Avg. Growth (%) 12-16	Growth (%) 15-16	World share %	Cum.
World	26 709.4	3.3	1.4	100.0	
USA	3 515.2	6.8	-2.6	13.2	13.2
France	2 549.6	-1.4	-0.6	9.5	22.7
Mexico	1 664.1	12.8	4.8	6.2	28.9
Germany	1 464.2	7.4	-10.8	5.5	34.4
United Kingdom	1 200.9	0.0	-11.0	4.5	38.9
Spain	916.9	4.1	-3.0	3.4	42.3
Italy	772.1	0.0	3.4	2.9	45.2
Netherlands	657.6	8.9	49.6	2.5	47.7
China	618.6	-0.4	-7.0	2.3	50.0
Canada	602.1	6.2	4.4	2.3	52.3
Thailand	566.0	4.1	7.7	2.1	54.4
Indonesia	554.7	7.1	9.0	2.1	56.5
Japan	544.1	-3.6	13.0	2.0	58.5
South Africa	477.2	0.5	0.1	1.8	60.3
Poland	473.9	2.3	3.5	1.8	62.1

Source: UN Comtrade

553 Perfumery, cosmetic or toilet preparations (excluding soaps)

In 2016, the value (in current US$) of exports of "perfumery, cosmetic or toilet preparations (excluding soaps)" (SITC group 553) increased by 6.4 percent (compared to 2.9 percent average growth rate from 2012-2016) to reach 89.1 bln US$ (see table 2), while imports increased by 5.5 percent to reach 87.9 bln US$ (see table 3). Exports of this commodity accounted for 5.0 percent of world exports of SITC section 5, and 0.6 percent of total world merchandise exports (see table 1). France, USA and Germany were the top exporters in 2016 (see table 2). They accounted for 14.8, 10.6 and 8.8 percent of world exports, respectively. USA, Germany and United Kingdom were the top destinations, with respectively 10.3, 6.1 and 5.7 percent of world imports (see table 3).

The top 15 countries/areas accounted for 78.0 and 61.4 percent of total world exports and imports, respectively (see tables 2 and 3). In 2016, France was the country/area with the highest value of net exports (+10.2 bln US$), followed by Rep. of Korea (+2.6 bln US$). By MDG regions (see graph 2), the largest surpluses in this product group were recorded by Developed Europe (+14.1 bln US$) and South-eastern Asia (+971.9 mln US$). The largest trade deficits were recorded by Western Asia (-4.0 bln US$), Commonwealth of Independent States (-2.5 bln US$) and Eastern Asia (-2.5 bln US$).

Table 1: Imports (Imp.) and exports (Exp.), 2002-2016, in current US$

		2002	2003	2004	2005	2006	2007	2008	2009	2010	2011	2012	2013	2014	2015	2016
Values in Bln US$	Imp.	27.6	33.1	38.9	42.9	47.8	56.4	63.9	58.6	65.0	74.1	77.3	83.6	87.6	83.4	87.9
	Exp.	28.5	34.5	40.2	43.9	49.4	58.3	65.8	59.8	67.4	78.0	79.4	86.5	89.7	83.7	89.1
As a percentage of SITC section (%)	Imp.	3.9	4.0	3.8	3.7	3.7	3.7	3.7	4.0	3.7	3.6	3.8	4.0	4.1	4.3	4.6
	Exp.	4.3	4.4	4.2	4.1	4.0	4.0	4.0	4.2	4.1	4.0	4.1	4.4	4.5	4.6	5.0
As a percentage of world trade (%)	Imp.	0.4	0.4	0.4	0.4	0.4	0.4	0.4	0.5	0.4	0.4	0.4	0.4	0.5	0.5	0.5
	Exp.	0.4	0.5	0.4	0.4	0.4	0.4	0.4	0.5	0.4	0.4	0.4	0.5	0.5	0.5	0.6

Graph 1: Annual growth rates of exports, 2002–2016
(In percentage by year)

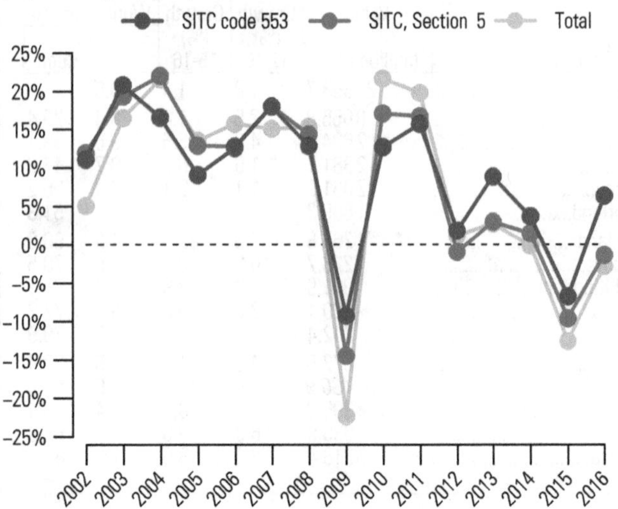

Graph 2: Trade Balance by MDG regions 2016
(Bln US$)

Imports Exports Trade balance

Developed Asia-Pacific
Developed Europe
Developed N. America
South-eastern Europe
CIS
Northern Africa
Sub-Saharan Africa
Latin Am, Caribbean
Eastern Asia
Southern Asia
South-eastern Asia
Western Asia
Oceania

-40 -30 -20 -10 0 10 20 30 40 50

Table 2: Top exporting countries or areas in 2016

Country or area	Value (million US$)	Avg. Growth (%) 12-16	Growth (%) 15-16	World share %	Cum.
World	89074.5	2.9	6.4	100.0	
France	13177.6	-0.6	1.9	14.8	14.8
USA	9414.1	3.5	1.1	10.6	25.4
Germany	7803.7	-2.1	2.6	8.8	34.1
Italy	4627.5	6.3	13.6	5.2	39.3
United Kingdom	4509.2	0.1	0.6	5.1	44.4
Rep. of Korea	4177.8	42.5	43.8	4.7	49.1
Singapore	3946.5	9.5	17.2	4.4	53.5
China	3544.8	6.4	-1.3	4.0	57.5
Spain	3349.4	3.7	6.3	3.8	61.2
Belgium	3036.6	7.4	10.3	3.4	64.7
Poland	2899.0	2.8	11.3	3.3	67.9
Netherlands	2567.7	9.1	23.9	2.9	70.8
Japan	2548.0	12.0	43.6	2.9	73.6
Mexico	1994.2	-0.3	-1.9	2.2	75.9
China, Hong Kong SAR	1911.6	7.4	8.3	2.1	78.0

Table 3: Top importing countries or areas in 2016

Country or area	Value (million US$)	Avg. Growth (%) 12-16	Growth (%) 15-16	World share %	Cum.
World	87931.0	3.3	5.5	100.0	
USA	9039.0	6.4	6.7	10.3	10.3
Germany	5401.8	1.9	4.2	6.1	16.4
United Kingdom	5030.4	2.9	-1.0	5.7	22.1
China	4888.2	33.8	27.2	5.6	27.7
China, Hong Kong SAR	4483.0	9.1	15.6	5.1	32.8
France	2941.2	2.3	7.5	3.3	36.1
Canada	2798.1	3.1	3.0	3.2	39.3
Singapore	2773.8	7.0	14.5	3.2	42.5
Netherlands	2726.2	7.1	13.5	3.1	45.6
Belgium	2603.5	8.9	16.2	3.0	48.5
Japan	2504.8	-2.8	8.1	2.8	51.4
Spain	2372.2	5.9	9.5	2.7	54.1
Italy	2202.3	0.9	8.4	2.5	56.6
Russian Federation	2137.0	-8.4	-1.9	2.4	59.0
United Arab Emirates	2110.8	-6.9	-4.8	2.4	61.4

In 2016, the value (in current US$) of exports of "soap, cleansing and polishing preparations" (SITC group 554) increased by 1.2 percent (compared to -0.5 percent average growth rate from 2012-2016) to reach 39.3 bln US$ (see table 2), while imports decreased by 1.4 percent to reach 38.5 bln US$ (see table 3). Exports of this commodity accounted for 2.2 percent of world exports of SITC section 5, and 0.2 percent of total world merchandise exports (see table 1). Germany, USA and Belgium were the top exporters in 2016 (see table 2). They accounted for 12.4, 11.5 and 5.9 percent of world exports, respectively. Germany, USA and France were the top destinations, with respectively 6.7, 5.3 and 4.9 percent of world imports (see table 3).

The top 15 countries/areas accounted for 71.4 and 51.9 percent of total world exports and imports, respectively (see tables 2 and 3). In 2016, USA was the country/area with the highest value of net exports (+2.5 bln US$), followed by Germany (+2.3 bln US$). By MDG regions (see graph 2), the largest surpluses in this product group were recorded by Developed Europe (+4.1 bln US$), Developed North America (+1.2 bln US$) and South-eastern Asia (+610.6 mln US$). The largest trade deficits were recorded by Western Asia (-1.2 bln US$), Latin America and the Caribbean (-1.1 bln US$) and Commonwealth of Independent States (-1.0 bln US$).

Table 1: Imports (Imp.) and exports (Exp.), 2002-2016, in current US$

		2002	2003	2004	2005	2006	2007	2008	2009	2010	2011	2012	2013	2014	2015	2016
Values in Bln US$	Imp.	15.2	18.0	20.3	22.2	24.7	28.4	33.5	30.8	33.9	39.2	39.3	41.3	43.0	39.1	38.5
	Exp.	15.4	18.4	20.9	22.3	25.0	28.8	34.5	31.4	34.4	40.0	40.0	42.0	43.5	38.8	39.3
As a percentage of SITC section (%)	Imp.	2.2	2.2	2.0	1.9	1.9	1.9	1.9	2.1	1.9	1.9	1.9	2.0	2.0	2.0	2.0
	Exp.	2.3	2.3	2.2	2.1	2.0	2.0	2.1	2.2	2.1	2.1	2.1	2.1	2.2	2.1	2.2
As a percentage of world trade (%)	Imp.	0.2	0.2	0.2	0.2	0.2	0.2	0.2	0.2	0.2	0.2	0.2	0.2	0.2	0.2	0.2
	Exp.	0.2	0.2	0.2	0.2	0.2	0.2	0.2	0.3	0.2	0.2	0.2	0.2	0.2	0.2	0.2

Graph 1: Annual growth rates of exports, 2002–2016

(In percentage by year)

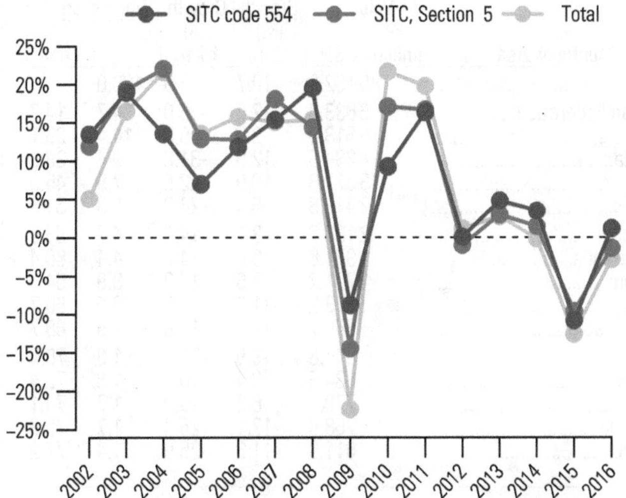

Graph 2: Trade Balance by MDG regions 2016

(Bln US$)

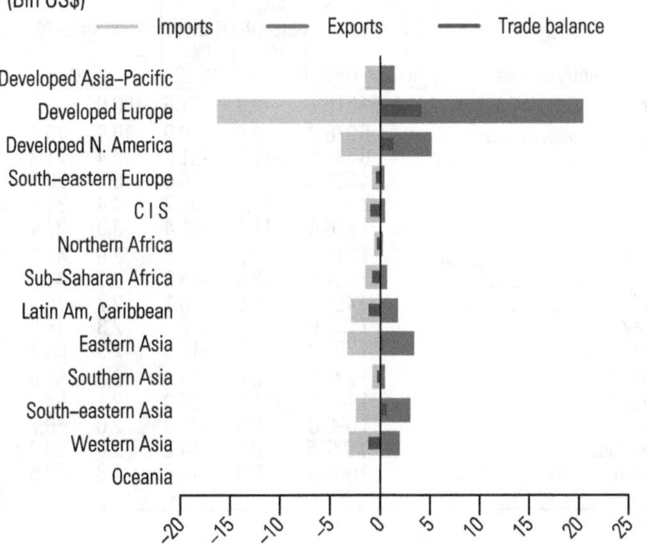

Table 2: Top exporting countries or areas in 2016

Country or area	Value (million US$)	Avg. Growth (%) 12-16	Growth (%) 15-16	World share %	Cum.
World	39280.5	-0.5	1.2	100.0	
Germany	4868.4	-0.7	3.0	12.4	12.4
USA	4536.0	-0.4	-1.7	11.5	23.9
Belgium	2330.5	6.1	7.8	5.9	29.9
China	2302.0	2.4	-0.7	5.9	35.7
France	2009.1	-3.1	4.0	5.1	40.8
Netherlands	1956.3	1.4	7.7	5.0	45.8
United Kingdom	1792.2	-2.8	-4.7	4.6	50.4
Italy	1678.6	-0.5	2.1	4.3	54.7
Poland	1314.8	4.7	12.8	3.3	58.0
Japan	1248.0	1.2	16.0	3.2	61.2
Spain	1034.9	1.1	-0.2	2.6	63.8
Indonesia	828.3	-1.6	1.4	2.1	65.9
Turkey	734.6	-2.9	-13.0	1.9	67.8
Malaysia	721.8	-1.6	-9.5	1.8	69.6
Rep. of Korea	673.4	8.9	10.6	1.7	71.4

Table 3: Top importing countries or areas in 2016

Country or area	Value (million US$)	Avg. Growth (%) 12-16	Growth (%) 15-16	World share %	Cum.
World	38531.7	-0.5	-1.4	100.0	
Germany	2599.0	-0.6	-0.9	6.7	6.7
USA	2061.2	2.1	0.3	5.3	12.1
France	1904.9	-2.9	0.3	4.9	17.0
Canada	1808.8	-0.5	-0.2	4.7	21.7
United Kingdom	1733.0	-1.1	-16.1	4.5	26.2
China	1725.4	3.9	5.7	4.5	30.7
Belgium	1499.6	3.6	9.8	3.9	34.6
Netherlands	1318.9	-0.9	4.4	3.4	38.0
Italy	970.6	-1.6	7.1	2.5	40.5
Poland	769.3	0.4	-2.1	2.0	42.5
Japan	748.8	-3.1	9.8	1.9	44.5
Spain	747.9	-1.8	3.3	1.9	46.4
United Arab Emirates	744.2	4.4	-2.7	1.9	48.4
Russian Federation	739.3	-6.5	-6.5	1.9	50.3
Austria	617.1	2.5	11.1	1.6	51.9

562 Fertilizers (other than those of group 272)

In 2016, the value (in current US$) of exports of "fertilizers (other than those of group 272)" (SITC group 562) decreased by 23.9 percent (compared to -10.7 percent average growth rate from 2012-2016) to reach 45.2 bln US$ (see table 2), while imports decreased by 21.6 percent to reach 54.6 bln US$ (see table 3). Exports of this commodity accounted for 2.5 percent of world exports of SITC section 5, and 0.3 percent of total world merchandise exports (see table 1). Russian Federation, China and Canada were the top exporters in 2016 (see table 2). They accounted for 14.7, 14.4 and 9.4 percent of world exports, respectively. Brazil, USA and India were the top destinations, with respectively 10.9, 10.4 and 8.4 percent of world imports (see table 3).

The top 15 countries/areas accounted for 77.2 and 60.5 percent of total world exports and imports, respectively (see tables 2 and 3). In 2016, Russian Federation was the country/area with the highest value of net exports (+6.6 bln US$), followed by China (+4.1 bln US$). By MDG regions (see graph 2), the largest surpluses in this product group were recorded by Commonwealth of Independent States (+8.9 bln US$), Eastern Asia (+3.8 bln US$) and Northern Africa (+3.3 bln US$). The largest trade deficits were recorded by Latin America and the Caribbean (-9.4 bln US$), Southern Asia (-6.0 bln US$) and South-eastern Asia (-5.2 bln US$).

Table 1: Imports (Imp.) and exports (Exp.), 2002-2016, in current US$

		2002	2003	2004	2005	2006	2007	2008	2009	2010	2011	2012	2013	2014	2015	2016
Values in Bln US$	Imp.	18.0	21.8	28.2	33.2	33.3	46.5	88.7	45.1	57.9	84.4	80.6	75.4	72.1	69.7	54.6
	Exp.	12.5	15.4	19.3	23.8	24.3	35.8	72.3	39.5	52.4	72.4	71.0	61.2	59.8	59.3	45.2
As a percentage of SITC section (%)	Imp.	2.6	2.6	2.8	2.9	2.6	3.1	5.1	3.0	3.3	4.1	4.0	3.6	3.4	3.6	2.9
	Exp.	1.9	2.0	2.0	2.2	2.0	2.5	4.4	2.8	3.2	3.7	3.7	3.1	3.0	3.3	2.5
As a percentage of world trade (%)	Imp.	0.3	0.3	0.3	0.3	0.3	0.3	0.5	0.4	0.4	0.5	0.4	0.4	0.4	0.4	0.3
	Exp.	0.2	0.2	0.2	0.2	0.2	0.3	0.5	0.3	0.3	0.4	0.4	0.3	0.3	0.4	0.3

Graph 1: Annual growth rates of exports, 2002–2016
(In percentage by year)

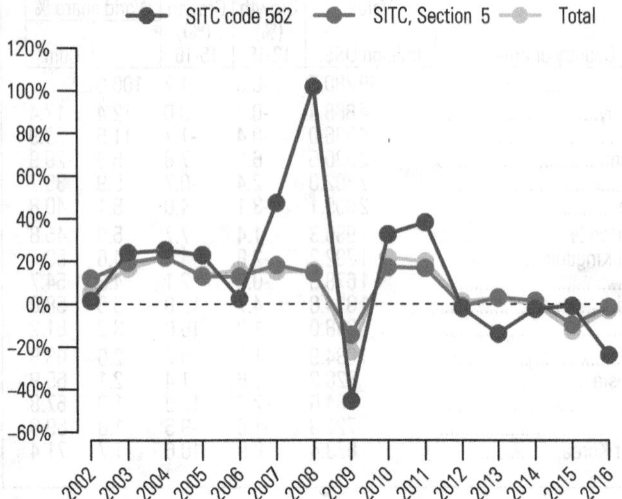

Table 2: Top exporting countries or areas in 2016

Country or area	Value (million US$)	Avg. Growth (%) 12-16	Growth (%) 15-16	World share %	Cum.
World	45182.3	-10.7	-23.9	100.0	
Russian Federation	6633.7	-12.2	-25.0	14.7	14.7
China	6513.0	-2.5	-39.9	14.4	29.1
Canada	4234.5	-12.9	-31.0	9.4	38.5
USA	3371.8	-10.9	-22.5	7.5	45.9
Belarus	2412.8	-5.4	-24.2	5.3	51.3
Morocco	2133.7	-3.1	14.2	4.7	56.0
Netherlands	1974.8	-9.0	-14.2	4.4	60.4
Belgium	1771.2	-7.6	-17.3	3.9	64.3
Israel	1113.2	-11.2	-7.5	2.5	66.7
Saudi Arabia	880.7	-14.1	-17.6	1.9	68.7
Egypt	847.8	-9.9	101.0	1.9	70.6
Germany	834.5	-9.4	-10.6	1.8	72.4
Spain	770.2	-6.2	-6.0	1.7	74.1
Lithuania	758.0	-12.1	-25.4	1.7	75.8
Jordan	611.8	-11.8	-25.9	1.4	77.2

Graph 2: Trade Balance by MDG regions 2016
(Bln US$)

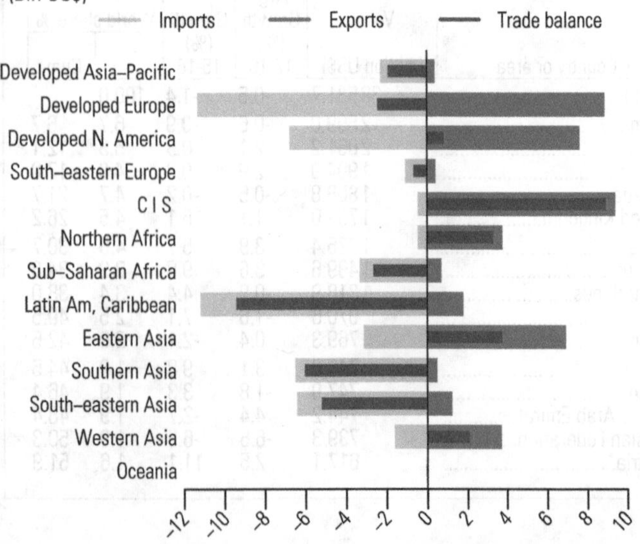

Table 3: Top importing countries or areas in 2016

Country or area	Value (million US$)	Avg. Growth (%) 12-16	Growth (%) 15-16	World share %	Cum.
World	54615.7	-9.3	-21.6	100.0	
Brazil	5976.3	-8.6	-9.0	10.9	10.9
USA	5664.6	-11.3	-31.6	10.4	21.3
India	4569.7	-12.7	-38.6	8.4	29.7
China	2404.7	-12.1	-38.7	4.4	34.1
France	1816.4	-11.6	-21.4	3.3	37.4
Indonesia	1548.4	-12.3	-22.8	2.8	40.2
Thailand	1501.6	-13.8	-15.3	2.7	43.0
Viet Nam	*1491.6*	-2.9	5.1	2.7	45.7
Turkey	1267.9	-2.0	2.0	2.3	48.0
Australia	1253.2	-7.4	-10.5	2.3	50.3
Mexico	1230.3	-6.8	-13.1	2.3	52.6
Germany	1144.3	-11.3	-24.0	2.1	54.7
Canada	1096.0	-5.8	-21.8	2.0	56.7
Bangladesh	*1077.5*	-0.7	-14.2	2.0	58.7
Belgium	1002.6	-9.9	-19.0	1.8	60.5

In 2016, the value (in current US$) of exports of "polymers of ethylene, in primary forms" (SITC group 571) decreased by 0.4 percent (compared to -1.4 percent average growth rate from 2012-2016) to reach 69.7 bln US$ (see table 2), while imports decreased by 3.6 percent to reach 72.6 bln US$ (see table 3). Exports of this commodity accounted for 3.9 percent of world exports of SITC section 5, and 0.4 percent of total world merchandise exports (see table 1). Saudi Arabia, USA and Belgium were the top exporters in 2016 (see table 2). They accounted for 11.6, 10.8 and 8.0 percent of world exports, respectively. China, USA and Germany were the top destinations, with respectively 19.4, 5.8 and 5.4 percent of world imports (see table 3).

The top 15 countries/areas accounted for 80.2 and 64.7 percent of total world exports and imports, respectively (see tables 2 and 3). In 2016, Saudi Arabia was the country/area with the highest value of net exports (+7.7 bln US$), followed by USA (+3.3 bln US$). By MDG regions (see graph 2), the largest surpluses in this product group were recorded by Western Asia (+7.6 bln US$), Developed North America (+6.2 bln US$) and South-eastern Asia (+1.9 bln US$). The largest trade deficits were recorded by Eastern Asia (-9.4 bln US$), Latin America and the Caribbean (-4.0 bln US$) and Sub-Saharan Africa (-1.8 bln US$).

Table 1: Imports (Imp.) and exports (Exp.), 2002-2016, in current US$

		2002	2003	2004	2005	2006	2007	2008	2009	2010	2011	2012	2013	2014	2015	2016
Values in Bln US$	Imp.	20.5	24.8	33.5	41.2	47.4	56.2	62.4	48.6	63.1	75.6	74.1	79.9	84.8	75.3	72.6
	Exp.	18.6	22.6	31.1	39.9	46.1	55.2	62.5	49.2	60.3	72.3	73.7	79.6	79.2	69.9	69.7
As a percentage of SITC section (%)	Imp.	2.9	3.0	3.3	3.6	3.7	3.7	3.6	3.3	3.6	3.7	3.7	3.9	4.0	3.9	3.8
	Exp.	2.8	2.9	3.3	3.7	3.8	3.8	3.8	3.5	3.6	3.7	3.8	4.0	4.0	3.9	3.9
As a percentage of world trade (%)	Imp.	0.3	0.3	0.4	0.4	0.4	0.4	0.4	0.4	0.4	0.4	0.4	0.4	0.5	0.5	0.5
	Exp.	0.3	0.3	0.3	0.4	0.4	0.4	0.4	0.4	0.4	0.4	0.4	0.4	0.4	0.4	0.4

Graph 1: Annual growth rates of exports, 2002–2016

(In percentage by year)

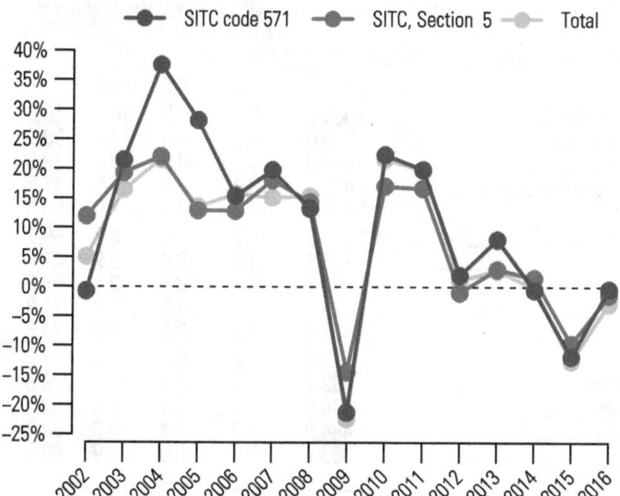

Graph 2: Trade Balance by MDG regions 2016

(Bln US$)

Imports — Exports — Trade balance

Developed Asia-Pacific
Developed Europe
Developed N. America
South-eastern Europe
CIS
Northern Africa
Sub-Saharan Africa
Latin Am, Caribbean
Eastern Asia
Southern Asia
South-eastern Asia
Western Asia
Oceania

-25 -20 -15 -10 -5 0 5 10 15 20 25

Table 2: Top exporting countries or areas in 2016

Country or area	Value (million US$)	Avg. Growth (%) 12-16	Growth (%) 15-16	World share %	Cum.
World	69659.1	-1.4	-0.4	100.0	
Saudi Arabia	8089.4	-0.5	-2.4	11.6	11.6
USA	7519.2	-0.1	-5.3	10.8	22.4
Belgium	5603.5	-2.7	-1.9	8.0	30.5
Singapore	5059.8	4.3	7.6	7.3	37.7
Canada	4148.0	1.9	-6.0	6.0	43.7
Rep. of Korea	3742.1	0.1	-7.5	5.4	49.0
Germany	3524.7	-2.8	0.4	5.1	54.1
Netherlands	3427.1	-0.4	8.2	4.9	59.0
United Arab Emirates	3292.7	15.9	86.4	4.7	63.7
Thailand	3016.2	-3.8	-11.4	4.3	68.1
Iran	*2367.7*	-1.3	-38.3	3.4	71.5
France	2199.4	-3.0	-1.9	3.2	74.6
Spain	1478.3	5.8	1.4	2.1	76.8
Brazil	1217.6	-3.3	-2.0	1.7	78.5
Uzbekistan	*1212.8*	95.8	963.1	1.7	80.2

Table 3: Top importing countries or areas in 2016

Country or area	Value (million US$)	Avg. Growth (%) 12-16	Growth (%) 15-16	World share %	Cum.
World	72578.8	-0.5	-3.6	100.0	
China	14046.4	2.4	-6.1	19.4	19.4
USA	4204.8	1.6	-4.7	5.8	25.1
Germany	3914.9	-3.6	-4.2	5.4	30.5
Belgium	3206.2	-1.2	13.4	4.4	35.0
Italy	2735.4	-0.4	2.0	3.8	38.7
India	2507.0	3.7	-6.7	3.5	42.2
Turkey	2340.6	0.4	-2.7	3.2	45.4
France	2083.9	-3.9	0.2	2.9	48.3
Mexico	2075.8	1.0	-5.7	2.9	51.1
Singapore	1911.3	-3.3	15.6	2.6	53.8
Viet Nam	*1877.7*	7.7	5.1	2.6	56.4
United Kingdom	1694.8	-6.3	-2.7	2.3	58.7
Spain	1565.4	2.6	1.5	2.2	60.8
Malaysia	1467.6	7.9	2.7	2.0	62.9
Netherlands	1355.8	0.3	14.4	1.9	64.7

 Source: UN Comtrade

572 Polymers of styrene, in primary forms

In 2016, the value (in current US$) of exports of "polymers of styrene, in primary forms" (SITC group 572) decreased by 4.2 percent (compared to -6.6 percent average growth rate from 2012-2016) to reach 18.7 bln US$ (see table 2), while imports decreased by 6.9 percent to reach 20.0 bln US$ (see table 3). Exports of this commodity accounted for 1.0 percent of world exports of SITC section 5, and 0.1 percent of total world merchandise exports (see table 1). Rep. of Korea, Other Asia, nes and Belgium were the top exporters in 2016 (see table 2). They accounted for 16.5, 14.4 and 9.0 percent of world exports, respectively. China, Germany and USA were the top destinations, with respectively 23.2, 6.2 and 5.8 percent of world imports (see table 3).

The top 15 countries/areas accounted for 86.6 and 68.7 percent of total world exports and imports, respectively (see tables 2 and 3). In 2016, Rep. of Korea was the country/area with the highest value of net exports (+2.9 bln US$), followed by Other Asia, nes (+2.6 bln US$). By MDG regions (see graph 2), the largest surpluses in this product group were recorded by Eastern Asia (+1.7 bln US$) and Developed Asia-Pacific (+300.2 mln US$). The largest trade deficits were recorded by Western Asia (-703.0 mln US$), Latin America and the Caribbean (-616.5 mln US$) and South-eastern Europe (-321.5 mln US$).

Table 1: Imports (Imp.) and exports (Exp.), 2002-2016, in current US$

		2002	2003	2004	2005	2006	2007	2008	2009	2010	2011	2012	2013	2014	2015	2016
Values in Bln US$	Imp.	11.8	13.3	16.8	18.7	22.8	23.9	24.5	18.5	24.3	27.1	26.1	26.9	26.3	21.5	20.0
	Exp.	11.3	13.0	16.9	19.1	20.9	24.5	24.2	17.5	23.7	25.9	24.6	25.6	24.5	19.5	18.7
As a percentage of SITC section (%)	Imp.	1.7	1.6	1.7	1.6	1.8	1.6	1.4	1.2	1.4	1.3	1.3	1.3	1.2	1.1	1.1
	Exp.	1.7	1.7	1.8	1.8	1.7	1.7	1.5	1.2	1.4	1.3	1.3	1.3	1.2	1.1	1.0
As a percentage of world trade (%)	Imp.	0.2	0.2	0.2	0.2	0.2	0.2	0.2	0.1	0.2	0.1	0.1	0.1	0.1	0.1	0.1
	Exp.	0.2	0.2	0.2	0.2	0.2	0.2	0.2	0.1	0.2	0.1	0.1	0.1	0.1	0.1	0.1

Graph 1: Annual growth rates of exports, 2002–2016

(In percentage by year)

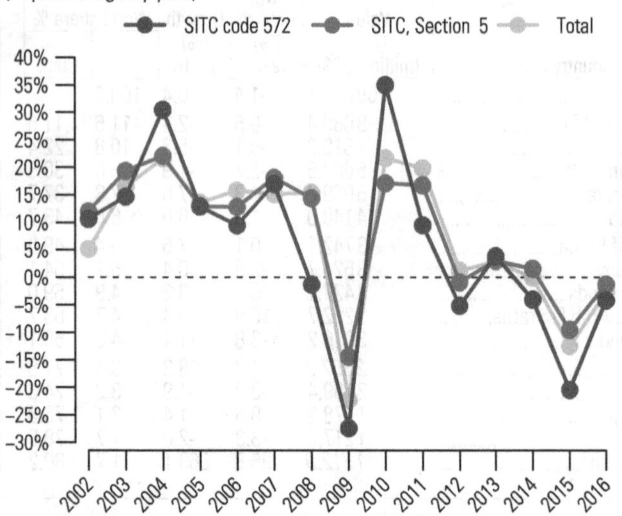

Graph 2: Trade Balance by MDG regions 2016

(Bln US$)

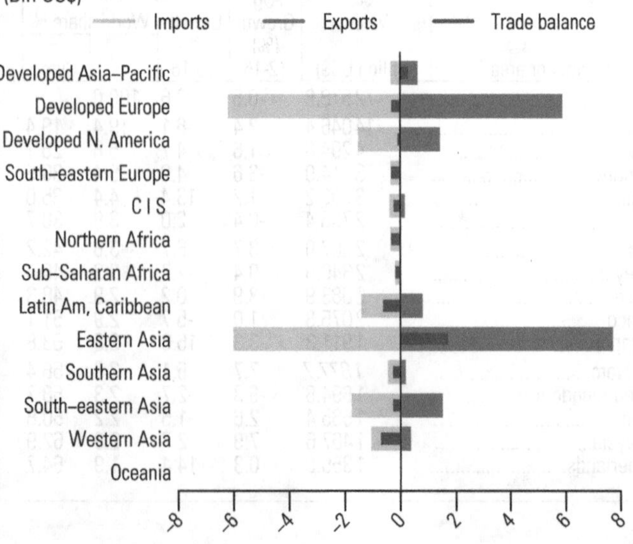

Table 2: Top exporting countries or areas in 2016

Country or area	Value (million US$)	Avg. Growth (%) 12-16	Growth (%) 15-16	World share %	Cum.
World	18690.2	-6.6	-4.2	100.0	
Rep. of Korea	3089.2	-6.3	-3.7	16.5	16.5
Other Asia, nes	2690.0	-8.6	-5.3	14.4	30.9
Belgium	1677.0	-6.2	-0.5	9.0	39.9
China, Hong Kong SAR	1423.3	-13.0	-16.5	7.6	47.5
USA	1302.5	-3.2	-4.9	7.0	54.5
Netherlands	1163.3	-0.7	2.5	6.2	60.7
France	723.4	-5.1	-10.4	3.9	64.6
Germany	640.3	-9.3	-6.1	3.4	68.0
Japan	623.2	-9.5	-3.5	3.3	71.3
Mexico	552.4	-1.1	-8.5	3.0	74.3
China	514.8	-8.2	-9.4	2.8	77.0
Singapore	482.2	-4.6	-4.6	2.6	79.6
Thailand	474.9	-3.1	6.1	2.5	82.2
Malaysia	464.9	-10.0	-7.4	2.5	84.7
Spain	363.7	-5.6	-8.0	1.9	86.6

Table 3: Top importing countries or areas in 2016

Country or area	Value (million US$)	Avg. Growth (%) 12-16	Growth (%) 15-16	World share %	Cum.
World	19978.2	-6.5	-6.9	100.0	
China	4639.5	-7.4	-8.0	23.2	23.2
Germany	1237.3	-6.5	-4.6	6.2	29.4
USA	1162.3	-1.0	-6.2	5.8	35.2
China, Hong Kong SAR	1090.9	-14.3	-18.9	5.5	40.7
Mexico	827.5	-1.6	-4.6	4.1	44.8
Italy	777.8	-6.6	1.0	3.9	48.7
Turkey	698.3	-8.8	-12.2	3.5	52.2
Poland	543.4	-3.9	-1.7	2.7	54.9
Thailand	476.6	-4.8	0.0	2.4	57.3
Viet Nam	*468.4*	-0.1	5.1	2.3	59.7
France	451.6	-10.7	-10.2	2.3	61.9
United Kingdom	370.2	-2.6	-14.2	1.9	63.8
Canada	349.3	-6.4	-8.6	1.7	65.5
Netherlands	320.1	-2.9	-8.5	1.6	67.1
Indonesia	317.6	-7.3	0.8	1.6	68.7

In 2016, the value (in current US$) of exports of "polymers of vinyl chloride or of other halogenated olefins" (SITC group 573) increased by 1.2 percent (compared to -3.1 percent average growth rate from 2012-2016) to reach 16.7 bln US$ (see table 2), while imports decreased by 1.6 percent to reach 17.4 bln US$ (see table 3). Exports of this commodity accounted for 0.9 percent of world exports of SITC section 5, and 0.1 percent of total world merchandise exports (see table 1). USA, Germany and China were the top exporters in 2016 (see table 2). They accounted for 20.0, 9.9 and 8.4 percent of world exports, respectively. India, China and Germany were the top destinations, with respectively 10.1, 7.3 and 6.3 percent of world imports (see table 3).

The top 15 countries/areas accounted for 84.1 and 63.4 percent of total world exports and imports, respectively (see tables 2 and 3). In 2016, USA was the country/area with the highest value of net exports (+2.4 bln US$), followed by Japan (+978.6 mln US$). By MDG regions (see graph 2), the largest surpluses in this product group were recorded by Developed North America (+2.0 bln US$), Eastern Asia (+1.1 bln US$) and Developed Europe (+1.0 bln US$). The largest trade deficits were recorded by Southern Asia (-2.0 bln US$), Western Asia (-1.1 bln US$) and Latin America and the Caribbean (-841.9 mln US$).

Table 1: Imports (Imp.) and exports (Exp.), 2002-2016, in current US$

		2002	2003	2004	2005	2006	2007	2008	2009	2010	2011	2012	2013	2014	2015	2016
Values in Bln US$	Imp.	8.3	9.3	11.8	12.6	13.8	16.1	17.8	13.5	17.5	20.8	19.6	20.4	20.7	17.7	17.4
	Exp.	7.9	8.9	11.6	12.3	13.4	16.0	17.3	13.0	17.1	19.9	19.0	18.9	19.6	16.5	16.7
As a percentage of SITC section (%)	Imp.	1.2	1.1	1.2	1.1	1.1	1.1	1.0	0.9	1.0	1.0	1.0	1.0	1.0	0.9	0.9
	Exp.	1.2	1.1	1.2	1.1	1.1	1.1	1.0	0.9	1.0	1.0	1.0	1.0	1.0	0.9	0.9
As a percentage of world trade (%)	Imp.	0.1	0.1	0.1	0.1	0.1	0.1	0.1	0.1	0.1	0.1	0.1	0.1	0.1	0.1	0.1
	Exp.	0.1	0.1	0.1	0.1	0.1	0.1	0.1	0.1	0.1	0.1	0.1	0.1	0.1	0.1	0.1

Graph 1: Annual growth rates of exports, 2002–2016
(In percentage by year)

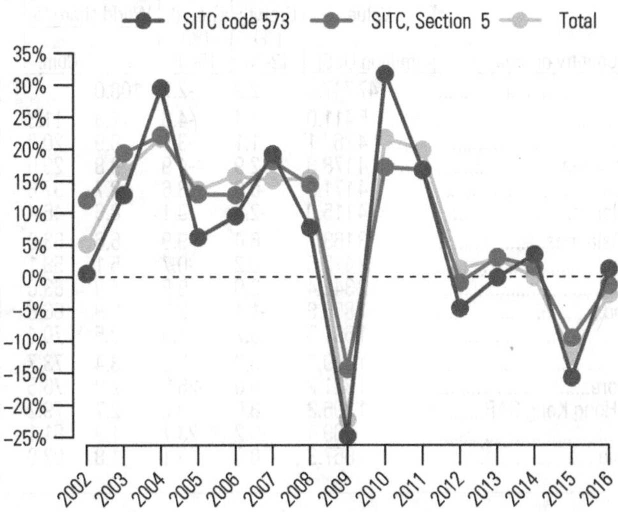

Table 2: Top exporting countries or areas in 2016

Country or area	Value (million US$)	Avg. Growth (%) 12-16	Growth (%) 15-16	World share %	Cum.
World	16699.9	-3.1	1.2	100.0	
USA	3335.0	-5.1	-4.0	20.0	20.0
Germany	1659.0	-6.5	-0.2	9.9	29.9
China	1408.9	12.2	13.9	8.4	38.3
Japan	1159.2	3.2	-0.5	6.9	45.3
Belgium	1057.2	-0.4	6.5	6.3	51.6
Other Asia, nes	1005.7	-1.0	3.1	6.0	57.6
Netherlands	975.8	-3.8	7.5	5.8	63.5
France	893.5	-2.2	7.8	5.4	68.8
Rep. of Korea	543.1	-9.6	-7.7	3.3	72.1
Italy	538.8	-1.1	-4.1	3.2	75.3
Thailand	373.9	-1.1	6.9	2.2	77.5
Spain	323.2	-1.5	3.8	1.9	79.5
Mexico	293.8	-4.8	-0.9	1.8	81.2
Colombia	248.5	-7.8	-12.4	1.5	82.7
United Kingdom	224.2	-10.8	-10.6	1.3	84.1

Graph 2: Trade Balance by MDG regions 2016
(Bln US$)

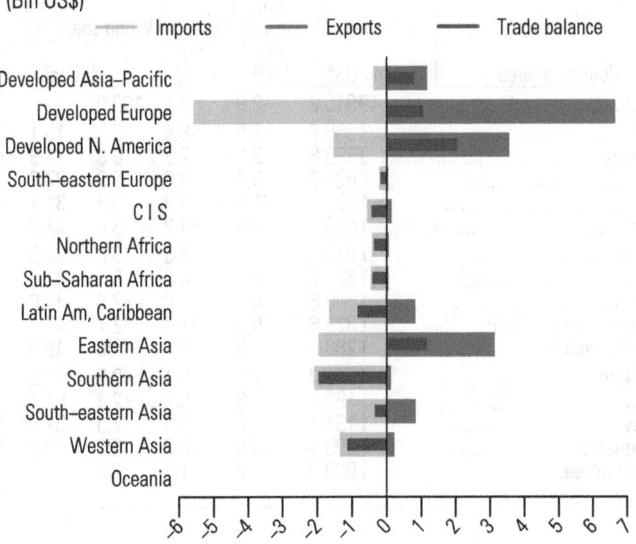

Table 3: Top importing countries or areas in 2016

Country or area	Value (million US$)	Avg. Growth (%) 12-16	Growth (%) 15-16	World share %	Cum.
World	17416.3	-3.0	-1.6	100.0	
India	1751.6	6.3	8.3	10.1	10.1
China	1268.5	-7.9	-5.5	7.3	17.3
Germany	1097.2	-3.4	1.0	6.3	23.6
USA	974.3	-1.1	-2.6	5.6	29.2
Belgium	892.0	3.6	24.6	5.1	34.4
Italy	878.6	-3.9	1.4	5.0	39.4
Turkey	705.4	-6.4	-13.6	4.1	43.5
Mexico	615.8	0.3	-4.3	3.5	47.0
Canada	557.6	-3.7	-3.6	3.2	50.2
France	455.1	-5.1	-1.5	2.6	52.8
United Kingdom	448.9	-0.9	-5.5	2.6	55.4
Rep. of Korea	399.6	0.3	5.0	2.3	57.7
Brazil	376.5	-11.0	-7.5	2.2	59.8
Poland	316.0	-4.2	3.1	1.8	61.7
Viet Nam	*308.5*	8.4	5.1	1.8	63.4

Source: UN Comtrade

574 Polyacetals, epoxide resins, etc, and other polyethers in primary forms

In 2016, the value (in current US$) of exports of "polyacetals, epoxide resins, etc, and other polyethers in primary forms" (SITC group 574) decreased by 2.7 percent (compared to -2.9 percent average growth rate from 2012-2016) to reach 47.7 bln US$ (see table 2), while imports decreased by 5.1 percent to reach 49.9 bln US$ (see table 3). Exports of this commodity accounted for 2.7 percent of world exports of SITC section 5, and 0.3 percent of total world merchandise exports (see table 1). USA, China and Rep. of Korea were the top exporters in 2016 (see table 2). They accounted for 11.3, 8.9 and 8.8 percent of world exports, respectively. China, Germany and USA were the top destinations, with respectively 15.1, 6.8 and 5.3 percent of world imports (see table 3).

The top 15 countries/areas accounted for 82.9 and 61.2 percent of total world exports and imports, respectively (see tables 2 and 3). In 2016, Rep. of Korea was the country/area with the highest value of net exports (+3.2 bln US$), followed by Netherlands (+3.0 bln US$). By MDG regions (see graph 2), the largest surpluses in this product group were recorded by Developed North America (+2.3 bln US$), Eastern Asia (+2.2 bln US$) and Developed Europe (+1.5 bln US$). The largest trade deficits were recorded by Latin America and the Caribbean (-2.8 bln US$), Western Asia (-1.4 bln US$) and Sub-Saharan Africa (-944.7 mln US$).

Table 1: Imports (Imp.) and exports (Exp.), 2002-2016, in current US$

		2002	2003	2004	2005	2006	2007	2008	2009	2010	2011	2012	2013	2014	2015	2016
Values in Bln US$	Imp.	20.3	24.5	30.4	36.9	41.2	47.7	49.6	37.4	49.2	57.9	56.3	58.1	59.7	52.6	49.9
	Exp.	19.4	23.4	29.2	35.4	39.6	45.5	46.8	37.1	48.0	56.3	53.7	55.5	56.5	49.1	47.7
As a percentage of SITC section (%)	Imp.	2.9	2.9	3.0	3.2	3.2	3.2	2.9	2.5	2.8	2.8	2.8	2.8	2.8	2.7	2.6
	Exp.	2.9	3.0	3.0	3.3	3.2	3.2	2.8	2.6	2.9	2.9	2.8	2.8	2.8	2.7	2.7
As a percentage of world trade (%)	Imp.	0.3	0.3	0.3	0.3	0.3	0.3	0.3	0.3	0.3	0.3	0.3	0.3	0.3	0.3	0.3
	Exp.	0.3	0.3	0.3	0.3	0.3	0.3	0.3	0.3	0.3	0.3	0.3	0.3	0.3	0.3	0.3

Graph 1: Annual growth rates of exports, 2002–2016

(In percentage by year)

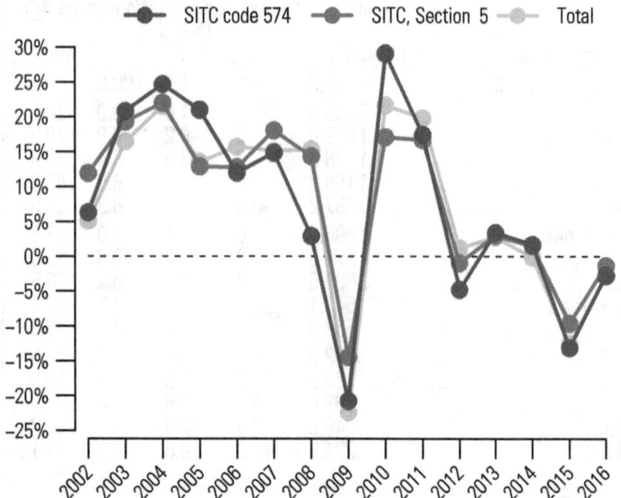

Table 2: Top exporting countries or areas in 2016

Country or area	Value (million US$)	Avg. Growth (%) 12-16	Growth (%) 15-16	World share %	Cum.
World	47747.6	-2.9	-2.7	100.0	
USA	5411.0	-1.4	-4.6	11.3	11.3
China	4267.1	1.1	-3.1	8.9	20.3
Rep. of Korea	4178.8	-2.9	-4.9	8.8	29.0
Germany	4171.9	-0.9	8.6	8.7	37.8
Netherlands	4115.0	-2.4	-3.1	8.6	46.4
Other Asia, nes	3163.7	-6.4	-9.9	6.6	53.0
Belgium	2412.5	0.2	-0.7	5.1	58.1
Japan	2342.4	-2.8	9.5	4.9	63.0
Thailand	1850.6	-1.4	-2.6	3.9	66.8
Italy	1691.5	-3.7	-1.5	3.5	70.4
Spain	1599.7	-5.3	-5.5	3.4	73.7
Singapore	1321.2	-10.0	-25.2	2.8	76.5
China, Hong Kong SAR	1296.3	-8.0	-9.2	2.7	79.2
India	909.4	15.2	23.7	1.9	81.1
Malaysia	867.3	0.0	13.1	1.8	82.9

Graph 2: Trade Balance by MDG regions 2016

(Bln US$)

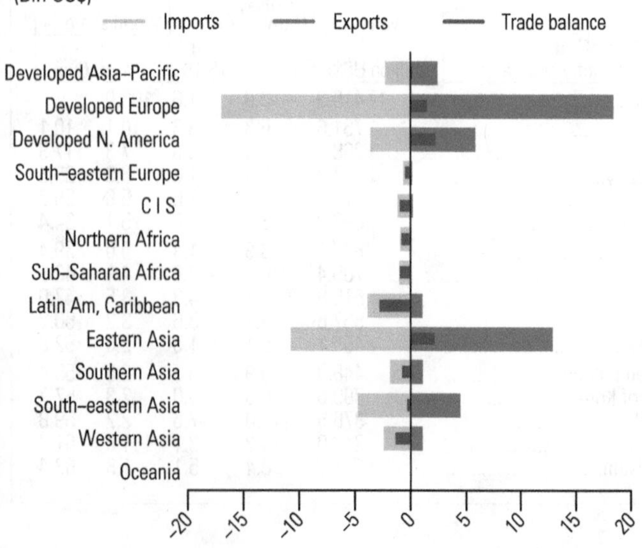

Table 3: Top importing countries or areas in 2016

Country or area	Value (million US$)	Avg. Growth (%) 12-16	Growth (%) 15-16	World share %	Cum.
World	49945.2	-2.9	-5.1	100.0	
China	7555.6	-2.5	-8.4	15.1	15.1
Germany	3390.8	-3.1	-2.7	6.8	21.9
USA	2629.7	0.6	-3.0	5.3	27.2
Italy	1939.5	-1.4	-4.3	3.9	31.1
Japan	1898.9	-3.9	-4.2	3.8	34.9
Mexico	1818.9	4.3	-1.3	3.6	38.5
France	1627.3	-5.2	-6.0	3.3	41.8
Belgium	1400.6	-4.5	1.8	2.8	44.6
China, Hong Kong SAR	1323.6	-9.3	-11.7	2.7	47.2
United Kingdom	1286.3	2.8	2.9	2.6	49.8
Viet Nam	*1263.1*	7.1	5.1	2.5	52.3
India	1193.1	0.8	-5.8	2.4	54.7
Turkey	1134.1	-3.0	-3.4	2.3	57.0
Netherlands	1093.1	-3.6	0.3	2.2	59.2
Rep. of Korea	1009.3	1.7	1.1	2.0	61.2

In 2016, the value (in current US$) of exports of "other plastics, in primary forms" (SITC group 575) decreased by 3.2 percent (compared to -2.6 percent average growth rate from 2012-2016) to reach 100.0 bln US$ (see table 2), while imports decreased by 4.4 percent to reach 105.5 bln US$ (see table 3). Exports of this commodity accounted for 5.6 percent of world exports of SITC section 5, and 0.6 percent of total world merchandise exports (see table 1). USA, Germany and Belgium were the top exporters in 2016 (see table 2). They accounted for 13.4, 12.2 and 8.6 percent of world exports, respectively. China, Germany and USA were the top destinations, with respectively 13.1, 7.0 and 5.3 percent of world imports (see table 3).

The top 15 countries/areas accounted for 82.1 and 61.8 percent of total world exports and imports, respectively (see tables 2 and 3). In 2016, USA was the country/area with the highest value of net exports (+7.8 bln US$), followed by Germany (+4.8 bln US$). By MDG regions (see graph 2), the largest surpluses in this product group were recorded by Developed North America (+5.9 bln US$), Developed Europe (+4.8 bln US$) and Developed Asia-Pacific (+2.5 bln US$). The largest trade deficits were recorded by Latin America and the Caribbean (-5.7 bln US$), Southern Asia (-3.4 bln US$) and Eastern Asia (-2.9 bln US$).

Table 1: Imports (Imp.) and exports (Exp.), 2002-2016, in current US$

		2002	2003	2004	2005	2006	2007	2008	2009	2010	2011	2012	2013	2014	2015	2016
Values in Bln US$	Imp.	37.8	45.0	55.8	64.7	73.5	87.3	95.3	75.7	99.2	117.5	115.2	120.5	127.0	110.3	105.5
	Exp.	36.5	44.2	55.2	64.9	74.6	87.5	94.6	72.0	94.3	110.8	111.3	117.7	121.8	103.3	100.0
As a percentage of SITC section (%)	Imp.	5.4	5.4	5.5	5.6	5.7	5.8	5.5	5.1	5.7	5.7	5.7	5.8	6.0	5.7	5.6
	Exp.	5.6	5.6	5.8	6.0	6.1	6.1	5.7	5.1	5.7	5.7	5.8	6.0	6.1	5.7	5.6
As a percentage of world trade (%)	Imp.	0.6	0.6	0.6	0.6	0.6	0.6	0.6	0.6	0.6	0.6	0.6	0.6	0.7	0.7	0.7
	Exp.	0.6	0.6	0.6	0.6	0.6	0.6	0.6	0.6	0.6	0.6	0.6	0.6	0.6	0.6	0.6

Graph 1: Annual growth rates of exports, 2002–2016
(In percentage by year)

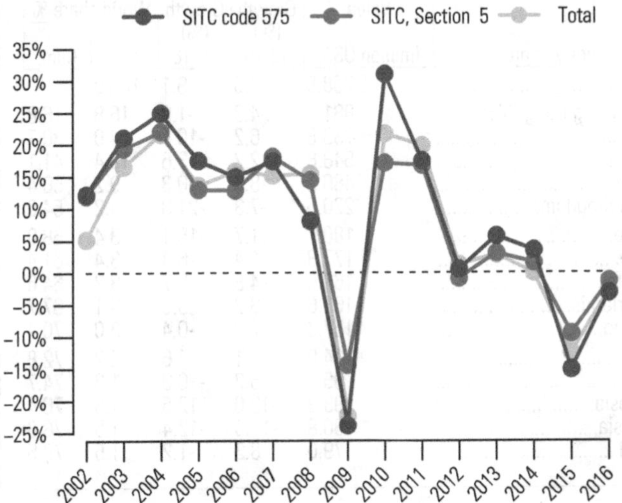

Graph 2: Trade Balance by MDG regions 2016
(Bln US$)

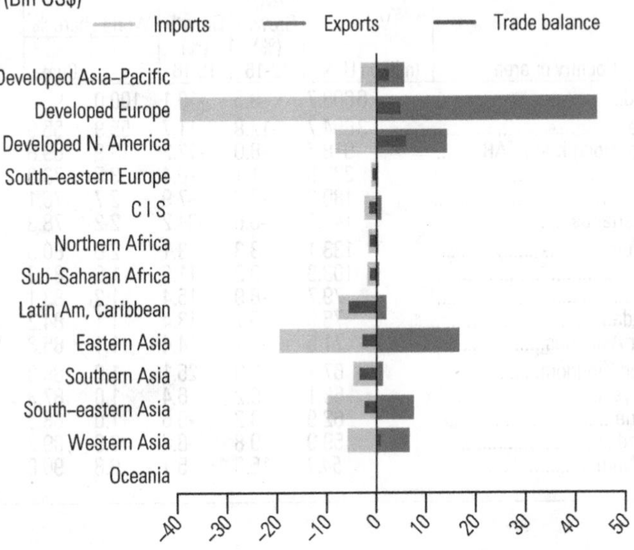

Table 2: Top exporting countries or areas in 2016

Country or area	Value (million US$)	Avg. Growth (%) 12-16	Growth (%) 15-16	World share %	Cum.
World	100043.1	-2.6	-3.2	100.0	
USA	13400.5	-2.3	-4.1	13.4	13.4
Germany	12194.8	-2.3	-1.0	12.2	25.6
Belgium	8642.7	-4.1	-3.0	8.6	34.2
Rep. of Korea	6709.0	-1.9	-4.9	6.7	40.9
Netherlands	5683.6	-1.2	6.3	5.7	46.6
Japan	5477.5	-3.2	2.7	5.5	52.1
China	5029.8	2.5	-6.0	5.0	57.1
Saudi Arabia	4573.9	-3.5	-12.8	4.6	61.7
Singapore	4212.1	-2.2	-4.5	4.2	65.9
France	4194.6	-3.9	-6.0	4.2	70.1
Other Asia, nes	3130.7	-4.6	-4.8	3.1	73.2
Italy	2849.3	-1.6	0.0	2.8	76.1
United Kingdom	2126.5	-5.3	-2.6	2.1	78.2
Spain	2078.2	-1.0	-4.8	2.1	80.3
China, Hong Kong SAR	1787.9	-6.4	-6.9	1.8	82.1

Table 3: Top importing countries or areas in 2016

Country or area	Value (million US$)	Avg. Growth (%) 12-16	Growth (%) 15-16	World share %	Cum.
World	105455.9	-2.2	-4.4	100.0	
China	13856.2	-5.0	-10.0	13.1	13.1
Germany	7434.5	-3.1	-3.1	7.0	20.2
USA	5559.3	3.6	1.2	5.3	25.5
Italy	4785.2	-3.4	-4.6	4.5	30.0
Belgium	4152.6	-3.2	4.8	3.9	33.9
France	3922.4	-4.0	-1.8	3.7	37.7
Turkey	3771.6	-3.7	-9.5	3.6	41.2
Mexico	3415.8	0.4	-1.6	3.2	44.5
India	2972.3	7.6	1.4	2.8	47.3
United Kingdom	2725.8	-3.0	-7.8	2.6	49.9
Canada	2714.8	-1.3	-1.2	2.6	52.4
Netherlands	2544.3	-4.0	0.6	2.4	54.9
Rep. of Korea	2544.0	1.7	-2.7	2.4	57.3
Japan	2375.3	-4.8	3.7	2.3	59.5
Poland	2362.5	1.9	5.0	2.2	61.8

Source: UN Comtrade

579 Waste, parings and scrap, of plastics

In 2016, the value (in current US$) of exports of "waste, parings and scrap, of plastics" (SITC group 579) decreased by 9.1 percent (compared to -7.5 percent average growth rate from 2012-2016) to reach 5.3 bln US$ (see table 2), while imports decreased by 10.1 percent to reach 6.6 bln US$ (see table 3). Exports of this commodity accounted for 0.3 percent of world exports of SITC section 5, and less than 0.1 percent of total world merchandise exports (see table 1). China, Hong Kong SAR, USA and Japan were the top exporters in 2016 (see table 2). They accounted for 16.8, 14.0 and 10.4 percent of world exports, respectively. China, China, Hong Kong SAR and USA were the top destinations, with respectively 55.9, 13.9 and 3.5 percent of world imports (see table 3).

The top 15 countries/areas accounted for 79.5 and 90.0 percent of total world exports and imports, respectively (see tables 2 and 3). In 2016, Japan was the country/area with the highest value of net exports (+546.8 mln US$), followed by USA (+500.0 mln US$). By MDG regions (see graph 2), the largest surpluses in this product group were recorded by Developed Europe (+779.6 mln US$), Developed Asia-Pacific (+596.9 mln US$) and Developed North America (+519.6 mln US$). The largest trade deficits were recorded by Eastern Asia (-3.6 bln US$), Southern Asia (-43.7 mln US$) and Commonwealth of Independent States (-13.0 mln US$).

Table 1: Imports (Imp.) and exports (Exp.), 2002-2016, in current US$

		2002	2003	2004	2005	2006	2007	2008	2009	2010	2011	2012	2013	2014	2015	2016
Values in Bln US$	Imp.	1.6	2.0	3.1	4.4	5.6	6.4	7.9	6.4	8.4	10.0	9.9	9.6	9.9	7.4	6.6
	Exp.	1.5	1.8	2.6	3.6	4.4	5.3	5.7	5.2	6.2	7.2	7.2	6.7	7.0	5.8	5.3
As a percentage of SITC section (%)	Imp.	0.2	0.2	0.3	0.4	0.4	0.4	0.5	0.4	0.5	0.5	0.5	0.5	0.5	0.4	0.3
	Exp.	0.2	0.2	0.3	0.3	0.4	0.4	0.3	0.4	0.4	0.4	0.4	0.3	0.3	0.3	0.3
As a percentage of world trade (%)	Imp.	0.0	0.0	0.0	0.0	0.0	0.0	0.0	0.1	0.1	0.1	0.1	0.1	0.1	0.0	0.0
	Exp.	0.0	0.0	0.0	0.0	0.0	0.0	0.0	0.0	0.0	0.0	0.0	0.0	0.0	0.0	0.0

Graph 1: Annual growth rates of exports, 2002–2016

(In percentage by year)

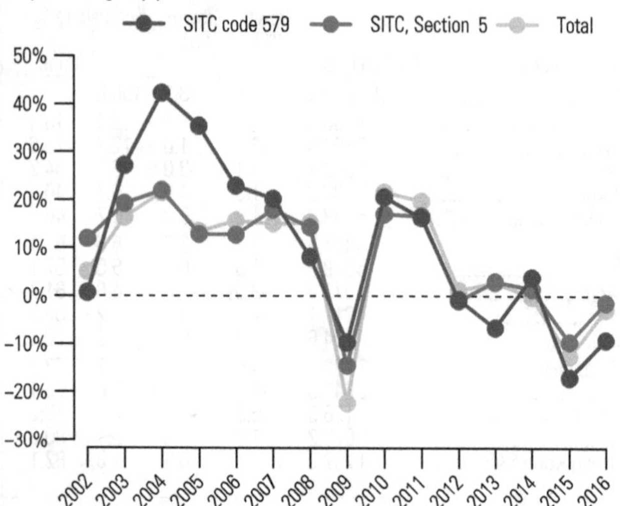

Table 2: Top exporting countries or areas in 2016

Country or area	Value (million US$)	Avg. Growth (%) 12-16	Growth (%) 15-16	World share %	Cum.
World	5258.5	-7.5	-9.1	100.0	
China, Hong Kong SAR	881.2	-4.3	-1.9	16.8	16.8
USA	733.8	-6.2	-10.1	14.0	30.7
Japan	548.8	-12.2	-12.6	10.4	41.1
Germany	486.2	-8.8	-10.3	9.2	50.4
United Kingdom	220.5	-7.3	-21.3	4.2	54.6
Mexico	180.1	-11.7	-15.1	3.4	58.0
France	177.8	-11.4	-16.4	3.4	61.4
Belgium	168.9	-4.8	-3.7	3.2	64.6
Netherlands	161.6	-9.2	-23.8	3.1	67.7
Thailand	157.3	-7.3	-0.4	3.0	70.7
Spain	114.0	3.1	-7.6	2.2	72.8
Canada	95.5	-5.2	-10.3	1.8	74.7
Indonesia	93.3	-12.0	12.5	1.8	76.4
Malaysia	80.8	-11.3	-12.4	1.5	78.0
Poland	79.0	8.3	-1.2	1.5	79.5

Graph 2: Trade Balance by MDG regions 2016

(Bln US$)

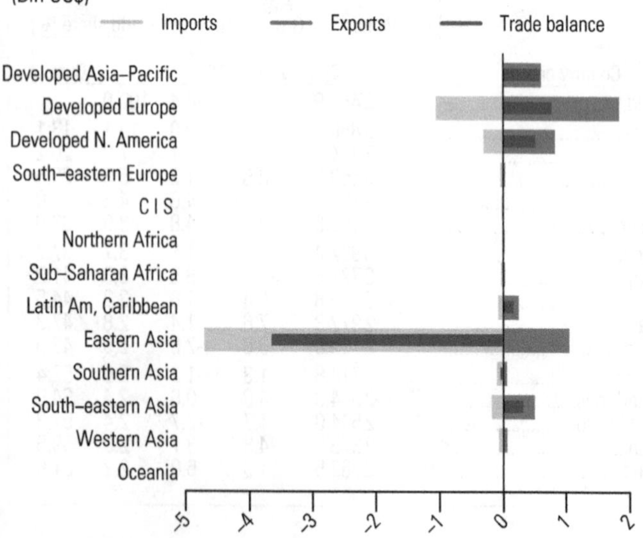

Table 3: Top importing countries or areas in 2016

Country or area	Value (million US$)	Avg. Growth (%) 12-16	Growth (%) 15-16	World share %	Cum.
World	6608.7	-9.5	-10.1	100.0	
China	3694.7	-12.8	-11.7	55.9	55.9
China, Hong Kong SAR	918.7	-8.0	-12.2	13.9	69.8
USA	233.8	1.1	-0.4	3.5	73.3
Germany	180.3	-2.9	-7.9	2.7	76.1
Netherlands	145.2	-8.6	-34.2	2.2	78.3
Belgium	133.1	-3.3	3.1	2.0	80.3
Italy	103.9	-0.2	11.9	1.6	81.9
India	79.7	-8.9	-15.4	1.2	83.1
Canada	75.9	-5.7	-13.4	1.1	84.2
Other Asia, nes	71.5	-1.1	-14.4	1.1	85.3
United Kingdom	67.7	3.9	25.1	1.0	86.3
Malaysia	66.1	0.2	6.4	1.0	87.3
Austria	62.9	-3.2	-9.5	1.0	88.3
Ireland	59.9	-9.8	-8.7	0.9	89.2
Viet Nam	*54.1*	15.6	5.1	0.8	90.0

In 2016, the value (in current US$) of exports of "tubes, pipes and hoses, and fittings therefore of plastics" (SITC group 581) decreased by 0.6 percent (compared to 0.3 percent average growth rate from 2012-2016) to reach 21.9 bln US$ (see table 2), while imports decreased by 0.9 percent to reach 21.3 bln US$ (see table 3). Exports of this commodity accounted for 1.2 percent of world exports of SITC section 5, and 0.1 percent of total world merchandise exports (see table 1). Germany, USA and China were the top exporters in 2016 (see table 2). They accounted for 17.2, 11.9 and 9.9 percent of world exports, respectively. USA, Germany and Mexico were the top destinations, with respectively 8.6, 7.3 and 6.3 percent of world imports (see table 3).

The top 15 countries/areas accounted for 76.1 and 55.2 percent of total world exports and imports, respectively (see tables 2 and 3). In 2016, Germany was the country/area with the highest value of net exports (+2.2 bln US$), followed by China (+1.3 bln US$). By MDG regions (see graph 2), the largest surpluses in this product group were recorded by Developed Europe (+2.9 bln US$), Eastern Asia (+1.3 bln US$) and Developed North America (+491.8 mln US$). The largest trade deficits were recorded by Latin America and the Caribbean (-1.5 bln US$), Commonwealth of Independent States (-619.1 mln US$) and South-eastern Asia (-609.4 mln US$).

Table 1: Imports (Imp.) and exports (Exp.), 2002-2016, in current US$

		2002	2003	2004	2005	2006	2007	2008	2009	2010	2011	2012	2013	2014	2015	2016
Values in Bln US$	Imp.	7.5	8.9	10.8	11.9	14.1	16.7	19.0	15.6	17.4	20.7	21.1	22.7	23.5	21.5	21.3
	Exp.	7.1	8.5	10.4	11.9	14.0	17.2	19.3	15.9	18.0	21.5	21.6	23.1	24.0	22.0	21.9
As a percentage of SITC section (%)	Imp.	1.1	1.1	1.1	1.0	1.1	1.1	1.1	1.1	1.0	1.0	1.0	1.1	1.1	1.1	1.1
	Exp.	1.1	1.1	1.1	1.1	1.1	1.2	1.2	1.1	1.1	1.1	1.1	1.2	1.2	1.2	1.2
As a percentage of world trade (%)	Imp.	0.1	0.1	0.1	0.1	0.1	0.1	0.1	0.1	0.1	0.1	0.1	0.1	0.1	0.1	0.1
	Exp.	0.1	0.1	0.1	0.1	0.1	0.1	0.1	0.1	0.1	0.1	0.1	0.1	0.1	0.1	0.1

Graph 1: Annual growth rates of exports, 2002–2016
(In percentage by year)

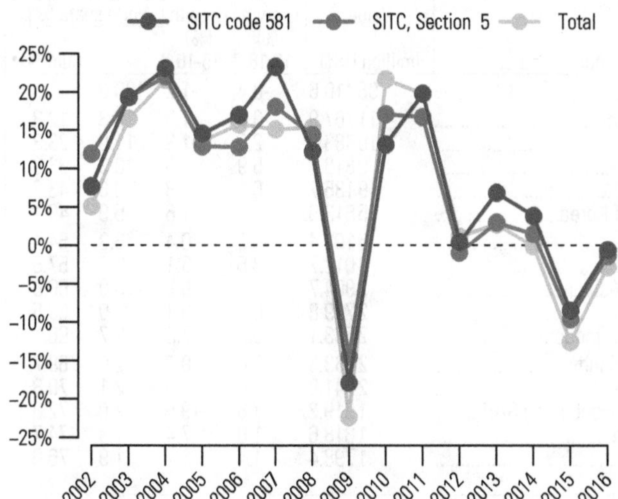

Graph 2: Trade Balance by MDG regions 2016
(Bln US$)

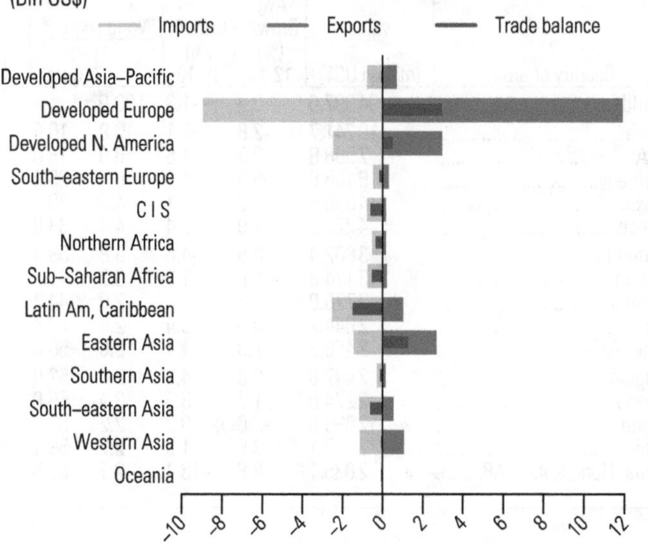

Table 2: Top exporting countries or areas in 2016

Country or area	Value (million US$)	Avg. Growth (%) 12-16	Growth (%) 15-16	World share %	Cum.
World	21861.3	0.3	-0.6	100.0	
Germany	3749.5	-0.5	2.6	17.2	17.2
USA	2606.0	1.7	-3.0	11.9	29.1
China	2169.1	3.6	-3.3	9.9	39.0
Italy	1344.0	0.7	3.0	6.1	45.1
Czechia	847.3	1.0	0.9	3.9	49.0
Poland	838.9	5.2	10.6	3.8	52.9
United Kingdom	786.7	0.7	4.3	3.6	56.5
France	629.5	2.9	7.5	2.9	59.3
Spain	574.1	1.4	2.9	2.6	62.0
Japan	562.0	-3.6	12.8	2.6	64.5
Turkey	552.4	-10.0	-22.0	2.5	67.1
Netherlands	530.1	-2.6	-3.5	2.4	69.5
Switzerland	491.1	-3.8	-7.6	2.2	71.7
Austria	475.1	1.9	9.2	2.2	73.9
Mexico	472.3	2.6	-1.2	2.2	76.1

Table 3: Top importing countries or areas in 2016

Country or area	Value (million US$)	Avg. Growth (%) 12-16	Growth (%) 15-16	World share %	Cum.
World	21316.7	0.3	-0.9	100.0	
USA	1842.6	4.3	-6.0	8.6	8.6
Germany	1560.2	0.3	-0.8	7.3	16.0
Mexico	1336.6	2.4	-2.7	6.3	22.2
France	1052.1	-1.0	3.2	4.9	27.2
China	911.9	5.4	9.2	4.3	31.4
Canada	615.4	-3.7	-3.3	2.9	34.3
Czechia	614.2	-0.1	0.2	2.9	37.2
Poland	570.0	2.8	8.2	2.7	39.9
United Kingdom	526.5	1.1	-9.4	2.5	42.4
Italy	521.0	0.0	2.7	2.4	44.8
Belgium	496.9	0.0	8.9	2.3	47.1
Switzerland	450.1	-1.0	2.7	2.1	49.2
Austria	427.1	1.3	14.0	2.0	51.2
Russian Federation	425.1	-17.2	-2.6	2.0	53.2
Netherlands	418.5	-2.5	-14.5	2.0	55.2

Source: UN Comtrade

582 Plates, sheets, film, foil and strip, of plastics

In 2016, the value (in current US$) of exports of "plates, sheets, film, foil and strip, of plastics" (SITC group 582) decreased by 1.2 percent (compared to -0.4 percent average growth rate from 2012-2016) to reach 95.4 bln US$ (see table 2), while imports decreased by 1.3 percent to reach 95.0 bln US$ (see table 3). Exports of this commodity accounted for 5.3 percent of world exports of SITC section 5, and 0.6 percent of total world merchandise exports (see table 1). Germany, USA and China were the top exporters in 2016 (see table 2). They accounted for 12.3, 11.0 and 10.3 percent of world exports, respectively. China, USA and Germany were the top destinations, with respectively 10.8, 8.0 and 6.4 percent of world imports (see table 3).

The top 15 countries/areas accounted for 76.6 and 61.5 percent of total world exports and imports, respectively (see tables 2 and 3). In 2016, Japan was the country/area with the highest value of net exports (+7.0 bln US$), followed by Germany (+5.7 bln US$). By MDG regions (see graph 2), the largest surpluses in this product group were recorded by Developed Asia-Pacific (+5.9 bln US$), Developed Europe (+5.1 bln US$) and Eastern Asia (+2.3 bln US$). The largest trade deficits were recorded by Latin America and the Caribbean (-5.8 bln US$), South-eastern Asia (-3.0 bln US$) and Commonwealth of Independent States (-2.0 bln US$).

Table 1: Imports (Imp.) and exports (Exp.), 2002-2016, in current US$

		2002	2003	2004	2005	2006	2007	2008	2009	2010	2011	2012	2013	2014	2015	2016
Values in Bln US$	Imp.	35.7	42.2	50.7	57.3	64.5	74.1	81.0	68.8	86.0	99.6	97.0	101.8	104.2	96.3	95.0
	Exp.	35.5	42.1	50.8	57.5	65.8	76.1	82.9	69.1	85.6	99.7	96.8	102.1	105.7	96.6	95.4
As a percentage of SITC section (%)	Imp.	5.1	5.0	5.0	5.0	5.0	4.9	4.7	4.6	4.9	4.9	4.8	4.9	4.9	5.0	5.0
	Exp.	5.4	5.4	5.3	5.3	5.4	5.3	5.0	4.9	5.2	5.2	5.1	5.2	5.3	5.3	5.3
As a percentage of world trade (%)	Imp.	0.5	0.5	0.5	0.5	0.5	0.5	0.5	0.5	0.6	0.5	0.5	0.5	0.6	0.6	0.6
	Exp.	0.6	0.6	0.6	0.6	0.5	0.6	0.5	0.6	0.6	0.6	0.5	0.5	0.6	0.6	0.6

Graph 1: Annual growth rates of exports, 2002–2016
(In percentage by year)

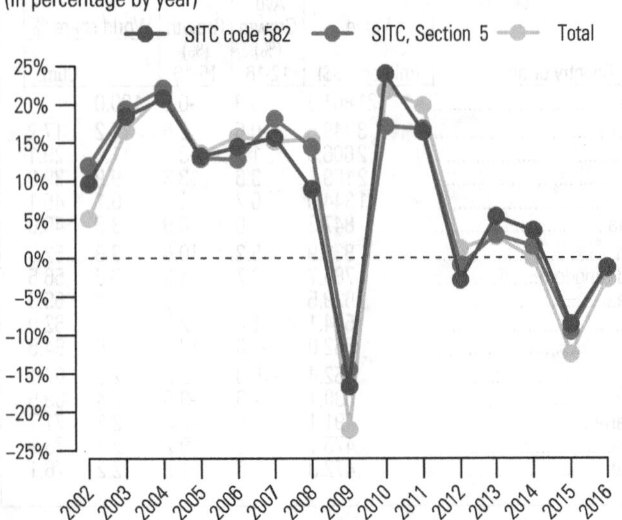

Table 2: Top exporting countries or areas in 2016

Country or area	Value (million US$)	Avg. Growth (%) 12-16	Growth (%) 15-16	World share %	Cum.
World	95410.6	-0.4	-1.2	100.0	
Germany	11767.9	-0.6	1.3	12.3	12.3
USA	10483.0	2.6	-1.3	11.0	23.3
China	9818.7	5.9	-5.5	10.3	33.6
Japan	9135.7	-6.5	4.8	9.6	43.2
Rep. of Korea	5613.9	3.6	1.6	5.9	49.1
Italy	5102.4	-1.2	0.4	5.3	54.4
Belgium	3012.7	-3.5	-3.1	3.2	57.6
Other Asia, nes	2904.7	-5.5	-6.8	3.0	60.6
France	2729.8	0.2	3.1	2.9	63.5
United Kingdom	2533.1	0.3	-7.3	2.7	66.1
Netherlands	2433.3	-2.4	0.7	2.6	68.7
Canada	2041.6	-0.6	-1.6	2.1	70.8
China, Hong Kong SAR	1919.2	-7.8	-19.5	2.0	72.8
Austria	1818.6	1.0	7.4	1.9	74.7
Spain	1798.4	1.4	3.7	1.9	76.6

Graph 2: Trade Balance by MDG regions 2016
(Bln US$)

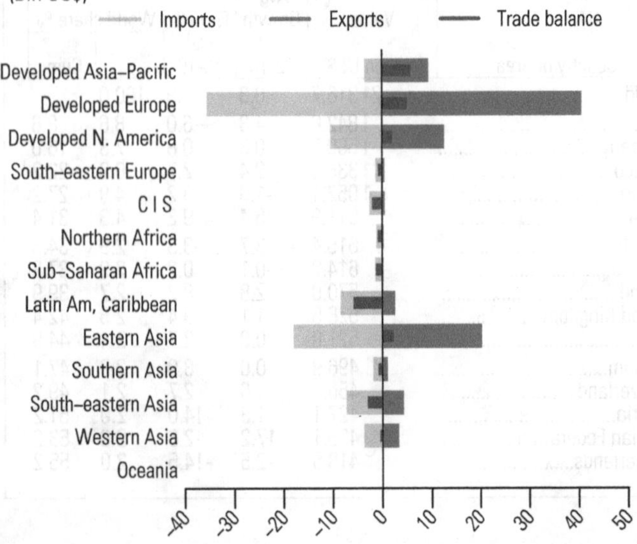

Table 3: Top importing countries or areas in 2016

Country or area	Value (million US$)	Avg. Growth (%) 12-16	Growth (%) 15-16	World share %	Cum.
World	94997.0	-0.5	-1.3	100.0	
China	10241.7	-2.8	-5.1	10.8	10.8
USA	7598.8	2.3	-1.5	8.0	18.8
Germany	6108.6	-0.8	-1.5	6.4	25.2
Mexico	4698.6	4.3	1.1	4.9	30.2
France	4221.2	-1.9	2.4	4.4	34.6
United Kingdom	3602.4	0.8	-4.6	3.8	38.4
Rep. of Korea	3174.3	-8.8	1.2	3.3	41.7
Canada	2778.0	2.4	2.5	2.9	44.7
Italy	2644.2	-0.5	-0.4	2.8	47.4
Other Asia, nes	2458.2	-7.9	-4.1	2.6	50.0
Belgium	2447.8	-0.6	4.2	2.6	52.6
Poland	2274.0	1.7	3.5	2.4	55.0
Japan	2090.8	-2.6	0.2	2.2	57.2
Spain	2073.1	3.5	1.5	2.2	59.4
China, Hong Kong SAR	2035.1	-8.8	-18.4	2.1	61.5

In 2016, the value (in current US$) of exports of "monofilament of any cross-sectional dimension exceed 1 mm, of plastics" (SITC group 583) increased by 2.0 percent (compared to -0.6 percent average growth rate from 2012-2016) to reach 5.0 bln US$ (see table 2), while imports increased by 0.6 percent to reach 4.4 bln US$ (see table 3). Exports of this commodity accounted for 0.3 percent of world exports of SITC section 5, and less than 0.1 percent of total world merchandise exports (see table 1). Germany, China and USA were the top exporters in 2016 (see table 2). They accounted for 32.5, 8.5 and 6.3 percent of world exports, respectively. USA, Germany and France were the top destinations, with respectively 9.5, 7.8 and 6.6 percent of world imports (see table 3).

The top 15 countries/areas accounted for 84.3 and 60.9 percent of total world exports and imports, respectively (see tables 2 and 3). In 2016, Germany was the country/area with the highest value of net exports (+1.3 bln US$), followed by China (+317.9 mln US$). By MDG regions (see graph 2), the largest surpluses in this product group were recorded by Developed Europe (+949.7 mln US$), Eastern Asia (+333.8 mln US$) and Western Asia (+136.6 mln US$). The largest trade deficits were recorded by South-eastern Europe (-253.3 mln US$), Latin America and the Caribbean (-153.5 mln US$) and Commonwealth of Independent States (-118.8 mln US$).

Table 1: Imports (Imp.) and exports (Exp.), 2002-2016, in current US$

		2002	2003	2004	2005	2006	2007	2008	2009	2010	2011	2012	2013	2014	2015	2016
Values in Bln US$	Imp.	2.2	2.7	3.2	3.5	4.2	4.8	5.4	3.8	4.2	4.8	4.5	4.8	4.9	4.4	4.4
	Exp.	2.2	2.7	3.3	3.7	4.2	4.8	5.2	4.3	4.7	5.6	5.1	5.3	5.5	4.9	5.0
As a percentage of SITC section (%)	Imp.	0.3	0.3	0.3	0.3	0.3	0.3	0.3	0.3	0.2	0.2	0.2	0.2	0.2	0.2	0.2
	Exp.	0.3	0.3	0.3	0.3	0.3	0.3	0.3	0.3	0.3	0.3	0.3	0.3	0.3	0.3	0.3
As a percentage of world trade (%)	Imp.	0.0	0.0	0.0	0.0	0.0	0.0	0.0	0.0	0.0	0.0	0.0	0.0	0.0	0.0	0.0
	Exp.	0.0	0.0	0.0	0.0	0.0	0.0	0.0	0.0	0.0	0.0	0.0	0.0	0.0	0.0	0.0

Graph 1: Annual growth rates of exports, 2002–2016

(In percentage by year)

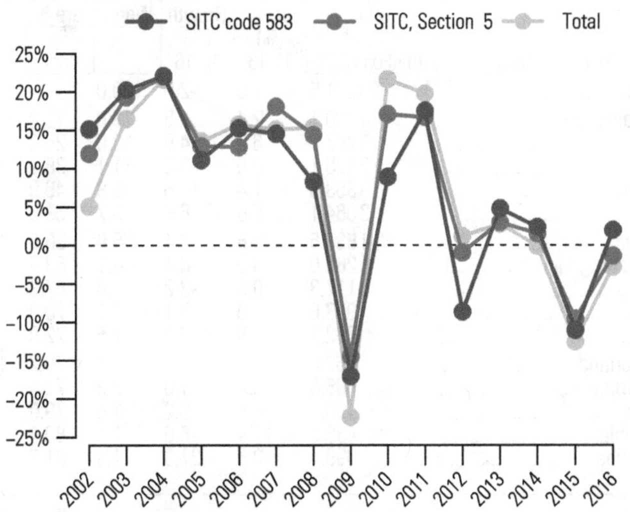

Graph 2: Trade Balance by MDG regions 2016

(Bln US$)

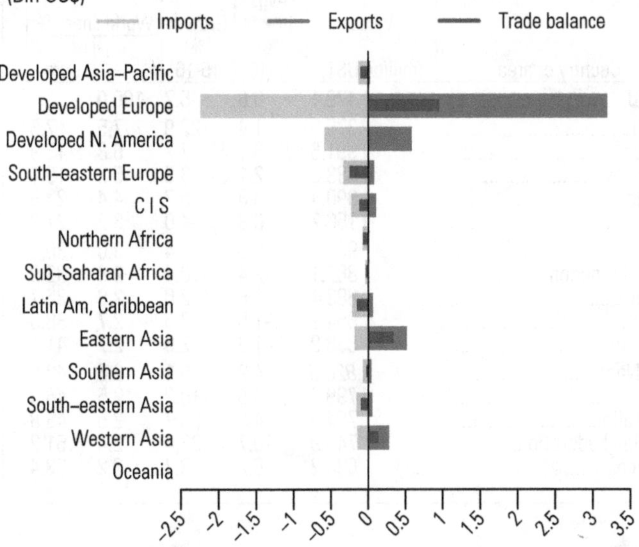

Table 2: Top exporting countries or areas in 2016

Country or area	Value (million US$)	Avg. Growth (%) 12-16	Growth (%) 15-16	World share %	Cum.
World	4955.5	-0.6	2.0	100.0	
Germany	1609.5	-2.8	2.5	32.5	32.5
China	419.9	6.7	3.5	8.5	41.0
USA	310.9	3.3	-5.5	6.3	47.2
Canada	273.8	11.3	7.1	5.5	52.8
Belgium	258.5	-4.8	-4.7	5.2	58.0
Turkey	250.1	-8.4	-15.6	5.0	63.0
Poland	217.8	-1.0	6.6	4.4	67.4
Italy	167.1	-1.8	12.1	3.4	70.8
United Kingdom	158.3	-0.1	-8.4	3.2	74.0
Austria	120.1	-7.1	31.4	2.4	76.4
Netherlands	104.1	6.0	16.5	2.1	78.5
France	96.0	-0.8	13.7	1.9	80.4
Spain	66.9	8.2	14.4	1.4	81.8
Slovakia	66.0	11.3	20.6	1.3	83.1
Czechia	59.2	-1.0	-5.0	1.2	84.3

Table 3: Top importing countries or areas in 2016

Country or area	Value (million US$)	Avg. Growth (%) 12-16	Growth (%) 15-16	World share %	Cum.
World	4389.9	-0.9	0.6	100.0	
USA	417.5	10.3	13.7	9.5	9.5
Germany	341.1	-2.1	3.5	7.8	17.3
France	291.8	-4.0	-0.6	6.6	23.9
Poland	202.6	-0.5	8.2	4.6	28.5
Romania	182.0	6.9	21.9	4.1	32.7
Italy	167.5	2.2	4.6	3.8	36.5
Canada	164.7	5.1	-3.2	3.8	40.3
United Kingdom	150.6	3.1	-0.9	3.4	43.7
Czechia	146.0	-7.0	-7.5	3.3	47.0
Austria	123.1	-3.2	3.5	2.8	49.8
Belgium	118.5	-1.7	7.2	2.7	52.5
China	102.0	2.9	2.4	2.3	54.8
Switzerland	92.9	-5.9	-4.0	2.1	57.0
Mexico	90.9	1.7	-18.2	2.1	59.0
Spain	82.5	3.6	3.7	1.9	60.9

591 Pesticides, disinfectant, put up in preparation, articles or packings for retail

In 2016, the value (in current US$) of exports of "pesticides, disinfectant, put up in preparation, articles or packings for retail" (SITC group 591) decreased by 2.9 percent (compared to 1.5 percent average growth rate from 2012-2016) to reach 30.9 bln US$ (see table 2), while imports decreased by 5.7 percent to reach 31.5 bln US$ (see table 3). Exports of this commodity accounted for 1.7 percent of world exports of SITC section 5, and 0.2 percent of total world merchandise exports (see table 1). Germany, China and USA were the top exporters in 2016 (see table 2). They accounted for 13.0, 12.0 and 11.1 percent of world exports, respectively. Brazil, France and Germany were the top destinations, with respectively 7.5, 6.3 and 5.2 percent of world imports (see table 3).

The top 15 countries/areas accounted for 81.7 and 53.4 percent of total world exports and imports, respectively (see tables 2 and 3). In 2016, China was the country/area with the highest value of net exports (+3.0 bln US$), followed by Germany (+2.4 bln US$). By MDG regions (see graph 2), the largest surpluses in this product group were recorded by Developed Europe (+4.5 bln US$), Eastern Asia (+3.0 bln US$) and Developed North America (+1.0 bln US$). The largest trade deficits were recorded by Latin America and the Caribbean (-4.4 bln US$), Sub-Saharan Africa (-1.5 bln US$) and South-eastern Asia (-1.4 bln US$).

Table 1: Imports (Imp.) and exports (Exp.), 2002-2016, in current US$

		2002	2003	2004	2005	2006	2007	2008	2009	2010	2011	2012	2013	2014	2015	2016
Values in Bln US$	Imp.	11.8	13.2	15.8	16.5	16.6	20.1	25.4	22.8	24.8	29.8	30.7	34.0	36.3	33.4	31.5
	Exp.	10.9	12.7	15.0	16.2	16.3	18.2	24.7	20.3	23.0	27.7	29.1	33.2	35.0	31.8	30.9
As a percentage of SITC section (%)	Imp.	1.7	1.6	1.6	1.4	1.3	1.3	1.5	1.5	1.4	1.5	1.5	1.6	1.7	1.7	1.7
	Exp.	1.7	1.6	1.6	1.5	1.3	1.3	1.5	1.4	1.4	1.4	1.5	1.7	1.7	1.8	1.7
As a percentage of world trade (%)	Imp.	0.2	0.2	0.2	0.2	0.1	0.1	0.2	0.2	0.2	0.2	0.2	0.2	0.2	0.2	0.2
	Exp.	0.2	0.2	0.2	0.2	0.1	0.1	0.2	0.2	0.2	0.2	0.2	0.2	0.2	0.2	0.2

Graph 1: Annual growth rates of exports, 2002–2016
(In percentage by year)

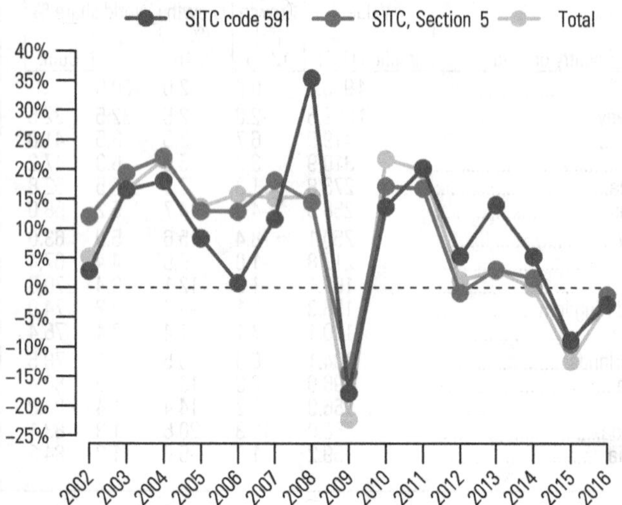

Table 2: Top exporting countries or areas in 2016

Country or area	Value (million US$)	Avg. Growth (%) 12-16	Growth (%) 15-16	World share %	Cum.
World	30931.5	1.5	-2.9	100.0	
Germany	4030.1	2.4	1.5	13.0	13.0
China	3707.8	6.8	4.6	12.0	25.0
USA	3428.1	0.9	-5.5	11.1	36.1
France	3353.8	-1.4	-14.5	10.8	46.9
India	2064.1	5.6	6.9	6.7	53.6
Belgium	1833.5	0.6	4.4	5.9	59.5
United Kingdom	1268.0	-3.9	-8.4	4.1	63.6
Spain	1117.3	-0.6	-3.2	3.6	67.3
Israel	943.6	6.0	-7.1	3.1	70.3
Italy	762.2	1.5	3.2	2.5	72.8
Switzerland	752.0	-6.2	-23.0	2.4	75.2
Netherlands	695.6	-5.8	-1.0	2.2	77.4
Japan	490.3	3.5	8.2	1.6	79.0
Colombia	433.8	11.4	-4.9	1.4	80.4
Argentina	399.4	-0.6	-27.3	1.3	81.7

Graph 2: Trade Balance by MDG regions 2016
(Bln US$)

Imports — Exports — Trade balance

Developed Asia-Pacific
Developed Europe
Developed N. America
South-eastern Europe
CIS
Northern Africa
Sub-Saharan Africa
Latin Am, Caribbean
Eastern Asia
Southern Asia
South-eastern Asia
Western Asia
Oceania

-15 -10 -5 0 5 10 15 20

Table 3: Top importing countries or areas in 2016

Country or area	Value (million US$)	Avg. Growth (%) 12-16	Growth (%) 15-16	World share %	Cum.
World	31479.1	0.6	-5.7	100.0	
Brazil	2375.5	1.4	-22.9	7.5	7.5
France	1991.6	-3.1	-7.7	6.3	13.9
Germany	1633.3	-2.1	-3.5	5.2	19.1
Canada	1390.4	3.8	5.7	4.4	23.5
USA	1156.2	6.9	-4.0	3.7	27.2
India	936.2	6.6	5.4	3.0	30.1
United Kingdom	887.1	-2.4	-10.4	2.8	32.9
Spain	883.4	1.8	-2.6	2.8	35.7
Italy	854.1	-1.5	3.5	2.7	38.5
Belgium	838.9	-1.3	2.5	2.7	41.1
Viet Nam	*826.3*	4.2	5.1	2.6	43.8
Poland	799.7	3.5	-10.3	2.5	46.3
Australia	794.3	4.9	28.7	2.5	48.8
Russian Federation	746.9	10.7	33.4	2.4	51.2
Mexico	694.2	6.2	3.7	2.2	53.4

In 2016, the value (in current US$) of exports of "starches, insulin and wheat gluten; albuminoidal substances; glues" (SITC group 592) increased by 0.3 percent (compared to 0.8 percent average growth rate from 2012-2016) to reach 25.9 bln US$ (see table 2), while imports decreased by 2.0 percent to reach 27.0 bln US$ (see table 3). Exports of this commodity accounted for 1.4 percent of world exports of SITC section 5, and 0.2 percent of total world merchandise exports (see table 1). Germany, USA and China were the top exporters in 2016 (see table 2). They accounted for 13.2, 10.8 and 9.3 percent of world exports, respectively. China, USA and Germany were the top destinations, with respectively 13.4, 9.3 and 7.0 percent of world imports (see table 3).

The top 15 countries/areas accounted for 78.9 and 63.9 percent of total world exports and imports, respectively (see tables 2 and 3). In 2016, Thailand was the country/area with the highest value of net exports (+1.5 bln US$), followed by Germany (+1.5 bln US$). By MDG regions (see graph 2), the largest surpluses in this product group were recorded by Developed Europe (+2.4 bln US$), South-eastern Asia (+1.1 bln US$) and Developed Asia-Pacific (+524.5 mln US$). The largest trade deficits were recorded by Eastern Asia (-1.4 bln US$), Latin America and the Caribbean (-1.1 bln US$) and Western Asia (-688.4 mln US$).

Table 1: Imports (Imp.) and exports (Exp.), 2002-2016, in current US$

		2002	2003	2004	2005	2006	2007	2008	2009	2010	2011	2012	2013	2014	2015	2016
Values in Bln US$	Imp.	10.2	11.8	14.0	15.1	16.4	19.5	22.6	19.3	22.4	27.1	27.5	29.4	30.4	27.6	27.0
	Exp.	9.7	11.0	12.7	13.7	14.9	17.8	20.3	17.9	20.8	24.9	25.1	27.4	28.7	25.8	25.9
As a percentage of SITC section (%)	Imp.	1.4	1.4	1.4	1.3	1.3	1.3	1.3	1.3	1.3	1.3	1.4	1.4	1.4	1.4	1.4
	Exp.	1.5	1.4	1.3	1.3	1.2	1.2	1.2	1.3	1.3	1.3	1.3	1.4	1.4	1.4	1.4
As a percentage of world trade (%)	Imp.	0.2	0.2	0.1	0.1	0.1	0.1	0.1	0.2	0.1	0.1	0.1	0.2	0.2	0.2	0.2
	Exp.	0.2	0.1	0.1	0.1	0.1	0.1	0.1	0.1	0.1	0.1	0.1	0.1	0.2	0.2	0.2

Graph 1: Annual growth rates of exports, 2002–2016
(In percentage by year)

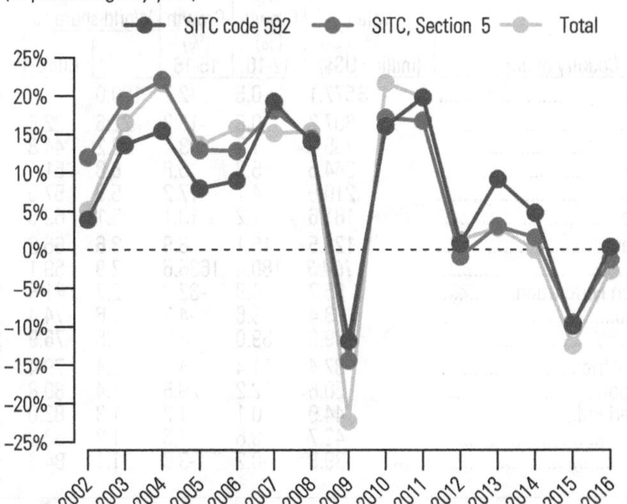

Table 2: Top exporting countries or areas in 2016

Country or area	Value (million US$)	Avg. Growth (%) 12-16	Growth (%) 15-16	World share %	Cum.
World	25914.2	0.8	0.3	100.0	
Germany	3408.0	-1.5	-1.4	13.2	13.2
USA	2808.3	0.5	-0.2	10.8	24.0
China	2421.8	3.1	-5.4	9.3	33.3
Netherlands	2045.6	12.6	21.8	7.9	41.2
Thailand	1827.7	1.6	-5.3	7.1	48.3
France	1606.6	-1.4	-1.2	6.2	54.5
Viet Nam	*1087.4*	5.9	8.9	4.2	58.7
Belgium	1067.2	9.4	9.9	4.1	62.8
New Zealand	848.9	-3.7	-18.7	3.3	66.1
Japan	720.9	-6.1	4.7	2.8	68.9
Italy	696.0	-1.8	-1.1	2.7	71.5
Other Asia, nes	519.9	-3.6	-6.5	2.0	73.5
Rep. of Korea	479.7	1.0	3.1	1.9	75.4
Ireland	454.6	-1.5	-4.1	1.8	77.1
China, Hong Kong SAR	446.9	1.4	-3.4	1.7	78.9

Graph 2: Trade Balance by MDG regions 2016
(Bln US$)

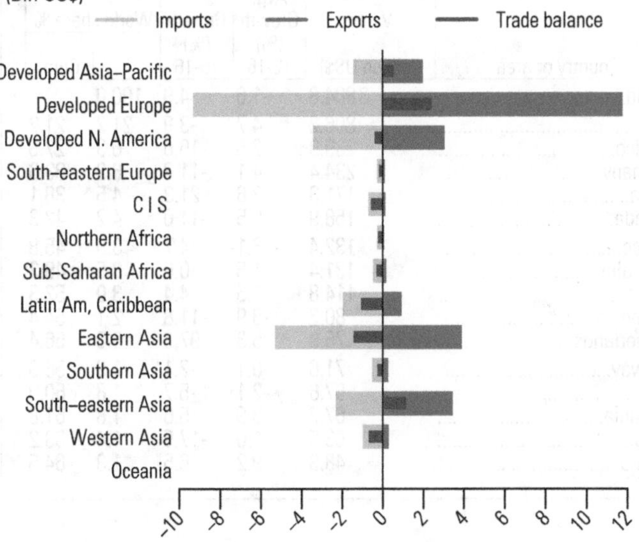

Table 3: Top importing countries or areas in 2016

Country or area	Value (million US$)	Avg. Growth (%) 12-16	Growth (%) 15-16	World share %	Cum.
World	27048.4	-0.5	-2.0	100.0	
China	3626.6	2.3	-0.5	13.4	13.4
USA	2514.8	1.8	-2.0	9.3	22.7
Germany	1885.2	-3.7	-8.2	7.0	29.7
Japan	1117.0	-4.5	-6.7	4.1	33.8
Canada	926.2	1.5	-1.8	3.4	37.2
France	911.7	-0.9	3.3	3.4	40.6
Netherlands	867.9	1.7	-5.8	3.2	43.8
United Kingdom	864.5	-0.2	-5.6	3.2	47.0
Mexico	808.2	1.1	1.7	3.0	50.0
Indonesia	717.5	-3.4	-6.5	2.7	52.6
Belgium	675.2	0.1	11.3	2.5	55.1
Rep. of Korea	659.8	-1.5	-2.8	2.4	57.6
Other Asia, nes	590.0	-5.7	-4.9	2.2	59.8
Spain	568.4	0.8	2.3	2.1	61.9
Poland	561.1	-2.8	3.4	2.1	63.9

593 Explosives and pyrotechnic products

In 2016, the value (in current US$) of exports of "explosives and pyrotechnic products" (SITC group 593) decreased by 2.7 percent (compared to -0.5 percent average growth rate from 2012-2016) to reach 3.6 bln US$ (see table 2), while imports decreased by 4.9 percent to reach 3.8 bln US$ (see table 3). Exports of this commodity accounted for 0.2 percent of world exports of SITC section 5, and less than 0.1 percent of total world merchandise exports (see table 1). China, USA and Czechia were the top exporters in 2016 (see table 2). They accounted for 22.6, 22.2 and 6.8 percent of world exports, respectively. USA, Mexico and Germany were the top destinations, with respectively 21.2, 6.3 and 6.2 percent of world imports (see table 3).

The top 15 countries/areas accounted for 84.3 and 64.5 percent of total world exports and imports, respectively (see tables 2 and 3). In 2016, China was the country/area with the highest value of net exports (+635.8 mln US$), followed by Czechia (+209.8 mln US$). By MDG regions (see graph 2), the largest surpluses in this product group were recorded by Eastern Asia (+575.1 mln US$), Developed North America (+36.5 mln US$) and Southern Asia (+24.9 mln US$). The largest trade deficits were recorded by Developed Asia-Pacific (-208.5 mln US$), Sub-Saharan Africa (-175.6 mln US$) and Latin America and the Caribbean (-165.1 mln US$).

Table 1: Imports (Imp.) and exports (Exp.), 2002-2016, in current US$

		2002	2003	2004	2005	2006	2007	2008	2009	2010	2011	2012	2013	2014	2015	2016
Values in Bln US$	Imp.	1.5	1.8	2.1	2.3	2.6	3.0	3.2	3.0	3.3	3.8	4.1	4.3	4.3	4.0	3.8
	Exp.	1.2	1.5	1.8	1.9	2.3	2.5	2.8	2.6	3.1	3.5	3.6	3.8	4.0	3.7	3.6
As a percentage of SITC section (%)	Imp.	0.2	0.2	0.2	0.2	0.2	0.2	0.2	0.2	0.2	0.2	0.2	0.2	0.2	0.2	0.2
	Exp.	0.2	0.2	0.2	0.2	0.2	0.2	0.2	0.2	0.2	0.2	0.2	0.2	0.2	0.2	0.2
As a percentage of world trade (%)	Imp.	0.0	0.0	0.0	0.0	0.0	0.0	0.0	0.0	0.0	0.0	0.0	0.0	0.0	0.0	0.0
	Exp.	0.0	0.0	0.0	0.0	0.0	0.0	0.0	0.0	0.0	0.0	0.0	0.0	0.0	0.0	0.0

Graph 1: Annual growth rates of exports, 2002–2016
(In percentage by year)

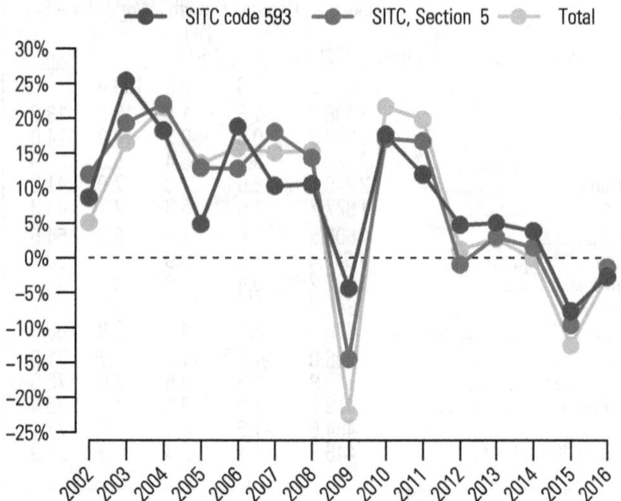

Table 2: Top exporting countries or areas in 2016

Country or area	Value (million US$)	Avg. Growth (%) 12-16	Growth (%) 15-16	World share %	Cum.
World	3577.1	-0.5	-2.7	100.0	
China	807.2	-0.6	-13.2	22.6	22.6
USA	795.5	-1.3	-3.7	22.2	44.8
Czechia	244.5	5.3	6.8	6.8	51.6
Canada	210.9	-4.1	-17.2	5.9	57.5
France	181.6	1.2	13.1	5.1	62.6
Germany	128.5	-15.1	8.9	3.6	66.2
Cuba	*104.3*	180.4	1636.6	2.9	69.1
Russian Federation	95.7	-4.9	-32.2	2.7	71.8
Mexico	93.4	-3.6	-4.3	2.6	74.4
Spain	89.6	59.0	3.9	2.5	76.9
South Africa	87.4	-11.4	4.5	2.4	79.4
Singapore	50.6	12.2	29.6	1.4	80.8
Switzerland	44.9	0.1	1.2	1.3	82.0
India	42.7	8.6	7.5	1.2	83.2
Italy	39.8	-0.2	-3.8	1.1	84.3

Graph 2: Trade Balance by MDG regions 2016
(Bln US$)

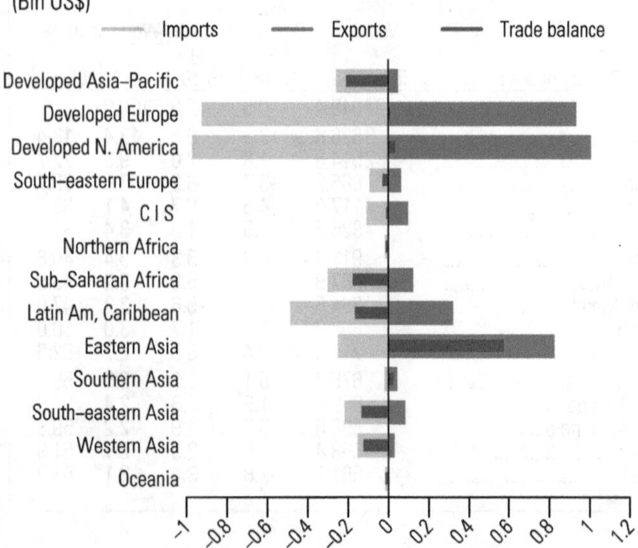

Table 3: Top importing countries or areas in 2016

Country or area	Value (million US$)	Avg. Growth (%) 12-16	Growth (%) 15-16	World share %	Cum.
World	3804.8	-1.6	-4.9	100.0	
USA	806.2	4.7	-3.9	21.2	21.2
Mexico	239.3	-2.5	-16.0	6.3	27.5
Germany	234.4	-4.1	-11.3	6.2	33.6
China	171.3	12.6	21.3	4.5	38.1
Canada	158.9	-5.5	-11.0	4.2	42.3
France	132.4	-18.1	34.7	3.5	45.8
Australia	131.4	-1.5	-0.6	3.5	49.3
Japan	114.8	1.5	4.4	3.0	52.3
Indonesia	80.2	-8.9	-11.8	2.1	54.4
Netherlands	75.9	5.3	97.3	2.0	56.4
Norway	71.6	-0.1	-2.1	1.9	58.3
Italy	67.6	-2.1	-5.7	1.8	60.0
Romania	67.2	3.9	5.6	1.8	61.8
Chile	53.5	1.0	-17.5	1.4	63.2
Poland	48.3	9.2	-6.5	1.3	64.5

In 2016, the value (in current US$) of exports of "prepared additives, de-icing and liquid for transmissions; lubricant, etc" (SITC group 597) decreased by 3.4 percent (compared to -2.8 percent average growth rate from 2012-2016) to reach 20.8 bln US$ (see table 2), while imports decreased by 2.7 percent to reach 22.5 bln US$ (see table 3). Exports of this commodity accounted for 1.2 percent of world exports of SITC section 5, and 0.1 percent of total world merchandise exports (see table 1). USA, Germany and France were the top exporters in 2016 (see table 2). They accounted for 21.6, 14.8 and 14.3 percent of world exports, respectively. China, Germany and Belgium were the top destinations, with respectively 13.3, 6.9 and 4.5 percent of world imports (see table 3).

The top 15 countries/areas accounted for 90.3 and 62.3 percent of total world exports and imports, respectively (see tables 2 and 3). In 2016, USA was the country/area with the highest value of net exports (+3.7 bln US$), followed by France (+2.0 bln US$). By MDG regions (see graph 2), the largest surpluses in this product group were recorded by Developed Europe (+3.4 bln US$), Developed North America (+3.2 bln US$) and Developed Asia-Pacific (+385.2 mln US$). The largest trade deficits were recorded by Eastern Asia (-3.5 bln US$), Latin America and the Caribbean (-1.5 bln US$) and Western Asia (-979.5 mln US$).

Table 1: Imports (Imp.) and exports (Exp.), 2002-2016, in current US$

		2002	2003	2004	2005	2006	2007	2008	2009	2010	2011	2012	2013	2014	2015	2016
Values in Bln US$	Imp.	7.9	8.8	10.5	12.0	13.9	16.2	19.1	16.5	19.8	23.5	23.6	25.0	25.8	23.2	22.5
	Exp.	7.2	8.2	9.8	11.2	13.0	15.2	18.2	15.6	19.0	22.9	23.3	23.5	24.4	21.5	20.8
As a percentage of SITC section (%)	Imp.	1.1	1.1	1.0	1.0	1.1	1.1	1.1	1.1	1.1	1.1	1.2	1.2	1.2	1.2	1.2
	Exp.	1.1	1.0	1.0	1.0	1.1	1.1	1.1	1.1	1.1	1.2	1.2	1.2	1.2	1.2	1.2
As a percentage of world trade (%)	Imp.	0.1	0.1	0.1	0.1	0.1	0.1	0.1	0.1	0.1	0.1	0.1	0.1	0.1	0.1	0.1
	Exp.	0.1	0.1	0.1	0.1	0.1	0.1	0.1	0.1	0.1	0.1	0.1	0.1	0.1	0.1	0.1

Graph 1: Annual growth rates of exports, 2002–2016

(In percentage by year)

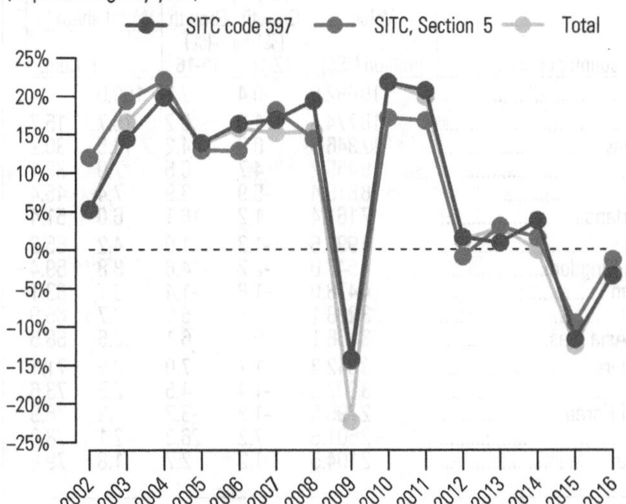

Graph 2: Trade Balance by MDG regions 2016

(Bln US$)

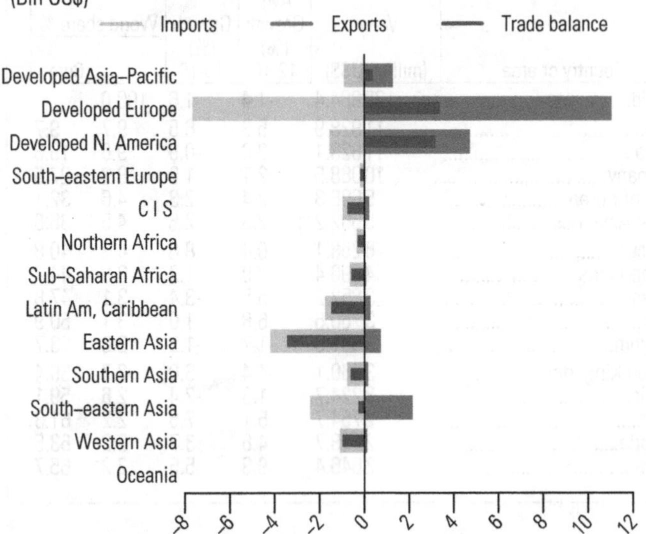

Table 2: Top exporting countries or areas in 2016

Country or area	Value (million US$)	Avg. Growth (%) 12-16	Growth (%) 15-16	World share %	Cum.
World	20800.9	-2.8	-3.4	100.0	
USA	4482.8	-3.3	-8.5	21.6	21.6
Germany	3069.4	0.9	1.7	14.8	36.3
France	2981.4	-1.3	-4.2	14.3	50.6
Singapore	2012.2	1.3	4.7	9.7	60.3
Belgium	1227.8	-2.9	-2.0	5.9	66.2
Italy	1198.7	-0.9	1.2	5.8	72.0
Japan	1197.4	-0.2	7.7	5.8	77.7
Netherlands	753.4	-5.3	0.1	3.6	81.4
United Kingdom	508.4	-8.2	-5.8	2.4	83.8
China	325.4	9.0	7.1	1.6	85.4
Spain	249.9	-2.7	2.0	1.2	86.6
Canada	242.6	-3.5	-2.9	1.2	87.7
Switzerland	222.3	2.4	-3.8	1.1	88.8
Rep. of Korea	154.4	-2.0	3.3	0.7	89.5
India	151.7	12.1	12.2	0.7	90.3

Table 3: Top importing countries or areas in 2016

Country or area	Value (million US$)	Avg. Growth (%) 12-16	Growth (%) 15-16	World share %	Cum.
World	22531.7	-1.2	-2.7	100.0	
China	2995.2	4.3	3.9	13.3	13.3
Germany	1561.8	1.2	0.1	6.9	20.2
Belgium	1009.5	-4.1	-6.4	4.5	24.7
Singapore	983.7	2.1	-4.1	4.4	29.1
France	972.9	-0.7	-1.7	4.3	33.4
USA	831.9	-0.6	-5.0	3.7	37.1
Russian Federation	734.6	-5.4	3.6	3.3	40.3
Canada	722.1	-3.9	-6.5	3.2	43.5
Rep. of Korea	689.5	0.1	-5.5	3.1	46.6
Italy	659.1	-3.3	-5.3	2.9	49.5
Mexico	651.7	6.6	8.9	2.9	52.4
Netherlands	639.6	-2.5	-7.2	2.8	55.3
Japan	603.4	-2.8	-0.2	2.7	57.9
India	530.9	2.8	5.9	2.4	60.3
Thailand	440.3	2.1	5.5	2.0	62.3

598 Miscellaneous chemical products, nes

In 2016, the value (in current US$) of exports of "miscellaneous chemical products, nes" (SITC group 598) increased by 2.9 percent (compared to -0.4 percent average growth rate from 2012-2016) to reach 119.7 bln US$ (see table 2), while imports increased by 1.6 percent to reach 122.9 bln US$ (see table 3). Exports of this commodity accounted for 6.7 percent of world exports of SITC section 5, and 0.7 percent of total world merchandise exports (see table 1). USA, Germany and China were the top exporters in 2016 (see table 2). They accounted for 15.7, 14.5 and 7.9 percent of world exports, respectively. USA, China and Germany were the top destinations, with respectively 9.7, 9.6 and 8.2 percent of world imports (see table 3).

The top 15 countries/areas accounted for 79.8 and 65.7 percent of total world exports and imports, respectively (see tables 2 and 3). In 2016, Germany was the country/area with the highest value of net exports (+7.3 bln US$), followed by USA (+6.8 bln US$). By MDG regions (see graph 2), the largest surpluses in this product group were recorded by Developed Europe (+11.3 bln US$), Developed North America (+6.2 bln US$) and Developed Asia-Pacific (+4.2 bln US$). The largest trade deficits were recorded by Eastern Asia (-7.6 bln US$), Latin America and the Caribbean (-4.6 bln US$) and Southern Asia (-3.0 bln US$).

Table 1: Imports (Imp.) and exports (Exp.), 2002-2016, in current US$

		2002	2003	2004	2005	2006	2007	2008	2009	2010	2011	2012	2013	2014	2015	2016
Values in Bln US$	Imp.	44.0	51.7	60.2	68.0	79.1	93.8	109.8	92.1	112.3	136.2	130.0	131.0	132.4	120.9	122.9
	Exp.	41.2	48.4	57.0	63.5	75.2	89.0	109.8	89.2	108.2	128.8	121.7	127.3	131.6	116.3	119.7
As a percentage of SITC section (%)	Imp.	6.2	6.2	5.9	5.9	6.2	6.2	6.3	6.2	6.5	6.6	6.4	6.3	6.3	6.3	6.5
	Exp.	6.3	6.2	6.0	5.9	6.2	6.2	6.6	6.3	6.5	6.7	6.4	6.4	6.6	6.4	6.7
As a percentage of world trade (%)	Imp.	0.7	0.7	0.6	0.6	0.6	0.7	0.7	0.7	0.7	0.7	0.7	0.7	0.7	0.7	0.8
	Exp.	0.6	0.6	0.6	0.6	0.6	0.6	0.7	0.7	0.7	0.7	0.7	0.7	0.7	0.7	0.7

Graph 1: Annual growth rates of exports, 2002–2016
(In percentage by year)

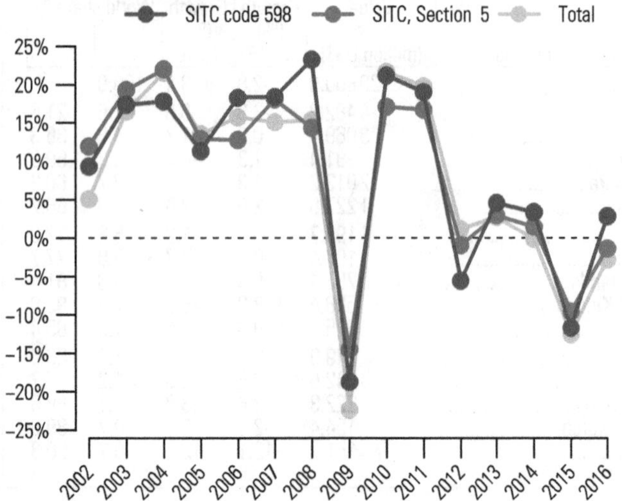

Graph 2: Trade Balance by MDG regions 2016
(Bln US$)

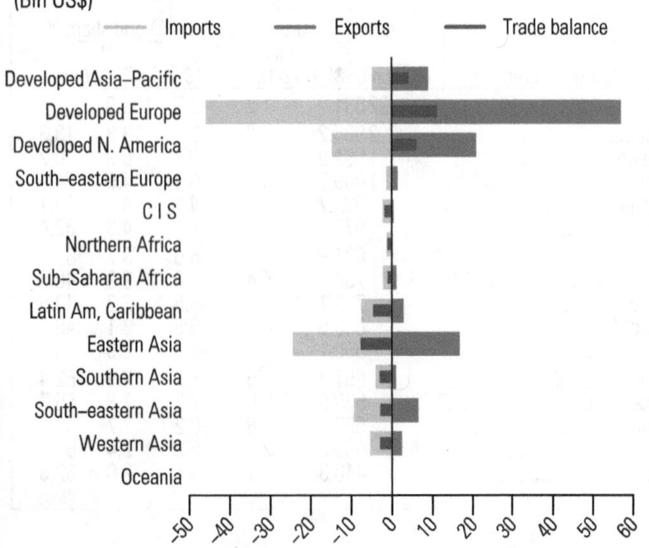

Table 2: Top exporting countries or areas in 2016

Country or area	Value (million US$)	Avg. Growth (%) 12-16	Growth (%) 15-16	World share %	Cum.
World	119692.0	-0.4	2.9	100.0	
USA	18774.4	1.0	0.2	15.7	15.7
Germany	17346.6	0.3	4.2	14.5	30.2
China	9455.2	4.7	0.5	7.9	38.1
Japan	8816.4	-5.9	3.9	7.4	45.4
Netherlands	7161.4	1.2	16.1	6.0	51.4
France	4996.5	-1.3	1.0	4.2	55.6
United Kingdom	4547.0	-2.2	-14.6	3.8	59.4
Belgium	4478.0	-1.6	-1.4	3.7	63.1
Ireland	3288.1	-2.1	5.5	2.7	65.9
Other Asia, nes	3158.1	0.7	-6.1	2.6	68.5
Singapore	3042.3	1.7	7.0	2.5	71.1
Italy	3007.3	-1.4	4.5	2.5	73.6
Rep. of Korea	2795.5	-1.3	-3.3	2.3	75.9
Spain	2501.5	7.2	26.3	2.1	78.0
Canada	2104.5	-1.2	2.7	1.8	79.8

Table 3: Top importing countries or areas in 2016

Country or area	Value (million US$)	Avg. Growth (%) 12-16	Growth (%) 15-16	World share %	Cum.
World	122884.4	-1.4	1.6	100.0	
USA	11928.9	5.3	6.5	9.7	9.7
China	11823.1	-2.0	-0.9	9.6	19.3
Germany	10068.5	-2.1	1.8	8.2	27.5
Rep. of Korea	5606.3	-2.4	2.3	4.6	32.1
Other Asia, nes	5502.2	-2.6	-2.5	4.5	36.6
France	5256.1	0.4	8.8	4.3	40.8
Netherlands	4696.4	-2.9	31.2	3.8	44.7
Japan	3852.2	-5.5	-3.4	3.1	47.8
Italy	3760.5	-6.8	1.0	3.1	50.9
Belgium	3501.5	-1.7	-1.9	2.8	53.7
United Kingdom	3360.1	-4.4	-8.0	2.7	56.4
Mexico	3224.7	1.3	-2.4	2.6	59.1
India	2754.7	5.1	7.5	2.2	61.3
Canada	2718.7	-4.6	-3.7	2.2	63.5
Spain	2646.4	-9.8	5.5	2.2	65.7

Manufactured goods classified chiefly by material

(SITC Section 6)

611 Leather

In 2016, the value (in current US$) of exports of "leather" (SITC group 611) decreased by 12.6 percent (compared to -3.7 percent average growth rate from 2012-2016) to reach 20.4 bln US$ (see table 2), while imports decreased by 12.1 percent to reach 20.5 bln US$ (see table 3). Exports of this commodity accounted for 1.0 percent of world exports of SITC section 6, and 0.1 percent of total world merchandise exports (see table 1). Italy, Brazil and China, Hong Kong SAR were the top exporters in 2016 (see table 2). They accounted for 20.3, 9.9 and 7.6 percent of world exports, respectively. China, Italy and China, Hong Kong SAR were the top destinations, with respectively 17.3, 10.7 and 8.5 percent of world imports (see table 3).

The top 15 countries/areas accounted for 75.7 and 75.4 percent of total world exports and imports, respectively (see tables 2 and 3). In 2016, Brazil was the country/area with the highest value of net exports (+2.0 bln US$), followed by Italy (+1.9 bln US$). By MDG regions (see graph 2), the largest surpluses in this product group were recorded by Latin America and the Caribbean (+2.4 bln US$), Developed Europe (+885.2 mln US$) and Southern Asia (+829.5 mln US$). The largest trade deficits were recorded by Eastern Asia (-2.5 bln US$), South-eastern Asia (-1.8 bln US$) and South-eastern Europe (-904.7 mln US$).

Table 1: Imports (Imp.) and exports (Exp.), 2002-2016, in current US$

		2002	2003	2004	2005	2006	2007	2008	2009	2010	2011	2012	2013	2014	2015	2016
Values in Bln US$	Imp.	16.2	18.0	19.8	19.9	21.7	23.2	21.7	15.2	19.8	23.3	22.0	24.5	26.5	23.3	20.5
	Exp.	16.9	18.5	20.5	20.6	22.8	24.9	23.1	16.5	23.5	24.2	23.8	26.2	27.3	23.4	20.4
As a percentage of SITC section (%)	Imp.	1.8	1.7	1.5	1.4	1.3	1.2	1.0	1.0	1.0	1.0	1.0	1.1	1.2	1.2	1.1
	Exp.	1.9	1.8	1.6	1.5	1.4	1.3	1.1	1.1	1.2	1.0	1.1	1.2	1.2	1.1	1.0
As a percentage of world trade (%)	Imp.	0.2	0.2	0.2	0.2	0.2	0.2	0.1	0.1	0.1	0.1	0.1	0.1	0.1	0.1	0.1
	Exp.	0.3	0.2	0.2	0.2	0.2	0.2	0.1	0.1	0.2	0.1	0.1	0.1	0.1	0.1	0.1

Graph 1: Annual growth rates of exports, 2002–2016
(In percentage by year)

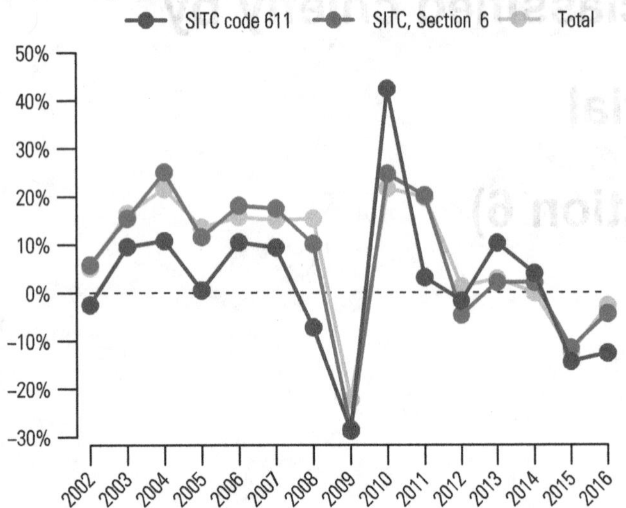

Table 2: Top exporting countries or areas in 2016

Country or area	Value (million US$)	Avg. Growth (%) 12-16	Growth (%) 15-16	World share %	Cum.
World	20420.8	-3.7	-12.6	100.0	
Italy	4143.2	-2.8	-4.9	20.3	20.3
Brazil	2027.3	-0.5	-10.2	9.9	30.2
China, Hong Kong SAR	1558.7	-9.5	-21.6	7.6	37.8
USA	1106.8	3.0	-9.7	5.4	43.3
India	908.0	-4.1	-17.1	4.4	47.7
Germany	724.0	-4.5	-8.9	3.5	51.3
Argentina	710.7	-3.7	-13.5	3.5	54.7
Rep. of Korea	682.7	-7.3	-25.1	3.3	58.1
China	606.2	8.8	-6.2	3.0	61.1
Austria	579.3	6.8	-2.3	2.8	63.9
Thailand	554.8	2.1	-6.8	2.7	66.6
Spain	515.2	-1.9	1.7	2.5	69.1
Viet Nam	*487.0*	17.9	8.9	2.4	71.5
Other Asia, nes	481.7	-9.3	-24.3	2.4	73.9
France	364.6	-3.3	1.2	1.8	75.7

Graph 2: Trade Balance by MDG regions 2016
(Bln US$)

Imports — Exports — Trade balance

Developed Asia-Pacific
Developed Europe
Developed N. America
South-eastern Europe
CIS
Northern Africa
Sub-Saharan Africa
Latin Am, Caribbean
Eastern Asia
Southern Asia
South-eastern Asia
Western Asia
Oceania

-8 -6 -4 -2 0 2 4 6 8

Table 3: Top importing countries or areas in 2016

Country or area	Value (million US$)	Avg. Growth (%) 12-16	Growth (%) 15-16	World share %	Cum.
World	20514.0	-1.7	-12.1	100.0	
China	3550.2	-3.6	-20.1	17.3	17.3
Italy	2199.3	-3.6	-13.1	10.7	28.0
China, Hong Kong SAR	1739.1	-12.7	-26.1	8.5	36.5
Viet Nam	*1685.7*	16.8	5.1	8.2	44.7
Mexico	963.4	7.7	0.6	4.7	49.4
USA	763.2	4.1	-0.4	3.7	53.1
Germany	574.4	-8.8	-13.2	2.8	55.9
Spain	566.3	-1.9	-22.7	2.8	58.7
India	552.3	7.2	-8.1	2.7	61.4
Romania	542.3	-3.7	-6.6	2.6	64.0
France	485.6	-4.2	2.9	2.4	66.4
Portugal	483.6	0.6	-6.2	2.4	68.8
Poland	473.5	0.3	-0.6	2.3	71.1
Thailand	442.4	1.1	-7.3	2.2	73.2
Indonesia	437.0	2.3	-5.4	2.1	75.4

In 2016, the value (in current US$) of exports of "manufactures of leather or of composition leather, nes; saddlery, harness" (SITC group 612) increased by 6.1 percent (compared to 6.6 percent average growth rate from 2012-2016) to reach 5.0 bln US$ (see table 2), while imports increased by 3.9 percent to reach 4.1 bln US$ (see table 3). Exports of this commodity accounted for 0.3 percent of world exports of SITC section 6, and less than 0.1 percent of total world merchandise exports (see table 1). China, Italy and France were the top exporters in 2016 (see table 2). They accounted for 21.9, 7.9 and 7.0 percent of world exports, respectively. USA, Romania and Germany were the top destinations, with respectively 16.0, 6.6 and 5.7 percent of world imports (see table 3).

The top 15 countries/areas accounted for 76.5 and 70.2 percent of total world exports and imports, respectively (see tables 2 and 3). In 2016, China was the country/area with the highest value of net exports (+988.4 mln US$), followed by Hungary (+264.2 mln US$). By MDG regions (see graph 2), the largest surpluses in this product group were recorded by Eastern Asia (+988.9 mln US$), Developed Europe (+633.8 mln US$) and Southern Asia (+231.7 mln US$). The largest trade deficits were recorded by Developed North America (-471.8 mln US$), South-eastern Europe (-280.3 mln US$) and Developed Asia-Pacific (-160.8 mln US$).

Table 1: Imports (Imp.) and exports (Exp.), 2002-2016, in current US$

		2002	2003	2004	2005	2006	2007	2008	2009	2010	2011	2012	2013	2014	2015	2016
Values in Bln US$	Imp.	1.6	1.9	2.4	2.4	2.5	2.8	2.8	2.2	2.7	3.2	3.2	3.5	4.1	4.0	4.1
	Exp.	2.0	2.3	2.9	3.1	3.4	3.5	3.4	2.7	3.1	3.6	3.8	4.2	4.6	4.7	5.0
As a percentage of SITC section (%)	Imp.	0.2	0.2	0.2	0.2	0.2	0.1	0.1	0.1	0.1	0.1	0.1	0.2	0.2	0.2	0.2
	Exp.	0.2	0.2	0.2	0.2	0.2	0.2	0.2	0.2	0.2	0.2	0.2	0.2	0.2	0.2	0.3
As a percentage of world trade (%)	Imp.	0.0	0.0	0.0	0.0	0.0	0.0	0.0	0.0	0.0	0.0	0.0	0.0	0.0	0.0	0.0
	Exp.	0.0	0.0	0.0	0.0	0.0	0.0	0.0	0.0	0.0	0.0	0.0	0.0	0.0	0.0	0.0

Graph 1: Annual growth rates of exports, 2002–2016
(In percentage by year)

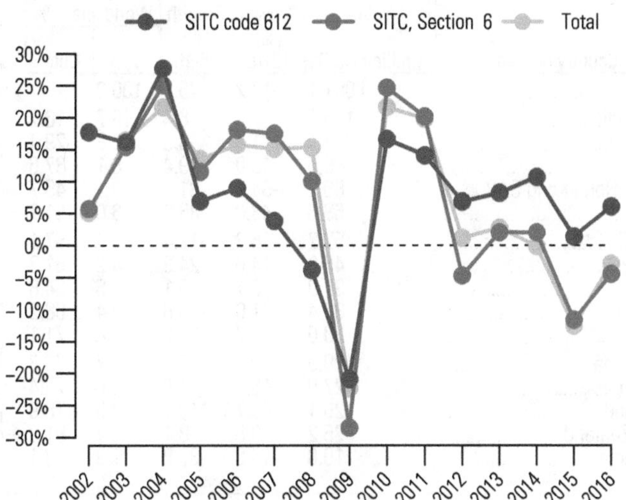

Table 2: Top exporting countries or areas in 2016

Country or area	Value (million US$)	Avg. Growth (%) 12-16	Growth (%) 15-16	World share %	Cum.
World	4955.1	6.6	6.1	100.0	
China	1087.3	8.2	-0.1	21.9	21.9
Italy	391.9	22.1	27.6	7.9	29.9
France	346.0	-3.9	8.0	7.0	36.8
Hungary	340.4	15.0	13.8	6.9	43.7
USA	239.1	0.9	1.6	4.8	48.5
Germany	222.7	1.7	6.6	4.5	53.0
India	209.7	7.7	-2.7	4.2	57.3
Croatia	156.0	7.8	-0.5	3.1	60.4
Poland	153.3	15.4	0.1	3.1	63.5
Mexico	125.1	-7.8	-5.1	2.5	66.0
Netherlands	111.2	16.2	44.7	2.2	68.3
Austria	110.6	2.3	3.8	2.2	70.5
Slovakia	107.1	11.1	27.6	2.2	72.7
Singapore	95.6	9.5	42.5	1.9	74.6
Romania	92.7	58.5	35.5	1.9	76.5

Graph 2: Trade Balance by MDG regions 2016
(Bln US$)

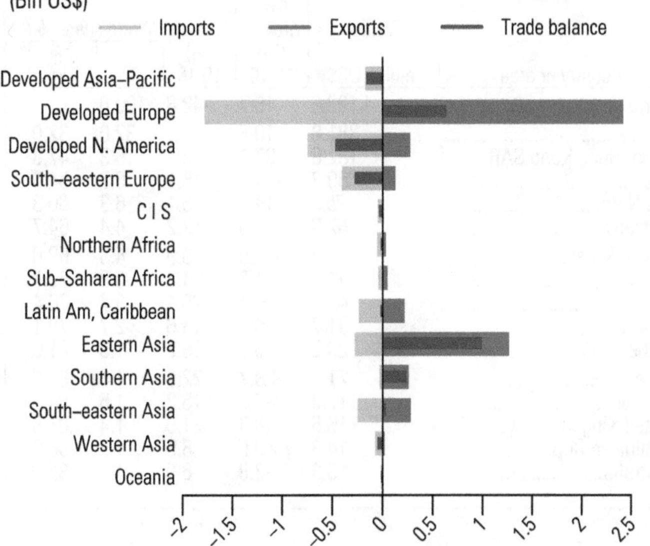

Table 3: Top importing countries or areas in 2016

Country or area	Value (million US$)	Avg. Growth (%) 12-16	Growth (%) 15-16	World share %	Cum.
World	4111.5	6.3	3.9	100.0	
USA	657.5	2.3	-1.6	16.0	16.0
Romania	273.3	27.2	21.8	6.6	22.6
Germany	232.6	5.4	-8.1	5.7	28.3
Italy	215.5	14.4	15.3	5.2	33.5
Mexico	200.4	6.2	7.3	4.9	38.4
France	184.4	0.8	7.2	4.5	42.9
United Kingdom	179.6	9.5	7.2	4.4	47.3
Singapore	150.8	11.1	-26.3	3.7	50.9
Poland	137.9	8.6	-9.3	3.4	54.3
Czechia	132.5	10.9	-11.2	3.2	57.5
Netherlands	124.5	15.2	20.9	3.0	60.5
China, Hong Kong SAR	106.5	-3.2	0.7	2.6	63.1
Japan	104.8	0.1	4.4	2.5	65.7
China	98.9	2.8	9.8	2.4	68.1
Canada	85.9	-2.9	-8.1	2.1	70.2

613 Furskins, tanned or dressed, other than those of heading 848.31

In 2016, the value (in current US$) of exports of "furskins, tanned or dressed, other than those of heading 848.31" (SITC group 613) decreased by 46.9 percent (compared to -17.2 percent average growth rate from 2012-2016) to reach 1.1 bln US$ (see table 2), while imports decreased by 42.8 percent to reach 1.2 bln US$ (see table 3). Exports of this commodity accounted for 0.1 percent of world exports of SITC section 6, and less than 0.1 percent of total world merchandise exports (see table 1). Cambodia, Viet Nam and Italy were the top exporters in 2016 (see table 2). They accounted for 16.7, 12.8 and 8.1 percent of world exports, respectively. China, China, Hong Kong SAR and Italy were the top destinations, with respectively 32.0, 15.3 and 6.7 percent of world imports (see table 3).

The top 15 countries/areas accounted for 83.1 and 87.9 percent of total world exports and imports, respectively (see tables 2 and 3). In 2016, Cambodia was the country/area with the highest value of net exports (+176.6 mln US$), followed by Viet Nam (+60.3 mln US$). By MDG regions (see graph 2), the largest surpluses in this product group were recorded by South-eastern Asia (+261.6 mln US$), Latin America and the Caribbean (+66.6 mln US$) and Western Asia (+23.2 mln US$). The largest trade deficits were recorded by Eastern Asia (-465.0 mln US$), Developed North America (-19.8 mln US$) and Commonwealth of Independent States (-13.1 mln US$).

Table 1: Imports (Imp.) and exports (Exp.), 2002-2016, in current US$

		2002	2003	2004	2005	2006	2007	2008	2009	2010	2011	2012	2013	2014	2015	2016
Values in Bln US$	Imp.	1.2	1.4	1.6	1.7	1.8	1.9	2.0	1.5	2.0	2.4	2.5	2.9	2.3	2.1	1.2
	Exp.	1.2	1.3	1.5	1.7	1.8	1.7	1.8	1.4	1.6	2.0	2.3	2.9	2.4	2.0	1.1
As a percentage of SITC section (%)	Imp.	0.1	0.1	0.1	0.1	0.1	0.1	0.1	0.1	0.1	0.1	0.1	0.1	0.1	0.1	0.1
	Exp.	0.1	0.1	0.1	0.1	0.1	0.1	0.1	0.1	0.1	0.1	0.1	0.1	0.1	0.1	0.1
As a percentage of world trade (%)	Imp.	0.0	0.0	0.0	0.0	0.0	0.0	0.0	0.0	0.0	0.0	0.0	0.0	0.0	0.0	0.0
	Exp.	0.0	0.0	0.0	0.0	0.0	0.0	0.0	0.0	0.0	0.0	0.0	0.0	0.0	0.0	0.0

Graph 1: Annual growth rates of exports, 2002–2016

(In percentage by year)

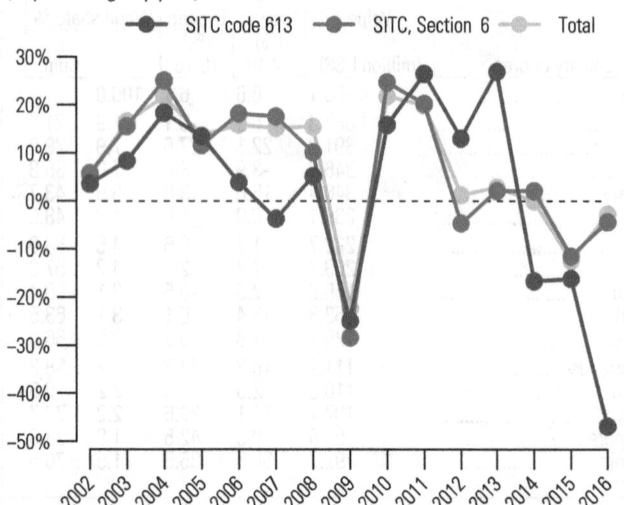

Table 2: Top exporting countries or areas in 2016

Country or area	Value (million US$)	Avg. Growth (%) 12-16	Growth (%) 15-16	World share %	Cum.
World	1061.1	-17.2	-46.9	100.0	
Cambodia	176.7	...	6.4	16.7	16.7
Viet Nam	*135.5*	131.4	8.9	12.8	29.4
Italy	86.5	-13.0	-19.4	8.1	37.6
China, Hong Kong SAR	86.2	-34.3	-81.4	8.1	45.7
China	63.5	-43.0	-86.0	6.0	51.7
Spain	57.2	-16.3	-12.4	5.4	57.1
Turkey	45.0	-14.6	-24.3	4.2	61.3
Brazil	37.0	3.1	10.1	3.5	64.8
Germany	36.4	-21.0	-35.8	3.4	68.2
Greece	30.0	-14.7	-37.8	2.8	71.1
Argentina	28.9	-10.5	-20.0	2.7	73.8
Poland	27.9	-15.9	-31.9	2.6	76.4
Thailand	26.1	208.7	11449.1	2.5	78.9
New Zealand	25.2	-0.8	-8.1	2.4	81.3
Lithuania	19.8	-16.3	-37.8	1.9	83.1

Graph 2: Trade Balance by MDG regions 2016

(Mln US$)

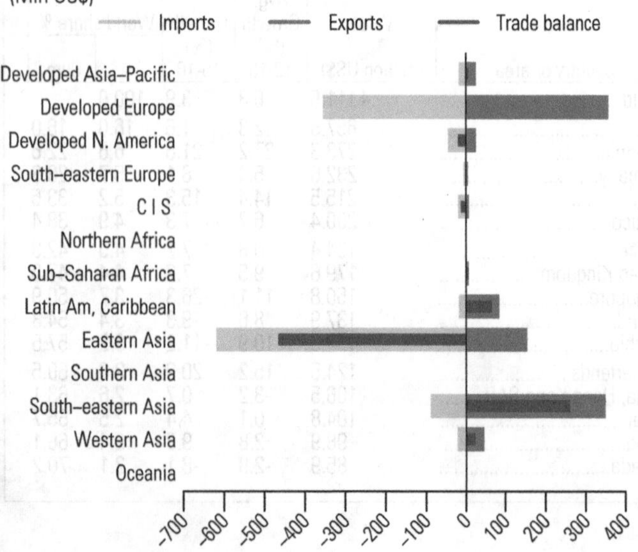

Table 3: Top importing countries or areas in 2016

Country or area	Value (million US$)	Avg. Growth (%) 12-16	Growth (%) 15-16	World share %	Cum.
World	1193.8	-16.7	-42.8	100.0	
China	381.8	10.8	-25.1	32.0	32.0
China, Hong Kong SAR	182.8	-37.1	-78.3	15.3	47.3
Italy	80.2	-14.6	-15.1	6.7	54.0
Viet Nam	*75.3*	14.1	5.1	6.3	60.3
Germany	52.3	-10.5	-12.2	4.4	64.7
Rep. of Korea	51.2	-16.0	-10.9	4.3	69.0
France	44.8	-1.6	24.3	3.8	72.7
Greece	43.6	-26.1	-25.4	3.7	76.4
USA	31.7	-0.3	-13.6	2.7	79.1
Netherlands	23.2	-10.3	-28.2	1.9	81.0
Turkey	21.1	-29.7	-22.6	1.8	82.8
Sweden	17.3	-7.6	-15.2	1.5	84.2
United Kingdom	16.5	-18.3	-21.0	1.4	85.6
Dominican Rep.	14.3	9.5	6.5	1.2	86.8
Australia	13.3	-2.8	-6.5	1.1	87.9

Source: UN Comtrade

In 2016, the value (in current US$) of exports of "materials of rubber (e.g., pastes, plates, rods, threads, tubes of rubber)" (SITC group 621) decreased by 4.5 percent (compared to -6.4 percent average growth rate from 2012-2016) to reach 19.6 bln US$ (see table 2), while imports decreased by 8.1 percent to reach 19.2 bln US$ (see table 3). Exports of this commodity accounted for 1.0 percent of world exports of SITC section 6, and 0.1 percent of total world merchandise exports (see table 1). Germany, USA and Italy were the top exporters in 2016 (see table 2). They accounted for 16.4, 10.9 and 6.6 percent of world exports, respectively. USA, Germany and China were the top destinations, with respectively 12.1, 9.2 and 7.7 percent of world imports (see table 3).

The top 15 countries/areas accounted for 77.4 and 67.2 percent of total world exports and imports, respectively (see tables 2 and 3). In 2016, Germany was the country/area with the highest value of net exports (+1.5 bln US$), followed by Italy (+693.5 mln US$). By MDG regions (see graph 2), the largest surpluses in this product group were recorded by Developed Europe (+2.0 bln US$), South-eastern Asia (+817.0 mln US$) and Developed Asia-Pacific (+297.1 mln US$). The largest trade deficits were recorded by Latin America and the Caribbean (-908.8 mln US$), Developed North America (-564.1 mln US$) and Commonwealth of Independent States (-378.4 mln US$).

Table 1: Imports (Imp.) and exports (Exp.), 2002-2016, in current US$

		2002	2003	2004	2005	2006	2007	2008	2009	2010	2011	2012	2013	2014	2015	2016
Values in Bln US$	Imp.	8.2	9.9	11.8	12.9	15.3	18.1	19.9	15.8	21.1	26.6	25.9	25.7	25.0	20.8	19.2
	Exp.	7.8	9.5	12.0	13.0	15.3	18.3	19.7	15.5	20.3	25.9	25.6	25.1	24.7	20.6	19.6
As a percentage of SITC section (%)	Imp.	0.9	1.0	0.9	0.9	0.9	0.9	0.9	1.0	1.1	1.2	1.2	1.2	1.1	1.0	1.0
	Exp.	0.9	0.9	0.9	0.9	0.9	0.9	0.9	1.0	1.0	1.1	1.2	1.1	1.1	1.0	1.0
As a percentage of world trade (%)	Imp.	0.1	0.1	0.1	0.1	0.1	0.1	0.1	0.1	0.1	0.1	0.1	0.1	0.1	0.1	0.1
	Exp.	0.1	0.1	0.1	0.1	0.1	0.1	0.1	0.1	0.1	0.1	0.1	0.1	0.1	0.1	0.1

Graph 1: Annual growth rates of exports, 2002–2016

(In percentage by year)

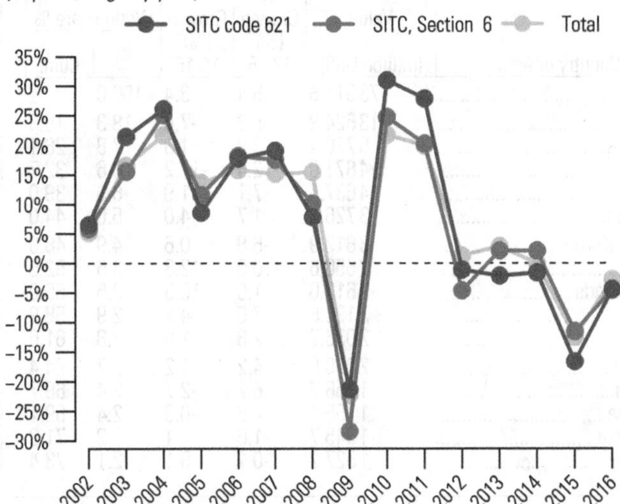

Table 2: Top exporting countries or areas in 2016

Country or area	Value (million US$)	Avg. Growth (%) 12-16	Growth (%) 15-16	World share %	Cum.
World	19625.1	-6.4	-4.5	100.0	
Germany	3217.6	-4.2	0.1	16.4	16.4
USA	2141.6	-0.5	-5.7	10.9	27.3
Italy	1294.5	-3.2	2.4	6.6	33.9
China	1149.0	0.6	-15.5	5.9	39.8
France	934.2	-3.2	3.3	4.8	44.5
Thailand	895.1	-24.5	-29.4	4.6	49.1
Japan	809.6	-8.5	0.2	4.1	53.2
Czechia	740.2	1.4	3.7	3.8	57.0
Belgium	681.3	-0.1	5.7	3.5	60.4
United Kingdom	676.8	-5.2	-11.3	3.4	63.9
Spain	610.6	1.9	2.5	3.1	67.0
Poland	608.4	3.4	19.9	3.1	70.1
Mexico	491.5	4.4	0.0	2.5	72.6
Canada	475.0	-7.5	-9.5	2.4	75.0
Turkey	472.5	-2.3	0.6	2.4	77.4

Graph 2: Trade Balance by MDG regions 2016

(Bln US$)

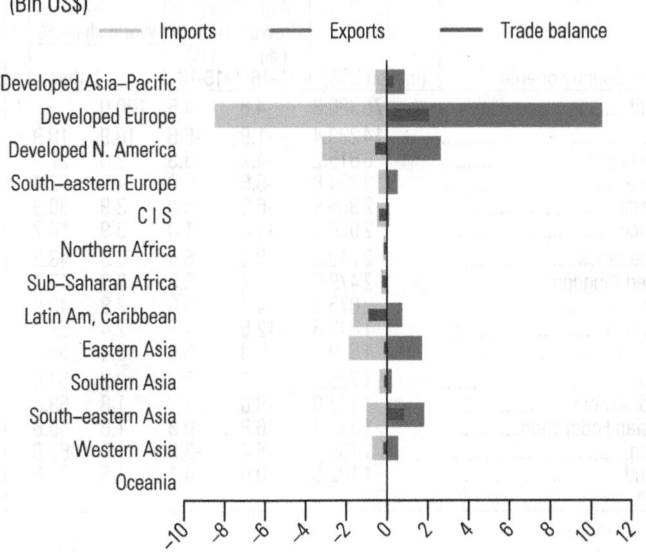

Table 3: Top importing countries or areas in 2016

Country or area	Value (million US$)	Avg. Growth (%) 12-16	Growth (%) 15-16	World share %	Cum.
World	19151.6	-7.3	-8.1	100.0	
USA	2311.2	-0.2	-5.3	12.1	12.1
Germany	1756.7	-2.6	0.4	9.2	21.2
China	1465.5	-28.1	-47.5	7.7	28.9
Mexico	884.5	4.2	-1.4	4.6	33.5
Canada	867.8	-1.9	-4.1	4.5	38.0
France	865.3	-5.8	-1.9	4.5	42.6
United Kingdom	766.2	-3.0	-5.9	4.0	46.6
Poland	730.0	2.1	6.7	3.8	50.4
Spain	685.4	-3.2	2.9	3.6	54.0
Italy	601.1	2.1	2.9	3.1	57.1
Belgium	549.4	-1.4	4.8	2.9	60.0
Czechia	480.3	0.5	9.1	2.5	62.5
Russian Federation	315.3	-11.5	1.2	1.6	64.1
Japan	298.9	-6.5	-5.7	1.6	65.7
Brazil	295.1	-12.2	-19.4	1.5	67.2

625 Rubber tyres, interchangeable tyre treads, tyre flaps and inner tubes

In 2016, the value (in current US$) of exports of "rubber tyres, interchangeable tyre treads, tyre flaps and inner tubes" (SITC group 625) decreased by 3.4 percent (compared to -5.4 percent average growth rate from 2012-2016) to reach 73.9 bln US$ (see table 2), while imports decreased by 4.5 percent to reach 75.4 bln US$ (see table 3). Exports of this commodity accounted for 3.8 percent of world exports of SITC section 6, and 0.5 percent of total world merchandise exports (see table 1). China, Germany and Japan were the top exporters in 2016 (see table 2). They accounted for 18.3, 7.8 and 6.6 percent of world exports, respectively. USA, Germany and France were the top destinations, with respectively 18.9, 9.0 and 4.5 percent of world imports (see table 3).

The top 15 countries/areas accounted for 73.4 and 63.5 percent of total world exports and imports, respectively (see tables 2 and 3). In 2016, China was the country/area with the highest value of net exports (+12.7 bln US$), followed by Japan (+3.8 bln US$). By MDG regions (see graph 2), the largest surpluses in this product group were recorded by Eastern Asia (+15.9 bln US$), South-eastern Asia (+4.1 bln US$) and Developed Asia-Pacific (+1.7 bln US$). The largest trade deficits were recorded by Developed North America (-10.8 bln US$), Latin America and the Caribbean (-4.4 bln US$) and Developed Europe (-2.4 bln US$).

Table 1: Imports (Imp.) and exports (Exp.), 2002-2016, in current US$

		2002	2003	2004	2005	2006	2007	2008	2009	2010	2011	2012	2013	2014	2015	2016
Values in Bln US$	Imp.	27.1	32.1	38.9	44.4	50.2	61.1	67.7	56.9	69.3	89.8	91.6	91.3	89.3	78.9	75.4
	Exp.	26.0	30.9	37.8	43.6	50.0	60.0	66.6	57.1	70.6	92.7	92.4	91.5	88.2	76.5	73.9
As a percentage of SITC section (%)	Imp.	3.0	3.1	3.0	3.1	3.0	3.1	3.1	3.7	3.6	3.9	4.2	4.1	3.9	3.9	3.9
	Exp.	3.0	3.0	3.0	3.1	3.0	3.0	3.1	3.7	3.6	4.0	4.1	4.0	3.8	3.7	3.8
As a percentage of world trade (%)	Imp.	0.4	0.4	0.4	0.4	0.4	0.4	0.4	0.5	0.5	0.5	0.5	0.5	0.5	0.5	0.5
	Exp.	0.4	0.4	0.4	0.4	0.4	0.4	0.4	0.5	0.5	0.5	0.5	0.5	0.5	0.5	0.5

Graph 1: Annual growth rates of exports, 2002–2016

(In percentage by year)

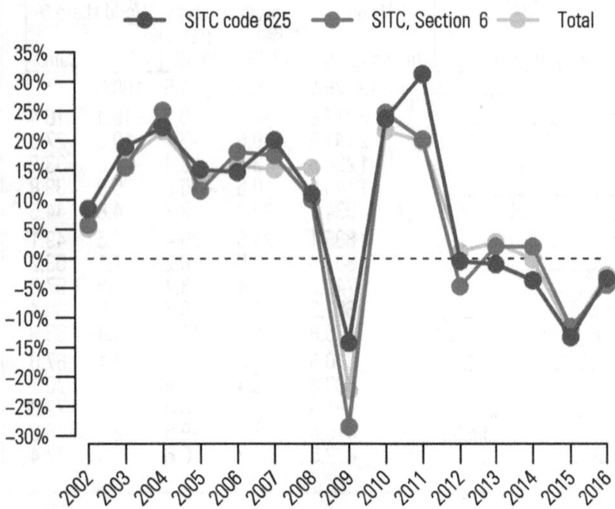

Graph 2: Trade Balance by MDG regions 2016

(Bln US$)

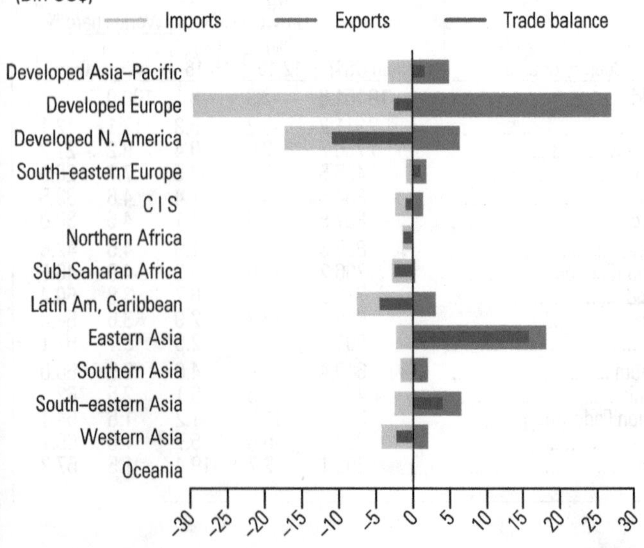

Table 2: Top exporting countries or areas in 2016

Country or area	Value (million US$)	Avg. Growth (%) 12-16	Growth (%) 15-16	World share %	Cum.
World	73911.6	-5.4	-3.4	100.0	
China	13524.9	-5.2	-7.0	18.3	18.3
Germany	5770.4	-3.9	1.3	7.8	26.1
Japan	4871.0	-12.4	-11.2	6.6	32.7
USA	4637.5	-7.1	-11.9	6.3	39.0
Thailand	3726.3	1.7	4.0	5.0	44.0
Rep. of Korea	3612.9	-6.8	0.6	4.9	48.9
France	2650.6	-10.9	-12.3	3.6	52.5
Netherlands	2612.6	1.6	10.3	3.5	56.0
Spain	2122.6	-7.0	-4.2	2.9	58.9
Poland	2036.7	-2.8	-1.8	2.8	61.6
Czechia	2000.0	-4.2	-1.2	2.7	64.4
Canada	1756.7	-6.2	-2.7	2.4	66.7
Slovakia	1755.1	4.6	-0.3	2.4	69.1
Indonesia	1645.7	-1.6	2.1	2.2	71.3
Hungary	1527.2	-0.1	5.1	2.1	73.4

Table 3: Top importing countries or areas in 2016

Country or area	Value (million US$)	Avg. Growth (%) 12-16	Growth (%) 15-16	World share %	Cum.
World	75380.3	-4.8	-4.5	100.0	
USA	14233.4	-1.9	-6.6	18.9	18.9
Germany	6815.2	-4.2	3.9	9.0	27.9
France	3354.8	-5.6	-6.0	4.5	32.4
Canada	2965.9	-6.0	-8.0	3.9	36.3
Mexico	2936.7	-1.8	-11.4	3.9	40.2
Netherlands	2740.3	0.6	6.4	3.6	43.8
United Kingdom	2479.5	-5.4	-5.8	3.3	47.1
Italy	2075.1	-4.8	-6.0	2.8	49.9
Australia	1842.8	-12.6	-1.7	2.4	52.3
Belgium	1809.1	-5.3	5.6	2.4	54.7
Spain	1725.3	-1.1	-2.7	2.3	57.0
Saudi Arabia	1343.0	-8.0	-21.3	1.8	58.8
Russian Federation	1325.8	-16.8	0.3	1.8	60.6
Japan	1109.8	-5.4	-3.5	1.5	62.0
Poland	1102.5	0.0	4.1	1.5	63.5

In 2016, the value (in current US$) of exports of "articles of rubber, nes" (SITC group 629) increased by 0.2 percent (compared to less than 0.1 percent average growth rate from 2012-2016) to reach 30.4 bln US$ (see table 2), while imports decreased by 1.7 percent to reach 33.3 bln US$ (see table 3). Exports of this commodity accounted for 1.5 percent of world exports of SITC section 6, and 0.2 percent of total world merchandise exports (see table 1). Germany, USA and China were the top exporters in 2016 (see table 2). They accounted for 14.2, 10.1 and 9.8 percent of world exports, respectively. USA, Germany and China were the top destinations, with respectively 13.7, 10.0 and 7.7 percent of world imports (see table 3).

The top 15 countries/areas accounted for 74.3 and 63.7 percent of total world exports and imports, respectively (see tables 2 and 3). In 2016, Japan was the country/area with the highest value of net exports (+1.0 bln US$), followed by Germany (+997.5 mln US$). By MDG regions (see graph 2), the largest surpluses in this product group were recorded by Developed Europe (+2.0 bln US$), Eastern Asia (+984.2 mln US$) and Developed Asia-Pacific (+555.8 mln US$). The largest trade deficits were recorded by Developed North America (-2.0 bln US$), Latin America and the Caribbean (-2.0 bln US$) and Commonwealth of Independent States (-885.1 mln US$).

Table 1: Imports (Imp.) and exports (Exp.), 2002-2016, in current US$

		2002	2003	2004	2005	2006	2007	2008	2009	2010	2011	2012	2013	2014	2015	2016
Values in Bln US$	Imp.	13.6	15.8	18.6	20.0	22.1	26.6	28.3	22.4	28.9	33.2	33.6	35.3	36.7	33.9	33.3
	Exp.	12.2	14.5	17.1	18.3	20.5	24.1	25.8	20.5	25.7	30.4	30.3	32.7	33.5	30.3	30.4
As a percentage of SITC section (%)	Imp.	1.5	1.5	1.4	1.4	1.3	1.3	1.3	1.4	1.5	1.4	1.5	1.6	1.6	1.7	1.7
	Exp.	1.4	1.4	1.3	1.3	1.2	1.2	1.2	1.3	1.3	1.3	1.4	1.4	1.4	1.5	1.5
As a percentage of world trade (%)	Imp.	0.2	0.2	0.2	0.2	0.2	0.2	0.2	0.2	0.2	0.2	0.2	0.2	0.2	0.2	0.2
	Exp.	0.2	0.2	0.2	0.2	0.2	0.2	0.2	0.2	0.2	0.2	0.2	0.2	0.2	0.2	0.2

Graph 1: Annual growth rates of exports, 2002–2016

(In percentage by year)

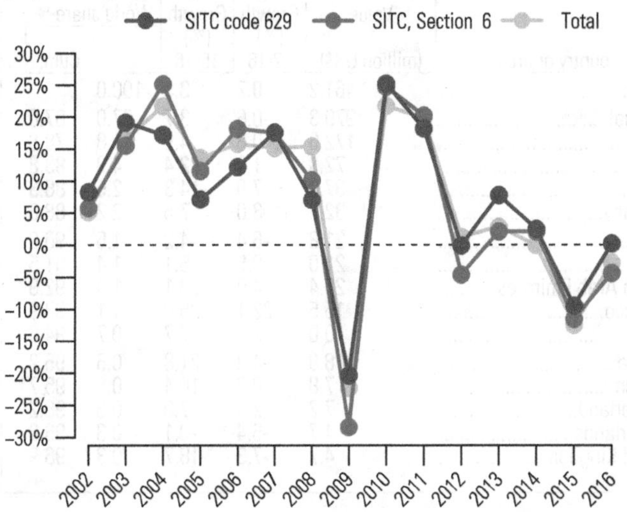

Table 2: Top exporting countries or areas in 2016

Country or area	Value (million US$)	Avg. Growth (%) 12-16	Growth (%) 15-16	World share %	Cum.
World	30394.5	0.0	0.2	100.0	
Germany	4320.1	0.9	2.7	14.2	14.2
USA	3074.7	1.0	-3.2	10.1	24.3
China	2980.1	1.0	-10.5	9.8	34.1
Japan	1904.8	-6.3	4.5	6.3	40.4
Poland	1525.2	4.5	0.2	5.0	45.4
France	1426.1	-2.3	2.3	4.7	50.1
Italy	1346.0	-1.6	0.7	4.4	54.5
Thailand	951.0	-0.8	2.9	3.1	57.7
Mexico	847.4	10.9	5.2	2.8	60.5
Belgium	790.0	-1.6	3.2	2.6	63.1
United Kingdom	730.7	-1.4	-6.0	2.4	65.5
Spain	688.4	-2.8	2.2	2.3	67.7
Turkey	686.8	3.2	2.9	2.3	70.0
Rep. of Korea	681.1	11.5	11.0	2.2	72.2
Canada	642.2	-2.9	-3.2	2.1	74.3

Graph 2: Trade Balance by MDG regions 2016

(Bln US$)

Imports — Exports — Trade balance

Developed Asia-Pacific
Developed Europe
Developed N. America
South-eastern Europe
CIS
Northern Africa
Sub-Saharan Africa
Latin Am, Caribbean
Eastern Asia
Southern Asia
South-eastern Asia
Western Asia
Oceania

-15 -10 -5 0 5 10 15

Table 3: Top importing countries or areas in 2016

Country or area	Value (million US$)	Avg. Growth (%) 12-16	Growth (%) 15-16	World share %	Cum.
World	33270.3	-0.2	-1.7	100.0	
USA	4570.5	1.6	-2.9	13.7	13.7
Germany	3322.6	0.5	2.0	10.0	23.7
China	2563.8	3.2	-0.8	7.7	31.4
Mexico	1707.3	2.5	-1.6	5.1	36.6
France	1214.8	-0.8	2.5	3.7	40.2
Canada	1162.5	-1.0	1.2	3.5	43.7
United Kingdom	1037.9	1.6	-0.5	3.1	46.8
Japan	904.0	-1.8	2.8	2.7	49.5
Italy	744.6	0.4	1.6	2.2	51.8
Czechia	740.6	1.6	4.1	2.2	54.0
Poland	718.9	1.7	0.1	2.2	56.2
Russian Federation	666.4	-6.2	8.7	2.0	58.2
Belgium	653.1	-2.1	9.4	2.0	60.1
Spain	597.0	2.0	5.5	1.8	61.9
India	576.8	-1.8	2.2	1.7	63.7

Source: UN Comtrade

633 Cork manufacture

In 2016, the value (in current US$) of exports of "cork manufacture" (SITC group 633) increased by 3.5 percent (compared to -0.7 percent average growth rate from 2012-2016) to reach 1.5 bln US$ (see table 2), while imports increased by 2.3 percent to reach 1.5 bln US$ (see table 3). Exports of this commodity accounted for 0.1 percent of world exports of SITC section 6, and less than 0.1 percent of total world merchandise exports (see table 1). Portugal, Spain and France were the top exporters in 2016 (see table 2). They accounted for 67.0, 11.8 and 4.9 percent of world exports, respectively. France, USA and Italy were the top destinations, with respectively 18.0, 17.1 and 11.4 percent of world imports (see table 3).

The top 15 countries/areas accounted for 96.9 and 81.1 percent of total world exports and imports, respectively (see tables 2 and 3). In 2016, Portugal was the country/area with the highest value of net exports (+934.7 mln US$), followed by Spain (+77.1 mln US$). By MDG regions (see graph 2), surpluses in this product group were recorded by Developed Europe (+526.9 mln US$) and Northern Africa (+16.4 mln US$). The largest trade deficits were recorded by Developed North America (-248.0 mln US$), Latin America and the Caribbean (-95.4 mln US$) and Commonwealth of Independent States (-57.2 mln US$).

Table 1: Imports (Imp.) and exports (Exp.), 2002-2016, in current US$

		2002	2003	2004	2005	2006	2007	2008	2009	2010	2011	2012	2013	2014	2015	2016
Values in Bln US$	Imp.	1.2	1.4	1.5	1.5	1.5	1.7	1.7	1.3	1.5	1.6	1.5	1.5	1.6	1.4	1.5
	Exp.	1.3	1.5	1.6	1.5	1.6	1.7	1.7	1.4	1.4	1.6	1.5	1.6	1.6	1.4	1.5
As a percentage of SITC section (%)	Imp.	0.1	0.1	0.1	0.1	0.1	0.1	0.1	0.1	0.1	0.1	0.1	0.1	0.1	0.1	0.1
	Exp.	0.1	0.1	0.1	0.1	0.1	0.1	0.1	0.1	0.1	0.1	0.1	0.1	0.1	0.1	0.1
As a percentage of world trade (%)	Imp.	0.0	0.0	0.0	0.0	0.0	0.0	0.0	0.0	0.0	0.0	0.0	0.0	0.0	0.0	0.0
	Exp.	0.0	0.0	0.0	0.0	0.0	0.0	0.0	0.0	0.0	0.0	0.0	0.0	0.0	0.0	0.0

Graph 1: Annual growth rates of exports, 2002–2016

(In percentage by year)

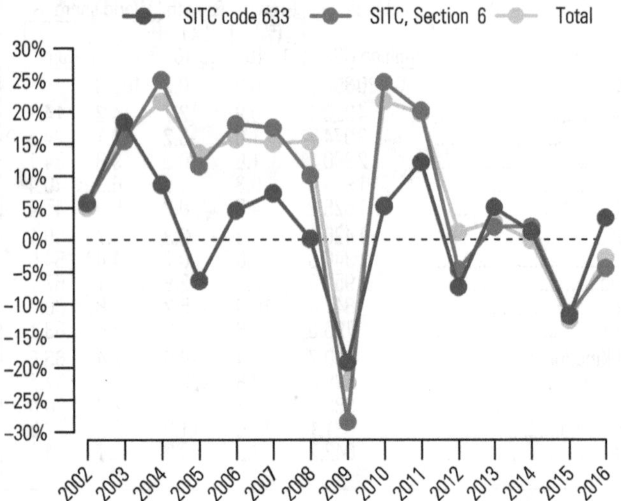

Table 2: Top exporting countries or areas in 2016

Country or area	Value (million US$)	Avg. Growth (%) 12-16	Growth (%) 15-16	World share %	Cum.
World	1461.2	-0.7	3.5	100.0	
Portugal	979.3	-0.6	3.7	67.0	67.0
Spain	172.6	-0.8	4.9	11.8	78.8
France	72.3	1.0	2.4	4.9	83.8
Italy	37.0	-7.9	-14.3	2.5	86.3
Germany	32.3	-3.0	7.5	2.2	88.5
USA	21.8	-6.4	-4.2	1.5	90.0
China	21.0	8.5	-5.1	1.4	91.5
United Arab Emirates	20.4	4.0	73.1	1.4	92.9
Morocco	15.5	22.1	25.0	1.1	93.9
Chile	10.0	2.5	7.7	0.7	94.6
Austria	8.9	-4.3	21.8	0.6	95.2
Belgium	7.8	-0.2	10.4	0.5	95.7
Switzerland	7.2	2.3	7.0	0.5	96.2
Netherlands	4.7	-5.4	-0.1	0.3	96.6
United Kingdom	4.7	-7.3	-18.7	0.3	96.9

Graph 2: Trade Balance by MDG regions 2016

(Bln US$)

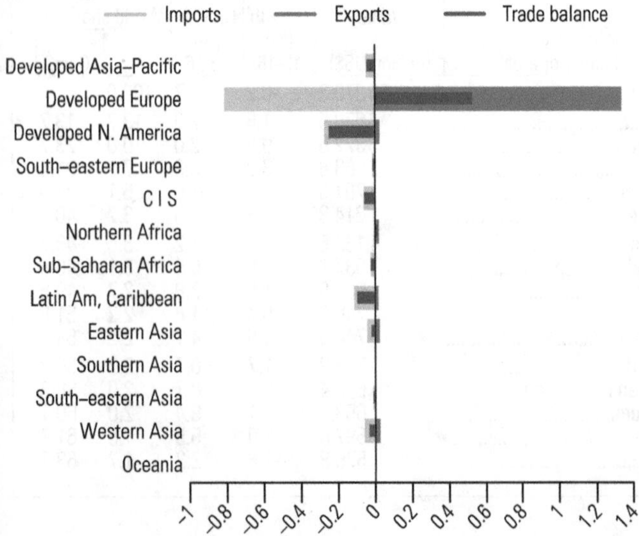

Table 3: Top importing countries or areas in 2016

Country or area	Value (million US$)	Avg. Growth (%) 12-16	Growth (%) 15-16	World share %	Cum.
World	1459.2	-0.8	2.3	100.0	
France	262.2	-1.7	8.0	18.0	18.0
USA	249.2	0.2	-13.4	17.1	35.0
Italy	166.3	3.0	8.7	11.4	46.4
Spain	95.5	3.3	12.1	6.5	53.0
Germany	88.7	-5.1	-4.4	6.1	59.1
Portugal	44.6	3.3	18.3	3.1	62.1
Russian Federation	41.2	-10.3	6.9	2.8	64.9
China	34.4	-0.5	11.6	2.4	67.3
Argentina	33.8	-4.9	-8.3	2.3	69.6
Chile	33.8	-0.6	-4.7	2.3	71.9
Mexico	30.1	2.2	9.6	2.1	74.0
United Kingdom	29.7	1.0	-17.0	2.0	76.0
Switzerland	26.0	-1.5	-1.0	1.8	77.8
Saudi Arabia	23.7	93.7	612.2	1.6	79.4
Canada	23.7	-7.7	-2.8	1.6	81.1

In 2016, the value (in current US$) of exports of "veneers, plywood, particle board,and other wood, worked, nes" (SITC group 634) increased by 1.4 percent (compared to 0.4 percent average growth rate from 2012-2016) to reach 35.0 bln US$ (see table 2), while imports increased by 0.1 percent to reach 33.7 bln US$ (see table 3). Exports of this commodity accounted for 1.8 percent of world exports of SITC section 6, and 0.2 percent of total world merchandise exports (see table 1). China, Germany and Canada were the top exporters in 2016 (see table 2). They accounted for 19.8, 8.5 and 7.1 percent of world exports, respectively. USA, Germany and Japan were the top destinations, with respectively 17.7, 6.3 and 6.1 percent of world imports (see table 3).

The top 15 countries/areas accounted for 76.1 and 60.4 percent of total world exports and imports, respectively (see tables 2 and 3). In 2016, China was the country/area with the highest value of net exports (+6.3 bln US$), followed by Indonesia (+2.2 bln US$). By MDG regions (see graph 2), the largest surpluses in this product group were recorded by Eastern Asia (+4.7 bln US$), South-eastern Asia (+3.5 bln US$) and Commonwealth of Independent States (+696.2 mln US$). The largest trade deficits were recorded by Developed North America (-3.4 bln US$), Developed Asia-Pacific (-2.0 bln US$) and Western Asia (-1.8 bln US$).

Table 1: Imports (Imp.) and exports (Exp.), 2002-2016, in current US$

		2002	2003	2004	2005	2006	2007	2008	2009	2010	2011	2012	2013	2014	2015	2016
Values in Bln US$	Imp.	19.3	22.7	29.0	30.0	32.4	35.2	33.8	23.8	29.1	33.3	33.6	34.8	36.8	33.7	33.7
	Exp.	18.8	21.8	27.8	29.8	32.2	35.7	34.6	25.8	30.0	34.0	34.4	36.2	38.3	34.5	35.0
As a percentage of SITC section (%)	Imp.	2.1	2.2	2.3	2.1	1.9	1.8	1.5	1.5	1.5	1.4	1.5	1.6	1.6	1.7	1.8
	Exp.	2.1	2.1	2.2	2.1	1.9	1.8	1.6	1.7	1.5	1.5	1.5	1.6	1.7	1.7	1.8
As a percentage of world trade (%)	Imp.	0.3	0.3	0.3	0.3	0.3	0.3	0.2	0.2	0.2	0.2	0.2	0.2	0.2	0.2	0.2
	Exp.	0.3	0.3	0.3	0.3	0.3	0.3	0.2	0.2	0.2	0.2	0.2	0.2	0.2	0.2	0.2

Graph 1: Annual growth rates of exports, 2002–2016
(In percentage by year)

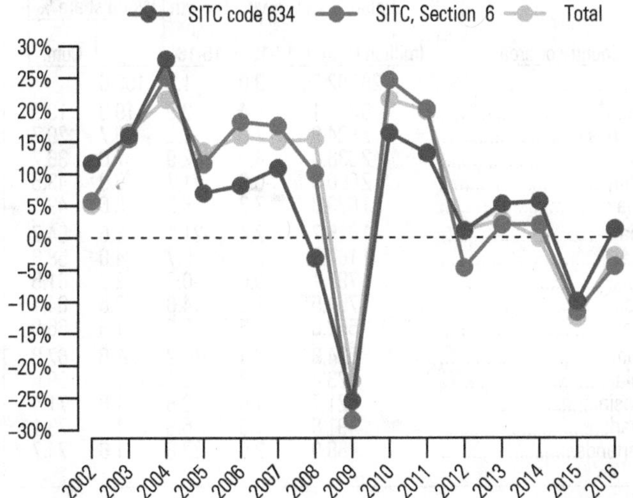

Table 2: Top exporting countries or areas in 2016

Country or area	Value (million US$)	Avg. Growth (%) 12-16	Growth (%) 15-16	World share %	Cum.
World	35008.4	0.4	1.4	100.0	
China	6917.4	0.7	-5.6	19.8	19.8
Germany	2958.6	-1.7	1.7	8.5	28.2
Canada	2495.9	9.8	17.3	7.1	35.3
Indonesia	2359.4	2.9	-5.1	6.7	42.1
Austria	1631.9	2.7	29.2	4.7	46.7
Malaysia	1532.4	-9.3	-9.4	4.4	51.1
Russian Federation	1451.9	2.1	3.9	4.1	55.3
Belgium	1087.2	-2.6	0.0	3.1	58.4
USA	1063.7	-3.4	-2.0	3.0	61.4
Poland	1002.6	3.5	7.2	2.9	64.3
France	989.1	-1.7	-1.2	2.8	67.1
Thailand	822.9	4.3	3.0	2.4	69.4
Spain	794.7	1.8	4.3	2.3	71.7
Brazil	787.8	8.8	7.0	2.3	74.0
Chile	751.8	3.8	-1.2	2.1	76.1

Graph 2: Trade Balance by MDG regions 2016
(Bln US$)

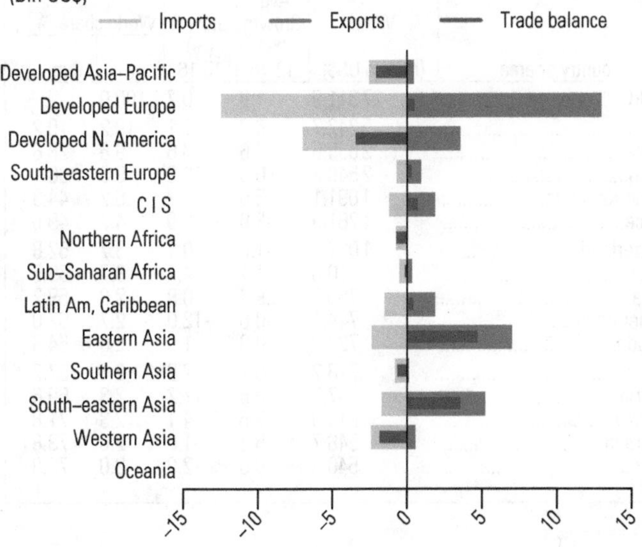

Table 3: Top importing countries or areas in 2016

Country or area	Value (million US$)	Avg. Growth (%) 12-16	Growth (%) 15-16	World share %	Cum.
World	33742.1	0.1	0.1	100.0	
USA	5986.5	9.7	8.8	17.7	17.7
Germany	2119.1	-1.9	-1.5	6.3	24.0
Japan	2055.4	-7.8	-6.1	6.1	30.1
United Kingdom	1400.7	3.5	-5.4	4.2	34.3
France	1169.1	-2.4	7.2	3.5	37.7
Rep. of Korea	1140.0	5.8	2.9	3.4	41.1
Canada	995.3	-0.9	4.7	2.9	44.1
Italy	979.2	1.7	-0.2	2.9	47.0
Netherlands	725.5	-5.2	-20.3	2.2	49.1
Belgium	692.2	-2.0	2.4	2.1	51.2
Austria	676.1	7.7	53.8	2.0	53.2
Mexico	638.6	0.9	-9.5	1.9	55.1
Poland	637.6	4.1	1.3	1.9	56.9
China	613.2	6.9	14.1	1.8	58.8
Turkey	546.8	-8.6	-11.0	1.6	60.4

635 Wood manufactures, nes

In 2016, the value (in current US$) of exports of "wood manufactures, nes" (SITC group 635) increased by 1.1 percent (compared to 3.0 percent average growth rate from 2012-2016) to reach 29.1 bln US$ (see table 2), while imports increased by 0.7 percent to reach 27.3 bln US$ (see table 3). Exports of this commodity accounted for 1.5 percent of world exports of SITC section 6, and 0.2 percent of total world merchandise exports (see table 1). China, Philippines and Poland were the top exporters in 2016 (see table 2). They accounted for 19.9, 9.7 and 7.0 percent of world exports, respectively. USA, Germany and Japan were the top destinations, with respectively 19.2, 9.6 and 9.3 percent of world imports (see table 3).

The top 15 countries/areas accounted for 74.7 and 75.8 percent of total world exports and imports, respectively (see tables 2 and 3). In 2016, China was the country/area with the highest value of net exports (+5.0 bln US$), followed by Philippines (+2.7 bln US$). By MDG regions (see graph 2), the largest surpluses in this product group were recorded by Eastern Asia (+4.7 bln US$), South-eastern Asia (+3.9 bln US$) and South-eastern Europe (+338.5 mln US$). The largest trade deficits were recorded by Developed North America (-3.2 bln US$), Developed Asia-Pacific (-3.0 bln US$) and Developed Europe (-562.0 mln US$).

Table 1: Imports (Imp.) and exports (Exp.), 2002-2016, in current US$

		2002	2003	2004	2005	2006	2007	2008	2009	2010	2011	2012	2013	2014	2015	2016
Values in Bln US$	Imp.	14.6	16.8	19.6	21.1	23.2	26.3	26.7	21.1	23.1	25.7	25.4	27.3	28.8	27.1	27.3
	Exp.	14.6	16.8	20.0	21.2	24.0	26.1	26.1	20.8	22.4	25.9	25.8	28.7	30.3	28.8	29.1
As a percentage of SITC section (%)	Imp.	1.6	1.6	1.5	1.5	1.4	1.3	1.2	1.4	1.2	1.1	1.2	1.2	1.3	1.3	1.4
	Exp.	1.7	1.7	1.6	1.5	1.4	1.3	1.2	1.3	1.2	1.1	1.2	1.3	1.3	1.4	1.5
As a percentage of world trade (%)	Imp.	0.2	0.2	0.2	0.2	0.2	0.2	0.2	0.2	0.2	0.1	0.1	0.1	0.2	0.2	0.2
	Exp.	0.2	0.2	0.2	0.2	0.2	0.2	0.2	0.2	0.1	0.1	0.1	0.2	0.2	0.2	0.2

Graph 1: Annual growth rates of exports, 2002–2016

(In percentage by year)

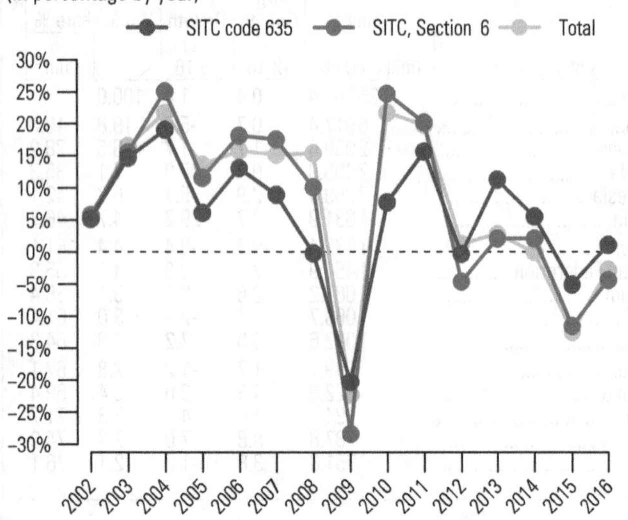

Graph 2: Trade Balance by MDG regions 2016

(Bln US$)

Imports — Exports — Trade balance

Developed Asia-Pacific
Developed Europe
Developed N. America
South-eastern Europe
CIS
Northern Africa
Sub-Saharan Africa
Latin Am, Caribbean
Eastern Asia
Southern Asia
South-eastern Asia
Western Asia
Oceania

-15 -10 -5 0 5 10 15

Table 2: Top exporting countries or areas in 2016

Country or area	Value (million US$)	Avg. Growth (%) 12-16	Growth (%) 15-16	World share %	Cum.
World	29082.2	3.0	1.1	100.0	
China	5800.1	6.4	-2.9	19.9	19.9
Philippines	2824.9	7.0	1.2	9.7	29.7
Poland	2038.4	4.9	2.9	7.0	36.7
Germany	2000.5	-0.6	1.7	6.9	43.5
Canada	1629.3	7.3	6.5	5.6	49.1
Austria	1625.7	2.4	21.1	5.6	54.7
USA	1167.8	2.3	0.7	4.0	58.8
Italy	787.1	0.0	-0.8	2.7	61.5
France	754.5	-1.2	4.8	2.6	64.1
Sweden	552.0	-3.5	-2.5	1.9	66.0
Belgium	534.3	2.4	10.2	1.8	67.8
Czechia	523.4	0.7	3.1	1.8	69.6
Indonesia	521.7	-1.0	0.8	1.8	71.4
Denmark	491.8	1.3	-5.9	1.7	73.1
Netherlands	468.0	-2.9	-22.8	1.6	74.7

Table 3: Top importing countries or areas in 2016

Country or area	Value (million US$)	Avg. Growth (%) 12-16	Growth (%) 15-16	World share %	Cum.
World	27311.9	1.8	0.7	100.0	
USA	5242.7	6.2	1.1	19.2	19.2
Germany	2635.6	0.6	0.6	9.6	28.8
Japan	2540.2	0.0	10.3	9.3	38.1
United Kingdom	1691.1	5.6	-7.2	6.2	44.3
France	1281.9	-3.0	5.0	4.7	49.0
Switzerland	1022.6	-1.0	-0.1	3.7	52.8
Italy	1010.6	-1.1	4.1	3.7	56.5
China	756.6	29.4	0.8	2.8	59.2
Netherlands	744.1	-0.8	-12.0	2.7	62.0
Canada	722.2	0.0	-1.9	2.6	64.6
Belgium	718.2	-0.1	2.8	2.6	67.2
Austria	637.7	0.6	17.2	2.3	69.6
Norway	614.9	-3.5	4.1	2.3	71.8
Australia	548.7	5.3	-1.0	2.0	73.8
Denmark	540.3	0.0	-2.0	2.0	75.8

In 2016, the value (in current US$) of exports of "paper and paperboard" (SITC group 641) decreased by 1.7 percent (compared to -3.0 percent average growth rate from 2012-2016) to reach 100.5 bln US$ (see table 2), while imports decreased by 3.5 percent to reach 101.5 bln US$ (see table 3). Exports of this commodity accounted for 5.1 percent of world exports of SITC section 6, and 0.6 percent of total world merchandise exports (see table 1). Germany, USA and China were the top exporters in 2016 (see table 2). They accounted for 12.6, 10.1 and 7.7 percent of world exports, respectively. USA, Germany and United Kingdom were the top destinations, with respectively 9.4, 8.6 and 5.0 percent of world imports (see table 3).

The top 15 countries/areas accounted for 77.2 and 58.5 percent of total world exports and imports, respectively (see tables 2 and 3). In 2016, Finland was the country/area with the highest value of net exports (+7.1 bln US$), followed by Sweden (+6.7 bln US$). By MDG regions (see graph 2), the largest surpluses in this product group were recorded by Developed Europe (+12.9 bln US$), Eastern Asia (+4.8 bln US$) and Developed North America (+3.0 bln US$). The largest trade deficits were recorded by Latin America and the Caribbean (-5.5 bln US$), Western Asia (-4.4 bln US$) and Southern Asia (-3.7 bln US$).

Table 1: Imports (Imp.) and exports (Exp.), 2002-2016, in current US$

		2002	2003	2004	2005	2006	2007	2008	2009	2010	2011	2012	2013	2014	2015	2016
Values in Bln US$	Imp.	76.4	86.2	96.6	100.3	106.6	116.8	124.8	101.8	113.2	125.6	117.3	118.9	120.0	105.2	101.5
	Exp.	73.8	83.0	93.1	96.5	104.0	113.7	120.6	98.7	110.9	123.3	113.4	116.3	116.9	102.3	100.5
As a percentage of SITC section (%)	Imp.	8.5	8.4	7.5	7.0	6.4	5.9	5.7	6.5	5.9	5.5	5.4	5.4	5.3	5.2	5.3
	Exp.	8.4	8.2	7.3	6.8	6.2	5.8	5.5	6.3	5.7	5.3	5.1	5.1	5.0	5.0	5.1
As a percentage of world trade (%)	Imp.	1.2	1.1	1.0	0.9	0.9	0.8	0.8	0.8	0.7	0.7	0.6	0.6	0.6	0.6	0.6
	Exp.	1.1	1.1	1.0	0.9	0.9	0.8	0.8	0.8	0.7	0.7	0.6	0.6	0.6	0.6	0.6

Graph 1: Annual growth rates of exports, 2002–2016
(In percentage by year)

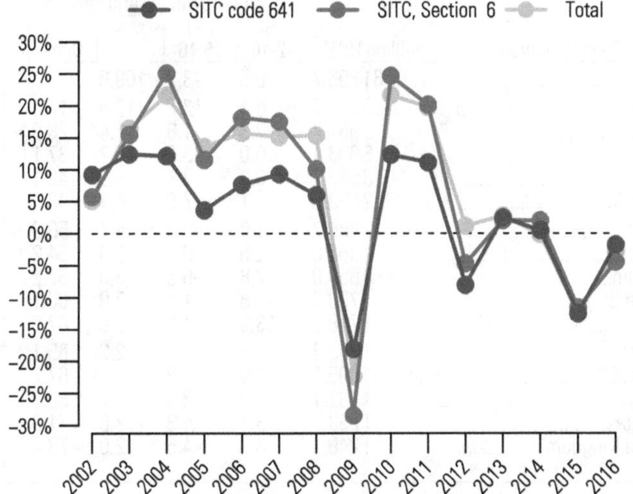

Graph 2: Trade Balance by MDG regions 2016
(Bln US$)

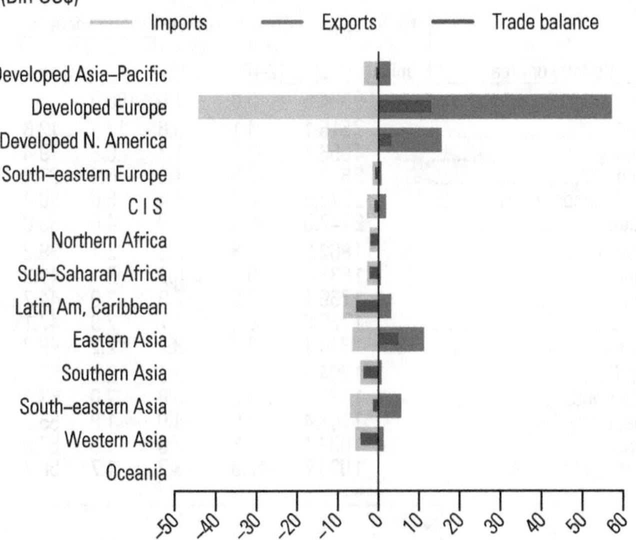

Table 2: Top exporting countries or areas in 2016

Country or area	Value (million US$)	Avg. Growth (%) 12-16	Growth (%) 15-16	World share %	Cum.
World	100514.6	-3.0	-1.7	100.0	
Germany	12690.8	-4.5	-1.1	12.6	12.6
USA	10115.9	-2.8	-6.1	10.1	22.7
China	7761.7	8.1	4.3	7.7	30.4
Sweden	7533.8	-6.3	-2.2	7.5	37.9
Finland	7455.0	-5.0	-3.9	7.4	45.3
Canada	5341.8	-5.8	-9.6	5.3	50.6
France	4127.0	-5.3	-1.9	4.1	54.7
Italy	3811.4	-2.8	-3.0	3.8	58.5
Austria	3281.7	-2.0	1.7	3.3	61.8
Indonesia	2978.2	-3.5	-4.6	3.0	64.8
Belgium	2685.9	-4.2	-4.3	2.7	67.4
Netherlands	2659.7	-1.6	5.8	2.6	70.1
Spain	2535.9	-3.2	-2.5	2.5	72.6
Rep. of Korea	2392.3	-2.2	0.1	2.4	75.0
Poland	2242.7	-2.0	3.6	2.2	77.2

Table 3: Top importing countries or areas in 2016

Country or area	Value (million US$)	Avg. Growth (%) 12-16	Growth (%) 15-16	World share %	Cum.
World	101490.1	-3.6	-3.5	100.0	
USA	9533.3	-1.7	-4.9	9.4	9.4
Germany	8706.7	-4.5	-3.0	8.6	18.0
United Kingdom	5083.7	-5.2	-11.8	5.0	23.0
France	4666.0	-6.3	-1.8	4.6	27.6
Italy	4132.7	-3.2	-0.2	4.1	31.7
Mexico	3294.5	1.2	-3.7	3.2	34.9
China	3280.4	-3.8	-2.0	3.2	38.1
Poland	3057.4	-0.3	1.7	3.0	41.1
Canada	2893.1	-1.5	-5.5	2.9	44.0
Belgium	2888.4	-6.1	1.5	2.8	46.8
Spain	2769.2	-2.2	0.0	2.7	49.6
Turkey	2437.4	-1.4	0.6	2.4	52.0
India	2415.7	5.1	9.9	2.4	54.3
Netherlands	2384.0	-6.2	-10.9	2.3	56.7
Japan	1816.5	-11.6	-3.1	1.8	58.5

Source: UN Comtrade

642 Paper and paperboard, cut to size or shape; articles of paper or paperboard

In 2016, the value (in current US$) of exports of "paper and paperboard, cut to size or shape; articles of paper or paperboard" (SITC group 642) decreased by 3.2 percent (compared to 0.5 percent average growth rate from 2012-2016) to reach 61.3 bln US$ (see table 2), while imports decreased by 1.6 percent to reach 59.6 bln US$ (see table 3). Exports of this commodity accounted for 3.1 percent of world exports of SITC section 6, and 0.4 percent of total world merchandise exports (see table 1). China, Germany and USA were the top exporters in 2016 (see table 2). They accounted for 17.5, 11.4 and 8.2 percent of world exports, respectively. USA, Germany and France were the top destinations, with respectively 12.6, 6.8 and 6.0 percent of world imports (see table 3).

The top 15 countries/areas accounted for 73.4 and 58.7 percent of total world exports and imports, respectively (see tables 2 and 3). In 2016, China was the country/area with the highest value of net exports (+9.0 bln US$), followed by Germany (+2.9 bln US$). By MDG regions (see graph 2), surpluses in this product group were recorded by Eastern Asia (+8.6 bln US$) and Developed Europe (+2.4 bln US$). The largest trade deficits were recorded by Developed North America (-2.9 bln US$), Commonwealth of Independent States (-1.4 bln US$) and Latin America and the Caribbean (-1.4 bln US$).

Table 1: Imports (Imp.) and exports (Exp.), 2002-2016, in current US$

		2002	2003	2004	2005	2006	2007	2008	2009	2010	2011	2012	2013	2014	2015	2016
Values in Bln US$	Imp.	27.1	31.1	34.9	37.1	39.9	48.3	54.2	48.8	52.7	59.1	59.6	62.5	65.2	60.5	59.6
	Exp.	26.9	30.7	34.2	36.3	39.5	47.2	52.3	47.9	51.9	59.2	60.0	64.1	67.1	63.3	61.3
As a percentage of SITC section (%)	Imp.	3.0	3.0	2.7	2.6	2.4	2.4	2.5	3.1	2.7	2.6	2.7	2.8	2.9	3.0	3.1
	Exp.	3.1	3.0	2.7	2.6	2.4	2.4	2.4	3.1	2.7	2.5	2.7	2.8	2.9	3.1	3.1
As a percentage of world trade (%)	Imp.	0.4	0.4	0.4	0.4	0.3	0.3	0.3	0.4	0.3	0.3	0.3	0.3	0.3	0.4	0.4
	Exp.	0.4	0.4	0.4	0.3	0.3	0.3	0.3	0.4	0.3	0.3	0.3	0.3	0.4	0.4	0.4

Graph 1: Annual growth rates of exports, 2002–2016
(In percentage by year)

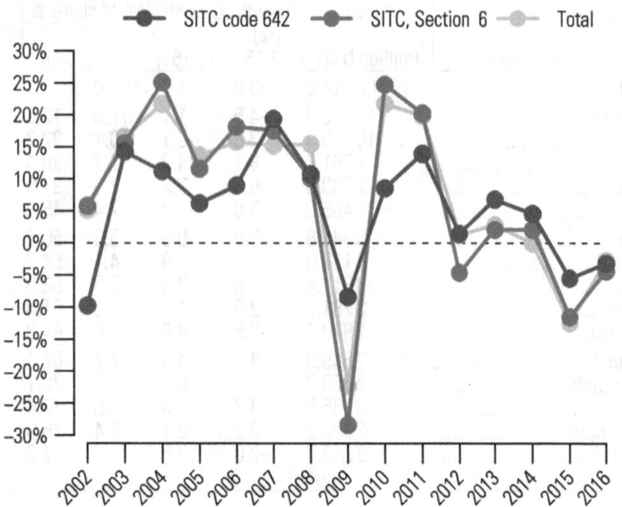

Table 2: Top exporting countries or areas in 2016

Country or area	Value (million US$)	Avg. Growth (%) 12-16	Growth (%) 15-16	World share %	Cum.
World	61305.7	0.5	-3.2	100.0	
China	10743.7	6.1	-12.2	17.5	17.5
Germany	6987.7	-2.3	1.8	11.4	28.9
USA	5006.4	0.0	-3.2	8.2	37.1
Italy	3088.2	0.2	2.1	5.0	42.1
Netherlands	2533.0	2.1	-7.0	4.1	46.3
Poland	2485.2	1.0	2.3	4.1	50.3
Canada	2362.6	2.5	-0.8	3.9	54.2
Belgium	1868.0	-2.8	-0.5	3.0	57.2
France	1750.6	-1.8	1.4	2.9	60.1
Japan	1718.2	13.9	-4.1	2.8	62.9
Mexico	1353.3	8.5	-5.7	2.2	65.1
Spain	1305.1	-1.0	4.3	2.1	67.2
Turkey	1282.1	2.0	-2.9	2.1	69.3
Czechia	1253.8	3.1	4.3	2.0	71.3
United Kingdom	1240.1	-3.7	-4.5	2.0	73.4

Graph 2: Trade Balance by MDG regions 2016
(Bln US$)

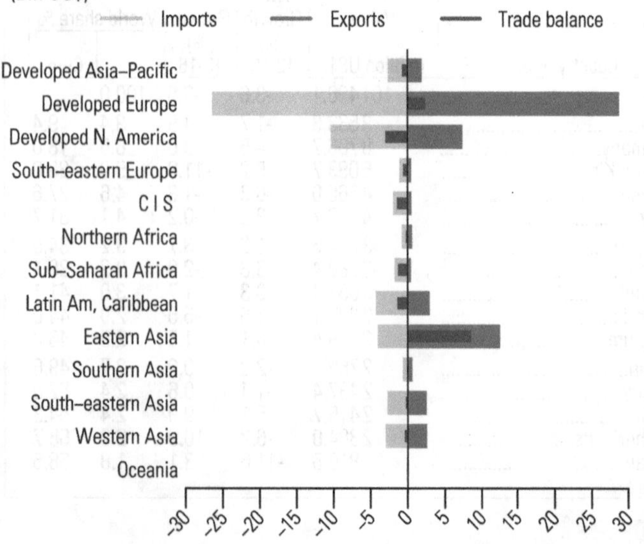

Table 3: Top importing countries or areas in 2016

Country or area	Value (million US$)	Avg. Growth (%) 12-16	Growth (%) 15-16	World share %	Cum.
World	59564.5	0.0	-1.6	100.0	
USA	7515.1	4.1	0.6	12.6	12.6
Germany	4056.1	-0.3	-1.3	6.8	19.4
France	3571.1	-2.5	1.2	6.0	25.4
United Kingdom	2973.6	0.7	-4.4	5.0	30.4
Canada	2747.0	-0.3	-1.9	4.6	35.0
Netherlands	1862.5	-3.6	-15.3	3.1	38.2
Belgium	1831.4	-0.9	6.7	3.1	41.2
China	1769.1	22.5	-2.8	3.0	44.2
Mexico	1725.0	-0.2	-4.7	2.9	47.1
Japan	1340.1	-0.7	3.4	2.2	49.3
Poland	1204.9	3.0	8.2	2.0	51.4
Switzerland	1170.2	-1.5	0.8	2.0	53.3
China, Hong Kong SAR	1101.4	-1.0	-4.0	1.8	55.2
Spain	1087.1	-1.5	-2.9	1.8	57.0
Russian Federation	1035.7	-10.8	-8.2	1.7	58.7

In 2016, the value (in current US$) of exports of "textile yarn" (SITC group 651) decreased by 5.0 percent (compared to -2.4 percent average growth rate from 2012-2016) to reach 49.6 bln US$ (see table 2), while imports decreased by 6.4 percent to reach 47.6 bln US$ (see table 3). Exports of this commodity accounted for 2.5 percent of world exports of SITC section 6, and 0.3 percent of total world merchandise exports (see table 1). China, India and USA were the top exporters in 2016 (see table 2). They accounted for 22.0, 10.2 and 6.4 percent of world exports, respectively. China, Turkey and USA were the top destinations, with respectively 15.6, 6.5 and 5.0 percent of world imports (see table 3).

The top 15 countries/areas accounted for 78.7 and 64.2 percent of total world exports and imports, respectively (see tables 2 and 3). In 2016, India was the country/area with the highest value of net exports (+4.0 bln US$), followed by China (+3.5 bln US$). By MDG regions (see graph 2), the largest surpluses in this product group were recorded by Eastern Asia (+3.9 bln US$), South-eastern Asia (+3.3 bln US$) and Southern Asia (+2.7 bln US$). The largest trade deficits were recorded by Developed Europe (-3.1 bln US$), Latin America and the Caribbean (-2.9 bln US$) and Western Asia (-1.6 bln US$).

Table 1: Imports (Imp.) and exports (Exp.), 2002-2016, in current US$

		2002	2003	2004	2005	2006	2007	2008	2009	2010	2011	2012	2013	2014	2015	2016
Values in Bln US$	Imp.	33.2	36.2	39.5	38.8	41.5	45.0	45.7	36.6	47.3	55.0	51.5	55.4	53.8	50.8	47.6
	Exp.	31.8	35.7	40.7	40.3	43.7	47.5	46.9	37.7	50.2	58.1	54.5	58.4	57.5	52.2	49.6
As a percentage of SITC section (%)	Imp.	3.7	3.5	3.1	2.7	2.5	2.3	2.1	2.3	2.5	2.4	2.4	2.5	2.4	2.5	2.5
	Exp.	3.6	3.5	3.2	2.8	2.6	2.4	2.2	2.4	2.6	2.5	2.4	2.6	2.5	2.5	2.5
As a percentage of world trade (%)	Imp.	0.5	0.5	0.4	0.4	0.3	0.3	0.3	0.3	0.3	0.3	0.3	0.3	0.3	0.3	0.3
	Exp.	0.5	0.5	0.4	0.4	0.4	0.3	0.3	0.3	0.3	0.3	0.3	0.3	0.3	0.3	0.3

Graph 1: Annual growth rates of exports, 2002–2016
(In percentage by year)

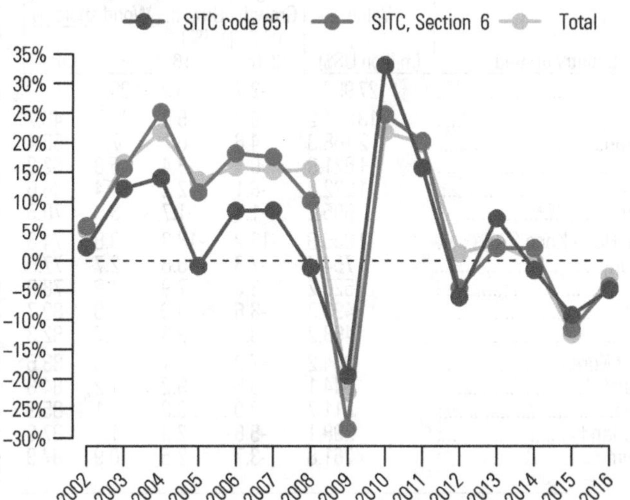

Table 2: Top exporting countries or areas in 2016

Country or area	Value (million US$)	Avg. Growth (%) 12-16	Growth (%) 15-16	World share %	Cum.
World	49570.7	-2.4	-5.0	100.0	
China	10904.8	-1.3	-1.8	22.0	22.0
India	5036.0	-1.3	-11.3	10.2	32.2
USA	3185.4	-1.3	-8.4	6.4	38.6
Viet Nam	*2700.8*	11.2	8.9	5.4	44.0
Indonesia	2220.0	0.0	-5.0	4.5	48.5
Italy	2080.8	-5.9	-3.6	4.2	52.7
China, Hong Kong SAR	1852.8	-10.4	-19.9	3.7	56.4
Uzbekistan	*1745.7*	26.7	-2.6	3.5	60.0
Turkey	1652.2	-0.2	0.9	3.3	63.3
Other Asia, nes	1541.5	-9.6	-8.9	3.1	66.4
Germany	1348.1	-5.7	-3.7	2.7	69.1
Rep. of Korea	1336.9	-6.7	-9.5	2.7	71.8
Pakistan	1272.9	-12.8	-20.8	2.6	74.4
Japan	1170.4	-4.8	-0.3	2.4	76.8
Netherlands	945.2	0.1	-0.5	1.9	78.7

Graph 2: Trade Balance by MDG regions 2016
(Bln US$)

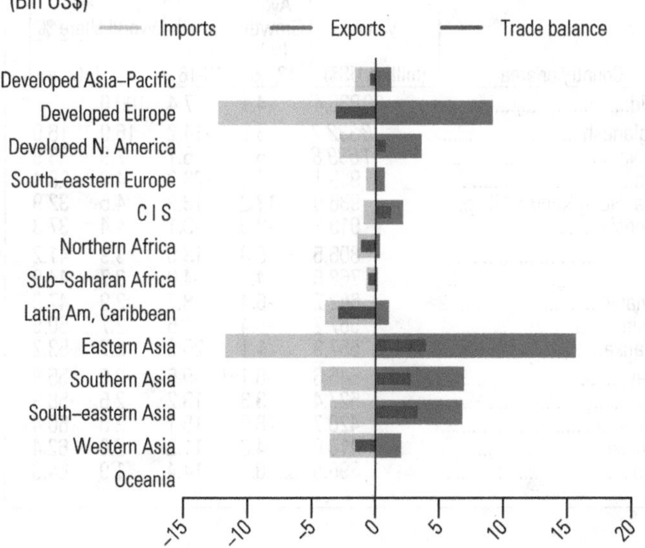

Table 3: Top importing countries or areas in 2016

Country or area	Value (million US$)	Avg. Growth (%) 12-16	Growth (%) 15-16	World share %	Cum.
World	47581.8	-2.0	-6.4	100.0	
China	7399.2	-0.9	-16.8	15.6	15.6
Turkey	3110.5	1.0	5.3	6.5	22.1
USA	2356.9	-2.9	-9.5	5.0	27.0
Italy	2345.3	-2.7	1.2	4.9	32.0
Germany	2183.9	-2.2	-2.2	4.6	36.6
Rep. of Korea	2017.7	-0.5	-1.7	4.2	40.8
China, Hong Kong SAR	1878.1	-12.5	-18.4	3.9	44.7
Bangladesh	*1737.9*	3.1	-14.2	3.7	48.4
Japan	1340.1	-2.5	-1.5	2.8	51.2
Viet Nam	*1335.2*	8.0	5.1	2.8	54.0
Brazil	1099.6	-9.7	-3.3	2.3	56.3
India	1016.7	0.9	-8.3	2.1	58.5
United Kingdom	918.2	-2.0	-9.8	1.9	60.4
France	909.7	-5.4	1.8	1.9	62.3
Belgium	886.7	0.0	5.9	1.9	64.2

652 Cotton fabrics, woven (not including narrow or special fabrics)

In 2016, the value (in current US$) of exports of "cotton fabrics, woven (not including narrow or special fabrics)" (SITC group 652) decreased by 5.9 percent (compared to -2.7 percent average growth rate from 2012-2016) to reach 28.0 bln US$ (see table 2), while imports decreased by 7.4 percent to reach 20.8 bln US$ (see table 3). Exports of this commodity accounted for 1.4 percent of world exports of SITC section 6, and 0.2 percent of total world merchandise exports (see table 1). China, Pakistan and India were the top exporters in 2016 (see table 2). They accounted for 48.7, 7.8 and 5.8 percent of world exports, respectively. Bangladesh, Viet Nam and China were the top destinations, with respectively 16.0, 7.9 and 4.6 percent of world imports (see table 3).

The top 15 countries/areas accounted for 87.9 and 64.3 percent of total world exports and imports, respectively (see tables 2 and 3). In 2016, China was the country/area with the highest value of net exports (+12.7 bln US$), followed by Pakistan (+2.1 bln US$). By MDG regions (see graph 2), the largest surpluses in this product group were recorded by Eastern Asia (+12.9 bln US$), Developed Europe (+476.8 mln US$) and Western Asia (+364.0 mln US$). The largest trade deficits were recorded by South-eastern Asia (-2.8 bln US$), Latin America and the Caribbean (-1.0 bln US$) and Northern Africa (-959.0 mln US$).

Table 1: Imports (Imp.) and exports (Exp.), 2002-2016, in current US$

		2002	2003	2004	2005	2006	2007	2008	2009	2010	2011	2012	2013	2014	2015	2016
Values in Bln US$	Imp.	21.2	22.7	25.0	24.9	24.3	24.7	26.9	20.5	23.6	28.1	24.6	25.3	21.5	22.5	20.8
	Exp.	24.5	26.5	28.9	28.9	30.2	30.0	30.8	24.1	28.6	33.6	31.3	34.0	32.2	29.7	28.0
As a percentage of SITC section (%)	Imp.	2.4	2.2	1.9	1.7	1.5	1.3	1.2	1.3	1.2	1.2	1.1	1.1	0.9	1.1	1.1
	Exp.	2.8	2.6	2.3	2.0	1.8	1.5	1.4	1.6	1.5	1.4	1.4	1.5	1.4	1.4	1.4
As a percentage of world trade (%)	Imp.	0.3	0.3	0.3	0.2	0.2	0.2	0.2	0.2	0.2	0.2	0.1	0.1	0.1	0.1	0.1
	Exp.	0.4	0.4	0.3	0.3	0.3	0.2	0.2	0.2	0.2	0.2	0.2	0.2	0.2	0.2	0.2

Graph 1: Annual growth rates of exports, 2002–2016
(In percentage by year)

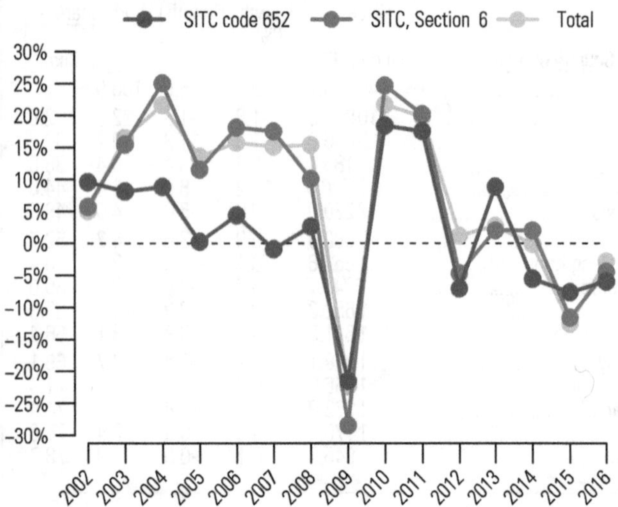

Table 2: Top exporting countries or areas in 2016

Country or area	Value (million US$)	Avg. Growth (%) 12-16	Growth (%) 15-16	World share %	Cum.
World	27 962.2	-2.7	-5.9	100.0	
China	13 614.2	0.7	-5.0	48.7	48.7
Pakistan	2 168.3	-4.6	-6.7	7.8	56.4
India	1 621.9	-0.1	-8.4	5.8	62.2
Italy	1 222.8	-8.1	-2.2	4.4	66.6
Turkey	1 095.2	-1.1	-1.7	3.9	70.5
China, Hong Kong SAR	1 056.9	-13.2	-18.3	3.8	74.3
Germany	754.7	-7.8	-5.8	2.7	77.0
Spain	526.2	-3.5	7.9	1.9	78.9
Japan	493.3	-8.6	-8.6	1.8	80.7
USA	463.2	-8.1	-19.3	1.7	82.3
Rep. of Korea	354.2	-7.0	-10.1	1.3	83.6
Thailand	344.1	-6.5	-9.2	1.2	84.8
Austria	311.7	10.0	26.8	1.1	85.9
Netherlands	298.1	-5.6	-2.3	1.1	87.0
Belgium	261.8	-3.7	-2.5	0.9	87.9

Graph 2: Trade Balance by MDG regions 2016
(Bln US$)

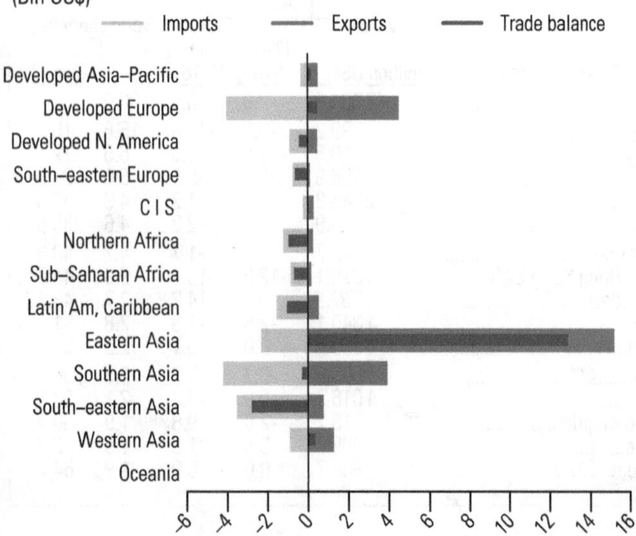

Table 3: Top importing countries or areas in 2016

Country or area	Value (million US$)	Avg. Growth (%) 12-16	Growth (%) 15-16	World share %	Cum.
World	20 836.4	-4.1	-7.4	100.0	
Bangladesh	*3 332.7*	3.5	-14.2	16.0	16.0
Viet Nam	*1 639.8*	5.2	5.1	7.9	23.9
China	953.1	-15.1	-23.3	4.6	28.4
China, Hong Kong SAR	936.9	-13.2	-18.9	4.5	32.9
Indonesia	918.7	-3.9	-3.1	4.4	37.3
USA	806.5	-5.3	-13.6	3.9	41.2
Italy	768.5	-4.1	-4.0	3.7	44.9
Germany	602.2	-6.4	-8.7	2.9	47.8
Tunisia	567.2	-5.4	-1.5	2.7	50.5
Sri Lanka	557.9	1.1	25.9	2.7	53.2
Turkey	546.6	-8.1	-9.5	2.6	55.8
Mexico	527.4	-3.3	-13.2	2.5	58.3
Cambodia	420.7	28.0	15.1	2.0	60.4
Morocco	418.0	-4.3	11.2	2.0	62.4
Spain	396.8	0.1	14.4	1.9	64.3

In 2016, the value (in current US$) of exports of "fabrics, woven, of man-made textile materials (not narrow or special fabrics)" (SITC group 653) decreased by 4.5 percent (compared to 0.3 percent average growth rate from 2012-2016) to reach 43.0 bln US$ (see table 2), while imports decreased by 1.6 percent to reach 35.0 bln US$ (see table 3). Exports of this commodity accounted for 2.2 percent of world exports of SITC section 6, and 0.3 percent of total world merchandise exports (see table 1). China, Rep. of Korea and Other Asia, nes were the top exporters in 2016 (see table 2). They accounted for 47.8, 5.1 and 4.3 percent of world exports, respectively. Viet Nam, China and Indonesia were the top destinations, with respectively 11.2, 5.7 and 4.2 percent of world imports (see table 3).

The top 15 countries/areas accounted for 88.9 and 53.2 percent of total world exports and imports, respectively (see tables 2 and 3). In 2016, China was the country/area with the highest value of net exports (+18.6 bln US$), followed by Rep. of Korea (+1.8 bln US$). By MDG regions (see graph 2), the largest surpluses in this product group were recorded by Eastern Asia (+21.9 bln US$), Developed Asia-Pacific (+893.0 mln US$) and Developed Europe (+414.8 mln US$). The largest trade deficits were recorded by South-eastern Asia (-5.7 bln US$), Latin America and the Caribbean (-2.9 bln US$) and Northern Africa (-1.6 bln US$).

Table 1: Imports (Imp.) and exports (Exp.), 2002-2016, in current US$

		2002	2003	2004	2005	2006	2007	2008	2009	2010	2011	2012	2013	2014	2015	2016
Values in Bln US$	Imp.	26.0	27.0	28.9	28.1	28.9	31.0	31.8	25.5	28.8	34.5	33.7	35.2	36.2	35.5	35.0
	Exp.	27.8	30.0	32.7	32.2	33.6	36.4	37.7	31.6	36.3	44.1	42.6	45.3	47.6	45.1	43.0
As a percentage of SITC section (%)	Imp.	2.9	2.6	2.2	2.0	1.7	1.6	1.5	1.6	1.5	1.5	1.5	1.6	1.6	1.8	1.8
	Exp.	3.2	2.9	2.6	2.3	2.0	1.8	1.7	2.0	1.9	1.9	1.9	2.0	2.1	2.2	2.2
As a percentage of world trade (%)	Imp.	0.4	0.4	0.3	0.3	0.2	0.2	0.2	0.2	0.2	0.2	0.2	0.2	0.2	0.2	0.2
	Exp.	0.4	0.4	0.4	0.3	0.3	0.3	0.2	0.3	0.2	0.2	0.2	0.2	0.3	0.3	0.3

Graph 1: Annual growth rates of exports, 2002–2016
(In percentage by year)

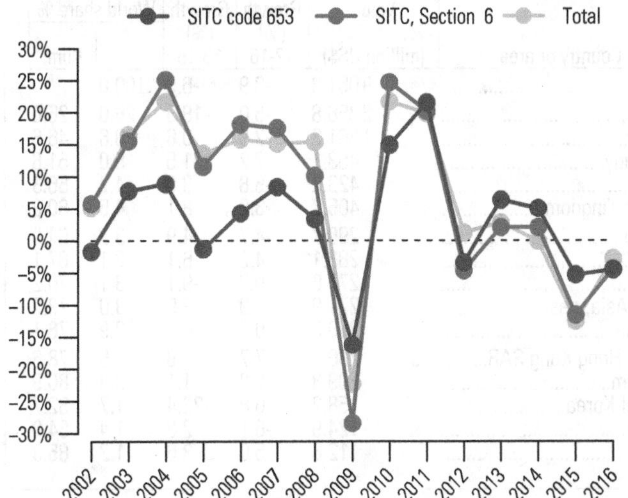

Table 2: Top exporting countries or areas in 2016

Country or area	Value (million US$)	Avg. Growth (%) 12-16	Growth (%) 15-16	World share %	Cum.
World	43021.2	0.3	-4.5	100.0	
China	20559.9	4.6	-4.2	47.8	47.8
Rep. of Korea	2215.1	-3.9	-8.6	5.1	52.9
Other Asia, nes	1859.1	-4.3	-9.0	4.3	57.3
India	1740.0	-1.2	-16.8	4.0	61.3
Italy	1692.1	-0.6	1.1	3.9	65.2
Japan	1543.1	-5.1	3.4	3.6	68.8
Turkey	1501.6	-1.4	-7.1	3.5	72.3
Germany	1295.1	-3.5	-1.8	3.0	75.3
United Arab Emirates	1127.8	1.0	8.2	2.6	77.9
USA	1051.4	0.4	-3.2	2.4	80.4
Indonesia	918.4	-8.2	-10.1	2.1	82.5
Spain	869.9	4.9	6.2	2.0	84.5
Belgium	649.7	-2.9	-1.0	1.5	86.1
France	644.1	-2.3	-3.5	1.5	87.6
Thailand	582.1	-4.8	-5.5	1.4	88.9

Graph 2: Trade Balance by MDG regions 2016
(Bln US$)

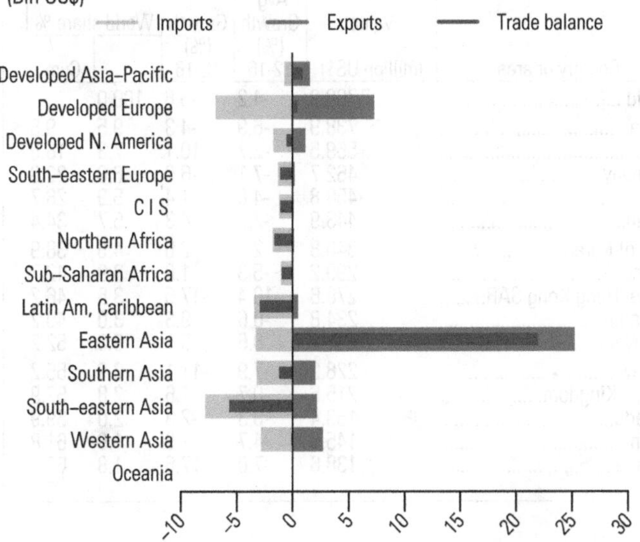

Table 3: Top importing countries or areas in 2016

Country or area	Value (million US$)	Avg. Growth (%) 12-16	Growth (%) 15-16	World share %	Cum.
World	34959.4	0.9	-1.6	100.0	
Viet Nam	*3918.3*	11.4	5.1	11.2	11.2
China	2000.4	-8.2	-9.2	5.7	16.9
Indonesia	1478.1	6.2	15.3	4.2	21.2
USA	1376.6	0.6	-10.3	3.9	25.1
Bangladesh	*1186.5*	8.9	-14.2	3.4	28.5
Germany	1039.5	-2.0	-4.1	3.0	31.5
United Arab Emirates	1030.6	-4.9	-16.1	2.9	34.4
Iran	*962.6*	9.5	-5.1	2.8	37.2
Mexico	916.7	0.2	-3.6	2.6	39.8
Italy	886.7	2.2	2.3	2.5	42.3
Cambodia	827.3	8.8	2.5	2.4	44.7
Morocco	764.0	5.1	11.1	2.2	46.9
United Kingdom	751.2	2.0	-7.3	2.1	49.0
Romania	732.4	0.8	-1.3	2.1	51.1
Spain	719.4	5.9	2.1	2.1	53.2

Source: UN Comtrade

654 Other textile fabrics, woven

In 2016, the value (in current US$) of exports of "other textile fabrics, woven" (SITC group 654) decreased by 6.5 percent (compared to -3.9 percent average growth rate from 2012-2016) to reach 9.1 bln US$ (see table 2), while imports decreased by 5.6 percent to reach 7.8 bln US$ (see table 3). Exports of this commodity accounted for 0.5 percent of world exports of SITC section 6, and 0.1 percent of total world merchandise exports (see table 1). China, Italy and Germany were the top exporters in 2016 (see table 2). They accounted for 26.0, 20.6 and 5.0 percent of world exports, respectively. China, USA and Germany were the top destinations, with respectively 9.5, 7.3 and 6.0 percent of world imports (see table 3).

The top 15 countries/areas accounted for 85.3 and 63.6 percent of total world exports and imports, respectively (see tables 2 and 3). In 2016, China was the country/area with the highest value of net exports (+1.6 bln US$), followed by Italy (+1.4 bln US$). By MDG regions (see graph 2), the largest surpluses in this product group were recorded by Developed Europe (+1.6 bln US$), Eastern Asia (+1.6 bln US$) and Southern Asia (+76.9 mln US$). The largest trade deficits were recorded by South-eastern Asia (-498.3 mln US$), Developed North America (-407.5 mln US$) and South-eastern Europe (-333.7 mln US$).

Table 1: Imports (Imp.) and exports (Exp.), 2002-2016, in current US$

		2002	2003	2004	2005	2006	2007	2008	2009	2010	2011	2012	2013	2014	2015	2016
Values in Bln US$	Imp.	7.9	8.5	10.1	10.4	10.7	11.1	11.3	8.1	8.7	10.1	9.2	9.0	9.2	8.2	7.8
	Exp.	8.6	9.3	11.1	11.1	11.5	11.9	12.0	8.9	9.9	11.3	10.6	10.5	10.7	9.7	9.1
As a percentage of SITC section (%)	Imp.	0.9	0.8	0.8	0.7	0.6	0.6	0.5	0.5	0.5	0.4	0.4	0.4	0.4	0.4	0.4
	Exp.	1.0	0.9	0.9	0.8	0.7	0.6	0.6	0.6	0.5	0.5	0.5	0.5	0.5	0.5	0.5
As a percentage of world trade (%)	Imp.	0.1	0.1	0.1	0.1	0.1	0.1	0.1	0.1	0.1	0.1	0.1	0.0	0.0	0.0	0.0
	Exp.	0.1	0.1	0.1	0.1	0.1	0.1	0.1	0.1	0.1	0.1	0.1	0.1	0.1	0.1	0.1

Graph 1: Annual growth rates of exports, 2002–2016
(In percentage by year)

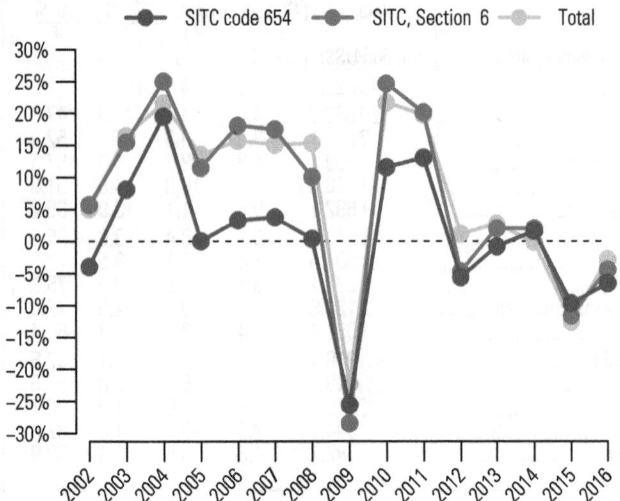

Table 2: Top exporting countries or areas in 2016

Country or area	Value (million US$)	Avg. Growth (%) 12-16	Growth (%) 15-16	World share %	Cum.
World	9051.3	-3.9	-6.5	100.0	
China	2356.8	-5.0	-18.5	26.0	26.0
Italy	1861.2	-2.9	0.6	20.6	46.6
Germany	453.1	-7.2	-1.5	5.0	51.6
Japan	423.2	-5.8	3.8	4.7	56.3
United Kingdom	405.7	-3.8	-8.1	4.5	60.8
France	290.7	-4.7	4.9	3.2	64.0
India	283.1	-4.2	-6.1	3.1	67.1
USA	277.6	-0.8	-9.1	3.1	70.2
Other Asia, nes	271.9	-1.9	2.6	3.0	73.2
Czechia	260.3	-0.7	6.7	2.9	76.1
China, Hong Kong SAR	230.1	-7.7	-12.8	2.5	78.6
Belgium	209.3	0.3	1.1	2.3	80.9
Rep. of Korea	158.2	-6.8	-22.4	1.7	82.7
Turkey	124.9	-6.1	2.8	1.4	84.0
Spain	112.6	-5.0	3.6	1.2	85.3

Graph 2: Trade Balance by MDG regions 2016
(Bln US$)

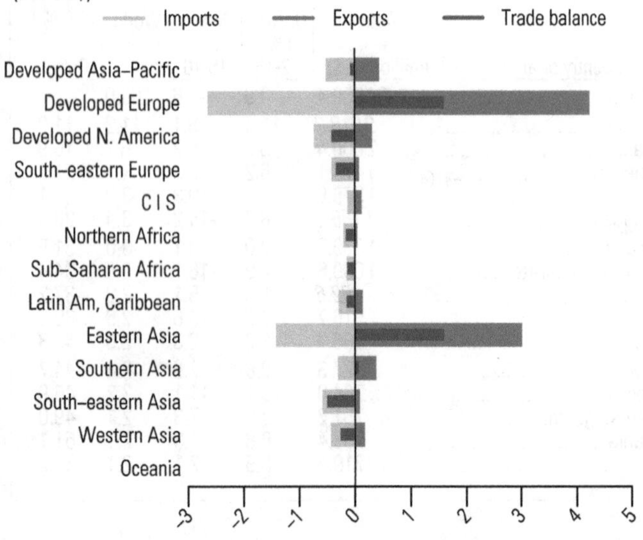

Table 3: Top importing countries or areas in 2016

Country or area	Value (million US$)	Avg. Growth (%) 12-16	Growth (%) 15-16	World share %	Cum.
World	7768.9	-4.2	-5.6	100.0	
China	738.9	-6.9	-4.3	9.5	9.5
USA	569.5	-2.7	-10.1	7.3	16.8
Germany	462.7	-7.1	-6.0	6.0	22.8
Italy	458.8	-4.8	-1.4	5.9	28.7
Japan	443.9	-2.2	4.3	5.7	34.4
Rep. of Korea	346.8	2.2	2.6	4.5	38.9
France	299.2	-5.3	-1.0	3.9	42.7
China, Hong Kong SAR	270.6	-10.4	-17.5	3.5	46.2
Romania	234.8	-0.6	9.3	3.0	49.2
Viet Nam	*231.4*	8.6	5.1	3.0	52.2
Turkey	228.2	-7.9	-11.1	2.9	55.2
United Kingdom	215.6	-0.7	-7.6	2.8	57.9
Canada	153.4	-0.3	-2.3	2.0	59.9
Spain	145.9	-4.7	7.9	1.9	61.8
India	138.6	-7.0	-17.6	1.8	63.6

In 2016, the value (in current US$) of exports of "knitted or crocheted fabrics, nes," (SITC group 655) decreased by 2.0 percent (compared to 2.0 percent average growth rate from 2012-2016) to reach 32.7 bln US$ (see table 2), while imports decreased by 0.8 percent to reach 25.6 bln US$ (see table 3). Exports of this commodity accounted for 1.7 percent of world exports of SITC section 6, and 0.2 percent of total world merchandise exports (see table 1). China, Rep. of Korea and Other Asia, nes were the top exporters in 2016 (see table 2). They accounted for 44.1, 10.4 and 7.9 percent of world exports, respectively. Viet Nam, Cambodia and China, Hong Kong SAR were the top destinations, with respectively 14.6, 8.6 and 7.6 percent of world imports (see table 3).

The top 15 countries/areas accounted for 90.7 and 66.5 percent of total world exports and imports, respectively (see tables 2 and 3). In 2016, China was the country/area with the highest value of net exports (+12.7 bln US$), followed by Rep. of Korea (+3.2 bln US$). By MDG regions (see graph 2), the largest surpluses in this product group were recorded by Eastern Asia (+18.6 bln US$), Developed Europe (+625.4 mln US$) and Developed Asia-Pacific (+393.1 mln US$). The largest trade deficits were recorded by South-eastern Asia (-7.0 bln US$), Latin America and the Caribbean (-1.8 bln US$) and Southern Asia (-1.8 bln US$).

Table 1: Imports (Imp.) and exports (Exp.), 2002-2016, in current US$

		2002	2003	2004	2005	2006	2007	2008	2009	2010	2011	2012	2013	2014	2015	2016
Values in Bln US$	Imp.	13.0	14.3	15.5	16.6	17.5	19.5	19.9	16.9	19.9	22.8	23.2	25.1	26.3	25.8	25.6
	Exp.	16.0	17.8	19.5	19.8	21.7	24.2	24.9	21.9	26.3	30.7	30.2	32.8	34.0	33.3	32.7
As a percentage of SITC section (%)	Imp.	1.4	1.4	1.2	1.2	1.1	1.0	0.9	1.1	1.0	1.0	1.1	1.1	1.2	1.3	1.3
	Exp.	1.8	1.7	1.5	1.4	1.3	1.2	1.1	1.4	1.4	1.3	1.4	1.4	1.5	1.6	1.7
As a percentage of world trade (%)	Imp.	0.2	0.2	0.2	0.2	0.1	0.1	0.1	0.1	0.1	0.1	0.1	0.1	0.1	0.2	0.2
	Exp.	0.2	0.2	0.2	0.2	0.2	0.2	0.2	0.2	0.2	0.2	0.2	0.2	0.2	0.2	0.2

Graph 1: Annual growth rates of exports, 2002–2016
(In percentage by year)

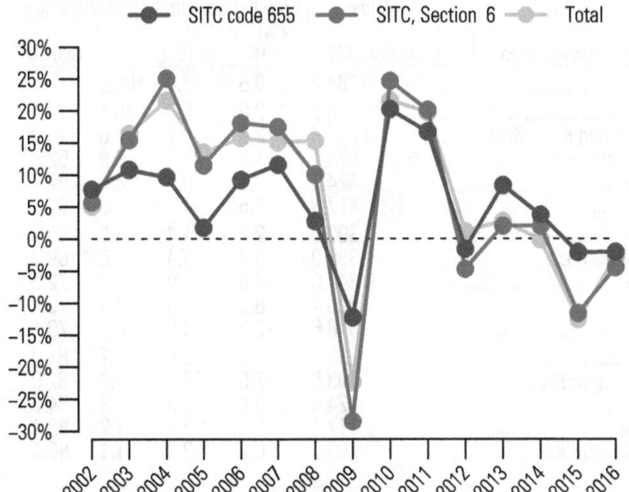

Graph 2: Trade Balance by MDG regions 2016
(Bln US$)

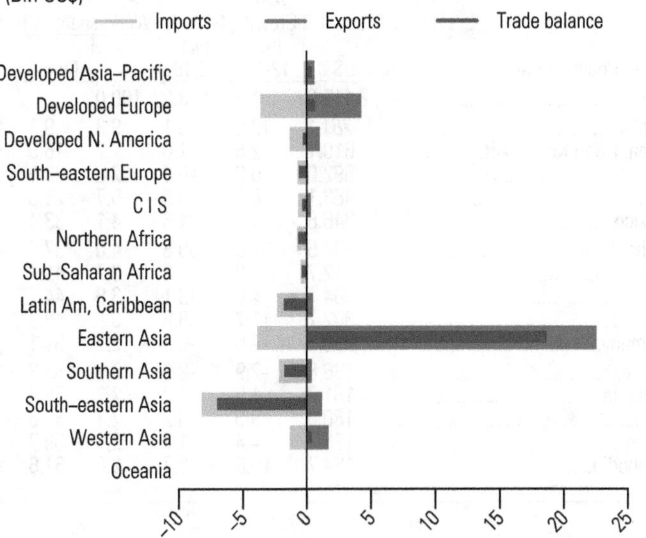

Table 2: Top exporting countries or areas in 2016

Country or area	Value (million US$)	Avg. Growth (%) 12-16	Growth (%) 15-16	World share %	Cum.
World	32670.2	2.0	-2.0	100.0	
China	14415.3	6.5	-1.4	44.1	44.1
Rep. of Korea	3385.5	-4.5	-3.7	10.4	54.5
Other Asia, nes	2583.1	1.4	-8.0	7.9	62.4
China, Hong Kong SAR	2119.6	-3.7	-11.3	6.5	68.9
Turkey	1497.9	-1.0	4.0	4.6	73.5
Italy	1047.0	-3.4	-4.1	3.2	76.7
USA	954.6	-1.9	-10.0	2.9	79.6
Germany	834.5	-3.5	0.9	2.6	82.1
Japan	584.0	-6.7	6.6	1.8	83.9
Viet Nam	*538.7*	24.4	8.9	1.6	85.6
France	438.4	-3.4	-2.8	1.3	86.9
Spain	390.1	3.8	20.6	1.2	88.1
Thailand	318.9	4.8	-1.3	1.0	89.1
India	265.9	6.2	11.7	0.8	89.9
Uzbekistan	*243.0*	50.8	46.1	0.7	90.7

Table 3: Top importing countries or areas in 2016

Country or area	Value (million US$)	Avg. Growth (%) 12-16	Growth (%) 15-16	World share %	Cum.
World	25562.2	2.4	-0.8	100.0	
Viet Nam	*3737.3*	14.7	5.1	14.6	14.6
Cambodia	2202.7	11.8	11.0	8.6	23.2
China, Hong Kong SAR	1933.2	-3.0	-9.1	7.6	30.8
China	1704.4	-7.8	-7.7	6.7	37.5
Indonesia	1329.9	0.7	-2.6	5.2	42.7
USA	1115.6	2.2	-2.0	4.4	47.0
Sri Lanka	797.1	4.4	15.5	3.1	50.2
Mexico	708.8	-0.8	-12.1	2.8	52.9
Italy	667.4	0.9	-4.6	2.6	55.5
Bangladesh	*506.5*	14.3	-14.2	2.0	57.5
India	499.5	8.0	5.1	2.0	59.5
Jordan	498.3	5.8	-5.2	1.9	61.4
Germany	455.4	-2.4	-3.2	1.8	63.2
Turkey	433.4	5.2	0.1	1.7	64.9
Morocco	411.3	-0.5	3.7	1.6	66.5

656 Tulles, lace, embroidery, ribbons, trimmings and other smallwares

In 2016, the value (in current US$) of exports of "tulles, lace, embroidery, ribbons, trimmings and other smallwares" (SITC group 656) decreased by 2.4 percent (compared to 0.5 percent average growth rate from 2012-2016) to reach 9.8 bln US$ (see table 2), while imports increased by 3.3 percent to reach 8.4 bln US$ (see table 3). Exports of this commodity accounted for 0.5 percent of world exports of SITC section 6, and 0.1 percent of total world merchandise exports (see table 1). China, China, Hong Kong SAR and Other Asia, nes were the top exporters in 2016 (see table 2). They accounted for 35.4, 10.6 and 6.9 percent of world exports, respectively. Viet Nam, China, Hong Kong SAR and USA were the top destinations, with respectively 9.3, 7.2 and 7.0 percent of world imports (see table 3).

The top 15 countries/areas accounted for 86.4 and 61.6 percent of total world exports and imports, respectively (see tables 2 and 3). In 2016, China was the country/area with the highest value of net exports (+3.0 bln US$), followed by Other Asia, nes (+649.6 mln US$). By MDG regions (see graph 2), surpluses in this product group were recorded by Eastern Asia (+4.3 bln US$), Developed Europe (+250.2 mln US$) and Developed Asia-Pacific (+19.9 mln US$). The largest trade deficits were recorded by South-eastern Asia (-1.2 bln US$), Southern Asia (-620.9 mln US$) and Latin America and the Caribbean (-508.0 mln US$).

Table 1: Imports (Imp.) and exports (Exp.), 2002-2016, in current US$

		2002	2003	2004	2005	2006	2007	2008	2009	2010	2011	2012	2013	2014	2015	2016
Values in Bln US$	Imp.	5.4	6.0	6.6	7.1	7.3	7.6	7.7	6.1	7.2	7.9	7.8	8.3	8.6	8.2	8.4
	Exp.	6.3	6.8	7.6	8.2	9.1	9.5	9.5	7.5	8.7	9.6	9.6	10.3	10.7	10.0	9.8
As a percentage of SITC section (%)	Imp.	0.6	0.6	0.5	0.5	0.4	0.4	0.4	0.4	0.4	0.3	0.4	0.4	0.4	0.4	0.4
	Exp.	0.7	0.7	0.6	0.6	0.5	0.5	0.4	0.5	0.4	0.4	0.4	0.5	0.5	0.5	0.5
As a percentage of world trade (%)	Imp.	0.1	0.1	0.1	0.1	0.1	0.1	0.0	0.0	0.0	0.0	0.0	0.0	0.0	0.0	0.1
	Exp.	0.1	0.1	0.1	0.1	0.1	0.1	0.1	0.1	0.1	0.1	0.1	0.1	0.1	0.1	0.1

Graph 1: Annual growth rates of exports, 2002–2016

(In percentage by year)

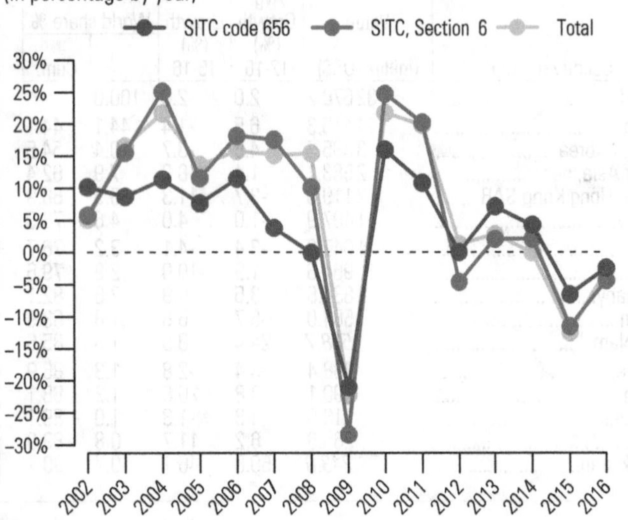

Table 2: Top exporting countries or areas in 2016

Country or area	Value (million US$)	Avg. Growth (%) 12-16	Growth (%) 15-16	World share %	Cum.
World	9784.3	0.5	-2.4	100.0	
China	3460.7	2.8	-5.0	35.4	35.4
China, Hong Kong SAR	1033.6	2.8	-1.7	10.6	45.9
Other Asia, nes	675.3	1.2	-3.2	6.9	52.8
Germany	424.2	0.5	-0.4	4.3	57.2
USA	417.3	-1.5	-7.1	4.3	61.4
Italy	392.0	-2.0	1.4	4.0	65.4
Rep. of Korea	350.0	-5.7	-6.4	3.6	69.0
France	344.0	-4.6	1.0	3.5	72.5
India	326.4	8.6	1.0	3.3	75.9
Turkey	318.6	-2.5	-4.0	3.3	79.1
Thailand	205.3	1.0	-2.6	2.1	81.2
Japan	163.5	-7.5	17.4	1.7	82.9
Spain	124.4	-0.4	5.3	1.3	84.2
Austria	117.4	-5.3	2.0	1.2	85.4
United Kingdom	103.8	0.2	-3.9	1.1	86.4

Graph 2: Trade Balance by MDG regions 2016

(Bln US$)

Imports — Exports — Trade balance

Developed Asia-Pacific
Developed Europe
Developed N. America
South-eastern Europe
CIS
Northern Africa
Sub-Saharan Africa
Latin Am, Caribbean
Eastern Asia
Southern Asia
South-eastern Asia
Western Asia
Oceania

-2 -1 0 1 2 3 4 5 6

Table 3: Top importing countries or areas in 2016

Country or area	Value (million US$)	Avg. Growth (%) 12-16	Growth (%) 15-16	World share %	Cum.
World	8417.6	1.8	3.3	100.0	
Viet Nam	*781.2*	12.0	5.1	9.3	9.3
China, Hong Kong SAR	610.1	2.5	-1.0	7.2	16.5
USA	592.0	-0.2	-6.0	7.0	23.6
China	483.1	-6.4	-4.9	5.7	29.3
Mexico	346.6	-1.8	-4.6	4.1	33.4
Afghanistan	334.5	32.0	39.8	4.0	37.4
Indonesia	312.7	5.8	12.6	3.7	41.1
Italy	304.4	4.6	13.1	3.6	44.7
Sri Lanka	302.7	11.7	58.6	3.6	48.3
Germany	230.5	-4.5	-0.8	2.7	51.1
France	186.8	-2.9	-2.9	2.2	53.3
Romania	181.7	1.5	1.2	2.2	55.4
India	180.0	8.5	-6.2	2.1	57.6
Turkey	176.2	4.4	-1.7	2.1	59.7
Cambodia	164.7	15.6	15.7	2.0	61.6

In 2016, the value (in current US$) of exports of "special yarns, special textile fabrics and related products" (SITC group 657) decreased by 1.2 percent (compared to 0.4 percent average growth rate from 2012-2016) to reach 46.3 bln US$ (see table 2), while imports decreased by 0.9 percent to reach 41.1 bln US$ (see table 3). Exports of this commodity accounted for 2.4 percent of world exports of SITC section 6, and 0.3 percent of total world merchandise exports (see table 1). China, Germany and USA were the top exporters in 2016 (see table 2). They accounted for 25.2, 10.4 and 9.6 percent of world exports, respectively. USA, China and Germany were the top destinations, with respectively 11.4, 7.0 and 5.9 percent of world imports (see table 3).

The top 15 countries/areas accounted for 77.7 and 59.5 percent of total world exports and imports, respectively (see tables 2 and 3). In 2016, China was the country/area with the highest value of net exports (+8.8 bln US$), followed by Germany (+2.4 bln US$). By MDG regions (see graph 2), surpluses in this product group were recorded by Eastern Asia (+10.9 bln US$) and Developed Europe (+3.8 bln US$). The largest trade deficits were recorded by Latin America and the Caribbean (-2.6 bln US$), South-eastern Asia (-2.1 bln US$) and South-eastern Europe (-1.1 bln US$).

Table 1: Imports (Imp.) and exports (Exp.), 2002-2016, in current US$

		2002	2003	2004	2005	2006	2007	2008	2009	2010	2011	2012	2013	2014	2015	2016
Values in Bln US$	Imp.	20.1	22.7	25.5	27.5	30.0	34.2	36.4	30.6	36.4	41.3	40.3	42.2	44.1	41.4	41.1
	Exp.	22.2	25.2	27.7	29.6	32.2	35.9	39.7	34.0	41.3	48.0	45.7	48.0	50.3	46.9	46.3
As a percentage of SITC section (%)	Imp.	2.2	2.2	2.0	1.9	1.8	1.7	1.7	2.0	1.9	1.8	1.8	1.9	1.9	2.1	2.1
	Exp.	2.5	2.5	2.2	2.1	1.9	1.8	1.8	2.2	2.1	2.1	2.1	2.1	2.2	2.3	2.4
As a percentage of world trade (%)	Imp.	0.3	0.3	0.3	0.3	0.2	0.2	0.2	0.2	0.2	0.2	0.2	0.2	0.2	0.3	0.3
	Exp.	0.3	0.3	0.3	0.3	0.3	0.3	0.2	0.3	0.3	0.3	0.2	0.3	0.3	0.3	0.3

Graph 1: Annual growth rates of exports, 2002–2016

(In percentage by year)

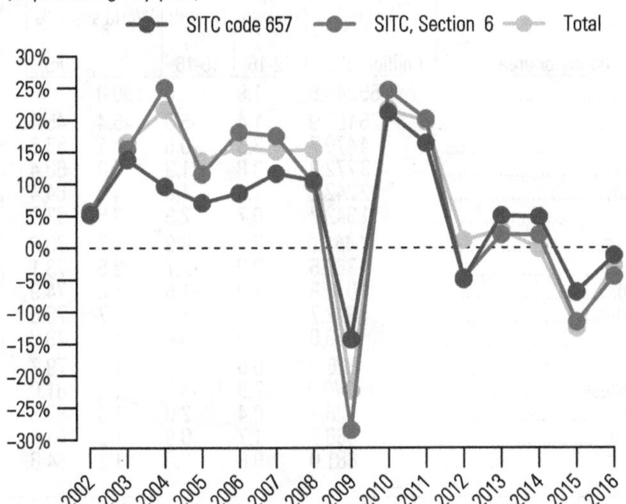

Table 2: Top exporting countries or areas in 2016

Country or area	Value (million US$)	Avg. Growth (%) 12-16	Growth (%) 15-16	World share %	Cum.
World	46318.2	0.4	-1.2	100.0	
China	11649.8	3.3	-1.4	25.2	25.2
Germany	4834.2	-0.5	3.4	10.4	35.6
USA	4425.6	0.7	-2.6	9.6	45.1
Italy	2521.5	0.2	2.5	5.4	50.6
Rep. of Korea	1967.3	-1.1	0.9	4.2	54.8
Japan	1856.9	-2.9	8.2	4.0	58.8
Other Asia, nes	1593.9	-3.5	-6.7	3.4	62.3
France	1150.4	-3.2	-0.5	2.5	64.8
Netherlands	1086.4	0.9	6.5	2.3	67.1
Turkey	865.8	6.1	9.3	1.9	69.0
Viet Nam	*859.2*	10.7	8.9	1.9	70.8
United Kingdom	844.3	-3.9	-8.7	1.8	72.7
Spain	816.8	-2.4	3.7	1.8	74.4
Czechia	784.9	0.1	2.3	1.7	76.1
China, Hong Kong SAR	719.7	-3.9	-5.9	1.6	77.7

Graph 2: Trade Balance by MDG regions 2016

(Bln US$)

Imports — Exports — Trade balance

Developed Asia-Pacific
Developed Europe
Developed N. America
South-eastern Europe
CIS
Northern Africa
Sub-Saharan Africa
Latin Am, Caribbean
Eastern Asia
Southern Asia
South-eastern Asia
Western Asia
Oceania

-15 -10 -5 0 5 10 15 20

Table 3: Top importing countries or areas in 2016

Country or area	Value (million US$)	Avg. Growth (%) 12-16	Growth (%) 15-16	World share %	Cum.
World	41053.5	0.5	-0.9	100.0	
USA	4661.7	4.0	-0.3	11.4	11.4
China	2892.1	-1.7	-3.2	7.0	18.4
Germany	2419.1	-2.3	-0.9	5.9	24.3
Mexico	1998.8	4.5	0.8	4.9	29.2
Viet Nam	*1720.1*	6.9	5.1	4.2	33.4
Japan	1521.8	2.4	4.3	3.7	37.1
France	1190.7	-2.8	1.2	2.9	40.0
United Kingdom	1118.2	-0.4	-7.2	2.7	42.7
Poland	1097.3	0.0	1.6	2.7	45.4
Italy	1047.3	1.6	2.6	2.6	47.9
Canada	1037.1	1.1	3.9	2.5	50.4
Rep. of Korea	995.2	2.4	5.0	2.4	52.9
India	978.2	2.0	-2.9	2.4	55.2
Indonesia	955.7	0.6	-3.6	2.3	57.6
Romania	796.3	9.4	1.3	1.9	59.5

Source: UN Comtrade

658 Made-up articles, wholly or chiefly of textile materials, nes

In 2016, the value (in current US$) of exports of "made-up articles, wholly or chiefly of textile materials, nes" (SITC group 658) decreased by 2.6 percent (compared to 2.0 percent average growth rate from 2012-2016) to reach 55.2 bln US$ (see table 2), while imports decreased by 0.4 percent to reach 49.3 bln US$ (see table 3). Exports of this commodity accounted for 2.8 percent of world exports of SITC section 6, and 0.3 percent of total world merchandise exports (see table 1). China, India and Pakistan were the top exporters in 2016 (see table 2). They accounted for 45.4, 8.1 and 6.8 percent of world exports, respectively. USA, Germany and Japan were the top destinations, with respectively 29.3, 7.8 and 6.8 percent of world imports (see table 3).

The top 15 countries/areas accounted for 84.8 and 74.2 percent of total world exports and imports, respectively (see tables 2 and 3). In 2016, China was the country/area with the highest value of net exports (+24.7 bln US$), followed by India (+4.2 bln US$). By MDG regions (see graph 2), the largest surpluses in this product group were recorded by Eastern Asia (+24.2 bln US$), Southern Asia (+8.5 bln US$) and South-eastern Asia (+1.4 bln US$). The largest trade deficits were recorded by Developed North America (-14.1 bln US$), Developed Europe (-8.5 bln US$) and Developed Asia-Pacific (-4.6 bln US$).

Table 1: Imports (Imp.) and exports (Exp.), 2002-2016, in current US$

		2002	2003	2004	2005	2006	2007	2008	2009	2010	2011	2012	2013	2014	2015	2016
Values in Bln US$	Imp.	19.4	23.2	27.1	29.9	33.4	37.4	40.1	36.8	41.2	47.1	45.6	48.1	51.3	49.5	49.3
	Exp.	19.3	23.6	27.2	31.4	34.6	37.6	41.7	39.1	44.6	51.2	51.2	56.7	59.8	56.7	55.2
As a percentage of SITC section (%)	Imp.	2.2	2.3	2.1	2.1	2.0	1.9	1.8	2.4	2.1	2.0	2.1	2.2	2.2	2.5	2.6
	Exp.	2.2	2.3	2.1	2.2	2.1	1.9	1.9	2.5	2.3	2.2	2.3	2.5	2.6	2.8	2.8
As a percentage of world trade (%)	Imp.	0.3	0.3	0.3	0.3	0.3	0.3	0.2	0.3	0.3	0.3	0.2	0.3	0.3	0.3	0.3
	Exp.	0.3	0.3	0.3	0.3	0.3	0.3	0.3	0.3	0.3	0.3	0.3	0.3	0.3	0.3	0.3

Graph 1: Annual growth rates of exports, 2002–2016

(In percentage by year)

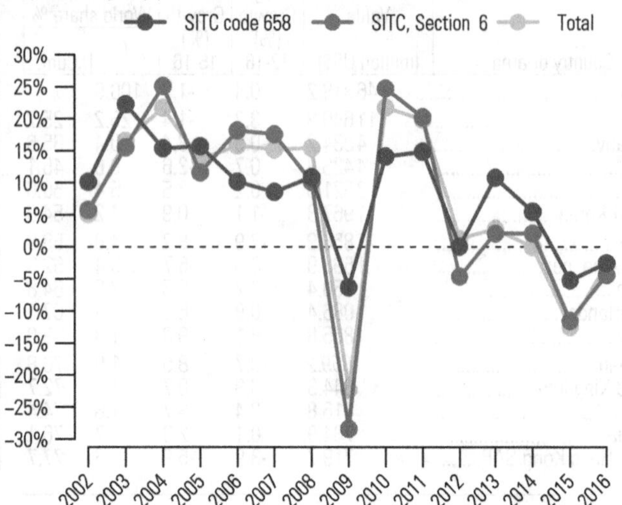

Table 2: Top exporting countries or areas in 2016

Country or area	Value (million US$)	Avg. Growth (%) 12-16	Growth (%) 15-16	World share %	Cum.
World	55245.8	1.9	-2.6	100.0	
China	25102.9	1.4	-5.0	45.4	45.4
India	4479.7	3.6	-0.5	8.1	53.5
Pakistan	3772.3	3.8	1.3	6.8	60.4
Germany	2242.2	1.4	1.0	4.1	64.4
Turkey	1942.2	0.7	2.9	3.5	67.9
Viet Nam	*1468.9*	13.7	8.9	2.7	70.6
USA	1360.5	2.0	-2.7	2.5	73.1
Mexico	1018.9	7.2	-1.5	1.8	74.9
Netherlands	942.7	6.7	18.2	1.7	76.6
Belgium	859.0	0.3	5.8	1.6	78.2
Poland	826.9	6.6	7.4	1.5	79.7
Bangladesh	*740.8*	-7.9	-4.9	1.3	81.0
France	726.7	0.4	2.9	1.3	82.3
Portugal	686.7	1.7	0.9	1.2	83.6
Spain	681.0	9.8	2.0	1.2	84.8

Graph 2: Trade Balance by MDG regions 2016

(Bln US$)

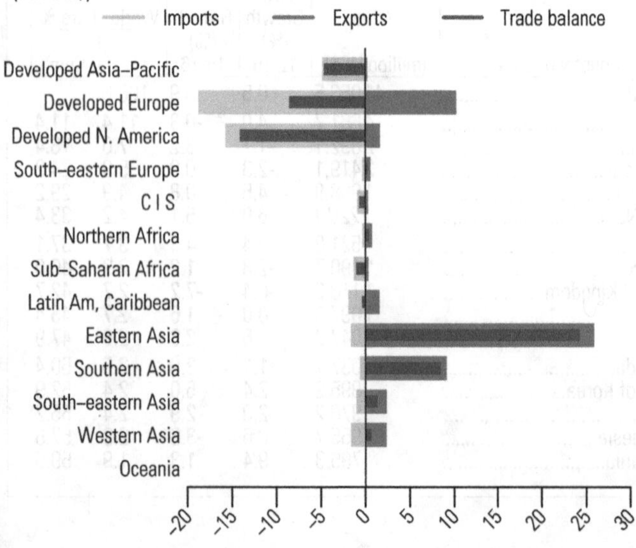

Table 3: Top importing countries or areas in 2016

Country or area	Value (million US$)	Avg. Growth (%) 12-16	Growth (%) 15-16	World share %	Cum.
World	49261.6	2.0	-0.4	100.0	
USA	14442.0	3.7	-1.7	29.3	29.3
Germany	3822.9	1.2	0.3	7.8	37.1
Japan	3346.9	-2.9	-0.6	6.8	43.9
France	2339.4	0.2	0.2	4.7	48.6
United Kingdom	2333.4	2.4	-7.0	4.7	53.4
Netherlands	1428.2	6.7	10.7	2.9	56.3
Spain	1307.4	8.7	0.4	2.7	58.9
Australia	1271.2	2.5	-0.8	2.6	61.5
Canada	1235.7	-0.4	-1.1	2.5	64.0
Italy	1141.1	2.6	7.6	2.3	66.3
Belgium	1021.6	-0.3	8.0	2.1	68.4
Poland	817.0	12.3	13.2	1.7	70.0
Austria	719.4	8.7	23.3	1.5	71.5
Rep. of Korea	686.8	6.9	-1.2	1.4	72.9
Switzerland	656.2	0.5	1.9	1.3	74.2

In 2016, the value (in current US$) of exports of "floor coverings, etc" (SITC group 659) decreased by 1.5 percent (compared to -0.3 percent average growth rate from 2012-2016) to reach 14.8 bln US$ (see table 2), while imports decreased by 0.5 percent to reach 13.3 bln US$ (see table 3). Exports of this commodity accounted for 0.8 percent of world exports of SITC section 6, and 0.1 percent of total world merchandise exports (see table 1). China, Turkey and Belgium were the top exporters in 2016 (see table 2). They accounted for 17.2, 12.9 and 11.8 percent of world exports, respectively. USA, United Kingdom and Germany were the top destinations, with respectively 21.3, 9.0 and 8.5 percent of world imports (see table 3).

The top 15 countries/areas accounted for 84.9 and 71.5 percent of total world exports and imports, respectively (see tables 2 and 3). In 2016, China was the country/area with the highest value of net exports (+2.4 bln US$), followed by Turkey (+1.8 bln US$). By MDG regions (see graph 2), the largest surpluses in this product group were recorded by Eastern Asia (+2.3 bln US$), Southern Asia (+1.9 bln US$) and Western Asia (+1.2 bln US$). The largest trade deficits were recorded by Developed North America (-2.4 bln US$), Developed Asia-Pacific (-935.4 mln US$) and Latin America and the Caribbean (-371.8 mln US$).

Table 1: Imports (Imp.) and exports (Exp.), 2002-2016, in current US$

		2002	2003	2004	2005	2006	2007	2008	2009	2010	2011	2012	2013	2014	2015	2016
Values in Bln US$	Imp.	8.2	9.1	10.4	11.1	12.0	13.2	13.5	11.1	12.3	13.5	13.4	14.0	14.7	13.4	13.3
	Exp.	8.4	9.5	10.7	11.6	12.6	14.1	15.3	12.6	14.1	15.7	15.0	16.2	16.7	15.0	14.8
As a percentage of SITC section (%)	Imp.	0.9	0.9	0.8	0.8	0.7	0.7	0.6	0.7	0.6	0.6	0.6	0.6	0.6	0.7	0.7
	Exp.	1.0	0.9	0.8	0.8	0.8	0.7	0.7	0.8	0.7	0.7	0.7	0.7	0.7	0.7	0.8
As a percentage of world trade (%)	Imp.	0.1	0.1	0.1	0.1	0.1	0.1	0.1	0.1	0.1	0.1	0.1	0.1	0.1	0.1	0.1
	Exp.	0.1	0.1	0.1	0.1	0.1	0.1	0.1	0.1	0.1	0.1	0.1	0.1	0.1	0.1	0.1

Graph 1: Annual growth rates of exports, 2002–2016
(In percentage by year)

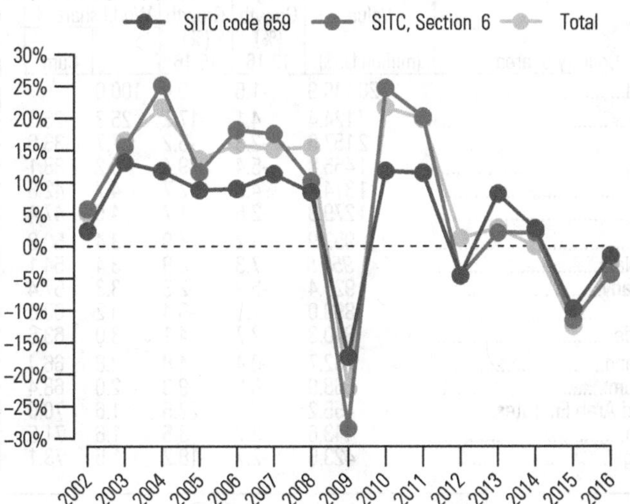

Table 2: Top exporting countries or areas in 2016

Country or area	Value (million US$)	Avg. Growth (%) 12-16	Growth (%) 15-16	World share %	Cum.
World	14802.1	-0.3	-1.5	100.0	
China	2540.1	1.1	-4.0	17.2	17.2
Turkey	1914.1	-1.1	-4.8	12.9	30.1
Belgium	1740.0	-1.7	0.4	11.8	41.8
India	1737.0	6.5	1.1	11.7	53.6
Netherlands	1146.7	1.3	-1.9	7.7	61.3
USA	982.2	-3.1	-5.5	6.6	68.0
Germany	629.9	-3.0	4.4	4.3	72.2
United Kingdom	333.7	-0.4	-4.4	2.3	74.5
Egypt	303.2	-6.1	-10.7	2.0	76.5
France	257.5	0.0	3.1	1.7	78.3
Poland	246.0	3.1	0.4	1.7	79.9
Italy	202.9	0.2	4.8	1.4	81.3
Austria	189.9	11.7	82.3	1.3	82.6
Denmark	188.9	0.8	7.8	1.3	83.9
Iran	*162.0*	-7.5	-19.0	1.1	84.9

Graph 2: Trade Balance by MDG regions 2016
(Bln US$)

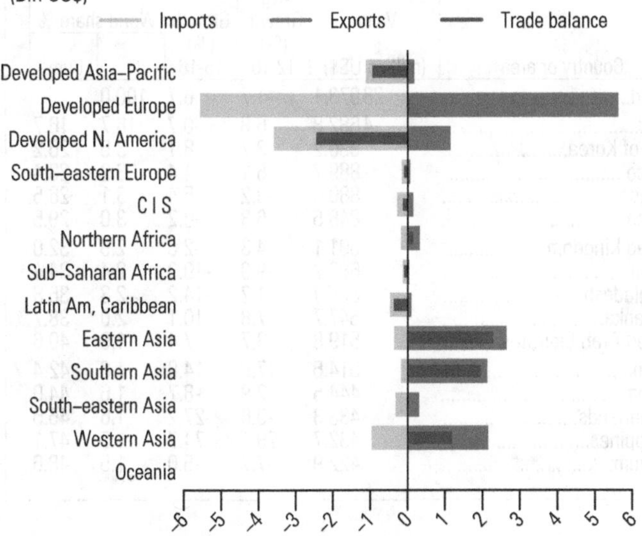

Table 3: Top importing countries or areas in 2016

Country or area	Value (million US$)	Avg. Growth (%) 12-16	Growth (%) 15-16	World share %	Cum.
World	13324.8	-0.2	-0.5	100.0	
USA	2831.9	6.5	5.2	21.3	21.3
United Kingdom	1201.3	1.9	-4.6	9.0	30.3
Germany	1138.1	-2.3	0.9	8.5	38.8
Canada	754.3	-3.4	-1.5	5.7	44.5
Japan	572.1	-5.9	4.3	4.3	48.8
France	468.8	-2.8	2.5	3.5	52.3
Australia	434.7	-0.4	1.1	3.3	55.5
Saudi Arabia	384.5	7.8	-21.3	2.9	58.4
Netherlands	336.4	-3.5	-10.8	2.5	61.0
Belgium	265.6	1.9	-0.1	2.0	62.9
Sweden	243.9	2.5	10.6	1.8	64.8
Austria	240.1	5.5	67.9	1.8	66.6
Poland	233.2	0.8	3.6	1.7	68.3
Italy	213.1	-0.1	4.0	1.6	69.9
Czechia	203.4	0.3	0.1	1.5	71.5

 Source: UN Comtrade

661 Lime, cement, and fabricated construction materials (except glass and clay)

In 2016, the value (in current US$) of exports of "lime, cement, and fabricated construction materials (except glass and clay)" (SITC group 661) decreased by 9.4 percent (compared to -1.5 percent average growth rate from 2012-2016) to reach 28.1 bln US$ (see table 2), while imports decreased by 6.7 percent to reach 28.1 bln US$ (see table 3). Exports of this commodity accounted for 1.4 percent of world exports of SITC section 6, and 0.2 percent of total world merchandise exports (see table 1). China, Italy and Turkey were the top exporters in 2016 (see table 2). They accounted for 25.3, 7.7 and 5.2 percent of world exports, respectively. USA, Rep. of Korea and France were the top destinations, with respectively 16.7, 3.5 and 3.2 percent of world imports (see table 3).

The top 15 countries/areas accounted for 73.1 and 48.6 percent of total world exports and imports, respectively (see tables 2 and 3). In 2016, China was the country/area with the highest value of net exports (+7.1 bln US$), followed by Italy (+1.9 bln US$). By MDG regions (see graph 2), the largest surpluses in this product group were recorded by Eastern Asia (+5.9 bln US$), Developed Europe (+2.2 bln US$) and South-eastern Asia (+328.5 mln US$). The largest trade deficits were recorded by Developed North America (-3.8 bln US$), Sub-Saharan Africa (-2.4 bln US$) and Western Asia (-791.4 mln US$).

Table 1: Imports (Imp.) and exports (Exp.), 2002-2016, in current US$

		2002	2003	2004	2005	2006	2007	2008	2009	2010	2011	2012	2013	2014	2015	2016
Values in Bln US$	Imp.	13.3	15.3	18.2	21.9	25.3	29.3	31.8	25.2	27.3	28.9	30.1	32.1	32.5	30.1	28.1
	Exp.	12.2	13.3	15.7	19.0	22.9	25.8	31.3	24.5	25.8	28.4	29.9	32.7	33.5	31.1	28.1
As a percentage of SITC section (%)	Imp.	1.5	1.5	1.4	1.5	1.5	1.5	1.5	1.6	1.4	1.3	1.4	1.5	1.4	1.5	1.5
	Exp.	1.4	1.3	1.2	1.3	1.4	1.3	1.4	1.6	1.3	1.2	1.3	1.4	1.4	1.5	1.4
As a percentage of world trade (%)	Imp.	0.2	0.2	0.2	0.2	0.2	0.2	0.2	0.2	0.2	0.2	0.2	0.2	0.2	0.2	0.2
	Exp.	0.2	0.2	0.2	0.2	0.2	0.2	0.2	0.2	0.2	0.2	0.2	0.2	0.2	0.2	0.2

Graph 1: Annual growth rates of exports, 2002–2016
(In percentage by year)

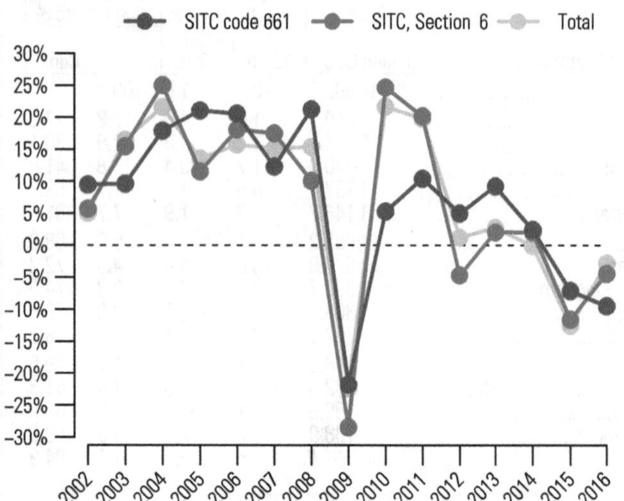

Table 2: Top exporting countries or areas in 2016

Country or area	Value (million US$)	Avg. Growth (%) 12-16	Growth (%) 15-16	World share %	Cum.
World	28146.9	-1.5	-9.4	100.0	
China	7124.4	4.1	-17.2	25.3	25.3
Italy	2157.6	-2.3	-5.2	7.7	33.0
Turkey	1455.8	-5.4	-9.4	5.2	38.1
India	1314.4	4.6	2.7	4.7	42.8
Spain	1279.9	-2.6	-1.7	4.5	47.4
Brazil	953.9	3.2	-6.9	3.4	50.8
Viet Nam	*953.5*	7.3	8.9	3.4	54.1
Germany	921.4	-5.9	-2.3	3.3	57.4
USA	898.0	-1.5	-5.4	3.2	60.6
Canada	840.3	2.7	4.1	3.0	63.6
Thailand	782.7	-0.4	-4.8	2.8	66.4
Belgium	568.9	-6.0	-9.3	2.0	68.4
United Arab Emirates	455.2	-2.6	-22.5	1.6	70.0
Japan	443.6	3.7	3.5	1.6	71.6
Portugal	423.5	-2.7	-18.2	1.5	73.1

Graph 2: Trade Balance by MDG regions 2016
(Bln US$)

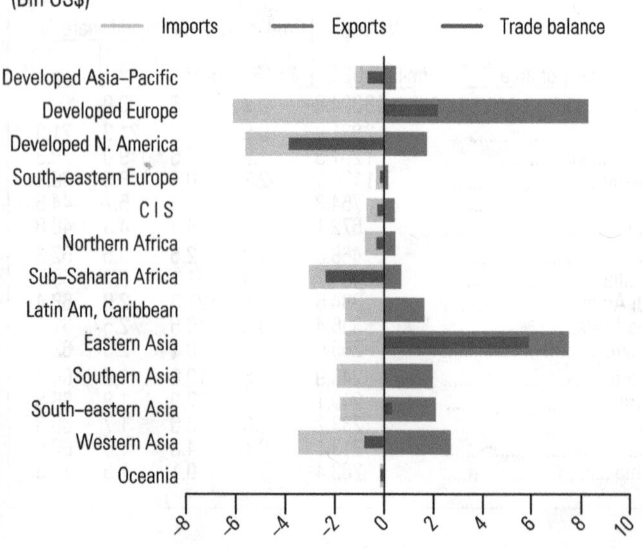

Table 3: Top importing countries or areas in 2016

Country or area	Value (million US$)	Avg. Growth (%) 12-16	Growth (%) 15-16	World share %	Cum.
World	28073.1	-1.7	-6.7	100.0	
USA	4682.8	6.8	-0.7	16.7	16.7
Rep. of Korea	990.2	3.7	8.1	3.5	20.2
France	889.7	-6.1	-4.4	3.2	23.4
Canada	880.0	-3.2	-5.4	3.1	26.5
Germany	848.5	-6.3	-8.2	3.0	29.5
United Kingdom	691.1	4.3	-2.0	2.5	32.0
Japan	682.7	-9.9	-10.3	2.4	34.4
Bangladesh	*656.1*	1.2	-14.2	2.3	36.8
Sri Lanka	547.7	7.8	10.1	2.0	38.7
United Arab Emirates	519.8	3.7	7.4	1.9	40.6
Oman	514.5	17.6	14.8	1.8	42.4
Ghana	444.5	2.9	-8.7	1.6	44.0
Netherlands	438.3	-9.6	-27.2	1.6	45.5
Philippines	432.7	29.1	74.7	1.5	47.1
Belgium	422.9	-7.7	-5.0	1.5	48.6

In 2016, the value (in current US$) of exports of "clay construction materials and refractory construction materials" (SITC group 662) decreased by 11.0 percent (compared to -1.6 percent average growth rate from 2012-2016) to reach 25.2 bln US$ (see table 2), while imports decreased by 2.9 percent to reach 23.2 bln US$ (see table 3). Exports of this commodity accounted for 1.3 percent of world exports of SITC section 6, and 0.2 percent of total world merchandise exports (see table 1). China, Italy and Spain were the top exporters in 2016 (see table 2). They accounted for 29.5, 18.5 and 12.3 percent of world exports, respectively. USA, France and Germany were the top destinations, with respectively 10.2, 5.3 and 4.8 percent of world imports (see table 3).

The top 15 countries/areas accounted for 86.6 and 46.7 percent of total world exports and imports, respectively (see tables 2 and 3). In 2016, China was the country/area with the highest value of net exports (+7.2 bln US$), followed by Italy (+4.3 bln US$). By MDG regions (see graph 2), the largest surpluses in this product group were recorded by Eastern Asia (+6.2 bln US$), Developed Europe (+5.6 bln US$) and Southern Asia (+122.5 mln US$). The largest trade deficits were recorded by Developed North America (-2.3 bln US$), Western Asia (-1.7 bln US$) and Sub-Saharan Africa (-1.4 bln US$).

Table 1: Imports (Imp.) and exports (Exp.), 2002-2016, in current US$

		2002	2003	2004	2005	2006	2007	2008	2009	2010	2011	2012	2013	2014	2015	2016
Values in Bln US$	Imp.	11.2	13.3	15.6	17.2	19.1	22.3	24.6	19.3	21.5	23.9	24.4	25.4	26.7	23.9	23.2
	Exp.	11.2	13.3	16.0	16.9	19.4	22.1	25.0	20.1	22.1	25.5	26.8	29.4	30.1	28.3	25.2
As a percentage of SITC section (%)	Imp.	1.2	1.3	1.2	1.2	1.2	1.1	1.1	1.2	1.1	1.0	1.1	1.2	1.2	1.2	1.2
	Exp.	1.3	1.3	1.3	1.2	1.2	1.1	1.2	1.3	1.1	1.1	1.2	1.3	1.3	1.4	1.3
As a percentage of world trade (%)	Imp.	0.2	0.2	0.2	0.2	0.2	0.2	0.2	0.2	0.1	0.1	0.1	0.1	0.1	0.1	0.1
	Exp.	0.2	0.2	0.2	0.2	0.2	0.2	0.2	0.2	0.1	0.1	0.1	0.2	0.2	0.2	0.2

Graph 1: Annual growth rates of exports, 2002–2016

(In percentage by year)

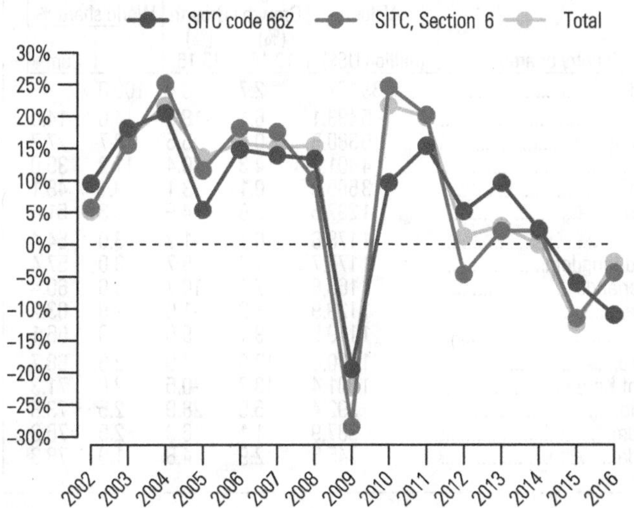

Table 2: Top exporting countries or areas in 2016

Country or area	Value (million US$)	Avg. Growth (%) 12-16	Growth (%) 15-16	World share %	Cum.
World	25163.1	-1.6	-11.0	100.0	
China	7425.9	-3.4	-31.9	29.5	29.5
Italy	4658.9	1.8	6.6	18.5	48.0
Spain	3089.4	1.4	4.0	12.3	60.3
Germany	1589.0	-5.0	-2.4	6.3	66.6
India	839.0	32.9	19.3	3.3	70.0
Turkey	624.4	-3.7	2.4	2.5	72.4
Austria	523.2	1.0	33.1	2.1	74.5
USA	507.3	-4.9	-13.2	2.0	76.5
Poland	433.8	0.4	3.9	1.7	78.3
Brazil	389.2	3.1	3.9	1.5	79.8
France	384.7	-8.3	5.2	1.5	81.3
Mexico	384.2	-3.1	-10.0	1.5	82.9
Netherlands	319.2	5.9	5.7	1.3	84.1
Portugal	317.4	-4.4	2.0	1.3	85.4
Belgium	299.2	-0.9	-6.0	1.2	86.6

Graph 2: Trade Balance by MDG regions 2016

(Bln US$)

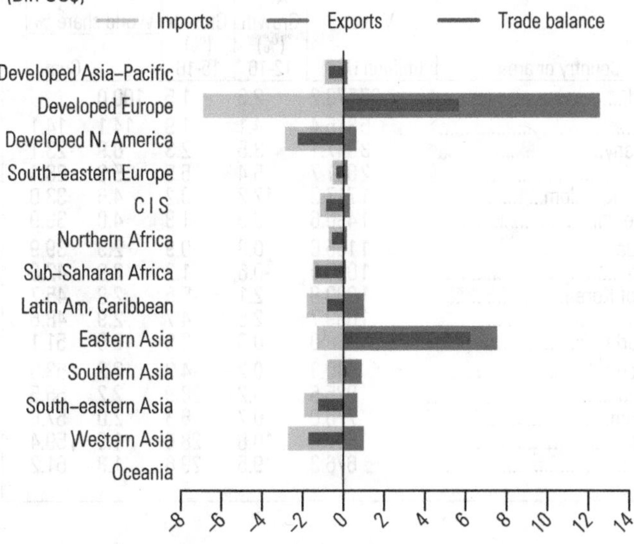

Table 3: Top importing countries or areas in 2016

Country or area	Value (million US$)	Avg. Growth (%) 12-16	Growth (%) 15-16	World share %	Cum.
World	23170.9	-1.3	-2.9	100.0	
USA	2357.2	8.0	3.3	10.2	10.2
France	1218.8	-4.3	4.3	5.3	15.4
Germany	1118.0	-0.4	5.9	4.8	20.3
Saudi Arabia	699.1	-4.1	-18.2	3.0	23.3
United Kingdom	662.3	3.2	-3.5	2.9	26.1
Rep. of Korea	662.2	3.1	11.3	2.9	29.0
Russian Federation	571.1	-13.9	-8.2	2.5	31.5
United Arab Emirates	520.7	12.3	46.8	2.2	33.7
Canada	511.1	-1.2	-7.1	2.2	35.9
Austria	486.9	7.9	58.4	2.1	38.0
Belgium	416.7	-3.6	4.8	1.8	39.8
Australia	413.5	6.4	2.4	1.8	41.6
Japan	410.9	-6.6	-4.7	1.8	43.4
Mexico	405.2	0.1	-7.1	1.7	45.1
Indonesia	366.5	0.8	19.9	1.6	46.7

Source: UN Comtrade

663 Mineral manufactures, nes

In 2016, the value (in current US$) of exports of "mineral manufactures, nes" (SITC group 663) decreased by 0.4 percent (compared to 2.7 percent average growth rate from 2012-2016) to reach 39.2 bln US$ (see table 2), while imports increased by 1.5 percent to reach 37.6 bln US$ (see table 3). Exports of this commodity accounted for 2.0 percent of world exports of SITC section 6, and 0.2 percent of total world merchandise exports (see table 1). China, Germany and USA were the top exporters in 2016 (see table 2). They accounted for 14.0, 13.7 and 11.2 percent of world exports, respectively. USA, Germany and China were the top destinations, with respectively 14.1, 8.9 and 5.3 percent of world imports (see table 3).

The top 15 countries/areas accounted for 78.3 and 61.2 percent of total world exports and imports, respectively (see tables 2 and 3). In 2016, China was the country/area with the highest value of net exports (+3.5 bln US$), followed by Japan (+2.5 bln US$). By MDG regions (see graph 2), the largest surpluses in this product group were recorded by Developed Europe (+3.0 bln US$), Eastern Asia (+2.6 bln US$) and Developed Asia-Pacific (+1.9 bln US$). The largest trade deficits were recorded by Developed North America (-1.3 bln US$), Western Asia (-760.8 mln US$) and Latin America and the Caribbean (-711.6 mln US$).

Table 1: Imports (Imp.) and exports (Exp.), 2002-2016, in current US$

		2002	2003	2004	2005	2006	2007	2008	2009	2010	2011	2012	2013	2014	2015	2016
Values in Bln US$	Imp.	14.0	15.8	18.9	21.1	24.3	28.8	31.1	23.8	28.8	34.8	34.3	36.0	39.7	37.0	37.6
	Exp.	13.6	15.7	19.2	21.4	25.0	29.5	31.8	24.2	29.4	35.3	35.3	38.2	41.7	39.3	39.2
As a percentage of SITC section (%)	Imp.	1.6	1.5	1.5	1.5	1.5	1.5	1.4	1.5	1.5	1.5	1.6	1.6	1.7	1.8	1.9
	Exp.	1.5	1.5	1.5	1.5	1.5	1.5	1.5	1.6	1.5	1.5	1.6	1.7	1.8	1.9	2.0
As a percentage of world trade (%)	Imp.	0.2	0.2	0.2	0.2	0.2	0.2	0.2	0.2	0.2	0.2	0.2	0.2	0.2	0.2	0.2
	Exp.	0.2	0.2	0.2	0.2	0.2	0.2	0.2	0.2	0.2	0.2	0.2	0.2	0.2	0.2	0.2

Graph 1: Annual growth rates of exports, 2002–2016

(In percentage by year)

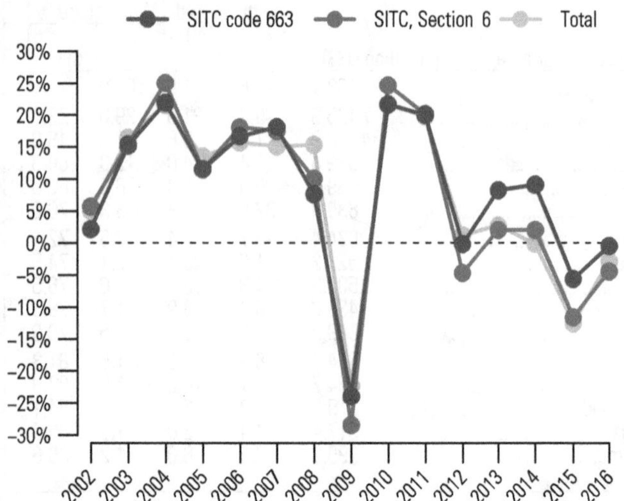

Table 2: Top exporting countries or areas in 2016

Country or area	Value (million US$)	Avg. Growth (%) 12-16	Growth (%) 15-16	World share %	Cum.
World	39171.4	2.7	-0.4	100.0	
China	5483.1	6.1	-18.5	14.0	14.0
Germany	5380.5	0.8	5.5	13.7	27.7
USA	4401.2	4.3	0.4	11.2	39.0
Japan	3565.9	0.1	3.1	9.1	48.1
Poland	1297.6	2.6	4.9	3.3	51.4
Italy	1178.6	0.1	-1.2	3.0	54.4
United Kingdom	1177.7	-1.3	-5.7	3.0	57.4
Netherlands	1160.8	7.1	16.7	3.0	60.4
France	1128.9	-1.2	-1.0	2.9	63.2
Spain	1119.5	9.1	9.0	2.9	66.1
Mexico	1030.8	13.0	4.0	2.6	68.7
Rep. of Korea	1001.4	13.2	-0.5	2.6	71.3
Austria	992.4	5.5	28.9	2.5	73.8
Belgium	987.9	-1.1	6.3	2.5	76.3
Canada	745.5	2.9	4.8	1.9	78.3

Graph 2: Trade Balance by MDG regions 2016

(Bln US$)

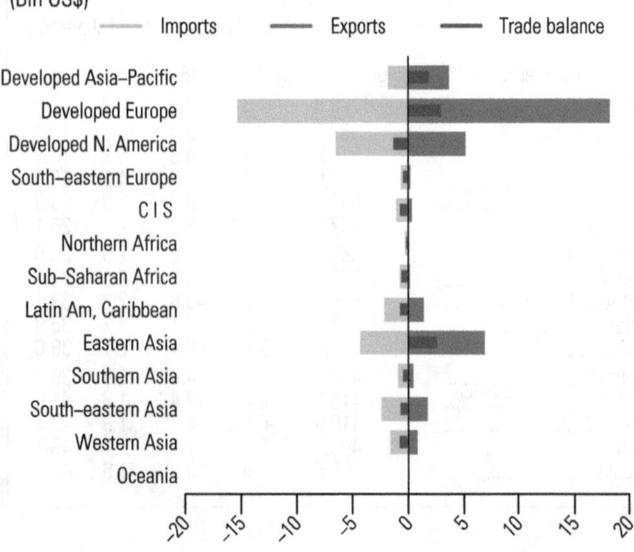

Table 3: Top importing countries or areas in 2016

Country or area	Value (million US$)	Avg. Growth (%) 12-16	Growth (%) 15-16	World share %	Cum.
World	37573.2	2.3	1.5	100.0	
USA	5315.4	4.1	1.9	14.1	14.1
Germany	3347.1	3.5	2.3	8.9	23.1
China	2001.7	5.4	5.5	5.3	28.4
United Kingdom	1717.3	12.2	0.2	4.6	33.0
France	1490.6	-0.9	-1.8	4.0	36.9
Canada	1105.6	0.8	-0.9	2.9	39.9
Japan	1095.0	-0.6	-1.2	2.9	42.8
Rep. of Korea	1090.8	2.1	-5.5	2.9	45.7
Italy	1089.7	2.5	4.7	2.9	48.6
Netherlands	938.0	-0.3	-3.9	2.5	51.1
Mexico	840.3	0.2	-4.3	2.2	53.3
Austria	825.5	6.2	28.9	2.2	55.5
Belgium	770.0	0.7	6.3	2.0	57.6
Spain	697.6	10.8	28.0	1.9	59.4
India	676.3	9.5	29.6	1.8	61.2

In 2016, the value (in current US$) of exports of "glass" (SITC group 664) increased by 3.5 percent (compared to -0.3 percent average growth rate from 2012-2016) to reach 37.7 bln US$ (see table 2), while imports increased by 3.9 percent to reach 40.5 bln US$ (see table 3). Exports of this commodity accounted for 1.9 percent of world exports of SITC section 6, and 0.2 percent of total world merchandise exports (see table 1). China, USA and Germany were the top exporters in 2016 (see table 2). They accounted for 20.4, 11.0 and 10.0 percent of world exports, respectively. China, USA and Germany were the top destinations, with respectively 13.3, 9.5 and 8.2 percent of world imports (see table 3).

The top 15 countries/areas accounted for 80.1 and 67.0 percent of total world exports and imports, respectively (see tables 2 and 3). In 2016, China was the country/area with the highest value of net exports (+2.3 bln US$), followed by Japan (+667.7 mln US$). By MDG regions (see graph 2), the largest surpluses in this product group were recorded by Eastern Asia (+2.6 bln US$) and Developed Asia-Pacific (+241.6 mln US$). The largest trade deficits were recorded by South-eastern Asia (-1.1 bln US$), Developed North America (-1.0 bln US$) and Latin America and the Caribbean (-862.0 mln US$).

Table 1: Imports (Imp.) and exports (Exp.), 2002-2016, in current US$

		2002	2003	2004	2005	2006	2007	2008	2009	2010	2011	2012	2013	2014	2015	2016
Values in Bln US$	Imp.	18.4	21.0	24.7	26.6	29.5	33.6	36.3	29.8	36.2	41.4	40.8	42.0	42.7	38.9	40.5
	Exp.	18.0	20.5	24.1	25.3	27.9	32.3	36.6	29.6	33.9	39.2	38.2	39.6	40.0	36.5	37.7
As a percentage of SITC section (%)	Imp.	2.0	2.0	1.9	1.9	1.8	1.7	1.7	1.9	1.9	1.8	1.9	1.9	1.9	1.9	2.1
	Exp.	2.0	2.0	1.9	1.8	1.7	1.6	1.7	1.9	1.7	1.7	1.7	1.7	1.7	1.8	1.9
As a percentage of world trade (%)	Imp.	0.3	0.3	0.3	0.3	0.2	0.2	0.2	0.2	0.2	0.2	0.2	0.2	0.2	0.2	0.3
	Exp.	0.3	0.3	0.3	0.2	0.2	0.2	0.2	0.2	0.2	0.2	0.2	0.2	0.2	0.2	0.2

Graph 1: Annual growth rates of exports, 2002–2016
(In percentage by year)

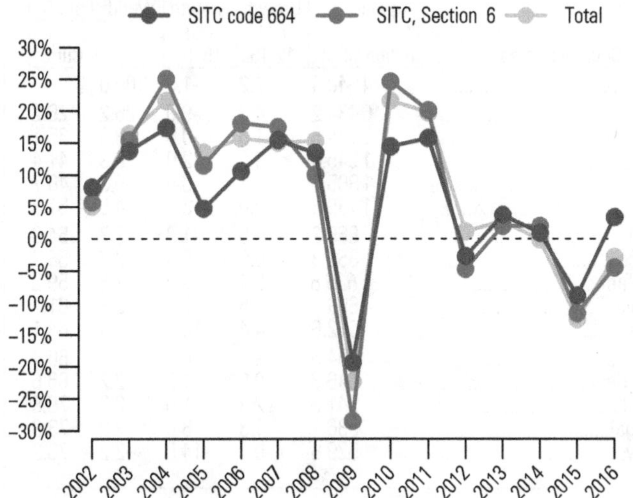

Table 2: Top exporting countries or areas in 2016

Country or area	Value (million US$)	Avg. Growth (%) 12-16	Growth (%) 15-16	World share %	Cum.
World	37749.1	-0.3	3.5	100.0	
China	7686.3	5.8	1.3	20.4	20.4
USA	4161.8	2.8	-0.4	11.0	31.4
Germany	3792.7	3.0	4.4	10.0	41.4
China, Hong Kong SAR	2256.4	8.8	7.7	6.0	47.4
Japan	2139.5	-18.2	3.7	5.7	53.1
Rep. of Korea	1252.0	11.5	9.2	3.3	56.4
Other Asia, nes	1250.0	-8.8	2.2	3.3	59.7
France	1234.9	-1.1	0.5	3.3	63.0
Poland	1213.8	7.4	3.4	3.2	66.2
Belgium	1142.9	-8.8	5.0	3.0	69.2
Italy	1077.3	-2.9	4.0	2.9	72.1
Czechia	859.6	1.2	8.7	2.3	74.4
Spain	852.5	5.6	9.4	2.3	76.6
United Kingdom	664.1	-2.2	8.6	1.8	78.4
Mexico	639.9	-2.5	0.3	1.7	80.1

Graph 2: Trade Balance by MDG regions 2016
(Bln US$)

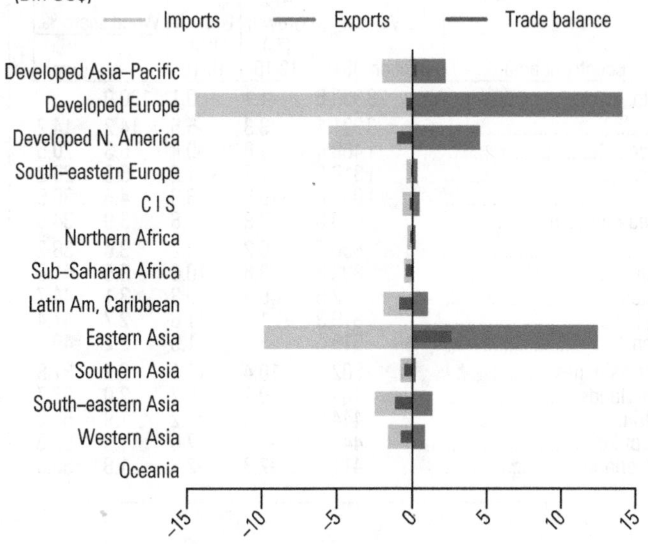

Table 3: Top importing countries or areas in 2016

Country or area	Value (million US$)	Avg. Growth (%) 12-16	Growth (%) 15-16	World share %	Cum.
World	40459.4	-0.2	3.9	100.0	
China	5362.8	3.4	8.5	13.3	13.3
USA	3826.5	7.3	3.6	9.5	22.7
Germany	3334.1	2.6	3.4	8.2	31.0
China, Hong Kong SAR	1939.5	11.4	25.3	4.8	35.7
Canada	1705.4	2.4	1.3	4.2	40.0
Rep. of Korea	1601.7	-15.5	-7.9	4.0	43.9
France	1537.2	-0.7	3.4	3.8	47.7
Japan	1471.8	-3.9	-3.4	3.6	51.4
United Kingdom	1348.8	1.9	4.7	3.3	54.7
Mexico	946.3	4.9	4.1	2.3	57.0
Belgium	936.6	-2.9	6.2	2.3	59.3
Other Asia, nes	906.8	-19.5	-18.0	2.2	61.6
Italy	782.1	-1.0	1.7	1.9	63.5
Spain	741.8	6.6	4.3	1.8	65.4
Poland	656.3	1.5	9.8	1.6	67.0

In 2016, the value (in current US$) of exports of "glassware" (SITC group 665) decreased by 1.5 percent (compared to -2.2 percent average growth rate from 2012-2016) to reach 24.5 bln US$ (see table 2), while imports increased by 0.1 percent to reach 23.3 bln US$ (see table 3). Exports of this commodity accounted for 1.3 percent of world exports of SITC section 6, and 0.2 percent of total world merchandise exports (see table 1). China, Germany and France were the top exporters in 2016 (see table 2). They accounted for 26.2, 8.9 and 6.3 percent of world exports, respectively. USA, France and Germany were the top destinations, with respectively 14.2, 6.3 and 5.6 percent of world imports (see table 3).

The top 15 countries/areas accounted for 75.2 and 59.3 percent of total world exports and imports, respectively (see tables 2 and 3). In 2016, China was the country/area with the highest value of net exports (+5.4 bln US$), followed by Germany (+858.5 mln US$). By MDG regions (see graph 2), the largest surpluses in this product group were recorded by Eastern Asia (+4.8 bln US$) and Developed Europe (+1.1 bln US$). The largest trade deficits were recorded by Developed North America (-2.7 bln US$), Sub-Saharan Africa (-561.2 mln US$) and Commonwealth of Independent States (-380.1 mln US$).

Table 1: Imports (Imp.) and exports (Exp.), 2002-2016, in current US$

		2002	2003	2004	2005	2006	2007	2008	2009	2010	2011	2012	2013	2014	2015	2016
Values in Bln US$	Imp.	11.5	13.3	15.7	16.7	18.2	21.7	23.4	19.2	22.3	24.9	24.4	24.8	25.6	23.3	23.3
	Exp.	11.7	13.6	16.1	17.2	19.6	21.8	22.5	19.4	23.1	25.9	26.8	28.1	27.3	24.9	24.5
As a percentage of SITC section (%)	Imp.	1.3	1.3	1.2	1.2	1.1	1.1	1.1	1.2	1.2	1.1	1.1	1.1	1.1	1.2	1.2
	Exp.	1.3	1.3	1.3	1.2	1.2	1.1	1.0	1.2	1.2	1.1	1.2	1.2	1.2	1.2	1.3
As a percentage of world trade (%)	Imp.	0.2	0.2	0.2	0.2	0.1	0.2	0.1	0.2	0.1	0.1	0.1	0.1	0.1	0.1	0.1
	Exp.	0.2	0.2	0.2	0.2	0.2	0.2	0.1	0.2	0.2	0.1	0.1	0.1	0.1	0.2	0.2

Graph 1: Annual growth rates of exports, 2002–2016

(In percentage by year)

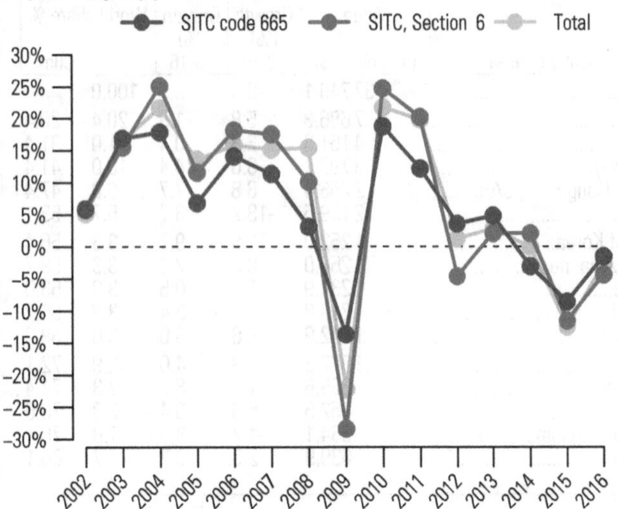

Table 2: Top exporting countries or areas in 2016

Country or area	Value (million US$)	Avg. Growth (%) 12-16	Growth (%) 15-16	World share %	Cum.
World	24 540.4	-2.2	-1.5	100.0	
China	6 434.2	-4.2	-9.0	26.2	26.2
Germany	2 174.5	-1.6	-0.6	8.9	35.1
France	1 545.8	-3.0	2.0	6.3	41.4
Italy	1 305.9	-2.1	-0.8	5.3	46.7
USA	1 139.8	0.0	3.7	4.6	51.3
Japan	656.2	-12.5	21.3	2.7	54.0
Mexico	652.3	-0.9	-5.4	2.7	56.7
Viet Nam	*639.6*	15.4	8.9	2.6	59.3
Czechia	603.9	-5.5	-7.4	2.5	61.7
Austria	582.6	4.4	16.5	2.4	64.1
Spain	554.6	2.8	4.6	2.3	66.4
Netherlands	546.3	0.5	1.6	2.2	68.6
Poland	541.5	2.4	1.0	2.2	70.8
Portugal	536.7	1.3	8.0	2.2	73.0
Turkey	529.6	-0.1	-14.5	2.2	75.2

Graph 2: Trade Balance by MDG regions 2016

(Bln US$)

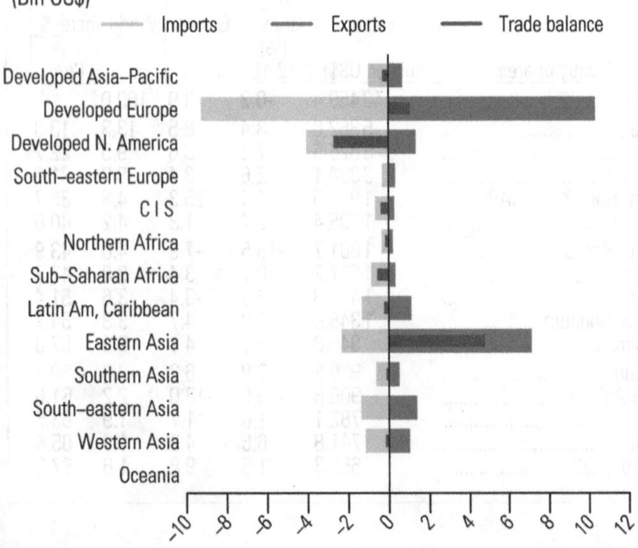

Table 3: Top importing countries or areas in 2016

Country or area	Value (million US$)	Avg. Growth (%) 12-16	Growth (%) 15-16	World share %	Cum.
World	23 339.6	-1.1	0.1	100.0	
USA	3 321.1	3.3	-5.5	14.2	14.2
France	1 468.4	-1.8	-0.4	6.3	20.5
Germany	1 316.0	1.7	1.2	5.6	26.2
China	1 043.0	-15.6	-8.8	4.5	30.6
United Kingdom	910.5	3.9	-7.8	3.9	34.5
Italy	850.5	0.2	3.2	3.6	38.2
Spain	806.8	3.6	10.0	3.5	41.6
Canada	722.5	0.3	-0.3	3.1	44.7
Belgium	619.3	1.3	11.6	2.7	47.4
Japan	519.5	-3.9	1.5	2.2	49.6
Other Asia, nes	502.7	10.4	-11.1	2.2	51.8
Netherlands	463.2	0.1	-9.2	2.0	53.7
Austria	444.5	6.3	21.2	1.9	55.6
Rep. of Korea	443.1	-1.3	7.0	1.9	57.5
Switzerland	411.0	-2.3	-2.3	1.8	59.3

In 2016, the value (in current US$) of exports of "pottery" (SITC group 666) decreased by 18.0 percent (compared to 2.8 percent average growth rate from 2012-2016) to reach 10.9 bln US$ (see table 2), while imports decreased by 4.2 percent to reach 8.1 bln US$ (see table 3). Exports of this commodity accounted for 0.6 percent of world exports of SITC section 6, and 0.1 percent of total world merchandise exports (see table 1). China, Germany and Portugal were the top exporters in 2016 (see table 2). They accounted for 63.4, 5.0 and 2.6 percent of world exports, respectively. USA, Germany and United Kingdom were the top destinations, with respectively 22.6, 6.5 and 4.9 percent of world imports (see table 3).

The top 15 countries/areas accounted for 89.5 and 64.0 percent of total world exports and imports, respectively (see tables 2 and 3). In 2016, China was the country/area with the highest value of net exports (+6.8 bln US$), followed by Portugal (+248.8 mln US$). By MDG regions (see graph 2), the largest surpluses in this product group were recorded by Eastern Asia (+6.5 bln US$), South-eastern Asia (+265.9 mln US$) and South-eastern Europe (+25.0 mln US$). The largest trade deficits were recorded by Developed North America (-1.9 bln US$), Developed Europe (-651.0 mln US$) and Developed Asia-Pacific (-333.9 mln US$).

Table 1: Imports (Imp.) and exports (Exp.), 2002-2016, in current US$

		2002	2003	2004	2005	2006	2007	2008	2009	2010	2011	2012	2013	2014	2015	2016
Values in Bln US$	Imp.	5.7	6.4	6.9	7.2	7.4	8.3	8.4	6.7	7.9	8.4	8.3	8.2	8.9	8.4	8.1
	Exp.	5.1	5.7	6.2	6.4	6.7	6.9	6.9	6.3	7.7	9.1	9.7	9.7	11.2	13.2	10.9
As a percentage of SITC section (%)	Imp.	0.6	0.6	0.5	0.5	0.4	0.4	0.4	0.4	0.4	0.4	0.4	0.4	0.4	0.4	0.4
	Exp.	0.6	0.6	0.5	0.4	0.4	0.3	0.3	0.4	0.4	0.4	0.4	0.4	0.5	0.6	0.6
As a percentage of world trade (%)	Imp.	0.1	0.1	0.1	0.1	0.1	0.1	0.1	0.1	0.1	0.0	0.0	0.0	0.0	0.1	0.1
	Exp.	0.1	0.1	0.1	0.1	0.1	0.0	0.0	0.1	0.1	0.1	0.1	0.1	0.1	0.1	0.1

Graph 1: Annual growth rates of exports, 2002–2016

(In percentage by year)

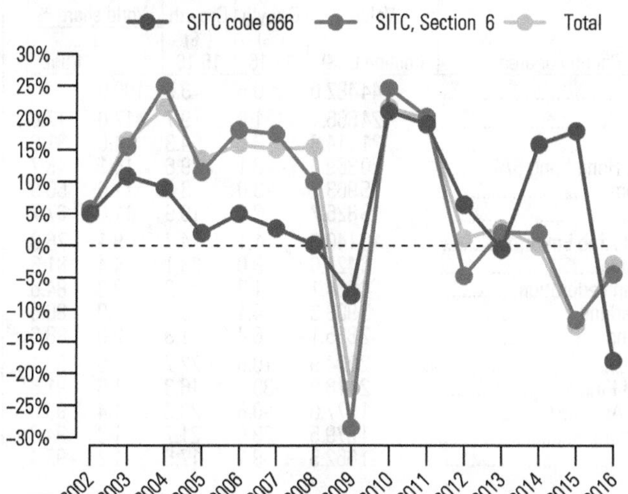

Table 2: Top exporting countries or areas in 2016

Country or area	Value (million US$)	Avg. Growth (%) 12-16	Growth (%) 15-16	World share %	Cum.
World	10854.6	2.8	-18.0	100.0	
China	6884.8	4.0	-26.1	63.4	63.4
Germany	546.8	-2.5	-1.4	5.0	68.5
Portugal	279.1	5.8	8.7	2.6	71.0
United Kingdom	274.9	1.2	-8.4	2.5	73.6
Thailand	223.1	1.2	-4.8	2.1	75.6
France	202.5	-3.1	8.9	1.9	77.5
Netherlands	200.5	6.7	15.9	1.8	79.3
Spain	164.0	10.5	52.4	1.5	80.8
USA	160.4	-0.3	-9.5	1.5	82.3
Italy	159.1	-1.4	-0.4	1.5	83.8
United Arab Emirates	139.9	-2.7	-2.8	1.3	85.1
Belgium	129.5	-2.1	-3.2	1.2	86.3
Poland	125.1	8.8	15.0	1.2	87.4
Indonesia	118.2	-1.7	-1.0	1.1	88.5
Japan	109.0	8.3	6.3	1.0	89.5

Graph 2: Trade Balance by MDG regions 2016

(Bln US$)

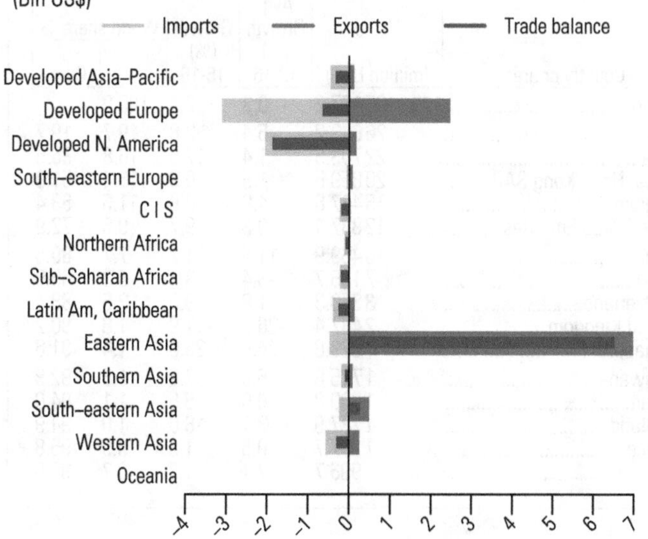

Table 3: Top importing countries or areas in 2016

Country or area	Value (million US$)	Avg. Growth (%) 12-16	Growth (%) 15-16	World share %	Cum.
World	8057.6	-0.9	-4.2	100.0	
USA	1817.4	2.2	-6.3	22.6	22.6
Germany	521.5	-3.1	-3.0	6.5	29.0
United Kingdom	394.0	-3.6	-12.1	4.9	33.9
France	327.7	-4.2	2.3	4.1	38.0
Italy	275.7	-3.2	12.0	3.4	41.4
Japan	266.7	-6.2	-2.8	3.3	44.7
Netherlands	248.9	3.4	12.2	3.1	47.8
Canada	225.8	-2.5	-3.4	2.8	50.6
Rep. of Korea	208.7	12.7	4.8	2.6	53.2
Spain	163.0	2.5	4.1	2.0	55.2
Turkey	162.3	-1.3	-34.7	2.0	57.2
Australia	153.2	-0.4	3.4	1.9	59.1
Belgium	137.8	-6.0	-8.5	1.7	60.8
Austria	137.7	0.8	14.3	1.7	62.6
Denmark	120.3	8.6	7.5	1.5	64.0

Source: UN Comtrade

667 Pearls and precious or semiprecious stones, unworked or worked

In 2016, the value (in current US$) of exports of "pearls and precious or semiprecious stones, unworked or worked" (SITC group 667) increased by 3.5 percent (compared to 0.5 percent average growth rate from 2012-2016) to reach 144.5 bln US$ (see table 2), while imports increased by 2.5 percent to reach 135.2 bln US$ (see table 3). Exports of this commodity accounted for 7.4 percent of world exports of SITC section 6, and 0.9 percent of total world merchandise exports (see table 1). India, USA and China, Hong Kong SAR were the top exporters in 2016 (see table 2). They accounted for 17.0, 14.6 and 14.1 percent of world exports, respectively. USA, India and China, Hong Kong SAR were the top destinations, with respectively 19.7, 16.8 and 15.4 percent of world imports (see table 3).

The top 15 countries/areas accounted for 95.4 and 96.6 percent of total world exports and imports, respectively (see tables 2 and 3). In 2016, Israel was the country/area with the highest value of net exports (+8.6 bln US$), followed by Russian Federation (+4.8 bln US$). By MDG regions (see graph 2), the largest surpluses in this product group were recorded by Western Asia (+8.7 bln US$), Sub-Saharan Africa (+7.6 bln US$) and Commonwealth of Independent States (+4.7 bln US$). The largest trade deficits were recorded by Eastern Asia (-8.9 bln US$), Developed North America (-4.3 bln US$) and Developed Europe (-1.8 bln US$).

Table 1: Imports (Imp.) and exports (Exp.), 2002-2016, in current US$

		2002	2003	2004	2005	2006	2007	2008	2009	2010	2011	2012	2013	2014	2015	2016
Values in Bln US$	Imp.	59.9	62.6	76.3	90.2	85.6	96.7	107.1	82.8	124.5	159.4	133.5	150.8	173.5	131.9	135.2
	Exp.	58.7	63.2	75.9	92.2	89.6	103.7	115.6	90.2	129.1	164.3	141.5	163.3	161.6	139.7	144.5
As a percentage of SITC section (%)	Imp.	6.7	6.1	5.9	6.3	5.1	4.9	4.9	5.3	6.5	6.9	6.1	6.8	7.6	6.5	7.0
	Exp.	6.7	6.2	6.0	6.5	5.3	5.3	5.3	5.8	6.7	7.0	6.4	7.2	7.0	6.8	7.4
As a percentage of world trade (%)	Imp.	0.9	0.8	0.8	0.9	0.7	0.7	0.7	0.7	0.8	0.9	0.7	0.8	0.9	0.8	0.8
	Exp.	0.9	0.8	0.8	0.9	0.7	0.7	0.7	0.7	0.9	0.9	0.8	0.9	0.9	0.8	0.9

Graph 1: Annual growth rates of exports, 2002–2016
(In percentage by year)

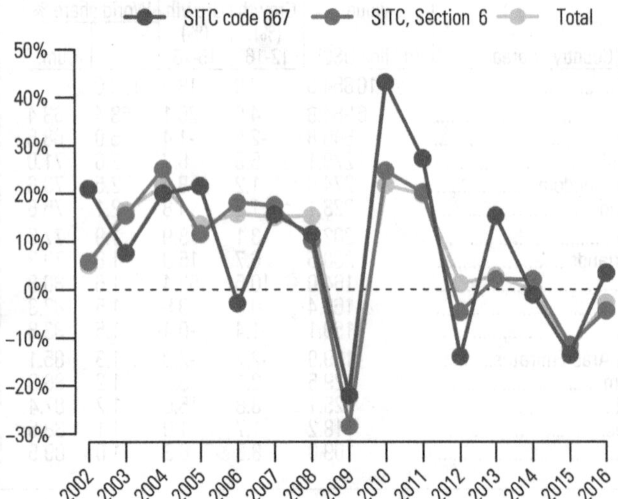

Table 2: Top exporting countries or areas in 2016

Country or area	Value (million US$)	Avg. Growth (%) 12-16	Growth (%) 15-16	World share %	Cum.
World	144482.0	0.5	3.5	100.0	
India	24566.1	1.9	9.7	17.0	17.0
USA	21114.9	3.8	4.3	14.6	31.6
China, Hong Kong SAR	20369.6	8.1	9.6	14.1	45.7
Belgium	15963.2	-3.0	3.0	11.0	56.8
Israel	15825.7	-2.6	-10.9	11.0	67.7
United Arab Emirates	13140.8	1.1	4.7	9.1	76.8
Botswana	6427.6	8.0	23.1	4.4	81.3
Russian Federation	4834.1	1.3	23.3	3.3	84.6
Switzerland	2908.3	4.4	-3.7	2.0	86.6
Thailand	2865.1	6.4	-1.3	2.0	88.6
China	2204.9	-10.6	-22.7	1.5	90.1
United Kingdom	2118.8	-30.2	-16.3	1.5	91.6
South Africa	1977.0	-0.6	23.0	1.4	93.0
Singapore	1879.5	29.0	21.7	1.3	94.3
Canada	1662.5	-9.1	-17.5	1.2	95.4

Graph 2: Trade Balance by MDG regions 2016
(Bln US$)

Imports — Exports — Trade balance

Developed Asia-Pacific
Developed Europe
Developed N. America
South-eastern Europe
C I S
Northern Africa
Sub-Saharan Africa
Latin Am, Caribbean
Eastern Asia
Southern Asia
South-eastern Asia
Western Asia
Oceania

-35 -30 -25 -20 -15 -10 -5 0 5 10 15 20 25 30

Table 3: Top importing countries or areas in 2016

Country or area	Value (million US$)	Avg. Growth (%) 12-16	Growth (%) 15-16	World share %	Cum.
World	135167.2	0.3	2.5	100.0	
USA	26643.2	5.4	2.8	19.7	19.7
India	22703.5	1.4	17.5	16.8	36.5
China, Hong Kong SAR	20859.5	1.5	0.3	15.4	51.9
Belgium	15487.6	-4.8	-0.8	11.5	63.4
United Arab Emirates	12837.4	0.3	9.7	9.5	72.9
China	10469.9	11.5	-11.2	7.7	80.6
Israel	7195.7	-3.4	3.4	5.3	86.0
Switzerland	3350.3	1.8	-9.5	2.5	88.4
United Kingdom	2437.4	-26.2	-11.9	1.8	90.2
Singapore	1829.8	24.5	25.0	1.4	91.6
Botswana	1725.8	-5.5	-37.6	1.3	92.9
Japan	1500.8	0.0	8.5	1.1	94.0
Thailand	1287.9	-3.1	-6.0	1.0	94.9
France	1207.7	0.5	1.8	0.9	95.8
Italy	996.7	7.1	1.2	0.7	96.6

In 2016, the value (in current US$) of exports of "pig iron, spiegeleisen, sponge iron, iron or steel granules and powders" (SITC group 671) decreased by 4.6 percent (compared to -9.7 percent average growth rate from 2012-2016) to reach 26.0 bln US$ (see table 2), while imports decreased by 9.5 percent to reach 29.3 bln US$ (see table 3). Exports of this commodity accounted for 1.3 percent of world exports of SITC section 6, and 0.2 percent of total world merchandise exports (see table 1). South Africa, Russian Federation and Brazil were the top exporters in 2016 (see table 2). They accounted for 13.9, 10.7 and 10.1 percent of world exports, respectively. China, USA and Japan were the top destinations, with respectively 16.7, 11.7 and 7.3 percent of world imports (see table 3).

The top 15 countries/areas accounted for 75.4 and 80.8 percent of total world exports and imports, respectively (see tables 2 and 3). In 2016, South Africa was the country/area with the highest value of net exports (+3.5 bln US$), followed by Brazil (+2.5 bln US$). By MDG regions (see graph 2), the largest surpluses in this product group were recorded by Commonwealth of Independent States (+4.0 bln US$), Sub-Saharan Africa (+3.6 bln US$) and Latin America and the Caribbean (+2.7 bln US$). The largest trade deficits were recorded by Eastern Asia (-6.3 bln US$), Developed Europe (-3.9 bln US$) and Developed North America (-2.9 bln US$).

Table 1: Imports (Imp.) and exports (Exp.), 2002-2016, in current US$

		2002	2003	2004	2005	2006	2007	2008	2009	2010	2011	2012	2013	2014	2015	2016
Values in Bln US$	Imp.	11.0	14.2	26.2	30.8	31.4	43.5	59.4	26.5	40.2	47.6	41.8	37.7	41.0	32.4	29.3
	Exp.	8.8	11.8	21.2	25.9	25.9	35.8	47.9	22.1	35.0	42.9	39.1	34.2	37.0	27.3	26.0
As a percentage of SITC section (%)	Imp.	1.2	1.4	2.0	2.1	1.9	2.2	2.7	1.7	2.1	2.1	1.9	1.7	1.8	1.6	1.5
	Exp.	1.0	1.2	1.7	1.8	1.5	1.8	2.2	1.4	1.8	1.8	1.8	1.5	1.6	1.3	1.3
As a percentage of world trade (%)	Imp.	0.2	0.2	0.3	0.3	0.3	0.3	0.4	0.2	0.3	0.3	0.2	0.2	0.2	0.2	0.2
	Exp.	0.1	0.2	0.2	0.2	0.2	0.3	0.3	0.2	0.2	0.2	0.2	0.2	0.2	0.2	0.2

Graph 1: Annual growth rates of exports, 2002–2016
(In percentage by year)

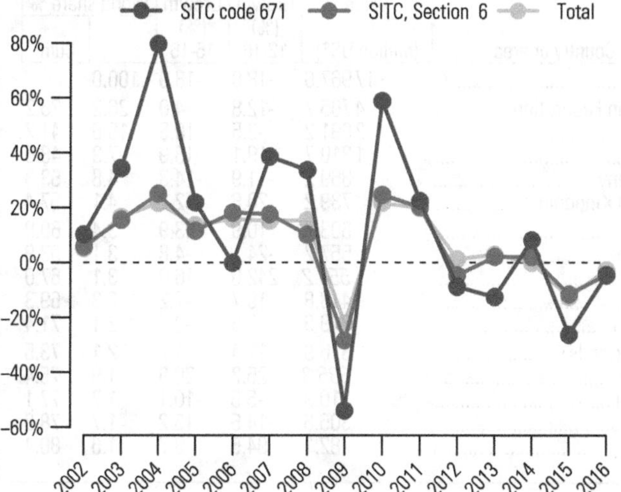

Graph 2: Trade Balance by MDG regions 2016
(Bln US$)

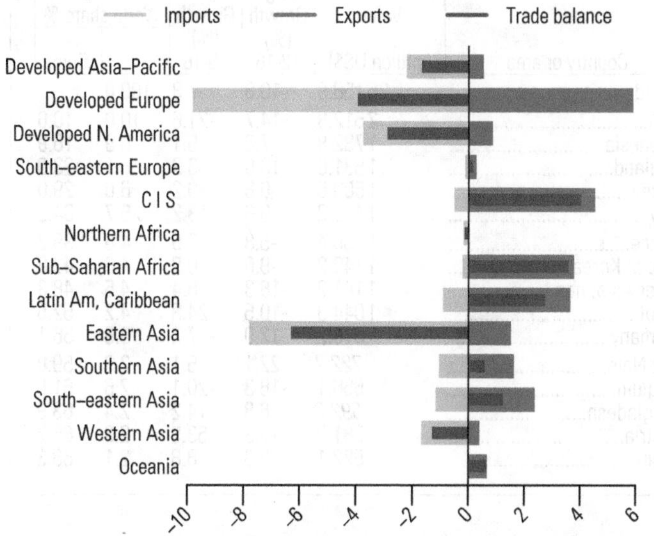

Table 2: Top exporting countries or areas in 2016

Country or area	Value (million US$)	Avg. Growth (%) 12-16	Growth (%) 15-16	World share %	Cum.
World	26015.6	-9.7	-4.6	100.0	
South Africa	3624.4	-1.8	22.4	13.9	13.9
Russian Federation	2780.1	-11.5	-11.0	10.7	24.6
Brazil	2636.6	-10.8	-13.5	10.1	34.8
Netherlands	2043.9	7.6	137.1	7.9	42.6
Kazakhstan	1405.8	-22.5	3.5	5.4	48.0
India	1308.7	-11.7	-13.5	5.0	53.0
Indonesia	1122.7	31.1	110.1	4.3	57.4
China	839.9	-22.6	-18.2	3.2	60.6
New Caledonia	*657.1*	-0.6	8.4	2.5	63.1
Sweden	608.7	-4.1	2.3	2.3	65.5
Norway	554.0	-7.4	-12.0	2.1	67.6
Viet Nam	*540.2*	26.3	8.9	2.1	69.7
Japan	518.2	-17.3	-24.7	2.0	71.7
Germany	494.0	-8.1	-12.5	1.9	73.5
Rep. of Korea	471.3	-8.0	-21.1	1.8	75.4

Table 3: Top importing countries or areas in 2016

Country or area	Value (million US$)	Avg. Growth (%) 12-16	Growth (%) 15-16	World share %	Cum.
World	29345.6	-8.5	-9.5	100.0	
China	4903.4	2.3	0.0	16.7	16.7
USA	3433.7	-14.0	-21.7	11.7	28.4
Japan	2139.2	-9.9	-15.1	7.3	35.7
Netherlands	2050.6	14.0	156.6	7.0	42.7
Germany	1793.7	-13.9	-19.7	6.1	48.8
Italy	1783.9	-10.5	-16.8	6.1	54.9
Rep. of Korea	1657.2	-12.9	-11.7	5.6	60.5
Other Asia, nes	1214.8	-7.8	-5.6	4.1	64.7
Belgium	918.1	-9.0	-18.4	3.1	67.8
India	836.7	-8.4	5.5	2.9	70.6
Spain	756.6	-8.8	-17.5	2.6	73.2
Turkey	735.9	-14.7	-22.1	2.5	75.7
Mexico	530.8	3.7	16.5	1.8	77.5
Saudi Arabia	496.8	-15.8	-24.5	1.7	79.2
France	472.3	-10.6	-20.1	1.6	80.8

672 Ingots and other primary forms, of iron or steel; semi-finished products

In 2016, the value (in current US$) of exports of "ingots and other primary forms, of iron or steel; semi-finished products" (SITC group 672) decreased by 18.9 percent (compared to -18.0 percent average growth rate from 2012-2016) to reach 18.0 bln US$ (see table 2), while imports decreased by 7.3 percent to reach 25.2 bln US$ (see table 3). Exports of this commodity accounted for 0.9 percent of world exports of SITC section 6, and 0.1 percent of total world merchandise exports (see table 1). Russian Federation, Brazil and Japan were the top exporters in 2016 (see table 2). They accounted for 26.2, 15.0 and 7.3 percent of world exports, respectively. USA, Indonesia and Thailand were the top destinations, with respectively 10.0, 6.9 and 6.1 percent of world imports (see table 3).

The top 15 countries/areas accounted for 80.4 and 68.3 percent of total world exports and imports, respectively (see tables 2 and 3). In 2016, Russian Federation was the country/area with the highest value of net exports (+4.7 bln US$), followed by Brazil (+2.6 bln US$). By MDG regions (see graph 2), the largest surpluses in this product group were recorded by Commonwealth of Independent States (+4.9 bln US$), Latin America and the Caribbean (+2.4 bln US$) and Developed Asia-Pacific (+1.2 bln US$). The largest trade deficits were recorded by South-eastern Asia (-4.1 bln US$), Developed Europe (-2.4 bln US$) and Developed North America (-2.3 bln US$).

Table 1: Imports (Imp.) and exports (Exp.), 2002-2016, in current US$

		2002	2003	2004	2005	2006	2007	2008	2009	2010	2011	2012	2013	2014	2015	2016
Values in Bln US$	Imp.	14.0	17.6	29.4	31.7	32.7	42.3	59.9	29.0	36.2	45.6	39.8	33.1	35.3	27.1	25.2
	Exp.	12.2	15.3	26.0	28.5	31.2	39.1	54.2	24.4	34.6	43.0	39.8	34.2	32.0	22.2	18.0
As a percentage of SITC section (%)	Imp.	1.6	1.7	2.3	2.2	2.0	2.1	2.7	1.9	1.9	2.0	1.8	1.5	1.5	1.3	1.3
	Exp.	1.4	1.5	2.0	2.0	1.9	2.0	2.5	1.6	1.8	1.8	1.8	1.5	1.4	1.1	0.9
As a percentage of world trade (%)	Imp.	0.2	0.2	0.3	0.3	0.3	0.3	0.4	0.2	0.2	0.2	0.2	0.2	0.2	0.2	0.2
	Exp.	0.2	0.2	0.3	0.3	0.3	0.3	0.3	0.2	0.2	0.2	0.2	0.2	0.2	0.1	0.1

Graph 1: Annual growth rates of exports, 2002–2016
(In percentage by year)

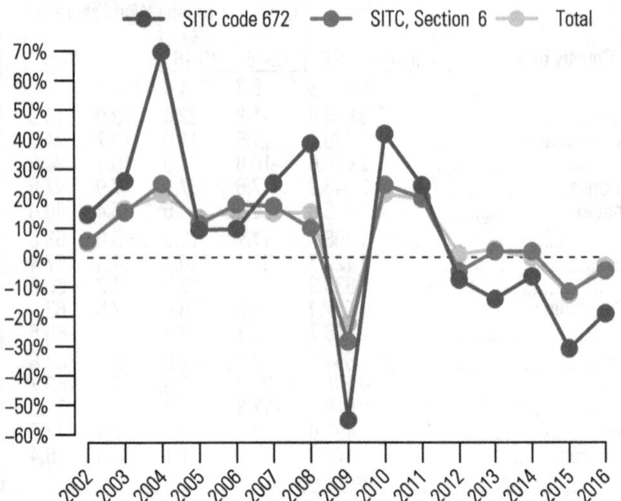

Table 2: Top exporting countries or areas in 2016

Country or area	Value (million US$)	Avg. Growth (%) 12-16	Growth (%) 15-16	World share %	Cum.
World	17967.6	-18.0	-18.9	100.0	
Russian Federation	4705.7	-12.8	-4.0	26.2	26.2
Brazil	2691.2	-8.5	-10.5	15.0	41.2
Japan	1310.7	-19.1	-18.9	7.3	48.5
Germany	869.2	-11.9	-14.3	4.8	53.3
United Kingdom	739.2	-20.6	-52.2	4.1	57.4
India	603.7	10.9	93.9	3.4	60.8
France	557.2	-24.1	-4.8	3.1	63.9
Iran	*554.2*	242.0	16.0	3.1	67.0
Italy	418.8	-19.7	-7.2	2.3	69.3
Austria	379.9	2.6	-0.5	2.1	71.4
Netherlands	376.9	-17.4	-1.2	2.1	73.5
Cuba	*335.3*	25.2	20.9	1.9	75.4
Poland	310.3	-5.5	-10.1	1.7	77.1
Mexico	305.6	-14.5	-15.2	1.7	78.8
Oman	282.1	94.5	8.7	1.6	80.4

Graph 2: Trade Balance by MDG regions 2016
(Bln US$)

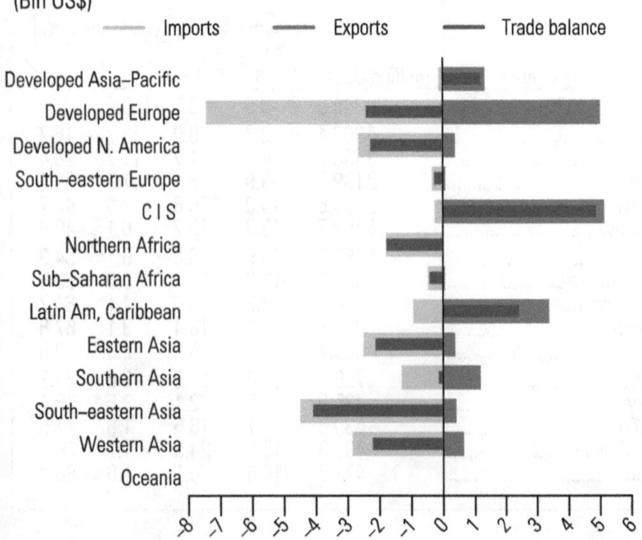

Table 3: Top importing countries or areas in 2016

Country or area	Value (million US$)	Avg. Growth (%) 12-16	Growth (%) 15-16	World share %	Cum.
World	25158.9	-10.8	-7.3	100.0	
USA	2512.9	-14.7	-21.6	10.0	10.0
Indonesia	1732.8	-7.8	5.1	6.9	16.9
Thailand	1531.0	-10.6	33.3	6.1	23.0
Turkey	1509.5	-6.8	-20.2	6.0	29.0
Italy	1423.2	-9.6	-13.2	5.7	34.6
France	1155.4	-5.8	-5.0	4.6	39.2
Rep. of Korea	1149.2	-9.6	0.9	4.6	43.8
Other Asia, nes	1141.2	-16.3	-8.4	4.5	48.3
Egypt	1044.9	-10.5	-24.8	4.2	52.5
Germany	910.2	-12.0	-17.2	3.6	56.1
Viet Nam	*722.7*	22.1	5.1	2.9	59.0
Belgium	656.1	-18.3	-20.1	2.6	61.6
Bangladesh	*592.2*	-6.8	-14.2	2.4	63.9
Austria	581.3	19.3	53.5	2.3	66.2
Spain	522.1	-8.6	8.8	2.1	68.3

In 2016, the value (in current US$) of exports of "flat-rolled products of iron or non-alloy steel, not clad, plated or coated" (SITC group 673) decreased by 10.8 percent (compared to -10.5 percent average growth rate from 2012-2016) to reach 50.6 bln US$ (see table 2), while imports decreased by 12.7 percent to reach 57.3 bln US$ (see table 3). Exports of this commodity accounted for 2.6 percent of world exports of SITC section 6, and 0.3 percent of total world merchandise exports (see table 1). Japan, Rep. of Korea and Germany were the top exporters in 2016 (see table 2). They accounted for 15.2, 12.6 and 6.8 percent of world exports, respectively. USA, Germany and Rep. of Korea were the top destinations, with respectively 6.2, 5.8 and 5.7 percent of world imports (see table 3).

The top 15 countries/areas accounted for 79.8 and 59.9 percent of total world exports and imports, respectively (see tables 2 and 3). In 2016, Japan was the country/area with the highest value of net exports (+6.3 bln US$), followed by Rep. of Korea (+3.1 bln US$). By MDG regions (see graph 2), the largest surpluses in this product group were recorded by Developed Asia-Pacific (+6.4 bln US$), Eastern Asia (+3.4 bln US$) and Commonwealth of Independent States (+2.4 bln US$). The largest trade deficits were recorded by South-eastern Asia (-6.4 bln US$), Developed Europe (-2.9 bln US$) and Western Asia (-2.8 bln US$).

Table 1: Imports (Imp.) and exports (Exp.), 2002-2016, in current US$

		2002	2003	2004	2005	2006	2007	2008	2009	2010	2011	2012	2013	2014	2015	2016
Values in Bln US$	Imp.	29.8	40.3	58.6	69.8	74.2	92.9	121.8	65.6	83.3	99.2	87.1	82.3	81.7	65.6	57.3
	Exp.	27.7	36.9	55.4	65.6	71.9	88.5	111.7	59.4	79.9	92.2	78.8	73.9	73.0	56.7	50.6
As a percentage of SITC section (%)	Imp.	3.3	3.9	4.6	4.9	4.5	4.7	5.6	4.2	4.3	4.3	4.0	3.7	3.6	3.3	3.0
	Exp.	3.1	3.6	4.4	4.6	4.3	4.5	5.1	3.8	4.1	4.0	3.5	3.3	3.1	2.8	2.6
As a percentage of world trade (%)	Imp.	0.5	0.5	0.6	0.7	0.6	0.7	0.7	0.5	0.5	0.5	0.5	0.4	0.4	0.4	0.4
	Exp.	0.4	0.5	0.6	0.6	0.6	0.6	0.7	0.5	0.5	0.5	0.4	0.4	0.4	0.3	0.3

Graph 1: Annual growth rates of exports, 2002–2016

(In percentage by year)

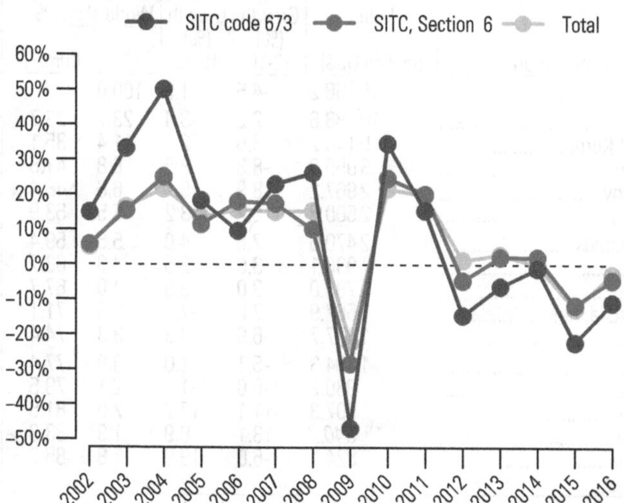

Graph 2: Trade Balance by MDG regions 2016

(Bln US$)

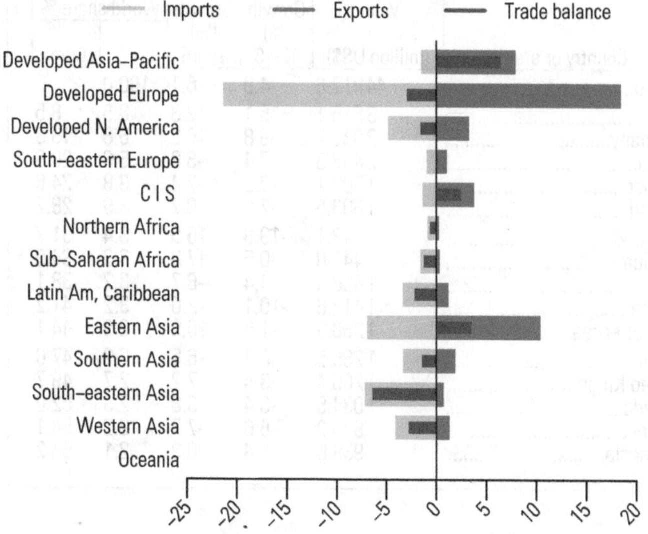

Table 2: Top exporting countries or areas in 2016

Country or area	Value (million US$)	Avg. Growth (%) 12-16	Growth (%) 15-16	World share %	Cum.
World	50 566.8	-10.5	-10.8	100.0	
Japan	7 688.6	-11.3	-13.6	15.2	15.2
Rep. of Korea	6 369.6	-10.8	-13.0	12.6	27.8
Germany	3 431.5	-11.2	-7.0	6.8	34.6
Belgium	3 293.8	-6.6	2.0	6.5	41.1
Russian Federation	2 988.2	-8.8	1.5	5.9	47.0
Other Asia, nes	2 313.4	-9.1	-8.3	4.6	51.6
France	2 081.4	-4.9	-12.8	4.1	55.7
USA	2 068.2	-9.1	-10.8	4.1	59.8
Italy	1 832.4	-15.1	1.3	3.6	63.4
Netherlands	1 712.6	-9.9	-7.0	3.4	66.8
China	1 617.9	-12.2	-37.6	3.2	70.0
India	1 393.6	0.2	21.6	2.8	72.8
Slovakia	1 203.6	-7.1	4.2	2.4	75.1
Austria	1 189.5	-8.4	7.4	2.4	77.5
Canada	1 183.0	-3.7	5.3	2.3	79.8

Table 3: Top importing countries or areas in 2016

Country or area	Value (million US$)	Avg. Growth (%) 12-16	Growth (%) 15-16	World share %	Cum.
World	57 269.1	-10.0	-12.7	100.0	
USA	3 573.1	-5.1	-28.0	6.2	6.2
Germany	3 331.2	-10.2	-7.0	5.8	12.1
Rep. of Korea	3 252.0	-16.1	-11.3	5.7	17.7
China	3 045.2	-11.1	-9.0	5.3	23.1
Italy	3 005.8	1.6	-12.2	5.2	28.3
Belgium	2 329.2	1.7	3.5	4.1	32.4
France	1 979.2	-10.4	-6.4	3.5	35.8
Turkey	1 957.9	-9.8	-12.7	3.4	39.2
Thailand	1 907.1	-10.3	-11.9	3.3	42.6
Viet Nam	1 885.4	-8.4	5.1	3.3	45.9
Mexico	1 878.5	-5.6	-18.8	3.3	49.1
Poland	1 702.0	-5.5	2.6	3.0	52.1
India	1 578.5	-14.6	-41.1	2.8	54.9
Spain	1 519.3	-6.2	-1.4	2.7	57.5
Japan	1 367.3	-13.7	-7.0	2.4	59.9

Source: UN Comtrade

674 Flat-rolled products of iron or non-alloy steel, clad, plated or coated

In 2016, the value (in current US$) of exports of "flat-rolled products of iron or non-alloy steel, clad, plated or coated" (SITC group 674) decreased by 1.9 percent (compared to -4.5 percent average growth rate from 2012-2016) to reach 45.2 bln US$ (see table 2), while imports decreased by 6.1 percent to reach 44.8 bln US$ (see table 3). Exports of this commodity accounted for 2.3 percent of world exports of SITC section 6, and 0.3 percent of total world merchandise exports (see table 1). China, Rep. of Korea and Belgium were the top exporters in 2016 (see table 2). They accounted for 23.7, 11.4 and 6.8 percent of world exports, respectively. USA, Germany and China were the top destinations, with respectively 8.5, 6.8 and 5.6 percent of world imports (see table 3).

The top 15 countries/areas accounted for 85.2 and 56.2 percent of total world exports and imports, respectively (see tables 2 and 3). In 2016, China was the country/area with the highest value of net exports (+8.2 bln US$), followed by Rep. of Korea (+3.9 bln US$). By MDG regions (see graph 2), the largest surpluses in this product group were recorded by Eastern Asia (+13.3 bln US$) and Developed Asia-Pacific (+1.8 bln US$). The largest trade deficits were recorded by South-eastern Asia (-3.8 bln US$), Latin America and the Caribbean (-2.7 bln US$) and Developed North America (-2.4 bln US$).

Table 1: Imports (Imp.) and exports (Exp.), 2002-2016, in current US$

		2002	2003	2004	2005	2006	2007	2008	2009	2010	2011	2012	2013	2014	2015	2016
Values in Bln US$	Imp.	19.9	25.2	33.1	36.2	41.4	50.8	57.8	38.6	51.1	59.5	54.7	54.3	56.0	47.7	44.8
	Exp.	18.7	23.5	30.9	34.2	40.2	48.2	56.2	36.1	49.4	58.7	54.4	54.1	55.2	46.1	45.2
As a percentage of SITC section (%)	Imp.	2.2	2.4	2.6	2.5	2.5	2.6	2.6	2.5	2.7	2.6	2.5	2.5	2.4	2.4	2.3
	Exp.	2.1	2.3	2.4	2.4	2.4	2.4	2.6	2.3	2.5	2.5	2.4	2.4	2.4	2.2	2.3
As a percentage of world trade (%)	Imp.	0.3	0.3	0.4	0.3	0.3	0.4	0.4	0.3	0.3	0.3	0.3	0.3	0.3	0.3	0.3
	Exp.	0.3	0.3	0.3	0.3	0.3	0.3	0.4	0.3	0.3	0.3	0.3	0.3	0.3	0.3	0.3

Graph 1: Annual growth rates of exports, 2002–2016

(In percentage by year)

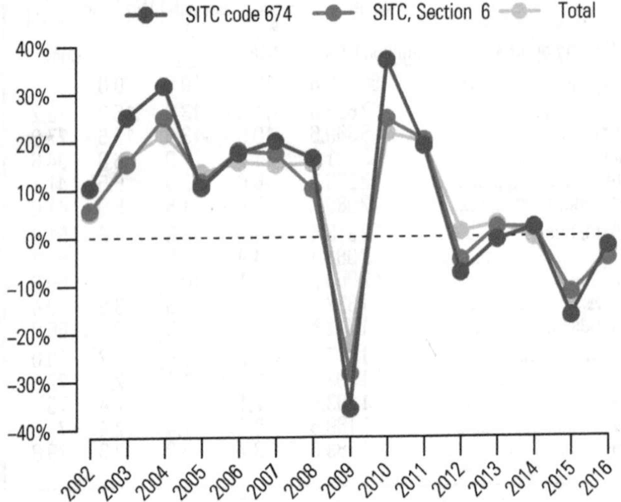

Table 2: Top exporting countries or areas in 2016

Country or area	Value (million US$)	Avg. Growth (%) 12-16	Growth (%) 15-16	World share %	Cum.
World	45168.2	-4.5	-1.9	100.0	
China	10688.6	2.2	-3.4	23.7	23.7
Rep. of Korea	5146.2	-3.6	2.1	11.4	35.1
Belgium	3059.0	-8.3	8.5	6.8	41.8
Germany	2967.2	-8.9	-5.1	6.6	48.4
Japan	2500.2	-15.2	-13.2	5.5	53.9
Netherlands	2470.6	2.8	4.0	5.5	59.4
Italy	1936.1	-3.6	2.5	4.3	63.7
France	1796.0	-3.0	-6.5	4.0	67.7
Other Asia, nes	1567.9	-7.6	-7.0	3.5	71.1
USA	1477.7	-6.9	-3.3	3.3	74.4
India	1354.3	-5.1	1.0	3.0	77.4
Canada	930.2	-0.6	-1.1	2.1	79.5
Austria	907.3	-11.1	-17.2	2.0	81.5
Viet Nam	*840.2*	13.1	8.9	1.9	83.3
Slovakia	824.1	-6.0	-19.0	1.8	85.2

Graph 2: Trade Balance by MDG regions 2016

(Bln US$)

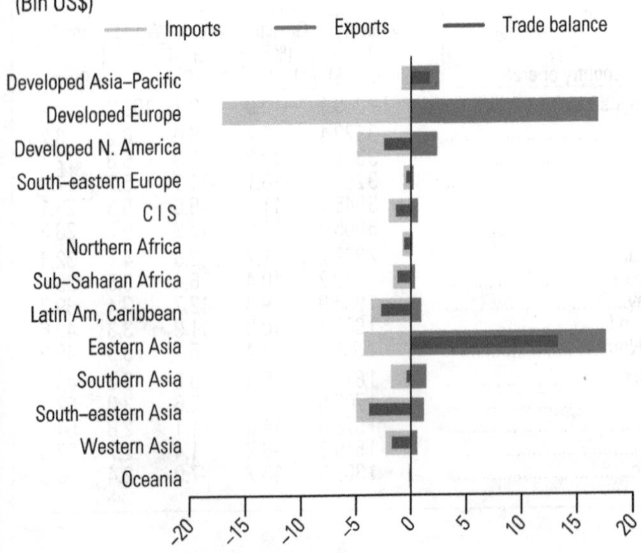

Table 3: Top importing countries or areas in 2016

Country or area	Value (million US$)	Avg. Growth (%) 12-16	Growth (%) 15-16	World share %	Cum.
World	44812.6	-4.9	-6.1	100.0	
USA	3815.1	5.1	-12.3	8.5	8.5
Germany	3032.4	-9.8	-16.2	6.8	15.3
China	2492.3	-7.4	-5.6	5.6	20.8
Mexico	1702.1	-2.9	-2.4	3.8	24.6
Poland	1603.5	-2.9	0.7	3.6	28.2
Thailand	1543.1	-13.9	-15.5	3.4	31.7
Belgium	1442.0	-0.5	17.8	3.2	34.9
Italy	1430.8	-4.4	-6.7	3.2	38.1
France	1412.6	-10.1	-2.0	3.2	41.2
Rep. of Korea	1288.3	-1.8	10.9	2.9	44.1
Spain	1286.5	-6.7	-6.5	2.9	47.0
United Kingdom	1206.4	-3.4	7.2	2.7	49.7
Canada	1034.5	-3.4	3.8	2.3	52.0
Czechia	976.0	-6.6	-7.7	2.2	54.1
Indonesia	938.6	-1.4	-0.3	2.1	56.2

Source: UN Comtrade

In 2016, the value (in current US$) of exports of "flat-rolled products of alloy steel" (SITC group 675) decreased by 6.0 percent (compared to -2.6 percent average growth rate from 2012-2016) to reach 59.0 bln US$ (see table 2), while imports decreased by 6.9 percent to reach 55.3 bln US$ (see table 3). Exports of this commodity accounted for 3.0 percent of world exports of SITC section 6, and 0.4 percent of total world merchandise exports (see table 1). China, Japan and Belgium were the top exporters in 2016 (see table 2). They accounted for 21.0, 10.3 and 7.9 percent of world exports, respectively. Germany, Italy and China were the top destinations, with respectively 9.9, 6.1 and 6.1 percent of world imports (see table 3).

The top 15 countries/areas accounted for 89.4 and 68.5 percent of total world exports and imports, respectively (see tables 2 and 3). In 2016, China was the country/area with the highest value of net exports (+9.0 bln US$), followed by Japan (+5.5 bln US$). By MDG regions (see graph 2), the largest surpluses in this product group were recorded by Eastern Asia (+10.8 bln US$), Developed Asia-Pacific (+5.3 bln US$) and Developed Europe (+3.5 bln US$). The largest trade deficits were recorded by South-eastern Asia (-6.4 bln US$), Latin America and the Caribbean (-3.1 bln US$) and Western Asia (-2.5 bln US$).

Table 1: Imports (Imp.) and exports (Exp.), 2002-2016, in current US$

		2002	2003	2004	2005	2006	2007	2008	2009	2010	2011	2012	2013	2014	2015	2016
Values in Bln US$	Imp.	20.4	26.5	37.7	43.0	54.3	70.5	69.7	41.2	55.6	68.4	60.9	57.7	65.1	59.4	55.3
	Exp.	21.3	28.0	39.4	44.2	56.6	72.2	73.0	43.0	59.4	75.0	65.5	61.1	72.2	62.8	59.0
As a percentage of SITC section (%)	Imp.	2.3	2.6	2.9	3.0	3.3	3.6	3.2	2.6	2.9	3.0	2.8	2.6	2.8	2.9	2.9
	Exp.	2.4	2.8	3.1	3.1	3.4	3.7	3.4	2.8	3.1	3.2	2.9	2.7	3.1	3.1	3.0
As a percentage of world trade (%)	Imp.	0.3	0.3	0.4	0.4	0.4	0.5	0.4	0.3	0.4	0.4	0.3	0.3	0.3	0.4	0.3
	Exp.	0.3	0.4	0.4	0.4	0.5	0.5	0.5	0.3	0.4	0.4	0.4	0.3	0.4	0.4	0.4

Graph 1: Annual growth rates of exports, 2002–2016
(In percentage by year)

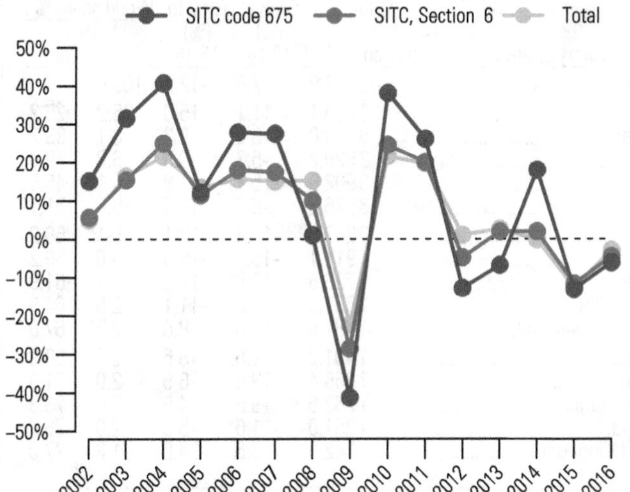

Table 2: Top exporting countries or areas in 2016

Country or area	Value (million US$)	Avg. Growth (%) 12-16	Growth (%) 15-16	World share %	Cum.
World	59000.5	-2.6	-6.0	100.0	
China	12367.1	5.9	-9.8	21.0	21.0
Japan	6080.1	-7.7	-6.1	10.3	31.3
Belgium	4675.0	-1.5	-10.0	7.9	39.2
Germany	4575.8	-5.3	-5.7	7.8	46.9
Rep. of Korea	3863.3	0.8	-5.7	6.5	53.5
France	3201.0	-7.0	-1.5	5.4	58.9
USA	2854.4	-1.2	-14.6	4.8	63.8
Netherlands	2745.1	2.2	6.5	4.7	68.4
Finland	2587.2	-6.0	-8.4	4.4	72.8
Sweden	2353.3	-6.8	-5.6	4.0	76.8
Other Asia, nes	2046.4	-6.7	-0.7	3.5	80.3
Austria	1879.0	6.9	17.8	3.2	83.4
Italy	1664.1	-11.2	-2.2	2.8	86.3
Spain	1159.2	-5.2	-13.4	2.0	88.2
India	675.9	-2.7	-7.3	1.1	89.4

Graph 2: Trade Balance by MDG regions 2016
(Bln US$)

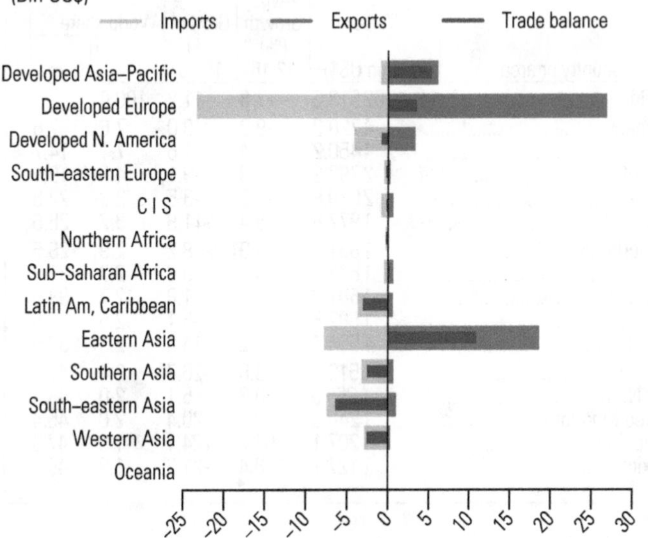

Table 3: Top importing countries or areas in 2016

Country or area	Value (million US$)	Avg. Growth (%) 12-16	Growth (%) 15-16	World share %	Cum.
World	55285.2	-2.4	-6.9	100.0	
Germany	5477.1	2.4	-6.0	9.9	9.9
Italy	3376.6	-3.4	-11.9	6.1	16.0
China	3347.6	-7.6	-11.3	6.1	22.1
Viet Nam	*2974.3*	17.2	5.1	5.4	27.4
USA	2774.5	-7.1	-15.8	5.0	32.5
Mexico	2458.1	-0.6	-3.7	4.4	36.9
Rep. of Korea	2448.7	0.3	-0.5	4.4	41.3
Netherlands	2389.2	-1.3	-3.1	4.3	45.7
India	2132.3	-3.5	-17.4	3.9	49.5
Turkey	2093.3	2.6	-13.1	3.8	53.3
Thailand	2052.7	-4.3	5.4	3.7	57.0
France	1935.2	-5.5	-6.9	3.5	60.5
Other Asia, nes	1692.0	-7.0	-3.7	3.1	63.6
Belgium	1400.5	-3.3	-0.3	2.5	66.1
Canada	1345.5	-1.8	-9.4	2.4	68.5

676 Iron and steel bars, rods, angles, shapes and sections

In 2016, the value (in current US$) of exports of "iron and steel bars, rods, angles, shapes and sections" (SITC group 676) decreased by 12.9 percent (compared to -7.6 percent average growth rate from 2012-2016) to reach 63.8 bln US$ (see table 2), while imports decreased by 11.2 percent to reach 62.5 bln US$ (see table 3). Exports of this commodity accounted for 3.3 percent of world exports of SITC section 6, and 0.4 percent of total world merchandise exports (see table 1). China, Germany and Italy were the top exporters in 2016 (see table 2). They accounted for 25.2, 8.1 and 6.2 percent of world exports, respectively. Germany, USA and Rep. of Korea were the top destinations, with respectively 7.6, 7.1 and 4.5 percent of world imports (see table 3).

The top 15 countries/areas accounted for 77.0 and 49.1 percent of total world exports and imports, respectively (see tables 2 and 3). In 2016, China was the country/area with the highest value of net exports (+14.4 bln US$), followed by Japan (+3.1 bln US$). By MDG regions (see graph 2), the largest surpluses in this product group were recorded by Eastern Asia (+12.8 bln US$), Developed Europe (+4.1 bln US$) and Developed Asia-Pacific (+2.7 bln US$). The largest trade deficits were recorded by South-eastern Asia (-7.0 bln US$), Developed North America (-3.1 bln US$) and Northern Africa (-2.6 bln US$).

Table 1: Imports (Imp.) and exports (Exp.), 2002-2016, in current US$

		2002	2003	2004	2005	2006	2007	2008	2009	2010	2011	2012	2013	2014	2015	2016
Values in Bln US$	Imp.	24.3	30.2	47.0	52.6	63.7	86.5	110.5	52.5	67.7	90.3	85.7	81.9	85.6	70.4	62.5
	Exp.	23.3	29.6	46.6	52.0	63.4	88.1	113.0	50.9	68.4	91.2	87.6	84.4	87.9	73.3	63.8
As a percentage of SITC section (%)	Imp.	2.7	2.9	3.7	3.7	3.8	4.4	5.1	3.4	3.5	3.9	3.9	3.7	3.7	3.5	3.2
	Exp.	2.6	2.9	3.7	3.7	3.8	4.5	5.2	3.3	3.5	3.9	3.9	3.7	3.8	3.6	3.3
As a percentage of world trade (%)	Imp.	0.4	0.4	0.5	0.5	0.5	0.6	0.7	0.4	0.4	0.5	0.5	0.4	0.5	0.4	0.4
	Exp.	0.4	0.4	0.5	0.5	0.5	0.6	0.7	0.4	0.5	0.5	0.5	0.4	0.5	0.4	0.4

Graph 1: Annual growth rates of exports, 2002–2016
(In percentage by year)

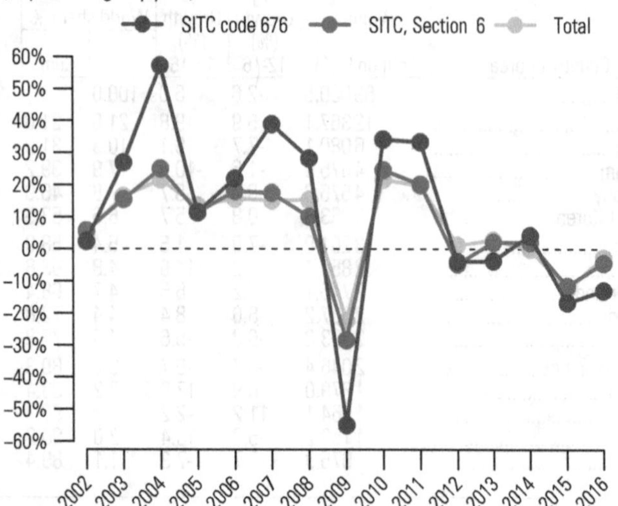

Table 2: Top exporting countries or areas in 2016

Country or area	Value (million US$)	Avg. Growth (%) 12-16	Growth (%) 15-16	World share %	Cum.
World	63813.9	-7.6	-12.9	100.0	
China	16069.1	11.1	-15.0	25.2	25.2
Germany	5143.0	-8.5	-9.2	8.1	33.2
Italy	3929.2	-5.7	-0.9	6.2	39.4
Turkey	3902.6	-15.1	-11.8	6.1	45.5
Japan	3576.5	-6.7	-10.8	5.6	51.1
Spain	3247.0	-11.4	-12.1	5.1	56.2
USA	1911.1	-15.7	-15.3	3.0	59.2
France	1728.5	-10.8	-12.0	2.7	61.9
Rep. of Korea	1657.8	-11.0	-11.1	2.6	64.5
Russian Federation	1581.8	-11.0	-8.0	2.5	67.0
Austria	1491.2	1.6	18.6	2.3	69.3
Poland	1265.4	-13.6	-6.5	2.0	71.3
Luxembourg	1262.6	-9.6	-4.9	2.0	73.3
Czechia	1251.0	-11.6	-5.9	2.0	75.2
United Kingdom	1142.5	-13.5	-24.8	1.8	77.0

Graph 2: Trade Balance by MDG regions 2016
(Bln US$)

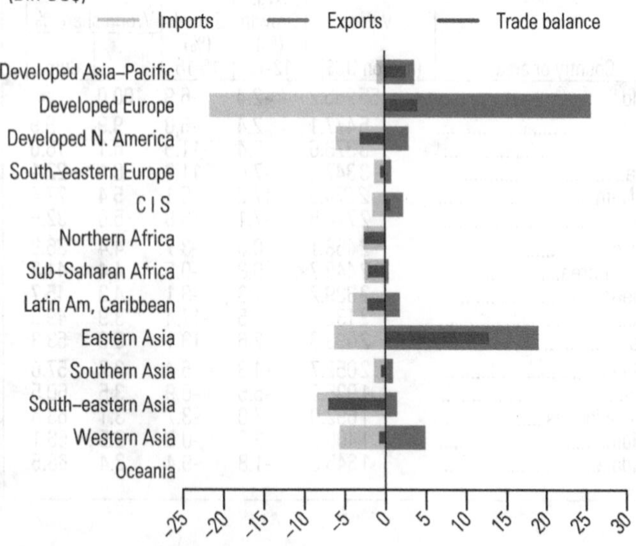

Table 3: Top importing countries or areas in 2016

Country or area	Value (million US$)	Avg. Growth (%) 12-16	Growth (%) 15-16	World share %	Cum.
World	62513.5	-7.6	-11.2	100.0	
Germany	4720.2	-9.2	-9.0	7.6	7.6
USA	4450.2	-5.4	-21.6	7.1	14.7
Rep. of Korea	2793.9	-6.8	-9.1	4.5	19.1
France	2070.8	-9.0	-3.5	3.3	22.5
Italy	1977.8	-5.4	-11.9	3.2	25.6
Netherlands	1831.7	-4.9	8.2	2.9	28.5
China	1693.9	-3.2	-3.6	2.7	31.3
Thailand	1681.0	-5.3	-1.8	2.7	33.9
Malaysia	1582.8	3.0	-5.1	2.5	36.5
Canada	1554.4	-13.2	-14.8	2.5	39.0
Algeria	1512.6	-13.8	-26.7	2.4	41.4
Viet Nam	*1255.3*	10.2	5.1	2.0	43.4
United Kingdom	1248.3	-9.5	-20.4	2.0	45.4
Philippines	1207.1	54.2	124.1	1.9	47.3
Mexico	1127.7	-8.4	-21.2	1.8	49.1

In 2016, the value (in current US$) of exports of "rails or railway track construction material, of iron or steel" (SITC group 677) decreased by 18.8 percent (compared to -7.9 percent average growth rate from 2012-2016) to reach 3.1 bln US$ (see table 2), while imports decreased by 17.5 percent to reach 3.6 bln US$ (see table 3). Exports of this commodity accounted for 0.2 percent of world exports of SITC section 6, and less than 0.1 percent of total world merchandise exports (see table 1). Austria, Japan and China were the top exporters in 2016 (see table 2). They accounted for 14.8, 13.6 and 12.3 percent of world exports, respectively. USA, Germany and Canada were the top destinations, with respectively 9.6, 7.8 and 7.6 percent of world imports (see table 3).

The top 15 countries/areas accounted for 89.8 and 58.7 percent of total world exports and imports, respectively (see tables 2 and 3). In 2016, Austria was the country/area with the highest value of net exports (+440.7 mln US$), followed by Japan (+417.8 mln US$). By MDG regions (see graph 2), the largest surpluses in this product group were recorded by Developed Europe (+502.3 mln US$), Developed Asia-Pacific (+356.7 mln US$) and Eastern Asia (+280.3 mln US$). The largest trade deficits were recorded by Developed North America (-334.0 mln US$), Latin America and the Caribbean (-295.0 mln US$) and Western Asia (-270.5 mln US$).

Table 1: Imports (Imp.) and exports (Exp.), 2002-2016, in current US$

		2002	2003	2004	2005	2006	2007	2008	2009	2010	2011	2012	2013	2014	2015	2016
Values in Bln US$	Imp.	1.5	1.8	2.1	2.6	3.0	3.8	5.4	4.2	4.3	4.7	4.8	4.9	4.8	4.4	3.6
	Exp.	1.3	1.6	2.0	2.2	2.5	3.3	4.3	3.8	3.8	4.4	4.4	4.3	4.2	3.9	3.1
As a percentage of SITC section (%)	Imp.	0.2	0.2	0.2	0.2	0.2	0.2	0.2	0.3	0.2	0.2	0.2	0.2	0.2	0.2	0.2
	Exp.	0.2	0.2	0.2	0.2	0.1	0.2	0.2	0.2	0.2	0.2	0.2	0.2	0.2	0.2	0.2
As a percentage of world trade (%)	Imp.	0.0	0.0	0.0	0.0	0.0	0.0	0.0	0.0	0.0	0.0	0.0	0.0	0.0	0.0	0.0
	Exp.	0.0	0.0	0.0	0.0	0.0	0.0	0.0	0.0	0.0	0.0	0.0	0.0	0.0	0.0	0.0

Graph 1: Annual growth rates of exports, 2002–2016

(In percentage by year)

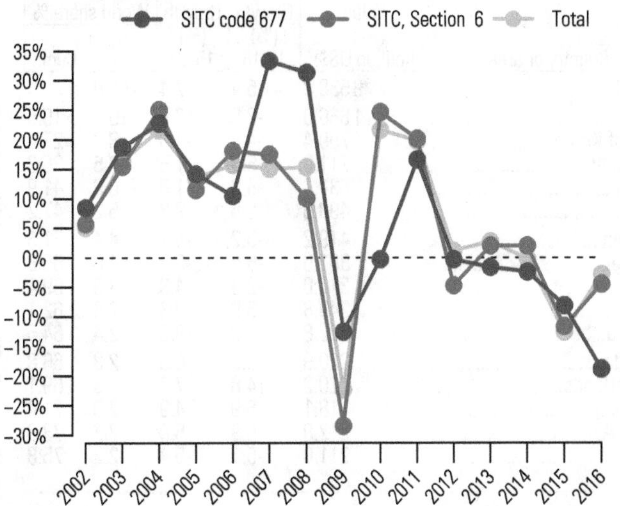

Table 2: Top exporting countries or areas in 2016

Country or area	Value (million US$)	Avg. Growth (%) 12-16	Growth (%) 15-16	World share %	Cum.
World	3147.6	-7.9	-18.8	100.0	
Austria	466.7	-7.2	-7.6	14.8	14.8
Japan	427.4	-10.6	-12.7	13.6	28.4
China	385.6	-7.1	-46.7	12.3	40.7
USA	242.2	-8.1	-18.8	7.7	48.4
Poland	196.6	21.4	-9.2	6.2	54.6
Czechia	190.9	-6.2	1.0	6.1	60.7
Germany	183.7	-9.5	2.0	5.8	66.5
Spain	146.3	-2.2	-33.9	4.6	71.1
Russian Federation	132.0	-7.2	0.8	4.2	75.3
United Kingdom	109.9	1.5	-29.3	3.5	78.8
Belgium	95.4	-8.7	-5.1	3.0	81.9
Luxembourg	71.4	-4.6	4.3	2.3	84.1
Italy	65.3	-26.8	-27.6	2.1	86.2
India	59.1	6.0	107.4	1.9	88.1
France	55.5	7.4	-4.3	1.8	89.8

Graph 2: Trade Balance by MDG regions 2016

(Bln US$)

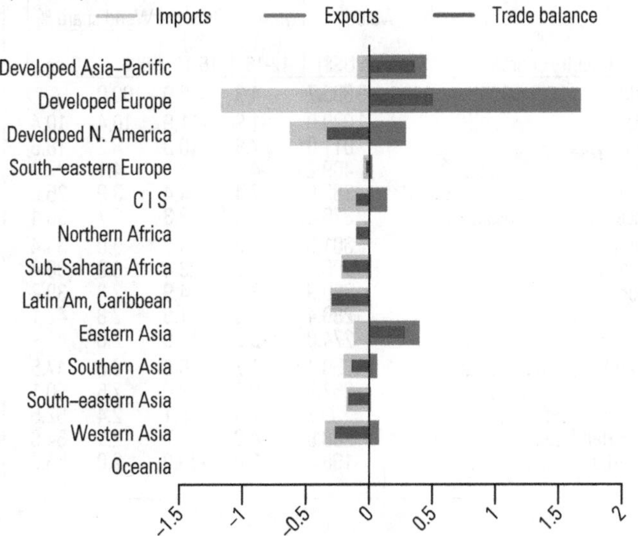

Table 3: Top importing countries or areas in 2016

Country or area	Value (million US$)	Avg. Growth (%) 12-16	Growth (%) 15-16	World share %	Cum.
World	3646.6	-6.4	-17.5	100.0	
USA	348.9	-7.4	-18.5	9.6	9.6
Germany	286.1	4.1	-13.9	7.8	17.4
Canada	275.8	-2.1	-13.4	7.6	25.0
Saudi Arabia	216.5	3.1	-16.5	5.9	30.9
Uzbekistan	*118.9*	39.2	105.5	3.3	34.2
Switzerland	114.1	-0.4	2.0	3.1	37.3
Brazil	104.1	-15.8	-61.1	2.9	40.2
France	99.6	3.7	-22.4	2.7	42.9
Belgium	92.3	-13.3	-8.9	2.5	45.4
Italy	92.1	19.3	113.6	2.5	47.9
Iran	*90.1*	54.8	122.2	2.5	50.4
Australia	80.2	-5.1	102.2	2.2	52.6
Mexico	79.2	-11.6	-38.6	2.2	54.8
Sweden	75.4	-3.9	-12.1	2.1	56.9
Argentina	68.6	-3.2	-59.1	1.9	58.7

Source: UN Comtrade

678 Wire of iron or steel

In 2016, the value (in current US$) of exports of "wire of iron or steel" (SITC group 678) decreased by 7.4 percent (compared to -5.4 percent average growth rate from 2012-2016) to reach 9.5 bln US$ (see table 2), while imports decreased by 6.0 percent to reach 9.9 bln US$ (see table 3). Exports of this commodity accounted for 0.5 percent of world exports of SITC section 6, and 0.1 percent of total world merchandise exports (see table 1). China, Rep. of Korea and Germany were the top exporters in 2016 (see table 2). They accounted for 19.6, 8.3 and 7.5 percent of world exports, respectively. USA, Germany and China were the top destinations, with respectively 10.4, 8.2 and 4.1 percent of world imports (see table 3).

The top 15 countries/areas accounted for 75.8 and 56.6 percent of total world exports and imports, respectively (see tables 2 and 3). In 2016, China was the country/area with the highest value of net exports (+1.5 bln US$), followed by Rep. of Korea (+515.6 mln US$). By MDG regions (see graph 2), the largest surpluses in this product group were recorded by Eastern Asia (+2.0 bln US$) and Developed Asia-Pacific (+129.5 mln US$). The largest trade deficits were recorded by Developed North America (-621.0 mln US$), South-eastern Asia (-564.3 mln US$) and Latin America and the Caribbean (-493.5 mln US$).

Table 1: Imports (Imp.) and exports (Exp.), 2002-2016, in current US$

		2002	2003	2004	2005	2006	2007	2008	2009	2010	2011	2012	2013	2014	2015	2016
Values in Bln US$	Imp.	4.5	5.3	7.4	7.9	8.7	10.9	13.1	8.0	10.7	13.2	11.8	11.6	12.1	10.5	9.9
	Exp.	3.8	4.5	6.6	7.2	8.2	10.3	12.7	7.8	10.8	13.3	11.9	11.6	12.1	10.3	9.5
As a percentage of SITC section (%)	Imp.	0.5	0.5	0.6	0.6	0.5	0.6	0.6	0.5	0.6	0.6	0.5	0.5	0.5	0.5	0.5
	Exp.	0.4	0.4	0.5	0.5	0.5	0.5	0.6	0.5	0.6	0.6	0.5	0.5	0.5	0.5	0.5
As a percentage of world trade (%)	Imp.	0.1	0.1	0.1	0.1	0.1	0.1	0.1	0.1	0.1	0.1	0.1	0.1	0.1	0.1	0.1
	Exp.	0.1	0.1	0.1	0.1	0.1	0.1	0.1	0.1	0.1	0.1	0.1	0.1	0.1	0.1	0.1

Graph 1: Annual growth rates of exports, 2002–2016
(In percentage by year)

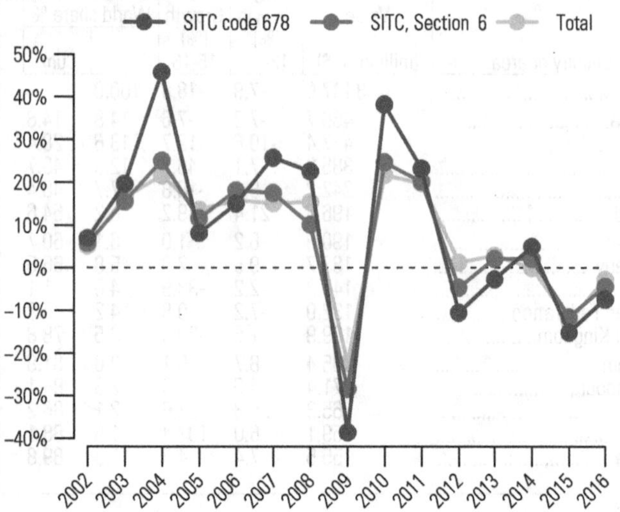

Table 2: Top exporting countries or areas in 2016

Country or area	Value (million US$)	Avg. Growth (%) 12-16	Growth (%) 15-16	World share %	Cum.
World	9 538.8	-5.4	-7.4	100.0	
China	1 866.0	-2.6	-12.5	19.6	19.6
Rep. of Korea	790.4	-4.8	-4.6	8.3	27.8
Germany	711.9	-6.3	-1.5	7.5	35.3
Japan	631.1	-6.0	1.9	6.6	41.9
Italy	498.6	-5.5	-2.3	5.2	47.2
Czechia	419.2	-5.2	-5.1	4.4	51.5
France	381.9	-6.6	-5.8	4.0	55.6
USA	370.0	-2.9	-4.8	3.9	59.4
India	249.8	-5.9	-10.3	2.6	62.1
Austria	232.8	1.3	18.9	2.4	64.5
Canada	220.9	-0.9	-6.9	2.3	66.8
Netherlands	220.2	14.8	17.2	2.3	69.1
Slovakia	218.1	-5.9	-4.9	2.3	71.4
Other Asia, nes	212.9	-5.9	-5.0	2.2	73.6
Sweden	211.0	-5.1	-5.4	2.2	75.8

Graph 2: Trade Balance by MDG regions 2016
(Bln US$)

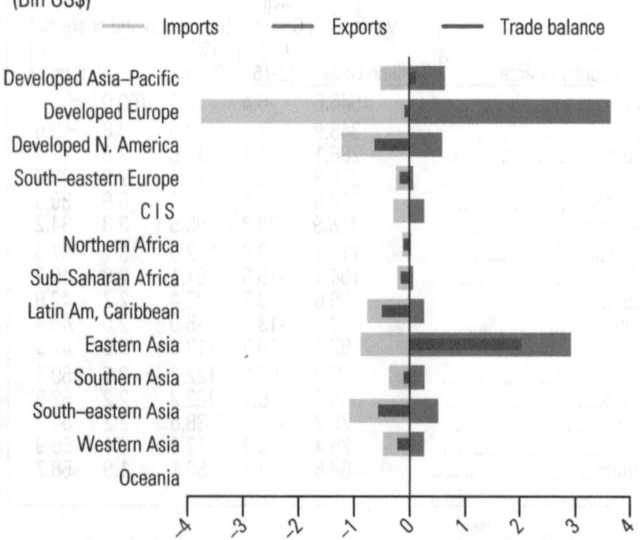

Table 3: Top importing countries or areas in 2016

Country or area	Value (million US$)	Avg. Growth (%) 12-16	Growth (%) 15-16	World share %	Cum.
World	9 896.7	-4.3	-6.0	100.0	
USA	1 029.9	-1.9	-11.9	10.4	10.4
Germany	811.0	-7.9	-10.3	8.2	18.6
China	409.2	-4.3	2.3	4.1	22.7
Japan	385.0	-7.4	4.4	3.9	26.6
France	370.8	-5.9	-3.3	3.7	30.4
Poland	301.5	-2.9	-4.2	3.0	33.4
Thailand	296.0	-0.8	23.4	3.0	36.4
Mexico	280.9	2.7	4.9	2.8	39.2
Italy	280.4	-1.6	-1.9	2.8	42.1
Rep. of Korea	274.8	-5.0	-16.0	2.8	44.9
United Kingdom	259.4	-1.7	-6.0	2.6	47.5
India	257.8	0.3	8.0	2.6	50.1
Viet Nam	*238.8*	2.3	5.1	2.4	52.5
Switzerland	208.6	-4.2	0.7	2.1	54.6
Netherlands	198.5	-5.8	-19.0	2.0	56.6

In 2016, the value (in current US$) of exports of "tubes, pipes and hollow profiles, and tube or pipe fittings of iron or steel" (SITC group 679) decreased by 17.1 percent (compared to -11.2 percent average growth rate from 2012-2016) to reach 60.8 bln US$ (see table 2), while imports decreased by 18.3 percent to reach 67.2 bln US$ (see table 3). Exports of this commodity accounted for 3.1 percent of world exports of SITC section 6, and 0.4 percent of total world merchandise exports (see table 1). China, Italy and Germany were the top exporters in 2016 (see table 2). They accounted for 18.9, 9.9 and 9.8 percent of world exports, respectively. USA, Germany and Iraq were the top destinations, with respectively 10.5, 5.3 and 5.0 percent of world imports (see table 3).

The top 15 countries/areas accounted for 76.8 and 51.3 percent of total world exports and imports, respectively (see tables 2 and 3). In 2016, China was the country/area with the highest value of net exports (+9.3 bln US$), followed by Italy (+4.5 bln US$). By MDG regions (see graph 2), the largest surpluses in this product group were recorded by Eastern Asia (+11.0 bln US$), Developed Europe (+5.1 bln US$) and Developed Asia-Pacific (+1.8 bln US$). The largest trade deficits were recorded by Western Asia (-8.2 bln US$), Developed North America (-4.1 bln US$) and South-eastern Asia (-3.1 bln US$).

Table 1: Imports (Imp.) and exports (Exp.), 2002-2016, in current US$

		2002	2003	2004	2005	2006	2007	2008	2009	2010	2011	2012	2013	2014	2015	2016
Values in Bln US$	Imp.	28.0	30.7	41.8	54.3	70.2	88.3	109.6	79.1	76.5	95.3	103.6	99.9	103.9	82.3	67.2
	Exp.	26.5	29.5	41.3	54.0	69.7	86.2	106.7	70.4	75.1	95.9	98.0	93.4	93.5	73.3	60.8
As a percentage of	Imp.	3.1	3.0	3.2	3.8	4.2	4.5	5.0	5.1	4.0	4.1	4.8	4.5	4.6	4.1	3.5
SITC section (%)	Exp.	3.0	2.9	3.2	3.8	4.1	4.4	4.9	4.5	3.9	4.1	4.4	4.1	4.0	3.6	3.1
As a percentage of	Imp.	0.4	0.4	0.4	0.5	0.6	0.6	0.7	0.6	0.5	0.5	0.6	0.5	0.6	0.5	0.4
world trade (%)	Exp.	0.4	0.4	0.5	0.5	0.6	0.6	0.7	0.6	0.5	0.5	0.5	0.5	0.5	0.4	0.4

Graph 1: Annual growth rates of exports, 2002–2016

(In percentage by year)

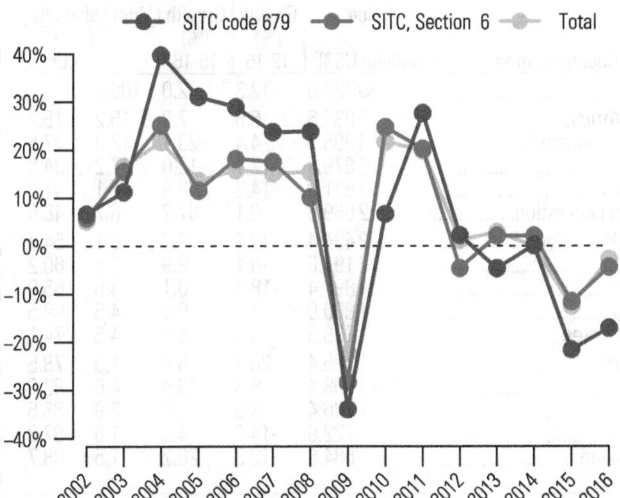

Graph 2: Trade Balance by MDG regions 2016

(Bln US$)

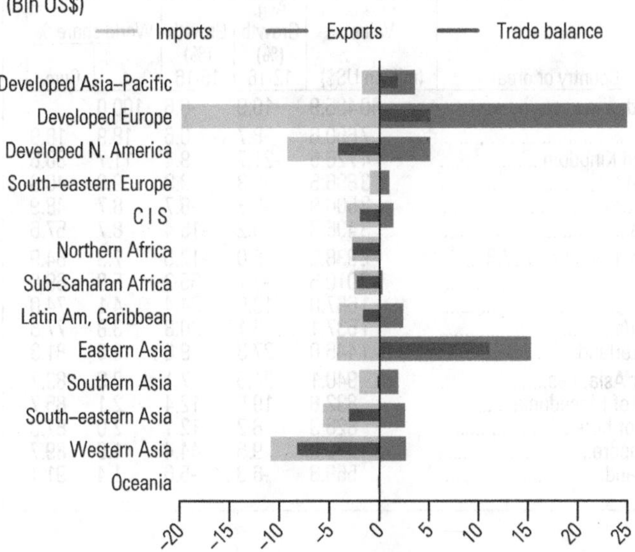

Table 2: Top exporting countries or areas in 2016

Country or area	Value (million US$)	Avg. Growth (%) 12-16	Growth (%) 15-16	World share %	Cum.
World	60806.2	-11.2	-17.1	100.0	
China	11479.1	-8.0	-16.0	18.9	18.9
Italy	6005.1	-6.7	-2.1	9.9	28.8
Germany	5983.0	-9.9	-10.6	9.8	38.6
USA	3937.5	-13.2	-22.9	6.5	45.1
Japan	3449.4	-18.4	-25.7	5.7	50.7
Rep. of Korea	2856.4	-13.2	-15.5	4.7	55.4
Netherlands	1850.0	0.1	9.6	3.0	58.5
India	1752.9	-13.6	-10.1	2.9	61.4
France	1587.0	-13.2	-37.2	2.6	64.0
Spain	1459.3	-5.5	-3.2	2.4	66.4
United Kingdom	1439.5	-12.5	-23.5	2.4	68.7
Mexico	1359.1	-6.7	-9.2	2.2	71.0
Austria	1231.7	-8.2	-8.0	2.0	73.0
Turkey	1160.2	-11.3	-17.3	1.9	74.9
Canada	1123.5	-14.6	-30.5	1.8	76.8

Table 3: Top importing countries or areas in 2016

Country or area	Value (million US$)	Avg. Growth (%) 12-16	Growth (%) 15-16	World share %	Cum.
World	67187.2	-10.3	-18.3	100.0	
USA	7077.0	-17.8	-39.3	10.5	10.5
Germany	3581.6	-6.6	-4.9	5.3	15.9
Iraq	*3366.3*	-5.3	-11.9	5.0	20.9
China	2129.9	-3.7	-10.2	3.2	24.0
Canada	2101.1	-18.4	-27.8	3.1	27.2
United Kingdom	1985.0	-4.0	-8.6	3.0	30.1
Saudi Arabia	1913.2	-13.1	-14.2	2.8	33.0
France	1899.8	-5.5	-21.5	2.8	35.8
United Arab Emirates	1850.5	-19.5	-14.0	2.8	38.6
Mexico	1570.8	-4.2	-13.8	2.3	40.9
Algeria	1552.0	18.6	28.3	2.3	43.2
Italy	1515.4	-4.6	-1.9	2.3	45.5
Netherlands	1448.6	-7.0	-4.0	2.2	47.6
Rep. of Korea	1344.8	-12.4	-26.0	2.0	49.6
India	1148.7	-8.2	-10.7	1.7	51.3

Source: UN Comtrade

681 Silver, platinum and other metals of the platinum group

In 2016, the value (in current US$) of exports of "silver, platinum and other metals of the platinum group" (SITC group 681) decreased by 2.0 percent (compared to -12.3 percent average growth rate from 2012-2016) to reach 39.7 bln US$ (see table 2), while imports decreased by 6.6 percent to reach 40.4 bln US$ (see table 3). Exports of this commodity accounted for 2.0 percent of world exports of SITC section 6, and 0.2 percent of total world merchandise exports (see table 1). South Africa, United Kingdom and USA were the top exporters in 2016 (see table 2). They accounted for 15.2, 12.3 and 7.2 percent of world exports, respectively. USA, United Kingdom and Japan were the top destinations, with respectively 18.9, 11.7 and 9.6 percent of world imports (see table 3).

The top 15 countries/areas accounted for 88.7 and 91.1 percent of total world exports and imports, respectively (see tables 2 and 3). In 2016, South Africa was the country/area with the highest value of net exports (+6.0 bln US$), followed by Russian Federation (+2.7 bln US$). By MDG regions (see graph 2), the largest surpluses in this product group were recorded by Sub-Saharan Africa (+6.1 bln US$), Commonwealth of Independent States (+3.3 bln US$) and Latin America and the Caribbean (+2.2 bln US$). The largest trade deficits were recorded by Developed North America (-4.5 bln US$), Eastern Asia (-2.5 bln US$) and Southern Asia (-2.2 bln US$).

Table 1: Imports (Imp.) and exports (Exp.), 2002-2016, in current US$

		2002	2003	2004	2005	2006	2007	2008	2009	2010	2011	2012	2013	2014	2015	2016
Values in Bln US$	Imp.	14.8	15.2	19.4	23.0	37.0	45.4	56.1	39.2	54.2	78.6	64.0	58.6	51.2	43.2	40.4
	Exp.	10.5	13.3	18.1	21.8	37.2	45.6	51.0	36.1	50.1	74.3	67.1	59.4	51.8	40.5	39.7
As a percentage of SITC section (%)	Imp.	1.7	1.5	1.5	1.6	2.2	2.3	2.6	2.5	2.8	3.4	2.9	2.7	2.2	2.1	2.1
	Exp.	1.2	1.3	1.4	1.5	2.2	2.3	2.3	2.3	2.6	3.2	3.0	2.6	2.2	2.0	2.0
As a percentage of world trade (%)	Imp.	0.2	0.2	0.2	0.2	0.3	0.3	0.3	0.3	0.4	0.4	0.3	0.3	0.3	0.3	0.3
	Exp.	0.2	0.2	0.2	0.2	0.3	0.3	0.3	0.3	0.3	0.4	0.4	0.3	0.3	0.2	0.2

Graph 1: Annual growth rates of exports, 2002–2016

(In percentage by year)

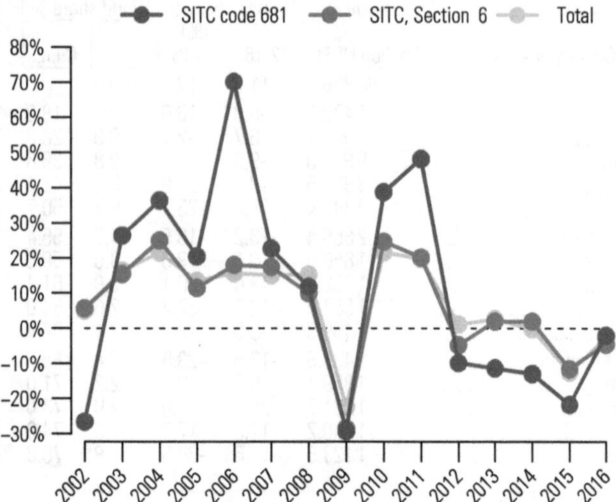

Graph 2: Trade Balance by MDG regions 2016

(Bln US$)

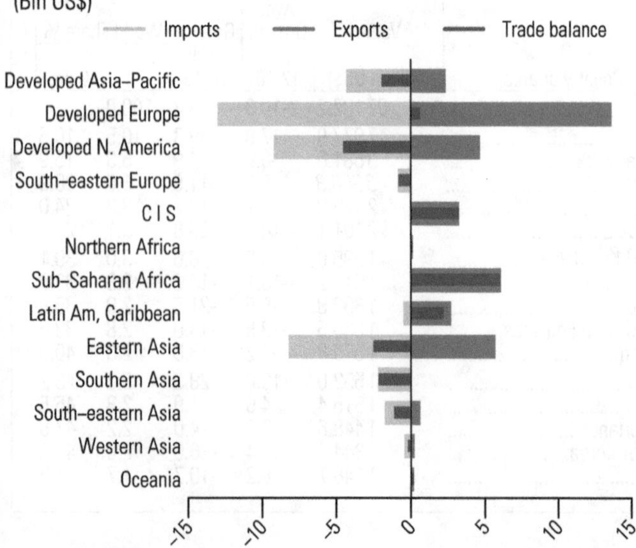

Table 2: Top exporting countries or areas in 2016

Country or area	Value (million US$)	Avg. Growth (%) 12-16	Growth (%) 15-16	World share %	Cum.
World	39738.9	-12.3	-2.0	100.0	
South Africa	6035.5	-6.6	-7.2	15.2	15.2
United Kingdom	4905.5	-4.4	-23.1	12.3	27.5
USA	2879.9	-12.1	-12.0	7.2	34.8
Germany	2821.9	-14.2	-3.5	7.1	41.9
Russian Federation	2669.8	-0.1	87.2	6.7	48.6
China, Hong Kong SAR	2434.4	-12.9	7.7	6.1	54.7
Japan	2191.0	-8.1	9.9	5.5	60.2
Mexico	1891.4	-18.5	0.1	4.8	65.0
Canada	1800.0	-7.1	6.0	4.5	69.5
Rep. of Korea	1799.3	-9.5	6.9	4.5	74.1
Switzerland	1785.4	-26.4	-9.6	4.5	78.5
Italy	1608.4	5.3	23.4	4.0	82.6
China	1136.4	3.9	-2.0	2.9	85.5
Poland	722.9	-14.6	-4.5	1.8	87.3
Kazakhstan	584.6	-12.3	20.2	1.5	88.7

Table 3: Top importing countries or areas in 2016

Country or area	Value (million US$)	Avg. Growth (%) 12-16	Growth (%) 15-16	World share %	Cum.
World	40405.9	-10.9	-6.6	100.0	
USA	7650.6	-8.7	0.6	18.9	18.9
United Kingdom	4726.5	-21.7	9.4	11.7	30.6
Japan	3896.5	-9.3	-3.3	9.6	40.3
Germany	3500.9	-5.8	-8.7	8.7	48.9
China	3496.3	-9.2	-15.4	8.7	57.6
China, Hong Kong SAR	2938.2	-5.0	-12.5	7.3	64.9
India	2010.5	-3.1	-55.2	5.0	69.8
Italy	1667.0	13.0	34.4	4.1	74.0
Canada	1537.1	-3.1	20.3	3.8	77.8
Switzerland	1446.0	-27.3	9.0	3.6	81.3
Other Asia, nes	940.1	-24.0	7.1	2.3	83.7
TFYR of Macedonia	832.6	19.5	12.4	2.1	85.7
Rep. of Korea	828.3	-8.2	-12.1	2.0	87.8
Singapore	770.0	9.5	44.4	1.9	89.7
Thailand	569.3	-6.3	-5.6	1.4	91.1

In 2016, the value (in current US$) of exports of "copper" (SITC group 682) decreased by 7.3 percent (compared to -8.4 percent average growth rate from 2012-2016) to reach 97.3 bln US$ (see table 2), while imports decreased by 7.1 percent to reach 100.1 bln US$ (see table 3). Exports of this commodity accounted for 5.0 percent of world exports of SITC section 6, and 0.6 percent of total world merchandise exports (see table 1). Chile, Germany and Japan were the top exporters in 2016 (see table 2). They accounted for 15.1, 8.0 and 5.8 percent of world exports, respectively. China, USA and Germany were the top destinations, with respectively 26.4, 6.4 and 5.8 percent of world imports (see table 3).

The top 15 countries/areas accounted for 66.9 and 72.1 percent of total world exports and imports, respectively (see tables 2 and 3). In 2016, Chile was the country/area with the highest value of net exports (+14.7 bln US$), followed by Zambia (+4.7 bln US$). By MDG regions (see graph 2), the largest surpluses in this product group were recorded by Latin America and the Caribbean (+14.8 bln US$), Sub-Saharan Africa (+7.1 bln US$) and Commonwealth of Independent States (+6.3 bln US$). The largest trade deficits were recorded by Eastern Asia (-22.4 bln US$), Western Asia (-5.9 bln US$) and South-eastern Asia (-3.8 bln US$).

Table 1: Imports (Imp.) and exports (Exp.), 2002-2016, in current US$

		2002	2003	2004	2005	2006	2007	2008	2009	2010	2011	2012	2013	2014	2015	2016
Values in Bln US$	Imp.	29.5	33.5	51.0	62.4	106.3	121.4	122.0	83.6	123.5	147.1	136.8	133.2	128.0	107.7	100.1
	Exp.	28.9	32.8	51.3	63.6	111.6	123.4	121.0	88.1	129.5	149.3	138.1	132.5	125.5	104.9	97.3
As a percentage of SITC section (%)	Imp.	3.3	3.3	4.0	4.4	6.4	6.1	5.6	5.4	6.4	6.4	6.3	6.0	5.6	5.3	5.2
	Exp.	3.3	3.2	4.0	4.5	6.6	6.3	5.6	5.7	6.7	6.4	6.2	5.8	5.4	5.1	5.0
As a percentage of world trade (%)	Imp.	0.4	0.4	0.5	0.6	0.9	0.9	0.7	0.7	0.8	0.8	0.7	0.7	0.7	0.7	0.6
	Exp.	0.4	0.4	0.6	0.6	0.9	0.9	0.8	0.7	0.9	0.8	0.8	0.7	0.7	0.6	0.6

Graph 1: Annual growth rates of exports, 2002–2016

(In percentage by year)

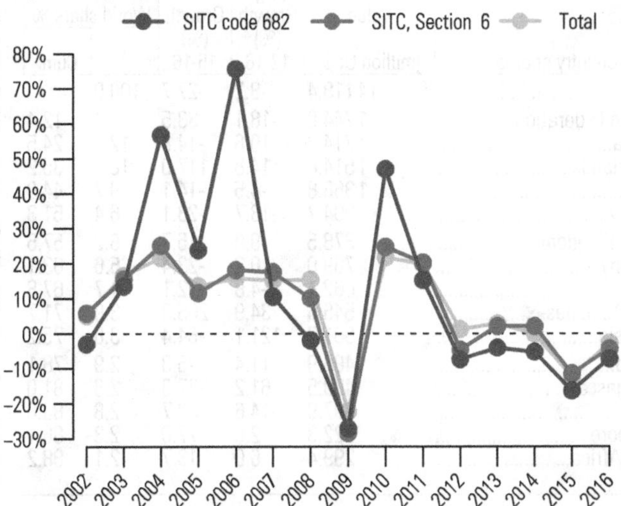

Table 2: Top exporting countries or areas in 2016

Country or area	Value (million US$)	Avg. Growth (%) 12-16	Growth (%) 15-16	World share %	Cum.
World	97 267.4	-8.4	-7.3	100.0	
Chile	14 723.1	-13.2	-13.2	15.1	15.1
Germany	7 770.2	-8.5	-5.4	8.0	23.1
Japan	5 640.1	-8.0	-4.3	5.8	28.9
China	5 146.2	-5.7	6.4	5.3	34.2
Zambia	*4806.0*	-6.8	-6.7	4.9	39.2
USA	3 330.0	-6.6	-3.5	3.4	42.6
Russian Federation	3 292.6	-12.7	-25.6	3.4	46.0
Rep. of Korea	3 292.1	-4.7	-13.5	3.4	49.3
Other Asia, nes	2 900.7	-1.2	4.0	3.0	52.3
Italy	2 712.6	-3.4	3.4	2.8	55.1
Dem.Rep. of the Congo	*2450.9*	-5.2	-15.0	2.5	57.6
Poland	2 353.3	-13.4	-19.5	2.4	60.1
Australia	2 268.8	-10.0	-11.8	2.3	62.4
Netherlands	2 236.1	19.6	199.6	2.3	64.7
Spain	2 182.5	-6.6	0.8	2.2	66.9

Graph 2: Trade Balance by MDG regions 2016

(Bln US$)

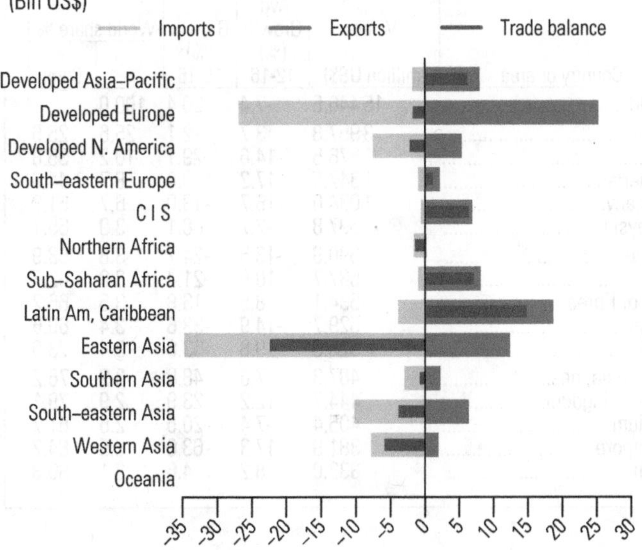

Table 3: Top importing countries or areas in 2016

Country or area	Value (million US$)	Avg. Growth (%) 12-16	Growth (%) 15-16	World share %	Cum.
World	100 120.6	-7.5	-7.1	100.0	
China	26 400.1	-9.1	-8.9	26.4	26.4
USA	6 397.4	-8.2	-11.2	6.4	32.8
Germany	5 791.2	-10.4	-10.1	5.8	38.5
Italy	4 879.5	-8.8	-10.9	4.9	43.4
Rep. of Korea	3 728.3	-3.8	0.7	3.7	47.1
Other Asia, nes	3 725.7	-6.8	-3.3	3.7	50.9
Thailand	2 790.4	-5.0	-1.9	2.8	53.6
Malaysia	2 600.0	-5.2	-13.4	2.6	56.2
France	2 574.1	-11.4	-7.0	2.6	58.8
Turkey	2 572.8	-9.4	-9.6	2.6	61.4
India	2 519.3	12.1	4.3	2.5	63.9
Netherlands	2 253.7	26.5	165.1	2.3	66.2
United Arab Emirates	2 042.4	-9.1	6.8	2.0	68.2
Mexico	1 953.1	-2.6	-7.1	2.0	70.1
Belgium	1 924.3	-10.5	-17.6	1.9	72.1

Source: UN Comtrade

683 Nickel

In 2016, the value (in current US$) of exports of "nickel" (SITC group 683) decreased by 27.7 percent (compared to -8.2 percent average growth rate from 2012-2016) to reach 14.1 bln US$ (see table 2), while imports decreased by 20.4 percent to reach 15.4 bln US$ (see table 3). Exports of this commodity accounted for 0.7 percent of world exports of SITC section 6, and 0.1 percent of total world merchandise exports (see table 1). Russian Federation, Canada and Netherlands were the top exporters in 2016 (see table 2). They accounted for 12.4, 12.1 and 10.7 percent of world exports, respectively. China, USA and Netherlands were the top destinations, with respectively 25.6, 10.2 and 8.7 percent of world imports (see table 3).

The top 15 countries/areas accounted for 88.2 and 86.3 percent of total world exports and imports, respectively (see tables 2 and 3). In 2016, Russian Federation was the country/area with the highest value of net exports (+1.7 bln US$), followed by Canada (+1.6 bln US$). By MDG regions (see graph 2), the largest surpluses in this product group were recorded by Commonwealth of Independent States (+1.7 bln US$), Developed North America (+1.4 bln US$) and Sub-Saharan Africa (+645.9 mln US$). The largest trade deficits were recorded by Eastern Asia (-4.0 bln US$), Southern Asia (-416.9 mln US$) and South-eastern Asia (-304.7 mln US$).

Table 1: Imports (Imp.) and exports (Exp.), 2002-2016, in current US$

		2002	2003	2004	2005	2006	2007	2008	2009	2010	2011	2012	2013	2014	2015	2016
Values in Bln US$	Imp.	6.7	9.1	13.0	14.6	21.9	32.9	22.6	13.8	20.3	25.8	21.0	20.9	22.5	19.4	15.4
	Exp.	7.0	8.0	12.2	13.3	20.9	31.7	20.9	13.3	19.2	23.1	19.9	21.0	23.5	19.5	14.1
As a percentage of SITC section (%)	Imp.	0.7	0.9	1.0	1.0	1.3	1.7	1.0	0.9	1.1	1.1	1.0	0.9	1.0	1.0	0.8
	Exp.	0.8	0.8	1.0	0.9	1.2	1.6	1.0	0.9	1.0	1.0	0.9	0.9	1.0	1.0	0.7
As a percentage of world trade (%)	Imp.	0.1	0.1	0.1	0.1	0.2	0.2	0.1	0.1	0.1	0.1	0.1	0.1	0.1	0.1	0.1
	Exp.	0.1	0.1	0.1	0.1	0.2	0.2	0.1	0.1	0.1	0.1	0.1	0.1	0.1	0.1	0.1

Graph 1: Annual growth rates of exports, 2002–2016
(In percentage by year)

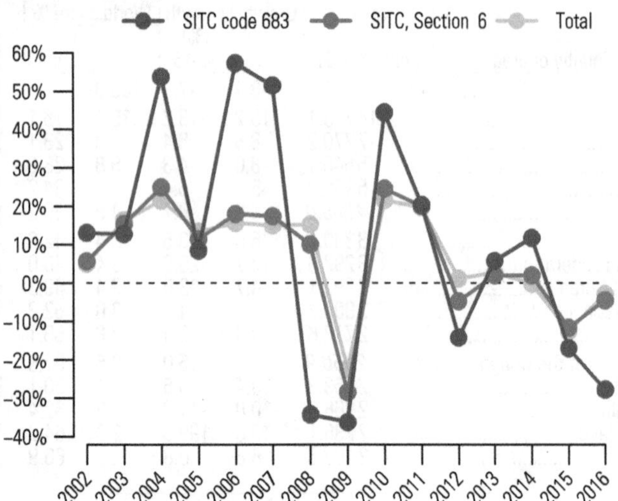

Graph 2: Trade Balance by MDG regions 2016
(Bln US$)

Imports — Exports — Trade balance

Developed Asia-Pacific
Developed Europe
Developed N. America
South-eastern Europe
C I S
Northern Africa
Sub-Saharan Africa
Latin Am, Caribbean
Eastern Asia
Southern Asia
South-eastern Asia
Western Asia
Oceania

-6 -5 -4 -3 -2 -1 0 1 2 3 4 5 6

Table 2: Top exporting countries or areas in 2016

Country or area	Value (million US$)	Avg. Growth (%) 12-16	Growth (%) 15-16	World share %	Cum.
World	14118.4	-8.2	-27.7	100.0	
Russian Federation	1744.0	-18.1	-33.5	12.4	12.4
Canada	1714.3	-10.6	-14.8	12.1	24.5
Netherlands	1514.8	14.8	117.0	10.7	35.2
USA	1366.8	-4.5	-14.1	9.7	44.9
Norway	904.7	-13.7	-23.1	6.4	51.3
United Kingdom	878.5	-9.0	-15.7	6.2	57.5
Germany	789.0	-10.2	-23.4	5.6	63.1
Japan	662.1	-4.8	-12.1	4.7	67.8
Other Asia, nes	546.6	34.9	205.3	3.9	71.7
Malaysia	501.7	121.1	-64.4	3.6	75.2
Finland	406.9	-11.4	-5.3	2.9	78.1
Madagascar	400.5	61.2	-27.3	2.8	81.0
France	397.9	-14.6	-32.7	2.8	83.8
Singapore	322.3	2.8	-77.0	2.3	86.1
South Africa	299.4	6.0	13.7	2.1	88.2

Table 3: Top importing countries or areas in 2016

Country or area	Value (million US$)	Avg. Growth (%) 12-16	Growth (%) 15-16	World share %	Cum.
World	15446.5	-7.4	-20.4	100.0	
China	3957.8	3.7	-2.1	25.6	25.6
USA	1576.5	-14.6	-29.1	10.2	35.8
Netherlands	1347.5	17.2	138.0	8.7	44.6
Germany	1034.0	-16.7	-18.0	6.7	51.2
Malaysia	597.8	-2.7	-68.1	3.9	55.1
France	590.9	-13.5	-24.7	3.8	58.9
Italy	587.7	-10.9	-21.4	3.8	62.7
Rep. of Korea	534.1	-8.5	-13.8	3.5	66.2
Japan	529.7	-14.9	-33.6	3.4	69.6
India	525.9	-9.8	-53.8	3.4	73.0
Other Asia, nes	487.3	7.6	48.8	3.2	76.2
United Kingdom	444.7	-12.2	-23.9	2.9	79.1
Belgium	405.4	-7.4	-20.5	2.6	81.7
Singapore	381.9	-17.3	-63.6	2.5	84.2
Spain	332.0	-8.2	-4.6	2.1	86.3

In 2016, the value (in current US$) of exports of "aluminium" (SITC group 684) decreased by 1.3 percent (compared to -0.1 percent average growth rate from 2012-2016) to reach 107.7 bln US$ (see table 2), while imports decreased by 3.4 percent to reach 106.3 bln US$ (see table 3). Exports of this commodity accounted for 5.5 percent of world exports of SITC section 6, and 0.7 percent of total world merchandise exports (see table 1). China, Germany and USA were the top exporters in 2016 (see table 2). They accounted for 11.5, 8.7 and 7.2 percent of world exports, respectively. USA, Germany and Netherlands were the top destinations, with respectively 12.8, 10.4 and 6.0 percent of world imports (see table 3).

The top 15 countries/areas accounted for 68.1 and 66.1 percent of total world exports and imports, respectively (see tables 2 and 3). In 2016, China was the country/area with the highest value of net exports (+9.5 bln US$), followed by Russian Federation (+5.3 bln US$). By MDG regions (see graph 2), the largest surpluses in this product group were recorded by Eastern Asia (+6.5 bln US$), Commonwealth of Independent States (+5.6 bln US$) and Western Asia (+4.4 bln US$). The largest trade deficits were recorded by South-eastern Asia (-4.4 bln US$), Developed Europe (-4.2 bln US$) and Latin America and the Caribbean (-3.7 bln US$).

Table 1: Imports (Imp.) and exports (Exp.), 2002-2016, in current US$

		2002	2003	2004	2005	2006	2007	2008	2009	2010	2011	2012	2013	2014	2015	2016
Values in Bln US$	Imp.	50.0	57.0	70.3	78.3	103.2	117.4	116.5	76.2	100.3	122.8	109.4	108.1	116.5	110.1	106.3
	Exp.	48.2	55.2	67.4	76.2	99.7	113.0	116.5	75.2	100.3	117.7	108.0	107.3	114.2	109.1	107.7
As a percentage of SITC section (%)	Imp.	5.6	5.5	5.5	5.5	6.2	5.9	5.3	4.9	5.2	5.3	5.0	4.9	5.1	5.5	5.5
	Exp.	5.5	5.4	5.3	5.4	5.9	5.7	5.4	4.8	5.2	5.0	4.9	4.7	4.9	5.3	5.5
As a percentage of world trade (%)	Imp.	0.8	0.7	0.8	0.7	0.8	0.8	0.7	0.6	0.7	0.7	0.6	0.6	0.6	0.7	0.7
	Exp.	0.7	0.7	0.7	0.7	0.8	0.8	0.7	0.6	0.7	0.7	0.6	0.6	0.6	0.7	0.7

Graph 1: Annual growth rates of exports, 2002–2016
(In percentage by year)

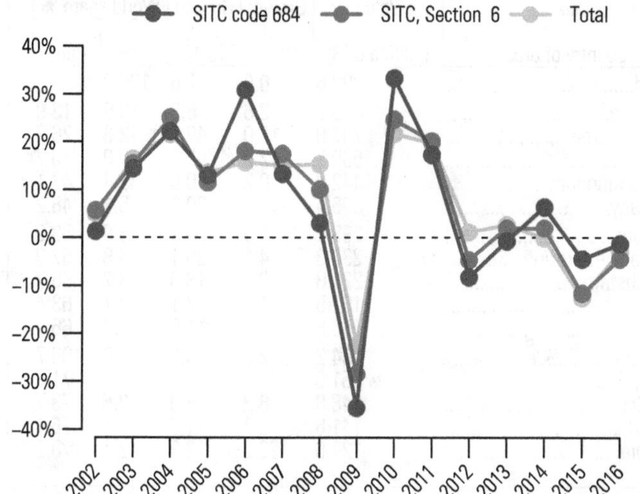

Graph 2: Trade Balance by MDG regions 2016
(Bln US$)

Imports | Exports | Trade balance

Developed Asia-Pacific
Developed Europe
Developed N. America
South-eastern Europe
C I S
Northern Africa
Sub-Saharan Africa
Latin Am, Caribbean
Eastern Asia
Southern Asia
South-eastern Asia
Western Asia
Oceania

-50 -40 -30 -20 -10 0 10 20 30 40 50

Table 2: Top exporting countries or areas in 2016

Country or area	Value (million US$)	Avg. Growth (%) 12-16	Growth (%) 15-16	World share %	Cum.
World	107736.0	-0.1	-1.3	100.0	
China	12370.8	2.4	-12.6	11.5	11.5
Germany	9324.8	-0.6	-2.6	8.7	20.1
USA	7766.7	2.2	9.9	7.2	27.3
Canada	6500.1	-2.2	-2.4	6.0	33.4
Netherlands	6140.6	23.9	117.2	5.7	39.1
Russian Federation	5804.2	-5.0	-16.0	5.4	44.5
United Arab Emirates	4739.8	30.3	-3.8	4.4	48.9
Italy	3103.9	-2.1	-2.0	2.9	51.7
Norway	3087.6	-7.1	-8.7	2.9	54.6
France	2906.1	-0.3	-0.1	2.7	57.3
Australia	2481.3	-10.9	-16.3	2.3	59.6
Spain	2389.4	2.3	-4.0	2.2	61.8
Austria	2327.5	-0.5	6.8	2.2	64.0
Malaysia	2314.7	17.4	55.7	2.1	66.1
Belgium	2117.1	0.1	-8.6	2.0	68.1

Table 3: Top importing countries or areas in 2016

Country or area	Value (million US$)	Avg. Growth (%) 12-16	Growth (%) 15-16	World share %	Cum.
World	106305.3	-0.7	-3.4	100.0	
USA	13563.8	4.1	4.4	12.8	12.8
Germany	11023.8	-2.8	-7.2	10.4	23.1
Netherlands	6348.2	16.0	125.0	6.0	29.1
Japan	5207.2	-6.3	-13.9	4.9	34.0
Mexico	4171.5	-1.9	-1.7	3.9	37.9
Rep. of Korea	4036.3	-0.4	-9.2	3.8	41.7
France	4033.3	-2.2	-5.5	3.8	45.5
Italy	3854.7	-0.2	-6.5	3.6	49.1
United Kingdom	3150.4	0.5	-10.7	3.0	52.1
China	2909.5	-11.7	-10.9	2.7	54.8
Turkey	2585.6	-1.7	-15.6	2.4	57.3
Poland	2552.3	2.2	-1.6	2.4	59.7
Canada	2325.7	-1.6	-8.0	2.2	61.9
Viet Nam	*2289.7*	19.3	5.1	2.2	64.0
Thailand	2202.5	-1.1	-4.0	2.1	66.1

In 2016, the value (in current US$) of exports of "lead" (SITC group 685) increased by 2.6 percent (compared to less than 0.1 percent average growth rate from 2012-2016) to reach 6.0 bln US$ (see table 2), while imports increased by 5.5 percent to reach 6.1 bln US$ (see table 3). Exports of this commodity accounted for 0.3 percent of world exports of SITC section 6, and less than 0.1 percent of total world merchandise exports (see table 1). Australia, Rep. of Korea and Canada were the top exporters in 2016 (see table 2). They accounted for 13.9, 12.8 and 9.0 percent of world exports, respectively. USA, India and United Kingdom were the top destinations, with respectively 17.6, 7.6 and 6.5 percent of world imports (see table 3).

The top 15 countries/areas accounted for 78.2 and 73.8 percent of total world exports and imports, respectively (see tables 2 and 3). In 2016, Australia was the country/area with the highest value of net exports (+829.3 mln US$), followed by Canada (+533.4 mln US$). By MDG regions (see graph 2), the largest surpluses in this product group were recorded by Developed Asia-Pacific (+786.6 mln US$), Commonwealth of Independent States (+469.5 mln US$) and Eastern Asia (+410.9 mln US$). The largest trade deficits were recorded by South-eastern Asia (-575.8 mln US$), Developed North America (-499.1 mln US$) and Southern Asia (-406.1 mln US$).

Table 1: Imports (Imp.) and exports (Exp.), 2002-2016, in current US$

		2002	2003	2004	2005	2006	2007	2008	2009	2010	2011	2012	2013	2014	2015	2016
Values in Bln US$	Imp.	1.5	1.5	2.6	3.0	3.9	6.4	6.3	4.6	5.8	7.0	6.0	6.7	6.7	5.8	6.1
	Exp.	1.4	1.5	2.3	2.8	3.8	6.3	5.9	4.5	5.6	6.9	6.0	6.6	6.6	5.8	6.0
As a percentage of SITC section (%)	Imp.	0.2	0.2	0.2	0.2	0.2	0.3	0.3	0.3	0.3	0.3	0.3	0.3	0.3	0.3	0.3
	Exp.	0.2	0.1	0.2	0.2	0.2	0.3	0.3	0.3	0.3	0.3	0.3	0.3	0.3	0.3	0.3
As a percentage of world trade (%)	Imp.	0.0	0.0	0.0	0.0	0.0	0.0	0.0	0.0	0.0	0.0	0.0	0.0	0.0	0.0	0.0
	Exp.	0.0	0.0	0.0	0.0	0.0	0.0	0.0	0.0	0.0	0.0	0.0	0.0	0.0	0.0	0.0

Graph 1: Annual growth rates of exports, 2002–2016

(In percentage by year)

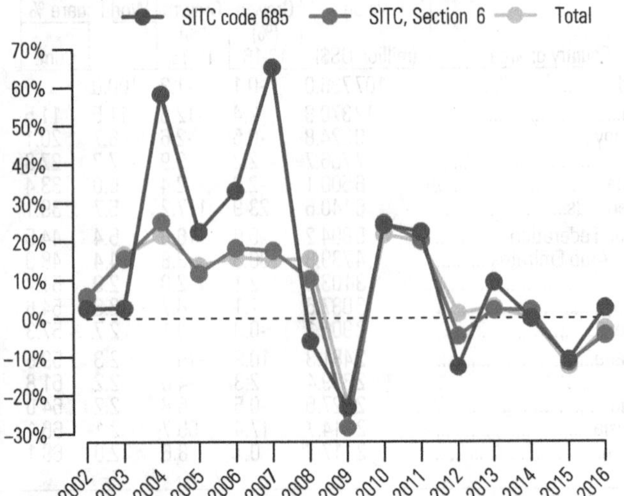

Table 2: Top exporting countries or areas in 2016

Country or area	Value (million US$)	Avg. Growth (%) 12-16	Growth (%) 15-16	World share %	Cum.
World	5992.6	0.0	2.6	100.0	
Australia	833.2	-2.6	6.9	13.9	13.9
Rep. of Korea	767.8	17.0	49.6	12.8	26.7
Canada	539.5	-2.2	3.9	9.0	35.7
United Kingdom	442.9	-0.2	0.6	7.4	43.1
Germany	305.4	-11.3	-20.9	5.1	48.2
Belgium	298.1	4.0	0.1	5.0	53.2
Russian Federation	230.3	4.1	28.1	3.8	57.0
Kazakhstan	221.8	-9.0	18.0	3.7	60.7
India	162.5	11.2	-7.1	2.7	63.4
Mexico	160.8	-7.3	-11.6	2.7	66.1
Bulgaria	154.2	2.6	-3.3	2.6	68.7
Malaysia	151.0	-1.0	-33.1	2.5	71.2
Sweden	148.8	8.2	18.9	2.5	73.7
Poland	141.6	2.7	-21.2	2.4	76.1
Czechia	127.6	22.2	12.3	2.1	78.2

Graph 2: Trade Balance by MDG regions 2016

(Bln US$)

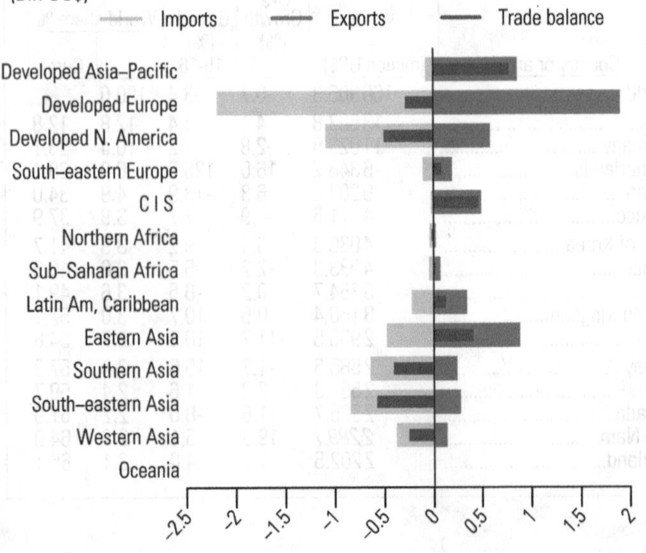

Table 3: Top importing countries or areas in 2016

Country or area	Value (million US$)	Avg. Growth (%) 12-16	Growth (%) 15-16	World share %	Cum.
World	6129.6	0.5	5.5	100.0	
USA	1081.5	10.7	6.5	17.6	17.6
India	464.4	2.4	14.3	7.6	25.2
United Kingdom	398.3	-8.0	-20.2	6.5	31.7
Germany	311.8	-1.8	4.9	5.1	36.8
Czechia	293.4	20.2	22.9	4.8	41.6
Rep. of Korea	266.6	-1.4	-23.5	4.3	45.9
Viet Nam	*256.7*	3.3	5.1	4.2	50.1
Thailand	232.3	2.0	27.0	3.8	53.9
Spain	219.0	-5.1	37.4	3.6	57.5
Turkey	212.3	-1.3	4.3	3.5	61.0
Italy	198.8	-0.7	0.9	3.2	64.2
Other Asia, nes	162.5	-6.0	4.3	2.7	66.8
Indonesia	155.5	-5.4	8.2	2.5	69.4
Poland	144.2	10.4	2.0	2.4	71.7
Brazil	125.0	-5.8	-1.5	2.0	73.8

In 2016, the value (in current US$) of exports of "zinc" (SITC group 686) increased by 0.2 percent (compared to 0.1 percent average growth rate from 2012-2016) to reach 12.4 bln US$ (see table 2), while imports decreased by 0.3 percent to reach 12.4 bln US$ (see table 3). Exports of this commodity accounted for 0.6 percent of world exports of SITC section 6, and 0.1 percent of total world merchandise exports (see table 1). Rep. of Korea, Canada and Netherlands were the top exporters in 2016 (see table 2). They accounted for 10.4, 9.4 and 8.2 percent of world exports, respectively. USA, China and Germany were the top destinations, with respectively 12.9, 9.1 and 9.1 percent of world imports (see table 3).

The top 15 countries/areas accounted for 79.7 and 74.6 percent of total world exports and imports, respectively (see tables 2 and 3). In 2016, Canada was the country/area with the highest value of net exports (+1.1 bln US$), followed by Rep. of Korea (+1.1 bln US$). By MDG regions (see graph 2), the largest surpluses in this product group were recorded by Commonwealth of Independent States (+983.1 mln US$), Developed Asia-Pacific (+937.4 mln US$) and Latin America and the Caribbean (+667.1 mln US$). The largest trade deficits were recorded by Western Asia (-865.7 mln US$), South-eastern Asia (-792.5 mln US$) and Eastern Asia (-332.7 mln US$).

Table 1: Imports (Imp.) and exports (Exp.), 2002-2016, in current US$

		2002	2003	2004	2005	2006	2007	2008	2009	2010	2011	2012	2013	2014	2015	2016
Values in Bln US$	Imp.	4.7	5.0	6.5	7.7	15.6	19.0	11.4	8.5	11.8	13.1	11.4	11.7	13.4	12.4	12.4
	Exp.	4.3	4.8	5.9	6.9	15.7	17.9	10.8	8.1	11.8	13.5	12.4	11.2	13.1	12.4	12.4
As a percentage of SITC section (%)	Imp.	0.5	0.5	0.5	0.5	0.9	1.0	0.5	0.5	0.6	0.6	0.5	0.5	0.6	0.6	0.6
	Exp.	0.5	0.5	0.5	0.5	0.9	0.9	0.5	0.5	0.6	0.6	0.6	0.5	0.6	0.6	0.6
As a percentage of world trade (%)	Imp.	0.1	0.1	0.1	0.1	0.1	0.1	0.1	0.1	0.1	0.1	0.1	0.1	0.1	0.1	0.1
	Exp.	0.1	0.1	0.1	0.1	0.1	0.1	0.1	0.1	0.1	0.1	0.1	0.1	0.1	0.1	0.1

Graph 1: Annual growth rates of exports, 2002–2016

(In percentage by year)

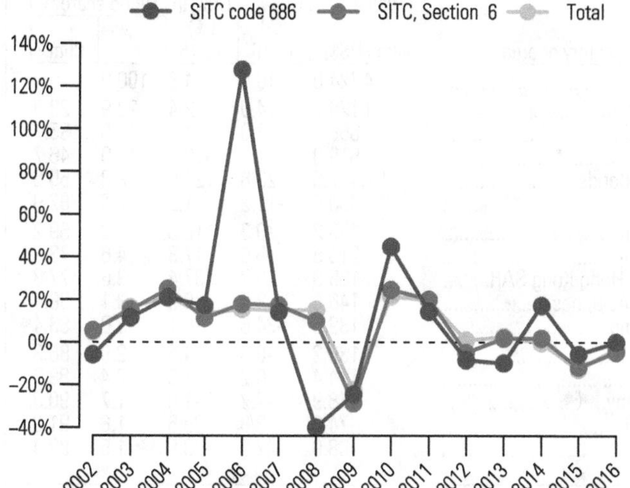

Graph 2: Trade Balance by MDG regions 2016

(Bln US$)

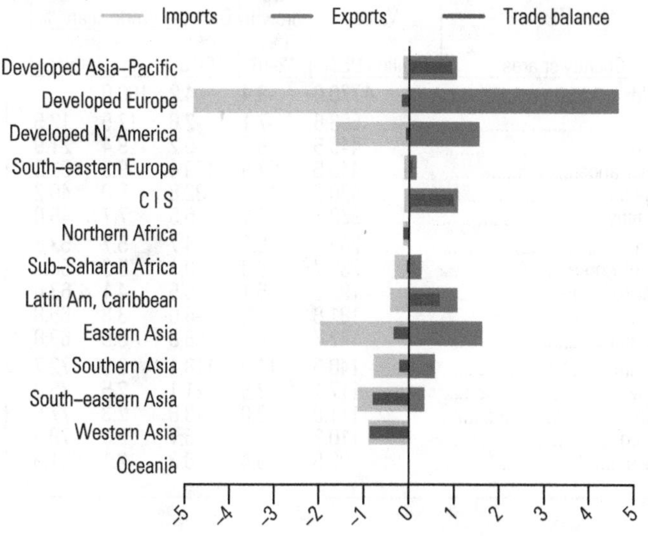

Table 2: Top exporting countries or areas in 2016

Country or area	Value (million US$)	Avg. Growth (%) 12-16	Growth (%) 15-16	World share %	Cum.
World	12430.1	0.1	0.2	100.0	
Rep. of Korea	1288.2	5.9	11.5	10.4	10.4
Canada	1169.9	1.7	3.5	9.4	19.8
Netherlands	1016.4	15.3	65.6	8.2	28.0
Belgium	982.7	-2.0	3.2	7.9	35.9
Australia	788.4	-3.0	-0.7	6.3	42.2
Spain	773.1	-2.2	-1.5	6.2	48.4
Peru	554.4	0.3	2.5	4.5	52.9
Kazakhstan	553.3	-14.4	-3.9	4.5	57.3
Finland	535.6	-2.2	-3.5	4.3	61.6
India	424.6	-3.8	-37.9	3.4	65.1
Uzbekistan	*424.3*	16.6	10.0	3.4	68.5
USA	387.6	14.9	94.3	3.1	71.6
Norway	381.6	5.6	10.9	3.1	74.7
Mexico	360.5	-2.3	-2.8	2.9	77.6
Japan	270.0	-5.0	-19.4	2.2	79.7

Table 3: Top importing countries or areas in 2016

Country or area	Value (million US$)	Avg. Growth (%) 12-16	Growth (%) 15-16	World share %	Cum.
World	12356.3	2.0	-0.3	100.0	
USA	1592.5	2.1	3.1	12.9	12.9
China	1128.7	-5.0	-18.4	9.1	22.0
Germany	1123.3	0.3	2.7	9.1	31.1
Belgium	755.7	0.9	15.7	6.1	37.2
Netherlands	615.0	6.6	45.3	5.0	42.2
India	576.6	29.2	80.5	4.7	46.9
Turkey	559.8	4.0	2.4	4.5	51.4
Italy	528.4	4.2	9.9	4.3	55.7
Other Asia, nes	504.3	1.9	-11.4	4.1	59.8
France	460.2	0.5	0.3	3.7	63.5
Indonesia	301.0	0.1	7.1	2.4	65.9
Viet Nam	*285.7*	15.7	5.1	2.3	68.2
Austria	285.0	8.6	17.0	2.3	70.5
United Kingdom	257.3	4.6	-4.1	2.1	72.6
Malaysia	246.1	3.4	-9.0	2.0	74.6

Source: UN Comtrade

In 2016, the value (in current US$) of exports of "tin" (SITC group 687) increased by 4.8 percent (compared to -10.4 percent average growth rate from 2012-2016) to reach 4.7 bln US$ (see table 2), while imports increased by 4.2 percent to reach 4.8 bln US$ (see table 3). Exports of this commodity accounted for 0.2 percent of world exports of SITC section 6, and less than 0.1 percent of total world merchandise exports (see table 1). Indonesia, Singapore and Malaysia were the top exporters in 2016 (see table 2). They accounted for 23.9, 11.8 and 11.0 percent of world exports, respectively. USA, Japan and Netherlands were the top destinations, with respectively 12.5, 9.4 and 9.3 percent of world imports (see table 3).

The top 15 countries/areas accounted for 93.4 and 81.9 percent of total world exports and imports, respectively (see tables 2 and 3). In 2016, Indonesia was the country/area with the highest value of net exports (+1.1 bln US$), followed by Malaysia (+402.8 mln US$). By MDG regions (see graph 2), the largest surpluses in this product group were recorded by South-eastern Asia (+1.6 bln US$) and Latin America and the Caribbean (+645.4 mln US$). The largest trade deficits were recorded by Developed Europe (-645.7 mln US$), Developed North America (-520.5 mln US$) and Eastern Asia (-414.0 mln US$).

Table 1: Imports (Imp.) and exports (Exp.), 2002-2016, in current US$

		2002	2003	2004	2005	2006	2007	2008	2009	2010	2011	2012	2013	2014	2015	2016
Values in Bln US$	Imp.	1.2	1.6	3.2	3.4	3.7	5.1	6.2	4.3	6.3	9.0	7.1	6.8	6.8	4.6	4.8
	Exp.	1.3	1.6	3.0	3.2	3.4	4.7	6.1	3.8	6.1	8.5	7.3	7.1	6.7	4.5	4.7
As a percentage of SITC section (%)	Imp.	0.1	0.2	0.3	0.2	0.2	0.3	0.3	0.3	0.3	0.4	0.3	0.3	0.3	0.2	0.2
	Exp.	0.1	0.2	0.2	0.2	0.2	0.2	0.3	0.2	0.3	0.4	0.3	0.3	0.3	0.2	0.2
As a percentage of world trade (%)	Imp.	0.0	0.0	0.0	0.0	0.0	0.0	0.0	0.0	0.0	0.0	0.0	0.0	0.0	0.0	0.0
	Exp.	0.0	0.0	0.0	0.0	0.0	0.0	0.0	0.0	0.0	0.0	0.0	0.0	0.0	0.0	0.0

Graph 1: Annual growth rates of exports, 2002–2016

(In percentage by year)

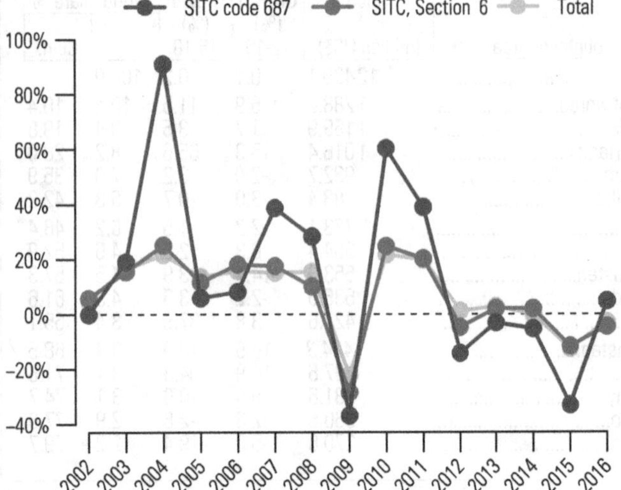

Table 2: Top exporting countries or areas in 2016

Country or area	Value (million US$)	Avg. Growth (%) 12-16	Growth (%) 15-16	World share %	Cum.
World	4724.0	-10.4	4.8	100.0	
Indonesia	1128.9	-14.0	-2.4	23.9	23.9
Singapore	556.7	-12.0	-4.1	11.8	35.7
Malaysia	519.9	-11.8	-19.4	11.0	46.7
Netherlands	417.5	23.8	121.9	8.8	55.5
Peru	350.5	-11.2	1.2	7.4	62.9
Bolivia	295.2	-0.3	15.8	6.2	69.2
Belgium	215.5	-5.6	17.8	4.6	73.8
China, Hong Kong SAR	168.3	5.7	37.4	3.6	77.3
Other Asia, nes	146.5	-3.0	0.9	3.1	80.4
Thailand	139.5	-24.6	18.1	3.0	83.4
Brazil	136.2	-0.6	4.5	2.9	86.3
USA	114.4	-6.2	7.9	2.4	88.7
Germany	78.9	-7.2	-1.0	1.7	90.3
Poland	74.5	3.8	20.5	1.6	91.9
Spain	68.9	42.6	173.6	1.5	93.4

Graph 2: Trade Balance by MDG regions 2016

(Bln US$)

Imports
Exports
Trade balance

Developed Asia-Pacific
Developed Europe
Developed N. America
South-eastern Europe
CIS
Northern Africa
Sub-Saharan Africa
Latin Am, Caribbean
Eastern Asia
Southern Asia
South-eastern Asia
Western Asia
Oceania

-2 -1.5 -1 -0.5 0 0.5 1 1.5 2 2.5

Table 3: Top importing countries or areas in 2016

Country or area	Value (million US$)	Avg. Growth (%) 12-16	Growth (%) 15-16	World share %	Cum.
World	4770.0	-9.4	4.2	100.0	
USA	596.6	-7.1	-2.6	12.5	12.5
Japan	446.5	-6.9	-0.2	9.4	21.9
Netherlands	445.5	27.9	179.4	9.3	31.2
Singapore	430.9	-15.3	-32.8	9.0	40.2
Germany	368.1	-4.1	5.5	7.7	48.0
China	269.5	-25.3	-4.7	5.7	53.6
Rep. of Korea	252.7	-8.9	-0.1	5.3	58.9
Other Asia, nes	193.8	-5.1	5.5	4.1	63.0
India	181.8	2.2	-6.0	3.8	66.8
Thailand	142.7	-26.7	58.8	3.0	69.8
Belgium	140.5	14.8	118.1	2.9	72.7
Malaysia	117.1	-32.8	21.1	2.5	75.2
Spain	111.0	-2.0	-3.8	2.3	77.5
Mexico	110.3	-1.3	5.1	2.3	79.8
France	99.5	-6.4	8.3	2.1	81.9

Source: UN Comtrade

In 2016, the value (in current US$) of exports of "miscellaneous non-ferrous base metals employed in metallurgy and cermets" (SITC group 689) decreased by 3.2 percent (compared to -4.1 percent average growth rate from 2012-2016) to reach 7.7 bln US$ (see table 2), while imports decreased by 1.9 percent to reach 9.1 bln US$ (see table 3). Exports of this commodity accounted for 0.4 percent of world exports of SITC section 6, and less than 0.1 percent of total world merchandise exports (see table 1). China, USA and Dem.Rep. of the Congo were the top exporters in 2016 (see table 2). They accounted for 22.2, 9.4 and 9.1 percent of world exports, respectively. USA, China and Germany were the top destinations, with respectively 17.6, 13.1 and 8.4 percent of world imports (see table 3).

The top 15 countries/areas accounted for 86.3 and 82.0 percent of total world exports and imports, respectively (see tables 2 and 3). In 2016, Dem.Rep. of the Congo was the country/area with the highest value of net exports (+698.2 mln US$), followed by China (+505.2 mln US$). By MDG regions (see graph 2), the largest surpluses in this product group were recorded by Sub-Saharan Africa (+847.5 mln US$), Commonwealth of Independent States (+272.8 mln US$) and Eastern Asia (+79.0 mln US$). The largest trade deficits were recorded by Developed Europe (-1.0 bln US$), Developed North America (-769.8 mln US$) and Latin America and the Caribbean (-255.7 mln US$).

Table 1: Imports (Imp.) and exports (Exp.), 2002-2016, in current US$

		2002	2003	2004	2005	2006	2007	2008	2009	2010	2011	2012	2013	2014	2015	2016
Values in Bln US$	Imp.	3.4	4.0	6.6	8.1	8.7	10.5	13.1	6.1	9.9	12.7	10.9	9.7	10.7	9.3	9.1
	Exp.	3.1	3.9	6.3	7.2	8.5	9.7	11.9	5.4	8.5	10.1	9.1	8.6	9.3	7.9	7.7
As a percentage of SITC section (%)	Imp.	0.4	0.4	0.5	0.6	0.5	0.5	0.6	0.4	0.5	0.6	0.5	0.4	0.5	0.5	0.5
	Exp.	0.4	0.4	0.5	0.5	0.5	0.5	0.5	0.3	0.4	0.4	0.4	0.4	0.4	0.4	0.4
As a percentage of world trade (%)	Imp.	0.1	0.1	0.1	0.1	0.1	0.1	0.1	0.0	0.1	0.1	0.1	0.1	0.1	0.1	0.1
	Exp.	0.0	0.1	0.1	0.1	0.1	0.1	0.1	0.0	0.1	0.1	0.0	0.0	0.0	0.0	0.0

Graph 1: Annual growth rates of exports, 2002–2016
(In percentage by year)

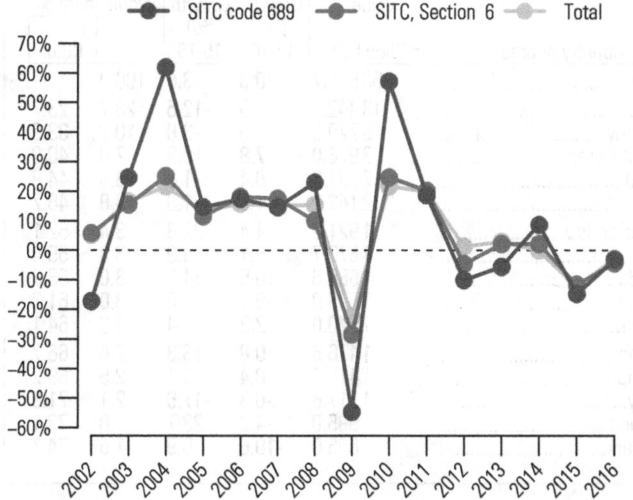

Table 2: Top exporting countries or areas in 2016

Country or area	Value (million US$)	Avg. Growth (%) 12-16	Growth (%) 15-16	World share %	Cum.
World	7665.0	-4.1	-3.2	100.0	
China	1699.4	-3.3	-11.6	22.2	22.2
USA	718.0	-2.4	-4.5	9.4	31.5
Dem.Rep. of the Congo	*698.2*	9.0	4.8	9.1	40.6
Germany	693.0	-1.0	-3.6	9.0	49.7
Netherlands	640.2	27.1	302.2	8.4	58.0
Japan	432.1	-11.8	-7.1	5.6	63.7
Canada	345.5	-4.1	-8.3	4.5	68.2
Russian Federation	278.1	-6.8	-0.8	3.6	71.8
United Kingdom	261.3	-7.2	-13.9	3.4	75.2
France	204.1	-6.2	-2.2	2.7	77.9
Austria	197.5	30.9	-0.5	2.6	80.5
Rep. of Korea	137.7	-8.2	-9.3	1.8	82.3
Kazakhstan	134.1	-19.2	-17.3	1.7	84.0
Other Asia, nes	89.1	-14.8	-8.6	1.2	85.2
Australia	84.7	-13.7	-47.0	1.1	86.3

Graph 2: Trade Balance by MDG regions 2016
(Bln US$)

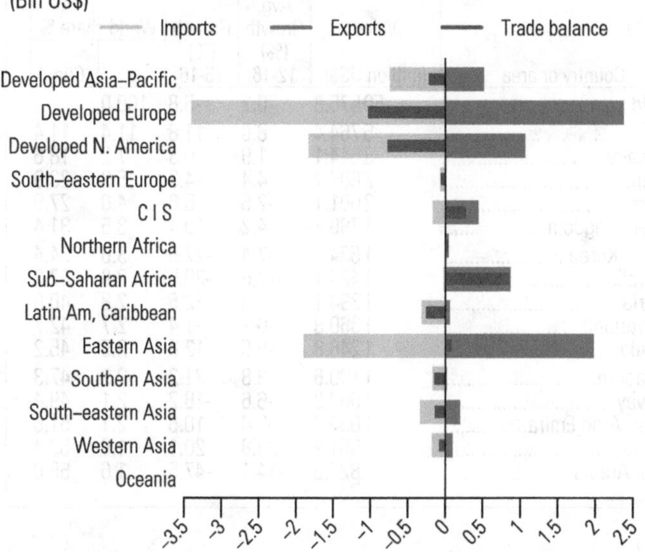

Table 3: Top importing countries or areas in 2016

Country or area	Value (million US$)	Avg. Growth (%) 12-16	Growth (%) 15-16	World share %	Cum.
World	9138.9	-4.2	-1.9	100.0	
USA	1610.9	-8.4	-11.8	17.6	17.6
China	1194.2	10.6	10.4	13.1	30.7
Germany	767.0	-9.1	-17.8	8.4	39.1
Japan	711.0	-10.0	-18.2	7.8	46.9
Netherlands	684.0	21.9	314.5	7.5	54.4
Rep. of Korea	488.7	-9.7	-10.9	5.3	59.7
United Kingdom	367.7	-13.7	-11.6	4.0	63.7
France	356.5	-0.7	-9.4	3.9	67.6
Canada	222.4	-3.2	-6.9	2.4	70.1
Austria	211.0	0.5	35.1	2.3	72.4
Finland	209.2	-0.5	2.8	2.3	74.7
Italy	188.8	2.9	12.1	2.1	76.7
Mexico	168.7	-5.6	-17.1	1.8	78.6
Other Asia, nes	166.2	-6.7	-14.5	1.8	80.4
India	151.5	-2.0	-6.3	1.7	82.0

In 2016, the value (in current US$) of exports of "structures and parts of structures, nes, of iron, steel or aluminium" (SITC group 691) decreased by 3.6 percent (compared to 0.3 percent average growth rate from 2012-2016) to reach 56.7 bln US$ (see table 2), while imports decreased by 5.8 percent to reach 50.6 bln US$ (see table 3). Exports of this commodity accounted for 2.9 percent of world exports of SITC section 6, and 0.4 percent of total world merchandise exports (see table 1). China, Germany and Rep. of Korea were the top exporters in 2016 (see table 2). They accounted for 23.7, 10.2 and 7.0 percent of world exports, respectively. USA, Germany and Japan were the top destinations, with respectively 11.4, 7.2 and 5.3 percent of world imports (see table 3).

The top 15 countries/areas accounted for 74.7 and 55.0 percent of total world exports and imports, respectively (see tables 2 and 3). In 2016, China was the country/area with the highest value of net exports (+12.8 bln US$), followed by Rep. of Korea (+2.4 bln US$). By MDG regions (see graph 2), the largest surpluses in this product group were recorded by Eastern Asia (+14.6 bln US$), Developed Europe (+7.2 bln US$) and South-eastern Europe (+126.8 mln US$). The largest trade deficits were recorded by Developed North America (-3.7 bln US$), Developed Asia-Pacific (-3.6 bln US$) and Sub-Saharan Africa (-2.4 bln US$).

Table 1: Imports (Imp.) and exports (Exp.), 2002-2016, in current US$

		2002	2003	2004	2005	2006	2007	2008	2009	2010	2011	2012	2013	2014	2015	2016
Values in Bln US$	Imp.	14.3	16.4	20.4	24.2	30.9	40.8	51.9	42.4	41.7	48.1	51.0	53.0	56.2	53.7	50.6
	Exp.	15.5	17.8	22.4	27.1	34.5	45.6	57.9	48.2	44.2	53.3	56.0	60.9	62.3	58.8	56.7
As a percentage of SITC section (%)	Imp.	1.6	1.6	1.6	1.7	1.9	2.1	2.4	2.7	2.2	2.1	2.3	2.4	2.5	2.7	2.6
	Exp.	1.8	1.7	1.8	1.9	2.1	2.3	2.7	3.1	2.3	2.3	2.5	2.7	2.7	2.9	2.9
As a percentage of world trade (%)	Imp.	0.2	0.2	0.2	0.2	0.3	0.3	0.3	0.3	0.3	0.3	0.3	0.3	0.3	0.3	0.3
	Exp.	0.2	0.2	0.2	0.3	0.3	0.3	0.4	0.4	0.3	0.3	0.3	0.3	0.3	0.4	0.4

Graph 1: Annual growth rates of exports, 2002–2016
(In percentage by year)

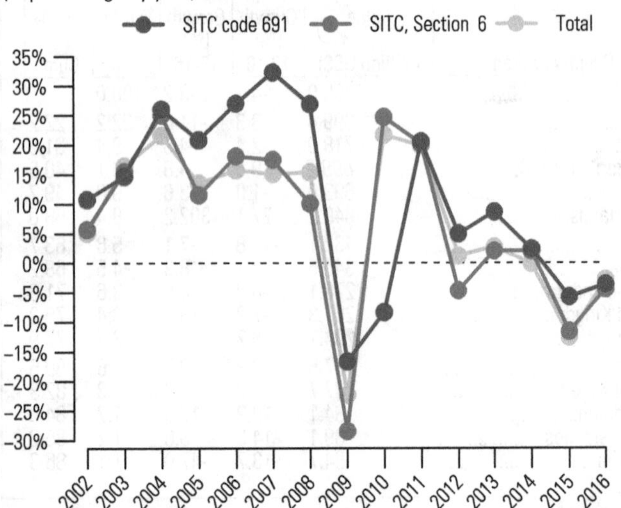

Table 2: Top exporting countries or areas in 2016

Country or area	Value (million US$)	Avg. Growth (%) 12-16	Growth (%) 15-16	World share %	Cum.
World	56 652.7	0.3	-3.6	100.0	
China	13 442.3	0.9	-12.5	23.7	23.7
Germany	5 779.9	-1.5	-3.8	10.2	33.9
Rep. of Korea	3 976.0	7.8	10.3	7.0	40.9
Poland	2 231.5	0.4	1.3	3.9	44.9
Italy	2 142.1	1.3	-1.9	3.8	48.7
Netherlands	1 921.8	4.4	22.8	3.4	52.1
Spain	1 873.7	5.1	-4.9	3.3	55.4
Canada	1 686.6	10.5	14.3	3.0	58.3
USA	1 675.0	-9.6	-15.0	3.0	61.3
Austria	1 570.0	2.3	13.4	2.8	64.1
Belgium	1 476.5	0.8	13.8	2.6	66.7
Czechia	1 418.0	0.4	3.1	2.5	69.2
Turkey	1 217.6	-6.3	-17.6	2.1	71.3
Thailand	995.0	-4.3	-23.7	1.8	73.1
Denmark	895.0	-10.6	5.9	1.6	74.7

Graph 2: Trade Balance by MDG regions 2016
(Bln US$)

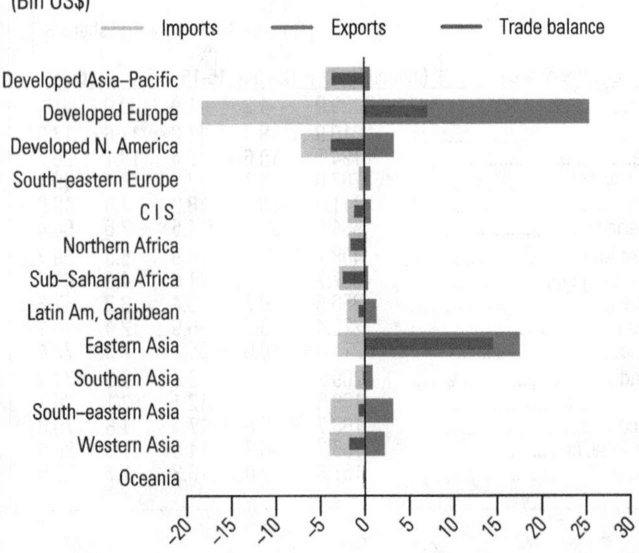

Table 3: Top importing countries or areas in 2016

Country or area	Value (million US$)	Avg. Growth (%) 12-16	Growth (%) 15-16	World share %	Cum.
World	50 575.3	-0.2	-5.8	100.0	
USA	5 764.4	8.0	11.8	11.4	11.4
Germany	3 644.1	-1.9	0.3	7.2	18.6
Japan	2 687.7	4.4	-4.3	5.3	23.9
France	2 001.1	-2.5	5.6	4.0	27.9
United Kingdom	1 780.7	4.2	10.4	3.5	31.4
Rep. of Korea	1 534.2	-7.4	-27.0	3.0	34.4
Australia	1 424.1	-7.6	-39.5	2.8	37.2
Austria	1 394.1	3.8	22.5	2.8	40.0
Switzerland	1 360.8	-0.1	-1.4	2.7	42.7
Canada	1 248.8	-5.5	-12.8	2.5	45.2
Singapore	1 100.6	3.8	21.2	2.2	47.3
Norway	1 062.3	-6.6	-18.2	2.1	49.4
United Arab Emirates	1 054.8	-2.4	10.5	2.1	51.5
Algeria	951.2	23.8	20.1	1.9	53.4
Saudi Arabia	827.5	-14.1	-47.5	1.6	55.0

In 2016, the value (in current US$) of exports of "metal containers for storage or transport" (SITC group 692) decreased by 6.0 percent (compared to -3.0 percent average growth rate from 2012-2016) to reach 17.5 bln US$ (see table 2), while imports decreased by 3.5 percent to reach 16.9 bln US$ (see table 3). Exports of this commodity accounted for 0.9 percent of world exports of SITC section 6, and 0.1 percent of total world merchandise exports (see table 1). USA, China and Germany were the top exporters in 2016 (see table 2). They accounted for 10.5, 10.4 and 9.4 percent of world exports, respectively. USA, Germany and France were the top destinations, with respectively 9.2, 5.9 and 5.0 percent of world imports (see table 3).

The top 15 countries/areas accounted for 70.1 and 54.5 percent of total world exports and imports, respectively (see tables 2 and 3). In 2016, China was the country/area with the highest value of net exports (+1.5 bln US$), followed by Italy (+665.6 mln US$). By MDG regions (see graph 2), the largest surpluses in this product group were recorded by Eastern Asia (+1.8 bln US$), Developed Europe (+1.7 bln US$) and South-eastern Europe (+40.0 mln US$). The largest trade deficits were recorded by Latin America and the Caribbean (-486.8 mln US$), Western Asia (-469.6 mln US$) and Sub-Saharan Africa (-465.4 mln US$).

Table 1: Imports (Imp.) and exports (Exp.), 2002-2016, in current US$

		2002	2003	2004	2005	2006	2007	2008	2009	2010	2011	2012	2013	2014	2015	2016
Values in Bln US$	Imp.	7.2	8.2	9.5	10.7	12.2	15.4	18.1	16.3	16.1	18.8	18.5	19.3	19.6	17.5	16.9
	Exp.	7.2	8.5	9.9	11.3	13.6	16.9	19.6	16.4	17.2	19.9	19.8	20.3	20.8	18.7	17.5
As a percentage of SITC section (%)	Imp.	0.8	0.8	0.7	0.7	0.7	0.8	0.8	1.0	0.8	0.8	0.8	0.9	0.9	0.9	0.9
	Exp.	0.8	0.8	0.8	0.8	0.8	0.9	0.9	1.1	0.9	0.9	0.9	0.9	0.9	0.9	0.9
As a percentage of world trade (%)	Imp.	0.1	0.1	0.1	0.1	0.1	0.1	0.1	0.1	0.1	0.1	0.1	0.1	0.1	0.1	0.1
	Exp.	0.1	0.1	0.1	0.1	0.1	0.1	0.1	0.1	0.1	0.1	0.1	0.1	0.1	0.1	0.1

Graph 1: Annual growth rates of exports, 2002–2016

(In percentage by year)

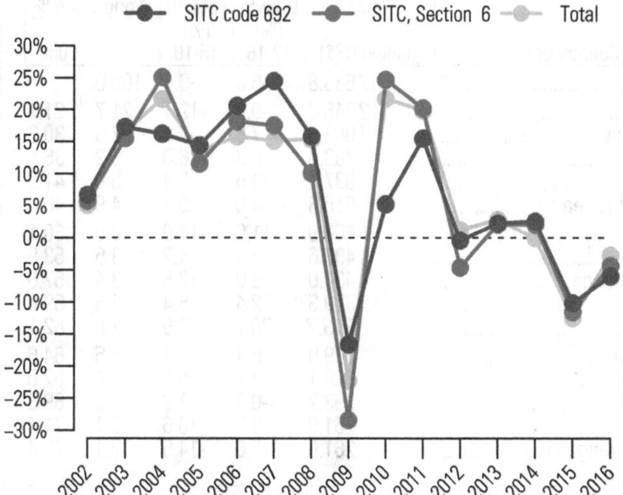

Table 2: Top exporting countries or areas in 2016

Country or area	Value (million US$)	Avg. Growth (%) 12-16	Growth (%) 15-16	World share %	Cum.
World	17541.9	-3.0	-6.0	100.0	
USA	1833.7	1.7	-5.4	10.5	10.5
China	1818.8	-1.0	-22.1	10.4	20.8
Germany	1646.0	-6.9	-10.8	9.4	30.2
Italy	948.7	-5.5	-4.8	5.4	35.6
Rep. of Korea	822.3	-6.2	-1.2	4.7	40.3
Spain	658.2	-4.5	-10.1	3.8	44.1
Czechia	599.5	-1.8	-1.3	3.4	47.5
Poland	592.1	-0.8	1.5	3.4	50.8
Thailand	585.0	8.1	4.1	3.3	54.2
United Kingdom	568.6	-5.0	-9.7	3.2	57.4
France	533.8	-10.4	-9.0	3.0	60.5
Austria	491.1	3.7	-0.4	2.8	63.3
Netherlands	461.5	-4.2	1.0	2.6	65.9
Turkey	399.8	-0.1	-8.8	2.3	68.2
Mexico	343.5	0.3	-4.4	2.0	70.1

Graph 2: Trade Balance by MDG regions 2016

(Bln US$)

Imports — Exports — Trade balance

Developed Asia-Pacific
Developed Europe
Developed N. America
South-eastern Europe
CIS
Northern Africa
Sub-Saharan Africa
Latin Am, Caribbean
Eastern Asia
Southern Asia
South-eastern Asia
Western Asia
Oceania

-8 -6 -4 -2 0 2 4 6 8 10

Table 3: Top importing countries or areas in 2016

Country or area	Value (million US$)	Avg. Growth (%) 12-16	Growth (%) 15-16	World share %	Cum.
World	16921.4	-2.2	-3.5	100.0	
USA	1563.8	1.6	-5.8	9.2	9.2
Germany	1002.9	-3.8	-4.5	5.9	15.2
France	843.7	-4.4	-0.2	5.0	20.2
Canada	826.9	-1.6	-5.6	4.9	25.0
Belgium	618.6	-2.0	8.4	3.7	28.7
Netherlands	591.4	-4.1	-10.5	3.5	32.2
United Kingdom	559.7	-1.5	-13.9	3.3	35.5
Rep. of Korea	486.1	3.7	-0.8	2.9	38.4
Thailand	429.1	0.1	-4.8	2.5	40.9
United Arab Emirates	421.0	-7.8	8.8	2.5	43.4
Spain	397.7	3.2	16.1	2.4	45.7
Mexico	396.2	11.5	14.6	2.3	48.1
China	365.4	1.4	-12.3	2.2	50.2
Poland	360.0	-0.6	5.7	2.1	52.4
Switzerland	358.3	-3.8	-15.6	2.1	54.5

693 Wire products (excluding insulated electrical wiring) and fencing grills

In 2016, the value (in current US$) of exports of "wire products (excluding insulated electrical wiring) and fencing grills" (SITC group 693) decreased by 9.4 percent (compared to -5.0 percent average growth rate from 2012-2016) to reach 12.6 bln US$ (see table 2), while imports decreased by 7.5 percent to reach 12.8 bln US$ (see table 3). Exports of this commodity accounted for 0.6 percent of world exports of SITC section 6, and 0.1 percent of total world merchandise exports (see table 1). China, Germany and USA were the top exporters in 2016 (see table 2). They accounted for 21.7, 8.6 and 6.2 percent of world exports, respectively. USA, Germany and France were the top destinations, with respectively 10.4, 6.4 and 4.7 percent of world imports (see table 3).

The top 15 countries/areas accounted for 73.4 and 51.7 percent of total world exports and imports, respectively (see tables 2 and 3). In 2016, China was the country/area with the highest value of net exports (+2.3 bln US$), followed by Rep. of Korea (+346.2 mln US$). By MDG regions (see graph 2), the largest surpluses in this product group were recorded by Eastern Asia (+2.5 bln US$), Western Asia (+42.7 mln US$) and South-eastern Europe (+16.2 mln US$). The largest trade deficits were recorded by Latin America and the Caribbean (-764.2 mln US$), Developed North America (-755.9 mln US$) and Sub-Saharan Africa (-564.6 mln US$).

Table 1: Imports (Imp.) and exports (Exp.), 2002-2016, in current US$

		2002	2003	2004	2005	2006	2007	2008	2009	2010	2011	2012	2013	2014	2015	2016
Values in Bln US$	Imp.	4.9	5.7	7.6	8.8	10.6	12.8	15.6	10.9	12.6	15.3	15.5	15.5	15.6	13.8	12.8
	Exp.	4.9	5.7	7.9	9.0	10.7	13.0	15.8	10.7	12.8	15.6	15.5	15.9	15.8	13.9	12.6
As a percentage of SITC section (%)	Imp.	0.5	0.6	0.6	0.6	0.6	0.6	0.7	0.7	0.7	0.7	0.7	0.7	0.7	0.7	0.7
	Exp.	0.6	0.6	0.6	0.6	0.6	0.7	0.7	0.7	0.7	0.7	0.7	0.7	0.7	0.7	0.6
As a percentage of world trade (%)	Imp.	0.1	0.1	0.1	0.1	0.1	0.1	0.1	0.1	0.1	0.1	0.1	0.1	0.1	0.1	0.1
	Exp.	0.1	0.1	0.1	0.1	0.1	0.1	0.1	0.1	0.1	0.1	0.1	0.1	0.1	0.1	0.1

Graph 1: Annual growth rates of exports, 2002–2016
(In percentage by year)

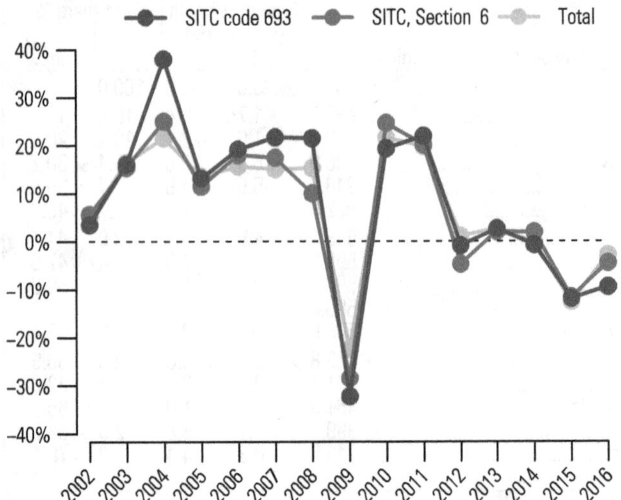

Graph 2: Trade Balance by MDG regions 2016
(Bln US$)

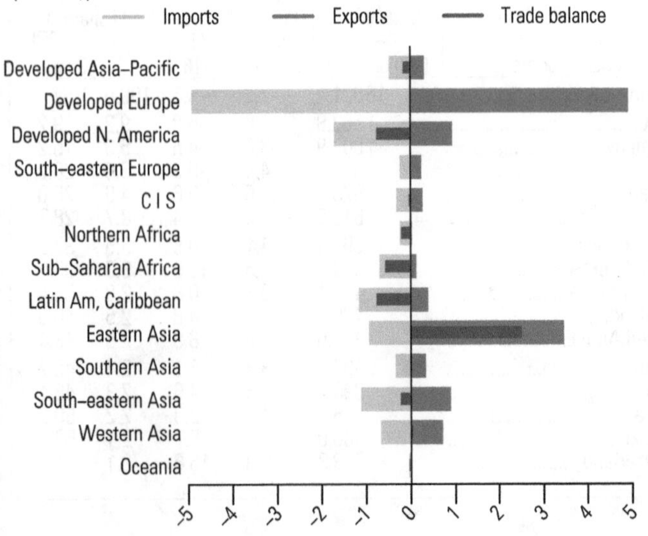

Table 2: Top exporting countries or areas in 2016

Country or area	Value (million US$)	Avg. Growth (%) 12-16	Growth (%) 15-16	World share %	Cum.
World	12 635.8	-5.0	-9.4	100.0	
China	2 746.3	-0.3	-12.1	21.7	21.7
Germany	1 083.6	-7.6	-4.9	8.6	30.3
USA	783.0	-6.3	-16.0	6.2	36.5
Italy	637.6	-4.5	-8.4	5.0	41.6
Rep. of Korea	615.3	-4.8	-9.1	4.9	46.4
Turkey	460.9	-11.0	-12.9	3.6	50.1
Spain	437.6	-5.0	4.2	3.5	53.5
Netherlands	434.0	-9.0	-12.5	3.4	57.0
India	329.3	2.4	-5.4	2.6	59.6
Viet Nam	*319.7*	20.1	8.9	2.5	62.1
Belgium	309.9	-6.4	4.4	2.5	64.6
France	306.1	-4.7	5.7	2.4	67.0
Poland	293.7	-0.2	-7.8	2.3	69.3
Japan	261.9	-6.3	10.6	2.1	71.4
United Kingdom	261.6	-5.0	-14.5	2.1	73.4

Table 3: Top importing countries or areas in 2016

Country or area	Value (million US$)	Avg. Growth (%) 12-16	Growth (%) 15-16	World share %	Cum.
World	12 799.2	-4.7	-7.5	100.0	
USA	1 334.9	-6.1	-10.9	10.4	10.4
Germany	813.3	-6.2	-6.0	6.4	16.8
France	606.1	-8.1	3.7	4.7	21.5
China	491.1	-2.9	-5.5	3.8	25.4
Mexico	475.1	-1.0	-6.8	3.7	29.1
United Kingdom	388.0	1.3	-4.3	3.0	32.1
Canada	360.9	-9.6	-12.0	2.8	34.9
Viet Nam	*310.2*	7.7	5.1	2.4	37.3
Italy	299.9	-1.8	-2.9	2.3	39.7
Belgium	275.2	-8.2	-2.2	2.1	41.8
Rep. of Korea	269.1	-2.7	-10.3	2.1	43.9
Netherlands	266.3	-7.6	-9.8	2.1	46.0
Spain	243.6	-15.8	6.2	1.9	47.9
Thailand	240.7	5.4	7.9	1.9	49.8
Japan	239.5	-8.7	-3.1	1.9	51.7

In 2016, the value (in current US$) of exports of "nails, screws, nuts, bolts, and the like of iron, steel, copper, aluminium" (SITC group 694) increased by 0.1 percent (compared to 0.4 percent average growth rate from 2012-2016) to reach 38.0 bln US$ (see table 2), while imports decreased by 2.3 percent to reach 41.8 bln US$ (see table 3). Exports of this commodity accounted for 1.9 percent of world exports of SITC section 6, and 0.2 percent of total world merchandise exports (see table 1). Germany, China and USA were the top exporters in 2016 (see table 2). They accounted for 15.4, 15.3 and 11.5 percent of world exports, respectively. USA, Germany and China were the top destinations, with respectively 13.7, 9.1 and 7.6 percent of world imports (see table 3).

The top 15 countries/areas accounted for 83.6 and 65.3 percent of total world exports and imports, respectively (see tables 2 and 3). In 2016, Other Asia, nes was the country/area with the highest value of net exports (+3.7 bln US$), followed by China (+2.6 bln US$). By MDG regions (see graph 2), the largest surpluses in this product group were recorded by Eastern Asia (+6.8 bln US$) and Developed Asia-Pacific (+1.3 bln US$). The largest trade deficits were recorded by Latin America and the Caribbean (-3.7 bln US$), Developed North America (-2.5 bln US$) and South-eastern Asia (-1.6 bln US$).

Table 1: Imports (Imp.) and exports (Exp.), 2002-2016, in current US$

		2002	2003	2004	2005	2006	2007	2008	2009	2010	2011	2012	2013	2014	2015	2016
Values in Bln US$	Imp.	14.8	17.4	22.0	25.0	28.2	33.9	38.5	27.7	35.2	42.4	42.1	43.5	45.7	42.8	41.8
	Exp.	12.5	14.8	18.8	21.3	24.4	29.3	33.2	23.3	30.8	37.8	37.4	39.1	41.7	38.0	38.0
As a percentage of SITC section (%)	Imp.	1.6	1.7	1.7	1.7	1.7	1.7	1.8	1.8	1.8	1.8	1.9	2.0	2.0	2.1	2.2
	Exp.	1.4	1.5	1.5	1.5	1.5	1.5	1.5	1.5	1.6	1.6	1.7	1.7	1.8	1.9	1.9
As a percentage of world trade (%)	Imp.	0.2	0.2	0.2	0.2	0.2	0.2	0.2	0.2	0.2	0.2	0.2	0.2	0.2	0.3	0.3
	Exp.	0.2	0.2	0.2	0.2	0.2	0.2	0.2	0.2	0.2	0.2	0.2	0.2	0.2	0.2	0.2

Graph 1: Annual growth rates of exports, 2002–2016
(In percentage by year)

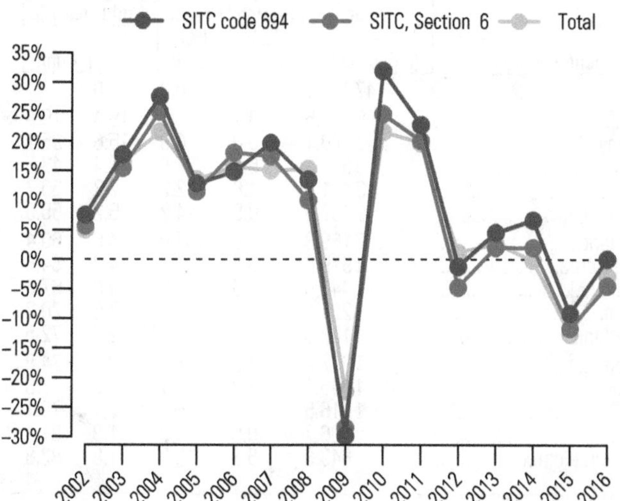

Table 2: Top exporting countries or areas in 2016

Country or area	Value (million US$)	Avg. Growth (%) 12-16	Growth (%) 15-16	World share %	Cum.
World	38008.7	0.4	0.1	100.0	
Germany	5856.5	0.6	3.3	15.4	15.4
China	5829.6	-0.4	-10.4	15.3	30.7
USA	4358.6	4.7	5.5	11.5	42.2
Other Asia, nes	3803.7	0.1	-6.9	10.0	52.2
Japan	2717.9	-5.6	8.2	7.2	59.4
Italy	1825.9	-0.4	1.2	4.8	64.2
France	1449.4	0.2	4.0	3.8	68.0
Switzerland	1034.5	0.0	1.6	2.7	70.7
Rep. of Korea	981.6	9.4	17.9	2.6	73.3
Netherlands	866.1	5.1	19.8	2.3	75.6
United Kingdom	837.3	0.5	-4.8	2.2	77.8
Spain	614.4	0.4	6.2	1.6	79.4
Austria	582.2	11.2	40.8	1.5	80.9
India	512.7	-4.0	-15.8	1.3	82.3
Thailand	508.9	1.5	6.3	1.3	83.6

Graph 2: Trade Balance by MDG regions 2016
(Bln US$)

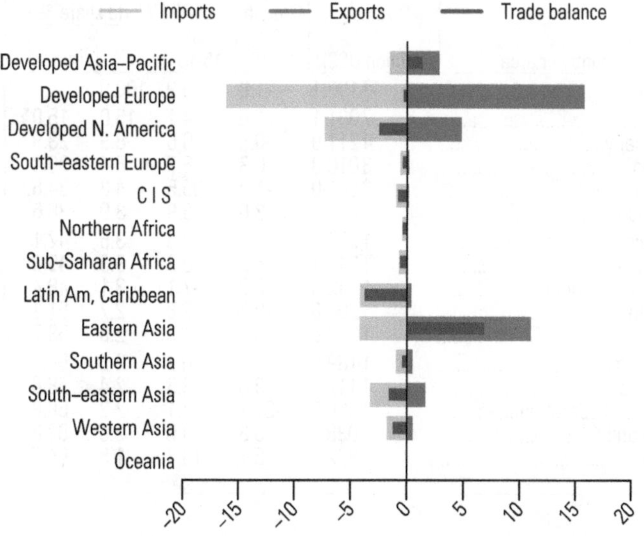

Table 3: Top importing countries or areas in 2016

Country or area	Value (million US$)	Avg. Growth (%) 12-16	Growth (%) 15-16	World share %	Cum.
World	41810.2	-0.1	-2.3	100.0	
USA	5711.7	-0.5	-9.6	13.7	13.7
Germany	3811.2	1.3	1.9	9.1	22.8
China	3183.9	0.3	2.8	7.6	30.4
Mexico	2672.0	3.3	-7.2	6.4	36.8
France	1758.8	0.7	1.0	4.2	41.0
Canada	1570.1	-2.1	-4.0	3.8	44.7
United Kingdom	1437.3	1.0	-3.2	3.4	48.2
Thailand	987.3	-5.8	0.8	2.4	50.5
Czechia	964.3	4.8	-2.0	2.3	52.9
Japan	947.6	-3.0	-4.2	2.3	55.1
Austria	934.4	6.6	27.8	2.2	57.4
Netherlands	931.0	1.5	2.9	2.2	59.6
Spain	845.1	5.1	10.1	2.0	61.6
Italy	833.4	1.2	-0.3	2.0	63.6
Turkey	732.7	7.4	5.5	1.8	65.3

695 Tools for use in the hand or in machines

In 2016, the value (in current US$) of exports of "tools for use in the hand or in machines" (SITC group 695) decreased by 0.3 percent (compared to -1.2 percent average growth rate from 2012-2016) to reach 47.5 bln US$ (see table 2), while imports decreased by 0.9 percent to reach 47.2 bln US$ (see table 3). Exports of this commodity accounted for 2.4 percent of world exports of SITC section 6, and 0.3 percent of total world merchandise exports (see table 1). China, Germany and USA were the top exporters in 2016 (see table 2). They accounted for 19.4, 15.6 and 8.4 percent of world exports, respectively. USA, Germany and China were the top destinations, with respectively 15.0, 8.9 and 6.4 percent of world imports (see table 3).

The top 15 countries/areas accounted for 82.8 and 64.7 percent of total world exports and imports, respectively (see tables 2 and 3). In 2016, China was the country/area with the highest value of net exports (+6.2 bln US$), followed by Germany (+3.2 bln US$). By MDG regions (see graph 2), the largest surpluses in this product group were recorded by Eastern Asia (+9.3 bln US$), Developed Asia-Pacific (+1.6 bln US$) and Developed Europe (+1.2 bln US$). The largest trade deficits were recorded by Developed North America (-3.9 bln US$), Latin America and the Caribbean (-2.5 bln US$) and South-eastern Asia (-1.7 bln US$).

Table 1: Imports (Imp.) and exports (Exp.), 2002-2016, in current US$

		2002	2003	2004	2005	2006	2007	2008	2009	2010	2011	2012	2013	2014	2015	2016
Values in Bln US$	Imp.	20.6	23.6	28.4	30.9	34.4	40.0	45.4	32.9	40.8	48.5	50.7	51.2	52.9	47.6	47.2
	Exp.	21.0	23.3	27.5	30.1	34.1	39.0	44.2	32.5	40.6	49.2	49.8	51.2	53.6	47.6	47.5
As a percentage of SITC section (%)	Imp.	2.3	2.3	2.2	2.2	2.1	2.0	2.1	2.1	2.1	2.1	2.3	2.3	2.3	2.4	2.4
	Exp.	2.4	2.3	2.2	2.1	2.0	2.0	2.0	2.1	2.1	2.1	2.2	2.3	2.3	2.3	2.4
As a percentage of world trade (%)	Imp.	0.3	0.3	0.3	0.3	0.3	0.3	0.3	0.3	0.3	0.3	0.3	0.3	0.3	0.3	0.3
	Exp.	0.3	0.3	0.3	0.3	0.3	0.3	0.3	0.3	0.3	0.3	0.3	0.3	0.3	0.3	0.3

Graph 1: Annual growth rates of exports, 2002–2016

(In percentage by year)

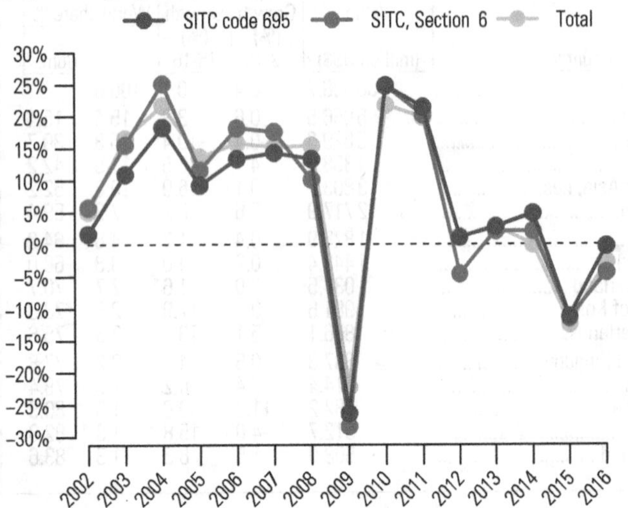

Table 2: Top exporting countries or areas in 2016

Country or area	Value (million US$)	Avg. Growth (%) 12-16	Growth (%) 15-16	World share %	Cum.
World	47 452.1	-1.2	-0.3	100.0	
China	9 213.5	3.7	-5.1	19.4	19.4
Germany	7 420.1	0.0	0.9	15.6	35.1
USA	3 994.3	-5.1	-7.8	8.4	43.5
Japan	3 421.9	-4.6	-2.2	7.2	50.7
Other Asia, nes	2 452.9	-0.5	-4.2	5.2	55.9
Netherlands	2 169.8	1.6	107.0	4.6	60.4
Rep. of Korea	1 979.8	3.3	-0.7	4.2	64.6
Italy	1 441.8	-1.6	0.5	3.0	67.6
Belgium	1 224.1	-1.0	-1.2	2.6	70.2
Switzerland	1 102.6	-1.3	-0.8	2.3	72.5
Sweden	1 072.0	-7.2	-8.5	2.3	74.8
Austria	1 046.1	3.2	37.1	2.2	77.0
France	1 016.6	-0.4	5.4	2.1	79.1
Israel	906.7	-0.5	-1.3	1.9	81.1
United Kingdom	843.8	-5.8	-13.3	1.8	82.8

Graph 2: Trade Balance by MDG regions 2016

(Bln US$)

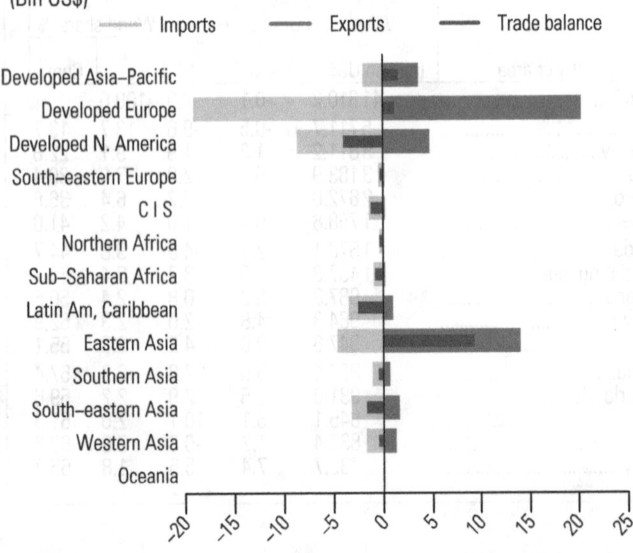

Table 3: Top importing countries or areas in 2016

Country or area	Value (million US$)	Avg. Growth (%) 12-16	Growth (%) 15-16	World share %	Cum.
World	47 196.1	-1.8	-0.9	100.0	
USA	7 061.1	1.6	-4.1	15.0	15.0
Germany	4 211.9	-0.8	-0.6	8.9	23.9
China	3 010.3	0.3	-6.7	6.4	30.3
Netherlands	2 041.0	-1.9	95.5	4.3	34.6
Mexico	1 861.6	3.6	5.9	3.9	38.5
France	1 684.9	-0.4	2.5	3.6	42.1
Canada	1 546.1	-4.9	-10.2	3.3	45.4
United Kingdom	1 442.3	0.2	-7.1	3.1	48.4
Japan	1 260.8	-0.7	2.8	2.7	51.1
Italy	1 233.6	0.2	1.3	2.6	53.7
Belgium	1 189.5	-1.1	0.7	2.5	56.2
Austria	1 117.3	9.0	38.3	2.4	58.6
Russian Federation	1 050.6	-21.1	-4.1	2.2	60.8
Thailand	938.0	-6.3	-3.0	2.0	62.8
Spain	872.1	5.7	13.7	1.8	64.7

In 2016, the value (in current US$) of exports of "cutlery" (SITC group 696) decreased by 4.1 percent (compared to -0.1 percent average growth rate from 2012-2016) to reach 11.6 bln US$ (see table 2), while imports decreased by 0.8 percent to reach 11.1 bln US$ (see table 3). Exports of this commodity accounted for 0.6 percent of world exports of SITC section 6, and 0.1 percent of total world merchandise exports (see table 1). China, Poland and Germany were the top exporters in 2016 (see table 2). They accounted for 34.1, 8.4 and 8.2 percent of world exports, respectively. USA, Germany and Czechia were the top destinations, with respectively 19.5, 6.3 and 4.9 percent of world imports (see table 3).

The top 15 countries/areas accounted for 86.2 and 65.5 percent of total world exports and imports, respectively (see tables 2 and 3). In 2016, China was the country/area with the highest value of net exports (+3.8 bln US$), followed by Poland (+616.8 mln US$). By MDG regions (see graph 2), the largest surpluses in this product group were recorded by Eastern Asia (+3.8 bln US$), South-eastern Asia (+60.5 mln US$) and Southern Asia (+18.7 mln US$). The largest trade deficits were recorded by Developed North America (-1.9 bln US$), Western Asia (-411.8 mln US$) and Developed Asia-Pacific (-329.9 mln US$).

Table 1: Imports (Imp.) and exports (Exp.), 2002-2016, in current US$

		2002	2003	2004	2005	2006	2007	2008	2009	2010	2011	2012	2013	2014	2015	2016
Values in Bln US$	Imp.	5.7	6.2	7.0	7.5	8.0	9.1	9.6	8.2	9.8	11.2	11.0	11.4	11.8	11.2	11.1
	Exp.	5.5	6.0	6.8	7.2	7.9	8.4	9.2	7.7	9.6	11.5	11.7	12.3	12.9	12.1	11.6
As a percentage of SITC section (%)	Imp.	0.6	0.6	0.5	0.5	0.5	0.5	0.4	0.5	0.5	0.5	0.5	0.5	0.5	0.6	0.6
	Exp.	0.6	0.6	0.5	0.5	0.5	0.4	0.4	0.5	0.5	0.5	0.5	0.5	0.6	0.6	0.6
As a percentage of world trade (%)	Imp.	0.1	0.1	0.1	0.1	0.1	0.1	0.1	0.1	0.1	0.1	0.1	0.1	0.1	0.1	0.1
	Exp.	0.1	0.1	0.1	0.1	0.1	0.1	0.1	0.1	0.1	0.1	0.1	0.1	0.1	0.1	0.1

Graph 1: Annual growth rates of exports, 2002–2016
(In percentage by year)

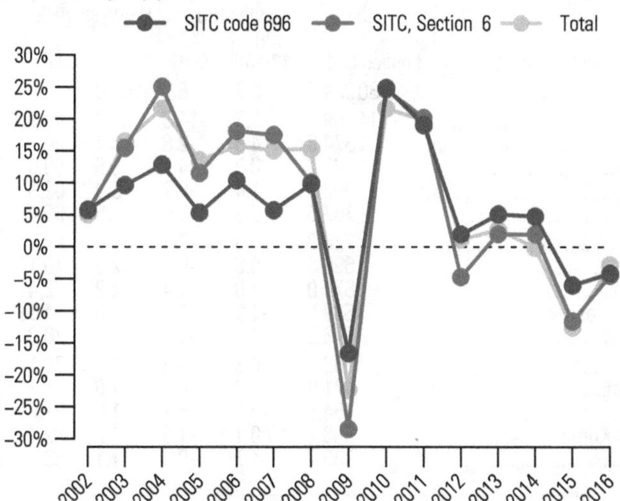

Graph 2: Trade Balance by MDG regions 2016
(Bln US$)

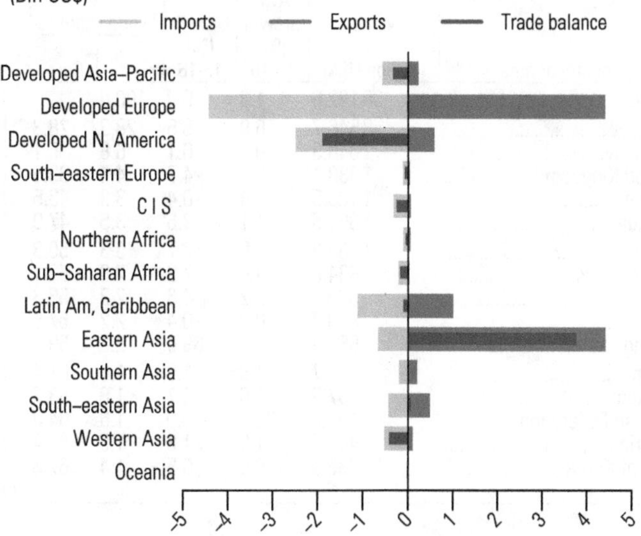

Table 2: Top exporting countries or areas in 2016

Country or area	Value (million US$)	Avg. Growth (%) 12-16	Growth (%) 15-16	World share %	Cum.
World	11629.6	-0.1	-4.1	100.0	
China	3967.3	-0.9	-15.0	34.1	34.1
Poland	972.9	-1.2	2.7	8.4	42.5
Germany	948.2	-2.4	0.8	8.2	50.6
Mexico	804.7	4.2	-8.3	6.9	57.6
Czechia	605.6	24.6	53.2	5.2	62.8
USA	568.2	3.0	-4.7	4.9	67.6
Belgium	486.6	6.7	6.0	4.2	71.8
Viet Nam	*295.7*	13.7	8.9	2.5	74.4
Netherlands	241.6	-2.8	12.7	2.1	76.4
France	238.7	2.1	6.9	2.1	78.5
Japan	217.5	0.3	10.3	1.9	80.4
China, Hong Kong SAR	192.4	-13.4	-10.8	1.7	82.0
Italy	170.2	2.5	9.0	1.5	83.5
Switzerland	158.4	-5.3	-5.6	1.4	84.9
Brazil	157.8	-8.3	-14.5	1.4	86.2

Table 3: Top importing countries or areas in 2016

Country or area	Value (million US$)	Avg. Growth (%) 12-16	Growth (%) 15-16	World share %	Cum.
World	11115.4	0.4	-0.8	100.0	
USA	2166.0	3.6	-5.0	19.5	19.5
Germany	699.9	-0.1	-5.9	6.3	25.8
Czechia	547.6	42.7	52.4	4.9	30.7
Mexico	463.4	5.4	1.9	4.2	34.9
United Kingdom	421.0	-2.8	-9.5	3.8	38.7
Belgium	378.1	2.5	23.6	3.4	42.1
France	370.5	-4.2	-2.0	3.3	45.4
Poland	356.1	-4.6	-4.5	3.2	48.6
Japan	351.6	-1.6	3.5	3.2	51.8
Netherlands	338.2	4.6	14.0	3.0	54.8
Canada	316.1	-1.4	-5.6	2.8	57.7
Italy	246.6	1.1	-0.6	2.2	59.9
Russian Federation	225.5	-11.3	-1.2	2.0	61.9
Spain	200.5	2.5	2.6	1.8	63.7
China	198.9	-0.6	0.2	1.8	65.5

697 Household equipment of base metal, nes

In 2016, the value (in current US$) of exports of "household equipment of base metal, nes" (SITC group 697) decreased by 8.7 percent (compared to -0.2 percent average growth rate from 2012-2016) to reach 30.2 bln US$ (see table 2), while imports increased by 0.9 percent to reach 30.2 bln US$ (see table 3). Exports of this commodity accounted for 1.5 percent of world exports of SITC section 6, and 0.2 percent of total world merchandise exports (see table 1). China, Italy and Germany were the top exporters in 2016 (see table 2). They accounted for 47.9, 6.2 and 5.6 percent of world exports, respectively. USA, Germany and United Kingdom were the top destinations, with respectively 28.3, 6.8 and 4.4 percent of world imports (see table 3).

The top 15 countries/areas accounted for 83.6 and 67.8 percent of total world exports and imports, respectively (see tables 2 and 3). In 2016, China was the country/area with the highest value of net exports (+14.2 bln US$), followed by Italy (+1.2 bln US$). By MDG regions (see graph 2), the largest surpluses in this product group were recorded by Eastern Asia (+14.4 bln US$), Southern Asia (+343.8 mln US$) and South-eastern Asia (+103.8 mln US$). The largest trade deficits were recorded by Developed North America (-8.4 bln US$), Developed Europe (-2.3 bln US$) and Developed Asia-Pacific (-1.6 bln US$).

Table 1: Imports (Imp.) and exports (Exp.), 2002-2016, in current US$

		2002	2003	2004	2005	2006	2007	2008	2009	2010	2011	2012	2013	2014	2015	2016
Values in Bln US$	Imp.	13.8	16.0	18.6	20.2	22.3	25.4	27.2	22.9	26.1	28.9	28.7	30.3	31.4	29.9	30.2
	Exp.	12.9	14.9	17.4	18.7	21.3	23.6	25.3	21.7	25.3	29.1	30.5	32.7	33.8	33.1	30.2
As a percentage of SITC section (%)	Imp.	1.5	1.6	1.4	1.4	1.3	1.3	1.2	1.5	1.4	1.3	1.3	1.4	1.4	1.5	1.6
	Exp.	1.5	1.5	1.4	1.3	1.3	1.2	1.2	1.4	1.3	1.2	1.4	1.4	1.5	1.6	1.5
As a percentage of world trade (%)	Imp.	0.2	0.2	0.2	0.2	0.2	0.2	0.2	0.2	0.2	0.2	0.2	0.2	0.2	0.2	0.2
	Exp.	0.2	0.2	0.2	0.2	0.2	0.2	0.2	0.2	0.2	0.2	0.2	0.2	0.2	0.2	0.2

Graph 1: Annual growth rates of exports, 2002–2016

(In percentage by year)

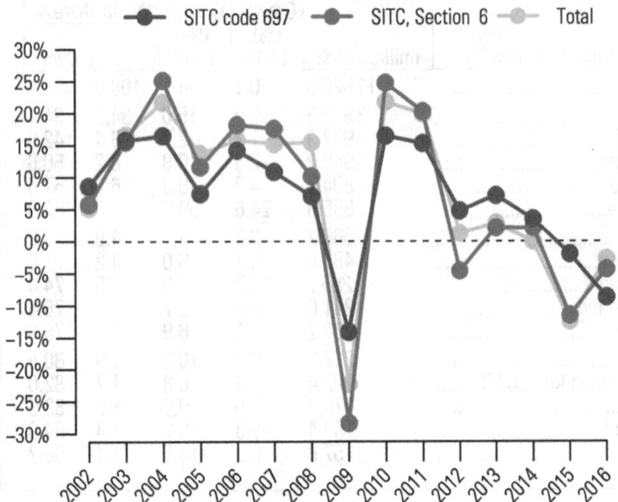

Table 2: Top exporting countries or areas in 2016

Country or area	Value (million US$)	Avg. Growth (%) 12-16	Growth (%) 15-16	World share %	Cum.
World	30234.5	-0.2	-8.7	100.0	
China	14469.7	1.7	-14.3	47.9	47.9
Italy	1874.5	-4.5	-2.8	6.2	54.1
Germany	1685.7	0.3	4.7	5.6	59.6
USA	982.9	-1.4	-6.7	3.3	62.9
France	767.5	-2.6	-3.6	2.5	65.4
Turkey	726.8	-1.3	-7.4	2.4	67.8
India	696.3	0.5	-6.1	2.3	70.1
Mexico	674.0	7.8	6.4	2.2	72.4
Other Asia, nes	588.5	-1.2	-1.2	1.9	74.3
Thailand	576.3	7.7	-5.6	1.9	76.2
Netherlands	568.5	0.3	0.8	1.9	78.1
Belgium	471.8	2.2	4.2	1.6	79.7
Spain	454.5	-2.1	6.1	1.5	81.2
Rep. of Korea	386.2	0.1	1.5	1.3	82.4
Poland	339.2	-4.7	-9.3	1.1	83.6

Graph 2: Trade Balance by MDG regions 2016

(Bln US$)

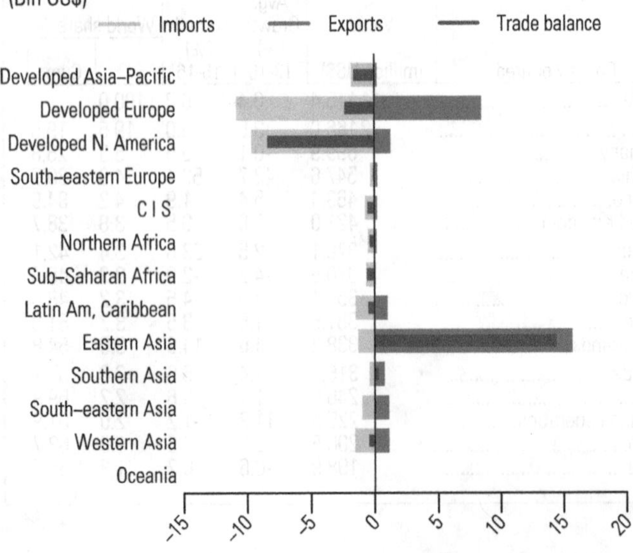

Table 3: Top importing countries or areas in 2016

Country or area	Value (million US$)	Avg. Growth (%) 12-16	Growth (%) 15-16	World share %	Cum.
World	30182.6	1.3	0.9	100.0	
USA	8546.7	6.9	5.5	28.3	28.3
Germany	2048.3	0.8	0.1	6.8	35.1
United Kingdom	1338.1	2.7	-4.7	4.4	39.5
France	1188.5	-2.4	-0.4	3.9	43.5
Canada	1051.5	-1.1	-3.5	3.5	47.0
Japan	1006.3	-1.8	2.7	3.3	50.3
Netherlands	834.8	4.6	7.9	2.8	53.1
Australia	669.8	-2.2	-4.6	2.2	55.3
Italy	659.7	0.9	-0.4	2.2	57.5
Poland	659.3	16.3	69.0	2.2	59.6
Spain	540.7	1.6	1.9	1.8	61.4
Belgium	537.9	-2.6	4.7	1.8	63.2
Russian Federation	480.0	-22.6	-30.0	1.6	64.8
Austria	465.7	1.8	21.8	1.5	66.4
Rep. of Korea	435.9	9.6	0.5	1.4	67.8

In 2016, the value (in current US$) of exports of "manufactures of base metal, nes" (SITC group 699) decreased by 2.7 percent (compared to less than 0.1 percent average growth rate from 2012-2016) to reach 145.6 bln US$ (see table 2), while imports decreased by 1.4 percent to reach 145.4 bln US$ (see table 3). Exports of this commodity accounted for 7.4 percent of world exports of SITC section 6, and 0.9 percent of total world merchandise exports (see table 1). China, Germany and USA were the top exporters in 2016 (see table 2). They accounted for 18.2, 11.9 and 9.4 percent of world exports, respectively. USA, Germany and Mexico were the top destinations, with respectively 13.7, 8.6 and 4.8 percent of world imports (see table 3).

The top 15 countries/areas accounted for 75.2 and 62.1 percent of total world exports and imports, respectively (see tables 2 and 3). In 2016, China was the country/area with the highest value of net exports (+20.4 bln US$), followed by Germany (+4.9 bln US$). By MDG regions (see graph 2), the largest surpluses in this product group were recorded by Eastern Asia (+23.7 bln US$), Developed Europe (+7.6 bln US$) and Southern Asia (+553.1 mln US$). The largest trade deficits were recorded by Developed North America (-8.2 bln US$), South-eastern Asia (-6.0 bln US$) and Latin America and the Caribbean (-4.2 bln US$).

Table 1: Imports (Imp.) and exports (Exp.), 2002-2016, in current US$

		2002	2003	2004	2005	2006	2007	2008	2009	2010	2011	2012	2013	2014	2015	2016
Values in Bln US$	Imp.	56.3	64.5	77.6	89.0	103.5	123.8	139.8	105.5	123.5	143.3	144.8	150.4	158.2	147.6	145.4
	Exp.	55.7	64.2	78.8	90.5	106.7	127.9	141.6	104.0	121.2	144.3	145.5	152.5	161.0	149.6	145.6
As a percentage of SITC section (%)	Imp.	6.3	6.3	6.0	6.2	6.2	6.3	6.4	6.8	6.4	6.2	6.6	6.8	6.9	7.3	7.5
	Exp.	6.3	6.3	6.2	6.4	6.4	6.5	6.5	6.7	6.2	6.2	6.5	6.7	6.9	7.3	7.4
As a percentage of world trade (%)	Imp.	0.9	0.8	0.8	0.8	0.8	0.9	0.9	0.8	0.8	0.8	0.8	0.8	0.8	0.9	0.9
	Exp.	0.9	0.9	0.9	0.9	0.9	0.9	0.9	0.8	0.8	0.8	0.8	0.8	0.9	0.9	0.9

Graph 1: Annual growth rates of exports, 2002–2016
(In percentage by year)

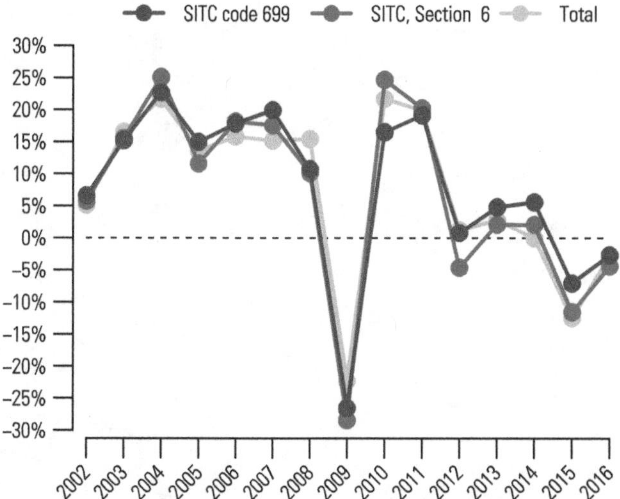

Graph 2: Trade Balance by MDG regions 2016
(Bln US$)

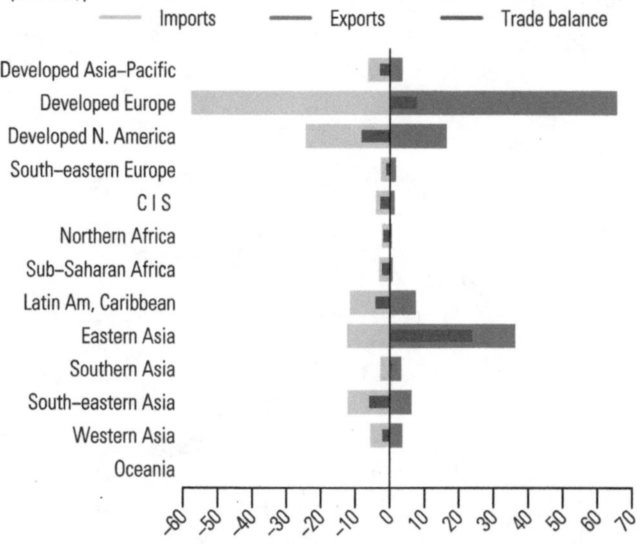

Table 2: Top exporting countries or areas in 2016

Country or area	Value (million US$)	Avg. Growth (%) 12-16	Growth (%) 15-16	World share %	Cum.
World	145609.5	0.0	-2.7	100.0	
China	26572.3	2.6	-13.0	18.2	18.2
Germany	17334.3	-1.4	1.0	11.9	30.2
USA	13675.9	0.7	-4.4	9.4	39.5
Italy	8584.3	-2.8	-1.7	5.9	45.4
Mexico	4700.5	4.5	-0.6	3.2	48.7
France	4676.9	-2.6	0.1	3.2	51.9
Austria	4622.5	1.8	14.7	3.2	55.1
Czechia	4377.1	0.7	1.8	3.0	58.1
Rep. of Korea	3970.7	2.4	4.9	2.7	60.8
Poland	3854.6	3.5	5.4	2.6	63.4
Other Asia, nes	3836.8	-1.9	-4.4	2.6	66.1
United Kingdom	3596.3	2.2	-1.9	2.5	68.5
Spain	3485.5	1.5	-3.3	2.4	70.9
India	3197.3	-0.3	-4.6	2.2	73.1
Japan	3074.2	-9.1	-0.5	2.1	75.2

Table 3: Top importing countries or areas in 2016

Country or area	Value (million US$)	Avg. Growth (%) 12-16	Growth (%) 15-16	World share %	Cum.
World	145422.9	0.1	-1.4	100.0	
USA	19926.9	2.2	-0.6	13.7	13.7
Germany	12453.8	0.0	2.0	8.6	22.3
Mexico	6920.4	1.6	-2.0	4.8	27.0
France	6546.2	-1.8	2.8	4.5	31.5
China	6209.5	-0.8	-0.6	4.3	35.8
United Kingdom	5280.3	1.9	-3.2	3.6	39.4
Thailand	4934.8	3.7	0.1	3.4	42.8
Canada	4535.9	-2.5	-4.2	3.1	45.9
Japan	3953.6	-1.7	-1.4	2.7	48.7
Italy	3733.3	-0.4	0.9	2.6	51.2
Rep. of Korea	3415.2	1.0	-5.4	2.3	53.6
Poland	3389.8	2.6	4.7	2.3	55.9
Austria	3173.7	2.1	20.4	2.2	58.1
Czechia	3042.4	2.3	4.4	2.1	60.2
Spain	2808.6	3.6	4.1	1.9	62.1

Source: UN Comtrade

Machinery and transport equipment

(SITC Section 7)

711 Steam boilers, superheated water boiler; auxiliary plants; parts thereof

In 2016, the value (in current US$) of exports of "steam boilers, superheated water boiler; auxiliary plants; parts thereof" (SITC group 711) decreased by 10.4 percent (compared to -7.7 percent average growth rate from 2012-2016) to reach 6.8 bln US$ (see table 2), while imports decreased by 7.7 percent to reach 7.9 bln US$ (see table 3). Exports of this commodity accounted for 0.1 percent of world exports of SITC section 7, and less than 0.1 percent of total world merchandise exports (see table 1). China, Rep. of Korea and USA were the top exporters in 2016 (see table 2). They accounted for 30.3, 14.5 and 6.1 percent of world exports, respectively. USA, Turkey and Viet Nam were the top destinations, with respectively 7.0, 6.7 and 6.6 percent of world imports (see table 3).

The top 15 countries/areas accounted for 85.9 and 61.7 percent of total world exports and imports, respectively (see tables 2 and 3). In 2016, China was the country/area with the highest value of net exports (+1.9 bln US$), followed by Rep. of Korea (+761.4 mln US$). By MDG regions (see graph 2), the largest surpluses in this product group were recorded by Eastern Asia (+2.6 bln US$), Developed Europe (+962.4 mln US$) and Developed Asia-Pacific (+157.0 mln US$). The largest trade deficits were recorded by South-eastern Asia (-1.3 bln US$), Western Asia (-1.2 bln US$) and Latin America and the Caribbean (-544.1 mln US$).

Table 1: Imports (Imp.) and exports (Exp.), 2002-2016, in current US$

		2002	2003	2004	2005	2006	2007	2008	2009	2010	2011	2012	2013	2014	2015	2016
Values in Bln US$	Imp.	2.9	2.6	2.9	3.6	3.6	5.4	8.3	8.9	6.8	7.4	7.5	9.3	8.3	8.5	7.9
	Exp.	2.5	2.7	3.1	3.9	4.1	5.8	9.1	9.1	8.1	9.8	9.3	9.1	8.4	7.5	6.8
As a percentage of SITC section (%)	Imp.	0.1	0.1	0.1	0.1	0.1	0.1	0.2	0.2	0.1	0.1	0.1	0.1	0.1	0.1	0.1
	Exp.	0.1	0.1	0.1	0.1	0.1	0.1	0.2	0.2	0.2	0.2	0.2	0.2	0.1	0.1	0.1
As a percentage of world trade (%)	Imp.	0.0	0.0	0.0	0.0	0.0	0.0	0.1	0.1	0.0	0.0	0.0	0.0	0.0	0.1	0.0
	Exp.	0.0	0.0	0.0	0.0	0.0	0.0	0.1	0.1	0.1	0.1	0.1	0.0	0.0	0.0	0.0

Graph 1: Annual growth rates of exports, 2002–2016
(In percentage by year)

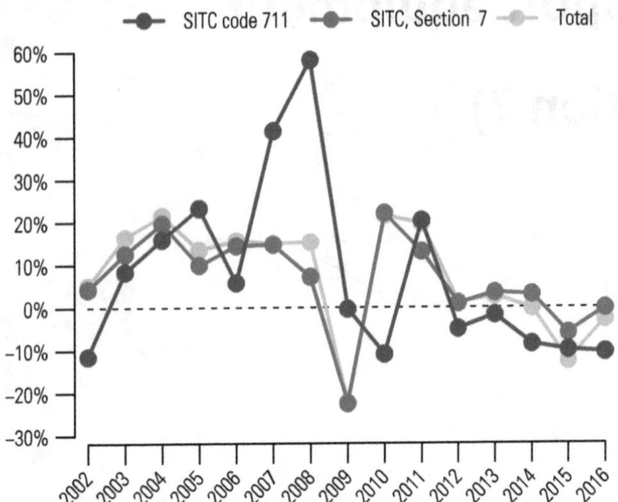

Table 2: Top exporting countries or areas in 2016

Country or area	Value (million US$)	Avg. Growth (%) 12-16	Growth (%) 15-16	World share %	Cum.
World	6756.8	-7.7	-10.4	100.0	
China	2048.3	-7.2	9.9	30.3	30.3
Rep. of Korea	981.2	-10.3	-18.8	14.5	44.8
USA	410.0	-9.9	-33.9	6.1	50.9
Italy	404.7	-7.3	14.8	6.0	56.9
India	357.6	7.0	7.2	5.3	62.2
Japan	333.1	-6.7	-28.8	4.9	67.1
Germany	297.6	-6.6	-20.2	4.4	71.5
Spain	176.4	-4.5	130.3	2.6	74.1
Finland	144.2	-11.5	-16.2	2.1	76.3
Denmark	140.8	1.4	-2.1	2.1	78.3
Other Asia, nes	139.2	4.7	-52.8	2.1	80.4
Canada	100.7	-10.3	-12.8	1.5	81.9
United Kingdom	97.0	-1.3	-9.1	1.4	83.3
Belgium	86.2	4.0	-51.5	1.3	84.6
Poland	84.9	-17.8	-4.3	1.3	85.9

Graph 2: Trade Balance by MDG regions 2016
(Bln US$)

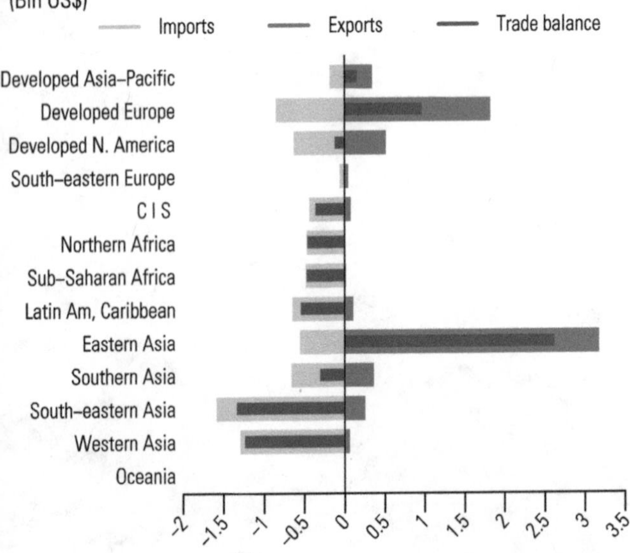

Table 3: Top importing countries or areas in 2016

Country or area	Value (million US$)	Avg. Growth (%) 12-16	Growth (%) 15-16	World share %	Cum.
World	7869.4	1.2	-7.7	100.0	
USA	550.7	5.0	-23.5	7.0	7.0
Turkey	526.5	7.1	64.1	6.7	13.7
Viet Nam	*516.2*	4.5	5.1	6.6	20.2
Pakistan	457.9	54.2	241.6	5.8	26.1
Saudi Arabia	358.8	-14.3	-69.4	4.6	30.6
Morocco	338.6	48.5	595.1	4.3	34.9
Indonesia	328.3	-14.4	-43.1	4.2	39.1
Philippines	320.3	78.0	37.7	4.1	43.2
United Arab Emirates	254.6	22.2	-20.6	3.2	46.4
Rep. of Korea	219.8	1.9	-8.1	2.8	49.2
Nigeria	213.9	79.6	879.3	2.7	51.9
Other Asia, nes	201.1	31.9	1.1	2.6	54.5
Uzbekistan	*196.7*	149.5	95.1	2.5	57.0
Malaysia	191.9	9.6	11.9	2.4	59.4
Brazil	180.5	11.2	708.7	2.3	61.7

In 2016, the value (in current US$) of exports of "steam turbines and other vapour turbines and parts thereof, nes" (SITC group 712) decreased by 10.4 percent (compared to -8.8 percent average growth rate from 2012-2016) to reach 5.3 bln US$ (see table 2), while imports increased by 3.6 percent to reach 6.1 bln US$ (see table 3). Exports of this commodity accounted for 0.1 percent of world exports of SITC section 7, and less than 0.1 percent of total world merchandise exports (see table 1). Japan, Germany and China were the top exporters in 2016 (see table 2). They accounted for 23.4, 15.7 and 14.3 percent of world exports, respectively. Indonesia, USA and Malaysia were the top destinations, with respectively 10.5, 6.2 and 5.9 percent of world imports (see table 3).

The top 15 countries/areas accounted for 91.9 and 63.7 percent of total world exports and imports, respectively (see tables 2 and 3). In 2016, Japan was the country/area with the highest value of net exports (+1.1 bln US$), followed by Germany (+633.3 mln US$). By MDG regions (see graph 2), the largest surpluses in this product group were recorded by Developed Europe (+1.3 bln US$), Developed Asia-Pacific (+1.1 bln US$) and Eastern Asia (+355.1 mln US$). The largest trade deficits were recorded by South-eastern Asia (-1.5 bln US$), Western Asia (-665.2 mln US$) and Southern Asia (-528.7 mln US$).

Table 1: Imports (Imp.) and exports (Exp.), 2002-2016, in current US$

		2002	2003	2004	2005	2006	2007	2008	2009	2010	2011	2012	2013	2014	2015	2016
Values in Bln US$	Imp.	3.3	2.7	3.3	4.6	4.6	4.9	6.3	8.0	7.8	8.5	8.2	7.4	6.2	5.9	6.1
	Exp.	3.1	2.7	3.2	4.1	4.3	5.1	6.8	8.3	8.1	8.7	7.7	7.5	7.3	5.9	5.3
As a percentage of SITC section (%)	Imp.	0.1	0.1	0.1	0.1	0.1	0.1	0.1	0.2	0.1	0.1	0.1	0.1	0.1	0.1	0.1
	Exp.	0.1	0.1	0.1	0.1	0.1	0.1	0.1	0.2	0.2	0.2	0.1	0.1	0.1	0.1	0.1
As a percentage of world trade (%)	Imp.	0.0	0.0	0.0	0.0	0.0	0.0	0.0	0.1	0.1	0.0	0.0	0.0	0.0	0.0	0.0
	Exp.	0.0	0.0	0.0	0.0	0.0	0.0	0.0	0.1	0.1	0.0	0.0	0.0	0.0	0.0	0.0

Graph 1: Annual growth rates of exports, 2002–2016
(In percentage by year)

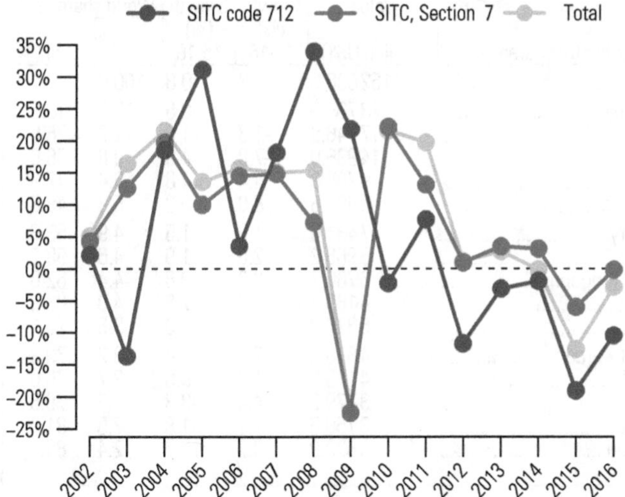

Graph 2: Trade Balance by MDG regions 2016
(Bln US$)

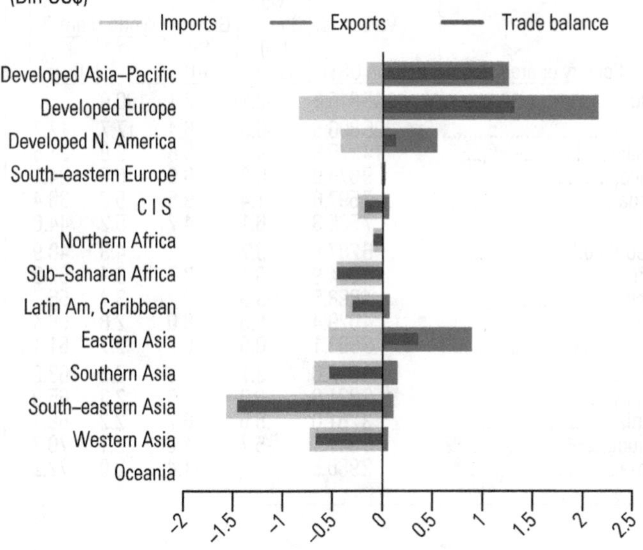

Table 2: Top exporting countries or areas in 2016

Country or area	Value (million US$)	Avg. Growth (%) 12-16	Growth (%) 15-16	World share %	Cum.
World	5318.6	-8.8	-10.4	100.0	
Japan	1247.1	-5.6	-14.1	23.4	23.4
Germany	833.2	-10.5	-1.2	15.7	39.1
China	762.6	-12.2	12.8	14.3	53.5
USA	525.7	-6.3	-28.1	9.9	63.3
Italy	306.9	-6.8	-10.8	5.8	69.1
Czechia	175.9	-7.5	-6.3	3.3	72.4
France	174.4	-14.3	49.3	3.3	75.7
Poland	164.4	5.0	-21.5	3.1	78.8
India	137.8	15.3	34.4	2.6	81.4
United Kingdom	127.2	-4.9	22.2	2.4	83.8
Rep. of Korea	126.5	-16.1	-23.1	2.4	86.1
Switzerland	99.4	10.5	2.0	1.9	88.0
Austria	80.6	-8.1	-19.1	1.5	89.5
Hungary	64.8	-0.8	9.8	1.2	90.7
Russian Federation	60.5	-3.1	-57.3	1.1	91.9

Table 3: Top importing countries or areas in 2016

Country or area	Value (million US$)	Avg. Growth (%) 12-16	Growth (%) 15-16	World share %	Cum.
World	6097.7	-7.1	3.6	100.0	
Indonesia	641.5	9.9	37.8	10.5	10.5
USA	378.9	-0.9	-7.4	6.2	16.7
Malaysia	359.4	34.2	532.2	5.9	22.6
Pakistan	310.9	35.2	407.2	5.1	27.7
South Africa	294.2	-27.0	43.7	4.8	32.6
Turkey	276.6	15.4	38.2	4.5	37.1
Viet Nam	*244.9*	6.3	5.1	4.0	41.1
China	233.5	-25.2	-33.4	3.8	44.9
Germany	199.9	-10.9	18.9	3.3	48.2
United Arab Emirates	183.3	48.7	-10.5	3.0	51.2
Rep. of Korea	160.9	-7.3	-59.9	2.6	53.9
Bangladesh	*157.4*	30.3	-14.2	2.6	56.4
Saudi Arabia	148.8	-1.9	-44.3	2.4	58.9
Philippines	148.5	57.5	25.3	2.4	61.3
India	148.0	-30.1	-25.5	2.4	63.7

713 Internal combustion piston engines and parts thereof, nes

In 2016, the value (in current US$) of exports of "internal combustion piston engines and parts thereof, nes" (SITC group 713) decreased by 0.8 percent (compared to -1.2 percent average growth rate from 2012-2016) to reach 152.6 bln US$ (see table 2), while imports decreased by 2.1 percent to reach 145.8 bln US$ (see table 3). Exports of this commodity accounted for 2.6 percent of world exports of SITC section 7, and 1.0 percent of total world merchandise exports (see table 1). Germany, USA and Japan were the top exporters in 2016 (see table 2). They accounted for 15.6, 11.2 and 9.8 percent of world exports, respectively. USA, Germany and Mexico were the top destinations, with respectively 17.7, 9.9 and 6.6 percent of world imports (see table 3).

The top 15 countries/areas accounted for 83.4 and 72.2 percent of total world exports and imports, respectively (see tables 2 and 3). In 2016, Japan was the country/area with the highest value of net exports (+11.3 bln US$), followed by Germany (+9.4 bln US$). By MDG regions (see graph 2), the largest surpluses in this product group were recorded by Developed Europe (+18.0 bln US$), Developed Asia-Pacific (+10.5 bln US$) and Eastern Asia (+3.0 bln US$). The largest trade deficits were recorded by Developed North America (-12.5 bln US$), Western Asia (-2.9 bln US$) and Latin America and the Caribbean (-2.5 bln US$).

Table 1: Imports (Imp.) and exports (Exp.), 2002-2016, in current US$

		2002	2003	2004	2005	2006	2007	2008	2009	2010	2011	2012	2013	2014	2015	2016
Values in Bln US$	Imp.	75.3	85.8	102.7	113.7	123.4	145.6	153.7	106.2	138.8	167.7	159.7	159.6	164.6	148.9	145.8
	Exp.	71.9	83.7	101.1	113.2	125.2	145.8	151.0	105.5	137.1	166.6	160.0	166.0	171.5	153.9	152.6
As a percentage of SITC section (%)	Imp.	2.9	2.9	2.9	2.9	2.8	2.9	2.8	2.5	2.7	2.8	2.7	2.6	2.6	2.5	2.4
	Exp.	2.8	2.9	2.9	3.0	2.9	2.9	2.8	2.5	2.7	2.9	2.7	2.7	2.7	2.6	2.6
As a percentage of world trade (%)	Imp.	1.1	1.1	1.1	1.1	1.0	1.0	0.9	0.8	0.9	0.9	0.9	0.9	0.9	0.9	0.9
	Exp.	1.1	1.1	1.1	1.1	1.0	1.1	0.9	0.9	0.9	0.9	0.9	0.9	0.9	0.9	1.0

Graph 1: Annual growth rates of exports, 2002–2016
(In percentage by year)

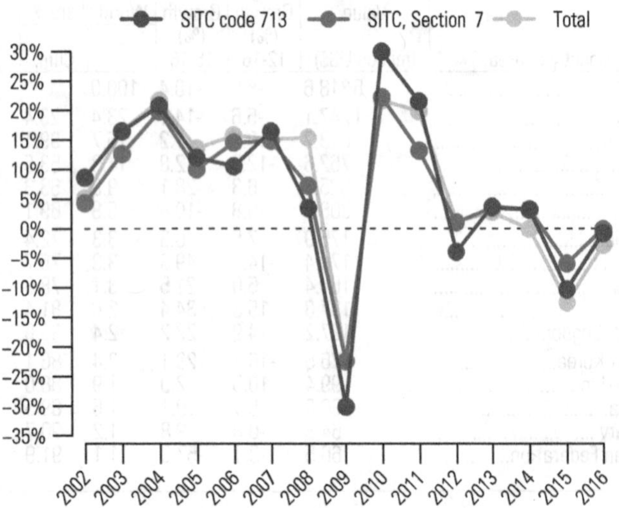

Table 2: Top exporting countries or areas in 2016

Country or area	Value (million US$)	Avg. Growth (%) 12-16	Growth (%) 15-16	World share %	Cum.
World	152 636.6	-1.2	-0.8	100.0	
Germany	23 735.6	-1.7	-6.5	15.6	15.6
USA	17 146.9	-1.3	-1.0	11.2	26.8
Japan	14 936.0	-7.0	4.8	9.8	36.6
Mexico	9 705.9	4.4	4.8	6.4	42.9
China	8 898.6	6.0	0.2	5.8	48.8
Hungary	7 431.0	1.8	1.5	4.9	53.6
France	6 965.2	-2.0	1.9	4.6	58.2
United Kingdom	6 700.7	-3.3	-9.8	4.4	62.6
Austria	6 169.7	1.0	7.5	4.0	66.6
Italy	5 377.2	-1.1	3.5	3.5	70.1
Rep. of Korea	4 816.5	-2.2	-7.4	3.2	73.3
Poland	4 179.8	-1.2	-0.5	2.7	76.0
Spain	3 779.2	4.4	-3.3	2.5	78.5
Canada	3 750.6	-1.1	-1.8	2.5	81.0
Thailand	3 633.9	3.2	16.2	2.4	83.4

Graph 2: Trade Balance by MDG regions 2016
(Bln US$)

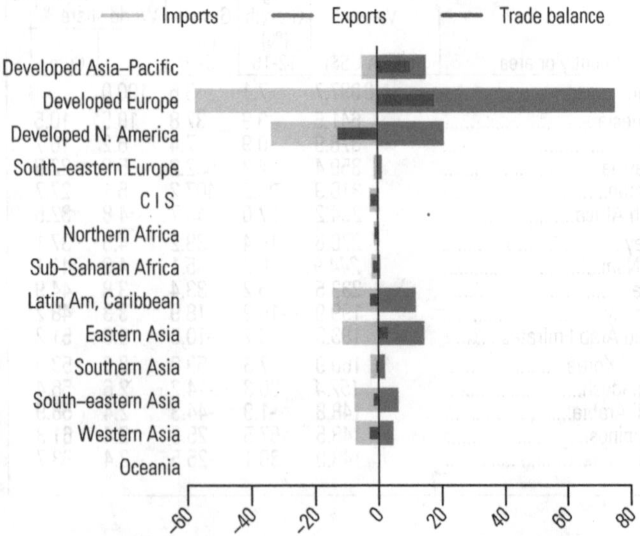

Table 3: Top importing countries or areas in 2016

Country or area	Value (million US$)	Avg. Growth (%) 12-16	Growth (%) 15-16	World share %	Cum.
World	145 815.3	-2.2	-2.1	100.0	
USA	25 806.5	-0.3	-6.4	17.7	17.7
Germany	14 370.8	-4.2	-5.6	9.9	27.6
Mexico	9 674.9	-0.3	-6.6	6.6	34.2
Canada	7 597.6	-1.4	9.5	5.2	39.4
China	7 585.3	-6.1	-4.2	5.2	44.6
United Kingdom	6 287.8	-3.7	-5.2	4.3	48.9
Spain	4 954.9	6.4	-2.7	3.4	52.3
France	4 898.5	-3.3	0.7	3.4	55.7
Turkey	4 029.4	5.5	8.0	2.8	58.4
Italy	3 903.1	0.9	-0.7	2.7	61.1
Japan	3 602.0	3.7	4.3	2.5	63.6
Hungary	3 321.8	6.3	1.8	2.3	65.9
Czechia	3 251.0	5.6	6.7	2.2	68.1
Belgium	3 041.1	-5.7	-4.2	2.1	70.2
Austria	2 986.5	1.7	11.4	2.0	72.2

In 2016, the value (in current US$) of exports of "engines and motors, non-electric; parts, nes (not those of 712, 713 and 718)" (SITC group 714) increased by 9.1 percent (compared to 3.0 percent average growth rate from 2012-2016) to reach 103.0 bln US$ (see table 2), while imports increased by 11.0 percent to reach 133.0 bln US$ (see table 3). Exports of this commodity accounted for 1.7 percent of world exports of SITC section 7, and 0.6 percent of total world merchandise exports (see table 1). United Kingdom, France and USA were the top exporters in 2016 (see table 2). They accounted for 18.8, 11.2 and 10.1 percent of world exports, respectively. USA, United Kingdom and France were the top destinations, with respectively 16.7, 13.2 and 8.0 percent of world imports (see table 3).

The top 15 countries/areas accounted for 86.4 and 80.7 percent of total world exports and imports, respectively (see tables 2 and 3). In 2016, United Kingdom was the country/area with the highest value of net exports (+1.9 bln US$), followed by Italy (+1.6 bln US$). By MDG regions (see graph 2), the largest surpluses in this product group were recorded by Developed Europe (+4.5 bln US$) and Commonwealth of Independent States (+738.3 mln US$). The largest trade deficits were recorded by Developed North America (-11.1 bln US$), Western Asia (-7.5 bln US$) and Eastern Asia (-5.1 bln US$).

Table 1: Imports (Imp.) and exports (Exp.), 2002-2016, in current US$

		2002	2003	2004	2005	2006	2007	2008	2009	2010	2011	2012	2013	2014	2015	2016
Values in Bln US$	Imp.	48.2	47.8	54.3	60.6	68.7	75.9	89.2	87.9	90.4	101.0	111.3	119.3	121.9	119.8	133.0
	Exp.	52.5	53.6	61.8	68.0	78.3	83.3	95.1	74.1	76.2	85.7	91.7	98.6	100.1	94.4	103.0
As a percentage of SITC section (%)	Imp.	1.9	1.6	1.5	1.6	1.6	1.5	1.6	2.1	1.7	1.7	1.9	1.9	1.9	2.0	2.2
	Exp.	2.0	1.8	1.8	1.8	1.8	1.7	1.8	1.8	1.5	1.5	1.6	1.6	1.6	1.6	1.7
As a percentage of world trade (%)	Imp.	0.7	0.6	0.6	0.6	0.6	0.5	0.5	0.7	0.6	0.6	0.6	0.6	0.7	0.7	0.8
	Exp.	0.8	0.7	0.7	0.7	0.7	0.6	0.6	0.6	0.5	0.5	0.5	0.5	0.5	0.6	0.6

Graph 1: Annual growth rates of exports, 2002–2016

(In percentage by year)

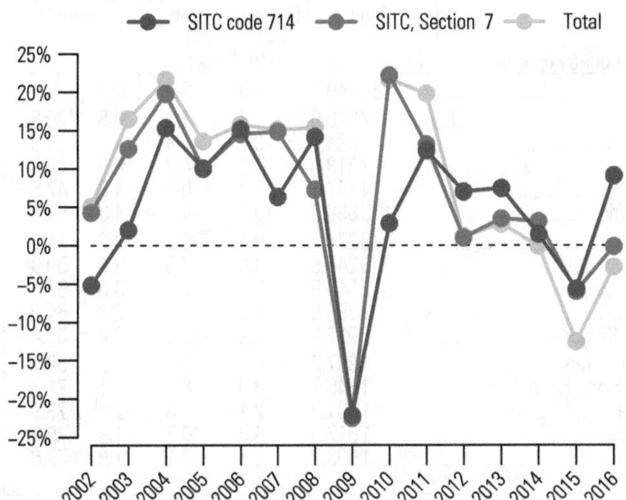

Graph 2: Trade Balance by MDG regions 2016

(Bln US$)

Imports — Exports — Trade balance

Developed Asia-Pacific
Developed Europe
Developed N. America
South-eastern Europe
C I S
Northern Africa
Sub-Saharan Africa
Latin Am, Caribbean
Eastern Asia
Southern Asia
South-eastern Asia
Western Asia
Oceania

-60 -50 -40 -30 -20 -10 0 10 20 30 40 50 60

Table 2: Top exporting countries or areas in 2016

Country or area	Value (million US$)	Avg. Growth (%) 12-16	Growth (%) 15-16	World share %	Cum.
World	103027.1	3.0	9.1	100.0	
United Kingdom	19377.2	-0.9	-1.0	18.8	18.8
France	11561.3	0.5	6.8	11.2	30.0
USA	10356.2	-0.7	-3.1	10.1	40.1
Germany	8181.0	-5.9	12.1	7.9	48.0
Singapore	5936.5	20.3	20.3	5.8	53.8
Canada	5213.4	3.9	8.9	5.1	58.8
Japan	4578.3	-0.2	8.6	4.4	63.3
China, Hong Kong SAR	3937.4	8.3	21.6	3.8	67.1
China	3855.5	19.3	14.4	3.7	70.9
Italy	3718.5	0.8	-2.7	3.6	74.5
Netherlands	3207.9	12.2	62.2	3.1	77.6
Mexico	2637.1	7.0	19.7	2.6	80.1
Brazil	2509.7	62.2	27.0	2.4	82.6
Poland	2127.0	15.4	18.2	2.1	84.6
Switzerland	1811.2	0.5	10.8	1.8	86.4

Table 3: Top importing countries or areas in 2016

Country or area	Value (million US$)	Avg. Growth (%) 12-16	Growth (%) 15-16	World share %	Cum.
World	132960.9	4.5	11.0	100.0	
USA	22191.6	3.2	-1.3	16.7	16.7
United Kingdom	17509.9	4.0	11.2	13.2	29.9
France	10675.6	6.5	12.5	8.0	37.9
Germany	9729.2	0.8	11.1	7.3	45.2
Singapore	7370.8	4.0	18.8	5.5	50.7
Japan	6253.7	8.9	23.1	4.7	55.5
China	5724.7	6.4	25.2	4.3	59.8
United Arab Emirates	5249.2	5.2	32.7	3.9	63.7
China, Hong Kong SAR	5168.1	0.9	16.7	3.9	67.6
Canada	4492.8	1.9	-10.7	3.4	71.0
Netherlands	2903.4	10.6	64.0	2.2	73.2
Brazil	2736.1	5.8	0.5	2.1	75.2
Other Asia, nes	2667.0	71.1	473.2	2.0	77.2
Mexico	2450.3	10.1	20.4	1.8	79.1
Italy	2117.8	4.6	9.1	1.6	80.7

Source: UN Comtrade

716 Rotating electric plant and parts thereof, nes

In 2016, the value (in current US$) of exports of "rotating electric plant and parts thereof, nes" (SITC group 716) decreased by 2.4 percent (compared to -3.3 percent average growth rate from 2012-2016) to reach 86.1 bln US$ (see table 2), while imports decreased by 3.4 percent to reach 88.0 bln US$ (see table 3). Exports of this commodity accounted for 1.5 percent of world exports of SITC section 7, and 0.5 percent of total world merchandise exports (see table 1). China, Germany and USA were the top exporters in 2016 (see table 2). They accounted for 20.5, 13.8 and 8.5 percent of world exports, respectively. USA, Germany and China were the top destinations, with respectively 14.0, 8.3 and 6.0 percent of world imports (see table 3).

The top 15 countries/areas accounted for 77.6 and 60.2 percent of total world exports and imports, respectively (see tables 2 and 3). In 2016, China was the country/area with the highest value of net exports (+12.3 bln US$), followed by Germany (+4.6 bln US$). By MDG regions (see graph 2), the largest surpluses in this product group were recorded by Developed Europe (+12.3 bln US$), Eastern Asia (+11.4 bln US$) and Developed Asia-Pacific (+1.2 bln US$). The largest trade deficits were recorded by Developed North America (-6.4 bln US$), Latin America and the Caribbean (-4.7 bln US$) and Western Asia (-4.2 bln US$).

Table 1: Imports (Imp.) and exports (Exp.), 2002-2016, in current US$

		2002	2003	2004	2005	2006	2007	2008	2009	2010	2011	2012	2013	2014	2015	2016
Values in Bln US$	Imp.	36.7	40.0	45.4	53.3	62.3	76.1	90.3	77.2	82.7	97.6	98.6	96.7	99.6	91.1	88.0
	Exp.	33.0	37.6	44.6	51.6	61.1	73.1	87.6	72.2	80.9	93.9	98.5	94.8	98.4	88.3	86.1
As a percentage of SITC section (%)	Imp.	1.4	1.4	1.3	1.4	1.4	1.5	1.7	1.8	1.6	1.7	1.6	1.6	1.6	1.5	1.4
	Exp.	1.3	1.3	1.3	1.3	1.4	1.5	1.6	1.7	1.6	1.6	1.7	1.6	1.6	1.5	1.5
As a percentage of world trade (%)	Imp.	0.6	0.5	0.5	0.5	0.5	0.5	0.6	0.6	0.5	0.5	0.5	0.5	0.5	0.6	0.5
	Exp.	0.5	0.5	0.5	0.5	0.5	0.5	0.5	0.6	0.5	0.5	0.5	0.5	0.5	0.5	0.5

Graph 1: Annual growth rates of exports, 2002–2016

(In percentage by year)

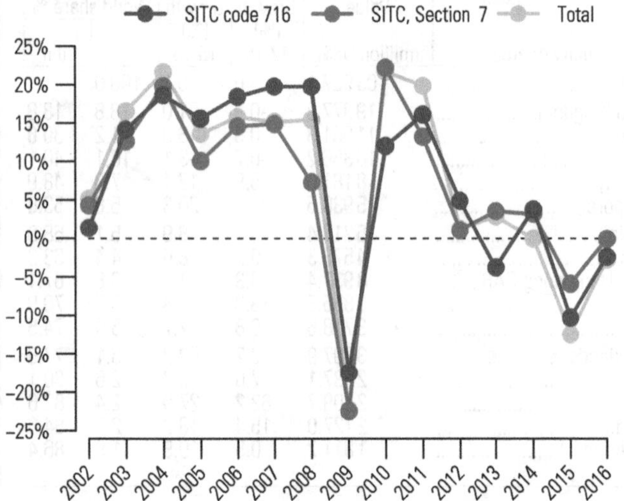

Table 2: Top exporting countries or areas in 2016

Country or area	Value (million US$)	Avg. Growth (%) 12-16	Growth (%) 15-16	World share %	Cum.
World	86 149.2	-3.3	-2.4	100.0	
China	17 626.6	1.1	-4.1	20.5	20.5
Germany	11 894.5	-3.7	5.4	13.8	34.3
USA	7 313.0	-7.2	-14.3	8.5	42.8
Japan	4 107.1	-9.2	-0.8	4.8	47.5
Denmark	3 666.5	10.1	-4.7	4.3	51.8
Mexico	3 274.2	0.1	-6.5	3.8	55.6
Italy	3 240.5	-3.8	-2.9	3.8	59.3
Spain	2 543.8	-8.6	-7.4	3.0	62.3
France	2 284.6	-6.0	-8.7	2.7	64.9
United Kingdom	2 097.6	-10.9	-15.9	2.4	67.4
Rep. of Korea	1 997.2	0.2	6.8	2.3	69.7
China, Hong Kong SAR	1 846.9	-8.6	-8.7	2.1	71.8
Austria	1 781.2	2.1	27.8	2.1	73.9
Hungary	1 617.3	4.8	40.7	1.9	75.8
Switzerland	1 603.3	-2.5	-3.1	1.9	77.6

Graph 2: Trade Balance by MDG regions 2016

(Bln US$)

Imports — Exports — Trade balance

Developed Asia-Pacific
Developed Europe
Developed N. America
South-eastern Europe
CIS
Northern Africa
Sub-Saharan Africa
Latin Am, Caribbean
Eastern Asia
Southern Asia
South-eastern Asia
Western Asia
Oceania

-30 -20 -10 0 10 20 30 40

Table 3: Top importing countries or areas in 2016

Country or area	Value (million US$)	Avg. Growth (%) 12-16	Growth (%) 15-16	World share %	Cum.
World	87 962.3	-2.8	-3.4	100.0	
USA	12 286.6	-0.3	-2.6	14.0	14.0
Germany	7 281.7	2.0	5.9	8.3	22.2
China	5 281.2	-6.4	-13.1	6.0	28.3
Mexico	4 042.0	3.6	2.6	4.6	32.8
France	2 614.5	-2.2	-0.4	3.0	35.8
Rep. of Korea	2 611.1	4.2	1.5	3.0	38.8
Thailand	2 484.6	-2.1	12.8	2.8	41.6
United Kingdom	2 388.0	-5.3	5.3	2.7	44.3
Turkey	2 312.6	3.0	22.4	2.6	47.0
China, Hong Kong SAR	2 246.0	-6.3	-9.1	2.6	49.5
Italy	2 182.7	-10.2	-6.0	2.5	52.0
Japan	2 156.6	-2.9	-1.3	2.5	54.4
Canada	2 028.8	-8.6	-19.5	2.3	56.7
Russian Federation	1 670.0	-16.0	-18.8	1.9	58.6
India	1 370.3	-2.8	8.6	1.6	60.2

In 2016, the value (in current US$) of exports of "power generating machinery and parts thereof, nes" (SITC group 718) decreased by less than 0.1 percent (compared to -1.7 percent average growth rate from 2012-2016) to reach 22.6 bln US$ (see table 2), while imports decreased by 8.8 percent to reach 22.3 bln US$ (see table 3). Exports of this commodity accounted for 0.4 percent of world exports of SITC section 7, and 0.1 percent of total world merchandise exports (see table 1). USA, Germany and China were the top exporters in 2016 (see table 2). They accounted for 15.4, 14.3 and 11.6 percent of world exports, respectively. USA, Germany and China were the top destinations, with respectively 20.0, 9.3 and 7.5 percent of world imports (see table 3).

The top 15 countries/areas accounted for 81.8 and 66.1 percent of total world exports and imports, respectively (see tables 2 and 3). In 2016, Germany was the country/area with the highest value of net exports (+1.2 bln US$), followed by Russian Federation (+1.0 bln US$). By MDG regions (see graph 2), the largest surpluses in this product group were recorded by Developed Europe (+2.0 bln US$), Eastern Asia (+844.6 mln US$) and Commonwealth of Independent States (+693.5 mln US$). The largest trade deficits were recorded by Developed North America (-1.3 bln US$), Latin America and the Caribbean (-766.8 mln US$) and Sub-Saharan Africa (-737.9 mln US$).

Table 1: Imports (Imp.) and exports (Exp.), 2002-2016, in current US$

		2002	2003	2004	2005	2006	2007	2008	2009	2010	2011	2012	2013	2014	2015	2016
Values in Bln US$	Imp.	7.6	9.2	10.6	11.8	13.3	17.0	22.2	18.7	22.2	26.2	26.8	26.1	26.7	24.5	22.3
	Exp.	6.7	8.1	9.7	11.4	13.1	16.2	20.7	17.1	20.7	24.5	24.3	24.7	25.2	22.6	22.6
As a percentage of SITC section (%)	Imp.	0.3	0.3	0.3	0.3	0.3	0.3	0.4	0.4	0.4	0.4	0.4	0.4	0.4	0.4	0.4
	Exp.	0.3	0.3	0.3	0.3	0.3	0.3	0.4	0.4	0.4	0.4	0.4	0.4	0.4	0.4	0.4
As a percentage of world trade (%)	Imp.	0.1	0.1	0.1	0.1	0.1	0.1	0.1	0.1	0.1	0.1	0.1	0.1	0.1	0.1	0.1
	Exp.	0.1	0.1	0.1	0.1	0.1	0.1	0.1	0.1	0.1	0.1	0.1	0.1	0.1	0.1	0.1

Graph 1: Annual growth rates of exports, 2002–2016
(In percentage by year)

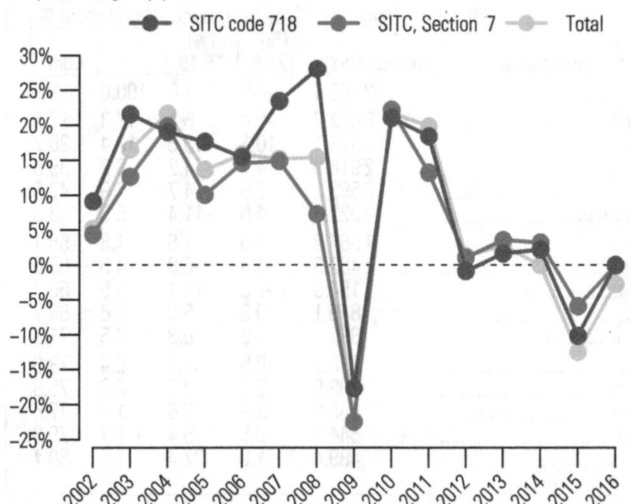

Table 2: Top exporting countries or areas in 2016

Country or area	Value (million US$)	Avg. Growth (%) 12-16	Growth (%) 15-16	World share %	Cum.
World	22635.7	-1.7	0.0	100.0	
USA	3484.2	2.6	5.7	15.4	15.4
Germany	3235.3	-0.1	4.7	14.3	29.7
China	2622.8	5.0	2.1	11.6	41.3
Russian Federation	1450.2	2.1	-6.5	6.4	47.7
Japan	1158.4	-9.9	13.0	5.1	52.8
Denmark	1011.7	-4.1	8.3	4.5	57.3
Sweden	985.7	-10.4	-7.5	4.4	61.6
Spain	808.9	-5.8	-26.3	3.6	65.2
France	658.5	-16.9	5.8	2.9	68.1
United Kingdom	611.5	-3.7	-7.3	2.7	70.8
Italy	568.7	-0.8	-5.1	2.5	73.3
Rep. of Korea	537.9	5.0	5.5	2.4	75.7
United Arab Emirates	505.1	53.5	51.8	2.2	77.9
Canada	466.1	-11.6	-17.5	2.1	80.0
Austria	417.0	4.0	21.6	1.8	81.8

Graph 2: Trade Balance by MDG regions 2016
(Bln US$)

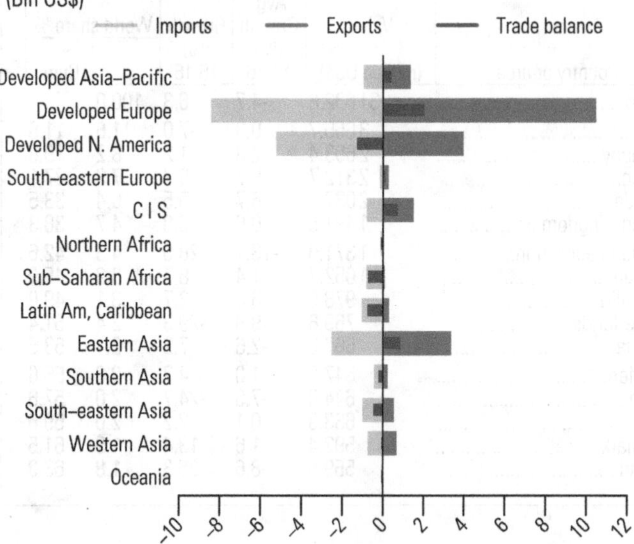

Table 3: Top importing countries or areas in 2016

Country or area	Value (million US$)	Avg. Growth (%) 12-16	Growth (%) 15-16	World share %	Cum.
World	22304.6	-4.5	-8.8	100.0	
USA	4471.4	-2.2	-4.8	20.0	20.0
Germany	2063.8	-9.7	-5.2	9.3	29.3
China	1683.5	-8.3	-8.4	7.5	36.8
France	1138.4	-9.6	-16.6	5.1	42.0
United Kingdom	873.7	-2.6	8.3	3.9	45.9
Canada	769.8	-9.5	-5.2	3.5	49.3
Japan	569.7	-3.2	4.7	2.6	51.9
Rep. of Korea	446.5	4.6	22.2	2.0	53.9
Italy	440.5	0.4	0.5	2.0	55.9
Russian Federation	436.5	-6.9	-4.0	2.0	57.8
Sweden	413.2	-4.1	1.6	1.9	59.7
Austria	399.4	5.2	5.1	1.8	61.5
Czechia	359.1	1.5	0.6	1.6	63.1
Finland	340.5	12.1	10.1	1.5	64.6
Australia	334.7	-3.1	27.5	1.5	66.1

721 Agricultural machinery (excluding tractors) and parts thereof

In 2016, the value (in current US$) of exports of "agricultural machinery (excluding tractors) and parts thereof" (SITC group 721) decreased by 1.6 percent (compared to -4.0 percent average growth rate from 2012-2016) to reach 32.8 bln US$ (see table 2), while imports decreased by 6.3 percent to reach 31.6 bln US$ (see table 3). Exports of this commodity accounted for 0.6 percent of world exports of SITC section 7, and 0.2 percent of total world merchandise exports (see table 1). Germany, USA and China were the top exporters in 2016 (see table 2). They accounted for 17.3, 13.4 and 8.9 percent of world exports, respectively. USA, Germany and France were the top destinations, with respectively 11.6, 8.2 and 7.3 percent of world imports (see table 3).

The top 15 countries/areas accounted for 80.7 and 63.3 percent of total world exports and imports, respectively (see tables 2 and 3). In 2016, Germany was the country/area with the highest value of net exports (+3.1 bln US$), followed by China (+2.3 bln US$). By MDG regions (see graph 2), the largest surpluses in this product group were recorded by Developed Europe (+5.3 bln US$) and Eastern Asia (+2.1 bln US$). The largest trade deficits were recorded by Commonwealth of Independent States (-1.8 bln US$), Latin America and the Caribbean (-980.4 mln US$) and Developed Asia-Pacific (-824.7 mln US$).

Table 1: Imports (Imp.) and exports (Exp.), 2002-2016, in current US$

		2002	2003	2004	2005	2006	2007	2008	2009	2010	2011	2012	2013	2014	2015	2016
Values in Bln US$	Imp.	12.6	15.0	17.7	20.1	22.1	27.1	34.9	26.0	28.2	37.3	38.4	39.1	38.5	33.7	31.6
	Exp.	12.5	14.9	17.9	20.5	22.5	27.8	35.6	26.4	28.8	37.1	38.6	39.6	38.7	33.3	32.8
As a percentage of SITC section (%)	Imp.	0.5	0.5	0.5	0.5	0.5	0.5	0.6	0.6	0.5	0.6	0.6	0.6	0.6	0.6	0.5
	Exp.	0.5	0.5	0.5	0.5	0.5	0.6	0.7	0.6	0.6	0.6	0.7	0.7	0.6	0.6	0.6
As a percentage of world trade (%)	Imp.	0.2	0.2	0.2	0.2	0.2	0.2	0.2	0.2	0.2	0.2	0.2	0.2	0.2	0.2	0.2
	Exp.	0.2	0.2	0.2	0.2	0.2	0.2	0.2	0.2	0.2	0.2	0.2	0.2	0.2	0.2	0.2

Graph 1: Annual growth rates of exports, 2002–2016
(In percentage by year)

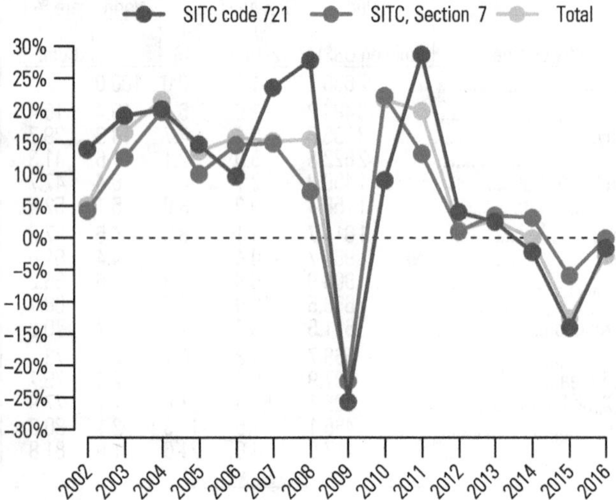

Graph 2: Trade Balance by MDG regions 2016
(Bln US$)

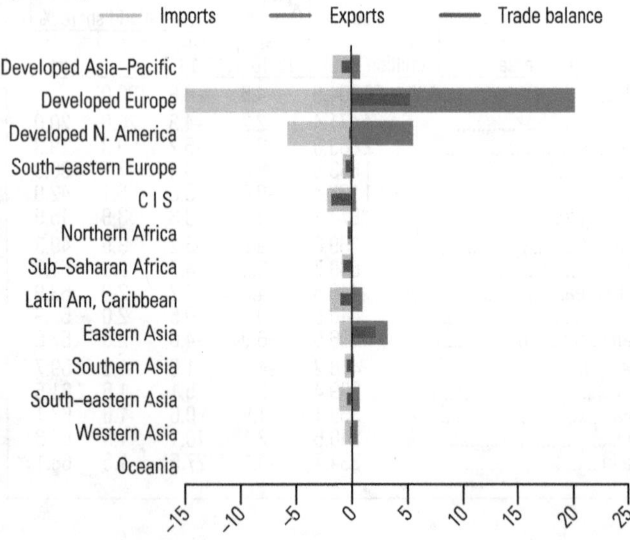

Table 2: Top exporting countries or areas in 2016

Country or area	Value (million US$)	Avg. Growth (%) 12-16	Growth (%) 15-16	World share %	Cum.
World	32762.4	-4.0	-1.6	100.0	
Germany	5672.7	-5.4	5.4	17.3	17.3
USA	4376.1	-10.1	-13.5	13.4	30.7
China	2916.8	4.7	4.2	8.9	39.6
Italy	2583.2	-2.9	-4.7	7.9	47.5
Netherlands	1922.6	-4.8	-11.4	5.9	53.3
France	1567.2	-4.8	-1.5	4.8	58.1
Belgium	1482.3	-4.4	-0.8	4.5	62.6
Canada	1154.0	-7.3	-10.1	3.5	66.2
Poland	849.1	-0.3	5.9	2.6	68.7
United Kingdom	830.9	2.2	6.3	2.5	71.3
Austria	770.7	-0.5	7.7	2.4	73.6
Denmark	709.0	-2.3	3.2	2.2	75.8
Sweden	565.8	-3.9	2.6	1.7	77.5
Czechia	544.0	-0.5	5.4	1.7	79.2
Japan	489.4	1.0	27.4	1.5	80.7

Table 3: Top importing countries or areas in 2016

Country or area	Value (million US$)	Avg. Growth (%) 12-16	Growth (%) 15-16	World share %	Cum.
World	31632.6	-4.7	-6.3	100.0	
USA	3655.7	0.3	-7.0	11.6	11.6
Germany	2603.4	-2.8	1.2	8.2	19.8
France	2312.7	-5.7	-5.7	7.3	27.1
Canada	2037.7	-6.7	-5.5	6.4	33.5
United Kingdom	1491.5	0.6	-6.8	4.7	38.3
Russian Federation	1371.5	-13.1	28.8	4.3	42.6
Belgium	1052.7	1.4	8.7	3.3	45.9
Australia	978.6	-3.5	12.7	3.1	49.0
Netherlands	769.6	-9.9	-29.3	2.4	51.4
Austria	667.5	-2.6	7.2	2.1	53.6
Sweden	647.5	-1.0	4.2	2.0	55.6
China	644.8	-7.5	-24.7	2.0	57.6
Italy	633.9	0.1	2.2	2.0	59.6
Denmark	592.4	1.6	13.4	1.9	61.5
Poland	559.6	-8.6	-25.3	1.8	63.3

In 2016, the value (in current US$) of exports of "tractors (other than those of headings 744.14 and 744.15)" (SITC group 722) decreased by 7.2 percent (compared to -7.5 percent average growth rate from 2012-2016) to reach 17.7 bln US$ (see table 2), while imports decreased by 9.1 percent to reach 18.6 bln US$ (see table 3). Exports of this commodity accounted for 0.3 percent of world exports of SITC section 7, and 0.1 percent of total world merchandise exports (see table 1). Germany, USA and Italy were the top exporters in 2016 (see table 2). They accounted for 18.4, 13.2 and 9.0 percent of world exports, respectively. USA, France and Canada were the top destinations, with respectively 17.8, 7.3 and 6.1 percent of world imports (see table 3).

The top 15 countries/areas accounted for 87.9 and 64.5 percent of total world exports and imports, respectively (see tables 2 and 3). In 2016, Germany was the country/area with the highest value of net exports (+2.2 bln US$), followed by Japan (+1.2 bln US$). By MDG regions (see graph 2), the largest surpluses in this product group were recorded by Developed Europe (+2.0 bln US$), Southern Asia (+671.1 mln US$) and Eastern Asia (+556.8 mln US$). The largest trade deficits were recorded by Developed North America (-1.8 bln US$), South-eastern Asia (-998.5 mln US$) and Sub-Saharan Africa (-687.7 mln US$).

Table 1: Imports (Imp.) and exports (Exp.), 2002-2016, in current US$

		2002	2003	2004	2005	2006	2007	2008	2009	2010	2011	2012	2013	2014	2015	2016
Values in Bln US$	Imp.	8.8	10.6	13.4	15.1	15.6	17.9	22.4	15.7	16.5	21.2	22.7	23.3	22.7	20.5	18.6
	Exp.	8.7	10.2	13.0	14.2	15.6	19.1	24.1	16.2	17.1	22.7	24.2	23.7	22.7	19.1	17.7
As a percentage of SITC section (%)	Imp.	0.3	0.4	0.4	0.4	0.4	0.4	0.4	0.4	0.3	0.4	0.4	0.4	0.4	0.3	0.3
	Exp.	0.3	0.3	0.4	0.4	0.4	0.4	0.4	0.4	0.3	0.4	0.4	0.4	0.4	0.3	0.3
As a percentage of world trade (%)	Imp.	0.1	0.1	0.1	0.1	0.1	0.1	0.1	0.1	0.1	0.1	0.1	0.1	0.1	0.1	0.1
	Exp.	0.1	0.1	0.1	0.1	0.1	0.1	0.2	0.1	0.1	0.1	0.1	0.1	0.1	0.1	0.1

Graph 1: Annual growth rates of exports, 2002–2016

(In percentage by year)

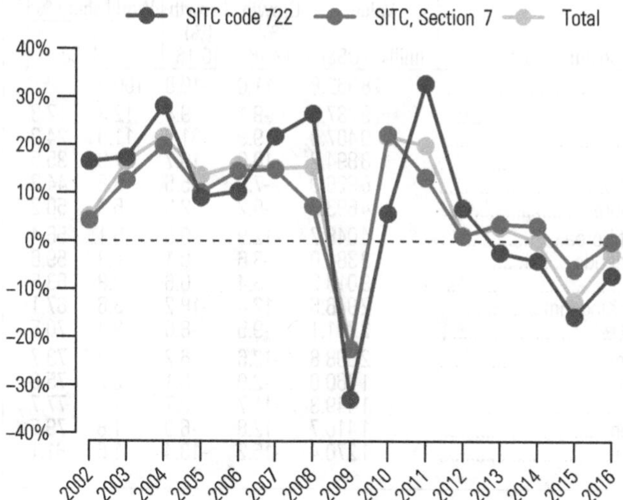

Table 2: Top exporting countries or areas in 2016

Country or area	Value (million US$)	Avg. Growth (%) 12-16	Growth (%) 15-16	World share %	Cum.
World	17747.0	-7.5	-7.2	100.0	
Germany	3265.9	-4.6	-7.9	18.4	18.4
USA	2340.4	-16.4	-11.7	13.2	31.6
Italy	1599.5	-7.2	-3.6	9.0	40.6
Japan	1409.1	-8.6	-9.8	7.9	48.5
France	1363.5	-3.5	10.0	7.7	56.2
United Kingdom	1311.6	-6.0	-5.9	7.4	63.6
India	868.4	2.4	-9.6	4.9	68.5
Austria	698.4	-5.5	0.7	3.9	72.4
Rep. of Korea	504.2	2.4	-18.8	2.8	75.3
Finland	476.4	0.4	10.1	2.7	78.0
Belarus	425.0	-20.2	-3.3	2.4	80.4
China	396.5	-4.4	-12.4	2.2	82.6
Turkey	340.3	1.0	-9.0	1.9	84.5
Belgium	321.9	-9.2	-22.0	1.8	86.3
Canada	286.7	-5.7	-12.0	1.6	87.9

Graph 2: Trade Balance by MDG regions 2016

(Bln US$)

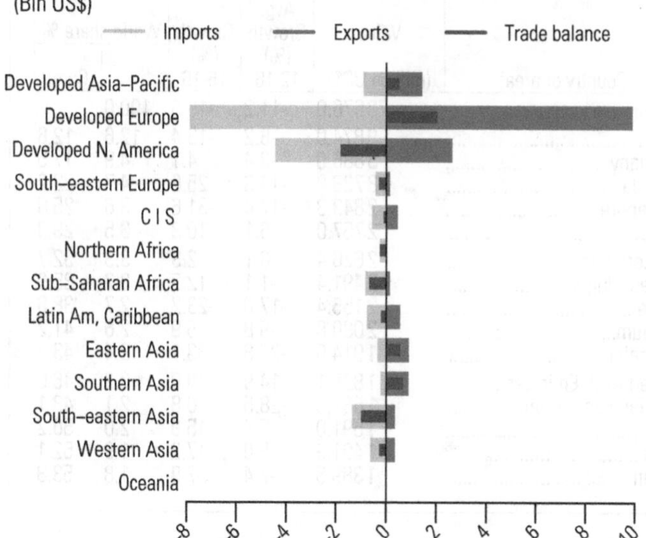

Table 3: Top importing countries or areas in 2016

Country or area	Value (million US$)	Avg. Growth (%) 12-16	Growth (%) 15-16	World share %	Cum.
World	18633.5	-4.8	-9.1	100.0	
USA	3313.1	-0.9	-16.1	17.8	17.8
France	1352.3	-9.3	-12.8	7.3	25.0
Canada	1134.1	-8.8	-10.4	6.1	31.1
Germany	1043.0	-6.8	-15.7	5.6	36.7
United Kingdom	768.3	-6.7	-1.7	4.1	40.8
Viet Nam	*746.7*	92.5	5.1	4.0	44.9
Australia	581.3	-6.5	4.1	3.1	48.0
Spain	561.8	10.3	6.3	3.0	51.0
Belgium	469.7	-9.4	-16.1	2.5	53.5
Italy	457.3	-3.8	-4.2	2.5	56.0
Turkey	393.9	10.1	-1.6	2.1	58.1
Austria	336.4	-4.3	4.7	1.8	59.9
Poland	300.3	-19.1	-39.8	1.6	61.5
Sweden	281.7	-4.7	11.7	1.5	63.0
Russian Federation	280.7	-12.8	17.0	1.5	64.5

Source: UN Comtrade

723 Civil engineering and contractors' plant and equipment; parts thereof

In 2016, the value (in current US$) of exports of "civil engineering and contractors' plant and equipment; parts thereof" (SITC group 723) decreased by 10.8 percent (compared to -11.0 percent average growth rate from 2012-2016) to reach 79.0 bln US$ (see table 2), while imports decreased by 15.5 percent to reach 78.7 bln US$ (see table 3). Exports of this commodity accounted for 1.3 percent of world exports of SITC section 7, and 0.5 percent of total world merchandise exports (see table 1). Japan, USA and China were the top exporters in 2016 (see table 2). They accounted for 12.3, 11.9 and 11.3 percent of world exports, respectively. USA, Germany and Canada were the top destinations, with respectively 12.6, 4.9 and 4.7 percent of world imports (see table 3).

The top 15 countries/areas accounted for 81.1 and 53.8 percent of total world exports and imports, respectively (see tables 2 and 3). In 2016, Japan was the country/area with the highest value of net exports (+8.3 bln US$), followed by China (+6.7 bln US$). By MDG regions (see graph 2), the largest surpluses in this product group were recorded by Eastern Asia (+9.8 bln US$), Developed Europe (+6.7 bln US$) and Developed Asia-Pacific (+6.6 bln US$). The largest trade deficits were recorded by Western Asia (-6.0 bln US$), Sub-Saharan Africa (-4.6 bln US$) and Developed North America (-2.9 bln US$).

Table 1: Imports (Imp.) and exports (Exp.), 2002-2016, in current US$

		2002	2003	2004	2005	2006	2007	2008	2009	2010	2011	2012	2013	2014	2015	2016
Values in Bln US$	Imp.	34.1	40.9	52.5	66.0	81.2	105.2	122.6	73.2	89.8	119.1	126.4	111.8	108.8	93.2	78.7
	Exp.	36.3	43.7	56.0	69.5	84.6	108.8	125.7	77.0	95.6	123.7	125.7	113.8	110.0	88.5	79.0
As a percentage of SITC section (%)	Imp.	1.3	1.4	1.5	1.7	1.8	2.1	2.3	1.7	1.7	2.0	2.1	1.8	1.7	1.5	1.3
	Exp.	1.4	1.5	1.6	1.8	1.9	2.2	2.3	1.8	1.9	2.1	2.1	1.9	1.8	1.5	1.3
As a percentage of world trade (%)	Imp.	0.5	0.5	0.6	0.6	0.7	0.7	0.8	0.6	0.6	0.7	0.7	0.6	0.6	0.6	0.5
	Exp.	0.6	0.6	0.6	0.7	0.7	0.8	0.8	0.6	0.6	0.7	0.7	0.6	0.6	0.5	0.5

Graph 1: Annual growth rates of exports, 2002–2016

(In percentage by year)

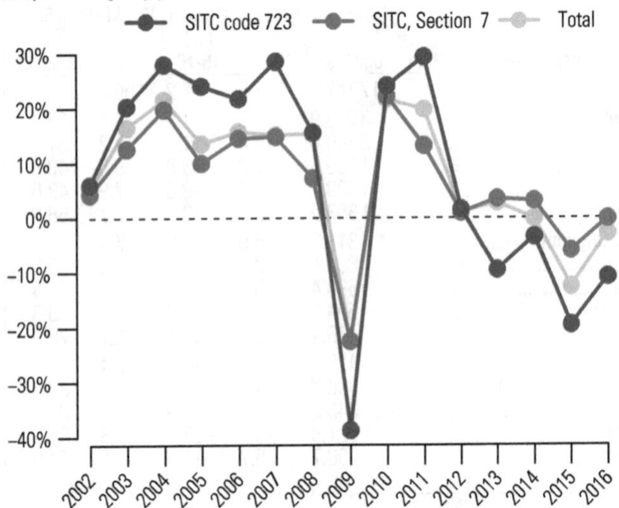

Graph 2: Trade Balance by MDG regions 2016

(Bln US$)

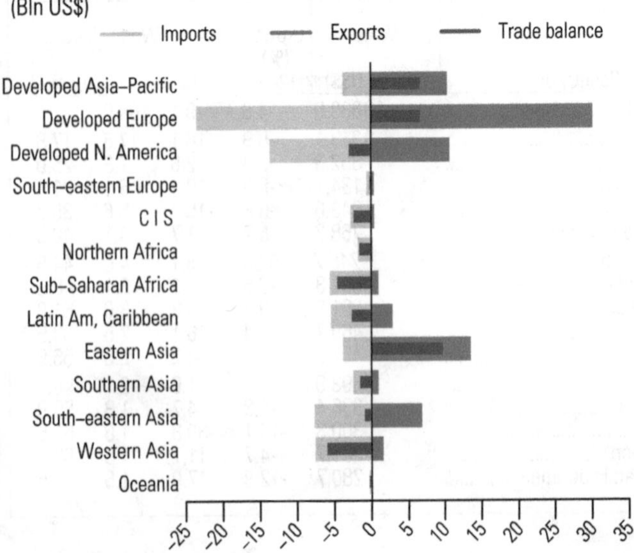

Table 2: Top exporting countries or areas in 2016

Country or area	Value (million US$)	Avg. Growth (%) 12-16	Growth (%) 15-16	World share %	Cum.
World	78962.8	-11.0	-10.8	100.0	
Japan	9737.6	-9.1	9.4	12.3	12.3
USA	9407.9	-19.9	-31.2	11.9	24.2
China	8894.2	-10.0	-15.7	11.3	35.5
Germany	6926.9	-7.9	-5.5	8.8	44.3
Singapore	4693.2	-6.2	-2.3	5.9	50.2
Rep. of Korea	4048.7	-12.9	-9.5	5.1	55.4
Netherlands	3384.0	-3.6	-8.1	4.3	59.6
Italy	3013.2	-3.4	0.6	3.8	63.5
United Kingdom	2846.6	-12.4	-18.2	3.6	67.1
France	2701.1	-9.5	-8.0	3.4	70.5
Belgium	2508.8	-12.6	-6.2	3.2	73.7
Austria	1760.0	-2.0	10.1	2.2	75.9
Brazil	1449.3	-11.7	3.7	1.8	77.7
Sweden	1416.7	-12.8	-6.0	1.8	79.5
Canada	1270.4	-15.2	-18.4	1.6	81.1

Table 3: Top importing countries or areas in 2016

Country or area	Value (million US$)	Avg. Growth (%) 12-16	Growth (%) 15-16	World share %	Cum.
World	78676.0	-11.2	-15.5	100.0	
USA	9874.0	-8.2	-13.4	12.6	12.6
Germany	3886.0	-3.4	4.1	4.9	17.5
Canada	3728.8	-14.3	-25.6	4.7	22.2
Singapore	2843.3	-17.4	-31.6	3.6	25.8
France	2757.0	-6.1	10.3	3.5	29.3
Netherlands	2626.4	0.1	2.3	3.3	32.7
United Kingdom	2491.4	-1.1	-12.2	3.2	35.9
China	2155.4	-17.0	-23.2	2.7	38.6
Belgium	2080.8	-8.8	5.9	2.6	41.2
Australia	1914.0	-27.8	-33.1	2.4	43.7
United Arab Emirates	1825.1	-14.9	-19.0	2.3	46.0
Russian Federation	1687.5	-28.5	0.8	2.1	48.1
Turkey	1591.0	-5.4	15.9	2.0	50.2
India	1491.9	-5.0	17.2	1.9	52.1
Japan	1389.5	-2.4	-7.9	1.8	53.8

In 2016, the value (in current US$) of exports of "textile and leather machinery and parts thereof, nes" (SITC group 724) decreased by 2.1 percent (compared to -0.1 percent average growth rate from 2012-2016) to reach 28.5 bln US$ (see table 2), while imports decreased by 2.6 percent to reach 30.6 bln US$ (see table 3). Exports of this commodity accounted for 0.5 percent of world exports of SITC section 7, and 0.2 percent of total world merchandise exports (see table 1). China, Germany and Italy were the top exporters in 2016 (see table 2). They accounted for 22.1, 12.5 and 9.5 percent of world exports, respectively. USA, China and India were the top destinations, with respectively 13.3, 9.5 and 7.8 percent of world imports (see table 3).

The top 15 countries/areas accounted for 87.0 and 65.9 percent of total world exports and imports, respectively (see tables 2 and 3). In 2016, China was the country/area with the highest value of net exports (+3.4 bln US$), followed by Germany (+2.6 bln US$). By MDG regions (see graph 2), the largest surpluses in this product group were recorded by Eastern Asia (+5.5 bln US$), Developed Europe (+5.3 bln US$) and Developed Asia-Pacific (+1.6 bln US$). The largest trade deficits were recorded by Southern Asia (-4.0 bln US$), Developed North America (-3.4 bln US$) and South-eastern Asia (-2.2 bln US$).

Table 1: Imports (Imp.) and exports (Exp.), 2002-2016, in current US$

		2002	2003	2004	2005	2006	2007	2008	2009	2010	2011	2012	2013	2014	2015	2016
Values in Bln US$	Imp.	21.3	23.9	25.5	26.0	27.7	31.0	29.9	20.8	27.9	33.4	30.4	32.5	33.1	31.4	30.6
	Exp.	20.2	23.0	24.5	24.8	26.8	29.9	27.3	19.3	26.6	31.4	28.6	30.9	31.8	29.2	28.5
As a percentage of SITC section (%)	Imp.	0.8	0.8	0.7	0.7	0.6	0.6	0.6	0.5	0.5	0.6	0.5	0.5	0.5	0.5	0.5
	Exp.	0.8	0.8	0.7	0.6	0.6	0.6	0.5	0.5	0.5	0.5	0.5	0.5	0.5	0.5	0.5
As a percentage of world trade (%)	Imp.	0.3	0.3	0.3	0.2	0.2	0.2	0.2	0.2	0.2	0.2	0.2	0.2	0.2	0.2	0.2
	Exp.	0.3	0.3	0.3	0.2	0.2	0.2	0.2	0.2	0.2	0.2	0.2	0.2	0.2	0.2	0.2

Graph 1: Annual growth rates of exports, 2002–2016

(In percentage by year)

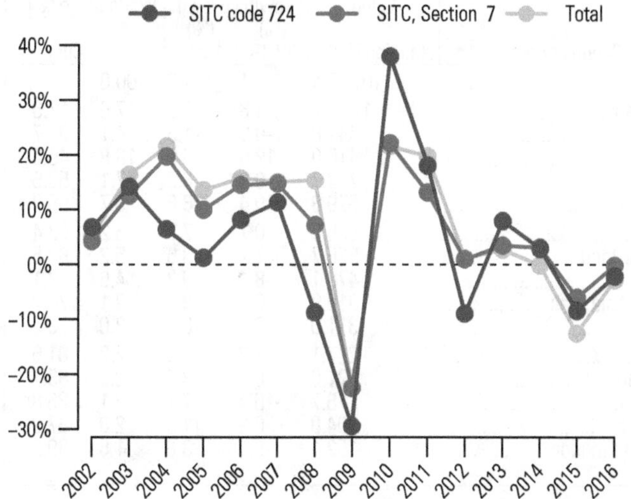

Graph 2: Trade Balance by MDG regions 2016

(Bln US$)

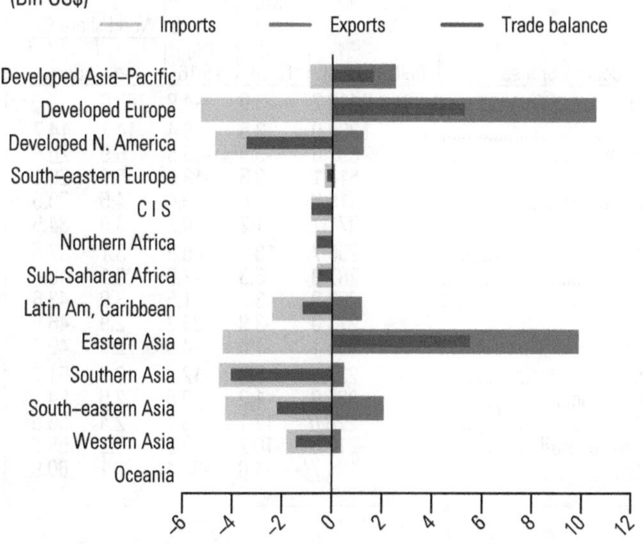

Table 2: Top exporting countries or areas in 2016

Country or area	Value (million US$)	Avg. Growth (%) 12-16	Growth (%) 15-16	World share %	Cum.
World	28539.6	-0.1	-2.1	100.0	
China	6303.0	7.8	-4.6	22.1	22.1
Germany	3578.4	-7.9	-5.6	12.5	34.6
Italy	2700.3	-1.0	1.7	9.5	44.1
Japan	2499.9	-3.9	9.7	8.8	52.8
Rep. of Korea	2010.2	-7.2	-5.0	7.0	59.9
USA	1220.2	-4.0	-11.4	4.3	64.2
Other Asia, nes	1049.9	-0.5	-2.1	3.7	67.8
Mexico	1039.0	5.3	-4.8	3.6	71.5
Singapore	836.1	11.6	2.9	2.9	74.4
Switzerland	817.2	-4.2	-11.5	2.9	77.3
France	779.2	0.5	2.3	2.7	80.0
Thailand	522.3	3.8	-1.4	1.8	81.8
China, Hong Kong SAR	510.6	-4.3	-11.4	1.8	83.6
Czechia	497.0	1.7	6.3	1.7	85.4
India	473.4	9.3	0.2	1.7	87.0

Table 3: Top importing countries or areas in 2016

Country or area	Value (million US$)	Avg. Growth (%) 12-16	Growth (%) 15-16	World share %	Cum.
World	30603.4	0.2	-2.6	100.0	
USA	4068.5	4.0	-5.0	13.3	13.3
China	2906.9	-10.8	-13.3	9.5	22.8
India	2373.3	5.0	-0.2	7.8	30.5
Viet Nam	*1728.3*	25.7	5.1	5.6	36.2
Turkey	1371.2	-7.9	-2.0	4.5	40.7
Bangladesh	*1223.9*	8.9	-14.2	4.0	44.7
Germany	1010.9	1.2	-5.7	3.3	48.0
Mexico	855.3	4.1	0.7	2.8	50.8
Indonesia	822.9	-5.3	2.3	2.7	53.5
Japan	739.3	0.5	6.9	2.4	55.9
Italy	719.7	3.7	7.0	2.4	58.2
Singapore	660.3	8.4	4.6	2.2	60.4
Canada	630.4	-1.6	-4.3	2.1	62.4
Pakistan	537.5	5.2	4.3	1.8	64.2
China, Hong Kong SAR	523.8	-7.9	-13.2	1.7	65.9

Source: UN Comtrade

725 Paper and paper manufacture machinery, and parts thereof

In 2016, the value (in current US$) of exports of "paper and paper manufacture machinery, and parts thereof" (SITC group 725) decreased by 1.8 percent (compared to -2.1 percent average growth rate from 2012-2016) to reach 10.2 bln US$ (see table 2), while imports decreased by 4.9 percent to reach 9.4 bln US$ (see table 3). Exports of this commodity accounted for 0.2 percent of world exports of SITC section 7, and 0.1 percent of total world merchandise exports (see table 1). Germany, Italy and China were the top exporters in 2016 (see table 2). They accounted for 17.6, 14.1 and 13.8 percent of world exports, respectively. USA, Germany and China were the top destinations, with respectively 14.7, 5.9 and 5.5 percent of world imports (see table 3).

The top 15 countries/areas accounted for 89.2 and 60.9 percent of total world exports and imports, respectively (see tables 2 and 3). In 2016, Germany was the country/area with the highest value of net exports (+1.3 bln US$), followed by Italy (+1.2 bln US$). By MDG regions (see graph 2), the largest surpluses in this product group were recorded by Developed Europe (+3.4 bln US$), Eastern Asia (+1.1 bln US$) and Developed Asia-Pacific (+59.5 mln US$). The largest trade deficits were recorded by South-eastern Asia (-882.6 mln US$), Latin America and the Caribbean (-773.3 mln US$) and Developed North America (-709.4 mln US$).

Table 1: Imports (Imp.) and exports (Exp.), 2002-2016, in current US$

		2002	2003	2004	2005	2006	2007	2008	2009	2010	2011	2012	2013	2014	2015	2016
Values in Bln US$	Imp.	6.1	7.6	8.3	9.1	9.2	11.5	12.6	9.3	9.4	11.0	10.6	10.1	10.3	9.9	9.4
	Exp.	6.6	7.7	8.7	9.3	10.0	11.8	12.1	9.2	10.1	11.5	11.2	10.9	11.1	10.4	10.2
As a percentage of SITC section (%)	Imp.	0.2	0.3	0.2	0.2	0.2	0.2	0.2	0.2	0.2	0.2	0.2	0.2	0.2	0.2	0.2
	Exp.	0.3	0.3	0.3	0.2	0.2	0.2	0.2	0.2	0.2	0.2	0.2	0.2	0.2	0.2	0.2
As a percentage of world trade (%)	Imp.	0.1	0.1	0.1	0.1	0.1	0.1	0.1	0.1	0.1	0.1	0.1	0.1	0.1	0.1	0.1
	Exp.	0.1	0.1	0.1	0.1	0.1	0.1	0.1	0.1	0.1	0.1	0.1	0.1	0.1	0.1	0.1

Graph 1: Annual growth rates of exports, 2002–2016

(In percentage by year)

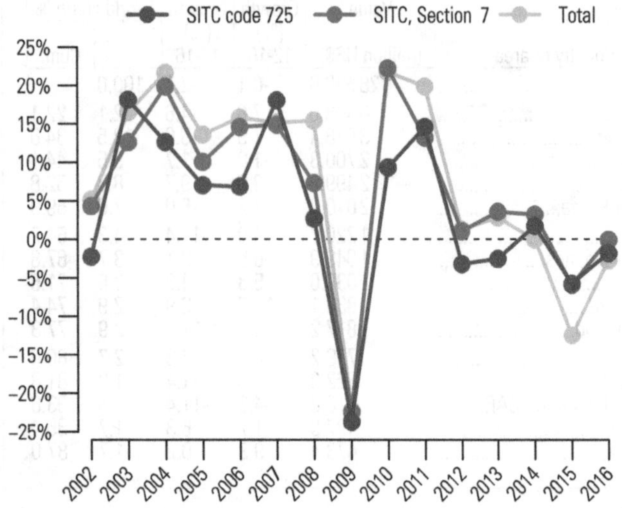

Table 2: Top exporting countries or areas in 2016

Country or area	Value (million US$)	Avg. Growth (%) 12-16	Growth (%) 15-16	World share %	Cum.
World	10246.4	-2.1	-1.8	100.0	
Germany	1805.2	-4.6	-5.0	17.6	17.6
Italy	1441.8	-0.3	11.5	14.1	31.7
China	1410.0	12.6	-6.9	13.8	45.5
USA	722.7	-0.3	6.2	7.1	52.5
Finland	579.8	-10.4	-6.8	5.7	58.2
France	535.0	0.7	7.7	5.2	63.4
Switzerland	528.7	1.2	3.5	5.2	68.5
Sweden	470.1	-8.4	0.2	4.6	73.1
Other Asia, nes	318.9	-0.6	-8.3	3.1	76.2
Japan	311.0	-7.0	10.1	3.0	79.3
Spain	227.1	-2.2	9.3	2.2	81.5
Netherlands	221.0	6.5	3.4	2.2	83.7
Austria	216.7	-16.4	-27.7	2.1	85.8
Canada	204.0	0.9	11.3	2.0	87.8
United Kingdom	152.1	-6.1	-3.6	1.5	89.2

Graph 2: Trade Balance by MDG regions 2016

(Bln US$)

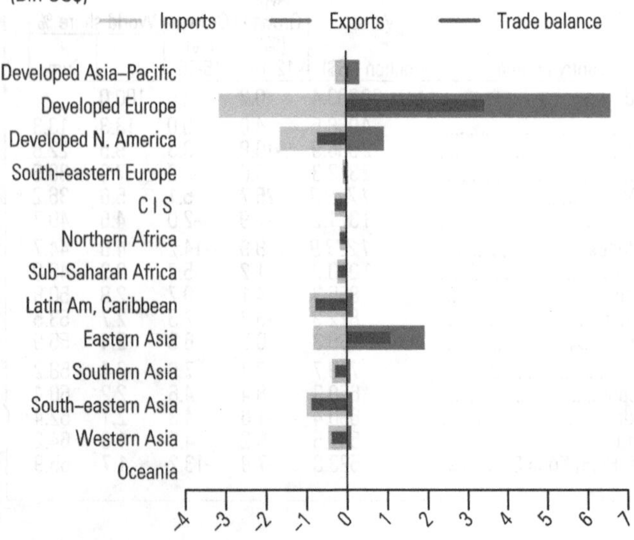

Table 3: Top importing countries or areas in 2016

Country or area	Value (million US$)	Avg. Growth (%) 12-16	Growth (%) 15-16	World share %	Cum.
World	9419.2	-3.0	-4.9	100.0	
USA	1388.0	3.5	6.4	14.7	14.7
Germany	552.6	-3.8	-15.5	5.9	20.6
China	514.1	-19.5	-13.9	5.5	26.1
Indonesia	419.6	-8.6	9.4	4.5	30.5
France	371.7	-1.2	-0.2	3.9	34.5
Spain	290.7	18.2	45.9	3.1	37.5
Mexico	287.9	5.3	-7.6	3.1	40.6
Italy	283.9	3.2	1.5	3.0	43.6
Brazil	273.0	-3.9	29.2	2.9	46.5
Canada	248.1	-1.0	-4.8	2.6	49.2
India	237.5	-5.8	-12.0	2.5	51.7
United Kingdom	235.9	1.2	0.6	2.5	54.2
Viet Nam	*228.0*	17.1	5.1	2.4	56.6
Russian Federation	211.5	-10.2	-12.0	2.2	58.8
Turkey	194.7	-4.0	-30.4	2.1	60.9

In 2016, the value (in current US$) of exports of "printing and bookbinding machinery and parts thereof" (SITC group 726) decreased by 1.9 percent (compared to -5.1 percent average growth rate from 2012-2016) to reach 11.9 bln US$ (see table 2), while imports decreased by 4.1 percent to reach 11.3 bln US$ (see table 3). Exports of this commodity accounted for 0.2 percent of world exports of SITC section 7, and 0.1 percent of total world merchandise exports (see table 1). Germany, Japan and USA were the top exporters in 2016 (see table 2). They accounted for 26.7, 6.8 and 6.8 percent of world exports, respectively. USA, China and Germany were the top destinations, with respectively 11.5, 6.3 and 5.6 percent of world imports (see table 3).

The top 15 countries/areas accounted for 84.3 and 58.8 percent of total world exports and imports, respectively (see tables 2 and 3). In 2016, Germany was the country/area with the highest value of net exports (+2.5 bln US$), followed by Japan (+581.1 mln US$). By MDG regions (see graph 2), the largest surpluses in this product group were recorded by Developed Europe (+3.5 bln US$), Developed Asia-Pacific (+494.6 mln US$) and Western Asia (+179.7 mln US$). The largest trade deficits were recorded by South-eastern Asia (-764.4 mln US$), Latin America and the Caribbean (-681.6 mln US$) and Developed North America (-578.5 mln US$).

Table 1: Imports (Imp.) and exports (Exp.), 2002-2016, in current US$

		2002	2003	2004	2005	2006	2007	2008	2009	2010	2011	2012	2013	2014	2015	2016
Values in Bln US$	Imp.	13.0	14.0	16.2	18.4	19.6	19.7	19.5	13.7	15.3	16.3	14.7	14.2	13.7	11.8	11.3
	Exp.	13.2	13.9	16.4	18.5	20.3	19.5	19.9	13.2	14.8	15.8	14.7	14.5	14.0	12.1	11.9
As a percentage of SITC section (%)	Imp.	0.5	0.5	0.5	0.5	0.4	0.4	0.4	0.3	0.3	0.3	0.2	0.2	0.2	0.2	0.2
	Exp.	0.5	0.5	0.5	0.5	0.5	0.4	0.4	0.3	0.3	0.3	0.3	0.2	0.2	0.2	0.2
As a percentage of world trade (%)	Imp.	0.2	0.2	0.2	0.2	0.2	0.1	0.1	0.1	0.1	0.1	0.1	0.1	0.1	0.1	0.1
	Exp.	0.2	0.2	0.2	0.2	0.2	0.1	0.1	0.1	0.1	0.1	0.1	0.1	0.1	0.1	0.1

Graph 1: Annual growth rates of exports, 2002–2016
(In percentage by year)

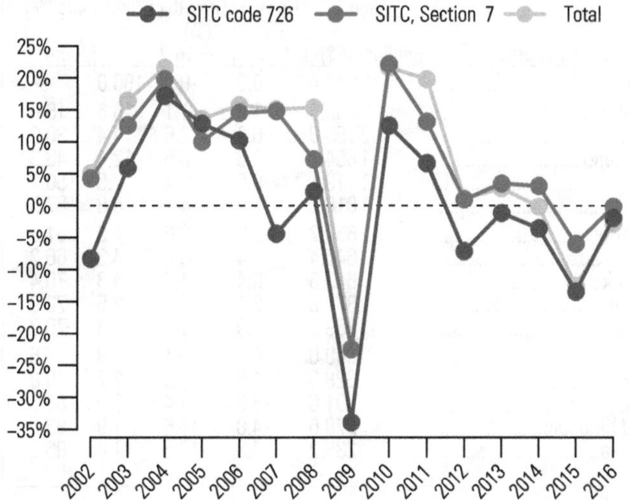

Graph 2: Trade Balance by MDG regions 2016
(Bln US$)

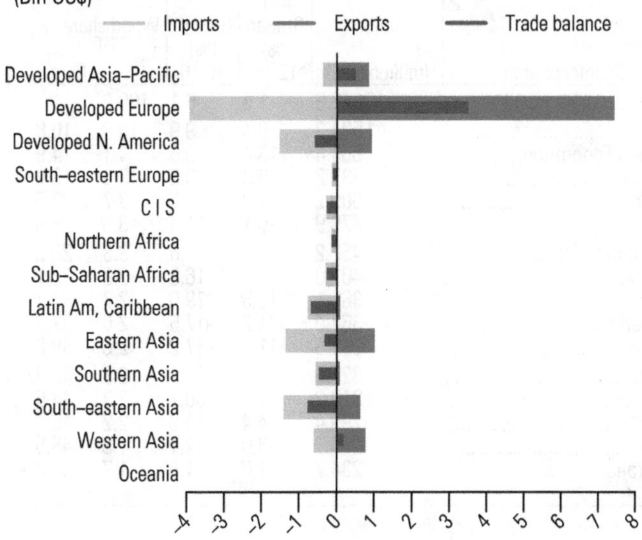

Table 2: Top exporting countries or areas in 2016

Country or area	Value (million US$)	Avg. Growth (%) 12-16	Growth (%) 15-16	World share %	Cum.
World	11896.0	-5.1	-1.9	100.0	
Germany	3180.5	-7.5	1.1	26.7	26.7
Japan	806.7	-4.8	-5.2	6.8	33.5
USA	806.4	-6.3	-12.2	6.8	40.3
Italy	774.5	-1.7	1.1	6.5	46.8
Israel	714.1	-0.1	6.0	6.0	52.8
Switzerland	633.8	-5.4	3.8	5.3	58.1
China	571.7	2.0	-3.0	4.8	62.9
United Kingdom	518.3	-5.3	-10.2	4.4	67.3
Belgium	485.6	-6.4	-0.3	4.1	71.4
Netherlands	353.3	-4.0	-6.6	3.0	74.4
France	347.6	-8.4	3.2	2.9	77.3
Singapore	237.9	7.5	12.3	2.0	79.3
Austria	233.5	-7.2	31.9	2.0	81.2
China, Hong Kong SAR	182.2	-15.5	-24.2	1.5	82.8
Spain	177.3	-5.7	0.0	1.5	84.3

Table 3: Top importing countries or areas in 2016

Country or area	Value (million US$)	Avg. Growth (%) 12-16	Growth (%) 15-16	World share %	Cum.
World	11325.7	-6.3	-4.1	100.0	
USA	1305.0	5.0	10.2	11.5	11.5
China	717.3	-18.6	-26.3	6.3	17.9
Germany	635.4	-10.5	0.9	5.6	23.5
Indonesia	610.1	-7.8	-4.3	5.4	28.9
Belgium	422.9	-6.1	9.9	3.7	32.6
France	422.6	-5.8	12.9	3.7	36.3
Italy	404.1	5.9	27.0	3.6	39.9
United Kingdom	368.2	-3.2	-6.3	3.3	43.1
India	343.2	-2.6	2.4	3.0	46.2
Mexico	298.3	5.2	5.7	2.6	48.8
China, Hong Kong SAR	254.4	-14.9	-22.7	2.2	51.0
Spain	232.1	6.5	4.0	2.0	53.1
Japan	225.6	-2.3	-13.6	2.0	55.1
Netherlands	210.8	-3.0	-17.0	1.9	56.9
Canada	207.1	-2.4	3.4	1.8	58.8

727 Food- processing machines (excluding domestic); parts thereof

In 2016, the value (in current US$) of exports of "food- processing machines (excluding domestic); parts thereof" (SITC group 727) decreased by 0.2 percent (compared to -0.3 percent average growth rate from 2012-2016) to reach 15.0 bln US$ (see table 2), while imports decreased by 6.1 percent to reach 13.9 bln US$ (see table 3). Exports of this commodity accounted for 0.3 percent of world exports of SITC section 7, and 0.1 percent of total world merchandise exports (see table 1). Germany, Italy and Netherlands were the top exporters in 2016 (see table 2). They accounted for 16.6, 14.4 and 12.4 percent of world exports, respectively. USA, Russian Federation and Germany were the top destinations, with respectively 10.8, 4.1 and 3.9 percent of world imports (see table 3).

The top 15 countries/areas accounted for 85.2 and 50.2 percent of total world exports and imports, respectively (see tables 2 and 3). In 2016, Germany was the country/area with the highest value of net exports (+2.0 bln US$), followed by Italy (+1.9 bln US$). By MDG regions (see graph 2), the largest surpluses in this product group were recorded by Developed Europe (+6.1 bln US$) and Eastern Asia (+675.2 mln US$). The largest trade deficits were recorded by Latin America and the Caribbean (-1.2 bln US$), Sub-Saharan Africa (-928.9 mln US$) and Commonwealth of Independent States (-827.9 mln US$).

Table 1: Imports (Imp.) and exports (Exp.), 2002-2016, in current US$

		2002	2003	2004	2005	2006	2007	2008	2009	2010	2011	2012	2013	2014	2015	2016
Values in Bln US$	Imp.	5.9	6.9	8.1	8.9	9.5	11.7	12.9	10.7	11.5	14.6	14.8	15.4	16.2	14.8	13.9
	Exp.	6.2	7.3	8.6	9.3	10.5	12.7	14.2	11.1	12.0	15.0	15.2	16.3	16.8	15.0	15.0
As a percentage of SITC section (%)	Imp.	0.2	0.2	0.2	0.2	0.2	0.2	0.2	0.3	0.2	0.2	0.2	0.2	0.3	0.2	0.2
	Exp.	0.2	0.3	0.2	0.2	0.2	0.3	0.3	0.3	0.2	0.3	0.3	0.3	0.3	0.3	0.3
As a percentage of world trade (%)	Imp.	0.1	0.1	0.1	0.1	0.1	0.1	0.1	0.1	0.1	0.1	0.1	0.1	0.1	0.1	0.1
	Exp.	0.1	0.1	0.1	0.1	0.1	0.1	0.1	0.1	0.1	0.1	0.1	0.1	0.1	0.1	0.1

Graph 1: Annual growth rates of exports, 2002–2016

(In percentage by year)

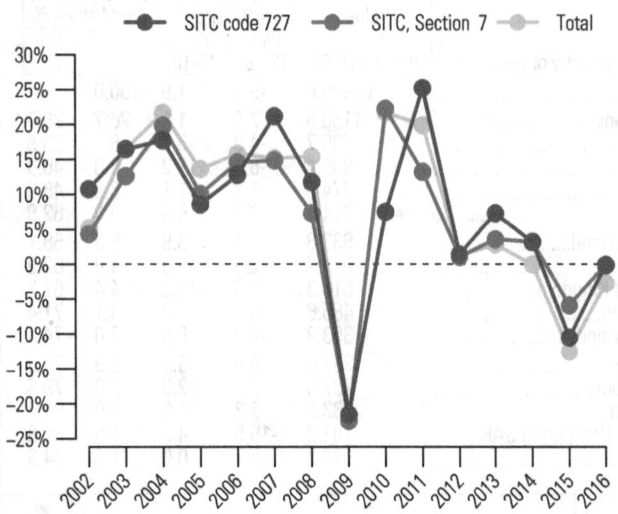

Graph 2: Trade Balance by MDG regions 2016

(Bln US$)

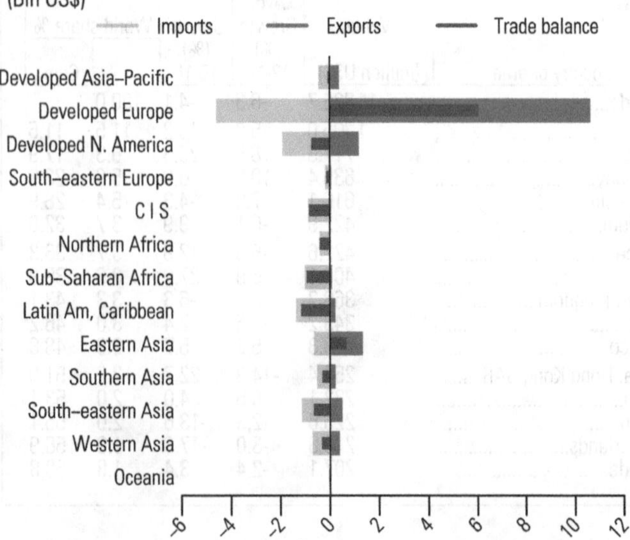

Table 2: Top exporting countries or areas in 2016

Country or area	Value (million US$)	Avg. Growth (%) 12-16	Growth (%) 15-16	World share %	Cum.
World	15013.4	-0.3	-0.2	100.0	
Germany	2488.5	-1.2	1.1	16.6	16.6
Italy	2156.8	0.3	2.6	14.4	30.9
Netherlands	1854.7	1.6	8.5	12.4	43.3
China	1119.1	6.6	0.4	7.5	50.7
USA	1018.2	-1.0	-4.7	6.8	57.5
Switzerland	650.2	-2.0	0.8	4.3	61.9
France	645.4	1.4	6.6	4.3	66.2
Denmark	643.5	0.4	4.5	4.3	70.4
Belgium	371.3	2.5	15.2	2.5	72.9
Austria	359.6	4.0	11.9	2.4	75.3
Spain	340.0	-0.2	-9.1	2.3	77.6
Turkey	328.5	1.6	-10.8	2.2	79.8
Japan	301.6	-3.8	-4.4	2.0	81.8
United Kingdom	278.6	-4.8	-11.6	1.9	83.6
Malaysia	235.2	-3.3	-16.3	1.6	85.2

Table 3: Top importing countries or areas in 2016

Country or area	Value (million US$)	Avg. Growth (%) 12-16	Growth (%) 15-16	World share %	Cum.
World	13866.8	-1.5	-6.1	100.0	
USA	1504.2	9.4	9.9	10.8	10.8
Russian Federation	563.4	-13.4	-9.5	4.1	14.9
Germany	537.2	-0.3	3.3	3.9	18.8
Mexico	509.2	17.2	-13.6	3.7	22.5
France	479.9	-0.1	11.4	3.5	25.9
United Kingdom	452.2	1.5	-4.6	3.3	29.2
Canada	401.0	6.3	16.3	2.9	32.1
Spain	368.1	12.5	19.0	2.7	34.7
Netherlands	364.0	-4.2	-17.5	2.6	37.3
Indonesia	363.5	-11.0	-17.2	2.6	40.0
China	325.0	-9.1	-17.1	2.3	42.3
Belgium	313.2	4.0	30.2	2.3	44.6
Italy	299.4	4.4	14.8	2.2	46.7
India	244.7	-3.0	-12.1	1.8	48.5
Australia	234.7	-1.0	1.5	1.7	50.2

"Other machinery, equipment, for specialized industries; parts nes" (SITC group 728) is amongst the top exported commodities in 2016 with 1.1 percent of total exports (see table 1). The value (in current US$) of exports of this commodity increased by 5.0 percent (compared to 0.7 percent average growth rate from 2012-2016) to reach 179.2 bln US$ (see table 2), while imports increased by 4.1 percent to reach 178.9 bln US$ (see table 3). Exports of this commodity accounted for 3.0 percent of world exports of SITC section 7 (see table 1). Japan, Germany and USA were the top exporters in 2016 (see table 2). They accounted for 16.2, 13.3 and 12.9 percent of world exports, respectively. China, USA and Other Asia, nes were the top destinations, with respectively 15.3, 10.4 and 8.9 percent of world imports (see table 3).

The top 15 countries/areas accounted for 86.8 and 68.5 percent of total world exports and imports, respectively (see tables 2 and 3). In 2016, Japan was the country/area with the highest value of net exports (+23.7 bln US$), followed by Germany (+16.1 bln US$). By MDG regions (see graph 2), the largest surpluses in this product group were recorded by Developed Europe (+36.8 bln US$), Developed Asia-Pacific (+22.5 bln US$) and Developed North America (+2.2 bln US$). The largest trade deficits were recorded by Eastern Asia (-27.1 bln US$), Latin America and the Caribbean (-7.7 bln US$) and South-eastern Asia (-6.4 bln US$).

Table 1: Imports (Imp.) and exports (Exp.), 2002-2016, in current US$

		2002	2003	2004	2005	2006	2007	2008	2009	2010	2011	2012	2013	2014	2015	2016
Values in Bln US$	Imp.	62.2	73.0	94.6	99.5	109.6	142.6	155.8	115.8	159.8	191.9	170.3	169.5	182.8	171.8	178.9
	Exp.	61.5	73.6	94.0	97.8	110.5	148.1	160.9	113.3	159.7	190.0	174.2	172.3	183.5	170.7	179.2
As a percentage of	Imp.	2.4	2.5	2.7	2.6	2.5	2.8	2.9	2.7	3.1	3.2	2.8	2.7	2.9	2.8	2.9
SITC section (%)	Exp.	2.4	2.5	2.7	2.6	2.5	2.9	3.0	2.7	3.1	3.3	3.0	2.8	2.9	2.9	3.0
As a percentage of	Imp.	0.9	1.0	1.0	0.9	0.9	1.0	1.0	0.9	1.0	1.1	0.9	0.9	1.0	1.0	1.1
world trade (%)	Exp.	1.0	1.0	1.0	0.9	0.9	1.1	1.0	0.9	1.1	1.1	1.0	0.9	1.0	1.0	1.1

Graph 1: Annual growth rates of exports, 2002–2016

(In percentage by year)

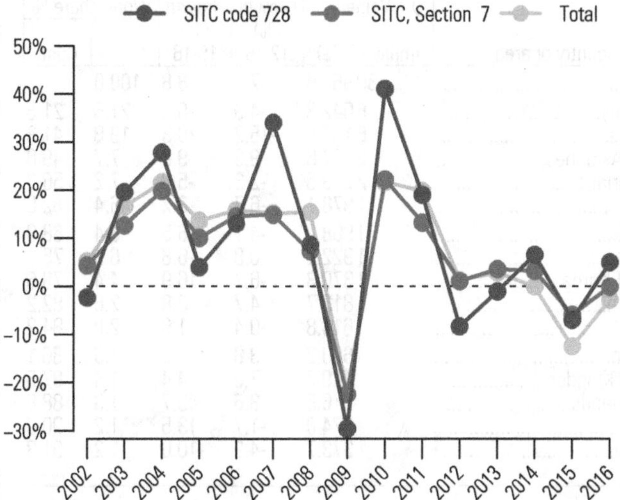

Table 2: Top exporting countries or areas in 2016

Country or area	Value (million US$)	Avg. Growth (%) 12-16	Growth (%) 15-16	World share %	Cum.
World	179194.2	0.7	5.0	100.0	
Japan	28962.0	-0.6	23.4	16.2	16.2
Germany	23892.9	-1.8	1.7	13.3	29.5
USA	23180.6	3.5	-0.2	12.9	42.4
China	14280.6	6.5	2.7	8.0	50.4
Italy	11427.5	-1.3	-0.5	6.4	56.8
Netherlands	10660.7	5.7	15.3	5.9	62.7
Rep. of Korea	10180.8	7.1	-7.9	5.7	68.4
Singapore	8277.2	1.2	15.4	4.6	73.0
Other Asia, nes	4908.5	1.9	11.1	2.7	75.8
Austria	4805.3	3.0	14.4	2.7	78.4
United Kingdom	3414.1	-2.6	-6.7	1.9	80.4
Switzerland	3317.4	-2.5	0.4	1.9	82.2
France	2986.8	-3.5	3.6	1.7	83.9
China, Hong Kong SAR	2677.1	-2.1	-3.1	1.5	85.4
Canada	2642.0	-3.4	-3.3	1.5	86.8

Graph 2: Trade Balance by MDG regions 2016

(Bln US$)

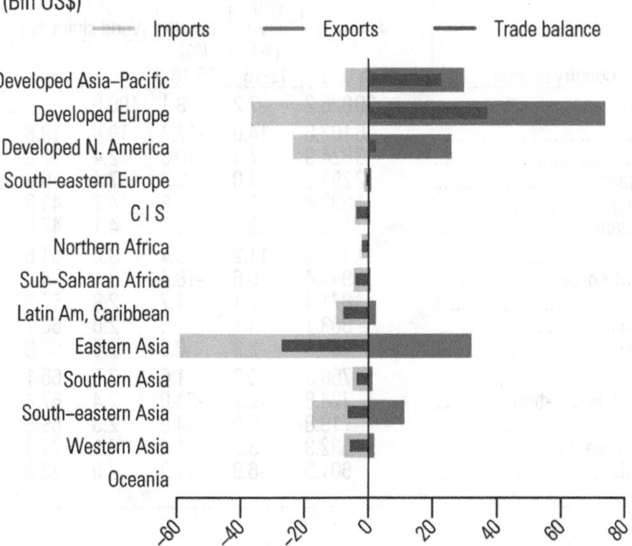

Table 3: Top importing countries or areas in 2016

Country or area	Value (million US$)	Avg. Growth (%) 12-16	Growth (%) 15-16	World share %	Cum.
World	178894.0	1.2	4.1	100.0	
China	27371.2	4.5	7.2	15.3	15.3
USA	18538.0	0.0	-2.7	10.4	25.7
Other Asia, nes	15953.9	7.1	28.9	8.9	34.6
Rep. of Korea	13325.2	1.1	5.9	7.4	42.0
Germany	7832.2	-0.7	2.4	4.4	46.4
Singapore	6262.8	5.5	34.9	3.5	49.9
Japan	5251.7	5.9	-14.8	2.9	52.8
Mexico	5173.8	6.6	2.5	2.9	55.7
Canada	5055.9	11.3	58.6	2.8	58.6
Netherlands	3455.8	1.8	-2.0	1.9	60.5
France	3051.7	-3.8	8.1	1.7	62.2
India	2994.9	-3.8	14.9	1.7	63.9
United Kingdom	2914.0	5.2	4.3	1.6	65.5
Viet Nam	*2751.2*	8.4	5.1	1.5	67.0
Russian Federation	2627.9	-17.8	-20.6	1.5	68.5

731 Machine tools working by removing metal or other material

In 2016, the value (in current US$) of exports of "machine tools working by removing metal or other material" (SITC group 731) decreased by 8.8 percent (compared to -7.1 percent average growth rate from 2012-2016) to reach 31.0 bln US$ (see table 2), while imports decreased by 8.1 percent to reach 30.8 bln US$ (see table 3). Exports of this commodity accounted for 0.5 percent of world exports of SITC section 7, and 0.2 percent of total world merchandise exports (see table 1). Germany, Japan and Other Asia, nes were the top exporters in 2016 (see table 2). They accounted for 21.5, 19.8 and 7.7 percent of world exports, respectively. China, USA and Germany were the top destinations, with respectively 19.8, 12.4 and 7.4 percent of world imports (see table 3).

The top 15 countries/areas accounted for 91.3 and 73.8 percent of total world exports and imports, respectively (see tables 2 and 3). In 2016, Japan was the country/area with the highest value of net exports (+5.4 bln US$), followed by Germany (+4.3 bln US$). By MDG regions (see graph 2), the largest surpluses in this product group were recorded by Developed Europe (+5.9 bln US$) and Developed Asia-Pacific (+5.3 bln US$). The largest trade deficits were recorded by Developed North America (-2.3 bln US$), Eastern Asia (-2.0 bln US$) and South-eastern Asia (-1.9 bln US$).

Table 1: Imports (Imp.) and exports (Exp.), 2002-2016, in current US$

		2002	2003	2004	2005	2006	2007	2008	2009	2010	2011	2012	2013	2014	2015	2016
Values in Bln US$	Imp.	16.1	18.1	23.8	27.3	31.8	33.7	37.2	21.2	26.3	38.2	41.6	35.7	38.1	33.5	30.8
	Exp.	15.9	18.1	23.7	27.3	32.0	32.7	36.8	21.4	26.9	38.3	41.5	36.2	39.2	33.9	31.0
As a percentage of SITC section (%)	Imp.	0.6	0.6	0.7	0.7	0.7	0.7	0.7	0.5	0.5	0.6	0.7	0.6	0.6	0.6	0.5
	Exp.	0.6	0.6	0.7	0.7	0.7	0.6	0.7	0.5	0.5	0.7	0.7	0.6	0.6	0.6	0.5
As a percentage of world trade (%)	Imp.	0.2	0.2	0.3	0.3	0.3	0.2	0.2	0.2	0.2	0.2	0.2	0.2	0.2	0.2	0.2
	Exp.	0.2	0.2	0.3	0.3	0.3	0.2	0.2	0.2	0.2	0.2	0.2	0.2	0.2	0.2	0.2

Graph 1: Annual growth rates of exports, 2002–2016
(In percentage by year)

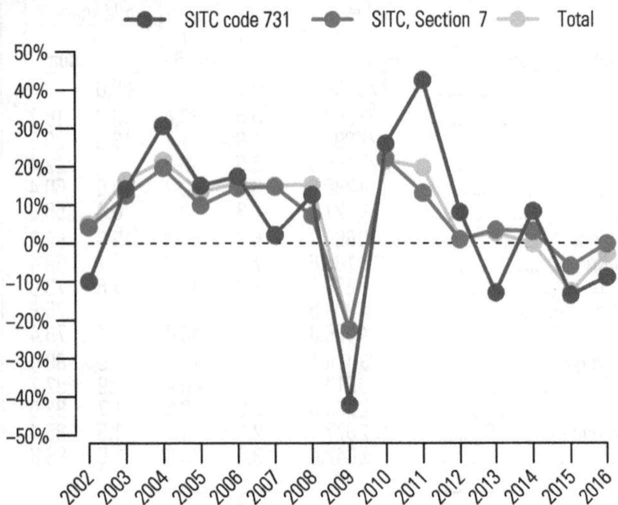

Table 2: Top exporting countries or areas in 2016

Country or area	Value (million US$)	Avg. Growth (%) 12-16	Growth (%) 15-16	World share %	Cum.
World	30 955.8	-7.1	-8.8	100.0	
Germany	6 642.3	-4.9	-5.3	21.5	21.5
Japan	6 137.8	-15.2	-20.3	19.8	41.3
Other Asia, nes	2 387.6	-9.5	-9.6	7.7	49.0
Switzerland	2 219.5	-2.3	-5.8	7.2	56.2
Italy	1 978.1	-6.7	-3.2	6.4	62.6
USA	1 968.2	-4.1	-6.5	6.4	68.9
China	1 922.2	0.8	-6.8	6.2	75.1
Rep. of Korea	1 370.3	-6.7	-16.9	4.4	79.6
Belgium	813.7	4.7	8.8	2.6	82.2
Spain	614.8	-0.4	1.9	2.0	84.2
Czechia	600.2	-3.8	-9.8	1.9	86.1
United Kingdom	429.7	-7.5	-14.4	1.4	87.5
Netherlands	416.6	8.6	43.7	1.3	88.8
France	374.0	-1.7	13.5	1.2	90.0
Austria	373.7	-4.2	-10.0	1.2	91.3

Graph 2: Trade Balance by MDG regions 2016
(Bln US$)

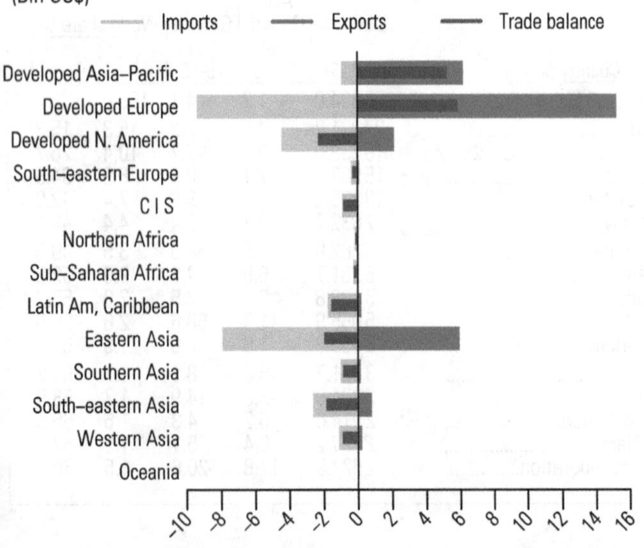

Table 3: Top importing countries or areas in 2016

Country or area	Value (million US$)	Avg. Growth (%) 12-16	Growth (%) 15-16	World share %	Cum.
World	30 825.2	-7.2	-8.1	100.0	
China	6 102.8	-14.0	-12.4	19.8	19.8
USA	3 824.9	-7.4	-10.3	12.4	32.2
Germany	2 293.2	-4.0	-3.3	7.4	39.6
Mexico	1 302.8	1.5	7.8	4.2	43.9
Viet Nam	*1 255.4*	33.6	5.1	4.1	47.9
Italy	1 124.5	11.2	-0.4	3.6	51.6
Rep. of Korea	941.4	-5.6	-18.4	3.1	54.6
India	871.4	-12.1	4.7	2.8	57.5
Belgium	803.1	4.1	4.9	2.6	60.1
Turkey	769.9	-2.2	0.9	2.5	62.6
France	768.3	0.2	1.6	2.5	65.1
Russian Federation	724.8	-12.7	-24.0	2.4	67.4
Japan	719.8	2.9	-4.9	2.3	69.8
Other Asia, nes	632.3	3.7	1.0	2.1	71.8
Canada	601.5	-6.9	-11.3	2.0	73.8

In 2016, the value (in current US$) of exports of "machine tools for working metal, sintered metal carbides or cermets" (SITC group 733) decreased by 3.3 percent (compared to -6.0 percent average growth rate from 2012-2016) to reach 10.7 bln US$ (see table 2), while imports decreased by 3.4 percent to reach 11.0 bln US$ (see table 3). Exports of this commodity accounted for 0.2 percent of world exports of SITC section 7, and 0.1 percent of total world merchandise exports (see table 1). Germany, Italy and Japan were the top exporters in 2016 (see table 2). They accounted for 17.3, 13.2 and 11.3 percent of world exports, respectively. China, USA and Mexico were the top destinations, with respectively 12.8, 10.8 and 9.9 percent of world imports (see table 3).

The top 15 countries/areas accounted for 88.4 and 67.5 percent of total world exports and imports, respectively (see tables 2 and 3). In 2016, Germany was the country/area with the highest value of net exports (+1.4 bln US$), followed by Italy (+1.2 bln US$). By MDG regions (see graph 2), the largest surpluses in this product group were recorded by Developed Europe (+3.1 bln US$), Developed Asia-Pacific (+954.6 mln US$) and Eastern Asia (+445.1 mln US$). The largest trade deficits were recorded by Latin America and the Caribbean (-1.3 bln US$), South-eastern Asia (-1.3 bln US$) and Developed North America (-572.1 mln US$).

Table 1: Imports (Imp.) and exports (Exp.), 2002-2016, in current US$

		2002	2003	2004	2005	2006	2007	2008	2009	2010	2011	2012	2013	2014	2015	2016
Values in Bln US$	Imp.	5.9	6.8	8.3	9.7	10.8	12.5	14.0	9.5	10.1	13.4	14.0	13.1	12.8	11.4	11.0
	Exp.	5.7	6.6	7.9	9.0	10.2	12.2	13.4	9.1	9.8	13.1	13.6	13.2	12.9	11.0	10.7
As a percentage of SITC section (%)	Imp.	0.2	0.2	0.2	0.3	0.2	0.2	0.3	0.2	0.2	0.2	0.2	0.2	0.2	0.2	0.2
	Exp.	0.2	0.2	0.2	0.2	0.2	0.2	0.2	0.2	0.2	0.2	0.2	0.2	0.2	0.2	0.2
As a percentage of world trade (%)	Imp.	0.1	0.1	0.1	0.1	0.1	0.1	0.1	0.1	0.1	0.1	0.1	0.1	0.1	0.1	0.1
	Exp.	0.1	0.1	0.1	0.1	0.1	0.1	0.1	0.1	0.1	0.1	0.1	0.1	0.1	0.1	0.1

Graph 1: Annual growth rates of exports, 2002–2016
(In percentage by year)

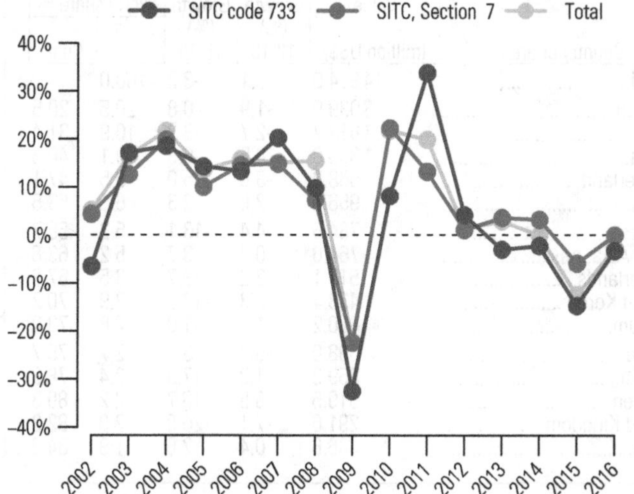

Graph 2: Trade Balance by MDG regions 2016
(Bln US$)

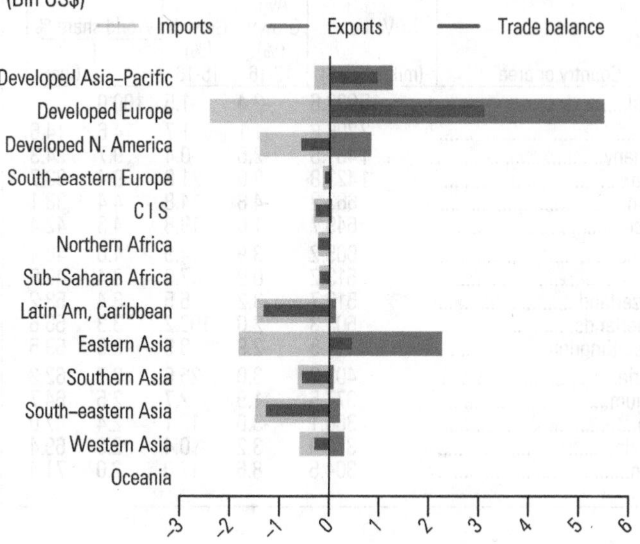

Table 2: Top exporting countries or areas in 2016

Country or area	Value (million US$)	Avg. Growth (%) 12-16	Growth (%) 15-16	World share %	Cum.
World	10662.9	-6.0	-3.3	100.0	
Germany	1849.7	-7.8	0.2	17.3	17.3
Italy	1410.3	-6.1	-6.1	13.2	30.6
Japan	1209.8	-12.0	-3.4	11.3	41.9
China	1028.9	3.9	-6.4	9.6	51.6
USA	713.2	-7.4	-14.2	6.7	58.3
Rep. of Korea	641.8	-3.4	-7.1	6.0	64.3
Other Asia, nes	510.0	-6.9	-5.2	4.8	69.1
Austria	367.1	-1.1	19.3	3.4	72.5
Switzerland	312.2	-6.7	-2.6	2.9	75.4
Spain	309.7	-5.1	22.6	2.9	78.3
Turkey	280.2	-3.1	-9.0	2.6	81.0
France	262.4	-2.2	8.6	2.5	83.4
Belgium	213.5	-1.8	-0.4	2.0	85.4
United Kingdom	197.6	-1.9	-0.1	1.9	87.3
Canada	120.7	2.1	6.5	1.1	88.4

Table 3: Top importing countries or areas in 2016

Country or area	Value (million US$)	Avg. Growth (%) 12-16	Growth (%) 15-16	World share %	Cum.
World	10986.5	-5.9	-3.4	100.0	
China	1410.7	-13.2	-14.6	12.8	12.8
USA	1189.7	3.1	2.6	10.8	23.7
Mexico	1084.9	18.4	9.7	9.9	33.5
Viet Nam	*529.0*	11.2	5.1	4.8	38.4
Germany	445.2	-5.0	2.3	4.1	42.4
India	436.1	-15.3	14.1	4.0	46.4
Thailand	368.7	-21.7	-7.6	3.4	49.7
Rep. of Korea	275.3	-1.2	9.3	2.5	52.2
United Kingdom	270.0	1.1	22.7	2.5	54.7
Turkey	269.6	-6.8	3.0	2.5	57.2
Indonesia	268.4	-12.8	-0.1	2.4	59.6
Italy	232.8	13.1	19.9	2.1	61.7
Canada	211.9	-1.0	-7.4	1.9	63.6
Russian Federation	211.8	-24.3	-28.5	1.9	65.6
France	209.7	-0.7	19.5	1.9	67.5

735 Parts, nes, accessories suitable for use with machines falling within 731&733

In 2016, the value (in current US$) of exports of "parts, nes, accessories suitable for use with machines falling within 731&733" (SITC group 735) decreased by 3.2 percent (compared to -3.1 percent average growth rate from 2012-2016) to reach 14.8 bln US$ (see table 2), while imports decreased by 1.5 percent to reach 15.1 bln US$ (see table 3). Exports of this commodity accounted for 0.3 percent of world exports of SITC section 7, and 0.1 percent of total world merchandise exports (see table 1). Germany, USA and Japan were the top exporters in 2016 (see table 2). They accounted for 20.5, 10.9 and 9.1 percent of world exports, respectively. USA, Germany and China were the top destinations, with respectively 14.6, 9.7 and 9.4 percent of world imports (see table 3).

The top 15 countries/areas accounted for 84.2 and 71.4 percent of total world exports and imports, respectively (see tables 2 and 3). In 2016, Germany was the country/area with the highest value of net exports (+1.6 bln US$), followed by Japan (+691.8 mln US$). By MDG regions (see graph 2), the largest surpluses in this product group were recorded by Developed Europe (+1.9 bln US$), Developed Asia-Pacific (+655.6 mln US$) and Eastern Asia (+22.1 mln US$). The largest trade deficits were recorded by Latin America and the Caribbean (-754.2 mln US$), Developed North America (-723.3 mln US$) and South-eastern Asia (-556.0 mln US$).

Table 1: Imports (Imp.) and exports (Exp.), 2002-2016, in current US$

		2002	2003	2004	2005	2006	2007	2008	2009	2010	2011	2012	2013	2014	2015	2016
Values in Bln US$	Imp.	6.9	8.1	10.0	11.0	12.4	13.5	15.7	9.6	12.3	16.6	16.6	15.7	17.2	15.3	15.1
	Exp.	7.5	8.6	10.5	11.8	13.1	13.7	16.4	10.4	13.0	16.9	16.8	15.8	17.2	15.3	14.8
As a percentage of SITC section (%)	Imp.	0.3	0.3	0.3	0.3	0.3	0.3	0.3	0.2	0.2	0.3	0.3	0.3	0.3	0.3	0.2
	Exp.	0.3	0.3	0.3	0.3	0.3	0.3	0.3	0.2	0.3	0.3	0.3	0.3	0.3	0.3	0.3
As a percentage of world trade (%)	Imp.	0.1	0.1	0.1	0.1	0.1	0.1	0.1	0.1	0.1	0.1	0.1	0.1	0.1	0.1	0.1
	Exp.	0.1	0.1	0.1	0.1	0.1	0.1	0.1	0.1	0.1	0.1	0.1	0.1	0.1	0.1	0.1

Graph 1: Annual growth rates of exports, 2002–2016
(In percentage by year)

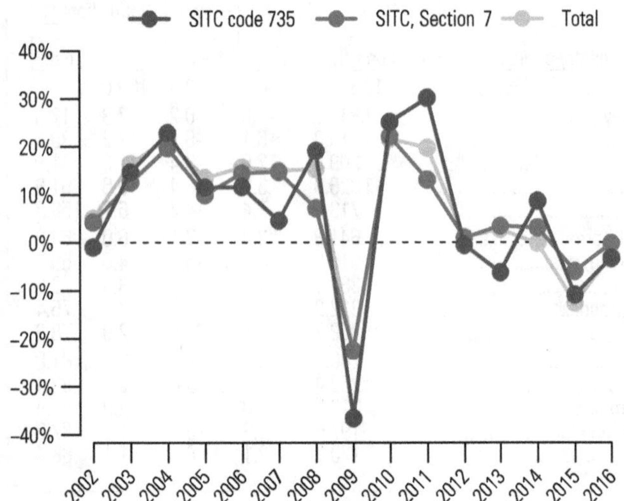

Table 2: Top exporting countries or areas in 2016

Country or area	Value (million US$)	Avg. Growth (%) 12-16	Growth (%) 15-16	World share %	Cum.
World	14824.0	-3.1	-3.2	100.0	
Germany	3039.9	-1.9	0.8	20.5	20.5
USA	1613.7	-2.7	-8.3	10.9	31.4
Japan	1355.0	-10.5	-6.9	9.1	40.5
Switzerland	968.3	-3.0	-5.0	6.5	47.1
Italy	956.6	-2.8	-3.3	6.5	53.5
China	764.6	-4.4	-13.1	5.2	58.7
Other Asia, nes	764.0	0.3	-3.7	5.2	63.8
Netherlands	513.1	-2.2	79.7	3.5	67.3
Rep. of Korea	433.4	0.3	-17.5	2.9	70.2
Belgium	420.2	1.8	-1.0	2.8	73.0
France	398.0	-8.4	3.7	2.7	75.7
Austria	359.3	1.2	17.3	2.4	78.2
Sweden	319.5	-6.5	-10.7	2.2	80.3
United Kingdom	291.6	-7.1	-20.8	2.0	82.3
Spain	286.6	0.4	2.6	1.9	84.2

Graph 2: Trade Balance by MDG regions 2016
(Bln US$)

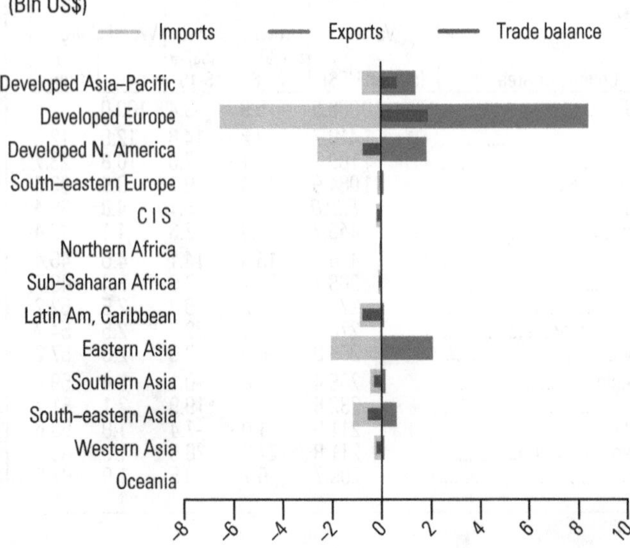

Table 3: Top importing countries or areas in 2016

Country or area	Value (million US$)	Avg. Growth (%) 12-16	Growth (%) 15-16	World share %	Cum.
World	15093.6	-2.4	-1.5	100.0	
USA	2206.8	1.1	-1.7	14.6	14.6
Germany	1461.8	-2.5	-0.4	9.7	24.3
China	1423.8	-8.0	-21.8	9.4	33.7
Japan	663.2	-4.8	-14.8	4.4	38.1
France	649.7	-1.6	13.8	4.3	42.4
Mexico	605.2	3.9	4.9	4.0	46.4
Italy	513.2	0.9	7.0	3.4	49.8
Switzerland	510.7	-3.2	-5.5	3.4	53.2
Netherlands	503.3	-2.0	193.2	3.3	56.6
United Kingdom	441.5	-2.9	-9.9	2.9	59.5
Austria	403.2	3.0	25.6	2.7	62.2
Belgium	377.5	1.9	2.7	2.5	64.7
India	360.1	-3.0	12.1	2.4	67.0
Canada	352.9	-3.2	0.4	2.3	69.4
Spain	304.5	8.6	17.0	2.0	71.4

In 2016, the value (in current US$) of exports of "metalworking machinery and parts thereof, nes" (SITC group 737) decreased by 4.6 percent (compared to -5.0 percent average growth rate from 2012-2016) to reach 17.7 bln US$ (see table 2), while imports decreased by 1.9 percent to reach 19.0 bln US$ (see table 3). Exports of this commodity accounted for 0.3 percent of world exports of SITC section 7, and 0.1 percent of total world merchandise exports (see table 1). Germany, China and Italy were the top exporters in 2016 (see table 2). They accounted for 15.8, 15.3 and 10.8 percent of world exports, respectively. USA, China and Mexico were the top destinations, with respectively 12.4, 8.8 and 6.5 percent of world imports (see table 3).

The top 15 countries/areas accounted for 85.5 and 61.9 percent of total world exports and imports, respectively (see tables 2 and 3). In 2016, Germany was the country/area with the highest value of net exports (+2.0 bln US$), followed by Italy (+1.5 bln US$). By MDG regions (see graph 2), the largest surpluses in this product group were recorded by Developed Europe (+3.7 bln US$), Developed Asia-Pacific (+1.3 bln US$) and Eastern Asia (+1.1 bln US$). The largest trade deficits were recorded by Latin America and the Caribbean (-1.9 bln US$), South-eastern Asia (-1.8 bln US$) and Developed North America (-916.0 mln US$).

Table 1: Imports (Imp.) and exports (Exp.), 2002-2016, in current US$

		2002	2003	2004	2005	2006	2007	2008	2009	2010	2011	2012	2013	2014	2015	2016
Values in Bln US$	Imp.	9.3	11.0	13.9	15.7	18.4	20.5	24.0	19.5	19.7	22.4	22.5	21.2	21.5	19.4	19.0
	Exp.	9.0	10.7	13.8	15.7	18.8	20.8	24.4	18.7	19.7	22.1	21.7	21.7	21.2	18.5	17.7
As a percentage of SITC section (%)	Imp.	0.4	0.4	0.4	0.4	0.4	0.4	0.4	0.5	0.4	0.4	0.4	0.3	0.3	0.3	0.3
	Exp.	0.3	0.4	0.4	0.4	0.4	0.4	0.5	0.4	0.4	0.4	0.4	0.4	0.3	0.3	0.3
As a percentage of world trade (%)	Imp.	0.1	0.1	0.1	0.1	0.2	0.1	0.1	0.2	0.1	0.1	0.1	0.1	0.1	0.1	0.1
	Exp.	0.1	0.1	0.2	0.2	0.2	0.2	0.2	0.2	0.1	0.1	0.1	0.1	0.1	0.1	0.1

Graph 1: Annual growth rates of exports, 2002–2016

(In percentage by year)

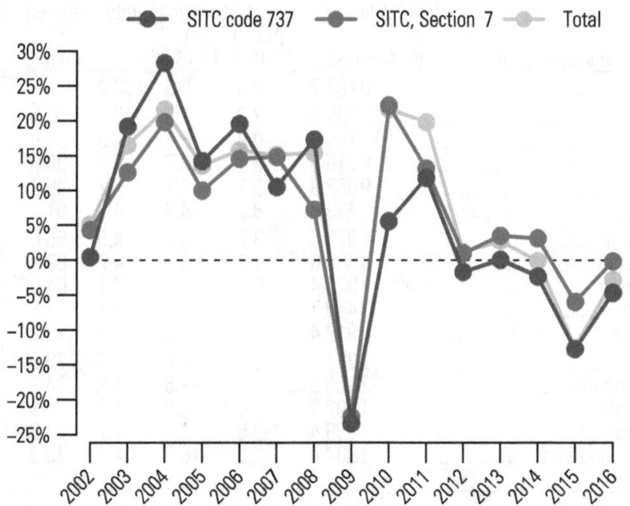

Graph 2: Trade Balance by MDG regions 2016

(Bln US$)

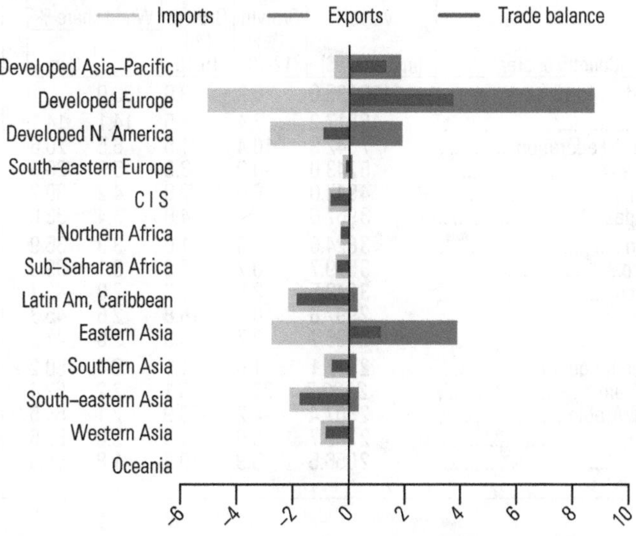

Table 2: Top exporting countries or areas in 2016

Country or area	Value (million US$)	Avg. Growth (%) 12-16	Growth (%) 15-16	World share %	Cum.
World	17680.3	-5.0	-4.6	100.0	
Germany	2800.8	-4.6	-6.0	15.8	15.8
China	2710.1	-4.4	-8.1	15.3	31.2
Italy	1913.0	-1.8	6.0	10.8	42.0
Japan	1797.8	-9.5	4.5	10.2	52.2
USA	1551.7	-7.1	-15.8	8.8	60.9
Rep. of Korea	824.5	8.9	14.8	4.7	65.6
Switzerland	735.4	0.0	-4.3	4.2	69.8
Austria	518.0	-4.2	-7.8	2.9	72.7
France	422.1	-7.2	-10.1	2.4	75.1
Sweden	386.4	-8.2	4.0	2.2	77.3
Canada	338.3	-3.0	-21.8	1.9	79.2
Netherlands	321.2	-6.1	-9.2	1.8	81.0
United Kingdom	286.7	-9.8	-18.4	1.6	82.6
Czechia	260.2	-0.4	5.4	1.5	84.1
India	254.2	3.1	13.9	1.4	85.5

Table 3: Top importing countries or areas in 2016

Country or area	Value (million US$)	Avg. Growth (%) 12-16	Growth (%) 15-16	World share %	Cum.
World	19008.1	-4.1	-1.9	100.0	
USA	2362.8	1.2	-1.0	12.4	12.4
China	1668.0	-10.0	-5.5	8.8	21.2
Mexico	1232.0	8.8	24.7	6.5	27.7
Germany	760.9	-7.0	-4.2	4.0	31.7
Viet Nam	*681.2*	21.4	5.1	3.6	35.3
India	595.3	-17.3	-2.6	3.1	38.4
Indonesia	570.7	9.0	30.1	3.0	41.4
Belgium	566.3	14.1	18.8	3.0	44.4
Russian Federation	566.3	-15.9	-30.7	3.0	47.4
Brazil	526.6	-15.8	15.2	2.8	50.1
Turkey	482.3	3.3	23.3	2.5	52.7
Rep. of Korea	478.9	-10.1	-21.4	2.5	55.2
Canada	441.4	-3.4	-36.6	2.3	57.5
Slovakia	424.9	26.6	142.4	2.2	59.8
France	401.3	-2.4	-6.7	2.1	61.9

Source: UN Comtrade

741 Heating and cooling equipment and parts thereof, nes

In 2016, the value (in current US$) of exports of "heating and cooling equipment and parts thereof, nes" (SITC group 741) increased by 0.5 percent (compared to -0.3 percent average growth rate from 2012-2016) to reach 110.1 bln US$ (see table 2), while imports increased by 3.0 percent to reach 116.7 bln US$ (see table 3). Exports of this commodity accounted for 1.9 percent of world exports of SITC section 7, and 0.7 percent of total world merchandise exports (see table 1). China, USA and Germany were the top exporters in 2016 (see table 2). They accounted for 20.5, 9.3 and 8.8 percent of world exports, respectively. USA, Russian Federation and Germany were the top destinations, with respectively 14.1, 6.5 and 5.3 percent of world imports (see table 3).

The top 15 countries/areas accounted for 79.3 and 58.3 percent of total world exports and imports, respectively (see tables 2 and 3). In 2016, China was the country/area with the highest value of net exports (+17.6 bln US$), followed by Italy (+6.1 bln US$). By MDG regions (see graph 2), the largest surpluses in this product group were recorded by Eastern Asia (+19.5 bln US$) and Developed Europe (+11.8 bln US$). The largest trade deficits were recorded by Commonwealth of Independent States (-9.1 bln US$), Developed North America (-8.5 bln US$) and Western Asia (-7.4 bln US$).

Table 1: Imports (Imp.) and exports (Exp.), 2002-2016, in current US$

		2002	2003	2004	2005	2006	2007	2008	2009	2010	2011	2012	2013	2014	2015	2016
Values in Bln US$	Imp.	43.3	51.4	64.0	70.8	80.7	99.0	114.4	90.4	96.1	113.1	112.5	116.8	120.5	113.4	116.7
	Exp.	42.8	50.6	63.0	68.4	80.3	99.1	112.6	88.2	94.6	111.1	111.3	115.5	117.8	109.5	110.1
As a percentage of SITC section (%)	Imp.	1.7	1.8	1.8	1.8	1.8	2.0	2.1	2.1	1.8	1.9	1.9	1.9	1.9	1.9	1.9
	Exp.	1.7	1.7	1.8	1.8	1.8	2.0	2.1	2.1	1.8	1.9	1.9	1.9	1.9	1.9	1.9
As a percentage of world trade (%)	Imp.	0.7	0.7	0.7	0.7	0.7	0.7	0.7	0.7	0.6	0.6	0.6	0.6	0.6	0.7	0.7
	Exp.	0.7	0.7	0.7	0.7	0.7	0.7	0.7	0.7	0.6	0.6	0.6	0.6	0.6	0.7	0.7

Graph 1: Annual growth rates of exports, 2002–2016

(In percentage by year)

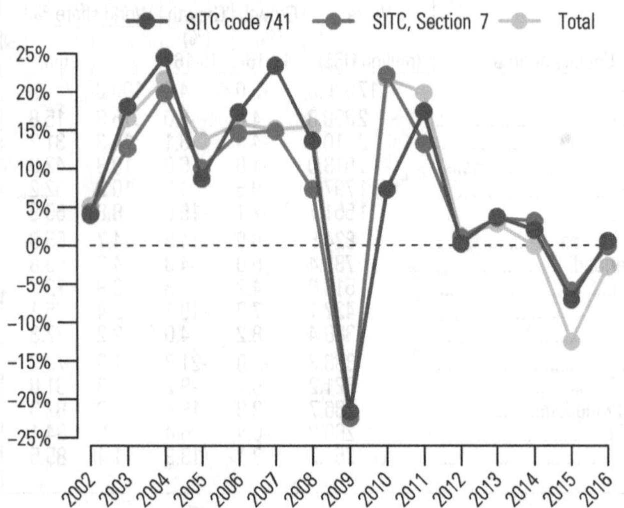

Table 2: Top exporting countries or areas in 2016

Country or area	Value (million US$)	Avg. Growth (%) 12-16	Growth (%) 15-16	World share %	Cum.
World	110107.7	-0.3	0.5	100.0	
China	22585.5	2.9	1.9	20.5	20.5
USA	10189.5	-0.9	-6.6	9.3	29.8
Germany	9718.6	-5.1	-3.7	8.8	38.6
Italy	9063.9	-0.1	4.1	8.2	46.8
Mexico	5439.3	8.3	4.4	4.9	51.8
Thailand	5373.5	3.7	5.2	4.9	56.6
Rep. of Korea	4580.6	-1.4	-6.9	4.2	60.8
Japan	4020.4	-6.9	3.5	3.7	64.5
France	3459.7	-2.7	-2.4	3.1	67.6
Czechia	2918.4	1.5	8.3	2.7	70.2
Belgium	2227.1	0.8	11.0	2.0	72.3
Netherlands	2126.3	-1.0	-3.5	1.9	74.2
Malaysia	1902.3	1.6	2.9	1.7	75.9
Sweden	1838.4	-3.5	3.9	1.7	77.6
United Kingdom	1837.4	-1.0	-16.3	1.7	79.3

Graph 2: Trade Balance by MDG regions 2016

(Bln US$)

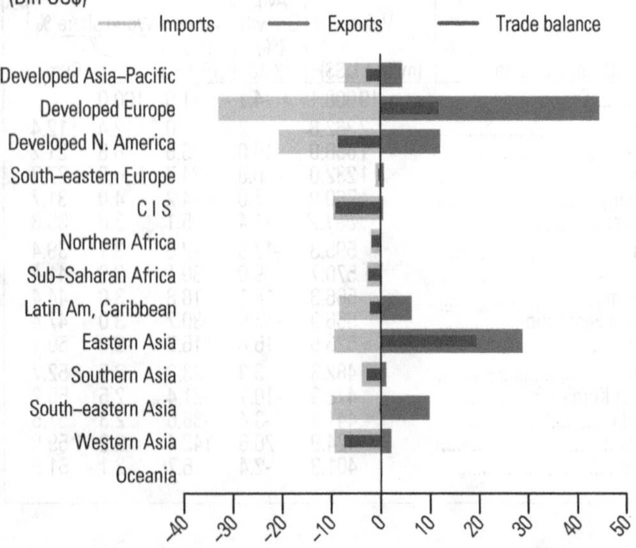

Table 3: Top importing countries or areas in 2016

Country or area	Value (million US$)	Avg. Growth (%) 12-16	Growth (%) 15-16	World share %	Cum.
World	116735.0	0.9	3.0	100.0	
USA	16517.2	7.4	3.5	14.1	14.1
Russian Federation	7542.9	10.4	71.5	6.5	20.6
Germany	6243.0	-0.9	3.8	5.3	26.0
China	4943.0	-8.0	-7.9	4.2	30.2
Canada	3967.0	1.2	-4.8	3.4	33.6
Japan	3824.6	-4.6	-1.0	3.3	36.9
France	3579.7	0.7	5.6	3.1	39.9
Mexico	3242.5	3.6	-2.3	2.8	42.7
Australia	2997.8	6.3	-16.8	2.6	45.3
Italy	2996.7	3.7	19.9	2.6	47.8
United Kingdom	2777.1	1.5	-1.5	2.4	50.2
Viet Nam	*2520.7*	26.4	5.1	2.2	52.4
Saudi Arabia	2507.4	-4.2	-23.9	2.1	54.5
Spain	2380.7	6.9	11.5	2.0	56.6
India	2056.5	-5.9	-10.6	1.8	58.3

In 2016, the value (in current US$) of exports of "pumps for liquids; liquid elevators; parts for such pumps and liquid elevators" (SITC group 742) decreased by 2.9 percent (compared to -1.7 percent average growth rate from 2012-2016) to reach 57.5 bln US$ (see table 2), while imports decreased by 4.6 percent to reach 59.9 bln US$ (see table 3). Exports of this commodity accounted for 1.0 percent of world exports of SITC section 7, and 0.4 percent of total world merchandise exports (see table 1). Germany, USA and China were the top exporters in 2016 (see table 2). They accounted for 16.8, 14.0 and 11.1 percent of world exports, respectively. USA, Germany and China were the top destinations, with respectively 16.0, 7.3 and 6.6 percent of world imports (see table 3).

The top 15 countries/areas accounted for 81.3 and 60.9 percent of total world exports and imports, respectively (see tables 2 and 3). In 2016, Germany was the country/area with the highest value of net exports (+5.2 bln US$), followed by Japan (+2.5 bln US$). By MDG regions (see graph 2), the largest surpluses in this product group were recorded by Developed Europe (+8.4 bln US$), Eastern Asia (+2.4 bln US$) and Developed Asia-Pacific (+1.9 bln US$). The largest trade deficits were recorded by Western Asia (-3.3 bln US$), Developed North America (-2.6 bln US$) and Latin America and the Caribbean (-2.3 bln US$).

Table 1: Imports (Imp.) and exports (Exp.), 2002-2016, in current US$

		2002	2003	2004	2005	2006	2007	2008	2009	2010	2011	2012	2013	2014	2015	2016
Values in Bln US$	Imp.	21.9	26.3	30.8	34.2	38.4	48.5	56.4	45.0	53.8	65.1	65.4	67.3	70.1	62.9	59.9
	Exp.	21.1	25.6	31.2	33.8	38.0	47.0	54.3	43.3	51.1	60.9	61.6	64.3	67.0	59.2	57.5
As a percentage of SITC section (%)	Imp.	0.8	0.9	0.9	0.9	0.9	1.0	1.0	1.1	1.0	1.1	1.1	1.1	1.1	1.0	1.0
	Exp.	0.8	0.9	0.9	0.9	0.9	0.9	1.0	1.0	1.0	1.0	1.0	1.1	1.1	1.0	1.0
As a percentage of world trade (%)	Imp.	0.3	0.3	0.3	0.3	0.3	0.3	0.3	0.4	0.4	0.4	0.4	0.4	0.4	0.4	0.4
	Exp.	0.3	0.3	0.3	0.3	0.3	0.3	0.3	0.3	0.3	0.3	0.3	0.3	0.4	0.4	0.4

Graph 1: Annual growth rates of exports, 2002–2016
(In percentage by year)

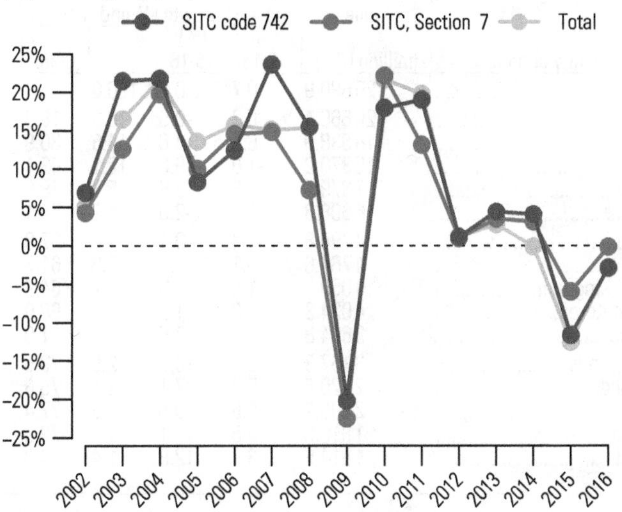

Graph 2: Trade Balance by MDG regions 2016
(Bln US$)

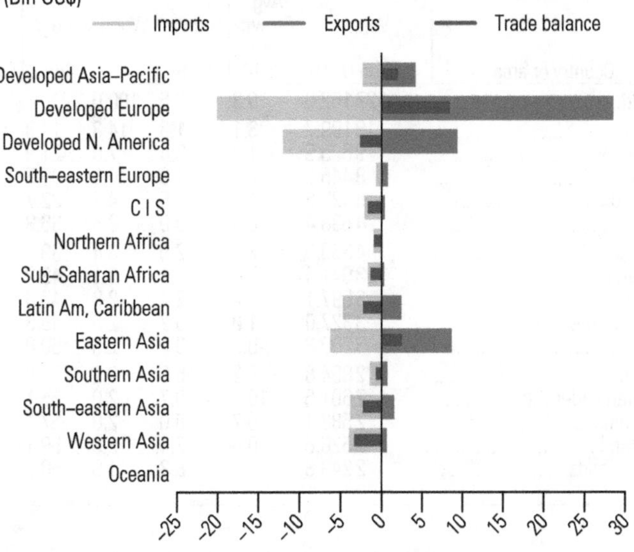

Table 2: Top exporting countries or areas in 2016

Country or area	Value (million US$)	Avg. Growth (%) 12-16	Growth (%) 15-16	World share %	Cum.
World	57503.2	-1.7	-2.9	100.0	
Germany	9643.9	-2.8	-2.2	16.8	16.8
USA	8026.5	-3.9	-11.2	14.0	30.7
China	6387.2	2.4	-2.6	11.1	41.8
Italy	3936.7	-1.0	1.4	6.8	48.7
Japan	3899.8	-5.1	5.1	6.8	55.5
France	2290.9	-1.3	-1.5	4.0	59.4
Czechia	2080.2	6.0	17.4	3.6	63.1
United Kingdom	1948.7	-5.5	-15.5	3.4	66.5
Mexico	1803.3	4.0	-1.3	3.1	69.6
Rep. of Korea	1549.9	3.9	2.7	2.7	72.3
Canada	1341.1	-6.0	-12.0	2.3	74.6
Netherlands	1220.2	-2.1	13.0	2.1	76.7
Denmark	926.8	-4.1	1.5	1.6	78.4
Belgium	887.5	1.3	5.4	1.5	79.9
Austria	794.7	-0.8	-6.1	1.4	81.3

Table 3: Top importing countries or areas in 2016

Country or area	Value (million US$)	Avg. Growth (%) 12-16	Growth (%) 15-16	World share %	Cum.
World	59942.0	-2.1	-4.6	100.0	
USA	9591.8	-1.3	-10.3	16.0	16.0
Germany	4396.7	-1.2	2.5	7.3	23.3
China	3969.0	-1.1	-1.4	6.6	30.0
Canada	2384.0	-7.6	-9.4	4.0	33.9
France	2238.7	-2.6	3.3	3.7	37.7
Mexico	2136.6	0.0	-2.5	3.6	41.2
United Kingdom	2127.4	-0.9	1.0	3.5	44.8
Rep. of Korea	1530.8	-4.6	-18.5	2.6	47.3
Italy	1498.6	0.8	3.2	2.5	49.8
Japan	1421.9	3.5	1.6	2.4	52.2
Russian Federation	1273.9	-11.0	-2.3	2.1	54.3
Belgium	1053.3	0.1	6.0	1.8	56.1
Spain	973.3	4.0	4.1	1.6	57.7
Czechia	963.4	2.6	-0.6	1.6	59.3
Saudi Arabia	945.6	-5.4	-32.8	1.6	60.9

Source: UN Comtrade

743 Pumps (other than liquid), air or other gas compressors and fans, etc; parts

In 2016, the value (in current US$) of exports of "pumps (other than liquid), air or other gas compressors and fans, etc; parts" (SITC group 743) increased by 0.3 percent (compared to 0.7 percent average growth rate from 2012-2016) to reach 126.7 bln US$ (see table 2), while imports decreased by 0.5 percent to reach 127.2 bln US$ (see table 3). Exports of this commodity accounted for 2.2 percent of world exports of SITC section 7, and 0.8 percent of total world merchandise exports (see table 1). Germany, China and USA were the top exporters in 2016 (see table 2). They accounted for 16.3, 14.6 and 12.1 percent of world exports, respectively. USA, Germany and China were the top destinations, with respectively 14.3, 7.6 and 6.6 percent of world imports (see table 3).

The top 15 countries/areas accounted for 80.3 and 60.9 percent of total world exports and imports, respectively (see tables 2 and 3). In 2016, Germany was the country/area with the highest value of net exports (+11.0 bln US$), followed by China (+10.1 bln US$). By MDG regions (see graph 2), the largest surpluses in this product group were recorded by Developed Europe (+14.6 bln US$), Eastern Asia (+10.3 bln US$) and Developed Asia-Pacific (+1.8 bln US$). The largest trade deficits were recorded by Developed North America (-5.7 bln US$), Western Asia (-5.4 bln US$) and Latin America and the Caribbean (-4.5 bln US$).

Table 1: Imports (Imp.) and exports (Exp.), 2002-2016, in current US$

		2002	2003	2004	2005	2006	2007	2008	2009	2010	2011	2012	2013	2014	2015	2016
Values in Bln US$	Imp.	47.4	54.5	66.2	72.3	82.8	98.8	111.5	92.8	107.9	126.3	125.6	133.6	140.6	127.8	127.2
	Exp.	44.5	53.0	65.2	69.4	80.0	96.5	107.1	88.8	105.4	123.7	123.4	131.2	138.9	126.3	126.7
As a percentage of SITC section (%)	Imp.	1.8	1.9	1.9	1.9	1.9	2.0	2.1	2.2	2.1	2.1	2.1	2.2	2.2	2.1	2.1
	Exp.	1.7	1.8	1.9	1.8	1.8	1.9	2.0	2.1	2.1	2.1	2.1	2.2	2.2	2.1	2.2
As a percentage of world trade (%)	Imp.	0.7	0.7	0.7	0.7	0.7	0.7	0.7	0.7	0.7	0.7	0.7	0.7	0.8	0.8	0.8
	Exp.	0.7	0.7	0.7	0.7	0.7	0.7	0.7	0.7	0.7	0.7	0.7	0.7	0.7	0.8	0.8

Graph 1: Annual growth rates of exports, 2002–2016

(In percentage by year)

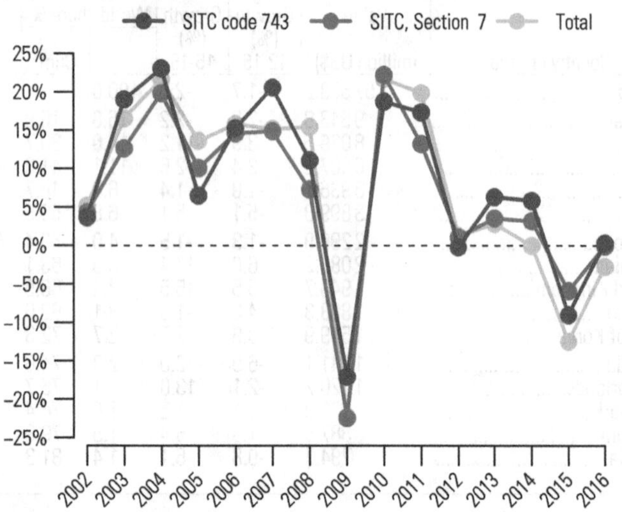

Table 2: Top exporting countries or areas in 2016

Country or area	Value (million US$)	Avg. Growth (%) 12-16	Growth (%) 15-16	World share %	Cum.
World	126 690.9	0.7	0.3	100.0	
Germany	20 666.4	0.2	-0.9	16.3	16.3
China	18 538.9	6.8	4.6	14.6	30.9
USA	15 370.2	-1.0	-9.0	12.1	43.1
Japan	7 379.1	-4.6	9.8	5.8	48.9
Italy	6 608.3	-1.0	-2.9	5.2	54.1
France	4 790.8	-2.4	-0.1	3.8	57.9
Mexico	4 764.6	5.1	0.6	3.8	61.7
United Kingdom	4 059.1	1.9	2.3	3.2	64.9
Rep. of Korea	4 024.3	5.8	1.2	3.2	68.0
Belgium	3 694.8	-3.7	2.5	2.9	71.0
Netherlands	3 167.3	2.6	16.7	2.5	73.5
Thailand	2 720.6	5.2	7.1	2.1	75.6
Czechia	2 298.7	5.6	10.6	1.8	77.4
Austria	1 818.5	6.6	16.1	1.4	78.9
Poland	1 814.9	3.9	12.8	1.4	80.3

Graph 2: Trade Balance by MDG regions 2016

(Bln US$)

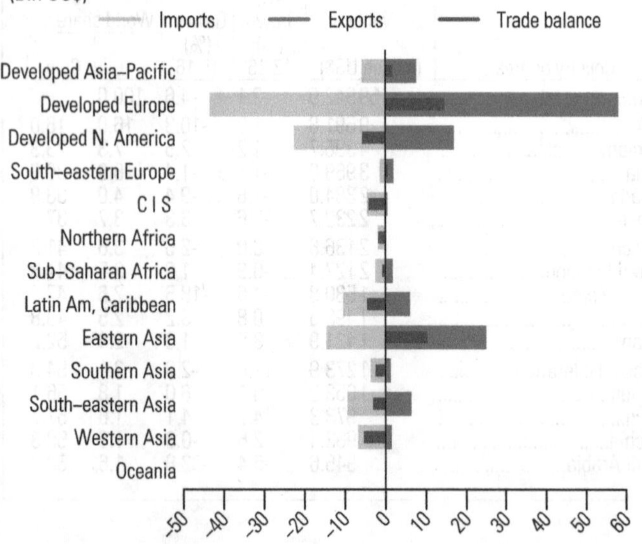

Table 3: Top importing countries or areas in 2016

Country or area	Value (million US$)	Avg. Growth (%) 12-16	Growth (%) 15-16	World share %	Cum.
World	127 152.0	0.3	-0.5	100.0	
USA	18 199.7	3.1	-1.3	14.3	14.3
Germany	9 625.5	1.7	3.4	7.6	21.9
China	8 445.6	-2.1	-4.6	6.6	28.5
Mexico	5 335.6	1.1	-2.6	4.2	32.7
France	4 538.4	-0.8	3.0	3.6	36.3
Canada	4 359.9	2.7	2.9	3.4	39.7
United Kingdom	3 941.4	3.9	-1.1	3.1	42.8
Japan	3 597.1	-3.4	2.4	2.8	45.6
Rep. of Korea	3 327.0	1.0	-5.2	2.6	48.3
Italy	3 200.8	-0.3	3.2	2.5	50.8
Spain	2 854.8	9.2	5.9	2.2	53.0
Russian Federation	2 601.5	-10.4	0.7	2.0	55.1
Belgium	2 588.1	-0.7	8.0	2.0	57.1
Thailand	2 528.6	0.8	7.4	2.0	59.1
Netherlands	2 249.8	-1.2	8.3	1.8	60.9

In 2016, the value (in current US$) of exports of "mechanical handling equipment and parts thereof, nes" (SITC group 744) decreased by 3.9 percent (compared to -1.2 percent average growth rate from 2012-2016) to reach 79.7 bln US$ (see table 2), while imports decreased by 4.8 percent to reach 81.0 bln US$ (see table 3). Exports of this commodity accounted for 1.4 percent of world exports of SITC section 7, and 0.5 percent of total world merchandise exports (see table 1). China, Germany and USA were the top exporters in 2016 (see table 2). They accounted for 17.7, 14.6 and 8.7 percent of world exports, respectively. USA, Germany and China were the top destinations, with respectively 14.4, 5.4 and 4.7 percent of world imports (see table 3).

The top 15 countries/areas accounted for 82.1 and 57.5 percent of total world exports and imports, respectively (see tables 2 and 3). In 2016, China was the country/area with the highest value of net exports (+10.3 bln US$), followed by Germany (+7.3 bln US$). By MDG regions (see graph 2), the largest surpluses in this product group were recorded by Developed Europe (+13.9 bln US$), Eastern Asia (+10.3 bln US$) and Developed Asia-Pacific (+1.2 bln US$). The largest trade deficits were recorded by Developed North America (-5.2 bln US$), South-eastern Asia (-5.0 bln US$) and Western Asia (-4.4 bln US$).

Table 1: Imports (Imp.) and exports (Exp.), 2002-2016, in current US$

		2002	2003	2004	2005	2006	2007	2008	2009	2010	2011	2012	2013	2014	2015	2016
Values in Bln US$	Imp.	28.8	33.7	42.1	51.4	60.8	74.7	88.4	60.2	62.9	78.7	83.8	87.6	91.6	85.1	81.0
	Exp.	30.1	34.9	44.3	52.1	62.3	77.4	92.0	62.8	65.1	80.4	83.6	86.8	90.1	83.0	79.7
As a percentage of SITC section (%)	Imp.	1.1	1.2	1.2	1.3	1.4	1.5	1.6	1.4	1.2	1.3	1.4	1.4	1.4	1.4	1.3
	Exp.	1.2	1.2	1.3	1.4	1.4	1.5	1.7	1.5	1.3	1.4	1.4	1.4	1.4	1.4	1.4
As a percentage of world trade (%)	Imp.	0.4	0.4	0.4	0.5	0.5	0.5	0.5	0.5	0.4	0.4	0.5	0.5	0.5	0.5	0.5
	Exp.	0.5	0.5	0.5	0.5	0.5	0.6	0.6	0.5	0.4	0.4	0.5	0.5	0.5	0.5	0.5

Graph 1: Annual growth rates of exports, 2002–2016
(In percentage by year)

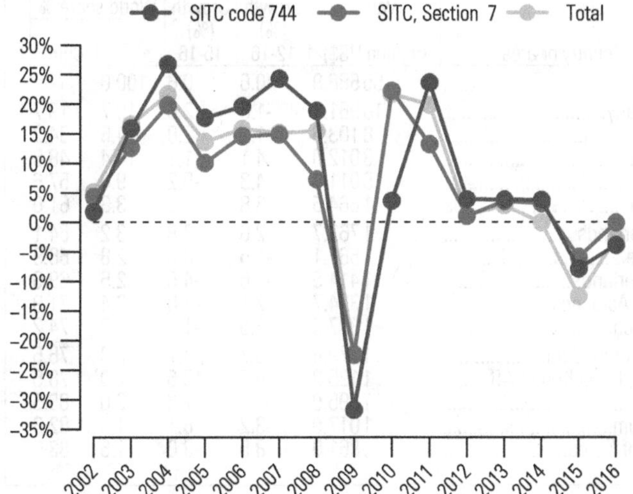

Table 2: Top exporting countries or areas in 2016

Country or area	Value (million US$)	Avg. Growth (%) 12-16	Growth (%) 15-16	World share %	Cum.
World	79746.2	-1.2	-3.9	100.0	
China	14117.6	5.0	-0.4	17.7	17.7
Germany	11676.7	-3.0	-3.2	14.6	32.3
USA	6927.8	-6.5	-18.0	8.7	41.0
Italy	5916.9	1.2	1.3	7.4	48.5
Japan	3929.4	-5.7	-9.0	4.9	53.4
France	3508.4	-1.0	-2.2	4.4	57.8
Netherlands	2977.0	-1.6	-1.4	3.7	61.5
Canada	2475.4	0.4	-6.4	3.1	64.6
United Kingdom	2411.8	-3.2	-13.1	3.0	67.6
Austria	2400.3	0.2	11.5	3.0	70.7
Spain	2184.0	0.1	3.5	2.7	73.4
Sweden	2177.9	-4.7	-0.8	2.7	76.1
Rep. of Korea	2081.3	-1.0	-9.5	2.6	78.7
Belgium	1491.5	-1.3	-6.3	1.9	80.6
Czechia	1219.2	4.1	13.3	1.5	82.1

Graph 2: Trade Balance by MDG regions 2016
(Bln US$)

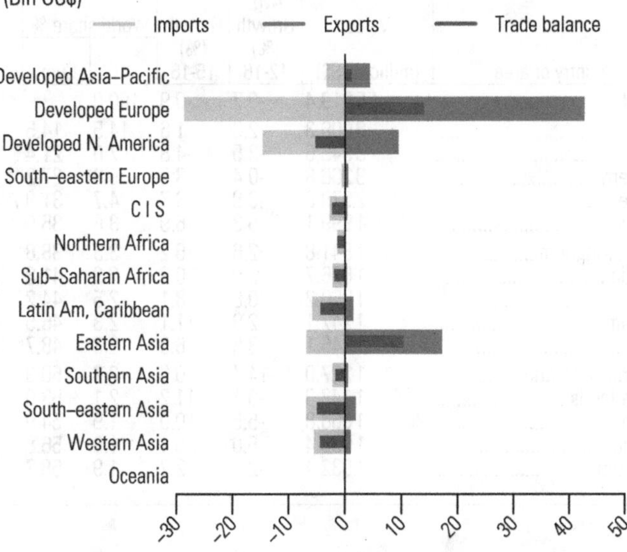

Table 3: Top importing countries or areas in 2016

Country or area	Value (million US$)	Avg. Growth (%) 12-16	Growth (%) 15-16	World share %	Cum.
World	80997.0	-0.8	-4.8	100.0	
USA	11677.6	4.3	-2.4	14.4	14.4
Germany	4371.0	-1.2	4.8	5.4	19.8
China	3797.9	-4.7	-27.4	4.7	24.5
France	3638.6	0.9	9.8	4.5	29.0
United Kingdom	3206.4	4.8	-0.9	4.0	33.0
Canada	2932.8	-3.9	-7.0	3.6	36.6
Netherlands	2403.3	-0.2	-17.7	3.0	39.5
Mexico	2143.9	5.6	-9.9	2.6	42.2
Belgium	2060.9	1.3	13.3	2.5	44.7
Italy	1927.3	5.7	13.0	2.4	47.1
Russian Federation	1871.0	-15.0	-1.8	2.3	49.4
Australia	1795.7	-9.1	-4.4	2.2	51.6
Rep. of Korea	1645.2	-2.8	-20.7	2.0	53.7
Singapore	1615.5	-5.6	-5.0	2.0	55.7
Turkey	1492.9	7.5	-2.7	1.8	57.5

745 Non-electrical machinery, tools and mechanical apparatus, parts thereof, nes

In 2016, the value (in current US$) of exports of "non-electrical machinery, tools and mechanical apparatus, parts thereof, nes" (SITC group 745) increased by 0.6 percent (compared to -0.6 percent average growth rate from 2012-2016) to reach 55.7 bln US$ (see table 2), while imports decreased by 0.9 percent to reach 55.3 bln US$ (see table 3). Exports of this commodity accounted for 0.9 percent of world exports of SITC section 7, and 0.3 percent of total world merchandise exports (see table 1). Germany, Italy and China were the top exporters in 2016 (see table 2). They accounted for 19.7, 14.6 and 14.4 percent of world exports, respectively. USA, China and Germany were the top destinations, with respectively 14.5, 7.0 and 5.8 percent of world imports (see table 3).

The top 15 countries/areas accounted for 83.9 and 58.7 percent of total world exports and imports, respectively (see tables 2 and 3). In 2016, Germany was the country/area with the highest value of net exports (+7.8 bln US$), followed by Italy (+6.7 bln US$). By MDG regions (see graph 2), the largest surpluses in this product group were recorded by Developed Europe (+12.4 bln US$) and Eastern Asia (+5.5 bln US$). The largest trade deficits were recorded by Developed North America (-3.8 bln US$), Latin America and the Caribbean (-3.5 bln US$) and South-eastern Asia (-2.5 bln US$).

Table 1: Imports (Imp.) and exports (Exp.), 2002-2016, in current US$

		2002	2003	2004	2005	2006	2007	2008	2009	2010	2011	2012	2013	2014	2015	2016
Values in Bln US$	Imp.	25.0	29.5	34.9	38.2	42.1	47.7	53.1	41.8	47.4	57.2	56.9	60.0	61.5	55.8	55.3
	Exp.	25.8	30.0	36.9	39.5	44.0	50.6	56.0	42.7	47.4	56.3	57.0	60.3	61.2	55.3	55.7
As a percentage of SITC section (%)	Imp.	1.0	1.0	1.0	1.0	1.0	0.9	1.0	1.0	0.9	1.0	0.9	1.0	1.0	0.9	0.9
	Exp.	1.0	1.0	1.1	1.0	1.0	1.0	1.0	1.0	0.9	1.0	1.0	1.0	1.0	0.9	0.9
As a percentage of world trade (%)	Imp.	0.4	0.4	0.4	0.4	0.3	0.3	0.3	0.3	0.3	0.3	0.3	0.3	0.3	0.3	0.3
	Exp.	0.4	0.4	0.4	0.4	0.4	0.4	0.4	0.3	0.3	0.3	0.3	0.3	0.3	0.3	0.3

Graph 1: Annual growth rates of exports, 2002–2016

(In percentage by year)

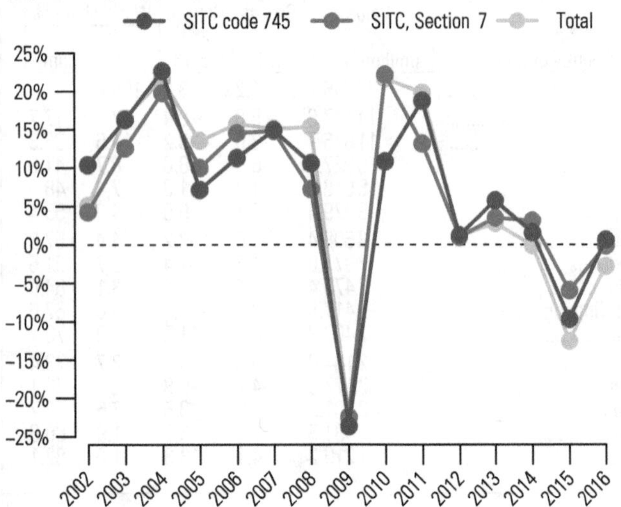

Graph 2: Trade Balance by MDG regions 2016

(Bln US$)

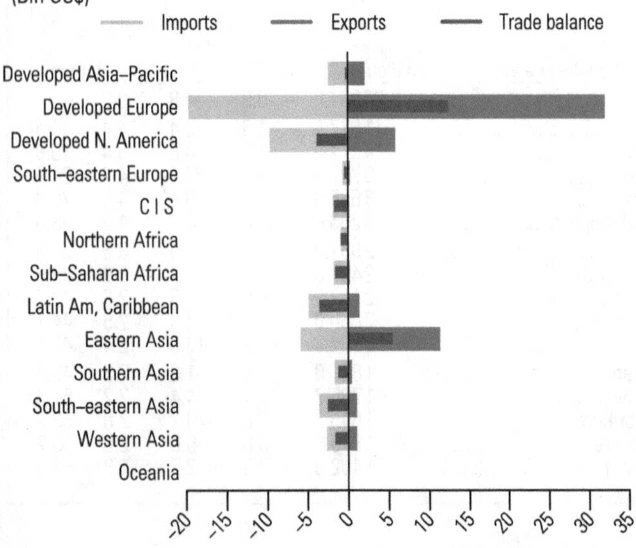

Table 2: Top exporting countries or areas in 2016

Country or area	Value (million US$)	Avg. Growth (%) 12-16	Growth (%) 15-16	World share %	Cum.
World	55 688.9	-0.6	0.6	100.0	
Germany	10 961.1	-1.6	2.6	19.7	19.7
Italy	8 103.6	-1.2	2.0	14.6	34.2
China	8 012.0	4.1	-1.1	14.4	48.6
USA	5 011.9	-4.3	-5.2	9.0	57.6
Japan	1 864.5	-3.8	7.5	3.3	61.0
Netherlands	1 762.7	2.0	-3.8	3.2	64.1
France	1 561.1	-1.6	8.8	2.8	66.9
Switzerland	1 414.5	-2.6	-4.5	2.5	69.5
Other Asia, nes	1 324.7	2.1	-1.8	2.4	71.9
Sweden	1 307.9	-3.5	-1.7	2.3	74.2
United Kingdom	1 279.4	-0.7	-4.7	2.3	76.5
China, Hong Kong SAR	1 125.3	6.6	13.5	2.0	78.5
Spain	1 095.0	-1.3	7.6	2.0	80.5
Belgium	1 017.9	-3.2	6.1	1.8	82.3
Rep. of Korea	861.0	8.5	-3.0	1.5	83.9

Table 3: Top importing countries or areas in 2016

Country or area	Value (million US$)	Avg. Growth (%) 12-16	Growth (%) 15-16	World share %	Cum.
World	55 319.4	-0.7	-0.9	100.0	
USA	8 006.3	2.3	1.6	14.5	14.5
China	3 845.6	-3.5	-4.8	7.0	21.4
Germany	3 206.8	-0.4	3.5	5.8	27.2
France	2 578.6	-0.8	3.7	4.7	31.9
Mexico	1 999.1	5.3	-6.9	3.6	35.5
United Kingdom	1 841.8	2.6	-6.2	3.3	38.8
Canada	1 626.7	-2.9	0.3	2.9	41.8
Italy	1 360.2	0.8	8.1	2.5	44.2
Belgium	1 247.1	-2.9	11.1	2.3	46.5
Spain	1 245.1	3.5	6.9	2.3	48.7
Russian Federation	1 227.0	-14.4	0.0	2.2	50.9
Netherlands	1 142.3	-0.1	-11.2	2.1	53.0
Japan	1 066.8	-5.5	0.0	1.9	54.9
Austria	1 038.4	5.0	25.1	1.9	56.8
Australia	1 032.4	-2.7	-2.2	1.9	58.7

In 2016, the value (in current US$) of exports of "ball or roller bearings" (SITC group 746) decreased by 2.3 percent (compared to -2.9 percent average growth rate from 2012-2016) to reach 29.3 bln US$ (see table 2), while imports decreased by 3.4 percent to reach 29.6 bln US$ (see table 3). Exports of this commodity accounted for 0.5 percent of world exports of SITC section 7, and 0.2 percent of total world merchandise exports (see table 1). China, Germany and Japan were the top exporters in 2016 (see table 2). They accounted for 15.6, 15.0 and 13.2 percent of world exports, respectively. Germany, China and USA were the top destinations, with respectively 12.9, 10.8 and 9.3 percent of world imports (see table 3).

The top 15 countries/areas accounted for 83.6 and 69.2 percent of total world exports and imports, respectively (see tables 2 and 3). In 2016, Japan was the country/area with the highest value of net exports (+3.3 bln US$), followed by China (+1.4 bln US$). By MDG regions (see graph 2), the largest surpluses in this product group were recorded by Developed Asia-Pacific (+3.0 bln US$), Eastern Asia (+1.2 bln US$) and Developed Europe (+704.2 mln US$). The largest trade deficits were recorded by Latin America and the Caribbean (-1.9 bln US$), Developed North America (-1.0 bln US$) and Southern Asia (-711.0 mln US$).

Table 1: Imports (Imp.) and exports (Exp.), 2002-2016, in current US$

		2002	2003	2004	2005	2006	2007	2008	2009	2010	2011	2012	2013	2014	2015	2016
Values in Bln US$	Imp.	13.0	15.5	18.5	20.7	22.9	26.9	31.8	23.6	30.3	36.2	33.9	33.4	34.6	30.6	29.6
	Exp.	12.5	14.8	17.6	19.7	21.9	26.0	30.9	22.0	29.4	35.6	32.9	33.0	34.3	30.0	29.3
As a percentage of SITC section (%)	Imp.	0.5	0.5	0.5	0.5	0.5	0.5	0.6	0.6	0.6	0.6	0.6	0.5	0.5	0.5	0.5
	Exp.	0.5	0.5	0.5	0.5	0.5	0.5	0.6	0.5	0.6	0.6	0.6	0.5	0.5	0.5	0.5
As a percentage of world trade (%)	Imp.	0.2	0.2	0.2	0.2	0.2	0.2	0.2	0.2	0.2	0.2	0.2	0.2	0.2	0.2	0.2
	Exp.	0.2	0.2	0.2	0.2	0.2	0.2	0.2	0.2	0.2	0.2	0.2	0.2	0.2	0.2	0.2

Graph 1: Annual growth rates of exports, 2002–2016
(In percentage by year)

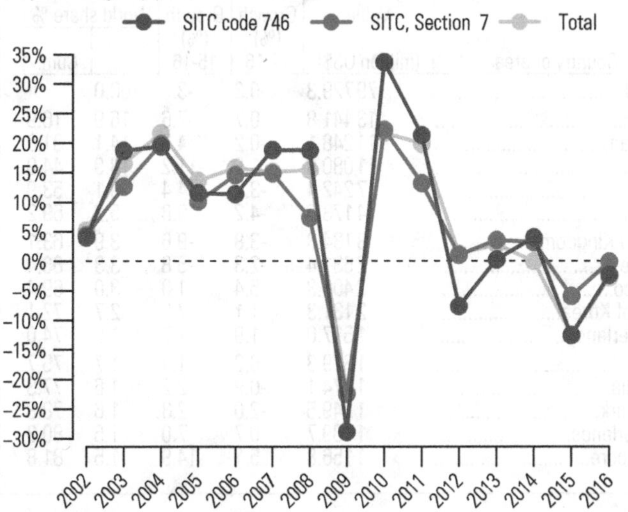

Table 2: Top exporting countries or areas in 2016

Country or area	Value (million US$)	Avg. Growth (%) 12-16	Growth (%) 15-16	World share %	Cum.
World	29315.0	-2.9	-2.3	100.0	
China	4564.5	2.1	-2.7	15.6	15.6
Germany	4399.6	-3.1	-1.0	15.0	30.6
Japan	3883.9	-6.5	-2.3	13.2	43.8
USA	2180.6	-1.1	-5.4	7.4	51.3
France	1654.9	-3.6	-6.0	5.6	56.9
Italy	1242.7	-2.8	-0.7	4.2	61.1
Singapore	1066.9	-7.5	-3.7	3.6	64.8
Netherlands	868.9	3.4	19.7	3.0	67.8
Rep. of Korea	862.6	11.3	12.6	2.9	70.7
Romania	754.7	1.5	1.9	2.6	73.3
Slovakia	726.6	-1.2	3.1	2.5	75.7
Belgium	684.4	-6.8	-12.6	2.3	78.1
Austria	610.1	-2.0	6.1	2.1	80.2
United Kingdom	508.7	-8.1	-14.3	1.7	81.9
Sweden	487.1	-13.6	-18.4	1.7	83.6

Graph 2: Trade Balance by MDG regions 2016
(Bln US$)

Imports — Exports — Trade balance

Developed Asia-Pacific
Developed Europe
Developed N. America
South-eastern Europe
CIS
Northern Africa
Sub-Saharan Africa
Latin Am, Caribbean
Eastern Asia
Southern Asia
South-eastern Asia
Western Asia
Oceania

-12 -10 -8 -6 -4 -2 0 2 4 6 8 10 12 14

Table 3: Top importing countries or areas in 2016

Country or area	Value (million US$)	Avg. Growth (%) 12-16	Growth (%) 15-16	World share %	Cum.
World	29571.1	-3.4	-3.4	100.0	
Germany	3829.2	-2.1	-0.8	12.9	12.9
China	3180.8	-1.5	-5.4	10.8	23.7
USA	2746.0	-3.7	-10.4	9.3	33.0
France	1506.9	-0.2	1.7	5.1	38.1
Mexico	1258.7	4.4	1.8	4.3	42.3
Italy	1149.1	-1.0	1.2	3.9	46.2
Rep. of Korea	976.6	-2.2	-0.4	3.3	49.5
Singapore	921.1	-9.0	-4.3	3.1	52.6
India	890.6	-1.4	2.7	3.0	55.7
Canada	772.4	-6.5	-10.2	2.6	58.3
Belgium	751.9	-7.1	-11.3	2.5	60.8
Netherlands	702.4	-0.1	12.8	2.4	63.2
Japan	626.9	-3.1	-4.8	2.1	65.3
Thailand	620.3	-6.5	-1.4	2.1	67.4
Brazil	536.3	-9.7	-10.7	1.8	69.2

747 Taps, cocks, valves, etc; pressure-reducing, thermostatically control valves

In 2016, the value (in current US$) of exports of "taps, cocks, valves, etc; pressure-reducing, thermostatically control valves" (SITC group 747) decreased by 3.5 percent (compared to -0.3 percent average growth rate from 2012-2016) to reach 79.7 bln US$ (see table 2), while imports decreased by 3.2 percent to reach 83.6 bln US$ (see table 3). Exports of this commodity accounted for 1.4 percent of world exports of SITC section 7, and 0.5 percent of total world merchandise exports (see table 1). China, Germany and USA were the top exporters in 2016 (see table 2). They accounted for 16.9, 14.1 and 13.9 percent of world exports, respectively. USA, China and Germany were the top destinations, with respectively 16.5, 8.3 and 6.6 percent of world imports (see table 3).

The top 15 countries/areas accounted for 81.8 and 63.7 percent of total world exports and imports, respectively (see tables 2 and 3). In 2016, China was the country/area with the highest value of net exports (+6.5 bln US$), followed by Germany (+5.7 bln US$). By MDG regions (see graph 2), the largest surpluses in this product group were recorded by Developed Europe (+10.7 bln US$), Eastern Asia (+6.5 bln US$) and Developed Asia-Pacific (+766.6 mln US$). The largest trade deficits were recorded by Western Asia (-5.0 bln US$), Developed North America (-4.7 bln US$) and Commonwealth of Independent States (-2.6 bln US$).

Table 1: Imports (Imp.) and exports (Exp.), 2002-2016, in current US$

		2002	2003	2004	2005	2006	2007	2008	2009	2010	2011	2012	2013	2014	2015	2016
Values in Bln US$	Imp.	27.9	33.0	40.4	44.0	54.1	64.4	73.9	59.8	68.5	80.9	85.8	89.9	94.7	86.4	83.6
	Exp.	25.4	29.9	36.4	40.8	50.0	62.3	70.7	56.9	65.2	77.1	80.8	86.5	90.9	82.6	79.7
As a percentage of SITC section (%)	Imp.	1.1	1.1	1.1	1.1	1.2	1.3	1.4	1.4	1.3	1.4	1.4	1.4	1.5	1.4	1.4
	Exp.	1.0	1.0	1.0	1.1	1.1	1.2	1.3	1.4	1.3	1.3	1.4	1.4	1.5	1.4	1.4
As a percentage of world trade (%)	Imp.	0.4	0.4	0.4	0.4	0.4	0.5	0.5	0.5	0.4	0.4	0.5	0.5	0.5	0.5	0.5
	Exp.	0.4	0.4	0.4	0.4	0.4	0.5	0.4	0.5	0.4	0.4	0.4	0.5	0.5	0.5	0.5

Graph 1: Annual growth rates of exports, 2002–2016
(In percentage by year)

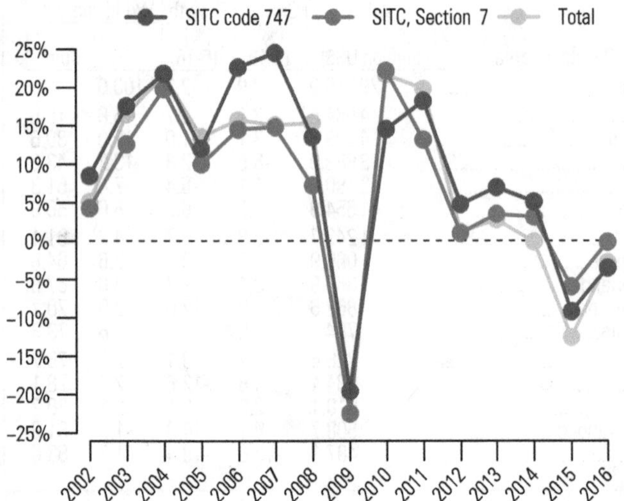

Graph 2: Trade Balance by MDG regions 2016
(Bln US$)

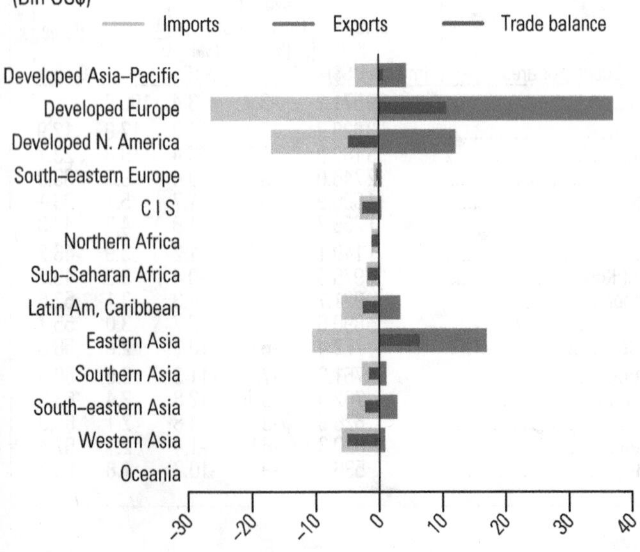

Table 2: Top exporting countries or areas in 2016

Country or area	Value (million US$)	Avg. Growth (%) 12-16	Growth (%) 15-16	World share %	Cum.
World	79729.3	-0.3	-3.5	100.0	
China	13441.8	0.7	-7.6	16.9	16.9
Germany	11248.1	-0.2	4.3	14.1	31.0
USA	11080.8	1.6	-11.2	13.9	44.9
Italy	7242.4	-3.2	-4.4	9.1	53.9
Japan	4173.6	-4.2	9.8	5.2	59.2
United Kingdom	3134.3	-3.8	-9.6	3.9	63.1
France	2631.4	-2.3	-5.8	3.3	66.4
Mexico	2406.3	5.4	-1.0	3.0	69.4
Rep. of Korea	2131.3	1.1	7.0	2.7	72.1
Switzerland	1517.0	1.9	7.7	1.9	74.0
Spain	1329.3	-0.2	1.4	1.7	75.7
Czechia	1274.1	-0.9	-2.2	1.6	77.3
Denmark	1249.5	-2.0	2.3	1.6	78.8
Netherlands	1189.7	0.7	7.0	1.5	80.3
Singapore	1156.8	5.1	-14.9	1.5	81.8

Table 3: Top importing countries or areas in 2016

Country or area	Value (million US$)	Avg. Growth (%) 12-16	Growth (%) 15-16	World share %	Cum.
World	83616.1	-0.6	-3.2	100.0	
USA	13772.1	0.6	-9.7	16.5	16.5
China	6973.8	-0.8	-2.8	8.3	24.8
Germany	5560.0	-0.1	4.4	6.6	31.5
United Kingdom	3206.0	0.4	-3.6	3.8	35.3
Mexico	3062.7	2.3	-5.7	3.7	39.0
Canada	3053.4	-4.3	-12.4	3.7	42.6
France	2961.7	-0.5	2.1	3.5	46.2
Rep. of Korea	2327.8	0.9	-7.6	2.8	48.9
Japan	2222.1	0.0	3.2	2.7	51.6
India	2126.4	15.4	86.2	2.5	54.1
Italy	1929.5	-0.8	1.7	2.3	56.4
Saudi Arabia	1625.6	-0.3	-11.4	1.9	58.4
Russian Federation	1586.0	-14.6	3.9	1.9	60.3
United Arab Emirates	1470.8	-9.1	-27.6	1.8	62.0
Netherlands	1385.3	1.1	-2.5	1.7	63.7

In 2016, the value (in current US$) of exports of "transmission shafts (camshafts, crankshafts) and cranks; parts thereof" (SITC group 748) decreased by 2.4 percent (compared to -0.8 percent average growth rate from 2012-2016) to reach 53.4 bln US$ (see table 2), while imports decreased by 2.9 percent to reach 56.4 bln US$ (see table 3). Exports of this commodity accounted for 0.9 percent of world exports of SITC section 7, and 0.3 percent of total world merchandise exports (see table 1). Germany, China and USA were the top exporters in 2016 (see table 2). They accounted for 21.0, 13.1 and 11.4 percent of world exports, respectively. USA, Germany and China were the top destinations, with respectively 15.1, 9.3 and 8.4 percent of world imports (see table 3).

The top 15 countries/areas accounted for 83.5 and 69.7 percent of total world exports and imports, respectively (see tables 2 and 3). In 2016, Germany was the country/area with the highest value of net exports (+6.0 bln US$), followed by Japan (+3.4 bln US$). By MDG regions (see graph 2), the largest surpluses in this product group were recorded by Developed Europe (+5.8 bln US$), Eastern Asia (+3.4 bln US$) and Developed Asia-Pacific (+2.9 bln US$). The largest trade deficits were recorded by Developed North America (-4.9 bln US$), Latin America and the Caribbean (-4.2 bln US$) and South-eastern Asia (-1.9 bln US$).

Table 1: Imports (Imp.) and exports (Exp.), 2002-2016, in current US$

		2002	2003	2004	2005	2006	2007	2008	2009	2010	2011	2012	2013	2014	2015	2016
Values in Bln US$	Imp.	19.1	22.3	27.4	31.1	35.1	43.1	51.9	38.7	46.9	57.9	57.6	57.8	63.0	58.0	56.4
	Exp.	17.7	20.7	25.4	29.6	33.6	40.4	48.3	36.7	44.5	54.8	55.1	56.2	60.5	54.7	53.4
As a percentage of SITC section (%)	Imp.	0.7	0.8	0.8	0.8	0.8	0.9	1.0	0.9	0.9	1.0	1.0	0.9	1.0	1.0	0.9
	Exp.	0.7	0.7	0.7	0.8	0.8	0.8	0.9	0.9	0.9	0.9	0.9	0.9	1.0	0.9	0.9
As a percentage of world trade (%)	Imp.	0.3	0.3	0.3	0.3	0.3	0.3	0.3	0.3	0.3	0.3	0.3	0.3	0.3	0.4	0.3
	Exp.	0.3	0.3	0.3	0.3	0.3	0.3	0.3	0.3	0.3	0.3	0.3	0.3	0.3	0.3	0.3

Graph 1: Annual growth rates of exports, 2002–2016
(In percentage by year)

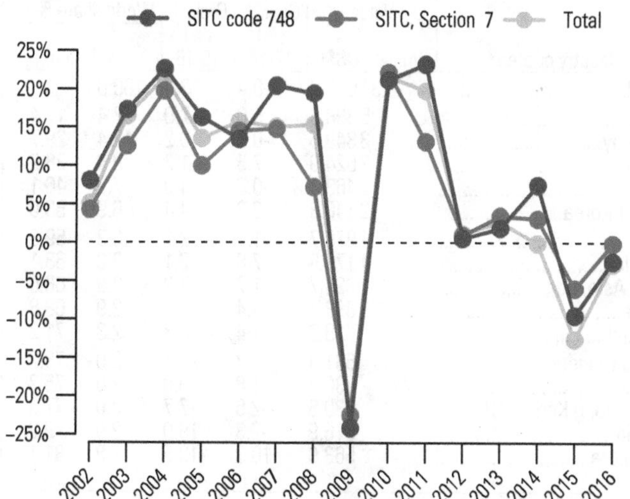

Graph 2: Trade Balance by MDG regions 2016
(Bln US$)

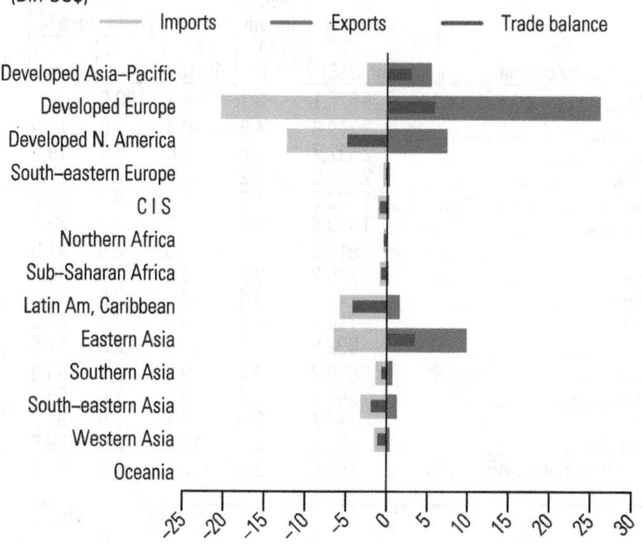

Table 2: Top exporting countries or areas in 2016

Country or area	Value (million US$)	Avg. Growth (%) 12-16	Growth (%) 15-16	World share %	Cum.
World	53415.4	-0.8	-2.4	100.0	
Germany	11216.0	-2.5	-0.1	21.0	21.0
China	7002.8	3.6	-3.7	13.1	34.1
USA	6068.5	2.4	-12.3	11.4	45.5
Japan	5252.4	-6.7	4.4	9.8	55.3
Italy	2990.7	-2.6	-0.3	5.6	60.9
France	1895.6	-1.3	1.1	3.5	64.4
Rep. of Korea	1495.5	6.6	6.9	2.8	67.2
Belgium	1492.3	-2.1	10.0	2.8	70.0
Canada	1304.3	1.9	-6.7	2.4	72.5
Other Asia, nes	1169.6	2.2	-2.7	2.2	74.7
United Kingdom	1043.8	-1.8	-7.8	2.0	76.6
Mexico	1030.1	4.0	2.2	1.9	78.6
Slovakia	1021.5	-0.3	8.3	1.9	80.5
Spain	830.3	-7.0	-7.0	1.6	82.0
Poland	803.3	7.0	8.6	1.5	83.5

Table 3: Top importing countries or areas in 2016

Country or area	Value (million US$)	Avg. Growth (%) 12-16	Growth (%) 15-16	World share %	Cum.
World	56362.1	-0.5	-2.9	100.0	
USA	8490.3	-0.6	-7.9	15.1	15.1
Germany	5223.2	0.6	0.7	9.3	24.3
China	4736.6	-3.4	-10.5	8.4	32.7
Canada	3830.6	13.1	-9.6	6.8	39.5
Mexico	3283.1	6.7	2.1	5.8	45.4
France	1953.4	-1.0	4.4	3.5	48.8
Japan	1847.2	0.0	-0.5	3.3	52.1
United Kingdom	1571.5	-1.2	-6.1	2.8	54.9
Italy	1528.5	0.3	1.0	2.7	57.6
Brazil	1258.2	-7.0	-11.0	2.2	59.8
Austria	1243.1	3.4	23.0	2.2	62.0
Rep. of Korea	1134.4	-7.6	-9.7	2.0	64.1
Hungary	1069.8	0.8	-3.6	1.9	65.9
India	1049.0	1.4	9.8	1.9	67.8
Thailand	1046.9	-4.1	2.4	1.9	69.7

Source: UN Comtrade

749 Non-electric parts and accessories of machinery, nes

In 2016, the value (in current US$) of exports of "non-electric parts and accessories of machinery, nes" (SITC group 749) decreased by 3.3 percent (compared to -0.4 percent average growth rate from 2012-2016) to reach 31.1 bln US$ (see table 2), while imports decreased by 4.1 percent to reach 29.5 bln US$ (see table 3). Exports of this commodity accounted for 0.5 percent of world exports of SITC section 7, and 0.2 percent of total world merchandise exports (see table 1). China, Germany and Japan were the top exporters in 2016 (see table 2). They accounted for 17.4, 12.4 and 8.4 percent of world exports, respectively. USA, China and Mexico were the top destinations, with respectively 11.0, 8.9 and 7.5 percent of world imports (see table 3).

The top 15 countries/areas accounted for 81.1 and 61.5 percent of total world exports and imports, respectively (see tables 2 and 3). In 2016, China was the country/area with the highest value of net exports (+2.8 bln US$), followed by Germany (+1.9 bln US$). By MDG regions (see graph 2), the largest surpluses in this product group were recorded by Eastern Asia (+5.0 bln US$), Developed Europe (+3.5 bln US$) and Developed Asia-Pacific (+1.1 bln US$). The largest trade deficits were recorded by Latin America and the Caribbean (-2.6 bln US$), South-eastern Asia (-1.7 bln US$) and Western Asia (-978.4 mln US$).

Table 1: Imports (Imp.) and exports (Exp.), 2002-2016, in current US$

		2002	2003	2004	2005	2006	2007	2008	2009	2010	2011	2012	2013	2014	2015	2016
Values in Bln US$	Imp.	14.4	16.2	19.0	20.6	22.2	24.0	27.1	23.1	25.0	29.0	29.7	31.6	32.8	30.8	29.5
	Exp.	16.0	18.2	21.1	21.9	24.3	25.9	28.6	23.1	25.5	30.4	31.6	33.3	34.4	32.2	31.1
As a percentage of SITC section (%)	Imp.	0.6	0.6	0.5	0.5	0.5	0.5	0.5	0.5	0.5	0.5	0.5	0.5	0.5	0.5	0.5
	Exp.	0.6	0.6	0.6	0.6	0.6	0.5	0.5	0.5	0.5	0.5	0.5	0.5	0.5	0.5	0.5
As a percentage of world trade (%)	Imp.	0.2	0.2	0.2	0.2	0.2	0.2	0.2	0.2	0.2	0.2	0.2	0.2	0.2	0.2	0.2
	Exp.	0.2	0.2	0.2	0.2	0.2	0.2	0.2	0.2	0.2	0.2	0.2	0.2	0.2	0.2	0.2

Graph 1: Annual growth rates of exports, 2002–2016

(In percentage by year)

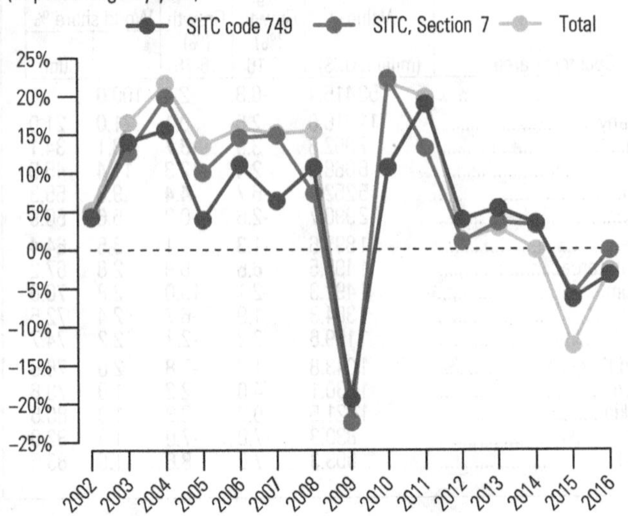

Table 2: Top exporting countries or areas in 2016

Country or area	Value (million US$)	Avg. Growth (%) 12-16	Growth (%) 15-16	World share %	Cum.
World	31 097.9	-0.4	-3.3	100.0	
China	5 398.5	5.0	-7.9	17.4	17.4
Germany	3 849.5	-0.6	0.2	12.4	29.7
Japan	2 624.9	-7.5	1.2	8.4	38.2
USA	2 463.4	-0.3	-4.0	7.9	46.1
Rep. of Korea	2 140.8	2.3	-4.4	6.9	53.0
Italy	1 970.7	1.1	2.1	6.3	59.3
Canada	1 170.5	7.8	2.1	3.8	63.1
Other Asia, nes	894.7	-1.7	-7.2	2.9	66.0
France	893.7	-4.4	-7.1	2.9	68.8
Portugal	729.2	1.4	4.3	2.3	71.2
United Kingdom	631.3	-6.2	-20.1	2.0	73.2
Mexico	630.8	1.8	9.0	2.0	75.2
China, Hong Kong SAR	630.5	-2.6	-7.7	2.0	77.3
Austria	616.9	-2.3	19.0	2.0	79.3
Singapore	563.6	-10.3	-13.5	1.8	81.1

Graph 2: Trade Balance by MDG regions 2016

(Bln US$)

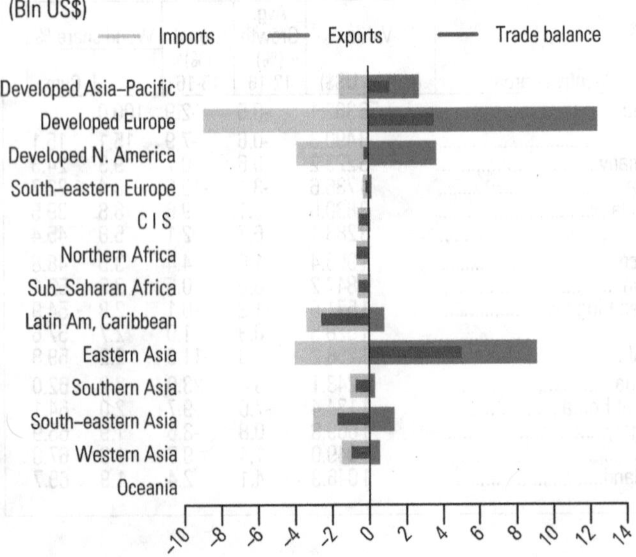

Table 3: Top importing countries or areas in 2016

Country or area	Value (million US$)	Avg. Growth (%) 12-16	Growth (%) 15-16	World share %	Cum.
World	29 528.1	-0.1	-4.1	100.0	
USA	3 249.6	4.2	-0.4	11.0	11.0
China	2 632.7	-3.6	-15.6	8.9	19.9
Mexico	2 225.8	4.2	10.0	7.5	27.5
Germany	1 992.2	1.2	2.5	6.7	34.2
Japan	1 319.6	2.6	9.6	4.5	38.7
Italy	819.6	0.7	-1.9	2.8	41.5
France	795.2	-3.8	0.6	2.7	44.1
Thailand	777.4	-9.4	-3.2	2.6	46.8
United Kingdom	714.9	-0.6	-9.6	2.4	49.2
India	692.5	1.3	-10.4	2.3	51.5
Canada	618.3	-3.7	-9.0	2.1	53.6
Malaysia	597.1	-0.4	0.2	2.0	55.7
Viet Nam	*591.6*	9.0	5.1	2.0	57.7
Rep. of Korea	580.5	-5.4	-11.5	2.0	59.6
China, Hong Kong SAR	561.8	-2.5	-12.0	1.9	61.5

In 2016, the value (in current US$) of exports of "office machines" (SITC group 751) decreased by 5.4 percent (compared to -5.1 percent average growth rate from 2012-2016) to reach 42.8 bln US$ (see table 2), while imports decreased by 4.9 percent to reach 42.9 bln US$ (see table 3). Exports of this commodity accounted for 0.7 percent of world exports of SITC section 7, and 0.3 percent of total world merchandise exports (see table 1). China, Netherlands and Germany were the top exporters in 2016 (see table 2). They accounted for 32.7, 10.3 and 7.3 percent of world exports, respectively. USA, Germany and Netherlands were the top destinations, with respectively 20.7, 8.6 and 8.1 percent of world imports (see table 3). See footnote.*

The top 15 countries/areas accounted for 88.9 and 72.4 percent of total world exports and imports, respectively (see tables 2 and 3). In 2016, China was the country/area with the highest value of net exports (+12.0 bln US$), followed by Viet Nam (+2.2 bln US$). By MDG regions (see graph 2), the largest surpluses in this product group were recorded by Eastern Asia (+12.7 bln US$) and South-eastern Asia (+5.8 bln US$). The largest trade deficits were recorded by Developed North America (-7.3 bln US$), Developed Europe (-3.8 bln US$) and Developed Asia-Pacific (-1.9 bln US$).

Table 1: Imports (Imp.) and exports (Exp.), 2002-2016, in current US$

		2002	2003	2004	2005	2006	2007	2008	2009	2010	2011	2012	2013	2014	2015	2016
Values in Bln US$	Imp.	12.3	14.0	16.1	17.1	19.4	49.3	52.7	41.4	49.7	50.6	50.9	50.1	50.9	45.1	42.9
	Exp.	11.6	11.6	12.7	15.0	18.2	45.0	49.4	41.4	50.1	51.1	52.7	51.1	50.4	45.3	42.8
As a percentage of SITC section (%)	Imp.	0.5	0.5	0.5	0.4	0.4	1.0	1.0	1.0	1.0	0.9	0.8	0.8	0.8	0.7	0.7
	Exp.	0.4	0.4	0.4	0.4	0.4	0.9	0.9	1.0	1.0	0.9	0.9	0.8	0.8	0.8	0.7
As a percentage of world trade (%)	Imp.	0.2	0.2	0.2	0.2	0.2	0.4	0.3	0.3	0.3	0.3	0.3	0.3	0.3	0.3	0.3
	Exp.	0.2	0.2	0.1	0.1	0.2	0.3	0.3	0.3	0.3	0.3	0.3	0.3	0.3	0.3	0.3

Graph 1: Annual growth rates of exports, 2002–2016
(In percentage by year)

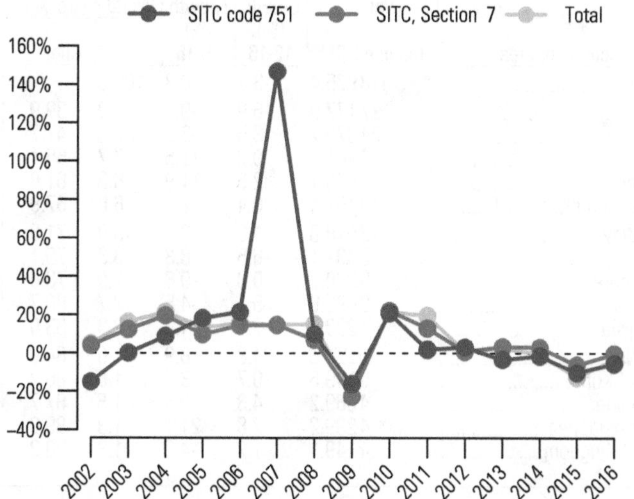

Graph 2: Trade Balance by MDG regions 2016
(Bln US$)

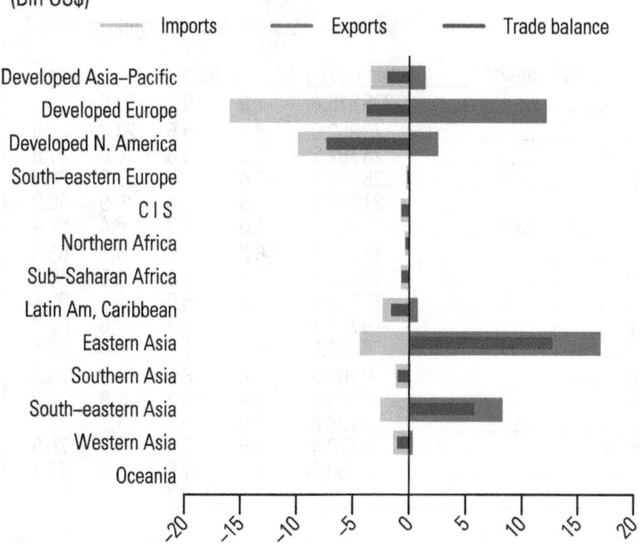

Table 2: Top exporting countries or areas in 2016

Country or area	Value (million US$)	Avg. Growth (%) 12-16	Growth (%) 15-16	World share %	Cum.
World	42846.9	-5.1	-5.4	100.0	
China	13993.3	-8.7	-13.5	32.7	32.7
Netherlands	4393.3	1.9	9.5	10.3	42.9
Germany	3118.4	-8.7	-3.9	7.3	50.2
Thailand	2672.7	15.6	0.1	6.2	56.4
Viet Nam	*2455.0*	3.5	8.9	5.7	62.2
USA	2292.0	-3.4	-11.3	5.3	67.5
China, Hong Kong SAR	1507.0	-12.4	-8.9	3.5	71.0
Japan	1323.7	-7.5	5.7	3.1	74.1
Indonesia	1200.1	-6.9	-5.6	2.8	76.9
Rep. of Korea	1097.9	-3.5	5.3	2.6	79.5
Hungary	1084.5	8.9	17.6	2.5	82.0
Singapore	972.5	-12.1	-10.2	2.3	84.3
Malaysia	759.4	-7.8	-10.1	1.8	86.1
Belgium	651.6	-5.1	-8.3	1.5	87.6
Mexico	552.3	-4.2	-24.7	1.3	88.9

Table 3: Top importing countries or areas in 2016

Country or area	Value (million US$)	Avg. Growth (%) 12-16	Growth (%) 15-16	World share %	Cum.
World	42871.0	-4.2	-4.9	100.0	
USA	8868.5	-0.5	-6.3	20.7	20.7
Germany	3678.7	-5.9	-4.7	8.6	29.3
Netherlands	3466.3	0.1	3.6	8.1	37.4
Japan	2468.8	-9.2	-8.2	5.8	43.1
China	2009.7	-10.6	-14.6	4.7	47.8
France	1707.2	-2.2	3.7	4.0	51.8
United Kingdom	1552.2	-2.1	-9.7	3.6	55.4
China, Hong Kong SAR	1369.4	-14.4	-12.0	3.2	58.6
Italy	1027.2	-0.6	2.9	2.4	61.0
Canada	970.7	-1.0	-12.7	2.3	63.3
Singapore	877.0	-11.1	-8.0	2.0	65.3
Mexico	815.9	-1.2	-14.1	1.9	67.2
Australia	772.6	-4.6	-6.2	1.8	69.0
India	753.0	1.0	-8.1	1.8	70.8
Spain	706.2	6.5	7.2	1.6	72.4

*Increase in 2007 was due to adoption of HS 2007 and its subsequent conversion to SITC Rev. 3

Source: UN Comtrade

752 Automatic data processing machines and units thereof

"Automatic data processing machines and units thereof" (SITC group 752) is amongst the top exported commodities in 2016 with 2.0 percent of total exports (see table 1). The value (in current US$) of exports of this commodity decreased by 0.3 percent (compared to -3.3 percent average growth rate from 2012-2016) to reach 318.9 bln US$ (see table 2), while imports decreased by 0.7 percent to reach 335.4 bln US$ (see table 3). Exports of this commodity accounted for 5.4 percent of world exports of SITC section 7 (see table 1). China, USA and Netherlands were the top exporters in 2016 (see table 2). They accounted for 39.9, 7.8 and 7.7 percent of world exports, respectively. USA, Netherlands and China were the top destinations, with respectively 23.8, 8.0 and 7.7 percent of world imports (see table 3).

The top 15 countries/areas accounted for 90.3 and 77.1 percent of total world exports and imports, respectively (see tables 2 and 3). In 2016, China was the country/area with the highest value of net exports (+101.3 bln US$), followed by Mexico (+10.3 bln US$). By MDG regions (see graph 2), the largest surpluses in this product group were recorded by Eastern Asia (+99.1 bln US$), South-eastern Asia (+21.5 bln US$) and Latin America and the Caribbean (+4.2 bln US$). The largest trade deficits were recorded by Developed North America (-61.7 bln US$), Developed Europe (-39.8 bln US$) and Developed Asia-Pacific (-17.8 bln US$).

Table 1: Imports (Imp.) and exports (Exp.), 2002-2016, in current US$

		2002	2003	2004	2005	2006	2007	2008	2009	2010	2011	2012	2013	2014	2015	2016
Values in Bln US$	Imp.	203.3	225.5	264.0	286.6	306.6	294.1	303.3	259.1	321.4	358.5	377.4	368.0	371.7	337.7	335.4
	Exp.	182.7	210.3	246.9	269.2	297.5	302.9	304.6	261.5	319.7	345.2	365.0	356.4	366.8	319.7	318.9
As a percentage of SITC section (%)	Imp.	7.9	7.7	7.5	7.4	7.0	5.8	5.6	6.1	6.2	6.1	6.3	5.9	5.8	5.6	5.5
	Exp.	7.1	7.2	7.1	7.0	6.8	6.0	5.6	6.2	6.2	5.9	6.2	5.9	5.9	5.4	5.4
As a percentage of world trade (%)	Imp.	3.1	2.9	2.8	2.7	2.5	2.1	1.9	2.1	2.1	2.0	2.1	2.0	2.0	2.0	2.1
	Exp.	2.8	2.8	2.7	2.6	2.5	2.2	1.9	2.1	2.1	1.9	2.0	1.9	1.9	1.9	2.0

Graph 1: Annual growth rates of exports, 2002–2016
(In percentage by year)

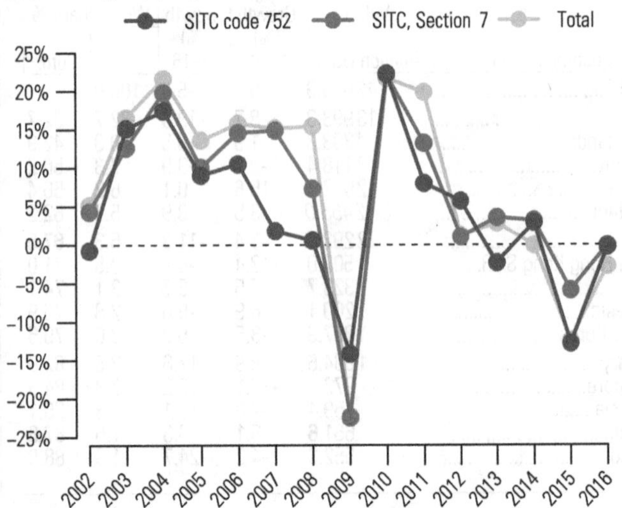

Table 2: Top exporting countries or areas in 2016

Country or area	Value (million US$)	Avg. Growth (%) 12-16	Growth (%) 15-16	World share %	Cum.
World	318925.4	-3.3	-0.3	100.0	
China	127177.0	-6.9	-9.3	39.9	39.9
USA	24975.7	-3.5	-3.3	7.8	47.7
Netherlands	24441.4	9.2	111.5	7.7	55.4
Mexico	20656.1	2.5	11.9	6.5	61.8
China, Hong Kong SAR	19157.4	-0.4	2.2	6.0	67.9
Germany	12578.8	1.5	-3.5	3.9	71.8
Thailand	10497.1	-6.5	-8.3	3.3	75.1
Singapore	9320.7	-0.8	-9.8	2.9	78.0
Czechia	8495.8	-5.1	-4.5	2.7	80.7
Malaysia	7333.5	-7.4	-4.9	2.3	83.0
Viet Nam	*5226.5*	34.8	8.9	1.6	84.6
Rep. of Korea	5149.5	-0.7	3.3	1.6	86.2
Philippines	4669.2	4.3	-0.4	1.5	87.7
Other Asia, nes	4299.2	2.8	21.1	1.3	89.0
United Kingdom	4149.1	1.2	-4.5	1.3	90.3

Graph 2: Trade Balance by MDG regions 2016
(Bln US$)

Imports — Exports — Trade balance

Developed Asia-Pacific
Developed Europe
Developed N. America
South-eastern Europe
CIS
Northern Africa
Sub-Saharan Africa
Latin Am, Caribbean
Eastern Asia
Southern Asia
South-eastern Asia
Western Asia
Oceania

-150 -100 -50 0 50 100 150 200

Table 3: Top importing countries or areas in 2016

Country or area	Value (million US$)	Avg. Growth (%) 12-16	Growth (%) 15-16	World share %	Cum.
World	335376.4	-2.9	-0.7	100.0	
USA	79852.8	-2.8	-5.5	23.8	23.8
Netherlands	26782.5	8.3	90.8	8.0	31.8
China	25833.3	-7.4	-1.2	7.7	39.5
Germany	21815.5	1.8	-2.4	6.5	46.0
China, Hong Kong SAR	21367.3	-1.9	-6.3	6.4	52.4
Japan	13879.9	-6.0	-1.6	4.1	56.5
United Kingdom	12854.7	-3.6	-8.9	3.8	60.3
Mexico	10352.8	3.7	6.9	3.1	63.4
France	8721.1	-4.3	-3.9	2.6	66.0
Canada	8202.1	-4.1	-1.2	2.4	68.5
Rep. of Korea	6209.5	2.4	6.1	1.9	70.3
Czechia	6139.0	-2.4	-10.3	1.8	72.2
Singapore	5794.6	-5.6	-10.5	1.7	73.9
Australia	5778.4	-5.9	-13.2	1.7	75.6
India	5000.7	1.1	-11.6	1.5	77.1

Source: UN Comtrade

Parts and accessories (not covers, carrying cases, etc) for machines of 751-752 759

In 2016, the value (in current US$) of exports of "parts and accessories (not covers, carrying cases, etc) for machines of 751-752" (SITC group 759) decreased by 7.5 percent (compared to -4.4 percent average growth rate from 2012-2016) to reach 156.5 bln US$ (see table 2), while imports decreased by 9.9 percent to reach 152.4 bln US$ (see table 3). Exports of this commodity accounted for 2.7 percent of world exports of SITC section 7, and 1.0 percent of total world merchandise exports (see table 1). China, China, Hong Kong SAR and USA were the top exporters in 2016 (see table 2). They accounted for 21.0, 17.0 and 12.1 percent of world exports, respectively. USA, China, Hong Kong SAR and China were the top destinations, with respectively 16.8, 12.4 and 11.8 percent of world imports (see table 3).

The top 15 countries/areas accounted for 91.8 and 79.2 percent of total world exports and imports, respectively (see tables 2 and 3). In 2016, China was the country/area with the highest value of net exports (+14.9 bln US$), followed by China, Hong Kong SAR (+7.7 bln US$). By MDG regions (see graph 2), the largest surpluses in this product group were recorded by Eastern Asia (+26.6 bln US$), Developed Asia-Pacific (+4.5 bln US$) and South-eastern Asia (+1.4 bln US$). The largest trade deficits were recorded by Latin America and the Caribbean (-8.2 bln US$), Developed North America (-7.7 bln US$) and Developed Europe (-7.5 bln US$).

Table 1: Imports (Imp.) and exports (Exp.), 2002-2016, in current US$

		2002	2003	2004	2005	2006	2007	2008	2009	2010	2011	2012	2013	2014	2015	2016
Values in Bln US$	Imp.	139.4	146.4	170.8	186.4	209.1	222.6	218.3	179.6	212.9	199.9	192.3	188.8	187.0	169.1	152.4
	Exp.	147.8	149.9	170.2	185.5	203.5	217.7	212.7	175.0	202.9	195.9	187.1	185.9	186.9	169.2	156.5
As a percentage of SITC section (%)	Imp.	5.4	5.0	4.8	4.8	4.8	4.4	4.0	4.2	4.1	3.4	3.2	3.0	2.9	2.8	2.5
	Exp.	5.7	5.2	4.9	4.8	4.6	4.3	3.9	4.2	4.0	3.4	3.2	3.1	3.0	2.9	2.7
As a percentage of world trade (%)	Imp.	2.1	1.9	1.8	1.8	1.7	1.6	1.3	1.4	1.4	1.1	1.0	1.0	1.0	1.0	0.9
	Exp.	2.3	2.0	1.9	1.8	1.7	1.6	1.3	1.4	1.3	1.1	1.0	1.0	1.0	1.0	1.0

Graph 1: Annual growth rates of exports, 2002–2016

(In percentage by year)

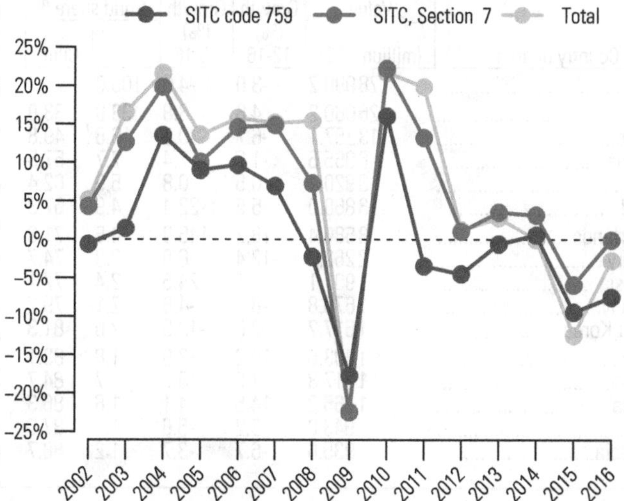

Table 2: Top exporting countries or areas in 2016

Country or area	Value (million US$)	Avg. Growth (%) 12-16	Growth (%) 15-16	World share %	Cum.
World	156493.4	-4.4	-7.5	100.0	
China	32919.5	-3.8	-9.9	21.0	21.0
China, Hong Kong SAR	26611.9	-5.8	-13.4	17.0	38.0
USA	18963.4	-0.6	-2.3	12.1	50.2
Netherlands	14621.3	-1.2	20.3	9.3	59.5
Japan	9608.3	-8.5	-7.7	6.1	65.6
Singapore	8326.1	-13.7	-12.4	5.3	71.0
Germany	6692.8	-6.3	-9.4	4.3	75.2
Other Asia, nes	5160.8	-1.2	-7.6	3.3	78.5
Malaysia	4888.9	-5.0	0.6	3.1	81.7
Rep. of Korea	4464.9	3.0	-23.0	2.9	84.5
Thailand	3543.2	-1.4	-4.1	2.3	86.8
United Kingdom	2499.8	1.7	-5.7	1.6	88.4
Czechia	1986.8	-4.1	-8.7	1.3	89.6
Philippines	1735.4	2.4	-11.4	1.1	90.8
Belgium	1631.0	-6.3	0.8	1.0	91.8

Graph 2: Trade Balance by MDG regions 2016

(Bln US$)

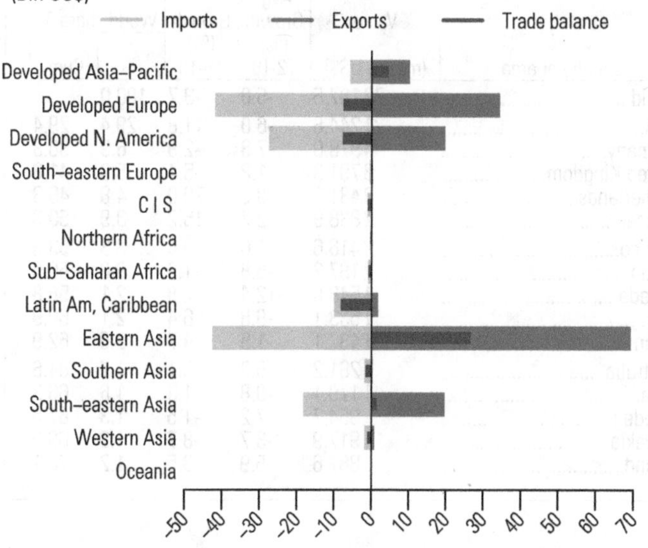

Table 3: Top importing countries or areas in 2016

Country or area	Value (million US$)	Avg. Growth (%) 12-16	Growth (%) 15-16	World share %	Cum.
World	152390.0	-5.6	-9.9	100.0	
USA	25528.0	-0.8	-7.1	16.8	16.8
China, Hong Kong SAR	18915.8	-9.1	-11.4	12.4	29.2
China	18030.5	-8.5	-18.4	11.8	41.0
Germany	8593.8	-5.3	-7.5	5.6	46.6
Netherlands	8576.5	-12.2	-31.6	5.6	52.3
Mexico	6980.3	0.1	1.9	4.6	56.8
Singapore	6694.4	-6.6	-7.3	4.4	61.2
Japan	4520.5	-5.7	0.3	3.0	64.2
United Kingdom	4309.1	-4.0	-8.9	2.8	67.0
Rep. of Korea	3410.2	5.7	11.0	2.2	69.3
Philippines	3329.9	1.3	59.4	2.2	71.5
France	3039.6	-7.0	-0.4	2.0	73.4
Czechia	3001.3	-4.8	-12.7	2.0	75.4
Thailand	2955.5	-9.4	-15.9	1.9	77.4
Malaysia	2878.5	-9.9	-11.2	1.9	79.2

761 Television receivers

In 2016, the value (in current US$) of exports of "television receivers" (SITC group 761) decreased by 4.9 percent (compared to -3.0 percent average growth rate from 2012-2016) to reach 79.0 bln US$ (see table 2), while imports decreased by 3.7 percent to reach 72.2 bln US$ (see table 3). Exports of this commodity accounted for 1.3 percent of world exports of SITC section 7, and 0.5 percent of total world merchandise exports (see table 1). China, Mexico and Slovakia were the top exporters in 2016 (see table 2). They accounted for 33.0, 16.8 and 7.7 percent of world exports, respectively. USA, Germany and United Kingdom were the top destinations, with respectively 29.4, 6.9 and 5.3 percent of world imports (see table 3).

The top 15 countries/areas accounted for 88.7 and 70.1 percent of total world exports and imports, respectively (see tables 2 and 3). In 2016, China was the country/area with the highest value of net exports (+25.6 bln US$), followed by Mexico (+10.8 bln US$). By MDG regions (see graph 2), the largest surpluses in this product group were recorded by Eastern Asia (+25.8 bln US$), Latin America and the Caribbean (+7.9 bln US$) and South-eastern Asia (+2.5 bln US$). The largest trade deficits were recorded by Developed North America (-18.6 bln US$), Developed Europe (-4.0 bln US$) and Developed Asia-Pacific (-2.7 bln US$).

Table 1: Imports (Imp.) and exports (Exp.), 2002-2016, in current US$

		2002	2003	2004	2005	2006	2007	2008	2009	2010	2011	2012	2013	2014	2015	2016
Values in Bln US$	Imp.	31.7	36.0	48.8	59.3	78.1	93.1	101.7	83.9	101.4	92.8	88.8	81.6	82.9	74.9	72.2
	Exp.	32.5	37.4	48.6	57.2	78.1	89.7	96.9	84.7	100.3	94.7	89.1	84.8	90.1	83.1	79.0
As a percentage of SITC section (%)	Imp.	1.2	1.2	1.4	1.5	1.8	1.8	1.9	2.0	1.9	1.6	1.5	1.3	1.3	1.2	1.2
	Exp.	1.3	1.3	1.4	1.5	1.8	1.8	1.8	2.0	2.0	1.6	1.5	1.4	1.4	1.4	1.3
As a percentage of world trade (%)	Imp.	0.5	0.5	0.5	0.6	0.6	0.7	0.6	0.7	0.7	0.5	0.5	0.4	0.4	0.5	0.4
	Exp.	0.5	0.5	0.5	0.6	0.7	0.6	0.6	0.7	0.7	0.5	0.5	0.5	0.5	0.5	0.5

Graph 1: Annual growth rates of exports, 2002–2016
(In percentage by year)

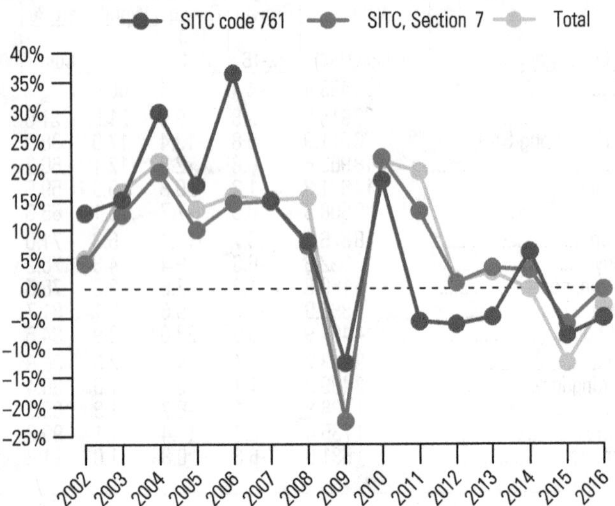

Table 2: Top exporting countries or areas in 2016

Country or area	Value (million US$)	Avg. Growth (%) 12-16	Growth (%) 15-16	World share %	Cum.
World	78990.2	-3.0	-4.9	100.0	
China	26060.2	4.6	3.8	33.0	33.0
Mexico	13257.1	-6.7	-20.6	16.8	49.8
Slovakia	6065.5	-1.5	7.4	7.7	57.5
USA	3920.4	0.5	0.8	5.0	62.4
Poland	3868.0	-5.5	-22.4	4.9	67.3
Netherlands	3580.4	18.2	145.8	4.5	71.8
Hungary	2262.3	-12.4	-6.8	2.9	74.7
Malaysia	1901.1	-15.5	-24.5	2.4	77.1
Germany	1679.8	-8.2	-4.8	2.1	79.2
Rep. of Korea	1617.2	-2.6	-12.5	2.0	81.3
Turkey	1403.6	-10.2	-12.9	1.8	83.1
Thailand	1317.8	-7.5	-18.5	1.7	84.7
Czechia	1265.2	-14.5	4.1	1.6	86.3
Japan	943.0	-3.2	-5.6	1.2	87.5
Indonesia	935.6	-6.7	-3.7	1.2	88.7

Graph 2: Trade Balance by MDG regions 2016
(Bln US$)

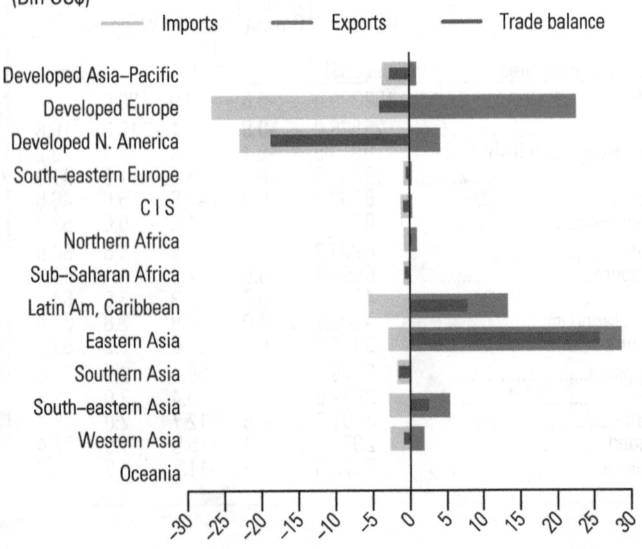

Table 3: Top importing countries or areas in 2016

Country or area	Value (million US$)	Avg. Growth (%) 12-16	Growth (%) 15-16	World share %	Cum.
World	72187.5	-5.0	-3.7	100.0	
USA	21244.8	-6.0	-11.8	29.4	29.4
Germany	4978.0	-7.8	-2.9	6.9	36.3
United Kingdom	3791.3	-1.8	-5.4	5.3	41.6
Netherlands	3431.3	9.5	79.0	4.8	46.3
France	2838.9	-2.2	15.2	3.9	50.3
Mexico	2416.6	1.0	-30.8	3.3	53.6
Japan	2187.2	-5.8	-1.9	3.0	56.6
Canada	1548.8	-12.4	2.8	2.1	58.8
Italy	1533.1	-6.8	6.4	2.1	60.9
Spain	1432.1	-1.5	4.7	2.0	62.9
Australia	1261.2	-5.3	-5.1	1.7	64.6
India	1179.1	-0.8	1.3	1.6	66.3
Sweden	954.7	-7.2	-1.5	1.3	67.6
Slovakia	917.9	-3.7	-8.7	1.3	68.9
Poland	887.6	-5.9	-23.5	1.2	70.1

In 2016, the value (in current US$) of exports of "radio-broadcast receivers" (SITC group 762) decreased by 4.9 percent (compared to -3.7 percent average growth rate from 2012-2016) to reach 14.6 bln US$ (see table 2), while imports decreased by 4.4 percent to reach 13.8 bln US$ (see table 3). Exports of this commodity accounted for 0.2 percent of world exports of SITC section 7, and 0.1 percent of total world merchandise exports (see table 1). China, Mexico and USA were the top exporters in 2016 (see table 2). They accounted for 32.5, 10.7 and 9.0 percent of world exports, respectively. USA, Germany and Canada were the top destinations, with respectively 32.1, 6.4 and 4.9 percent of world imports (see table 3).

The top 15 countries/areas accounted for 89.7 and 77.3 percent of total world exports and imports, respectively (see tables 2 and 3). In 2016, China was the country/area with the highest value of net exports (+4.5 bln US$), followed by Mexico (+1.0 bln US$). By MDG regions (see graph 2), the largest surpluses in this product group were recorded by Eastern Asia (+5.0 bln US$), South-eastern Asia (+1.7 bln US$) and Latin America and the Caribbean (+326.7 mln US$). The largest trade deficits were recorded by Developed North America (-3.8 bln US$), Developed Europe (-786.0 mln US$) and Developed Asia-Pacific (-674.8 mln US$).

Table 1: Imports (Imp.) and exports (Exp.), 2002-2016, in current US$

		2002	2003	2004	2005	2006	2007	2008	2009	2010	2011	2012	2013	2014	2015	2016
Values in Bln US$	Imp.	21.2	20.4	21.1	21.3	21.4	21.7	19.0	14.5	17.7	18.6	18.6	17.0	16.2	14.5	13.8
	Exp.	16.9	16.7	17.7	18.6	18.9	19.5	18.1	13.2	16.1	16.6	17.0	16.4	16.6	15.4	14.6
As a percentage of SITC section (%)	Imp.	0.8	0.7	0.6	0.5	0.5	0.4	0.4	0.3	0.3	0.3	0.3	0.3	0.3	0.2	0.2
	Exp.	0.7	0.6	0.5	0.5	0.4	0.4	0.3	0.3	0.3	0.3	0.3	0.3	0.3	0.3	0.2
As a percentage of world trade (%)	Imp.	0.3	0.3	0.2	0.2	0.2	0.2	0.1	0.1	0.1	0.1	0.1	0.1	0.1	0.1	0.1
	Exp.	0.3	0.2	0.2	0.2	0.2	0.1	0.1	0.1	0.1	0.1	0.1	0.1	0.1	0.1	0.1

Graph 1: Annual growth rates of exports, 2002–2016
(In percentage by year)

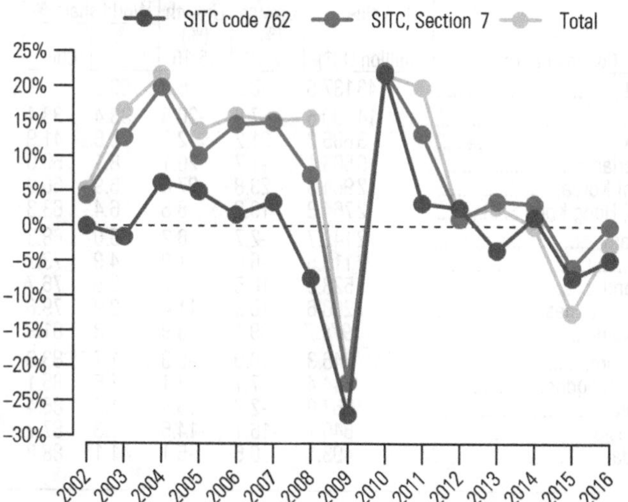

Table 2: Top exporting countries or areas in 2016

Country or area	Value (million US$)	Avg. Growth (%) 12-16	Growth (%) 15-16	World share %	Cum.
World	14636.9	-3.7	-4.9	100.0	
China	4759.9	-0.1	-4.7	32.5	32.5
Mexico	1563.8	8.5	-4.2	10.7	43.2
USA	1318.7	-2.6	-7.4	9.0	52.2
Thailand	965.8	-3.0	-26.2	6.6	58.8
Malaysia	673.8	-17.1	-15.0	4.6	63.4
Portugal	635.7	-10.5	46.1	4.3	67.8
Czechia	565.9	-3.3	-18.4	3.9	71.6
China, Hong Kong SAR	456.6	-18.0	-13.9	3.1	74.7
Germany	396.1	-13.5	-24.9	2.7	77.5
Rep. of Korea	379.7	5.4	11.7	2.6	80.0
Belgium	366.4	-6.4	6.2	2.5	82.5
Poland	300.6	52.4	0.2	2.1	84.6
Spain	282.4	30.3	46.1	1.9	86.5
Hungary	233.2	-3.7	18.9	1.6	88.1
Other Asia, nes	228.4	17.4	39.1	1.6	89.7

Graph 2: Trade Balance by MDG regions 2016
(Bln US$)

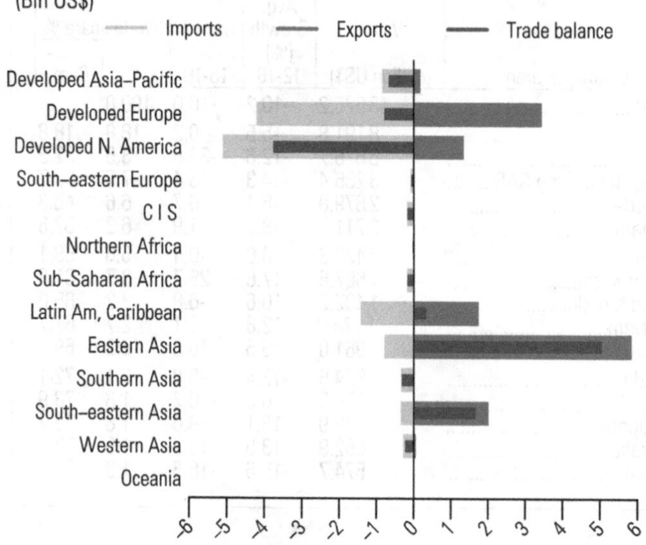

Table 3: Top importing countries or areas in 2016

Country or area	Value (million US$)	Avg. Growth (%) 12-16	Growth (%) 15-16	World share %	Cum.
World	13832.6	-7.1	-4.4	100.0	
USA	4440.0	-4.1	-5.2	32.1	32.1
Germany	879.2	-11.4	-8.1	6.4	38.5
Canada	674.4	-11.2	-10.9	4.9	43.3
Japan	640.3	-12.6	-13.2	4.6	48.0
United Kingdom	563.4	-5.7	9.9	4.1	52.0
Mexico	560.2	1.8	-7.2	4.0	56.1
Spain	412.0	13.7	45.7	3.0	59.1
Belgium	396.5	-12.1	-3.9	2.9	61.9
France	391.7	-5.4	-7.4	2.8	64.8
Italy	344.6	13.4	0.4	2.5	67.2
China, Hong Kong SAR	335.7	-18.4	-14.6	2.4	69.7
India	281.3	17.6	11.2	2.0	71.7
Netherlands	271.5	-7.6	56.9	2.0	73.7
China	252.5	3.9	-16.6	1.8	75.5
Brazil	243.5	-6.4	-2.2	1.8	77.3

763 Sound recorders or reproducers; television image and sound recorders

In 2016, the value (in current US$) of exports of "sound recorders or reproducers; television image and sound recorders" (SITC group 763) decreased by 6.2 percent (compared to -8.2 percent average growth rate from 2012-2016) to reach 43.1 bln US$ (see table 2), while imports decreased by 10.0 percent to reach 43.6 bln US$ (see table 3). Exports of this commodity accounted for 0.7 percent of world exports of SITC section 7, and 0.3 percent of total world merchandise exports (see table 1). China, Japan and Netherlands were the top exporters in 2016 (see table 2). They accounted for 33.4, 8.6 and 8.1 percent of world exports, respectively. USA, China and China, Hong Kong SAR were the top destinations, with respectively 18.8, 13.5 and 7.5 percent of world imports (see table 3).

The top 15 countries/areas accounted for 88.8 and 78.5 percent of total world exports and imports, respectively (see tables 2 and 3). In 2016, China was the country/area with the highest value of net exports (+8.5 bln US$), followed by Rep. of Korea (+1.4 bln US$). By MDG regions (see graph 2), the largest surpluses in this product group were recorded by Eastern Asia (+10.1 bln US$), South-eastern Asia (+1.6 bln US$) and Developed Asia-Pacific (+644.6 mln US$). The largest trade deficits were recorded by Developed North America (-6.5 bln US$), Developed Europe (-2.7 bln US$) and Latin America and the Caribbean (-938.0 mln US$).

Table 1: Imports (Imp.) and exports (Exp.), 2002-2016, in current US$

		2002	2003	2004	2005	2006	2007	2008	2009	2010	2011	2012	2013	2014	2015	2016
Values in Bln US$	Imp.	36.7	46.3	60.4	66.2	66.8	72.4	71.3	57.0	68.0	67.8	67.0	61.8	53.3	48.5	43.6
	Exp.	32.6	42.2	55.3	61.0	61.6	65.0	67.1	58.5	63.2	61.5	60.7	56.5	48.2	46.0	43.1
As a percentage of SITC section (%)	Imp.	1.4	1.6	1.7	1.7	1.5	1.4	1.3	1.3	1.3	1.1	1.1	1.0	0.8	0.8	0.7
	Exp.	1.3	1.5	1.6	1.6	1.4	1.3	1.2	1.4	1.2	1.1	1.0	0.9	0.8	0.8	0.7
As a percentage of world trade (%)	Imp.	0.6	0.6	0.6	0.6	0.5	0.5	0.4	0.5	0.4	0.4	0.4	0.3	0.3	0.3	0.3
	Exp.	0.5	0.6	0.6	0.6	0.5	0.5	0.4	0.5	0.4	0.3	0.3	0.3	0.3	0.3	0.3

Graph 1: Annual growth rates of exports, 2002–2016

(In percentage by year)

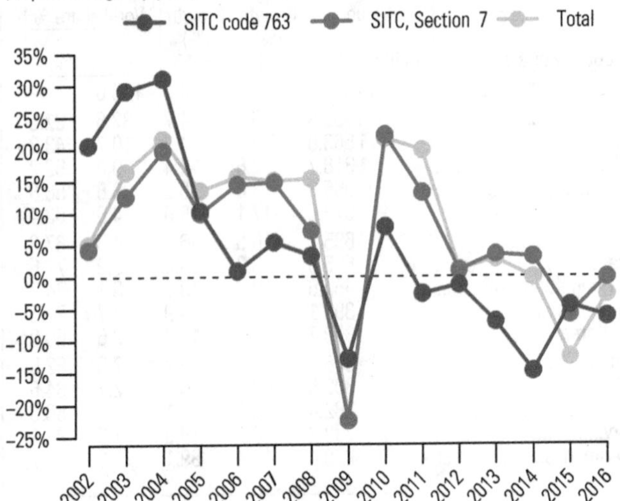

Table 2: Top exporting countries or areas in 2016

Country or area	Value (million US$)	Avg. Growth (%) 12-16	Growth (%) 15-16	World share %	Cum.
World	43 137.5	-8.2	-6.2	100.0	
China	14 390.6	-7.9	-20.5	33.4	33.4
Japan	3 695.3	-21.2	-2.2	8.6	41.9
Netherlands	3 503.1	-1.7	26.1	8.1	50.0
Rep. of Korea	2 964.3	29.8	87.6	6.9	56.9
China, Hong Kong SAR	2 764.3	-13.2	-8.5	6.4	63.3
Germany	2 142.7	-2.7	6.2	5.0	68.3
USA	2 111.5	-6.0	1.0	4.9	73.2
Thailand	1 523.3	-10.5	-16.2	3.5	76.7
Other Asia, nes	1 260.6	-10.3	-11.4	2.9	79.6
Viet Nam	*978.7*	89.1	8.9	2.3	81.9
Singapore	746.3	-10.9	-5.9	1.7	83.6
United Kingdom	644.4	-7.1	7.1	1.5	85.1
Czechia	557.9	-2.2	16.4	1.3	86.4
Indonesia	540.7	-16.1	-14.5	1.3	87.7
Canada	493.1	0.6	-5.1	1.1	88.8

Graph 2: Trade Balance by MDG regions 2016

(Bln US$)

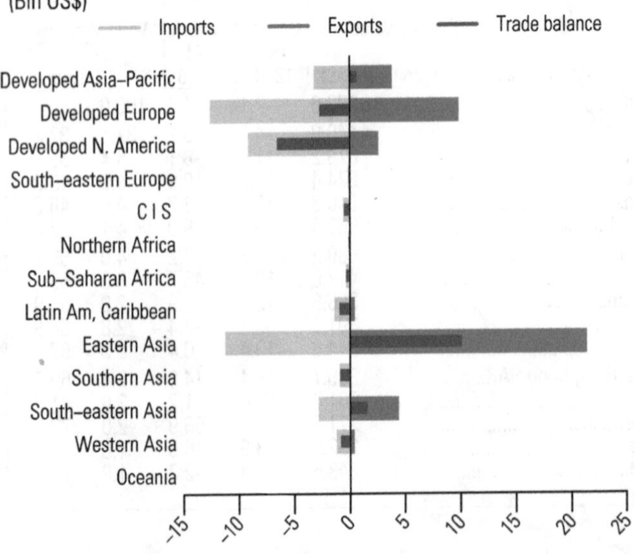

Table 3: Top importing countries or areas in 2016

Country or area	Value (million US$)	Avg. Growth (%) 12-16	Growth (%) 15-16	World share %	Cum.
World	43 625.2	-10.2	-10.0	100.0	
USA	8 191.8	-5.5	0.2	18.8	18.8
China	5 878.7	-12.6	-39.6	13.5	32.3
China, Hong Kong SAR	3 266.4	-14.3	-13.4	7.5	39.7
Netherlands	2 879.8	-6.1	16.7	6.6	46.3
Germany	2 711.3	-8.0	1.9	6.2	52.6
Japan	2 423.3	-8.6	-0.4	5.6	58.1
Rep. of Korea	1 607.6	17.6	26.7	3.7	61.8
United Kingdom	1 402.2	-10.6	-6.8	3.2	65.0
Viet Nam	*1 178.9*	12.8	5.1	2.7	67.7
France	961.0	-15.5	-18.6	2.2	69.9
Canada	934.6	-12.4	-5.8	2.1	72.1
India	796.5	0.0	-10.2	1.8	73.9
Singapore	776.9	-15.1	-9.0	1.8	75.7
Australia	662.9	-13.5	-13.7	1.5	77.2
Mexico	574.7	-15.6	-18.5	1.3	78.5

Source: UN Comtrade

"Telecommunications equipment, nes, and parts, nes, and accessories of 76" (SITC group 764) is amongst the top exported commodities in 2016 with 4.0 percent of total exports (see table 1). The value (in current US$) of exports of this commodity increased by 1.4 percent (compared to 4.3 percent average growth rate from 2012-2016) to reach 639.6 bln US$ (see table 2), while imports increased by 1.3 percent to reach 688.1 bln US$ (see table 3). Exports of this commodity accounted for 10.9 percent of world exports of SITC section 7 (see table 1). China, China, Hong Kong SAR and USA were the top exporters in 2016 (see table 2). They accounted for 36.3, 14.3 and 6.8 percent of world exports, respectively. USA, China, Hong Kong SAR and China were the top destinations, with respectively 18.0, 12.9 and 8.8 percent of world imports (see table 3).

The top 15 countries/areas accounted for 89.8 and 73.4 percent of total world exports and imports, respectively (see tables 2 and 3). In 2016, China was the country/area with the highest value of net exports (+171.7 bln US$), followed by Viet Nam (+20.8 bln US$). By MDG regions (see graph 2), the largest surpluses in this product group were recorded by Eastern Asia (+198.3 bln US$) and South-eastern Asia (+13.7 bln US$). The largest trade deficits were recorded by Developed North America (-88.1 bln US$), Developed Europe (-58.7 bln US$) and Developed Asia-Pacific (-29.4 bln US$).

Table 1: Imports (Imp.) and exports (Exp.), 2002-2016, in current US$

		2002	2003	2004	2005	2006	2007	2008	2009	2010	2011	2012	2013	2014	2015	2016
Values in Bln US$	Imp.	193.5	218.5	285.7	340.6	406.1	433.2	473.1	396.7	494.6	562.3	603.6	655.9	681.8	679.2	688.1
	Exp.	207.6	228.9	294.5	350.7	423.2	417.5	451.3	378.3	446.7	510.7	539.6	597.0	630.7	631.0	639.6
As a percentage of SITC section (%)	Imp.	7.5	7.5	8.1	8.8	9.2	8.6	8.7	9.3	9.5	9.5	10.0	10.6	10.7	11.2	11.3
	Exp.	8.1	7.9	8.5	9.2	9.6	8.3	8.3	9.0	8.7	8.8	9.2	9.8	10.1	10.7	10.9
As a percentage of world trade (%)	Imp.	2.9	2.8	3.0	3.2	3.3	3.1	2.9	3.2	3.2	3.1	3.3	3.5	3.6	4.1	4.3
	Exp.	3.2	3.0	3.2	3.4	3.5	3.0	2.8	3.0	3.0	2.8	2.9	3.2	3.4	3.8	4.0

Graph 1: Annual growth rates of exports, 2002–2016
(In percentage by year)

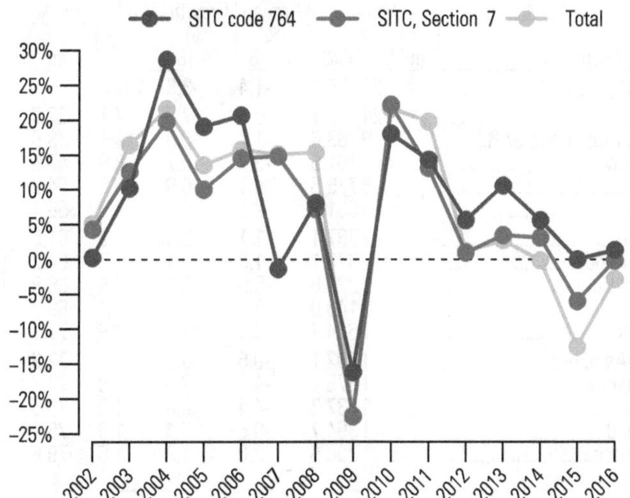

Graph 2: Trade Balance by MDG regions 2016
(Bln US$)

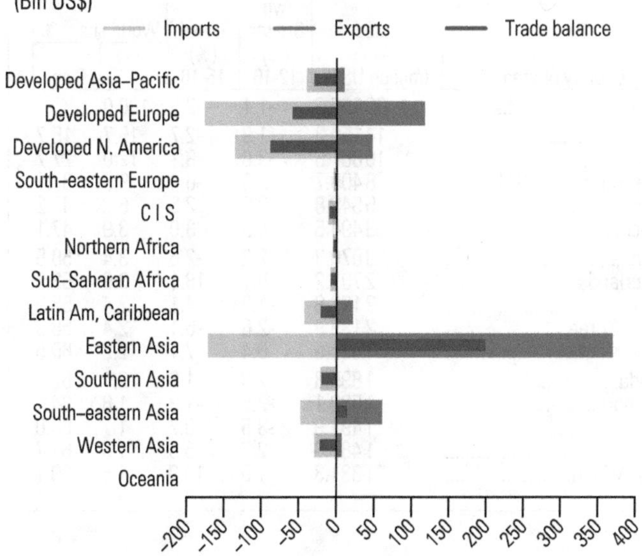

Table 2: Top exporting countries or areas in 2016

Country or area	Value (million US$)	Avg. Growth (%) 12-16	Growth (%) 15-16	World share %	Cum.
World	639609.3	4.3	1.4	100.0	
China	232363.5	6.2	-4.9	36.3	36.3
China, Hong Kong SAR	91406.0	5.6	-1.3	14.3	50.6
USA	43631.1	2.1	-3.0	6.8	57.4
Netherlands	37452.7	24.8	110.0	5.9	63.3
Viet Nam	*36006.3*	26.3	8.9	5.6	68.9
Rep. of Korea	32172.6	2.4	-13.3	5.0	74.0
Mexico	20330.6	-0.2	1.1	3.2	77.1
Germany	19901.2	1.5	9.0	3.1	80.2
Other Asia, nes	13731.4	0.9	24.6	2.1	82.4
Singapore	11815.5	2.2	-1.9	1.8	84.2
Japan	8766.0	-6.2	-4.7	1.4	85.6
United Kingdom	7193.6	-3.1	-3.8	1.1	86.7
Malaysia	6666.4	2.9	1.8	1.0	87.8
France	6532.4	-3.8	-1.5	1.0	88.8
Sweden	6230.4	-4.1	-5.8	1.0	89.8

Table 3: Top importing countries or areas in 2016

Country or area	Value (million US$)	Avg. Growth (%) 12-16	Growth (%) 15-16	World share %	Cum.
World	688102.0	3.3	1.3	100.0	
USA	123520.5	5.6	1.7	18.0	18.0
China, Hong Kong SAR	89017.7	5.4	-3.1	12.9	30.9
China	60622.5	3.8	-0.9	8.8	39.7
Netherlands	38254.6	21.6	76.7	5.6	45.3
Japan	29816.5	-2.9	3.1	4.3	49.6
Germany	28847.9	2.4	5.3	4.2	53.8
Mexico	22151.9	-3.4	-4.5	3.2	57.0
United Kingdom	20270.2	1.8	-3.6	2.9	59.9
India	16783.0	10.2	-4.8	2.4	62.4
Viet Nam	*15208.4*	23.9	5.1	2.2	64.6
Rep. of Korea	14779.7	19.0	2.9	2.1	66.7
France	13810.0	1.1	5.3	2.0	68.8
Canada	11979.9	-1.1	-5.5	1.7	70.5
United Arab Emirates	10400.3	-8.2	10.1	1.5	72.0
Singapore	9711.3	-5.1	-2.4	1.4	73.4

771 Electric power machinery, and parts thereof

In 2016, the value (in current US$) of exports of "electric power machinery, and parts thereof" (SITC group 771) decreased by 3.5 percent (compared to -1.4 percent average growth rate from 2012-2016) to reach 87.8 bln US$ (see table 2), while imports decreased by 2.5 percent to reach 90.0 bln US$ (see table 3). Exports of this commodity accounted for 1.5 percent of world exports of SITC section 7, and 0.5 percent of total world merchandise exports (see table 1). China, China, Hong Kong SAR and Germany were the top exporters in 2016 (see table 2). They accounted for 27.7, 11.1 and 8.8 percent of world exports, respectively. USA, China and China, Hong Kong SAR were the top destinations, with respectively 15.7, 12.0 and 9.3 percent of world imports (see table 3).

The top 15 countries/areas accounted for 79.6 and 69.1 percent of total world exports and imports, respectively (see tables 2 and 3). In 2016, China was the country/area with the highest value of net exports (+13.5 bln US$), followed by Germany (+2.2 bln US$). By MDG regions (see graph 2), the largest surpluses in this product group were recorded by Eastern Asia (+15.2 bln US$), Developed Europe (+2.2 bln US$) and South-eastern Asia (+286.3 mln US$). The largest trade deficits were recorded by Developed North America (-9.4 bln US$), Western Asia (-2.9 bln US$) and Latin America and the Caribbean (-2.7 bln US$).

Table 1: Imports (Imp.) and exports (Exp.), 2002-2016, in current US$

		2002	2003	2004	2005	2006	2007	2008	2009	2010	2011	2012	2013	2014	2015	2016
Values in Bln US$	Imp.	34.6	38.3	45.2	49.9	58.5	71.0	80.6	69.3	88.3	96.5	94.0	98.7	100.1	92.3	90.0
	Exp.	31.8	35.6	41.8	45.7	55.8	69.1	79.7	68.2	85.6	92.6	92.9	98.2	97.2	90.9	87.8
As a percentage of SITC section (%)	Imp.	1.3	1.3	1.3	1.3	1.3	1.4	1.5	1.6	1.7	1.6	1.6	1.6	1.6	1.5	1.5
	Exp.	1.2	1.2	1.2	1.2	1.3	1.4	1.5	1.6	1.7	1.6	1.6	1.6	1.6	1.5	1.5
As a percentage of world trade (%)	Imp.	0.5	0.5	0.5	0.5	0.5	0.5	0.5	0.6	0.6	0.5	0.5	0.5	0.5	0.6	0.6
	Exp.	0.5	0.5	0.5	0.4	0.5	0.5	0.5	0.5	0.6	0.5	0.5	0.5	0.5	0.6	0.5

Graph 1: Annual growth rates of exports, 2002–2016

(In percentage by year)

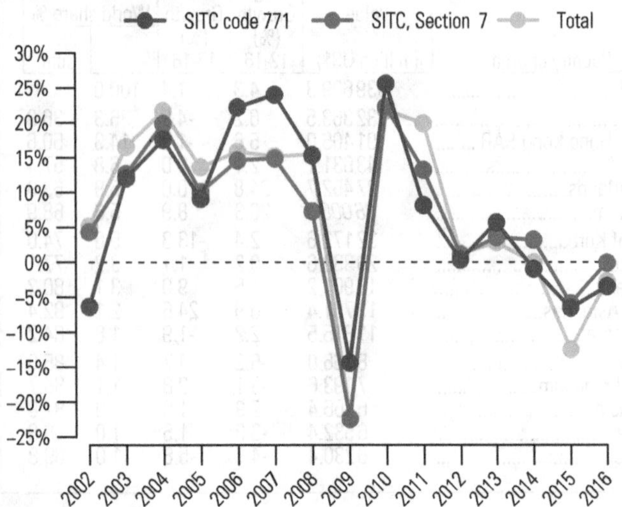

Table 2: Top exporting countries or areas in 2016

Country or area	Value (million US$)	Avg. Growth (%) 12-16	Growth (%) 15-16	World share %	Cum.
World	87756.4	-1.4	-3.5	100.0	
China	24318.1	0.6	-7.7	27.7	27.7
China, Hong Kong SAR	9763.6	-1.7	-6.3	11.1	38.8
Germany	7701.5	-3.7	0.7	8.8	47.6
USA	5775.5	0.1	-10.9	6.6	54.2
Japan	3651.2	-2.1	0.4	4.2	58.4
Mexico	2787.1	1.1	0.3	3.2	61.5
Netherlands	2378.1	1.0	15.1	2.7	64.2
Rep. of Korea	2221.6	-5.5	-5.6	2.5	66.8
Italy	2143.0	-3.7	-6.2	2.4	69.2
Austria	1684.7	-0.1	14.8	1.9	71.1
Other Asia, nes	1592.1	-0.6	3.5	1.8	72.9
Philippines	1575.2	-4.0	2.0	1.8	74.7
France	1537.3	-4.4	0.8	1.8	76.5
Thailand	1394.7	-0.6	-6.4	1.6	78.1
Singapore	1308.5	-2.0	-1.3	1.5	79.6

Graph 2: Trade Balance by MDG regions 2016

(Bln US$)

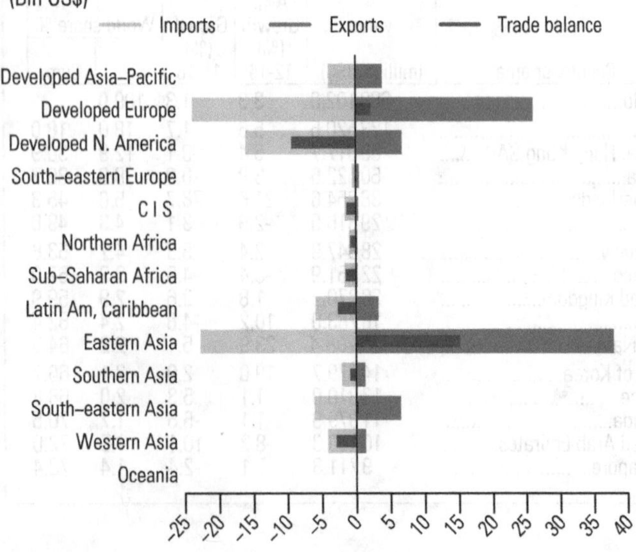

Table 3: Top importing countries or areas in 2016

Country or area	Value (million US$)	Avg. Growth (%) 12-16	Growth (%) 15-16	World share %	Cum.
World	90005.6	-1.1	-2.5	100.0	
USA	14150.2	1.9	-2.7	15.7	15.7
China	10801.6	-3.0	-8.1	12.0	27.7
China, Hong Kong SAR	8400.7	-2.0	-6.4	9.3	37.1
Germany	5548.8	-2.2	2.5	6.2	43.2
Mexico	3494.5	4.3	3.0	3.9	47.1
Japan	3070.3	-2.2	-2.6	3.4	50.5
Netherlands	2701.2	9.1	18.1	3.0	53.5
France	2152.8	-1.3	4.1	2.4	55.9
Rep. of Korea	2139.9	-2.6	-5.1	2.4	58.3
United Kingdom	1990.5	-0.4	-7.1	2.2	60.5
Canada	1895.3	-1.0	1.6	2.1	62.6
Singapore	1580.1	-2.5	-1.3	1.8	64.4
Italy	1491.9	-3.5	-0.7	1.7	66.0
India	1481.6	2.2	5.8	1.6	67.7
Other Asia, nes	1331.3	1.0	10.9	1.5	69.1

"Electrical apparatus for switching, protecting or connecting electrical circuits" (SITC group 772) is amongst the top exported commodities in 2016 with 1.5 percent of total exports (see table 1). The value (in current US$) of exports of this commodity increased by 0.4 percent (compared to 0.7 percent average growth rate from 2012-2016) to reach 244.6 bln US$ (see table 2), while imports decreased by 0.1 percent to reach 245.6 bln US$ (see table 3). Exports of this commodity accounted for 4.2 percent of world exports of SITC section 7 (see table 1). China, Germany and USA were the top exporters in 2016 (see table 2). They accounted for 16.0, 12.8 and 9.5 percent of world exports, respectively. China, USA and China, Hong Kong SAR were the top destinations, with respectively 14.4, 11.4 and 7.8 percent of world imports (see table 3).

The top 15 countries/areas accounted for 80.8 and 69.0 percent of total world exports and imports, respectively (see tables 2 and 3). In 2016, Germany was the country/area with the highest value of net exports (+13.3 bln US$), followed by Japan (+9.8 bln US$). By MDG regions (see graph 2), the largest surpluses in this product group were recorded by Developed Europe (+14.8 bln US$), Eastern Asia (+14.4 bln US$) and Developed Asia-Pacific (+8.5 bln US$). The largest trade deficits were recorded by Latin America and the Caribbean (-9.2 bln US$), Developed North America (-7.7 bln US$) and Western Asia (-7.0 bln US$).

Table 1: Imports (Imp.) and exports (Exp.), 2002-2016, in current US$

		2002	2003	2004	2005	2006	2007	2008	2009	2010	2011	2012	2013	2014	2015	2016
Values in Bln US$	Imp.	89.1	103.6	127.5	142.0	165.6	189.6	205.0	165.4	208.5	238.1	244.2	254.3	259.6	245.8	245.6
	Exp.	89.2	104.5	128.2	142.4	164.1	185.9	200.1	161.7	204.9	232.0	238.0	249.8	259.9	243.5	244.6
As a percentage of SITC section (%)	Imp.	3.4	3.5	3.6	3.7	3.8	3.8	3.8	3.9	4.0	4.0	4.1	4.1	4.1	4.1	4.0
	Exp.	3.5	3.6	3.7	3.7	3.7	3.7	3.7	3.9	4.0	4.0	4.1	4.1	4.1	4.1	4.2
As a percentage of world trade (%)	Imp.	1.4	1.4	1.4	1.3	1.4	1.4	1.3	1.3	1.4	1.3	1.3	1.4	1.4	1.5	1.5
	Exp.	1.4	1.4	1.4	1.4	1.4	1.3	1.3	1.3	1.4	1.3	1.3	1.3	1.4	1.5	1.5

Graph 1: Annual growth rates of exports, 2002–2016
(In percentage by year)

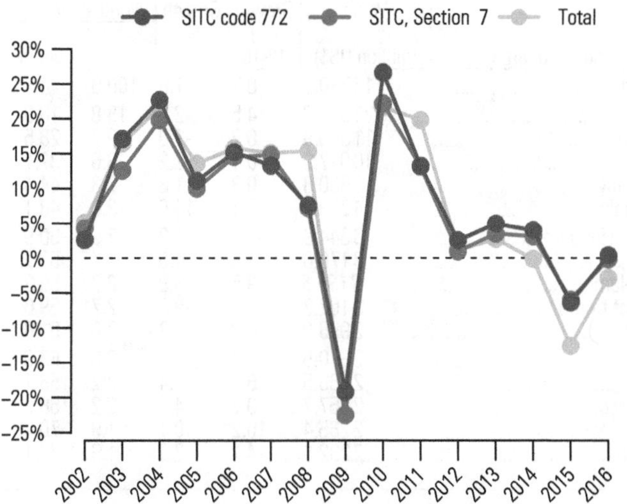

Graph 2: Trade Balance by MDG regions 2016
(Bln US$)

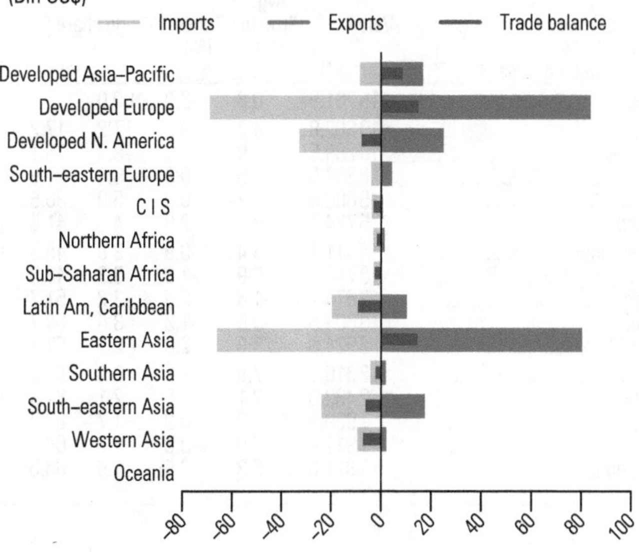

Table 2: Top exporting countries or areas in 2016

Country or area	Value (million US$)	Avg. Growth (%) 12-16	Growth (%) 15-16	World share %	Cum.
World	244570.3	0.7	0.4	100.0	
China	39135.4	2.9	-3.4	16.0	16.0
Germany	31379.0	0.6	5.2	12.8	28.8
USA	23238.4	3.2	-2.2	9.5	38.3
China, Hong Kong SAR	20627.4	-0.1	-2.6	8.4	46.8
Japan	16373.7	-5.3	6.5	6.7	53.5
Rep. of Korea	12483.4	3.2	0.0	5.1	58.6
Mexico	9015.6	4.0	1.2	3.7	62.3
France	8004.2	-3.3	-1.2	3.3	65.5
Other Asia, nes	7980.1	-3.1	-6.2	3.3	68.8
Singapore	5296.7	-6.4	-1.3	2.2	71.0
Italy	5234.5	0.4	2.6	2.1	73.1
Czechia	5035.2	3.9	2.4	2.1	75.2
Hungary	5031.9	8.7	4.6	2.1	77.2
Malaysia	4526.9	-6.3	-5.2	1.9	79.1
Thailand	4298.1	11.4	7.6	1.8	80.8

Table 3: Top importing countries or areas in 2016

Country or area	Value (million US$)	Avg. Growth (%) 12-16	Growth (%) 15-16	World share %	Cum.
World	245585.0	0.1	-0.1	100.0	
China	35485.4	-2.1	-4.7	14.4	14.4
USA	28098.2	3.9	2.2	11.4	25.9
China, Hong Kong SAR	19086.7	-2.4	-5.5	7.8	33.7
Germany	18093.1	2.9	6.7	7.4	41.0
Mexico	13920.0	4.8	0.2	5.7	46.7
Rep. of Korea	7337.4	-7.9	-8.9	3.0	49.7
Japan	6598.8	1.5	2.1	2.7	52.4
France	6465.8	-0.4	1.7	2.6	55.0
United Kingdom	5783.2	4.6	2.4	2.4	57.4
Thailand	5306.2	-1.5	-1.7	2.2	59.5
Malaysia	4783.9	-2.6	2.1	1.9	61.5
Singapore	4706.0	-3.0	-5.3	1.9	63.4
Viet Nam	*4694.0*	14.1	5.1	1.9	65.3
Italy	4616.0	2.6	4.1	1.9	67.2
Canada	4565.8	-1.8	-0.3	1.9	69.0

773 Equipment for distributing electricity, nes

In 2016, the value (in current US$) of exports of "equipment for distributing electricity, nes" (SITC group 773) decreased by 1.8 percent (compared to 0.7 percent average growth rate from 2012-2016) to reach 116.7 bln US$ (see table 2), while imports decreased by 2.0 percent to reach 115.8 bln US$ (see table 3). Exports of this commodity accounted for 2.0 percent of world exports of SITC section 7, and 0.7 percent of total world merchandise exports (see table 1). China, Mexico and USA were the top exporters in 2016 (see table 2). They accounted for 18.8, 9.7 and 8.6 percent of world exports, respectively. USA, Germany and Japan were the top destinations, with respectively 17.2, 8.9 and 5.4 percent of world imports (see table 3).

The top 15 countries/areas accounted for 72.1 and 66.5 percent of total world exports and imports, respectively (see tables 2 and 3). In 2016, China was the country/area with the highest value of net exports (+16.1 bln US$), followed by Mexico (+5.6 bln US$). By MDG regions (see graph 2), the largest surpluses in this product group were recorded by Eastern Asia (+15.9 bln US$), Latin America and the Caribbean (+4.4 bln US$) and South-eastern Europe (+3.0 bln US$). The largest trade deficits were recorded by Developed North America (-12.6 bln US$), Developed Asia-Pacific (-4.8 bln US$) and Developed Europe (-3.8 bln US$).

Table 1: Imports (Imp.) and exports (Exp.), 2002-2016, in current US$

		2002	2003	2004	2005	2006	2007	2008	2009	2010	2011	2012	2013	2014	2015	2016
Values in Bln US$	Imp.	42.8	47.3	55.4	62.4	77.5	92.9	102.1	73.8	94.3	113.9	113.2	119.0	125.5	118.1	115.8
	Exp.	39.9	44.7	54.0	61.3	76.9	91.7	101.8	73.3	93.0	111.2	113.3	120.3	127.8	118.9	116.7
As a percentage of SITC section (%)	Imp.	1.7	1.6	1.6	1.6	1.8	1.8	1.9	1.7	1.8	1.9	1.9	1.9	2.0	1.9	1.9
	Exp.	1.5	1.5	1.6	1.6	1.8	1.8	1.9	1.7	1.8	1.9	1.9	2.0	2.0	2.0	2.0
As a percentage of world trade (%)	Imp.	0.6	0.6	0.6	0.6	0.6	0.7	0.6	0.6	0.6	0.6	0.6	0.6	0.7	0.7	0.7
	Exp.	0.6	0.6	0.6	0.6	0.6	0.7	0.6	0.6	0.6	0.6	0.6	0.6	0.7	0.7	0.7

Graph 1: Annual growth rates of exports, 2002–2016

(In percentage by year)

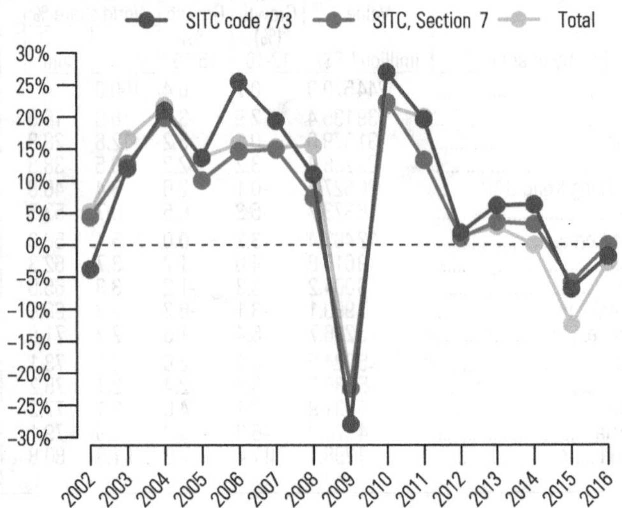

Graph 2: Trade Balance by MDG regions 2016

(Bln US$)

Imports
Exports
Trade balance

Developed Asia-Pacific
Developed Europe
Developed N. America
South-eastern Europe
CIS
Northern Africa
Sub-Saharan Africa
Latin Am, Caribbean
Eastern Asia
Southern Asia
South-eastern Asia
Western Asia
Oceania

-40 -30 -20 -10 0 10 20 30 40

Table 2: Top exporting countries or areas in 2016

Country or area	Value (million US$)	Avg. Growth (%) 12-16	Growth (%) 15-16	World share %	Cum.
World	116730.3	0.7	-1.8	100.0	
China	21936.2	4.5	-2.7	18.8	18.8
Mexico	11365.9	6.2	-1.0	9.7	28.5
USA	10047.3	-0.1	-2.2	8.6	37.1
Germany	8530.8	0.3	1.8	7.3	44.4
Romania	4238.3	7.1	14.0	3.6	48.1
China, Hong Kong SAR	3344.9	-3.5	-9.2	2.9	50.9
Italy	3170.0	-1.8	4.5	2.7	53.7
Viet Nam	*3135.5*	9.5	8.9	2.7	56.3
Rep. of Korea	3102.2	-4.9	-9.8	2.7	59.0
Czechia	2998.0	0.8	1.2	2.6	61.6
Poland	2670.5	1.7	0.1	2.3	63.9
Japan	2565.5	-6.1	7.4	2.2	66.1
Morocco	2557.7	9.7	4.6	2.2	68.2
Philippines	2265.4	10.2	0.1	1.9	70.2
France	2232.6	-4.1	2.3	1.9	72.1

Table 3: Top importing countries or areas in 2016

Country or area	Value (million US$)	Avg. Growth (%) 12-16	Growth (%) 15-16	World share %	Cum.
World	115761.9	0.6	-2.0	100.0	
USA	19882.8	4.2	-3.5	17.2	17.2
Germany	10289.5	1.0	-0.6	8.9	26.1
Japan	6287.0	-1.5	-0.6	5.4	31.5
China	5806.4	-2.3	-6.0	5.0	36.5
Mexico	5724.1	3.1	-2.9	4.9	41.5
United Kingdom	4411.1	3.4	-0.9	3.8	45.3
China, Hong Kong SAR	3749.5	0.9	-1.5	3.2	48.5
France	3674.1	-1.6	3.5	3.2	51.7
Canada	3503.5	-3.6	-1.2	3.0	54.7
Rep. of Korea	2924.6	3.0	2.8	2.5	57.2
Spain	2610.9	7.8	-1.8	2.3	59.5
Czechia	2432.5	2.1	1.8	2.1	61.6
Romania	1969.9	5.7	10.9	1.7	63.3
Italy	1911.4	3.0	-3.8	1.7	64.9
Thailand	1811.6	2.3	-2.5	1.6	66.5

In 2016, the value (in current US$) of exports of "electro-medical and radiological equipment" (SITC group 774) increased by 3.5 percent (compared to -0.5 percent average growth rate from 2012-2016) to reach 41.9 bln US$ (see table 2), while imports increased by 1.1 percent to reach 40.4 bln US$ (see table 3). Exports of this commodity accounted for 0.7 percent of world exports of SITC section 7, and 0.3 percent of total world merchandise exports (see table 1). USA, Germany and Netherlands were the top exporters in 2016 (see table 2). They accounted for 22.0, 18.2 and 10.5 percent of world exports, respectively. USA, China and Japan were the top destinations, with respectively 22.5, 13.1 and 6.1 percent of world imports (see table 3).

The top 15 countries/areas accounted for 89.3 and 73.8 percent of total world exports and imports, respectively (see tables 2 and 3). In 2016, Germany was the country/area with the highest value of net exports (+5.2 bln US$), followed by Netherlands (+2.2 bln US$). By MDG regions (see graph 2), the largest surpluses in this product group were recorded by Developed Europe (+7.9 bln US$) and Developed Asia-Pacific (+462.5 mln US$). The largest trade deficits were recorded by Eastern Asia (-2.1 bln US$), Latin America and the Caribbean (-1.1 bln US$) and Southern Asia (-876.6 mln US$).

Table 1: Imports (Imp.) and exports (Exp.), 2002-2016, in current US$

		2002	2003	2004	2005	2006	2007	2008	2009	2010	2011	2012	2013	2014	2015	2016
Values in Bln US$	Imp.	17.0	19.2	22.1	25.1	28.9	32.5	36.0	33.0	36.6	41.1	42.7	41.5	42.1	40.0	40.4
	Exp.	17.2	20.3	23.1	25.9	29.4	33.7	36.9	34.0	37.7	41.8	42.7	42.1	42.6	40.5	41.9
As a percentage of	Imp.	0.7	0.7	0.6	0.6	0.7	0.6	0.7	0.8	0.7	0.7	0.7	0.7	0.7	0.7	0.7
SITC section (%)	Exp.	0.7	0.7	0.7	0.7	0.7	0.7	0.7	0.8	0.7	0.7	0.7	0.7	0.7	0.7	0.7
As a percentage of	Imp.	0.3	0.3	0.2	0.2	0.2	0.2	0.2	0.3	0.2	0.2	0.2	0.2	0.2	0.2	0.3
world trade (%)	Exp.	0.3	0.3	0.3	0.2	0.2	0.2	0.2	0.3	0.2	0.2	0.2	0.2	0.2	0.2	0.3

Graph 1: Annual growth rates of exports, 2002–2016

(In percentage by year)

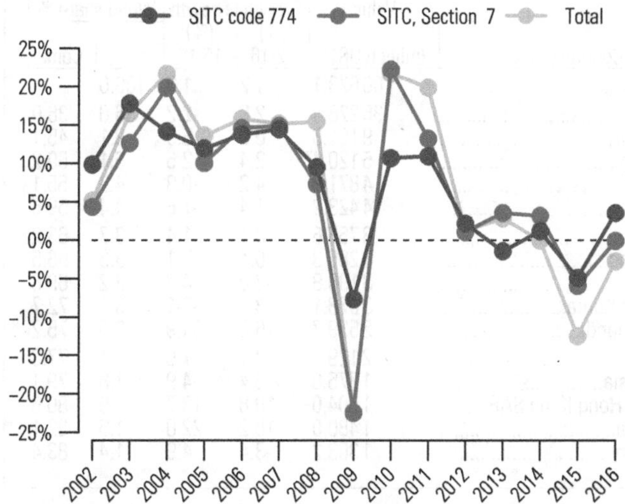

Table 2: Top exporting countries or areas in 2016

Country or area	Value (million US$)	Avg. Growth (%) 12-16	Growth (%) 15-16	World share %	Cum.
World	41 883.4	-0.5	3.5	100.0	
USA	9 233.7	-1.9	0.2	22.0	22.0
Germany	7 635.7	-3.3	0.3	18.2	40.3
Netherlands	4 398.3	0.8	41.9	10.5	50.8
Japan	3 597.5	-0.3	1.5	8.6	59.4
China	3 056.3	3.5	-4.3	7.3	66.7
France	1 790.9	-4.1	2.4	4.3	70.9
United Kingdom	1 591.5	-1.8	-11.6	3.8	74.7
Rep. of Korea	1 212.4	4.6	3.0	2.9	77.6
Singapore	960.9	10.5	1.8	2.3	79.9
Mexico	748.4	8.5	7.2	1.8	81.7
Italy	722.4	0.6	5.9	1.7	83.4
Israel	709.9	-4.6	-8.9	1.7	85.1
Finland	631.7	2.6	12.0	1.5	86.6
Switzerland	575.4	-0.6	22.4	1.4	88.0
China, Hong Kong SAR	555.5	1.6	0.5	1.3	89.3

Graph 2: Trade Balance by MDG regions 2016

(Bln US$)

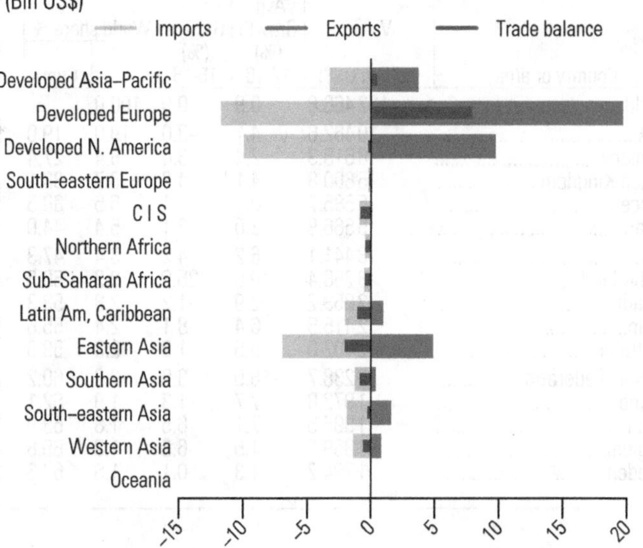

Table 3: Top importing countries or areas in 2016

Country or area	Value (million US$)	Avg. Growth (%) 12-16	Growth (%) 15-16	World share %	Cum.
World	40 433.4	-1.4	1.1	100.0	
USA	9 091.6	2.3	2.8	22.5	22.5
China	5 283.5	1.3	6.7	13.1	35.6
Japan	2 482.2	-3.3	7.2	6.1	41.7
Germany	2 469.2	-4.6	-3.0	6.1	47.8
Netherlands	2 196.5	-2.0	16.0	5.4	53.2
France	1 457.2	-3.3	7.4	3.6	56.8
United Kingdom	1 171.6	-0.6	-9.2	2.9	59.7
Canada	836.0	-3.5	-6.5	2.1	61.8
India	829.0	1.8	-4.2	2.1	63.9
Rep. of Korea	786.8	-0.8	1.9	1.9	65.8
Italy	784.3	-1.3	9.3	1.9	67.7
Australia	659.4	-2.1	-3.0	1.6	69.4
Mexico	628.3	5.5	8.3	1.6	70.9
Singapore	624.3	-0.7	12.0	1.5	72.5
Belgium	545.7	2.2	-6.2	1.3	73.8

Source: UN Comtrade

775 Household-type electrical and non-electrical equipment, nes

In 2016, the value (in current US$) of exports of "household-type electrical and non-electrical equipment, nes" (SITC group 775) increased by 1.3 percent (compared to 1.2 percent average growth rate from 2012-2016) to reach 100.6 bln US$ (see table 2), while imports increased by 0.9 percent to reach 102.5 bln US$ (see table 3). Exports of this commodity accounted for 1.7 percent of world exports of SITC section 7, and 0.6 percent of total world merchandise exports (see table 1). China, Germany and Mexico were the top exporters in 2016 (see table 2). They accounted for 36.0, 9.1 and 5.1 percent of world exports, respectively. USA, Germany and United Kingdom were the top destinations, with respectively 19.0, 8.4 and 5.7 percent of world imports (see table 3).

The top 15 countries/areas accounted for 83.4 and 67.5 percent of total world exports and imports, respectively (see tables 2 and 3). In 2016, China was the country/area with the highest value of net exports (+34.3 bln US$), followed by Mexico (+4.1 bln US$). By MDG regions (see graph 2), the largest surpluses in this product group were recorded by Eastern Asia (+35.1 bln US$), South-eastern Asia (+2.9 bln US$) and Latin America and the Caribbean (+1.3 bln US$). The largest trade deficits were recorded by Developed North America (-18.9 bln US$), Developed Europe (-9.8 bln US$) and Developed Asia-Pacific (-7.3 bln US$).

Table 1: Imports (Imp.) and exports (Exp.), 2002-2016, in current US$

		2002	2003	2004	2005	2006	2007	2008	2009	2010	2011	2012	2013	2014	2015	2016
Values in Bln US$	Imp.	42.2	49.5	57.7	64.3	71.8	83.1	88.8	76.4	88.1	96.9	99.0	102.6	107.3	101.6	102.5
	Exp.	41.7	48.9	58.2	63.7	70.9	81.2	86.1	74.0	84.9	94.4	95.8	101.7	106.2	99.3	100.6
As a percentage of SITC section (%)	Imp.	1.6	1.7	1.6	1.7	1.6	1.6	1.6	1.8	1.7	1.6	1.6	1.7	1.7	1.7	1.7
	Exp.	1.6	1.7	1.7	1.7	1.6	1.6	1.6	1.8	1.7	1.6	1.6	1.7	1.7	1.7	1.7
As a percentage of world trade (%)	Imp.	0.6	0.6	0.6	0.6	0.6	0.6	0.5	0.6	0.6	0.5	0.5	0.5	0.6	0.6	0.6
	Exp.	0.6	0.7	0.6	0.6	0.6	0.6	0.5	0.6	0.6	0.5	0.5	0.5	0.6	0.6	0.6

Graph 1: Annual growth rates of exports, 2002–2016

(In percentage by year)

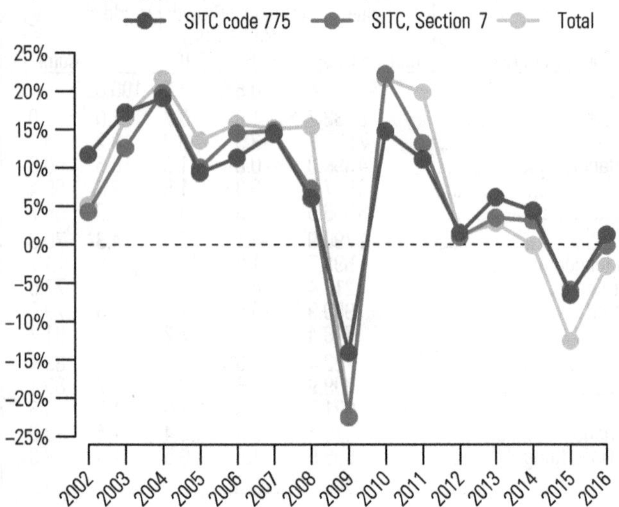

Table 2: Top exporting countries or areas in 2016

Country or area	Value (million US$)	Avg. Growth (%) 12-16	Growth (%) 15-16	World share %	Cum.
World	100623.1	1.2	1.3	100.0	
China	36228.4	2.8	-2.2	36.0	36.0
Germany	9191.6	0.6	5.9	9.1	45.1
Mexico	5120.4	2.4	2.5	5.1	50.2
Poland	4871.9	4.2	-0.8	4.8	55.1
Italy	4423.2	-1.4	-1.6	4.4	59.5
Turkey	3755.6	0.1	1.4	3.7	63.2
Thailand	3285.3	0.4	5.1	3.3	66.5
USA	3190.8	-2.0	-4.8	3.2	69.6
Rep. of Korea	3078.1	-3.6	-3.1	3.1	72.7
Netherlands	2539.7	16.3	34.9	2.5	75.2
France	2129.1	2.1	7.5	2.1	77.3
Malaysia	1775.0	6.4	-4.9	1.8	79.1
China, Hong Kong SAR	1504.0	-10.8	-13.7	1.5	80.6
Czechia	1480.0	10.2	22.0	1.5	82.1
Hungary	1363.2	-3.4	4.9	1.4	83.4

Graph 2: Trade Balance by MDG regions 2016

(Bln US$)

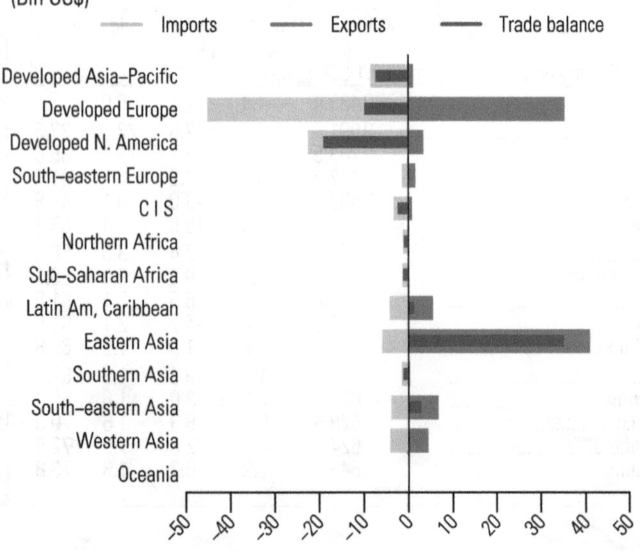

Table 3: Top importing countries or areas in 2016

Country or area	Value (million US$)	Avg. Growth (%) 12-16	Growth (%) 15-16	World share %	Cum.
World	102466.8	0.9	0.9	100.0	
USA	19462.6	4.1	-3.0	19.0	19.0
Germany	8618.3	2.4	3.4	8.4	27.4
United Kingdom	5800.8	4.1	-4.9	5.7	33.1
France	5585.7	-0.1	2.1	5.5	38.5
Japan	5566.9	-2.0	2.1	5.4	44.0
Italy	3441.1	6.2	4.2	3.4	47.3
Netherlands	3258.4	10.5	25.9	3.2	50.5
Canada	2853.2	-2.9	-1.2	2.8	53.3
Spain	2415.5	6.4	8.1	2.4	55.6
Australia	2402.0	0.5	1.9	2.3	58.0
Russian Federation	2238.7	-16.5	3.9	2.2	60.2
Poland	1972.8	7.7	-1.3	1.9	62.1
China	1895.5	7.1	6.5	1.8	63.9
Belgium	1869.2	-1.5	6.6	1.8	65.8
Sweden	1794.2	1.3	0.1	1.8	67.5

"Thermionic, microcircuits, transistors, valves, cathodes, diodes, etc" (SITC group 776) is amongst the top exported commodities in 2016 with 4.0 percent of total exports (see table 1). The value (in current US$) of exports of this commodity increased by 2.6 percent (compared to 3.7 percent average growth rate from 2012-2016) to reach 638.6 bln US$ (see table 2). Exports of this commodity accounted for 10.8 percent of world exports of SITC section 7 (see table 1). China, Hong Kong SAR, China and Other Asia, nes were the top exporters in 2016 (see table 2). They accounted for 17.5, 14.0 and 13.5 percent of world exports, respectively. China, China, Hong Kong SAR and Singapore were the top destinations, with respectively 33.5, 17.3 and 7.7 percent of world imports (see table 3).

The top 15 countries/areas accounted for 95.9 and 92.7 percent of total world exports and imports, respectively (see tables 2 and 3). In 2016, Other Asia, nes was the country/area with the highest value of net exports (+46.7 bln US$), followed by Rep. of Korea (+23.7 bln US$). By MDG regions (see graph 2), the largest surpluses in this product group were recorded by South-eastern Asia (+20.0 bln US$) and Developed Asia-Pacific (+9.2 bln US$). The largest trade deficits were recorded by Eastern Asia (-116.6 bln US$), Latin America and the Caribbean (-19.5 bln US$) and Southern Asia (-5.9 bln US$).

Table 1: Imports (Imp.) and exports (Exp.), 2002-2016, in current US$

		2002	2003	2004	2005	2006	2007	2008	2009	2010	2011	2012	2013	2014	2015	2016
Values in Bln US$	Imp.	278.1	298.8	367.4	394.5	448.1	526.9	530.3	465.9	633.9	655.6	658.4	721.7	740.9	740.4	764.7
	Exp.	252.4	263.6	307.1	320.6	367.5	456.7	449.5	401.2	535.8	551.5	552.8	613.7	623.4	622.5	638.6
As a percentage of SITC section (%)	Imp.	10.8	10.2	10.4	10.2	10.2	10.5	9.8	10.9	12.1	11.1	11.0	11.6	11.6	12.2	12.6
	Exp.	9.8	9.1	8.8	8.4	8.4	9.1	8.3	9.6	10.4	9.5	9.4	10.1	9.9	10.6	10.8
As a percentage of world trade (%)	Imp.	4.2	3.9	3.9	3.7	3.7	3.8	3.3	3.7	4.2	3.6	3.6	3.9	4.0	4.5	4.7
	Exp.	3.9	3.5	3.4	3.1	3.1	3.3	2.8	3.2	3.5	3.0	3.0	3.3	3.3	3.8	4.0

Graph 1: Annual growth rates of exports, 2002–2016

(In percentage by year)

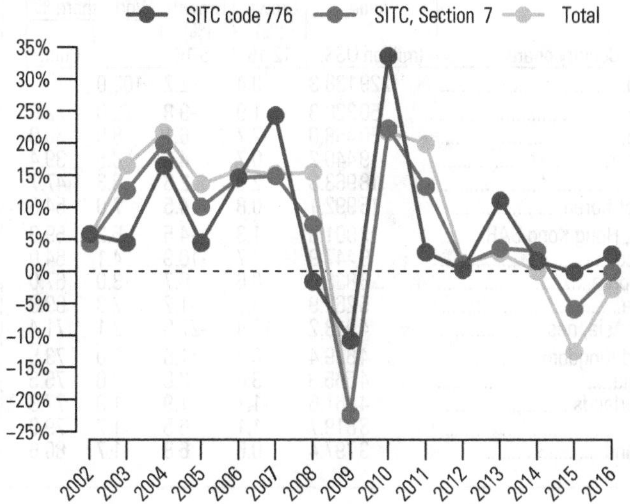

Table 2: Top exporting countries or areas in 2016

Country or area	Value (million US$)	Avg. Growth (%) 12-16	Growth (%) 15-16	World share %	Cum.
World	638627.2	3.7	2.6	100.0	
China, Hong Kong SAR	111861.3	12.8	14.8	17.5	17.5
China	89453.1	2.1	-13.1	14.0	31.5
Other Asia, nes	86117.8	6.8	-10.6	13.5	45.0
Singapore	80948.1	-0.3	-4.2	12.7	57.7
Rep. of Korea	57993.1	5.5	1.1	9.1	66.8
USA	42864.1	0.8	2.9	6.7	73.5
Malaysia	34984.4	1.4	-1.3	5.5	79.0
Japan	33227.2	-5.6	2.7	5.2	84.2
Germany	18900.2	0.8	0.5	3.0	87.1
Philippines	17139.2	8.6	-1.5	2.7	89.8
Netherlands	9652.9	13.8	74.1	1.5	91.3
Thailand	9328.4	5.0	9.0	1.5	92.8
France	8511.7	-2.9	-2.9	1.3	94.1
Ireland	6391.6	41.8	279.1	1.0	95.1
Viet Nam	*5145.5*	24.7	8.9	0.8	95.9

Graph 2: Trade Balance by MDG regions 2016

(Bln US$)

Imports — Exports — Trade balance

Developed Asia-Pacific
Developed Europe
Developed N. America
South-eastern Europe
CIS
Northern Africa
Sub-Saharan Africa
Latin Am, Caribbean
Eastern Asia
Southern Asia
South-eastern Asia
Western Asia
Oceania

-500 -400 -300 -200 -100 0 100 200 300 400

Table 3: Top importing countries or areas in 2016

Country or area	Value (million US$)	Avg. Growth (%) 12-16	Growth (%) 15-16	World share %	Cum.
World	764727.1	3.8	3.3	100.0	
China	256293.7	3.9	-1.8	33.5	33.5
China, Hong Kong SAR	131999.9	12.2	14.5	17.3	50.8
Singapore	58565.5	0.0	0.6	7.7	58.4
USA	45307.3	4.1	9.9	5.9	64.4
Other Asia, nes	39385.2	3.4	14.0	5.2	69.5
Rep. of Korea	34259.1	3.0	-5.3	4.5	74.0
Malaysia	28543.5	-0.5	-0.5	3.7	77.7
Japan	23129.6	0.9	-6.6	3.0	80.7
Germany	19563.0	-1.9	0.6	2.6	83.3
Mexico	18335.4	6.3	0.3	2.4	85.7
Viet Nam	*14993.2*	17.1	5.1	2.0	87.7
Philippines	12838.3	4.1	-10.2	1.7	89.3
Thailand	11082.5	0.6	2.4	1.4	90.8
Netherlands	8689.4	13.6	90.6	1.1	91.9
France	6062.9	-6.3	-6.8	0.8	92.7

778 Electrical machinery and apparatus, nes

"Electrical machinery and apparatus, nes" (SITC group 778) is amongst the top exported commodities in 2016 with 1.4 percent of total exports (see table 1). The value (in current US$) of exports of this commodity decreased by 2.2 percent (compared to 0.4 percent average growth rate from 2012-2016) to reach 229.1 bln US$ (see table 2), while imports increased by less than 0.1 percent to reach 225.3 bln US$ (see table 3). Exports of this commodity accounted for 3.9 percent of world exports of SITC section 7 (see table 1). China, Japan and Germany were the top exporters in 2016 (see table 2). They accounted for 22.0, 8.9 and 8.5 percent of world exports, respectively. USA, China and Germany were the top destinations, with respectively 16.1, 10.7 and 8.4 percent of world imports (see table 3).

The top 15 countries/areas accounted for 80.6 and 69.6 percent of total world exports and imports, respectively (see tables 2 and 3). In 2016, China was the country/area with the highest value of net exports (+26.1 bln US$), followed by Japan (+13.3 bln US$). By MDG regions (see graph 2), the largest surpluses in this product group were recorded by Eastern Asia (+38.5 bln US$), Developed Asia-Pacific (+11.0 bln US$) and South-eastern Asia (+529.1 mln US$). The largest trade deficits were recorded by Developed North America (-21.6 bln US$), Developed Europe (-6.2 bln US$) and Latin America and the Caribbean (-5.7 bln US$).

Table 1: Imports (Imp.) and exports (Exp.), 2002-2016, in current US$

		2002	2003	2004	2005	2006	2007	2008	2009	2010	2011	2012	2013	2014	2015	2016
Values in Bln US$	Imp.	97.0	113.1	139.8	148.8	163.1	178.4	194.4	158.8	196.9	224.2	219.3	228.3	236.1	225.2	225.3
	Exp.	94.2	109.0	135.0	147.1	166.3	180.1	195.0	157.2	198.0	224.4	225.3	238.9	243.8	234.2	229.1
As a percentage of SITC section (%)	Imp.	3.8	3.9	4.0	3.8	3.7	3.5	3.6	3.7	3.8	3.8	3.6	3.7	3.7	3.7	3.7
	Exp.	3.7	3.8	3.9	3.8	3.8	3.6	3.6	3.7	3.9	3.9	3.8	3.9	3.9	4.0	3.9
As a percentage of world trade (%)	Imp.	1.5	1.5	1.5	1.4	1.3	1.3	1.2	1.3	1.3	1.2	1.2	1.2	1.3	1.4	1.4
	Exp.	1.5	1.5	1.5	1.4	1.4	1.3	1.2	1.3	1.3	1.2	1.2	1.3	1.3	1.4	1.4

Graph 1: Annual growth rates of exports, 2002–2016

(In percentage by year)

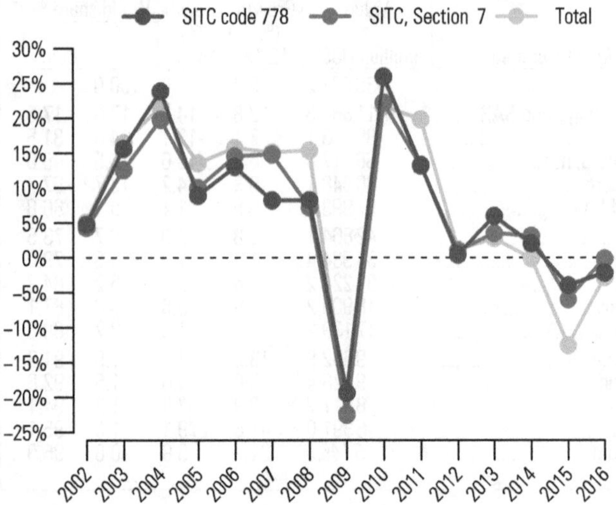

Table 2: Top exporting countries or areas in 2016

Country or area	Value (million US$)	Avg. Growth (%) 12-16	Growth (%) 15-16	World share %	Cum.
World	229 138.3	0.4	-2.2	100.0	
China	50 326.3	1.9	-9.8	22.0	22.0
Japan	20 488.0	-2.7	6.1	8.9	30.9
Germany	19 440.2	0.7	4.6	8.5	39.4
USA	18 963.3	2.5	2.6	8.3	47.7
Rep. of Korea	15 992.1	-0.8	-4.5	7.0	54.6
China, Hong Kong SAR	12 001.8	1.3	-4.5	5.2	59.9
Mexico	9 447.9	4.7	-10.9	4.1	64.0
Singapore	6 836.0	0.6	0.7	3.0	67.0
France	5 262.9	-3.2	-1.2	2.3	69.3
Other Asia, nes	4 913.2	-10.4	-27.8	2.1	71.4
United Kingdom	4 669.4	0.3	-11.8	2.0	73.5
Czechia	4 565.9	3.6	8.8	2.0	75.5
Netherlands	4 261.6	-1.7	1.9	1.9	77.3
Italy	3 819.7	1.1	6.5	1.7	79.0
Thailand	3 797.4	0.6	6.8	1.7	80.6

Graph 2: Trade Balance by MDG regions 2016

(Bln US$)

Imports — Exports — Trade balance

Developed Asia-Pacific
Developed Europe
Developed N. America
South-eastern Europe
C I S
Northern Africa
Sub-Saharan Africa
Latin Am, Caribbean
Eastern Asia
Southern Asia
South-eastern Asia
Western Asia
Oceania

-80 -60 -40 -20 0 20 40 60 80 100

Table 3: Top importing countries or areas in 2016

Country or area	Value (million US$)	Avg. Growth (%) 12-16	Growth (%) 15-16	World share %	Cum.
World	225 280.1	0.7	0.0	100.0	
USA	36 214.6	4.6	0.9	16.1	16.1
China	24 196.1	-0.6	-8.3	10.7	26.8
Germany	18 837.6	3.1	4.3	8.4	35.2
China, Hong Kong SAR	11 937.3	1.2	-4.1	5.3	40.5
Mexico	9 863.4	5.6	8.3	4.4	44.9
France	7 536.0	0.3	-1.5	3.3	48.2
Japan	7 154.4	-1.6	4.1	3.2	51.4
United Kingdom	7 136.3	2.1	-4.8	3.2	54.5
Canada	6 336.7	2.9	2.9	2.8	57.4
Rep. of Korea	5 592.4	-5.2	-14.0	2.5	59.8
Netherlands	4 888.4	2.8	7.5	2.2	62.0
Thailand	4 623.4	-3.1	7.9	2.1	64.1
Singapore	4 504.7	-1.9	0.1	2.0	66.1
Italy	4 030.5	0.2	1.5	1.8	67.8
Spain	4 020.2	6.5	4.4	1.8	69.6

"Cars, other motor vehicles principally designed for the transports of persons" (SITC group 781) is amongst the top exported commodities in 2016 with 4.4 percent of total exports (see table 1). The value (in current US$) of exports of this commodity increased by 4.0 percent (compared to 2.0 percent average growth rate from 2012-2016) to reach 704.7 bln US$ (see table 2), while imports increased by 3.5 percent to reach 707.2 bln US$ (see table 3). Exports of this commodity accounted for 12.0 percent of world exports of SITC section 7 (see table 1). Germany, Japan and USA were the top exporters in 2016 (see table 2). They accounted for 21.6, 13.0 and 7.6 percent of world exports, respectively. USA, Germany and United Kingdom were the top destinations, with respectively 24.5, 7.3 and 6.4 percent of world imports (see table 3).

The top 15 countries/areas accounted for 86.9 and 73.9 percent of total world exports and imports, respectively (see tables 2 and 3). In 2016, Germany was the country/area with the highest value of net exports (+100.6 bln US$), followed by Japan (+81.6 bln US$). By MDG regions (see graph 2), the largest surpluses in this product group were recorded by Developed Europe (+83.5 bln US$), Developed Asia-Pacific (+63.7 bln US$) and Latin America and the Caribbean (+8.2 bln US$). The largest trade deficits were recorded by Developed North America (-97.1 bln US$), Western Asia (-34.8 bln US$) and Eastern Asia (-16.4 bln US$).

Table 1: Imports (Imp.) and exports (Exp.), 2002-2016, in current US$

		2002	2003	2004	2005	2006	2007	2008	2009	2010	2011	2012	2013	2014	2015	2016
Values in Bln US$	Imp.	347.8	398.0	463.6	484.6	541.1	626.6	632.8	445.2	553.2	637.0	652.0	678.8	710.4	683.0	707.2
	Exp.	344.3	393.9	455.7	487.0	536.9	623.3	636.8	438.5	558.5	640.2	651.7	679.6	710.1	677.5	704.7
As a percentage of SITC section (%)	Imp.	13.5	13.6	13.2	12.5	12.3	12.4	11.7	10.4	10.6	10.8	10.8	10.9	11.1	11.3	11.6
	Exp.	13.4	13.6	13.1	12.7	12.2	12.4	11.8	10.5	10.9	11.0	11.1	11.2	11.3	11.5	12.0
As a percentage of world trade (%)	Imp.	5.3	5.2	4.9	4.6	4.4	4.5	3.9	3.5	3.6	3.5	3.5	3.6	3.8	4.1	4.4
	Exp.	5.3	5.2	5.0	4.7	4.5	4.5	4.0	3.5	3.7	3.5	3.6	3.6	3.8	4.1	4.4

Graph 1: Annual growth rates of exports, 2002–2016

(In percentage by year)

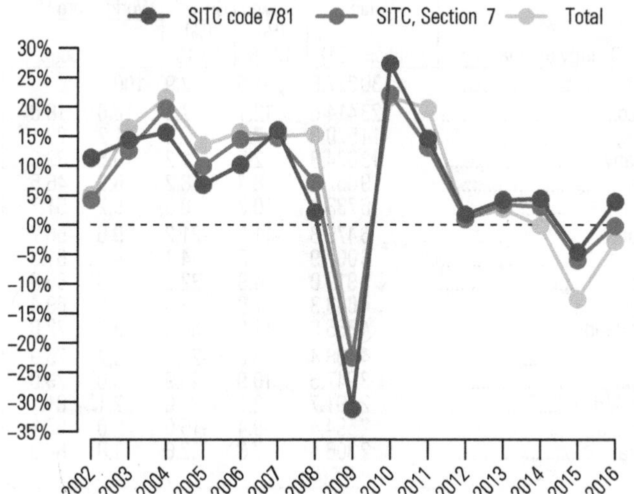

Table 2: Top exporting countries or areas in 2016

Country or area	Value (million US$)	Avg. Growth (%) 12-16	Growth (%) 15-16	World share %	Cum.
World	704674.7	2.0	4.0	100.0	
Germany	151920.8	0.9	-0.8	21.6	21.6
Japan	91900.0	-1.5	6.8	13.0	34.6
USA	53861.2	-0.3	-2.8	7.6	42.2
Canada	48835.0	1.0	8.8	6.9	49.2
United Kingdom	40785.8	4.7	4.7	5.8	55.0
Rep. of Korea	37496.4	-3.0	-10.1	5.3	60.3
Spain	35563.8	9.1	7.3	5.0	65.3
Mexico	31417.6	1.9	-4.3	4.5	69.8
Belgium	30330.3	2.5	9.3	4.3	74.1
Czechia	18799.5	5.5	10.0	2.7	76.8
France	18372.5	-2.5	4.3	2.6	79.4
Slovakia	15483.0	4.0	11.8	2.2	81.6
Italy	15169.9	13.3	8.5	2.2	83.7
Thailand	11623.0	19.6	23.7	1.6	85.4
Hungary	11052.8	21.4	-1.4	1.6	86.9

Graph 2: Trade Balance by MDG regions 2016

(Bln US$)

Imports — Exports — Trade balance

Developed Asia-Pacific
Developed Europe
Developed N. America
South-eastern Europe
CIS
Northern Africa
Sub-Saharan Africa
Latin Am, Caribbean
Eastern Asia
Southern Asia
South-eastern Asia
Western Asia
Oceania

-300 -200 -100 0 100 200 300 400

Table 3: Top importing countries or areas in 2016

Country or area	Value (million US$)	Avg. Growth (%) 12-16	Growth (%) 15-16	World share %	Cum.
World	707163.7	2.1	3.5	100.0	
USA	173287.7	3.8	2.4	24.5	24.5
Germany	51274.6	5.0	11.3	7.3	31.8
United Kingdom	45585.0	7.2	-6.4	6.4	38.2
China	44005.2	-0.8	-0.5	6.2	44.4
France	31893.3	1.6	9.2	4.5	48.9
Belgium	31446.5	5.3	10.7	4.4	53.4
Italy	27480.9	7.9	21.7	3.9	57.3
Canada	26437.7	0.5	0.5	3.7	61.0
Spain	18271.5	16.1	12.5	2.6	63.6
Australia	15961.4	-2.3	4.3	2.3	65.8
Saudi Arabia	12875.9	-5.3	-27.0	1.8	67.7
Netherlands	11791.1	1.3	24.0	1.7	69.3
United Arab Emirates	11697.9	-1.8	-15.0	1.7	71.0
Japan	10328.6	-1.3	15.0	1.5	72.4
Switzerland	10295.6	-1.6	-2.0	1.5	73.9

In 2016, the value (in current US$) of exports of "motor vehicles for the transport of goods; special-purpose motor vehicles" (SITC group 782) increased by 2.9 percent (compared to -1.5 percent average growth rate from 2012-2016) to reach 130.3 bln US$ (see table 2), while imports increased by 3.1 percent to reach 134.9 bln US$ (see table 3). Exports of this commodity accounted for 2.2 percent of world exports of SITC section 7, and 0.8 percent of total world merchandise exports (see table 1). Mexico, USA and Germany were the top exporters in 2016 (see table 2). They accounted for 18.0, 11.2 and 10.5 percent of world exports, respectively. USA, Canada and United Kingdom were the top destinations, with respectively 19.1, 10.1 and 5.4 percent of world imports (see table 3).

The top 15 countries/areas accounted for 84.9 and 64.9 percent of total world exports and imports, respectively (see tables 2 and 3). In 2016, Mexico was the country/area with the highest value of net exports (+21.1 bln US$), followed by Japan (+8.6 bln US$). By MDG regions (see graph 2), the largest surpluses in this product group were recorded by Latin America and the Caribbean (+16.9 bln US$), Developed Europe (+5.1 bln US$) and Eastern Asia (+4.2 bln US$). The largest trade deficits were recorded by Developed North America (-22.7 bln US$), Western Asia (-2.8 bln US$) and Sub-Saharan Africa (-2.5 bln US$).

Table 1: Imports (Imp.) and exports (Exp.), 2002-2016, in current US$

		2002	2003	2004	2005	2006	2007	2008	2009	2010	2011	2012	2013	2014	2015	2016
Values in Bln US$	Imp.	64.5	72.0	84.7	94.5	107.7	133.4	140.3	84.6	109.3	131.3	140.6	139.7	140.5	130.8	134.9
	Exp.	60.2	68.2	80.2	89.8	103.2	127.9	134.3	79.9	105.1	128.5	138.6	137.4	139.0	126.6	130.3
As a percentage of SITC section (%)	Imp.	2.5	2.5	2.4	2.4	2.5	2.6	2.6	2.0	2.1	2.2	2.3	2.3	2.2	2.2	2.2
	Exp.	2.3	2.4	2.3	2.3	2.4	2.5	2.5	1.9	2.0	2.2	2.4	2.3	2.2	2.1	2.2
As a percentage of world trade (%)	Imp.	1.0	0.9	0.9	0.9	0.9	1.0	0.9	0.7	0.7	0.7	0.8	0.7	0.8	0.8	0.8
	Exp.	0.9	0.9	0.9	0.9	0.9	0.9	0.8	0.6	0.7	0.7	0.8	0.7	0.7	0.8	0.8

Graph 1: Annual growth rates of exports, 2002–2016
(In percentage by year)

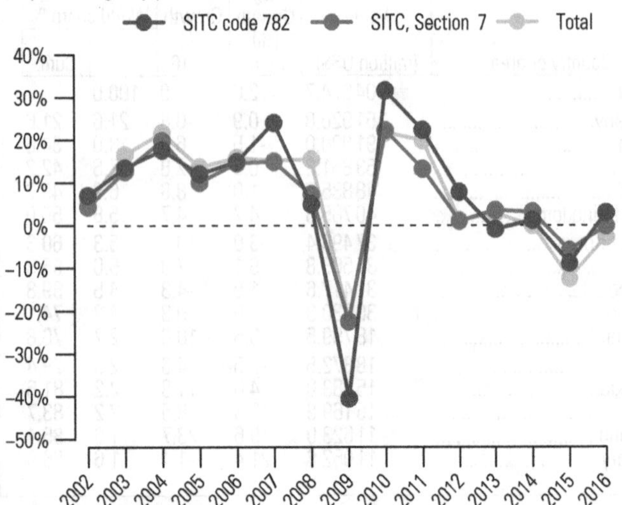

Table 2: Top exporting countries or areas in 2016

Country or area	Value (million US$)	Avg. Growth (%) 12-16	Growth (%) 15-16	World share %	Cum.
World	130327.5	-1.5	2.9	100.0	
Mexico	23414.6	12.1	7.5	18.0	18.0
USA	14570.8	-7.3	2.4	11.2	29.1
Germany	13624.3	-2.5	1.2	10.5	39.6
Japan	9057.4	-8.4	-8.2	6.9	46.5
France	6733.4	10.2	8.0	5.2	51.7
Thailand	6479.3	-11.5	-21.2	5.0	56.7
Italy	6007.9	1.8	4.4	4.6	61.3
Spain	5919.0	4.9	32.3	4.5	65.8
Turkey	4683.3	7.0	6.3	3.6	69.4
Netherlands	4355.5	11.8	56.6	3.3	72.8
China	4108.4	-10.6	-23.0	3.2	75.9
Belgium	3947.5	10.9	49.9	3.0	79.0
South Africa	2791.7	-2.7	23.0	2.1	81.1
Argentina	2584.4	-9.4	-15.0	2.0	83.1
Austria	2306.4	7.3	32.6	1.8	84.9

Graph 2: Trade Balance by MDG regions 2016
(Bln US$)

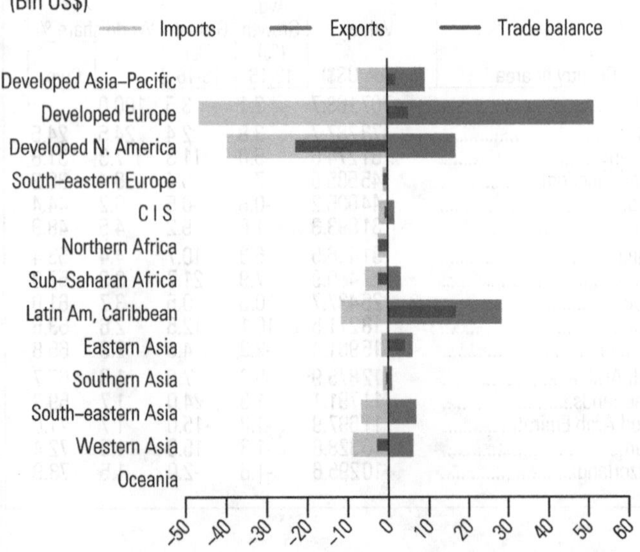

Table 3: Top importing countries or areas in 2016

Country or area	Value (million US$)	Avg. Growth (%) 12-16	Growth (%) 15-16	World share %	Cum.
World	134873.7	-1.0	3.1	100.0	
USA	25763.6	10.5	6.0	19.1	19.1
Canada	13662.5	-0.8	7.9	10.1	29.2
United Kingdom	7251.8	7.7	-11.0	5.4	34.6
France	6070.3	2.7	14.1	4.5	39.1
Germany	5856.9	-0.7	6.1	4.3	43.5
Australia	5618.4	-10.8	11.1	4.2	47.6
Belgium	4362.6	7.5	31.7	3.2	50.9
Netherlands	3192.9	4.3	37.2	2.4	53.2
Italy	3161.0	13.0	42.4	2.3	55.6
Saudi Arabia	2516.6	-9.6	-36.6	1.9	57.4
Spain	2371.6	31.6	17.7	1.8	59.2
Mexico	2297.2	-0.9	4.4	1.7	60.9
Viet Nam	*1884.9*	49.0	5.1	1.4	62.3
Chile	1856.0	-12.8	0.6	1.4	63.7
Austria	1655.0	10.2	22.4	1.2	64.9

Source: UN Comtrade

In 2016, the value (in current US$) of exports of "road motor vehicles, nes" (SITC group 783) decreased by 11.3 percent (compared to -1.5 percent average growth rate from 2012-2016) to reach 43.3 bln US$ (see table 2), while imports decreased by 7.0 percent to reach 40.6 bln US$ (see table 3). Exports of this commodity accounted for 0.7 percent of world exports of SITC section 7, and 0.3 percent of total world merchandise exports (see table 1). Germany, Netherlands and Mexico were the top exporters in 2016 (see table 2). They accounted for 14.8, 12.9 and 12.3 percent of world exports, respectively. USA, France and Germany were the top destinations, with respectively 14.3, 5.9 and 5.6 percent of world imports (see table 3).

The top 15 countries/areas accounted for 89.6 and 58.3 percent of total world exports and imports, respectively (see tables 2 and 3). In 2016, Mexico was the country/area with the highest value of net exports (+4.9 bln US$), followed by Netherlands (+4.8 bln US$). By MDG regions (see graph 2), the largest surpluses in this product group were recorded by Developed Europe (+6.4 bln US$), Latin America and the Caribbean (+3.1 bln US$) and Eastern Asia (+2.5 bln US$). The largest trade deficits were recorded by Developed North America (-5.1 bln US$), South-eastern Asia (-1.8 bln US$) and Sub-Saharan Africa (-1.7 bln US$).

Table 1: Imports (Imp.) and exports (Exp.), 2002-2016, in current US$

		2002	2003	2004	2005	2006	2007	2008	2009	2010	2011	2012	2013	2014	2015	2016
Values in Bln US$	Imp.	14.9	17.7	23.6	25.8	31.1	39.6	45.5	25.4	30.3	42.2	40.9	42.4	45.2	43.7	40.6
	Exp.	16.6	20.9	27.7	30.2	34.3	41.5	49.9	25.1	32.7	46.3	45.9	46.8	50.6	48.8	43.3
As a percentage of SITC section (%)	Imp.	0.6	0.6	0.7	0.7	0.7	0.8	0.8	0.6	0.6	0.7	0.7	0.7	0.7	0.7	0.7
	Exp.	0.6	0.7	0.8	0.8	0.8	0.8	0.9	0.6	0.6	0.8	0.8	0.8	0.8	0.8	0.7
As a percentage of world trade (%)	Imp.	0.2	0.2	0.3	0.2	0.3	0.3	0.3	0.2	0.2	0.2	0.2	0.2	0.2	0.3	0.3
	Exp.	0.3	0.3	0.3	0.3	0.3	0.3	0.3	0.2	0.2	0.3	0.3	0.2	0.3	0.3	0.3

Graph 1: Annual growth rates of exports, 2002–2016
(In percentage by year)

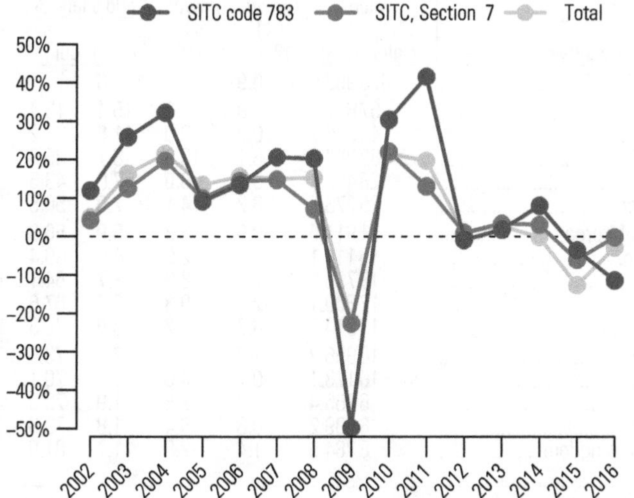

Graph 2: Trade Balance by MDG regions 2016
(Bln US$)

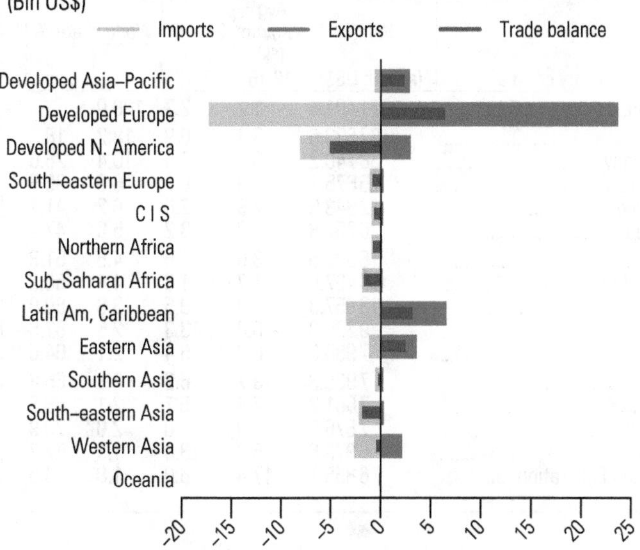

Table 2: Top exporting countries or areas in 2016

Country or area	Value (million US$)	Avg. Growth (%) 12-16	Growth (%) 15-16	World share %	Cum.
World	43305.8	-1.5	-11.3	100.0	
Germany	6404.8	-1.4	-8.7	14.8	14.8
Netherlands	5573.7	5.2	11.8	12.9	27.7
Mexico	5311.4	-1.8	-38.1	12.3	39.9
Japan	2870.8	-6.2	-9.8	6.6	46.6
China	2794.1	-1.3	-18.7	6.5	53.0
Belgium	2446.7	-5.2	-20.8	5.6	58.7
USA	2360.2	-12.5	-20.9	5.5	64.1
France	2149.2	1.3	-2.3	5.0	69.1
Turkey	1819.8	13.4	45.3	4.2	73.3
Poland	1663.1	1.7	0.9	3.8	77.1
Spain	1465.8	15.9	-6.9	3.4	80.5
Sweden	1456.1	-3.3	-4.5	3.4	83.9
Brazil	917.2	-3.1	2.6	2.1	86.0
Rep. of Korea	801.1	-15.6	-31.8	1.8	87.8
Czechia	766.0	6.1	-1.2	1.8	89.6

Table 3: Top importing countries or areas in 2016

Country or area	Value (million US$)	Avg. Growth (%) 12-16	Growth (%) 15-16	World share %	Cum.
World	40633.7	-0.2	-7.0	100.0	
USA	5804.6	2.6	-35.8	14.3	14.3
France	2386.7	6.4	11.4	5.9	20.2
Germany	2273.9	6.2	9.8	5.6	25.8
Canada	2260.3	-7.6	-22.6	5.6	31.3
Italy	1657.1	17.7	45.9	4.1	35.4
Poland	1555.5	8.6	23.2	3.8	39.2
United Kingdom	1118.8	13.1	10.6	2.8	42.0
Spain	1079.9	14.0	4.6	2.7	44.6
Belgium	1072.8	2.7	13.9	2.6	47.3
Austria	883.1	13.9	56.5	2.2	49.4
Philippines	792.4	20.4	17.7	2.0	51.4
Netherlands	764.0	1.9	9.1	1.9	53.3
Czechia	716.0	11.2	0.0	1.8	55.0
United Arab Emirates	688.3	-1.7	-29.7	1.7	56.7
Chile	641.9	-9.4	3.6	1.6	58.3

784 Parts and accessories of the motor vehicles of 722, 781, 782 and 783

"Parts and accessories of the motor vehicles of 722, 781, 782 and 783" (SITC group 784) is amongst the top exported commodities in 2016 with 2.3 percent of total exports (see table 1). The value (in current US$) of exports of this commodity increased by 3.1 percent (compared to 0.9 percent average growth rate from 2012-2016) to reach 374.0 bln US$ (see table 2), while imports increased by 2.7 percent to reach 371.4 bln US$ (see table 3). Exports of this commodity accounted for 6.3 percent of world exports of SITC section 7 (see table 1). Germany, USA and Japan were the top exporters in 2016 (see table 2). They accounted for 15.4, 11.8 and 8.7 percent of world exports, respectively. USA, Germany and China were the top destinations, with respectively 18.2, 10.4 and 6.9 percent of world imports (see table 3).

The top 15 countries/areas accounted for 81.5 and 74.6 percent of total world exports and imports, respectively (see tables 2 and 3). In 2016, Japan was the country/area with the highest value of net exports (+24.7 bln US$), followed by Germany (+18.9 bln US$). By MDG regions (see graph 2), the largest surpluses in this product group were recorded by Eastern Asia (+22.7 bln US$), Developed Asia-Pacific (+22.7 bln US$) and Developed Europe (+12.1 bln US$). The largest trade deficits were recorded by Developed North America (-33.3 bln US$), Commonwealth of Independent States (-8.2 bln US$) and Western Asia (-4.9 bln US$).

Table 1: Imports (Imp.) and exports (Exp.), 2002-2016, in current US$

		2002	2003	2004	2005	2006	2007	2008	2009	2010	2011	2012	2013	2014	2015	2016
Values in Bln US$	Imp.	156.5	182.8	216.2	231.4	255.6	296.7	307.7	223.5	292.6	347.4	354.4	375.2	388.0	361.6	371.4
	Exp.	152.8	179.5	214.2	234.4	258.3	296.5	309.9	227.9	301.4	355.3	360.9	377.9	385.9	362.7	374.0
As a percentage of SITC section (%)	Imp.	6.1	6.3	6.1	6.0	5.8	5.9	5.7	5.2	5.6	5.9	5.9	6.0	6.1	6.0	6.1
	Exp.	5.9	6.2	6.2	6.1	5.9	5.9	5.7	5.4	5.9	6.1	6.2	6.2	6.2	6.2	6.3
As a percentage of world trade (%)	Imp.	2.4	2.4	2.3	2.2	2.1	2.1	1.9	1.8	1.9	1.9	1.9	2.0	2.1	2.2	2.3
	Exp.	2.4	2.4	2.3	2.3	2.2	2.1	1.9	1.8	2.0	2.0	2.0	2.0	2.1	2.2	2.3

Graph 1: Annual growth rates of exports, 2002–2016

(In percentage by year)

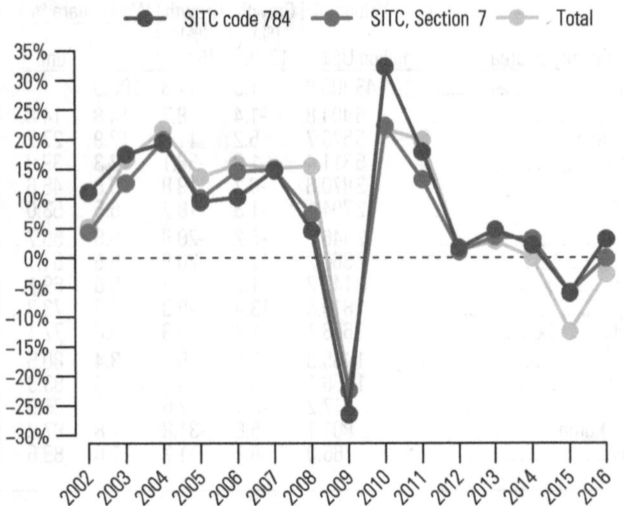

Graph 2: Trade Balance by MDG regions 2016

(Bln US$)

Imports — Exports — Trade balance

Developed Asia-Pacific
Developed Europe
Developed N. America
South-eastern Europe
CIS
Northern Africa
Sub-Saharan Africa
Latin Am, Caribbean
Eastern Asia
Southern Asia
South-eastern Asia
Western Asia
Oceania

-200 -150 -100 -50 0 50 100 150 200

Table 2: Top exporting countries or areas in 2016

Country or area	Value (million US$)	Avg. Growth (%) 12-16	Growth (%) 15-16	World share %	Cum.
World	373 952.0	0.9	3.1	100.0	
Germany	57 617.2	1.8	5.2	15.4	15.4
USA	43 996.7	0.9	-2.0	11.8	27.2
Japan	32 387.9	-6.1	10.8	8.7	35.8
China	28 492.1	5.7	0.0	7.6	43.5
Mexico	26 273.2	8.2	4.1	7.0	50.5
Rep. of Korea	21 911.5	-0.9	-5.3	5.9	56.3
France	15 118.1	-3.5	2.0	4.0	60.4
Czechia	13 735.9	7.1	8.6	3.7	64.1
Italy	12 800.1	-2.3	-0.3	3.4	67.5
Poland	11 314.7	6.7	12.2	3.0	70.5
Canada	10 956.3	1.2	-2.8	2.9	73.4
Spain	10 123.1	-0.7	4.0	2.7	76.1
Thailand	6 955.4	4.2	2.8	1.9	78.0
Sweden	6 709.2	0.8	16.4	1.8	79.8
United Kingdom	6 384.5	-1.4	-2.5	1.7	81.5

Table 3: Top importing countries or areas in 2016

Country or area	Value (million US$)	Avg. Growth (%) 12-16	Growth (%) 15-16	World share %	Cum.
World	371 401.4	1.2	2.7	100.0	
USA	67 533.6	3.4	-0.9	18.2	18.2
Germany	38 740.2	3.2	7.6	10.4	28.6
China	25 675.7	3.9	8.7	6.9	35.5
Mexico	22 943.9	2.5	-2.6	6.2	41.7
Canada	20 652.8	-1.2	3.2	5.6	47.3
Spain	16 808.5	3.0	-3.0	4.5	51.8
United Kingdom	16 467.5	1.7	1.6	4.4	56.2
France	13 957.3	1.9	9.5	3.8	60.0
Czechia	9 225.8	6.0	13.3	2.5	62.5
Italy	7 980.3	6.8	6.4	2.1	64.6
Slovakia	7 938.3	3.7	6.2	2.1	66.8
Japan	7 661.2	2.4	5.7	2.1	68.8
Belgium	7 576.5	-6.0	3.0	2.0	70.9
Poland	6 973.6	6.3	13.3	1.9	72.7
Russian Federation	6 855.7	-17.4	6.0	1.8	74.6

In 2016, the value (in current US$) of exports of "motorcycles and cycles motorized and non-motorized; invalid carriages" (SITC group 785) decreased by 1.0 percent (compared to 1.1 percent average growth rate from 2012-2016) to reach 50.1 bln US$ (see table 2), while imports decreased by 1.7 percent to reach 45.4 bln US$ (see table 3). Exports of this commodity accounted for 0.9 percent of world exports of SITC section 7, and 0.3 percent of total world merchandise exports (see table 1). China, Other Asia, nes and Japan were the top exporters in 2016 (see table 2). They accounted for 29.9, 8.9 and 8.1 percent of world exports, respectively. USA, Germany and Netherlands were the top destinations, with respectively 11.5, 9.4 and 5.5 percent of world imports (see table 3).

The top 15 countries/areas accounted for 87.6 and 62.7 percent of total world exports and imports, respectively (see tables 2 and 3). In 2016, China was the country/area with the highest value of net exports (+14.2 bln US$), followed by Other Asia, nes (+3.3 bln US$). By MDG regions (see graph 2), the largest surpluses in this product group were recorded by Eastern Asia (+16.8 bln US$), Developed Asia-Pacific (+1.2 bln US$) and South-eastern Asia (+989.1 mln US$). The largest trade deficits were recorded by Developed Europe (-5.6 bln US$), Developed North America (-3.7 bln US$) and Latin America and the Caribbean (-2.9 bln US$).

Table 1: Imports (Imp.) and exports (Exp.), 2002-2016, in current US$

		2002	2003	2004	2005	2006	2007	2008	2009	2010	2011	2012	2013	2014	2015	2016
Values in Bln US$	Imp.	21.1	24.8	29.2	32.1	34.9	41.2	45.5	35.2	38.4	44.2	44.9	45.3	47.8	46.1	45.4
	Exp.	21.1	25.0	29.7	32.5	35.5	40.5	46.6	35.2	39.9	46.8	47.9	49.0	52.6	50.6	50.1
As a percentage of SITC section (%)	Imp.	0.8	0.8	0.8	0.8	0.8	0.8	0.8	0.8	0.7	0.7	0.7	0.7	0.7	0.8	0.7
	Exp.	0.8	0.9	0.9	0.8	0.8	0.8	0.9	0.8	0.8	0.8	0.8	0.8	0.8	0.9	0.9
As a percentage of world trade (%)	Imp.	0.3	0.3	0.3	0.3	0.3	0.3	0.3	0.3	0.3	0.2	0.2	0.2	0.3	0.3	0.3
	Exp.	0.3	0.3	0.3	0.3	0.3	0.3	0.3	0.3	0.3	0.3	0.3	0.3	0.3	0.3	0.3

Graph 1: Annual growth rates of exports, 2002–2016
(In percentage by year)

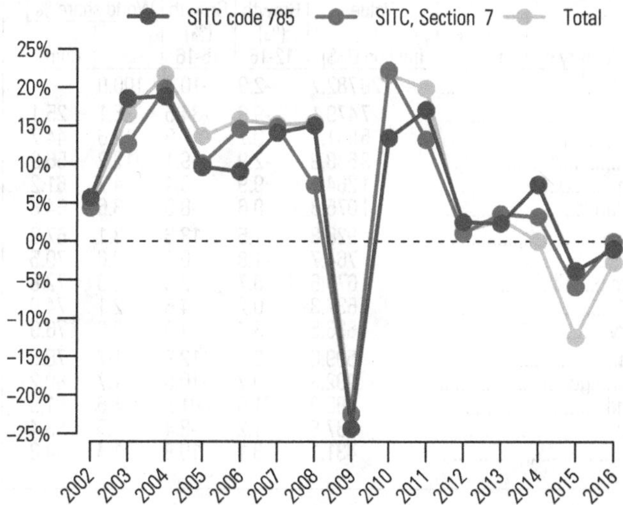

Table 2: Top exporting countries or areas in 2016

Country or area	Value (million US$)	Avg. Growth (%) 12-16	Growth (%) 15-16	World share %	Cum.
World	50081.0	1.1	-1.0	100.0	
China	14964.3	2.3	-5.0	29.9	29.9
Other Asia, nes	4459.5	-1.6	-8.6	8.9	38.8
Japan	4059.0	-5.4	0.0	8.1	46.9
Germany	3263.1	6.1	4.8	6.5	53.4
Italy	2720.7	-2.5	-0.3	5.4	58.8
USA	2173.4	-1.3	-1.8	4.3	63.2
India	2057.9	4.5	-8.3	4.1	67.3
Netherlands	1832.2	4.8	7.5	3.7	70.9
Thailand	1775.4	-1.6	-1.6	3.5	74.5
Austria	1450.4	12.9	21.6	2.9	77.4
Belgium	1261.1	3.2	19.5	2.5	79.9
Indonesia	1034.1	6.8	18.2	2.1	82.0
Viet Nam	*993.0*	19.7	8.9	2.0	84.0
Singapore	963.4	-5.2	-14.4	1.9	85.9
France	869.2	4.3	6.3	1.7	87.6

Graph 2: Trade Balance by MDG regions 2016
(Bln US$)

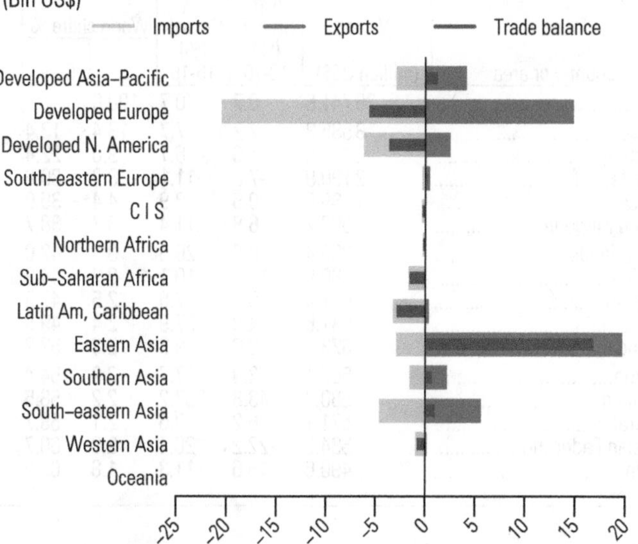

Table 3: Top importing countries or areas in 2016

Country or area	Value (million US$)	Avg. Growth (%) 12-16	Growth (%) 15-16	World share %	Cum.
World	45350.8	0.3	-1.7	100.0	
USA	5217.2	-2.1	-8.0	11.5	11.5
Germany	4254.2	3.7	5.1	9.4	20.9
Netherlands	2491.3	6.4	13.5	5.5	26.4
France	2448.1	1.2	8.0	5.4	31.8
United Kingdom	1881.7	2.0	-1.0	4.1	35.9
Japan	1840.1	-5.6	-7.0	4.1	40.0
Italy	1820.9	1.3	4.9	4.0	44.0
Belgium	1423.0	-1.9	11.2	3.1	47.1
Spain	1250.4	4.7	9.1	2.8	49.9
Other Asia, nes	1137.4	-2.2	-14.9	2.5	52.4
Philippines	1009.5	20.9	34.7	2.2	54.6
Austria	987.9	7.1	30.8	2.2	56.8
Canada	939.0	-2.5	-4.8	2.1	58.9
Australia	876.7	-4.6	-4.6	1.9	60.8
Switzerland	869.4	2.1	4.7	1.9	62.7

786 Trailers, semi-trailers; other vehicles, not mechanically propelled

In 2016, the value (in current US$) of exports of "trailers, semi-trailers; other vehicles, not mechanically propelled" (SITC group 786) decreased by 10.4 percent (compared to -2.9 percent average growth rate from 2012-2016) to reach 29.8 bln US$ (see table 2), while imports decreased by 0.7 percent to reach 26.7 bln US$ (see table 3). Exports of this commodity accounted for 0.5 percent of world exports of SITC section 7, and 0.2 percent of total world merchandise exports (see table 1). China, Germany and USA were the top exporters in 2016 (see table 2). They accounted for 25.1, 19.6 and 12.2 percent of world exports, respectively. USA, Germany and Canada were the top destinations, with respectively 13.4, 9.0 and 8.2 percent of world imports (see table 3).

The top 15 countries/areas accounted for 84.8 and 62.5 percent of total world exports and imports, respectively (see tables 2 and 3). In 2016, China was the country/area with the highest value of net exports (+7.3 bln US$), followed by Germany (+3.4 bln US$). By MDG regions (see graph 2), the largest surpluses in this product group were recorded by Eastern Asia (+7.2 bln US$) and Developed Europe (+1.7 bln US$). The largest trade deficits were recorded by Developed North America (-1.7 bln US$), Developed Asia-Pacific (-964.7 mln US$) and Western Asia (-834.1 mln US$).

Table 1: Imports (Imp.) and exports (Exp.), 2002-2016, in current US$

		2002	2003	2004	2005	2006	2007	2008	2009	2010	2011	2012	2013	2014	2015	2016
Values in Bln US$	Imp.	8.9	11.0	14.4	16.9	20.6	26.7	28.7	15.6	18.6	25.3	26.0	27.6	29.3	26.9	26.7
	Exp.	11.1	14.9	20.0	23.2	26.7	34.9	37.2	17.4	25.7	36.4	33.5	33.9	36.5	33.2	29.8
As a percentage of SITC section (%)	Imp.	0.3	0.4	0.4	0.4	0.5	0.5	0.5	0.4	0.4	0.4	0.4	0.4	0.5	0.4	0.4
	Exp.	0.4	0.5	0.6	0.6	0.6	0.7	0.7	0.4	0.5	0.6	0.6	0.6	0.6	0.6	0.5
As a percentage of world trade (%)	Imp.	0.1	0.1	0.2	0.2	0.2	0.2	0.2	0.1	0.1	0.1	0.1	0.1	0.2	0.2	0.2
	Exp.	0.2	0.2	0.2	0.2	0.2	0.3	0.2	0.1	0.2	0.2	0.2	0.2	0.2	0.2	0.2

Graph 1: Annual growth rates of exports, 2002–2016

(In percentage by year)

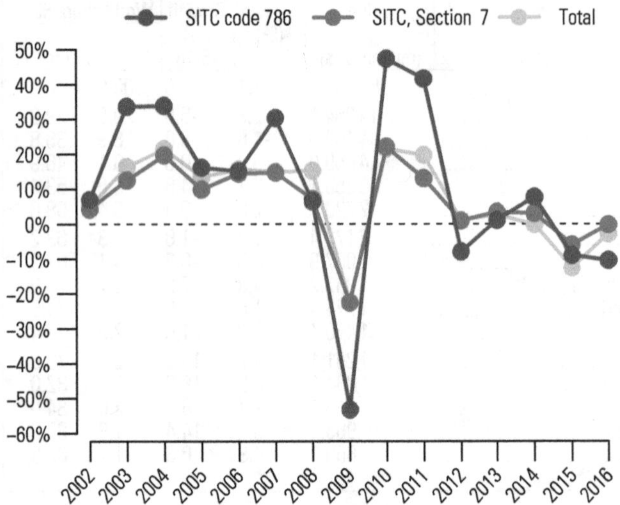

Graph 2: Trade Balance by MDG regions 2016

(Bln US$)

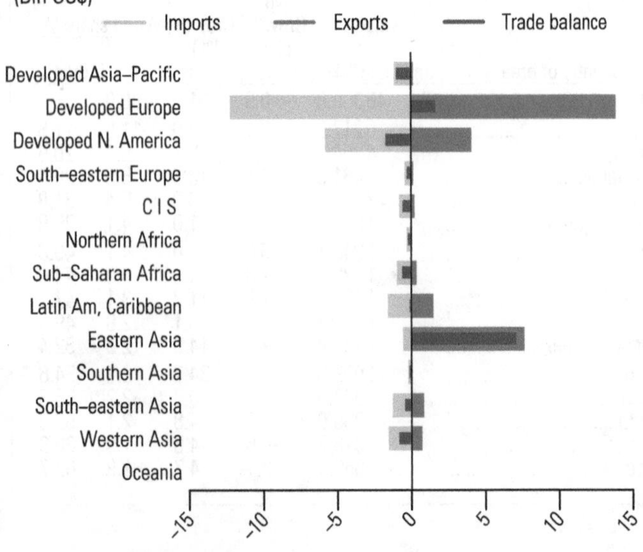

Table 2: Top exporting countries or areas in 2016

Country or area	Value (million US$)	Avg. Growth (%) 12-16	Growth (%) 15-16	World share %	Cum.
World	29782.7	-2.9	-10.4	100.0	
China	7479.1	-9.9	-34.5	25.1	25.1
Germany	5841.7	0.7	7.9	19.6	44.7
USA	3638.9	-2.9	-9.1	12.2	56.9
Mexico	1264.1	9.9	-8.4	4.2	61.2
Netherlands	1075.3	0.6	-8.5	3.6	64.8
Poland	928.8	1.5	13.6	3.1	67.9
France	764.7	-1.8	-0.5	2.6	70.5
Belgium	679.6	0.7	-2.5	2.3	72.8
Italy	637.3	0.2	4.6	2.1	74.9
Hungary	586.5	3.4	4.8	2.0	76.9
Austria	509.8	0.9	12.9	1.7	78.6
United Kingdom	492.3	0.2	-10.5	1.7	80.2
Thailand	490.0	71.6	801.8	1.6	81.9
Canada	437.5	1.2	-3.4	1.5	83.4
Turkey	431.1	8.1	10.8	1.4	84.8

Table 3: Top importing countries or areas in 2016

Country or area	Value (million US$)	Avg. Growth (%) 12-16	Growth (%) 15-16	World share %	Cum.
World	26741.6	0.7	-0.7	100.0	
USA	3585.3	7.2	-7.7	13.4	13.4
Germany	2408.5	1.9	6.1	9.0	22.4
Canada	2190.9	-7.8	-11.1	8.2	30.6
France	1165.6	0.5	8.9	4.4	35.0
United Kingdom	992.2	6.8	-11.4	3.7	38.7
Netherlands	890.4	-0.8	-26.5	3.3	42.0
Mexico	780.8	11.5	10.1	2.9	44.9
Belgium	681.4	0.9	7.5	2.5	47.5
Italy	631.6	14.9	27.9	2.4	49.8
Poland	623.4	3.6	9.3	2.3	52.2
Austria	587.1	3.9	17.7	2.2	54.4
Thailand	580.7	43.8	357.2	2.2	56.5
Australia	571.1	-6.2	-13.6	2.1	58.7
Russian Federation	534.2	-22.2	28.4	2.0	60.7
Spain	490.6	15.6	11.3	1.8	62.5

In 2016, the value (in current US$) of exports of "railway vehicles (including hovertrains) and associated equipment" (SITC group 791) decreased by 9.8 percent (compared to -6.9 percent average growth rate from 2012-2016) to reach 25.1 bln US$ (see table 2), while imports decreased by 10.8 percent to reach 22.5 bln US$ (see table 3). Exports of this commodity accounted for 0.4 percent of world exports of SITC section 7, and 0.2 percent of total world merchandise exports (see table 1). Germany, Mexico and USA were the top exporters in 2016 (see table 2). They accounted for 16.9, 12.4 and 12.0 percent of world exports, respectively. Germany, United Kingdom and Mexico were the top destinations, with respectively 9.8, 7.6 and 5.3 percent of world imports (see table 3).

The top 15 countries/areas accounted for 88.2 and 61.9 percent of total world exports and imports, respectively (see tables 2 and 3). In 2016, Germany was the country/area with the highest value of net exports (+2.0 bln US$), followed by Mexico (+1.9 bln US$). By MDG regions (see graph 2), the largest surpluses in this product group were recorded by Developed Europe (+2.2 bln US$), Eastern Asia (+1.7 bln US$) and Developed North America (+936.0 mln US$). The largest trade deficits were recorded by Western Asia (-903.7 mln US$), South-eastern Asia (-859.2 mln US$) and Sub-Saharan Africa (-585.9 mln US$).

Table 1: Imports (Imp.) and exports (Exp.), 2002-2016, in current US$

		2002	2003	2004	2005	2006	2007	2008	2009	2010	2011	2012	2013	2014	2015	2016
Values in Bln US$	Imp.	8.3	11.6	14.3	15.3	16.5	19.0	24.6	21.4	23.4	28.3	31.5	28.2	28.2	25.2	22.5
	Exp.	9.2	12.5	15.8	16.3	18.4	21.6	26.2	21.8	24.5	29.0	33.4	29.7	31.4	27.8	25.1
As a percentage of SITC section (%)	Imp.	0.3	0.4	0.4	0.4	0.4	0.4	0.5	0.5	0.4	0.5	0.5	0.5	0.4	0.4	0.4
	Exp.	0.4	0.4	0.5	0.4	0.4	0.4	0.5	0.5	0.5	0.5	0.6	0.5	0.5	0.5	0.4
As a percentage of world trade (%)	Imp.	0.1	0.2	0.2	0.1	0.1	0.1	0.2	0.2	0.2	0.2	0.2	0.2	0.2	0.2	0.1
	Exp.	0.1	0.2	0.2	0.2	0.2	0.2	0.2	0.2	0.2	0.2	0.2	0.2	0.2	0.2	0.2

Graph 1: Annual growth rates of exports, 2002–2016

(In percentage by year)

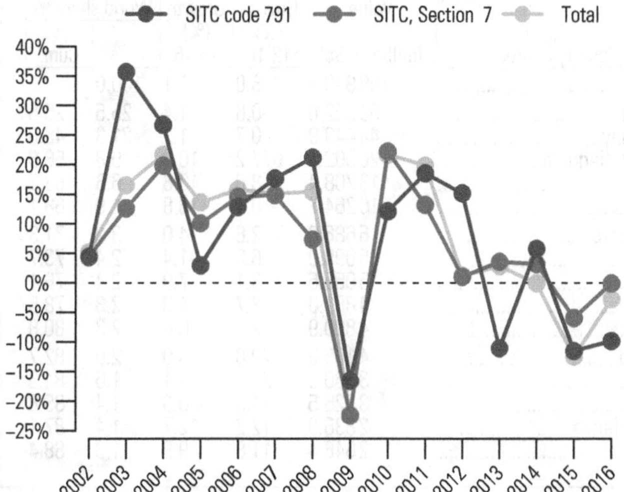

Table 2: Top exporting countries or areas in 2016

Country or area	Value (million US$)	Avg. Growth (%) 12-16	Growth (%) 15-16	World share %	Cum.
World	25073.1	-6.9	-9.8	100.0	
Germany	4246.2	-3.2	28.3	16.9	16.9
Mexico	3119.0	9.6	-14.8	12.4	29.4
USA	3015.8	-3.7	-17.3	12.0	41.4
China	2628.9	-12.4	-43.5	10.5	51.9
Austria	1332.1	-4.9	-5.4	5.3	57.2
Japan	1291.8	15.0	46.3	5.2	62.4
Spain	1278.5	-6.1	5.5	5.1	67.5
France	960.5	-4.6	20.0	3.8	71.3
Switzerland	877.1	-4.4	-10.3	3.5	74.8
Italy	780.3	-5.3	-12.9	3.1	77.9
Czechia	721.1	-8.5	-21.6	2.9	80.8
Poland	601.2	-3.2	-25.9	2.4	83.2
Rep. of Korea	459.1	-12.5	-34.5	1.8	85.0
Russian Federation	458.6	-25.2	-17.7	1.8	86.8
Hungary	343.2	0.4	2.9	1.4	88.2

Graph 2: Trade Balance by MDG regions 2016

(Bln US$)

Imports — Exports — Trade balance

Developed Asia-Pacific
Developed Europe
Developed N. America
South-eastern Europe
C I S
Northern Africa
Sub-Saharan Africa
Latin Am, Caribbean
Eastern Asia
Southern Asia
South-eastern Asia
Western Asia
Oceania

-12 -10 -8 -6 -4 -2 0 2 4 6 8 10 12 14

Table 3: Top importing countries or areas in 2016

Country or area	Value (million US$)	Avg. Growth (%) 12-16	Growth (%) 15-16	World share %	Cum.
World	22509.8	-8.1	-10.8	100.0	
Germany	2213.5	3.2	-2.0	9.8	9.8
United Kingdom	1706.7	27.1	161.2	7.6	17.4
Mexico	1203.4	2.3	-16.0	5.3	22.8
Canada	1178.4	0.1	-3.8	5.2	28.0
Italy	1111.2	8.9	-1.5	4.9	32.9
USA	1110.4	-8.4	-35.9	4.9	37.9
China	1018.2	-3.4	-22.8	4.5	42.4
Austria	1000.7	5.2	48.7	4.4	46.8
France	675.5	-4.8	8.2	3.0	49.8
Switzerland	625.2	0.5	-15.8	2.8	52.6
Argentina	464.9	38.6	-26.6	2.1	54.7
Brazil	438.4	-11.1	-53.3	1.9	56.6
Turkey	410.8	-6.7	14.1	1.8	58.5
India	385.8	3.0	-11.5	1.7	60.2
Kazakhstan	380.8	-36.5	74.9	1.7	61.9

"Aircraft and associated equipment; spacecraft and their launch vehicles; parts" (SITC group 792) is amongst the top exported commodities in 2016 with 1.3 percent of total exports (see table 1). The value (in current US$) of exports of this commodity decreased by 1.1 percent (compared to 5.0 percent average growth rate from 2012-2016) to reach 209.0 bln US$ (see table 2), while imports decreased by 0.3 percent to reach 246.3 bln US$ (see table 3). Exports of this commodity accounted for 3.5 percent of world exports of SITC section 7 (see table 1). France, Germany and United Kingdom were the top exporters in 2016 (see table 2). They accounted for 25.5, 21.3 and 9.8 percent of world exports, respectively. France, USA and China were the top destinations, with respectively 13.7, 12.6 and 9.3 percent of world imports (see table 3).

The top 15 countries/areas accounted for 88.4 and 78.4 percent of total world exports and imports, respectively (see tables 2 and 3). In 2016, Germany was the country/area with the highest value of net exports (+24.7 bln US$), followed by France (+19.6 bln US$). By MDG regions (see graph 2), the largest surpluses in this product group were recorded by Developed Europe (+34.0 bln US$) and Latin America and the Caribbean (+671.5 mln US$). The largest trade deficits were recorded by Eastern Asia (-25.6 bln US$), Western Asia (-16.8 bln US$) and Developed North America (-14.1 bln US$).

Table 1: Imports (Imp.) and exports (Exp.), 2002-2016, in current US$

		2002	2003	2004	2005	2006	2007	2008	2009	2010	2011	2012	2013	2014	2015	2016
Values in Bln US$	Imp.	84.1	88.0	104.7	110.8	130.9	144.1	171.0	149.9	156.9	175.3	194.6	207.5	239.1	247.0	246.3
	Exp.	109.6	108.4	120.7	128.9	161.5	183.0	195.8	126.9	136.8	154.3	172.0	186.2	208.1	211.2	209.0
As a percentage of SITC section (%)	Imp.	3.3	3.0	3.0	2.9	3.0	2.9	3.2	3.5	3.0	3.0	3.2	3.3	3.7	4.1	4.1
	Exp.	4.3	3.7	3.5	3.4	3.7	3.6	3.6	3.0	2.7	2.7	2.9	3.1	3.3	3.6	3.5
As a percentage of world trade (%)	Imp.	1.3	1.1	1.1	1.0	1.1	1.0	1.1	1.2	1.0	1.0	1.1	1.1	1.3	1.5	1.5
	Exp.	1.7	1.4	1.3	1.2	1.3	1.3	1.2	1.0	0.9	0.9	0.9	1.0	1.1	1.3	1.3

Graph 1: Annual growth rates of exports, 2002–2016

(In percentage by year)

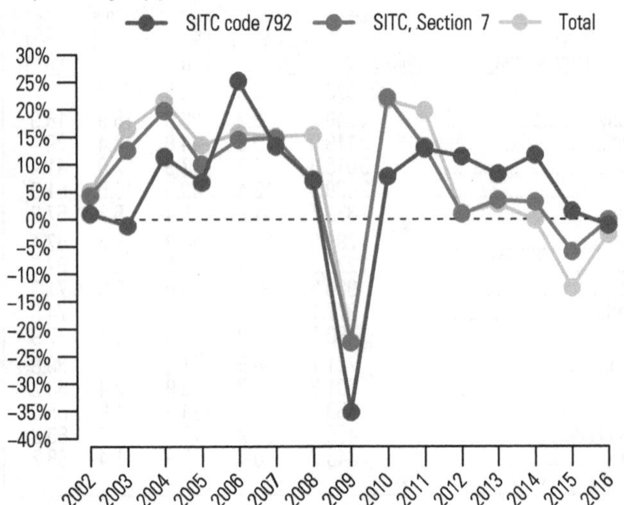

Table 2: Top exporting countries or areas in 2016

Country or area	Value (million US$)	Avg. Growth (%) 12-16	Growth (%) 15-16	World share %	Cum.
World	208973.3	5.0	-1.1	100.0	
France	53352.0	-0.6	-1.4	25.5	25.5
Germany	44443.9	0.7	1.2	21.3	46.8
United Kingdom	20502.4	677.2	10.8	9.8	56.6
USA	13708.4	8.0	13.6	6.6	63.2
Canada	10264.7	0.1	-16.8	4.9	68.1
Singapore	6686.0	2.8	4.0	3.2	71.3
Japan	5095.0	6.3	-1.4	2.4	73.7
Spain	5055.5	3.1	7.9	2.4	76.1
Italy	4881.0	-3.7	-4.9	2.3	78.5
Brazil	4800.9	-2.1	6.6	2.3	80.8
Ireland	4105.9	70.8	-33.0	2.0	82.7
China	3360.3	21.3	-3.1	1.6	84.3
India	3025.5	14.3	-20.0	1.4	85.8
Netherlands	2836.9	12.2	12.7	1.4	87.1
Israel	2646.4	11.8	-9.9	1.3	88.4

Graph 2: Trade Balance by MDG regions 2016

(Bln US$)

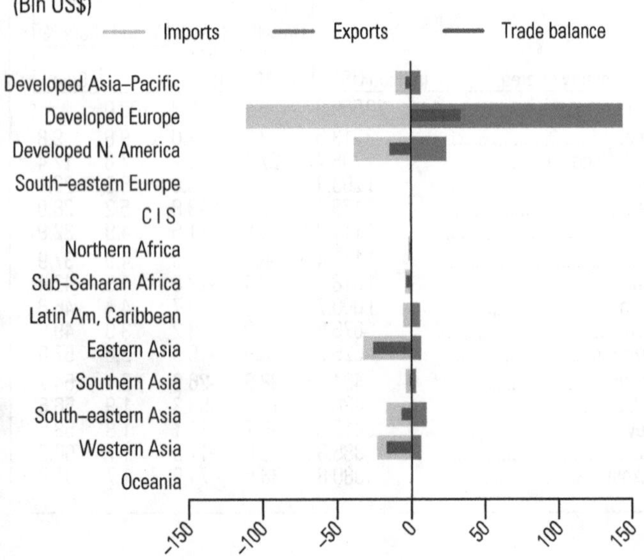

Table 3: Top importing countries or areas in 2016

Country or area	Value (million US$)	Avg. Growth (%) 12-16	Growth (%) 15-16	World share %	Cum.
World	246262.3	6.1	-0.3	100.0	
France	33743.8	2.0	9.4	13.7	13.7
USA	31027.8	6.2	-12.1	12.6	26.3
China	22839.3	6.7	-12.0	9.3	35.6
Germany	19725.9	-4.8	-21.8	8.0	43.6
United Kingdom	18701.2	2828.7	20.6	7.6	51.2
Ireland	13636.2	44.1	4.9	5.5	56.7
United Arab Emirates	12405.1	4.2	44.4	5.0	61.8
Canada	7066.6	5.8	-20.0	2.9	64.6
Japan	6730.9	-1.9	9.2	2.7	67.4
Singapore	6721.2	4.9	-12.1	2.7	70.1
Turkey	4308.8	8.1	12.5	1.7	71.8
Spain	4210.5	20.8	43.9	1.7	73.5
Rep. of Korea	4065.2	8.1	9.4	1.7	75.2
Netherlands	4050.8	21.7	47.7	1.6	76.8
Switzerland	3918.2	16.3	115.0	1.6	78.4

In 2016, the value (in current US$) of exports of "ships, boats (including hovercraft) and floating structures" (SITC group 793) decreased by 9.8 percent (compared to -5.7 percent average growth rate from 2012-2016) to reach 121.7 bln US$ (see table 2), while imports decreased by 3.4 percent to reach 54.8 bln US$ (see table 3). Exports of this commodity accounted for 2.1 percent of world exports of SITC section 7, and 0.8 percent of total world merchandise exports (see table 1). Rep. of Korea, China and Japan were the top exporters in 2016 (see table 2). They accounted for 27.2, 18.5 and 10.6 percent of world exports, respectively. India, Norway and Germany were the top destinations, with respectively 10.0, 5.3 and 5.1 percent of world imports (see table 3).

The top 15 countries/areas accounted for 88.1 and 57.0 percent of total world exports and imports, respectively (see tables 2 and 3). In 2016, Rep. of Korea was the country/area with the highest value of net exports (+31.3 bln US$), followed by China (+20.6 bln US$). By MDG regions (see graph 2), the largest surpluses in this product group were recorded by Eastern Asia (+51.7 bln US$), Developed Asia-Pacific (+11.7 bln US$) and Developed Europe (+9.6 bln US$). The largest trade deficits were recorded by Southern Asia (-4.1 bln US$), Sub-Saharan Africa (-2.4 bln US$) and Northern Africa (-1.6 bln US$).

Table 1: Imports (Imp.) and exports (Exp.), 2002-2016, in current US$

		2002	2003	2004	2005	2006	2007	2008	2009	2010	2011	2012	2013	2014	2015	2016
Values in Bln US$	Imp.	21.5	30.4	36.7	42.3	53.4	51.2	71.2	62.4	75.9	76.9	70.4	75.7	55.7	56.7	54.8
	Exp.	46.4	52.9	63.1	68.7	86.5	105.1	142.6	144.5	170.9	187.4	153.9	142.9	136.3	135.0	121.7
As a percentage of SITC section (%)	Imp.	0.8	1.0	1.0	1.1	1.2	1.0	1.3	1.5	1.5	1.3	1.2	1.2	0.9	0.9	0.9
	Exp.	1.8	1.8	1.8	1.8	2.0	2.1	2.6	3.4	3.3	3.2	2.6	2.4	2.2	2.3	2.1
As a percentage of world trade (%)	Imp.	0.3	0.4	0.4	0.4	0.4	0.4	0.4	0.5	0.5	0.4	0.4	0.4	0.3	0.3	0.3
	Exp.	0.7	0.7	0.7	0.7	0.7	0.8	0.9	1.2	1.1	1.0	0.8	0.8	0.7	0.8	0.8

Graph 1: Annual growth rates of exports, 2002–2016
(In percentage by year)

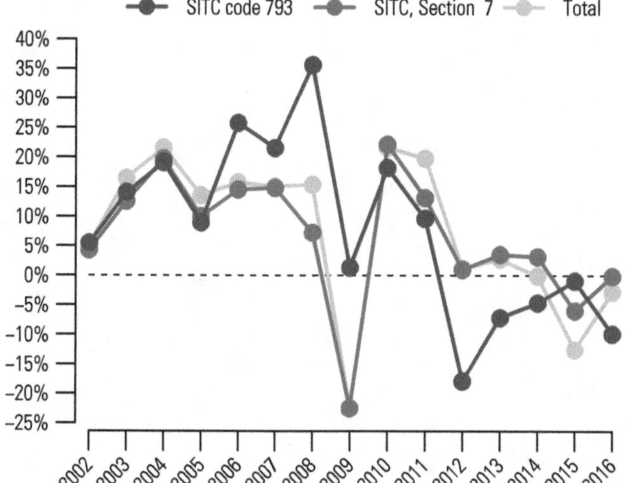

Graph 2: Trade Balance by MDG regions 2016
(Bln US$)

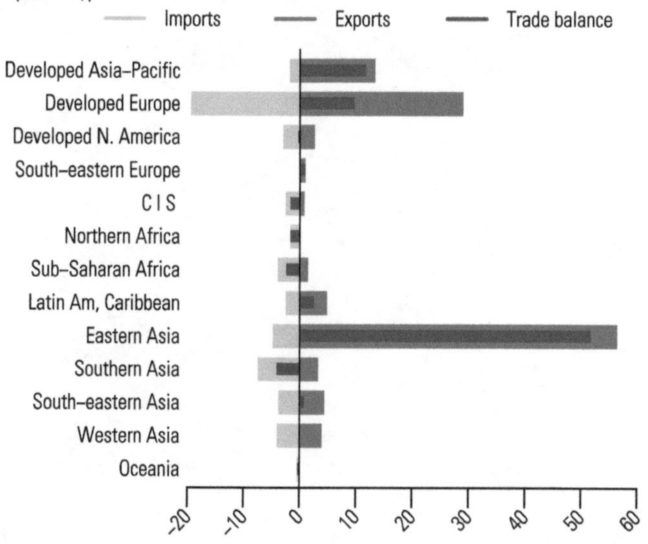

Table 2: Top exporting countries or areas in 2016

Country or area	Value (million US$)	Avg. Growth (%) 12-16	Growth (%) 15-16	World share %	Cum.
World	121741.4	-5.7	-9.8	100.0	
Rep. of Korea	33143.8	-3.3	-13.7	27.2	27.2
China	22514.9	-12.7	-21.9	18.5	45.7
Japan	12895.3	-12.7	13.1	10.6	56.3
Germany	5641.9	2.7	-0.8	4.6	60.9
Netherlands	5093.1	24.2	30.5	4.2	65.1
Italy	4721.1	9.9	37.4	3.9	69.0
Brazil	3841.4	25.5	93.5	3.2	72.2
Poland	3697.6	-1.9	-32.3	3.0	75.2
India	3221.9	-6.0	-20.7	2.6	77.8
France	2771.8	9.5	76.0	2.3	80.1
Saudi Arabia	2365.2	11.2	-4.1	1.9	82.1
USA	2341.9	-9.8	-25.2	1.9	84.0
United Kingdom	1944.4	8.8	34.4	1.6	85.6
Norway	1870.7	9.1	49.4	1.5	87.1
Thailand	1184.4	-6.9	12.8	1.0	88.1

Table 3: Top importing countries or areas in 2016

Country or area	Value (million US$)	Avg. Growth (%) 12-16	Growth (%) 15-16	World share %	Cum.
World	54770.5	-6.1	-3.4	100.0	
India	5480.6	-2.9	15.6	10.0	10.0
Norway	2904.3	6.5	-30.7	5.3	15.3
Germany	2774.2	-17.8	40.5	5.1	20.4
United Kingdom	2197.1	37.4	26.5	4.0	24.4
Greece	2146.7	-4.0	20.5	3.9	28.3
Poland	2098.3	-10.0	-52.1	3.8	32.1
USA	2033.5	1.8	-25.6	3.7	35.8
Russian Federation	1995.1	9.4	-6.2	3.6	39.5
China	1924.4	1.9	91.8	3.5	43.0
Rep. of Korea	1849.5	-7.6	-21.5	3.4	46.4
Netherlands	1314.6	22.7	136.0	2.4	48.8
Denmark	1203.5	22.4	-37.6	2.2	51.0
Malta	1145.6	34.1	34.2	2.1	53.1
Egypt	1082.4	72.2	255.9	2.0	55.0
Malaysia	1069.4	10.4	160.4	2.0	57.0

Source: UN Comtrade

Miscellaneous manufactured articles
(SITC Section 8)

811 Prefabricated buildings

In 2016, the value (in current US$) of exports of "prefabricated buildings" (SITC group 811) decreased by less than 0.1 percent (compared to -2.5 percent average growth rate from 2012-2016) to reach 8.2 bln US$ (see table 2), while imports decreased by 0.3 percent to reach 7.3 bln US$ (see table 3). Exports of this commodity accounted for 0.4 percent of world exports of SITC section 8, and 0.1 percent of total world merchandise exports (see table 1). China, USA and Netherlands were the top exporters in 2016 (see table 2). They accounted for 17.3, 7.0 and 6.2 percent of world exports, respectively. Germany, Norway and USA were the top destinations, with respectively 10.6, 6.9 and 4.4 percent of world imports (see table 3).

The top 15 countries/areas accounted for 72.1 and 54.1 percent of total world exports and imports, respectively (see tables 2 and 3). In 2016, China was the country/area with the highest value of net exports (+1.4 bln US$), followed by Netherlands (+433.6 mln US$). By MDG regions (see graph 2), the largest surpluses in this product group were recorded by Developed Europe (+1.4 bln US$), Eastern Asia (+1.2 bln US$) and South-eastern Europe (+84.8 mln US$). The largest trade deficits were recorded by Sub-Saharan Africa (-521.5 mln US$), Latin America and the Caribbean (-395.7 mln US$) and Commonwealth of Independent States (-357.9 mln US$).

Table 1: Imports (Imp.) and exports (Exp.), 2002-2016, in current US$

		2002	2003	2004	2005	2006	2007	2008	2009	2010	2011	2012	2013	2014	2015	2016
Values in Bln US$	Imp.	2.7	3.2	4.0	4.6	5.5	6.6	7.8	5.6	6.0	7.5	8.3	8.2	8.0	7.3	7.3
	Exp.	3.1	3.8	4.7	5.4	6.3	8.0	9.5	6.6	7.3	8.6	9.1	10.4	9.2	8.2	8.2
As a percentage of SITC section (%)	Imp.	0.3	0.3	0.4	0.4	0.4	0.4	0.5	0.4	0.4	0.4	0.4	0.4	0.4	0.4	0.4
	Exp.	0.4	0.4	0.4	0.5	0.5	0.5	0.6	0.5	0.4	0.5	0.5	0.5	0.4	0.4	0.4
As a percentage of world trade (%)	Imp.	0.0	0.0	0.0	0.0	0.0	0.0	0.0	0.0	0.0	0.0	0.0	0.0	0.0	0.0	0.0
	Exp.	0.0	0.1	0.1	0.1	0.1	0.1	0.1	0.1	0.0	0.0	0.0	0.1	0.0	0.1	0.1

Graph 1: Annual growth rates of exports, 2002–2016

(In percentage by year)

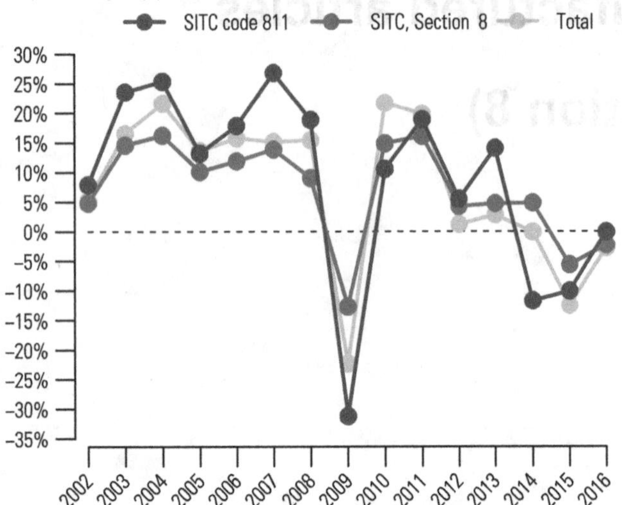

Table 2: Top exporting countries or areas in 2016

Country or area	Value (million US$)	Avg. Growth (%) 12-16	Growth (%) 15-16	World share %	Cum.
World	8 244.5	-2.5	0.0	100.0	
China	1 426.1	-3.2	-3.1	17.3	17.3
USA	573.0	-14.8	-26.3	7.0	24.2
Netherlands	512.2	6.1	-23.0	6.2	30.5
Germany	456.9	-6.7	1.4	5.5	36.0
Czechia	445.5	10.4	18.4	5.4	41.4
Italy	397.9	12.3	50.7	4.8	46.2
Estonia	355.9	8.4	8.6	4.3	50.5
Slovenia	278.5	11.4	44.6	3.4	53.9
Poland	244.2	17.6	25.6	3.0	56.9
Spain	237.2	4.9	65.8	2.9	59.8
France	236.3	-1.7	11.6	2.9	62.6
Belgium	213.7	-2.4	-2.9	2.6	65.2
Canada	203.8	-2.1	11.0	2.5	67.7
Lithuania	190.1	15.7	24.4	2.3	70.0
Israel	176.8	8.0	30.9	2.1	72.1

Graph 2: Trade Balance by MDG regions 2016

(Bln US$)

Imports — Exports — Trade balance

Developed Asia-Pacific
Developed Europe
Developed N. America
South-eastern Europe
C I S
Northern Africa
Sub-Saharan Africa
Latin Am, Caribbean
Eastern Asia
Southern Asia
South-eastern Asia
Western Asia
Oceania

-4 -3 -2 -1 0 1 2 3 4 5

Table 3: Top importing countries or areas in 2016

Country or area	Value (million US$)	Avg. Growth (%) 12-16	Growth (%) 15-16	World share %	Cum.
World	7 299.5	-3.1	-0.3	100.0	
Germany	772.3	12.1	22.8	10.6	10.6
Norway	501.6	3.6	10.6	6.9	17.5
USA	323.8	6.4	13.6	4.4	21.9
Canada	312.2	-18.0	-27.5	4.3	26.2
France	276.9	-4.5	-4.7	3.8	30.0
Switzerland	274.8	-2.4	1.8	3.8	33.7
United Kingdom	255.4	14.4	-3.7	3.5	37.2
Russian Federation	194.8	-9.3	76.3	2.7	39.9
Mexico	181.6	-5.0	19.0	2.5	42.4
Sweden	180.6	34.7	48.1	2.5	44.9
Rep. of Korea	164.4	55.1	309.0	2.3	47.1
Austria	151.4	-0.4	12.9	2.1	49.2
Indonesia	135.8	23.5	49.0	1.9	51.0
Saudi Arabia	113.8	4.1	-21.8	1.6	52.6
Kazakhstan	107.2	-1.6	-35.0	1.5	54.1

In 2016, the value (in current US$) of exports of "sanitary, plumbing and heating fixtures and fittings, nes" (SITC group 812) decreased by 10.7 percent (compared to 1.0 percent average growth rate from 2012-2016) to reach 15.3 bln US$ (see table 2), while imports decreased by 3.9 percent to reach 14.5 bln US$ (see table 3). Exports of this commodity accounted for 0.8 percent of world exports of SITC section 8, and 0.1 percent of total world merchandise exports (see table 1). China, Germany and Italy were the top exporters in 2016 (see table 2). They accounted for 21.4, 13.0 and 8.0 percent of world exports, respectively. USA, Germany and United Kingdom were the top destinations, with respectively 13.5, 11.1 and 9.6 percent of world imports (see table 3).

The top 15 countries/areas accounted for 83.2 and 70.9 percent of total world exports and imports, respectively (see tables 2 and 3). In 2016, China was the country/area with the highest value of net exports (+2.9 bln US$), followed by Turkey (+810.9 mln US$). By MDG regions (see graph 2), the largest surpluses in this product group were recorded by Eastern Asia (+2.9 bln US$), Western Asia (+569.8 mln US$) and Latin America and the Caribbean (+500.4 mln US$). The largest trade deficits were recorded by Developed North America (-1.8 bln US$), Commonwealth of Independent States (-565.2 mln US$) and Sub-Saharan Africa (-305.1 mln US$).

Table 1: Imports (Imp.) and exports (Exp.), 2002-2016, in current US$

		2002	2003	2004	2005	2006	2007	2008	2009	2010	2011	2012	2013	2014	2015	2016
Values in Bln US$	Imp.	6.6	8.4	10.2	11.4	13.2	14.9	16.3	13.4	14.1	15.8	15.6	16.3	16.6	15.1	14.5
	Exp.	6.6	8.5	10.2	11.3	13.5	15.0	16.4	13.1	13.6	15.2	14.8	16.6	17.8	17.2	15.3
As a percentage of SITC section (%)	Imp.	0.8	0.9	0.9	0.9	1.0	1.0	1.0	0.9	0.9	0.9	0.8	0.8	0.8	0.8	0.8
	Exp.	0.8	0.9	1.0	1.0	1.0	1.0	1.0	0.9	0.8	0.8	0.7	0.8	0.8	0.8	0.8
As a percentage of world trade (%)	Imp.	0.1	0.1	0.1	0.1	0.1	0.1	0.1	0.1	0.1	0.1	0.1	0.1	0.1	0.1	0.1
	Exp.	0.1	0.1	0.1	0.1	0.1	0.1	0.1	0.1	0.1	0.1	0.1	0.1	0.1	0.1	0.1

Graph 1: Annual growth rates of exports, 2002–2016
(In percentage by year)

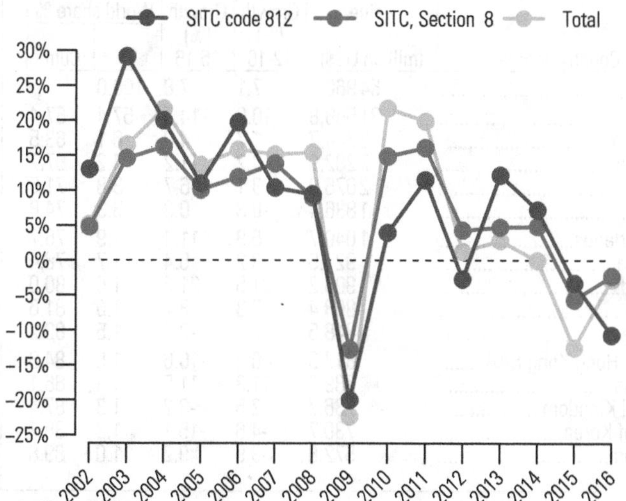

Graph 2: Trade Balance by MDG regions 2016
(Bln US$)

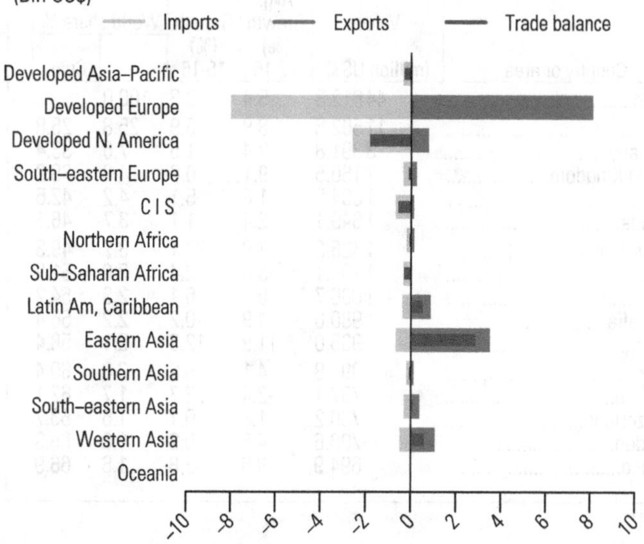

Table 2: Top exporting countries or areas in 2016

Country or area	Value (million US$)	Avg. Growth (%) 12-16	Growth (%) 15-16	World share %	Cum.
World	15337.6	1.0	-10.7	100.0	
China	3276.2	27.2	-32.2	21.4	21.4
Germany	1993.6	-5.1	-3.2	13.0	34.4
Italy	1224.3	-7.0	-6.1	8.0	42.3
Turkey	965.0	-0.7	0.1	6.3	48.6
Mexico	749.3	13.0	-5.7	4.9	53.5
Slovakia	609.9	-1.2	-3.2	4.0	57.5
Netherlands	599.9	-1.7	8.6	3.9	61.4
Austria	577.2	-3.2	-1.0	3.8	65.2
Poland	558.5	-1.2	8.0	3.6	68.8
USA	545.5	-0.9	-9.8	3.6	72.4
France	541.2	-5.4	-4.3	3.5	75.9
Czechia	364.8	-4.9	-0.2	2.4	78.3
Belgium	264.4	-12.1	-2.6	1.7	80.0
United Kingdom	260.8	7.5	20.5	1.7	81.7
Canada	223.0	4.0	-14.2	1.5	83.2

Table 3: Top importing countries or areas in 2016

Country or area	Value (million US$)	Avg. Growth (%) 12-16	Growth (%) 15-16	World share %	Cum.
World	14480.7	-1.9	-3.9	100.0	
USA	1951.5	8.2	-6.5	13.5	13.5
Germany	1601.9	-1.2	-2.4	11.1	24.5
United Kingdom	1395.5	0.6	-5.7	9.6	34.2
France	917.2	-6.1	-3.1	6.3	40.5
Canada	625.3	-1.4	-7.2	4.3	44.8
Italy	582.8	-2.6	7.3	4.0	48.9
Belgium	479.2	-6.3	-1.1	3.3	52.2
Netherlands	440.5	-5.6	-3.7	3.0	55.2
Spain	397.5	-0.6	-3.0	2.7	57.9
Russian Federation	394.2	-17.1	-15.9	2.7	60.7
China	363.8	10.5	18.3	2.5	63.2
Poland	343.7	-0.2	9.6	2.4	65.6
Austria	323.1	-3.8	-2.5	2.2	67.8
Switzerland	228.5	-4.7	-3.1	1.6	69.4
Romania	228.4	-0.2	-8.7	1.6	70.9

813 Lighting fixtures and fittings, nes

In 2016, the value (in current US$) of exports of "lighting fixtures and fittings, nes" (SITC group 813) decreased by 7.8 percent (compared to 7.1 percent average growth rate from 2012-2016) to reach 55.0 bln US$ (see table 2), while imports increased by 2.3 percent to reach 44.6 bln US$ (see table 3). Exports of this commodity accounted for 2.7 percent of world exports of SITC section 8, and 0.3 percent of total world merchandise exports (see table 1). China, Germany and Mexico were the top exporters in 2016 (see table 2). They accounted for 57.4, 6.1 and 4.2 percent of world exports, respectively. USA, Germany and United Kingdom were the top destinations, with respectively 25.8, 7.6 and 4.8 percent of world imports (see table 3).

The top 15 countries/areas accounted for 89.8 and 66.9 percent of total world exports and imports, respectively (see tables 2 and 3). In 2016, China was the country/area with the highest value of net exports (+31.1 bln US$), followed by Mexico (+1.6 bln US$). By MDG regions (see graph 2), the largest surpluses in this product group were recorded by Eastern Asia (+31.5 bln US$) and Latin America and the Caribbean (+497.3 mln US$). The largest trade deficits were recorded by Developed North America (-10.3 bln US$), Developed Europe (-3.9 bln US$) and Developed Asia-Pacific (-2.1 bln US$).

Table 1: Imports (Imp.) and exports (Exp.), 2002-2016, in current US$

		2002	2003	2004	2005	2006	2007	2008	2009	2010	2011	2012	2013	2014	2015	2016
Values in Bln US$	Imp.	15.5	17.7	20.3	22.3	24.4	28.0	29.9	24.9	29.9	33.6	36.1	39.7	44.7	43.6	44.6
	Exp.	13.4	15.3	17.2	19.1	21.1	24.9	28.6	23.6	27.8	34.1	41.8	48.4	56.7	59.6	55.0
As a percentage of SITC section (%)	Imp.	1.8	1.8	1.8	1.8	1.8	1.8	1.8	1.7	1.8	1.8	1.9	2.1	2.2	2.3	2.3
	Exp.	1.7	1.7	1.6	1.6	1.6	1.7	1.7	1.7	1.7	1.8	2.1	2.3	2.6	2.9	2.7
As a percentage of world trade (%)	Imp.	0.2	0.2	0.2	0.2	0.2	0.2	0.2	0.2	0.2	0.2	0.2	0.2	0.2	0.3	0.3
	Exp.	0.2	0.2	0.2	0.2	0.2	0.2	0.2	0.2	0.2	0.2	0.2	0.3	0.3	0.4	0.3

Graph 1: Annual growth rates of exports, 2002–2016
(In percentage by year)

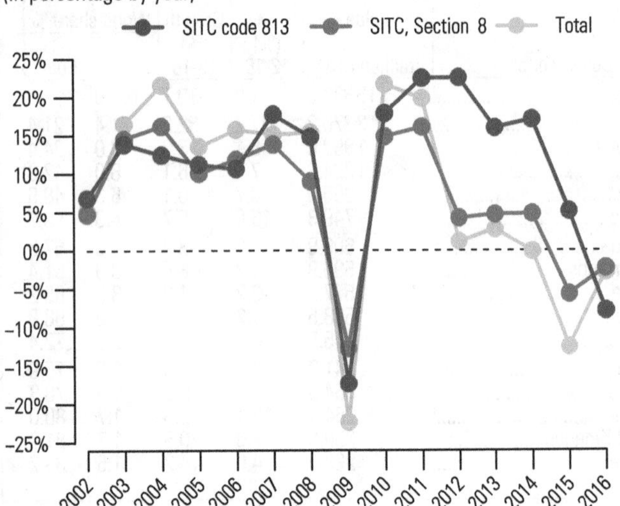

Table 2: Top exporting countries or areas in 2016

Country or area	Value (million US$)	Avg. Growth (%) 12-16	Growth (%) 15-16	World share %	Cum.
World	54960.2	7.1	-7.8	100.0	
China	31568.8	10.6	-14.7	57.4	57.4
Germany	3344.7	1.7	4.0	6.1	63.5
Mexico	2282.9	14.2	11.2	4.2	67.7
USA	2075.9	3.1	-6.7	3.8	71.5
Italy	1836.4	-0.3	0.3	3.3	74.8
Netherlands	1040.7	5.9	11.4	1.9	76.7
Austria	927.5	3.2	5.4	1.7	78.4
Poland	906.2	21.5	21.5	1.6	80.0
Spain	868.4	8.3	8.7	1.6	81.6
France	848.5	-2.5	-2.9	1.5	83.2
China, Hong Kong SAR	817.3	0.0	-10.6	1.5	84.6
Canada	789.3	11.3	11.5	1.4	86.1
United Kingdom	736.7	2.5	-3.2	1.3	87.4
Rep. of Korea	730.7	-4.6	-15.1	1.3	88.7
Belgium	572.8	-3.9	9.2	1.0	89.8

Graph 2: Trade Balance by MDG regions 2016
(Bln US$)

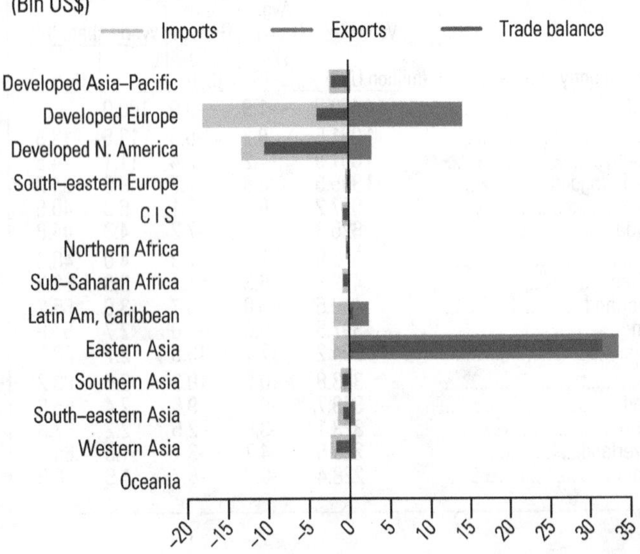

Table 3: Top importing countries or areas in 2016

Country or area	Value (million US$)	Avg. Growth (%) 12-16	Growth (%) 15-16	World share %	Cum.
World	44612.3	5.4	2.3	100.0	
USA	11502.5	8.9	5.9	25.8	25.8
Germany	3391.8	3.4	1.5	7.6	33.4
United Kingdom	2150.5	9.1	-0.6	4.8	38.2
France	1894.5	1.8	5.1	4.2	42.5
Canada	1649.1	2.4	1.1	3.7	46.1
Netherlands	1425.3	7.9	27.1	3.2	49.3
Japan	1139.1	-3.6	2.4	2.6	51.9
Italy	1006.7	6.1	6.1	2.3	54.2
Australia	980.0	4.9	-0.2	2.2	56.4
Spain	935.0	11.9	-12.3	2.1	58.4
Austria	891.8	4.1	5.8	2.0	60.4
Belgium	737.1	-2.4	3.7	1.7	62.1
Switzerland	730.2	1.8	0.1	1.6	63.7
Sweden	708.6	4.5	-0.2	1.6	65.3
Mexico	694.9	8.6	-3.8	1.6	66.9

"Furniture and parts thereof; stuffed furnishings" (SITC group 821) is amongst the top exported commodities in 2016 with 1.0 percent of total exports (see table 1). The value (in current US$) of exports of this commodity decreased by 0.9 percent (compared to 1.4 percent average growth rate from 2012-2016) to reach 165.5 bln US$ (see table 2), while imports increased by 1.0 percent to reach 161.9 bln US$ (see table 3). Exports of this commodity accounted for 8.2 percent of world exports of SITC section 8 (see table 1). China, Germany and Italy were the top exporters in 2016 (see table 2). They accounted for 33.6, 7.1 and 6.4 percent of world exports, respectively. USA, Germany and United Kingdom were the top destinations, with respectively 31.3, 8.9 and 5.3 percent of world imports (see table 3).

The top 15 countries/areas accounted for 80.2 and 74.6 percent of total world exports and imports, respectively (see tables 2 and 3). In 2016, China was the country/area with the highest value of net exports (+53.0 bln US$), followed by Poland (+8.6 bln US$). By MDG regions (see graph 2), the largest surpluses in this product group were recorded by Eastern Asia (+51.8 bln US$), South-eastern Asia (+8.1 bln US$) and Latin America and the Caribbean (+2.9 bln US$). The largest trade deficits were recorded by Developed North America (-45.0 bln US$), Developed Asia-Pacific (-9.1 bln US$) and Western Asia (-3.0 bln US$).

Table 1: Imports (Imp.) and exports (Exp.), 2002-2016, in current US$

		2002	2003	2004	2005	2006	2007	2008	2009	2010	2011	2012	2013	2014	2015	2016
Values in Bln US$	Imp.	70.2	82.7	97.3	107.2	117.8	135.6	142.0	113.6	130.6	143.6	146.0	152.7	164.2	160.4	161.9
	Exp.	65.3	76.1	89.8	97.6	108.4	127.0	136.6	112.6	129.1	145.9	156.6	166.3	173.8	167.0	165.5
As a percentage of SITC section (%)	Imp.	8.3	8.5	8.7	8.7	8.6	8.8	8.5	7.9	8.0	7.7	7.8	7.9	8.2	8.4	8.5
	Exp.	8.1	8.3	8.4	8.3	8.2	8.5	8.4	7.9	7.9	7.7	7.9	8.0	8.0	8.1	8.2
As a percentage of world trade (%)	Imp.	1.1	1.1	1.0	1.0	1.0	1.0	0.9	0.9	0.9	0.8	0.8	0.8	0.9	1.0	1.0
	Exp.	1.0	1.0	1.0	0.9	0.9	0.9	0.9	0.9	0.9	0.8	0.9	0.9	0.9	1.0	1.0

Graph 1: Annual growth rates of exports, 2002–2016
(In percentage by year)

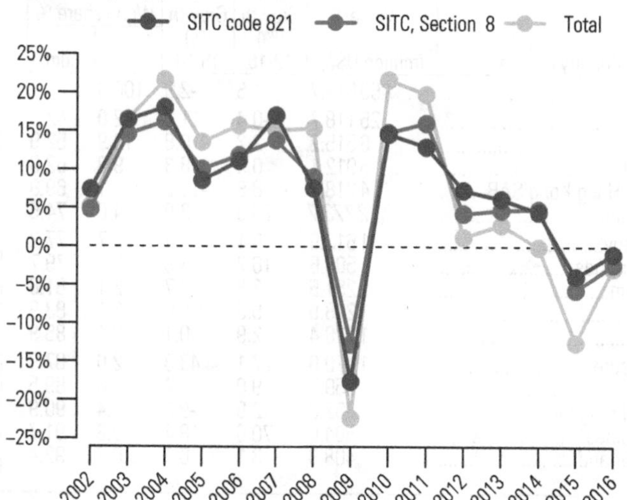

Table 2: Top exporting countries or areas in 2016

Country or area	Value (million US$)	Avg. Growth (%) 12-16	Growth (%) 15-16	World share %	Cum.
World	165456.5	1.4	-0.9	100.0	
China	55516.3	-0.3	-8.4	33.6	33.6
Germany	11817.9	-1.0	1.0	7.1	40.7
Italy	10538.5	-0.6	0.5	6.4	47.1
Poland	10500.5	5.2	6.7	6.3	53.4
USA	7901.7	2.4	-1.6	4.8	58.2
Mexico	7809.5	7.7	3.1	4.7	62.9
Viet Nam	*5646.7*	11.6	8.9	3.4	66.3
Canada	4587.8	4.5	6.8	2.8	69.1
Czechia	3821.6	11.3	13.0	2.3	71.4
France	2673.0	-0.3	2.1	1.6	73.0
United Kingdom	2671.2	6.7	2.1	1.6	74.6
Malaysia	2372.5	-2.9	-2.1	1.4	76.1
Romania	2353.0	7.3	7.0	1.4	77.5
Spain	2284.5	6.4	11.0	1.4	78.9
Denmark	2271.6	0.9	3.6	1.4	80.2

Graph 2: Trade Balance by MDG regions 2016
(Bln US$)

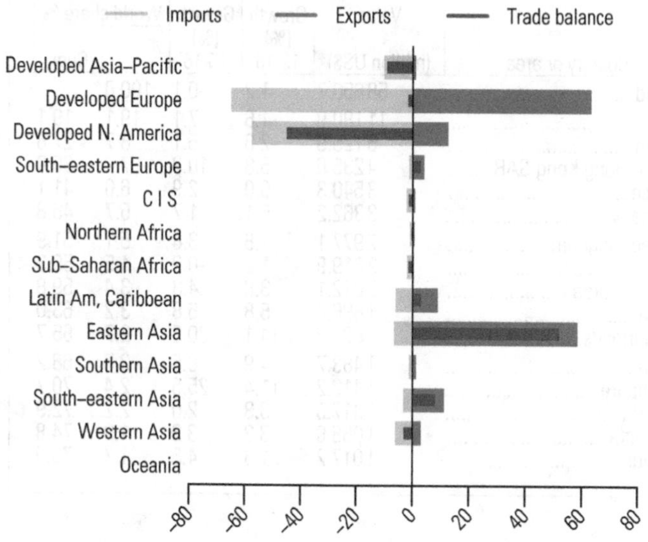

Table 3: Top importing countries or areas in 2016

Country or area	Value (million US$)	Avg. Growth (%) 12-16	Growth (%) 15-16	World share %	Cum.
World	161917.9	2.6	1.0	100.0	
USA	50657.1	7.0	2.9	31.3	31.3
Germany	14478.2	1.7	1.4	8.9	40.2
United Kingdom	8553.5	3.7	-3.3	5.3	45.5
France	7911.5	-1.7	6.4	4.9	50.4
Canada	6695.1	0.1	2.3	4.1	54.5
Japan	6441.4	-1.8	1.6	4.0	58.5
Switzerland	3270.9	-0.6	-0.6	2.0	60.5
Australia	3186.2	1.5	-2.2	2.0	62.5
Netherlands	3184.8	-2.1	-14.9	2.0	64.5
Spain	3163.5	6.0	7.5	2.0	66.4
Mexico	2799.4	4.7	-4.1	1.7	68.1
Belgium	2751.8	-3.0	5.3	1.7	69.8
Austria	2679.9	1.4	21.8	1.7	71.5
China	2558.6	3.7	6.5	1.6	73.1
Czechia	2530.1	15.5	18.6	1.6	74.6

Source: UN Comtrade

831 Travel goods, handbags, etc, of leather, plastics, textile, others

In 2016, the value (in current US$) of exports of "travel goods, handbags, etc, of leather, plastics, textile, others" (SITC group 831) decreased by 2.9 percent (compared to 1.5 percent average growth rate from 2012-2016) to reach 59.8 bln US$ (see table 2), while imports decreased by 0.1 percent to reach 58.7 bln US$ (see table 3). Exports of this commodity accounted for 3.0 percent of world exports of SITC section 8, and 0.4 percent of total world merchandise exports (see table 1). China, Italy and France were the top exporters in 2016 (see table 2). They accounted for 42.0, 10.9 and 9.9 percent of world exports, respectively. USA, Japan and China, Hong Kong SAR were the top destinations, with respectively 19.1, 8.7 and 7.2 percent of world imports (see table 3).

The top 15 countries/areas accounted for 92.4 and 76.5 percent of total world exports and imports, respectively (see tables 2 and 3). In 2016, China was the country/area with the highest value of net exports (+23.2 bln US$), followed by Italy (+3.9 bln US$). By MDG regions (see graph 2), the largest surpluses in this product group were recorded by Eastern Asia (+20.6 bln US$), South-eastern Asia (+2.4 bln US$) and Southern Asia (+1.0 bln US$). The largest trade deficits were recorded by Developed North America (-11.1 bln US$), Developed Asia-Pacific (-6.2 bln US$) and Western Asia (-2.0 bln US$).

Table 1: Imports (Imp.) and exports (Exp.), 2002-2016, in current US$

		2002	2003	2004	2005	2006	2007	2008	2009	2010	2011	2012	2013	2014	2015	2016
Values in Bln US$	Imp.	19.8	22.1	26.2	29.2	32.9	38.8	43.4	37.2	43.8	52.9	55.8	58.2	61.1	58.7	58.7
	Exp.	16.1	17.8	21.3	23.7	27.1	32.3	37.7	33.2	40.8	53.2	56.3	61.2	62.3	61.6	59.8
As a percentage of SITC section (%)	Imp.	2.3	2.3	2.3	2.4	2.4	2.5	2.6	2.6	2.7	2.9	3.0	3.0	3.0	3.1	3.1
	Exp.	2.0	1.9	2.0	2.0	2.1	2.2	2.3	2.3	2.5	2.8	2.8	2.9	2.9	3.0	3.0
As a percentage of world trade (%)	Imp.	0.3	0.3	0.3	0.3	0.3	0.3	0.3	0.3	0.3	0.3	0.3	0.3	0.3	0.4	0.4
	Exp.	0.2	0.2	0.2	0.2	0.2	0.2	0.2	0.3	0.3	0.3	0.3	0.3	0.3	0.4	0.4

Graph 1: Annual growth rates of exports, 2002–2016
(In percentage by year)

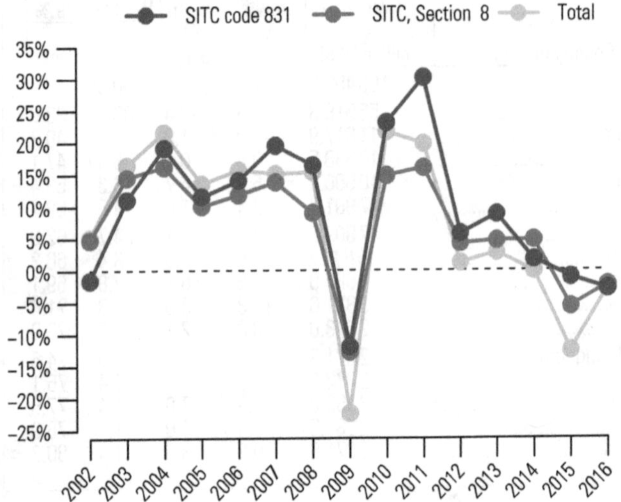

Table 2: Top exporting countries or areas in 2016

Country or area	Value (million US$)	Avg. Growth (%) 12-16	Growth (%) 15-16	World share %	Cum.
World	59813.7	1.5	-2.9	100.0	
China	25118.7	-0.4	-11.5	42.0	42.0
Italy	6515.2	2.2	0.8	10.9	52.9
France	5912.1	0.9	8.3	9.9	62.8
China, Hong Kong SAR	4218.7	-8.8	-11.2	7.1	69.8
Viet Nam	*2773.7*	20.9	8.9	4.6	74.5
Germany	1613.9	5.1	8.4	2.7	77.2
Netherlands	1505.6	16.2	33.8	2.5	79.7
Belgium	1251.5	2.6	7.7	2.1	81.8
India	1248.6	5.6	0.6	2.1	83.9
USA	1228.4	2.9	-0.1	2.1	85.9
Singapore	1170.6	27.1	43.3	2.0	87.9
Spain	959.7	9.0	7.4	1.6	89.5
United Kingdom	852.3	2.5	-9.2	1.4	90.9
Philippines	504.6	70.0	18.4	0.8	91.7
Switzerland	408.9	3.1	6.1	0.7	92.4

Graph 2: Trade Balance by MDG regions 2016
(Bln US$)

Imports — Exports — Trade balance

Developed Asia-Pacific
Developed Europe
Developed N. America
South-eastern Europe
C I S
Northern Africa
Sub-Saharan Africa
Latin Am, Caribbean
Eastern Asia
Southern Asia
South-eastern Asia
Western Asia
Oceania

-25 -20 -15 -10 -5 0 5 10 15 20 25 30

Table 3: Top importing countries or areas in 2016

Country or area	Value (million US$)	Avg. Growth (%) 12-16	Growth (%) 15-16	World share %	Cum.
World	58650.7	1.2	-0.1	100.0	
USA	11180.9	1.6	-7.1	19.1	19.1
Japan	5125.9	-2.8	5.1	8.7	27.8
China, Hong Kong SAR	4235.6	-5.8	-10.3	7.2	35.0
France	3540.3	0.0	2.9	6.0	41.1
Germany	3362.2	5.1	1.7	5.7	46.8
United Kingdom	2977.1	1.8	-3.8	5.1	51.9
Italy	2619.9	1.2	-0.9	4.5	56.3
Rep. of Korea	2012.1	3.8	4.3	3.4	59.8
China	1886.0	5.8	6.8	3.2	63.0
Netherlands	1601.2	14.1	30.3	2.7	65.7
Spain	1483.7	4.9	6.5	2.5	68.2
Singapore	1412.2	11.4	25.5	2.4	70.7
Canada	1317.5	3.3	2.0	2.2	72.9
Australia	1088.6	3.2	3.3	1.9	74.8
Belgium	1017.2	1.3	4.5	1.7	76.5

In 2016, the value (in current US$) of exports of "men's or boys' outerwear, of textile fabrics, not knitted or crocheted" (SITC group 841) decreased by 2.8 percent (compared to 1.9 percent average growth rate from 2012-2016) to reach 75.6 bln US$ (see table 2), while imports decreased by 2.0 percent to reach 68.7 bln US$ (see table 3). Exports of this commodity accounted for 3.8 percent of world exports of SITC section 8, and 0.5 percent of total world merchandise exports (see table 1). China, Bangladesh and Viet Nam were the top exporters in 2016 (see table 2). They accounted for 28.3, 11.0 and 7.0 percent of world exports, respectively. USA, Germany and Japan were the top destinations, with respectively 20.7, 9.9 and 6.8 percent of world imports (see table 3).

The top 15 countries/areas accounted for 79.6 and 75.9 percent of total world exports and imports, respectively (see tables 2 and 3). In 2016, China was the country/area with the highest value of net exports (+19.9 bln US$), followed by Bangladesh (+8.3 bln US$). By MDG regions (see graph 2), the largest surpluses in this product group were recorded by Eastern Asia (+17.8 bln US$), Southern Asia (+12.7 bln US$) and South-eastern Asia (+7.9 bln US$). The largest trade deficits were recorded by Developed North America (-14.7 bln US$), Developed Europe (-12.8 bln US$) and Developed Asia-Pacific (-5.8 bln US$).

Table 1: Imports (Imp.) and exports (Exp.), 2002-2016, in current US$

		2002	2003	2004	2005	2006	2007	2008	2009	2010	2011	2012	2013	2014	2015	2016
Values in Bln US$	Imp.	39.8	44.2	48.2	51.1	54.8	59.5	63.7	54.9	58.9	71.0	67.9	70.5	74.1	70.1	68.7
	Exp.	40.5	45.5	49.3	53.1	57.1	60.6	65.0	55.6	59.7	72.0	70.3	74.4	76.8	77.8	75.6
As a percentage of	Imp.	4.7	4.6	4.3	4.1	4.0	3.8	3.8	3.8	3.6	3.8	3.6	3.7	3.7	3.7	3.6
SITC section (%)	Exp.	5.1	4.9	4.6	4.5	4.3	4.0	4.0	3.9	3.6	3.8	3.5	3.6	3.5	3.8	3.8
As a percentage of	Imp.	0.6	0.6	0.5	0.5	0.4	0.4	0.4	0.4	0.4	0.4	0.4	0.4	0.4	0.4	0.4
world trade (%)	Exp.	0.6	0.6	0.5	0.5	0.5	0.4	0.4	0.4	0.4	0.4	0.4	0.4	0.4	0.5	0.5

Graph 1: Annual growth rates of exports, 2002–2016
(In percentage by year)

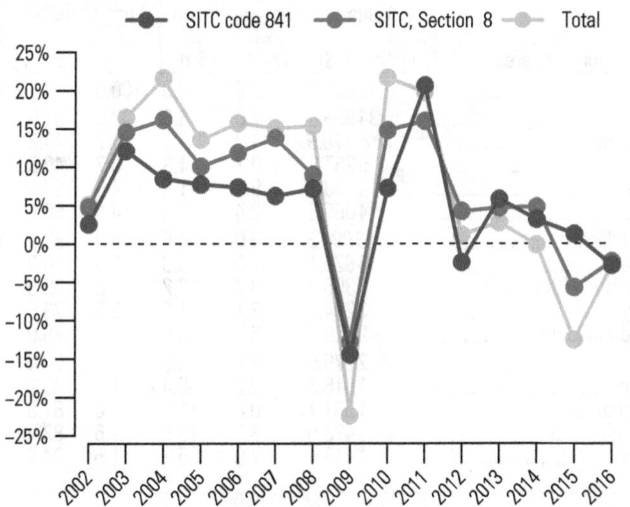

Graph 2: Trade Balance by MDG regions 2016
(Bln US$)

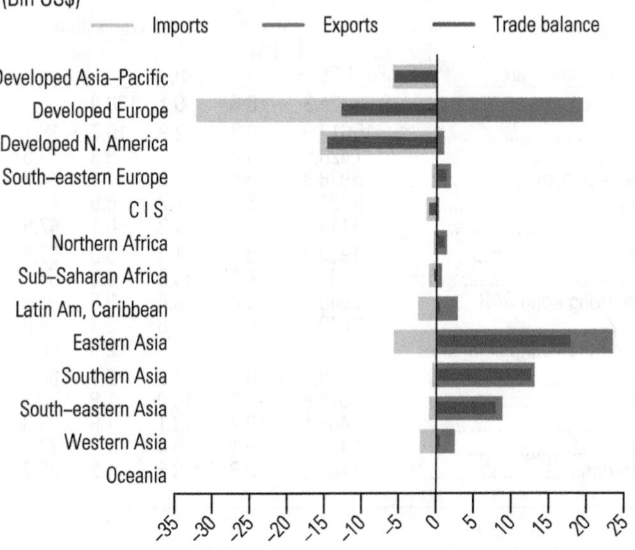

Table 2: Top exporting countries or areas in 2016

Country or area	Value (million US$)	Avg. Growth (%) 12-16	Growth (%) 15-16	World share %	Cum.
World	75644.5	1.9	-2.8	100.0	
China	21373.0	1.6	-10.6	28.3	28.3
Bangladesh	*8323.0*	5.4	-4.9	11.0	39.3
Viet Nam	*5263.4*	12.3	8.9	7.0	46.2
Italy	3839.7	-0.9	0.5	5.1	51.3
Germany	3635.5	-1.9	1.4	4.8	56.1
India	2641.7	7.5	7.0	3.5	59.6
Turkey	2216.9	1.0	-1.3	2.9	62.5
Spain	2039.1	11.4	3.4	2.7	65.2
China, Hong Kong SAR	1884.5	-9.7	-18.3	2.5	67.7
Mexico	1701.4	-3.4	-7.6	2.2	70.0
Netherlands	1618.1	0.7	2.6	2.1	72.1
Indonesia	1575.1	-0.6	3.7	2.1	74.2
Pakistan	1558.0	11.9	24.8	2.1	76.2
United Kingdom	1279.9	2.6	-2.7	1.7	77.9
Belgium	1260.5	1.3	-5.5	1.7	79.6

Table 3: Top importing countries or areas in 2016

Country or area	Value (million US$)	Avg. Growth (%) 12-16	Growth (%) 15-16	World share %	Cum.
World	68677.2	0.3	-2.0	100.0	
USA	14218.1	-0.2	-6.0	20.7	20.7
Germany	6824.0	0.1	2.7	9.9	30.6
Japan	4681.7	-5.2	-4.2	6.8	37.5
United Kingdom	4054.4	0.3	-10.6	5.9	43.4
France	3513.0	0.3	-1.9	5.1	48.5
Spain	2981.1	5.7	-3.2	4.3	52.8
Italy	2979.9	-1.0	-0.5	4.3	57.2
Netherlands	2611.7	7.9	27.9	3.8	61.0
Rep. of Korea	1972.1	6.2	-4.0	2.9	63.8
China, Hong Kong SAR	1766.5	-5.5	-15.3	2.6	66.4
Canada	1467.4	0.4	-2.8	2.1	68.5
China	1458.6	4.6	-6.3	2.1	70.7
Belgium	1352.0	0.0	9.4	2.0	72.6
Austria	1136.2	4.5	20.6	1.7	74.3
Switzerland	1110.1	1.3	10.4	1.6	75.9

Source: UN Comtrade

842 Women's or girls' outerwear, of textile fabrics, not knitted or crocheted

In 2016, the value (in current US$) of exports of "women's or girls' outerwear, of textile fabrics, not knitted or crocheted" (SITC group 842) decreased by 2.9 percent (compared to 3.9 percent average growth rate from 2012-2016) to reach 92.9 bln US$ (see table 2), while imports decreased by 0.1 percent to reach 83.7 bln US$ (see table 3). Exports of this commodity accounted for 4.6 percent of world exports of SITC section 8, and 0.6 percent of total world merchandise exports (see table 1). China, Viet Nam and Italy were the top exporters in 2016 (see table 2). They accounted for 37.6, 5.7 and 5.7 percent of world exports, respectively. USA, Germany and United Kingdom were the top destinations, with respectively 18.7, 8.9 and 7.1 percent of world imports (see table 3).

The top 15 countries/areas accounted for 84.9 and 75.9 percent of total world exports and imports, respectively (see tables 2 and 3). In 2016, China was the country/area with the highest value of net exports (+33.4 bln US$), followed by Viet Nam (+5.3 bln US$). By MDG regions (see graph 2), the largest surpluses in this product group were recorded by Eastern Asia (+31.4 bln US$), Southern Asia (+9.1 bln US$) and South-eastern Asia (+6.9 bln US$). The largest trade deficits were recorded by Developed North America (-16.4 bln US$), Developed Europe (-14.7 bln US$) and Developed Asia-Pacific (-7.2 bln US$).

Table 1: Imports (Imp.) and exports (Exp.), 2002-2016, in current US$

		2002	2003	2004	2005	2006	2007	2008	2009	2010	2011	2012	2013	2014	2015	2016
Values in Bln US$	Imp.	50.3	57.1	63.4	69.0	74.2	79.8	82.7	72.0	75.8	85.5	82.1	85.3	87.8	83.8	83.7
	Exp.	47.1	52.7	59.2	64.6	70.3	75.5	78.9	68.0	72.2	82.4	79.7	87.2	97.0	95.6	92.9
As a percentage of SITC section (%)	Imp.	5.9	5.9	5.6	5.6	5.4	5.2	4.9	5.0	4.6	4.6	4.4	4.4	4.4	4.4	4.4
	Exp.	5.9	5.7	5.5	5.5	5.3	5.0	4.8	4.8	4.4	4.3	4.0	4.2	4.5	4.6	4.6
As a percentage of world trade (%)	Imp.	0.8	0.7	0.7	0.7	0.6	0.6	0.5	0.6	0.5	0.5	0.4	0.5	0.5	0.5	0.5
	Exp.	0.7	0.7	0.6	0.6	0.6	0.5	0.5	0.5	0.5	0.5	0.4	0.5	0.5	0.6	0.6

Graph 1: Annual growth rates of exports, 2002–2016

(In percentage by year)

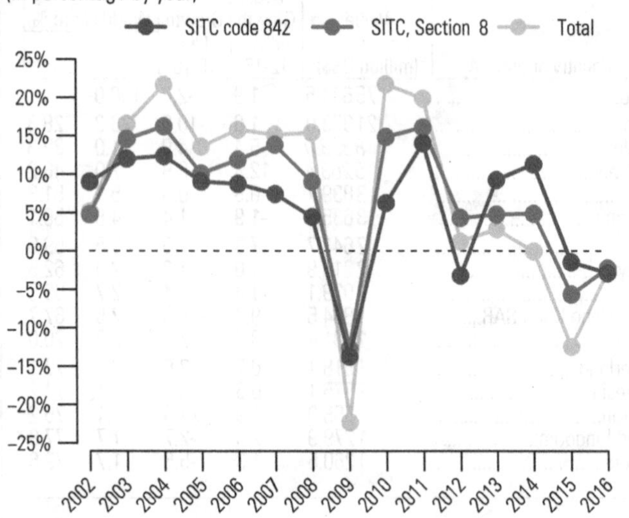

Table 2: Top exporting countries or areas in 2016

Country or area	Value (million US$)	Avg. Growth (%) 12-16	Growth (%) 15-16	World share %	Cum.
World	92854.3	3.9	-2.9	100.0	
China	34899.6	7.8	-6.6	37.6	37.6
Viet Nam	*5318.9*	14.2	8.9	5.7	43.3
Italy	5257.2	0.2	4.3	5.7	49.0
Spain	4439.3	9.9	-1.8	4.8	53.8
India	4065.8	2.4	-10.3	4.4	58.1
Bangladesh	*3996.2*	10.0	-4.9	4.3	62.4
Germany	3626.4	-1.0	3.9	3.9	66.3
China, Hong Kong SAR	3306.7	-8.7	-12.2	3.6	69.9
Turkey	3294.1	2.1	1.0	3.5	73.5
United Kingdom	2328.7	6.7	-6.0	2.5	76.0
France	2279.5	3.6	5.5	2.5	78.4
Indonesia	1615.3	2.2	-5.4	1.7	80.2
Netherlands	1531.1	0.6	11.9	1.6	81.8
Morocco	1473.9	3.3	13.6	1.6	83.4
Poland	1413.4	7.0	5.2	1.5	84.9

Graph 2: Trade Balance by MDG regions 2016

(Bln US$)

Imports — Exports — Trade balance

Developed Asia-Pacific
Developed Europe
Developed N. America
South-eastern Europe
CIS
Northern Africa
Sub-Saharan Africa
Latin Am, Caribbean
Eastern Asia
Southern Asia
South-eastern Asia
Western Asia
Oceania

-50 -40 -30 -20 -10 0 10 20 30 40

Table 3: Top importing countries or areas in 2016

Country or area	Value (million US$)	Avg. Growth (%) 12-16	Growth (%) 15-16	World share %	Cum.
World	83724.3	0.5	-0.1	100.0	
USA	15617.9	-0.3	-2.9	18.7	18.7
Germany	7426.5	0.6	1.5	8.9	27.5
United Kingdom	5978.3	0.8	-6.0	7.1	34.7
Japan	5731.9	-5.6	-1.2	6.8	41.5
France	5114.3	2.2	1.3	6.1	47.6
Spain	4953.8	8.5	1.3	5.9	53.5
Netherlands	2962.2	8.2	33.3	3.5	57.1
China, Hong Kong SAR	2940.1	-3.8	-6.4	3.5	60.6
Italy	2840.7	-0.5	0.8	3.4	64.0
Rep. of Korea	2205.2	8.7	1.2	2.6	66.6
Canada	1788.7	0.1	1.2	2.1	68.7
Belgium	1512.8	-1.2	13.0	1.8	70.6
China	1485.1	10.7	-3.1	1.8	72.3
Poland	1482.8	10.1	6.4	1.8	74.1
Switzerland	1481.5	3.6	9.5	1.8	75.9

In 2016, the value (in current US$) of exports of "men's or boys' outerwear, of textile fabrics, knitted or crocheted" (SITC group 843) decreased by 3.6 percent (compared to -0.5 percent average growth rate from 2012-2016) to reach 30.2 bln US$ (see table 2), while imports decreased by 0.1 percent to reach 23.6 bln US$ (see table 3). Exports of this commodity accounted for 1.5 percent of world exports of SITC section 8, and 0.2 percent of total world merchandise exports (see table 1). China, Viet Nam and India were the top exporters in 2016 (see table 2). They accounted for 35.0, 6.1 and 6.0 percent of world exports, respectively. USA, United Kingdom and Germany were the top destinations, with respectively 26.7, 6.8 and 6.2 percent of world imports (see table 3).

The top 15 countries/areas accounted for 81.1 and 75.1 percent of total world exports and imports, respectively (see tables 2 and 3). In 2016, China was the country/area with the highest value of net exports (+10.2 bln US$), followed by Viet Nam (+1.8 bln US$). By MDG regions (see graph 2), the largest surpluses in this product group were recorded by Eastern Asia (+9.7 bln US$), Southern Asia (+4.7 bln US$) and South-eastern Asia (+4.1 bln US$). The largest trade deficits were recorded by Developed North America (-6.6 bln US$), Developed Europe (-3.9 bln US$) and Developed Asia-Pacific (-1.8 bln US$).

Table 1: Imports (Imp.) and exports (Exp.), 2002-2016, in current US$

		2002	2003	2004	2005	2006	2007	2008	2009	2010	2011	2012	2013	2014	2015	2016
Values in Bln US$	Imp.	10.1	11.1	12.0	13.0	14.7	16.8	18.2	16.2	18.4	22.0	21.2	22.3	23.7	23.6	23.6
	Exp.	11.0	12.9	14.2	15.1	18.2	24.0	24.4	21.3	24.5	29.9	30.8	34.5	32.3	31.3	30.2
As a percentage of SITC section (%)	Imp.	1.2	1.1	1.1	1.1	1.1	1.1	1.1	1.1	1.1	1.2	1.1	1.2	1.2	1.2	1.2
	Exp.	1.4	1.4	1.3	1.3	1.4	1.6	1.5	1.5	1.5	1.6	1.6	1.7	1.5	1.5	1.5
As a percentage of world trade (%)	Imp.	0.2	0.1	0.1	0.1	0.1	0.1	0.1	0.1	0.1	0.1	0.1	0.1	0.1	0.1	0.1
	Exp.	0.2	0.2	0.2	0.1	0.2	0.2	0.2	0.2	0.2	0.2	0.2	0.2	0.2	0.2	0.2

Graph 1: Annual growth rates of exports, 2002–2016

(In percentage by year)

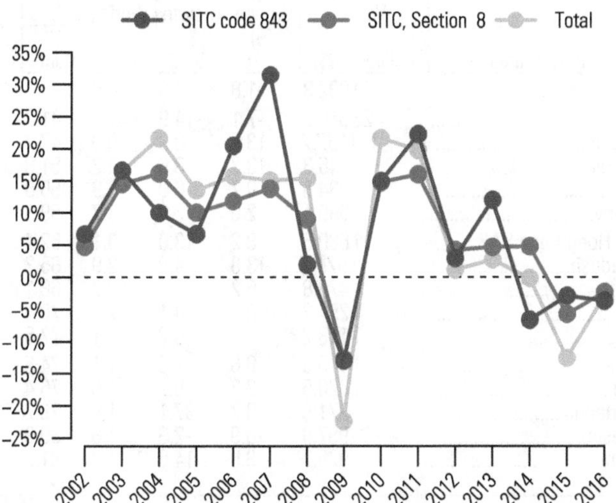

Table 2: Top exporting countries or areas in 2016

Country or area	Value (million US$)	Avg. Growth (%) 12-16	Growth (%) 15-16	World share %	Cum.
World	30212.6	-0.5	-3.6	100.0	
China	10578.0	-8.1	-12.9	35.0	35.0
Viet Nam	*1835.4*	12.3	8.9	6.1	41.1
India	1804.7	13.0	9.5	6.0	47.1
Bangladesh	*1696.6*	7.3	-4.9	5.6	52.7
Cambodia	1503.3	13.1	11.8	5.0	57.7
Pakistan	1041.6	3.6	-1.2	3.4	61.1
Belgium	860.7	12.1	17.3	2.8	63.9
Turkey	793.9	6.3	1.9	2.6	66.6
China, Hong Kong SAR	783.9	-8.7	-14.0	2.6	69.2
Italy	775.1	1.1	4.5	2.6	71.7
Netherlands	703.8	11.1	26.0	2.3	74.1
Germany	684.9	2.0	3.6	2.3	76.3
Indonesia	551.4	0.4	-11.4	1.8	78.2
Spain	467.1	16.7	20.3	1.5	79.7
United Kingdom	413.6	8.8	1.8	1.4	81.1

Graph 2: Trade Balance by MDG regions 2016

(Bln US$)

Imports — Exports — Trade balance

Developed Asia-Pacific
Developed Europe
Developed N. America
South-eastern Europe
CIS
Northern Africa
Sub-Saharan Africa
Latin Am, Caribbean
Eastern Asia
Southern Asia
South-eastern Asia
Western Asia
Oceania

-10 -8 -6 -4 -2 0 2 4 6 8 10 12

Table 3: Top importing countries or areas in 2016

Country or area	Value (million US$)	Avg. Growth (%) 12-16	Growth (%) 15-16	World share %	Cum.
World	23577.0	2.7	-0.1	100.0	
USA	6284.5	2.9	-7.8	26.7	26.7
United Kingdom	1604.8	2.3	-6.4	6.8	33.5
Germany	1470.6	3.1	2.8	6.2	39.7
Japan	1430.7	-3.8	-0.5	6.1	45.8
France	1036.2	1.0	1.7	4.4	50.2
Italy	942.2	0.5	0.3	4.0	54.2
Spain	850.2	7.8	10.2	3.6	57.8
Netherlands	770.1	9.2	35.0	3.3	61.0
China, Hong Kong SAR	693.6	-6.9	-14.0	2.9	64.0
Belgium	551.8	3.1	17.4	2.3	66.3
Canada	540.7	2.6	-3.7	2.3	68.6
Rep. of Korea	450.9	14.5	13.0	1.9	70.5
China	379.3	12.6	4.2	1.6	72.1
Australia	362.1	5.2	-2.2	1.5	73.7
Austria	343.6	11.1	24.4	1.5	75.1

844 Women's or girls' outerwear, of textile fabrics, knitted or crocheted

In 2016, the value (in current US$) of exports of "women's or girls' outerwear, of textile fabrics, knitted or crocheted" (SITC group 844) decreased by 5.9 percent (compared to -1.8 percent average growth rate from 2012-2016) to reach 54.1 bln US$ (see table 2), while imports increased by 0.3 percent to reach 44.9 bln US$ (see table 3). Exports of this commodity accounted for 2.7 percent of world exports of SITC section 8, and 0.3 percent of total world merchandise exports (see table 1). China, Viet Nam and Cambodia were the top exporters in 2016 (see table 2). They accounted for 41.7, 6.0 and 4.2 percent of world exports, respectively. USA, Germany and Japan were the top destinations, with respectively 24.9, 9.0 and 6.8 percent of world imports (see table 3).

The top 15 countries/areas accounted for 81.7 and 77.8 percent of total world exports and imports, respectively (see tables 2 and 3). In 2016, China was the country/area with the highest value of net exports (+22.1 bln US$), followed by Viet Nam (+3.2 bln US$). By MDG regions (see graph 2), the largest surpluses in this product group were recorded by Eastern Asia (+21.7 bln US$), South-eastern Asia (+6.7 bln US$) and Southern Asia (+4.3 bln US$). The largest trade deficits were recorded by Developed North America (-11.6 bln US$), Developed Europe (-9.2 bln US$) and Developed Asia-Pacific (-3.8 bln US$).

Table 1: Imports (Imp.) and exports (Exp.), 2002-2016, in current US$

		2002	2003	2004	2005	2006	2007	2008	2009	2010	2011	2012	2013	2014	2015	2016
Values in Bln US$	Imp.	18.2	20.8	22.9	24.2	27.1	32.5	35.1	32.6	37.2	42.1	41.7	44.1	47.2	44.7	44.9
	Exp.	19.3	23.2	25.9	26.5	32.3	41.8	41.7	38.5	45.0	53.2	58.2	65.2	62.2	57.5	54.1
As a percentage of SITC section (%)	Imp.	2.1	2.1	2.0	2.0	2.0	2.1	2.1	2.3	2.3	2.3	2.2	2.3	2.4	2.3	2.4
	Exp.	2.4	2.5	2.4	2.3	2.5	2.8	2.6	2.7	2.7	2.8	2.9	3.1	2.9	2.8	2.7
As a percentage of world trade (%)	Imp.	0.3	0.3	0.2	0.2	0.2	0.2	0.2	0.3	0.2	0.2	0.2	0.2	0.3	0.3	0.3
	Exp.	0.3	0.3	0.3	0.3	0.3	0.3	0.3	0.3	0.3	0.3	0.3	0.3	0.3	0.3	0.3

Graph 1: Annual growth rates of exports, 2002–2016

(In percentage by year)

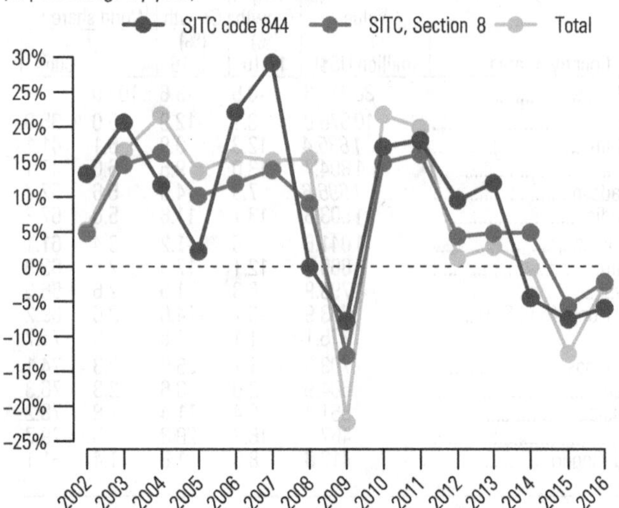

Table 2: Top exporting countries or areas in 2016

Country or area	Value (million US$)	Avg. Growth (%) 12-16	Growth (%) 15-16	World share %	Cum.
World	54 092.3	-1.8	-5.9	100.0	
China	22 568.2	-7.1	-14.9	41.7	41.7
Viet Nam	*3237.7*	13.6	8.9	6.0	47.7
Cambodia	2 246.3	13.2	8.6	4.2	51.9
Turkey	2 034.5	0.7	-6.0	3.8	55.6
Germany	1 995.1	2.0	2.3	3.7	59.3
China, Hong Kong SAR	1 680.6	-8.2	-13.0	3.1	62.4
Bangladesh	*1575.7*	13.0	-4.9	2.9	65.3
India	1 478.8	6.2	0.9	2.7	68.1
Italy	1 254.2	0.2	4.1	2.3	70.4
Spain	1 123.2	7.5	-0.2	2.1	72.5
Sri Lanka	1 115.8	8.6	7.6	2.1	74.5
France	1 028.5	2.2	5.7	1.9	76.4
Netherlands	971.5	9.7	37.1	1.8	78.2
Indonesia	957.9	-0.9	-2.9	1.8	80.0
Belgium	926.7	9.5	14.6	1.7	81.7

Graph 2: Trade Balance by MDG regions 2016

(Bln US$)

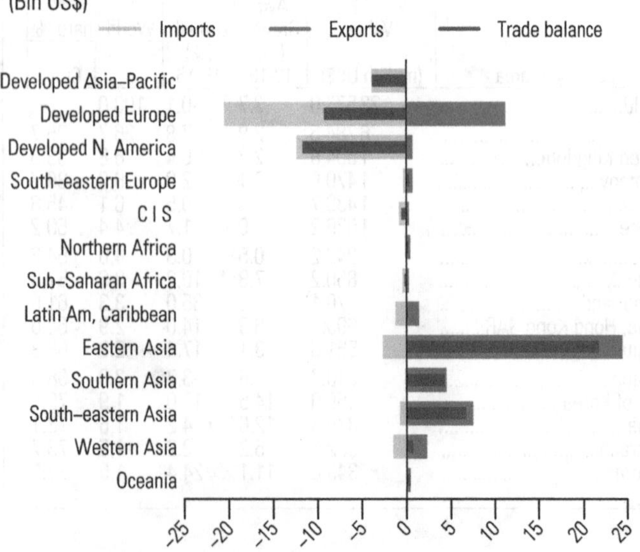

Table 3: Top importing countries or areas in 2016

Country or area	Value (million US$)	Avg. Growth (%) 12-16	Growth (%) 15-16	World share %	Cum.
World	44 866.9	1.8	0.3	100.0	
USA	11 166.9	2.6	-5.9	24.9	24.9
Germany	4 042.5	2.8	2.7	9.0	33.9
Japan	3 037.8	-6.0	-3.2	6.8	40.7
United Kingdom	3 033.6	1.8	-7.2	6.8	47.4
France	2 343.7	1.5	-1.4	5.2	52.7
Netherlands	1 889.2	15.4	63.5	4.2	56.9
Spain	1 692.4	6.8	5.9	3.8	60.6
China, Hong Kong SAR	1 452.9	-4.5	-10.0	3.2	63.9
Italy	1 371.0	-0.2	0.7	3.1	66.9
Canada	1 171.2	3.1	-2.9	2.6	69.5
Belgium	893.5	3.5	23.7	2.0	71.5
Austria	819.3	8.2	23.6	1.8	73.4
Australia	704.7	1.6	-4.4	1.6	74.9
Poland	681.8	13.4	11.8	1.5	76.4
Switzerland	619.7	2.8	9.9	1.4	77.8

In 2016, the value (in current US$) of exports of "articles of apparel, of textile fabrics, whether or not knitted or crocheted, nes" (SITC group 845) decreased by 2.6 percent (compared to 1.4 percent average growth rate from 2012-2016) to reach 143.6 bln US$ (see table 2), while imports decreased by 0.4 percent to reach 139.4 bln US$ (see table 3). Exports of this commodity accounted for 7.1 percent of world exports of SITC section 8, and 0.9 percent of total world merchandise exports (see table 1). China, Bangladesh and Viet Nam were the top exporters in 2016 (see table 2). They accounted for 31.0, 6.7 and 5.1 percent of world exports, respectively. USA, Germany and Japan were the top destinations, with respectively 23.0, 8.8 and 6.7 percent of world imports (see table 3).

The top 15 countries/areas accounted for 79.1 and 77.2 percent of total world exports and imports, respectively (see tables 2 and 3). In 2016, China was the country/area with the highest value of net exports (+42.7 bln US$), followed by Bangladesh (+9.5 bln US$). By MDG regions (see graph 2), the largest surpluses in this product group were recorded by Eastern Asia (+41.5 bln US$), Southern Asia (+17.3 bln US$) and South-eastern Asia (+12.5 bln US$). The largest trade deficits were recorded by Developed North America (-32.9 bln US$), Developed Europe (-25.7 bln US$) and Developed Asia-Pacific (-11.6 bln US$).

Table 1: Imports (Imp.) and exports (Exp.), 2002-2016, in current US$

		2002	2003	2004	2005	2006	2007	2008	2009	2010	2011	2012	2013	2014	2015	2016
Values in Bln US$	Imp.	73.9	82.9	93.1	99.4	108.3	117.5	126.2	114.1	122.8	139.6	131.8	139.3	147.1	139.9	139.4
	Exp.	65.3	74.7	84.5	92.7	108.7	119.9	126.5	110.9	121.4	139.9	135.6	146.5	151.7	147.4	143.6
As a percentage of SITC section (%)	Imp.	8.7	8.5	8.3	8.1	7.9	7.6	7.5	8.0	7.5	7.5	7.1	7.2	7.3	7.3	7.3
	Exp.	8.1	8.1	7.9	7.9	8.3	8.0	7.7	7.8	7.4	7.4	6.8	7.0	7.0	7.2	7.1
As a percentage of world trade (%)	Imp.	1.1	1.1	1.0	0.9	0.9	0.8	0.8	0.9	0.8	0.8	0.7	0.7	0.8	0.8	0.9
	Exp.	1.0	1.0	0.9	0.9	0.9	0.9	0.8	0.9	0.8	0.8	0.7	0.8	0.8	0.9	0.9

Graph 1: Annual growth rates of exports, 2002–2016
(In percentage by year)

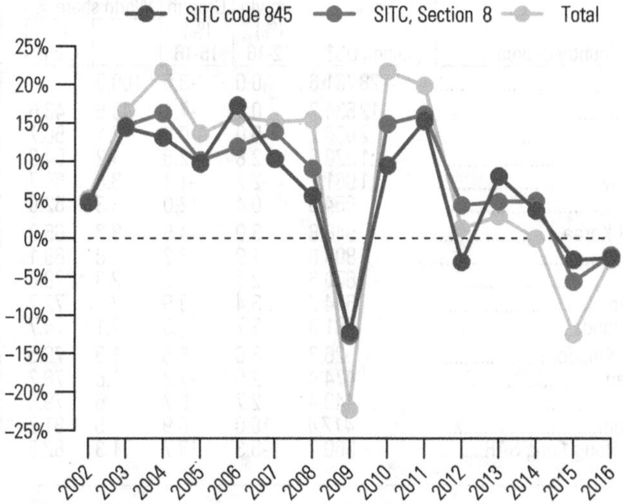

Table 2: Top exporting countries or areas in 2016

Country or area	Value (million US$)	Avg. Growth (%) 12-16	Growth (%) 15-16	World share %	Cum.
World	143565.6	1.4	-2.6	100.0	
China	44524.7	-0.2	-8.7	31.0	31.0
Bangladesh	*9557.0*	6.3	-4.9	6.7	37.7
Viet Nam	*7265.7*	13.9	8.9	5.1	42.7
China, Hong Kong SAR	6899.8	-8.2	-14.9	4.8	47.5
Italy	6672.1	0.6	3.8	4.6	52.2
India	6016.2	10.7	1.4	4.2	56.4
Germany	5472.1	-0.2	0.1	3.8	60.2
Turkey	5215.0	1.1	0.2	3.6	63.8
France	4409.0	-0.4	-0.2	3.1	66.9
Spain	3764.9	2.5	9.2	2.6	69.5
Belgium	3547.8	2.7	10.2	2.5	72.0
Netherlands	3071.1	4.1	24.6	2.1	74.1
United Kingdom	2480.9	5.8	-4.4	1.7	75.9
Cambodia	2464.5	12.5	9.5	1.7	77.6
Indonesia	2205.7	-1.2	0.5	1.5	79.1

Graph 2: Trade Balance by MDG regions 2016
(Bln US$)

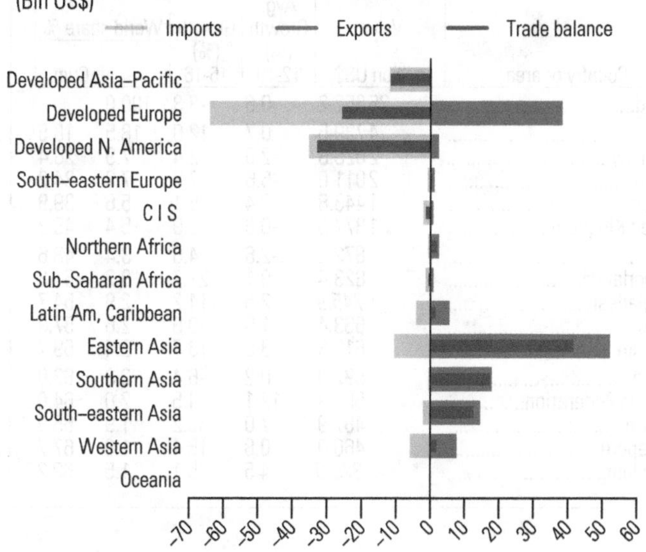

Table 3: Top importing countries or areas in 2016

Country or area	Value (million US$)	Avg. Growth (%) 12-16	Growth (%) 15-16	World share %	Cum.
World	139364.5	1.4	-0.4	100.0	
USA	31984.6	1.4	-5.4	23.0	23.0
Germany	12281.1	2.0	0.7	8.8	31.8
Japan	9356.2	-3.9	-0.5	6.7	38.5
United Kingdom	8467.8	0.6	-6.4	6.1	44.6
France	8066.8	0.2	0.0	5.8	50.3
Spain	5716.7	4.8	6.4	4.1	54.4
Italy	5521.2	-0.2	0.7	4.0	58.4
China, Hong Kong SAR	5274.7	-4.9	-11.2	3.8	62.2
Netherlands	5226.1	11.9	43.4	3.7	65.9
Belgium	3350.7	0.8	14.1	2.4	68.3
Canada	3226.0	0.5	-3.2	2.3	70.7
Rep. of Korea	2701.2	9.4	3.5	1.9	72.6
Austria	2321.5	5.3	18.5	1.7	74.3
Australia	2107.6	2.7	-1.2	1.5	75.8
Poland	1972.3	12.9	10.6	1.4	77.2

846 Clothing accessories, of textile fabrics, whether or not knitted or crocheted

In 2016, the value (in current US$) of exports of "clothing accessories, of textile fabrics, whether or not knitted or crocheted" (SITC group 846) decreased by 3.5 percent (compared to less than 0.1 percent average growth rate from 2012-2016) to reach 28.8 bln US$ (see table 2), while imports decreased by 3.3 percent to reach 25.7 bln US$ (see table 3). Exports of this commodity accounted for 1.4 percent of world exports of SITC section 8, and 0.2 percent of total world merchandise exports (see table 1). China, Italy and Turkey were the top exporters in 2016 (see table 2). They accounted for 43.6, 7.1 and 4.2 percent of world exports, respectively. USA, Germany and Japan were the top destinations, with respectively 18.5, 7.9 and 7.8 percent of world imports (see table 3).

The top 15 countries/areas accounted for 82.5 and 69.2 percent of total world exports and imports, respectively (see tables 2 and 3). In 2016, China was the country/area with the highest value of net exports (+12.2 bln US$), followed by Italy (+1.2 bln US$). By MDG regions (see graph 2), the largest surpluses in this product group were recorded by Eastern Asia (+13.0 bln US$), Southern Asia (+874.4 mln US$) and Western Asia (+435.0 mln US$). The largest trade deficits were recorded by Developed North America (-4.6 bln US$), Developed Europe (-3.0 bln US$) and Developed Asia-Pacific (-2.3 bln US$).

Table 1: Imports (Imp.) and exports (Exp.), 2002-2016, in current US$

		2002	2003	2004	2005	2006	2007	2008	2009	2010	2011	2012	2013	2014	2015	2016
Values in Bln US$	Imp.	12.7	14.2	16.2	17.0	17.7	19.4	22.1	19.4	23.3	27.3	26.3	27.8	28.1	26.5	25.7
	Exp.	12.9	14.5	16.3	17.5	18.8	20.2	23.7	21.3	24.5	29.1	28.8	31.3	32.2	29.8	28.8
As a percentage of SITC section (%)	Imp.	1.5	1.5	1.4	1.4	1.3	1.3	1.3	1.4	1.4	1.5	1.4	1.4	1.4	1.4	1.3
	Exp.	1.6	1.6	1.5	1.5	1.4	1.3	1.5	1.5	1.5	1.5	1.4	1.5	1.5	1.4	1.4
As a percentage of world trade (%)	Imp.	0.2	0.2	0.2	0.2	0.1	0.1	0.1	0.2	0.2	0.2	0.1	0.1	0.1	0.2	0.2
	Exp.	0.2	0.2	0.2	0.2	0.2	0.1	0.1	0.2	0.2	0.2	0.2	0.2	0.2	0.2	0.2

Graph 1: Annual growth rates of exports, 2002–2016
(In percentage by year)

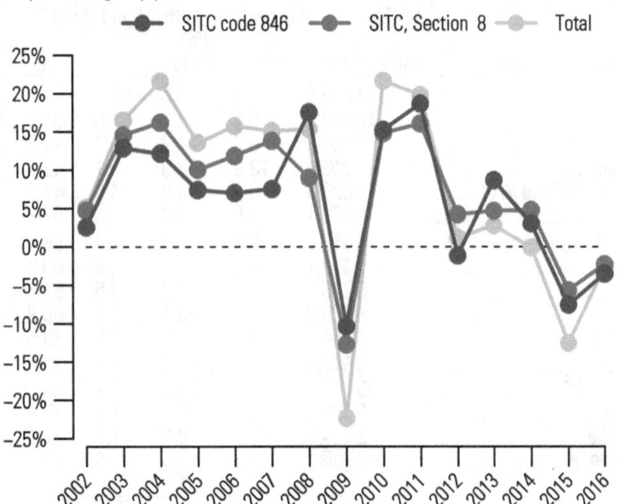

Graph 2: Trade Balance by MDG regions 2016
(Bln US$)

Imports — Exports — Trade balance

Developed Asia-Pacific
Developed Europe
Developed N. America
South-eastern Europe
C I S
Northern Africa
Sub-Saharan Africa
Latin Am, Caribbean
Eastern Asia
Southern Asia
South-eastern Asia
Western Asia
Oceania

-12 -10 -8 -6 -4 -2 0 2 4 6 8 10 12 14 16

Table 2: Top exporting countries or areas in 2016

Country or area	Value (million US$)	Avg. Growth (%) 12-16	Growth (%) 15-16	World share %	Cum.
World	28761.6	0.0	-3.5	100.0	
China	12534.7	0.4	-7.4	43.6	43.6
Italy	2036.2	-5.0	0.5	7.1	50.7
Turkey	1220.3	2.8	2.8	4.2	54.9
Germany	1081.7	-2.2	-1.4	3.8	58.7
India	954.0	0.4	-12.0	3.3	62.0
Rep. of Korea	946.8	3.0	-4.6	3.3	65.3
France	808.6	1.9	3.2	2.8	68.1
USA	670.6	-2.3	-1.7	2.3	70.4
Belgium	644.2	3.4	13.9	2.2	72.7
Netherlands	591.6	3.7	7.0	2.1	74.7
United Kingdom	526.3	3.6	-5.5	1.8	76.5
Pakistan	474.4	2.6	-7.2	1.6	78.2
Spain	449.4	2.7	6.7	1.6	79.8
Viet Nam	*417.4*	16.0	8.9	1.5	81.2
China, Hong Kong SAR	360.2	-8.3	-13.7	1.3	82.5

Table 3: Top importing countries or areas in 2016

Country or area	Value (million US$)	Avg. Growth (%) 12-16	Growth (%) 15-16	World share %	Cum.
World	25652.2	-0.6	-3.3	100.0	
USA	4739.5	0.7	-12.0	18.5	18.5
Germany	2028.8	-2.0	-2.4	7.9	26.4
Japan	2011.0	-5.6	-7.8	7.8	34.2
France	1443.8	0.4	5.1	5.6	39.9
United Kingdom	1377.9	-0.6	-13.9	5.4	45.2
Italy	872.2	-2.6	4.6	3.4	48.6
Netherlands	823.4	9.1	21.7	3.2	51.8
Bangladesh	*745.9*	2.5	-14.2	2.9	54.7
Spain	663.4	1.5	-0.9	2.6	57.3
Belgium	613.8	3.5	13.7	2.4	59.7
Canada	592.9	0.2	-6.4	2.3	62.0
Russian Federation	506.9	-12.1	4.5	2.0	64.0
Austria	487.9	7.0	33.2	1.9	65.9
Singapore	460.0	-0.8	15.4	1.8	67.7
Viet Nam	*375.0*	4.5	5.1	1.5	69.2

In 2016, the value (in current US$) of exports of "articles of apparel, and clothing accessories not textile fabrics; headgear" (SITC group 848) decreased by 3.8 percent (compared to -0.6 percent average growth rate from 2012-2016) to reach 29.7 bln US$ (see table 2), while imports decreased by 4.9 percent to reach 27.5 bln US$ (see table 3). Exports of this commodity accounted for 1.5 percent of world exports of SITC section 8, and 0.2 percent of total world merchandise exports (see table 1). China, Malaysia and Italy were the top exporters in 2016 (see table 2). They accounted for 39.4, 11.0 and 6.2 percent of world exports, respectively. USA, Germany and Japan were the top destinations, with respectively 25.9, 7.2 and 6.0 percent of world imports (see table 3).

The top 15 countries/areas accounted for 86.5 and 72.6 percent of total world exports and imports, respectively (see tables 2 and 3). In 2016, China was the country/area with the highest value of net exports (+11.2 bln US$), followed by Malaysia (+3.1 bln US$). By MDG regions (see graph 2), the largest surpluses in this product group were recorded by Eastern Asia (+11.0 bln US$), South-eastern Asia (+4.3 bln US$) and Southern Asia (+1.6 bln US$). The largest trade deficits were recorded by Developed North America (-6.9 bln US$), Developed Europe (-3.2 bln US$) and Developed Asia-Pacific (-2.0 bln US$).

Table 1: Imports (Imp.) and exports (Exp.), 2002-2016, in current US$

		2002	2003	2004	2005	2006	2007	2008	2009	2010	2011	2012	2013	2014	2015	2016
Values in Bln US$	Imp.	15.3	16.4	17.9	19.4	20.8	22.2	24.7	21.8	25.1	29.2	29.1	29.4	30.6	28.9	27.5
	Exp.	14.5	17.0	19.0	21.1	20.7	21.5	23.3	20.8	24.7	29.7	30.4	32.3	33.5	30.9	29.7
As a percentage of SITC section (%)	Imp.	1.8	1.7	1.6	1.6	1.5	1.4	1.5	1.5	1.5	1.6	1.6	1.5	1.5	1.5	1.4
	Exp.	1.8	1.8	1.8	1.8	1.6	1.4	1.4	1.5	1.5	1.6	1.5	1.6	1.5	1.5	1.5
As a percentage of world trade (%)	Imp.	0.2	0.2	0.2	0.2	0.2	0.2	0.2	0.2	0.2	0.2	0.2	0.2	0.2	0.2	0.2
	Exp.	0.2	0.2	0.2	0.2	0.2	0.2	0.1	0.2	0.2	0.2	0.2	0.2	0.2	0.2	0.2

Graph 1: Annual growth rates of exports, 2002–2016
(In percentage by year)

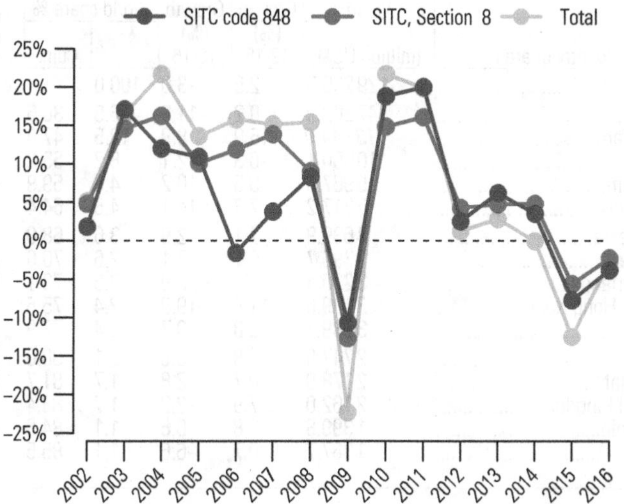

Table 2: Top exporting countries or areas in 2016

Country or area	Value (million US$)	Avg. Growth (%) 12-16	Growth (%) 15-16	World share %	Cum.
World	29704.3	-0.6	-3.8	100.0	
China	11701.3	0.8	-5.2	39.4	39.4
Malaysia	3270.3	-1.6	-4.9	11.0	50.4
Italy	1855.8	-1.5	-4.8	6.2	56.6
Germany	1138.1	-1.7	0.3	3.8	60.5
Thailand	1056.7	-4.9	-0.9	3.6	64.0
India	970.4	0.9	-6.4	3.3	67.3
France	965.5	1.0	-1.6	3.3	70.6
China, Hong Kong SAR	772.6	-12.1	-20.4	2.6	73.2
USA	758.6	-1.5	-5.1	2.6	75.7
Netherlands	594.9	1.4	5.8	2.0	77.7
Belgium	592.9	2.5	11.9	2.0	79.7
Viet Nam	*560.0*	11.4	8.9	1.9	81.6
Pakistan	502.4	-0.5	-6.3	1.7	83.3
United Kingdom	489.9	5.8	-5.8	1.6	84.9
Spain	468.3	9.3	2.0	1.6	86.5

Graph 2: Trade Balance by MDG regions 2016
(Bln US$)

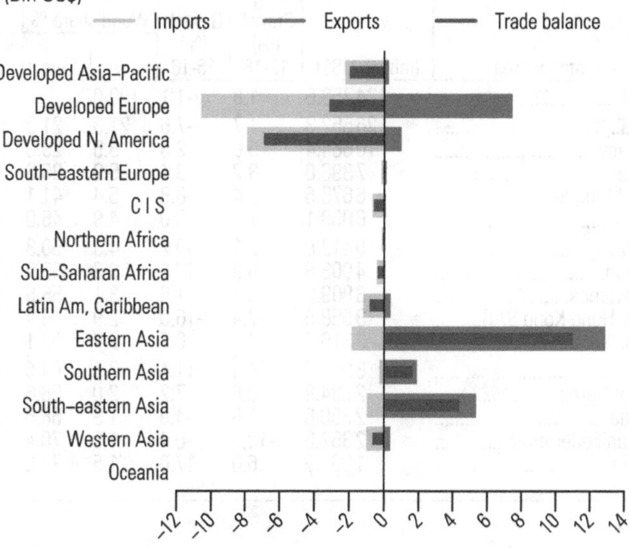

Table 3: Top importing countries or areas in 2016

Country or area	Value (million US$)	Avg. Growth (%) 12-16	Growth (%) 15-16	World share %	Cum.
World	27465.0	-1.5	-4.9	100.0	
USA	7127.1	-0.5	-8.7	25.9	25.9
Germany	1973.6	-1.8	-4.5	7.2	33.1
Japan	1650.7	-3.5	-3.6	6.0	39.1
France	1441.0	-2.0	-2.7	5.2	44.4
United Kingdom	1284.2	-0.2	-10.1	4.7	49.1
Italy	962.2	-0.8	-0.6	3.5	52.6
Canada	781.3	-2.5	-11.6	2.8	55.4
Spain	772.4	4.8	4.3	2.8	58.2
Netherlands	729.2	2.4	5.8	2.7	60.9
China, Hong Kong SAR	719.2	-10.7	-20.1	2.6	63.5
Belgium	527.3	-1.1	6.4	1.9	65.4
Russian Federation	509.0	-16.5	3.7	1.9	67.3
China	495.6	-0.9	-8.2	1.8	69.1
Australia	484.3	-0.6	-1.7	1.8	70.8
Rep. of Korea	470.1	6.6	2.5	1.7	72.6

851 Footwear

In 2016, the value (in current US$) of exports of "footwear" (SITC group 851) decreased by 3.0 percent (compared to 2.5 percent average growth rate from 2012-2016) to reach 129.2 bln US$ (see table 2), while imports decreased by 1.1 percent to reach 124.8 bln US$ (see table 3). Exports of this commodity accounted for 6.4 percent of world exports of SITC section 8, and 0.8 percent of total world merchandise exports (see table 1). China, Viet Nam and Italy were the top exporters in 2016 (see table 2). They accounted for 36.5, 10.5 and 8.2 percent of world exports, respectively. USA, Germany and France were the top destinations, with respectively 21.3, 8.5 and 5.9 percent of world imports (see table 3).

The top 15 countries/areas accounted for 85.5 and 71.8 percent of total world exports and imports, respectively (see tables 2 and 3). In 2016, China was the country/area with the highest value of net exports (+44.1 bln US$), followed by Viet Nam (+12.9 bln US$). By MDG regions (see graph 2), the largest surpluses in this product group were recorded by Eastern Asia (+41.1 bln US$), South-eastern Asia (+17.2 bln US$) and Southern Asia (+2.6 bln US$). The largest trade deficits were recorded by Developed North America (-27.3 bln US$), Developed Europe (-12.2 bln US$) and Developed Asia-Pacific (-7.2 bln US$).

Table 1: Imports (Imp.) and exports (Exp.), 2002-2016, in current US$

		2002	2003	2004	2005	2006	2007	2008	2009	2010	2011	2012	2013	2014	2015	2016
Values in Bln US$	Imp.	55.1	60.5	66.3	73.1	80.8	88.8	97.2	86.8	100.7	115.1	116.0	123.0	130.7	126.2	124.8
	Exp.	48.8	54.3	60.0	66.1	73.6	82.6	91.9	81.7	96.2	113.7	117.0	128.1	140.6	133.3	129.2
As a percentage of SITC section (%)	Imp.	6.5	6.2	5.9	5.9	5.9	5.7	5.8	6.1	6.1	6.2	6.2	6.4	6.5	6.6	6.6
	Exp.	6.1	5.9	5.6	5.6	5.6	5.5	5.6	5.7	5.9	6.0	5.9	6.2	6.4	6.5	6.4
As a percentage of world trade (%)	Imp.	0.8	0.8	0.7	0.7	0.7	0.6	0.6	0.7	0.7	0.6	0.6	0.7	0.7	0.8	0.8
	Exp.	0.8	0.7	0.7	0.6	0.6	0.6	0.6	0.7	0.6	0.6	0.6	0.7	0.7	0.8	0.8

Graph 1: Annual growth rates of exports, 2002–2016
(In percentage by year)

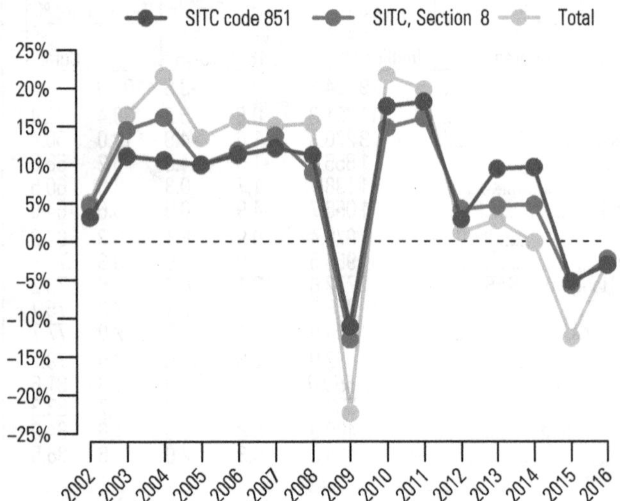

Table 2: Top exporting countries or areas in 2016

Country or area	Value (million US$)	Avg. Growth (%) 12-16	Growth (%) 15-16	World share %	Cum.
World	129236.5	2.5	-3.0	100.0	
China	47202.9	0.2	-11.8	36.5	36.5
Viet Nam	*13544.0*	15.9	8.9	10.5	47.0
Italy	10650.1	-0.3	2.1	8.2	55.2
Belgium	5967.6	8.5	10.2	4.6	59.9
Germany	5817.2	7.3	14.1	4.5	64.4
Indonesia	4639.9	7.1	2.9	3.6	68.0
France	3396.7	6.1	7.1	2.6	70.6
Netherlands	3229.4	1.4	5.9	2.5	73.1
China, Hong Kong SAR	3139.0	-11.8	-19.8	2.4	75.5
Spain	3089.7	2.8	-9.7	2.4	77.9
India	2747.9	8.8	-0.8	2.1	80.0
Portugal	2178.0	0.7	2.8	1.7	81.7
United Kingdom	2162.0	7.9	-2.2	1.7	83.4
Romania	1399.8	-2.8	-0.6	1.1	84.5
USA	1367.7	0.7	-6.6	1.1	85.5

Graph 2: Trade Balance by MDG regions 2016
(Bln US$)

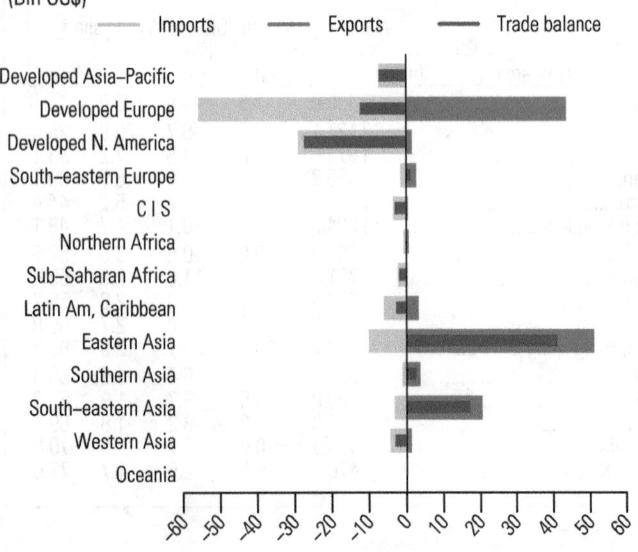

Table 3: Top importing countries or areas in 2016

Country or area	Value (million US$)	Avg. Growth (%) 12-16	Growth (%) 15-16	World share %	Cum.
World	124753.5	1.8	-1.1	100.0	
USA	26552.3	1.7	-7.6	21.3	21.3
Germany	10664.4	5.0	2.5	8.5	29.8
France	7396.0	3.2	3.4	5.9	35.8
United Kingdom	6675.5	2.4	-8.8	5.4	41.1
Italy	6069.1	1.2	3.0	4.9	46.0
Japan	5412.8	-2.1	-0.2	4.3	50.3
Belgium	4003.8	6.9	10.9	3.2	53.5
Netherlands	3809.8	3.1	-1.6	3.1	56.6
China, Hong Kong SAR	3558.5	-7.4	-16.0	2.9	59.4
Spain	3316.7	4.7	6.7	2.7	62.1
China	3062.8	14.4	11.4	2.5	64.5
Rep. of Korea	2534.8	8.6	7.2	2.0	66.6
Canada	2356.6	1.6	-4.9	1.9	68.5
Russian Federation	2352.8	-13.8	-0.4	1.9	70.4
Austria	1868.9	6.0	17.0	1.5	71.8

In 2016, the value (in current US$) of exports of "optical instruments and apparatus, nes" (SITC group 871) decreased by 15.4 percent (compared to -8.5 percent average growth rate from 2012-2016) to reach 76.3 bln US$ (see table 2), while imports decreased by 13.0 percent to reach 67.3 bln US$ (see table 3). Exports of this commodity accounted for 3.8 percent of world exports of SITC section 8, and 0.5 percent of total world merchandise exports (see table 1). China, Rep. of Korea and Other Asia, nes were the top exporters in 2016 (see table 2). They accounted for 38.4, 21.2 and 9.8 percent of world exports, respectively. China, China, Hong Kong SAR and USA were the top destinations, with respectively 58.0, 6.1 and 5.9 percent of world imports (see table 3).

The top 15 countries/areas accounted for 97.2 and 92.4 percent of total world exports and imports, respectively (see tables 2 and 3). In 2016, Rep. of Korea was the country/area with the highest value of net exports (+13.0 bln US$), followed by Other Asia, nes (+6.5 bln US$). By MDG regions (see graph 2), the largest surpluses in this product group were recorded by Eastern Asia (+8.8 bln US$), Developed Asia-Pacific (+3.9 bln US$) and Developed Europe (+788.5 mln US$). The largest trade deficits were recorded by Latin America and the Caribbean (-3.5 bln US$), Western Asia (-719.0 mln US$) and Southern Asia (-661.7 mln US$).

Table 1: Imports (Imp.) and exports (Exp.), 2002-2016, in current US$

		2002	2003	2004	2005	2006	2007	2008	2009	2010	2011	2012	2013	2014	2015	2016
Values in Bln US$	Imp.	13.8	25.3	39.9	49.8	63.1	75.8	80.8	62.0	80.2	85.7	87.6	87.8	81.9	77.4	67.3
	Exp.	12.5	20.3	32.6	44.7	57.3	71.8	81.5	72.3	97.4	102.8	109.1	105.7	99.4	90.2	76.3
As a percentage of SITC section (%)	Imp.	1.6	2.6	3.6	4.0	4.6	4.9	4.8	4.3	4.9	4.6	4.7	4.6	4.1	4.0	3.5
	Exp.	1.6	2.2	3.0	3.8	4.4	4.8	5.0	5.1	5.9	5.4	5.5	5.1	4.6	4.4	3.8
As a percentage of world trade (%)	Imp.	0.2	0.3	0.4	0.5	0.5	0.5	0.5	0.5	0.5	0.5	0.5	0.5	0.4	0.5	0.4
	Exp.	0.2	0.3	0.4	0.4	0.5	0.5	0.5	0.6	0.6	0.6	0.6	0.6	0.5	0.5	0.5

Graph 1: Annual growth rates of exports, 2002–2016
(In percentage by year)

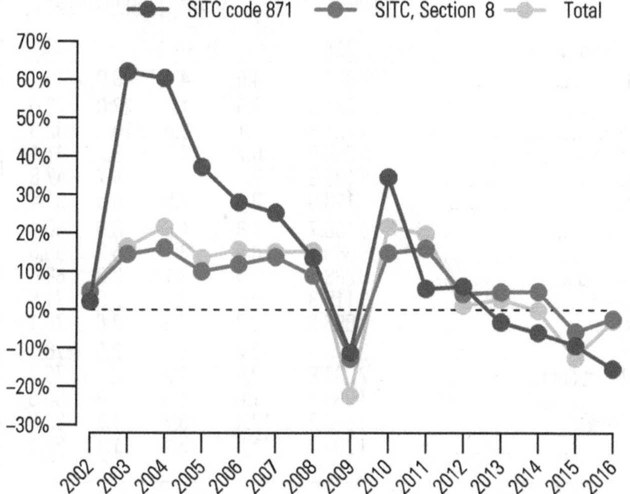

Table 2: Top exporting countries or areas in 2016

Country or area	Value (million US$)	Avg. Growth (%) 12-16	Growth (%) 15-16	World share %	Cum.
World	76345.7	-8.5	-15.4	100.0	
China	29312.4	-7.0	-15.1	38.4	38.4
Rep. of Korea	16183.5	-12.5	-24.8	21.2	59.6
Other Asia, nes	7505.8	-18.2	-28.8	9.8	69.4
Japan	5533.4	-11.1	-16.9	7.2	76.7
USA	3808.8	4.1	2.6	5.0	81.7
Germany	3296.9	0.9	6.4	4.3	86.0
China, Hong Kong SAR	3133.2	-6.1	12.0	4.1	90.1
Thailand	1659.0	43.4	13.6	2.2	92.3
United Kingdom	763.9	1.8	-6.8	1.0	93.3
Netherlands	698.3	12.3	15.4	0.9	94.2
Mexico	608.5	18.6	48.5	0.8	95.0
Singapore	579.7	2.8	1.1	0.8	95.7
Czechia	424.4	-1.9	2.7	0.6	96.3
Canada	407.3	-10.6	-18.9	0.5	96.8
France	315.4	-7.5	1.1	0.4	97.2

Graph 2: Trade Balance by MDG regions 2016
(Bln US$)

Imports — Exports — Trade balance

Developed Asia-Pacific
Developed Europe
Developed N. America
South-eastern Europe
C I S
Northern Africa
Sub-Saharan Africa
Latin Am, Caribbean
Eastern Asia
Southern Asia
South-eastern Asia
Western Asia
Oceania

-50 -40 -30 -20 -10 0 10 20 30 40 50 60

Table 3: Top importing countries or areas in 2016

Country or area	Value (million US$)	Avg. Growth (%) 12-16	Growth (%) 15-16	World share %	Cum.
World	67345.4	-6.4	-13.0	100.0	
China	39072.5	-8.8	-17.3	58.0	58.0
China, Hong Kong SAR	4085.1	-6.6	-0.8	6.1	64.1
USA	3971.5	3.9	8.9	5.9	70.0
Mexico	3857.8	4.5	-17.3	5.7	75.7
Rep. of Korea	3174.7	-4.2	-15.7	4.7	80.4
Japan	1415.2	-8.9	-2.9	2.1	82.5
Slovakia	1379.9	-8.4	-8.3	2.0	84.6
Germany	1222.2	-2.3	0.6	1.8	86.4
Other Asia, nes	1019.6	-6.6	-37.2	1.5	87.9
Malaysia	713.6	-0.5	-15.2	1.1	89.0
United Kingdom	533.5	-1.0	7.0	0.8	89.8
India	502.2	0.8	-10.5	0.7	90.5
Netherlands	453.9	-0.7	-1.3	0.7	91.2
Singapore	445.2	-5.6	10.0	0.7	91.8
Canada	395.7	-1.6	4.4	0.6	92.4

 Source: UN Comtrade

872 Instruments and appliances, nes, for medical and veterinary sciences

In 2016, the value (in current US$) of exports of "instruments and appliances, nes, for medical and veterinary sciences" (SITC group 872) increased by 4.4 percent (compared to 4.0 percent average growth rate from 2012-2016) to reach 107.8 bln US$ (see table 2), while imports increased by 5.2 percent to reach 107.2 bln US$ (see table 3). Exports of this commodity accounted for 5.4 percent of world exports of SITC section 8, and 0.7 percent of total world merchandise exports (see table 1). USA, Germany and Netherlands were the top exporters in 2016 (see table 2). They accounted for 22.0, 10.9 and 8.2 percent of world exports, respectively. USA, Germany and Netherlands were the top destinations, with respectively 20.0, 7.6 and 7.3 percent of world imports (see table 3).

The top 15 countries/areas accounted for 83.4 and 73.8 percent of total world exports and imports, respectively (see tables 2 and 3). In 2016, Mexico was the country/area with the highest value of net exports (+4.4 bln US$), followed by Ireland (+4.2 bln US$). By MDG regions (see graph 2), the largest surpluses in this product group were recorded by Developed Europe (+4.7 bln US$), Latin America and the Caribbean (+4.2 bln US$) and South-eastern Asia (+1.1 bln US$). The largest trade deficits were recorded by Developed Asia-Pacific (-3.7 bln US$), Commonwealth of Independent States (-2.0 bln US$) and Western Asia (-1.7 bln US$).

Table 1: Imports (Imp.) and exports (Exp.), 2002-2016, in current US$

		2002	2003	2004	2005	2006	2007	2008	2009	2010	2011	2012	2013	2014	2015	2016
Values in Bln US$	Imp.	32.9	39.3	47.4	54.7	60.0	67.0	77.2	74.1	80.5	89.8	93.2	99.5	104.7	101.9	107.2
	Exp.	32.5	39.9	46.5	53.2	56.6	63.7	74.8	72.7	79.0	88.3	92.2	99.0	105.5	103.3	107.8
As a percentage of SITC section (%)	Imp.	3.9	4.1	4.2	4.4	4.4	4.3	4.6	5.2	4.9	4.8	5.0	5.2	5.2	5.3	5.6
	Exp.	4.1	4.3	4.4	4.5	4.3	4.3	4.6	5.1	4.8	4.6	4.6	4.8	4.8	5.0	5.4
As a percentage of world trade (%)	Imp.	0.5	0.5	0.5	0.5	0.5	0.5	0.5	0.6	0.5	0.5	0.5	0.5	0.6	0.6	0.7
	Exp.	0.5	0.5	0.5	0.5	0.5	0.5	0.5	0.6	0.5	0.5	0.5	0.5	0.6	0.6	0.7

Graph 1: Annual growth rates of exports, 2002–2016
(In percentage by year)

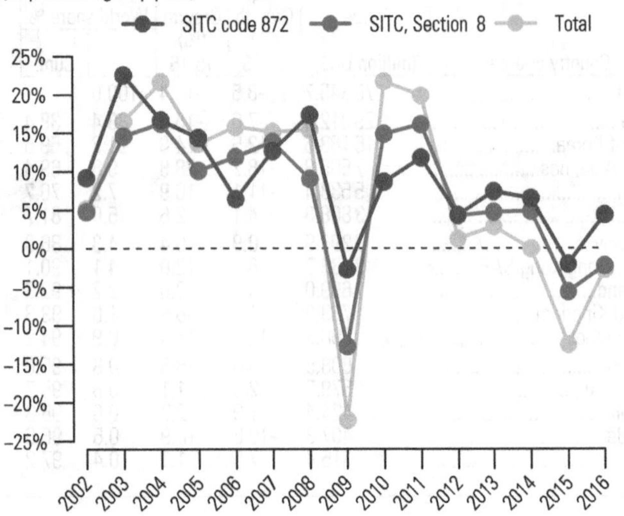

Table 2: Top exporting countries or areas in 2016

Country or area	Value (million US$)	Avg. Growth (%) 12-16	Growth (%) 15-16	World share %	Cum.
World	107 827.5	4.0	4.4	100.0	
USA	23 731.3	2.5	1.8	22.0	22.0
Germany	11 721.8	1.1	2.5	10.9	32.9
Netherlands	8 855.8	6.7	24.3	8.2	41.1
China	7 196.9	7.1	-1.0	6.7	47.8
Mexico	7 113.0	9.9	7.5	6.6	54.4
Belgium	6 496.7	4.8	4.6	6.0	60.4
Ireland	5 569.5	10.8	-3.1	5.2	65.6
Switzerland	3 288.3	3.4	3.1	3.0	68.6
Singapore	3 115.3	0.5	-2.7	2.9	71.5
Japan	2 856.6	0.2	7.6	2.6	74.1
France	2 675.4	-3.2	5.1	2.5	76.6
United Kingdom	2 237.8	0.0	-3.3	2.1	78.7
Italy	1 983.1	1.0	4.6	1.8	80.5
Costa Rica	1 876.2	17.4	15.7	1.7	82.3
Israel	1 204.7	11.9	15.1	1.1	83.4

Graph 2: Trade Balance by MDG regions 2016
(Bln US$)

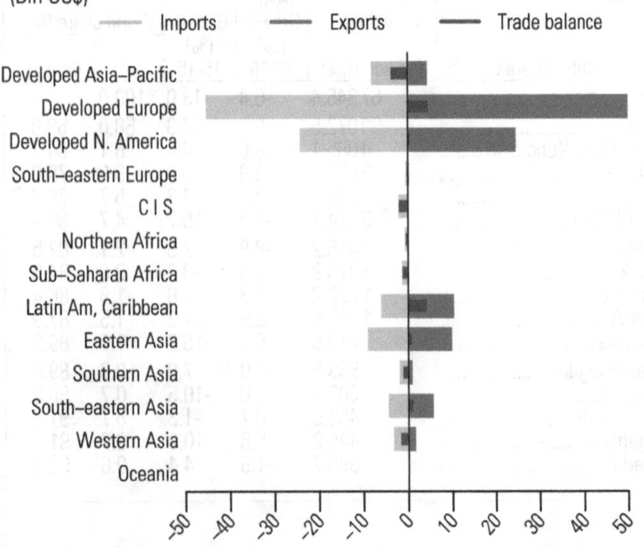

Table 3: Top importing countries or areas in 2016

Country or area	Value (million US$)	Avg. Growth (%) 12-16	Growth (%) 15-16	World share %	Cum.
World	107 223.3	3.6	5.2	100.0	
USA	21 410.6	7.2	8.4	20.0	20.0
Germany	8 180.5	2.7	4.4	7.6	27.6
Netherlands	7 798.0	10.4	29.3	7.3	34.9
Japan	5 462.6	-2.5	6.4	5.1	40.0
Belgium	5 453.5	1.9	-0.8	5.1	45.1
China	5 155.3	11.6	12.7	4.8	49.9
France	4 656.5	1.4	6.0	4.3	54.2
United Kingdom	3 893.1	2.8	-6.8	3.6	57.8
Italy	2 856.5	1.1	3.3	2.7	60.5
Canada	2 757.9	-0.9	0.0	2.6	63.1
Mexico	2 745.9	9.1	9.0	2.6	65.6
Australia	2 283.0	3.0	8.7	2.1	67.8
Singapore	2 240.3	7.1	4.9	2.1	69.8
Spain	2 211.4	5.7	12.5	2.1	71.9
Switzerland	2 034.9	4.1	3.3	1.9	73.8

In 2016, the value (in current US$) of exports of "meters and counters, nes." (SITC group 873) increased by 6.4 percent (compared to 3.9 percent average growth rate from 2012-2016) to reach 14.8 bln US$ (see table 2), while imports increased by 3.5 percent to reach 14.6 bln US$ (see table 3). Exports of this commodity accounted for 0.7 percent of world exports of SITC section 8, and 0.1 percent of total world merchandise exports (see table 1). Mexico, China and Germany were the top exporters in 2016 (see table 2). They accounted for 12.9, 11.6 and 10.8 percent of world exports, respectively. USA, Germany and United Kingdom were the top destinations, with respectively 20.3, 10.0 and 5.8 percent of world imports (see table 3).

The top 15 countries/areas accounted for 75.5 and 69.2 percent of total world exports and imports, respectively (see tables 2 and 3). In 2016, China was the country/area with the highest value of net exports (+1.4 bln US$), followed by Mexico (+1.2 bln US$). By MDG regions (see graph 2), the largest surpluses in this product group were recorded by Eastern Asia (+1.6 bln US$), Latin America and the Caribbean (+857.0 mln US$) and Commonwealth of Independent States (+367.3 mln US$). The largest trade deficits were recorded by Developed North America (-2.4 bln US$), Sub-Saharan Africa (-298.3 mln US$) and Western Asia (-288.9 mln US$).

Table 1: Imports (Imp.) and exports (Exp.), 2002-2016, in current US$

		2002	2003	2004	2005	2006	2007	2008	2009	2010	2011	2012	2013	2014	2015	2016
Values in Bln US$	Imp.	5.1	6.0	6.8	7.2	7.7	9.1	10.0	8.5	10.1	12.1	13.1	13.8	14.6	14.2	14.6
	Exp.	4.7	5.4	6.2	6.6	7.1	8.6	9.7	8.3	10.1	12.1	12.7	13.2	14.7	13.9	14.8
As a percentage of SITC section (%)	Imp.	0.6	0.6	0.6	0.6	0.6	0.6	0.6	0.6	0.6	0.7	0.7	0.7	0.7	0.7	0.8
	Exp.	0.6	0.6	0.6	0.6	0.5	0.6	0.6	0.6	0.6	0.6	0.6	0.6	0.7	0.7	0.7
As a percentage of world trade (%)	Imp.	0.1	0.1	0.1	0.1	0.1	0.1	0.1	0.1	0.1	0.1	0.1	0.1	0.1	0.1	0.1
	Exp.	0.1	0.1	0.1	0.1	0.1	0.1	0.1	0.1	0.1	0.1	0.1	0.1	0.1	0.1	0.1

Graph 1: Annual growth rates of exports, 2002–2016
(In percentage by year)

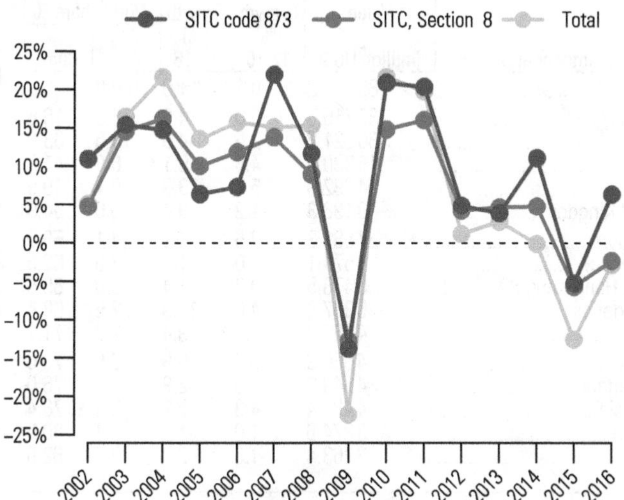

Table 2: Top exporting countries or areas in 2016

Country or area	Value (million US$)	Avg. Growth (%) 12-16	Growth (%) 15-16	World share %	Cum.
World	14812.1	3.9	6.4	100.0	
Mexico	1908.2	11.1	5.6	12.9	12.9
China	1721.6	-2.7	-15.7	11.6	24.5
Germany	1602.2	-0.6	2.3	10.8	35.3
USA	1266.1	0.2	2.7	8.5	43.9
Japan	634.9	2.7	52.0	4.3	48.2
France	608.2	1.9	2.3	4.1	52.3
Uzbekistan	*518.8*	613.9	>	3.5	55.8
China, Hong Kong SAR	450.7	7.3	-23.6	3.0	58.8
United Kingdom	446.6	3.8	-3.5	3.0	61.8
Italy	433.4	2.2	0.7	2.9	64.7
Hungary	348.6	-9.6	0.8	2.4	67.1
Poland	333.0	12.2	52.9	2.2	69.4
Spain	331.6	17.7	27.2	2.2	71.6
Romania	295.3	35.1	28.6	2.0	73.6
Czechia	277.0	8.5	40.2	1.9	75.5

Graph 2: Trade Balance by MDG regions 2016
(Bln US$)

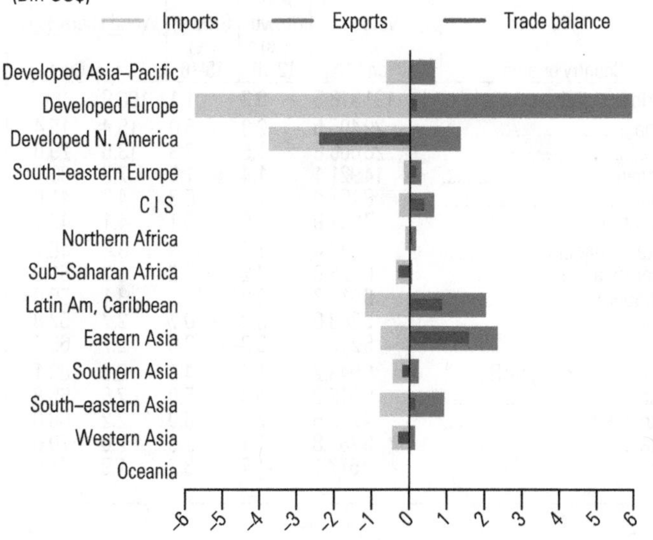

Table 3: Top importing countries or areas in 2016

Country or area	Value (million US$)	Avg. Growth (%) 12-16	Growth (%) 15-16	World share %	Cum.
World	14643.4	2.8	3.5	100.0	
USA	2975.6	5.0	-6.3	20.3	20.3
Germany	1465.9	6.5	18.3	10.0	30.3
United Kingdom	851.5	12.5	32.1	5.8	36.1
Canada	784.4	2.6	19.9	5.4	41.5
Mexico	732.1	10.3	1.3	5.0	46.5
France	611.5	2.5	11.3	4.2	50.7
Spain	419.2	8.1	-0.5	2.9	53.5
Japan	412.5	0.6	12.4	2.8	56.4
Italy	365.7	7.4	14.2	2.5	58.9
China	297.0	-16.0	-33.8	2.0	60.9
Netherlands	286.0	-1.3	-0.1	2.0	62.8
Afghanistan	261.0	...	21.0	1.8	64.6
China, Hong Kong SAR	244.0	3.4	-10.9	1.7	66.3
Thailand	215.4	-3.7	11.5	1.5	67.8
Poland	208.9	0.9	1.4	1.4	69.2

874 Measuring, checking, analyzing and controlling instruments, apparatus nes

"Measuring, checking, analyzing and controlling instruments, apparatus nes" (SITC group 874) is amongst the top exported commodities in 2016 with 1.2 percent of total exports (see table 1). The value (in current US$) of exports of this commodity increased by 1.9 percent (compared to -0.1 percent average growth rate from 2012-2016) to reach 185.4 bln US$ (see table 2), while imports increased by 1.1 percent to reach 191.3 bln US$ (see table 3). Exports of this commodity accounted for 9.2 percent of world exports of SITC section 8 (see table 1). Germany, USA and Japan were the top exporters in 2016 (see table 2). They accounted for 16.6, 16.5 and 8.8 percent of world exports, respectively. China, USA and Germany were the top destinations, with respectively 15.4, 13.6 and 7.8 percent of world imports (see table 3).

The top 15 countries/areas accounted for 82.6 and 71.8 percent of total world exports and imports, respectively (see tables 2 and 3). In 2016, Germany was the country/area with the highest value of net exports (+15.8 bln US$), followed by Japan (+8.2 bln US$). By MDG regions (see graph 2), the largest surpluses in this product group were recorded by Developed Europe (+23.7 bln US$), Developed Asia-Pacific (+6.3 bln US$) and Developed North America (+3.4 bln US$). The largest trade deficits were recorded by Eastern Asia (-20.3 bln US$), Latin America and the Caribbean (-5.0 bln US$) and Western Asia (-4.4 bln US$).

Table 1: Imports (Imp.) and exports (Exp.), 2002-2016, in current US$

		2002	2003	2004	2005	2006	2007	2008	2009	2010	2011	2012	2013	2014	2015	2016
Values in Bln US$	Imp.	74.9	86.2	106.3	112.5	127.7	143.1	153.9	125.6	155.1	182.1	188.7	191.4	199.1	189.2	191.3
	Exp.	72.8	83.5	103.4	110.8	125.8	140.3	149.5	123.8	153.3	179.2	186.1	188.5	195.3	182.0	185.4
As a percentage of SITC section (%)	Imp.	8.8	8.9	9.5	9.1	9.4	9.2	9.2	8.8	9.5	9.8	10.1	9.9	9.9	9.9	10.1
	Exp.	9.1	9.1	9.7	9.4	9.6	9.4	9.1	8.7	9.4	9.4	9.4	9.1	9.0	8.8	9.2
As a percentage of world trade (%)	Imp.	1.1	1.1	1.1	1.1	1.0	1.0	0.9	1.0	1.0	1.0	1.0	1.0	1.1	1.1	1.2
	Exp.	1.1	1.1	1.1	1.1	1.0	1.0	0.9	1.0	1.0	1.0	1.0	1.0	1.0	1.1	1.2

Graph 1: Annual growth rates of exports, 2002–2016

(In percentage by year)

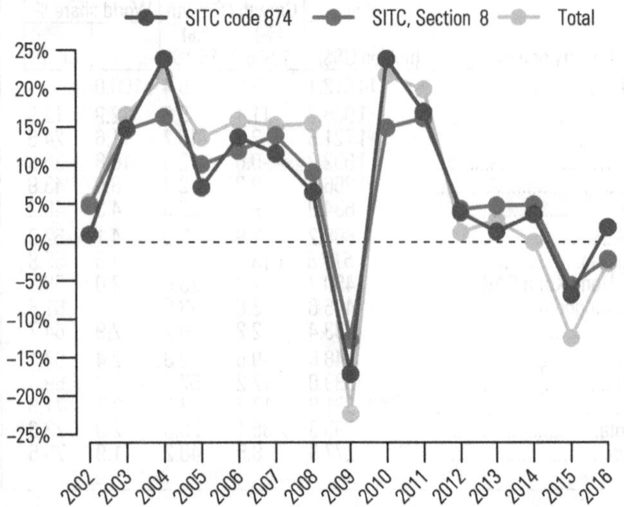

Table 2: Top exporting countries or areas in 2016

Country or area	Value (million US$)	Avg. Growth (%) 12-16	Growth (%) 15-16	World share %	Cum.
World	185401.2	-0.1	1.9	100.0	
Germany	30715.5	0.0	4.9	16.6	16.6
USA	30521.2	-2.5	-4.9	16.5	33.0
Japan	16330.5	-4.4	6.1	8.8	41.8
China	14992.9	5.7	3.3	8.1	49.9
United Kingdom	9196.3	-1.2	-9.4	5.0	54.9
Singapore	7581.3	2.5	4.2	4.1	59.0
France	6574.1	-2.0	-1.7	3.5	62.5
China, Hong Kong SAR	5478.5	0.2	1.4	3.0	65.5
Netherlands	5357.8	4.6	14.9	2.9	68.4
Rep. of Korea	4988.6	9.7	9.4	2.7	71.1
Mexico	4656.3	5.0	0.8	2.5	73.6
Switzerland	4549.3	-1.0	2.9	2.5	76.0
Malaysia	4482.4	-4.3	5.2	2.4	78.4
Canada	3874.6	1.0	-1.9	2.1	80.5
Italy	3763.4	-1.6	2.3	2.0	82.6

Graph 2: Trade Balance by MDG regions 2016

(Bln US$)

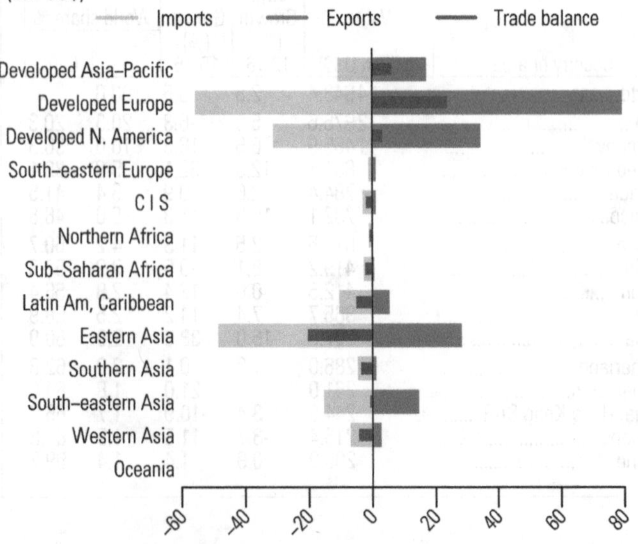

Table 3: Top importing countries or areas in 2016

Country or area	Value (million US$)	Avg. Growth (%) 12-16	Growth (%) 15-16	World share %	Cum.
World	191318.5	0.3	1.1	100.0	
China	29405.5	2.3	5.0	15.4	15.4
USA	26006.8	1.5	-2.3	13.6	29.0
Germany	14921.1	1.4	1.3	7.8	36.8
Japan	8102.0	1.2	0.3	4.2	41.0
Rep. of Korea	7861.9	-0.6	0.1	4.1	45.1
United Kingdom	6847.4	-1.3	-7.9	3.6	48.7
Other Asia, nes	6125.6	4.2	9.9	3.2	51.9
Singapore	6011.7	2.9	14.3	3.1	55.0
France	5248.6	-3.2	-0.7	2.7	57.8
Mexico	5212.4	3.3	-3.0	2.7	60.5
China, Hong Kong SAR	5043.2	1.4	4.8	2.6	63.1
Canada	5012.2	-5.4	-5.0	2.6	65.8
Netherlands	4272.6	2.5	6.0	2.2	68.0
India	3782.8	1.1	2.5	2.0	70.0
Italy	3577.1	-1.7	3.2	1.9	71.8

In 2016, the value (in current US$) of exports of "photographic apparatus and equipments, nes" (SITC group 881) increased by 4.7 percent (compared to -1.8 percent average growth rate from 2012-2016) to reach 7.3 bln US$ (see table 2), while imports decreased by 6.0 percent to reach 4.6 bln US$ (see table 3). Exports of this commodity accounted for 0.4 percent of world exports of SITC section 8, and less than 0.1 percent of total world merchandise exports (see table 1). Viet Nam, China and Philippines were the top exporters in 2016 (see table 2). They accounted for 32.3, 11.8 and 8.9 percent of world exports, respectively. USA, Viet Nam and China were the top destinations, with respectively 13.4, 12.6 and 10.7 percent of world imports (see table 3).

The top 15 countries/areas accounted for 87.4 and 73.1 percent of total world exports and imports, respectively (see tables 2 and 3). In 2016, Viet Nam was the country/area with the highest value of net exports (+1.8 bln US$), followed by Philippines (+565.0 mln US$). By MDG regions (see graph 2), the largest surpluses in this product group were recorded by South-eastern Asia (+2.7 bln US$), Eastern Asia (+414.8 mln US$) and Developed Asia-Pacific (+20.4 mln US$). The largest trade deficits were recorded by Developed North America (-181.9 mln US$), Latin America and the Caribbean (-65.3 mln US$) and Southern Asia (-49.6 mln US$).

Table 1: Imports (Imp.) and exports (Exp.), 2002-2016, in current US$

		2002	2003	2004	2005	2006	2007	2008	2009	2010	2011	2012	2013	2014	2015	2016
Values in Bln US$	Imp.	14.8	15.3	17.6	15.9	16.0	10.2	8.8	5.1	5.9	6.0	6.1	5.6	5.3	4.9	4.6
	Exp.	15.5	15.9	18.5	16.8	17.4	8.5	8.0	6.3	6.2	6.7	7.8	7.5	7.2	6.9	7.3
As a percentage of SITC section (%)	Imp.	1.7	1.6	1.6	1.3	1.2	0.7	0.5	0.4	0.4	0.3	0.3	0.3	0.3	0.3	0.2
	Exp.	1.9	1.7	1.7	1.4	1.3	0.6	0.5	0.4	0.4	0.4	0.4	0.4	0.3	0.3	0.4
As a percentage of world trade (%)	Imp.	0.2	0.2	0.2	0.2	0.1	0.1	0.1	0.0	0.0	0.0	0.0	0.0	0.0	0.0	0.0
	Exp.	0.2	0.2	0.2	0.2	0.1	0.1	0.1	0.1	0.0	0.0	0.0	0.0	0.0	0.0	0.0

Graph 1: Annual growth rates of exports, 2002-2016
(In percentage by year)

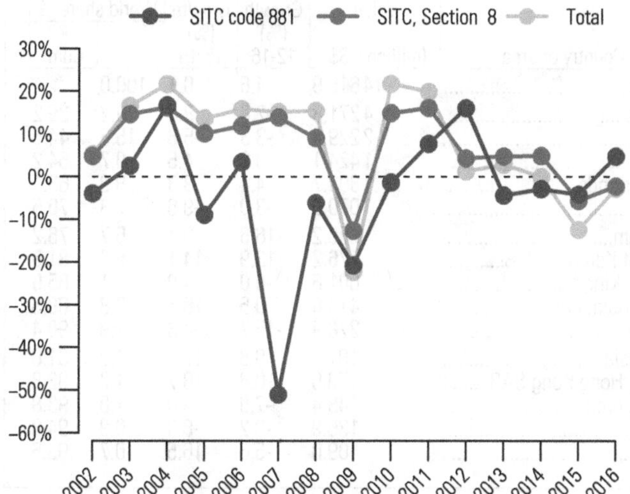

Graph 2: Trade Balance by MDG regions 2016
(Bln US$)

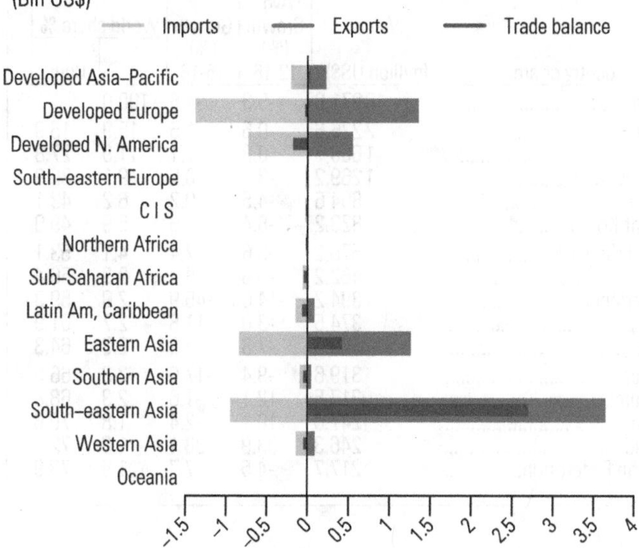

Table 2: Top exporting countries or areas in 2016

Country or area	Value (million US$)	Avg. Growth (%) 12-16	Growth (%) 15-16	World share %	Cum.
World	7259.8	-1.8	4.7	100.0	
Viet Nam	*2347.9*	9.8	8.9	32.3	32.3
China	857.9	-1.5	-0.7	11.8	44.2
Philippines	646.7	3.5	164.8	8.9	53.1
USA	420.3	-15.6	-19.1	5.8	58.9
Singapore	338.4	-1.0	-25.6	4.7	63.5
Germany	239.7	-8.6	-6.5	3.3	66.8
China, Hong Kong SAR	229.7	-17.5	-24.3	3.2	70.0
United Kingdom	212.4	10.6	21.7	2.9	72.9
Italy	189.0	-0.7	8.4	2.6	75.5
Japan	176.0	-12.6	-7.9	2.4	77.9
Netherlands	170.8	3.5	15.1	2.4	80.3
Thailand	168.6	-11.5	6.5	2.3	82.6
Malaysia	129.4	-22.7	-17.6	1.8	84.4
Canada	128.4	12.8	29.9	1.8	86.2
Rep. of Korea	92.7	8.9	20.0	1.3	87.4

Table 3: Top importing countries or areas in 2016

Country or area	Value (million US$)	Avg. Growth (%) 12-16	Growth (%) 15-16	World share %	Cum.
World	4623.4	-6.5	-6.0	100.0	
USA	619.4	1.1	12.9	13.4	13.4
Viet Nam	*581.0*	11.6	5.1	12.6	26.0
China	492.8	-5.3	11.7	10.7	36.6
Germany	287.9	-8.1	-8.1	6.2	42.8
United Kingdom	214.3	8.0	-9.5	4.6	47.5
France	204.8	5.6	4.9	4.4	51.9
China, Hong Kong SAR	164.2	-24.6	-41.5	3.6	55.5
Singapore	126.8	-16.7	-17.6	2.7	58.2
Netherlands	119.9	-8.3	-18.7	2.6	60.8
Rep. of Korea	115.4	-16.9	3.8	2.5	63.3
Canada	110.5	-3.0	-10.0	2.4	65.7
Japan	107.5	-10.6	-23.7	2.3	68.0
Philippines	81.7	-11.3	-8.6	1.8	69.8
India	78.6	-4.4	17.2	1.7	71.5
Italy	76.8	1.1	7.7	1.7	73.1

882 Photographic and cinematographic supplies

In 2016, the value (in current US$) of exports of "photographic and cinematographic supplies" (SITC group 882) increased by 0.1 percent (compared to -4.6 percent average growth rate from 2012-2016) to reach 14.6 bln US$ (see table 2), while imports decreased by 4.6 percent to reach 14.0 bln US$ (see table 3). Exports of this commodity accounted for 0.7 percent of world exports of SITC section 8, and 0.1 percent of total world merchandise exports (see table 1). Japan, USA and Germany were the top exporters in 2016 (see table 2). They accounted for 29.2, 15.3 and 9.7 percent of world exports, respectively. China, USA and Other Asia, nes were the top destinations, with respectively 15.9, 11.9 and 9.1 percent of world imports (see table 3).

The top 15 countries/areas accounted for 95.5 and 73.9 percent of total world exports and imports, respectively (see tables 2 and 3). In 2016, Japan was the country/area with the highest value of net exports (+4.0 bln US$), followed by Netherlands (+909.5 mln US$). By MDG regions (see graph 2), the largest surpluses in this product group were recorded by Developed Asia-Pacific (+3.9 bln US$), Developed Europe (+877.9 mln US$) and Developed North America (+476.6 mln US$). The largest trade deficits were recorded by Eastern Asia (-2.1 bln US$), Latin America and the Caribbean (-616.4 mln US$) and Western Asia (-515.2 mln US$).

Table 1: Imports (Imp.) and exports (Exp.), 2002-2016, in current US$

		2002	2003	2004	2005	2006	2007	2008	2009	2010	2011	2012	2013	2014	2015	2016
Values in Bln US$	Imp.	17.2	18.3	19.6	19.5	19.5	19.7	19.3	16.4	17.1	18.1	17.4	17.0	16.3	14.6	14.0
	Exp.	16.9	18.8	19.8	19.2	19.0	18.7	18.4	16.0	17.1	18.2	17.7	17.1	16.4	14.6	14.6
As a percentage of SITC section (%)	Imp.	2.0	1.9	1.7	1.6	1.4	1.3	1.2	1.1	1.0	1.0	0.9	0.9	0.8	0.8	0.7
	Exp.	2.1	2.0	1.9	1.6	1.4	1.2	1.1	1.1	1.0	1.0	0.9	0.8	0.8	0.7	0.7
As a percentage of world trade (%)	Imp.	0.3	0.2	0.2	0.2	0.2	0.1	0.1	0.1	0.1	0.1	0.1	0.1	0.1	0.1	0.1
	Exp.	0.3	0.3	0.2	0.2	0.2	0.1	0.1	0.1	0.1	0.1	0.1	0.1	0.1	0.1	0.1

Graph 1: Annual growth rates of exports, 2002–2016
(In percentage by year)

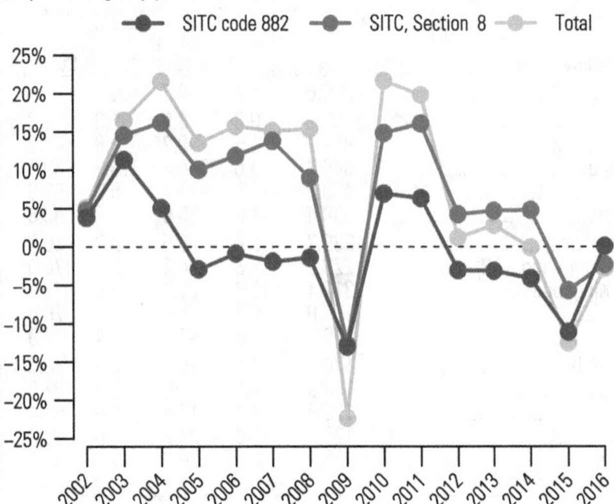

Graph 2: Trade Balance by MDG regions 2016
(Bln US$)

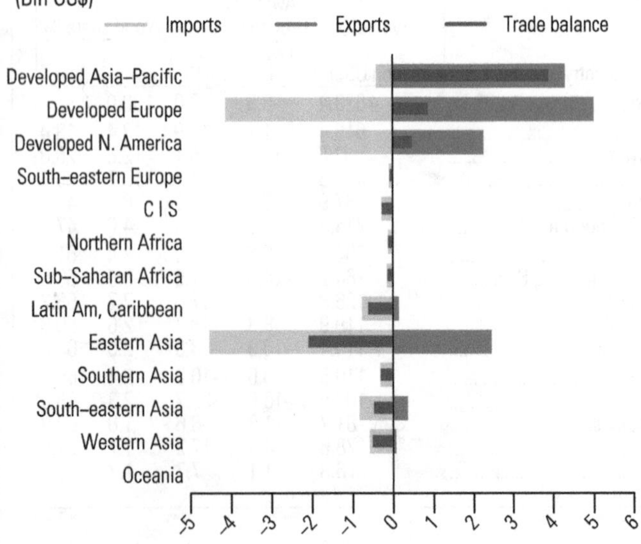

Table 2: Top exporting countries or areas in 2016

Country or area	Value (million US$)	Avg. Growth (%) 12-16	Growth (%) 15-16	World share %	Cum.
World	14615.9	-4.6	0.1	100.0	
Japan	4271.8	-2.8	8.5	29.2	29.2
USA	2229.6	-3.3	-5.6	15.3	44.5
Germany	1424.1	-0.9	4.5	9.7	54.2
Netherlands	1303.7	-4.4	3.3	8.9	63.1
China	1070.6	-3.0	-9.6	7.3	70.5
Belgium	835.2	-16.6	-9.1	5.7	76.2
Rep. of Korea	776.2	13.9	14.1	5.3	81.5
United Kingdom	601.6	-6.0	-4.9	4.1	85.6
Other Asia, nes	415.6	0.5	18.5	2.8	88.5
France	278.9	-15.7	-4.3	1.9	90.4
Malaysia	181.2	6.8	-17.1	1.2	91.6
China, Hong Kong SAR	179.6	-10.8	-18.7	1.2	92.8
Singapore	148.4	-7.9	-8.0	1.0	93.8
Italy	135.9	-9.2	-6.3	0.9	94.8
Spain	109.0	-5.6	16.5	0.7	95.5

Table 3: Top importing countries or areas in 2016

Country or area	Value (million US$)	Avg. Growth (%) 12-16	Growth (%) 15-16	World share %	Cum.
World	13971.0	-5.3	-4.6	100.0	
China	2226.6	-0.5	1.5	15.9	15.9
USA	1660.7	0.8	1.1	11.9	27.8
Other Asia, nes	1269.2	-3.1	-0.5	9.1	36.9
Germany	864.6	-4.5	0.2	6.2	43.1
Rep. of Korea	823.2	-8.4	-1.6	5.9	49.0
United Kingdom	579.2	-3.6	-7.4	4.1	53.1
France	462.2	-5.8	8.8	3.3	56.4
Netherlands	394.2	-14.6	-45.9	2.8	59.3
Singapore	374.5	-3.0	11.8	2.7	61.9
Italy	323.1	-7.8	4.9	2.3	64.3
Mexico	319.6	-9.4	-17.0	2.3	66.5
Belgium	317.5	-12.1	-1.6	2.3	68.8
Japan	247.0	-10.1	-2.4	1.8	70.6
Ireland	246.3	33.9	38.1	1.8	72.3
Russian Federation	217.7	-4.5	7.7	1.6	73.9

In 2016, the value (in current US$) of exports of "cinematographic film, exposed and developed" (SITC group 883) decreased by 22.8 percent (compared to -47.0 percent average growth rate from 2012-2016) to reach 12.8 mln US$ (see table 2), while imports decreased by 33.5 percent to reach 11.3 mln US$ (see table 3). Exports of this commodity accounted for less than 0.1 percent of world exports of SITC section 8, and less than 0.1 percent of total world merchandise exports (see table 1). India, China, Hong Kong SAR and United Kingdom were the top exporters in 2016 (see table 2). They accounted for 37.5, 12.4 and 9.1 percent of world exports, respectively. Qatar, Thailand and USA were the top destinations, with respectively 28.5, 15.6 and 10.9 percent of world imports (see table 3).

The top 15 countries/areas accounted for 96.1 and 89.0 percent of total world exports and imports, respectively (see tables 2 and 3). In 2016, India was the country/area with the highest value of net exports (+4.8 mln US$), followed by China, Hong Kong SAR (+1.6 mln US$). By MDG regions (see graph 2), the largest surpluses in this product group were recorded by Southern Asia (+4.3 mln US$), Developed Europe (+2.0 mln US$) and Eastern Asia (+0.4 mln US$). The largest trade deficits were recorded by Western Asia (-3.3 mln US$), South-eastern Asia (-1.3 mln US$) and Developed North America (-0.2 mln US$).

Table 1: Imports (Imp.) and exports (Exp.), 2002-2016, in current US$

		2002	2003	2004	2005	2006	2007	2008	2009	2010	2011	2012	2013	2014	2015	2016
Values in Mln US$	Imp.	430.0	537.7	607.2	662.8	706.2	711.4	708.9	720.0	613.1	504.2	154.3	84.1	36.4	17.0	11.3
	Exp.	472.0	572.3	665.3	668.2	737.8	819.3	796.4	737.7	637.3	495.4	163.0	78.8	39.7	16.6	12.8
As a percentage of SITC section (%)	Imp.	0.1	0.1	0.1	0.1	0.1	0.0	0.0	0.1	0.0	0.0	0.0	0.0	0.0	0.0	0.0
	Exp.	0.1	0.1	0.1	0.1	0.1	0.1	0.0	0.1	0.0	0.0	0.0	0.0	0.0	0.0	0.0
As a percentage of world trade (%)	Imp.	0.0	0.0	0.0	0.0	0.0	0.0	0.0	0.0	0.0	0.0	0.0	0.0	0.0	0.0	0.0
	Exp.	0.0	0.0	0.0	0.0	0.0	0.0	0.0	0.0	0.0	0.0	0.0	0.0	0.0	0.0	0.0

Graph 1: Annual growth rates of exports, 2002–2016
(In percentage by year)

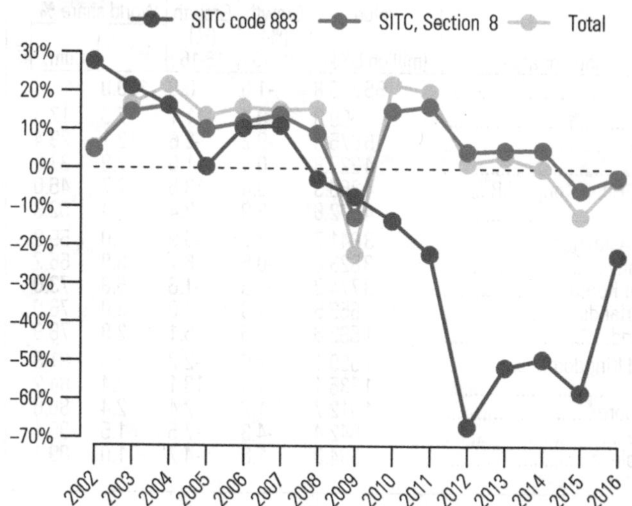

Table 2: Top exporting countries or areas in 2016

Country or area	Value (million US$)	Avg. Growth (%) 12-16	Growth (%) 15-16	World share %	Cum.
World	12.8	-47.0	-22.8	100.0	
India	4.8	-26.7	-4.0	37.5	37.5
China, Hong Kong SAR	1.6	-12.3	-2.2	12.4	49.9
United Kingdom	1.2	-41.0	133.2	9.1	59.0
Belgium	1.1	2.3	-19.3	8.7	67.7
USA	1.1	-54.8	-66.3	8.3	76.0
Greece	0.8	307.0	>	6.1	82.1
Ireland	0.5	353.3		3.9	86.0
France	0.4	-45.0	-80.0	3.4	89.3
Singapore	0.2	5.9	25.7	1.9	91.3
Thailand	0.2	-71.3	-23.5	1.5	92.8
Italy	0.1	-73.7	14.4	0.8	93.6
Indonesia	0.1	12.3	375.9	0.8	94.4
Spain	0.1	-69.0	364.6	0.6	95.0
Russian Federation	0.1	-52.0	488.2	0.6	95.5
Other Asia, nes	0.1	32.1		0.6	96.1

Graph 2: Trade Balance by MDG regions 2016
(Mln US$)

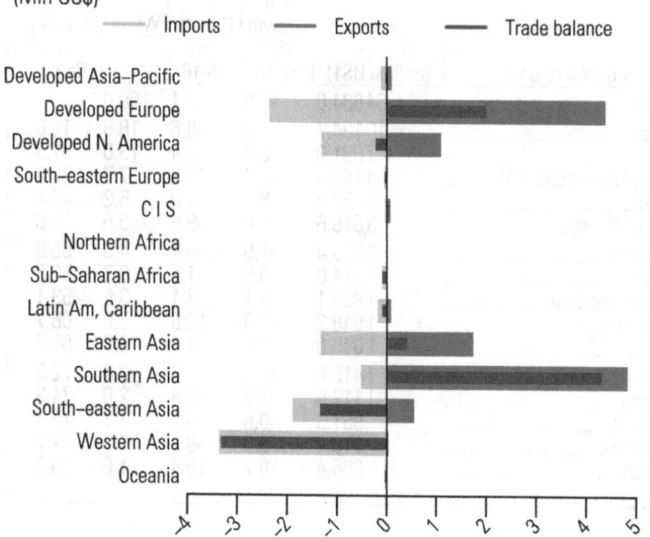

Table 3: Top importing countries or areas in 2016

Country or area	Value (million US$)	Avg. Growth (%) 12-16	Growth (%) 15-16	World share %	Cum.
World	11.3	-48.0	-33.5	100.0	
Qatar	3.2	6.4	974.7	28.5	28.5
Thailand	1.8	-26.7	14.9	15.6	44.2
USA	1.2	-48.4	53.0	10.9	55.1
China	1.2	-29.7	-29.5	10.6	65.7
Switzerland	0.5	0.2	63.1	4.5	70.2
France	0.5	-41.8	-18.7	4.5	74.7
Austria	0.4	-57.3	101.0	3.1	77.8
Sri Lanka	0.3	-20.1	-36.7	2.7	80.6
Spain	0.3	-43.9	-91.6	2.6	83.1
Greece	0.2	-43.5	-6.3	1.6	84.8
Belgium	0.1	-15.3	11.2	1.3	86.1
United Kingdom	0.1	-57.5	24.2	0.8	86.9
Pakistan	0.1	-29.7	13.8	0.7	87.6
Canada	0.1	-64.7	-73.5	0.7	88.3
Nepal	*0.1*	-3.2	-20.6	0.7	89.0

Source: UN Comtrade

884 Optical goods, nes

In 2016, the value (in current US$) of exports of "optical goods, nes" (SITC group 884) decreased by 0.8 percent (compared to -1.0 percent average growth rate from 2012-2016) to reach 55.2 bln US$ (see table 2), while imports increased by 0.1 percent to reach 54.7 bln US$ (see table 3). Exports of this commodity accounted for 2.7 percent of world exports of SITC section 8, and 0.3 percent of total world merchandise exports (see table 1). China, Japan and USA were the top exporters in 2016 (see table 2). They accounted for 17.3, 12.1 and 7.8 percent of world exports, respectively. China, USA and China, Hong Kong SAR were the top destinations, with respectively 18.6, 13.0 and 7.7 percent of world imports (see table 3).

The top 15 countries/areas accounted for 89.1 and 79.3 percent of total world exports and imports, respectively (see tables 2 and 3). In 2016, Japan was the country/area with the highest value of net exports (+3.3 bln US$), followed by Italy (+2.4 bln US$). By MDG regions (see graph 2), the largest surpluses in this product group were recorded by Developed Asia-Pacific (+2.7 bln US$), Eastern Asia (+2.6 bln US$) and South-eastern Asia (+997.8 mln US$). The largest trade deficits were recorded by Developed North America (-3.7 bln US$), Latin America and the Caribbean (-1.1 bln US$) and Western Asia (-948.8 mln US$).

Table 1: Imports (Imp.) and exports (Exp.), 2002-2016, in current US$

		2002	2003	2004	2005	2006	2007	2008	2009	2010	2011	2012	2013	2014	2015	2016
Values in Bln US$	Imp.	16.5	20.0	25.0	28.9	34.2	39.7	44.4	40.2	50.2	54.7	56.4	57.1	58.5	54.6	54.7
	Exp.	17.8	21.0	26.7	30.7	35.2	40.4	43.5	40.0	50.3	55.3	57.6	58.7	59.6	55.7	55.2
As a percentage of SITC section (%)	Imp.	1.9	2.1	2.2	2.3	2.5	2.6	2.7	2.8	3.1	3.0	3.0	3.0	2.9	2.9	2.9
	Exp.	2.2	2.3	2.5	2.6	2.7	2.7	2.7	2.8	3.1	2.9	2.9	2.8	2.7	2.7	2.7
As a percentage of world trade (%)	Imp.	0.3	0.3	0.3	0.3	0.3	0.3	0.3	0.3	0.3	0.3	0.3	0.3	0.3	0.3	0.3
	Exp.	0.3	0.3	0.3	0.3	0.3	0.3	0.3	0.3	0.3	0.3	0.3	0.3	0.3	0.3	0.3

Graph 1: Annual growth rates of exports, 2002–2016
(In percentage by year)

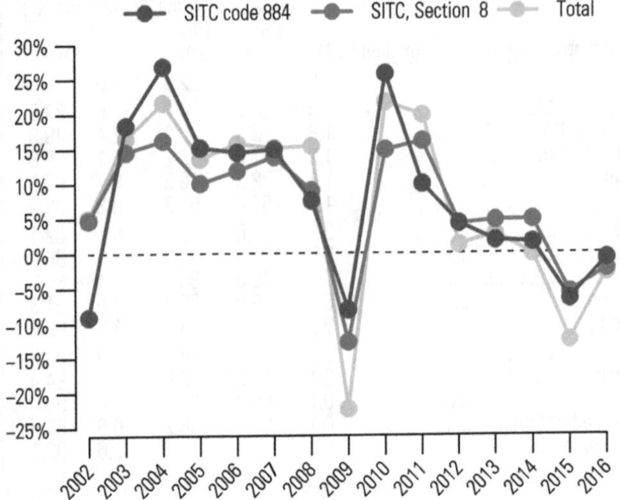

Graph 2: Trade Balance by MDG regions 2016
(Bln US$)

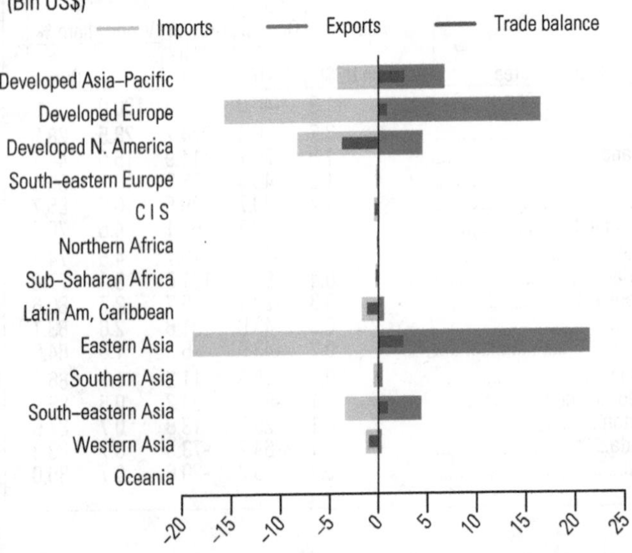

Table 2: Top exporting countries or areas in 2016

Country or area	Value (million US$)	Avg. Growth (%) 12-16	Growth (%) 15-16	World share %	Cum.
World	55235.8	-1.0	-0.8	100.0	
China	9559.0	-0.4	-11.1	17.3	17.3
Japan	6675.3	-9.2	-2.6	12.1	29.4
USA	4327.8	0.4	-1.0	7.8	37.2
China, Hong Kong SAR	4268.3	-0.4	13.5	7.7	45.0
Italy	4072.6	3.9	3.4	7.4	52.3
Other Asia, nes	3841.7	2.7	-5.9	7.0	59.3
Germany	3823.8	-0.5	6.7	6.9	66.2
Rep. of Korea	3774.2	-3.8	-1.6	6.8	73.0
Netherlands	1652.5	1.3	7.0	3.0	76.0
Thailand	1595.6	-2.5	-5.1	2.9	78.9
United Kingdom	1589.1	2.0	-2.2	2.9	81.8
Ireland	1335.1	-1.3	13.1	2.4	84.2
Singapore	1312.7	1.2	-2.4	2.4	86.6
France	842.4	-4.3	-7.5	1.5	88.1
Philippines	534.3	1.8	-4.7	1.0	89.1

Table 3: Top importing countries or areas in 2016

Country or area	Value (million US$)	Avg. Growth (%) 12-16	Growth (%) 15-16	World share %	Cum.
World	54684.0	-0.8	0.1	100.0	
China	10194.7	-2.9	-9.6	18.6	18.6
USA	7091.0	3.4	4.4	13.0	31.6
China, Hong Kong SAR	4190.4	-0.4	15.9	7.7	39.3
Japan	3376.3	-5.7	4.0	6.2	45.4
Rep. of Korea	3018.6	-5.8	-9.9	5.5	51.0
Germany	2656.4	-1.9	-5.1	4.9	55.8
France	2014.0	0.5	1.9	3.7	59.5
United Kingdom	1969.1	5.1	-3.1	3.6	63.1
Netherlands	1948.2	-1.3	13.8	3.6	66.7
Italy	1645.0	3.5	-1.1	3.0	69.7
Other Asia, nes	1415.6	-7.9	0.4	2.6	72.3
Canada	1117.5	1.7	-4.4	2.0	74.3
Thailand	951.3	0.6	4.5	1.7	76.1
Singapore	916.4	-3.0	-8.2	1.7	77.7
Mexico	866.4	10.7	19.4	1.6	79.3

Source: UN Comtrade

In 2016, the value (in current US$) of exports of "watches and clocks" (SITC group 885) decreased by 9.4 percent (compared to -1.3 percent average growth rate from 2012-2016) to reach 50.0 bln US$ (see table 2), while imports decreased by 8.6 percent to reach 48.5 bln US$ (see table 3). Exports of this commodity accounted for 2.5 percent of world exports of SITC section 8, and 0.3 percent of total world merchandise exports (see table 1). Switzerland, China, Hong Kong SAR and China were the top exporters in 2016 (see table 2). They accounted for 39.6, 17.6 and 10.7 percent of world exports, respectively. China, Hong Kong SAR, USA and Switzerland were the top destinations, with respectively 17.1, 10.6 and 8.1 percent of world imports (see table 3).

The top 15 countries/areas accounted for 94.0 and 79.9 percent of total world exports and imports, respectively (see tables 2 and 3). In 2016, Switzerland was the country/area with the highest value of net exports (+15.9 bln US$), followed by China (+2.2 bln US$). By MDG regions (see graph 2), the largest surpluses in this product group were recorded by Developed Europe (+12.1 bln US$) and Eastern Asia (+1.3 bln US$). The largest trade deficits were recorded by Developed North America (-4.3 bln US$), Developed Asia-Pacific (-2.7 bln US$) and Western Asia (-2.3 bln US$).

Table 1: Imports (Imp.) and exports (Exp.), 2002-2016, in current US$

		2002	2003	2004	2005	2006	2007	2008	2009	2010	2011	2012	2013	2014	2015	2016
Values in Bln US$	Imp.	19.6	21.6	24.3	25.4	27.1	31.5	35.7	28.8	36.0	46.6	50.5	52.1	55.0	53.0	48.5
	Exp.	19.4	21.4	24.2	25.2	27.4	31.4	35.9	29.2	36.9	47.9	52.7	55.1	57.4	55.2	50.0
As a percentage of SITC section (%)	Imp.	2.3	2.2	2.2	2.1	2.0	2.0	2.1	2.0	2.2	2.5	2.7	2.7	2.7	2.8	2.5
	Exp.	2.4	2.3	2.3	2.1	2.1	2.1	2.2	2.0	2.2	2.5	2.7	2.7	2.6	2.7	2.5
As a percentage of world trade (%)	Imp.	0.3	0.3	0.3	0.2	0.2	0.2	0.2	0.2	0.2	0.3	0.3	0.3	0.3	0.3	0.3
	Exp.	0.3	0.3	0.3	0.2	0.2	0.2	0.2	0.2	0.2	0.3	0.3	0.3	0.3	0.3	0.3

Graph 1: Annual growth rates of exports, 2002–2016
(In percentage by year)

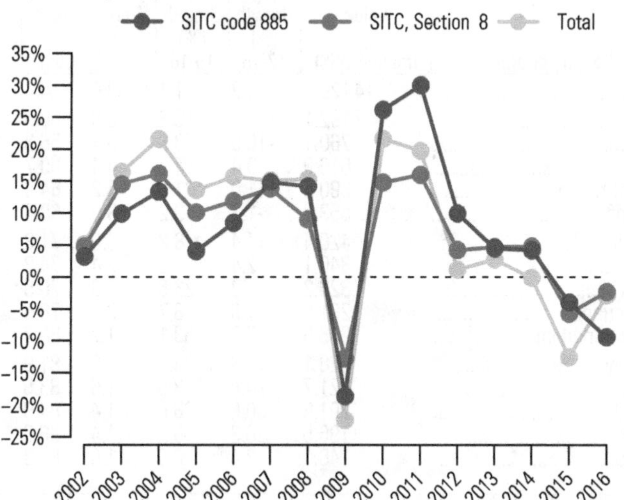

Graph 2: Trade Balance by MDG regions 2016
(Bln US$)

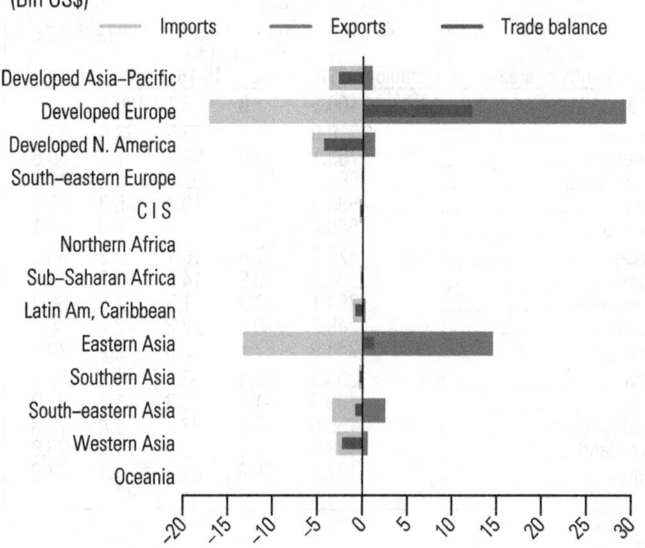

Table 2: Top exporting countries or areas in 2016

Country or area	Value (million US$)	Avg. Growth (%) 12-16	Growth (%) 15-16	World share %	Cum.
World	50011.1	-1.3	-9.4	100.0	
Switzerland	19827.0	-3.5	-12.0	39.6	39.6
China, Hong Kong SAR	8817.5	-2.1	-11.1	17.6	57.3
China	5331.0	1.3	-7.0	10.7	67.9
France	2676.3	5.4	-5.8	5.4	73.3
Germany	2029.7	-0.4	-14.2	4.1	77.3
Singapore	1597.0	-1.0	-10.2	3.2	80.5
Italy	1425.4	-4.2	-10.6	2.9	83.4
USA	1251.0	-0.1	-5.0	2.5	85.9
United Kingdom	984.7	11.3	-0.9	2.0	87.9
Japan	938.4	-8.5	-5.0	1.9	89.7
Thailand	520.7	3.1	-12.0	1.0	90.8
Spain	485.3	5.5	-2.5	1.0	91.7
Austria	382.9	2.5	6.8	0.8	92.5
Netherlands	367.2	8.1	23.5	0.7	93.2
United Arab Emirates	361.4	-15.5	-3.2	0.7	94.0

Table 3: Top importing countries or areas in 2016

Country or area	Value (million US$)	Avg. Growth (%) 12-16	Growth (%) 15-16	World share %	Cum.
World	48480.9	-1.0	-8.6	100.0	
China, Hong Kong SAR	8303.5	-5.7	-12.9	17.1	17.1
USA	5140.9	1.0	-11.6	10.6	27.7
Switzerland	3944.2	2.4	-2.2	8.1	35.9
Japan	3162.0	0.9	-4.2	6.5	42.4
China	3127.7	-6.8	-10.2	6.5	48.8
France	2997.9	1.1	-11.9	6.2	55.0
Germany	2439.3	-2.5	-12.8	5.0	60.1
United Kingdom	1990.0	6.6	-5.2	4.1	64.2
Singapore	1760.8	-2.7	-15.2	3.6	67.8
Italy	1706.1	0.7	-12.2	3.5	71.3
United Arab Emirates	1152.0	-6.7	3.1	2.4	73.7
Spain	869.2	1.9	-7.8	1.8	75.5
Thailand	750.8	4.7	-14.3	1.5	77.0
Netherlands	707.9	13.7	11.8	1.5	78.5
Rep. of Korea	681.0	4.6	2.6	1.4	79.9

891 Arms and ammunition

In 2016, the value (in current US$) of exports of "arms and ammunition" (SITC group 891) increased by 1.1 percent (compared to 4.3 percent average growth rate from 2012-2016) to reach 14.1 bln US$ (see table 2), while imports increased by 6.1 percent to reach 11.1 bln US$ (see table 3). Exports of this commodity accounted for 0.7 percent of world exports of SITC section 8, and 0.1 percent of total world merchandise exports (see table 1). USA, Canada and Italy were the top exporters in 2016 (see table 2). They accounted for 50.9, 5.4 and 4.4 percent of world exports, respectively. USA, Indonesia and Rep. of Korea were the top destinations, with respectively 33.5, 7.1 and 6.2 percent of world imports (see table 3).

The top 15 countries/areas accounted for 87.3 and 77.9 percent of total world exports and imports, respectively (see tables 2 and 3). In 2016, USA was the country/area with the highest value of net exports (+3.5 bln US$), followed by Italy (+495.7 mln US$). By MDG regions (see graph 2), the largest surpluses in this product group were recorded by Developed North America (+3.6 bln US$), Developed Europe (+1.0 bln US$) and Eastern Asia (+96.2 mln US$). The largest trade deficits were recorded by South-eastern Asia (-1.1 bln US$), Developed Asia-Pacific (-511.1 mln US$) and Sub-Saharan Africa (-327.4 mln US$).

Table 1: Imports (Imp.) and exports (Exp.), 2002-2016, in current US$

		2002	2003	2004	2005	2006	2007	2008	2009	2010	2011	2012	2013	2014	2015	2016
Values in Bln US$	Imp.	4.5	5.6	6.5	7.0	7.0	8.5	9.8	9.8	10.9	11.1	10.3	11.2	10.1	10.5	11.1
	Exp.	5.9	6.3	7.5	7.3	8.2	9.7	10.5	11.3	11.9	11.3	11.9	13.2	12.7	14.0	14.1
As a percentage of SITC section (%)	Imp.	0.5	0.6	0.6	0.6	0.5	0.5	0.6	0.7	0.7	0.6	0.6	0.6	0.5	0.5	0.6
	Exp.	0.7	0.7	0.7	0.6	0.6	0.6	0.6	0.8	0.7	0.6	0.6	0.6	0.6	0.7	0.7
As a percentage of world trade (%)	Imp.	0.1	0.1	0.1	0.1	0.1	0.1	0.1	0.1	0.1	0.1	0.1	0.1	0.1	0.1	0.1
	Exp.	0.1	0.1	0.1	0.1	0.1	0.1	0.1	0.1	0.1	0.1	0.1	0.1	0.1	0.1	0.1

Graph 1: Annual growth rates of exports, 2002–2016

(In percentage by year)

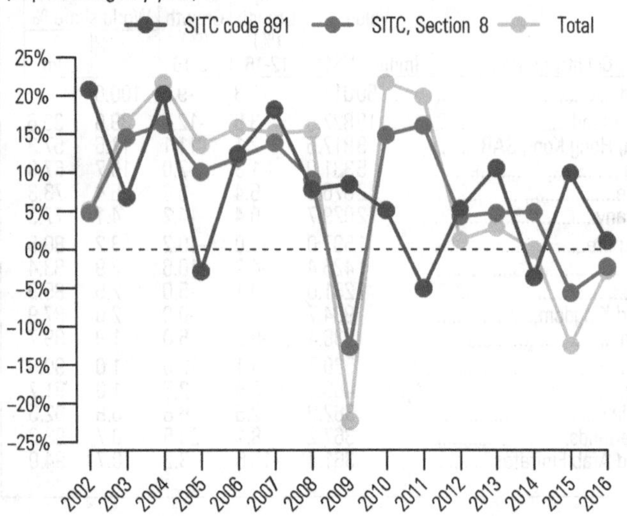

Table 2: Top exporting countries or areas in 2016

Country or area	Value (million US$)	Avg. Growth (%) 12-16	Growth (%) 15-16	World share %	Cum.
World	14 120.5	4.3	1.1	100.0	
USA	7 192.1	9.6	15.8	50.9	50.9
Canada	760.1	-10.5	53.8	5.4	56.3
Italy	616.9	0.4	4.2	4.4	60.7
Rep. of Korea	590.5	11.0	31.8	4.2	64.9
Germany	553.2	-1.2	13.2	3.9	68.8
Czechia	420.4	14.4	8.2	3.0	71.8
Brazil	340.1	2.4	-5.2	2.4	74.2
Turkey	326.2	16.2	23.5	2.3	76.5
Switzerland	291.6	-11.0	-8.7	2.1	78.5
United Kingdom	243.5	17.9	53.1	1.7	80.3
Norway	228.1	-14.8	-24.1	1.6	81.9
Croatia	221.7	24.8	113.5	1.6	83.5
Poland	201.9	60.6	68.6	1.4	84.9
Spain	196.5	6.3	-6.2	1.4	86.3
France	146.1	-3.4	-8.6	1.0	87.3

Graph 2: Trade Balance by MDG regions 2016

(Bln US$)

Imports — Exports — Trade balance

Developed Asia-Pacific
Developed Europe
Developed N. America
South-eastern Europe
CIS
Northern Africa
Sub-Saharan Africa
Latin Am, Caribbean
Eastern Asia
Southern Asia
South-eastern Asia
Western Asia
Oceania

-5 -4 -3 -2 -1 0 1 2 3 4 5 6 7 8

Table 3: Top importing countries or areas in 2016

Country or area	Value (million US$)	Avg. Growth (%) 12-16	Growth (%) 15-16	World share %	Cum.
World	11 100.5	1.8	6.1	100.0	
USA	3 718.8	-1.7	13.5	33.5	33.5
Indonesia	793.1	48.9	54.3	7.1	40.6
Rep. of Korea	684.7	21.1	92.8	6.2	46.8
Canada	590.9	-7.7	-10.4	5.3	52.1
Australia	546.4	3.8	51.0	4.9	57.1
Norway	426.5	7.8	16.7	3.8	60.9
Thailand	300.3	-0.9	14.5	2.7	63.6
Netherlands	284.1	7.9	1.5	2.6	66.2
Germany	248.2	-0.3	22.2	2.2	68.4
Poland	244.9	7.8	2.5	2.2	70.6
Ghana	204.3	102.4	-8.7	1.8	72.4
France	189.3	-1.6	3.3	1.7	74.2
United Kingdom	150.0	-8.2	-23.1	1.4	75.5
Switzerland	138.3	-1.0	20.2	1.2	76.8
Qatar	127.4	58.8	-64.2	1.1	77.9

In 2016, the value (in current US$) of exports of "printed matter" (SITC group 892) decreased by 2.8 percent (compared to -3.4 percent average growth rate from 2012-2016) to reach 41.5 bln US$ (see table 2), while imports decreased by 4.4 percent to reach 40.4 bln US$ (see table 3). Exports of this commodity accounted for 2.1 percent of world exports of SITC section 8, and 0.3 percent of total world merchandise exports (see table 1). USA, Germany and China were the top exporters in 2016 (see table 2). They accounted for 12.3, 11.5 and 10.2 percent of world exports, respectively. USA, Germany and United Kingdom were the top destinations, with respectively 12.2, 6.9 and 6.1 percent of world imports (see table 3).

The top 15 countries/areas accounted for 79.3 and 64.9 percent of total world exports and imports, respectively (see tables 2 and 3). In 2016, China was the country/area with the highest value of net exports (+2.4 bln US$), followed by Germany (+1.9 bln US$). By MDG regions (see graph 2), the largest surpluses in this product group were recorded by Developed Europe (+4.1 bln US$), Eastern Asia (+3.1 bln US$) and Western Asia (+586.3 mln US$). The largest trade deficits were recorded by Latin America and the Caribbean (-1.5 bln US$), Developed North America (-1.4 bln US$) and Developed Asia-Pacific (-1.1 bln US$).

Table 1: Imports (Imp.) and exports (Exp.), 2002-2016, in current US$

		2002	2003	2004	2005	2006	2007	2008	2009	2010	2011	2012	2013	2014	2015	2016
Values in Bln US$	Imp.	29.2	32.9	36.9	39.7	42.1	48.3	51.2	44.7	45.8	50.1	47.0	47.1	47.4	42.3	40.4
	Exp.	28.7	32.6	36.7	39.7	42.2	48.6	52.9	47.7	49.9	54.8	47.6	50.0	50.7	42.7	41.5
As a percentage of SITC section (%)	Imp.	3.4	3.4	3.3	3.2	3.1	3.1	3.1	3.1	2.8	2.7	2.5	2.4	2.4	2.2	2.1
	Exp.	3.6	3.5	3.4	3.4	3.2	3.2	3.2	3.3	3.0	2.9	2.4	2.4	2.3	2.1	2.1
As a percentage of world trade (%)	Imp.	0.4	0.4	0.4	0.4	0.3	0.3	0.3	0.4	0.3	0.3	0.3	0.3	0.3	0.3	0.3
	Exp.	0.4	0.4	0.4	0.4	0.4	0.4	0.3	0.4	0.3	0.3	0.3	0.3	0.3	0.3	0.3

Graph 1: Annual growth rates of exports, 2002–2016

(In percentage by year)

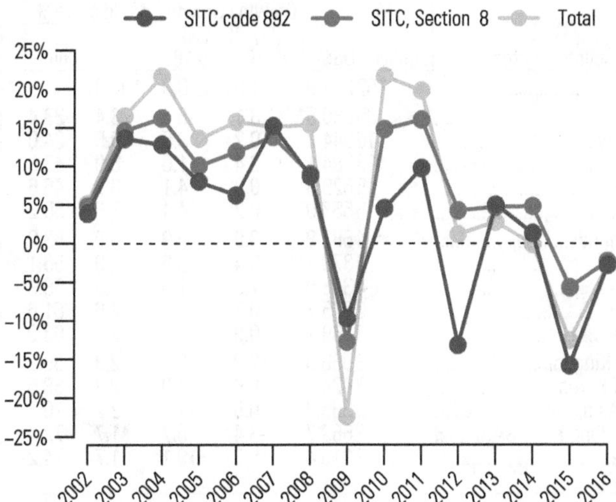

Table 2: Top exporting countries or areas in 2016

Country or area	Value (million US$)	Avg. Growth (%) 12-16	Growth (%) 15-16	World share %	Cum.
World	41494.9	-3.4	-2.8	100.0	
USA	5094.7	-5.0	-6.4	12.3	12.3
Germany	4751.7	-3.4	-1.9	11.5	23.7
China	4246.9	1.3	-7.0	10.2	34.0
United Kingdom	3797.6	-3.8	-12.6	9.2	43.1
China, Hong Kong SAR	2376.9	0.9	-5.3	5.7	48.8
Netherlands	1664.3	-2.0	8.8	4.0	52.9
France	1636.6	-7.0	-4.1	3.9	56.8
Poland	1498.0	16.2	7.0	3.6	60.4
Italy	1445.0	-6.4	1.7	3.5	63.9
Belgium	1215.9	-6.1	2.8	2.9	66.8
United Arab Emirates	1210.1	22.5	45.3	2.9	69.7
Czechia	1155.3	2.2	21.1	2.8	72.5
Canada	1004.1	-2.6	-9.6	2.4	74.9
Spain	930.2	-1.2	5.4	2.2	77.2
Singapore	867.3	-23.0	-8.3	2.1	79.3

Graph 2: Trade Balance by MDG regions 2016

(Bln US$)

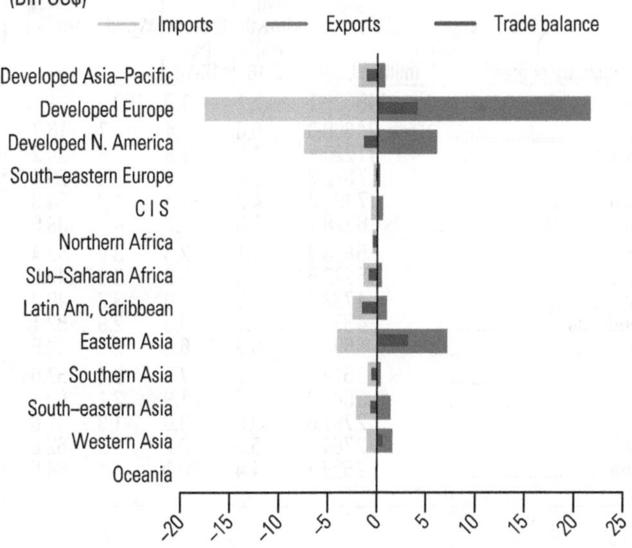

Table 3: Top importing countries or areas in 2016

Country or area	Value (million US$)	Avg. Growth (%) 12-16	Growth (%) 15-16	World share %	Cum.
World	40402.5	-3.7	-4.4	100.0	
USA	4933.5	1.0	-2.6	12.2	12.2
Germany	2802.8	3.3	6.3	6.9	19.1
United Kingdom	2451.6	-4.6	-13.4	6.1	25.2
Canada	2422.5	-7.1	-6.8	6.0	31.2
France	2175.8	-6.1	0.7	5.4	36.6
China	1852.5	0.4	-2.5	4.6	41.2
China, Hong Kong SAR	1694.2	0.8	-5.3	4.2	45.4
Switzerland	1624.2	-4.4	-2.7	4.0	49.4
Austria	1153.0	-1.1	18.4	2.9	52.2
Mexico	956.0	-2.4	-7.9	2.4	54.6
Belgium	952.1	-9.6	-2.5	2.4	57.0
Japan	837.3	-9.6	0.4	2.1	59.0
Netherlands	821.8	-11.8	-32.6	2.0	61.1
Australia	784.9	-7.1	-6.7	1.9	63.0
Italy	739.3	-3.8	-4.3	1.8	64.9

893 Articles, nes, of plastics

In 2016, the value (in current US$) of exports of "articles, nes, of plastics" (SITC group 893) increased by 0.9 percent (compared to 1.6 percent average growth rate from 2012-2016) to reach 152.3 bln US$ (see table 2), while imports increased by 1.9 percent to reach 148.0 bln US$ (see table 3). Exports of this commodity accounted for 7.6 percent of world exports of SITC section 8, and 1.0 percent of total world merchandise exports (see table 1). China, Germany and USA were the top exporters in 2016 (see table 2). They accounted for 23.4, 10.5 and 8.9 percent of world exports, respectively. USA, Germany and France were the top destinations, with respectively 16.7, 7.6 and 5.2 percent of world imports (see table 3).

The top 15 countries/areas accounted for 74.2 and 64.5 percent of total world exports and imports, respectively (see tables 2 and 3). In 2016, China was the country/area with the highest value of net exports (+31.0 bln US$), followed by Germany (+4.8 bln US$). By MDG regions (see graph 2), the largest surpluses in this product group were recorded by Eastern Asia (+35.2 bln US$) and Developed Europe (+1.1 bln US$). The largest trade deficits were recorded by Developed North America (-12.9 bln US$), Latin America and the Caribbean (-6.2 bln US$) and Developed Asia-Pacific (-5.8 bln US$).

Table 1: Imports (Imp.) and exports (Exp.), 2002-2016, in current US$

		2002	2003	2004	2005	2006	2007	2008	2009	2010	2011	2012	2013	2014	2015	2016
Values in Bln US$	Imp.	59.6	68.5	79.0	87.8	97.8	110.8	121.3	103.1	119.4	134.7	136.4	145.3	153.1	145.2	148.0
	Exp.	57.5	66.2	77.0	85.6	95.3	107.6	116.5	99.5	115.0	133.7	142.7	153.1	159.4	150.9	152.3
As a percentage of SITC section (%)	Imp.	7.0	7.1	7.0	7.1	7.2	7.2	7.3	7.2	7.3	7.3	7.3	7.5	7.6	7.6	7.8
	Exp.	7.2	7.2	7.2	7.3	7.2	7.2	7.1	7.0	7.0	7.0	7.2	7.4	7.3	7.3	7.6
As a percentage of world trade (%)	Imp.	0.9	0.9	0.8	0.8	0.8	0.8	0.7	0.8	0.8	0.7	0.7	0.8	0.8	0.9	0.9
	Exp.	0.9	0.9	0.8	0.8	0.8	0.8	0.7	0.8	0.8	0.7	0.8	0.8	0.8	0.9	1.0

Graph 1: Annual growth rates of exports, 2002–2016

(In percentage by year)

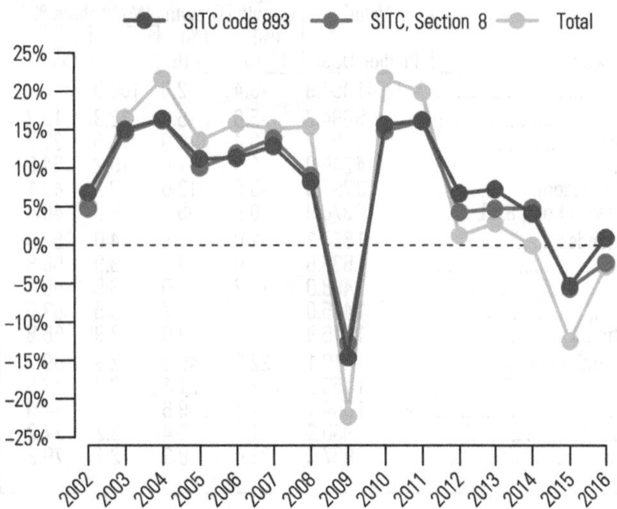

Graph 2: Trade Balance by MDG regions 2016

(Bln US$)

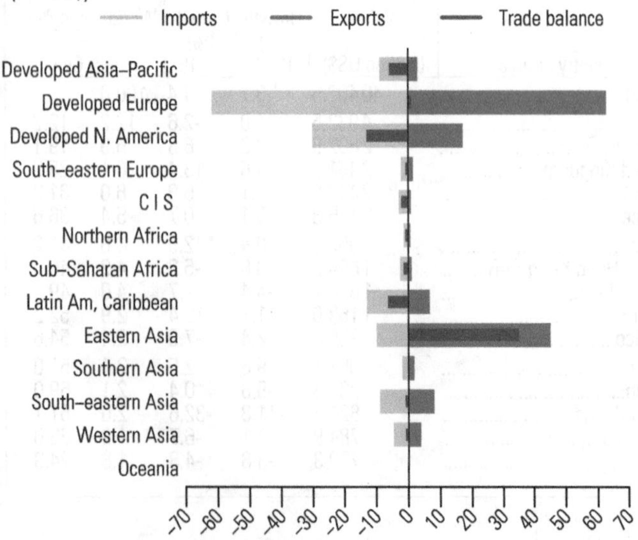

Table 2: Top exporting countries or areas in 2016

Country or area	Value (million US$)	Avg. Growth (%) 12-16	Growth (%) 15-16	World share %	Cum.
World	152277.6	1.6	0.9	100.0	
China	35680.5	3.1	-5.4	23.4	23.4
Germany	16044.0	0.2	3.5	10.5	34.0
USA	13584.1	2.4	1.0	8.9	42.9
France	5623.8	0.3	4.1	3.7	46.6
Italy	5557.0	0.2	4.4	3.6	50.2
Netherlands	4582.8	3.8	9.9	3.0	53.2
Poland	4378.7	5.4	6.6	2.9	56.1
Mexico	4303.0	7.5	1.5	2.8	58.9
Belgium	3975.7	0.7	3.7	2.6	61.6
Canada	3569.1	0.9	1.8	2.3	63.9
United Kingdom	3566.5	2.8	-3.7	2.3	66.2
Rep. of Korea	3424.5	6.6	11.9	2.2	68.5
Other Asia, nes	3355.7	0.6	-1.5	2.2	70.7
China, Hong Kong SAR	2662.7	-3.4	-6.7	1.7	72.4
Austria	2615.4	5.3	19.1	1.7	74.2

Table 3: Top importing countries or areas in 2016

Country or area	Value (million US$)	Avg. Growth (%) 12-16	Growth (%) 15-16	World share %	Cum.
World	148029.1	2.1	1.9	100.0	
USA	24668.3	5.0	3.4	16.7	16.7
Germany	11220.1	1.8	1.8	7.6	24.2
France	7672.2	-0.1	3.3	5.2	29.4
Mexico	7195.3	4.2	1.8	4.9	34.3
United Kingdom	6228.7	2.3	-2.2	4.2	38.5
Japan	5826.3	-1.1	2.6	3.9	42.4
Canada	5272.5	0.4	0.6	3.6	46.0
China	4722.2	1.2	2.0	3.2	49.2
Netherlands	4335.8	2.1	-3.5	2.9	52.1
Belgium	3694.2	-0.3	6.5	2.5	54.6
Italy	3519.4	3.7	7.5	2.4	57.0
Spain	3084.3	6.8	1.9	2.1	59.1
Poland	2791.6	3.5	3.0	1.9	61.0
Czechia	2784.4	5.5	10.2	1.9	62.8
Austria	2528.3	4.4	20.1	1.7	64.5

In 2016, the value (in current US$) of exports of "baby carriages, toys, games and sporting goods" (SITC group 894) increased by 3.1 percent (compared to 1.8 percent average growth rate from 2012-2016) to reach 100.2 bln US$ (see table 2), while imports increased by 1.0 percent to reach 110.0 bln US$ (see table 3). Exports of this commodity accounted for 5.0 percent of world exports of SITC section 8, and 0.6 percent of total world merchandise exports (see table 1). China, USA and China, Hong Kong SAR were the top exporters in 2016 (see table 2). They accounted for 46.3, 6.3 and 5.8 percent of world exports, respectively. USA, Germany and United Kingdom were the top destinations, with respectively 28.6, 5.9 and 5.8 percent of world imports (see table 3).

The top 15 countries/areas accounted for 87.3 and 76.2 percent of total world exports and imports, respectively (see tables 2 and 3). In 2016, China was the country/area with the highest value of net exports (+44.4 bln US$), followed by Czechia (+1.7 bln US$). By MDG regions (see graph 2), the largest surpluses in this product group were recorded by Eastern Asia (+45.5 bln US$) and South-eastern Asia (+1.1 bln US$). The largest trade deficits were recorded by Developed North America (-28.2 bln US$), Developed Europe (-13.3 bln US$) and Developed Asia-Pacific (-6.0 bln US$).

Table 1: Imports (Imp.) and exports (Exp.), 2002-2016, in current US$

		2002	2003	2004	2005	2006	2007	2008	2009	2010	2011	2012	2013	2014	2015	2016
Values in Bln US$	Imp.	62.7	67.3	73.8	83.6	91.5	113.9	128.1	107.5	112.9	115.8	110.0	108.1	113.6	109.0	110.0
	Exp.	49.1	52.1	56.7	64.2	71.1	86.4	100.9	84.1	86.9	95.4	93.2	92.8	96.6	97.2	100.2
As a percentage of SITC section (%)	Imp.	7.4	6.9	6.6	6.8	6.7	7.4	7.7	7.5	6.9	6.2	5.9	5.6	5.7	5.7	5.8
	Exp.	6.1	5.7	5.3	5.5	5.4	5.8	6.2	5.9	5.3	5.0	4.7	4.5	4.4	4.7	5.0
As a percentage of world trade (%)	Imp.	1.0	0.9	0.8	0.8	0.7	0.8	0.8	0.9	0.7	0.6	0.6	0.6	0.6	0.7	0.7
	Exp.	0.8	0.7	0.6	0.6	0.6	0.6	0.6	0.7	0.6	0.5	0.5	0.5	0.5	0.6	0.6

Graph 1: Annual growth rates of exports, 2002–2016
(In percentage by year)

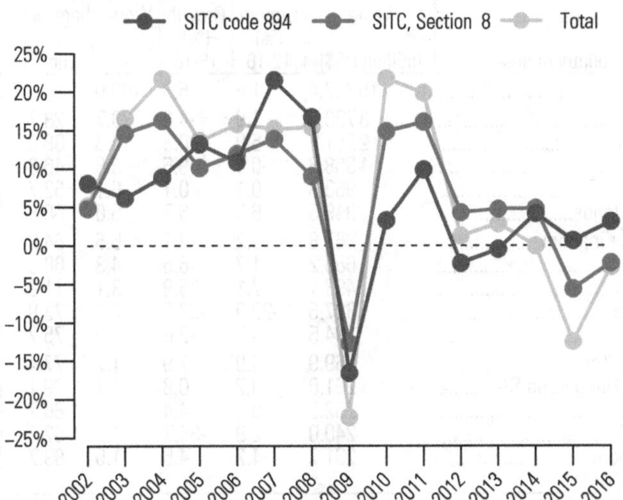

Table 2: Top exporting countries or areas in 2016

Country or area	Value (million US$)	Avg. Growth (%) 12-16	Growth (%) 15-16	World share %	Cum.
World	100240.3	1.8	3.1	100.0	
China	46373.1	5.1	1.5	46.3	46.3
USA	6281.7	-3.0	0.5	6.3	52.5
China, Hong Kong SAR	5792.1	-16.1	-22.5	5.8	58.3
Netherlands	5604.3	27.7	117.3	5.6	63.9
Germany	4492.2	-2.9	0.0	4.5	68.4
Czechia	3324.2	5.6	4.2	3.3	71.7
Other Asia, nes	2144.0	-0.6	0.1	2.1	73.8
United Kingdom	2060.5	3.0	3.1	2.1	75.9
Italy	1898.8	1.6	5.9	1.9	77.8
Belgium	1763.6	2.2	8.3	1.8	79.5
France	1728.8	1.3	3.3	1.7	81.3
Japan	1688.7	-5.4	13.5	1.7	83.0
Mexico	1466.6	3.2	-10.5	1.5	84.4
Poland	1423.5	26.7	9.0	1.4	85.8
Austria	1419.4	1.2	14.8	1.4	87.3

Graph 2: Trade Balance by MDG regions 2016
(Bln US$)

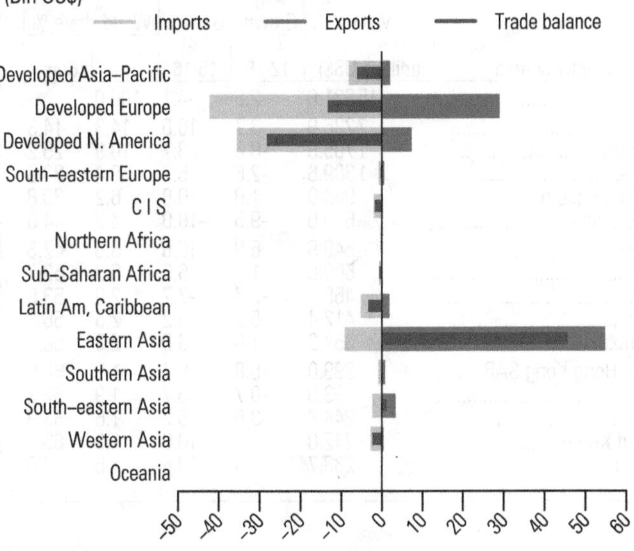

Table 3: Top importing countries or areas in 2016

Country or area	Value (million US$)	Avg. Growth (%) 12-16	Growth (%) 15-16	World share %	Cum.
World	110049.9	0.0	1.0	100.0	
USA	31507.7	1.8	-2.8	28.6	28.6
Germany	6524.4	-0.1	-2.3	5.9	34.6
United Kingdom	6437.8	3.0	-3.4	5.8	40.4
Japan	5346.9	-7.6	0.6	4.9	45.3
Netherlands	5231.3	23.7	99.9	4.8	50.0
France	4695.2	-0.1	0.9	4.3	54.3
China, Hong Kong SAR	4537.7	-17.3	-22.5	4.1	58.4
Canada	4000.6	-1.8	-4.8	3.6	62.0
Spain	2754.9	8.2	19.9	2.5	64.5
Italy	2553.1	-1.1	4.4	2.3	66.9
Australia	2337.5	-0.6	-1.1	2.1	69.0
Mexico	2030.9	1.4	-7.1	1.8	70.8
Belgium	2001.6	0.5	11.2	1.8	72.7
China	1932.9	7.6	1.7	1.8	74.4
Poland	1914.0	18.7	17.3	1.7	76.2

895 Office and stationery supplies, nes

In 2016, the value (in current US$) of exports of "office and stationery supplies, nes" (SITC group 895) decreased by 5.3 percent (compared to -1.9 percent average growth rate from 2012-2016) to reach 15.8 bln US$ (see table 2), while imports decreased by 4.1 percent to reach 15.6 bln US$ (see table 3). Exports of this commodity accounted for 0.8 percent of world exports of SITC section 8, and 0.1 percent of total world merchandise exports (see table 1). China, Germany and Japan were the top exporters in 2016 (see table 2). They accounted for 23.7, 14.3 and 8.6 percent of world exports, respectively. USA, Germany and France were the top destinations, with respectively 14.3, 10.9 and 8.4 percent of world imports (see table 3).

The top 15 countries/areas accounted for 83.7 and 67.0 percent of total world exports and imports, respectively (see tables 2 and 3). In 2016, China was the country/area with the highest value of net exports (+3.2 bln US$), followed by Japan (+1.0 bln US$). By MDG regions (see graph 2), the largest surpluses in this product group were recorded by Eastern Asia (+3.3 bln US$) and Developed Asia-Pacific (+799.1 mln US$). The largest trade deficits were recorded by Developed North America (-1.8 bln US$), Western Asia (-509.9 mln US$) and Latin America and the Caribbean (-458.2 mln US$).

Table 1: Imports (Imp.) and exports (Exp.), 2002-2016, in current US$

		2002	2003	2004	2005	2006	2007	2008	2009	2010	2011	2012	2013	2014	2015	2016
Values in Bln US$	Imp.	9.1	9.7	11.1	11.7	12.6	14.1	14.8	13.2	15.4	16.9	17.4	18.0	18.1	16.3	15.6
	Exp.	7.9	8.9	9.8	10.5	11.6	12.9	13.6	11.7	14.0	16.3	17.0	18.1	18.6	16.6	15.8
As a percentage of SITC section (%)	Imp.	1.1	1.0	1.0	0.9	0.9	0.9	0.9	0.9	0.9	0.9	0.9	0.9	0.9	0.9	0.8
	Exp.	1.0	1.0	0.9	0.9	0.9	0.9	0.8	0.8	0.9	0.9	0.9	0.9	0.9	0.8	0.8
As a percentage of world trade (%)	Imp.	0.1	0.1	0.1	0.1	0.1	0.1	0.1	0.1	0.1	0.1	0.1	0.1	0.1	0.1	0.1
	Exp.	0.1	0.1	0.1	0.1	0.1	0.1	0.1	0.1	0.1	0.1	0.1	0.1	0.1	0.1	0.1

Graph 1: Annual growth rates of exports, 2002–2016

(In percentage by year)

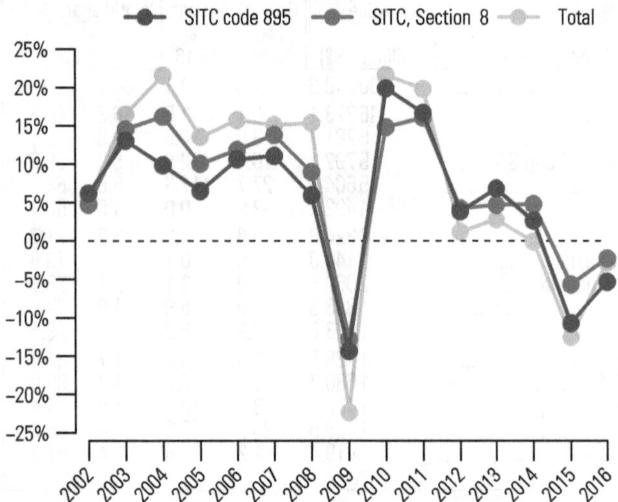

Table 2: Top exporting countries or areas in 2016

Country or area	Value (million US$)	Avg. Growth (%) 12-16	Growth (%) 15-16	World share %	Cum.
World	15752.4	-1.9	-5.3	100.0	
China	3733.9	1.9	-4.0	23.7	23.7
Germany	2251.6	-5.8	-20.3	14.3	38.0
Japan	1358.8	-0.1	9.5	8.6	46.6
France	963.3	0.1	0.1	6.1	52.7
Netherlands	949.5	-6.5	-6.7	6.0	58.8
United Kingdom	867.8	5.2	-4.1	5.5	64.3
USA	685.2	1.7	6.5	4.3	68.6
Mexico	493.1	7.1	25.9	3.1	71.8
Czechia	327.5	-22.9	-37.2	2.1	73.8
India	294.5	4.5	-2.6	1.9	75.7
Rep. of Korea	269.9	4.0	7.9	1.7	77.4
China, Hong Kong SAR	261.0	-3.2	0.8	1.7	79.1
Italy	252.5	0.1	4.4	1.6	80.7
Ireland	240.0	2.9	-34.7	1.5	82.2
Singapore	231.7	-4.2	4.5	1.5	83.7

Graph 2: Trade Balance by MDG regions 2016

(Bln US$)

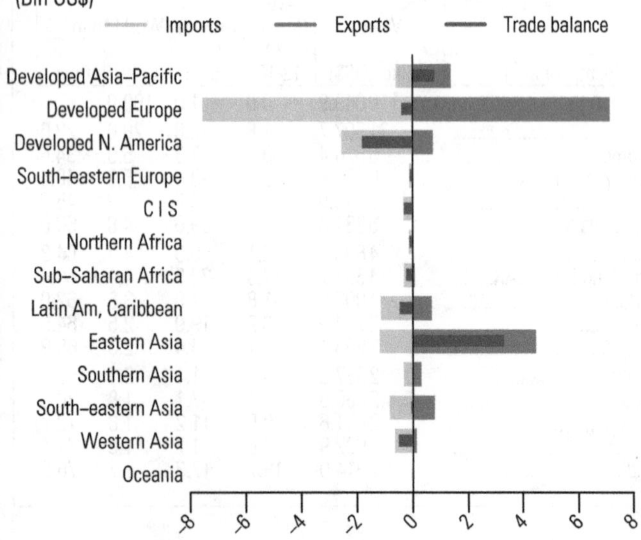

Table 3: Top importing countries or areas in 2016

Country or area	Value (million US$)	Avg. Growth (%) 12-16	Growth (%) 15-16	World share %	Cum.
World	15621.0	-2.6	-4.1	100.0	
USA	2236.9	3.7	10.0	14.3	14.3
Germany	1705.8	-8.6	-28.7	10.9	25.2
France	1309.6	-2.6	-5.7	8.4	33.6
United Kingdom	963.0	1.0	-10.8	6.2	39.8
Netherlands	659.0	-9.5	-10.0	4.2	44.0
Mexico	546.9	6.9	16.6	3.5	47.5
China	500.6	1.3	6.9	3.2	50.7
Italy	455.2	-3.7	-7.7	2.9	53.6
Spain	412.4	-5.3	9.2	2.6	56.3
Japan	357.2	-1.8	3.0	2.3	58.6
China, Hong Kong SAR	299.0	-5.8	0.7	1.9	60.5
Canada	293.9	-0.7	5.7	1.9	62.3
Czechia	244.8	-3.6	-6.2	1.6	63.9
Rep. of Korea	242.0	2.5	10.0	1.5	65.5
Austria	233.7	3.6	18.6	1.5	67.0

In 2016, the value (in current US$) of exports of "works of art, collectors' pieces and antiques" (SITC group 896) decreased by 3.4 percent (compared to 4.7 percent average growth rate from 2012-2016) to reach 28.1 bln US$ (see table 2), while imports decreased by 15.7 percent to reach 23.9 bln US$ (see table 3). Exports of this commodity accounted for 1.4 percent of world exports of SITC section 8, and 0.2 percent of total world merchandise exports (see table 1). USA, United Kingdom and Switzerland were the top exporters in 2016 (see table 2). They accounted for 39.9, 25.5 and 7.2 percent of world exports, respectively. USA, United Kingdom and Switzerland were the top destinations, with respectively 41.3, 15.9 and 9.1 percent of world imports (see table 3).

The top 15 countries/areas accounted for 95.0 and 92.8 percent of total world exports and imports, respectively (see tables 2 and 3). In 2016, United Kingdom was the country/area with the highest value of net exports (+3.4 bln US$), followed by USA (+1.3 bln US$). By MDG regions (see graph 2), the largest surpluses in this product group were recorded by Developed Europe (+4.7 bln US$), Developed North America (+1.4 bln US$) and Southern Asia (+150.1 mln US$). The largest trade deficits were recorded by Eastern Asia (-1.3 bln US$), Western Asia (-300.7 mln US$) and Developed Asia-Pacific (-253.6 mln US$).

Table 1: Imports (Imp.) and exports (Exp.), 2002-2016, in current US$

		2002	2003	2004	2005	2006	2007	2008	2009	2010	2011	2012	2013	2014	2015	2016
Values in Bln US$	Imp.	11.6	10.4	12.9	14.3	16.6	23.7	20.9	13.8	17.6	22.2	23.0	23.8	24.6	28.3	23.9
	Exp.	9.8	11.2	12.7	14.7	17.1	20.9	21.2	15.3	17.6	20.1	23.4	24.5	27.6	29.1	28.1
As a percentage of SITC section (%)	Imp.	1.4	1.1	1.1	1.2	1.2	1.5	1.2	1.0	1.1	1.2	1.2	1.2	1.2	1.5	1.3
	Exp.	1.2	1.2	1.2	1.2	1.3	1.4	1.3	1.1	1.1	1.1	1.2	1.2	1.3	1.4	1.4
As a percentage of world trade (%)	Imp.	0.2	0.1	0.1	0.1	0.1	0.2	0.1	0.1	0.1	0.1	0.1	0.1	0.1	0.2	0.1
	Exp.	0.2	0.1	0.1	0.1	0.1	0.2	0.1	0.1	0.1	0.1	0.1	0.1	0.1	0.2	0.2

Graph 1: Annual growth rates of exports, 2002–2016
(In percentage by year)

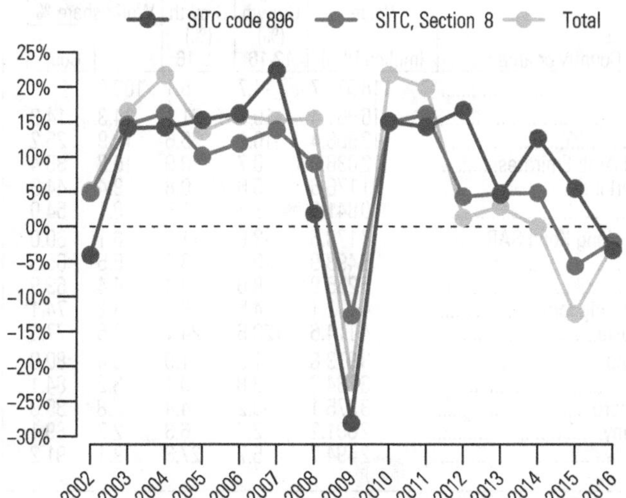

Table 2: Top exporting countries or areas in 2016

Country or area	Value (million US$)	Avg. Growth (%) 12-16	Growth (%) 15-16	World share %	Cum.
World	28129.2	4.7	-3.4	100.0	
USA	11216.6	11.0	1.7	39.9	39.9
United Kingdom	7167.2	-1.0	-22.4	25.5	65.4
Switzerland	2022.5	6.8	15.7	7.2	72.5
France	1990.4	1.7	44.1	7.1	79.6
Germany	807.1	-8.9	-16.2	2.9	82.5
China, Hong Kong SAR	725.1	11.1	5.4	2.6	85.1
Singapore	382.2	25.8	14.7	1.4	86.4
Japan	368.6	21.1	17.5	1.3	87.7
Austria	353.9	29.3	66.8	1.3	89.0
Italy	344.1	-3.9	-23.6	1.2	90.2
Canada	334.0	13.0	39.1	1.2	91.4
India	319.8	7.0	90.7	1.1	92.5
Rep. of Korea	291.3	24.0	-33.7	1.0	93.6
China	215.4	-20.3	-61.9	0.8	94.3
Brazil	198.1	43.8	75.5	0.7	95.0

Graph 2: Trade Balance by MDG regions 2016
(Bln US$)

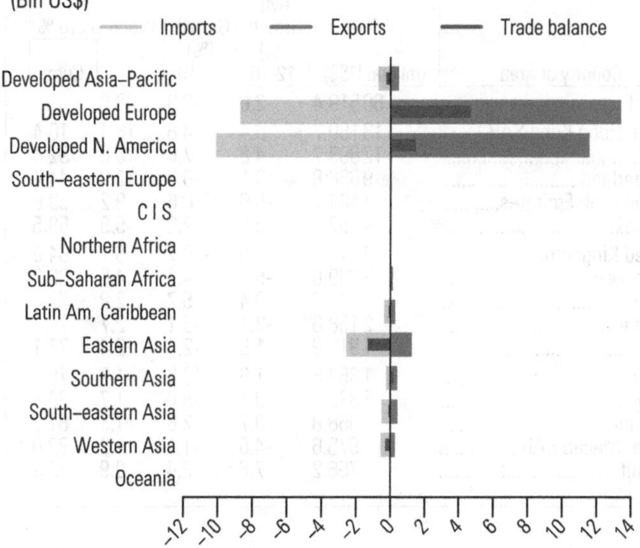

Table 3: Top importing countries or areas in 2016

Country or area	Value (million US$)	Avg. Growth (%) 12-16	Growth (%) 15-16	World share %	Cum.
World	23885.7	0.9	-15.7	100.0	
USA	9875.6	6.0	-15.9	41.3	41.3
United Kingdom	3787.8	-16.6	-40.0	15.9	57.2
Switzerland	2163.2	5.5	-10.3	9.1	66.3
China, Hong Kong SAR	1980.1	12.3	-19.1	8.3	74.5
Germany	736.7	0.5	-12.8	3.1	77.6
France	661.8	1.5	-10.7	2.8	80.4
Japan	513.2	21.1	23.0	2.1	82.6
Singapore	485.0	26.6	59.0	2.0	84.6
Netherlands	386.3	23.3	-2.8	1.6	86.2
Rep. of Korea	360.0	21.4	81.9	1.5	87.7
Qatar	322.0	35.4	516.3	1.3	89.1
Austria	257.2	11.7	-1.7	1.1	90.1
Canada	231.6	-1.1	-29.9	1.0	91.1
India	213.1	73.1	142.5	0.9	92.0
Venezuela	*188.0*	30.3	23517.5	0.8	92.8

897 Gold, silverware, jewellery and articles of precious materials, nes

In 2016, the value (in current US$) of exports of "gold, silverware, jewellery and articles of precious materials, nes" (SITC group 897) decreased by 5.1 percent (compared to -4.7 percent average growth rate from 2012-2016) to reach 118.6 bln US$ (see table 2), while imports decreased by 2.3 percent to reach 80.5 bln US$ (see table 3). Exports of this commodity accounted for 5.9 percent of world exports of SITC section 8, and 0.7 percent of total world merchandise exports (see table 1). China, India and United Arab Emirates were the top exporters in 2016 (see table 2). They accounted for 14.3, 10.9 and 10.2 percent of world exports, respectively. China, Hong Kong SAR, USA and Switzerland were the top destinations, with respectively 16.4, 16.0 and 12.0 percent of world imports (see table 3).

The top 15 countries/areas accounted for 91.2 and 83.9 percent of total world exports and imports, respectively (see tables 2 and 3). In 2016, China was the country/area with the highest value of net exports (+15.6 bln US$), followed by India (+12.5 bln US$). By MDG regions (see graph 2), the largest surpluses in this product group were recorded by Southern Asia (+11.9 bln US$), South-eastern Asia (+8.4 bln US$) and Eastern Asia (+8.4 bln US$). The largest trade deficits were recorded by Developed North America (-2.4 bln US$), Developed Asia-Pacific (-608.3 mln US$) and Latin America and the Caribbean (-209.9 mln US$).

Table 1: Imports (Imp.) and exports (Exp.), 2002-2016, in current US$

		2002	2003	2004	2005	2006	2007	2008	2009	2010	2011	2012	2013	2014	2015	2016
Values in Bln US$	Imp.	23.3	26.5	31.5	36.5	42.3	49.4	53.6	48.4	61.6	74.9	89.3	87.6	91.4	82.5	80.5
	Exp.	25.8	28.7	35.8	40.9	48.9	58.0	65.3	66.0	77.9	112.4	144.0	140.8	166.4	124.9	118.6
As a percentage of	Imp.	2.7	2.7	2.8	3.0	3.1	3.2	3.2	3.4	3.8	4.0	4.8	4.5	4.6	4.3	4.2
SITC section (%)	Exp.	3.2	3.1	3.4	3.5	3.7	3.9	4.0	4.6	4.8	5.9	7.3	6.8	7.6	6.1	5.9
As a percentage of	Imp.	0.4	0.3	0.3	0.3	0.3	0.4	0.3	0.4	0.4	0.4	0.5	0.5	0.5	0.5	0.5
world trade (%)	Exp.	0.4	0.4	0.4	0.4	0.4	0.4	0.4	0.5	0.5	0.6	0.8	0.7	0.9	0.8	0.7

Graph 1: Annual growth rates of exports, 2002–2016

(In percentage by year)

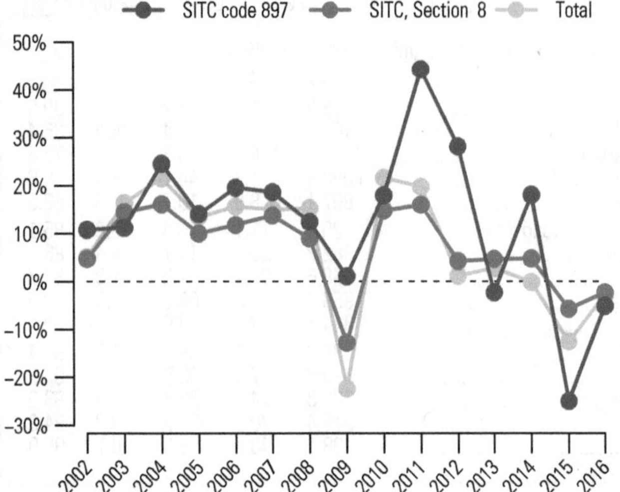

Table 2: Top exporting countries or areas in 2016

Country or area	Value (million US$)	Avg. Growth (%) 12-16	Growth (%) 15-16	World share %	Cum.
World	118573.7	-4.7	-5.1	100.0	
China	16961.4	-19.7	-31.1	14.3	14.3
India	12958.4	-10.0	25.6	10.9	25.2
United Arab Emirates	12036.8	0.7	8.9	10.2	35.4
Switzerland	11176.6	5.6	-0.8	9.4	44.8
USA	10841.6	3.7	-1.9	9.1	54.0
China, Hong Kong SAR	7178.6	-3.0	-11.8	6.1	60.0
Italy	6493.9	-0.9	-3.6	5.5	65.5
France	5255.8	8.0	3.4	4.4	69.9
United Kingdom	4932.1	-4.5	-26.7	4.2	74.1
Indonesia	4114.6	120.6	24.1	3.5	77.5
Thailand	3973.8	-1.2	-1.9	3.4	80.9
Turkey	3784.6	8.8	0.1	3.2	84.1
Singapore	3375.1	-0.2	4.4	2.8	86.9
Germany	2601.2	2.7	6.3	2.2	89.1
Japan	2494.7	5.7	27.3	2.1	91.2

Graph 2: Trade Balance by MDG regions 2016

(Bln US$)

Imports — Exports — Trade balance

Developed Asia-Pacific
Developed Europe
Developed N. America
South-eastern Europe
C I S
Northern Africa
Sub-Saharan Africa
Latin Am, Caribbean
Eastern Asia
Southern Asia
South-eastern Asia
Western Asia
Oceania

-30 -25 -20 -15 -10 -5 0 5 10 15 20 25 30 35

Table 3: Top importing countries or areas in 2016

Country or area	Value (million US$)	Avg. Growth (%) 12-16	Growth (%) 15-16	World share %	Cum.
World	80519.4	-2.6	-2.3	100.0	
China, Hong Kong SAR	13180.7	0.4	4.6	16.4	16.4
USA	12893.7	4.8	7.5	16.0	32.4
Switzerland	9666.8	0.1	-6.0	12.0	44.4
United Arab Emirates	7404.7	-5.6	0.6	9.2	53.6
France	4782.7	6.5	2.3	5.9	59.5
United Kingdom	4112.8	-2.9	-10.7	5.1	64.6
Singapore	3699.0	-5.2	-4.7	4.6	69.2
Japan	2247.0	-0.4	5.7	2.8	72.0
Germany	2158.6	-3.1	-3.1	2.7	74.7
Italy	1916.9	1.5	-2.4	2.4	77.1
China	1352.8	1.6	-18.3	1.7	78.8
Canada	1332.7	0.1	-8.0	1.7	80.4
Australia	1068.8	0.7	2.8	1.3	81.7
China, Macao SAR	975.6	-4.0	-11.1	1.2	83.0
Kuwait	756.2	7.6	2.4	0.9	83.9

In 2016, the value (in current US$) of exports of "musical instruments, parts/accessories; records, tapes and similar recordings" (SITC group 898) decreased by 0.4 percent (compared to -3.2 percent average growth rate from 2012-2016) to reach 49.5 bln US$ (see table 2), while imports increased by 2.6 percent to reach 56.4 bln US$ (see table 3). Exports of this commodity accounted for 2.5 percent of world exports of SITC section 8, and 0.3 percent of total world merchandise exports (see table 1). Other Asia, nes, China and Singapore were the top exporters in 2016 (see table 2). They accounted for 11.4, 11.1 and 9.5 percent of world exports, respectively. USA, China and China, Hong Kong SAR were the top destinations, with respectively 16.9, 8.6 and 7.1 percent of world imports (see table 3).

The top 15 countries/areas accounted for 87.7 and 72.8 percent of total world exports and imports, respectively (see tables 2 and 3). In 2016, Other Asia, nes was the country/area with the highest value of net exports (+4.4 bln US$), followed by Singapore (+3.5 bln US$). By MDG regions (see graph 2), the largest surpluses in this product group were recorded by Eastern Asia (+4.2 bln US$) and South-eastern Asia (+3.5 bln US$). The largest trade deficits were recorded by Developed North America (-6.1 bln US$), Developed Europe (-2.1 bln US$) and Southern Asia (-1.8 bln US$).

Table 1: Imports (Imp.) and exports (Exp.), 2002-2016, in current US$

		2002	2003	2004	2005	2006	2007	2008	2009	2010	2011	2012	2013	2014	2015	2016
Values in Bln US$	Imp.	34.4	38.1	44.3	50.3	53.8	63.8	65.6	55.1	61.3	65.9	60.1	58.0	58.8	55.0	56.4
	Exp.	33.7	36.8	41.7	47.4	49.6	60.7	61.7	51.0	55.4	60.7	56.3	50.5	51.8	49.7	49.5
As a percentage of SITC section (%)	Imp.	4.0	3.9	3.9	4.1	3.9	4.1	3.9	3.8	3.7	3.6	3.2	3.0	2.9	2.9	3.0
	Exp.	4.2	4.0	3.9	4.0	3.8	4.1	3.8	3.6	3.4	3.2	2.8	2.4	2.4	2.4	2.5
As a percentage of world trade (%)	Imp.	0.5	0.5	0.5	0.5	0.4	0.5	0.4	0.4	0.4	0.4	0.3	0.3	0.3	0.3	0.4
	Exp.	0.5	0.5	0.5	0.5	0.4	0.4	0.4	0.4	0.4	0.3	0.3	0.3	0.3	0.3	0.3

Graph 1: Annual growth rates of exports, 2002–2016
(In percentage by year)

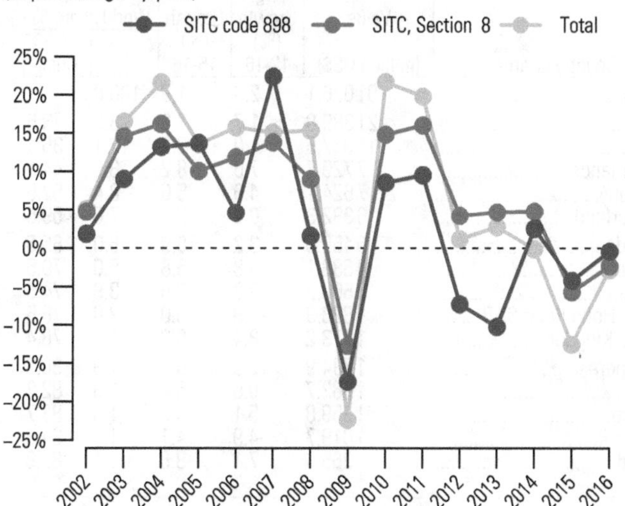

Table 2: Top exporting countries or areas in 2016

Country or area	Value (million US$)	Avg. Growth (%) 12-16	Growth (%) 15-16	World share %	Cum.
World	49481.0	-3.2	-0.4	100.0	
Other Asia, nes	5628.8	-1.1	-0.7	11.4	11.4
China	5482.3	-7.8	-15.3	11.1	22.5
Singapore	4723.2	-3.6	3.7	9.5	32.0
Germany	4709.5	-5.0	-1.7	9.5	41.5
USA	4392.2	-5.2	-0.8	8.9	50.4
China, Hong Kong SAR	3056.4	-5.3	2.5	6.2	56.6
Netherlands	3015.6	3.2	16.7	6.1	62.7
Japan	2292.7	-8.3	-8.0	4.6	67.3
Malaysia	2214.8	12.4	15.4	4.5	71.8
United Kingdom	1723.5	1.0	5.9	3.5	75.3
Czechia	1610.0	8.1	17.1	3.3	78.5
Poland	1457.9	27.2	10.4	2.9	81.5
Rep. of Korea	1199.8	0.0	3.3	2.4	83.9
France	1120.6	-4.2	0.9	2.3	86.1
Ireland	769.9	-9.2	-5.3	1.6	87.7

Graph 2: Trade Balance by MDG regions 2016
(Bln US$)

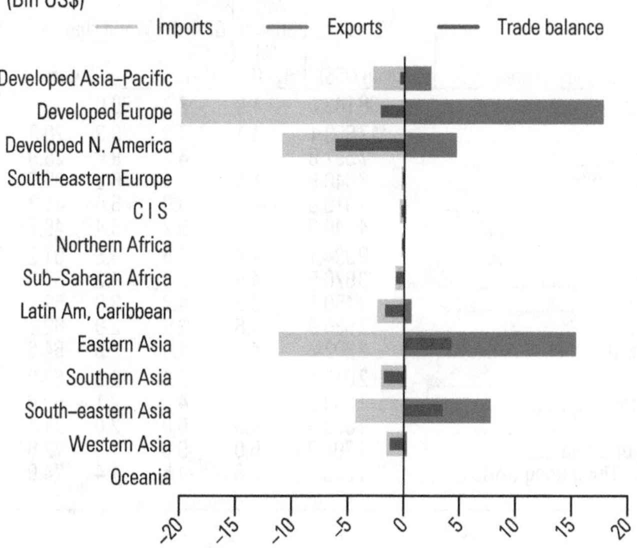

Table 3: Top importing countries or areas in 2016

Country or area	Value (million US$)	Avg. Growth (%) 12-16	Growth (%) 15-16	World share %	Cum.
World	56418.3	-1.6	2.6	100.0	
USA	9556.9	14.1	15.9	16.9	16.9
China	4868.8	-7.0	-13.0	8.6	25.6
China, Hong Kong SAR	4020.5	-6.3	-0.6	7.1	32.7
Germany	3787.3	-3.9	0.2	6.7	39.4
United Kingdom	2706.3	0.3	5.3	4.8	44.2
Netherlands	2074.0	-3.9	-3.4	3.7	47.9
Japan	1983.1	-9.5	2.6	3.5	51.4
Thailand	1966.3	0.8	1.8	3.5	54.9
France	1924.6	-4.0	-1.5	3.4	58.3
India	1695.3	9.9	23.1	3.0	61.3
Poland	1570.7	25.1	1.8	2.8	64.1
Canada	1278.7	-10.5	-7.5	2.3	66.3
Singapore	1246.4	-3.8	11.6	2.2	68.6
Other Asia, nes	1233.6	-9.4	13.5	2.2	70.7
Mexico	1172.0	10.6	12.5	2.1	72.8

899 Miscellaneous manufactured articles, nes

In 2016, the value (in current US$) of exports of "miscellaneous manufactured articles, nes" (SITC group 899) decreased by 1.9 percent (compared to 2.3 percent average growth rate from 2012-2016) to reach 91.0 bln US$ (see table 2), while imports increased by 2.7 percent to reach 88.1 bln US$ (see table 3). Exports of this commodity accounted for 4.5 percent of world exports of SITC section 8, and 0.6 percent of total world merchandise exports (see table 1). China, USA and Netherlands were the top exporters in 2016 (see table 2). They accounted for 23.5, 12.1 and 8.5 percent of world exports, respectively. USA, Germany and Netherlands were the top destinations, with respectively 20.3, 8.6 and 6.9 percent of world imports (see table 3).

The top 15 countries/areas accounted for 85.9 and 74.0 percent of total world exports and imports, respectively (see tables 2 and 3). In 2016, China was the country/area with the highest value of net exports (+17.5 bln US$), followed by Ireland (+4.6 bln US$). By MDG regions (see graph 2), the largest surpluses in this product group were recorded by Eastern Asia (+17.5 bln US$), Developed Europe (+5.2 bln US$) and South-eastern Asia (+879.7 mln US$). The largest trade deficits were recorded by Developed North America (-8.4 bln US$), Developed Asia-Pacific (-5.3 bln US$) and Western Asia (-2.1 bln US$).

Table 1: Imports (Imp.) and exports (Exp.), 2002-2016, in current US$

		2002	2003	2004	2005	2006	2007	2008	2009	2010	2011	2012	2013	2014	2015	2016
Values in Bln US$	Imp.	30.5	37.1	43.0	46.8	51.3	58.4	67.1	64.2	71.7	80.8	81.7	85.6	89.1	85.9	88.1
	Exp.	27.2	33.4	40.0	44.5	49.7	56.5	65.9	63.9	72.9	80.4	83.2	88.6	94.3	92.7	91.0
As a percentage of SITC section (%)	Imp.	3.6	3.8	3.8	3.8	3.8	3.8	4.0	4.5	4.4	4.4	4.4	4.4	4.4	4.5	4.6
	Exp.	3.4	3.6	3.7	3.8	3.8	3.8	4.0	4.5	4.4	4.2	4.2	4.3	4.3	4.5	4.5
As a percentage of world trade (%)	Imp.	0.5	0.5	0.5	0.4	0.4	0.4	0.4	0.5	0.5	0.4	0.4	0.5	0.5	0.5	0.5
	Exp.	0.4	0.4	0.4	0.4	0.4	0.4	0.4	0.5	0.5	0.4	0.5	0.5	0.5	0.6	0.6

Graph 1: Annual growth rates of exports, 2002–2016
(In percentage by year)

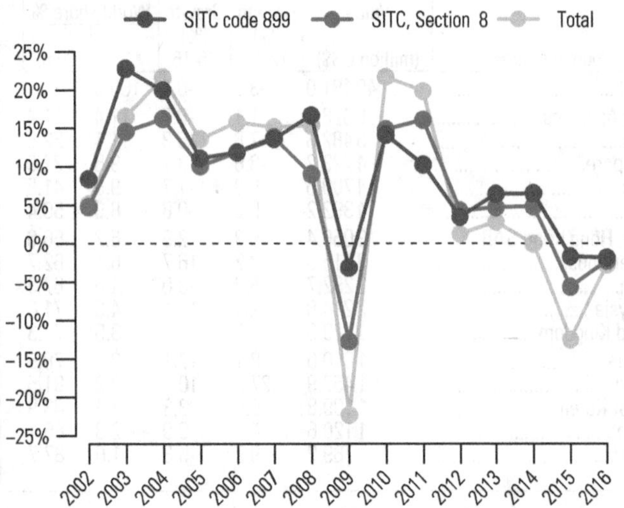

Table 2: Top exporting countries or areas in 2016

Country or area	Value (million US$)	Avg. Growth (%) 12-16	Growth (%) 15-16	World share %	Cum.
World	91 026.1	2.3	-1.9	100.0	
China	21 389.0	1.7	-7.9	23.5	23.5
USA	11 037.5	1.0	-3.1	12.1	35.6
Netherlands	7 729.7	7.6	18.2	8.5	44.1
Germany	7 624.1	4.9	5.6	8.4	52.5
Switzerland	6 392.3	0.2	-2.1	7.0	59.5
Ireland	5 453.9	3.2	10.9	6.0	65.5
Belgium	4 589.1	6.8	-5.8	5.0	70.5
France	3 569.3	-3.3	-0.6	3.9	74.5
China, Hong Kong SAR	1 828.3	-4.8	-5.0	2.0	76.5
United Kingdom	1 773.2	3.4	0.3	1.9	78.4
Singapore	1 734.9	12.3	6.7	1.9	80.3
Italy	1 682.7	-0.6	5.4	1.8	82.2
Mexico	1 359.8	5.1	6.2	1.5	83.7
Denmark	1 019.7	-4.9	4.1	1.1	84.8
Poland	965.6	7.1	-8.6	1.1	85.9

Graph 2: Trade Balance by MDG regions 2016
(Bln US$)

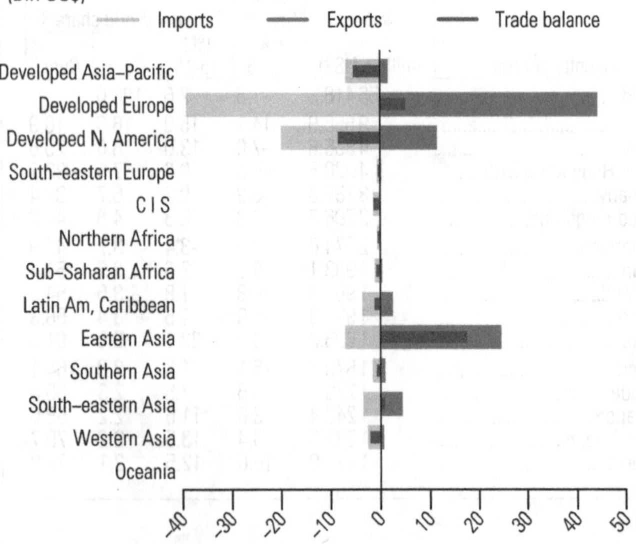

Table 3: Top importing countries or areas in 2016

Country or area	Value (million US$)	Avg. Growth (%) 12-16	Growth (%) 15-16	World share %	Cum.
World	88 143.0	1.9	2.7	100.0	
USA	17 863.1	4.1	3.9	20.3	20.3
Germany	7 592.0	4.2	4.7	8.6	28.9
Netherlands	6 040.6	1.5	3.1	6.9	35.7
France	4 918.6	-1.7	3.9	5.6	41.3
Japan	4 740.3	-2.8	5.2	5.4	46.7
China	3 934.1	7.8	1.5	4.5	51.2
United Kingdom	3 670.5	4.9	-2.3	4.2	55.3
Belgium	3 450.1	6.2	-4.2	3.9	59.2
Italy	2 536.9	0.6	2.9	2.9	62.1
Switzerland	2 202.8	4.0	4.0	2.5	64.6
Canada	2 010.0	-0.9	-2.2	2.3	66.9
Australia	1 893.0	1.7	4.5	2.1	69.0
Spain	1 806.3	0.8	6.0	2.0	71.1
Rep. of Korea	1 291.2	5.0	5.0	1.5	72.6
China, Hong Kong SAR	1 256.1	-7.8	-4.6	1.4	74.0

Commodities and transactions not classified elsewhere in the SITC

(SITC Section 9)

961 Coin (other than gold coin), not being legal tender

In 2016, the value (in current US$) of exports of "coin (other than gold coin), not being legal tender" (SITC group 961) decreased by 14.4 percent (compared to -6.1 percent average growth rate from 2012-2016) to reach 283.7 mln US$ (see table 2), while imports decreased by 1.3 percent to reach 543.3 mln US$ (see table 3). Exports of this commodity accounted for less than 0.1 percent of world exports of SITC section 9, and less than 0.1 percent of total world merchandise exports (see table 1). Poland, Germany and Canada were the top exporters in 2016 (see table 2). They accounted for 16.0, 14.8 and 13.4 percent of world exports, respectively. Germany, Singapore and Other Asia, nes were the top destinations, with respectively 68.9, 3.7 and 3.6 percent of world imports (see table 3).

The top 15 countries/areas accounted for 91.7 and 93.7 percent of total world exports and imports, respectively (see tables 2 and 3). In 2016, Poland was the country/area with the highest value of net exports (+42.8 mln US$), followed by Canada (+36.6 mln US$). By MDG regions (see graph 2), the largest surpluses in this product group were recorded by Developed North America (+40.0 mln US$), Commonwealth of Independent States (+5.1 mln US$) and Oceania (+1.4 mln US$). The largest trade deficits were recorded by Developed Europe (-257.1 mln US$), Eastern Asia (-21.4 mln US$) and South-eastern Asia (-11.4 mln US$).

Table 1: Imports (Imp.) and exports (Exp.), 2002-2016, in current US$

		2002	2003	2004	2005	2006	2007	2008	2009	2010	2011	2012	2013	2014	2015	2016
Values in Mln US$	Imp.	94.0	118.4	108.1	106.6	106.0	145.3	186.6	438.5	552.2	930.6	719.8	682.4	504.4	550.3	543.3
	Exp.	105.8	156.0	217.4	186.7	233.7	334.2	360.9	442.2	578.4	416.4	365.6	344.3	387.6	331.2	283.7
As a percentage of SITC section (%)	Imp.	0.0	0.0	0.0	0.0	0.0	0.0	0.0	0.1	0.1	0.1	0.1	0.1	0.1	0.1	0.1
	Exp.	0.0	0.0	0.0	0.0	0.0	0.1	0.1	0.1	0.1	0.0	0.0	0.0	0.0	0.0	0.0
As a percentage of world trade (%)	Imp.	0.0	0.0	0.0	0.0	0.0	0.0	0.0	0.0	0.0	0.0	0.0	0.0	0.0	0.0	0.0
	Exp.	0.0	0.0	0.0	0.0	0.0	0.0	0.0	0.0	0.0	0.0	0.0	0.0	0.0	0.0	0.0

Graph 1: Annual growth rates of exports, 2002–2016

(In percentage by year)

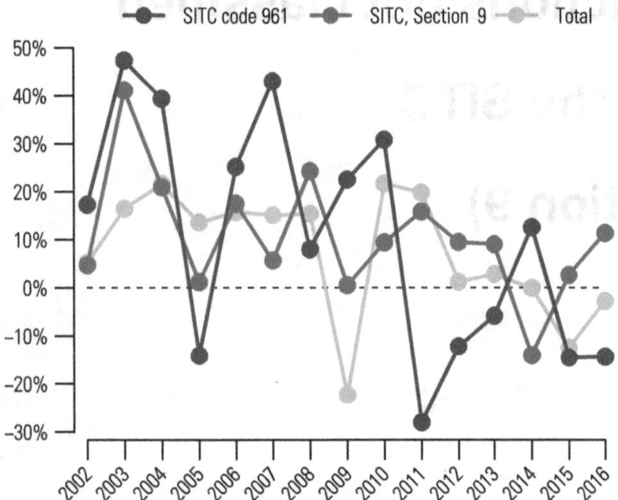

Table 2: Top exporting countries or areas in 2016

Country or area	Value (million US$)	Avg. Growth (%) 12-16	Growth (%) 15-16	World share %	Cum.
World	283.7	-6.1	-14.4	100.0	
Poland	45.3	58.7	512.3	16.0	16.0
Germany	42.0	-7.3	-6.6	14.8	30.8
Canada	37.9	10.0	51.3	13.4	44.1
Slovakia	26.2	19.5	-25.1	9.2	53.4
Finland	23.0	-3.2	27.4	8.1	61.5
USA	19.5	-29.5	-62.5	6.9	68.3
France	19.3	-14.7	127.5	6.8	75.1
United Kingdom	13.2	-9.8	-70.5	4.7	79.8
Singapore	8.3	24.4	55.1	2.9	82.8
Russian Federation	5.4	48.3	-9.3	1.9	84.7
Netherlands	5.3	7.5	-84.7	1.9	86.5
India	5.1	21.6	7149.2	1.8	88.3
South Africa	4.2	-14.5	402.6	1.5	89.8
Chile	2.7	...	4479.4	1.0	90.8
Italy	2.7	-17.6	-5.6	0.9	91.7

Graph 2: Trade Balance by MDG regions 2016

(Mln US$)

Imports
Exports
Trade balance

Developed Asia-Pacific
Developed Europe
Developed N. America
South-eastern Europe
C I S
Northern Africa
Sub-Saharan Africa
Latin Am, Caribbean
Eastern Asia
Southern Asia
South-eastern Asia
Western Asia
Oceania

-500 -400 -300 -200 -100 0 100 200

Table 3: Top importing countries or areas in 2016

Country or area	Value (million US$)	Avg. Growth (%) 12-16	Growth (%) 15-16	World share %	Cum.
World	543.3	-6.8	-1.3	100.0	
Germany	374.3	-3.6	22.4	68.9	68.9
Singapore	20.0	-0.6	1.0	3.7	72.6
Other Asia, nes	19.4	19.8	-21.8	3.6	76.1
Slovakia	15.9	69.5	-20.1	2.9	79.1
France	15.7	1.4	0.7	2.9	82.0
USA	13.1	-24.8	-49.4	2.4	84.4
Sri Lanka	12.6	17.5	127.2	2.3	86.7
Luxembourg	9.3	3.3	501.7	1.7	88.4
United Kingdom	6.9	-19.8	-39.8	1.3	89.7
Australia	4.7	-6.6	7.8	0.9	90.6
Netherlands	3.8	-25.5	7.3	0.7	91.3
Qatar	3.5	-23.5	-28.9	0.6	91.9
Chile	3.4	151.3	-91.5	0.6	92.5
Denmark	3.1	33.4	25.3	0.6	93.1
Switzerland	3.0	-40.7	-69.9	0.6	93.7

"Gold, non-monetary (excluding gold ores and concentrates)" (SITC group 971) is amongst the top exported commodities in 2016 with 2.1 percent of total exports (see table 1). The value (in current US$) of exports of this commodity increased by 9.8 percent (compared to -3.3 percent average growth rate from 2012-2016) to reach 343.0 bln US$ (see table 2), while imports increased by 12.3 percent to reach 378.7 bln US$ (see table 3). Exports of this commodity accounted for 32.0 percent of world exports of SITC section 9 (see table 1). Switzerland, China, Hong Kong SAR and USA were the top exporters in 2016 (see table 2). They accounted for 24.0, 15.8 and 5.8 percent of world exports, respectively. Switzerland, China and United Kingdom were the top destinations, with respectively 22.5, 16.9 and 15.4 percent of world imports (see table 3).

The top 15 countries/areas accounted for 81.2 and 95.2 percent of total world exports and imports, respectively (see tables 2 and 3). In 2016, China, Hong Kong SAR was the country/area with the highest value of net exports (+23.9 bln US$), followed by Uzbekistan (+10.5 bln US$). By MDG regions (see graph 2), the largest surpluses in this product group were recorded by Latin America and the Caribbean (+24.2 bln US$), Sub-Saharan Africa (+18.1 bln US$) and Developed Asia-Pacific (+17.0 bln US$). The largest trade deficits were recorded by Developed Europe (-44.4 bln US$), Eastern Asia (-38.9 bln US$) and Southern Asia (-19.9 bln US$).

Table 1: Imports (Imp.) and exports (Exp.), 2002-2016, in current US$

		2002	2003	2004	2005	2006	2007	2008	2009	2010	2011	2012	2013	2014	2015	2016
Values in Bln US$	Imp.	32.2	40.1	49.5	50.1	63.3	75.9	113.7	99.0	142.9	214.6	346.8	417.5	286.8	337.2	378.7
	Exp.	24.3	35.5	41.0	39.7	63.4	75.7	110.7	125.1	157.5	241.1	392.8	483.4	315.4	312.4	343.0
As a percentage of SITC section (%)	Imp.	13.4	12.3	12.2	12.7	12.0	14.1	17.0	15.9	21.4	28.8	40.0	45.1	39.4	42.2	41.3
	Exp.	9.1	9.4	8.9	8.6	11.6	13.1	15.5	17.4	20.0	26.4	39.3	44.3	33.7	32.5	32.0
As a percentage of world trade (%)	Imp.	0.5	0.5	0.5	0.5	0.5	0.5	0.7	0.8	0.9	1.2	1.9	2.2	1.5	2.0	2.4
	Exp.	0.4	0.5	0.4	0.4	0.5	0.5	0.7	1.0	1.0	1.3	2.1	2.6	1.7	1.9	2.1

Graph 1: Annual growth rates of exports, 2002–2016
(In percentage by year)

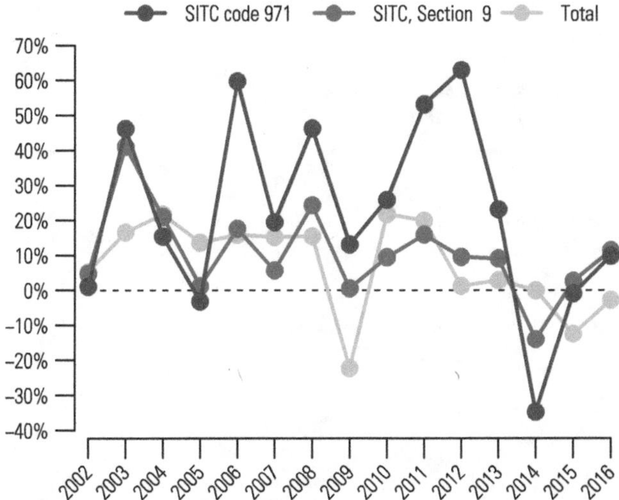

Table 2: Top exporting countries or areas in 2016

Country or area	Value (million US$)	Avg. Growth (%) 12-16	Growth (%) 15-16	World share %	Cum.
World	343000.6	-3.3	9.8	100.0	
Switzerland	82409.0	-1.6	13.5	24.0	24.0
China, Hong Kong SAR	54070.7	1.9	20.1	15.8	39.8
USA	20049.4	-14.0	-4.0	5.8	45.6
United Arab Emirates	16643.5	-16.4	2.0	4.9	50.5
United Kingdom	16048.4	40.0	-58.6	4.7	55.2
Australia	14066.8	-3.3	28.6	4.1	59.3
Canada	12891.9	-5.6	-0.1	3.8	63.0
Singapore	11059.2	45.0	726.6	3.2	66.3
Uzbekistan	*10482.3*	66.0	52.8	3.1	69.3
Japan	8618.0	5.2	59.6	2.5	71.8
Turkey	8248.5	-11.3	11.8	2.4	74.2
Thailand	7317.2	2.3	93.3	2.1	76.4
Peru	6430.5	-10.0	13.7	1.9	78.2
Germany	5232.7	-13.9	11.5	1.5	79.8
Mexico	4926.0	-11.8	12.7	1.4	81.2

Graph 2: Trade Balance by MDG regions 2016
(Bln US$)

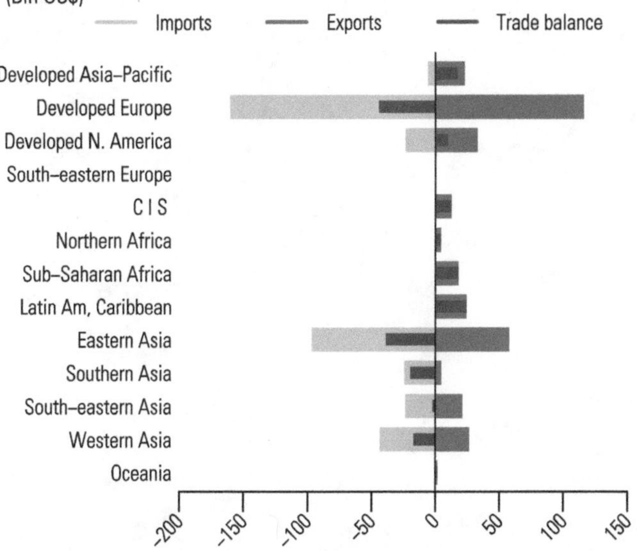

Table 3: Top importing countries or areas in 2016

Country or area	Value (million US$)	Avg. Growth (%) 12-16	Growth (%) 15-16	World share %	Cum.
World	378727.6	2.2	12.3	100.0	
Switzerland	85070.9	-3.0	18.8	22.5	22.5
China	63985.3	...	-19.0	16.9	39.4
United Kingdom	58473.6	77.7	205.3	15.4	54.8
United Arab Emirates	32175.0	-6.4	26.1	8.5	63.3
China, Hong Kong SAR	30193.6	-11.4	-17.7	8.0	71.3
India	22944.6	-18.7	-34.4	6.1	77.3
USA	16973.7	-1.2	47.8	4.5	81.8
Singapore	13880.6	55.6	342.4	3.7	85.5
Canada	6609.8	-12.2	-7.7	1.7	87.2
Turkey	6459.1	-4.1	88.5	1.7	88.9
Germany	6205.4	-5.9	18.4	1.6	90.6
Thailand	6055.9	-13.3	-15.9	1.6	92.2
Australia	5569.5	-2.0	66.4	1.5	93.6
Italy	3805.4	-16.3	-9.7	1.0	94.6
Malaysia	2314.7	-5.7	-20.6	0.6	95.2

2016 International Trade Statistics Yearbook

Volume II
Trade by Product

Part 3 – Service Trade Profiles

- Transportation (EBOPS code 205)
- Travel (EBOPS code 236)
- Communications services (EBOPS code 245)
- Construction services (EBOPS code 249)
- Insurance services (EBOPS code 253)
- Financial services (EBOPS code 260)
- Computer and information services (EBOPS code 262)
- Royalties and license fees (EBOPS code 266)
- Other business services (EBOPS code 268)
- Personal, cultural and recreational services (EBOPS code 287)
- Government services, n.i.e. (EBOPS code 291)

Transportation (EBOPS 2002 code 205)

In 2015, the value (in current US$) of exports of "transportation" (EBOPS 2002 code 205) decreased by 13.6 percent (compared to -0.5 percent average growth rate from 2011-2015) to reach 801.9 bln US$ (see table 2), while imports decreased by 13.1 percent to reach 942.7 bln US$ (see table 3). Exports of this service accounted for 16.8 percent of total world services exports (see table 1). USA, Germany and Singapore were the top exporters in 2015 (see table 2). They accounted for 10.9, 6.4 and 5.9 percent of world exports, respectively. USA, China and Germany were the top importers, with respectively 10.3, 8.0 and 6.9 percent of world imports (see table 3).

The top 15 countries/areas accounted for 67.6 and 62.5 percent of total world exports and imports, respectively (see tables 2 and 3). In 2015, Netherlands was the country/area with the highest value of net exports (+13.1 bln US$), followed by China, Hong Kong SAR (+12.5 bln US$). By MDG regions (see graph 2), the largest surpluses in this product group were recorded by Developed Europe (+28.2 bln US$), Commonwealth of Independent States (+8.7 bln US$) and South-eastern Europe (+4.6 bln US$). The largest trade deficits were recorded by South-eastern Asia (-37.0 bln US$), Latin America and the Caribbean (-30.2 bln US$) and Western Asia (-29.9 bln US$).

Table 1: Imports (Imp.) and exports (Exp.), 2003-2015, in current US$

		2003	2004	2005	2006	2007	2008	2009	2010	2011	2012	2013	2014	2015
Values in Bln US$	Imp.	477.3	588.0	638.1	740.4	887.5	968.4	792.2	1 031.4	1 013.2	1 011.1	1 039.2	1 084.6	942.7
	Exp.	409.8	507.4	549.5	648.5	789.6	858.3	701.7	946.2	818.4	843.1	857.2	928.2	801.9
As a percentage of world trade (%)	Imp.	24.3	25.5	26.9	26.6	26.6	27.1	23.4	21.1	24.7	24.0	23.2	22.8	21.1
	Exp.	20.4	21.1	22.3	22.0	21.9	22.7	19.5	16.1	18.7	18.8	18.0	18.4	16.8

Graph 1: Annual growth rates of exports, 2004–2015
(In percentage by year)

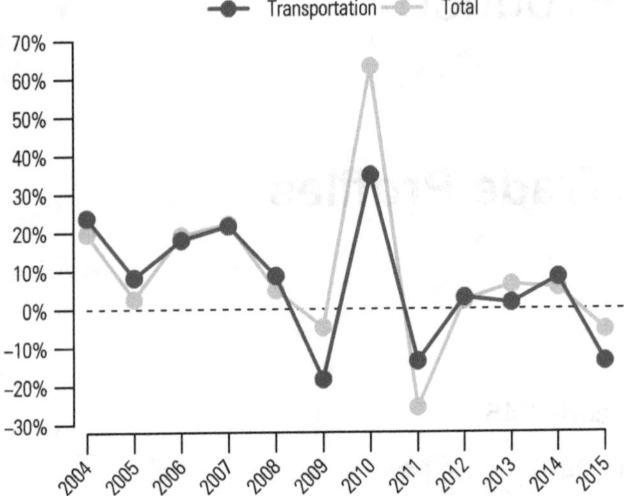

Table 2: Top exporting countries or areas in 2015

Country or area	Value (million US$)	Avg. Growth (%) 11-15	Growth (%) 14-15	World share %	Cum.
World	801 854.7	-0.5	-13.6	100.0	
USA	87 221.0	2.2	-3.8	10.9	10.9
Germany	51 216.7	-2.8	-9.0	6.4	17.3
Singapore	47 420.1	2.8	-7.6	5.9	23.2
France	42 132.4	-3.6	-11.7	5.3	28.4
China	38 594.3	2.1	0.9	4.8	33.2
United Kingdom	36 819.5	2.0	-16.2	4.6	37.8
Denmark	36 501.0	-2.5	-17.7	4.6	42.4
Japan	35 518.6	-0.1	-10.2	4.4	46.8
Netherlands	34 462.8	...	-16.5	4.3	51.1
Rep. of Korea	32 364.9	-3.2	-14.8	4.0	55.2
China, Hong Kong SAR	29 783.7	-1.6	-8.4	3.7	58.9
Belgium	23 361.4	-3.0	-6.0	2.9	61.8
Russian Federation	16 498.8	-1.1	-19.7	2.1	63.8
Spain	15 824.8	...	-8.1	2.0	65.8
India	14 298.1	-5.2	-23.2	1.8	67.6

Graph 2: Trade Balance by MDG regions 2015
(Bln US$)

Imports — Exports — Trade balance

Developed Asia-Pacific
Developed Europe
Developed N. America
South-eastern Europe
CIS
Northern Africa
Sub-Saharan Africa
Latin Am, Caribbean
Eastern Asia
Southern Asia
South-eastern Asia
Western Asia
Oceania

-400 -300 -200 -100 0 100 200 300 400

Table 3: Top importing countries or areas in 2015

Country or area	Value (million US$)	Avg. Growth (%) 11-15	Growth (%) 14-15	World share %	Cum.
World	942 669.3	-1.8	-13.1	100.0	
USA	97 050.0	4.5	3.1	10.3	10.3
China	75 614.4	-1.5	-21.4	8.0	18.3
Germany	64 902.6	-1.6	-11.9	6.9	25.2
France	46 340.2	-1.8	-10.3	4.9	30.1
Singapore	44 268.0	7.4	-3.0	4.7	34.8
Japan	40 986.9	-2.9	-10.6	4.3	39.2
United Kingdom	33 212.4	4.0	4.2	3.5	42.7
Rep. of Korea	29 001.9	-1.0	-7.5	3.1	45.8
Denmark	28 427.2	-2.0	-11.9	3.0	48.8
Thailand	23 895.7	-2.8	-10.5	2.5	51.3
Italy	23 529.7	-3.8	-11.9	2.5	53.8
Netherlands	21 333.9	...	-11.0	2.3	56.1
Belgium	20 551.0	-1.2	-9.5	2.2	58.3
Canada	20 176.6	-3.5	-10.4	2.1	60.4
Saudi Arabia	20 096.7	7.0	0.9	2.1	62.5

Source: UN Comtrade

In 2015, the value (in current US$) of exports of "travel" (EBOPS 2002 code 236) decreased by 3.0 percent (compared to 2.8 percent average growth rate from 2011-2015) to reach 1178.5 bln US$ (see table 2), while imports increased by 3.1 percent to reach 1145.4 bln US$ (see table 3). Exports of this service accounted for 24.7 percent of total world services exports (see table 1). USA, China and Spain were the top exporters in 2015 (see table 2). They accounted for 17.4, 9.7 and 4.8 percent of world exports, respectively. China, USA and Germany were the top importers, with respectively 25.5, 9.9 and 6.8 percent of world imports (see table 3).

The top 15 countries/areas accounted for 65.0 and 71.9 percent of total world exports and imports, respectively (see tables 2 and 3). In 2015, USA was the country/area with the highest value of net exports (+91.7 bln US$), followed by Spain (+39.1 bln US$). By MDG regions (see graph 2), the largest surpluses in this product group were recorded by Developed North America (+78.2 bln US$), South-eastern Asia (+44.4 bln US$) and Developed Europe (+33.1 bln US$). The largest trade deficits were recorded by Eastern Asia (-145.1 bln US$), Commonwealth of Independent States (-25.7 bln US$) and Western Asia (-17.9 bln US$).

Table 1: Imports (Imp.) and exports (Exp.), 2003-2015, in current US$

		2003	2004	2005	2006	2007	2008	2009	2010	2011	2012	2013	2014	2015
Values in Bln US$	Imp.	524.1	610.3	628.5	705.0	827.8	838.8	796.7	1218.7	938.8	984.4	1050.3	1110.9	1145.4
	Exp.	558.2	660.5	674.1	767.8	898.8	928.8	881.6	1194.5	1056.1	1074.3	1171.0	1214.6	1178.5
As a percentage of world trade (%)	Imp.	26.7	26.4	26.5	25.3	24.8	23.5	23.5	24.9	22.9	23.4	23.4	23.4	25.6
	Exp.	27.8	27.5	27.3	26.1	25.0	24.6	24.4	20.3	24.1	24.0	24.6	24.1	24.7

Graph 1: Annual growth rates of exports, 2004–2015

(In percentage by year)

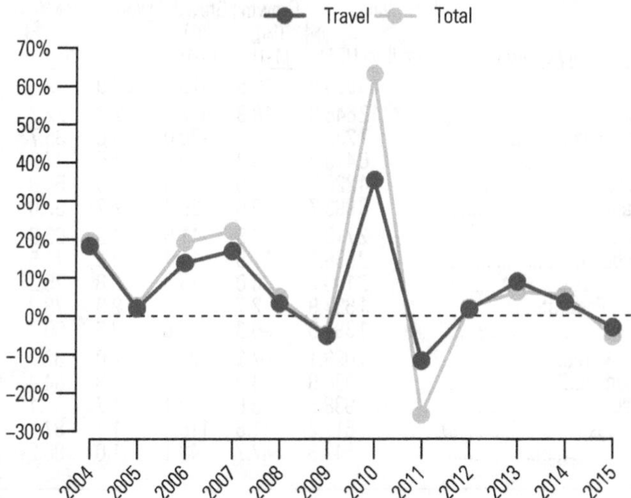

Graph 2: Trade Balance by MDG regions 2015

(Bln US$)

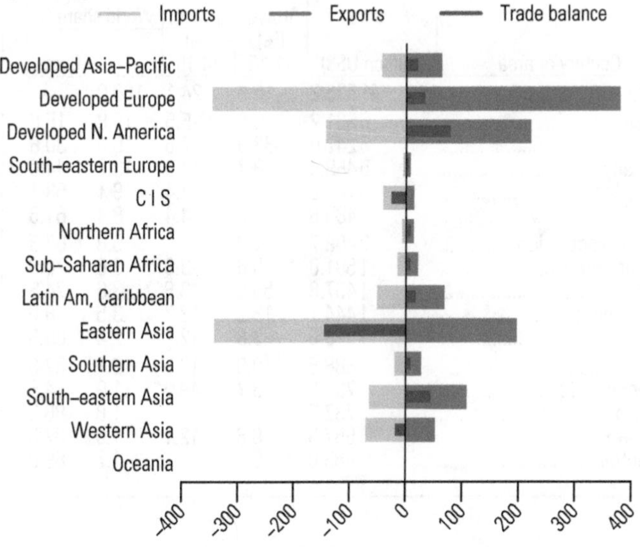

Table 2: Top exporting countries or areas in 2015

Country or area	Value (million US$)	Avg. Growth (%) 11-15	Growth (%) 14-15	World share %	Cum.
World	1178458.8	2.8	-3.0	100.0	
USA	204523.0	7.9	6.9	17.4	17.4
China	114109.4	23.9	100.5	9.7	27.0
Spain	56465.8	-2.4	-13.3	4.8	31.8
France	45900.9	-4.3	-21.1	3.9	35.7
United Kingdom	45463.6	6.2	-2.5	3.9	39.6
Thailand	44552.7	13.1	16.0	3.8	43.4
Italy	39449.3	-2.1	-13.3	3.3	46.7
Germany	36853.2	-1.3	-14.9	3.1	49.8
China, Hong Kong SAR	36150.2	6.2	-8.9	3.1	52.9
China, Macao SAR	30985.1	0.3	-27.5	2.6	55.5
Australia	29481.5	-1.9	-7.8	2.5	58.0
Japan	24968.0	25.1	32.4	2.1	60.2
India	21012.7	4.4	6.7	1.8	61.9
Austria	18219.1	-2.1	-12.5	1.5	63.5
Malaysia	17510.9	-2.8	-22.6	1.5	65.0

Table 3: Top importing countries or areas in 2015

Country or area	Value (million US$)	Avg. Growth (%) 11-15	Growth (%) 14-15	World share %	Cum.
World	1145407.9	5.1	3.1	100.0	
China	292199.9	41.6	77.2	25.5	25.5
USA	112873.0	5.9	7.0	9.9	35.4
Germany	77480.5	-2.5	-17.0	6.8	42.1
United Kingdom	63272.9	2.8	0.1	5.5	47.7
France	38404.8	-3.7	-21.2	3.4	51.0
Russian Federation	34934.2	1.5	-30.7	3.0	54.1
Canada	30089.8	-2.7	-12.1	2.6	56.7
Rep. of Korea	24957.9	5.8	7.6	2.2	58.9
Italy	24422.4	-3.9	-15.3	2.1	61.0
Australia	23541.7	-3.7	-10.9	2.1	63.0
China, Hong Kong SAR	23059.4	5.0	1.3	2.0	65.1
Singapore	22133.7	0.8	-8.9	1.9	67.0
Saudi Arabia	19345.7	2.9	-19.8	1.7	68.7
Belgium	18927.3	-2.0	-20.5	1.7	70.3
Netherlands	17552.1	-4.0	-14.0	1.5	71.9

Communications services (EBOPS 2002 code 245)

In 2015, the value (in current US$) of exports of "communications services" (EBOPS 2002 code 245) decreased by 18.1 percent (compared to -10.6 percent average growth rate from 2011-2015) to reach 55.7 bln US$ (see table 2), while imports decreased by 24.1 percent to reach 41.5 bln US$ (see table 3). Exports of this service accounted for 1.2 percent of total world services exports (see table 1). USA, Netherlands and France were the top exporters in 2015 (see table 2). They accounted for 22.7, 13.0 and 11.5 percent of world exports, respectively. France, USA and Germany were the top importers, with respectively 15.8, 15.0 and 13.2 percent of world imports (see table 3).

The top 15 countries/areas accounted for 88.2 and 89.0 percent of total world exports and imports, respectively (see tables 2 and 3). In 2015, USA was the country/area with the highest value of net exports (+6.4 bln US$), followed by Netherlands (+3.4 bln US$). By MDG regions (see graph 2), the largest surpluses in this product group were recorded by Developed North America (+6.4 bln US$), Developed Europe (+3.9 bln US$) and Southern Asia (+1.9 bln US$). The largest trade deficits were recorded by Sub-Saharan Africa (-690.6 mln US$), Commonwealth of Independent States (-559.0 mln US$) and Eastern Asia (-448.2 mln US$).

Table 1: Imports (Imp.) and exports (Exp.), 2003-2015, in current US$

		2003	2004	2005	2006	2007	2008	2009	2010	2011	2012	2013	2014	2015
Values in Bln US$	Imp.	38.4	46.2	46.1	61.3	71.3	75.0	78.6	69.7	83.0	80.4	52.5	54.7	41.5
	Exp.	39.0	49.8	53.0	70.1	83.6	84.6	88.9	68.1	87.2	84.4	62.5	68.0	55.7
As a percentage of world trade (%)	Imp.	2.0	2.0	1.9	2.2	2.1	2.1	2.3	1.4	2.0	1.9	1.2	1.1	0.9
	Exp.	1.9	2.1	2.1	2.4	2.3	2.2	2.5	1.2	2.0	1.9	1.3	1.3	1.2

Graph 1: Annual growth rates of exports, 2004–2015

(In percentage by year)

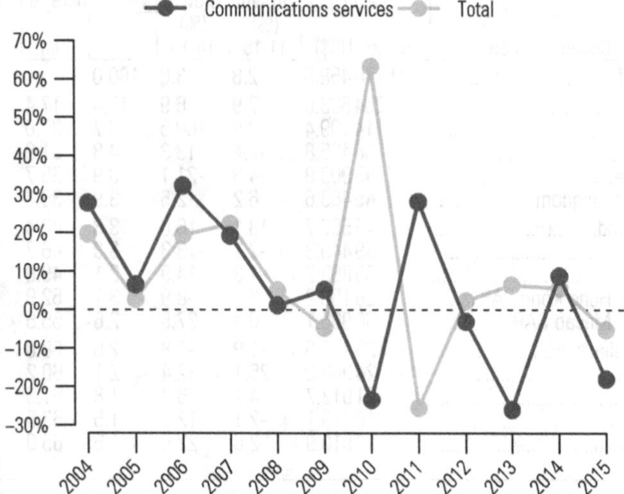

Table 2: Top exporting countries or areas in 2015

Country or area	Value (million US$)	Avg. Growth (%) 11-15	Growth (%) 14-15	World share %	Cum.
World	55684.5	-10.6	-18.1	100.0	
USA	12645.0	-18.9	-7.9	22.7	22.7
Netherlands	7233.3	...	-20.0	13.0	35.7
France	6419.2	-3.8	-5.4	11.5	47.2
Belgium	4226.7	-4.0	-7.8	7.6	54.8
Germany	3993.7	-9.9	-20.4	7.2	62.0
Kuwait	2713.1	-6.9	-11.5	4.9	66.9
Luxembourg	2558.6	-17.6	-12.7	4.6	71.5
India	2109.2	6.0	-3.3	3.8	75.2
Russian Federation	1637.9	2.7		2.9	78.2
Austria	1394.6	-0.3	-8.6	2.5	80.7
Rep. of Korea	1098.1	7.3	21.7	2.0	82.7
Lebanon	976.9	4.3	12.3	1.8	84.4
Morocco	938.5	5.6	-14.1	1.7	86.1
Bangladesh	617.2	11.8	118.4	1.1	87.2
Qatar	542.3	47.7	43.1	1.0	88.2

Graph 2: Trade Balance by MDG regions 2015

(Bln US$)

Imports — Exports — Trade balance

Developed Asia-Pacific
Developed Europe
Developed N. America
South-eastern Europe
CIS
Northern Africa
Sub-Saharan Africa
Latin Am, Caribbean
Eastern Asia
Southern Asia
South-eastern Asia
Western Asia
Oceania

-25 -20 -15 -10 -5 0 5 10 15 20 25 30

Table 3: Top importing countries or areas in 2015

Country or area	Value (million US$)	Avg. Growth (%) 11-15	Growth (%) 14-15	World share %	Cum.
World	41525.2	-15.9	-24.1	100.0	
France	6561.2	5.8	-5.5	15.8	15.8
USA	6242.0	-33.9	-7.6	15.0	30.8
Germany	5469.9	-8.7	-17.6	13.2	44.0
Netherlands	3787.2	...	-12.4	9.1	53.1
Belgium	3485.8	-2.0	-4.4	8.4	61.5
Russian Federation	2408.7	-1.2		5.8	67.3
Rep. of Korea	1501.0	-0.6	-3.3	3.6	70.9
Qatar	1497.8	55.9	-43.8	3.6	74.5
Luxembourg	1444.1	-13.2	-12.7	3.5	78.0
Austria	1013.0	-3.8	-12.7	2.4	80.5
India	888.5	-10.9	-18.9	2.1	82.6
Lebanon	791.5	3.7	49.9	1.9	84.5
Nigeria	732.6	...		1.8	86.3
Denmark	657.5	-6.8	-12.1	1.6	87.9
Argentina	483.0	0.8		1.2	89.0

In 2015, the value (in current US$) of exports of "construction services" (EBOPS 2002 code 249) decreased by 12.6 percent (compared to 0.9 percent average growth rate from 2011-2015) to reach 88.9 bln US$ (see table 2), while imports decreased by 14.7 percent to reach 77.4 bln US$ (see table 3). Exports of this service accounted for 1.9 percent of total world services exports (see table 1). China, Rep. of Korea and Japan were the top exporters in 2015 (see table 2). They accounted for 18.7, 15.2 and 11.9 percent of world exports, respectively. China, Japan and Saudi Arabia were the top importers, with respectively 13.2, 10.5 and 6.4 percent of world imports (see table 3).

The top 15 countries/areas accounted for 82.5 and 74.0 percent of total world exports and imports, respectively (see tables 2 and 3). In 2015, Rep. of Korea was the country/area with the highest value of net exports (+10.5 bln US$), followed by China (+6.5 bln US$). By MDG regions (see graph 2), the largest surpluses in this product group were recorded by Eastern Asia (+16.9 bln US$), Developed Europe (+10.1 bln US$) and Developed Asia-Pacific (+2.6 bln US$). The largest trade deficits were recorded by Western Asia (-5.0 bln US$), Commonwealth of Independent States (-4.3 bln US$) and Sub-Saharan Africa (-3.5 bln US$).

Table 1: Imports (Imp.) and exports (Exp.), 2003-2015, in current US$

		2003	2004	2005	2006	2007	2008	2009	2010	2011	2012	2013	2014	2015
Values in Bln US$	Imp.	32.4	42.9	46.8	59.6	81.6	91.8	90.0	79.4	71.5	70.7	82.0	90.7	77.4
	Exp.	38.3	47.0	52.2	67.5	86.6	104.3	105.4	92.8	85.7	90.4	91.6	101.8	88.9
As a percentage of world trade (%)	Imp.	1.7	1.9	2.0	2.1	2.4	2.6	2.7	1.6	1.7	1.7	1.8	1.9	1.7
	Exp.	1.9	2.0	2.1	2.3	2.4	2.8	2.9	1.6	2.0	2.0	1.9	2.0	1.9

Graph 1: Annual growth rates of exports, 2004–2015
(In percentage by year)

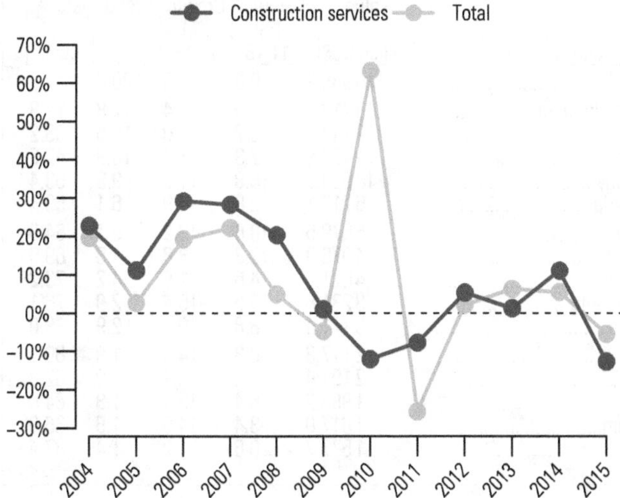

Table 2: Top exporting countries or areas in 2015

Country or area	Value (million US$)	Avg. Growth (%) 11-15	Growth (%) 14-15	World share %	Cum.
World	88922.1	0.9	-12.6	100.0	
China	16652.5	3.1	8.4	18.7	18.7
Rep. of Korea	13492.3	-3.4	-30.3	15.2	33.9
Japan	10558.7	0.9	-6.7	11.9	45.8
Denmark	5084.5	11.2	50.1	5.7	51.5
Russian Federation	3664.2	-4.5	-22.5	4.1	55.6
Belgium	3466.9	3.0	-31.1	3.9	59.5
Netherlands	3248.2	...	-18.5	3.7	63.2
France	3143.1	-4.9	-6.6	3.5	66.7
USA	2526.0	-5.0	39.1	2.8	69.5
United Kingdom	2404.7	-0.2	-25.6	2.7	72.2
Germany	2154.9	...	-23.2	2.4	74.7
Finland	2053.2	30.1	37.3	2.3	77.0
Israel	1973.2	78.2	527.9	2.2	79.2
India	1483.1	15.3	-8.1	1.7	80.9
Poland	1471.5	-2.5	-15.4	1.7	82.5

Graph 2: Trade Balance by MDG regions 2015
(Bln US$)

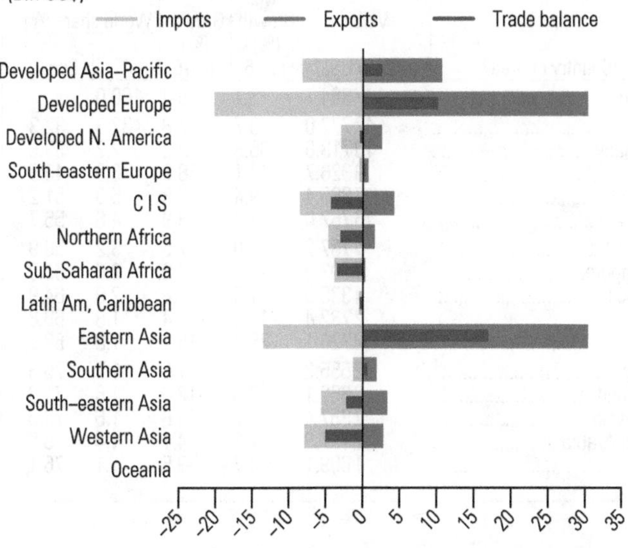

Table 3: Top importing countries or areas in 2015

Country or area	Value (million US$)	Avg. Growth (%) 11-15	Growth (%) 14-15	World share %	Cum.
World	77366.3	2.0	-14.7	100.0	
China	10197.3	28.6	109.4	13.2	13.2
Japan	8105.8	3.1	-22.5	10.5	23.7
Saudi Arabia	4952.1	17.7	15.7	6.4	30.1
Russian Federation	4831.3	-3.6	-35.8	6.2	36.3
Azerbaijan	3519.7	61.8	-10.5	4.5	40.9
Angola	3107.4	-20.9	-53.4	4.0	44.9
Rep. of Korea	3000.0	-5.7	-26.3	3.9	48.7
USA	2942.0	0.1	35.9	3.8	52.5
Belgium	2831.4	2.6	-14.9	3.7	56.2
Malaysia	2707.6	19.0	2.1	3.5	59.7
Netherlands	2502.5	...	-16.7	3.2	62.9
Kuwait	2333.1	12.3	-1.9	3.0	66.0
Algeria	2233.6	1.5	3.6	2.9	68.8
Denmark	2108.7	3.2	2.4	2.7	71.6
France	1896.5	-7.1	-34.8	2.5	74.0

Insurance services (EBOPS 2002 code 253)

In 2015, the value (in current US$) of exports of "insurance services" (EBOPS 2002 code 253) decreased by 16.3 percent (compared to 0.8 percent average growth rate from 2011-2015) to reach 110.9 bln US$ (see table 2), while imports decreased by 16.4 percent to reach 147.9 bln US$ (see table 3). Exports of this service accounted for 2.3 percent of total world services exports (see table 1). United Kingdom, USA and Ireland were the top exporters in 2015 (see table 2). They accounted for 17.8, 15.5 and 10.3 percent of world exports, respectively. USA, Germany and China were the top importers, with respectively 32.3, 7.2 and 6.3 percent of world imports (see table 3).

The top 15 countries/areas accounted for 87.4 and 76.1 percent of total world exports and imports, respectively (see tables 2 and 3). In 2015, United Kingdom was the country/area with the highest value of net exports (+19.5 bln US$), followed by Switzerland (+5.0 bln US$). By MDG regions (see graph 2), the largest surpluses in this product group were recorded by Developed Europe (+26.3 bln US$) and Southern Asia (+453.6 mln US$). The largest trade deficits were recorded by Developed North America (-30.7 bln US$), South-eastern Asia (-7.1 bln US$) and Western Asia (-6.2 bln US$).

Table 1: Imports (Imp.) and exports (Exp.), 2003-2015, in current US$

		2003	2004	2005	2006	2007	2008	2009	2010	2011	2012	2013	2014	2015
Values in Bln US$	Imp.	74.9	87.3	86.8	111.5	133.1	151.8	159.1	174.4	171.7	175.0	181.9	176.9	147.9
	Exp.	51.8	54.5	43.0	59.6	75.6	77.2	97.7	234.0	107.3	110.8	123.9	132.5	110.9
As a percentage of world trade (%)	Imp.	3.8	3.8	3.7	4.0	4.0	4.2	4.7	3.6	4.2	4.2	4.1	3.7	3.3
	Exp.	2.6	2.3	1.7	2.0	2.1	2.0	2.7	4.0	2.4	2.5	2.6	2.6	2.3

Graph 1: Annual growth rates of exports, 2004–2015
(In percentage by year)

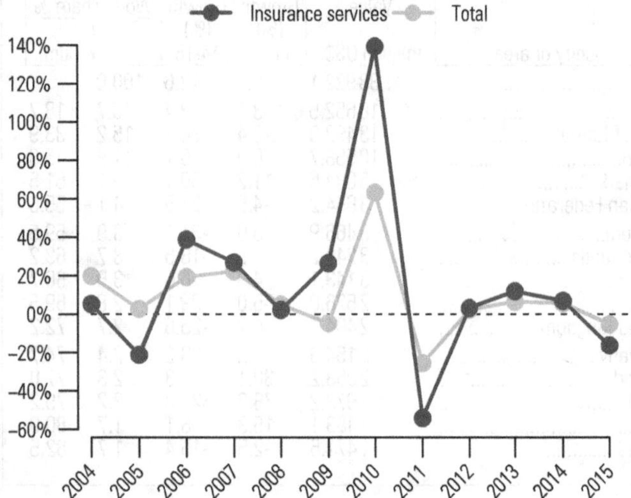

Table 2: Top exporting countries or areas in 2015

Country or area	Value (million US$)	Avg. Growth (%) 11-15	Growth (%) 14-15	World share %	Cum.
World	110 935.7	0.8	-16.3	100.0	
United Kingdom	19 719.1	-4.0	-40.4	17.8	17.8
USA	17 142.0	3.2	-1.0	15.5	33.2
Ireland	11 427.9	2.3	-1.4	10.3	43.5
Germany	10 923.2	16.8	-11.0	9.8	53.4
Switzerland	6 716.1	5.8	-5.9	6.1	59.4
France	5 679.5	-10.6	-19.2	5.1	64.5
China	4 976.3	13.3	8.8	4.5	69.0
Singapore	4 621.0	4.6	-1.6	4.2	73.2
Luxembourg	3 231.8	-15.5	-15.4	2.9	76.1
Mexico	3 171.4	8.8	-10.8	2.9	79.0
Italy	2 117.3	-0.3	-14.5	1.9	80.9
Spain	2 101.4	...	-3.1	1.9	82.8
India	1 985.2	-6.4	-13.1	1.8	84.6
Belgium	1 617.0	-3.4	-14.9	1.5	86.0
Japan	1 577.7	0.6	1.2	1.4	87.4

Graph 2: Trade Balance by MDG regions 2015
(Bln US$)

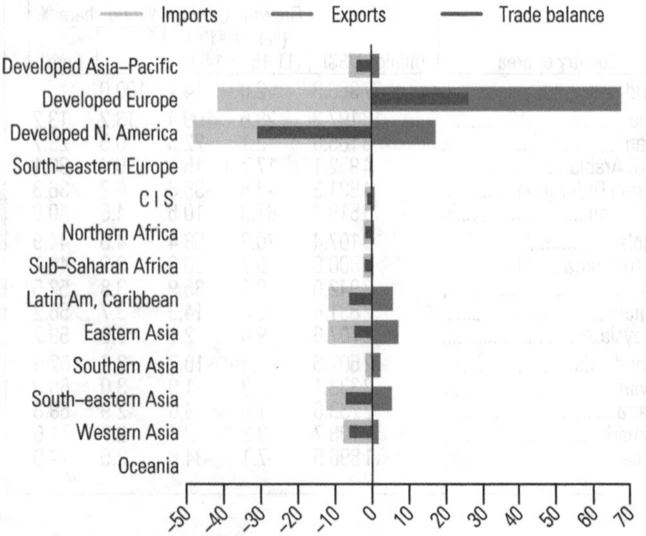

Table 3: Top importing countries or areas in 2015

Country or area	Value (million US$)	Avg. Growth (%) 11-15	Growth (%) 14-15	World share %	Cum.
World	147 884.7	-3.7	-16.4	100.0	
USA	47 772.0	-3.7	-7.8	32.3	32.3
Germany	10 713.6	35.8	-3.2	7.2	39.5
China	9 326.7	-17.1	-58.5	6.3	45.9
Ireland	7 866.4	0.4	3.8	5.3	51.2
France	6 762.0	7.0	-13.9	4.6	55.7
Japan	4 737.2	-7.0	-7.6	3.2	58.9
Singapore	4 503.9	-0.1	0.9	3.0	62.0
Mexico	4 338.6	1.5	2.8	2.9	64.9
Italy	2 732.4	-11.0	-17.4	1.8	66.8
Qatar	2 720.1	25.2	15.2	1.8	68.6
Spain	2 555.2	...	-11.6	1.7	70.3
Thailand	2 362.1	-3.8	-12.6	1.6	71.9
Malaysia	2 357.4	-1.7	-14.8	1.6	73.5
Saudi Arabia	2 137.9	2.3	4.1	1.4	75.0
Egypt	1 689.1	3.7	-3.5	1.1	76.1

In 2015, the value (in current US$) of exports of "financial services" (EBOPS 2002 code 260) decreased by 2.3 percent (compared to -2.5 percent average growth rate from 2011-2015) to reach 266.9 bln US$ (see table 2), while imports increased by 0.7 percent to reach 135.4 bln US$ (see table 3). Exports of this service accounted for 5.6 percent of total world services exports (see table 1). USA, Luxembourg and Singapore were the top exporters in 2015 (see table 2). They accounted for 38.4, 20.0 and 7.6 percent of world exports, respectively. Luxembourg, USA and Germany were the top importers, with respectively 29.0, 18.6 and 6.0 percent of world imports (see table 3).

The top 15 countries/areas accounted for 94.8 and 87.7 percent of total world exports and imports, respectively (see tables 2 and 3). In 2015, USA was the country/area with the highest value of net exports (+77.3 bln US$), followed by Singapore (+15.8 bln US$). By MDG regions (see graph 2), the largest surpluses in this product group were recorded by Developed North America (+77.4 bln US$), Developed Europe (+22.9 bln US$) and South-eastern Asia (+15.5 bln US$). The largest trade deficits were recorded by Latin America and the Caribbean (-2.4 bln US$), Commonwealth of Independent States (-1.5 bln US$) and Sub-Saharan Africa (-974.0 mln US$).

Table 1: Imports (Imp.) and exports (Exp.), 2003-2015, in current US$

		2003	2004	2005	2006	2007	2008	2009	2010	2011	2012	2013	2014	2015
Values in Bln US$	Imp.	52.4	67.6	75.4	104.4	126.9	118.6	107.0	130.6	160.9	100.9	148.4	134.5	135.4
	Exp.	117.5	148.8	166.2	225.6	308.2	284.4	265.0	232.9	295.6	203.6	235.0	273.1	266.9
As a percentage of world trade (%)	Imp.	2.7	2.9	3.2	3.7	3.8	3.3	3.2	2.7	3.9	2.4	3.3	2.8	3.0
	Exp.	5.9	6.2	6.7	7.7	8.6	7.5	7.3	4.0	6.7	4.5	4.9	5.4	5.6

Graph 1: Annual growth rates of exports, 2004–2015
(In percentage by year)

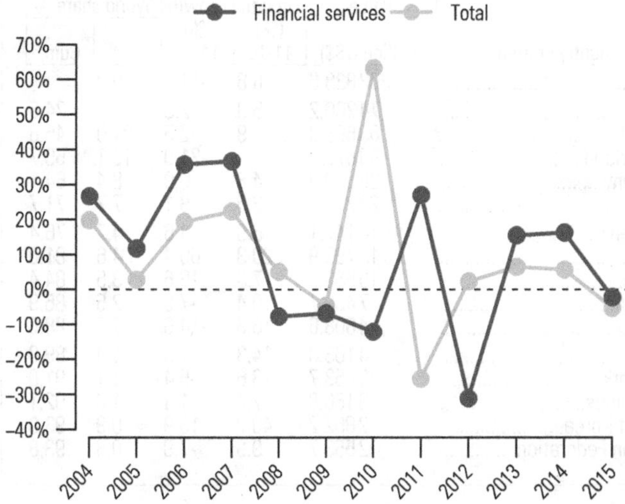

Table 2: Top exporting countries or areas in 2015

Country or area	Value (million US$)	Avg. Growth (%) 11-15	Growth (%) 14-15	World share %	Cum.
World	266905.8	-2.5	-2.3	100.0	
USA	102461.0	7.0	-4.9	38.4	38.4
Luxembourg	53362.7	-9.9	-1.5	20.0	58.4
Singapore	20332.9	7.6	0.1	7.6	66.0
China, Hong Kong SAR	15552.9	6.4	10.1	5.8	71.8
Germany	15062.2	-0.3	109.8	5.6	77.5
Japan	10281.5	28.0	42.1	3.9	81.3
France	7098.0	-14.9	19.4	2.7	84.0
India	5344.1	-3.8	5.9	2.0	86.0
Belgium	4892.1	6.0	-13.9	1.8	87.8
Netherlands	4876.9	...	-3.2	1.8	89.6
Italy	3562.6	8.5	-13.9	1.3	91.0
Australia	2835.1	16.7	-0.9	1.1	92.0
Sweden	2707.8	15.8	-2.8	1.0	93.1
Lebanon	2360.0	-4.0	28.9	0.9	93.9
China	2334.4	28.8	-48.5	0.9	94.8

Graph 2: Trade Balance by MDG regions 2015
(Bln US$)

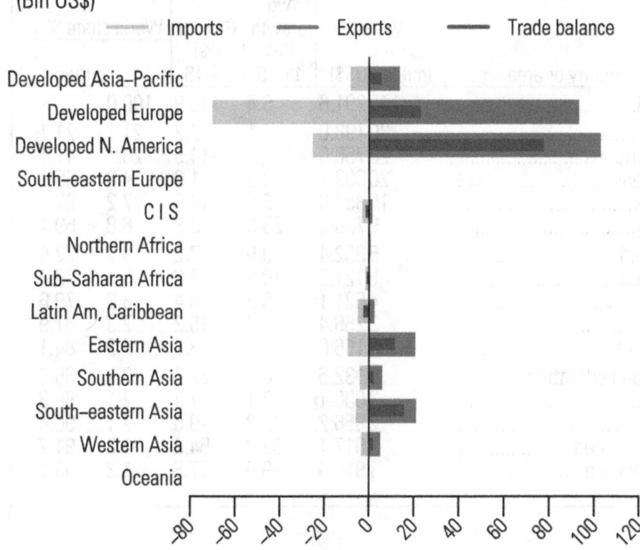

Table 3: Top importing countries or areas in 2015

Country or area	Value (million US$)	Avg. Growth (%) 11-15	Growth (%) 14-15	World share %	Cum.
World	135430.5	-4.2	0.7	100.0	
Luxembourg	39252.1	-8.7	0.3	29.0	29.0
USA	25162.0	9.7	1.0	18.6	47.6
Germany	8171.6	-0.2	79.0	6.0	53.6
Japan	5994.3	17.8	13.7	4.4	58.0
Italy	5675.4	2.3	-15.5	4.2	62.2
France	4960.9	-11.0	10.3	3.7	65.9
Belgium	4843.3	3.1	-6.8	3.6	69.5
Singapore	4483.1	9.6	4.3	3.3	72.8
Netherlands	4356.9	...	1.7	3.2	76.0
China, Hong Kong SAR	4306.3	4.9	5.6	3.2	79.2
India	3116.6	-21.7	-15.5	2.3	81.5
China	2644.7	37.2	-46.5	2.0	83.4
Russian Federation	1997.9	-4.8	-16.7	1.5	84.9
Australia	1936.8	17.9	1.0	1.4	86.3
Rep. of Korea	1913.2	-1.4	8.4	1.4	87.7

Computer and information services (EBOPS 2002 code 262)

In 2015, the value (in current US$) of exports of "computer and information services" (EBOPS 2002 code 262) decreased by 11.1 percent (compared to 6.8 percent average growth rate from 2011-2015) to reach 302.8 bln US$ (see table 2), while imports decreased by 16.9 percent to reach 143.3 bln US$ (see table 3). Exports of this service accounted for 6.3 percent of total world services exports (see table 1). India, Ireland and Netherlands were the top exporters in 2015 (see table 2). They accounted for 24.5, 21.0 and 10.1 percent of world exports, respectively. USA, Netherlands and Germany were the top importers, with respectively 21.1, 20.1 and 14.0 percent of world imports (see table 3).

The top 15 countries/areas accounted for 93.8 and 93.1 percent of total world exports and imports, respectively (see tables 2 and 3). In 2015, India was the country/area with the highest value of net exports (+71.3 bln US$), followed by Ireland (+62.7 bln US$). By MDG regions (see graph 2), the largest surpluses in this product group were recorded by Developed Europe (+84.7 bln US$), Southern Asia (+72.1 bln US$) and Western Asia (+13.0 bln US$). The largest trade deficits were recorded by Developed Asia-Pacific (-7.5 bln US$), Developed North America (-7.0 bln US$) and Sub-Saharan Africa (-638.2 mln US$).

Table 1: Imports (Imp.) and exports (Exp.), 2003-2015, in current US$

		2003	2004	2005	2006	2007	2008	2009	2010	2011	2012	2013	2014	2015
Values in Bln US$	Imp.	40.1	50.4	54.6	70.8	87.8	97.0	102.2	88.5	111.9	116.8	132.4	172.5	143.3
	Exp.	73.3	96.9	100.7	134.0	169.8	208.8	207.8	195.7	233.0	256.7	279.9	340.8	302.8
As a percentage of world trade (%)	Imp.	2.0	2.2	2.3	2.5	2.6	2.7	3.0	1.8	2.7	2.8	3.0	3.6	3.2
	Exp.	3.7	4.0	4.1	4.6	4.7	5.5	5.8	3.3	5.3	5.7	5.9	6.8	6.3

Graph 1: Annual growth rates of exports, 2004–2015

(In percentage by year)

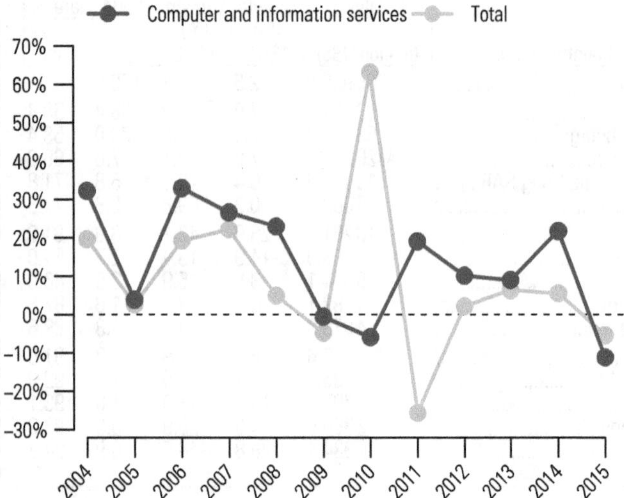

Table 2: Top exporting countries or areas in 2015

Country or area	Value (million US$)	Avg. Growth (%) 11-15	Growth (%) 14-15	World share %	Cum.
World	302 838.6	6.8	-11.1	100.0	
India	74 280.2	5.3	2.3	24.5	24.5
Ireland	63 695.3	11.9	-2.5	21.0	45.6
Netherlands	30 675.0	...	-21.0	10.1	55.7
Germany	25 339.9	4.8	0.9	8.4	64.1
USA	23 250.0	8.5	9.1	7.7	71.7
Sweden	14 147.1	6.9	-4.6	4.7	76.4
Israel	13 799.9	20.3	60.4	4.6	81.0
France	10 553.9	7.3	-16.6	3.5	84.4
Belgium	7 450.7	10.4	-7.9	2.5	86.9
Austria	4 808.6	16.6	-14.6	1.6	88.5
Italy	4 163.8	14.3	-1.3	1.4	89.9
Denmark	3 453.7	13.6	-5.4	1.1	91.0
Philippines	3 166.8	7.4	1.4	1.0	92.1
Rep. of Korea	2 852.2	40.2	16.9	0.9	93.0
Russian Federation	2 553.7	9.9	-7.9	0.8	93.8

Graph 2: Trade Balance by MDG regions 2015

(Bln US$)

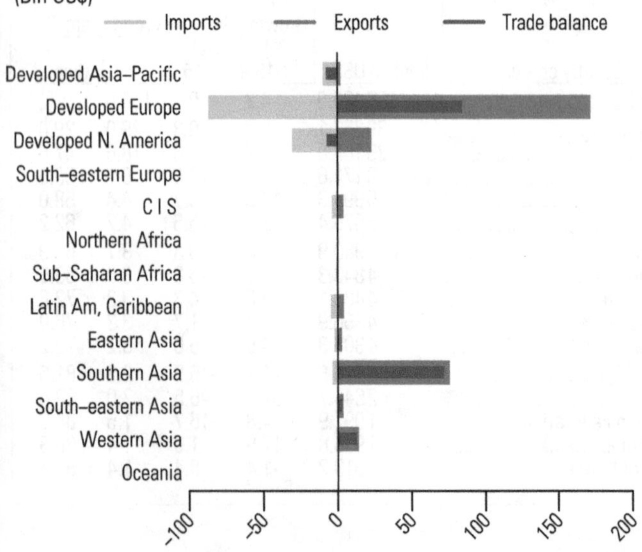

Table 3: Top importing countries or areas in 2015

Country or area	Value (million US$)	Avg. Growth (%) 11-15	Growth (%) 14-15	World share %	Cum.
World	143 291.6	6.4	-16.9	100.0	
USA	30 198.0	4.1	2.2	21.1	21.1
Netherlands	28 750.6	...	-14.5	20.1	41.1
Germany	20 003.1	2.3	-1.2	14.0	55.1
France	10 357.6	2.6	-14.6	7.2	62.3
Japan	9 736.2	25.5	3.8	6.8	69.1
Belgium	5 352.4	9.5	-7.2	3.7	72.9
Sweden	5 121.0	10.8	-7.6	3.6	76.4
Italy	4 521.1	-0.2	-2.4	3.2	79.6
Austria	3 256.4	16.6	-15.2	2.3	81.9
Denmark	3 156.0	0.3	-8.3	2.2	84.1
Russian Federation	3 132.5	6.5	-22.0	2.2	86.2
Brazil	3 000.1	-7.1	-7.3	2.1	88.3
India	2 956.2	12.3	-9.5	2.1	90.4
Rep. of Korea	1 917.1	33.2	54.9	1.3	91.7
Luxembourg	1 915.3	-9.9	-37.8	1.3	93.1

In 2015, the value (in current US$) of exports of "royalties and license fees" (EBOPS 2002 code 266) decreased by 1.2 percent (compared to 4.0 percent average growth rate from 2011-2015) to reach 300.9 bln US$ (see table 2), while imports decreased by 0.8 percent to reach 338.9 bln US$ (see table 3). Exports of this service accounted for 6.3 percent of total world services exports (see table 1). USA, Japan and Netherlands were the top exporters in 2015 (see table 2). They accounted for 41.4, 12.2 and 8.4 percent of world exports, respectively. Ireland, USA and Netherlands were the top importers, with respectively 22.2, 11.7 and 10.4 percent of world imports (see table 3).

The top 15 countries/areas accounted for 95.2 and 84.1 percent of total world exports and imports, respectively (see tables 2 and 3). In 2015, USA was the country/area with the highest value of net exports (+85.2 bln US$), followed by Japan (+19.6 bln US$). By MDG regions (see graph 2), the largest surpluses in this product group were recorded by Developed North America (+85.2 bln US$) and Developed Asia-Pacific (+16.4 bln US$). The largest trade deficits were recorded by Developed Europe (-66.7 bln US$), Eastern Asia (-25.8 bln US$) and South-eastern Asia (-22.2 bln US$).

Table 1: Imports (Imp.) and exports (Exp.), 2003-2015, in current US$

		2003	2004	2005	2006	2007	2008	2009	2010	2011	2012	2013	2014	2015
Values in Bln US$	Imp.	112.2	145.3	147.4	171.3	198.4	230.0	254.7	297.2	264.5	264.0	296.5	341.5	338.9
	Exp.	114.1	144.5	152.6	178.6	211.1	223.0	240.4	310.8	257.0	244.6	277.7	304.7	300.9
As a percentage of world trade (%)	Imp.	5.7	6.3	6.2	6.1	5.9	6.4	7.5	6.1	6.5	6.3	6.6	7.2	7.6
	Exp.	5.7	6.0	6.2	6.1	5.9	5.9	6.7	5.3	5.9	5.5	5.8	6.1	6.3

Graph 1: Annual growth rates of exports, 2004–2015
(In percentage by year)

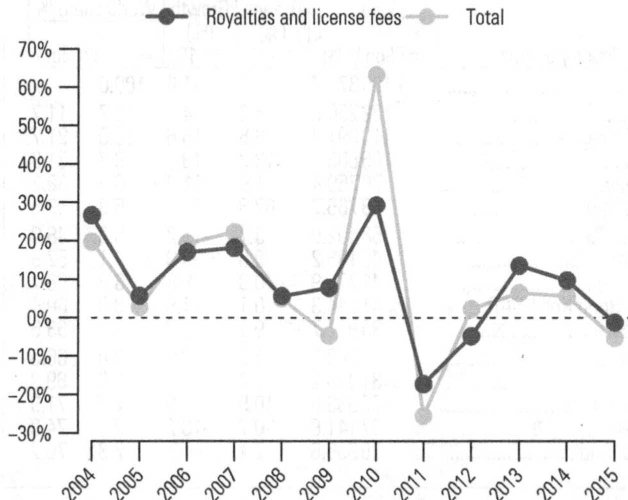

Table 2: Top exporting countries or areas in 2015

Country or area	Value (million US$)	Avg. Growth (%) 11-15	Growth (%) 14-15	World share %	Cum.
World	300 880.6	4.0	-1.2	100.0	
USA	124 664.0	0.3	-4.0	41.4	41.4
Japan	36 631.1	7.9	-0.7	12.2	53.6
Netherlands	25 344.5	...	28.7	8.4	62.0
United Kingdom	17 538.9	0.8	-2.6	5.8	67.9
Switzerland	16 205.1	-3.0	-10.8	5.4	73.2
France	14 975.7	-0.6	4.6	5.0	78.2
Germany	14 596.4	8.0	-2.8	4.9	83.1
Sweden	8 837.8	7.4	-3.9	2.9	86.0
Ireland	7 459.2	12.5	7.1	2.5	88.5
Rep. of Korea	6 198.6	9.0	20.0	2.1	90.6
Singapore	3 313.6	18.9	-12.1	1.1	91.7
Belgium	3 195.2	5.9	-5.4	1.1	92.7
Italy	3 052.1	-6.8	-7.8	1.0	93.7
Finland	2 401.6	-5.4	-9.7	0.8	94.5
Denmark	2 133.3	-3.7	-15.6	0.7	95.2

Graph 2: Trade Balance by MDG regions 2015
(Bln US$)

Imports — Exports — Trade balance

Developed Asia-Pacific
Developed Europe
Developed N. America
South-eastern Europe
CIS
Northern Africa
Sub-Saharan Africa
Latin Am, Caribbean
Eastern Asia
Southern Asia
South-eastern Asia
Western Asia
Oceania

-200 -150 -100 -50 0 50 100 150

Table 3: Top importing countries or areas in 2015

Country or area	Value (million US$)	Avg. Growth (%) 11-15	Growth (%) 14-15	World share %	Cum.
World	338 922.4	6.4	-0.8	100.0	
Ireland	75 185.3	18.6	17.2	22.2	22.2
USA	39 495.0	2.3	-6.4	11.7	33.8
Netherlands	35 389.8	...	18.3	10.4	44.3
China	22 022.4	10.6	-2.6	6.5	50.8
Singapore	17 345.6	-2.9	-12.1	5.1	55.9
Japan	16 989.6	-1.2	-18.5	5.0	60.9
France	13 966.5	7.3	13.2	4.1	65.0
Switzerland	12 940.3	-11.0	-8.1	3.8	68.8
United Kingdom	12 423.9	2.9	27.5	3.7	72.5
Rep. of Korea	9 831.1	7.3	-6.8	2.9	75.4
Germany	8 920.2	4.7	-4.5	2.6	78.0
Russian Federation	5 633.8	-0.9	-29.8	1.7	79.7
Brazil	5 250.5	8.8	-11.3	1.5	81.3
India	5 009.0	15.4	3.3	1.5	82.7
Spain	4 523.4	...	1.0	1.3	84.1

Source: UN Comtrade

Other business services (EBOPS 2002 code 268)

In 2015, the value (in current US$) of exports of "other business services" (EBOPS 2002 code 268) decreased by 1.6 percent (compared to 3.2 percent average growth rate from 2011-2015) to reach 1105.4 bln US$ (see table 2), while imports decreased by 4.4 percent to reach 979.4 bln US$ (see table 3). Exports of this service accounted for 23.2 percent of total world services exports (see table 1). USA, United Kingdom and France were the top exporters in 2015 (see table 2). They accounted for 11.7, 10.0 and 9.7 percent of world exports, respectively. USA, France and Germany were the top importers, with respectively 9.6, 8.4 and 8.2 percent of world imports (see table 3).

The top 15 countries/areas accounted for 76.7 and 75.7 percent of total world exports and imports, respectively (see tables 2 and 3). In 2015, United Kingdom was the country/area with the highest value of net exports (+48.4 bln US$), followed by USA (+35.2 bln US$). By MDG regions (see graph 2), the largest surpluses in this product group were recorded by Developed Europe (+113.6 bln US$), Eastern Asia (+45.6 bln US$) and Developed North America (+35.5 bln US$). The largest trade deficits were recorded by Developed Asia-Pacific (-22.1 bln US$), Sub-Saharan Africa (-12.9 bln US$) and Latin America and the Caribbean (-12.1 bln US$).

Table 1: Imports (Imp.) and exports (Exp.), 2003-2015, in current US$

		2003	2004	2005	2006	2007	2008	2009	2010	2011	2012	2013	2014	2015
Values in Bln US$	Imp.	407.8	472.6	469.4	590.3	731.6	785.1	790.7	995.8	888.2	913.9	934.4	1 024.5	979.4
	Exp.	418.3	489.0	534.3	667.7	836.7	871.6	879.6	1 243.6	975.0	1 004.5	1 052.1	1 123.6	1 105.4
As a percentage of world trade (%)	Imp.	20.8	20.5	19.8	21.2	21.9	22.0	23.3	20.4	21.7	21.7	20.8	21.5	21.9
	Exp.	20.9	20.4	21.7	22.7	23.2	23.0	24.4	21.1	22.2	22.4	22.1	22.3	23.2

Graph 1: Annual growth rates of exports, 2004–2015
(In percentage by year)

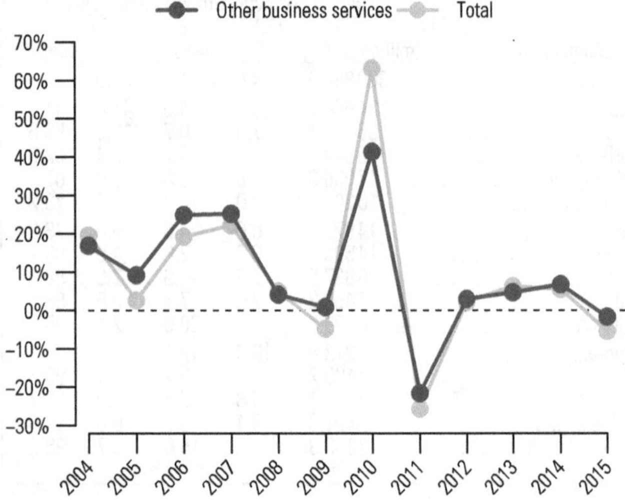

Table 2: Top exporting countries or areas in 2015

Country or area	Value (million US$)	Avg. Growth (%) 11-15	Growth (%) 14-15	World share %	Cum.
World	1 105 374.7	3.2	-1.6	100.0	
USA	129 290.0	4.3	4.2	11.7	11.7
United Kingdom	110 091.7	6.5	15.6	10.0	21.7
France	106 803.1	13.2	18.9	9.7	31.3
Germany	76 259.4	1.9	-11.4	6.9	38.2
Netherlands	58 765.7	62.8	10.2	5.3	43.5
China	58 402.9	-3.7	-15.2	5.3	48.8
Belgium	45 185.2	9.5	-9.3	4.1	52.9
Japan	41 735.9	-0.3	-9.8	3.8	56.7
China, Hong Kong SAR	41 544.3	0.1	-11.9	3.8	60.4
Singapore	33 927.7	9.1	-6.7	3.1	63.5
Ireland	32 943.3	2.2	-2.9	3.0	66.5
India	31 390.2	7.0	2.2	2.8	69.3
Rep. of Korea	27 938.0	10.5	-16.0	2.5	71.9
Sweden	27 141.8	-0.7	-13.2	2.5	74.3
Switzerland	25 956.6	2.1		2.3	76.7

Graph 2: Trade Balance by MDG regions 2015
(Bln US$)

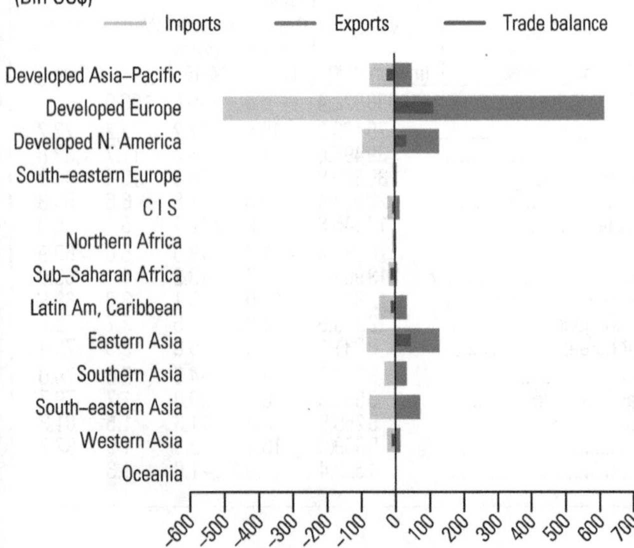

Table 3: Top importing countries or areas in 2015

Country or area	Value (million US$)	Avg. Growth (%) 11-15	Growth (%) 14-15	World share %	Cum.
World	979 395.2	2.5	-4.4	100.0	
USA	94 099.0	4.2	4.3	9.6	9.6
France	82 522.3	8.0	-1.3	8.4	18.0
Germany	80 317.5	0.1	-9.2	8.2	26.2
Ireland	64 242.3	9.1	19.6	6.6	32.8
United Kingdom	61 739.1	3.7	5.7	6.3	39.1
Japan	60 991.2	9.3	3.5	6.2	45.3
Netherlands	45 650.4	...	6.5	4.7	50.0
Singapore	41 498.2	9.2	-10.8	4.2	54.2
China	39 542.1	-5.3	-25.9	4.0	58.3
Belgium	39 331.9	9.0	-5.7	4.0	62.3
Rep. of Korea	29 981.5	3.8	-1.7	3.1	65.3
India	29 809.6	-0.6	-4.5	3.0	68.4
Brazil	28 774.7	3.9	-8.2	2.9	71.3
Italy	23 825.6	-5.0	-12.3	2.4	73.8
Sweden	19 190.6	-0.9	-13.5	2.0	75.7

In 2015, the value (in current US$) of exports of "personal, cultural, and recreational services" (EBOPS 2002 code 287) decreased by 19.6 percent (compared to -1.6 percent average growth rate from 2011-2015) to reach 34.0 bln US$ (see table 2), while imports decreased by 11.8 percent to reach 45.6 bln US$ (see table 3). Exports of this service accounted for 0.7 percent of total world services exports (see table 1). Luxembourg, United Kingdom and USA were the top exporters in 2015 (see table 2). They accounted for 15.2, 11.3 and 9.1 percent of world exports, respectively. United Kingdom, Luxembourg and France were the top importers, with respectively 10.8, 10.6 and 9.9 percent of world imports (see table 3).

The top 15 countries/areas accounted for 78.5 and 76.2 percent of total world exports and imports, respectively (see tables 2 and 3). In 2015, Malta was the country/area with the highest value of net exports (+2.2 bln US$), followed by USA (+778.0 mln US$). By MDG regions (see graph 2), the largest surpluses in this product group were recorded by Developed North America (+778.7 mln US$), South-eastern Europe (+69.1 mln US$) and Northern Africa (+68.8 mln US$). The largest trade deficits were recorded by Latin America and the Caribbean (-4.5 bln US$), Developed Europe (-3.7 bln US$) and Developed Asia-Pacific (-1.2 bln US$).

Table 1: Imports (Imp.) and exports (Exp.), 2003-2015, in current US$

		2003	2004	2005	2006	2007	2008	2009	2010	2011	2012	2013	2014	2015
Values in Bln US$	Imp.	19.2	25.2	24.0	30.5	33.8	35.0	33.0	53.9	43.7	43.6	47.4	51.7	45.6
	Exp.	15.0	20.1	19.9	23.0	26.2	25.9	25.8	46.1	36.3	36.1	40.7	42.3	34.0
As a percentage of world trade (%)	Imp.	1.0	1.1	1.0	1.1	1.0	1.0	1.0	1.1	1.1	1.0	1.1	1.1	1.0
	Exp.	0.7	0.8	0.8	0.8	0.7	0.7	0.7	0.8	0.8	0.8	0.9	0.8	0.7

Graph 1: Annual growth rates of exports, 2004–2015

(In percentage by year)

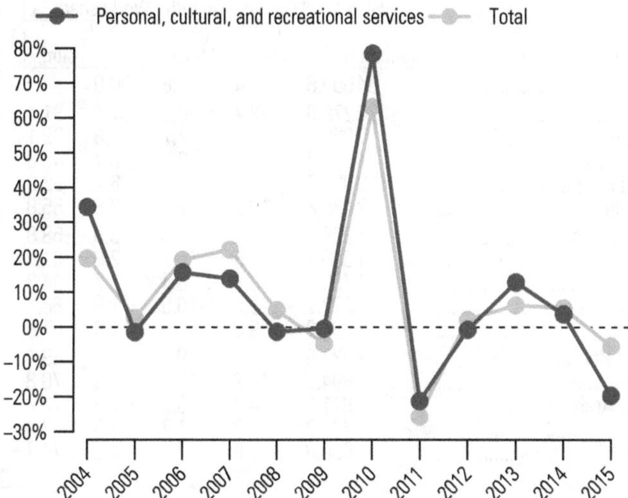

Graph 2: Trade Balance by MDG regions 2015

(Bln US$)

Imports — Exports — Trade balance

Developed Asia-Pacific
Developed Europe
Developed N. America
South-eastern Europe
C I S
Northern Africa
Sub-Saharan Africa
Latin Am, Caribbean
Eastern Asia
Southern Asia
South-eastern Asia
Western Asia
Oceania

-30 -25 -20 -15 -10 -5 0 5 10 15 20 25

Table 2: Top exporting countries or areas in 2015

Country or area	Value (million US$)	Avg. Growth (%) 11-15	Growth (%) 14-15	World share %	Cum.
World	33 999.1	-1.6	-19.6	100.0	
Luxembourg	5 164.9	-5.2	-20.2	15.2	15.2
United Kingdom	3 827.1	-6.5	9.4	11.3	26.4
USA	3 091.0	39.4	-5.4	9.1	35.5
France	2 966.8	5.3	-13.5	8.7	44.3
Malta	2 246.7	-0.9	-9.7	6.6	50.9
Germany	1 798.9	12.9	-6.1	5.3	56.2
India	1 265.8	38.3	0.0	3.7	59.9
Belgium	1 235.5	12.2	-11.7	3.6	63.5
Netherlands	992.2	...	-63.8	2.9	66.4
Rep. of Korea	895.2	14.5	-2.9	2.6	69.1
China	731.4	56.2	318.3	2.2	71.2
Australia	717.6	-3.5	-18.5	2.1	73.3
Japan	648.9	44.6	37.8	1.9	75.2
Qatar	558.8	...	9.0	1.6	76.9
Singapore	536.1	0.9	-5.8	1.6	78.5

Table 3: Top importing countries or areas in 2015

Country or area	Value (million US$)	Avg. Growth (%) 11-15	Growth (%) 14-15	World share %	Cum.
World	45 560.1	1.1	-11.8	100.0	
United Kingdom	4 901.1	7.0	-5.2	10.8	10.8
Luxembourg	4 842.2	-4.2	1.4	10.6	21.4
France	4 499.5	11.5	-1.5	9.9	31.3
Venezuela	3 114.0	-5.9	-6.4	6.8	38.1
Germany	2 769.3	-0.7	-20.1	6.1	44.2
USA	2 313.0	35.4	6.5	5.1	49.3
China	1 894.4	47.6	116.9	4.2	53.4
Australia	1 512.1	-2.5	-3.2	3.3	56.7
Denmark	1 432.7	9.8	-5.4	3.1	59.9
India	1 369.4	41.1	-1.5	3.0	62.9
Qatar	1 345.6	-1.5	-9.1	3.0	65.8
Japan	1 281.2	8.9	50.7	2.8	68.6
Netherlands	1 260.1	...	-52.3	2.8	71.4
Belgium	1 095.8	0.1	-15.2	2.4	73.8
Russian Federation	1 092.4	0.8	-32.2	2.4	76.2

Source: UN Comtrade

Government services, n.i.e. (EBOPS 2002 code 291)

In 2015, the value (in current US$) of exports of "government services, n.i.e." (EBOPS 2002 code 291) decreased by 7.8 percent (compared to -2.4 percent average growth rate from 2011-2015) to reach 64.6 bln US$ (see table 2), while imports decreased by 18.0 percent to reach 96.0 bln US$ (see table 3). Exports of this service accounted for 1.4 percent of total world services exports (see table 1). USA, Germany and Japan were the top exporters in 2015 (see table 2). They accounted for 31.4, 7.8 and 6.7 percent of world exports, respectively. Saudi Arabia, USA and United Kingdom were the top importers, with respectively 33.7, 22.4 and 4.2 percent of world imports (see table 3).

The top 15 countries/areas accounted for 74.7 and 82.6 percent of total world exports and imports, respectively (see tables 2 and 3). In 2015, Germany was the country/area with the highest value of net exports (+3.4 bln US$), followed by Japan (+2.4 bln US$). By MDG regions (see graph 2), the largest surpluses in this product group were recorded by Developed Europe (+8.3 bln US$), Southern Asia (+3.6 bln US$) and Developed Asia-Pacific (+2.2 bln US$). The largest trade deficits were recorded by Western Asia (-34.4 bln US$), Latin America and the Caribbean (-3.9 bln US$) and Commonwealth of Independent States (-1.9 bln US$).

Table 1: Imports (Imp.) and exports (Exp.), 2003-2015, in current US$

		2003	2004	2005	2006	2007	2008	2009	2010	2011	2012	2013	2014	2015
Values in Bln US$	Imp.	68.7	74.0	77.5	91.0	96.8	106.2	112.8	137.9	111.0	104.0	107.0	117.1	96.0
	Exp.	45.0	49.9	52.8	62.6	69.1	65.7	66.2	81.5	71.3	70.2	68.2	70.1	64.6
As a percentage of world trade (%)	Imp.	3.5	3.2	3.3	3.3	2.9	3.0	3.3	2.8	2.7	2.5	2.4	2.5	2.1
	Exp.	2.2	2.1	2.1	2.1	1.9	1.7	1.8	1.4	1.6	1.6	1.4	1.4	1.4

Graph 1: Annual growth rates of exports, 2004–2015

(In percentage by year)

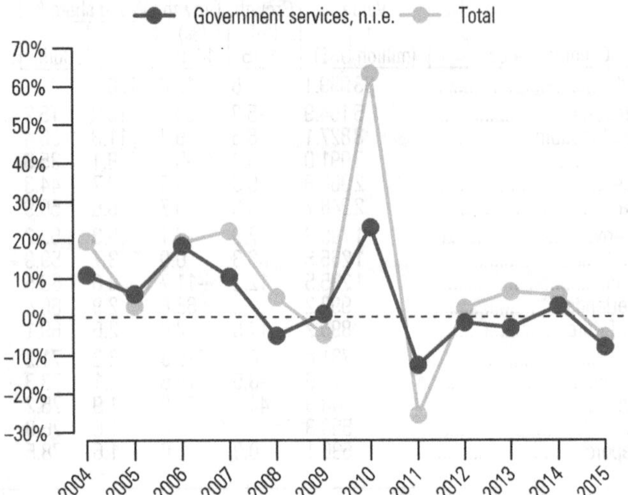

Table 2: Top exporting countries or areas in 2015

Country or area	Value (million US$)	Avg. Growth (%) 11-15	Growth (%) 14-15	World share %	Cum.
World	64609.8	-2.4	-7.8	100.0	
USA	20270.0	-2.2	-0.3	31.4	31.4
Germany	5020.7	-1.2	-7.7	7.8	39.1
Japan	4324.2	12.0	-2.8	6.7	45.8
United Kingdom	3998.2	1.9	-1.7	6.2	52.0
Pakistan	2436.8	10.3	7.6	3.8	55.8
Netherlands	1929.4	...	-9.5	3.0	58.8
Bangladesh	1805.2	17.5	45.7	2.8	61.6
Belgium	1760.1	-3.6	-6.4	2.7	64.3
Canada	1222.7	-6.5	-10.9	1.9	66.2
China	1064.2	9.0	0.9	1.6	67.8
Rep. of Korea	1033.5	-3.6	-9.7	1.6	69.4
Qatar	894.2	-16.2	19.0	1.4	70.8
United Arab Emirates	871.3	4.3	3.2	1.3	72.2
Italy	824.2	-9.2	-1.7	1.3	73.4
Russian Federation	806.8	3.8	-12.9	1.2	74.7

Graph 2: Trade Balance by MDG regions 2015

(Bln US$)

Imports — Exports — Trade balance

Developed Asia-Pacific
Developed Europe
Developed N. America
South-eastern Europe
CIS
Northern Africa
Sub-Saharan Africa
Latin Am, Caribbean
Eastern Asia
Southern Asia
South-eastern Asia
Western Asia
Oceania

-40 -35 -30 -25 -20 -15 -10 -5 0 5 10 15 20 25

Table 3: Top importing countries or areas in 2015

Country or area	Value (million US$)	Avg. Growth (%) 11-15	Growth (%) 14-15	World share %	Cum.
World	95999.5	-3.6	-18.0	100.0	
Saudi Arabia	32345.9	8.8	-14.6	33.7	33.7
USA	21515.0	-8.9	-11.2	22.4	56.1
United Kingdom	4002.8	-11.6	-42.1	4.2	60.3
China	2565.7	24.6	26.6	2.7	62.9
Mexico	2562.3	-12.0	-19.8	2.7	65.6
Qatar	2385.2	16.0	-16.4	2.5	68.1
Japan	1961.9	3.3	0.0	2.0	70.1
Brazil	1833.9	-12.7	-15.0	1.9	72.1
Kuwait	1670.0	4.0	15.2	1.7	73.8
Italy	1582.0	-9.5	-24.7	1.6	75.4
Germany	1581.5	7.6	12.3	1.6	77.1
Russian Federation	1534.0	-7.6	-27.4	1.6	78.7
Nigeria	1354.4	-10.4	-21.0	1.4	80.1
Rep. of Korea	1239.7	2.2	18.8	1.3	81.4
United Arab Emirates	1198.1	10.0	7.3	1.2	82.6

Product Trade Profiles
Profils de produits de commerce

General notes:

For further information on Sources, Method of Estimation, Currency Conversion, Period, Country Nomenclature and Country Grouping of this table, as well as for a brief table description, please see the Introduction.

Remarque générale:

Pour plus d'information en ce qui concerne les sources, la méthode d'estimation, taux d'exchange, période, nomenclature des pays et groupement de pays, ainsi que pour une brève description de ce tableau, veuillez voir l'introduction.